The Bible Guide

THE
BIBLE
GUIDE

Andrew Knowles

A LION BOOK

For

Penny Whiting,

and in honour of

G.R. Buchanan

Copyright © 2001 Andrew Knowles

This edition copyright © 2001 Lion Publishing

The author asserts the moral right
to be identified as the author of this work

Published by
Lion Publishing plc
Sandy Lane West, Oxford, England
www.lion-publishing.co.uk
ISBN 0 7459 1908 1 (hardback)
ISBN 0 7459 5090 6 (paperback)

First edition 2001
10 9 8 7 6 5 4 3 2 1 0

Acknowledgments
The scripture quotations have been taken from The New
Revised Standard Version of the Bible, Anglicized Edition,
copyright © 1989, 1995 by the Division of Christian Education
of the National Council of the Churches of Christ in the
United States of America, and are used by permission; all rights
reserved; and from the *Holy Bible, New International Version*,
copyright © 1973, 1978, 1984 by International Bible Society.
Used by permission of Hodder & Stoughton Limited. All rights
reserved. 'NIV' is a registered trademark of International Bible
Society. UK trademark number 1448790.

A catalogue record for this book is available
from the British Library

Typeset in 10/12 Goudy Oldstyle
Printed and bound in China

Contents

Author's Preface

It was Michael Ramsey, a great archbishop of Canterbury, who said, 'We must study to be simple.' This is what I have tried to do in preparing this companion guide to the Bible.

Many people who need access to the scriptures have little background scholarship or time to read. They are teaching or leading study groups and sometimes require a resource which will quickly give them their bearings and provide some essential information. I hope that my colleagues in ministry – clergy and pastors – will also find this book useful when time for preparation is short and something straightforward and immediate is appropriate.

This book is the product of many hearts and minds and hands. Its roots are in the ministry of my own Bible-class teacher, Gordon Buchanan, who first showed me the labour, reverence and reward of Bible study. It was conceived by a chance remark of my commissioning editor, Becky Winter, late in 1992. It was gestated by the dedicated scholars on whose books and articles I have relied. I have often found myself 'on giants' shoulders'.

In particular I am indebted to two friends from my student days, Dr Chris Wright of All Nations' College, Ware, and Dr Stephen Travis of St John's College Nottingham. They read the Old and New Testament sections respectively and made many important amendments, covering my ignorance with their fine understanding and gentle tact. I am also grateful to Dr John Bimson and Revd Mike Butterworth, who provided me with valuable notes on the Old Testament. Martin Manser gave painstaking attention to a myriad of tiny details and encouraged me to fill many gaps. David Winter, an outstanding communicator, read the entire manuscript to challenge me with his keen perceptions. For Lion Publishing, Angela Handley has overseen the project with the greatest care, patience and goodwill, Nick Rous has been the genius behind the design and illustration, and Jenni Dutton has made the final preparations for publication.

I would like to thank those who have shared the labour pains of bringing this book to birth. Peter and Fiona Beer provided generous hospitality and much-needed sanctuary in their successive homes at Innsworth and Southmoor. Derek Osborne loaned his study at Lee Abbey through two summer vacations. Becky Winter's promptings and Jo Dale's prayers revived the project when all vital signs were absent. And Gwen Potter, my co-leader of the Normandy Crusaders, typed the manuscript with infectious enthusiasm and skill.

Finally my family, Diane, Hannah and Matthew, have sustained me with the love and forbearance that I so greatly need, whether writing a book or not. For everyone, and to the Lord, who provides, I give my heartfelt thanks.

Andrew Knowles
Chelmsford
Easter 2001

What is the Bible?

The Bible began with a collection of stories, passed on by word of mouth. They were stories of how God chose and blessed a nomadic group of people, the Israelites, and gave them a land of their own.

In due course, the history of Israel and the messages of her prophets were written down. These scriptures became a treasured library of Jewish literature: history, folklore, wisdom and prayers, written on parchment and stored in rolls. This was the Hebrew Bible, the Old Testament.

If the Old Testament is the history of the Jews, then the New Testament is the story of the Christian church. It begins with the four Gospels, each of which narrates the life and significance of Jesus of Nazareth. Then follows an account of how the gospel (the good news) of Jesus spread from Jerusalem to Rome in a single generation. There are also letters which were written in those early years.

Eventually, the Bible documents were collected together, transcribed on vellum (calf or sheep skin) and bound in books.

BOOKS OF THE BIBLE

The Old Testament

- Law
- History
- Poetry and wisdom
- Prophecy

The New Testament

- Gospels and Acts
- Letters and Revelation

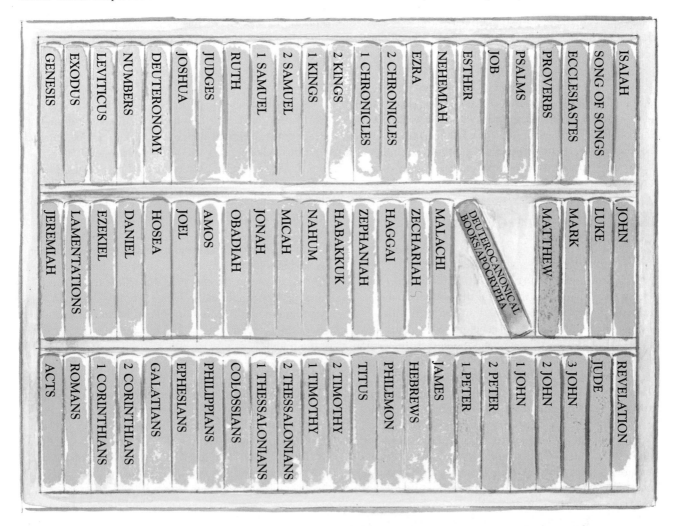

GENESIS · EXODUS · LEVITICUS · NUMBERS · DEUTERONOMY · JOSHUA · JUDGES · RUTH · 1 SAMUEL · 2 SAMUEL · 1 KINGS · 2 KINGS · 1 CHRONICLES · 2 CHRONICLES · EZRA · NEHEMIAH · ESTHER · JOB · PSALMS · PROVERBS · ECCLESIASTES · SONG OF SONGS · ISAIAH

JEREMIAH · LAMENTATIONS · EZEKIEL · DANIEL · HOSEA · JOEL · AMOS · OBADIAH · JONAH · MICAH · NAHUM · HABAKKUK · ZEPHANIAH · HAGGAI · ZECHARIAH · MALACHI · DEUTEROCANONICAL BOOKS/APOCRYPHA · MATTHEW · MARK · LUKE · JOHN

ACTS · ROMANS · 1 CORINTHIANS · 2 CORINTHIANS · GALATIANS · EPHESIANS · PHILIPPIANS · COLOSSIANS · 1 THESSALONIANS · 2 THESSALONIANS · 1 TIMOTHY · 2 TIMOTHY · TITUS · PHILEMON · HEBREWS · JAMES · 1 PETER · 2 PETER · 1 JOHN · 2 JOHN · 3 JOHN · JUDE · REVELATION

The volumes were rare and precious, kept in the libraries of monasteries or chained in churches. Then, in the 15th century, the printing press was invented. The Bible was finally released from the limitation of being copied out by hand, and embarked on mass production.

Now the Bible has been translated into a multitude of languages and taken to every part of the world. It is stored on microchip, recorded on tape, produced on CD-ROMs and accessed via the Internet. There are versions to suit all sorts of people and groups, and levels of understanding.

Wherever and however the Bible is read, people find it to be the word of God. Here, more than anywhere else, we discover what God is like and what it is that he offers us. He is our creator, Saviour and judge. He is righteous and merciful and loving. He is perfectly portrayed in the life, death and resurrection of his Son, Jesus Christ.

The Bible is made up of two main parts: the Old Testament and the New Testament. Both these parts are themselves collections of books.

In a remarkable way, all the books in the Bible contribute to the same overall story and message. Although written at different times by a number of authors, each book contributes its own perspective to the others. Together they build a complete picture of God's holiness and love, our human rebellion against him, and his wonderful plan to rescue us from sin and death and to restore us to eternal life.

The Old Testament story

'In the beginning...'

The earliest stories in the Bible are of Adam and Eve, Cain and Abel, Noah's flood and the tower of Babel (Genesis 1–11). They have much in common with myths, as they portray the ages before recorded history. They deal with how things began and depict the tension between God's holiness and human sin.

Then comes the story of Abram who became Abraham – the ancestor of the nation of Israel. Abram responds to God's call to leave his home and become a wandering shepherd. By a solemn covenant, God promises to make Abraham the father of a great nation and to bless the world through his descendants. He also promises to give him the land of Canaan. It is because Abraham believes God against all odds that he is known as 'the father of the faithful'.

The whole Bible story flows from God's covenant with Abraham, to bless him and the whole world through him (Genesis 12–36).

Abraham's son is Isaac and his grandson is Jacob. They are the promise-bearers, the heirs of the covenant, the ancestors of the nation of Israel. It is Jacob who is given the name Israel.

Jacob has twelve sons, who become the patriarchs of the twelve tribes of Israel. One of these sons is Jacob's favourite, Joseph. Joseph becomes a slave and prisoner in Egypt, but rises to become the country's first minister (Genesis 37–50).

'Let my people go!'

In Egypt, the Israelites (Hebrews) sink into slavery. God rescues them through the leadership of Moses, who is a Hebrew brought up as an Egyptian prince. God inflicts a series of plagues on the Egyptians, climaxing in the death of all their first-born sons in a single night. The Hebrews are spared when the angel of death 'passes over' their homes – hence the night and its special meal are called 'Passover'.

Moses leads the Israelites out of Egypt across the Red Sea (or Sea of Reeds). This is the exodus – the dramatic escape from slavery by which God rescues his people and begins to make them a nation (Exodus 1–15).

Moses is to lead the Israelites to their Promised Land of Canaan. It is a short journey, but it takes forty years. God gives the people his law (the Ten Commandments) at Mount Sinai, but they rebel by making and worshipping a golden calf.

An entire generation dies in the wilderness and even Moses himself is not allowed to enter the Promised Land. He does, however, receive God's instructions for the building of the tabernacle. This is a tent where God dwells among his people, surrounded by an enclosure where they offer sacrifices. The tabernacle is a forerunner of the temple (Exodus 16–40).

God's plans for his people

God gives Moses instructions on how to appoint priests, offer sacrifices and celebrate festivals (the book of Leviticus). Israel's experiences in the wilderness and the approach to Canaan are narrated (the book of Numbers). As they are about to enter Canaan, the 'Promised Land', Moses reviews the lessons God has taught them and the law he has given them (the book of Deuteronomy). Moses is not permitted to go into the Promised Land.

The conquest of Canaan

Moses is succeeded by Joshua ('God saves'), who leads the campaign to conquer the land of Canaan (Joshua 1–12). It is a campaign in which God fights for his people, most famously in the collapsing of the walls of Jericho.

At the end of his life, Joshua divides the land between the tribes of Israel. The Israelites are exposed to the customs and religion of the Canaanites, who worship the fertility gods of Baal. Joshua challenges them to be faithful to the Lord their God. The land is never completely conquered until the reign of King David.

The judges

After Joshua there is no clear leader. Israel is ruled by 'judges' who emerge from time to time to tackle a crisis or fight an enemy (the book of Judges). The best-known judge is Samson, to whom God gives great strength to fight the Philistines. The nation disintegrates into social and moral chaos.

The bloodthirsty adventures of the judges are offset by the love story of Ruth and Boaz. They are the ancestors of King David (the book of Ruth).

Prophets and kings

SAMUEL AND DAVID

The last of the judges is Samuel, who is also a prophet. Samuel is brought up at the shrine at Shiloh, where he sees the corruption of the priests. When he is old, the people ask him to appoint a king (1 Samuel).

Samuel believes that only God is Israel's king. He tries to persuade them against having a human king, but the people want to be like the other nations. God guides Samuel to anoint Saul as Israel's first king.

Saul is a man of royal appearance, but he is not completely obedient to God. He suffers from depression and becomes jealous of the young hero, David. It is David who shows true faith in God by slaying the Philistine giant, Goliath. Samuel seeks out David and anoints him to be Israel's next king.

DAVID AND SOLOMON

David is Israel's greatest king, reigning around 1000 BC. He is able to unite the rival tribes of Israel and protect the nation from her enemies. He captures the city of Jebus and makes it Jerusalem, 'city of peace'. He brings the ark of the covenant, the symbol of God's presence, to Jerusalem. He establishes peace and justice for all, and makes preparations to build a temple (2 Samuel).

David is a man who listens to God and obeys God. His many psalms express a wide range of feelings towards God, from high praise to near despair (the book of Psalms). In a tragic error of judgment David has an affair with Bathsheba, the wife of one of his soldiers. He loses his moral authority, fails to govern his sons and suffers the rebellion of one of them, Absalom.

David is succeeded by Solomon, who is his son by Bathsheba. Solomon asks God for wisdom to rule Israel well. His wisdom becomes legendary and he is an author and collector of wise sayings (the book of Proverbs, Song of Songs).

Solomon establishes a wealthy and well-organized kingdom. He builds and dedicates a fine temple for God. However, he contracts many marriages with foreign women, who introduce him to their pagan gods. He also disrupts Israel's rural society. He presses large numbers of people into the army and building projects. He imposes heavy taxation to pay for his lavish lifestyle and grandiose schemes.

THE TWO KINGDOMS

After the reign of Solomon, the nation of Israel splits into two kingdoms (the books of Kings and Chronicles). The northern kingdom is composed of ten tribes and keeps the name Israel. The southern kingdom retains Jerusalem and the temple and is ruled by the descendants of David and Solomon. It is called Judah.

The northern kingdom of Israel

The first ruler of the northern kingdom is Jeroboam. He prevents his people worshipping in Jerusalem by building rival sanctuaries at Dan (in the north) and Beersheba (in the south). He sets up calf idols and claims that they are Israel's true gods.

Israel has a succession of kings, of whom the greatest is Omri. He establishes Samaria as a strong capital. He also marries his son, Ahab, to a Phoenician princess called Jezebel. Jezebel introduces worship of the Baal-god Melkart as a major religion in Israel and has many of God's prophets killed.

Jezebel is opposed by the prophet Elijah. Elijah predicts a long drought (the Baals are supposed to send rain) and defeats the Baal prophets in a contest at Mount Carmel. Elijah is succeeded by Elisha, whose ministry includes the extraordinary healing of Naaman, an enemy commander, from leprosy. The evil reign of Ahab is ended by Jehu. Jehu establishes Israel's longest dynasty, lasting almost 100 years.

During the 9th century BC, Israel's powerful neighbour is Syria, with her capital Damascus. Syria takes territory from a weak Israel, until she herself is invaded by Assyria (803 BC).

Jehu's grandson is Jeroboam II (about 841–753 BC). He is able to recapture lost ground and restore Israel's borders. During his reign Israel becomes secure and prosperous. There are signs of religious enthusiasm, too, as pilgrims journey to worship at sanctuaries such as Bethel and Gilgal.

A prophet arrives from the south with a revolutionary message. He is Amos, a shepherd, and he condemns both the wealth and the worship of Israel. It is wealth which is made by exploiting the poor. It is worship which makes no difference to an immoral and unjust society.

Another prophet, Hosea, likens Israel to an unfaithful wife. She plays the whore with other gods. Hosea should know, as this is the story of his own marriage. Both Hosea and God long to win back their loved ones.

The last thirty years of the northern kingdom are overshadowed by the threat of the powerful Assyrian empire. Both Ahab and Jehu pay tribute to prevent Assyria invading, as does a later king, Menahem.

In 735 BC Israel forms an alliance with Syria against Assyria. Together, they invade Judah, which in turn calls on Assyria for help. The Assyrian emperor, Tiglath-Pileser, conquers Syria and cripples Israel. Israel's capital, Samaria, attempts a further rebellion and is besieged. After a three-year siege Samaria is captured by the new Assyrian king, Shalmaneser V.

This is the end of the northern kingdom. Amos had predicted such a fate as God's punishment for Israel's unfaithfulness. The people of Israel are deported and replaced by a mixture of Syrians and Babylonians. This new population, so mixed in race and religion, will become the Samaritans.

The southern kingdom of Judah

When the nation splits, Judah keeps the capital city of Jerusalem, with its temple and priesthood. Judah's kings are the royal line descending from David. These factors give the people of the southern kingdom a great sense of security, because they believe that God will always protect his temple and his king. The truth is that Judah is poor and unattractive to a conqueror.

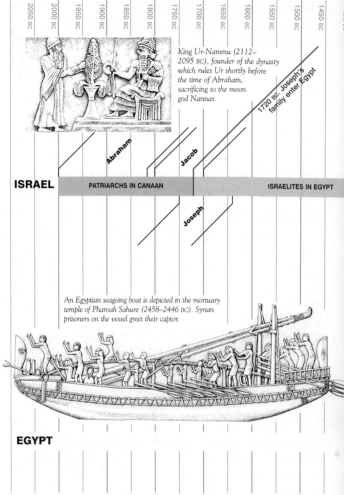

King Ur-Nammu (2112–2095 BC), founder of the dynasty which rules Ur shortly before the time of Abraham, sacrificing to the moon god Nannar.

1720 BC: Joseph's family enter Egypt

Abraham

Jacob

ISRAEL · PATRIARCHS IN CANAAN · ISRAELITES IN EGYPT

Joseph

An Egyptian seagoing boat is depicted in the mortuary temple of Pharoah Sahure (2458–2446 BC). Syrian prisoners on the vessel greet their captor.

EGYPT

During the 8th century BC, Judah's most successful king is Uzziah. He reigns for fifty-two years, and is able to strengthen Judah's defences and fortify Jerusalem. Judah gains prosperity and confidence at this time. In the uncertainty which follows Uzziah's death, the prophet Isaiah has a magnificent vision of Judah's true king, the Holy One of Israel (Isaiah 6).

After the fall of the northern kingdom, the southern kingdom continues for 135 years.

Judah is blessed with a good king in Hezekiah. He restores the temple and purges the nation of idols. The leading prophets at this time are Isaiah and Micah, both of whom live in Jerusalem.

Judah is a small country, overshadowed by Assyria to the north and Egypt to the south. Isaiah and Micah advise King Hezekiah to stay neutral and rely on God;

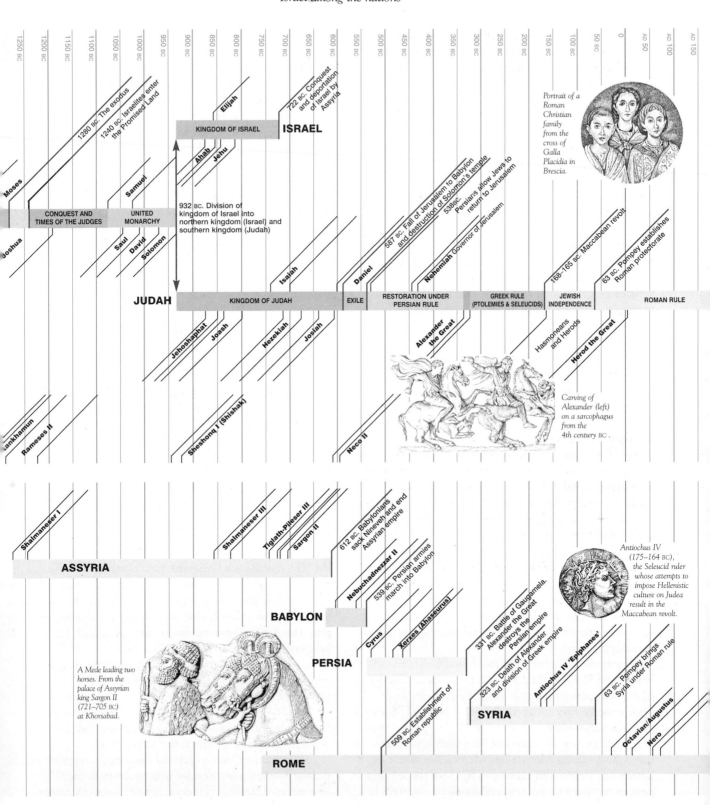

Timeline scale (top): 1250 BC · 1200 BC · 1150 BC · 1100 BC · 1050 BC · 1000 BC · 950 BC · 900 BC · 850 BC · 800 BC · 750 BC · 700 BC · 650 BC · 600 BC · 550 BC · 500 BC · 450 BC · 400 BC · 350 BC · 300 BC · 250 BC · 200 BC · 150 BC · 100 BC · 50 BC · 0 · AD 50 · AD 100 · AD 150

1280 BC. The exodus

1240 BC. Israelites enter the Promised Land

Elijah

KINGDOM OF ISRAEL   **ISRAEL**

722 BC. Conquest and deportation of Israel by Assyria

Ahab   Jehu

Moses

Samuel

Joshua

Saul   David   Solomon

CONQUEST AND TIMES OF THE JUDGES   UNITED MONARCHY

932 BC. Division of kingdom of Israel into northern kingdom (Israel) and southern kingdom (Judah)

Isaiah

Daniel

587 BC. Fall of Jerusalem to Babylon and destruction of Solomon's temple

538BC. Persians allow Jews to return to Jerusalem

Nehemiah Governor of Jerusalem

168–165 BC. Maccabean revolt

63 BC. Pompey establishes Roman protectorate

JUDAH   KINGDOM OF JUDAH   EXILE   RESTORATION UNDER PERSIAN RULE   GREEK RULE (PTOLEMIES & SELEUCIDS)   JEWISH INDEPENDENCE   ROMAN RULE

Jehoshaphat   Joash   Hezekiah   Josiah

Alexander the Great

Hasmoneans and Herods

Herod the Great

Sheshonq I (Shishak)

Neco II

Tutankhamun   Rameses II

Portrait of a Roman Christian family from the cross of Galla Placidia in Brescia.

Carving of Alexander (left) on a sarcophagus from the 4th century BC.

Shalmaneser I

Shalmaneser III   Tiglath-Pileser III   Sargon II

612 BC. Babylonians sack Nineveh and end Assyrian empire

ASSYRIA

Nebuchadnezzar II

539 BC. Persian armies march into Babylon

BABYLON

Cyrus   Xerxes (Ahasuerus)

331 BC. Battle of Gaugamela. Alexander the Great destroys the Persian empire

323 BC. Death of Alexander and division of Greek empire

Antiochus IV (175–164 BC), the Seleucid ruler whose attempts to impose Hellenistic culture on Judea result in the Maccabean revolt.

PERSIA

A Mede leading two horses. From the palace of Assyrian king Sargon II (721–705 BC) at Khorsabad.

Antiochus IV 'Epiphanes'

63 BC. Pompey brings Syria under Roman rule

SYRIA

509 BC. Establishment of Roman republic

Octavian/Augustus   Nero

ROME

but the king pays tribute to appease Assyria and considers a rebellion in alliance with Egypt.

In 701 BC the Assyrian king, Sennacherib, besieges Jerusalem. The city is saved by a miracle when the Assyrian army is stricken by plague. Isaiah's advice was proved to be correct.

Hezekiah is succeeded by his son, Manasseh. He is an evil king who reintroduces the Baal-gods and other occult practices.

Manasseh's grandson is Josiah, who is only eight years old when he becomes king. When he comes of age, Josiah turns his nation to God once again. Zephaniah is prophesying at this time, and in 627 BC the young Jeremiah is also called to be a prophet.

During repairs to the temple, in 622 BC, the Book of the Law is found. This may be a copy of Deuteronomy. Josiah has it read aloud in public. He then leads his people in renewing their covenant with God, destroying pagan idols throughout the land and celebrating the Passover in Jerusalem.

Meanwhile, Jeremiah is certain that Judah is about to fall. This will be God's judgment, despite the reforms of recent years. Another prophet, Habakkuk, receives the astonishing message that God will use the power of Babylon to punish Judah.

To most people the destruction of Jerusalem and the temple is unthinkable. God will never allow it to happen. When King Jehoiakim has a scroll of Jeremiah's prophecies read to him, he shreds it into a fire, piece by piece.

In 616 BC the international scene undergoes a major change. The Babylonians invade Assyria and, in 612 BC, destroy her capital, Nineveh. A story about the prophet Jonah describes Nineveh repenting; but another prophet, Nahum, rejoices at her downfall.

In 609 BC Pharaoh Neco of Egypt tries to assist Assyria against the Babylonians. He is defeated and killed at the Battle of Carchemish on the River Euphrates. So Babylon becomes the reigning superpower in the region.

The book of Daniel describes how Daniel, an exiled Jew who remains faithful to God, becomes a valued adviser to successive pagan kings. His bravery and wisdom make him a role model for all persecuted Jews in future generations.

In 597 BC, on the orders of King Nebuchadnezzar, the Babylonian armies capture Jerusalem. They take King Jehoiachin (Jehoiakim's son) and 3,000 of the leading citizens as prisoners into exile. Among the captives is a young priest who will also become a prophet. His name is Ezekiel.

Ezekiel shares the years of exile with God's people, confronting them with the reality of God's holiness and judgment. He has a vision that the Lord, the God of Israel, is with them even in Babylon. He also sees God's glory depart from the temple and the total destruction of Jerusalem. This comes about in 587 BC.

Once the worst has happened, Ezekiel begins to deliver prophecies of renewal and hope. One day God will give his people new, obedient hearts. They will be restored to a new covenant relationship, a new Jerusalem and a perfect temple.

Jeremiah, in Jerusalem, preaches the unpopular message that this disaster is God's judgment. He also predicts a return from exile one day, and buys a plot of land in Jerusalem as a sign of hope for the future. He writes to the exiles to warn them that they will be in Babylon for some time. They are to settle down and seek to be a blessing to their oppressors.

When Jerusalem is destroyed and its population deported, Jeremiah stays behind with the survivors. They even seek refuge in Egypt, which is the last place someone like Jeremiah would ever want to go. His 'Lamentations' describe his grief at the destruction of Jerusalem.

THE RETURN FROM EXILE

The exiles are held captive in Babylon for fifty years. At the end of this time a new power arises: that of Persia. In 559 BC a brilliant military leader becomes king. He is Cyrus II. In 550 BC he conquers the armies of Media, and becomes emperor of the Medes and Persians.

God uses Cyrus to defeat the Babylonians and release the Jews. Isaiah calls Cyrus the Lord's 'anointed' – the word which signifies a chosen ruler or 'christ' (Isaiah 42:1).

In 539 BC the Persians take King Belshazzar by surprise and capture Babylon. Cyrus is quick to issue decrees of liberation for the Jews and other subject nations. He believes in and encourages religious freedom. The Jews are free to return to Jerusalem and rebuild the temple.

The Jews return to Jerusalem in stages and over a number of years. The precise sequence is not entirely clear.

The first and main group is led by Zerubbabel, who is the grandson of King Jehoiachin. He leaves Babylon in 537 BC. With him is Joshua, the high priest.

The returnees start to rebuild the temple, but progress is slow. Resources are slender, opposition from the Samaritans is fierce and morale is low. The work comes to a standstill until 520 BC, when the prophets Haggai and Zechariah encourage a fresh start. The new temple (a poor replacement for the first) is completed by 515 BC – seventy years after Solomon's temple was destroyed.

The little community continues to struggle until further help arrives. In 445 BC Nehemiah comes to Jerusalem with the permission of King Artaxerxes to rebuild the walls. Nehemiah is an excellent organizer and the task is completed in fifty-two days, despite some very unpleasant opposition. After nearly 150 years, Jerusalem becomes a fortified city once again.

At some other point (perhaps 458 BC) Ezra brings another group of returning exiles. Ezra is both a priest and a scribe. He is also an expert in the law of Moses.

Ezra leads the Jerusalem community in an act of repentance and renewal of the covenant. He teaches God's law and establishes a regime of strict obedience to it. A particular concern is the forbidding of marriage to people outside the Jewish community.

The prophecy of Malachi may belong to this time. He too is concerned with mixed marriages, as well as the payment of tithes and the offering of worthy sacrifices.

At this point the Old Testament history ends. There is a silence of 400 years until the New Testament begins.

God's story

The Old Testament is more than a history of Israel. It is the story of God's revelation of himself.

FAR OFF AND CLOSE

God is the supreme creator. He is holy, 'above' and separate from his creation. And yet he is most intimately aware of, and concerned about, every detail of life. He loves genuine worship. He is angered by injustice and corruption. He looks for faithful relationships, honest trading, protection for the weak and generosity to the poor.

SEEN IN ACTION

God cares deeply about how a nation and its individuals behave. He holds people responsible for their actions. He promises to bless obedience and punish wickedness. The Old Testament stories show God in action: in compassion and rescue, anger and punishment, judgment, mercy and renewal. God is ultimately committed to forgiving, restoring and recreating all things.

REIGNING SUPREME

The Lord reigns over all. He is the creator of the universe and the Lord of history. Even Israel's formidable enemies and conquerors, the tyrants of Egypt, Assyria, Babylon and Persia, are God's subjects. He uses them to fulfil his great purposes.

FAITHFUL WITH THE FAITHFUL

God loves to work with humble and responsive people. Abraham, Moses and David are the great examples.

Abraham dies without seeing the multitude of his descendants or possessing his land. Moses is not allowed to enter the Promised Land, nor David to build the temple. All leave 'unfinished business', yet their lives are completed by faith. God treated them as friends and gave them honoured places in his plan.

And the story continues. The Old Testament promises that Abraham's 'seed' will bless the world; a prophet 'like Moses' will appear one day; and a king 'like David' will rule over everything in the end.

The New Testament story

The New Testament tells how God sends his Son, Jesus, to be born into the nation of Israel. Jesus shows God's total commitment to defeat evil and win the world to his love. This commitment is expressed by 'incarnation' – God actually becoming a human being.

Jesus shows what God is like, by his teaching, healing and power to overcome evil. He gives his life as a sacrifice for the sins of the world, by dying on a cross. He is raised from death by God, as a sign that sin is forgiven and death is conquered. Jesus' followers are filled with his Spirit and take the good news of his victory to other parts of the world.

While the story of the Old Testament covers thousands of years, the story of the New Testament covers less than a century. The New Testament begins with the birth of Jesus and ends with his promise, in the book of Revelation, that he will return 'soon'.

The New Testament, like the Old, is a collection of books. There are four accounts of Jesus' life (the Gospels), a record of the life and mission of the early church (the Acts of the Apostles) and some letters written by Paul and others. The New Testament ends with the 'Apocalypse', or book of Revelation.

The four Gospels

The story of Jesus is told in four Gospels. In the early years of the church, they were known simply as 'the gospel'.

Three of the Gospels are similar – those of Matthew, Mark and Luke. Because they follow the same storyline and contain some of the same material, they are called the 'Synoptic' Gospels. The fourth Gospel is named after John. This Gospel is arranged around a series of 'signs' that Jesus did, with teaching and commentary in the form of lengthy discourses.

'Gospel' means 'good news'. Whether preached or written, the gospel proclaims the life, death and resurrection of Jesus. The purpose of a Gospel is that people may hear about Jesus Christ and put their faith in him.

The Gospels are the record of the eyewitness accounts of Jesus. At first the stories about Jesus were passed on by word of mouth ('oral' tradition). This was a very safe way of communicating his teaching, as Jesus was a rabbi who taught in a rhythmic and colourful style. The Jews especially had well-trained memories, for that was how the law was learned. Jesus also promised his apostles that the Holy Spirit would remind them of his

teaching and lead them into all truth.

When the eyewitnesses of Jesus' resurrection started to die out, it became necessary to collect the stories about Jesus and his teachings and write them down. Such collections were used in the early church for worship, teaching and evangelism. The Gospels included some of these collections. The first Gospel to be written was Mark, in the AD 50s. The Gospels of Matthew and Luke followed, using Mark's outline, but adding material of their own. The last Gospel to be written was John, around AD 90.

Acts

The book of Acts begins with the ascension of Jesus into heaven and the sending of his Holy Spirit upon his apostles.

The Holy Spirit enables the apostles to preach the gospel boldly. A lively, loving community of believers is established in Jerusalem. This is disrupted and dispersed by persecution from the authorities. The result is that the gospel starts to travel to other regions and cultures.

One of the leading persecutors of the church is Saul of Tarsus. He is dramatically converted on the Damascus road, where he encounters the risen Christ. As the apostle Paul, he makes three extensive missionary journeys. He travels to Cyprus and through areas which today are Turkey and Greece. His final journey is to Rome, where he is sent for trial before the emperor. So the book of Acts sees the gospel travel from Jerusalem, the centre of the Jewish religion, to Rome, the capital of the world.

The letters

The New Testament includes twenty-one letters. Most of them are by Paul, while others bear the names of Peter, James, Jude and John. A letter 'to the Hebrews' has no author's name.

Paul writes to the churches he has founded in the course of his travels. His letters are vitally important, because they are written before the Gospels. They give us the earliest evidence of the impact of Jesus.

Paul is born a Jew and educated as a Pharisee – someone committed to holy living by keeping God's law. He is also, through his family, a Roman citizen. Paul is not one of the original group of apostles, but has his own life-changing encounter with the risen Christ. He is converted from persecuting the church to preaching the gospel.

Paul brings to the church's mission a combination of physical energy, intellectual brilliance and sheer willpower.

He spends years digesting the implications of Jesus: the consequences of the gospel for Jews and their law, and for Gentiles and their morals. With others, Paul travels and preaches, teaches and writes. He suffers hardship, brutal punishment and imprisonment for his faith.

In his letters, Paul raises issues with the churches, clarifies the gospel and deals with problems. The longest letters begin with Christian doctrine, then give practical application and close with personal messages.

Some of Paul's letters are named after the places where the churches were established: Rome, Corinth, the region of Galatia, Ephesus, Philippi, Colosse and Thessalonica. Others are written to church leaders: Timothy and Titus. One short letter is addressed to Philemon, asking him to be good to a slave. The letters are placed in the New Testament in approximate order of length – not in the order in which they were written!

Revelation

The early church suffered periods of severe persecution. The first letter of Peter was written during the Emperor Nero's persecution of Christians in Rome. The church's tradition is that Paul and Peter were executed at this time – Peter crucified upside down (AD 64–65) and Paul beheaded (AD 67).

A more terrible and widespread persecution occurred during the reign of the Emperor Domitian (AD 81–96). This is the background to the book of Revelation, which brings the New Testament to a close.

In Revelation, John has visions of the cosmic battle which is being waged between God and Satan. These visions are like those of the book of Daniel, which was also written in time of persecution. They form a coded message to believers, that God will give them victory despite all their present troubles.

The victory of Revelation is centred on Jesus, 'the Lamb who was slain'. He is now enthroned in heaven, at the heart of its glorious worship and eternal peace. From heaven will come the New Jerusalem, God's perfect community, where God himself will live for ever among his people.

In conclusion

The New Testament presents us not only with the life, death and resurrection of Jesus, but also with his amazing power to heal disease, challenge legalism, break down social barriers, and conquer death. His gospel of God's love offers a new freedom for Jews and an open invitation to Gentiles.

The New Testament shows us how people come to faith in Jesus from all sorts of backgrounds and in all kinds of circumstance. These believers form Christian communities in which they worship Jesus as Lord, face the challenges of persecution and heresy, and deal with the internal conflicts of pride, disobedience, ignorance and lack of vision. Their priorities are to commit themselves to God and each other in Christian love, to be an influence for good in their society, and to look forward to Christ's return.

Dates

Most dates are approximate. Those which are confirmed by information outside the New Testament are in bold type.

5 BC	*Jesus is born*
4 BC	**The death of Herod the Great**
AD 27	*The death and resurrection of Jesus*
33	*The conversion of Paul*
44	**The death of Herod Agrippa (Acts 12:19–23)**
47–48	*Paul's first missionary journey (Acts 13 and 14)*
49	*The Council of Jerusalem (Acts 15)*
49–52	*Paul's second missionary journey (Acts 15:36 – 18:22)*
52–56	*Paul's third missionary journey (Acts 18:23 – 21:16)*
57	*Paul is arrested in Jerusalem (Acts 21:27 – 23:22)*
60–61	*Paul under house arrest in Rome (Acts 28:14–31)*
64	**The Great Fire of Rome**
67	*Paul is executed*
70	**Jerusalem is destroyed by the Romans**

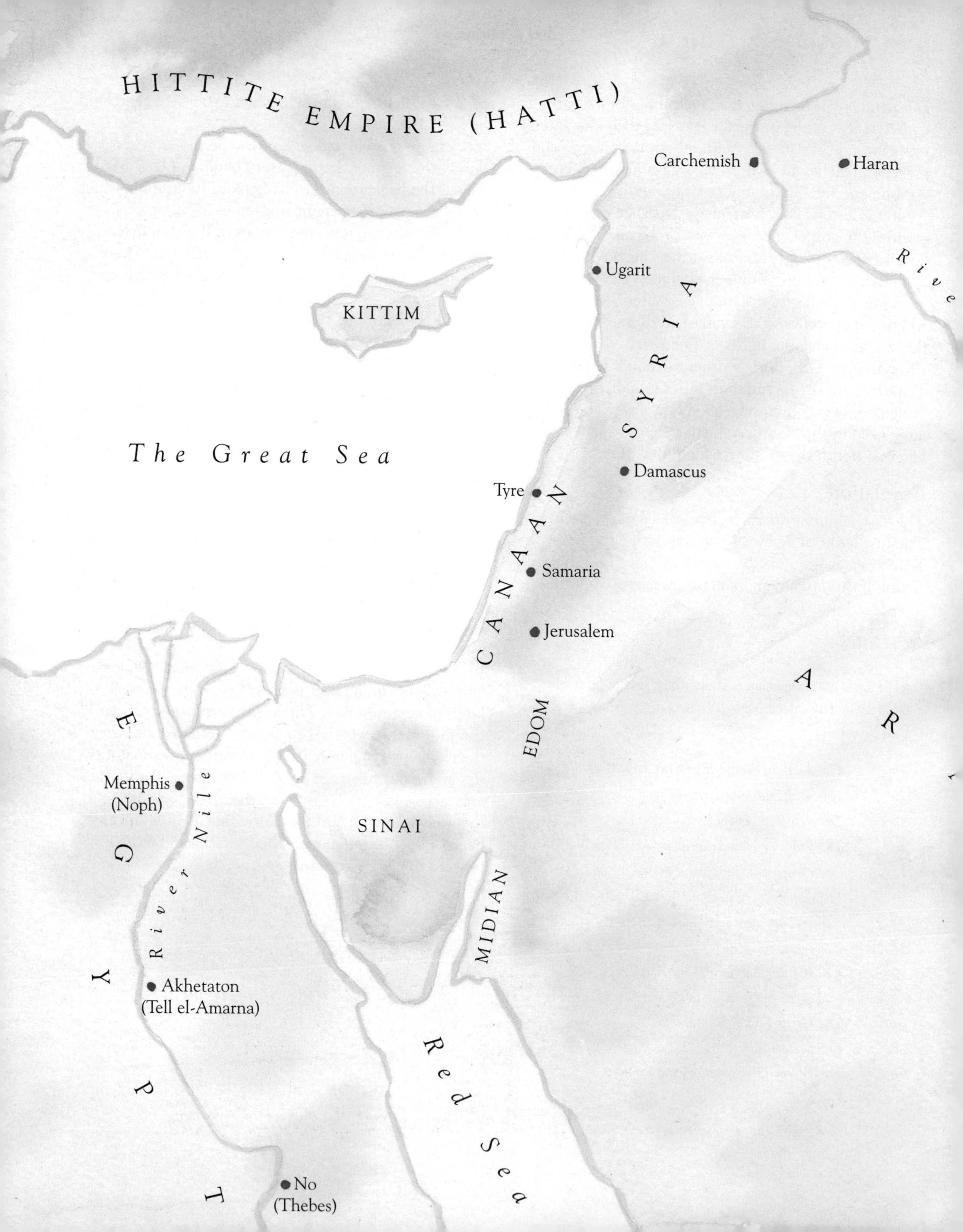

HITTITE EMPIRE (HATTI)

Carchemish ●   ● Haran

● Ugarit

River

KITTIM

S
Y
R
I
A

The Great Sea

Damascus ●

Tyre ●

C
A
N
A
A
N

● Samaria

● Jerusalem

A
R

EDOM

E
G
Y
P
T

Memphis
(Noph) ●

River Nile

SINAI

MIDIAN

● Akhetaton
(Tell el-Amarna)

R
e
d

S
e
a

● No
(Thebes)

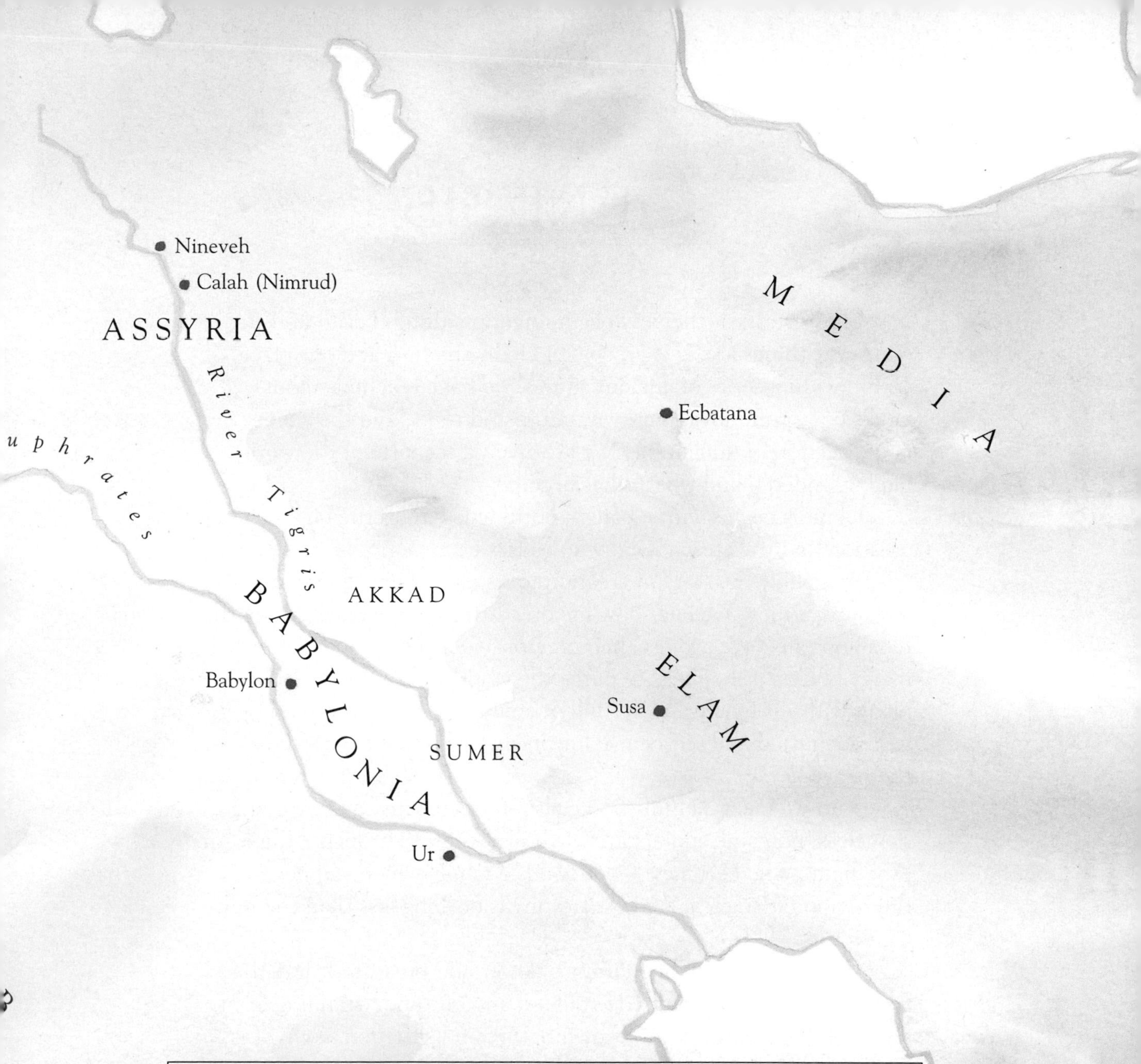

Nineveh

Calah (Nimrud)

ASSYRIA

MEDIA

Ecbatana

River Tigris

Euphrates

AKKAD

ELAM

BABYLON

Babylon

Susa

SUMER

BABYLONIA

Ur

I A

THE OLD TESTAMENT

GENESIS

Genesis starts at the very beginning: how things began and the way things are. It is an epic of God's creation and our place within it. In a series of ancient stories, we have teaching about God's power and love, our own nature and roots, and the shape and direction of human life. We are given a scenario of the world God intended – and what it has become.

Genesis begins with a bang – nothing less than the big bang of creation and the eternal God who causes it.

We follow the story of creation to its climax in the making of the human race. We hear how life on earth is fatally damaged by the rebellion of people against their creator. We meet the judgment and mercy of God as he seeks to purge the world with a flood, but saves Noah with his family and ark full of animals. We see how God deals with the proud and self-centred people who build a tower to reach the heavens…

And we meet Abram. God calls Abram to trust him by living a homeless, nomadic and apparently hopeless life. Through Abram (or 'Abraham' as he becomes) God founds a family which will become the nation of Israel, and whose destiny is nothing less than the new creation.

Genesis is a book of enormous power and breadth. It lays the foundations for our knowledge of God and our understanding of his purpose. It explains to us our own nature and situation – why it is that we are at odds with God, each other and the world around. But Genesis doesn't abandon us to our fate, because it shows us a God who doesn't give up. In Genesis, God embarks on the long and painstaking task of winning people back to the loving, joyful, eternal life he always intended.

Outline

INTRODUCTION

Genesis means 'origin'. It is the glorious account of how things began.

Genesis wasn't the first book ever written – nor is it the oldest part of the Bible. But when the Bible was put together, this book had an obvious claim to come first.

The book of Genesis is in two parts: ancient stories from the mists of time (1:1 – 11:32) and the stories of the patriarchs (12:1 – 50:26).

Ancient stories from the mists of time

These stories are beautiful in their telling and simple in their teaching. They cover the creation of the world and early human history – but with a difference. They tell the tale from God's point of view.

Genesis is a book about God. It tells us something we can never guess: that there is only one God. He has personality, power and opinion – and he creates to perfection.

The first story tells how God created the universe, stage by stage. He made something from nothing, and brought order out of chaos. Although the story doesn't give scientific details, it describes creation being shaped in a purposeful way. In other words, we're living in a designer universe and not a chance accident.

The universe is not an accident. It was conceived, wanted and brought into existence by God. He originated the design, generated the power and executed the production. And he worked it all from nothing.

As the story of Genesis unfolds, we see God's heartfelt love for the people he has made. Human beings are the crown of his creation. We are made to show the world what God is like: God said, 'Let us make humankind in our image, according to our likeness; and let them have dominion... over all the earth' (1:26).

So the story of creation leads into the story of the first humans: Adam and Eve. The couple are made for each other and can commune with God. They are set in a perfect environment, the Garden of Eden. They are different from the rest of creation, because they alone are 'the image' of God. They can influence the world around them, and are given the mandate to govern it.

God's intention is that human beings should enjoy his creation and care for it, wisely managing its resources and tending its species. God gives men and women, uniquely in all creation, a mind and will of their own. But Adam and Eve use their free will to defy God. Human beings have independence of choice, and the freedom even to reject God's love. When Adam and Eve, the first couple, disobey God's instruction, the entire creation is tragically spoiled. This moment is called 'the fall'. They are expelled from the Garden. Their life becomes one of hard work, sorrow, discomfort, conflict and death. Because they disobey God, they lose their hope of eternal life.

From humanity's fall onwards, Genesis is the story of a dreadful falling-out. All the relationships are damaged and distorted – between God and humanity, between humanity and creation, between partners, siblings, families, communities and nations. God intervenes to punish people and correct situations. His love, justice and desire to help are always evident. He makes himself known, guides those who turn to him and shapes the course of history. But, by the end of the book, the situation is in no way resolved. Already the world needs a Saviour.

The story of the first human beings is followed by that of the first murder. Adam and Eve have two sons, Cain and Abel. Cain is jealous of Abel and kills him – only to be challenged and condemned by God. Cain becomes an outcast, bearing for ever his burden of guilt. This story shows how easily jealousy leads to murder. But human life is precious to God – and he holds us responsible for our actions.

Then comes the longer story of Noah and the flood. God decides to drown the corrupt and sinful world and start again. He warns Noah of a coming flood, and commands him to build a huge wooden vessel – the ark. Noah builds the ark with the help of his sons, and they take refuge from the flood. With them are their wives, and a large assortment of animals in breeding pairs. This story describes how God passes judgment on the corruption of the world, but spares just one faithful man and his family. It closes with God promising a safe and reliable world in the future, and signing his word with a rainbow.

The last of these ancient tales is of the tower of Babel. It dates from the founding of communities and the development of building skills. One such community attempts to build a tower to reach the heavens, to establish its prestige and permanence. But God judges their pride, confuses their language and scatters them far and wide. It's a story against the Jews' old enemy, Babylon ('babble town'!). It reminds us of our human littleness and futility. And it tells, in a quaint but astute way, how different nations and languages came to be.

Genesis contains a sparkling collection of stories. These stories teach us that God loves us as children but treats us as adults. Our disobedience hurts him and provokes his anger. But, even as he judges us, he softens his sentence with mercy. But Genesis is more than just stories. Here is food for thought to engage the finest minds. How did the universe come to exist? Was it by accident or design? And how can we understand ourselves within it? Are we up-market apes or low-grade angels?

Genesis answers questions like this with a bold presentation of God, in all his power and holiness, justice and love. It holds up God's world like a mirror, so we can see ourselves in all our dignity and deviousness.

The stories of Adam and Eve and Cain and Abel probe the deepest recesses of our nature. They expose the shabbiness of our motives and the poverty of our love. Greed and jealousy, anger and guilt are the driving forces of our lives. The account of creation, with God commissioning humanity to care for planet earth, takes us to the heart of the debate about conservation and our present ecological crisis. It is only for love of God – and with his help – that we can change our ways and reverse

Favourite stories

In the Bible's top-ten stories, Genesis must supply half the favourites. The creation, Adam and Eve, Noah's ark, the tower of Babel, Jacob's ladder and Joseph's coat all jostle for attention. This one book has inspired the imagination of painters, poets, playwrights and producers in every age. Milton's epic poem 'Paradise Lost', Michelangelo's majestic portrayal of 'The Creation of Adam' on the ceiling of the Sistine Chapel, and the fun-filled productions of 'Joseph and the Amazing Technicolor Dreamcoat' in theatres around the world bear witness to the power and fascination of these ancient tales. And what children's store is complete without a whole range of posters, toys and story books depicting Noah's ark?

the exploitation and pollution which is plunging us towards extinction.

The stories of the patriarchs

The patriarchs are the founding fathers – the ancestors of the Jewish race and the pioneers of their faith.

The first of them is Abram, who becomes Abraham, 'the Father of Nations'. God calls one man, Abram, to live a life of faith. God promises him a multitude of descendants and a land of his own. The idea of a chosen race (Israel) in a Promised Land (Canaan) is born.

Genesis is a source book for three of the world's great religions. Jews, Muslims and Christians all look back to Abraham as their ancestor.

With Abraham a tender seed of faith is planted. From this seed will grow a family and a nation to which God will always be committed. Eventually, and despite many failures, setbacks and betrayals, this nation will be the people who receive God's Son, the Messiah.

After Abraham come his sons Isaac and Ishmael. Some people trace the hostility between Israeli and Arab to the rivalry between Isaac and Ishmael. Today's bloody disputes over territory spring from God's promise of a land for his people.

Then come Abraham's grandsons Esau and Jacob. Esau and Jacob are twins, with Esau the elder. In theory, it is Esau who should inherit the special relationship with God, but in fact this falls to the devious and self-seeking Jacob. After many adventures, Jacob becomes 'Israel' – a

Genesis ends with Joseph in Egypt, where he occupies a position of great authority.

name of strenuous defiance meaning 'He Struggles with God'. With the help of two wives and two maidservants, Jacob has twelve sons. They are the forefathers of the twelve tribes which later make up the nation of Israel.

Jacob's favourite son is Joseph. Joseph is a spoilt brat who dreams of lording it over his family. Sold into slavery by his jealous brothers, he ends up in prison in Egypt. But, thanks to his gift for interpreting dreams, he emerges to become Egypt's prime minister.

Not only does Joseph correctly forecast years of famine, but he takes charge of the operation to store and ration food. When his brothers come from Canaan to get grain, Joseph is in the very position of dominance he had predicted! But Joseph's pride has been softened through his sufferings, and he greets his brothers with tears – and a gracious explanation of events.

The story of Genesis draws to a close with Jacob and his family moving to Egypt. They survive the famine, but are a long way from the Promised Land. Rather eerily, the book ends with the death of Joseph and the closing of his coffin – as if the promises of God have gone to ground and passed from sight.

The story of Joseph helps us prepare for the story of Jesus. Jesus, too, was rejected by his own people and put to death. But God raised him to glory, to bring deliverance and forgiveness to all.

Who wrote the book of Genesis?

For many centuries it was assumed that Moses wrote the book of Genesis. He is the main character in four of the first five books of the Bible, which are known as the 'books of Moses'. He also has the Hebrew background and Egyptian education to enable him to write them.

We read of Moses writing down God's laws and keeping a record of Israel's journey from Egypt to Canaan.

Some of the stories in Genesis are very old, and must have been passed from parents to children for many generations before they were collected or written down. Again, Moses was the sort of person who could have gathered and edited them. If it wasn't Moses, then

we don't know who shaped and organized this material. Whoever it was, the result is a flowing story of God's people and a clear picture of God's purpose for them.

DISCOVERING GENESIS

Ancient stories from the mists of time

The story of creation
(1:1 – 2:3)

The Bible, and the story of creation, begins with God.

We cannot see God, for he is spirit. But we can *know* God by his actions – just as our own character is revealed by our behaviour.

The words 'in the beginning' (1:1) tell us straight away that God is embarking on a project which he will develop, sustain and bring to completion. It is a vast project – nothing less than the creation of 'the heavens and the earth', the universe.

The earth is 'formless' (1:2) and God gives it shape and meaning. It is 'empty' and he starts to fill it. It is dark and he commands light.

As we wonder whether it is right to call God 'he', the writer introduces the Spirit of God. The Spirit hovers over the waters, attentive, thoughtful and poised for action. The picture is more like a mother bird tending her chicks than an old man in the sky.

There is nothing remote or detached about the way God works. He is a 'hands-on' creator, keenly committed to this marvellous work, absorbed in concentration and fizzing with enthusiasm. His Spirit moves to shape the chaos, fill the void, lighten the darkness and bring a universe to life.

'Let there be light,' says God (1:3), and his words have power to bring light into existence. As the story unfolds, we see that God's word is his deed. When God speaks, it happens.

Centuries later, the Gospel of John begins with an echo of Genesis. Speaking about Jesus Christ, the Gospel introduces him as 'the Word' of God: 'In the beginning was the Word, and the Word was with God, and the Word was God… Through him all things were made…' (John 1:1–3).

In a few sentences, we are introduced to God, his Spirit and his word. We have a matter-of-fact statement that the universe was made by God, with the kind of power that turns nothing to something, and darkness to light. As the Bible story unfolds, we will discover God as the one who makes everything new, even forgiving sins, healing sickness and bringing the dead to life.

WHAT A DIFFERENCE A 'DAY' MAKES!

Science has revealed that the universe was formed over a period of billions of years. The book of Genesis seems to simplify the entire process into a single week! However, there's no need to dismiss the creation story just because it is told in 'days'. It is the shrinking of the timescales that enables our limited minds to handle the immense scope of God's achievement.

Did God make the universe in six days?

Some people say that the story of creation is scientifically true, and that God really did create the universe in six days. Others dismiss both the story and God as flights of fancy. This is an argument that should never have happened!

We must be careful not to make the Genesis story something it isn't. It isn't a scientific account of physics, cosmology and biology. It is a statement that 'God did it all – and it was very good'.

The simplicity and sequence of the creation story is impressive. The bursting forth of light is followed by water and space, land and seas. Then come plants, animals and humans. The cosmos emerges from chaos in an ordered way. The text provides an excellent screenplay. Through the eye of an earthbound camera we watch the panorama of events – including the realistic detail of the sun, moon and stars appearing through water vapour and smoke on the 'fourth day'.

The modern physicist sees more clearly than anyone that the universe is positively designed for living. If gravity were stronger, stars would burn out too quickly for life to evolve on their planets. If protons and neutrons were different by even a fraction, there could be no hydrogen, no stars – and you would not be reading this. It takes a lot of faith to say that all this is a meaningless accident.

Genesis gives us the big picture of God and his creation – without losing us in the infinities of light years and the abstractions of particle physics. Science can stun us with statistics, or bury us in facts, but leave us no wiser about God.

It's good to have the Bible's unique perspective on the universe – that it is God-made and God-given. Genesis deals with the mighty process in a single chapter – and gets on to the main business of God's purpose for humankind.

In recent years it has been popular to compare the history of the world to an hour, with human life occurring only in the closing seconds. Such a timescale puts us in our place as a brief and fleeting species – 'last in and first out'.

The Bible's view is quite the opposite. The book of Genesis gives just a few seconds to the countless aeons of prehistory, and devotes the rest of its pages to God and us. We learn that human beings are not a chance and feeble speck, but the summit of God's creation and the key to his purpose.

THEN GOD SAID, 'LET US MAKE HUMANKIND IN OUR IMAGE...'

Our modern knowledge provides us with many images of primitive people. We discover them as ape-like creatures which gradually become more resourceful, sociable and physically upright. Increasingly, like ourselves, they hunt, live in caves, make tools, paint walls, erect landmarks and bury their dead.

Genesis describes God creating human beings 'in his own image'. The emphasis is not on men and women being ape-like, but how *like God* they are. Humankind, in mint condition, is a divine hologram. Because of sin, the image of God is now spoilt. But we can still detect traces of God's likeness – in our creativity, decision-making, compassion, love of company and sense of humour.

'MALE AND FEMALE HE CREATED THEM'

The division into 'male and female' comes after the basic creation of 'humankind'. God makes human beings for

The Creation of Heaven and Earth from the Chaos; mosaic (12th–13th century AD), Monreale Cathedral, Sicily.

'one-anotherness' – and this, too, is a glimpse of God himself. There is a one-anotherness in God, when he says 'Let us make...' God, his Spirit and his Word are all introduced in the opening sentences of Genesis.

As the Bible's teaching unfolds, we will see the emergence of the three-in-one description of God. He is 'Father, Son and Holy Spirit'. We will hear of the love *within* God, and the longing of Jesus that human beings should share it: 'That all of them may be one, Father, just as you are in me and I am in you. May they also be in us...' (John 17:21).

'GOD BLESSED THEM...'

God gives human beings the unique responsibility of ruling the earth and its creatures. Everything is given for discovery, enjoyment and satisfaction – although it seems, at this stage, that the menu is strictly vegetarian!

As God completes the heavens and the earth, his verdict is that it is 'very good' (1:31). And if God is perfect and his judgment true, it must have been very good indeed.

'ON THE SEVENTH DAY [GOD] RESTED FROM ALL HIS WORK'

God stops work, not because he is tired, but because he has finished (2:2). The result is a universe full of infinite variety and yet completely integrated. 'God blessed the seventh day and made it holy, because on it he rested...' (2:3). The seventh day becomes the 'sabbath', from the Hebrew word for 'ceased'. In years to come a commandment will declare it a day of rest for men and women, families, households and animals. By blessing the day, God invites the whole of creation to share his satisfaction and enjoy his peace.

Jews keep Saturday as their day of rest, their sabbath, while Christians have merged it with Sunday – the day of Christ's resurrection. Taken seriously, with joy and imagination, it is the perfect antidote to the rat race of modern life.

Of course, God's work of maintaining and renewing

the creation continues, irrespective of the sabbath. 'My Father is always at his work to this very day,' says Jesus, when criticized for healing an invalid on that day (John 5:17). Without God's authority, attention and sustaining love, the universe would revert to chaos.

Adam and Eve
(2:4–25)

The Lord God forms human beings from the dust of the ground – the same material he has used for the plants and animals. But to humanity he gives the special dimension of relationship. From the beginning humankind is 'a living being' – a seamless body–soul. A person, wanted and loved.

God sets man in the Garden of Eden. Eden means 'delight', and 'Garden' has a sense of spaciousness, pleasure and peace. Rivers flow from Eden to water the world around. This lovely place is somewhere north of today's Persian Gulf, in an area known as the 'Fertile Crescent'.

At the centre of the Garden are two trees – one the tree of life and the other the tree of the knowledge of good and evil. God gives the human beings the fruit of all the trees, except these two. If they take fruit from the forbidden trees, they will forfeit the life-sustaining love of God. They will die.

Why does God forbid human beings the fruit of the trees of life, and the knowledge of good and evil? Is he afraid that they will get above themselves and start to experiment with test-tube babies and deep-frozen corpses? Is he worried that they will see through God, call his bluff and hijack his world?

Although human beings have conquered the world, split the atom and landed on the moon, we have only the merest glimmer of God's creativity and wisdom. The 'trees' in this story are a test of whether we will accept God's authority. Will we accept that God's limits are for our good?

'THE LORD GOD FORMED MAN...'

The more we discover and understand about the human body, the more amazing it seems. Eye and foot, tongue and brain, fingerprint and eardrum are all uniquely formed and coordinated. And what about imagination, reason, passion, laughter and self-awareness? 'I am fearfully and wonderfully made,' says the writer of one of the psalms.

As Genesis tells the story, the first man gives names to all his fellow creatures. He has the care of them; but none of them is his equal. So God makes a woman for the man as he sleeps. When he wakes, the man recognizes his 'other half'. At last he can name someone after himself:

The Fall from Grace; detail from the Verdun Altar (AD 1181) by Nicholas of Verdun. Champlevé enamel on gilded copper.

This is now bone of my bones and flesh of my flesh; she shall be called 'woman', for she was taken out of man (2:23).

'FOR THIS REASON...'

The partnership of a man and his wife is not to be split by any other loyalty – not even to parents. Father and mother are excluded as a new creation takes place: husband and wife become 'one flesh', one new 'self' in marriage.

The man and the woman belong together and complete each other. They're different, but they match. Their bodies fit. Heart to heart, they correspond. They are at ease with each other. They aren't embarrassed or self-conscious about their bodies. They are comfortable in their one-anotherness. Sadly, it is not to last.

The fall
(3:1–24)

Enter the serpent – crafty and critical. He is a picture of the devil, Satan, who seeks to spoil God's relationship with humankind. He raises questions in the woman's mind. What did God *actually* say? And to what extent did he really mean it? Surely God is keeping a few privileges for himself! He doesn't want human beings becoming too enlightened. And so the most damaging idea is born: that God is somehow against humanity. He doesn't want any competition.

The woman's eyes and imagination (and hands and mouth) do the rest. She eats the fruit and shares it with

The tragedy of sin

In the New Testament, Paul points out that 'it was the woman who was deceived' – as though the man, left to himself, would have known better. If he did know better, then his disobedience was all the more wilful. He defied God with the full intent of a clear head and a rebellious heart.

Jesus takes this story to be about the reason we die. We are all sinful, because we share Adam's rebellious nature. It is a story about the tragedy of sin – and the spiritual deadness which results from it. It was this kind of death (a complete inability to respond to God) that Jesus Christ came to defeat.

Think of a deadly virus, easily caught and incurable. Originally it came from just one person, Adam, but it has spread throughout the world.

The Bible sees sin in a similar way. It came from a single act of disobedience and has contaminated the entire human race. Paul says there are no exceptions, for 'All have sinned and fall short of the glory of God' (Romans 3:23).

Jesus came to deal with the deadly virus of sin, and restore us to spiritual life. From one person, Jesus Christ, eternal life is spreading to the whole of creation. For this reason Jesus is sometimes called 'the Second Adam'. While the first Adam was the cause of death, Jesus Christ is the source of life: 'For as in Adam all die, so in Christ all will be made alive' (1 Corinthians 15:22).

---

her husband. As the serpent promised, their eyes are opened – to see each other naked and ashamed. Their security vanishes; so does their trust in each other. They try to cover up with leaves. When God comes calling, they hide from him. They lie to him. They blame each other – and the serpent.

God deals with each in turn. He questions the man first and then the woman. The man is defiant. As far as he's concerned, it was God who gave him the woman and the woman who gave him the fruit. His only fault had been to eat what was put in front of him. The woman blames the serpent. She explains she's been cunningly tricked.

God curses the serpent. From now on his place will be in the dust. He will be for ever at odds with humankind. God forecasts that the woman's offspring will crush his head – a prediction that will be fulfilled when Christ inflicts crushing defeat on Satan.

To the woman, God says that childbirth will be painful and marriage will become a power struggle. She will need her husband, and he will rule her.

The fall of humanity spoils the relationship with the rest of creation as well. God says that the very ground is cursed by their disobedience. The easy, gentle partnership of human beings and the world of nature is gone. From now on, if people want to eat, they must scratch a living from the earth, until they die and become part of that earth themselves.

Cain and Abel
(4:1–26)

When Adam and Eve disobey God, they are banished from the Garden of Eden. They become farmers.

Their first son, Cain, is also a farmer. Their second

The first people

Adam and Eve are presented as the first man and woman to be conscious of God and responsive to him. They are the crown of God's creation, and their fall into sin is a tragedy.

But clearly there are other humans around, as the wider world is already populated. Cain in his wanderings finds a wife and founds a city. Soon we read of generations that have the skills to make music and work with bronze and iron.

Putting these clues together, we can date the people of these stories as living between the Neolithic and Bronze Ages – from 6000 to 2500 BC.

It may seem an anticlimax to think of Adam and Eve in a world in which there are already other people. But this doesn't prevent us taking the main point – that God made human beings with individual personalities and sensitive consciences. These people are 'new' in their awareness of themselves, in their responsibility for their actions and in their relationship with God.

son, Abel, is a shepherd. We may detect some rivalry between their two ways of life in their choices of sacrifice. Cain brings a cereal offering, but Abel brings meat. We learn that God prefers Abel's gift.

It isn't that God likes meat rather than grain. The point is that he prefers a cheerful offering to a grudging one. A sacrifice is only pleasing to God if it comes with love.

Abel brings select portions of the first young animals from his flocks – and finds joy in doing so. Cain brings some grain, but his heart is hostile. He is the first person in the Bible to pretend religion – but it gives him no pleasure.

When the phoney sacrifice is rejected, Cain is angry and jealous. God warns him that evil is waiting to invade him. Cain can let jealousy take control and become a murderer, or he can resist it. Either way, God will hold him responsible for his action, and his brother's welfare.

Cain yields to anger and kills Abel. When God asks him where his brother is, Cain snubs him. But God knows what has happened, and is deeply outraged. Not only has the first murder occurred between brothers, but lifeblood has been shed on God's earth. God declares Cain guilty, and curses him with a hard and homeless life. But Cain isn't to be killed in turn. God's way is not to recycle evil, but to contain it, and, whenever he is asked, to forgive.

From Adam to Noah
(5:1 – 6:8)

Genesis lists the ancestors from Adam to Noah, including some remarkably long-lived people:

When Enoch had lived 65 years, he became the father of Methuselah. And after he became the father of Methuselah, Enoch walked with God 300 years and had other sons and daughters. Altogether, Enoch lived

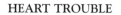

Noah Building the Ark; from the Bedford Hours (c. 1423). Vellum.

365 years. Enoch walked with God; then he was no more, because God took him away (5:21–24).

These astonishing ages (of which Methuselah holds the record at 969) provide plenty of scope for discussion. In those days, great ages were attributed to great people as a mark of honour. It may be that entire branches of a family tree were named after one person. Or perhaps their lifestyle was healthy, their environment unpolluted and their family free of disease. We don't know.

The memory that Enoch didn't die (but 'God took him') reminds us that God never intended death to touch us.

HEART TROUBLE

Humankind is the pits! As God surveys the human race, he finds everyone planning evil all the time (6:5–8). But, while human hearts are full of wickedness, God's heart is full of pain. He alone knows our true glory and the paradise we have lost.

It is because God's heart aches for lost humanity that he will one day send his Son to be our Saviour. Jesus will show, by his suffering and death, exactly what our sin costs God.

Noah and the flood
(6:9 – 9:17)

Noah is a good man in a wicked world. While other people are violent and corrupt, Noah keeps company with God and shares his thoughts. When God resolves to destroy all life with a flood, he makes an exception of Noah. He tells him to make an ark – a giant coffin-like structure, the length of a football field and three storeys high. This is to be a refuge for Noah and his family when the flood of God's judgment comes.

Noah and his three sons build the ark from wood plastered with reeds and waterproofed with tar. It's a magnificent act of faith in a region of little rain and far from the sea. They believe that God will do as he says and spare their family. They hope that life on earth and the knowledge of God will survive through them and be re-established in a clean new world.

When the ark is completed, they stock it with a huge selection of animals and birds and a supply of food. Like Adam before him, Noah seems to have a special affinity with God's creatures, tending animals and handling birds. They come in pairs and board the ark as the storm clouds gather. The story records that the flood begins when Noah is 600 years, two months and seventeen days old. An unforgettable day.

Soon the ark is engulfed in a deluge of water – as though God is throwing creation into reverse, drowning all in a soup of ocean and vapour. Inside the ark, people and animals are buried alive, but safe – a model of God's saving power for every generation to come.

The ark rides the flood for five months, until the waters begin to subside. It finally comes to rest on Mount Ararat. Noah sends first a raven and then a dove to search for land. The raven doesn't return – probably because it finds plenty of floating corpses to live on. But the dove comes back with a freshly picked olive leaf – the very first sign that life will continue and all will be well.

Months later, the land is dry enough for the company to leave the ark. Noah makes sacrifices to God even from among the few animals they have. He is determined to put God first in this brave new world.

And God in turn makes a vow:

I will never again curse the ground because of humankind, for the inclination of the human heart is evil from youth; nor will I ever again destroy every living creature as I have done (8:21).

God promises Noah:

As long as the earth endures,
seedtime and harvest,
cold and heat,
summer and winter,
day and night
will never cease (8:22).

The story of the flood leaves us with many questions. If God wanted to wipe out all corruption, he clearly didn't succeed. But the story conveys the seriousness of sin, the reality of God's judgment and the certainty of his power to save.

In centuries to come, the ark will be a picture of the church. It is a place of safety and deliverance in the midst of a wicked world.

God blesses Noah and his family. They are to repopulate the earth. Sadly, humans and animals will now be afraid of each other. Humans will be meat-eaters, but they must respect blood. Blood is the liquid of life and belongs to God. Human blood is doubly sacred, because humankind is the image of God.

Of course, the people who boarded the ark took with

What about other flood stories?

The early chapters of Genesis are about the people of Mesopotamia – a fertile area where early humans settle and build communities. Mesopotamia means 'between rivers'. It is the fertile land which lies between the great rivers, the Tigris and the Euphrates. To the south is Babylonia, to be known in the future for its power, wealth and pagan pride. Both regions have folk memories of great floods, and stories of the heroes who built vessels and survived. Traces of these floods have been found in the ruins of some of the ancient cities, but nothing as vast and totally devastating as Noah's flood.

In one famous flood story from Babylonia, the hero is a man called Atrahasis. He is at the mercy of a multitude of petty and quarrelsome gods. The gods regard humans as unpleasant and noisy neighbours, and resolve to wipe them out. But then they miss the delicious smell of burnt offerings!

This and other pagan stories, dating from around 3000 BC, show a very different understanding of 'god' and the reasons for flooding. There is nothing about awesome judgment, life-saving faith or the merciful promise that it won't happen again.

The Genesis story tells of one creator-God, who is holy and just. He is determined to save the righteous and punish the wicked. There are various simple details (such as the actual date of the downpour) which a family could have remembered and handed down. It is possible that Noah's story is told to put the record straight about the flood and why it happened.

them their old human nature. Noah's sons and their wives aren't perfect and their experience doesn't change them. Soon the world will be seeded again with selfishness and pride. But God's word stands. All disasters of flood, fire, famine or disease will now be restricted. God will never again destroy the whole world.

THE RAINBOW COVENANT

God gives his word that all natural disasters will now be local and limited (9:1–17). He will never again destroy the whole world. It is a promise to every creature on earth in every place and for all time. This is God's free and generous assurance, which he signs as only he can – with a rainbow.

The spread of nations
(10:1–32)

After the great flood, the world is populated by Noah's sons, Shem, Ham and Japheth. Japheth is the eldest, but Shem is the most important to the Bible story.

JAPHETH

Japheth's descendants spread north of the Fertile Crescent, to the Caspian Sea in the east and the Aegean Sea in the west (10:2–4). They become several nations, some of which will be a threat to Israel in the future. Gomer, Magog, Tubal and Meschech are described by the prophet Ezekiel as warlike nations to the far north (Ezekiel 38:1–6). The Madai are probably the Medes living south of the Caspian Sea. Javan refers to a Greek people beyond the Aegean, and Tiras may be the Etruscans. The names of individual people can become the name of a clan, nation, race or place. It is thought that Ashkenaz becomes the Scythians, the Kittim inhabit Cyprus and the Rodanim live on the island of Rhodes.

HAM

Ham's descendants occupy Canaan and the territories to the south, including parts of Africa and Arabia (10:5–20). They develop as four main groups – Cush, Mizraim, Put and Canaan. The 'sons of Cush' are Ethiopians in Africa, to the west of the Red Sea. Another segment of Cush becomes the Kassite people who (perhaps led by Nimrod) settle far away, east of Assyria beyond the Fertile Crescent. Seba and Sheba are similar peoples who settle on the eastern shore of the Red Sea. With Havilah and Dedan, they occupy part of

Arabia. Mizraim is a plural word which may refer to Upper and Lower Egypt. The Philistines are listed as coming from Egypt, although it is from Crete that they will later invade Palestine (and give it their name). The Caphtorites also come from Crete.

SHEM

Shem's descendants are the Semites or Semitic peoples (10:21–32). Although Japheth is the eldest son, it is Shem who receives a special blessing from Noah (9:26); and it is through Shem that the line of God's promise passes from Adam to Abraham.

It is Shem's son Eber who is the ancestor of Abraham. Abraham is called 'the Hebrew' (14:13) – a name which might come from 'eber' (meaning 'passing through'), or from the word 'habiru' (meaning 'a wandering, insignificant people'). The Bible story now concentrates on these descendants of Shem. They will be the Hebrews who are rescued by God from landless slavery in Egypt, to become his 'chosen race' of Israel, living in the 'Promised Land' of Canaan. Another of Shem's sons is Joktan, who is the ancestor of many Arab races.

Seventy nations spring from the sons of Noah – or seventy-two in the Septuagint (Greek) version of the Old Testament. Although God has special dealings with the descendants of Shem, he has an ultimate purpose for all the nations. His plan is to draw the whole earth into his perfect kingdom and saving love. Jesus echoes God's mission to all nations when he sends out seventy (or seventy-two) disciples to announce that God's kingdom is coming (Luke 10:1).

The tower of Babel
(11:1–32)

This is the last of the ancient folk tales of 'how things began'. It tells of the founding of Babylon, not as a 'gate of heaven', but as a proud and misguided folly.

The story tells of an ambitious community which tries its strength against God. The people want to build a city which will be the centre of the world and a stairway to the sky. Using the very latest construction materials (bricks and tar), they set about building a tower.

God, 'coming down' to investigate, is hardly afraid of their competition. But he is greatly concerned by the emergence of a united, godless society. To confound the project, God confuses the people's language so that they can no longer work together. They are scattered far and wide, leaving the tower half-built.

The name 'Babylon' means 'gate of God'. In the story of the tower, the name is changed to 'Babel', which sounds like the Hebrew word for 'confusion' or 'mixing'.

The ruins of sacred towers have been discovered throughout the area of Mesopotamia. These multi-storey landmarks are called 'ziggurats', and were built more than 2,000 years BC. They have ramps or stairways to enable people to climb to the top and talk with the gods.

The stories of the patriarchs

Abraham
(12:1 – 25:11)

The scene and the tone change. We leave the mists of prehistory to arrive at a particular time and place. We focus on a particular man. His name is Abram.

GOD'S CALL TO ABRAM

Abram lives in a well-established city called Ur. God calls him to leave this comfortable home and venture out on a life of faith (12:1–9). Abram is to receive a new land and found a great nation.

Building the tower of Babel. From Aelfric's *Pentateuch*, an early 11th-century English manuscript. A community plans a landmark to establish its fame. But God opposes the arrogance of the project, and scatters the people by confusing their language.

It is to Abram that God makes the keynote promise that will shape the whole story of God's people. God declares his covenant plan to bless Abram and his descendants. All other nations will be blessed through this nation and judged by their response to its people. Already God has a plan to bless and reunite the races he has scattered from the tower of Babel (11:1–9). Here we glimpse for the first time the good news that God will one day restore the world and bless its peoples.

Abram becomes a nomadic shepherd, seeking to discover God through his experiences. With his wife Sarai and nephew Lot, he travels from Mesopotamia down through Canaan to the Negev desert. At Shechem, the heart of the future 'Promised Land', Abram builds an altar to the Lord, much as astronauts might plant their national flag on the moon.

Shechem is at the crossroads of Palestine. At Shechem the main roads meet – between north and south, east and west. Here stands the great tree of Moreh – perhaps the site of a pagan shrine. And here Abram builds an altar to the Lord.

God's people will return to this place in centuries to

A tale of two cities

Throughout the Bible, Babylon is the capital of all that is anti-God. It is a centre of ruthless power and gross immorality. In every way it is the opposite of Jerusalem – the city of God whose name means 'peace'.

At the end of the Bible, God utterly destroys Babylon and gives humankind a 'new Jerusalem'. It is the perfect city, not built by human effort (like Babel), but given by God. Instead of human beings trying to get to God, God comes to live with them. Instead of confusion and scattering, this city gives light and unity to the nations:

I saw the holy city, the new Jerusalem, coming down out of heaven from God… And I heard a loud voice from the throne saying,

'See, the home of God is among mortals. He will dwell with them… The nations will walk by its light, and the kings of the earth will bring their glory into it' (Revelation 21:2–3, 24).

come. Joshua will summon the twelve tribes – six to one side of him on Mount Ebal; six to the other side on Mount Gerizim. Here they must choose between obeying God or serving idols, between blessing and curse, between life and death. Shechem is a place of decision; a place to make up your mind.

AN EMBARRASSING EPISODE

When famine causes Abram and Sarai to move to Egypt, Abram pretends Sarai is his sister (12:10–20). Pharaoh, the king of Egypt, takes her into his household, and finds himself punished by God for doing so.

Pharaoh reproaches Abram for not being honest with him, but sends them away with generous gifts of servants and cattle. There is a similar episode some years later, with a king named Abimelech.

THE PARTING WITH LOT

As their herds increase, Abram and Lot have to split and go separate ways (13:1–18). Abram gives Lot first choice of the land. Lot chooses the fertile plain of the River Jordan, with its infamously

An alabaster figure dedicated to the god Ishtar. It was found at Mari, one of the most influential cities of Mesopotamia during Abram's time.

wicked cities of Sodom and Gomorrah.

Does Abram feel dispirited when Lot takes the best land, camps near Sodom, and then returns to city life? Not at all! Abram doesn't pilot his life by human bearings. He moves in God's magnetic field (although not without mistakes – as we have already seen).

Abram has learned the great lesson of 'letting go'. He settles at the oak of Mamre – about twenty miles south of Bethlehem.

VICTORY AND BLESSING

When the cities of the plain are ransacked by rival kings, Abram becomes a military leader. He raises an army and rescues Lot (14:1–24).

There are many alliances and power struggles between the city states of Middle Bronze Age Palestine, about 2000 BC. Genesis describes the Valley of Siddim as 'full of tar pits' (14:10). That valley was to disappear under the Dead Sea, which the Romans later called 'Asphaltites', because of the lumps of tar they found floating in the salty water.

On his triumphant return from battle, Abram is given bread and wine and blessed by Melchizedek, the priest–king of Salem. Abram

Justification by faith

Abram is the first to trust God's promises against all the odds. From now on, faith means believing what God says. This simple trust in God's word counts as 'righteousness' – being right with God.

The apostle Paul looks back to Abram as the father of all who have faith. Abram wasn't at peace with God because he was circumcised or had kept God's law. These developments came later. Abram was right with God because he believed God's promises. He was old and his wife was past childbearing, but he believed God would give him an heir. He was homeless and a nomad, but he believed God would give him a land:

He did not waver through unbelief regarding the promise of God, but was strengthened in his faith and gave glory to God, being fully persuaded that God had power to do what he had promised (Romans 4:20–21).

In the time of the Reformation, this important truth of 'justification by faith' was rediscovered by Martin Luther and others. It became a crucial weapon in the fight against fanciful traditions and superstitious practices in the church.

We are justified (made right with God) by faith alone – not by good deeds, religious devotion or the prayers of others. Such actions may be important ways of expressing our faith; but faith itself is trusting only in what God has done for us, not what we have done for him.

gives him a tenth of the wealth he has won in the fighting. But when the king of Sodom tries to strike a deal, Abram will have none of it. He wants only the wealth God gives.

Salem will become Jerusalem in the future. Melchizedek appears from nowhere. His name means 'King of Righteousness'. The New Testament describes him as, 'Without father or mother, without gen...
without beginning of days ...
God, he r...
unique ble...
Jesus Chris...

GOD'S CO...

God speaks ...
to protect A...
Abram is cor...
How can he h...
son to succeed...

An heir

God promises ...
a faithful serva...
son (15:1–6). H...
night sky, and p...
numerous to cou...

A land

The conversatio...
give Abram (15:...
he will take possess...
to bring animals a...

The covena...

God makes a covena...
contract by which Go...
The ceremony of God's...
sacrifices symbolizes th...
In future, a covenant b...
by sharing a meal or exc...
covenant', which God m...
sacrifice of Jesus on the c...
fellowship meal of Holy C...

and cuts the animals in half. He arranges them and stands guard to prevent them being disturbed.

At sunset, Abram falls asleep and is enveloped in deep darkness. God tells him of things that are to come – the slavery of the Hebrews in Egypt and their great escape; the return of Abram's descendants (in the time of Josh... ...liver God's judgment on the wickedness

... smoking brazier and a blazing torch
...ces of the sacrifices. This is the
... God in smoke and fire and deep
...itions will appear again in the
...cends on Mount Sinai to give
...ndments (Exodus 19:18).
...ises Abram that he will give his
...n which he is lying, from Egypt in
...River Euphrates in the east. This
...el's empire when David is king.

...rous, but has neither the land
...ised him. In desperation, Abram
...uld sleep with their Egyptian
... becomes pregnant with Ishmael
...ealousy (16:1–16).

...CUMCISION

...nant with Abram (17:1–27).
...to 'Abraham', and promises
... name means – the 'Father

...aham and all the men and
...ncised. In the future, all
... when they are eight days
...me. She is to be 'Sarah',
... she will give birth to
... she is ninety! Ishmael
...ng with Abraham. He
... great nation (the
... covenant and the land.

... strangers (18:1–15).
... encounter with
...two angels. The Lord
... Abraham that Sarah will bear a son. Sarah overhears – and bursts out laughing, much to her own embarrassment! When the baby is born, he will

Love the Lord your God
& your neighbour as yourself
Being brave.

Do good to those who
hate you.

Turn the other cheek

loyalty.
Being kind to animals
caring for the environment
not wasting.
no Waste
Caring for the animals

Respecting other people's
beliefs
not being Greedy
A christian prays &
glorifies God & Jesus

be called Isaac, which means 'He Laughs'.

It's hard to imagine Sarah at antenatal class when she should be in the old folks' home. We can try dividing her age by two – making her attractive to Pharaoh at thirty-five and the happy mother of Isaac in her forties. Or we can accept that Abraham and Sarah have exceptionally long lives, and that Isaac's birth is a miracle. The emphasis of the story is on the helplessness of Sarah in her barren old age. Why else would Abraham's divine visitor say, 'Is anything too hard for the Lord?' (18:14).

THE DESTRUCTION OF SODOM AND GOMORRAH

The three strangers are on their way to judge the wickedness of Sodom and Gomorrah (18:16 – 19:29). Abraham begs that Sodom may be spared, for the sake of any good people there (such as Lot). The Lord agrees that if there are even as few as ten good men in Sodom he will not destroy it.

The strangers (now 'angels') stay with Lot in Sodom, where a mob threatens to rape them that night. With the angels' help, Lot and his daughters manage to escape to the small town of Zoar. But Lot's wife, pausing to look back, is caught in the terrible volcanic disaster that engulfs the cities. She becomes a pillar of salt.

The Hospitality of Abraham (16th-century AD). Cupola fresco in the Sucevita Monastery, Moldavia, Romania.

LOT AND HIS DAUGHTERS

The end of Lot's story is pathetic and degrading (19:30–38). He is afraid to settle in Zoar and takes his daughters to live in a cave in the mountains. After his ambition for security and prosperity in the wicked cities of the plain, this is a terrible humiliation. We can't help but compare his miserable fate with the outcome of Abraham's humble faith.

Without husbands, Lot's daughters decide to make their father drunk and have sex with him. In this way they become pregnant. Their descendants will be the peoples of Moab and Ammon, who will bring shame and disgrace on Israel in the future. Moabite women will seduce God's people into immorality and idolatry (Numbers 25:1–3). The Ammonites will sacrifice their children to the pagan god Molech (Leviticus 18:21).

ABRAHAM AND ABIMELECH

Lot is not perfect, but neither is Abraham. Abraham settles in Gerar, where he becomes afraid that the local king, Abimelech, will kill him for his wife (20:1–18). Sarah is very beautiful, and Abraham has long ago decided to avoid trouble by saying she is his sister; which is partly true, as they have the same father (20:12).

There has already been a similar episode with the king of Egypt (Genesis 12:10–20). On both occasions, the sin of taking another man's wife brings suffering on the ruler's people. On both occasions, the ruler reproaches Abraham and Abraham apologizes and explains his lie. Some scholars believe that these two stories are in fact the same; but it's quite possible (and very human) that Abraham hasn't learned from his first mistake. His old fear has led to his old deceit. He is saved by the forgiveness of God and the generous understanding of a pagan ruler.

THE BIRTH OF ISAAC

At last, and despite her old age, Sarah gives birth to Isaac (21:1–21). Sarah puts pressure on Abraham to get rid of Hagar and Ishmael. He sends them away with great sadness. But God is with them, and they survive their desert journey to start a new life.

THE TREATY AT BEERSHEBA

Abraham now makes a treaty with Abimelech, who is a powerful neighbour – perhaps one of the early Philistine immigrants into the south of Canaan (21:22–34). As we have already seen (20:1–18), Abimelech is an open and honest man who respects Abraham's faith and has given him permission to live in this area of the Negev. Now they come to an agreement over the use of a well, which Abraham has dug, but Abimelech's servants have seized. The treaty is probably marked by sacrifices of animals, but also by Abraham giving seven ewe lambs to Abimelech and the two men swearing an oath.

The place is called Beersheba, which means 'well of seven' or 'well of the oath'. Abraham plants a tamarisk tree as a landmark and worships God there. Beersheba will be an important base for both Abraham and his son Isaac, and mark the southern boundary of the Promised Land.

ABRAHAM IS TESTED

Some time later, when Isaac is an older child or teenager, God tells Abraham to take him to Mount Moriah (22:1–24). There he is to offer him as a sacrifice. Child sacrifice is practised by some pagan religions, and Abraham might well think it is the ultimate sign of commitment. Isaac is his dearest possession. However, with the fire laid, Isaac bound and the knife raised, God calls to Abraham to stop. Nearby is a ram, caught by its horns in a thicket. The Lord has provided a sacrifice, and Abraham's faith in God has passed its greatest test.

In the future, Solomon will build his great temple on the site of Mount Moriah. Today Abraham's rock is covered by the 'Dome of the Rock' Mosque in Jerusalem. It is near here, also, that God will offer his only son, Jesus, as a sacrifice for the sins of the world. Jesus will

be described by John the Baptist as 'the Lamb of God' (John 1:29).

THE DEATH OF SARAH

Sarah dies and Abraham buries her in the land of Canaan (23:1–20). He negotiates a burial plot at Hebron, and insists on paying the Hittites the proper (perhaps even a high) price for it. It is a cave in a field, and by purchasing it Abraham becomes a landowner.

This is the only piece of the Promised Land that Abraham will possess in his lifetime; but it is a marker, by faith, of all that God has vowed to give him and his descendants. The place is called Machpelah. Abraham will also be buried here, as will Isaac and his wife Rebekah, and Jacob and his first wife Leah (49:29–32).

ISAAC AND REBEKAH

Isaac is the promise-bearer. He is the link between Abraham and the future. It is crucial that he should marry within the family of faith, and have a son.

Abraham sends his most trusted servant to find a wife for Isaac from among his relatives (24:1–67). We might think Isaac is weak, to let someone else do his courting. But Abraham is taking no risks. It would be dangerous for Isaac to be attracted to Canaanite women or distracted by their pagan religion. He remembers what happened to Lot.

The servant (perhaps Eliezer) asks God to guide him to the right woman. His prayer is wonderfully answered. He meets the beautiful, youthful Rebekah at a well outside Nahor. She gives him a drink, carries water to his camels – and turns out to be the daughter of Abraham's nephew.

Abraham – father of the faithful

As we follow Abraham's story, we become aware that the supreme quality of his life is his faith. He has wandered in an unknown land, worshipped an invisible God and believed in an unfulfilled promise. By the time he dies, Abraham owns no more of the Promised Land than a cave in a field, which he has bought for Sarah's grave. For descendants he has just two sons, of whom one has

been sent away. But God is committed to Abraham. His plan is to bless him and make a nation out of him. This nation is to be a blessing to the whole world.

God is showing in Abraham's life what he can do in every life. But he can only work where there is faith. Abraham is the spiritual father of all who have faith in God.

The apostle Paul writes of Abraham:

He is our father in the sight of God, in whom he believed – the God who

gives life to the dead and calls things that are not as though they were (Romans 4:17).

Rebekah's father is Nahor, and her brother is Laban. They try to delay the proposed marriage, but the servant handles the situation faithfully and well. Soon he is taking Rebekah home to Isaac, who happily marries her.

ABRAHAM'S LAST DAYS

Abraham has another wife besides Sarah. Her name is Keturah and she bears him six sons. The family tree will list Abraham's sons by three women: Sarah, Hagar and Keturah, who is called a concubine or secondary wife (1 Chronicles 1:28–34). Through Keturah, Abraham is the ancestor of many Arab peoples, of whom the most famous mentioned here is Midian.

Of all Abraham's sons, Isaac is the one who is to inherit God's promise – to bless the world through him, make him a great nation and give him a land. Before he dies, Abraham is careful to give a fair inheritance to each of his other sons, and to send them away from the region which is to be occupied by Isaac (25:1–11). When Abraham dies, Isaac and Ishmael (his half-brother and rival) are united in burying him at Mechpelah, in the cave he had purchased as a tomb for Sarah (23:19).

The descendants of Ishmael
(25:12–18)

Ishmael is Abraham's son by Hagar, who was Sarah's Egyptian maidservant. He in turn has twelve sons who become the rulers of tribes. The Arab nations today trace their ancestry to him.

Isaac (Abraham's son)
(25:19 – 26:35)

ISAAC'S SONS: JACOB AND ESAU

At first it seems that Rebekah is unable to have children. Then God gives her twin boys. They start fighting even before they are born! God explains to Rebekah: 'Two nations are in your womb' (25:23). These two nations will always be at odds with each other. When the twins are born, the first is called Esau, which means 'Hairy', and the second is named Jacob, which means 'Cheat'. This is because Jacob is born clinging to Esau's heel, as though trying to overtake him to be born first.

The twins grow up. Esau becomes a man of the great outdoors. He brings home wild game from his hunting trips. This pleases Isaac, who loves his food. Jacob is a mother's boy. He stays home and helps with the cooking.

One day, when Esau returns hungry, Jacob has some delicious stew prepared. Before he lets Esau taste any, he makes him resign his rights as the elder son. Esau, faced with the choice of food or future, takes the food without a second thought.

The full meaning of 'Jacob' is 'Took by the Heel'. It has the sense of 'coming from behind, catching, spoiling, being determined to get what isn't his'. In later life, God will name Jacob 'Israel' – which means 'Wrestled'. Jacob is a man who will never give up, and nor will the people who descend from him.

ISAAC PROSPERS

Like his father Abraham, Isaac lives as a herdsman. God renews the promise to give him the land of Canaan, and descendants 'as numerous as the stars in the sky'.

They live among the Philistines – a vigorous, pagan people. Like Abraham before him, Isaac is afraid he might be killed by someone who wants to take his beautiful wife. For a long time he pretends that Rebekah is his sister. He is challenged by the Philistine king, Abimelech, who sees Isaac being more than brotherly to Rebekah.

Isaac is prosperous and has large herds, but no land. He has a constant problem getting water for his people and animals. He digs wells, but then has to move on.

Something about Isaac's wealth and peaceableness impresses his neighbours. 'We saw clearly that the Lord was with you' (26:28), they say when they come to make a treaty. They agree to give Isaac some land at Beersheba.

Meanwhile, Esau grows to manhood and marries pagan women. This distresses his parents, whose own marriage was so clearly guided by God. Isaac expects Esau to inherit the promise, and his choice of wife will be important. But Esau doesn't care about such things.

Jacob (Abraham's grandson)
(27:1 – 35:29)

Jacob is cunning and hard-working; the underdog who somehow comes out on top. He is an unpleasant and selfish young man, but God blesses him. In due course he will become 'Israel' and give his name to a nation.

JACOB STEALS HIS BROTHER'S BLESSING

When Isaac is old and blind, the time comes for him to bless his successor (27:1–40). He sends Esau to catch something tasty for a meal. After he has eaten, he will give him the special blessing which passes the promises of God from father to first-born son.

Rebekah has other ideas. While Esau is away, she dresses Jacob in Esau's clothes, disguises his arms and neck with goatskin, and sends him to Isaac with a tasty dish. Isaac is suspicious, but accepts the food and drink. By the time Esau returns, Jacob has received the blessing.

The blessing is unique and non-transferable. There is no question of Isaac taking it back. All he can promise Esau is a life of conflict and discontent. Esau resolves to murder Jacob as soon as he gets the chance.

JACOB'S DREAM AT BETHEL

Jacob has to run for his life. Isaac and Rebekah send him north to marry one of his uncle Laban's daughters. He goes with the promise ringing in his ears: 'May God Almighty bless you and make you fruitful and increase in numbers until you become a community of peoples.' The word 'community' will become the Old Testament's word for 'church'.

Travelling up through the hills, Jacob stops for the night. Lonely and homeless, he lies down with his head on a stone. As he sleeps, he dreams (28:10–22). He sees a stairway, reaching all the way from earth to heaven – with angels coming and going on God's business. The Lord speaks to him.

Young Jacob is stopped in his tracks. God is real. God is here. God knows all about him, and has a plan for his life. In the morning, Jacob takes the stone he used as a pillow and stands it as a landmark. He strikes a bargain with God. In return for food, clothes and safe travel, he will worship God, make this place a shrine and give God a tenth of his wealth. It's a shrewd deal. This is Jacob, after all!

JACOB AND RACHEL

Jacob continues his journey and arrives in Haran. There he asks for his uncle Laban, and meets Laban's daughter Rachel. We have encountered Laban once before – in the negotiation for his sister Rebekah to marry Isaac. In those days he drove a hard bargain and tried to play for time. We find he hasn't changed.

Laban welcomes Jacob with open arms. He has two daughters he wishes to marry off. Leah is the elder. She has a problem with her eyes. Rachel is the younger. She is shapely and beautiful. Jacob agrees to work for Laban for seven years in return for marrying Rachel.

But uncle Laban is too sharp to be left with an elder, unmarried daughter on his hands. When Jacob wakes up after a wedding feast and a rather dimly lit marriage ceremony, he finds Leah lying beside him! Laban explains that it's their custom to marry the older daughter first – and signs up Jacob to work *another* seven years for Rachel. In uncle Laban, the crafty Jacob has met his match.

In later years the Jewish law forbids the marrying of sisters while both are alive. It can only result in jealousy, rejection and hurt. But God has a purpose for Leah. While Rachel struggles to get pregnant, Leah gives birth to six sons and a daughter. Half the tribes of Israel, including the royal tribe of Judah and the priestly tribe of Levi, will honour Leah as their mother.

Jacob also has four sons through his wives' maids, Bilhah and Zilpah. Only after many years of barrenness does Rachel give birth to Joseph and Benjamin.

Jacob proves to be a good and businesslike shepherd. Under his management, Laban's flocks increase. When Jacob has completed the fourteen years of service for his wives, Laban persuades him to stay on. His payment is to keep any speckled or spotted sheep that are born in the flock; Laban immediately withdraws the goats that might father such offspring. Jacob breeds them anyway. He gets

---

Bethel – 'house of God'

Jacob calls the place of his dream 'Bethel'. It had also been known as Luz. Most scholars think this is at or near Tell Beitin, eleven miles north of Jerusalem, where there are remains of an Early Bronze Age city.

Abraham had visited Bethel, and Jacob will return here. In future years, when the land is conquered by Joshua, it will be captured by Ephraim, one of the Joseph tribes. The ark of the covenant will be kept here for a while, and it will become a sanctuary and place of pilgrimage. Samuel will include it in his annual judge's tour.

When the northern kingdom of Israel is formed, King Jeroboam will make Bethel his religious centre. He will build a shrine to rival the temple in Jerusalem, and create his own priests. The prophet Amos will arrive to condemn the practices there. The worship may be impressive, but the worshippers are wicked (Amos 5:5–13).

the animals to mate while looking at branches he has speckled – a doubtful but God-blessed technique. Over a period of six years Jacob becomes very rich.

Jacob and Laban have now lost all respect for each other. The Lord tells Jacob it is time to return home. Without telling Laban, Jacob gathers his wives and children and flocks – and leaves. For extra protection, Rachel steals her father's gods.

It takes Laban a week to catch up with them. When he does, he makes a tear-jerking speech about wanting to kiss his grandchildren goodbye. He also wants his gods back. Laban is allowed to search for the gods, but doesn't find them because Rachel is sitting on them. Jacob doesn't know that the gods are in Rachel's baggage, and makes a speech of fiery indignation. How can Laban possibly accuse him of theft?

Eventually Laban and Jacob agree to live separate lives, and mark the boundary between them. They call the place 'Mizpah', which means 'watchtower'. God will watch over them when they're apart.

JACOB AND ESAU ARE REUNITED

Jacob has left Laban behind, but Esau lies ahead. He sends news of himself to Esau, and asks for a kindly welcome home. The message comes back that Esau is heading towards them with a small army (32:1 – 33:20).

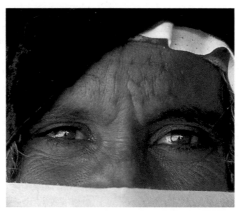

An Eastern woman wearing a veil, which gives modesty, and protection from the sun and wind. Of Jacob's two wives, Rachel was reckoned the more beautiful but Leah was known for her eyes. Scholars are not sure whether they were 'lovely' or 'weak' – but they were striking!

With a breaking heart, Jacob divides up his family and flocks – so that some may escape the coming massacre. He begs God to keep his promise and protect them. The following day he sends animals and servants ahead in groups. Each is briefed to say they are a gift to Esau from Jacob; and that Jacob himself is following. In this way Jacob hopes to buy enough goodwill for Esau to spare them. Finally, he sends his family on ahead.

Jacob is in torment. There is nothing more he can do. He doesn't know which way to turn for escape. All night he wrestles with someone – a dark angel, or his fear of death, or his uneasy conscience.

As dawn breaks, the strange opponent dislocates Jacob's hip. Jacob clings on, refusing to admit defeat. He won't let go without a blessing to resolve this terrible conflict.

The One wrestling with Jacob gives him a new name: 'Israel', meaning 'He Struggles with God'. Then he blesses him.

Only then does Jacob realize he has been fighting God. It wasn't a dream. He has a permanent limp to prove it.

So Jacob comes of age. This is the supreme crisis of his life, as he struggles with Esau and God, past and future, fear and faith. He wins through to a new identity and peace.

In the morning Esau appears, galloping towards them with 400 men. As Jacob prepares for death, Esau runs forward – and hugs him! Jacob is overwhelmed. His new-found peace with God is echoed in his reconciliation with his brother.

Jacob and his family settle at Shechem in Canaan – a day's journey from Bethel, where his long journey of faith began.

DINAH

God's chosen family are living among pagans. Jacob's daughter, Dinah, is raped by a man called Shechem, a Hivite, who wants to marry her (34:1–31). Hiding their rage, Dinah's brothers pretend friendship and agree to the marriage. In fact they hold out hope of many marriages between the two peoples in years to come. All they ask is that the Hivite men should be circumcised.

The Hivites agree. While they are still sore, Simeon and Levi (Dinah's actual brothers) attack the city and kill Shechem and his father. Jacob's other sons join in, seizing cattle, carrying off women and children and looting houses. So rape is avenged by deceit and cruelty, to everyone's discredit.

JACOB'S RETURN TO BETHEL

It is time to get right with God. The Lord calls Jacob back to Bethel, the place of his first commitment (35:1–29). The family purges itself of all superstition by burying its foreign gods and lucky charms. For his part,

God renews his promise that Jacob will become a great nation and receive the land of Canaan. Jacob sets up a stone and pours out an offering – just as he did twenty years before. In those days God's blessings were just a dream. Now they are his daily experience.

On the way south towards Ephrath, Rachel dies while struggling to give birth. The baby survives and is called Benjamin, which means 'Son of My Right Hand'. Rachel is buried about twelve miles north of Ephrath (Bethlehem). So Jacob comes home to his father Isaac in Mamre. When Isaac dies at a great age, Esau and Jacob bury him there. It's the end of an era.

The descendants of Esau

(36:1–43)

The writer narrates the wives and children of Esau and the generations of Edom that flowed from them.

'Edom' is Esau's nickname. It means 'red' – the colour of the stew that Jacob traded for the birthright. It is also the name of Esau's descendants, the Edomites, and their land – which stretches south from the Dead Sea to the Red Sea.

The story of the Edomites runs parallel to that of the Israelites throughout the Old Testament. When the Israelites are on the move from Egypt, Edom refuses to allow them to pass along its border. In later centuries, David conquers Edom, and Solomon builds a port and exports its copper. There is suspicion and hatred between the two nations. The psalmist says that Edom cheered when Jerusalem was destroyed.

Joseph (Abraham's great-grandson)

(37:1 – 50:26)

Joseph is Jacob's favourite son. He shows his favouritism by making Joseph a princely robe. When Joseph dreams, he sees himself as superior to the rest of his family, and that they bow down before him. The other brothers are angered by Jacob's bias and Joseph's boastings.

One day, far from home, the brothers seize Joseph. They strip him of his precious robe and sell him as a slave to some Midianite merchants. Brutally, they stain the costly coat with goat's blood and show it to Jacob. Jacob is heartbroken at the evidence that Joseph is dead.

Meanwhile, Joseph is very much alive. He is taken to market in Egypt and sold to Potiphar, who works for Pharaoh. Pharaoh is the king of Egypt and Potiphar is captain of the king's guard. Between 1720 and 1550 BC Egypt is ruled by the Hyksos pharaohs who, like Joseph, have come from Canaan. They favour servants and administrators from Semitic (that is, Asiatic or 'foreign') backgrounds.

The Lord blesses Joseph, and soon the young man is trusted to manage Potiphar's entire household. Everything goes terribly wrong when Potiphar's wife tries to seduce him. Joseph refuses her, explaining that this would be a betrayal of his master, and a sin against God.

Potiphar's wife is obsessed with Joseph, and her lust turns to rage. She snatches his cloak and later tells her husband that she obtained it when Joseph tried to force himself on her. Joseph is thrown into prison.

In prison, the Lord's favour (and Joseph's charm and competence) work wonders. He runs the place for the warder and interprets dreams for his fellow prisoners. The king's chief cupbearer and the royal baker both have their curious dreams explained. Two years later, when Pharaoh himself is troubled by nightmares, the cupbearer remembers Joseph and recommends him to his master.

Pharaoh's dreams are of thin corn consuming full corn and lean cows devouring fat cows. Everything comes in sevens! Joseph explains that the two dreams carry the same message, and that God is showing Pharaoh the future. Seven years of plenty will be followed by seven years of famine.

God and 'brother or sister'

There is a close relationship between God and 'brother or sister'. Jacob discovers that to be at odds with one is to be out of sorts with the other. Jesus teaches that we must make peace with a brother or sister before bringing a gift to God:

Leave your gift there before the altar and go; first be reconciled to your brother or sister, and then come and offer your gift (Matthew 5:24).

One of the letters of John makes a similar point:

Those who say, 'I love God', and hate their brothers or sisters, are liars; for those who do not love a brother or sister whom they have seen, cannot love God whom they have not seen (1 John 4:20).

Joseph goes on to suggest how Pharaoh might meet the crisis. He should appoint a suitable person to prepare for the famine and administer the relief supplies. With the help of area commissioners, this man will ensure that surplus food is stored during the good years and distributed during the bad years.

Not surprisingly, Joseph gets the job. Pharaoh makes him his chief minister. At the age of thirty, Joseph is in charge of all Egypt. He marries and has two children – Manasseh (meaning 'Forget') and Ephraim (meaning 'Twice Fruitful'). He feels that God has helped him forget his troubles and flourish in spite of them. During the years of plenty, Joseph organizes the storage of vast quantities of grain. Then the years of famine bite – just as Joseph had predicted.

JOSEPH'S FAMILY COME TO EGYPT

Among those who travel to Egypt to buy grain are Joseph's brothers. Joseph is now completely Egyptian in appearance and manner. He stands before them dressed in fine linen, wearing his gold chain of office and the Pharaoh's ring. The brothers have changed very little and Joseph recognizes them immediately. They bow before him with their faces to the ground – and Joseph remembers his boyhood dream.

Speaking through an interpreter, Joseph accuses his brothers of being spies. He gets them to admit that their youngest brother is still at home, and another is dead. He orders them to go and bring Benjamin to prove their story, while he holds Simeon as a hostage.

Although it is twenty years since the brothers sold Joseph, he is still on their consciences. As soon as they get into trouble, they guess they are being punished for what they did.

Meanwhile Joseph isn't the spoilt and bossy brat of years ago. His own sufferings have changed him. He is deeply moved to see his brothers, and has to turn away to weep even while he cross-questions them. Without revealing his true identity, he has their bags filled with grain, puts their money back in their sacks and supplies them with food for their journey.

As they return home, the brothers discover their money has been returned to their sacks. Their hearts sink. God is doing something very strange here. When Jacob hears their story, he is panic-stricken and refuses to let Benjamin go with them to Egypt. But the family faces starvation, and he is forced to agree.

When the brothers arrive back in Egypt, Joseph has them shown to his house for lunch. They fear they are under arrest and explain to Joseph's steward that there has been some misunderstanding. When Joseph arrives he continues to astonish them by asking after their father – and sitting them at table in order of age! When he sees his young brother Benjamin, he has to hurry out to weep.

The following morning the brothers are sent on their way – but not before Joseph has supplied them with grain, returned their money and had his own silver cup planted in Benjamin's sack. Joseph orders his steward to catch them up and charge them with theft.

Sure enough, the cup is found hidden in Benjamin's grain.

Back at Joseph's house, Judah makes an impassioned appeal for Benjamin to be spared. If anything happens to Benjamin, their father will die. Judah offers to take

Benjamin's punishment and become Joseph's slave. Finally Joseph relents. He clears the room of attendants, and makes himself known to his brothers. He explains that God has been at work throughout this long adventure:

Tomb of Menna, Thebes (c. 1420–1411 BC); Joseph's policy to deal with the impending famine in Egypt was to buy up all the productive land on behalf of Pharoah. The result was that the Egyptians were effectively reduced to servitude, working the land they once owned. Joseph provided the people with seed, allowing them to keep 80 per cent of the resulting crop. The remainder went to Pharoah.

I am your brother Joseph, the one you sold into Egypt! And now, do not be distressed and do not be angry with yourselves for selling me here, because it was to save lives that God sent me ahead of you... to save your lives by a great deliverance... it was not you who sent me here, but God (45:5, 7–8).

Joseph has it all worked out. They must fetch their father and bring their families and flocks to Egypt. Pharaoh sends wagons for them and promises that 'the best of all Egypt' will be theirs. They are settled in the fertile land of Goshen.

THE LAST DAYS OF JACOB AND JOSEPH

As Jacob prepares to die, he makes Joseph promise that his body will be taken from Egypt and buried with Abraham and Sarah in the Promised Land. He blesses Joseph's sons, Ephraim and Manasseh. Jacob crosses his hands to give priority to Ephraim, the younger of the two – just as Jacob had himself been given the first-born's blessing instead of Esau. The God of Jacob is One who makes the first last and the last first.

Jacob blesses each of his sons. He has great insight into their character and destiny. He has particular condemnation for Reuben, and blessings for the royal line of Judah and the godliness of Joseph. When Jacob dies, Joseph has his body embalmed and carried in solemn state to Canaan for burial.

Genesis closes with Joseph's own death and the placing of his body in an Egyptian coffin. In due course this coffin, too, will be taken to the Promised Land.

Life in ancient Egypt depended totally on the River Nile. It was the main route of communication, and its fertile banks provided most of the country's agricultural land.

EXODUS

The book of Exodus describes how God rescues his people, the Israelites, from slavery in Egypt. The climax of their escape comes when God causes a wind to part the waters of the Red Sea. The Israelites cross in safety, but the Egyptian army is drowned. This is the defining moment of the 'Exodus' which means 'way out'. (The same idea is in our word 'exit'.)

God leads his people through the desert to Mount Sinai, where he gives them his law and prepares them for their new life in Canaan, the Promised Land.

The Israelite leader is Moses. He is born a Hebrew, raised as an Egyptian prince and works as a shepherd on the slopes of Sinai. He is assisted by his brother Aaron, who acts as spokesman and later becomes Israel's first high priest.

Outline

The slavery of the Israelites and the birth of Moses (1:1 – 2:25)

God calls Moses (3:1 – 4:31)

The great escape (5:1 – 15:21)

The desert journey (15:22 – 18:27)

The giving of the law (19:1 – 24:18)

The tabernacle and the priests (25:1 – 31:18)

Rebellion and judgment (32:1 – 34:35)

The climax of Exodus (35:1 – 40:38)

INTRODUCTION

The story so far

The family of Jacob (also known as 'Israel') has migrated to Egypt to escape a famine in their homeland, Canaan. One of Jacob's sons, Joseph, was already in Egypt – serving as the minister in charge of famine relief.

Out of gratitude to Joseph, the king of Egypt ('Pharaoh'), invited Jacob and his other sons to settle with their families and herds in the fertile district of Goshen.

Now times have changed. Jacob and Joseph have been dead for many years and their memory forgotten. Meanwhile, the Egyptians have become anxious at the large number of Israelites in their country. They fear that this powerful minority will cause trouble.

The exodus

The book of Exodus continues the story which began in Genesis. It tells how God's people, the Israelites, are trapped in Egypt where they work as slaves. But God calls Moses, who is Hebrew by birth and Egyptian by upbringing, to lead Israel out of slavery. He reveals himself to Moses by telling him his name, 'Yahweh', which means 'I Am Who I Am', or 'I Will Be Who I Will Be'. The Israelites are to leave Egypt and move to Canaan, the land God promised to Abraham. In all this, Moses is to be assisted by his brother Aaron.

God works wonderful signs through Moses, and inflicts terrible plagues on Egypt. In the end, God kills all Egypt's eldest sons in a single night, but 'passes over' the Israelites. This becomes the Passover, which is remembered for all time as the moment Israel became a nation.

The Egyptian king, Pharaoh, has no choice but to allow the Israelites to leave. But then he changes his mind and pursues them with his army. In a dramatic intervention, God parts the waters of the Red Sea, so that the Israelites can escape, but the Egyptians are drowned. This is the exodus.

As the Israelites journey through the desert, the joy of freedom evaporates and they start to grumble. God provides them with water, and the strange 'manna' – their daily bread. After three months they come to Mount Sinai. This is where Moses had worked as a shepherd and first met God. Now God gives Moses the Ten Commandments and the other laws by which Israel is to live.

The people swear that they will obey God's commands. In return, God makes a covenant with them. They are to be a holy nation, with God as their king. Their way of life will set them apart from all other nations.

But while Moses is away on the mountain, receiving further laws from God, the people rebel. They persuade Aaron to make a golden calf – a god they can see. Moses returns to find the Israelites engaged in a wild pagan orgy. He calls the tribe of Levi to use force to bring the people under control. Then he begs God to forgive them.

God gives Moses detailed instructions for the building of a special tent. This is the tabernacle where God will live among his people. The tabernacle is to house an ark or box containing God's law. Outside the tabernacle, in a screened compound, will be an altar for sacrifices. Aaron and his sons are to be set apart, robed and consecrated as priests.

The book of Exodus closes with the tabernacle being completed with its furniture, its fittings and its

priesthood. All is consecrated to the Lord, who dwells there in a cloud of glory.

God's power to rescue his people

Exodus shows God in control of history and of the whole world. He is not just a family god, the focus of superstition and nostalgia. He is the One and Only – the Lord.

God has chosen Israel to be his people. He breaks the power of a cruel tyrant, Pharaoh, to set them free. He leads the Israelites through the desert, gives them his law and instructs them in worship. The climax of the exodus is the building and dedication of the tabernacle, the tented enclosure where God dwells among his people.

Exodus is a book about God's power to rescue his people however desperate their situation. Many oppressed groups have taken courage from this story. God

---

Statues from the temple at Luxor. To the captive Israelites, the splendour and scale of Egypt's civilization must have been overwhelming. Was there any force on earth powerful enough to deliver them from such mighty oppressors?

hears the cry of the poor and weak. Freedom fighters in South America and civil rights leaders in the United States have alike echoed Moses' mighty command to Pharaoh: 'Let my people go!'

The exodus is a very human story. We follow the career of Moses, who is called to challenge Pharaoh and lead the people. He feels totally inadequate for the task. The people themselves are first fearful, then fickle. Their slavery has seeped into their souls, making them coarse, suspicious and angry.

But Moses is not the hero of the story. The vision and the end result are God's. Moses is in fact a reluctant leader and an unimpressive speaker. It is only his trust in God that makes him great.

Exodus is a story of God's goodwill and power; the story of how he rescues his people against all odds and gives them freedom and dignity. It is the story of Israel becoming a nation for God.

Israel, too, has many failures. The people are often ungrateful and rebellious. Nevertheless, it is with them that God makes a covenant, and to them he commits his law. They have been rescued from slavery. Now the law will teach them how to be truly free. The appalling lapse when they abandon God and worship a golden calf is a solemn reminder of the weakness of human nature. Moses' prayer for the people in their disgrace, and their developing friendship with God, are among the Bible's greatest treasures.

The final part of the book is about the building of the tabernacle – the mobile sanctuary where God will dwell. The special nature of God is expressed in the detailed and orderly structure, the choice of materials and the skill of the craftspeople. The people are given ways of expressing God's holiness and sharing it. Their worship is focused in sacrifices and offerings. The book ends on a high note, with the tabernacle being dedicated by Moses and filled with the cloud of God's glory.

The heart of the Old Testament

The book of Exodus gives the Jewish people their roots. God rescued them when they were down and out. To this day they celebrate the Passover with the sense and thrill of their God-given freedom.

The exodus became Israel's prime example of God's overwhelming power and perfect timing. The great moment when the Red Sea parted for the Israelites and then engulfed their enemies reverberates throughout the Bible. Centuries later, when the Jews return from exile in

Babylon, they see their deliverance as a new exodus.

And then there is the law. At Sinai, God gives guidelines for the good life. The Ten Commandments put God first and others next. They tackle human behaviour at source – in the mind and imagination.

In the building of the tabernacle, Exodus provides a model for every holy place. Here is an attempt to use design and space, materials and skills, to speak of God. Every detail of the tabernacle points to God. All subsequent temples and churches owe something to the tabernacle as their prototype.

For Christians, Exodus marks the beginning of many exciting trails. Luke's Gospel says that when Jesus prayed about his approaching death, he was joined by Moses and Elijah. They talked about his departure ('exodus') and so looked forward to God's mighty rescue beyond the suffering of the cross (Luke 9:31).

There are unmistakable links between Passover and the death of Jesus. Jesus shared the Last Supper with his disciples at Passover time. John's Gospel actually has Jesus dying on the cross while the Passover lambs are being sacrificed in the temple. Certainly Paul makes the connection when he writes, 'Christ, our Passover lamb, has been sacrificed.' Jesus was remembered as saying, as he passed the wine at the Last Supper, 'This cup is the new covenant in my blood.'

Matthew's Gospel tells us that when Jesus died, the curtain of the temple – like the tabernacle curtain hiding the Most Holy Place – 'was torn in two from top to bottom'. So, through the sacrifice of Jesus, people are no longer excluded from God's holy presence.

The letter to the Hebrews explains that, through his death, Jesus offered himself as the perfect sacrifice and acted as the perfect high priest (Hebrews 9:11–12).

Paul teaches that every Christian is like a tabernacle – a place where the Holy Spirit dwells, and where others may meet with God. Our body is a temporary tent, which looks forward to eternal life with God (2 Corinthians 5:1–5).

Who wrote Exodus?

The book of Exodus is the second of five books, which together are called 'the Pentateuch'. They are also known as the 'books of Moses', because Moses is the main character in four of them (Exodus, Leviticus, Numbers and Deuteronomy).

The old Jewish tradition is that Moses actually wrote these books, apart from the description of his own death (the end of Deuteronomy) and the events which took

place afterwards. Sometimes it has even been said that he wrote these passages too, as he was a very great prophet. However, there is nothing in the books themselves to say that Moses wrote them. They contain stories, poetry and laws which are extremely old. They might have been passed on by word of mouth for several generations, before being written down in (say) the early years of David's reign.

Some scholars believe that the final versions of these books were put together from several different sources. Two major strands have been identified by the different names used for God: 'J' material calls God 'Yahweh' (the Lord), and 'E' material refers to God as 'Elohim'. In fact, 'Yahweh' is a verb meaning 'I AM' – expressing the ever-present reality of the living God. Another kind of material is information and regulations for priests, and is known as 'P'. More recently, there has been attention to the people who might have preserved these stories – and so 'J' has stood for Judah and 'E' for Ephraim.

Of these five books, Exodus contains the greatest mixture of contents. It includes the story of Moses in Egypt as well as the desert journey to Canaan, the giving of the Ten Commandments and the construction of the tabernacle. The exultant song of Miriam after the crossing of the Red Sea is particularly old, while some of the laws are not about desert life so much as the society of towns and farms which lies in the future.

However the material has come to take its present form, the story is the same. Moses is the central character and he is the most likely person to have written the basic, original material. He had a sophisticated Egyptian education as well as a deep understanding of Hebrew culture and origins; and he was an eyewitness. There is reference to him keeping a written record of events (Exodus 17:14), and writing God's law in a book for the Levites to keep in the covenant box (Deuteronomy 31:24).

The revelation that there is one holy, personal, covenanting God must have come through a very great mind. We know of no one greater than Moses, and Exodus is very much his story.

DISCOVERING EXODUS

The slavery of the Israelites and the birth of Moses

The book of Exodus continues the story which began in Genesis. It begins by listing the twelve sons of Jacob. These are the men who will give their names to the twelve tribes of Israel. The Israelites are also known by a gypsy-like name for wandering Semites: the 'Hebrews'.

The Israelites become slaves
(1:1–22)

The Israelites have multiplied in the generations since Joseph. The Egyptians are alarmed at their growing numbers and decide to suppress them. They force them to become slaves and put them to work building store cities for Pharaoh. When this makes no impression on this sturdy race, the king embarks on a programme of ethnic cleansing. All Hebrew boys are to be killed at birth, or thrown in the river.

The store cities (1:11) of Pithom and Rameses were built to house the treasures of Pharaoh Rameses II, in the 13th century BC. This suggests a date for the exodus at about 1250 BC, although some scholars date it to the 15th century BC.

Moses is born – and hidden
(2:1–10)

In this desperate situation, one baby boy survives. His parents are from the tribe of Levi, which will one day become the priestly tribe. The baby is placed in a mini-ark and hidden in the reeds by the River Nile. There his loud cries, which had made it impossible to hide him at home,

Moses near the burning thorn bush from the *Golden Haggada*, a Jewish book illustration from Catalonia (c. AD 1320–30).

become an asset. He is found and adopted by none other then Pharaoh's daughter. She asks his own mother to care for him through babyhood, and then adopts him. She names him 'Moses', which means 'Draw Out', because she drew him out of the water. Moses is brought up in the royal household, with the double advantages of an Egyptian education and his mother's love.

Moses murders an Egyptian
(2:11–25)

As a young man, Moses is moved by the terrible hardship of his people. One day he loses his temper and kills an Egyptian who is beating a Hebrew. As a result, he has to flee the country. He goes to live in Midian where he marries a priest's daughter, Zipporah. They start a family and for many years Moses works as a shepherd for his father-in-law.

Moses is passionately concerned for justice, but he is impetuous. In his years as a shepherd he learns patience, discovers the ways of the desert – and meets with God.

God calls Moses

The burning bush
(3:1–12)

One day, Moses is feeding his flock on the slopes of Horeb, 'the mountain of God'. Mount Horeb is also called Mount Sinai. Both names are used in Exodus. Horeb may come from a Hebrew word for 'desert', and Sinai may be linked with the desert of Sin. Although it is clearly to the south of Canaan (and Elijah went there in later years), the actual mountain is not known. It wasn't a holy mountain in terms of God living there. It was simply the place where Moses met with God.

On Mount Horeb Moses catches sight of a bush which is on fire but not burning up. When he goes over to look more closely, God calls him by name.

God warns Moses not to come any closer and to take off his sandals. The very ground is 'holy', because God is present. The book of Exodus will teach us much about holiness. Holiness is always to do with God. Only God is holy and to be in his presence is an overwhelming experience. A sinful person can no more approach a holy God than a tissue can survive in a furnace.

The God who had been missing, presumed dead, now makes himself known to Moses. 'I am the God of your father, the God of Abraham, the God of Isaac and the God of Jacob' (3:6). After the years of silence and the hardship endured by the Israelites, this is a stunning revelation.

God tells Moses that he, too, is moved by the plight of his people. He intends to rescue them and bring them out of Egypt to Canaan – 'a good and spacious land, a land flowing with milk and honey' (3:9). And the leader of this epic adventure is to be – Moses!

God's name
(3:13–22)

When asked his name, God replies, 'I Am Who I Am.' The Hebrew YHWH (pronounced 'Yahweh') means 'I Will Be What I Will Be'.

God is alive, immediate, and present. He *is*! In the past he was known by what he did for the patriarchs: Abraham, Isaac, Jacob and Joseph. Now he will be known by what he does for the Israelites. The proof that he *is* will be that his people will be rescued from slavery – and worship him on this mountain.

'The LORD' is the English translation of Yahweh or 'Jehovah'. It comes from the days when strict Jews would not pronounce God's name, because their lips were unholy. Instead, they took the letters of YHWH and the vowels from 'Adonai' ('my Lord') to make 'Jehovah'.

Signs for Moses – and Aaron
(4:1–31)

Moses asks for more definite signs that the Lord is at work. God turns Moses' shepherd staff into a snake and makes his hand leprous. If the people don't believe Moses, he is to pour Nile water on the ground and it will become blood. Such Bible miracles are always grouped around special

This statue at Luxor is of Rameses II, who may have been the pharaoh confronted reluctantly by Moses and Aaron.

events. They are the pointers to some mighty work of God.

Desperately, Moses pleads that he isn't a good speaker. But this is no problem to God. The Lord of creation, who gave people their mouths and all their senses, is well able to help Moses speak. So in the end Moses has to tell the truth. He simply doesn't want to go. He isn't good at leadership. No one will believe him. He is happy where he is. He's a coward.

God agrees that Moses' brother Aaron will assist him and speak for him. Reluctantly, Moses returns to Egypt. On the way he has a fierce struggle with God, which is resolved when Zipporah circumcises their son. Perhaps Moses is bringing his covenant commitment up to date, before calling on others to do the same.

The great escape

'Let my people go!'
(5:1–21)

Moses and Aaron go to Pharaoh with the reasonable request that the Hebrews should be allowed a three-day pilgrimage into the desert. They have their own God, who is calling them to hold a festival.

But Pharaoh does not acknowledge this Lord, the God of Israel. His answer is to make life even harder for the slaves. From now on, they will have to find the straw for making bricks, while still producing the same number. The Hebrews obviously have too much time on their hands if they're planning a pilgrimage!

And so the Israelites make bricks with a mixture of mud, sand and straw. This is shaped in wooden moulds and dried by the sun. The straw is vital for bonding the mud, as it decays in the clay and improves the plasticity of the brick.

'I will free you'
(5:22 – 6:27)

The Israelites blame Moses and Aaron for getting them into deeper trouble. Moses (for the first time, but not the last) turns his discouragement into prayer.

The Lord reassures Moses of his overwhelming commitment to rescue the Israelites from Egypt. He states again that he is the very same God who made covenant promises to Abraham, Isaac and Jacob. Now he has 'remembered' his covenant. He is Israel's next of kin, and can be relied on to 'redeem' her – to rescue her from trouble.

Moses faithfully relays God's message to the Israelites – but they are too angry and disillusioned to take it in.

'I will harden Pharaoh's heart'
(6:28 – 7:13)

Moses is feeling totally inadequate. He is also tongue-tied. But God tells him to challenge Pharaoh with complete confidence. God is in control. He is even going to 'harden Pharaoh's heart' so that Pharaoh will become set in his resistance. Then, when the climax comes, the full contrast between Israel's God and the gods of Egypt will be clearly seen.

Moses is now eighty. He was forty when he killed the Egyptian, and he has been a further forty years working as a shepherd. Forty years is 'a generation' – the time it takes to grow up and have children. When Moses dies at the age of 120 his life will have spanned three generations.

Despite their sense of utter weakness, Moses and Aaron obey God. When Pharaoh demands some proof that God is on their side, Aaron throws down his staff and it turns into a snake. Pharaoh is unimpressed. He gets his own people to do the same. Even when Aaron's snake eats the rest, Pharaoh won't change his mind.

The plagues
(7:14 – 11:10)

The River Nile is worshipped as a god in Egypt. It is the country's lifeline. Without its waters, Egypt would die. Now Moses commands Aaron to strike the water and it turns to blood. It becomes thick, red and undrinkable. Pharaoh's magicians can conjure the same effect, but they can't produce a cure.

This is the first of ten plagues which God inflicts on Egypt. The Nile and all water flowing from it are turned 'to blood'. Thousands of fish die – and rot. Multitudes of frogs leave their swamps and take to the houses. Pharaoh promises to let the Israelites go, if only Moses will ask the Lord to get rid of the frogs. But once they're dead and heaped in piles, he changes his mind.

The frogs are followed by plagues of gnats and flies, animal sickness, and boils on humans and cattle. There is a storm of thunder and hail in which branches are stripped from trees and the crops are ruined. But the storm doesn't hit Goshen, where the Israelites live, and it stops when Moses prays. Meanwhile, Pharaoh's magicians manage to conjure up some frogs, but admit defeat with the gnats. When it comes to boils, they themselves can hardly walk!

After the hail, a strong east wind brings clouds of locusts. They eat all that's left after the storm. Moses had warned Pharaoh that the Lord would do this and the

---

The plagues

The plagues seem to have occurred over a period of several months, from the flooding of the Nile in July to the Israelites' departure from Egypt in the following spring.

The Nile rises each year in July and August, reaching its high point in September and subsiding in October and November. When the waters are particularly high, they bring down red clay from Ethiopia. Sometimes the plankton and bacteria multiply, to give a dramatic reddish effect.

Decomposing fish could have driven the frogs inshore – where they might have died of anthrax, which would also kill the cattle. Swarms of mosquitoes would breed on the stagnant water, while flies would incubate in the piles of rotting frogs. Together they would carry disease from animals to humans, causing bites and skin sores.

Storms that flattened barley and flax (but not wheat and spelt), would have come in January or February. Such weather was more likely in Upper Egypt than in Goshen, which is near the sea. Locusts come in dense clouds in March, blown on the east wind up the Nile Valley. It was wind, too, which would complete the drying of the red clay and whip it into a dust storm. The resulting dense darkness could last for several days.

The plagues can all be explained by natural events, but God's mighty power is evident in their intensity and timing.

wind had risen when Moses raised his staff.

When Pharaoh asks forgiveness, Moses prays to the Lord and a west wind drives the locusts away.

Finally there is total darkness throughout the land – except, of course, where the Israelites live. It's a darkness that can be *felt* and it lasts for three days.

Each of the plagues can be explained by natural causes, but it is the fact that they happened *when* they did – and on such a scale – that indicates God at work.

The tenth and final plague is truly terrible. The eldest sons of all Egyptian families – humans and animals – are to die in a single night. But the Lord will 'pass over' the families of the Israelites and spare them.

The Passover

(12:1–30)

Moses tells the Israelites to prepare for this 'Passover'. Every family is to kill a lamb and daub its blood on the outside door. This is a sign for the Lord to pass over the home. The people are to pack their possessions, get dressed for a journey and eat a hasty meal.

At midnight the first-born of the Egyptians start to die, from Pharaoh's son to the child of the lowest slave. While desolate cries are heard from the Egyptian houses, the Israelite homes are secure and calm. Nobody stirs, not even the dogs.

At midnight, a new age begins for the Israelites. Passover is to be their New Year's Day; their birth as a nation.

The first month of the year has the Canaanite name 'Abib', which means 'ripening corn'. Later the Jews will call it 'Nisan', a name from Babylonia. In Western months, it comes towards the end of March and the beginning of April. The Jewish Passover sometimes coincides with the Christian Maundy Thursday.

Moses tells the whole community of Israel what to do. This 'gathering for God' is our first glimpse of a word which will later be used for 'church'. Such a 'community' or 'church' is a group of people who are 'called together' to hear the word of God.

On the tenth day of the first month, each household is to take a lamb. It must be a year-old male and can be a sheep or a goat. On the fourteenth day the animal is to be killed. This is halfway through the month, when the moon is full. The Passover is a festival timed by the new moon, but not in honour of it. In later years, the Passover date will be announced when the new moon is seen in the sky above Jerusalem.

The blood of the lamb is a sign rather than a sacrifice. The animal's life is paid by a family so that the first-born son will be spared. But this isn't a payment for any sin. There is no priest, no ceremony and no confession. The lamb is simply killed and its blood painted on the sides and tops of the Hebrew door frames.

A bunch of 'hyssop' is used for painting the lamb's blood on the doorposts. This isn't the plant we call hyssop today. It may be a common shrub or herb, such as Syrian marjoram.

The lamb is roasted whole on a spit over an open fire. It is eaten with bitter herbs and bread made without yeast. Everything is to be eaten up. Nothing of this holy meal is to be left as if it doesn't matter, or taken away for use in magic. And all is to be done in a hurry, because God's time for action has come.

When the Passover is eaten in Jewish homes today there is no lamb, because there is no temple in Jerusalem and therefore no sacrifices. Instead, there is the shank bone of a sheep as a token. The bitter herbs have become a reminder of the bitterness of slavery.

The Feast of Unleavened Bread includes Passover and lasts for a week. Perhaps Moses orders bread without yeast because there is no time for the dough to rise. If some is for the journey, it will pack flat and last well.

The exodus

(12:31 – 14:31)

Pharaoh commands Moses and Aaron to leave Egypt. The Israelites ask the Egyptians for silver, gold and clothing. No doubt some gifts are made with goodwill, and others given just to get rid of the terror. In any case, the Israelites leave Egypt laden with treasure just as God had promised.

The departure is so sudden that the Israelites travel with unleavened bread still in their kneading bowls. The Lord goes ahead of them in a pillar of cloud. At night the cloud moves behind them, to shield them from the Egyptians.

The quickest route, along the coast, is also the most dangerous. Instead, God leads the Israelites inland on a desert road to the Red Sea, or 'Sea of Reeds'. This is not the 'Red Sea' of the Persian Gulf, but a marshy area of papyrus or other reedy plants.

The exact place of the exodus and the route through the wilderness is not known. It isn't even certain which mountain is Sinai. One theory has the Israelites travelling a long way south to Mount Horeb, and then up to Kadesh Barnea. Another takes a more direct route across to Kadesh, with Jebel Helal as the holy mountain.

Once the Israelites have left, Pharaoh changes his mind. But God is at work in Pharaoh's defiance. He is hardening Pharaoh's attitudes and preparing him for total defeat.

Pharaoh pursues the Hebrews with horses and chariots. He catches up with them as they camp by the Red Sea. The Israelites fear that all is lost, but Moses speaks to them with authority and confidence. They must stand firm in their faith in God and watch what he will do to deliver them once and for all.

The Lord tells Moses to stretch out his hand over the sea. Then, throughout the night, the Lord causes a strong east wind to divide the water and create a dry path for the people to cross.

It is unlikely that the waters are stacked up each side of the fleeing Israelites, as in a Hollywood epic. This great deliverance is more in the timing than the special effects. But the water to either side certainly protects the Israelites from being outflanked by the Egyptian forces. When the chariots use the same route in the early hours of the morning, they are doomed.

As Pharaoh's finest battalion charges, the God of Israel intervenes. In fire and cloud he throws them into muddy, panic-stricken chaos. The chariot wheels stick, the horses rear, the drivers fight for control and then turn back. As they do so, the Lord tells Moses to stretch out his hand again. The first rays of daylight reveal the waters flooding back to drown the pride of Egypt. Israel's awesome and pitiless enemy is routed, without a blow being struck. This is God's mighty act of deliverance.

The song of Moses and Miriam
(15:1–21)

Moses and the Israelites sing a song which tells the story of God's thrilling victory. It has strong rhythms, and uses ancient words and phrases. There is a great sense of God surging up powerfully like a wave, to toss Pharaoh's soldiers and swallow the chariots. The Lord is supreme as both God and king. The exodus is his sovereign act to rescue his people from tyranny and slavery. He is Israel's redeemer.

Miriam, Moses' sister or half-sister, leads the women in a song and dance of victory. The words are particularly old:

> *I will sing to the Lord,*
> *for he is highly exalted.*
> *The horse and its rider*
> *he has hurled into the sea (15:1).*

The exodus becomes an important image in later psalms and prophecies, for example Psalm 106:9–12:

> *He rebuked the Red Sea, and it dried up;*
> *he led them through the depths as through a desert.*
> *He saved them from the hand of the foe;*
> *from the hand of the enemy he redeemed them.*
> *The waters covered their adversaries;*
> *not one of them survived.*
> *Then they believed his promises and sang his praise.*

The desert journey

Once in the desert, the Israelites have to learn to trust God. The route and pace of their journey depend on finding pasture and water for their flocks and herds.

The waters of Marah and Elim
(15:22–27)

The Desert of Shur is barren and sandy. When they get to Marah (meaning 'bitter' – like myrrh), they find the water unpleasant. Marah may have been today's Ain Hawarah, which has an artesian well tainted by mineral salts.

The people grumble. The joy of freedom evaporates in the heat of hardship. This is the first of many occasions when they blame Moses for their troubles. Moses, in despair, cries out to God.

The Lord 'shows' Moses a piece of wood. Moses throws the wood in the water and it becomes sweet. The Hebrew word for 'show' is 'torah'. It means 'instruction' – the way to something good. It will be used for the 'Torah', the law of God, which the psalmist will describe as 'sweeter than honey' (Psalm 119:103).

The wood may have been a shrub such as a barberry bush, which would have a strong enough flavour to make the water drinkable. The Lord reveals himself as One who can give his people a healthy life, if they follow his way.

The Israelites move on some seven miles to Elim, which means 'terebinths' or 'oak trees'. This could have been the modern Wadi Gharandel, which is a more comfortable oasis. These places are hard to trace, because the names have been changed so often by nomads passing through.

Quail and manna
(16:1–36)

The grumbling goes on. The people wish they were back in Egypt, sitting round pots of stew. But the Lord is going to provide them with daily bread.

That evening, fresh meat arrives, in the form of a flock of quail. Quails are small game birds, like partridges, which fly low and roost on the ground. They migrate north across the Sinai peninsular between March and April, on their way from Arabia to southern Europe. And they are tasty to eat.

The following morning, when the dew has dried, the Israelites find the ground covered with thin flakes, like frost. They say in Hebrew, 'Manna?' ('What's-its-name?') – and the phrase sticks.

Manna is to be the Israelites' basic food for the next

forty years. It is 'white like coriander seeds and tastes like wafers made with honey' (16:31). Moses tells the people to collect an omer (probably about four pints) per person every morning, except the sabbath. On the day before the sabbath they must collect enough for two days and cook or bake it to make it last.

Water from the rock
(17:1–7)

When the Israelites camp at Rephidim, they are again short of water. Rephidim is today's Wadi Feiran, the principal oasis in southern Sinai. It may be that the Israelites were prevented from getting to water by the Amalekites.

Kibbutz Qalia, an oasis near Qumran. God led his people from one oasis to another as they journeyed through the desert. It is now difficult to identify many of them precisely, as generations of nomads have altered their names.

Moses feels that his life is in danger, because the people are so angry with him. The Lord leads Moses to a rock at Horeb, and tells him to strike it. Water gushes out, as it does when the smooth surface of limestone is split. Moses may have been familiar with this extraordinary method of finding water, as he had been a shepherd for forty years in a nearby region.

The place is given two names: Massah ('testing'), because the people doubt whether the Lord is with them, and Meribah ('quarrelling'), because the Israelites quarrel with Moses. In a similar episode, Moses is commanded simply to speak to the rock. In the event he strikes it twice with his rod, and God is angry with him. Again, the place is called Meribah (Numbers 20:9–12).

Prayer battle
(17:8–16)

The Amalekites attack the Israelites. They are probably anxious to keep Rephidim for themselves. It is known by Arabs today as the 'Pearl of Sinai', a mini-paradise of palm trees and pasture.

At this point we meet Joshua. He is later described as Moses' assistant. Here he is commanding a contingent fighting the Amalekites. The Israelites must learn to rely on God in battle just as they have done for food and water. Moses prays from a vantage point overlooking the conflict, with Aaron and Hur either side to support his hands as they are raised in prayer.

When the enemy is defeated, the Lord tells Moses to declare a lasting ban on the Amalekites. This is to be both in writing on a scroll and by word of mouth to Joshua. In years to come, the Amalekites will be defeated and destroyed by Saul (1 Samuel 15:7–8).

Jethro visits Moses
(18:1–27)

Moses' father-in-law, Jethro, arrives with Moses' wife and sons. He sees how overburdened Moses is with the care of so many people and offers him sound advice on how to share the load. Jethro's principles of selection and delegation have never been surpassed and are valued and applied to this day.

The giving of the law

Mount Sinai
(19:1–25)

The Israelites arrive at the Desert of Sinai and camp near God's holy mountain. Moses goes up to speak with God and God gives him a solemn message for the people.

Israel has been given her freedom to become a nation. Now she receives her calling to belong to God. She is singled out from all the nations of the world to be God's priests: his pure, distinct, holy representatives. The Israelites will represent God to the nations and bring the nations to God. God's reputation is to depend on Israel's example.

It is a solemn moment. The people are to focus on God's holiness by washing their clothes and abstaining

---

What is manna?

There are various theories about manna, but in the end it remains a mystery and a miracle. Certain insects in the Sinai peninsular secrete drops of honeydew on tamarisk bushes overnight. The drops melt in the sunshine and fall to the ground, where they are carried off by ants. The substance sounds like manna, but is only produced for a few weeks of the year, round about June. Only by a miracle could food be provided on the scale and with the regularity required to feed the Israelites. Relying on manna is a major

step in Israel's learning to trust in God and his promises (Deuteronomy 8:3).

Manna is God's food supply: 'bread from heaven'. It is a daily proof to the Israelites that God cares for them and will provide for their needs as each day comes. This theme is found in the Lord's Prayer, when Jesus teaches his disciples to pray, 'Give us today our daily bread' (Matthew 6:11).

When Jesus feeds a multitude by blessing and breaking five small barley loaves, the people are excited that a new Moses has appeared to lead them. Jesus explains that he isn't like Moses, whose

manna lasted only a day. The Israelites who ate that manna died in the desert. Jesus declares himself as God, the provider and life-giver, when he says, 'I am the bread of life... the bread that comes down from heaven, so that one may eat of it and not die' (John 6:47–50).

from sex. Sex is not dirty, but it is engrossing. The Israelites are to devote themselves entirely to the task in hand. Even so, they must keep their distance from the holy mountain.

The presence of God is awesome. The Lord descends on the mountain with fire, smoke billows up, the landscape shudders, a ram's horn trumpet sounds a crescendo… and God speaks.

It is tempting to think that Mount Sinai is an active volcano, but it may not be so. There are volcanoes to the east of the gulf of Aqaba, but the traditional Mount Sinai is today's Gebel Mosa, one of three fine peaks near modern Feiran (Rephidim). It isn't volcanic.

The Ten Commandments
(20:1–17)

The keynote of Israel's relationship with God is to be obedience. The people's commitment to God is to be shown by keeping his laws. The Lord reveals these laws to Moses, beginning with the Ten Commandments. They are firm, clear and concise. Although several begin with the words 'You shall not…' their effect is very positive and liberating. In their simplicity and directness they apply to everyone, without exception, for all time.

The first commandments deal with respect for God:

'I am the Lord your God, who brought you out of Egypt… You shall have no other gods before me' (20:2–3). The Lord is identified as the One who alone rescued his people from Egypt. The Israelites are not to worship any other god. To take another god is idolatry, just as to take another sexual partner outside marriage is adultery.

'You shall not make for yourself an idol' (20:4). The Israelites are not to make images of any god, nor even to attempt to portray the true One. Any carving or painting, however sincere, can only have the effect of shrinking the concept of God and misleading his worshippers. God is invisible.

'You shall not misuse the name of the Lord your God' (20:7). God's people are not to abuse or misuse God's name. They must not empty it of meaning by using it lightly, or by making vows which they then break.

Mount Sinai, where Moses received the Ten Commandments. Many scholars think this is the mountain known today as Jebel Musa (2,244 m high). In the Old Testament it is also known as Mount Horeb.

'*Remember the Sabbath day by keeping it holy*' (20:8). The sabbath, every seventh day, is to be kept for rest and enjoyment of God's blessing. It is to be a day of freedom and fresh perspective.

The last commandments have to do with people's behaviour towards each other. Every person's life is to be respected. So are marriages, possessions and reputations.

'*Honour your father and your mother*' (20:12). Parents are to be honoured. This is God's social structure, which will enable the nation to survive. The word 'honour' means more than just respect for parents. It implies giving money or an allowance to provide for your parents in their old age. Jesus rebukes some Pharisees for breaking this commandment. They have set aside for 'religious' use the money which should be maintaining their parents (Matthew 15:1–6).

'*You shall not murder*' (20:13). This is just two words in Hebrew: 'No killing!' It means that there is to be no violent murder of a personal enemy. Later laws understand that death is sometimes accidental. The death penalty, as well as killing enemies in battle, are an accepted part of Jewish life.

'*You shall not commit adultery*' (20:14). A man is not to have sex with another man's wife. It is the worst kind of stealing, short of murder.

'*You shall not steal*' (20:15). A person has a right to life, freedom and property. These rights are respected and protected by the commandment not to steal. No society can establish trust when theft and burglary are rife. Terrible pain and disruption come from such crimes as kidnapping and slavery. Death itself can result from the theft of someone's livelihood or savings.

'*You shall not give false testimony against your neighbour*' (20:16). This is again about stealing. This time the theft is of someone's reputation. With so many laws carrying the death penalty, a lie may cause a person to be executed for something they didn't do. Even gossip can be lethal and result in a living death for someone who can't prove the truth.

'*You shall not covet*' (20:17). God forbids jealousy of someone else's possessions. This is a law against mental theft and a warning against being discontented. It is also a 'threshold' commandment. To cross it may lead to breaking one of the other commandments as well.

Other laws
(20:18 – 23:13)

After the Ten Commandments, God gives Moses a variety of laws. Here, and in the books of Leviticus, Numbers and Deuteronomy, there are as many as seven groups of laws. They are collections of rules and detailed procedures.

Here we find guidance for owning servants and settling quarrels. There is compensation for injuries to people or damage to property. The weaker members of society – orphans, widows, the poor and the stranger – are given special protection. And just as people are to rest on every seventh day, so cultivated land is to rest every seventh year.

'EYE FOR EYE, TOOTH FOR TOOTH'

This regulation sounds brutal and vindictive (21:24). In fact it is simply an attempt to be fair. Someone who inflicts hurt is to receive an equal hurt as his penalty. Nothing more and nothing less. *Only* an eye for an eye, and *only* a tooth for a tooth. It is a restriction on unlimited vengeance.

In the Sermon on the Mount, Jesus teaches a better way, which is forgiveness: 'Do not resist an evildoer. If anyone strikes you on the right cheek, turn the other also' (Matthew 5:39). In forgiving, hurt is absorbed by the wronged person, and not recycled in revenge. This is what Jesus himself did on the cross.

Three annual festivals
(23:14–17)

Three times a year there are to be festivals. So God declares three weeks of official holiday every year.

The Feast of Unleavened Bread falls at the beginning of the barley harvest. It is a week in which

---

Jesus and the law

Jesus teaches that obedience to God starts with our thoughts. This is already at the heart of the law, as the tenth commandment shows, but Jesus makes it particularly clear.

In the Sermon on the Mount, Jesus says of murder, 'Don't even nurse anger' (Matthew 5:22–23). On adultery, he says, 'Don't even give her that "look"' (Matthew 5:28). This is a fascinating glimpse of Jesus' own self-discovery and self-control, as well as being essential guidance for our own thoughts.

A covenant is made when God commits himself to bless and protect his people. He does so of his own free will and keeps his promise despite his people's failures and rebellions. By the time of this covenant at Sinai, God has already made binding promises to Noah and Abraham. In the future he will also make a solemn commitment to preserve the royal line of David.

the Israelites eat bread made without yeast. It celebrates the Passover, when they remember their escape from Egypt. The Feast of Harvest (or 'Weeks') comes seven weeks later, while the wheat harvest is being gathered. The Feast of Ingathering is in the autumn when the last crops, including the grapes and olives, are safely stored.

'Do not cook a young goat in its mother's milk'
(23:18–19)

To those who love pets, this command goes without saying. We may think it's a ban on a tasteless and cruel act, but it probably refers to a pagan ritual or fertility spell.

'If...'
(23:20–33)

The laws which begin with the Ten Commandments are rounded off with a wonderful promise. Chapters 21 to 23 form a mini-book, dealing with the terms, conditions and benefits of the covenant.

If the Israelites will honour God in every aspect of their life, he will give them health and security. He will also go ahead of them into Canaan, to drive out their enemies and give them the land.

The covenant confirmed
(24:1–12)

The covenant is the agreement by which the Lord becomes Israel's God, and Israel commits herself to be God's people and keep his law. The Lord calls Moses and Aaron, together with Aaron's sons Nadab and Abihu, and seventy elders. They are to worship God at a distance, while Moses alone approaches the Lord.

Moses tells the people God's laws and writes them down as a permanent record. The Israelites promise obedience and Moses builds an altar at the foot of the mountain. They offer sacrifices and Moses reads them the book of the covenant. This book may be the same three chapters we have just read.

The people swear: 'Everything the Lord has said we will do.' The rest of the Old Testament will be the story of their failure to keep this promise.

Moses sprinkles the people with blood from the sacrifices. Then the select group, Moses and the elders, share a meal in God's presence. It is a time-honoured way of marking an agreement.

Moses on the mountain
(24:13–18)

Moses spends forty days and nights alone on the mountain top, enveloped in the cloud of God's presence and glory. The glory of the Lord 'settles' on Mount Sinai – a word which has the sense of pitching a tent, or staying for a while.

God's glory is his 'weight' or worth. The signs of his presence are dense cloud and raging fire.

Moses is one of the Old Testament's 'mountain men'. Both he and Elijah have awesome encounters with God at Sinai. One day Jesus will meet with them in the cloud of God's glory on the Mount of Transfiguration. He will talk with them about his own 'exodus' or departure (Luke 9:30). Unlike Elijah, there will be no fiery chariot for Jesus. His path to glory must pass through death on a cross.

The tabernacle and the priests

Offerings for the tabernacle
(25:1–9)

The Lord asks that the Israelites, of their own free will, may give the materials for building a tabernacle. This is to be God's own tent, so that he can live among his people. It is to be made with extraordinary care and attention to detail. In the tent there will be special furniture: an ark, a table and a lampstand.

The ark
(25:10–22)

The ark is a wooden chest, about a yard long and two feet in width and height. It is overlaid with gold and

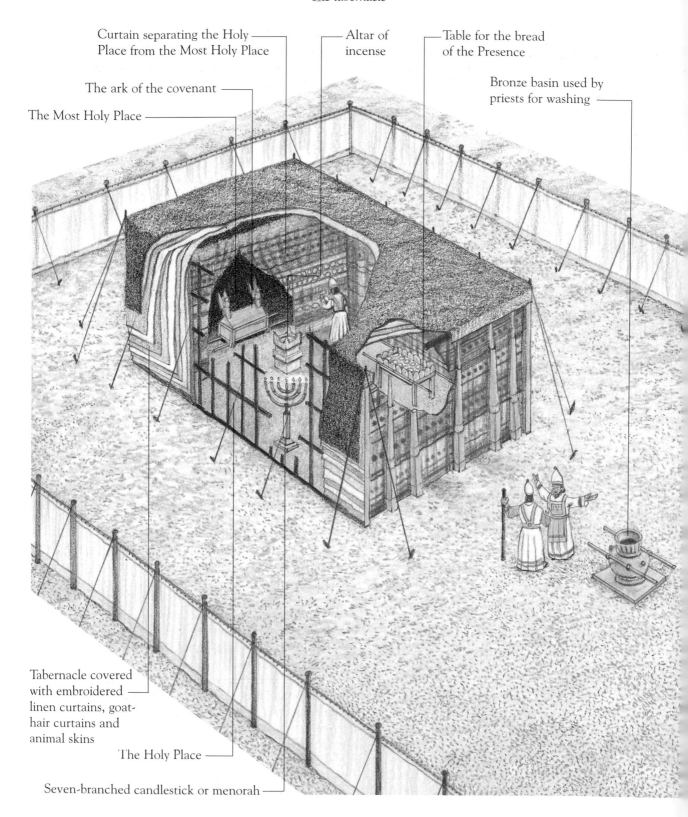

Curtain separating the Holy
Place from the Most Holy Place

The ark of the covenant

The Most Holy Place

Altar of
incense

Table for the bread
of the Presence

Bronze basin used by
priests for washing

Tabernacle covered
with embroidered
linen curtains, goat-
hair curtains and
animal skins

The Holy Place

Seven-branched candlestick or menorah

The tabernacle was a symbol to the Israelites of the presence of God accompanying them as they travelled through the wilderness. It provided a focus for worship and sacrifice. The materials for its construction – dyed yarn, wood, animal skins, spices, precious stones and metals – came in the form of gifts donated by people. Designers and craftsman were anointed by God to work on the tabernacle. Its construction and the specification of its furnishings were given in detail by God, and its basic layout was followed by Solomon in building Israel's first temple (p. 183).

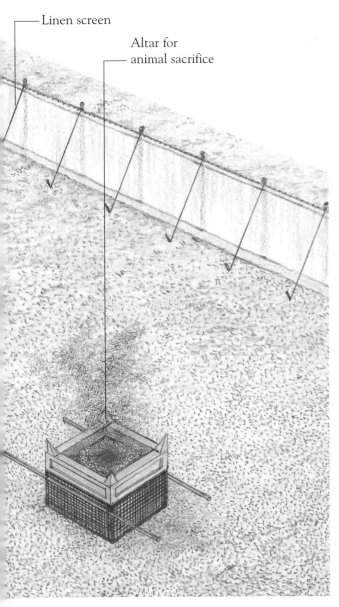

Linen screen

Altar for animal sacrifice

topped with cherubim. This is the ark of the testimony, where the stone tablets containing the Ten Commandments will be kept. Although Noah's boat and Moses' basket are both called arks, a different word is used here.

The table
(25:23–30)

The table is for 'the bread of the Presence'. These are twelve loaves (one for each tribe), freshly baked and placed in the presence of God.

The lampstand
(25:31–40)

There is to be a six-branched lampstand which, with its centre stem, will provide seven lamps. It is to be decorated with almond buds and blossoms in gold.

The tabernacle
(26:1–37)

The first tabernacle is a 'tent of meeting' which Moses pitches outside the camp. Anyone can seek God there. Moses himself speaks with God 'face to face, as one speaks to a friend'.

Now the tabernacle is to be a curtained sanctuary *within* the camp. It can be assembled and dismantled to travel with the Israelites on their journey, as God himself does.

There is considerable detail about how the tabernacle is to be made and furnished. Mobile meeting tents and pavilions were well known in Egypt long before the time of Moses. Incense altars, too, have been discovered from various Canaanite sites dating from the 10th century BC.

The basic structure of the tabernacle is a wooden frame, about 45 feet long by 15 feet wide. It is covered with ten linen curtains. The material is gorgeously embroidered with blue, purple and scarlet thread. It is then protected from the weather by eleven goat-hair curtains and layers of animal skins.

Inside the tabernacle it is cool, dark and airless. There are two sections or compartments. The first is the heart of the tabernacle, the 'Most Holy Place'. Here stands the ark of the covenant. The ark has an 'atonement cover' of pure gold, on which blood from the sacrifices is sprinkled. This is a sign that sin has been covered and cancelled.

The second compartment is the 'Holy Place'. It is

'The Lord is here'

The tabernacle is the prototype of all later temples and churches. It is a place to meet with God.

When Jesus is born, John's Gospel says, 'The Word became flesh and lived ['tabernacled'] for a while among us.' Paul teaches that every Christian is a tabernacle of the Holy Spirit.

The tabernacle has many links with the New Testament and what Jesus comes to do. The letter to the Hebrews says that Jesus, in offering his life as a sacrifice for the sin of the world, 'entered heaven itself, now to appear for us in God's presence' (Hebrews 9:24).

separated from the Most Holy Place by a curtain. This is the curtain which, in Herod's temple, will be torn from top to bottom when Jesus dies (Matthew 27:51).

In front of the curtain is the altar of incense, covered with gold and with horns projecting at the four corners. The altar stands directly opposite the ark.

On the north side of the altar is the table for the 'bread of the Presence'. On it are twelve loaves, specially baked from fine flour and arranged in the presence of God. They remind the twelve tribes that they are always living in God's sight.

Every sabbath, the priests place fresh bread on the table and eat the old bread in the Holy Place. One day the young hero David will, rather shockingly, ask for the bread of the Presence to feed his men (1 Samuel 21:2–6). A thousand years later, Jesus will approve what David did. He lets his own men pick ears of corn on the sabbath, because he puts people before protocol (Mark 2:23–28).

On the south side of the altar is the lampstand.

The courtyard
(27:1–21)

The tabernacle is set in a courtyard, about 50 yards long and 25 yards wide. The area is marked out by a high linen screen, hung on posts and held by guy ropes and pegs. This is where the people can assemble when sacrifices are offered or for other special occasions.

In the eastern half of the courtyard stands the altar of burnt offering. It has no top, but is hollow to form an

incinerator. It is covered in copper and, like the altar of incense, has horns at the corners. The burnt offering from the main sacrifice is offered here. The horns can be for tying animals, or for a person to cling to when making a request.

Between the altar and the door of the tabernacle stands a bronze basin. This is for Aaron and his sons to wash their hands and feet, before entering the tabernacle or approaching the altar. God's work is holy and must be done with clean bodies and pure hearts.

The priestly garments
(28:1–43)

Aaron and his sons are to have special robes. Aaron, as high priest, is to be magnificently dressed in breastplate, ephod, robe, tunic, turban and sash. The instructions are full of symbolic detail, although the meaning isn't always clear to us today.

Like the linen drapes of the tabernacle, the garments are to be finely embroidered – this time with the addition of gold thread. Gold is the colour of God's glory.

The consecration of the priests
(29:1–46)

Aaron and his sons are to be consecrated – set apart from everyone else to serve God as priests. They must be made clean, by washing and sacrifice, before they can take on their holy work.

Moses washes the priests and dresses them in their robes. He anoints Aaron with holy oil, pouring it over his head. This is the sign of the outpouring of God's spirit for a special task. Then Moses makes a sacrifice for their sins.

The priests lay their hands on a bull. In this way they identify themselves with the animal that is to be killed on their behalf. The bull is then slaughtered in God's presence, at the entrance to the tabernacle. The bull's blood is smeared on the horns of the altar and poured out at the base. Some of its fat, liver and kidneys are burned on the altar. The bulk of the carcass is burned outside the camp. It is an awesome symbol of the damage and cost of sin.

Next a ram is chosen. Aaron and his sons lay their hands on its head. It is slaughtered, cut up and the pieces washed. This time the whole animal is burned on the altar. This means that the priests are wholly acceptable, no longer torn apart by sin. Now they are pleasing to God.

Another ram is killed. Some of its blood is smeared on the priests – on their right ear lobes, right thumbs and right big toes. Some is sprinkled on the altar and some over the priests and their robes. Now they are entirely embraced in the life and work of God at the altar.

Parts of the ram – the breast and thigh – are waved before the Lord, together with the sacred bread. The meat is cooked for the priests to eat. This, with the sacred bread, is their ordination meal.

For a week, Aaron and his sons offer sacrifices to consecrate the altar. When these are completed, the routine of morning and evening sacrifice begins. Each day, at dawn and dusk, a year-old lamb is offered, with flour, oil and wine.

The sequence of washing and bloodshed is complete. Each sacrifice and ceremony has played a part in opening the way to God. Now a holy bridgehead has been established between God and his people. The poured-out blood is the focus. The priests are the live links. The purpose is that the Israelites will enjoy communion with God for ever.

The altar of incense
(30:1–10)

Inside the tabernacle there is a small altar. It stands in front of the curtain in the Holy Place and is used only for burning incense. The incense itself is made to a unique recipe. Aaron burns it twice a day as he tends the lamps. Once a year he cleanses and rededicates the altar, with blood from the annual Day of Atonement sacrifice.

A holy poll tax
(30:11–16)

Every man over twenty years old is to pay half a shekel for 'atonement money'. Although the rescue from Egypt is God's free gift, this holy tax acknowledges what God has done for each person. The amount is the same for rich and poor alike and the money is used to maintain the tabernacle. Centuries later, this becomes the two-drachma temple tax collected from Jesus and Peter in Capernaum (Matthew 17:24–27).

The basin
(30:17–21)

There is a bronze basin for the priests to wash their hands and feet. They must do this before entering the tent of meeting or approaching the altar for sacrifice. Their hands and feet will often be spattered with blood. But, more importantly, the washing will help them focus their minds and hearts on the seriousness of approaching God.

The anointing oil
(30:22–33)

Moses is told to make the anointing oil. The base is olive oil and the spices are rare and expensive. This oil could have many uses, such as treating wounds or sunburn, or perfuming hair and skin. The Lord tells Moses that this particular formula is to be kept exclusively for the priests.

Incense
(30:34–38)

The incense, too, is made to a special recipe. It contains rare and expensive spices, together with salt to preserve it and help it burn.

Incense is burned as a sign of prayer. It gives a fragrant smell and clouds of smoke. With so many other strong smells around (animal dung, burning fat, hot blood and crowds of humans in desert heat) the incense will soothe the senses and condition the air.

The skilled workers
(31:1–11)

God is providing a gifted worker to head up the design and manufacture of all the sacred furniture, fittings and robes. His name is Bezalel, which means 'Overshadowed by God'. His skills are inspired by God.

The sabbath
(31:12–18)

The Lord reminds Moses of the importance of keeping the sabbath. By setting aside every seventh day, Israel acknowledges God as Lord over work and time.

Although work is necessary and even exciting, it must never become an end in itself. It must not come between the Israelites and their God. To observe the sabbath as a holy day of rest must be for ever a distinctive aspect of Jewish life.

The Lord concludes his instructions to Moses by giving him the two 'tablets of the testimony'. These are stone plaques on which God has written the law, probably in the form of the Ten Commandments.

Rebellion and judgment

The golden calf

(32:1 – 33:6)

Moses has been away from the camp for more than a month. The Israelites begin to assume that he has had an accident, or simply gone away and left them. They were never very impressed with him anyway.

The people put pressure on Aaron. Sullen, impatient and boorish, they want a god they can see. Aaron gives in to their demands. He collects all the gold earrings, melts them down and fashions a golden calf. Then he builds an altar for the worship of the calf-idol and announces a festival.

This a tragic lapse, but it is very true to human nature and our own experience. The high points of commitment are often followed by shameful failure. This is why Jesus is so impressive in resisting the devil's temptations just after his baptism.

The calf is a young bull. The bull is a favourite with all fertility cults, because of its strength and power to reproduce. Baal, chief of the many gods of Canaan, is sometimes depicted as a bull. The Israelites feel defenceless and rather inferior without something similar. And pagan rites are great fun. Let the party begin!

The Lord is seething with anger at this terrible betrayal. He tells Moses to stand aside so that he can destroy the people and start again. But Moses pleads with God. He appeals to God's promises, his name and his reputation. He argues that the Egyptians will say that God has rescued his people only to kill them in the desert. He reminds God of his promise to multiply the descendants of Abraham, Isaac and Jacob.

For his part, God seems almost to *want* Moses to pray in this way. He agrees to spare the people and decides on a different course of action.

Long before he arrives at the camp, Moses hears the shouting and singing. Joshua, who is with him, thinks there must be a battle going on. Moses knows it's the sound of a drunken celebration.

Seeing the calf and the dancing, Moses flares with

Bronze bull (12th century BC), Samaria.

anger. He smashes the tablets of the law. He destroys the calf. He grinds the gold to powder, scatters it on water and makes the people drink it. This is like the later punishment for adultery. Israel has betrayed God, her husband, and must drink 'the waters of bitterness'.

Moses turns to Aaron for an explanation. Aaron pleads that the people have bullied him. All he did was throw their gold jewellery in the fire and there was a miracle. The calf made itself!

Moses calls on his own tribe, the Levites, to arm themselves and bring the people under control. Their faithfulness in this crisis will lead to them becoming the priestly tribe.

Moses tries to repair the damage with God. Unlike Aaron, he takes full responsibility for what has happened. He offers himself as a sacrifice for the people's sin, even if it means that he must be blotted out of God's book of life.

The Lord answers that each person will be responsible for his or her own sin. But, in any case, they must now travel on without him. The land of the Canaanites awaits them but the special relationship with God is over. The covenant is cancelled.

The people are chastened and go into mourning. Once and for all they discard their ornaments as a sign of repentance.

The tent of meeting

(33:7–11)

Moses has a tent outside the camp. It is known as the 'tent of meeting' and is a forerunner of the larger tabernacle which is to be built inside the camp. The people stand in their tent doors as Moses goes to pray for them. When they see the cloud of God's presence, they worship from a distance.

Moses has a direct experience of talking with God. He doesn't rely on visions, dreams or inspired guesses. 'The Lord used to speak to Moses face to face, as one speaks to a friend' (33:11).

Moses begs to know God more closely. He puts it to the Lord: 'If your Presence does not go with us, do not send us up from here' (33:15). The Lord is pleased with his prayer and agrees to continue with the people.

Moses asks if he may be allowed actually to see God. The request is impossible, because the force of God's glory would destroy Moses instantly. But the Lord hides him in the cleft of a rock and passes by. Moses is allowed to catch a glimpse of God's 'back'.

'When my glory passes by'

(33:12–23)

God is to be known by his name and his word.

Moses can only see God's 'back'. He can only know God through what has just happened – by what God has *done*. An example from the world around us is that we can only see the wind by what it has just done.

When Jesus comes, he will be the perfect image of God in human life. All of God's nature and personality will be seen in him. But the full, revealed, unleashed glory of God? We would be safer standing beside an atomic explosion.

The new stone tablets

(34:1–28)

The Lord instructs Moses to cut new tablets of stone. Moses returns to the mountain and receives the law afresh.

God describes himself to Moses as:

The Lord, the Lord,
a God merciful and gracious,
slow to anger,
and abounding in steadfast love and faithfulness,
keeping steadfast love for the thousandth generation,
forgiving iniquity and transgression and sin,
yet by no means clearing the guilty,
but visiting the iniquity of the parents
upon the children
and the children's children,
to the third and the fourth generation
        (34:6–7).

This is a glorious definition of God, which is often repeated in the Old Testament (Psalm 103:6–8; Jonah 4:2).

Moses begs God's forgiveness for the people and asks that they might go on to their Promised Land. The Lord makes a covenant with him and promises to do great deeds through the people. They are to advance on the Promised Land and drive out all the pagan tribes, smashing their idols, altars and fertility poles. There is

to be no compromise with pagan religion or intermarriage with pagan people.

The radiant face of Moses

(34:29–35)

Moses returns to the people with the new tablets of the law. His face is so radiant with the afterglow of God's glory that for a while he has to wear a veil.

The climax of Exodus

The climax of the book of Exodus is not the escape from Egypt or the giving of the law at Sinai. It is the construction and dedication of the tabernacle, where God will dwell among his people in the beauty of holiness.

Moses calls the people together. He reminds them again not to work on the sabbath – not even to labour in lighting a fire. It is the keeping of sabbath which will mark out Israel as different from other nations.

Materials for the tabernacle

(35:1–29)

Now Moses invites the people to bring materials for the building of the tabernacle. They come with precious metals, coloured yarn, fine linen, goat hair, rams' skins, acacia wood, olive oil and spices. There are even precious stones for the high priest's garments, the ephod and breastpiece.

The tabernacle is constructed

(35:30 – 40:33)

The skilled worker Bezalel and his assistant Oholiab embark on the great project.

Bezalel has the power of God's Spirit upon him to do this sacred work. In the New Testament, too, spiritual gifts will enable very practical ministries. The skilled workers, designers, embroiderers and weavers are all worshipping God with their skills, just as the people are with their overflowing generosity.

The ark, the table and the lampstand are each made as the Lord instructed Moses. So, too, the altar of incense, the anointing oil and the fragrant incense. Everything is assembled for the glory of God.

The altar of burnt offering is built of acacia wood, with horns on the corners, and overlaid with bronze. There are bronze utensils to match: pots, shovels, sprinkling bowls, meat forks and firepans. And there is the bronze basin on its stand.

The priestly garments are made with the greatest care and attention to detail; the ephod of gold, with blue, purple and scarlet yarn and fine twisted linen. Precious stones are mounted in gold settings. Nothing but the best is good enough for God.

Moses inspects the work and sees that all has been done to the Lord's specification. So he blesses the Israelites.

The Lord tells Moses to set up the tabernacle, the tent of meeting, and bring in the ark of the testimony, the table and the lampstand. The altar of incense is to be placed in front of the ark and the entrance is to be covered with the curtain.

The altar of burnt offering is to be placed in front of the entrance of the tabernacle, and the courtyard area screened off around it. All the items are to be anointed. The tabernacle and all its furnishings are to be holy.

Aaron and his sons are brought to the entrance of the tabernacle. They are washed and clothed. Aaron is robed in his sacred garments, anointed and consecrated to serve the Lord as priest. His sons are also robed and anointed for priesthood.

The glory of the Lord
(40:34–38)

When all is finished, the Lord comes to hallow the place. The cloud of his presence covers the tabernacle, and the glory of the Lord fills it. Now whenever the cloud lifts, the Israelites will know it is time to move on. And wherever they go, the Lord will be with his people in cloud and fire.

LEVITICUS

The book of Leviticus gives detailed instructions for carrying out sacrifices and other religious ceremonies in ancient Israel.

God is holy, and every aspect of the life of his people must reflect his holiness. By sacrifice, sin can be cleansed or covered. Through the other regulations, the whole of life can be related to the holiness of God.

The name 'Leviticus' comes from the first word of this book in the Hebrew Bible. It means 'and he called' and refers to the Lord calling Moses to give him these instructions. Inevitably, the name 'Leviticus' has a strong association with 'Levi' – the name of the tribe set apart to be priests.

The best-known words from the book, found in 19:18, are those which Jesus calls the second great commandment: 'Love your neighbour as you love yourself.'

Outline

Instructions for priests (1:1 – 16:34)
Everyday holiness (17:1 – 27:34)

INTRODUCTION

The story so far

The people of Israel, Jacob's descendants, have been rescued from slavery in Egypt. Led by Moses, they have journeyed across the desert to Mount Sinai, where God has made a covenant with them and given them his law. Now Moses is given further instruction on how the people can maintain their unique relationship with God.

Leviticus – a well-planned book

At Mount Sinai, God gave Israel a special identity and role in the world. They are to be a priestly people and a holy nation (Exodus 19:6). The book of Leviticus falls into two halves reflecting each of these.

Chapters 1 to 17 are mainly to do with the priestly tasks of sacrifice and getting right with God. 'Love the Lord your God with all your heart, soul, mind and strength.'

Chapters 18 to 27 are a call to Israel to be holy in every practical area of life. 'Love your neighbour as yourself.' These chapters are sometimes known as the 'holiness code'.

The first half of the book leads up to the great climax of the Day of Atonement in chapter 16, when a right relationship is restored between the nation and God. The second half reaches its high point with the Jubilee in chapter 25, when right relationships are restored in the community and nation.

God rescued his people from Egypt by a mighty act of grace. They didn't earn, deserve or (at times) even want their freedom. Now God's goodness to them is to be fully shared – and shown to the world. It is to fill every part of their lives.

To this end, the law and the sacrifices are major ways of staying in tune with God. The rules of diet, health and hygiene are a guide to living life in his honour.

Who wrote Leviticus?

Leviticus is the third of the five books of the 'Pentateuch' (the 'Five Scrolls') which are also known as the 'books of Moses'.

The original instructions for priests come from Moses himself, but in his day there is no temple. Moses' instructions are for the worship at the 'tent of meeting', where God meets with him in the years of travelling through the wilderness from Egypt to Canaan (1:1). Other priestly authors have added their insights and regulations in later years, to provide the more elaborate rituals of Solomon's temple and the second temple which was built after Israel's return from exile in Babylon. The leading priest at the time of the return is Ezra. It may be during his time, around 400 BC, that Leviticus reaches its final version.

The importance of sacrifice

'AT-ONEMENT'

Sacrifice is a way of approaching God, to mark an occasion, thank him for a blessing or ask his protection

---

Living with a holy God

Leviticus begins with 'how to make sacrifices'. It provides a manual for all kinds of ritual for the time when the Jews will have a temple in Jerusalem. The slaying of large numbers of animals is alien and disgusting to many people today. Such bloodshed is an awesome image of the seriousness of sin and the cost of salvation.

When the last temple is destroyed, in AD 70, all sacrifices cease. But Jews and Christians continue to read Leviticus because of its teaching about the holiness of God and the everyday life of the believer. For Christians, Leviticus also gives many pointers to Jesus, who is the perfect high priest and sacrifice. The letter to the Hebrews, towards the end of the New Testament, gives a Christian interpretation of the themes we first meet here.

Leviticus goes on to teach 'holiness for everyone'. It covers all the many-sidedness of human life, from sabbath to sex and from murder to menstruation. Holiness extends to all God's people – not just the priests; and to every place – not just the tabernacle or temple. Everyone who belongs to God is called to be holy in every way.

or forgiveness. Because God is holy, anyone approaching him must first be cleansed from their sin. Sacrifice is the way God provides for a person or group to receive forgiveness. This process is called 'atonement' or covering, from the idea that the blood hides sin by covering it and so enables God and sinners to be 'at one' again.

IS SACRIFICE PAGAN?

The sacrificing of animals is common to many religions. It is only when we look at the reasons for Israel's sacrifices that we see a clear difference from pagan practices.

In Israel, the sacrifice is for the benefit of the ordinary person who brings it. It is he who places his hand on the sacrifice, kills it and receives the words of forgiveness. There are no sex acts or fertility rites, and no attempts to contact the dead or pray to ancestors. There is no casting of spells, studying of entrails or fortune-telling. There are no self-inflicted wounds to prove sorrow to God, and there is no sacrificing of children.

In Jewish sacrifice there is no attempt to bribe God or manipulate his favours. People can't impress God with a large sacrifice, because they aren't graded according to wealth and power. There is no special offering required of a king, for example. Every person or family is expected simply to bring the best sacrifice they can manage, without reducing themselves to poverty. If a family is poor, then a pigeon or a cup of flour is enough.

Where there *is* a larger sacrifice, it is to indicate a greater responsibility for sin. The high priest offers the largest, because of everyone he has sinned most knowingly! In all this, the only purpose is to be made right with God and receive his forgiveness.

HOW DOES THE THEME OF SACRIFICE DEVELOP?

In Isaiah 53, the prophet describes the innocent suffering and death of the 'servant of the Lord'. This servant dies, not for his own sin, but for the sin of others. In other words, he is a sacrifice – 'led like a lamb to the slaughter'. His death is a 'guilt offering' to cover the wrongs of others, so that they may become right with God.

When Jesus comes, he is this 'suffering servant'. Matthew's Gospel says that Jesus fulfils Isaiah's words: 'He took up our infirmities and carried our sorrows' (Isaiah 53:4). Peter writes in his first letter: 'He himself bore our sins in his body on the tree, so that we might die to sins and live for righteousness; by his wounds you have been healed' (1 Peter 2:24). This understanding comes from Jesus himself.

In Luke's account of the Last Supper, Jesus warns his friends that he will be 'numbered with the transgressors'. After his resurrection, he explains everything to the two people he meets on the road to Emmaus:

Beginning with Moses and all the Prophets, he explained to them what was said in all the Scriptures concerning himself (Luke 24:25–27).

The death of Jesus includes every aspect of sacrifice. He is a ransom for our guilt. He cleanses our dirty lives. He pays the debt we owe for our wrongdoing. In Mark's Gospel Jesus says he must give his life 'as a ransom for many'. This is the function of the burnt offering in Leviticus – to provide atonement for sin and deal with guilt.

The fullest explanation of the death of Jesus is found in the letter to the Hebrews. The writer tells us that Jesus' death on the cross is the supreme sacrifice of all time – a sacrifice to end all sacrifices.

The sacrifices described in Leviticus are solemn, costly and moving. But they are never enough. They are for ever being repeated, because sin is never fully dealt with. The letter to the Hebrews describes this weary and repetitive process:

Day after day every priest stands and performs his religious duties; again and again he offers the same sacrifices, which can never take away sins (Hebrews 10:11).

The writer expresses the painful knowledge that all the sacrificing of animals has never really dealt with sin. Jesus, on the cross, at last makes a sacrifice which works for everyone for all time. He dies shouting triumphantly, 'It is finished!' As the letter to the Hebrews explains:

When this priest [Christ] had offered for all time one sacrifice for sins, he sat down at the right hand of God (Hebrews 10:12).

Like the 'sin offering', the blood of Christ has power to cleanse. It not only removes the guilt of sin, but also purges away its pollution. When we accept the death of Jesus for us, we can approach God with confidence.

Our sins are forgiven. Our consciences are clear:

> *Therefore... since we have confidence to enter the Most Holy Place by the blood of Jesus, by a new and living way opened for us through the curtain, that is, his body... let us draw near to God with a sincere heart in full assurance of faith, having our hearts sprinkled to cleanse us from a guilty conscience and having our bodies washed with pure water (Hebrews 10:19–22).*

The 'fellowship offering' of Leviticus is a sacrifice which becomes a shared meal. It expresses a joyful unity of life, between God and people and between the worshippers themselves. In the New Testament this becomes the agape, Eucharist or Lord's Supper. By breaking bread and sharing it, believers give thanks for the sacrifice of Jesus, broken for them. By pouring wine and drinking it, they remember his blood shed for the sins of the world.

The New Testament writers encourage believers to care for one another because of their fellowship with Christ. Paul warns the Christians at Corinth that if they don't share their meal (if the wealthy eat while the poor go hungry), then it isn't the Lord's Supper.

> *When you come together, it is not the Lord's Supper you eat, for as you eat, each of you goes ahead without waiting for anybody else. One remains hungry, another gets drunk (1 Corinthians 11:20–21).*

'LIVING' SACRIFICES

The most exciting development in the New Testament is that we ourselves are now temples, priests and offerings. Peter writes, 'You... like living stones, are being built into a spiritual house to be a holy priesthood, offering spiritual sacrifices acceptable to God through Jesus Christ' (1 Peter 2:5). Paul encourages Christians at Rome to offer themselves 'as living sacrifices, holy and pleasing to God' (Romans 12:1).

Our offering of ourselves is not to pay for our sin. Only the death of Jesus can do that. But we can become 'living sacrifices' – offering our bodies and minds, time, gifts and daily life to God. What a glorious development, from the dead animals in Leviticus to our own total commitment today! Jesus looked forward to the time when 'true worshippers will worship the Father in spirit and truth' (John 4:23).

A FAIR SHARE

The New Testament writers don't forget that the old system of sacrifice supported God's priests. Grain, meat and bread from offerings went to feed the priestly tribe of Levi, which had no land or income.

In the New Testament, the ministers of Christ are to be provided for in a comparable way. Paul was prepared to support himself by his tentmaking, but he still insisted that 'those who preach the gospel should receive their living from the gospel' (1 Corinthians 9:13–14).

DISCOVERING LEVITICUS

Instructions for priests

How to make offerings and sacrifices
(1:1 – 7:38)

In the opening chapters of Leviticus, God provides a range of sacrifices and offerings. Animals and birds, grain and fruit can all be used, each with their proper occasion and meaning.

Sacrifice is a way of approaching God by making a costly gift. We first meet it when Cain brings his produce and Abel offers an animal. Later, Noah burns a whole animal on an altar. Abraham makes burnt offerings, but also uses sacrificed animals for special meals – to express a friendship or seal an agreement. When Moses introduces the Passover, it is both a sacrifice and a meal.

WHAT MAKES A SUITABLE SACRIFICE?

A sacrifice has to be a person's own property – not a wild animal, and not stolen. It must be something the person has cared for or cultivated – and so is a part of him in some way. And it must be the best – healthy, mature and valuable. But if the person is poor, then even a cup of flour will be acceptable, and the resulting forgiveness will be as complete as if the finest bullock has been offered.

WHEN ARE THE SACRIFICES MADE?

Sacrifices are made by the priests every day at dawn and dusk, with a special emphasis on the sabbath. There are

---

A Bedouin baking bread on the ancient Spice Road through the Negev ('dry land'). Bread became part of the staple diet once the Israelites settled in Canaan and could cultivate cereal crops.

also monthly (new moon) and yearly sacrifices. The natural points of celebration are the changing seasons and the harvest festivals, when the firstfruits are offered to God, and the rest released for human consumption. The harvest offerings are used afterwards to feed the priests. But the most important religious festival isn't agricultural at all. It is the annual Day of Atonement – a day of national repentance with fasting and prayer.

At Passover, lambs are sacrificed for each family, and shared at home. Other sacrifices are more personal still – to mark a vow, to thank God for healing or to purify a mother after childbirth. At the other extreme, there will be sacrifices on a grand scale for the dedication of a temple or the coronation of a king.

HOW IS A SACRIFICE OFFERED?

Making a sacrifice involves both the priest and the worshipper. The worshipper brings his sacrifice to the altar in front of the tent of meeting. He connects with the animal or bird by laying his hand on it. This offering is his, and is to die on his behalf. He then kills the creature himself. After this the priest takes over to deal with the blood, and to butcher and burn the body. If the sacrifice is for a dreadful and wilful sin, the carcass is burnt completely, away from the altar.

In animal sacrifice, the fat of the kidneys, liver and intestines is burnt for God, while the rest of the meat is eaten by the priests and worshippers. Some food, such as the showbread, may only be eaten by the priests within the Holy Place.

The 'burnt offering' (1:1–17; 6:8–13) is a bullock, sheep or goat, and must be a perfect male animal. Poorer people may offer a dove or young pigeon. Sacrifice is costly, solemn and serious. The life of an innocent creature is being paid for human sin. The commitment is total – the blood poured out and the body completely burnt up.

The 'grain offering' (2:1–16; 6:14–23) is fine flour, made into a cake with oil and incense. These ingredients help it burn and give off a fragrant smell. The smell of sacrifices is thought of as reaching God and pleasing him. It is a reminder that God's anger with sin is being taken out on the sacrifice.

The grain offering is to be mixed with salt – a preservative which is a token of friendship. Yeast or honey are not allowed, because they ferment and are symbols of spreading sin. Part of the grain offering is burnt as a 'memorial portion', to remind God of his promise to protect his people. The rest of the offering is kept by the priest for his wages and livelihood.

The 'fellowship offering' (3:1–17; 7:11–34) is for making peace. It is like a burnt offering, but part of the sacrifice is eaten by the worshipper. It is a meal shared with God, as an expression of harmony.

IT'S THE HEART THAT COUNTS

It must have been a dreadful experience to watch a fellow creature die on your behalf. Even so, sacrifices could become mechanical and thoughtless. In later years the prophet Isaiah will warn against 'meaningless' sacrifices – that is, offerings which are made without any commitment to lead a better life.

The 'sin offering' (4:1 – 5:13; 6:24–30) provides for unintentional wrongdoing. Some sins are committed through ignorance (and sometimes damage is done to

---

Holy Communion

The sacrifices of the Old Testament are the background to the cross of Christ in the New Testament. Jesus is the perfect offering, provided by God to bear the guilt of the entire human race. Jesus takes upon himself the sin of the world and the punishment it deserves. His sacrifice is accepted. As Jesus dies, the temple curtain is torn apart to show an open door to God. Afterwards, God raises his Son to new life – to declare the forgiveness of sins and the defeat of death.

The sacrifice of Jesus is celebrated in a fellowship meal – called the agape, Eucharist, Lord's Supper or Holy Communion. Here bread and wine are offered in memory of what Jesus did. The bread is broken, just as Jesus' body was broken. The wine is poured out, just as his blood was shed. The bread and wine are then shared by all, to identify each person with the death and life of Jesus. For Christians this is the central act of worship – a shared and uniting experience, with all realizing God's forgiveness, enjoying fellowship with each other and expressing love.

people or property by accident), but there is still guilt. This kind of sin is described in a word which means 'missing the mark'. The examples given are both sacred and secular (the Jews make no distinction). They range from withholding information to touching something unclean.

The 'guilt offering' (5:14 – 6:7; 7:1–6) has a strong sense of repairing damage between God and people. It is a substantial, expensive sacrifice to emphasize the person's fault for what has happened. The offence has hurt both God and a fellow human being, so the sacrifice is designed to 'mend' holiness and make good the relationships.

How to ordain priests

(8:1 – 10:20)

The Lord said to Moses, 'Bring Aaron and his sons, their garments, the anointing oil, the bull for the sin offering, the two rams, and the basket containing bread without yeast, and gather the entire assembly at the entrance to the Tent of Meeting' (8:2–4).

God chooses Aaron and his sons to be his priests. They are to be responsible for the tent of meeting and the sacrifices – to ensure that everything is done decently and with reverence. They are to be both teachers and living examples of God's holy ways.

In a series of sacrifices and ceremonies, Moses clothes the priests and consecrates them for their special task.

AARON'S HIGH PRIESTLY ROBES

Aaron wears a tunic as an undergarment. It is long and full, tied with a sash. Over this he wears a bright blue robe and an 'ephod', secured by a woven waistband. We have to guess at the appearance of the ephod, which may have been a kind of apron. Over this is worn a breastpiece with a pocket for the 'Urim and Thummim'. The exact description of these has been lost; but they are a kind of holy dice. They are thrown after prayer for guidance, and give God's 'yes' or 'no'. Finally, Aaron wears a turban, with a gold plate on the front of it. This is to honour his head and holy leadership. Moses pours oil over Aaron's head to consecrate him – that is, to set him apart for his sacred role.

HOLINESS – YOU PUT YOUR WHOLE SELF IN!

Aaron and his sons are washed, clothed in their priestly robes and marked with sacrificial blood on their right ears, hands and toes. They are sprinkled, robes and all, with oil and blood. They remain at the door of the tent of meeting for seven days – the timescale of God's creation. After this, Aaron carries out the sacrifices – a calf for his own sins, followed by a goat for the sins of the people. Finally a cow and a ram are killed as a fellowship offering, to celebrate peace between God and Israel. The Lord glorifies the occasion with his presence and consuming fire.

THE DEATH OF NADAB AND ABIHU

Aaron's sons Nadab and Abihu took their censers, put fire in them and added incense; and they offered unauthorised fire before the Lord, contrary to his command (10:1).

The holiness which consecrates can also destroy. When two of Aaron's sons produce their own flame for the burning of incense, holy fire flares up to consume them. They have wilfully breached God's command to keep every detail of sacrifice separate from everyday use – and they pay with their lives.

THE HOLY AND THE COMMON

Aaron's sons should have known better than to confuse the 'holy' and the 'common'. Something is 'holy' when it is associated with God. Everything else is 'common' – that is, a part of everyday life. 'Common' things are clean, unless something has happened to spoil or pollute them. In this case they have become 'unclean', but can be restored through an appropriate sacrifice.

The priests are supposed to prevent the 'common' coming into contact with the 'holy'. Such an event produces a spiritual short circuit and a fatal shock. When Aaron's sons introduce common fire, they are themselves consumed.

TOUGH LOVE

Israel is to be holy. Holiness is to be the lifestyle of God's people, in sanctuary and sacrifice, marriage and money, food and sex.

This holiness isn't voluntary – it's a command. It is enforced in the sudden death of Aaron's sons when they casually break God's rule. It is spelt out in the many regulations – straightforward in their wording and stark in their consequences.

God's love is tough. If Israel is to continue in freedom, she must beware of the reality and danger of sin. Anything that undermines her relationship with God must be rigorously dealt with.

For the Christian, the teaching of Leviticus is fulfilled in Jesus Christ. He is the perfect, once-for-all sacrifice who brings forgiveness of sin and peace with God. It is through him and for him that we seek to live a life of purity, love and service.

Jesus, too, is tough on sin and tough on the causes of sin. He develops the laws of Leviticus in the Sermon on the Mount. He holds us personally responsible for our thoughts and actions: 'You have heard that it was said to those of ancient times, "You shall not murder"; and "whoever murders shall be liable to judgment." But I say to you that if you are angry with a brother or sister, you will be liable to judgment' (Matthew 5:21–22).

How to deal with dirt and disease
(11:1 – 15:33)

CLEAN AND UNCLEAN FOOD

The Lord said to Moses and Aaron, 'Say to the Israelites: "Of all the animals that live on land, these are the ones you may eat: You may eat any animal that has a split hoof completely divided and that chews the cud"' (11:2–3).

Here is guidance as to which animals are wholesome to eat. The distinctions are very simple, and generally follow lines of safety and good taste. Usually there is a health hazard or an instinctive shudder behind these food laws. Animals and birds which have themselves fed on dead meat will almost certainly carry infection. Pork harbours tapeworm and is dangerous when undercooked. Shellfish can cause food poisoning. All eating of blood is forbidden, because it is the very liquid of life and belongs to God.

God's people are to reflect his holiness. What they do with their bodies will influence their minds and spirits. What they believe in their hearts will affect their actions. So, in matters of food and diet, they are to live clean and well-ordered lives.

The overall purpose of the rules is that Israel shall be distinctive and disciplined – living in God's world, God's way. God's own summary of the situation is this: 'I... brought you up out of Egypt to be your God; therefore be holy, because I am holy' (11:45).

HEALTH REGULATIONS

The Lord said to Moses, 'Say to the Israelites: "A woman who becomes pregnant and gives birth to a son will be ceremonially unclean for seven days, just as she is unclean during her monthly period"' (12:1–2).

A woman's monthly period and the act of giving birth are bloody and harrowing experiences. Women are to be treated as 'unclean' at these times, although 'unclean' doesn't mean immoral or sinful. They are to be left alone, to allow body and mind to recover. One day Jesus will heal a woman whose life has been ruined by constant menstrual bleeding. In a desperate gesture of faith, she who is 'unclean' dares to reach out to touch him – to catch his holiness and healing (Luke 8:43–48).

While sex is exciting, the actual business of

'Holy' and 'common'

You must distinguish between the holy and the common, between the unclean and the clean (10:10).

The Israelites are to make a clear distinction between things that are 'holy' and things that are 'common'. Then again, a common article can be either 'clean' or 'unclean'.

God is holy, and any person or thing associated with him is also holy. The opposite of holy is 'common', or 'profane'. This doesn't necessarily mean 'dirty' or 'sinful'. It simply means 'ordinary, normal and everyday'.

When ordinary people or things become polluted, they are 'unclean'. Certain animals – and death itself – are permanently unclean. But most other conditions can be restored to normality ('made clean') through the appropriate sacrifice. The main task of a blood sacrifice is to make holy something which is common, or cleanse something which is polluted.

It was the priest's task to teach people these distinctions, so that they could lead a clean life in the everyday circumstances of family, home and farm. The laws in Leviticus are the means to this end. Their purpose is to enable God to dwell with his people.

reproduction is messy and even repulsive. The law provides for the trauma of childbirth to be followed by rest – and completed with a simple offering to God. So a woman can be assured of God's love, cleansing and peace.

The Lord said to Moses and Aaron, 'If some of the people notice a swelling or a rash or a shiny patch on their skin that develops into a contagious skin disease, they must be brought to Aaron the priest or to one of his sons' (13:1–2).

The priests are also the doctors. By observation and experience, they build up their knowledge of a whole variety of rashes and skin disorders. Some of these can be passed on by touch, so the sufferer must be isolated to protect the rest of the community.

The most dreadful of the skin diseases is leprosy. It begins with loss of feeling, which means that a person can be cut or burnt without noticing. It develops to deform and rot whole areas of the body and is easily passed on to other people.

The law provides ways of diagnosing and isolating these diseases. There are routines of washing and shaving and recommended periods of quarantine. With these rules it is clear when someone is infectious – and when they have recovered.

Sickness, sin and sacrifice

The priest offers the same sacrifices for both healing and forgiveness. This highlights the likeness between sickness and sin.

Because a human being is a harmony of body, mind and spirit, Leviticus assumes that disease is a symptom of sin. Later, in the book of Job, we will read that the two are not necessarily connected, and that sometimes suffering is completely undeserved.

Leprosy is contagious, crippling and (in Bible times) incurable. Jesus is unusual in his readiness to touch lepers and counter their disease with God's health. While Jesus never assumes that sickness is a person's own fault, he sometimes makes the connection. On one occasion, he discerns the guilt behind a man's paralysis (Mark 2:3–5). And he often declares forgiveness of sin as well as physical healing.

Cleanliness and godliness

The Lord said to Moses and Aaron, 'Speak to the Israelites and say to them: "When any man has a bodily discharge, the discharge is unclean"' (15:1–2).

God's law is for the whole of life, and here it deals with some very intimate details. When a man ejects semen or discharges any other body fluid, there are regulations for his cleansing and precautions against any infection. Similarly, a woman is to cope with her period bleeding by keeping away from other people, being careful to wash herself and the everyday things she touches. There is equality here in the way men and women are treated.

All this is practical holiness – the good life. Human beings are made in the image of God and are not to live at the level of squalor and basic instinct. As Paul says, 'Your body is a temple of the Holy Spirit, who is in you' (1 Corinthians 6:19).

The Day of Atonement
(16:1–34)

The supreme sacrifice is to take place on the Day of Atonement. It falls on the tenth day of the seventh month, towards the end of September. On this day Aaron, the high priest, makes sacrifices for all the sins of all the people. It is also a ceremony by which the tent of meeting itself and the altar outside are made holy again.

This is the only day of the year that Aaron may enter the Most Holy Place. He goes behind the curtain which divides the tent of meeting and separates off the presence of God. This is where God dwells in deep holiness, and where the covenant box (the ark of the covenant) is kept.

The covenant box is called the 'testimony'. It contains the stone tablets which are engraved with the Ten Commandments. Its lid is the atonement cover: the place where atonement is made. Martin Luther called it the 'mercy seat', the earthly throne of God.

Aaron is not to come thoughtlessly or casually into God's holy presence. He is to lay aside his ornate high-priestly robes, wash himself and dress in linen – the garment of an ordinary priest. It is a sign of humility and purity.

He is to select three animals for sacrifice. One is a bull, which he is to kill for his own sin and the sins of his family. The other animals are goats. He is to cast lots, so that God will decide which goat is to be killed and which is to be sent away into the desert. The goat that is to be killed is a sacrifice for the sins of the people. The goat that is sent away into the desert is the 'scapegoat', carrying off the people's sins so that they are separated from them for ever.

Aaron is to sacrifice the bull and take some of its blood into the Most Holy Place. He is to burn a large amount of fine incense, so that the smoke will protect him from seeing God and being killed by the power of his holiness.

Aaron splashes the bull's blood on the front of the covenant box and on the ground in front of it – sprinkling it with his finger, so that he doesn't actually touch the holy box. He does the same with the blood of the goat, making a 'cover' of blood between the holy God and his sinful people. All their sins are 'covered' or painted out by the blood of the lives which have been paid in sacrifice.

Next Aaron comes out of the tent of meeting to sprinkle blood on the altar. This cleanses and consecrates it afresh for holy use. He also lays his hands on the scapegoat, to heap all the people's sins on its head, and then banishes it to wander in the desert. Finally, he takes off his linen clothes, washes himself again and puts on his fine high-priestly robes. He completes the sacrifices by offering the bodies of the bull and the goat on the altar, burning them up completely, because they are sin offerings.

The Day of Atonement is to be kept every year. It is a day of rest, like the sabbath, and the people are to deny themselves. This means that they are to fast, to show their sorrow for their sins. It is the most solemn of festivals, and very different from the Feast of Tabernacles, when there is joyful dancing.

The Day of Atonement isn't mentioned again in the Old Testament, but by the time of the New Testament it has become known as 'the Fast' (Acts 27:9). Today it is Yom Kippur, which strict Jews keep as one of the holiest days in the year. They no longer have the temple or the covenant box, but they keep the day with prayers and tears, and prepare for it with ten days of careful self-examination.

For Christians, the Day of Atonement is fulfilled in the death of Jesus. He went into the holy presence of God with his own blood – not needing to make sacrifice for his own sins, but offering his life for the sins of all people (Hebrews 9). Jesus is both the perfect high priest *and* the perfect sacrifice.

Everyday holiness

The Day of Atonement is a high point and halfway mark in the book of Leviticus. The chapters which follow are sometimes called the 'holiness code'. They contain the laws which express God's holiness in the details of everyday life. Holiness is to be the distinguishing mark of God's people.

The importance of blood
(17:1–16)

Blood is sacred to the Jews, because it is the essence of an animal's life. It is also the means that God has given for paying for sin.

From now on the Israelites must bring their animals to the priests to be killed. Even providing meat for the family is an act of worship, because it involves the shedding of a life which belongs to God. The animals are to be brought to the door of the tent of meeting as a peace offering between God and his people.

The Israelites are forbidden to make random killings out in the fields, like pagans making sacrifices to their goat idols, the demon spirits of nature worship. This law is relaxed in Deuteronomy, where it is accepted that people needing meat may live too far from an official place of sacrifice. Even so, the eating of blood is forbidden (Deuteronomy 12:20–25). To this day, Jews will only eat meat which is 'kosher' – that is, carefully drained of blood and reverently prepared for the table.

The limits of sex
(18:1–30)

Among the Egyptians, when the Israelites were slaves, sex was a family affair. The Pharaohs often married their close relatives, and suffered the dreadful effects of inbreeding.

Among the Canaanites, where the Israelites are heading, sex is a free-for-all. There is sex between family members, sex between people of the same sex, and sex between people and animals. Sex is also involved in the worship of pagan gods, which are themselves sexually permissive and perverted.

God tells his people that they are to be very different. They are to be holy, with their holiness rooted in God's own holiness.

Moses teaches that sex between parents and children,

and between brothers and sisters, is wrong. The whole family is to be a network of honour, decency and mutual respect – not spoilt and destroyed by sexual scheming and abuse. These rules are not because sex is dirty, but because it is such a vital and powerful part of our nature. Wrong sex unleashes enormous forces of guilt, depression, jealousy and hatred. We do well to believe God's warnings and accept his boundaries.

These sex regulations will be adopted in Christian cultures as 'prohibited relationships'. It is strange to think that Abraham would not have been allowed to marry his sister Sarah, and Jacob would have been unable to marry the sisters Leah and Rachel. God blessed and used those relationships; but we see in their stories the pain, suspicion and anger that flares up in such marriages.

CHILD SACRIFICE

Moses forbids the sacrifice of children (18:21). This was practised by the Ammonites, who worshipped the god Molech. His name is a mixture of the words for 'king' and 'shame'.

For some, to offer up a child must have seemed like the ultimate act of commitment – costly and heartbreaking. Thank God it is so clearly forbidden!

WRONG SEX

Moses forbids unnatural and perverted sex (18:22–30). Men are not to have sex with other men, or with animals. It is because of such degrading behaviour that God is judging the Canaanites and driving them out of their land. The land itself is disgusted with them and ejecting them like vomit. But God warns the Israelites that he will expel them, too, if they sin in the same way. God's standards do not vary and he makes no exceptions for the Israelites.

How to live wisely and well

(19:1–37)
Here is a fascinating selection of laws. They are listed almost at random, although all their roots can be traced

Ruth gleaning grain in the field belonging to Boaz; from the Lambeth Bible, Canterbury (c. 1140–50). The law commanded reapers to leave some of the crop for the poor to gather.

to the Ten Commandments. The common link is that they are all grounded in the holiness of God. 'I am the Lord' is repeated, as God endorses each regulation with his own character and authority. We see, too, that holiness is not just about religion. It is deeply practical, affecting every area of life.

Some of these commands echo the Ten Commandments quite directly: respect your father and mother, observe the sabbath and do not make or worship idols.

Others are practical ways to provide for the needy: leave some gleanings behind when you harvest your grain or grapes, so that poor people and strangers may gather some food. Pay your workers on the day of their labour, so that they can provide for themselves and their families.

The deaf and the blind are to be protected; you are not to take advantage by abusing them or playing tricks.

Some commands deal with the motives that guide our actions: do not be swayed by self-interest when you judge between rich and poor; do not hate your brother or sister in your heart.

There are laws against causing confusion in the world of nature: do not mate different kinds of animals, or mix the crops in a field, or weave clothes from different materials. These laws commend practical purity and holiness – a reminder not to mix the worship of God with pagan idolatry.

And what about the owner who sleeps with his slave girl, despite the fact that she is promised to another man? This is not counted as serious as adultery, but it is wrong nevertheless. A woman is not to be treated as a prostitute, just because she is unfortunate enough to be a slave. A way is provided for the man to atone for his sin and deal with his guilt.

The godly way of life is described in dozens of fascinating and inspiring examples – about fruit trees and fortune-tellers, mediums and migrant-workers, tattoos and traders…

The secret of understanding a law is to ask which commandment it follows, what principle it upholds or what kind of person it protects. The keynote is found at the heart of this chapter: 'Love your neighbour as yourself' (19:18). This will become known as the Golden Rule, and Jesus will rate it as the second of the great commandments (Matthew 22:39). The first is 'Love the Lord your God with all your heart and with all your soul and with all your strength' (Deuteronomy 6:5) – to which Jesus adds 'and with all your mind' (Mark 12:30).

The Israelites come to regard their neighbour as anyone who is a fellow Jew (as opposed to a pagan or foreigner). Jesus will show, in his parable of the Good Samaritan, that our neighbour is anyone we have the chance to help – irrespective of race, religion or convenience (Luke 10:25–37). Leviticus anticipates this attitude with the command: 'Love the alien as yourself' (Leviticus 19:34).

Controls and consequences
(20:1–27)

God speaks to Moses not only of laws but also of punishments. When people are responsible for their sin, they must bear the consequence. Sometimes the punishment must be death – as when an Israelite sacrifices his child to Molech, or consults mediums, or curses his parents.

Sexual sins such as adultery, incest, homosexuality and bestiality all carry the death penalty. Such behaviour must be cut like a cancer from the body of God's people. Some of the laws actually speak of being 'cut off' – the guilty person being expelled or excommunicated, to prevent infecting others.

Why is God so strict? Because he wants Israel to model true worship, justice and holy living to the world. To do this she must be a dedicated and disciplined nation – devoted to God's law in heart and home, in dress and diet, in relationships and responses.

Many of these laws are warnings against the cruelty and moral chaos of the Canaanites. Israel is to be different, set apart for God, and holy for him.

The purity of priests
(21:1 – 22:33)

From speaking to the people, God now tells Moses to speak to the priests. The prime function of the priest is to perform his holy duties. For this he must be clean and ready in body and spirit. He is to avoid touching a corpse, unless it is that of a close relative, because death is linked with sin.

Priests must not shave their heads (a sign of mourning), nor trim their beards, nor cut themselves (as pagans do). They must honour God in their speech. They must be devoted and fit for their privileged task of offering food to God.

Priests are to be holy in their family relationships, too. They must not marry prostitutes or divorcees (people who have already been sexually united with someone else), and their daughters must not sink into prostitution. If this should happen, the punishment (for the daughter) is death.

There are similar, but stricter, rules for a high priest. He has been set apart from his priestly colleagues by anointing with oil and clothing with special robes. He is also to be distinguished by his extra degree of holiness.

The high priest must avoid touching the dead bodies of even his nearest and dearest relatives. Nor must he leave the sanctuary to pay his respects to the dead, in case he defiles it on his return. His whole orientation is to purity and life. He may get married, of course, but only to a virgin from a priestly family, so that his children will be born with an unblemished moral pedigree.

PHYSICAL DEFORMITY

Priests are to be perfect, not only in their choice of wife and way of life, but in their physical well-being (21:16–24). Just as the sacrifices are to be perfect specimens, so must the priests be who are offering them. Priests who are disabled, deformed, diseased or mutilated are excluded from the work of the sanctuary, although they may still eat the holy food. The idea is not to discriminate against the disfigured, but to reflect the perfection of God.

HOW TO TREAT HOLY OFFERINGS

The priests may eat food which has been sacrificed, and so may their families, but the food is to be treated with respect, and eaten only by those who realize its worth (22:1–16).

There will be times when the priest himself is unfit to touch the offerings, because he is suffering from a disease or has become unclean. He must be very careful not to treat the sacred offerings casually or with contempt.

The priest's family may eat food that has been offered in sacrifice, but a guest or occasional worker may not. A slave may eat, because he or she is a permanent member of the household and is treated as part of the family.

These regulations are to ensure that gifts to God are not misused or discarded behind the scenes once the worshipper has gone home. Those who live off the faith of others must be mindful that they enjoy a very special privilege.

QUALITY CONTROL

What kind of sacrifice is acceptable? God tells Moses that the animals must be perfect (22:17–33).

It might be tempting to offer as a sacrifice an animal that is diseased or deformed. After all, it's only going to be destroyed. But only the best is good enough for God. If the sacrifice is a freewill offering, over and above a necessary sacrifice, then an inferior animal is acceptable – but not if it's an attempt to cheat on a vow.

God shows his concern for all his creatures. A newborn animal is not to be taken straight from its mother and offered as a sacrifice. Nor are a mother and her young to be slaughtered on the same day. As with the law forbidding the boiling of a kid in its mother's milk, this command respects the right and dignity of animals.

A thank-offering is to be eaten on the same day. Once something has been offered in sacrifice, it becomes holy. It is important to treat it with reverence and put it to its proper use. If offerings are treated carelessly, then the worshippers lose their sense of reverence. When something is offered to the Lord, it becomes associated with his holiness – and must be treated accordingly.

Festivals and assemblies

(23:1 – 24:9)

God appoints a series of festivals. They are God's own festivals on which the Israelites are to gather for worship – summoned by the blowing of silver trumpets.

Most of the festivals mark a particular day in the farming year, but they also celebrate great events in Israel's history. They each have their spiritual meaning. They celebrate some aspect of God's greatness and goodness and enable his people to respond to him in celebration and sacrifice.

The feasts are listed in the order in which they occur during the year.

THE SABBATH

The sabbath is the first festival to be mentioned (23:3). It is unique among the feasts, in that it occurs every week, while the other festivals come only once a year.

Sabbath is the most important of the feasts, and the other festivals tend to include it.

The word 'sabbath' means 'stop'. The sabbath is a day of rest as well as a day of assembly and sacrifice.

The sabbath falls on the seventh day of the week. This is the day on which God rested after his work of creation (Genesis 2:2), and the day on which the Israelites rested during their journey through the wilderness from Egypt to Canaan. God provided for their rest by giving a double measure of manna on the previous day, so that no one needed to work.

THE PASSOVER AND FEAST OF UNLEAVENED BREAD

The Passover is the most important of the annual feasts (23:5). It celebrates the rescue of the Israelites from slavery in Egypt, when God caused the angel of death to 'pass over' the homes of the Hebrews and spare the lives of their first-born sons.

Passover falls on the fourteenth day of the month of Abib – later called Nisan. It marks the birth of the nation of Israel and the Jewish New Year. Once Jerusalem and the temple are established, the Passover becomes an occasion of pilgrimage; but it is always a festival to be celebrated at home and in a family group.

The first Passover is described in Exodus 12. The special sacrifices are described in Numbers 28:16–25.

The Passover is closely linked with the Feast of Unleavened Bread, which takes place the following day (23:6). It celebrates the escape of the Israelites from Egypt, when God commanded the people to make bread without leaven (yeast). Such bread was made quickly, as it needed no time for the dough to rise – and became a symbol of the haste with which the Israelites made their escape.

The Feast of Unleavened Bread lasts a whole week, starting on 15th Abib (Nisan). It begins and ends with a day of rest and solemn assembly, and during it the people bake their bread without yeast.

THE FIRSTFRUITS

This festival looks forward to the Israelites settling in their own land and producing harvests. The first sheaf of the harvest is to be brought to the priest, who will wave it before God on the sabbath day (23:9–14).

The sheaf is probably barley, which ripens two or three weeks before wheat. Waving it before God means that the whole harvest is offered to him. Only after this is done are the people allowed to enjoy the produce themselves. Special sacrifices are made of lamb and grain – and for the first time in Leviticus a drink offering is mentioned. This is probably wine poured out on the ground in front of the altar.

By the time of Jesus, Firstfruits is celebrated on 16th Nisan – two days after Passover. This is the day of Christ's resurrection. Paul describes Jesus as 'the firstfruits of those who have fallen asleep' – the prototype of all who, by God's mighty power, will be harvested from the grave (1 Corinthians 15:20–23).

Jesus, Paul – and yeast

For Jesus, yeast is an image of something that spreads very slowly, but affects a huge area of life. He warns his disciples against 'the leaven' of the Pharisees and Sadducees – the legalism and unbelief which denies and spoils God's work of grace (Matthew 16:6–12). But he also describes the kingdom of God as like yeast 'mixed into a large amount of flour' – gradually and certainly spreading until the whole mass is transformed. His kingdom will win (Matthew 13:33)!

Paul understands that Jesus Christ is the true Passover lamb – and yeast is a picture of sin. Christians are to clear the sin out of their lives and be like unleavened bread, sincere and truthful (1 Corinthians 5:7–8).

Christians and the Jewish festivals

After the time of Jesus, many of the Jewish festivals take on a new meaning for Christians. The Passover is the day of the Last Supper and the eve of Jesus' death on the cross. 'Firstfruits' is the day of his resurrection. Pentecost is the day on which the Holy Spirit is poured out on his apostles.

The Christian church is a mixture of Jews and Gentiles, so there is not much emphasis on keeping the Jewish feasts. By the end of the first century, the first day of the week (the day of the resurrection of Jesus) has taken over from the sabbath as the focal day of worship.

THE FEAST OF WEEKS

The Feast of Weeks is a harvest festival, marking the end of the wheat harvest (23:15–22). Two loaves are baked from fine flour and leaven, and waved before the Lord. This is an offering of the 'finished product' of the harvest – the daily food of the people of God.

The Feast of Weeks gets its name from coming seven 'full weeks' (fifty days) after the offering of the firstfruits. Because the fifty days could be counted from either a normal sabbath or a special one, the calculation was a matter of great debate!

In later centuries, the Greek for 'fifty' gives this festival the name 'Pentecost'. It falls in the third month, Sivan. This is the time of year when the Israelites received God's law at Sinai, and the day of Pentecost becomes a joyful celebration of that great event.

As well as the harvest offering, there are sacrifices for sin and to express fellowship. As the grain harvest comes to an end, God reminds the reapers to leave some gleanings for the poor.

THE FEAST OF TRUMPETS

The number seven has special significance for Israel, and the seventh month is marked by three special occasions: the Feast of Trumpets, the Day of Atonement and the Feast of Tabernacles.

The Feast of Trumpets falls on the first day of the seventh month (23:23–25). It comes at the end of the grape harvest – the close of the old farming year and the beginning of the new.

This is a special sabbath, heralded by the blowing of trumpets. The Jewish tradition is that these trumpets are the rams' horns – the ones which are used to announce the Year of Jubilee. They sound a more solemn note than the usual silver trumpets.

This feast is a landmark day of rest, sacred assembly and sacrifice. It is a day to pause and prepare for the great festivals which are approaching.

THE DAY OF ATONEMENT

This is the most important of all the festivals described in Leviticus, and is a fast rather than a feast (23:26–32).

The Day of Atonement falls on the tenth day of the seventh month. On this day the high priest makes sacrifice for his own sin and the sins of the people. He re-consecrates the entire tent of meeting and its surrounds for the worship and service of God.

This is the only day of the year that the high priest is

allowed to enter the Most Holy Place and sprinkle blood for the atonement of sin. The ceremony is described in chapter 16.

God's repeated instruction to the people is that they are to deny themselves. They must abstain from food and other pleasures, to fast in sorrow for their sins. This is not a time for joyful celebration, but for deep repentance and solemn sacrifice.

THE FEAST OF TABERNACLES

On the fifteenth day of the seventh month, the Feast of Tabernacles begins (23:33–44). This feast lasts for eight days, beginning and ending with a day of rest. It is party time, with feasting and dancing to celebrate the 'ingathering' – the end of all the harvests.

During this festival, the Israelites remember how their ancestors lived in tents in the wilderness. They build shelters or booths with palm fronds and leafy branches, and live in them for the week.

A great number of sacrifices are offered in careful sequence. Each day, two rams and fourteen lambs are sacrificed as burnt offerings, and a single goat is sacrificed as a sin offering. Bulls are also sacrificed as burnt offerings – beginning with thirteen on the first day and reducing to seven on the seventh. On the eighth day just one bull is offered, to bring the total to seventy (Numbers 28:12–28).

In the time of Jesus, the climax of the Feast of Tabernacles comes on its closing day. The high priest brings a golden pitcher of water in procession from the Pool of Siloam, and pours it out in front of the altar in the temple. He asks God to give rain for the coming growing season – and prays that he will pour out his Spirit on his people. It is a dramatic moment when Jesus stands forward and cries, 'Let anyone who is thirsty come to me, and… drink' (John 7:37–38)!

OIL AND BREAD

In the tent of meeting stands a pure gold lampstand, with seven branches bearing seven oil lamps. The oil is clear, made from pressed olives (24:1–9). It is brought by the people to provide light for God's sanctuary. The lamps are tended and their wicks trimmed by Aaron and his sons. The flames burn continually, day and night, as a symbol of God's constant presence among his people.

God commands that twelve large loaves are to be baked from fine flour. The flour, like the oil, is the very best that can be produced. The loaves are to be placed on the gold table in the tent of meeting, arranged in two rows of six. They represent the twelve tribes of Israel, and are known as the bread of the Presence (Exodus 25:23–30).

The loaves are an offering to the Lord and are accompanied by incense in bowls or spoons. After the loaves have been on display for seven days, they are eaten by Aaron and his sons. This is the most holy portion of all the food which they are allowed to consume from the people's offerings.

The custom for providing bread for the gods was practised by the Babylonians. They liked their gods to eat the same food as they did – although their priests had to consume the bread in secret to make sure it disappeared! Israel's custom is different. God doesn't need human food. Rather, the loaves are offered as a sign that he provides his people with their daily bread.

A tabernacle shelter: the Jews build booths once every year from the branches of trees, and live in them for a week as a reminder of the tents used in the wilderness.

The death penalty for blasphemy

(24:10–23)

Moses has to decide a difficult case. A man who is only half-Israelite (his mother is an Israelite but his father an Egyptian) has blasphemed the name of God with a curse. One of the commandments forbids such blasphemy but doesn't prescribe a punishment (Exodus 20:7). Should the man be excused altogether, as he is not a full Israelite?

God's command is that the man shall be taken outside the camp and stoned to death. It is no excuse that he is only half-Israelite. He has blasphemed God's name, which is an act of violence against God and a denial of his presence and purpose in the world. It makes no difference whether he is a native Israelite or a foreigner; he is responsible for his outburst and must bear the penalty.

God also gives Moses directions on how to deal with other violent crimes. Anyone who murders a fellow human being must be put to death. Anyone who kills an animal must replace it in kind. Anyone who inflicts an injury must have a similar injury inflicted in return.

These penalties are intended to be exactly fair, and apply to Israelites and foreigners alike. The victims of crime won't need to take personal revenge, but can rely on the law to give them justice. It also ensures that the punishment fits the crime, and doesn't become an excuse for excessive violence or cruelty. Despite the fairness of 'eye for eye, tooth for tooth', it seems likely that fines and compensations were soon allowed as an alternative.

Sabbaths and Jubilees
(25:1–55)

THE SABBATH YEAR

During their years in the wilderness, the Israelites have become used to 'keeping the sabbath' – that is, resting on the seventh (and last) day of the week.

Sabbath means 'cease' or 'stop'. The sabbath is a day of rest for everyone, when work stops for both people and animals. To enable this absolute rest, God provides a double amount of manna on the previous day (Exodus 16:22–26).

The sabbath rest echoes the story of creation, when God rested from all his work on the seventh day (Genesis 2:2). It was revealed as one of God's laws, when it was given as the fourth commandment (Exodus 20:8–11).

Moses tells the Israelites that, when they have their own land, they are to give the land itself a sabbath rest (25:1–7). Every seventh year, the farmers are to leave the fields unploughed and the vines untended. God promises that the crops which grow naturally, without human labour, will be enough for everyone to eat.

The sabbath year makes good sense from a farming point of view. It allows the land to recover and so renew its fertility. But a far more important point is being made – that God is the real owner of the land and his people are only tenants.

Clear olive oil was used to fuel the lamps which stood in the tabernacle.

It is God who provides the needs of his people. He has already shown his power and rewarded the people's trust by providing them with daily manna. Now the 'manna principle' is to be applied to a whole year!

THE YEAR OF JUBILEE

If every seventh year is a sabbath, then seven *times* seven (forty-nine) years must herald a very special celebration. The fiftieth year is to be a Jubilee (25:8–55).

The word 'jubilee' comes from the Hebrew for 'ram', because the Jubilee Year is announced by the blowing of rams' horn trumpets. They are sounded across the country on the Day of Atonement. The Day of Atonement restores harmony between God and his people. Now, through the Jubilee, the peace of God is to enfold the natural world as well.

The Year of Jubilee is the time for rest, restoration and return. As with the forty-ninth year (a sabbath) there is to be no hard labour on the land. Those who have lost their land through debt or bad luck will now have their inheritance restored to them. Families will be relieved of all their usual duties, so that they can be reunited and spend time together.

The land belongs to God, and is only leased by its human owners as their God-given inheritance. Because the land will revert to these original owners (or their families) every fifty years, its price must be adjusted as the Jubilee approaches. It is the number of harvests that give the land its value. The land is most valuable when there are still many years to go until the Jubilee.

Laws for redeeming property

Various laws are provided for redeeming property (25:25–34).

Sometimes the land that has been lost can be redeemed by the nearest relative (the next of kin), who will step in to rescue the person who has fallen into poverty. Boaz was the next of kin to his cousin Ruth, who was both a foreigner and a widow. As her 'redeemer', he first helped her to survive and later married her (Ruth 4:1–4).

The Jubilee laws are clearly for a rural community.

They are not expected to work in a town. If someone is forced to sell his town house, then he has only a year to reclaim it. After that it belongs to the new owner.

The Levites (the priestly tribe) can buy and sell houses in their own towns, but the properties will revert to their original owners at Jubilee. Levites are not to sell their pastureland, because God has given it to them for ever.

Special treatment for the poor

Israel's care for the poor and the stranger is based on the fact that the whole nation was once rescued from slavery by God (25:35–55).

Israelites who become poor are to be lent money without being charged interest, and are to be sold food at cost price. This enables them and their families to continue to live in the same community. Israelites are never to become slaves to other Israelites. If they are forced to become servants, then they must be released at the Jubilee.

Foreigners and immigrants may be bought by Israelites as slaves. There is no law that such slaves must be released at the Jubilee. They and their children are the property of their Israelite owners, and can be handed on to the next generation.

If Israelites become the slaves of wealthy foreigners, they have the right to be redeemed from slavery at a later date. Near relatives may act as their redeemer and buy them back, or they may earn enough to purchase their own freedom. Failing this, the Jubilee will release the Israelite slaves and their families when it comes round.

Israelite slaves are to be released at the Jubilee, but foreign slaves are not. This is because the Israelites belong to God, who redeemed them from slavery in Egypt.

Blessings and curses
(26:1–46)

God promises great blessings if his people keep his commands, and terrible punishments if they reject them. These rewards and penalties are the consequences of the covenant – like the outcomes of a treaty. It is the stark choice between a way of life or a way of death (Deuteronomy 30:15).

THE BLESSINGS OF OBEDIENCE

The Israelites are not to carve images of God, or set up sacred stones as pillars. Jacob did this with his stone pillow after his dream of God (Genesis 28:18) – but the Canaanites do the same for their pagan rites.

The Israelites are to keep the sabbath rests and reverence God's sanctuary (the tent of meeting and, later, the temple). These are the special ways by which they will honour God in time and place.

God describes the life he will give his people if they keep his commands. They will live in perfect harmony with nature, with times of harvest so long and full that they will overlap each other. God will also protect them from wild beasts and give them victory over their enemies (26:1–13).

God will bless the Israelites with growing numbers. He will walk among them, as he once did with Adam and Eve in the Garden of Eden (Genesis 3:8). They will be his own free people, secure and confident in his purpose and love.

THE PENALTIES FOR DISOBEDIENCE

If the Israelites disobey God, they will face disease, death and defeat (26:14–45). The climate and the land will be hostile to them, and their enemies will overwhelm them. God himself will be against them, punishing them with sevenfold intensity.

Instead of protecting and strengthening his people, God will attack and scatter them. This prediction will come true when they are divided and defeated, dispersed

---

Jesus and the Jubilee

The prophet Isaiah proclaims rescue and release for God's people (Isaiah 60:1–3). This is to be a glorious Jubilee. God will do this great work through his servant, who will be the redeemer of his poor, broken and enslaved people.

When Jesus begins his public ministry, he teaches in the synagogue at Nazareth. He takes this scripture from Isaiah for his text, and astounds his hearers by proclaiming that the prophet's words have now come true.

Jesus claims that he is the servant described in Isaiah's prophecy, whose mission is to proclaim and demonstrate God's Jubilee (Luke 4:16–30). His hearers in Nazareth are outraged by what seems to them a blasphemy. They try to kill him.

and exiled. Without the burden of farming, the land will at last be able to take its sabbath rest!

But with the warning of judgment comes the promise of mercy. If the Israelites will turn to God again and confess their sin, then he will honour his covenant and restore them.

The price of keeping faith

(27:1–34)

The people of Israel express their commitment to God through vows and gifts. Such a gift may be a person, an animal, a house or a field. If the offerers change their mind, then the gifts can be bought back (redeemed) with a sum of money.

God gives Moses a way of valuing gifts in terms of money. People who have been dedicated to God are valued according to their age and sex. This is a measure of the work they will be able to do. Men are worth more than women. The very young and the very old are worth less than those in their prime. If the price of redeeming a person is too high, then the priest will help to work out an amount that is reasonable.

The priest also helps in valuing houses. A field is valued by the amount of seed it takes to sow it, or the number of harvests it will yield before the next Jubilee. If worshippers want to repossess their houses or fields, they must pay an extra 20 per cent for them. All land reverts to its original owner at the Jubilee.

First-born animals already belong to the Lord, so they can't be offered twice (Exodus 13:2, 12). If the animal is 'clean' (a cow or sheep suitable for sacrifice), it can never be repossessed by the worshipper. If it is an 'unclean' animal, the worshipper may buy it back for 20 per cent extra, or it can be sold to someone else.

A tithe (tenth) of all produce belongs to God, and is to be offered to him. Again, the worshipper can buy it back for its value, plus a fifth.

One in ten of the animals in every herd and flock belongs to the Lord and is to be offered to him. When selecting these animals, the worshippers must not pick out the best or worst, or seek to substitute one for another. And, unlike the crops, they can't buy them back.

These rules show the importance of keeping a vow to God. A gift must be of real value and express a real commitment.

Behind all sacrifice is the seriousness of sin. Sin is so dreadful that it can only be paid for with a pure life,

completely offered. So Leviticus points us to the perfect, once-for-all sacrifice of Jesus on the cross.

NUMBERS

The book of Numbers describes the years that the Israelites spend in the Sinai Desert. Between leaving Mount Sinai with the tabernacle and embarking on the conquest of Canaan, an entire generation lives and dies in the wilderness. The book of Numbers counts them, tells us how they were organized, records their laws and narrates their adventures.

The wilderness years have been hard. The people have grumbled against God and rebelled against Moses – and there have been some devastating setbacks. An entire generation has forfeited the right to enter the Promised Land. But through this great shared adventure, the Israelites have experienced for themselves the power and love and mercy of God. They have realized the force of his holiness. They have learned obedience. They are ready for victory.

Outline

The tribes at Mount Sinai (1:1 – 9:23)
The journey from Sinai to Moab (10:1 – 21:35)
Events in Moab (22:1 – 32:42)
A log of the journey (33:1–56)
Preparing for settlement (34:1 – 36:13)

INTRODUCTION

Numbers is one of the five 'books of Moses'. Moses is the central character, leading the Israelites throughout this period. 'Numbers' is almost a nickname, referring to the fact that people are counted both at the beginning and towards the end of the book.

The wilderness years are tough. The Israelites are often hungry and thirsty. At times they wish they were back in Egypt. There are frequent complaints about Moses' leadership and even some attempts to overthrow him. In it all, God is faithful to his promise to protect and preserve his people. It is an aspect of his love for them that, on occasions, he disciplines his people severely.

When was Numbers written?

Numbers is about Moses rather than by him. Although he was in a position to record all this information (33:2 has Moses noting the stages of the desert journey), he would hardly describe himself as 'more humble than anyone else on the face of the earth' (12:3)! The book contains some very old poetry, especially in the story of Balaam. The details of history and geography are true to the 13th century BC.

The book of Numbers may not have been written in its final form until some 200 years later, perhaps during the reign of Saul or David. By then there may have been some 'tidying up' of the organization and rules of the wilderness years, as well as some interpretation of what God was doing with his people at this time.

DISCOVERING NUMBERS

The tribes at Mount Sinai

The first census
(1:1–54)

It is just over a year since the Israelites escaped from Egypt. That great event is narrated in the book of Exodus. Moses has a tent of meeting where he speaks with God. It is during one of these times of prayer and listening that God tells Moses to take a census of all the men who are twenty or over. The aim is to register everyone who can serve in the army. The people are counted by tribes; each tribe is named after one of the sons of Jacob.

The resulting total is astonishing: 603,550! This number has been eagerly discussed by scholars because it is so large as to be almost unbelievable. The Hebrew word for 'thousand' can also mean simply 'a clan of families' or even 'a company of soldiers'. It may be that a translator confused the terms and came up with a rather large estimate of the numbers involved.

The Levites are treated as a special case. They aren't counted, as they are to be excused military service. Their sacred responsibility is to assemble and dismantle the tabernacle and to care for its furnishings. They are even to pitch their tents round the tabernacle to provide a protective screen between the Israelites and the wrath of God. The tabernacle is called the tabernacle of the testimony, because it contains the ark in which are kept the Ten Commandments.

A fighting force
(2:1–34)

The Israelites are now a highly organized force. The panic-stricken and argumentative rabble that scrambled out of Egypt has become a disciplined and well-organized army.

The Levites
(3:1–51)

Aaron, the brother of Moses, serves as high priest. In this he is assisted by his sons. They in turn are served by the Levites. Instead of taking the first-born son from every Israelite family, God chooses the Levites as his dedicated tribe. As there aren't enough Levites to account for all the Israelites' first-born, a sum of five shekels per head is collected to cover the rest.

Special responsibilities
(4:1–49)

Within the tribe of Levi, different families and clans are responsible for caring for different parts of the tabernacle. The Kohathite clans have the care of the sanctuary. The Gershonites are responsible for the tenting, curtains and ropes. The Merarites look after frames, posts and pegs.

Although the Kohathites are responsible for the furniture of the sanctuary, only Aaron and his sons are allowed to dismantle the shielding curtain and pack the sacred furnishings. If the Kohathites touch the holy articles, they will die. They are, however, allowed to carry them once they are reverently packed.

A holy place
(5:1–31)

The Israelite camp is a holy place. Everything is to be clean. Every person is to be pure in body and mind. God tells Moses how to keep the camp free of disease by putting certain people in quarantine. People with infectious skin diseases (such as lepers), together with those suffering from discharges, or who have been in contact with a dead body, are to be excluded from the camp. This includes women during the time of their period and men after they have ejaculated semen.

There are regulations for compensating someone who has been wronged. Any offence must be put right, not just between the people concerned, but also with God. There is a special test for a woman whose husband suspects her of being unfaithful to him. She is to swallow bitter water in the presence of the priest. If she is guilty, she will take ill and become barren. This is a very humane law which protects women from quick-tempered or jealous husbands.

The Nazirite
(6:1–21)

A man or woman wishing to be dedicated to God for a particular time or task can become a Nazirite. 'Nazirite' simply means 'one who has taken a vow'. It means that the person concerned is set apart from ordinary life for a while.

The Nazirite is not to drink alcohol, have a haircut or touch a dead body while the vow is in force. When we come to the story of Samson in the book of Judges, we will see how he wilfully breaks all these conditions. Here, in Numbers, the ceremony for becoming a Nazirite brings to mind the words of Paul to the Christians at Rome: 'Offer your bodies as living sacrifices, holy and pleasing to God – this is your spiritual act of worship' (Romans 12:1).

The priestly blessing
(6:22–27)

God gives Moses a form of words by which the priests may bless people. The blessing has an almost overwhelming sense of God's goodwill:

> *The Lord bless you and keep you;*
> *The Lord make his face shine upon you and be*
> *gracious to you;*
> *The Lord turn his face towards you and give you*
> *peace (6:24–26).*

This beautiful blessing is echoed in Psalm 67, where it becomes a prayer that God will bless all the nations through Israel.

Offerings for the tabernacle
(7:1–89)

As Moses completes the work on the tabernacle, the tribal leaders bring their offerings. They come one at a time, on successive days, with an abundance of costly gifts. These include silver and gold plates and bowls, grain, flour and oil, bulls, rams, lambs, oxen and goats. Everything is weighed, measured, counted and recorded. The heads of families are leading by example in their generosity to God. Their gifts will be used to equip the tabernacle for its ceremonies and supply its sacrifices.

At the heart of the tabernacle is the tent of meeting. Here is the ark of the testimony. It is a box containing the two stone slabs which are engraved with the Ten Commandments. On top of the box, at each end, are two cherubim. Between them is the 'atonement cover', where the blood of the sacrifice is to be poured once a year on the Day of Atonement. This is the very place where Moses hears God speak – and speaks with him.

Setting apart the Levites
(8:1–26)

The Levites are commissioned with a special ceremony. After they have been sprinkled with water, they shave themselves all over and wash their clothes and bodies. This is a systematic 'de-sinning'! They offer special

sacrifices. In particular, they have hands laid on them. This is to identify them as representing the whole Israelite community. The Levites in turn lay their hands on the animals that are to be offered in sacrifice for them. The Levites are dedicated to God as substitutes for the first-born sons of every family. There is a contrast here with the first-born sons of Egypt, who died when Israel was rescued from slavery at the first Passover.

The Passover
(9:1–14)

People who miss the Passover because they are away on a journey, or ceremonially unclean, are allowed to celebrate it a month later. However, it is regarded as a very serious matter if someone is able to celebrate the Passover at the proper time but fails to do so. There is a generous rule that non-Israelites can join in the Passover celebration on the same terms as everyone else. Israelites may be exclusive but they are not to be racist.

The cloud above the tabernacle
(9:15–23)

A cloud covers the tent of testimony. It shrouds it during the day and glows like fire at night. This is the symbol of the Lord's presence. In later years it will be called the 'Shekinah'. The Israelites live in such harmony with the will of God that when the cloud lifts they strike camp and move on; where the cloud settles, they stay.

The journey from Sinai to Moab

The silver trumpets
(10:1–10)

God instructs Moses to make two silver trumpets. They are to be used to call people to assembly, to declare war and to proclaim feasts. They are a different kind of trumpet from the rams' horns which are blown to announce the Year of Jubilee.

> The Sinai Desert – God's classroom. The Israelites arrived in this barren region just three months after leaving the irrigated land of Egypt. The wilderness was to be their home for forty years as they learned to rely on God for food and water and protection from enemies. It was on Mount Sinai that Moses received God's law.

The Israelites leave Sinai

(10:11–36)

At last the Israelites move on from Sinai. They travel in good order, in their tribal and family groups. From here on, the story looks forward to the Promised Land.

Moses' father-in-law is thinking of returning home, but Moses persuades him to continue with them. There is a puzzle about his name. Here he is called Hobab, but elsewhere his name is Jethro. He is a much-valued counsellor to Moses, with an unrivalled knowledge of the area and an instinct for good management.

Fire from the Lord

(11:1–3)

Journeying through the desert, the stresses start to show. The people complain about their hardships – and God scorches them for their ingratitude.

Complaints

(11:4–23)

There are complaints about the manna – and dreams of the cool salads of Egypt. No one is sure what 'manna' is, but there is a tamarisk plant which produces sweet sticky globules overnight. These fall to the ground and are melted by the morning sun. This could be the substance that the Israelites collected day by day and prepared as food in a variety of ways.

Moses is exasperated by the people's complaints. They are clamouring for meat and Moses feels unable to take their grumbling any longer. He wishes he could die.

Seventy elders

(11:24–35)

God guides Moses to appoint seventy elders to share in the tasks of leadership. God will give them a share of his Spirit to enable them to do the work. God also promises to give the people meat until they are sick of it!

When the elders are gathered and commissioned, they receive God's Spirit and prophesy. Two of those chosen are still in the camp, some distance from the tent of meeting. They also prophesy, to the delight of Moses (and the jealousy of Joshua!). Moses is not jealous for his own status, but only for God's authority.

The Lord raises a wind which blows in from the Gulf of Aqabah, bringing flocks of quail from the sea. They arrive in astonishing numbers, flying low or falling exhausted. The Israelites gather and eat them, only to be struck down by some kind of disease. This is God's punishment on them for their discontent. As many people die and are buried, the place is named Kibroth Hattaavah, which means 'graves of craving'. They have gorged themselves to death.

Opposition

(12:1–16)

For some reason Miriam and Aaron are jealous of Moses. They criticize him for marrying a Cushite. They also doubt whether he is really that special. Doesn't God also work through them, his brother and sister? This is a crisis brought on by Moses' low-key style of leadership. So far his troubles have included organizational difficulties, food shortages, outbreaks of spiritual gifts, family jealousies and marriage problems.

God takes Aaron and Miriam to task for daring to speak against Moses. Moses does in fact have a unique relationship with God: one that is an open friendship, 'face to face', without deception or defence.

Miriam is punished with a terrible outbreak of skin disease. She has to spend a week in isolation outside the camp.

Exploring Canaan

(13:1–33)

The Israelites have now arrived in the Desert of Paran. They are just a few days' march from Canaan and God tells Moses to send spies on ahead. They are to assess the landscape, the local people and the strength of the defences. The group is made up from a member of each tribe. The significant members are Joshua, son of Nun, and Caleb, son of Jephunneh. In the Valley of Eshcol the spies find such a huge cluster of grapes that it takes two of them to carry it on a pole between them. The name Eshcol means 'cluster'.

After forty days, the twelve spies return. They report to Moses at Kadesh. They give an exciting account of the land and its resources, but feel there is no chance of dislodging its powerful people. Strong tribes occupy the hills and the Canaanites occupy the land between the River Jordan and the sea.

Caleb disagrees with the rest. In his opinion the Israelites are well able to capture the land. The others begin to exaggerate their case – claiming that the land is occupied by giants ('descendants of Anak', 13:33). The Israelites are like 'grasshoppers' compared with them.

The people rebel

(14:1–45)

The spies' report plunges the community into crisis. No one gets any sleep that night as the Israelites bewail their fate. They complain to Moses that they were better off in Egypt. If they go forward from here, they are certain to walk into the jaws of death.

Joshua and Caleb speak to the people. They emphasize again that the land is good and that the Lord will give it to them if they obey him. With God on their side, there is no need to be afraid of any enemy, however tall or strong.

The people are about to stone Joshua and Caleb, when the Lord himself appears at the tent of meeting. He is angry and threatens to destroy the people and make a new nation from Moses. This must have been a very great temptation for Moses, but he rejects it – and even rebukes God for suggesting it. Moses begs God not to destroy his people, because the Egyptians will think that the Lord has failed to rescue them. He pleads that God will forgive the Israelites as he has done before. He describes God in an unforgettable way:

'The Lord is slow to anger, abounding in love and forgiving sin and rebellion. Yet he does not leave the guilty unpunished' (14:18).

God agrees to forgive. But there is a penalty. Of all those who left Egypt, only two will survive to enter the Promised Land. They are the faithful spies, Caleb and Joshua. The Israelites must turn back and wander through the desert until an entire generation has died.

Further offerings

(15:1–21)

God gives Moses some further details about life in the Promised Land. When animals are offered in sacrifice, they are to be accompanied by offerings of grain and wine. The grain will probably take the form of fine flour mixed with oil. The point is not that God needs food, but that flour and oil and wine make a wonderful smell when they burn on the altar. The smell pleases the Lord.

Tassels along the fringe of a garment are a sign of dedication to God. To tug at a rabbi's robe is a child's request for prayer (Luke 8:44).

As a smell is invisible, it is thought of as reaching God, who is invisible.

Israel's law is God's teaching. It is revealed to Israel by God, not devised by the people themselves. A statute is a lasting rule. It comes from the word 'to engrave'. An ordinance (15:15) is a detail of God's law, applied in a particular situation.

Accidental sins

(15:22–31)

God deals with the difference between sins which are committed on purpose and sins which are done by accident. There are sacrifices that can be made when a group or individual causes damage or loss of life by accident. It is far more serious when someone sins on purpose.

A sabbath-breaker is put to death

(15:32–36)

An example is given of a man who is found gathering wood on the sabbath. This is a wilful breach of God's commandment not to do any work on the sabbath day. The Lord tells Moses that the man must be put to death. The whole community takes part in the execution, which is done by stoning outside the camp. This punishment is extreme because the law it enforces is so crucial for the health of society.

Tassels

(15:37–41)

God tells Moses that the Israelites are to wear tassels on the corners of their clothes. These will be a visible reminder of God's law in years to come – and catch the eye when temptations loom!

Rebels

(16:1–50)

Two rebellions flare up against Moses and Aaron. Korah, who is a Levite, challenges the fact that only Aaron and his sons are allowed to be priests. Surely the whole people of God are holy! Korah has a large following. Moses suggests that they each bring a censer (incense burner) and try acting as priests the following day.

Meanwhile, Dathan and Abiram start to disobey Moses. They are Reubenites. In their opinion, Moses has brought them out of a land of plenty and stranded them in a desert. By what right does he give them orders?

The following morning, Korah and his followers waft incense to the Lord. Moses warns everyone else to stand well back from the tents of the rebels. The ground splits open to swallow Korah and everyone who belonged to him, their families and possessions. The Lord sends fire to consume the 250 men who are presuming to offer incense. When the horrifying act of judgment is over, the bronze censers are retrieved from the ashes and beaten into the overlay of the altar. As God's holy anger continues to break out, Aaron offers incense to stem the tide of a plague. Even so, 14,700 people die that day.

The budding of Aaron's staff
(17:1–13)

The challenge to Aaron's status continues and God tells Moses how to handle it. The leader of each of the twelve tribes is to write his name on a staff and place it in the tent of meeting. God will prove to everyone that Aaron is his chosen priest by causing Aaron's staff to send out shoots. The following morning, Aaron's staff has not only sprouted, but budded, blossomed – and produced almonds!

The duties of priests and Levites
(18:1–7)

God tells Aaron that he and his family are to have the care of the sanctuary. The Levites – the wider tribe to which Aaron belongs – are to look after the tent of meeting. After the recent rebellions and testing of holiness, the priesthood is to be exclusive to Aaron and his sons.

Offerings for priests and Levites
(18:8–32)

The priests and their families will be provided for from the offerings brought by the people. The same will be done for the Levites. When the tribes arrive in Canaan

Aaron's staff was made from an almond branch, which blossomed and fruited in a single night to show God's choice of a high priest.

and the territory is divided up, there will be no allocation of land for priests and Levites. God explains to Aaron: 'I am your share.'

The uniqueness of Aaron and his special status is emphasized again. God tells Moses that the Levites must offer a tenth of all that they receive to the Lord, with the best of all (the Lord's portion) given to Aaron.

The water of cleansing
(19:1–22)

God tells Moses and Aaron to prepare 'water of cleansing'. This is to be done by sacrificing and burning a heifer and making a solution of the ashes by mixing them with water. This water is to be sprinkled on anyone who has contact with a dead body or a grave. This gives the Israelites a clear procedure for dealing with death and the risk of infection.

Water from the rock
(20:1–13)

The Israelites arrive at the Desert of Zin and camp at Kadesh. They will settle here for nearly forty years. The people complain at the lack of water and reproach Moses for stranding them in the desert. Egypt now seems to them a place of pleasure and plenty.

God tells Moses to take his staff, gather the people and call water out of the rock. Moses vents some of his anger by striking the rock twice with the rod. Water gushes out in plenty, but God is angry with Moses and Aaron. The spirit and manner in which Moses has worked the miracle have dishonoured God. In a devastating judgment, God declares that Moses and Aaron will not be allowed to lead the Israelites into the new land. The place is named Meribah, which means 'quarrelling'.

Edom bars the way
(20:14–21)

Moses sends messengers to the king of Edom. The Edomites are descended from Esau, just as the Israelites are descended from Jacob. Moses asks permission for the Israelites to use the 'King's Highway' – the caravan track which provides their most direct route to Canaan. The

Edomites refuse permission – a snub which Israel will remember for many generations to come.

The death of Aaron
(20:22–29)
The Lord tells Moses and Aaron that the time has come for Aaron to die. With Aaron's son Eleazar, they climb Mount Hor. At the summit, Moses transfers Aaron's garments to Eleazar; and Aaron dies.

The destruction of Arad
(21:1–3)
The nations and tribes of the area are now on guard against Israel's advance. The king of Arad attacks them – and is completely destroyed.

The bronze snake
(21:4–9)
Taking the long route round Edom, the Israelites continue to complain about God's plan and Moses' leadership. God punishes them with an infestation

of venomous snakes. When they beg for forgiveness and Moses prays for them, God instructs him to make a snake and put it on a pole.

Moses makes the snake of bronze and hangs it high on a pole. Anyone suffering from snake-bites can look at it and be healed. One day Jesus will take this as an image of himself – nailed to the cross in the sight of, and for the sake of, the whole world (John 3:14–15).

The journey from Kadesh to Pisgah
(21:10–20)
The Israelites are now nearing the end of the journey. After a lengthy stay at Kadesh, they move their camp to Oboth and then on to Iye-abarim (the 'ruins of Abarim'). At this point they are about fifteen miles south of the Dead Sea and journeying east. When they come to the arid valley of the Arabah, they join a trade route which takes them north, along the western boundary of Edom. Reaching the Zered Valley, they follow it east through Edom, and then travel north again along Edom's western boundary. Arriving at the River Arnon, which runs swiftly westward to the Dead Sea, the Israelites cross from Moab into the territory of the Amorites and the kingdom of Sihon. The journey is simply summarized in Judges 11:16–18.

We hear snatches of two songs which survive in an ancient saga called *The Book of the Wars of the Lord*. They speak of the slopes and wadis (river beds) encountered on the desert journey, and recall the official opening of a well at a place called Beer! In later years, this 'Song of Israel' was sung every third sabbath, along with Moses' great 'Song of the Sea' (Exodus 15:1–19).

The Israelites travel on through places whose names are unknown today, until they come to the heights of Pisgah in Moab, with a panoramic view of Canaan to the west. This is their first sight of the Promised Land.

The defeat of Sihon and Og
(21:21–35)
Continuing their journey, the Israelites again ask permission to use the King's Highway. This time it is Sihon, king of the Amorites, who obstructs them. The Israelites defeat him in pitched battle and capture his capital, Heshbon. The mention of various towns and settlements at this point in the journey helps us to date the time of the exodus. Permanent settlements only began in this area after 1350 BC. By the time Israel encounters them, they are already well established – leading us to a date around 1250 BC for Israel's desert journey.

Balaam's donkey

The wonderful, hilarious story of Balaam is a treasure of wit and wisdom – and features some of the oldest poetry in the Bible. It is written by someone who knows all about donkeys – although not many of us have met one that talks!

Balaam delivers four oracles about Israel, but is completely unable to curse them – much to Balak's annoyance. Balaam is a genuine prophet, who can only say the words God gives him. He proclaims the mystery of Israel:

> *I see people who live apart*
> *and do not consider themselves one of the nations (23:9).*

Balaam's fourth oracle attains the very heights of prophecy. As he declares the future victories of Israel, we have a tingling recognition of the coming Messiah:

> *I see him, but not now;*
> *I behold him, but not near.*
> *A star will come out of Jacob;*
> *A sceptre will rise out of Israel (24:17).*

Having conquered the Amorites, the Israelites take the main road towards Bashan. Here they defeat King Og and his army and capture the land. So Israel makes her first gains in the area we now know as Trans-Jordan.

Events in Moab

The story of Balaam
(22:1 – 24:25)

The Israelites arrive in the plains of Moab and camp along the banks of the River Jordan, opposite Jericho. At last they are out of the desert, in a kinder landscape of woods and water, north of the Dead Sea. The king of Moab, Balak, is so alarmed that he sends all the way to the Euphrates for a prophet. So we meet Balaam, who is hired to curse the Israelites and prevent any further advance.

Balaam consults God and discovers that the Israelites are his chosen people. He refuses to curse them. God allows Balaam to return with the messengers (now augmented by a delegation of princes), but proceeds to give him a very rough time with his donkey. With Balaam, God uses a foreigner to bless Israel, although it is Israel who is to bless the nations.

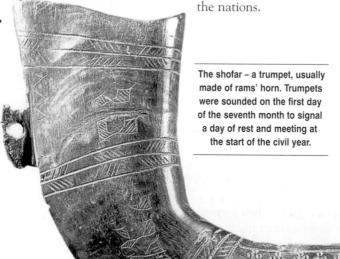

The shofar – a trumpet, usually made of rams' horn. Trumpets were sounded on the first day of the seventh month to signal a day of rest and meeting at the start of the civil year.

Trouble with Moabite women
(25:1–18)

Some Israelite men get involved with Moabite women. Soon the potent mixture of sex and paganism is compromising Israel's holiness. God tells Moses to stop the rot by executing the leaders and hanging their bodies. This will avert God's anger.

One particular Israelite, Zimri, takes a Midianite woman to his tent in full view of everyone. Aaron's son, Phinehas, follows them and runs them both through with a spear. This puts a stop to a plague which has already claimed 24,000 lives. One day the priestly line of Zadok will trace its descent from the zealous Phinehas, who acted out of a passion for God's holiness. But a young Midianite widow, Ruth, will become an ancestor of King David – and Jesus.

The second census
(26:1–65)

As the Israelites approach the end of their journey, God tells Moses to take another census. Moses and Eleazar are to count the people over twenty, to assess the military strength of Israel and prepare for the dividing up of Canaan. As we found with the first census, it is difficult to be sure of these figures. The Hebrew term for a thousand can also be used for a much smaller group, such as a company of soldiers, an extended family or a clan. Certainly the numbers as they stand are huge.

God tells Moses to allocate the new land according to the size of the tribes. Larger groups will have more territory than others, but the actual decisions are to be made by lottery. The Levites are also counted, but they will not receive a share of land, because they are a tribe set aside for the service of God.

None of the people counted by Moses and Aaron in the first census has survived to be counted by Moses and Eleazar in the second. Only Caleb and Joshua remain of the generation that grumbled its way across the desert from Egypt to the borders of Canaan.

Equal rights for women

(27:1–11)

From now on, the ownership of land will become an issue. An important legal point is raised with Moses. The daughters of Zelophehad want to know if they can inherit property, because their father had no sons. God tells Moses that they must certainly be allowed their father's inheritance.

Joshua to succeed Moses

(27:12–23)

God tells Moses that the time is approaching for him to die. Moses asks God to appoint a faithful leader in his place. The Lord tells Moses to choose Joshua, a man God has already blessed with his Spirit. Joshua is commissioned by Moses in the presence of Eleazar the priest and the whole community. From now on Joshua is recognized as Moses' successor.

Offerings and festivals

(28:1–31)

God gives Moses detailed instructions about sacrifices and festivals. All this is important information for the priests, as they lead and regulate the life of the community.

These chapters in the book of Numbers show us the holiness of God and the seriousness of sin. They warn against half-hearted or casual worship. They encourage us to come to God for forgiveness and cleansing. Although we live in a different time, place and culture, the principle of reverence is still all-important.

Sacrifices are offered every day at morning and evening. In addition, there are special sacrifices on the sabbath day and on the first day of every month. Regulations are given here for the Passover, when the Israelites celebrate their deliverance from Egypt, and the Feast of Weeks, which is a harvest festival. Jews no longer offer sacrifices, because they have no temple in

Jerusalem. Christians believe that the death of Jesus put an end to the sacrificing of animals, because he was the all-sufficient sacrifice for all time.

Three great feasts

(29:1–40)

God gives Moses details of the sacrifices and offerings to be made at the Feast of Trumpets, the Day of Atonement and the Feast of Tabernacles. While the Feast of Trumpets is a time of celebration, the Day of Atonement is one of fasting, reflection and repentance. The Feast of Tabernacles lasts for a whole week and includes an extensive pattern of sacrifices. In centuries to come it will be celebrated by families camping out, to recall the tents and shelters of those wilderness years.

Vows

(30:1–16)

When making vows, the word of an Israelite man is to be his bond. A young Israelite woman is entitled to make a vow, but her father may veto it. When she is married, her husband can disallow her pledges. In both cases, the vow must be cancelled promptly, as soon as the father or husband first hears of it.

A holy war

(31:1–54)

God commissions Moses for a last campaign. Israel is to destroy the Midianites, who are immoral and pagan. Moses stops his officers sparing the Midianite women.

This is a holy war. God has commanded it, and it is fought in his strength. There are strict rules whereby the soldiers must clean up afterwards. If they have killed anyone or touched a dead body, they must stay outside the camp for a week. They must scrupulously wash themselves and their clothes – and clean their equipment. Even the plunder must be thoroughly cleansed: the precious metals through fire, and the other goods with water. Everything belongs to the Lord and is either carefully saved or utterly destroyed.

The Trans-Jordan tribes

(32:1–42)

Two of the tribes, the Reubenites and the Gadites, ask if they can settle in the land already captured, on the east side of the Jordan. At first Moses thinks they are backing out of the campaign. The two tribes assure him that they will actually lead the advance and not rest until all the land is conquered. Moses agrees to their proposal and grants these two tribes, together with the half-tribe of Manasseh (one of Joseph's sons), the land captured from Sihon and Og. This great desire for unity among the tribes does not last long after the conquest of Canaan.

A log of the journey

Moses has been keeping a record of all the stages and stopping places of the journey. We get some idea of his sophisticated Egyptian education as we read the entries made over many years. There is a vivid note of the day they left Egypt – marching out boldly while the Egyptians were burying their first-born. There is a postcard view of Elim, with its twelve springs and seventy palm trees. There is the bitter memory that there was no water to drink at Rephidim. The day and place of Aaron's death are recorded, together with his age. But this is mainly a list of places. While we can trace the broad outline of the route – from Rameses to Mount Sinai, and from Sinai to Ezion Geber on the coast of the Gulf of Aqaba; from there to the oasis of Kadesh in the Desert of Zin, and then on to the Plains of Moab – it is impossible to pinpoint the places today. Place names change frequently, especially in the desert.

God gives Moses a summary of his instructions. When the Israelites enter Canaan, they must expel its inhabitants and destroy their pagan gods and hilltop shrines. The land is to be divided among the Israelite tribes by size and by lot. It is not to be owned by a wealthy few, but by everyone as equally as possible. Moses must warn the people that if they fail to purge the land of its old inhabitants, they will bring pain and judgment on themselves in the future.

Preparing for settlement

The boundaries of Canaan
(34:1–29)
God gives Moses the boundaries of Canaan, the Promised Land. The boundary runs from the southern end of the Dead Sea, takes in Edom and Kadesh Barnea, and stretches to the Mediterranean coastline. The sea then forms the western boundary. In the north, the limit of the Israelite territory is marked by Hazar Enan. From

there the boundary runs south where it joins the River Jordan. The river forms the eastern boundary. These are the ideal dimensions of Israel and will only be achieved in the reigns of David and Solomon.

Towns for the Levites
(35:1–5)
The Levites are to be a tribe devoted to the Lord, and won't have a tribal land of their own. Instead, they are to be given forty-eight cities, scattered around the country, each with some pasture for their cattle and flocks. Israel is not to be ruled by powerful religious leaders who control most of the wealth.

Cities of refuge
(35:6–34)
Six of the Levites' towns are to be 'cities of refuge'. Anyone accused of murder can claim sanctuary in one of these places until their case is brought to trial. When there has been a violent death, it is important to establish whether it was a murder or an accident. A high value is set on human life and great care is to be taken to ensure that judgments are true and penalties fair. An 'avenger of blood' is the next of kin of someone who has been killed. The avenger of blood makes sure that justice is done.

Land for everyone
(36:1–13)
It is intended that the tribal lands will be permanent. They are not to be fragmented by trade or marriage. This means that the daughters of Zelophehad must marry within their tribe, to keep the land for the clans of Manasseh. The Promised Land is not for the profit of great landowners but for the benefit and survival of all Israel's families.

DEUTERONOMY

The Israelites have completed their journey from Egypt. They stand on the threshold of the Promised Land. For Moses this is a poignant moment, for he himself is about to die.

The book of Deuteronomy is Moses' farewell to the people. He encourages them to go on and occupy the land which God promised to their ancestors long ago. He reviews their journey together and spells out in simple language the terms of their covenant with God. A 'covenant' is a formal agreement, like a treaty.

Much of Deuteronomy is made out like an agreement between God and Israel. If they keep God's law, he will continue to bless them with peace and prosperity as he has promised. If not, they will fall under his curse.

Deuteronomy is a warm-hearted, forward-looking book. It contains brilliant rules for a full and happy life – a life based on a total commitment to God. At its heart are the words which Jesus himself took as the finest summary of the law:

Love the Lord your God with all your heart and with all your soul and with all your strength (6:5; Mark 12:30).

Outline

The wilderness years (1:1 – 4:49)
God's law and other instructions (5:1 – 26:19)
Blessings and curses (27:1 – 28:68)
Israel renews the covenant (29:1 – 30:20)
Farewell, Moses (31:1 – 34:12)

INTRODUCTION

Deuteronomy is the fifth of the 'books of Moses' at the beginning of the Bible. The title 'Deuteronomy' means 'a copy of this law' and comes from the Greek translation of a phrase in 17:18. Much of Deuteronomy can be found in parts of Exodus, Leviticus and Numbers, but this is far more than just an extra copy. Deuteronomy is laid out like one of the treaties of those days. It sets out, in everyday language, the terms and conditions of Israel's relationship with God. While Exodus and Leviticus provide information for the priests, Deuteronomy gives instruction and inspiration for everyone else.

Almost the whole of the book is presented in Moses' own words. This is the teaching he gave the new generation of the Israelites as they camped in the Plains of Moab and prepared to invade and capture the Promised Land of Canaan.

Moses has kept notes during the journey through the desert. He has thought deeply about God's dealings with them. Now he recalls and relates and interprets all that God has done.

The Israelites are God's own people. God has rescued Israel from Egypt and given her his law. She is the only nation in the world who has first-hand experience of the one and only God as her Saviour and king. With these great privileges comes the solemn responsibility to love and honour God in return.

Israel is to be a holy nation. This theme will be of enormous importance to the Christian church in centuries to come. Peter will write:

You are a chosen people, a royal priesthood, a holy nation, a people belonging to God, that you may declare the praises of him who called you out of darkness into his wonderful light. Once you were not a people, but now you are the people of God; once you had not received mercy, but now you have received mercy (1 Peter 2:9–10).

Indeed, there are over eighty quotations from the book of Deuteronomy in the New Testament.

In many ways, Deuteronomy is a handbook to go with the covenant of Sinai. It gives detailed examples of how the Ten Commandments are to be lived out in everyday life. It warns of the deadly dangers of getting involved in the paganism of nearby nations. It teaches that obedience to God is good, wise, safe, liberating – and joyful. It deals in detail with right relationships – how people can live at peace with one another and care for the poor. It makes goodness attractive. When we are right with God, then we can get right with one another. When we are right with one another, then the whole world – earth, sky, people, plants and animals – will enjoy peace and plenty, harmony and happiness. In all this, the blessings of God depend on, but are not deserved by, the people's obedience to God.

Bedouin with goats in the desert. The Israelites learned dependence on God in this tough environment, but many of the laws of Deuteronomy look forward to their settlement in towns.

DISCOVERING DEUTERONOMY

The wilderness years

It is forty years since the exodus. Only Moses, Caleb and Joshua remember the great day when Israel escaped from slavery in Egypt. Now Moses tells the story again for the next generation. He remembers how God called them at Horeb (Mount Sinai) to cross the desert, challenge and defeat the tribes of Canaan and occupy the land between the Mediterranean Sea and the River Euphrates. This is the Promised Land that God swore to give their ancestor Abraham, and which they are now about to possess.

The delay of disobedience
(1:1–46)

Moses recalls the terrible burden of trying to care for so many people, and how the problem was resolved by sharing leadership. He describes how the spies were sent ahead and how they brought back reports of a good land but a powerful enemy. It was when the Israelites refused to trust God and go on to victory that they were sentenced to spend the rest of their lives in the desert. A journey that should have taken eleven days in fact lasted forty years. Moses was included in this failure and it is Joshua who will now lead the invasion of Canaan.

Learning to trust God
(2:1 – 3:29)

Moses tells how the extra time in the desert has been used to build up Israel's trust in God. The people have discovered how God guides and provides. He gave them resounding victories over Sihon and the daunting Amorites, and over Og, the giant king of Bashan. Og's bed (made of iron) was thirteen feet long and six feet wide! All this is important experience for the campaign ahead. If God could defeat Sihon and Og, then he can give victory over the strongholds of Canaan.

'The Lord is God'
(4:1–49)

Moses tells Israel that her strength lies in obedience to God. She must never forget the darkness and fire of Mount Sinai, when God gave her the Ten Commandments. The law is Israel's greatest treasure. It is to be learned, digested, lived – and taught to the children of every future generation. God is invisible and not to be imaged or modelled as an idol. It will be Israel's privileged task, by her obedience, to show the reality of God to the nations of the world. Moses warns the Israelites that if they turn to idol-worship they will lose their land and not regain it until they repent.

God's law and other instructions

The Ten Commandments
(5:1–33)

Moses recites the Ten Commandments. These laws are for the people here and now. They are not to be dismissed as applying only to the old days.

God identifies himself by what he has done. He brought his people out of Egypt. They are to have no other gods. He is invisible. They must not try to make an image of God or express him in terms of heavenly bodies or earthly creatures. Any idol of God would be pitifully inadequate and dangerously misleading. Instead, God wishes to be known by his passion for his people: his jealousy for their love, his hatred of their wickedness and his lasting commitment to their well-being.

God's name is utterly holy. It sums up his personality and purpose. It is a serious thing to abuse God's name, by taking it lightly or using it to endorse empty promises.

The sabbath day is to be kept holy. It is a day when the whole community – including servants, animals, visitors and strangers – has time and space to rest and reflect.

Children are to honour their parents. Families are to be bonded by obedience as well as affection. Elderly parents are to be provided for by their children. Soundly built families make a strong and stable society.

Human life, marriage, possessions and reputations are all to be respected. In particular, jealousy is to be tackled at source – in the heart. A neighbour is any fellow human being – not just a person who lives nearby. Another person's partner and possessions are not negotiable. Don't even think it!

'Love the Lord your God'
(6:1–25)

God's law is a guide for living in total commitment to God. God's law is to be Israel's delight and magnificent obsession:

Love the Lord your God with all your heart and with all your soul and with all your strength. These commandments that I give you today are to be upon your hearts. Impress them on your children. Talk about them when you sit at home and when you walk along the road, when you lie down and when you get up. Tie them as symbols on your hands, and bind

These Phoenician figurines of pregnant women may depict fertility goddesses (7th–6th century BC). The Israelites were to destroy the idols of paganism, because the true God is holy and invisible, not to be reduced to a model in metal or stone.

them on your foreheads. Write them on the doorframes of your houses and on your gates (6:5–9).

These verses are the Hebrew 'Shema', which pious Jews recite twice a day.

'Tie them as symbols on your hands and bind them on your foreheads.' Orthodox Jews take these words literally and have copies of the law in containers (phylacteries), tied to their wrists and foreheads. God's law is to govern their personal, family and public life.

In later centuries there will be much debate about which is the most important law. Many people choose this verse as their summary: 'Love the Lord your God with all your heart and with all your soul and with all your strength.' Jesus agrees, adding the phrase, 'with all your mind'. In Hebrew, the 'heart' is the centre of the mind and will – not just the emotions. For Jesus this is 'the most important' commandment (Mark 12:28–34).

Destroying pagan nations
(7:1–26)

The Israelites are told to destroy the pagan tribes of Canaan. They are to break down their altars, cut down their Asherah poles (fertility symbols) and burn their idols. All temptations to compromise with paganism by preserving idols, intermarrying with the people or even sparing their lives is strictly forbidden. This is not an ethnic cleansing as much as a spiritual purge. It is vital that God's holy people have a new start in a clean land. Even things as neutral as silver and gold are to be rejected, in case Israel relies on them instead of God. All their attitudes, standards and dealings are to reflect the holiness of God, because he has saved and loved them – and because that's what he is like.

'Do not forget...'
(8:1–20)

Moses warns the Israelites not to forget the lessons of the desert. It was here that they learned that the Lord provides – and that there is more to life than filling your stomach.

Jesus quotes this chapter when the devil tempts him to turn stones into bread: 'One does not live by bread alone, but by every word that comes from the mouth of God' (Matthew 4:4, quoting Deuteronomy 8:3).

Moses is here a superb teacher and pastor. He is interpreting the hard lessons of the desert as examples of God's love. He also sees that when life gets easier, faith in God will become harder. It will seem to the Israelites that they have deserved their good life, by luck, prowess or hard work. In fact it is God's gift to them. The earth's natural resources and human ability to produce wealth are both aspects of God's covenant care. They should be grateful rather than proud.

'Not because of your righteousness'
(9:1–29)

When the Israelites enter Canaan, God will enable them to defeat even the legendary Anakites, who are like giants. They will be able to do this, not because they themselves are powerful or good, but because God is with them. They will conquer Canaan because they are executing God's judgment on the Canaanites' wickedness, not because the Israelites are righteous. The Israelites are 'stiff-necked' – resistant to guidance and almost impossible to train. They made and worshipped an idol, a golden calf, even while Moses was on Sinai

Staying loyal to God

Moses warns the people not to forget God when they come into the wealth and comfort of the new land. They are to depend on God just as much as they did in the desert, when they relied on him for every crumb of food and every sip of water. In the future Jesus will quote these verses to counter the temptations of the devil (Matthew 4:1–11). When challenged to throw himself from the highest point of the temple, Jesus answers, 'Do not put the Lord your God to the test' (Matthew 4:7, quoting Deuteronomy 6:16). When invited to worship the devil in return for a world empire, Jesus replies, 'Worship the Lord your God, and serve him only' (Matthew 4:10, quoting Deuteronomy 6:13). These commandments are not only to do with trusting and obeying God, but also about being loyal to him.

receiving God's law. The Israelites smashed the Ten Commandments from the start. It was only Moses' earnest prayer that dissuaded God from destroying them there and then.

'Fear the Lord your God'
(10:1–22)

Moses recalls how he cut two new stone tablets for the law and made a wooden chest, the ark of the covenant, for their safe keeping. There is a note in brackets that Aaron died and Eleazar became high priest, and that the tribe of Levi was given the task of carrying the ark and pronouncing blessings. Perhaps this was added in later years by an editor who was himself a priest.

Moses comes to one of the great conclusions of his story:

> *And now, O Israel, what does the Lord your God ask of you but to fear the Lord your God, to walk in all his ways, to love him, to serve the Lord your God with all your heart and with all your soul, and to observe the Lord's commands and decrees that I am giving you today (10:12–13)?*

God is supreme over his creation, and greater than all he has made. By an almost incredible act of grace, he has set his heart on this little, obstinate people of Israel. The Israelites must 'circumcise their hearts' – change their minds about God and cut away their resistance to him. They must realize that God is absolutely fair in all his dealings, protecting the weak and providing for the outsider. The Israelites should always remember what it was like to be helpless, when they were slaves in Egypt.

The blessings of obedience
(11:1–32)

The land of Canaan is fertile and watered by rains and rivers – unlike Egypt, which was laboriously irrigated by channels from the Nile. Moses warns the Israelites that if they lapse into paganism, then God will punish them with drought and dearth. The Israelites have a choice. If they keep God's commands, he will continue to bless them. If they disobey God's commands, he will curse them. When they come into the land they will hold a ceremony on the twin mountains of Gerizim and Ebal, proclaiming God's blessings from one and his curses from the other.

One place of worship

(12:1–32)

Now Moses gives more detailed rules for life in Canaan. Every sign of paganism is to be destroyed – especially the altars on the summits of mountains, on the tops of hills and under trees. God will show the Israelites one central place of worship, where they are to offer sacrifices and bring gifts to the one and only God. As time goes by, there will be a number of major shrines. An altar will be built on Mount Ebal. Shiloh and Shechem will both become places of pilgrimage. Finally, Jerusalem will be the spiritual centre, established by King David and with the temple built by his son Solomon.

Even so, what matters is not where 'the place' is, but whose name is worshipped there. Moses warns the Israelites that they must have nothing to do with the pagan practices of other nations – not even be curious to know what they do. Pagan worship is savage and senseless, including the killing and burning of children.

Warnings against other gods

(13:1–18)

Purity of faith is crucial. Anyone who preaches lies about God is to be put to death even if that person is your own wife. Any town which switches its allegiance to other gods is to be destroyed and left as a ruin. These drastic rules show the seriousness with which God takes false belief and misguided religion.

Clean and unclean food

(14:1–21)

Moses repeats the laws of diet and hygiene which are also found in the book of Leviticus. He gives again the guidelines for knowing which animals, birds and fish are 'clean' and which are 'unclean'.

These food laws show that Israel is distinct from other nations in her belief and behaviour. One day this distinctiveness will be based on Christ, and food laws will no longer matter (Mark 7:18–19; Acts 10:11–16).

Tithes

(14:22–29)

A tenth of the harvest each year is to be taken to God's centre (a shrine, or the temple) and used for a festival in his presence. The Levites and all who have no means of support, such as foreigners, orphans and widows, are to enjoy a share of the produce.

Every three years, the tithe is to be stored and used to feed those who are destitute. Providing for the poor is an important aspect of Israel's economy.

Cancelling debts and freeing slaves

(15:1–23)

Once every seven years, all debts are to be cancelled. Ideally, there will be no poor people at all. If God provides and his people are generous, the causes of poverty will be removed. However, God is also a realist. He knows that there will always be those who are poor, and so he commands his people to be generous to them (15:11).

In the same way as debts are cancelled, so is slavery. A slave must be released after six years of service, unless he or she wishes to stay in the owner's employment. These laws reflect the forgiveness and generosity which are at the heart of God. He will bless those who treat others in this way.

Celebrating the feasts

(16:1–17)

The rules for calculating and keeping the main festivals are repeated from the books of Exodus, Leviticus and Numbers: the Feast of Unleavened Bread (Passover), the Feast of Weeks and the Feast of Tabernacles.

Appointing judges

(16:18–20)

Judges are to be appointed who will make decisions fairly, and not be influenced by favouritism or bribes.

Fair trial

(16:21 – 17:13)

It will be important to stamp out paganism, but there are to be no hysterical witch-hunts. If anyone is suspected of occult practice, he or she may only be found guilty after proper investigation and the evidence of more than one witness. Any difficult cases may be taken to the priests, whose decisions will be binding. To deny or ignore their ruling is a capital offence.

A king who is under the law

(17:14–20)

Moses anticipates that one day the Israelites will want a king. When this happens, they must choose a fellow Israelite who will himself be under God's law. He mustn't build up a large personal army or allow himself to be distracted by acquiring wives or wealth. The first thing he must do is sit down and write out his own copy of the law. This scroll is to be his constant companion. These rules about kingship are so appropriate to Solomon that many scholars have wondered whether they were added as a result of his reign. They would, in fact, apply to any oriental king, even long before Solomon's time.

Offerings for priests and Levites
(18:1–8)

Just as the king is to be regulated in the liberties and privileges of his office, so are the priests. The priests belong to the tribe of Levi. Their special work is to offer sacrifices and to teach God's law.

Unlike the other tribes of Israel, the Levites have no area of the Promised Land to call their own. Instead, they have forty-eight cities in the territories of the other tribes, together with some pastureland for cattle or crops. They are set aside for God's work and must depend on the other tribes for their food and drink. This comes from the offerings and sacrifices of the people, to which the priests have the right to a portion or share. So God himself is the inheritance of the Levites. They live by faith and blessing rather than land and livelihood.

The rights of a Levite are not restricted to his home town. If he moves to serve God in a sanctuary, he is to receive his share of food there, along with the other priests.

Warning against pagan practices
(18:9–13)

Moses issues another stern warning against paganism. This time he is quite specific about child sacrifice and all aspects of the occult. Israel is to be a no-go area for the black arts of witchcraft and spiritism. On the contrary, the whole nation is to live in the light of God's word.

A prophet like Moses
(18:14–22)

One day God will raise up another prophet like Moses, who will stand between God and the people to reveal his truth. The apostle Peter will quote these words in his Pentecost sermon, showing that Jesus Christ fulfils this ancient promise (Acts 3:22). Stephen, in a brilliant speech to the Jewish Council, will make the same point (Acts 7:37).

Moses gives a simple test to tell if a prophet is genuine. If things turn out as a prophet has said, then his message was from the Lord. There is no need to take a prophet seriously if he might be an impostor. Time will tell. Jesus warns that many false prophets will appear towards the end of the age (Matthew 24:11).

Cities of refuge
(19:1–14)

Three cities are to be set aside as 'cities of refuge'. Anyone who kills another person by accident can run to one of these centres for sanctuary. If Israel's territory increases, then three more cities are to be set aside for this purpose. There is always to be one within easy reach, so that the next of kin doesn't add to tragic accidents by murdering innocent people. If the death was intentional, then the murderer is to be handed over for trial and execution.

Witnesses
(19:15–21)

A person can only be convicted of a crime if there is evidence from more than one witness. Such witnesses are to be carefully cross-examined. A false witness is to be given whatever punishment he was trying to inflict on another. 'Eye for eye, tooth for tooth' is known as the 'lex talionis' – the law by which a penalty is absolutely fair: no more and no less. Jesus quotes these words in the Sermon on the Mount. Instead of precise penalty or fair compensation, he teaches non-retaliation and generous forgiveness: giving grace rather than taking revenge (Matthew 5:38–42).

Going to war
(20:1–20)

There are special guidelines for going to war. The priests are to tell the soldiers not to be afraid, because God will be fighting for them. Anyone who is worried or scared can go home! Before an enemy city is attacked, its people are to be invited to surrender. If they do so, they are to be spared and taken as slaves. However, if the captured people have vile pagan practices, they are to be completely destroyed before they infect Israel. When laying siege to a city and destroying the surrounding woodland, the fruit trees are to be spared. They have offended no one and they produce food. The natural world is often the first victim of war.

Dealing with bloodshed

(21:1–9)

Blood is always important. Blood is the essence of life – and life is God's creation and gift. If someone is found murdered in open country and no one knows who did it, then the people in the nearest town are to make an atoning sacrifice. This doesn't cover the guilt of the murderer, but it protects the innocent people nearby.

Marrying a captive woman

(21:10–14)

If a soldier is attracted to a woman who has been captured, he is to treat her with all respect. He may take her to his home, where she must shave her head, trim her nails and change her clothes. This reminds us of the ceremony for becoming a priest. She must be allowed a month to grieve for her loved ones and the passing of her old life. After this, the soldier may marry her. If he later changes his mind, he must set his wife free – not simply make her a slave. These guidelines have a respect for women which was unheard of in other cultures – is rare in war even today.

Justice for sons

(21:15–21)

A first-born son is to have special honour and a double share of his father's property. This is his right by birth and does not depend on whether he is the favourite son. A delinquent son is to be presented to the elders of the town, publicly accused and sentenced to death by

Ours to reason 'why?'

These laws come to us from a different time and culture. They often seem primitive and out of date. To understand them, we need to look for their underlying purpose.

Behind every law is the desire to reflect and express God's justice and generosity.

It may help to ask such questions as: 'Who will benefit from this law?' 'Whose interest is being protected?' 'Whose power is being restricted?' and 'What is this law trying to promote – or prevent?'

stoning. A father does not have power of life and death over his children. Such cases are to be referred to the civil authorities. If a criminal is executed by hanging, his body must be buried at nightfall. There is to be dignity, not savagery, in applying God's law.

God in the detail

(21:22 – 22:30)

Here is a cluster of rules to encourage kindness and holiness. People are to respect one another's possessions – returning stray animals or lost property. Some actions are forbidden because they are a confusion of God's created order. For example, men and women must not wear each other's clothes. A mother bird is not to be taken from her nest. There is to be no mixing of seeds, crops or animals – nor of the fabrics used in making clothes. All these are little practical details which together express a wholeness of heart and life.

Sex and marriage are also holy. A woman is to remain a virgin until she is married. If it turns out that she is not a virgin, then she is to be executed by stoning. Sex before or outside marriage carries the death penalty. Promiscuous behaviour is a confusion of God's order. Being engaged ('betrothed') is just as binding as marriage. We see this in Joseph's dilemma when Mary is found to be pregnant (Matthew 1:19). Those who commit adultery are to be put to death. There is no such thing as sex without responsibility. Rape is as serious as murder. A man who rapes a woman who is neither married nor engaged is to pay a fine to her father and marry her. Sex between parents and children, or between close relatives, is expressly forbidden.

Staying clear and keeping clean

(23:1–14)

Certain people are to be excluded from Israel's assembly. There is a ban on men with damaged testicles, illegitimate children and foreign enemies. These laws prevent confusions and highlight consequences. God's holiness extends to the whole of life, and there are simple guidelines for such normal functions as having wet dreams or going to the bathroom.

Finding the right balance

(23:15 – 25:19)

Some of these laws find a precise balance between severity and generosity. Divorce is allowed to resolve ruined marriages, but not to license promiscuity. Newly-weds are excused all other duties, so that they can establish their marriage. Taking security for a loan must not wreck another person's business or deprive them of their only clothes. Some of the harvest is to be left in the fields and on the trees, so that the poor can find food. Israelites are never to forget what it is like to be helpless and in trouble – as they were themselves, when they were slaves in Egypt.

Legal punishments are to be administered with dignity, under proper supervision and within maximum limitations. They are penalties, not humiliations.

An ox is to be allowed to eat while it is working. This is a principle Paul applies to Christian ministers and missionaries (1 Corinthians 9:3–12). If possible, a widow is to be married to one of her husband's brothers, and have a son to continue the dead man's name. This is sometimes known as Levirate marriage. There is a public non-marriage ceremony if the brother-in-law refuses to do his duty! (See also Ruth 4:7.)

Firstfruits and family roots
(26:1–19)

The Promised Land is God's gift to Israel. At harvest time, the first basket of produce is to be taken to the priest and presented as a thank-offering to God. The person bringing the gift is to recite a brief history of Israel, from the time God called Abraham ('a wandering Aramean'), to the present day. In this way, individual Israelites take their very own place in the story and life of God's people.

Every third year, a tithe (10 per cent) of the harvest is to be given to the Levites and to the poor. Israel is to remember that obedience and blessing go together. Responsibility to God is fulfilled through practical care for the poor.

Melons from the Jordan Valley. The Israelites are to bring the 'firstfruits' of their harvest as a thank-offering to God for their freedom and their land. After prayer, the produce is used for a harvest feast.

Blessings and curses

The altar on Mount Ebal
(27:1–8)

In the centre of Canaan there are two prominent hills – Mount Ebal and Mount Gerizim. Moses gives instructions that large stones are to be coated with plaster and inscribed with God's law. The stones are to be set up on Mount Ebal, and sacrifices are to be offered on an altar there.

Curses for disobedience
(27:9–26)

Half the tribes (or perhaps their representatives) are to stand on Mount Gerizim, and half on Mount Ebal. Those on Mount Gerizim are to pronounce the blessings. They are all the tribes which have descended from Jacob's wives, Leah and Rachel. Those on Mount Ebal are to pronounce curses. They are (apart from Reuben) the tribes which have descended from Jacob's maidservants, Bilhah and Zilpah. The curses are for those who break God's commands, by making idols, harming defenceless people or having forbidden sex.

Blessings for obedience
(28:1–14)

For those who obey the Lord fully, there are many wonderful blessings. God's love will be experienced in the quiet enjoyment of everyday life – families, farms, shopping and housework, comings and goings. A basket is used for carrying produce, and is the symbol of harvest. A kneading trough is used for working dough – and is a symbol of daily bread. God will protect his people from

their enemies, provide rain for their crops and promote their businesses. The fear and frenzy of fertility rites are not for Israel! All this is conditional on Israel's faithful obedience to God's commands.

Further curses
(28:15–68)
Disobedience will trigger distress, disease, disaster, drought, darkness, destruction and despair. Moses outlines the tragedy that awaits a faithless Israel:

> *In hunger and thirst, in nakedness and dire poverty, you will serve the enemies the Lord sends against you (28:48).*

Such curses were a standard feature of ancient treaties.

Israel renews the covenant

When God first made a covenant with Israel at Mount Sinai, it was broken immediately. Even as God was giving Moses the Ten Commandments, the Israelites were making and worshipping a golden calf-idol. Now the next generation is to renew its commitment to the living God.

'Carefully follow the terms of this covenant'
(29:1–29)
Moses calls the whole community together. He reminds them of the great things God has done for them. He has rescued, guided and protected them – and supplied all their needs for forty years. They have experienced God's power and discovered that his ways are true. The alternative is terrible. Disobedience provokes God's anger and brings destruction.

'The Lord is your life'
(30:1–20)
Moses knows that one day Israel will abandon God's way and be defeated and dispersed. But there is no place or situation from which God is unable to bring them back and restore them. Despair and desolation will be followed by delight. Now Moses delivers his final challenge – and gives the people full responsibility for their choice:

> *I call heaven and earth as witnesses against you that I have set before you life and death, blessings and curses. Now choose life, so that you and your children may live, and that you may love the Lord your God, listen to his voice, and hold fast to him (30:19–20).*

Farewell, Moses

Joshua to succeed Moses
(31:1–8)
Moses knows that he is about to die. He puts his affairs in order. He exhorts the Israelites to take possession of Canaan. He encourages Joshua to take on the leadership with the strength that God will give him.

The wonderful panorama of the Promised Land, looking west from Mount Nebo. It was here that Moses stood when God 'showed him the whole land'.

The reading of the law

(31:9–13)

Moses writes out a copy of the law and commits it to the care of the priests. It is to be kept beside the ark of the covenant. He knows in his heart that the agreement will soon be broken. Nevertheless, he commands that it be read every seven years, during the week when Israel gathers for the Feast of Tabernacles.

Scholars have discovered many ancient agreements – known as 'Suzerainty treaties' – which date from the Near East at this time. They list the terms and conditions, benefits and penalties which govern the relationships between masters and servants, lords and slaves. Such agreements were to be kept safely and read in public from time to time.

A song of judgment

(31:14 – 32:47)

Moses writes a song and recites it to the people so that they can learn it by heart. He begins with words of praise:

> *I will proclaim the name of the Lord.*
> *Oh, praise the greatness of our God!*
> *He is the Rock, his works are perfect,*
> *and all his ways are just.*
> *A faithful God who does no wrong,*
> *upright and just is he (32:3–4).*

The song goes on to describe Israel's behaviour in the most unflattering terms. They are 'a warped and crooked generation... a nation without sense' (32:5, 28). But God has chosen them, loved them, and treated them with both severity and compassion.

Moses knows that betrayals, disasters and difficulties lie ahead for his people. The song is a means of lodging God's truth in their hearts for generations to come.

God tells Moses that he is to die on Mount Nebo – a part of the Abarim Range in north-west Moab, overlooking Canaan. Moses is not to enter the Promised Land, because of what happened when he struck the rock at Meribah Kadesh. Moses and Aaron failed God that day, with their anger and lack of faith.

Moses blesses the tribes

(32:48 – 33:29)

Moses blesses each of the tribes in turn – as Jacob had done before his death. For each tribe, Moses has words of praise and encouragement. Some of his words to 'Jeshurun' (an old, poetic name for Israel) have provided comfort for every generation of believers:

> *The eternal God is your refuge,*
> *and underneath are the everlasting arms (33:27).*

The tribe of Simeon isn't mentioned. It may have become part of the tribe of Judah.

The death of Moses

(34:1–12)

Moses climbs Mount Nebo and surveys the Promised Land. His prayer to see it is granted. He can die content that his mission is accomplished.

Muslims identify Mount Nebo with Jebel Osha.

Moses dies at the age of 120. In Egypt, such an age would be attributed to a person of great distinction. In the Bible, his epitaph is even finer: 'Moses, whom the Lord knew face to face' (34:10).

Moses was the greatest leader Israel ever had. Despite his sense of inadequacy, he accepted God's call to confront Pharaoh and head up the exodus. In a quiet, self-effacing way, he discerned God's will and made it known to others. He encountered all kinds of difficulty and discouragement during the trek across the desert – but met every crisis with honest passion and unfailing prayer. His enduring achievement was that he received the revelation of God's law, and made every effort to record it, teach it and establish it for future generations.

JOSHUA

The book of Joshua tells how the Israelites capture the rest of the land of Canaan – the land God had promised to their ancestor Abraham.

Joshua succeeds Moses as the leader of Israel. Like Moses, he tells the people what God wants them to do. In the course of the military campaign, the Israelites discover that victory depends on obeying God. When they obey God, they are successful. When they try to fight in their own strength, they fail.

At the end of his life, Joshua commits himself and his family to obey God – and challenges all the tribes of Israel to do the same.

Outline

Israel prepares to invade Canaan (1:1 – 5:12)

The conquest of Canaan (5:13 – 13:7)

The land is divided (13:8 – 22:34)

Epilogue (23:1 – 24:33)

INTRODUCTION

Joshua is the sixth book of the Bible. It links the first five books ('the Pentateuch'), which narrate the beginning of the nation of Israel, with the later books, which tell of Israel's longing for a king.

The hero of the book is Joshua, whose name means 'The Lord Saves'! This is the same name as 'Jesus' in the New Testament. Joshua is a worthy successor to Moses, listening to God and leading the people in much the same way. He has a difficult task, because the land of Canaan cannot be conquered by military might. It can only be captured through a venture of faith. The disobedience of even a single person can lead to disaster for everyone. Above all, there is to be no compromise with the pagan nations who live in Canaan, or their gross fertility gods.

Who wrote Joshua – and when?

We aren't told who wrote this book, but parts of it are very personal to Joshua himself. The story of the conquest is told by someone who was clearly there to see it – and some of the people involved (such as Rahab) are still alive at the time of writing. The practice of making a pile of stones – to mark the crossing of the River Jordan, or the site of an important grave – is typical of this time in history. An important clue to the date is to be found in a reference to three Canaanite towns: Gaza, Gad and Ashdod. Their inhabitants are called Anakites. This could mean that the events described took place before 1200 BC, because after that time Philistines settled in these towns. Some scholars believe that the Philistines arrived some 200 years earlier.

Have historians found any signs of ancient battles? Those who have dug in the foundations of the old Canaanite cities have discovered that many of them were destroyed towards the end of the 13th century BC. In some places a thick layer of ash is a sign that the whole community was wiped out. This may have been the work

Canaanite bronze dagger (c. 15th century BC) found at Kadum, Samaria.

of the invading Israelites, or the debris of later battles. We must remember that the conquest of Canaan took a long time. Jerusalem isn't captured until the days of David, around 1000 BC.

The campaign to capture Canaan

Joshua begins his campaign in the south of Canaan by laying siege to Jericho, which lies in the Jordan Valley. Once Jericho is captured, he attacks Ai, which sits high in the hills about fifteen miles to the west of Jericho. The next obvious target would have been Gibeon, but the Gibeonites trick Israel into a peace treaty. This treaty commits Israel to fight for Gibeon against an alliance of five Amorite kings. Joshua surprises the Amorites by marching through the night to attack them – and God gives an extra-long day for their destruction. In the following months, Israel captures and destroys all the major cities in the southern part of Canaan.

In the north, the king of Hazor unites several Canaanite tribes to resist Israel's advance. But they are no match for Joshua, who destroys both them and their cities. (In fact, chapter 12 lists thirty-one defeated kings and their towns.) It is typical of the writer to note that all this is in accordance with God's plan. 'It was the Lord himself who hardened their hearts to wage war against Israel, so that he might destroy them totally, exterminating them without mercy, as the Lord had commanded Moses' (11:20). For us, such a view of God's will is very unsatisfactory. His people still have a long way to go before they discover the true balance of his justice and mercy.

As Joshua comes to the end of his active life, it is clear that there is still much land to be conquered. However, God instructs him to allocate a territory to each tribe, even if they do not yet possess the areas concerned. So Joshua divides the land, in faith that one day Israel's victory will be complete. In fact this won't happen until the heady days of David's reign. It will be David who finally captures Jerusalem, the last stronghold, from the Jebusites.

The importance of obedience

The secret of success is to love God totally. Such love will be shown by obeying his law. God urges Joshua to obey the law of Moses carefully – like a straight path, from which it is dangerous to stray. The law is to govern his speech, thought and behaviour. If Joshua obeys God's law, then he will be prosperous and successful.

Israel learns that disobedience to God results in failure when her troops are routed at Ai. One of the Israelites, Achan, has disobeyed God and deceived his fellow Israelites by keeping and hiding some of the plunder from the capture of Jericho. The result is an alarming defeat for Israel's army. In his farewell speech at the end of the book, Joshua calls on the people of Israel to make a clear choice for God. Some of them are still harbouring the old household gods from Mesopotamia and Egypt. Many are tempted by the fertility gods of the Amorites. 'But as for me and my household,' says Joshua, 'we will serve the Lord' (24:25).

Spiritual lessons

For Christians, the lessons of the book of Joshua are spiritual. Our Joshua (Jesus) has won a great victory over the powers of sin and death. Like the people of Israel, we must live in the light of this victory and allow God to establish his rule in every part of our lives.

DISCOVERING JOSHUA

Israel prepares to invade Canaan

The Lord commands Joshua to 'be strong'
(1:1–18)

God speaks to Joshua. He gives Joshua his own personal call to lead the people after Moses' death. The promise of the land has not died with Moses, nor has the principle of obedience. Joshua is to be strong, courageous – and devoted to God's law. And God makes him this solemn promise: 'As I was with Moses, so I will be with you; I will never leave you nor forsake you' (1:5).

Like Moses, Joshua has the faith to translate his conversation with God into commands to his officers. The people are to strike camp and prepare to cross the Jordan and enter their Promised Land.

Some of the tribes – the Reubenites, the Gadites and the half-tribe of Mannaseh – are allowed to settle their women, children and animals in the land that has already been won. However, their warriors are to continue in the army until the whole country is conquered. They are to lead the advance – perhaps because they will be the keenest to complete the task and return home. It is a sign of the unity and good discipline of the Israelites that they readily agree.

The spies stay with Rahab
(2:1–24)

Joshua sends two spies ahead to reconnoitre Jericho. Jericho is an oasis town, often called the 'city of palms', and has been the site of a settlement from the earliest times. Built on a mound, and defended by walls and towers, it bars Israel's way into the Promised Land. The capture of Jericho must be the first objective of Joshua's campaign.

Cleverly, the spies stay with a prostitute or innkeeper. Her name is Rahab. She hides them under the flax which she is drying on the flat roof of her house. She tells them she knows that the Lord, the God of Israel, has brought his people from Egypt and is now giving them this land. Rahab begs that she and her family may be spared. The spies agree, and Rahab helps them escape by a rope from her window, which is set in the city wall. They arrange that she will tie a scarlet cord in the window as a sign to the invading army.

When the spies return to Joshua, they are able to report that the walls of Jericho may be high, but the morale of its people is low.

Crossing the River Jordan
(3:1 – 4:18)

This is a holy war. Joshua tells the people that the ark of the covenant – the symbol of God's commitment to them – will lead the way. They are to consecrate themselves, devoting themselves completely to the task ahead. The priests carry the ark into the waters of the Jordan, and immediately the water ceases to flow from upstream.

The same God who brought his people through the Red Sea is now bringing the next generation through the Jordan – despite the fact that the river is normally swollen at this time of year by melted snow. We don't know how the waters were dammed – only that it took place some twenty miles upriver. At the exodus, the drying of the river bed was attributed to the blowing of a strong east wind. Whatever is happening at the Jordan, God is behind it. His timing is deliberate and precise.

The standing stones at Gilgal
(4:19–24)

God speaks to Joshua, and Joshua instructs the people. Joshua is being established as a leader in the style of Moses, a leader whose word proves to be true.

A representative from each tribe is chosen to bring a stone from the bed of the River Jordan. The stones are set up at Gilgal, as a sign to future generations of the miraculous crossing. This is a permanent tribute to the power of God and a reminder that all the tribes entered the land together.

Circumcision at Gilgal
(5:1–12)

The Israelites are now just sixteen miles from Jericho. The Amorite and Canaanite kings are terrified at their approach. This is the moment for the new generation of fighting men to be circumcised. In circumcision, the

The ark of the covenant being carried through the River Jordan; book illumination from Westphalia (c. AD 1360). The heap of twelve boulders represents the twelve tribes of Israel.

foreskin is cut right round in a circle and rolled back. This is a considerable act of faith and courage, as the Israelite soldiers will be unable to fight for several days.

Gilgal means 'circle' or 'rolling'. God says to Joshua that he is now rolling away the reproach of Egypt. The people are no longer being punished for their breach of the covenant at Sinai. They are back in relationship with God.

This is a new beginning. The families of Israel celebrate the Passover with unleavened bread and roasted grain – the produce of Canaan. The next morning, there is no manna on the ground outside the tents. The wilderness journey is over.

A 'holy war'?

The campaign to capture Canaan is sometimes described as a 'holy war'. The idea of a 'holy war' has been wrongly used to justify many acts of cruelty. It inspired the Crusaders who fought for possession of Jerusalem in the Middle Ages. It was a central theme in the American Civil War, when both sides claimed they were fighting God's cause. It was used by white South Africans to dispossess their black neighbours, and by extreme Zionists to expel Palestinians from modern Israel. This has been a terrible and shameful use of the Bible to justify human self-interest.

Jericho, the 'city of palms'. Jericho is one of the lowest places on the earth's surface, well below sea level.

The conquest of Canaan

The commander of the Lord's army
(5:13–15)

On the approach to Jericho, Joshua has a visible encounter with God. A man stands before him with a drawn sword and announces himself as 'commander of the army of the Lord'. Joshua bows before him. This is the Lord's battle, and Joshua submits to his supreme commander. The tiny nation of Israel will be joining far greater forces: the mighty powers of nature and the angelic hosts of heaven.

Stage one: the capture of Jericho and Ai
(6:1 – 8:35)

The campaign to capture Canaan will be in three stages. In the first phase, the Israelites will cut the land in half from east to west, capturing the strategic towns of Jericho and Ai (6:1 – 8:35). In the second phase, they

will defeat an alliance of Amorite kings in the south and take their cities (9:1 – 10:43). The third phase will see the capture of the northern part of the country, by defeating an alliance of pagan tribes under the leadership of the king of Hazor (11:1–23).

THE FALL OF JERICHO

The strategy for capturing Jericho is unique in the history of warfare (6:1–27). For once, God's will and Israel's obedience are in perfect harmony. God tells Joshua that the Israelites must march around the city, with the ark of the covenant leading the way and the priests blowing trumpets. This march is to take place each day for six days. On the seventh day, the Israelites are to march seven times round the city before giving a sustained blast on the trumpets and a loud shout. The city wall will collapse and the Israelites will be able to march straight in.

This 'perfect plan' is shaped on the number seven. There are to be seven priests with seven trumpets; the people are to march around Jericho on seven days – including seven times on the seventh. The trumpets which the priests blow are rams' horns. They are the same trumpets that are used to announce a Jubilee Year – the fiftieth year when debts are cancelled, slaves and prisoners are released, and all land is returned to its original family. The number fifty is significant because it marks the completion of seven lots of seven years.

Joshua and the Israelites fulfil God's instructions and the walls of Jericho collapse. Whether this happens because God intervenes with an earth tremor, we don't know. Historians investigating the site of Jericho have not found any particular signs of this great event – but then the destruction was complete. Jericho is not rebuilt until King Ahab restores it 500 years later. In that time, sun and wind may have erased much of the evidence.

Although the population of Jericho is destroyed, Rahab and her family are spared, as the spies had promised. The elderly Rahab is still living at the time this account is written. Is she the same Rahab who becomes an ancestor of David – and Jesus (Matthew 1:5)?

ACHAN'S SIN

Israel's next target is Ai. This is a town set in the hills about fifteen miles to the west of Jericho. While Jericho lies below sea level (the lowest town in the world), Ai is nearly 1,000 feet up. Joshua's spies report that the capture of Ai will be a fairly simple task. They won't require the whole army. It comes as a shock when the Israelite task force is unexpectedly defeated. Suddenly, Israel's confidence vanishes.

God reveals to Joshua that the defeat is because of sin. Someone has taken and hidden some of the plunder from Jericho. God's express command had been that Jericho's treasures were to be either devoted to the Lord

Does God want to massacre his enemies?

The conquest of Canaan is unique. It does not give permission for any person or race to commit mass murder or ethnic cleansing.

In Canaan there were certainly some dreadful pagan practices to be purged and diseases to be eradicated. And clearly the Israelites believed that God wanted them to exterminate their enemies. But this is not the whole truth.

We see in the Bible that a true picture of God only emerges gradually. At various stages, it was possible for people to be wrong about God – his nature, plan or way of doing things. In particular, the policy of wiping out entire nations in a violent bloodbath is very different from the approach we later see in Jesus.

How can we understand the killing fields of the days of Moses, Joshua, Samuel, Saul and David? Did God really command such bloodshed, or were even these great men affected by the times in which they lived? Did they slay their enemies believing it was God's will – or assume that God approved because he gave them victory?

One thing is certain. Our picture of God gets clearer as the Bible story unfolds. It becomes perfectly clear only when we see the life and example of Jesus. It isn't that God has changed, but our understanding of him has developed.

When Jesus is asked by James and John if they may destroy a Samaritan village, he rebukes them (Luke 9:54–55). God's way is not to destroy but to save; not to take life but to give it; not to wreak vengeance, but to forgive and make peace.

or destroyed. The fact that even one person has disobeyed has brought defeat on the whole nation.

The fault is traced to Achan (7:1–26). He has kept a beautiful robe and some silver and gold and buried them in the ground beneath his tent. This is such a serious breach of Israel's pure relationship with God that Achan and his family are stoned to death. The place of execution is called the Valley of Achor, which means 'trouble' or 'bitterness'.

There is a similar terrible episode in the early days of the church in Jerusalem, when a couple named Ananias and Sapphira are struck dead for deceiving the Apostles over money (Acts 5:1–11). These punishments seem out of all proportion to the crimes. We have to understand that both acts of disobedience are enough to pollute the purity of God's people at a time of great spiritual advance. The offenders must be cut out like a cancer, to prevent the disease of disobedience from spreading.

At the crossroads of the Promised Land of Canaan, between the peaks of Ebal and Gerizim, the Israelites renew their covenant with God.

THE DESTRUCTION OF AI

Joshua now uses his entire army to attack Ai (8:1–29). He sets up camp with 5,000 of his troops across the valley within sight of Ai, but conceals a further 30,000 in the hills. When the king of Ai confidently attacks the smaller force, the Israelites pretend to flee. The army from Ai gives chase, leaving the city defenceless. Joshua turns and signals his men in the hills to come down and destroy the place. This time God allows the Israelites to keep the livestock and plunder.

THE COVENANT IS RENEWED

At Mount Ebal, in the centre of Canaan, Joshua builds an altar. He summons the people to offer sacrifices to God and renew their covenant commitment to him (8:30–35). This great assembly probably takes place at Shechem, between the twin peaks of Gerizim and Ebal. Joshua makes replicas of the tablets of the law by coating large stones with plaster and writing on them the Ten Commandments.

Moses had given instructions for the renewal of the covenant (Deuteronomy 27–28). Half the tribes are to stand on the slopes of Mount Gerizim. These are the tribes descended from Jacob's wives Leah and Rachel. They are to recite the blessings which come from keeping faith with God. The rest of the people – the tribes descended from Jacob's slave girls – are to stand on the slopes of Mount Ebal. They are to pronounce the curses that will befall those who disobey God's commandments.

Stage two: the conquest of the south
(9:1 – 10:43)

A CUNNING PLAN

One of the tribes of Canaan, the Gibeonites, develop a plan to avoid being destroyed by Israel (9:1–27). They send a delegation to Joshua at Gilgal, dressed and equipped as though they have travelled a great distance. They explain that they have heard of Israel's victories and have come to make a treaty. Without consulting God, Joshua agrees terms of peace – only to discover that they are a neighbouring tribe! Finding himself bound by his own solemn word, Joshua strikes a compromise. He forces the Gibeonites to become woodcutters and water-carriers in the service of the altar and tabernacle.

We are told that Gibeon is an important city, larger than Ai, and that its men are good fighters. Historians have discovered a large well in the centre of Gibeon. It is 80 feet deep with access by a staircase. How appropriate that the Gibeonites are set to draw water!

THE SUN STANDS STILL

The king of Jerusalem calls on four other Amorite kings to join him in attacking Gibeon. The Gibeonites call for Joshua to rescue them. Joshua marches quickly through the night to take the enemy by surprise. As the Amorites flee, God bombards them with large hailstones, and makes the sun stand still until the victory is complete (10:1–15).

'O sun, stand still over Gibeon…' (10:12) is a quotation from the Book of Jashar – a collection of songs which is now lost to us but tells of the great deeds of Israel's early heroes. Joshua calls on God to hold the sun and moon in the sky, and so extend the daylight for the work of slaughter. Some people think it was the darkness of the hailstorm that merged day with night while the killing went on.

THE CONQUERED KINGS AND CITIES

Joshua assures Israel that God will always give such victories. Joshua now completes the conquest of the southern part of Canaan (10:16–43). He attacks each

Aerial view of Hazor, bastion of the north. The defeat and destruction of Hazor by Joshua was the key to victory in the northern campaign.

of the major cities except Jerusalem and destroys them, leaving no survivors. The writer is careful to record that 'all these kings and their lands Joshua conquered in one campaign, because the Lord, the God of Israel, fought for Israel' (10:42). When we consider that the Canaanites were strong and good fighters and that their cities were well fortified, we realize that Israel's success was a God-given miracle. Historians have confirmed that the cities of southern Canaan, Lachish, Eglon and Debir were completely destroyed at about this time.

Stage three: the conquest of the north
(11:1–23)

Now the northern kings unite to resist the Israelites. They are led by Jabin, king of Hazor. He masses a considerable force at the waters of Merom, about ten miles west of the Jordan, between two lakes. God tells Joshua not to fear the enemy's superior equipment of chariots and horses. The horses will be hamstrung and the chariots burned. The Israelites won't even need to salvage them, because the only resource they need is the presence of God.

A hot spring in the Negev. Caleb's daughter requested springs of water as a wedding gift from her father.

As in the southern campaign, Joshua uses speed of approach and surprise attack. He routs the northern army, pressing home his advantage until every enemy soldier is killed and all the chariots and horses destroyed.

Joshua consolidates the victory by capturing Hazor. This is a large city covering about 200 acres and with about 40,000 inhabitants. In recent years, excavation of Hazor shows that it was destroyed around the middle of the 13th century BC. In its ruins are the remains of Canaanite temples, with signs of the astrology and nature worship which were practised in them.

The power of the north is now broken and the land is at Joshua's mercy. He destroys Hazor and overruns the other centres of population. The writer emphasizes that the destruction is complete and that Joshua is carrying out the commands that God had given to Moses. The Canaanites are being destroyed because of their all-pervading paganism. The whole area is being purged of fertility cults and magic. Instead, it is to become God's land and the home of his people.

Last of all, the Anakites are destroyed. They were the race of giants which had so frightened the Israelites and sapped their morale just forty years earlier.

A catalogue of victory
(12:1–12)

The writer lists all the kings that Israel has defeated, including Og and Sihon who were defeated by Moses.

He describes the main features of the land west of the Jordan. By the 'hill country' he means the Judean highlands. The 'western foothills' lie between the central highlands and the coastal plain. The Arabah (whose name has a sense of 'burned up') is the dry rift valley which runs south of the Dead Sea to the Gulf of Aqabah. The 'mountain slopes' are probably those which border the Dead Sea. The Negev (which means 'the dry') is the semi-arid land which stretches off to the desert in the south. All this territory is divided between the tribes and given to them as a permanent inheritance.

The land still to be taken
(13:1–7)

The years have passed and Joshua is now an old man. Despite his successes, large areas of Canaan are still unconquered. We have the first mention of the Philistines – a seafaring people who have come from the Mediterranean island of Crete and occupied the coastal towns of Canaan. They will have a long-running enmity with Israel, but eventually give Canaan its most enduring name – 'Palestine'.

God promises to drive out the Sidonians. Their land is to be divided between the tribes of Israel and is allocated in faith that it will one day become theirs. The mention of the half-tribes of Manasseh goes back to the days of Joseph. Joseph had two sons – Ephraim and Manasseh, whose descendants are counted as half-tribes. They are the tribe of Joseph by another name (Genesis 48:11–20).

The land is divided

A summary of settlements

(13:8 – 19:51)

The land of Canaan is divided between the tribes of Israel. Their territories and towns are listed here with careful attention to detail. The whole land was not in fact conquered until the time of David, but it is here allocated in faith. The broad picture is that the tribes of Judah and Joseph are given most of the south of Canaan, with Benjamin between them. The tribe of Dan is given the coastal plain, which proves impossible to occupy because of the presence of the powerful Philistines. The remaining tribes are awarded land in the northern area of Canaan which is not yet completely conquered. It will be many years before they enter into all that has been promised.

In detail, the tribes of Reuben and Gad, and the half-tribe of Manasseh, settle in the area that was first conquered, to the east of the River Jordan. The land on the other side of the Jordan is divided between the tribes of Judah and Joseph. Judah is given the southern section – the territory won from the five kings. Caleb, still vigorous at eighty-five, begs for the privilege of driving the Anakites from the hill country and so winning Hebron for his inheritance. Joshua (like Caleb, one of the original spies) is pleased to grant his request. Joseph (the half-tribes of Ephraim and Manasseh) receives the fertile land at the heart of Canaan. North of this, the territory is still unconquered – and guarded by fortresses. Joshua urges the Israelites to clear the forests and press on to complete the conquest.

At the end of chapter 19 we learn that the task of dividing the land was undertaken by Eleazar the priest,

Caleb requested land in the hill country of Judah, promising to drive out the inhabitants. Joshua gave him the city of Hebron (above), which was also designated as a city of refuge.

Joshua and the heads of the tribal clans. They allocate it by casting lots – perhaps something like throwing dice – at the entrance to the tent of meeting. This is a way of letting God make the decisions. Although he is the leader, Joshua is under the authority of this group and given his share of the land last of all. He asks for the town of Timnath Serah in the hill country of Ephraim.

Cities of refuge

(20:1–9)

Certain cities are named 'cities of refuge'. They are to act as a sanctuary for anyone accused of murder. Such people are to be protected from anyone seeking revenge (usually the next of kin) until they can be given a fair trial.

Towns for the Levites

(21:1–45)

The tribe of Levi has no land of its own, as a sign that it belongs to the Lord. God himself is Levi's inheritance. Now the other tribes allocate some of their towns and pastures to the Levites to provide them with homes and a livelihood.

The eastern tribes go home

(22:1–34)

With the main task of conquest completed, Joshua allows the Reubenites, the Gadites and the half-tribe of Manasseh to go home. They immediately perplex the other tribes by building their own impressive altar on the east side of the Jordan! When challenged about this they explain that the altar is not for sacrifices; nor is it intended as a rival to the central altar of all Israel. They explain it as 'a witness' – a sign of continuing faith in

Tyre

Dan

Hazor

The Great Sea

*Sea of
Chinnereth*

Mount Carmel

▲ Mount Tabor

Megiddo

Jezreel

Mount Gilboa

Beth-shean

Ramoth-gilead

Jabesh-gilead

I   S   R   A   E   L

Samaria

Shechem

▲ Mount Gerizim

*HILL
COUNTRY OF
EPHRAIM*

Shiloh

River Jordan

G   I   L   E   A   D

A   M   M   O   N

Mizpah

Gilgal

Gibeon

Gezer

Michmash

Gibeah

Jericho

Heshbon

Jerusalem

▲ Mount Nebo

Ashdod

Ekron

Bethlehem

Timnah

WILDERNESS OF JUDAH

*Salt
Sea*

Ashkelon

J   U   D   A   H

M   O   A   B

Gath

Mamre

Gaza

Lachish

Hebron

En-gedi

Arad

Beersheba

T H E   N E G E V

P   H   I   L   I   S   T   I   A

Israel's God, and solidarity with the other tribes, even though the Jordan forms a boundary between them.

Epilogue

Joshua's farewell

(23:1–16)

Joshua bids farewell to the people. He urges them to continue to obey God's law and have nothing to do with the pagan peoples who are still living in the land. If the Israelites mix their worship with that of the Canaanites, or marry them, they will perish.

Joshua reviews Israel's history from the time of Abraham. God has given them, by his amazing power, victory over every enemy. Now, in his goodness, he is giving them a land of beauty and plenty, ready cultivated to provide their needs.

Back to basics

(24:1–27)

Joshua calls the tribes of Israel to Shechem – the place of decision at the crossroads of Canaan. Here he challenges them to commit themselves afresh to the Lord. He challenges them to renew the covenant that was first made with God and Moses at Mount Sinai. If they decline to do this, they must decide whom they *will* serve – the pagan gods of Egypt, Canaan or Mesopotamia.

Joshua leaves the people in no doubt about his own decision. He boldly declares that he and his family will serve the Lord. The people protest that they will do the same; but Joshua warns them not to take the decision lightly. If they choose the Lord, they must get rid of their idols. If they fail to do so, the consequences will be terrible.

The book of Joshua may have been written at a time when the law of Moses was being rejected and the Israelites were intermarrying with pagans. Some families or clans may have reverted to ancient household gods and superstitions – or taken up with new ones. Joshua's speech is a ringing call to repent and commit themselves to the Lord, the only true God of Israel.

Home at last

(24:28–33)

The book of Joshua closes with the burials of three great leaders. Joshua dies and is buried at Timnath Serah – the place he chose for his inheritance. Joseph's coffin, brought all the way from Egypt (Genesis 50:26), is committed to a family grave at Shechem in the heart of the Promised Land. And Eleazar, Israel's second high priest, is laid to rest on his family's land in the hills of Ephraim. All God's promises have been fulfilled. They are home at last.

JUDGES

The book of Judges tells the story of Israel after the tribes have settled in the land of Canaan. During this time they are guided by 'judges', who lead them in battle against their enemies.

In Hebrew, 'to judge' means 'to put things right'. The judges are the community leaders who get things done.

The judges don't only give legal rulings, but take whatever action is necessary, including going to war. They 'judge' Israel's enemies by overpowering them in the name of God.

This is a dangerous, lawless time, with Israelite society fragmented, her enemies aggressive and her morals in decline. At the beginning of the period there is no clear leader to follow Joshua, and by the end there is no leader at all. The book closes with the grim words: 'In those days there was no king in Israel; all the people did what was right in their own eyes' (21:25). But this is also a book about God's readiness to save his people and to forgive them when they repent and turn to him.

Outline

The partial conquest of Canaan and the death of Joshua (1:1 – 3:6)
The great deeds of the judges (3:7 – 16:31)
Israel in decline (17:1 – 21:25)

INTRODUCTION

When Joshua dies, there is no clear leader for the people of Israel. The land of Canaan is not completely conquered, so several of the tribes find themselves living among pagan neighbours. After Joshua's death, the people begin to stray from their commitment to the God who brought them out of Egypt. They worship the Baals and the Ashtoreths, the fertility gods of the neighbouring tribes. Because of this disobedience, God stops protecting his people and they suffer defeat and oppression.

However, there are some fine acts of faith and heroism. Gideon wins great victories with God's help. Samson, too, although he is a weak character, is given superhuman strength to overcome the Philistines.

The book of Judges shows us that human beings are hopeless without God. The people of Israel are in great danger of collapsing as a nation and culture because of their idolatry. We see how leadership plays an important part in the life of any people, and that Israel needs a strong and godly leader.

At the end of the book, Israel is sinking by spiritual decline into moral chaos. Defenceless people are hurt or killed, and civil war threatens an end to the tribe of Benjamin. Here is a depressing record of human depravity, as well as the wonderful reality of God's grace.

Who wrote Judges?

We don't know who wrote the book of Judges. If an editor compiled these stories, then perhaps we hear him speaking in these words:

> Then the Lord raised up judges, who delivered them [the Israelites] out of the power of those who plundered them. Yet they did not listen even to their judges; for they lusted after other gods and bowed down to them. They soon turned aside from the way in which their ancestors had walked, who had obeyed the commandments of the Lord; they did not follow their example (2:16–17).

The writer explains that God is angry with the tribes of Israel because they have not pressed on to defeat their enemies and occupy the whole land. In the end God allows the pagan peoples to remain, to be 'thorns in Israel's side' – to test whether the Israelites will be faithful to their God.

We begin to notice a pattern in Israel's behaviour. The people disobey God and fall into the hands of their enemies. They cry out to the Lord for help and he rescues them. Then there are some years of peace before they fall into sin again. In all this, God uses a number of imperfect leaders to rescue his people at times of crisis.

Where does Judges come in the Bible?

In the Bible, the book of Judges is included among the history books. The Hebrew Bible calls these books 'the Former Prophets'. Bible history is about what God is doing in the lives of his people. Judges may be part of a 'deuteronomic history' which includes the books of Deuteronomy, Joshua, Judges, Samuel and Kings. The writers or editors of these books judge everything by the principle set out in the book of Deuteronomy: that God honours those who honour him.

A particular sentence keeps cropping up: 'In those days there was no king in Israel; all the people did what was right in their own eyes.' This is a clue that the writer is looking back from a time when the people of Israel finally have a king, and can see the disasters that befell them when there was no clear leader.

DISCOVERING JUDGES

The partial conquest of Canaan and the death of Joshua

'Their gods will be a snare to you' (2:3). God warns the Israelites that the Canaanite gods will tempt and trap them. They will be attracted to the bloody, violent and sexually permissive practices of their pagan neighbours. Like birds winging their way into a trap, they will be captured, hurt and killed.

When Joshua dies, at the age of 110, he is described as 'the servant of the Lord' (2:8). He is buried some ten miles north-west of Bethel, in the land he has won from the Canaanites. He was born into slavery in Egypt, shared in the exodus as a young man, and was one of the brave spies who went ahead into the Promised Land. After the death of Moses, Joshua led the military campaigns which captured much of Canaan. When the push for victory faltered and the people were tempted by paganism, Joshua continued to stand by his faith in the living God.

A Canaanite stone altar at Megiddo (c. 2200 BC).
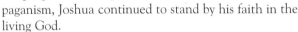

The unfinished conquest of Canaan
(1:1 – 2:5)

The tribes of Israel have each been allotted an area of Canaan, their Promised Land. Now they must go in and conquer their territories.

THE SUCCESSES OF JUDAH IN THE SOUTH

The tribes of Judah and Simeon fight together, as their ancestors were brothers. Judah is successful in defeating the Canaanites, together with another local people, the Perizzites (1:2–21). They capture and mutilate a local king, Adoni-Bezek. They also burn the ancient city of Jerusalem, but a later note (1:21) has the Benjaminites living there alongside the Jebusites, who are the original inhabitants. Jerusalem lies between the territories of Judah and Benjamin and will become King David's capital for the united tribes.

Judah's forces advance south and west of Jerusalem. To the south is the hill country around Hebron and, beyond, the dry wastes of the Negev. To the west lie the foothills which run between the central mountain range of Canaan and the coastal plain.

Particular stories are recorded of how people receive their share of the land. Caleb gives his daughter in marriage to Othniel; and she asks her father for a water supply in the desert. Caleb himself is given the city of Hebron (which means 'alliance'), which will become Judah's centre and David's first capital. Judah's army also tackles the cities of the coastal plain (Gaza, Ashkelon and Ekron), but is unable to hold them against the iron chariots of their enemies. Israel's weaponry is still in the Bronze Age.

THE CAPTURE OF BETHEL

The Joseph tribes (the half-tribes of Ephraim and Manasseh) are successful in taking Bethel (1:22–26). This is where Jacob had his famous dream (Genesis 28:19), and where there will be an important shrine for the northern kingdom in years to come. 'Beth-el' means 'house of God'.

AN UNFINISHED TASK

Despite Judah's successes, there are many failures to note as well (1:27–36). Some tribes are unable to expel the Canaanites and have to live alongside them. This will be a constant tension and source of corruption, as the Israelites feel the attractions of moral compromise, intermarriage and idolatry. It is King Ahab's marriage to Jezebel, a princess from Phoenicia, which plunges Israel into Baal-worship in the time of the prophet Elijah.

CONFRONTATION AT BOKIM

God confronts his people. They are failing to keep their part of the covenant bargain (2:1–5).

God has been faithful to them in rescuing them from Egypt. He has brought them to the land of Canaan. But Israel should be destroying the pagan religions of the Canaanites, not settling down to live with them. Now the Canaanite idols will be an ongoing problem – like painful thorns and a deadly trap.

When the people hear God's verdict, they weep. The place is called Bokim, which means 'weepers'.

The death of Joshua

(2:6–9)

When Joshua dies, at the age of 110, he is described as 'the servant of the Lord' (2:8). He is buried some ten miles north-west of Bethel, in the land he has won from the Canaanites.

Joshua's life has spanned the history of the exodus, the wilderness wanderings and the conquest of Canaan. He was born into slavery in Egypt, took part in the exodus as a young man and was one of the brave spies who went ahead into the Promised Land. After the death of Moses, Joshua led the military campaigns which captured the heart of Canaan. When the push for complete occupation faltered and the people began to compromise with paganism, Joshua continued to stand by his faith in the living God.

The reason for judges

(2:10 – 3:6)

After the death of Joshua, Israel's faith and unity breaks down. The tribes merge with their Canaanite neighbours and accept the local forms of Baal-worship. They no longer live by faith in God, and suffer defeat at the hands of their enemies.

God does not abandon his people, but gives them 'judges' – leaders who are gifted with faith, strength and wisdom. These judges rescue the Israelites from a series

Ehud, the left-handed 'judge' assassinates the Moabite king, Eglon. Illuminated manuscript from Westphalia (c. AD 1350).

of desperate situations, so that they continue to experience God's power to save them. However, they repeatedly lapse back into their old ways. Once a crisis is passed, they forget God again. They return to the attractions of paganism until another defeat brings them to their senses. This pattern is repeated throughout the era of the judges.

The great deeds of the judges

The book of Judges has stories of twelve of Israel's judges or rescuers. The main attention is given to Deborah and her general Barak, Gideon, Jephthah and Samson. Their stories are full of energy and interest. A minor judge, Ehud, is left-handed – a gift which he uses to assassinate an enemy king (3:21).

Each of the judges is associated with a particular enemy. Ehud fights for Israel against the Moabites. Deborah and Barak fight the Canaanites. Gideon delivers Israel from the Midianites. Jephthah rescues Israel from the oppression of Ammon. Samson is the Israelites' champion against the Philistines.

Othniel

(3:7–11)

For the first time (but not the last) we read the author's refrain: 'The Israelites did evil in the eyes of the Lord' (3:7).

God is angry and jealous (perfectly angry and perfectly jealous) because his people are serving the pagan Baals and Asherahs. These are the male and female fertility gods, through which the Canaanites try to control the natural world of seasons, weather and crops. They are human idols which have no reality or power in themselves, but the people who believe in them are in bondage to superstition and fear. The stories of these gods are full of violence, cruelty and lust – which are re-enacted by their worshippers in real life.

Asherah, in Canaanite mythology, is the goddess wife of the chief god El. When there are several Asherahs (or Asherim), they are the female gods of the Baals.

Because of their idolatry, Israel's God allows his people to be defeated and oppressed by Cushan-Rishathaim. Cushan is the king of Aram, in north-west Mesopotamia. His added title, 'Rishathaim', means 'doubly wicked'.

After eight years of misery, the Israelites plead with God to rescue them. He empowers Othniel to be their champion. Othniel is a nephew of Caleb, who was the colleague of Joshua in the days of the invasion of Canaan. God's Spirit gives Othniel the inspiration, courage and strength he needs to become a successful military leader (or 'judge') and defeat Cushan.

Ehud
(3:12–30)

Again the Israelites commit themselves to idol-worship, and God allows them to be defeated. This time their oppressor is Eglon, king of Moab. Moab is to the south of Canaan and east of the Dead Sea. Eglon joins forces with the neighbouring tribes of Ammon and Amalek to attack Israel and capture the city of palms (the ruined site of Jericho).

After eighteen years of oppression, the Israelites cry to God for help. This time God gives them Ehud, who is remarkable in that he is left-handed. He uses his left hand to assassinate Eglon, king of Moab, by thrusting a double-edged sword into him. Ehud hid the sword by strapping it to his thigh when he went to pay tribute to the enemy king.

Shamgar
(3:31)

After Ehud, another judge delivers Israel. He is Shamgar, who defeats 600 Philistines by striking them down with an ox-goad (3:31). An ox-goad is sharp, metal-tipped like a spear and up to ten feet long! It seems to be a makeshift instrument at a time when weapons are

The Jezreel Plain viewed from Mount Tabor. Here Barak's army routed the Canaanite army of Sisera.

banned. Samson makes similar use of a donkey's jawbone (15:16).

Deborah and Barak
(4:1 – 5:31)

After the time of Ehud, the Israelites again commit evil. Now God allows Jabin, king of Canaan, to make them his subjects. Jabin's army commander is Sisera, who has a force of 900 iron chariots at his disposal.

After twenty years of oppression, the Israelites cry out to God for help. Their leader ('judge') at this time is Deborah, whose name means 'Bee'. She sends for Barak ('Lightning') and outlines a plan to defeat Sisera by luring his chariots into the River Kishon. The Kishon is a wadi which is flooded by torrential rain at a certain time of year. Barak is reluctant to attempt this battle unless Deborah goes with him. She agrees, but predicts that the fame of slaying Sisera will go to a woman.

Sisera's chariots get bogged down in the Kishon and are overwhelmed by Barak's forces, just as Deborah has planned. Sisera flees on foot, and takes refuge in the tent of a woman called Jael. He assumes she will protect him, but in fact she kills him by driving a tent peg through his temple while he is asleep. This great victory,

with its grisly detail, is celebrated in the vivid and rhythmic 'Song of Deborah' (5:1–31). The song is very old and was probably written soon after the great deeds it records.

Gideon

(6:1 – 8:35)

The Israelites have been driven out of their settlements by Midianite raiders. Their animals have been killed and their crops trampled.

Gideon is secretly threshing wheat in an underground cellar when an angel visits him. Gideon finds himself

commissioned to be Israel's deliverer – although he explains that he is a very junior member of a very weak clan. Even his tribe, Manasseh, is only a half-tribe!

But in God's sight Gideon is a mighty warrior. In a night raid the reluctant hero pulls down his father's Baal altar and cuts down an Asherah pole – a pagan fertility symbol. In their place he builds an altar to the God of Israel and (using the Asherah pole for firewood) sacrifices a bullock.

Gideon is now to fight the Midianites. He makes doubly sure that this is what God wants by seeking guidance in an unusual way. He asks God for a sign that dew will settle on a fleece overnight, but the surrounding ground will remain dry. Just to make sure, the following night he asks for the opposite to happen.

Then God tests Gideon. He tells him to reduce his fighting force from 32,000 to 300, by sending home those who are afraid and by ruling out those who kneel down to drink. The few who stay on their feet and lap the water are worth all the rest – because they are always ready for battle and on guard against surprise attack.

One night, Gideon spies on the enemy camp. He finds that God is undermining the Midianite morale by sending them dreams of defeat. Encouraged, Gideon splits his force into three groups and gives each man a trumpet – and a flaming torch in an earthenware jar.

The head of a camel bedecked with tassels. Such ornaments were seized as trophies of war.

The Midianites and Amalekites were a formidable fighting force, 'their camels, countless as the sand on the seashore' (7:12).

Who are the Baals?

The Baals are an extensive family of Canaanite gods. They are nature idols, worshipped to bring rain and fertility for crops, cattle and humans.

The leading figure is Baal the son of El, the god of storm and rain. His name can also mean 'husband' or 'Lord' – which makes him sound similar to Israel's God. We can understand Israel's confusion – and the temptation to experiment with paganism.

Baal's wife or partner is Ashtoreth, the goddess of war and fertility. Together, they are a terrifying partnership. The attempts of their worshippers to please them may range from acts of gross indecency to child sacrifice. The degradation and cruelty of Canaanite religion is a major reason for the judgment of God in the conquest by Israel.

Normally only an officer would carry a torch – so the Midianites are going to think themselves surrounded by thousands of men.

With the blowing of trumpets, smashing of jars and brandishing of torches, Gideon and his mini-army rout their terrified and demoralized enemy.

Abimelech
(9:1–56)

Abimelech is not a judge. He is one of the sons of Gideon ('Jerub-Baal'), whose mother is a Canaanite from Shechem. His story is included as a brief, violent and unsuccessful attempt at kingship.

Shechem is a city at the centre of Palestine. 'Shechem' means 'shoulder', because the town lies on the shoulder of land between two mountains, Ebal and Gerizim. This is where Joshua had called the Israelites to renew their covenant with God (Joshua 8:30–35). It is also the burial place of Joseph, whose coffin was brought from Egypt (Joshua 24:32).

Abimelech is ambitious to rule. He persuades his Canaanite relatives in Shechem to help him murder his seventy brothers who are the other sons of Gideon. Only Jotham, the youngest, escapes the public execution, which is carried out on a particular stone. Abimelech is then crowned king beside the great tree at the sacred pillar in Shechem.

The survivor of the massacre, Jotham, climbs to the top of Gerizim. There he makes an impassioned speech to the people of Shechem, telling them they have made a worthless choice. Abimelech is like a thornbush – useless, treacherous and inflammable.

Abimelech's kingdom is small (about four towns) and his reign short (just three years). In suppressing a rebellion at Shechem he destroys the city and burns down its tower. When he besieges the tower at Thebez, his skull is cracked by an upper millstone dropped on him by a woman, and he dies.

Tola and Jair
(10:1–5)

Tola and Jair are both judges who lead Israel for a number of years. Like Shamgar before them (and Ibzan, Elon and Abdon afterwards), we know very little of their lives and achievements. But Jair was clearly prominent and prosperous in his day – with his thirty sons riding thirty donkeys!

Jephthah
(10:6 – 12:7)

The Israelites continue to indulge in Baal-worship, and God punishes them through crushing defeats at the hands of the Philistines and Ammonites. The Ammonites not only dominate the Israelite settlements to the east of the River Jordan, but also cross over to oppress the great tribes to the west.

In this grim situation, Jephthah emerges to lead the fight against the Ammonites. He has been rejected by his family because of his illegitimate birth, but has become the head of a band of dissidents. Now his clan turns to him for help.

Jephthah argues with the Ammonites that the disputed land belongs to Israel. It was given them by God, who helped them drive out the Amorites. However, the matter comes to war.

Jephthah is filled with God's Spirit for the task of leading the military campaign. Rashly and unnecessarily, he vows to sacrifice the first person who greets him on his successful return home. It is strange that Jephthah is both filled with the Spirit of the Lord and yet misguided about the Lord's demands. God is adamantly opposed to human sacrifice.

Tragically, the person who meets Jephthah on his return home is his only daughter. She insists that he fulfil his vow, asking only a delay of two months so that she can spend time in the hills and with her friends. Jephthah's action means that he kills off his own family line.

Men from the tribe of Ephraim ask why Jephthah didn't summon them to the fight against the Ammonites. Jephthah replies that he did, but they didn't respond. An exchange of insults leads to civil war between Gilead and Ephraim. The Ephraimites are defeated and flee for home, but the Gileadites seize them as they try to ford the Jordan. They identify the Ephraimites by their accents, because they can't pronounce the word 'shibboleth', which means 'ear of corn'.

The tribe of Ephraim is permanently weakened by the massacre at the hands of Gilead. Until now they have been the leading group in central and northern Israel. When the tribes of Israel finally choose a king, he will be Saul, from the weak tribe of Benjamin.

Samson

(13:1 – 16:31)

Now the Israelites fall under the power of the Philistines. They are a warlike, seagoing people who have arrived from Crete and settled along the coastal strip of Canaan. They are pressing inland to give trouble to the Israelites. God raises up a champion for Israel in Samson.

Samson is the only son of an elderly, hitherto childless couple. His birth is a miracle. He is brought up as a Nazirite, dedicated to God. He doesn't eat meat or drink wine. He lets his hair grow long. He abstains from sex and avoids touching dead bodies. In other words, Samson is as pure and holy as possible. In addition, he is given a special gift of superhuman strength.

But, for all his physical prowess, Samson is a weak character. He wilfully chooses a Philistine woman for his wife. He flaunts his great strength to tease, taunt and hurt his enemies. He always sails close to danger.

One by one, Samson breaks all his Nazirite vows. On one occasion, he kills a lion with his bare hands – but keeps it a secret. Sometime later he finds that bees have nested in the lion's carcass, so he scoops out and eats the honey. At his wedding feast he turns the episode into a riddle:

***Samson Defeats the Lion**; altar decoration (AD 1151) by Nicholas of Verdun. Champlevé enamel on gilded copper.*

Out of the eater, something to eat,
Out of the strong, something sweet (14:14).

The Philistines ask Samson's wife to find out the secret of his great strength. When he realizes that they are trying to trick him, he kills dozens of Philistines and destroys their crops. In the end the Philistines use another woman, Delilah, to coax the truth out of him. He gets closer and closer to telling his secret.

Eventually Delilah wears Samson down with her begging, and he tells her his secret. His strength is in the Lord, and his commitment to the Lord is expressed in his long hair. As soon as she can, Delilah betrays Samson to his enemies and has his hair cut while he sleeps.

Deprived of his strength, Samson is captured, blinded and sentenced to hard labour by the Philistines. But his hair grows – and his relationship with God is restored. One day, when the Philistines make sport of him in their pagan temple, he prays for his strength to return. Hauling at the pillars which support the temple roof, Samson collapses the building, killing thousands of his enemies.

Samson is a mighty, tragic figure. He has abandoned his calling, broken all his vows, made a fool of himself with women and misused his spiritual gift. He reminds us of Esau, who treated holy things lightly because he was so confident of his prowess and privileges (Genesis 25:29–34). Samson's life is a warning against taking God for granted. A holy calling must be matched by a holy life.

Israel in decline

The writer shows us Israel in a state of anarchy. Here is religion corroded by superstition and society corrupted by cruelty. Might is right and the weakest go to the wall. The great sense of Israel being a nation under God has broken down.

Micah's idols

(17:1–13)

Micah has stolen some silver from his mother. Not realizing that her son has done this, she utters curses on the thief. When he returns the silver to her, she tries to cancel the curse by offering part of it to God.

Micah has the silver made into an idol. This is a curious mixture of true and false religion – offering something precious to God (which is encouraged) and making an idol (which is forbidden).

Micah enjoys being religious. He sets up his own shrine, with an ephod and idols. An ephod was, in Aaron's time, an ornate garment covering the chest and stomach. It may have had a pouch containing the Urim and Thummim which were used to discover God's will. By now the ephod may have become something that could be carried – but still associated with seeking God's guidance and blessing.

Micah appoints one of his sons as the priest. This is the kind of 'do-it-yourself' religion which will be banned in Israel in the future. The worship of God is not to be reduced to an exclusive, private, local action. There is only one God, and he is to be worshipped by everyone in one place – the temple in Jerusalem. When Micah takes on another priest, who is actually from the priestly tribe of Levi, he feels God will show him special favour. This is also a sign of his superstition.

The Danite migration

(18:1–31)

One of the tribes, the descendants of Dan, are still looking for a place to settle. In their search, some of them arrive at the house of Micah and recognize the young Levite who is the priest there. He directs them to Laish, which is a beautiful stretch of country occupied by peaceful and unsuspecting people.

The advance guard returns with the full force of Danites. They take the contents of Micah's shrine, the ephod, the idols and the young Levite, to give them good luck in conquering Laish. Although Micah protests and makes as if to fight, there is nothing he can do. The people of Laish are equally defenceless in the face of the Danite onslaught. So Dan wins some territory in the northernmost part of the land of Canaan, and keeps Micah's idols in the shrine at Shiloh. The young priest is named as Jonathan, a descendant of Moses. But all has been done by deceit, superstition and brute force. No one has tried to discover and do God's will.

A Levite and his concubine

(19:1–30)

A Levite (a member of the priestly tribe) is living with his concubine or slave girl. On their way from Bethlehem to Ephraim, they take special care to stay with fellow Israelites – at the town of Gibeah which belongs to the tribe of Benjamin. They expect shelter and hospitality, but receive none.

Eventually an old man takes them into his home. During the evening some local men come pounding on the door, demanding sex with the Levite. The Levite saves himself by sending out his girl to them. They gang-rape her all night, and in the morning she lies dead on the threshold of the house.

The Levite is appalled at what has happened. The security and respect which the tribes of Israel owe each other has been breached. An innocent woman has been unspeakably abused and done to death. To convey the brutality and shame to all Israel, he cuts his slave girl's body into twelve pieces and sends a grisly and stinking segment to every tribe – including Benjamin, which has been responsible for the deed.

This is a sign of the times! This is what Israel has come to! Without God's law, there are no healthy relationships, no safe communities and there is no hope of justice.

The Israelites fight the Benjaminites

(20:1–48)

When the tribes of Israel receive the dreadful evidence of the woman's severed corpse, they gather together at Mizpah. 'Mizpah' means 'watchtower', and the place is not far from Jerusalem. The eleven tribes of Israel resolve to raise a united army to discipline the offending tribe of Benjamin.

At first the Israelites demand that the Benjaminites hand over the men who committed the rape and murder, but this request is refused. Instead, the Benjaminites gather an army, which includes 700 formidable slingsmen. A sling is a fearsome weapon, jettisoning a stone of up to a pound in weight at very high speed and with enormous accuracy – as Goliath will find out to his cost when he is confronted by the shepherd-boy David.

The numbers of men gathering for battle are extremely large, and it is uncertain how to translate or interpret this information. Sometimes a number can refer to a clan or family, or to a contingent under the command of an officer.

The Benjaminites are hopelessly outnumbered, but they are great fighters. This is the tribe that produced Ehud – and will produce Saul. For two days they defend Gibeah and inflict death and destruction on the Israelites with their slings. The Israelites seek God's guidance with increasing earnestness – tears of penitence, fasting for grief and sacrifices for forgiveness and peace. They worship God at Bethel, where Phineas is the priest guarding the ark of the covenant. Phineas has been a great man of action himself in the past.

On the third day of the battle, the Israelites adopt a different strategy. They retreat from Gibeah in two directions, drawing out and splitting up the Benjaminites who pursue them. But an extra force of Israelites then emerges from hiding to capture Gibeah and set fire to it. The Benjaminites turn to see their city going up in flames, and are routed. Some escape to the rock of Rimmon, a few miles from Bethel, where they manage to survive, but the rest of the Benjaminite men and their cities are destroyed.

The tribe of Benjamin is spared
(21:1–25)

Once the battle is over, the full horror of the situation sinks in. The tribes of Israel have been torn apart by civil war, and one of them, Benjamin, has been brought to the brink of extinction. The Benjaminites will die out because the other tribes have vowed never to let their daughters marry them.

As they weep and worship, the Israelites realize that the men of Jabesh Gilead have failed to help in the crisis. The people of Jabesh Gilead are descended from Joseph, and so have a close relationship with the Benjaminites, who are descended from Joseph's much-loved brother. Nevertheless, they have withheld their support from the common cause of Israel and must be punished.

A force is sent to destroy Jabesh Gilead and to seize its young women to be wives for the surviving Benjaminites. When there is still a shortage of females, the Benjaminites are encouraged to kidnap the girls they need from a festival at Shiloh. This outrage is agreed by all the tribes and any protest will fall on deaf ears. The important thing is that the tribe of Benjamin will continue to exist.

So God's holy people lurch from moral disaster to impetuous bloodshed and high-handed injustice. There is no wisdom, sanity or restraint. The writer explains that the Israelites lack a king – by which he means a powerful and godly leader such as David or Solomon. But the first sign of hope in this desperate and divided situation will be Samuel, the last and greatest of the judges.

RUTH

The little book of Ruth is a love story. Ruth is a foreigner to Israel. She comes from Moab. Ruth and her sister were both married to Israelite men, but they are widowed. Ruth shows great love and loyalty to her mother-in-law, Naomi, who is also a widow. Together they travel from Moab to Naomi's home in Bethlehem. There Ruth meets Boaz, her husband's next of kin. Boaz is a good man who deals kindly with them. In due course, Boaz marries Ruth. Their great-grandson will be King David.

Outline

Naomi and Ruth travel to Bethlehem (1:1–22)

Ruth meets Boaz, a local farmer (2:1 – 3:18)

Boaz and Ruth are married (4:1–22)

INTRODUCTION

This gentle story comes from the days of the judges and is a contrast to their bloodthirsty adventures. We see that God cares for strangers and widows – and weaves even our tragedies into his perfect plan.

Throughout the story, Boaz stands out as a man of truth and generosity. He lives out the laws of Moses in their true spirit – which is to show the character of God.

Boaz is kind to a stranger. He has compassion on two widows. He allows his crops to be gleaned by the needy. He respects and protects Ruth when others might abuse her. He makes a wise decision, acts on it promptly and deals openly and fairly with all concerned.

Although Boaz is the saviour who brings about a happy ending, it is Naomi who is the hero and driving force of the story. It is she who has faith, and takes the initiative, to return to Bethlehem – and steer Ruth in Boaz's direction! And when baby Obed is born, he is (as everyone says) really a son for her.

Who wrote the story of Ruth?

We do not know who wrote this story. It is set in the days when the judges were leading Israel, but has a much more peaceful atmosphere than the tales of their exploits. It tells how God can guide and bless people even in the midst of personal tragedy. It shows how a righteous man, Boaz, protects and provides for two widows. It also has a special interest as background to the story of David. It seems to be told as a true story and is therefore one of the Bible's history books.

DISCOVERING RUTH

Naomi and Ruth travel to Bethlehem
(1:1–22)

There is a famine in Israel. A man called Elimelech takes his wife, Naomi, and their two sons to find food in Moab.

In the old days, the people of Moab had been hostile to the Israelites on their journey to Canaan. Their women were also blamed for seducing Israelite men and persuading them to worship the Baal-gods (Numbers 25:1–3). As a result, Moabites were banned from marrying Israelites for ten generations (Deuteronomy 23:3)!

After the family have lived in Moab for ten years, Elimelech and his sons die. Naomi and her daughters-in-law, Orpah and Ruth, are left as widows. Naomi feels abandoned by God – without protection or livelihood in a foreign land. Hearing that the famine has ended, she decides to return to her people in Bethlehem.

Naomi realizes that her daughters-in-law will be foreigners in Bethlehem. She tries to persuade them to go back to their own family homes and find husbands there. Orpah agrees, but Ruth insists on staying with Naomi. With moving words she commits herself to her mother-in-law and to Israel's God:

Where you go, I will go…
your people shall be my people,
*   and your God my God.*
Where you die, I will die –
*   there will I be buried (1:16–17).*

Ruth's choice is remarkable, because all she has known is tragedy and loss. Yet she, a foreigner to Israel, still puts her trust in the Lord.

When Naomi arrives in Bethlehem, she tells everyone of her loss. When she left she had a family, but now she is alone. Her name means 'Pleasant', but her life has turned bitter. Then a ray of hope breaks into the story. The barley harvest is beginning.

Ruth meets Boaz, a local farmer
(2:1 – 3:18)

Naomi has a relative named Boaz. He is a leading member of the Bethlehem community. When Ruth goes to glean – gathering grain the harvesters have left – she finds herself in one of Boaz's fields. When Boaz comes to visit his workers, he notices Ruth and makes her welcome.

Boaz is a godly man. He shows God's love in his kindness to her, although she is a foreigner. He prays that God will reward her for her loyalty to Naomi. At the meal he shares his food with Ruth – and afterwards he tells his men to leave plenty of stalks in the field for Ruth to glean. She collects and threshes an ephah of barley – about four gallons.

When Ruth arrives home to tell Naomi of her successful day, her mother-in-law explains that Boaz is one of their kinsman-redeemers. In other words, he is a close relative on whom they can rely for help.

One night Naomi sends Ruth to the threshing-floor, where the harvesters are sleeping. She lies at Boaz's feet and wakes him. They talk about her situation and he promises to help. He treats her with the utmost respect – moved that she has come to him and not gone after one of the younger men. But there is a kinsman-redeemer who is a closer relative than Boaz, and he must have first opportunity to look after Naomi and Ruth.

Boaz and Ruth are married
(4:1–22)

The following morning, at the town gate, Boaz meets with the other kinsman-redeemer. He invites him to buy Elimelech's land and marry Ruth. There is a law that a man should marry his brother's widow and enable her to have a son to continue the family line (Deuteronomy 25:5–6).

The closer relative declines the offer. Either he doesn't want to marry a foreigner, or he can't afford to buy a field just to leave it to someone else. The way is open for Boaz to purchase the field and marry Ruth.

Boaz marries Ruth and they have a son, Obed. His name means 'Servant'. Proudly Naomi takes her grandson and nurses him. Now *she* has a kinsman! Obed will be the father of Jesse; and he in turn will be father of the great King David.

Ruth comes to the attention of Boaz, a Bethlehem farmer, as she gleans corn from the edges of his field. The law instructs reapers not to go back over a field a second time, so that any grain that is left can be collected by the poor.

Boaz meets his relative at the town gate to discuss which of them shall care for Naomi and Ruth. It is at the gate of a town that the elders sit and important business is transacted.

1 AND 2 SAMUEL

The first book of Samuel continues the story of Israel from the time of the judges to the end of the reign of King Saul. At the beginning the Israelites are a loose association of tribes. By the end they are a united nation with their own king.

Samuel is the last judge. He tries to persuade the Israelites not to have a king, but they insist. The first king, Saul, is a disappointment. He disobeys God. He is also jealous of a popular young hero – David. Samuel anoints David as Saul's successor; but for many years David has to flee from Saul for fear of his life. The first book of Samuel ends with Saul's death.

The second book of Samuel continues the story of God's people, Israel. Its main theme is the reign of King David, who is Israel's greatest king.

When David comes to power, he brings unity and peace to a divided nation and a troubled land. He defeats Israel's enemies and establishes Jerusalem as his political and religious centre. He receives God's promise that his descendants will rule for ever.

But David is far from perfect. In mid-life he commits adultery with Bathsheba, the wife of one of his soldiers – and then tries to hide his crime by arranging the man's death. This episode proves to be a turning point in David's fortunes. He loses the respect of his own sons, and they cause both him and the nation great grief.

Outline

Samuel (1 Samuel 1:1 – 7:17)
Saul (1 Samuel 8:1 – 15:35)
David (1 Samuel 16:1 – 31:13)
David becomes king (2 Samuel 1:1 – 10:19)
David's weaknesses and failures (2 Samuel 11:1 – 18:33)
The final period of David's reign (2 Samuel 19:1 – 24:25)

INTRODUCTION

In the Hebrew Bible, the two books of Samuel were a single book. When the Septuagint (the Greek version of the Hebrew Bible) was compiled, the books of Samuel and Kings were called the 'books of the kingdoms'. In the famous English 'Authorized (King James) Version' they are numbered as four books of Kings. They tell a continuous history from the time of Samuel (the last of the judges), through the reigns of three great kings (Saul, David and Solomon), to the division of Israel and Judah and their eventual fall.

The books of Joshua, Judges, Samuel and Kings tell the ongoing story of Israel, from the triumphant conquest of Canaan to the bitter exile in Babylon. The writers and editors show how God is at work in the lives of his people. God rewards faithfulness with success – and punishes disobedience with failure.

Samuel

Samuel is the last and greatest of the judges. He is a key figure at a time when Israel's priesthood is corrupt, its enemies are strong and the people are demanding to have a king. Samuel warns Israel of the dangers of having a human king, but follows God's guidance in choosing and anointing two great kings – Saul and David.

Three kings

Saul, David and Solomon are Israel's first three kings. They are each said to reign for forty years – the Bible's clue to a 'complete' period of time. If Saul dies around 1010 BC, we have some possible dates for their reigns:

Saul	1045 to 1010 BC
David	1010 to 970 BC
Solomon	970 to 930 BC

SAUL

Saul is Israel's first king. He seems to be the right choice. He is tall, with a striking appearance and a desire to lead well.

However, there are occasions when he does the wrong thing – showing that he has no true sense of God's will. God rejects him as king, and his leadership begins to fail. Saul is a picture of our human impulse to run our lives without God.

DAVID

David is Israel's second and most famous king.

As a boy, he slays a giant Philistine, Goliath. Goliath symbolizes the threat and awesome power of Israel's pagan enemies. But David simply puts his trust in God – and his skill with a shepherd's sling.

As 'king-in-waiting', David gives protection and leadership to poor and disaffected people. He refuses to seize the throne by force, and twice spares King Saul's life.

When he eventually becomes king, David will defeat all Israel's enemies and protect her borders. His reign will be the only time in Israel's history when she actually occupies all the land which God promised to Abraham.

SOLOMON

See 1 Kings.

An incense burner found at Shiloh.

Who wrote the books of Samuel and Kings?

We don't know who wrote these books. Certainly it wasn't Samuel. Although he is a leading character, he dies before the end of the first volume (1 Samuel 25:1)! Most of the material was written by the end of the reign of Solomon, around 900 BC. A tell-tale verse (1 Samuel 27:6) hints that the final editing took place many years later, during or after the exile of Judah in Babylon.

Mixed doubles

Sometimes the author (or editor) tells the same story twice – or even gives two different accounts of the same story. For example, it's hard to tell whether Samuel was the most famous leader of his day or just a local circuit judge. And when exactly did David first meet Saul? Was the young man well known to the king as a musician and armour bearer – or was he a likely lad who suddenly volunteered to fight Goliath? The author gives us the stories and leaves the choice to us.

DISCOVERING 1 AND 2 SAMUEL

Samuel

The birth and call of Samuel
(1 Samuel 1:1 – 3:21)

Samuel is the son of Hannah. Hannah has been childless for many years – feeling abandoned by God and a failure to her husband. At last God gives her a longed-for son. She sings a song of praise – that God can turn despair to hope and failure to triumph. He lifts the lowly and humbles the proud. This song will be echoed, centuries later, by Mary the mother of Jesus (Luke 1:46–55). Out of gratitude, Hannah gives her son Samuel, while he is still a small boy, to serve God at the shrine in Shiloh.

The priest at Shiloh is Eli. He is old and his sons, also priests, are decadent. They feed themselves from the choicest portions of the

The 'tent of meeting' was the focus of God's presence with his people while they wandered in the desert. Once they were settled in Canaan, the tent was pitched on a permanent site at Shiloh.

sacrifices, and sleep around with the women on their staff. Eli is warned by a prophet that God will judge this scandalous situation.

One night, God speaks to Samuel. The voice is so clear that at first Samuel thinks Eli is calling him. God tells Samuel that he is about to judge Eli and his sons – the sons for their wicked behaviour and Eli for not controlling them.

The ark is captured – and returned
(1 Samuel 4:1 – 7:1)

Eli's sons, Hophni and Phinehas, take the ark of the covenant into battle against the Philistines. The ark is captured and they are killed. When Eli receives the terrible news, he topples off his chair and dies. The shock also causes Phinehas' wife to go into labour. As she dies giving birth, she calls her baby 'Ichabod', – which means 'No Glory'. The presence of God has departed from Eli and his family.

The Philistines take the ark of the covenant to the temple of Dagon, their pagan idol. Next morning they find the giant statue flat on its face. After that the presence of the ark brings disease and panic to the Philistines – and they resolve to return it to Israel.

Samuel conquers the Philistines
(1 Samuel 7:2–17)

The ark of the Lord is returned to Israel. The Philistines have found that its holy presence brings death and destruction; but the Israelites aren't worthy of it either. For twenty years it remains in a kind of quarantine at the house of Abinadab at Kiriath Jearim, the 'city of woods' between the tribes of Benjamin and Judah. The Israelites mourn the loss of the presence of God, and begin to turn to him again.

Eventually, Samuel sends out a message to all Israel. He says that if they are ready to return to the Lord and will reject all foreign gods (especially Astarte, the Baal-goddess of fertility and war) then God will rescue them from the domination of the Philistines.

Samuel calls the tribes of Israel to assemble at Mizpah

A mixed blessing

Sometimes God gives us what we want – but it's not always for the best. The monarchy is a mixed blessing for Israel – a flawed human invention which God can sometimes bless.

Although human kingship is not God's choice, he guides Samuel to anoint Saul – a man with an impressive physique but a weak character. In time, God will bless the monarchy by raising up David – a wise, strong and caring king. David's reign will look forward to the perfect rule of Christ. The love and justice of David's kingdom will foreshadow the kingdom of God.

– west of the River Jordan in the territory of the tribe of Benjamin. There they pour out water in the presence of God, as a sign that he alone can wash away their sins. They fast, confess their guilt and receive God's judgment through Samuel. He is the last and greatest of the judges, ministering to the people as their military leader, prophet and priest.

'Mizpah' means 'watchtower'. It is a small settlement only a few miles north of Jerusalem, whose height above the valleys makes it a good rallying point.

The Philistines hear that the Israelites are massing at Mizpah and assume that they are about to be attacked. They decide to advance their own army, and the Israelites plead with Samuel to secure God's help. This is a very different attitude from the Israel of the past, which assumed that the presence of the ark would give automatic victory.

Samuel offers a sacrifice and prays for God's help in the crisis. As the smoke rises from the burnt offering, the Lord sends a great thunderstorm upon the Philistines, which throws them into confusion and forces them to flee. The Israelites pursue them, having the advantage of chasing them downhill. To mark such a great deliverance, Samuel sets up a memorial stone. He calls it Ebenezer, which means 'stone of help'. It was a place called Ebenezer which had been the site of Israel's last defeat (4:1), but now God has granted repentance and success.

The Philistines capture the ark of the covenant but, wherever they take it, it seems to cause death and destruction. Eventually, they put it onto a new cart and send it back in the direction of the Israelites. From a 13th-century fresco in Anagni Cathedral, Italy.

The Philistines

Israel's chief enemy at this time is Philistia. The Philistines are a seafaring people who have settled in the coastal region between Israel and the Mediterranean Sea. Their technology is more advanced than Israel's, and they make their weapons and armour from iron. Meanwhile, Israel is still in the Bronze Age, and her weapons are less effective.

The Philistines cause no further trouble to Israel during Samuel's lifetime. He makes an annual circuit, spending time at Bethel, Gilgal and Mizpah to hear cases and make judgments. By so doing, he restores and sustains the relationship of the people with their God. Each of the places is a sanctuary where God is worshipped; and Samuel builds an altar in his home town of Ramah as well. There is stability and peace throughout Israel under the ministry of Samuel and the government of God. But it isn't to last.

An Egyptian relief, depicting captured Philistine soldiers.

Rough justice?

It is hard for us to accept that God commands the complete destruction of the Amalekites and their possessions. Is this really the fate he demands for the vile and perverted peoples of Canaan? Certainly he would want Israel to be uncompromising with the beliefs and practices of paganism. Even keeping some plunder from a battle can sow the seeds of greed in God's holy people. Ethnic cleansing may have been the Israelites' best guess at what God wanted them to do. Jesus will show God as merciful towards traditional enemies. On one occasion he forbids James and John to call down fire from heaven on a Samaritan village (Luke 9:54–55).

Saul

Israel asks for a king
(1 Samuel 8:1–22)

As Samuel grows old, the question arises as to who will succeed him. Other nations have a king to unite and protect them, and the leaders of Israel feel that the time has come for Israel to do the same. Samuel believes that God is the true king of Israel, and the one who appoints leaders and judges for his people. It is also true that no human king is perfect, and some become tyrants who bully and exploit their people. After much heart-searching and debate, Samuel agrees to select and anoint a human king – an impressive young man called Saul. But it is against Samuel's better judgment, and he will live to regret it.

Saul begins his reign well, by leading his people to victory over their enemies. But he is strong-headed and does not always wait for or heed God's advice. He also suffers from periods of black depression and is jealous of the people's hero, David. In the end, he becomes a sad picture – a fine man who has become estranged from God and so is unable to control either himself or his destiny.

Saul becomes king
(1 Samuel 9:1 – 11:15)

We first meet Saul as he searches for his father's donkeys. Saul goes to ask Samuel for help because Samuel is a 'seer' – a holy man who may be able to 'see' where the donkeys are.

But Samuel is interested in Saul for other reasons. He reveals that Saul is to become the king of Israel. Saul is reluctant. He pleads that he and his tribe are very insignificant. Gideon said the same in his day (Judges 6:15).

Samuel anoints Saul and tells him the special signs which will confirm that he is God's choice. One by one they take place – including the outpouring of God's Spirit so that Saul becomes a frenzied prophet. But when the tribes gather to choose and confirm Saul as their king, he is still unwilling. They find him hiding under a pile of baggage!

Although he is king, Saul has limited power. Samuel writes down certain guidelines and restrictions, which are kept with the ark of the covenant. Saul may be ruler of Israel, but he himself is to be ruled by God.

Samuel's farewell speech

(1 Samuel 12:1–25)

Saul is now Israel's king. He is God's anointed leader and the people's united choice. It remains for Samuel to let go of his own great influence. As he does so, he reminds all Israel that he has not burdened or cheated them in any way. He is the last of the judges, who have been God's means of delivering them from powerful and pagan enemies.

Samuel warns the people to be faithful to the Lord – and his solemn words are endorsed by an unseasonal

Samuel anoints David, to signify that God has chosen him to be king of Israel one day. This mural is from Dura Europus, in Syria.

thunderstorm. They have been wrong to demand a king, but God will not abandon them – and nor will Samuel. Samuel will continue to act as God's prophet and fulfil his responsibility to pray for and teach God's people.

The relationship between Samuel and Saul will always be difficult. Samuel has not wanted to anoint a king, and Saul has not wanted to be one. Now Saul must rule Israel with Samuel still around to criticize and correct him. Ideally, Saul should make Samuel his close adviser and friend – but they simply don't get on that well. Saul is proud and increasingly independent. Samuel will never accept anyone between himself and God.

Saul's disobedience

(1 Samuel 13:1 – 15:35)

Saul and his son Jonathan are successful army commanders, driving back Israel's enemies. But there are two occasions when Saul offends God greatly. The first is when he offers a sacrifice without waiting for Samuel. In so doing he usurps the work of a priest and treats the sacrifice as a token of good luck. On another occasion Saul disobeys God by failing to destroy the Amalekites (15:7–9). He makes the excuse that he is saving the Amalekite cattle for sacrifices. But Samuel points out that it is more important to do what God wants (15:22):

*Does the Lord delight
in burnt offerings
and sacrifices as
much as in obeying
the voice of the Lord?*

This is a vital insight into Samuel's understanding of God. In years to come it will be echoed by other prophets and by Jesus himself.

From this point Samuel and Saul part company. They live only ten miles apart, but they never see each other again.

David

Samuel anoints David

(1 Samuel 16:1–23)

God sends Samuel to Bethlehem. There he discovers David, the youngest of the sons of Jesse. It doesn't occur to anyone in the family that this shepherd lad might be a future king. But God sees things differently. In another remarkable statement, Samuel shows his deep awareness of the presence and perception of God:

Mortals look on the outward appearance, but the Lord looks on the heart (16:7).

Samuel anoints David by pouring oil over his head. The young man is filled with God's Spirit for the task of leadership. As the Spirit of the Lord comes upon David, so the Spirit leaves Saul. It is almost as though there is not enough Spirit to go round. But one day there will be. As Joel prophesies:

And afterwards,
I will pour out my Spirit on all people.
Your sons and daughters will prophesy,
your old men will dream dreams,
your young men will see visions.
Even on my servants, both men
and women,
I will pour out my Spirit in those
days (Joel 2:28–29).

Joel looks forward to the era of Jesus. There will come a Day of Pentecost when God's Spirit will no longer be rationed to an occasional priest or prophet or king, but freely given to all God's people (Acts 2:1–11).

From now on Saul is rejected by God. He suffers fits of depression. Young David is summoned to court to play the harp and ease the king's black moods.

David and Goliath
(1 Samuel 17:1–58)

A champion is needed to fight a giant Philistine called Goliath. David volunteers. This should be Saul's task, as he is a head taller than any of his men – and has one of the few suits of armour! But David goes out to meet Goliath, armed only with faith in the living God – and his shepherd's sling. This is more than a test of bravery. It is a brave declaration that the God of Israel is greater than all other gods. As David says:

The whole world will know that there is a God in Israel. All those gathered here will know that it is not by sword or spear that the Lord saves; for the battle is the Lord's (17:46–47).

This is God's war! The lad with faith takes on the giant of fear. Goliath stands for all the pride and power of paganism. David and his sling are so puny that victory can only be an act of God.

David, the king-in-waiting
(1 Samuel 18:1 – 27:12)

David is now married to Saul's daughter Michal, and has Saul's son Jonathan as his closest friend. But the king himself is mad with jealousy. He is determined to take David's life.

The shepherd boy David slays the giant Goliath.
From a 12th-century Spanish wall-painting.

David becomes an outlaw. At first he hides out at the cave of Adullam, where he is joined by the outcasts and rebels of Israelite society. Later he makes the town of Ziklag his centre; and on another occasion he takes refuge with the Philistines.

Saul pursues David, killing the priests who have given him sanctuary. On two occasions David actually spares the king's life. He comes close enough to cut a piece from Saul's robe, and take his spear and water jug.

David believes that Saul is God's anointed king. His life and status are sacred, and no one but God may remove him. David himself will not become king before God's time.

DAVID TAKES REFUGE WITH THE PHILISTINES

David's life is threatened and he must live by his wits. He goes to Nob, where the ark of the Lord is kept. He asks the priest for bread, but the only food available is the special batch of loaves which are laid out in the presence of God. Only priests are allowed to eat this 'bread of the Presence'. However, David manages to persuade the priest that his mission is very urgent and his men are ritually pure. He allows them to eat the loaves.

David hides from Saul in the limestone caves of this bleak landscape – the Desert of Maon, on the edge of the Dead Sea.

David has rare insight and understanding. He knows the worlds of politics and of the human heart. Of course, the two go together. Understanding human nature and need is an important part of good government.

Our attitude to monarchy and leadership is still shaped by David's ideals and example. What a shame he was not as skilled at governing his own family!

In the future, Jesus will agree with the priest's decision. Human need is more important than religious formality. Jesus recalls this episode when he confronts the legalistic Pharisees about keeping or breaking the sabbath (Matthew 12:1–8).

After food, David's next need is for a weapon. He persuades the priest to let him take the sword of the giant Goliath – the very sword with which David himself had cut off the great Philistine's head.

To escape Saul, David makes for the very last place he would be expected to go – the Philistine city of Gath. It is an outrageous ploy! Carrying Goliath's sword, he goes to Goliath's home town and becomes a servant of King Achish. Inevitably, the other servants recognize him, but he averts their anger by pretending to be mad. It is a humiliating experience, but later David will look back on it as a God-given means of escape:

An example of decorated Philistine pottery from about the 11th century BC.

I sought the Lord and he answered me;
  he delivered me from all my fears (Psalm 34:4).

Achish takes a look at David and decides he has enough madmen already. So David is able to escape.

Saul and the witch of Endor
(1 Samuel 28:1–25)
Samuel dies. Even though they are no longer friends, Saul misses his old adviser. His own relationship with God is dead as well. In terror of the Philistines, Saul decides to consult a medium. She summons the spirit of Samuel. Whether this is really the spirit of Samuel or a demonic impersonation, we don't know. Certainly the message from Samuel in death is the same as it was in life:

The Lord has torn the kingdom out of your hands and given it to one of your neighbours – to David (28:17).

Grimly, the medium predicts the death of Saul and his sons in battle with the Philistines the following day. Saul has been extremely foolish to seek help by occult means – a form of guidance which God expressly forbids. And no good has come of it.

Achish sends David back to Ziklag
(1 Samuel 29:1–11)
The Philistine forces are gathering at Aphek, about thirty miles to the north of Gath. The Israelite army is at Jezreel, on the slopes of Mount Gilboa. David and his men have supported Achish in many military campaigns; but this battle will be different, because it is against Israel and her king. The Philistine commanders don't trust David to be loyal to them. They suspect that he may use the opportunity to change sides and win the battle for Israel – perhaps even seizing Saul's throne. Achish has complete confidence in David, but for his own sake dismisses him from the Philistine force. This is a great mercy, because David is spared having to fight Saul, the Lord's anointed king.

David destroys the Amalekites
(1 Samuel 30:1–31)
Meanwhile, an Amalekite raiding party has attacked David's centre at Ziklag, and taken the families, livestock and possessions of all his men. David's reaction is a model of good leadership. He seeks God's guidance, acts wisely and decisively, and secures complete success. In victory he shares the plunder fairly and generously with everyone. We can't help comparing David's confident judgment with Saul's dangerous instability.

The death of Saul

(1 Samuel 31:1–13)

Saul and his army are defeated by the Philistines. The royal sons – including David's friend Jonathan – are killed, and Saul takes his own life. It is a degrading death for the king the people demanded, but God rejected.

David becomes king

David's lament for Saul and Jonathan

(2 Samuel 1:1–27)

David receives the news that King Saul and his son Jonathan have been killed in battle with the Philistines. He is heartbroken. Although Saul has long treated David as a rival and tried to kill him, David has never wished him harm. When the messenger claims to have helped the stricken Saul to end his life, David has him killed on the spot. Saul was the Lord's anointed king. His life was sacred.

David sings a lament which has been famous ever since. He forbids the news of Saul's death to be published, in case the Philistines celebrate. He curses the mountains of Gilboa where the great men died. He remembers Saul and Jonathan in their prime, as princes, soldiers and friends.

The Book of Jashar ('The Upright') (1:18) seems to have been a collection of well-known poems and songs. No copies have survived but it provides a clue to how the Bible books must have been written, using historical records, songs and stories. The Book of Jashar is also mentioned in Joshua 10:13.

The mountains of Gilboa are well known to this day, simply because they are the place where Saul and Jonathan died.

David becomes king of Judah

(2 Samuel 2:1 – 5:5)

Saul has died – and so has his son Jonathan. The way is now open for David to become king – except that there are other contenders. There is sure to be a candidate from among Saul's sons or from his tribe of Benjamin. This could lead to further bloodshed and civil war.

David seeks God's guidance before he takes any step – and then makes the short journey to Hebron. Hebron is where Abraham and the patriarchs are buried, and the

place where a king might be anointed, at least over the tribe of Judah.

David is duly anointed as king over Judah, the leading tribe of Israel.

Meanwhile Abner, Saul's general, has made someone else king at Mahanaim. This king is Ish-Bosheth. He is Saul's son, and he reigns over parts of Israel for two years. His name may mean 'Strong Man' – but the real trial of strength is going on between two rival army commanders – Abner (for Ish-Bosheth and the tribe of Benjamin) and Joab (for David and the tribe of Judah).

Joab, David's general, wants revenge on Abner, who has killed his brother Asahel. When Abner holds talks with David to make peace, Joab moves swiftly to seize and murder him. David mourns the death of Abner – a fine leader who was already working to unite the nation. This is just the start of trouble with Joab, who becomes David's hit man whether David likes it or not. Joab is a violent enemy and an unscrupulous friend.

Ish-Bosheth is also murdered, by two of his own supporters who have changed sides. David is appalled at their deed and has them executed.

At last David is anointed king over the united tribes of Israel. He is thirty years old and will reign until he is seventy.

David makes Jerusalem his capital

(2 Samuel 5:6 – 6:23)

David's first action is to capture Jerusalem from the Jebusites. Throughout the years of the Canaan campaign, Jerusalem has resisted all attempts to be captured. Now David makes her his own capital: 'the city of David'. By doing this he gives Israel a centre which has no previous link with any of the tribes.

Next, David defeats the Philistines. Unlike Saul, David only goes to battle if God gives him the command. Like Jesus, he only does what God tells him to do (John 6:38).

David sees life as a whole. The tribes of Israel should be united as the people of God. Politics and religion belong together. He decides to show this by bringing the ark of the covenant (the symbol of God's presence) to Jerusalem (the centre of government).

The ark is carried in procession towards Jerusalem, with great celebration – until Uzzah touches it unthinkingly and is struck dead. The ark is holy and not

Second best?

Both the monarchy and the temple are second best. God is the real king of Israel, and he needs no earthly house. But God accepts Israel's need for a king and a temple, to act as a focus for his divine rule and holy presence.

to be handled roughly – not even touched, except by the appointed priests. David is angry and perplexed by this unexpected tragedy. He leaves the ark in the care of a man called Obed-Edom for three months, until it is clearly safe to proceed.

As the ark arrives in Jerusalem, David dances before it, dressed only in an ephod – a kind of priestly apron. He has an enormous sense of joy in the Lord, but his wife, Michal, thinks he looks ridiculous. Her father, Saul, was far more kingly. But David is not ashamed. He is dancing for the Lord, not for anyone else.

God's promise to David

(2 Samuel 7:1–29))

David and the prophet Nathan are thinking how strange it is that the king now lives in a palace, but God remains in a tent. The tent is the old tabernacle shelter of the wilderness years.

Nathan receives a message from the Lord. God doesn't want or need a house. There is even some danger in building a temple, because it will seem to 'fix' God in one place. The Israelites have always experienced God 'on the move', leading them forward on a journey of faith. He does not live in a temple or shrine, but with his people, wherever they are.

Far from David needing to establish God's house, God is going to establish David's 'house' or dynasty. He promises to be a father to David. He will make David very great, and his descendants will reign for ever. One day a son of David (Solomon) will build 'a house for the Lord' – a beautiful temple.

God's promise to David becomes the central pillar of

Israel's hope for survival. The people believe that God will never fail them. He has committed himself to preserving David's descendants as kings for ever. This promise echoes God's ancient covenant with Abraham, which included the promise of a land and a great nation of descendants. Now God's promise to Abraham is being fulfilled and continued through the promise to David. God's plan is to bless the whole world through them.

The royal line of David continues to reign in Jerusalem for 400 years – until the destruction of Jerusalem and the exile in Babylon in 586 BC. Even now, the Jews continue to look forward to the coming of their Messiah – a son of David, who will conquer their

Modern Jerusalem. In the foreground is the city of David, which is the oldest part of the settlement. It is built on the spur of land leading up to the temple mount. Herod the Great constructed a vast platform to support his temple, which was being built during the lifetime of Jesus. Today the temple site is dominated by the golden Dome of the Rock, one of Islam's most important mosques.

enemies and establish a universal kingdom of justice and peace.

After the exile, the royal line of David is still carefully traced – until it eventually leads to Jesus. Two Gospel writers, Matthew and Luke, record Jesus' descent from David, through his earthly father, Joseph (Matthew 1:5–6; Luke 3:31).

DAVID'S PRAYER

David expresses his trust in God (7:18–29). He describes himself as God's servant ten times over. It is God who has done everything for him, from his days as a shepherd to his anointing as king. Now he begs God to keep the

great promises he has made. His prayer is a mixture of humble submission and urgent demand. He prays success for the temple and for all God's work in the world.

David's victories

(2 Samuel 8:1 – 10:19)

David has many years of success. He unites his people, defeats his enemies and secures the borders of Israel. He acts justly, without fear or favour. He is kind to Mephibosheth, the crippled son of his friend Jonathan. He goes out to battle with his soldiers, sharing their hardships and triumphs.

The king and the commandments

In Israel God is king, and everyone is subject to his law. David, God's earthly king, must keep the Ten Commandments along with everyone else.

As David lusts after Bathsheba, commits adultery with her, deceives her husband and has him killed, God's law is tossed aside. In Israel a man may take another wife – but not if she is already married to someone else. Everyone knows this is wrong.

David has wronged God, Bathsheba, Uriah and himself. There will be far-reaching consequences for his family and nation. David sets a bad example for his sons – two of whom, Amnon and Absalom, abuse their royal power to commit sexual outrage.

David is guilty, but he repents. He gives himself totally to prayer and fasting, spending a week without food or sleep, and pleading for the baby's life to be spared.

In his attitude, David is very different from Saul. Where Saul would have blustered excuses and brazened his way out, David completely admits his wrong. He submits to God and asks for forgiveness, cleansing and a new heart.

In doing so he pioneers new paths for the human spirit – across deserts of despair to the oases of repentance, and the heights of forgiveness.

After the child dies, David resumes normal life. He has fully expressed his great grief. He has accepted the Lord's judgment.

David's weaknesses and failures

David and Bathsheba

(2 Samuel 11:1 – 12:25)

One spring, David decides not to go to war. No doubt he feels that he deserves a rest – a chance to take a well-earned break and leave the fighting to others.

In his idleness, David starts an affair with the beautiful wife of one of his soldiers. Her name is Bathsheba. Her husband, Uriah the Hittite, is one of David's finest men. Her father Eliam is also one of David's famous 'Thirty': mighty warriors. Her grandfather is the wise and subtle counsellor, Ahithophel.

Bathsheba becomes pregnant. David brings Uriah home from battle and encourages him to spend a few nights with his wife. But this man is a professional soldier and he sleeps in the guardhouse. So David tries another plan. He sends a letter to his commander, Joab, with instructions that Uriah be sent where the fighting is fiercest and then left to die.

One thing has led to another. David's lack of self-discipline has resulted in adultery, deceit and murder. At first David thinks he has hidden his crime; but God knows – and so does his prophet Nathan. Sin is always found out.

NATHAN REBUKES DAVID

David is the most powerful person in the land – and yet Nathan can challenge him in the name of the Lord (2 Samuel 12:1–12). He tells him an innocent little story about a rich man who has flocks of sheep, but stoops to take a poor man's only lamb – to cook for a visitor.

David is furious that such a thing can happen – until Nathan says, 'It's you!' David – a king with wives and mistresses to spare – has stolen a soldier's only wife and taken his life as well.

This is a turning point for David's reign. Until now everything has gone right. After this everything goes wrong. David repents before God with all his heart. We have his words (Psalm 51:1, 4, 10):

> Have mercy on me, O God,
> according to your unfailing love…
> Against you, you only, have I sinned…
> Create in me a pure heart, O God,
> and renew a steadfast spirit within me.

Bathsheba's baby dies; but soon she and David have another son. They name him Solomon.

Solomon will inherit his father's throne and become a king of legendary wealth and wisdom. He will fulfil David's dream of building a temple for the Lord in Jerusalem. We see how God takes even our disobedience and failure and works them into his perfect plan.

Solomon's name comes from the Hebrew word 'Shalom', which means 'Peace'. Nathan arrives with another name as well – 'Jedidiah', which means 'Loved by the Lord'. This baby will not die.

Defeating the Ammonites

(2 Samuel 12:26–31)

The conquest of the Ammonites and their capital Rabbah is a considerable success. Joab is a loyal general, and he wants his king to have the honour of capturing the city.

The sins of the father...

(2 Samuel 13:1 – 18:33)

David's adultery with Bathsheba and his murder of Uriah make it very difficult for him to correct his own sons. They know too much about him. We now see how two of David's sons, Amnon and Absalom, also behave disgracefully.

AMNON RAPES HIS HALF-SISTER

Amnon is David's eldest son, and heir to the throne. He is infatuated with princess Tamar, but can't marry her because she is his half-sister. A crafty cousin, Jonadab, advises Amnon to pretend to be sick. The king will then send Tamar to look after him!

All goes according to plan – and Tamar finds herself alone in Amnon's bedroom. Despite her pleas, he seizes her, rapes her and throws her out.

Tamar's brother is Absalom. When he finds her in mourning, with ashes on her head and her royal robe torn, he immediately plans revenge. He is a patient man. It takes two years; but eventually Amnon is killed – and Absalom goes into hiding.

ABSALOM REBELS

The king and Absalom don't see each other for three years, until Joab devises a way of bringing them together. He gets a wise old woman to come to King David with a moving story of a son who needs forgiveness. David sees that she is describing Absalom, and allows him to return home. But David ignores his son for another two years – and Absalom grows angry and rebellious.

Absalom is strikingly good-looking. He is especially proud of his long hair. One day he acquires a chariot and fifty men, and starts to pose as king-in-waiting.

Absalom encourages dissatisfied people to turn to him for help. If only he were king, he would give them their rights! He is over-friendly – stopping people bowing to him and shaking their hands or kissing them instead. This continues for four years – and then Absalom declares himself king in Hebron.

Absalom's following is large and growing. As he advances on Jerusalem, David decides to leave. He has no desire for bloodshed or civil war.

Absalom takes control of Jerusalem. He has Ahithophel, one of David's best counsellors, on his side. Ahithophel is Bathsheba's grandfather. He will advise Absalom to sleep with David's concubines. Does he want to humiliate the king for what was done to his granddaughter?

David leaves ten concubines (royal mistresses) in charge of his palace. As he reviews his troops, we notice that the foreign soldiers are loyal to David, although his own son is a rebel. Ittai the Gittite, for example, is a Philistine from Gath, the home town of the giant Goliath.

The people weep as the king crosses the Kidron Valley and journeys towards the desert. David gives instructions for the ark of the covenant to stay in the city. God is in control of everything, and well able to look after himself.

On the brow of the Mount of Olives, with a magnificent view of his royal city, David weeps. Jerusalem is rejecting her king, and no good can come of it. One day Jesus, too, will weep on this spot – and for the same reason (Matthew 23:37–39).

David sends some priests, including Zadok and Abiathar and their two sons, back into Jerusalem to act as informers.

David's behaviour in this crisis is calm and dignified. He has only ever been king by God's authority and the people's assent. If they don't want him any longer, so be it. He does not retaliate when the fiery Shimei curses him and throws stones!

HUSHAI VERSUS AHITHOPHEL

Meanwhile Absalom and Ahithophel are getting established in Jerusalem. Hushai the Archite appears to join them. Little does Absalom realize that when Hushai says, 'Long live the king!' he means King David.

The two counsellors, Hushai and Ahithophel, give Absalom conflicting advice. Ahithophel encourages Absalom to sleep with the king's concubines. Absalom agrees. He commits this outrage on the roof of the palace, for all to see.

Next Ahithophel advises Absalom to attack David quickly, overtaking his soldiers while they are tired. But Absalom consults Hushai as well.

Hushai points out that David and his men are

experienced campaigners. Absalom would do well to marshal all his troops. This will take a while, but they will then surely overwhelm the king by force of numbers. This suggestion appeals to Absalom's pride, and he delays attacking David.

Hushai's advice to Absalom gives David time to organize his forces. He deploys his men in three sections, with Joab, Abishai and Ittai the Gittite as commanders. He gives strict orders to everyone that Absalom is not to be harmed.

In a running battle through the forest of Ephraim, David's units rout Absalom's men. The young prince himself is caught in a tree by his famous hair. Joab, true to form and against David's orders, kills him. When David hears the news, he is broken-hearted.

The final period of David's reign

David returns to Jerusalem; Sheba's rebellion
(2 Samuel 19:1 – 20:25)

Slowly the country unites again under David's rule. He is forgiving and fair as he deals with those who have rejected him; and those whose loyalty has been suspect.

There is friction between the ten northern tribes of Israel and the southern tribe of Judah. The leaders of Judah take David back to Jerusalem as 'their' king. David is, after all, from the tribe of Judah. The tribes of Israel feel left out, and this flares into a rebellion led by Sheba. The rebellion is crushed when Joab negotiates Sheba's execution in the northern town of Abel Beth Maacah.

Joab is listed as commander 'over Israel's entire army'. He has always been loyal to David – and always beyond his control. David has never checked him for his high-handed murder of rivals – including Absalom, the king's own son. But then, Joab knows how Uriah met his death! In the end, David passes the problem on to Solomon (1 Kings 2:6).

The great David – musician, warrior and king. A 17th-century Armenian Bible shows David on his throne playing a harp.

Vengeance for the Gibeonites
(2 Samuel 21:1–14)

David accepts that, long ago, Saul wronged the Gibeonites. He hated them as foreigners and put some of them to death. God has sent drought as a result. Now David agrees an 'expiation' – that seven members of Saul's family shall be sacrificed. This act of revenge is requested by the Gibeonites, not commanded by God.

Great deeds
(2 Samuel 21:15–22)

The names of great heroes are recorded, and especially those who were 'mentioned in dispatches' during skirmishes with the Philistines. David values the qualities and achievements of his warriors – some of them giant-killers like himself.

David's song of praise
(2 Samuel 22:1–51)

David sings of the God who saves. God is a rock, a fortress, a shield and a Saviour. David has found himself protected from so many enemies and rescued from so many dangerous situations. He concludes that the Lord is the living God, with whom he has an ongoing relationship of honour and trust: 'The Lord lives!' (22:47). This psalm appears in a very similar version as Psalm 18 in the book of Psalms.

The last words of David
(2 Samuel 23:1–7)

David speaks of the privilege of being the Lord's anointed king. He has found the beauty of reigning with righteousness and in the fear of God. Now he is sure that his royal line will continue after him.

David's mighty warriors
(2 Samuel 23:8–39)

Some more of David's mighty warriors are listed, with brief descriptions of their exploits. Three of them stole through Philistine lines to get a drink of water for David from his favourite well at Bethlehem. Kabzeel, 'went down into a pit on a snowy day and killed a lion' (23:20)! But how poignant to see listed last among the 'Thirty' none other than Uriah the Hittite (23:39).

David's folly

(2 Samuel 24:1–25)

For some reason David decides to count his armed forces. This is an affront to God, because it implies that David relies on his army for protection, instead of on the living God. Really he knows better, for he writes in a psalm:

> *Some trust in chariots and some in horses,*
> *but we trust in the name of the Lord our God*
> *(Psalm 20:7).*

God punishes David's pride by sending a plague on Israel. The disease cuts down a large part of the population and threatens Jerusalem. David is guided to buy a particular threshing-floor which belongs to Araunah, one of the conquered Jebusites. Here he builds an altar and offers sacrifices to halt the plague, and the danger is averted. Araunah's threshing-floor is high up, overlooking the Kidron Valley. It will become the site of Solomon's temple.

1 AND 2 KINGS

The books of Kings continue the story of Israel with the reign of Solomon and the building of the temple in Jerusalem. After Solomon's death the nation divides, with a northern kingdom of Israel and a southern kingdom of Judah.

We follow the parallel stories of both kingdoms, until the northern kingdom is defeated by the Assyrians with the capture of Samaria in 722 BC. After that we follow the history of Judah until Jerusalem is captured and destroyed by the Babylonians in 587 BC. The whole story covers a period of 500 years.

Most of Israel's kings fail her. Even Solomon, who asks God for wisdom and builds the temple, makes foolish compromises with paganism. During this period, the challenge to remain faithful to God is upheld by the prophets – especially Elijah and his younger companion and successor, Elisha.

Outline

The reign of King Solomon (1 Kings 1:1 – 11:43)

The kingdom is divided (1 Kings 12:1 – 16:34)

The prophets Elijah and Elisha (1 Kings 17:1 – 2 Kings 8:15)

The rulers of Judah and Israel (2 Kings 8:16 – 16:20)

The fall of Israel, the northern kingdom (2 Kings 17:1–41)

Judah, the southern kingdom, until the fall of Jerusalem (2 Kings 18:1 – 25:30)

INTRODUCTION

The books of Kings

The books of Kings follow on from the books of Samuel, and are intended to be read together with them. In the Hebrew Bible, the books of Kings complete a story which began way back in the time of Joshua.

The books of Joshua, Judges, Samuel and Kings are known as 'the Former Prophets'. These are the history books which tell the story of Israel from the arrival of the tribes in the Promised Land to the eventual loss of the land and Judah's exile in Babylon. They may have been written, edited or compiled during the years of exile.

The author has old songs, stories and other documents to hand. He mentions some of them, such as the 'Annals of the Kings of Israel and Judah'. None of them has survived for us to study today. The books we call 1 and 2 Chronicles were written after the Jews returned from exile and are not the same as the 'Chronicles' mentioned in 1 Kings 14.

Running through this history is a strong sense of God's purpose for his people. God has made a covenant with Israel, giving his law and promising his blessing. But, as the book of Deuteronomy points out, obedience and blessing go together. The author of these books is showing us how disobedience and idolatry lead to failure and God's judgment. Some scholars call these books the 'deuteronomic history', because of the strong influence of themes which come from the book of Deuteronomy.

When were the books of Kings written?

The books of Kings were written some time after 561 BC. King Jehoiachin is released from prison about halfway through the time of the Jewish exile in Babylon. This is the last event recorded in the books, which stop short of telling us how the Jewish exiles return to Jerusalem in 538 BC.

All the books from Joshua to 2 Kings may be the work of one author or editor, who is using older writings and records to retell the whole story. If so, he may be one of the people exiled with King Jehoiachin in 597 BC, just ten years before the temple is destroyed.

With their king in exile, their city in ruins and their land taken from them, the Israelites' faith in God has suffered a devastating blow. Perhaps the editor is compiling the work for friends and colleagues in the exiled royal court, to try to make sense of the tragedy which has overtaken them. The prophets had warned that wicked and idolatrous behaviour would bring God's judgment upon them. This is the reason for the present disaster:

The Lord became angry with Solomon because his heart had turned away from the Lord, the God of Israel, who had appeared to him twice. Although he had forbidden Solomon to follow other gods, Solomon did not keep the Lord's command.

So the Lord said to Solomon, 'Since this is your attitude and you have not kept my covenant and my decrees, which I commanded you, I will most certainly tear the kingdom away from you and give it to one of your subordinates. Nevertheless, for the sake of David your father, I will not do it during your lifetime. I will tear it out of the hand of your son. Yet I will not tear the whole kingdom from him, but will give him one tribe for the sake of David my servant and for the sake of Jerusalem, which I have chosen.' (1 Kings 11:11–13)

The books of Kings give a long account of the reign of Solomon – and then a brief account of the reign of Joash. Yet both kings are said to have reigned for forty years. King Omri is an important figure on the international scene – but his reign is summed up in a few verses: 'Omri did evil in the eyes of the Lord and sinned more than all those before him' (1 Kings 16:25).

Every king in these books is assessed by the same standard: is he faithful to God or not? Does he build pagan altars on the hilltops (the 'high places') or pull them down? The kings that encourage idolatry are leading their people astray, and bringing destruction on their kingdoms.

Two great prophets

The books of Kings also tell the stories of two great prophets, Elijah and Elisha. Elijah dominates 1 Kings 17–19 and 2 Kings 1–2. His successor, Elisha, is the major prophetic figure in 2 Kings 2–8, with further appearances in chapters 9 and 13.

Stories of other prophets are also included in 1 Kings 20 and 22.

DISCOVERING 1 AND 2 KINGS

The reign of King Solomon

Solomon's reign
(1 Kings 1:1 – 4:34)

There is some doubt as to who will succeed David as king. Adonijah puts himself forward, but both Bathsheba and Nathan make sure that Solomon is chosen. Solomon is David's son by Bathsheba. He is anointed by Zadok the priest and Nathan the prophet. David advises him to walk in God's ways, and commissions him to repay favours and settle old scores.

The reigns of David and Solomon are the high point of Israel's history. Solomon asks God for wisdom, and becomes a man of great insight and judgment. He establishes a lavish royal household, supplied by twelve districts. He builds up a large army and, with the help of the seagoing Phoenicians, develops foreign trade. All this is expensive in money and human resources. Samuel had warned that a king would be a burden to his people (1 Samuel 8:10–18).

Solomon's building projects
(1 Kings 5:1 – 9:28)

BUILDING THE TEMPLE AND THE PALACE

Solomon starts to build the temple. Hiram king of Tyre sends cedar and pine from Lebanon, floated on rafts by sea to Joppa. The quarrying and cutting of stone is another major task, involving an army of workers and the advice of foreign experts. All the stone dressing is done at the quarry, so that there is no violent action on the site.

The temple is built on the threshing-floor of Araunah, which David bought to make a sacrifice when Jerusalem was threatened by plague (2 Samuel 24:18–25). Today the Muslim Dome of the Rock stands there – the 'rock' being the place where Abraham was told to sacrifice Isaac (Genesis 22:2). Both Jews and Muslims honour Abraham as a patriarch.

The temple is similar in layout to the old tabernacle, but larger. It has an entrance hall (portico), a sanctuary (the 'Holy Place') and an inner sanctuary (the 'Most Holy Place'). It is in the inner sanctuary that the ark of the covenant will be housed. The ark contains the tablets of stone on which are written the Ten Commandments. The inner sanctuary is shaped like a cube, to provide the 'perfect' space for a holy God.

The writer tells us that it takes seven years to build Solomon's temple. The temple which is built by Herod the Great in Jesus' time takes far longer. It is scarcely completed before it is destroyed by the Romans in AD 70.

Solomon also builds a palace for himself, which is called the 'Palace of the Forest of Lebanon' because of its fine cedar pillars and beams. The throne hall is larger than the temple and provides an impressive court, in which Solomon delivers his famous judgments. It takes thirteen years to build this palace – which is perhaps an indication of Solomon's real priorities.

One of Solomon's most famous judgments was between two women both claiming to be the mother of the same baby. The scene is depicted here in a 14th-century English psalter.

A SKILLED WORKER CALLED HURAM

The bronze furnishings for the temple are all the work of Huram, whom Solomon brings from the Phoenician port

Solomon's building projects were not confined to Jerusalem. These remains at Megiddo are thought to have been his stable blocks or storehouses.

of Tyre. Two mighty bronze pillars are given the names 'Jakin' ('solid') and 'Boaz' ('strong') – although their exact position is not known.

A great bronze basin, called 'the sea', is the successor to the tabernacle basin. It is used by the priests for washing their hands and feet. It is a superb feat of engineering, measuring fifteen feet across and holding about 10,000 gallons of water.

Solomon doesn't weigh the bronze furnishings, but they are all carefully listed, and their detail lovingly remembered. Tragically, they will one day become plunder for the Babylonians, who will cart them away in triumph (Jeremiah 52:17–23).

THE TEMPLE IS DEDICATED

The dedication of the temple is the greatest moment of Solomon's reign (8:1–66). The ark of the covenant is carried into the temple by the priests. It is brought from Zion, the southern hill of Jerusalem. The ark unites the days of God's guidance in the wilderness with the grace of his presence now – and the whole city becomes known as 'Zion'. So Jerusalem becomes the centre for both the worship of God and the reign of David's descendants.

The cloud of God's presence fills the temple. This is the cloud which once surrounded the tabernacle. Sometimes it is thick and dark, cloaking God's presence. Sometimes it is dazzlingly bright, denoting his glory. This same cloud will surround Jesus at his transfiguration (Luke 9:34) and receive him at his ascension (Acts 1:9).

Standing before the people, Solomon declares that he has fulfilled the plans of God and his father David. Kneeling before the altar, he prays. He asks that the new building may always be a focal point of God's care, and a place of justice, mercy and new beginnings for his people. He includes a remarkable plea that foreigners will come to this place and receive God's healing and help. Solomon truly shares God's vision that the whole world may find God through the witness of Israel (8:60).

The dedication of the temple is celebrated in a series of offerings and sacrifices, and with a great festival lasting for two weeks.

GOD APPEARS TO SOLOMON

The writer tells us that God appears to Solomon on two occasions. The first is at Gibeon, where the young king goes to make sacrifices in the early days of his reign. It is at Gibeon that Solomon asks God to give him the wisdom he needs to rule his people well (3:7–12).

Now (again, after a period of commitment and sacrifice), God appears to Solomon a second time (9:1–9). He tells Solomon that the temple is nothing without obedience and faith. He promises Solomon that his royal line will continue. However, he also warns that if Israel worships other gods, disaster will surely follow. The books of Kings are the story of how these words come true.

The queen of Sheba visits Solomon
(1 Kings 10:1–13)

Solomon is now internationally famous. His wealth and wisdom make him a living legend. Not only has he built a fine temple and palace, but he has developed trade routes and built a fleet of ships on the Red Sea.

The queen of Sheba comes from Arabia to visit Solomon. Today her country is Yemen. She comes to trade both goods and ideas, and is deeply impressed by all she sees. She praises the God who has done all this for Solomon.

Solomon's downfall
(1 Kings 11:1–43)

God has clearly honoured Solomon's request for wisdom and has also given him great wealth. Sadly, the king's confidence now starts to shift from God to his riches. His wisdom also is undermined by his marriages to foreign princesses.

Solomon's problems begin when he uses marriage to make treaties with other nations. This results in him taking wives who bring their pagan gods and practices into his palace and the life of the nation. Although it was usual for kings to have several wives (David had fifteen!), God has expressly forbidden the marrying of foreigners (Deuteronomy 7:1–4) and the taking of many wives (Deuteronomy 17:14–20). Solomon systematically disobeys all these commands, with his wives, weapons and wealth.

Solomon loses his desire to serve God, and becomes a slave to his lust for women. Their gods are the old Canaanite gods. Ashtoreth is the goddess of fertility, who is worshipped in bloodshed and sex. Molech is a god who is worshipped with child sacrifice. Solomon provides places of worship for them, and then joins in himself.

All this makes God angry. For judgment, he resolves that the kingdom will not pass intact to Solomon's descendants. However, because of David's faithfulness (and his promise to him) God grants that one tribe will continue to be ruled by Solomon's line. This will be the southern kingdom of Judah, which includes the capital, Jerusalem, and the temple.

Solomon's problems start to mount up. He has two particular enemies in Hadad and Rezon. Hadad is a survivor of one of Joab's massacres who now has the backing of the king of Egypt. Rezon is a rebel who seizes control of the area around Damascus in the northern part of the kingdom. But the greatest threat to Solomon's reign is much closer. His trusted servant Jeroboam turns traitor.

Jeroboam's ambition to be king is awakened by a prophet, Ahijah. Ahijah dramatically tears his own new cloak into twelve pieces. He predicts that the twelve tribes of Israel will be divided up – ten to Jeroboam and two to the descendants of David and Solomon. It seems that Jeroboam attempts a coup but then flees to Egypt. The king of Egypt, Shishak, is called Sheshonq I in other records. He rules from 945 to 924 BC.

Solomon dies in 932 BC, after a reign of forty years. He is succeeded by his son Rehoboam.

Solomon had asked God for wisdom, but his son takes the advice of hot-headed friends. The result is that Jeroboam wins the support of the northern tribes, while the southern kingdom shrinks to the tribes of Judah and Benjamin. Both stray from God's way. Rehoboam chooses oppression and Jeroboam chooses idolatry.

King Jeroboam worships idols
(1 Kings 12:25–33)

Jeroboam begins his reign in the north by making Shechem his capital. Shechem is in Ephraim, which is Jeroboam's home country. It has been a religious site since the days of the Canaanites, and a place of dedication and decision since the time of Abraham.

Jeroboam is insecure. He fears that his people will still be drawn to worship in Jerusalem, and then revert to a king of David's line. To avert this, he sets up a religion of his own, with idols, shrines and priests. He strengthens his control of his people by providing worship centres at Dan in the far north and at Bethel in the south. The shrine at Bethel blocks the way to Jerusalem. The whole state of Israel is idolatrous from the start (Amos 7:13).

Israel was under constant pressure to adopt the idolatrous practices of her neighbours. These clay figurines from the 9th to the 7th centuries BC represent the fertility goddess Asherah.

The kingdom is divided

After the reign of Solomon, the kingdom of Israel splits in two. Ten northern tribes, led by Jeroboam, become the nation of Israel. The remaining and largest tribe, Judah-with-Benjamin, is ruled by Solomon's son, Rehoboam.

Israel rebels against King Rehoboam
(1 Kings 12:1–24)

Solomon's reign has been harsh on many Israelites. They have become slaves to his building projects, which have taken them away from their families and land. Now the people ask Rehoboam for an easier life – but he refuses. The narrative sounds rather like the story of Exodus, with Rehoboam as Pharaoh and Jeroboam as a new Moses, calling for justice and liberation.

The idolatry continues
(1 Kings 13:1 – 14:31)

A 'man of God' arrives at Bethel from Judah. He condemns what Jeroboam is doing. He is a true prophet, and his message is confirmed by the withering of the king's hand and the splitting of the altar. However, he is distracted and misled by a rival prophet, and dies.

From now on, the work of the prophets becomes increasingly important. They take their stand and declare God's word; but they are only proved true if their message is fulfilled. There will be a constant rivalry between true and false prophets – with the added twist that God can even use false prophets to reveal his truth!

AHIJAH'S PROPHECY AGAINST JEROBOAM

When Jeroboam's son falls dangerously ill, he sends his wife to seek advice from the prophet Ahijah. The queen disguises herself in the hope of getting a favourable message, but the prophet knows who she is before she even enters his house. Ahijah delivers a message of judgment which foretells death for her son and disaster for her husband (14:1–20). Jeroboam has failed to be a king like David, and so his line will die out.

Kings of Judah and Israel
(1 Kings 15:1 – 16:34)

The writer now gives a parallel account of the northern and southern kingdoms. He briefly describes each king, giving his name, age, date of succession and length of rule.

The writer always notes whether a king does 'right' or 'evil' in the sight of God, and points out the consequences. David is the standard by which all other kings are judged – although even he failed to keep God's commands, when he committed adultery with Bathsheba (15:5).

The ten kings who do 'right' are all kings of Judah. They continue the line of David and enjoy longer reigns than the kings of Israel. Meanwhile, there are thirty-three kings of Israel who do 'evil'. They follow the idolatrous ways of Jeroboam and cause their people to do the same. There is little continuity of reign from father to son and several meet their deaths by rebellion or assassination.

KING ABIJAH OF JUDAH

Abijah (15:1–8) is the son of Rehoboam and his name means 'My Father is the Lord'. He takes after his father both in idolatry and war-mongering. He continues to promote pagan worship in Judah and also maintains the struggle against Jeroboam in their contest for the kingship of Israel. The royal line of David has fallen on hard times, but God keeps faith with Abijah, for the sake of the good things David did and to honour his promise to bless the heirs to David's throne.

KING ASA OF JUDAH

Abijah reigns a mere three years before he dies and is succeeded by Asa (15:9–24). Asa reigns for forty-one years, during which time he tries to purge pagan religions from Jerusalem and Judah. He even cuts down and burns his mother's (or, more likely, grandmother's) Asherah pole, which is a symbol for fertility rites. The historian describes Asa as 'true to the Lord all his days'.

Asa continues the war with Israel, which is now ruled by King Baasha. He bribes the king of Damascus to help him by invading Israel. This attack in the north takes pressure off Judah in the south, and the stronghold which Baasha has been building at Ramah is dismantled. Asa uses the materials of stone and timber to fortify two centres of his own at Geba and Mizpah.

King Omri turned the hilltop town of Samaria into his capital. These excavations are of his palace, or that of his successor, Ahab.

In his old age, Asa suffers from a disease in his feet. This may be gout, or even a sexual disease. 'Feet' can be a polite word for private parts!

Although Asa is recorded as being a good man, he makes a fatal alliance in his dealings with the Arameans of Damascus. It is this kind of reliance upon a foreign power rather than God which will at last result in defeat for both Israel and Judah.

KING NADAB OF ISRAEL

Nadab is the king of Israel while Asa is king of Judah (15:25–31). He is the son of Jeroboam and his rule is short and wicked. He is killed by Baasha during the siege of a Philistine stronghold. Baasha seizes the throne and eliminates all Nadab's relatives, thus putting an end to the descendants of Jeroboam. This is seen as a judgment on Jeroboam and the fulfilment of a prophecy by Ahijah of Shiloh (not to be confused with Ahijah the father of Baasha!).

KING BAASHA OF ISRAEL

After so violently seizing power, Baasha rules Israel for twenty-four years (15:32 – 16:7). Although he has overthrown the line of Jeroboam, he continues with the same damaging idolatry. In God's sight he is doubly guilty, because he has destroyed a royal line which God had set up. A prophet called Jehu declares that God's judgment will fall on Baasha and his family.

KING ELAH OF ISRAEL

Baasha is succeeded by his son Elah, whose reign is a mere two years (16:8–14). He is assassinated by one of his senior commanders, Zimri, while he is too drunk to defend himself.

KING ZIMRI OF ISRAEL

Zimri (16:15–20) himself takes the throne and makes his first act to kill off all Elah's male relatives and friends. There are to be no reprisals. Jehu's prophecy against Baasha's family has been fulfilled.

Zimri has only been king a week when the troops besieging Gibbethon hear of his rebellion and murder of Elah. They make their commander, Omri, king instead. Omri marches on Zimri's capital at Tirzah; but Zimri takes matters into his own hands and commits suicide by setting fire to his house with himself in it.

KING OMRI AND SAMARIA

King Omri of Israel (16:21–28) is a powerful figure whose name is mentioned on Assyrian inscriptions. He rules for twelve years, making the hill town of Samaria his capital, and so founding a country which has kept the same name ever since. Our writer says that 'Omri sinned more than all those before him' (16:25) and became the father of another wicked king, Ahab.

AHAB BECOMES KING OF ISRAEL

Ahab is a king like Jeroboam (16:29–34). He rules Israel from about 874 to 854 BC. In Samaria he builds a temple to the nature god Baal, whose name means 'Lord' or 'husband'. He also marries a pagan princess of legendary wickedness, called Jezebel.

The prophets Elijah and Elisha

Elijah and King Ahab

(1 Kings 17:1 – 2 Kings 2:18)

ELIJAH PROCLAIMS A DROUGHT

One of the greatest prophets in the Old Testament emerges to oppose Ahab. His name is Elijah.

Elijah steps forward to confront Ahab with the word and power of Israel's true God. He declares that the whole land will suffer drought – until Elijah himself gives the word for rain to fall again (17:1–6).

Elijah is challenging the widespread faith in Baal. Baal is the old Canaanite god of rain, whose dying brings drought and whose rising brings new life. Now the Lord, the God of Israel, will be shown to be the true God.

As the drought takes hold, God protects Elijah in hiding by the Kerith Ravine. There the prophet has a steady supply of water, and ravens bring him food.

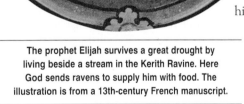

The prophet Elijah survives a great drought by living beside a stream in the Kerith Ravine. Here God sends ravens to supply him with food. The illustration is from a 13th-century French manuscript.

ELIJAH AND THE WIDOW AT ZAREPHATH

When the Kerith brook dries up, God guides Elijah to a widow who lives at Zarephath, which today is Sarafand, near Sidon (17:7–24).

Sidon is a Phoenician city on the coast – well away from the attentions of Ahab and Jezebel! The widow is foreign, pagan and living in Jezebel's own country; but Elijah has to depend on her for refuge.

When Elijah first meets the widow she is about to prepare a last meal for herself and her son. He tests her faith by asking her first to prepare some food for him. She does so. In the months that follow, her small supply of flour and oil never runs out. The writer tells us that this is to show that Elijah speaks for God and that his word is true.

Elijah is able to help the widow in an even more

wonderful way, when her son dies. The woman assumes that she is being punished for some secret sin, and reproaches the prophet for exposing her to God's justice. But Elijah stretches himself on the boy and calls on God to return his life. The child is restored, and his mother declares her faith that Elijah is God's true messenger. The miracle is an encouragement to Elijah, too. His is a lone voice in a hostile situation.

CONTEST AT CARMEL

After three years of drought, Elijah presents himself to Ahab again. The king has been sending out search parties for him, while Jezebel has been slaughtering all the prophets she can find. Elijah makes contact with Ahab through a royal servant, Obadiah. This man has remained faithful to God (and protected his prophets) during the dangerous days of Jezebel's persecution.

Elijah challenges Ahab to meet him on the summit of Mount Carmel. He is to bring with him the people of Israel and the prophets of Baal (18:1–46).

Mount Carmel is on the coast, overlooking the sea. Once there, Elijah urges God's people to stop wavering in their faith between God and Baal. There is only one true God, and they must make their choice.

To prove his point, Elijah invites the prophets of Baal to build an altar and prepare a sacrifice. When all is ready, they must call on Baal to light the fire.

The Baal prophets accept the challenge. They cry to their 'Lord' from dawn to dusk – capering round the altar and cutting themselves in frenzy. As they do so, Elijah teases them. Perhaps Baal's attention has wandered? He may be thinking of something else, or locked in the bathroom, or away on business? He's obviously not the kind of god who can handle too much at any one time. Better shout louder!

Then Elijah takes his turn. He repairs the altar of the Lord, which has fallen into disrepair. He uses twelve stones to remind the people that they are the twelve tribes of Israel. He avoids any cheating by digging a trench around the altar and drenching the wood and sacrifice with water – three times over. And then he prays.

God's fire doesn't just lick up from the heart of the wood – it falls from heaven! The people also fall – face down – to acknowledge the true God. Then they round up the Baal prophets and kill them. This is not cruel vengeance, but the punishment laid down for false prophets (Deuteronomy 13:1–5).

Now Elijah takes charge. He tells the king to have a meal, while he himself prays for rain. When a small cloud appears on the horizon, far out to sea, Elijah sends word that Ahab must take shelter. The king drives his chariot seventeen miles – to his summer palace in Jezreel. Elijah – on a spiritual 'high' – runs ahead of him all the way!

ELIJAH AT HOREB

Suddenly, after the triumph of Carmel, Elijah realizes he has Jezebel to reckon with. All his energy drains from him, and terror strikes his heart. He flees for his life – south to Beersheba, where he leaves his servant, and on into the desert (19:1–18).

Exhausted, Elijah sits down under a broom tree and begs to die. Instead, he sleeps; and when he wakes there is hot food and fresh water awaiting him. He eats and sleeps and eats again. Then he travels for forty days and nights – to Horeb, the mountain of God.

The number (forty) and the place (Sinai) show us that Elijah is following in the steps of Moses. Moses led the Israelites for forty years in this wilderness, and met with God at this mountain. Does Elijah spend the night in the same cave in which Moses hid his face while God passed by (Exodus 33:22–23)?

At last, God speaks: 'What are you doing here, Elijah?' (19:9). Is Elijah scared of Jezebel, even though he has so recently seen the far greater power of God? Is he consumed with self-pity, sunk in depression or breaking under stress? Elijah expresses all these conditions as he confesses that he feels persecuted and totally alone.

God invites his prophet to stand outside the cave. He demonstrates the titanic forces of nature in whirlwind, earthquake and fire. But God himself is not in any of these, which are merely his creations. And then there is a gentle whisper. Perhaps even silence.

Again, God asks the question. Again, Elijah pours out his complaint and fear. Then God, clearly and firmly, shows the way ahead. He directs Elijah to anoint two kings, Hazael and Jehu, and to appoint Elisha as his own successor.

Elijah is to take heart. God's purposes will continue to unfold and triumph. He is preparing a new generation of leaders to do his work – and 7,000 faithful Israelites (a perfect number) are praying that it will be accomplished.

THE CALL OF ELISHA

As far as we know, Elijah never anoints Hazael or Jehu. Perhaps it is enough that God has revealed them to

An age of miracles

The stories of Elijah and Elisha feature several miracles. The coming of drought and the feeding by ravens are the first of many ways in which God honours, protects and vindicates his prophets.

Miracles in the Bible are clustered around the key points of the story. They occur first at the exodus, when God rescues his people from Egypt and provides them with food and water in the desert. Now there is another season of miracles in the time of the prophets. God's people are again in deep trouble, with their faith almost extinguished by a sexually debauched and superstitious pagan culture.

Elijah as key people for the future. Instead, he journeys back to Judah and to Abel Meholah in the Jordan Valley – the home of Elisha (19:19–21).

The young Elisha is ploughing with oxen when Elijah claims his life by throwing his cloak around him. Elisha begs to say goodbye to his parents, but Elijah is offended by any delay. A backward-looking disciple is useless, as Jesus himself will say one day – and with a ploughing image to match (Luke 9:62).

In the event, Elisha *does* delay – but only long enough to chop up his plough for firewood and roast the oxen for a farewell feast.

The first two tasks which God gives to Elijah – the anointing of Hazael (2 Kings 8:15) and of Jehu (2 Kings 9) – are in fact performed by Elisha. Hazael is anointed to be king of Syria in place of Ben-Hadad. Jehu is anointed to be king in Israel in place of Jehoram (Ahab's son).

AHAB'S WARS

The writer now turns from the story of Elijah and Elisha, and narrates Ahab's military campaigns against Syria (20:1–34). The issue is whether Ahab will now trust God or not.

Ahab's capital, Samaria, is under attack from his northern neighbour, King Ben-Hadad of Aram (Syria). Ben-Hadad's forces are considerably stronger, and he makes oppressive demands on Ahab and the Israelites. However, Ahab takes the advice of a prophet and sends his young officers against the Arameans, ahead of the main Israelite force. The plan meets with unexpected success, as they defeat their enemy in the hills.

The following year, God again gives Ahab victory against huge odds – this time on a plain. Ben-Hadad is trapped in a city called Aphek and forced to beg Ahab for mercy. Ahab agrees, releasing his enemy and making a trading agreement with him.

Ahab, like Saul, has acted without consulting God and obeying him. Through one of his prophets, God tells Ahab that his own life is now forfeit for sparing Ben-Hadad.

It suits Ahab to make an alliance with Ben-Hadad. They need each other against the rising power of Assyria. Israel and the Arameans will join forces to fight Assyria in the battle of Qarqar in 853 BC – the year before Ahab's death. This battle is known from Assyrian records, although it is not mentioned in the Old Testament.

NABOTH'S VINEYARD

King Ahab makes Naboth an offer for his vineyard, which is next door to the summer palace in Jezreel. Naboth refuses. He has every right to do so, for this is his family's land for all time (21:1–29).

While Ahab sulks, his wife Jezebel gets to work. She sets up a neighbourhood feast, at which Naboth is accused of blasphemy and stoned to death. Ahab wastes no time in going to take possession of the vacant vineyard, but is confronted on the road by Elijah. Elijah is just as passionate for justice for Naboth as he was for God's reputation at Mount Carmel. He declares that Ahab and Jezebel will die for their sins and their dynasty will end. But Ahab repents and God spares him this immediate disaster.

MICAIAH PROPHESIES AGAINST AHAB

The king of Judah, Jehoshaphat, makes an alliance with Ahab, the king of Israel. They hope to recapture the city of Ramoth Gilead from Aram (the Syrians). Ramoth Gilead is important for trade, because it protects the caravan route to the east.

The kings agree to seek God's guidance by consulting the prophets (22:1–28). They summon 400 prophets – all of whom predict victory over Aram. But Ahab insists that they consult one last prophet, Micaiah, although he dislikes both the man and his messages.

At first Micaiah, with heavy sarcasm, repeats the assurance of victory. But when Ahab presses him for the truth, Micaiah declares that God has inspired the other prophets with a lie. The allies are heading for disaster and Ahab is being lured to his death.

Micaiah is thrown into prison for his insolence; but events prove him right. The episode is a warning. We cannot lightly discover God's will, without honest listening and wise judgment. Ahab asks for God's guidance and then refuses it. He goes to his death knowing full well that he is rejecting the prophet's message.

THE DEATH OF AHAB

King Ahab dies in the battle of Ramoth Gilead (22:29–40). In spite of disguising himself, he is mortally wounded by an arrow fired at random. When Ahab's blood is washed out of his chariot, the dogs lick it up – as Elijah had predicted. The writer closes the record of Ahab's reign by noting his various building projects and the style and wealth of his palace. Ahab is succeeded by his son Ahaziah, who reigns for only two years.

KING JEHOSHAPHAT

Jehoshaphat's reign in Judah runs parallel to Ahab's reign in Israel (22:41–50). As we know from his desire to seek God's guidance, he is one of the rare kings who tries to do what is right (22:7).

Jehoshaphat clears the country of male shrine-prostitutes, but neither he nor his father removes the 'high places'. These are the hill altars and platforms at which people worship pagan gods.

ELIJAH AND KING AHAZIAH

Ahaziah is the new king of Samaria (the northern kingdom of Israel) (2 Kings 1:1–8). He takes after his father, Ahab. He and the prophet Elijah quickly fall out.

When Ahaziah is severely injured, he seeks hope for recovery from a pagan idol, Baal-Zebub. Elijah meets the king's messengers on the way to the idol's shrine, and turns them back! Ahaziah should be asking for help from the God of Israel.

The king threatens Elijah by sending two companies of soldiers to arrest him; but the old prophet calls down fire from heaven to consume them. This fierce act of judgment reveals the true struggle between God's prophet and the new king. It is a trial of strength just as serious as the contest on Mount Carmel.

Only when God assures Elijah of his safety does he agree to appear before the king. There he repeats his sentence and the king dies.

ELIJAH IS TAKEN INTO HEAVEN

Elijah is one of the greatest of the Old Testament prophets. He does not die in the usual way, but is taken into heaven by a whirlwind (2 Kings 2:1–18).

On the day of Elijah's departure, he and his younger companion Elisha visit three groups of prophets. They go to Bethel, Jericho and Gilgal. In each place Elijah urges Elisha to stay – perhaps to make a new home there; but Elisha refuses.

Finally, Elijah strikes the River Jordan with his cloak. The waters part and the two prophets cross the dry river bed together.

In their final conversation, Elisha asks his master if he might inherit 'a double portion' of his spirit. He is asking Elijah to treat him as his eldest son. Elijah has no power to give God's gift to someone else; but he knows that if Elisha is able to see him pass into heaven, then the same spirit is being given to him.

Elijah is taken up to heaven in a fiery chariot. Elisha receives Elijah's cloak, confirming his inheritance of the prophetic ministry. From a 17th-century Russian icon.

Suddenly a fiery chariot and horses separate the two men, and Elijah is taken up to heaven in a whirlwind. Elisha is left alone – with the cloak which has fallen from Elijah's shoulders. The first sign that he has inherited Elijah's spirit is that he is able to part the River Jordan as his master had done.

Elijah's ascension is a great honour. It was said of Enoch that he 'walked with God; then he was no more, because God took him away' (Genesis 5:24). There is also a legend that Moses didn't die, because his body was never found. It is Moses and Elijah who appear to talk with Jesus at his transfiguration (Mark 9:4). They are with Jesus on that occasion because Moses stands for the Law and Elijah for the Prophets – the two great strands of teaching which lead to Christ.

The stories of Elisha

(2 Kings 2:19 – 8:15)

ELISHA'S MIRACLES

There are a number of miracles associated with Elisha – some of them quite different from other miracles in the Bible.

He helps a community in Jericho by curing their foul spring water with salt (2:19–22).

He curses young hooligans who insult him. They challenge him to ascend into heaven – and tease him for his baldness; but his curse results in them being mauled by bears (2:23–24)! This is not just a fit of temper on Elisha's part. The youngsters are attacking and mocking the authority of God in him.

He advises the kings of Israel and Judah how to trap rain from a flash flood, and so provide water for their armies (3:14–20).

He helps a prophet's widow pay off her debts by telling her to pour her small amount of oil into her neighbours' empty jars (4:1–7).

He promises a wealthy but childless woman of Shunem that she will have a son in a year's time – and she does (4:8–17).

Some years later, the child dies suddenly. The mother rides to Carmel to find Elisha. For immediate help, the prophet sends his servant Gehazi with his staff to lay on the boy's face. Then he follows, and stretches himself on the child and restores his life (4:18–37).

When a group of prophets fear their stew is poisoned, Elisha tells them how to make it safe (4:38–41).

He assures his servant that twenty loaves of barley bread and some ears of corn will be enough to feed 100 men. It is so – and there is some left over (4:42–44). This miracle is imitated and amplified by Jesus when he feeds a multitude. In John's Gospel they call Jesus 'the Prophet' because of it.

All these miracles demonstrate God's power to heal, help or judge. They are all linked with particular people or places as though they were valued and remembered by these communities for many years.

Some of Elisha's miracles (such as curing a water supply or using a staff for power) echo the great deeds of Moses. Others (like the supply of oil for the widow or raising a child to life) are similar to the works of Elijah. Most of all, they foreshadow some of the miracles of Jesus, who raises Jairus' daughter to life and feeds a large crowd of people from a few barley loaves.

Unlike Elisha, Jesus does not use curses and acts of revenge – except in his condemnation of the Pharisees for their hypocrisy, and the cursing of a fig tree for its lack of fruit. On both occasions he is expressing God's frustration with pretence. When Jesus' disciples want to call down fire from heaven on a Samaritan village, he rebukes them (Luke 9:54–55). While Jesus preaches that God will certainly judge people, his own miracles are acts of mercy. As the Bible record unfolds, people get an ever-clearer concept of what God is really like.

Naaman is healed of leprosy

Naaman (5:1–27) is the supreme commander of the army of Aram – that is, Syria. Syria is Israel's northern neighbour, with whom she has recently been at war. Naaman's fame rests on the fact that God granted him victory. His wife's serving girl is an Israelite who was captured in a raid across the border.

Naaman is his nation's strong man – and yet he is a leper. Leprosy is an incurable skin disease, which will certainly isolate him from other people, and may eventually kill him. But the Israelite serving girl advises her master to seek help from Elisha.

Naaman travels to Israel. He takes with him a large amount of silver and gold, together with valuable clothes or rolls of cloth. He also bears a letter addressed to the king of Israel, requesting a cure.

The king of Israel is dismayed and powerless, but Elisha offers help. When Naaman and his impressive company arrive at Elisha's house, the prophet merely sends out a message. The Syrian commander is to wash himself seven times in Israel's river! Naaman feels grossly insulted and starts for home in a rage, but his servants persuade him to do as the prophet says.

Naaman washes himself in the River Jordan and is healed. He tries to reward Elisha from his treasury of gifts, but the holy man refuses. This is God's work and he wants no payment. Naaman resolves to worship the God of Israel – and takes some local soil to make a place of prayer at home.

Elisha's servant Gehazi can't bear to see so much wealth on offer without taking any of it. He runs after

Naaman with a story that some silver and clothes are needed after all – and then lies to Elisha that he hasn't been anywhere.

Elisha confronts Gehazi with the truth. This is a serious abuse of God's grace as well as a breach of trust between them. He condemns Gehazi to contract Naaman's leprosy and dismisses him from his service. A mighty act of God has been spoilt by human sin. A similar greed corrupted Achan after Israel's conquest of Jericho (Joshua 7:20) – and he was just as severely punished.

Naaman is mentioned by Jesus when he preaches in Nazareth. Naaman's cure is an example of God responding to true faith, wherever he finds it, even if the person is an enemy, a foreigner and a leper. God has the right to bless and heal whoever he chooses, however much popular opinion may disapprove (Luke 4:27)!

More stories about Elisha

The writer gives us many more stories of Elisha's miraculous powers and perceptions.

He retrieves an iron axe-head from a river (6:1–7).

He keeps the king of Israel informed of his enemy's most secret plans (6:8–12).

He trusts absolutely in God's protection, whatever the odds (6:13–18).

He prays that enemy soldiers will be blinded, leads them into captivity and then advises that they be fed and sent home (6:18–23)!

He predicts the precise day when a siege of Samaria will be unexpectedly lifted (6:24 – 7:20).

He warns the Shunammite woman that a famine is coming, so that she and her family can move to safety. His influence enables her to have her land restored when she returns (8:1–6).

He foresees that Hazael, the king of Aram's trusted servant, will murder his master and become a cruel enemy of Israel (8:7–15).

The rulers of Judah and Israel

Our historian now returns to his account of the rulers of Israel and Judah. There is a strange coincidence in that both nations have kings called Jehoram, although the name of Israel's king is helpfully shortened to 'Joram'.

The writer gives us a history of Judah and Israel in parallel. He tells us the names and ages of kings, the years of their reigns and (in the case of the kings of Judah) the names of their mothers. As before, he is most concerned to record whether or not they do 'right' or 'evil' in the eyes of God.

Jehu, king of Israel

(2 Kings 9:1 – 10:36)

The first mention of Jehu is when God tells Elijah to anoint him as king of Israel (1 Kings 19:16). Elisha sends one of the young prophets to anoint Jehu when the reigning king, Joram, is wounded in battle. Jehu's task is to avenge God's prophets, whom Ahab and Jezebel have killed. Ahab has died, but his queen lives on, and it is their son Joram who is now on the throne of Israel.

Jehu rides with his fellow army officers to Jezreel, where Joram and Jezebel have a summer palace. Next to it is the vineyard for which Jezebel had Naboth murdered.

Jehu ('driving like a madman'!) meets Joram at the vineyard and kills him. He mortally wounds Joram's ally – Ahaziah, king of Judah. Then he rides on to Jezreel, where he calls on Jezebel's attendants to throw her from an upper window. They do so, and she is trampled to death by the horses' hoofs.

Later, when they come to bury Jezebel, they find that dogs have already devoured her corpse – just as Elijah had predicted (1 Kings 21:23).

JEHU'S PURGE

Jehu has killed Ahab's son Joram and widow Jezebel. Now he has seventy other sons of Ahab executed, to prevent any further challenge to the throne (10:1–36). He puts an end to the evil 'house of Omri' which has ruled Israel for three generations.

Jehu also slaughters forty-two relatives of Ahaziah, who is king of Judah and Jezebel's grandson. He summons all the prophets of Baal to their temple in Samaria, leads them in an act of sacrifice and then has them massacred. These bloodthirsty actions are condemned by Hosea. Jehu may be fulfilling prophecy but he incurs God's anger by the way he does it.

Jehu has completed a revolution in Israel and Judah. He has purged two royal families and wiped out Baal-worship. He becomes king himself and reigns for twenty-eight years. His dynasty will last for four generations. Sadly, the historian tells us that Jehu himself worships idols at the shrines of Bethel and Dan. Israel also loses territory to Hazael and the Arameans during his reign.

King Hazael of Aram

Hazael has a long and important reign in Aram (Syria), from 843 to 796 BC. He becomes king after suffocating Ben-Hadad II and makes Damascus his capital. He is a tormentor of Israel through three reigns – those of Joram, Jehu and Jehoahaz. He is at various times both a vassal of and a rebel against the mighty empire of Assyria. Assyria at this time is ruled by Shalmaneser III.

Queen Athaliah reigns in Judah
(2 Kings 11:1–21)

The historian takes up the story of the southern kingdom of Judah. Jehu has killed the king, Ahaziah, but his mother Athaliah now seizes power. She is Jezebel's daughter.

Queen Athaliah tries to destroy Judah's royal family, the line of David. Fortunately, one of her half-sisters resists her, and manages to save Ahaziah's infant son, Joash. He is kept hidden with his nurse in the temple for six years. It is by this slender link that the line of David survives.

King Joash repairs the temple
(2 Kings 12:1–21)

When Joash is seven years old, the priest Jehoiada proclaims him king. Athaliah is overthrown and killed. Joash begins a forty-year reign in which the covenant is renewed, Baal-worship is partly suppressed and the temple of Solomon is repaired.

Our historian judges that Joash does 'right' in the eyes of the Lord until Jehoiada dies, although the 'high places' are still left and used for pagan worship. At one point, Joash has to prevent the Aramean king Hazael marching on Jerusalem, by giving him many of the temple treasures. In the end, Joash is murdered by his own officials.

The death of Elisha
(2 Kings 13:1–25)

In Israel, Jehu's son becomes king. His name is Jehoahaz, and he is infected by the paganism of Jeroboam. He is under constant pressure from Hazael, the strong king of Aram, but he seeks God's help and is granted some respite. After a reign of seventeen years he is succeeded by his son Jehoash.

It is during Jehoash's reign that Elisha dies. He has been a prophet in Israel for sixty years and has seen the reigns of six kings. When the king visits Elisha on his deathbed, the old prophet promises him some success against the forces of Aram (Syria).

One last miracle is associated with Elisha after he is buried. His bones raise a dead man to life.

King Amaziah versus Jehoash
(2 Kings 14:1–22)

Soon after Jehoash becomes king in Israel, Amaziah becomes king in Judah. Amaziah is a good king – though not as good as David. He avenges his father's murder and leads a successful campaign against the Edomites in the desert to the south.

Flushed with success, and with Edomite gods to boost his confidence, Amaziah challenges Jehoash to hold talks. Jehoash refuses – likening himself to a great cedar and Amaziah to a little thistle. To assert his strength, Jehoash attacks Judah. He captures Amaziah, breaks down a section of Jerusalem's defences, ransacks the temple and royal palace, and takes hostages back to Samaria.

At some point in Amaziah's reign there is a rebellion against him. The details are unclear. It seems that his son Azariah is made either regent or king in about 790 BC, while his father is still alive. Azariah is also known as Uzziah, which may be his first name. Azariah may be a 'throne name' given him at his coronation.

Jeroboam II, king of Israel
(2 Kings 14:23–29)

Jeroboam's long reign in Israel is mentioned only briefly. He rules for forty years, from 793 to 753 BC. He is the third generation of the line of Jehu and inherits the family's military prowess.

Israel's old enemy, Aram, is now much weaker, and the powerful Assyrians are busy fighting elsewhere. Jeroboam wins back land that has been lost in recent years, and restores Israel's boundaries as they were in the days of David and Solomon. The prophet Jonah (born a few miles north of Nazareth) predicts that God will give Jeroboam success.

Although Israel is strong and prosperous, the historian records that this is an evil reign. For him it is not power or wealth that counts, but faithfulness to God. The rich (especially the royal family) are living in luxury by crushing the poor. Idolatry is rife, with Baal-worship far more popular than the worship of the Lord, the God of Israel.

The prophet Amos is not mentioned here, but he travels north from Judah to preach in Israel at this time. He denounces the shallow faith and cruel injustice of Israelite society. This could have been a reign of peace and spiritual renewal. Instead, the northern kingdom continues on a course which will lead to its destruction.

Azariah, king of Judah
(2 Kings 15:1–7)

Azariah (Uzziah) comes to the throne as co-regent with his father, in about 790 BC. This arrangement continues for twenty-four years, until he becomes king in his own right, in about 767 BC.

Azariah is often called Uzziah and is the greatest king of Israel since David. He reigns for a total of fifty-two years, including his years as regent. Although our historian says that Azariah does 'right', he notes that he fails to demolish the 'high places' – the hilltop shrines used for pagan worship.

Azariah (Uzziah) suffers from leprosy – a highly contagious skin disease. He has to live in isolation for the last years of his life. His son Jotham becomes regent and takes over the day-to-day government of the kingdom.

We know more about Azariah from 2 Chronicles. He has a well-trained, well-equipped army, which he uses to defeat both Philistines and Arabs. He strengthens the defences of Jerusalem. He also builds watchtowers to warn of approaching enemies and digs wells in the desert to provide water for people, cattle and crops.

A bronze figure of a Baal-god dating from about 1400 to 1300 BC.

But Azariah grows proud. He tries to act as a priest by burning incense in the temple. It is for this that God punishes him with leprosy (2 Chronicles 26:6–23). Isaiah mentions the year that Azariah dies, using the name Uzziah, as though an era of strength and stability is coming to an end (Isaiah 6:1).

The final kings of Israel
(2 Kings 15:8–31)

The kings of Israel now follow one another in quick succession. There are six of them in twenty years, and all but one are assassinated.

The 'sins of Jeroboam I' still shape the nation's religion. Jeroboam had made two gold calf idols for worshipping the Baal-gods. He installed them in shrines in the north and south of Israel, to divert attention from the one true temple in Jerusalem. He also appointed his own order of priests.

Zechariah is assassinated by Shallum, bringing to an end the line of Jehu. Shallum reigns for only one month, before himself being assassinated by Menahem. Menahem is a tyrant who is capable of merciless cruelty.

The king of Assyria is Tiglath-Pileser III, whose personal name is Pul. From 743 BC he leads campaigns on the western borders of his empire. If paid enough, he will leave a people in peace.

Menahem of Israel reigns for a decade – clinging to power by paying tribute to Assyria. He passes on the cost to his people. Menahem manages to save both his life and his throne, and is the only king of this period to die of natural causes.

Menahem is succeeded by his son Pekahiah. He reigns for two years at the time Uzziah's reign is drawing to a close in Judah. Pekahiah is assassinated by Pekah, one of his leading generals, who then becomes king.

Our historian says that Pekah reigns for twenty years, but it is difficult to know how this is calculated. Some scholars think he reigned for only two years. Pekah resists Assyria's demands for tribute, and in the end refuses to pay. In reply, Assyria starts to invade Israel.

The first Assyrian campaign captures northern Galilee and Gilead (Trans-Jordan). The area becomes part of an Assyrian province ruled from Megiddo. Many leading Israelites are taken into exile in Assyria, so weakening the nation's power to recover.

Pekah is attacked and killed by Hoshea, who succeeds him as king. Tiglath-Pileser records how he puts Hoshea on the throne and makes him pay tribute in gold and silver.

The narrative of the fall of Israel continues at 17:1.

Meanwhile, in Judah...
(2 Kings 15:32 – 16:20)

In the southern kingdom of Judah, we read of two more kings – Jotham and his son Ahaz.

KING JOTHAM OF JUDAH

Jotham (15:32–38) is the son of the great Azariah (Uzziah) who has been regent and then king for a total of fifty-two years.

Jotham is twenty-five. He is regent for most of his reign – the twelve years during which his father is still alive, but suffering from leprosy. After Uzziah's death, Jotham is king in his own right for only four years.

The writer of Chronicles tells us that Jotham is a good king (2 Chronicles 27:2). He avoids the pride that made Uzziah try to act as a priest. He defeats the Ammonites and forces them to pay a large amount of tribute money. He defends Judah against an invasion of Syrians and Ephraimites (Aram and Israel) from the north. But he fails to demolish the 'high places' of pagan worship.

KING AHAZ OF JUDAH

Ahaz becomes king at the age of twenty (16:1–20). He plunges Judah into further acts of idolatry. He even burns his own sons as sacrifices.

The writer of Chronicles tells how God punishes Ahaz with defeat by both Aram and Israel. There is terrible loss of life, and thousands of his people are taken to be slaves. However, a prophet challenges Israel to be merciful. Many of the hostages are well treated and allowed to return home (2 Chronicles 28:5–15).

Ahaz asks the king of Assyria, Tiglath-Pileser, for help against Aram (Syria) and Israel. He pays him with treasures from the temple and palace. Tiglath-Pileser invades Judah's northern enemies, capturing Damascus and sending its people into exile. It is this event which is the context of the 'Immanuel' prophecy: that a young woman will give birth to a son as a sign of hope for the future (Isaiah 7:14).

Ahaz visits Damascus – perhaps to pay tribute to his Assyrian master. There he sees an altar which he greatly admires. He has a similar one made for the temple in Jerusalem – moving the old altar to the side of the new.

The new Assyrian altar is larger than the old bronze altar. It is used for offering sacrifices to the gods of Assyria, which seem to be at least as powerful as the God of Israel and Judah.

Ahaz makes many outrageous changes to the temple and its worship. He himself acts as a priest, offering every kind of sacrifice as Solomon once did. He also breaks up much of the bronze furniture to cash its wealth – either for his own treasury or to pay tribute to Assyria.

Judah's worship is now in chaos. Through all the years that the northern kingdom has had pagan shrines at Dan and Bethel, the southern kingdom has kept its temple for the exclusive worship of the living God. Now pagan practices are brought into the very heart of the Jerusalem temple. The God of Israel is worshipped alongside the gods of Assyria.

The fall of Israel, the northern kingdom

Hoshea, the last king of Israel

(2 Kings 17:1–6)

Hoshea reigns for nine years. He tries to escape from Assyrian rule by making an alliance with Egypt. This provokes a second Assyrian campaign against Israel.

Assyria, now ruled by Shalmaneser, overruns the northern kingdom and lays siege to its capital, Samaria. After three years, Samaria falls and the Israelites are taken away from their land into captivity.

So ends the history of the northern kingdom of Israel. Her people are in exile in Assyria. In time they will be dispersed among people of other races and religions – and be lost without trace.

The reason why

(2 Kings 17:7–23)

The writer explains that the fall of Israel is God's punishment for her sin.

Despite many warnings to turn back to God, the Israelites have been no different from the other nations. They have worshipped the fertility gods of their pagan neighbours. They have indulged in astrology, witchcraft and child sacrifice.

The Israelites have rejected the life of holiness to which God called them through his law and prophets. As the writer says: 'They followed worthless idols and themselves became worthless' (17:15).

With the tribes of the northern kingdom dispersed, there is now only the tribe of Judah left. Judah, the southern kingdom, must bear the name of God alone, and be his people among the nations.

The Samaritans

(2 Kings 17:24–41)

People from various races are brought into Samaria to replace the Israelites. At first there is some fear of the God of Israel, because they believe that he still has power in the land – and because they are attacked by lions! Gradually the new 'Samaritans' adopt a mixture of religions, worshipping their various national gods rather than the Lord.

In later centuries the Samaritans will worship the God of the Old Testament. Their sacred books will be the books of Moses – the first five books of our Bible. But their mixed race and incomplete religion will make the Jews regard them as enemies.

Jesus sees Samaritans differently. He travels through Samaria on his way between Galilee and Jerusalem. He has a famous talk with a Samaritan woman whom he meets by a well, and makes a 'good' Samaritan the surprise hero of a well-known parable (Luke 10:25–37).

Judah, the southern kingdom, until the fall of Jerusalem

The historian tells us of the last 100 years of the southern kingdom of Judah. Although his story will end in disaster, he begins with the reign of a great and good king, Hezekiah.

King Hezekiah of Judah
(2 Kings 18:1 – 20:21)

Hezekiah is twenty-five years old when he becomes king. The historian describes him as doing 'right' in the eyes of the Lord, as his ancestor David had done.

HEZEKIAH'S REFORMS

Hezekiah does what so many of Judah's kings have failed to do. He tackles paganism. He removes the 'high places' of Baal-worship from rural hilltops and the platforms in towns and villages. He smashes the sacred stones which are used for altars. He chops up the poles of the goddess Asherah, which are fertility symbols. He even destroys the bronze snake which Moses once made for healing in

The conquering Assyrians deported many of the Israelites and imported people from other parts of their empire. The resulting mixture of races became the Samaritans. Even today, they continue to worship the God of the Old Testament.

the wilderness (Numbers 21:9), because people regard it as magical.

THE ASSYRIAN THREAT

Great events now overtake the reign of good king Hezekiah. Assyria is on the march (18:5 – 19:8).

The king of Assyria, Sennacherib, invades and conquers Samaria (the northern kingdom of Israel). From there he continues to move south, besieging and capturing the population of Judah. His own account of the campaign survives, with his record of forty-six walled cities captured and 200,150 people taken prisoner.

Sennacherib threatens to besiege Jerusalem. Hezekiah desperately tries to pay him off with large amounts of silver and gold, national treasures from the temple and palace, and the gold linings of the temple doors. But it isn't enough.

The Assyrian king sends a delegation to the outskirts of Jerusalem. His field commander speaks to the people of Jerusalem in their own language, and calls on them to surrender. He promises them safety and a new life. If they refuse, they will be destroyed.

The big question is whether the Lord God of Israel has enough power to defend his people. So far the armies of Assyria have proved stronger than every foreign god. Even the northern kingdom has been defeated...

In grief and near-despair, King Hezekiah seeks advice from the prophet Isaiah. This is the first we hear of Isaiah in the history books of the Bible. We know from his prophecies (in the book of Isaiah) that he is against turning to Egypt for help against Assyria (Isaiah 30:1–7).

Isaiah urges a straightforward trust in God. He sends a message to his king that there is no need to be afraid. The Assyrians will suddenly withdraw!

Isaiah is right. The Assyrians lift their siege of Jerusalem. Our historian explains that they were afraid of being attacked by the king of Egypt. Sennacherib's own record says that he has already defeated the Egyptians at the battle of Eltekah (701 BC). It seems more likely that the Assyrians receive news of trouble at home and go to attend to it. However this deliverance comes about, we see God's action in its perfect timing and completeness.

HEZEKIAH'S PRAYER

King Hezekiah receives a threatening letter from the Assyrian king, Sennacherib. In it he says that Jerusalem's fate is sealed. Hezekiah needn't think that the God of Israel will be strong enough to save him.

Hezekiah spreads out the letter in the temple, in God's presence. He prays to God, who is the Lord of heaven and earth and king of all kingdoms. He begs him to help and deliver his people (19:9–19).

ISAIAH'S TAUNT SONG

God answers Hezekiah through his prophet Isaiah. Isaiah delivers a poem or chant which taunts Sennacherib for his pride (19:20–37).

Isaiah says that the Assyrian king has only been allowed such conquests as God permits. Now Sennacherib will be forced to withdraw from Judah. The land will recover from his invasion and the survivors will be able to harvest it once again in three years' time. Jerusalem is being protected for God's own sake, and for the sake of David, the faithful king who established it.

That night the Assyrian army suffers a disaster. Some kind of plague or dysentery sweeps through the camp. Our historian says that God does this – his angel killing 185,000 men. Sennacherib has no choice but to return to Nineveh. It is in Nineveh, some years later, that he is assassinated by his own sons.

The Assyrian threat to Jerusalem is terrifying. In 701 BC, the Assyrian king Sennacherib attacks the fortified cities of Judah, taking all except Jerusalem. This relief from his palace at Nineveh depicts archers and slingers engaged in the successful siege of Lachish, just 28 miles from King Hezekiah's capital.

The prophecies of Isaiah

Isaiah's early prophecies date from Jotham's reign. It is a time of pride and prosperity, but Isaiah sees disaster looming, because of Judah's resistance to God. He predicts a terrible destruction, but beyond it will come God's perfect reign. God will establish a new society, founded on the truth, justice and peace which he alone can give (Isaiah 2–5).

HEZEKIAH'S ILLNESS

Hezekiah is gravely ill – perhaps with a blood disease which has caused the eruption of a painful boil (20:1–11). Isaiah's verdict is that the king will die.

Hezekiah 'turns his face to the wall' and prepares to die. He asks God to remember the good deeds of his life, and weeps over his fate.

Suddenly God prompts Isaiah to return to the king. He promises him fifteen more years of life, and deliverance from the threat of Assyria. He also applies a poultice of figs to heal the boil. No doubt Isaiah has faith in the power of prayer – but medicine can do wonders, too!

As a sign that he will recover, the king is allowed to ask that the sun's shadow will move back ten steps on King Ahaz's stairway. Is this a miracle to show that God is giving Hezekiah extra time?

THE SHADOW OF BABYLON

Hezekiah receives a delegation from Babylon – the power which will dominate the region after Assyria declines (20:12–21). Hezekiah treats his visitors as potential allies and shows them all his treasures. Isaiah warns that one

The aqueduct of the Upper Pool

The aqueduct where the Assyrian commander calls on Jerusalem to surrender (2 Kings 18:17) is the same place that Isaiah had once met King Ahaz. He urged him on that occasion to trust God against the threats of Rezin and Pekah, the kings of Aram and Israel (Isaiah 7:3–4). The Upper Pool is probably the Gihon spring on the east side of Jerusalem. It waters the fields as the stream follows the conduit (aqueduct) to a lower pool.

day all this wealth will be carried off to Babylon, together with members of the royal family.

The historian closes his account of Hezekiah's reign. He mentions the tunnel which Hezekiah has built, to supply Jerusalem with water during a siege. Hezekiah's Tunnel was discovered in 1880, running from the Gihon spring to the Upper Pool near Ophel and the Lower Pool in Jerusalem.

Manasseh, king of Judah

(2 Kings 21:1–18)

Hezekiah, one of the best kings, is succeeded by his son Manasseh, who is one of the worst.

Manasseh has the longest reign of any king in Judah. As regent and king he rules for a total of fifty-five years. Assyria is strong and prosperous at this time, and there is peace for Judah because she is subject to Assyria.

Manasseh reverses the good work of Hezekiah. He brings back the worship of the Baal-gods. He rebuilds the 'high places' for pagan worship. He puts altars in the temple in honour of the stars. He encourages all kinds of occult practice, including witchcraft, communication with spirits and child sacrifice.

Manasseh's sins are as dreadful as anything that was done by the Canaanites in the past and for this reason Judah will be punished as they were. It is because of these sins that Judah is to suffer the same fate as Samaria (the northern kingdom of Israel) and the line of Ahab (Israel's most wicked king). She will be measured and judged by the same standard. Jerusalem will be wiped out and left upside down, like an empty dish, when she is sacked of people and property in 587 BC.

This is the only time that a king of Judah is compared to a king of Israel. Like Ahab, Manasseh slaughters innocent people, including God's prophets. There is a story among the Jews that Manasseh had Isaiah sawn in two (Hebrews 11:37).

Amon, king of Judah

(2 Kings 21:19–26)

Amon's evil reign lasts for only two years. He sets out to be as wicked as his father, but his rule is cut short when he is assassinated by his own officials.

The reforms of King Josiah

(2 Kings 22:1 – 23:30)

Josiah becomes king of Judah at the age of eight. He is the ideal king – ranking with his great-grandfather

Hezekiah as a fitting descendant of King David.

Assyria's power is fading, which leaves Josiah free to make religious reforms. He organizes some repair work on the temple. It is while this work is being carried out that the old Book of the Law is found.

THE BOOK OF THE LAW

We don't know what the Book of the Law contains. It seems likely to be at least a large part of the book of Deuteronomy (22:8–13).

Deuteronomy contains Moses' farewell speech to the Israelites, when they are about to enter the Promised Land of Canaan. It lists the blessings that will come with obeying God's law and the curses that will result when it is broken (Deuteronomy 28:1–68). The final curse is that Israel will be uprooted from her land and her people scattered as slaves in exile (Deuteronomy 28:63–64).

When King Josiah hears this he tears his clothes in dismay. Judah has fallen so far from God's standard and committed so many of the sins that are forbidden. A prophetess called Huldah confirms that God is going to punish Judah – but not in Josiah's time, because of his humility and repentance.

KING JOSIAH RENEWS THE COVENANT

Josiah calls everyone together. They meet in the temple – king, priests, prophets, leaders and ordinary folk.

Josiah reads aloud from the Book of the Covenant – the newly discovered Book of the Law. Then he leads his people in making a new commitment to God (23:1–3). This is a covenant – a marriage between God and his holy people Israel. He will always provide for them and protect them. They will always worship and obey him.

JOSIAH PURGES PAGANISM

Now Josiah clears Judah of every trace of pagan worship (23:4–25). He pulls down shrines and altars, dismisses priests and prostitutes, and destroys the paraphernalia of fertility rites and astrology.

The Asherah pole (the symbol of Astarte, Baal's goddess) is removed from the temple, burned to ashes, ground to dust and scattered on graves. The grisly altar of Topheth, where children have been sacrificed to Molech, is desecrated and destroyed. The valley of Topheth, called Ben Hinnom, becomes Jerusalem's ever-burning rubbish tip. It will be known as 'Gehenna', and used by Jesus as an image of hell.

Josiah goes north across the border to Samaria and Bethel. Here Jeroboam built one of two shrines for golden Baal-calves. This is where so much trouble began, with Jeroboam preventing his people from worshipping God in Jerusalem. The Bethel shrine is now demolished, burned and littered with dead men's bones.

When all is ready, Josiah summons his people to celebrate the Passover. This is the meal by which the Jews remember how God rescued them from Egypt in the time of Moses.

NEVERTHELESS…

Josiah's reforms have been thorough and complete. Nevertheless, God will still judge Judah for her sins. Her king, people, city and temple will soon be conquered and crushed (23:26–30).

The political balance of the region is shifting as the power of Assyria fades. Nineveh, the capital of the Assyrian empire, is defeated by the combined armies of the Medes and the Babylonians in 612 BC. This creates a power vacuum which will be quickly filled by Babylon.

Pharaoh Neco II, seeking some advantage for Egypt, marches north. He intends to join forces with Assyria against Babylon. Josiah also campaigns to the north to prevent any help getting through to Assyria. At Megiddo, Egypt and Judah engage in battle, and King Josiah is killed. Mount Megiddo gives its name to 'Armageddon' – a great battle between the powers of good and evil.

The fall of Judah
(2 Kings 23:31 – 25:30)

Now events rush to their terrible conclusion. In a mere twenty-two years Judah will have four kings and Jerusalem will suffer three invasions. God's judgment is breaking over his own people.

JEHOAHAZ AND JEHOIAKIM

Jehoahaz is a popular choice for king. His personal name is Shallum. His reign is evil and short. Pharaoh Neco takes him captive, demands tribute from Judah and makes Eliakim king instead. Eliakim is Jehoahaz's elder brother – they are both Josiah's sons. He is given a throne-name, Jehoiakim, and rules for eleven years.

JEHOIAKIM, KING OF JUDAH

Nebuchadnezzar invades Judah around the time he becomes king of Babylon in 605 BC. For three years Jehoiakim becomes a vassal of Nebuchadnezzar, but then he rebels. The writer of Chronicles tells us that

Nebuchadnezzar takes Jehoiakim captive to Babylon. Our historian merely says that Jehoiakim 'rested with his fathers'. Jeremiah predicts that he will have 'the burial of a donkey' – his body thrown out of Jerusalem and left to rot (Jeremiah 22:19).

Judah suffers invasion by a number of enemy raiders. The writer explains that this is God's punishment for her sins. When the prophets Jeremiah and Uriah predict this situation, Uriah is executed for his message. Jeremiah narrowly escapes the same fate (Jeremiah 26:20–24).

JEHOIACHIN, KING OF JUDAH

Jehoiachin is Jehoiakim's eighteen-year-old son. He reigns for only three months, during which Jerusalem is besieged by Nebuchadnezzar and the Babylonian army (24:8–17).

Our historian now starts to date history by the years of a foreign reign – the reign of Nebuchadnezzar. In the eighth year of his reign, Nebuchadnezzar captures and ransacks Jerusalem and starts to deport her leading citizens. A Babylonian tablet records the date as 15/16 March (2nd Adar) 597 BC. The Jewish exile has begun.

Nebuchadnezzar leaves only the poorest people in Judah, and appoints Jehoiachin's uncle to be their king. His name is Mattaniah, and he is given the throne-name Zedekiah.

ZEDEKIAH AND THE FALL OF JERUSALEM

Judah is now weakened by the loss of her leaders. She is also divided in her opinions and loyalties. Some people want to rely on Egypt to rescue them. Others (like Jeremiah) preach dependence on God alone. False prophets (like Hananiah) advise that the grip of Babylon will soon be broken (Jeremiah 28:10–11).

The prophet Jeremiah supports King Zedekiah and writes letters to the exiles in Babylon. Our historian sees Zedekiah as king of all the Jews and not just those left in Judah. But Zedekiah fails in several ways. He doesn't listen to Jeremiah. He actively seeks to join Egypt in rebellion against Babylon – so breaking a solemn vow he has made to Nebuchadnezzar. He allows idolatry to seep back into Judah's worship.

The siege of Jerusalem

On 15 January 588 BC, Nebuchadnezzar again lays siege to Jerusalem (25:1–12). He plans to starve the inhabitants into surrender, and does so over a period of nineteen months. At the end of this time Zedekiah and his army try to break out. They are defeated by the Babylonians on the plains of Jericho.

Zedekiah is forced to watch while his sons are killed. He is then blinded and taken to Babylon where he will die. The temple, palace and all Jerusalem's main buildings are destroyed by fire. The Babylonian soldiers break down the city walls. Everyone is deported, except for some very poor people who are left to work the fields and tend the vineyards.

The temple is ransacked

The writer describes how the temple bronze is broken up and carted away to Babylon (25:13–17). It is the dismantling of David and Solomon's dream. It is also the final evidence that God has withdrawn his presence and support from his people. The leading citizens are rounded up, taken to Riblah, and executed. Every source of resistance is snuffed out.

Gedaliah

Nebuchadnezzar appoints Gedaliah as governor of Judah (25:22–26). Gedaliah advises his people to settle down and cooperate with the Babylonians. His approach is gentle and wise, and agrees with the advice of Jeremiah to the exiles. But this is too tame for a small group of resistance fighters. They assassinate Gedaliah and his pro-Babylonian friends, and flee with the remaining survivors to Egypt.

JEHOIACHIN IS RELEASED

After thirty-seven years of exile, a new king comes to the throne of Babylon. He releases Jehoiachin from prison and gives him a place at the royal table (25:27–30).

So the history of the Kings ends on a note of hope. The Jews have no homeland, no city, no temple and no royal throne. But there is a descendant of David – alive and well, and living in Babylon.

1 AND 2 CHRONICLES

The books of Chronicles are the 'Family Bible' of the Jewish scriptures. They trace the whole story of Israel from Adam to the present day.

The Chronicles are written some time after the Jews return from exile in Babylon. They look back 500 years to the golden age of Israel's history: the reigns of the great kings, David and Solomon, and the building of the temple.

These are books which record family names, listing people by their tribes and roles. There is particular interest in the history of the royal tribes of Judah and Benjamin, and in the priestly tribe of Levi.

The person or group who wrote the Chronicles (sometimes called 'the Chronicler') wants to show how God has dealt with his people throughout their history. The great kings and the temple may be long gone, but God's promises and purpose for Israel still continue.

Outline

The family lines of Israel (1 Chronicles 1:1 – 9:44)

The reign of King David (1 Chronicles 10:1 – 29:30)

The reign of King Solomon (2 Chronicles 1:1 – 9:31)

The kings of Judah (2 Chronicles 10:1 – 36:23)

INTRODUCTION

The books of Chronicles are really one book. Together they tell the whole story of God's people, Israel, from earliest times to the years following the return from exile in Babylonia. Their story continues in the books of Ezra and Nehemiah.

The Chronicles were originally the last books in the Hebrew scriptures. They give the overall view of God's dealings with his people and inspire readers to continue the great adventure of faith.

Who wrote the Chronicles?

We don't know who wrote or edited the Chronicles. For convenience, the writer is called 'the Chronicler', and for a long time it was thought the writer might be Ezra.

Ezra would have been an expert in the long list of ancestors. He would also have understood the history of Israel in the light of God's purpose for his people. However, the story continues after the time of Ezra, and is obviously the work of another person or group as well.

The Chronicler shows that God is the true king of his people Israel. He blesses them when they are faithful to him and punishes them when they worship other gods.

When were the Chronicles written?

We don't know exactly when the Chronicles were written. The most likely time is around 430 BC – about 500 years after the reign of King David. The last episode

in the history is the decree of Cyrus, king of Persia, by which the Israelites can return from exile in Babylon to rebuild their temple in Jerusalem. This is in 537 BC.

The last people listed as descendants of King David are Elioenai and his sons. They are probably still alive as the Chronicles are written (1 Chronicles 3:24).

The message of the Chronicles

The high point of Israel's history is when they have a king who is faithful to God. This is the reign of David. After David comes Solomon, who is granted God's wisdom and builds the temple. Again, God is at the very centre of Israel's life.

The Chronicles begin with long lists of names. These names trace the family lines of the tribes of Israel from earliest times. Some of the tribes, such as Dan and Naphtali, are barely mentioned. However, the royal tribes of Judah and Benjamin and the priestly tribe of Levi are recorded in considerable detail.

The Chronicler then gives special attention to the reigns of David and his son Solomon. This is Israel's golden age when the kingdom is made secure, the capital city of Jerusalem is established and the temple is built and dedicated.

After Solomon's reign, the nation is divided. The Chronicler follows the history of the southern kingdom of Judah. He records the reigns of all the kings who are descended from David, until the fall of Jerusalem in 587 BC. He then deals very briefly with the years of exile in Babylon until the decree of King Cyrus that the people can return to their land.

Chronicles is a book of 'roots'. It is compiled and written for the Israelites who have returned from exile, to remind them who they are. It may seem that Israel is a poor, small, weak nation on the fringes of the Persian empire. However, the reality is that God is still their king and he has a continuing calling and mission for his people.

The message of the Chronicles is that God is with Israel, just as much as he was in the days of David and the ark of the covenant, or Solomon and the temple. The royal and priestly lines continue to the present day, and so does God's promise to bless his people if they are faithful to him.

Saul, David and Solomon

The Chronicles are written to inspire the people of Israel with the story of their past. God has been guiding,

A range of names

The books we call 'Chronicles' have had various names. The Septuagint version of the Old Testament divided the Chronicles into two parts and called them the 'Annals'. Roman Catholic versions of the Bible have called the Chronicles 'Paralipomena', meaning 'Things which were left out'. This is because the Chronicles provide extra information which is missing from the books of Kings.

blessing and judging them from the very beginning. Their greatest successes and most terrible failures can all be understood in the light of their obedience or disobedience to God's law and God's calling.

The first king, Saul, is a failure, because he is disobedient to God (1 Chronicles 10). David, who succeeds Saul, is Israel's greatest king. He brings the ark of God to Jerusalem, conquers Israel's enemies and prepares for the building of the temple. God is pleased with David and promises him that his royal line will continue for ever (1 Chronicles 17). There is no mention of David's failings, such as his adultery with Bathsheba, the wife of one of his soldiers.

David is succeeded by his son Solomon. The Chronicler presents Solomon as a magnificent king who reigns with all the wisdom and wealth that God gives him. It is he who builds and dedicates the temple as the focus of God's presence among his people. There is no mention of Solomon's failings – his many foreign wives, his experiments with idolatry or the lifestyle which causes many of his people to become slaves.

The kings of Judah

After Solomon's death, the nation of Israel divides, with a northern kingdom of Israel and a southern kingdom of Judah. The Chronicler blames the split on the rebellion of the northern tribes against the southern tribe of Judah, which is the royal house of David (2 Chronicles 13).

The Chronicler follows the history of Judah, measuring each king by the standard of David. He records a small amount of detail about each reign and especially notes whether the king is obedient to God or not. The worst king of all, at least according to the Chronicler, is Ahaz (2 Chronicles 28).

Although the Chronicler is telling the same history as the books of Kings, the writer has his own way of presenting the story. He is portraying people and events from God's point of view. His many extra items of information and insight are used to highlight the shape and meaning of events.

The Chronicler shows how God blesses those who obey him, but disobedience results in judgment and disaster. The Chronicler is using history to highlight spiritual truths. For example, Manasseh is one of the worst rulers in the books of Kings. In the Chronicles, however, he is taken captive to Babylon where he repents and turns to God. He then returns to Jerusalem to strengthen the city and purge it of foreign gods. This is a picture to inspire the exiles. If Manasseh can change, then so can they (2 Chronicles 33)!

The Chronicles end with the fall of Jerusalem, the city of David. The temple is completely destroyed by the armies of Babylon, and the people are carried away into exile. The royal line survives, but with the kings in captivity. The land of Judah is left to rest for seventy years, catching up on the sabbaths it has missed (2 Chronicles 36:17–21). God is merciful. The Chronicles close with the Persian king's decree that the Israelites can return to their land.

DISCOVERING 1 AND 2 CHRONICLES

The family lines of Israel

The Chronicler begins with lists of ancestors. He traces the ancient nation of Israel from Adam, the first man, all the way to the 5th century BC, when he himself is writing.

From Adam to the sons of Israel (Jacob)
(1 Chronicles 1:1 – 2:2)

Here are some famous names: Enoch who 'walked with God', Methuselah who lived for 969 years, Noah from the time of the flood. The family line continues from Noah through his son Shem, until it arrives eventually at another famous name – Abraham.

With Abraham we step from 'prehistory' into history. God calls Abraham to be the father of a nation through whom the whole world will be blessed.

Abraham's first son, Ishmael, is the ancestor of the Arab nations. His second son, Isaac, is the father of the twins, Esau and Jacob. Esau, the elder twin, is the ancestor of the nation of Edom. The younger twin is Jacob, whom the Chronicler calls Israel. Israel is the father of twelve sons. Their descendants become the twelve tribes which make up the nation of Israel.

The 'twelve' tribes
(1 Chronicles 2:3 – 9:44)

The Chronicler takes each of the tribes in turn. He gives the most attention to the royal tribe of Judah, while Naphtali has only one verse.

JUDAH

Judah is the most important of the tribes, because it produces the royal line of David. The Chronicler traces the family line from fathers to sons, and the branching off of families and clans (2:3 – 4:23). Some men have given their names to places (Bethlehem and Tekoa), while some places have become known for their trades or crafts.

The Chronicler occasionally brightens his lists of names with colourful comments. We meet Hezron who got married at sixty (2:21), Sheshan who enlisted his Egyptian servant as a son-in-law (2:34), and we learn how Jebez got his name (4:9). We also discover the names of David's nine lawful sons and his one daughter (3:5–9).

SIMEON

Among the descendants of Simeon (4:24–43), Shimei has sixteen sons. He is the exception, however, as the Simeonites are not very successful breeders. Until David's reign they live in towns and villages around the area of Beersheba, where they are outnumbered by the more successful tribe of Judah. More recently, they have won some land from the Amalekites, and are currently living on it.

REUBEN, GAD AND MANASSEH

The Chronicler explains why Reuben is not listed first among the tribes, although he is the eldest son of Jacob. Reuben lost his rights as the first-born son when he slept with his mother's maid, Bilhah (Genesis 35:22). The birthright passed instead to the sons of Joseph, who were called Ephraim and Manasseh. Manasseh exists as two 'half-tribes', on the east and west banks of the Jordan.

Three tribes live to the east of the River Jordan. They are the Reubenites, the Gadites and the eastern branch of Manasseh (5:1–26). It was Moses who decided their allocation of land (Joshua 13:8).

These tribes once enjoyed military strength and success. Centuries ago, they won a famous victory over the Hagrites. They cried to God for help in the battle, and he answered their prayers (5:20). More recently, however, they have worshipped pagan gods and been defeated and carried off by the Assyrians. This was God's punishment for their idolatry (5:25–26).

LEVI

The Chronicler has a special interest in the Levites, because they are the priestly tribe (6:1–81).

Levi has three sons. It is from the second son, Kohath, that Aaron, Moses and Miriam are descended (6:2–3). Aaron becomes the first high priest of Israel, and the father of the high-priestly line.

The Chronicler also traces the descendants of Levi's other sons, Gershom and Merari.

The Levites are musicians. King David appoints them to provide music for the worship of the tabernacle. The tabernacle is the tent of meeting which houses the ark of God in the years before the temple is built. Meanwhile, it is the descendants of Aaron who become the priests and offer sacrifices in the Most Holy Place.

When the land of Canaan is divided between the tribes, the Levites are not given any territory of their own. This is to show that God himself is their inheritance. Instead, they are given a number of towns and villages throughout the land. The Levites are to be holy – set apart as a spiritual sign and influence among all the other tribes.

ISSACHAR AND BENJAMIN

The tribe of Issachar was known as a fighting force in the days of King David. Benjamin, too, was a tribe which was proud of its military muscle. Now those days are gone. But God isn't weak or captive, and his purposes have not expired.

THE REMAINING TRIBES

The Chronicler traces the ancestors of the remaining tribes (7:13–40): Naphtali, the western branch of Manasseh, Ephraim and Asher. Dan and Zebulun are not mentioned, and the total number of 'twelve' tribes is in fact only eleven.

BENJAMIN

The Chronicler turns his attention again to the tribe of Benjamin (8:1–40). He provides a much longer list of ancestors, a list which has little in common with his previous one! The family lines can omit several generations; or a single name can represent an entire branch of the family tree. The Chronicler now brings us to Saul, who is the first king of Israel.

The Benjaminites have had their moment as a royal tribe, and their present descendants can take pride in their pedigree. There is some further detail of Saul's descendants at the end of chapter 9.

THE FAMILIES NOW RESETTLED IN JERUSALEM

The Chronicler explains that the people of Judah were captured by the Babylonians and taken into exile. This was God's punishment for their unfaithfulness. However, they have now returned (9:1–34).

Among the returnees are descendants of the main tribal groups. There are people from the tribes of Judah and Benjamin, which had formed the southern kingdom of Judah. There are also survivors of the tribes of Ephraim and Manasseh, which had broken off to form the northern kingdom of Israel. Now they are a united nation once again, as they return to inhabit Jerusalem.

The Chronicler lists the names of the priests and Levites, and outlines their duties. He records gatekeepers, keyholders, sanctuary attendants, spice-mixers, bread-bakers and music-makers. Some of the gatekeepers of the past were great people, responsible for the security and dignity of the temple precincts. Now their descendants are once again taking up these historic tasks.

The priests and Levites are a living link with the past. The holy work of the Levites was first planned by King David and the prophet Samuel. Now times have changed and the temple is different, but the worshipping heart of Israel is starting to beat again.

THE FAMILY LINE OF SAUL

The family line of Saul has been listed already (8:29–40), but is now repeated as the Chronicler prepares to narrate

---

How many tribes are there?

The calculation and listing of the twelve tribes has many variations in the Old Testament. Most lists of the tribes have eleven or twelve names, but they aren't always the names of the original sons of Jacob.

Jacob's (Israel's) twelve sons give their names to the tribes in theory. There is in fact no tribe named after Joseph. Instead,

there are two tribes named after Joseph's sons, Ephraim and Manasseh. This gives the possibility of thirteen tribal names.

When the tribes settle in Canaan, the Levites have no land of their own. This reduces the number of tribal territories to twelve. Of these, Simeon seems to get absorbed into Judah, and Dan and Zebulun have also disappeared by the time of the Chronicler's list. However, Manasseh is divided into two half-tribes, and its territories count for two.

The 'twelve tribes of Israel' is perhaps an ideal picture of completeness rather than a factual description.

Saul's death (9:35–44). It is strange to see 'baal' appearing as part of an Israelite name. Baal means 'lord' and is used by the Canaanites for their pagan gods. The Jewish scribes who dislike writing 'baal' replace it with 'bosheth', which means 'shame'. So Saul's son Esh-baal becomes 'Ishbosheth'. Jonathan's son Merib-baal is 'Mephibosheth', who was disabled as a child and befriended by David in later life (2 Samuel 9).

The reign of King David

The Chronicler begins his presentation of the reign of King David. He uses much of the material we already have in the books of Samuel and Kings. He also has other stories and documents to hand. However, he is not setting out to tell again a story that his readers already know.

The Chronicler's interest is in the lasting importance of kingship and priesthood. Human kings represent God's authority over people. Human priests represent the people's worship of God. One day these imperfect examples of kings and priests will find their perfect expression in Jesus Christ. He is the king of kings and the great high priest.

The death of Saul
(1 Chronicles 10:1–14)

The Chronicler tells us that King Saul dies because 'the Lord put him to death' (10:14). Saul has become completely out of touch with God. He is unfaithful to the Lord, he does not obey the Lord's word and he has even called on an occult medium for guidance.

This is how our writer is going to handle this history. He will show us how God rules. It is God who puts Saul to death. It is God who gives the kingdom to David.

David becomes king
(1 Chronicles 11:1 – 12:40)

David becomes king because God has appointed him and because the people want him. David has shown himself to be at one with the people, fighting for them against their enemies.

David wastes no time in capturing Jebus – the last stronghold in Canaan to resist the Israelites. Jebus becomes Jerusalem, the city of David. The 'Mount Zion' on which Jerusalem is built will become an earthly image of the eternal city of God.

David is an outstanding leader. He draws warriors to him, inviting their loyalties, enlisting their skills and releasing their strengths. They will give their lives for him.

Three of David's finest champions break through enemy lines at night to fetch him some water from the well at Bethlehem. But David is too moved to drink it. Instead, he pours it out as an offering to the Lord.

It is a mark of David's leadership style that so many of his warriors are remembered by name. He prizes their commitment and brave deeds. Now their descendants can read their names on the roll of honour, and reflect on their own potential for greatness.

David and the ark
(1 Chronicles 13:1 – 17:27)

David consults his people about bringing the ark of the covenant to Jerusalem. It will be an act of supreme importance, because it will unite the symbol of God's presence with the throne of David and his capital city. David is only willing to do this if the people want it.

The ark of the covenant, or the 'covenant box', has

The ark

The ark was made in the days of Moses. It was constructed of acacia wood, overlaid with gold, and with two golden cherubim standing at each end. Its solid gold cover is God's throne, the 'mercy seat', where forgiveness or 'atonement' is granted for sins. Inside the ark are the stone tablets on which are engraved the Ten Commandments.

The ark symbolizes God's presence among his people. It was carried ahead of them on their wilderness journey and rested in the tent of meeting when they camped. It stood guard when they crossed the River Jordan, and led them into battle in the days of the judges.

been kept in the southern town of Kiriath Jearim for twenty years – ever since the Philistines captured it but found it too dangerous to keep (1 Samuel 4:17 – 7:2). From Kiriath Jearim to Jerusalem is a journey of eight or nine miles.

The ark is brought to Jerusalem, but not without a shocking accident. One of the attendants, Uzzah, tries to steady the ark on its ox cart, and is struck dead. The Chronicler is showing us that the holiness of God is not to be treated casually. The ark is left to rest in the house of Obed-Edom for three months, where it brings great blessing to his family. Obed-Edom is a Levite. When the ark is finally transported to Jerusalem, only the Levites are allowed to handle the precious cargo.

The ark is brought into Jerusalem with music and dancing. The Chronicler describes David as dressed in a linen ephod like a priest, dancing and celebrating with the rest. He also notes that David's wife despises him. She is Saul's daughter and expects her king to behave with more dignity.

David has the ark installed in the tent that he has prepared. He takes great care to make appropriate sacrifices and offerings, and to appoint suitable attendants and musicians. This is the kind of attention to detail which David will one day give to the planning of the temple and its worship.

David praises the God who keeps his covenant promises. His song is a combination of the Psalms we know as 96, 105 and 106:

> *Give thanks to the Lord, for he is good;*
> *his love endures for ever (16:34).*

Meanwhile, the original tabernacle, or tent of meeting, is at 'the high place in Gibeon'. There is an altar there, and Zadok the priest is in attendance to offer sacrifices.

The ark and the tabernacle do not need to be in the same place. There is a growing understanding that God can be worshipped anywhere, with or without an ark or tabernacle. This is an important insight for the Israelites who are living after the exile, because they have lost both.

David begins to ponder an irony. He is living in a

Bethlehem – birthplace of King David and his descendant Jesus.

175

palace, while the ark of the Lord is housed in a tent. He talks it over with the prophet Nathan.

That night, God speaks to Nathan with a message for David. He says that he has no need for a permanent house. The tent of meeting perfectly expresses his desire to be with his people wherever they are. But God himself will build an enduring house for David – a kingdom and a line of successors that will never end. As for a physical house or temple, the son who succeeds David will build it.

David is deeply moved by Nathan's message. He goes into the tent where the ark is and prays. He wonders at the uniqueness of such a God, who loves and saves a people like Israel. He asks God to fulfil his promise: that the royal house of David will be established and honour the Lord for ever.

David's victories
(1 Chronicles 18:1 – 20:8)

God gives David victories over all his enemies. The Philistines are conquered and Gath is captured. Gath was the home of the giant Goliath. The Moabites are defeated and made to pay tribute. The Aramaean (Syrian) peoples of Zobah, Damascus, Maacah and Mesopotamia are soundly beaten.

The Chronicler repeats that it is God who gives David these victories. In return, David devotes all his captured treasure and tribute to the Lord.

This is very different from Saul's approach to his plunder from the Amalekites (1 Samuel 15:19). The superb haul of bronze that David takes from Tebah and Cun will be used to make the famous bronze 'sea' for ablutions in Solomon's temple.

Preparing to build the temple
(1 Chronicles 21:1 – 22:19)

Satan comes in the wake of David's victories. This is a rather different explanation to the account in the book of Kings. Perhaps the idea is to lessen the blame on David.

Satan tempts David to take a census of his armed forces, to see just how strong he is. Joab, the army commander, knows this is foolish. Israel's triumphs are not because her armies are numerous, but because God is on her side.

God is angry. Through his prophet Gad, he offers David a choice of punishment – famine, defeat in battle or plague. Because plague is 'the sword of the Lord',

David chooses to endure God's wrath and hopes also for his mercy.

The plague takes a tremendous toll of life, but the Lord calls the angel of death to halt before it ravages Jerusalem. The point at which the plague stops is the threshing-floor of Araunah. Here, where judgment and mercy meet, David offers a sacrifice.

This story is puzzling. Why should God give David a choice of punishment? Is the Chronicler himself making 'faith' connections between a series of dramatic events?

The threshing-floor of Araunah has been used by the Jebusites for centuries. It is on Mount Moriah, at the northern end of Jerusalem, where Abraham once prepared to sacrifice Isaac. In 1,000 years' time the same place will be Golgotha, where Jesus will offer up his life for the sins of the world. But for now, this is to be the site of the new temple. Although the owner is a Jebusite whom David has defeated, he insists on paying fifteen pounds of gold for the land – the full price.

Soon David is busy with the preparations for a magnificent building. He is not allowed to build the temple himself, because he has been a warrior and has shed blood. This will be a task for his son Solomon, who is a man of peace.

Before he dies, David assembles the materials and workforce that are needed for the huge task. He gives Solomon a careful briefing. The key to success is to obey the law of the Lord, and to proceed boldly in faith. He assures Solomon that God will secure Israel's peace while the work is going on. He also commands all the leaders of Israel to support his son. All is to be done in, and for, the name of the Lord.

The special role of the Levites
(1 Chronicles 23:1 – 26:32)

David introduces Solomon to the work of kingship. For the last period of David's life, their reigns will overlap.

The Chronicler outlines the part the Levites are to play in the building and administration of the temple. David decides that they will have four main functions: supervisors of the building work, gatekeepers, musicians, and 'officials and judges'.

The numbers of Levites are huge, but so is the task. The Levites are to provide all the practical support needed for the smooth running of the temple and the sacred work of the priests. They themselves are to be active worshippers, joining in the morning and evening prayers, as well as the other occasions when sacrifices are offered.

David organizes rotas of duties which will still be used 1,000 years later. Zechariah will be taking his turn in his division's tour of duty when the angel appears to announce the birth of John the Baptist (Luke 1:8).

All the duties of the temple are outlined with great care. The purpose is that the worship will be well-ordered and deeply honouring to God. In case there is too little room for God's Spirit to move, there are singers whose ministry is to prophesy (25:1–3).

The long lists of names, and the fascinating personal details, convey the involvement of real people in this great work. No doubt the apostle Peter had this picture in his mind when he wrote to the early Christians:

You also, like living stones, are being built into a spiritual house to be a holy priesthood, offering spiritual sacrifices acceptable to God through Jesus Christ (1 Peter 2:5).

The day will come when the temple is no more. But God's people have never relied on a temple or any other building to enable them to worship God (John 4:23).

The leading Israelites
(1 Chronicles 27:1–34)

The Chronicler lists the twelve army divisions which each serve for one month of the year. Their commanders are named and come from a number of different tribes. We recognize Behaiah, one of David's Thirty 'mighty warriors', and Asahel, the brother of Joab.

The idea of serving for a month in the year enables the men to continue to live with their families and attend to their farms or businesses. It also reduces the size of any standing army, which can be both expensive and a source of rebellion.

The officers responsible for each tribe are listed. There are thirteen tribes by this count, with Aaron, Ephraim, and both half-tribes of Manasseh included, but Gad and Asher left out. Dan makes a reappearance, having been omitted from a previous list.

There is a move to count the people, but this provokes God's anger. Joab has advised David against this before, and was proved right (21:3). Now it is Joab who starts to number those under twenty years old, but stops in the face of God's wrath. It is the Lord's protection, not the number of warriors, that guards Israel.

The Chronicler lists the individuals who are in charge of David's property. There are twelve of them (of course!) and they have oversight of his farmlands, vineyards, animals, produce and provisions. Here is a well-ordered royal household.

Finally, we have the names of David's close circle of advisers. Including David, they form a group of six. When Ahithophel turns traitor and then hangs himself, he is replaced by Jehoiada (2 Samuel 17:23). Joab is an uncomfortable colleague who must be included because of his power. His influence is balanced by Hushai, who is there simply as David's friend.

David is a leader of genius, a shepherd of people. He is a master of team-building, organizational structure and delegation. He knows his people, trusts them and gets the best from them. Everyone knows where they belong in the life of the nation, what is expected of them and when. They know to whom they are responsible, who they are working with and why they are doing what they do.

The measure of David's success is that he is able to unite the tribes of Israel and enlist a large number of incomers and foreigners in his service. People of differing backgrounds, abilities and temperaments work together for the common good, and many an enemy becomes a friend. We will see these gifts at work again in the approach of Jesus to his disciples, and in the mission of the early church.

Solomon is made king
(1 Chronicles 28:1 – 29:30)

David summons a great assembly. He is old and nearing death. He does everything in his power to ensure a safe transfer of authority to his son Solomon.

David opens his heart to his people. He tells them how God has barred him from building a temple, because he has been a warrior and has shed blood. Nevertheless, God has chosen one of his sons to reign after him and to build the house of the Lord.

David commissions Solomon for the task ahead. He charges him to follow God's commands. This is the first principle of security and success, for himself, for his people and for the future. The Lord has chosen Solomon for a great work. Now the young man must respond with an open heart, strong determination and a humble dependence on God.

David hands the plans for the temple to Solomon. He explains that God's Spirit has inspired him with the vision of it, and guided him in every detail. He assures him that the same God will be with him, together with all the people, to see the work completed.

Now David turns to the people. He invites them to commit themselves to the building of the temple. This is not to be a grandiose project for the glory of an extravagant king. This is to be a fine and fitting place, provided by all the people for the praise of their God. In response to David's invitation, the nation's leaders give willingly, with generosity and joy.

David praises God. He acknowledges that all glory belongs to him and all gifts come from him. These same words are used around the world to this day, especially for the presentation of offerings to God:

All things come from you, and of your own have we given you (29:14).

The following day, in a great festival, Solomon is acknowledged and anointed as king. The Chronicler says this is Solomon's second anointing. There has already been a hasty ceremony, to confirm his right to the throne. This was to counter a claim from Adonijah, another of David's sons (1 Kings 1:39).

As Solomon starts to emerge as the most glorious of Israel's kings, David dies full of years and honour.

The Chronicler has spared us the mistakes, failures and gossip of David's reign. They are there for all to see in the books of Samuel and Kings, and were as well known in the Chronicler's day as they are in our own.

Instead, the Chronicler shows us the ideals and dignities of kingship. He reveals the ultimate reign and purposes of our only true king, which is God. He awakens in us a longing for that just and gentle rule, which will be Christ's at his coming. Jesus is 'Great David's greater Son'.

The reign of King Solomon

Solomon inherits the throne of Israel from his father David.

David's reign has been outstanding. He has won security for his people and given structure to their government. But David's rule involved him in many

Solomon offers sacrifices at Gibeon. This is where the tent of the meeting which had accompanied the people of Israel on their desert wanderings is pitched. Solomon expresses his concern to govern his people well, and God promises him a gift of exceptional wisdom.

battles and much bloodshed. Solomon's reign, by contrast, will be a time of peace.

The new king will be free from powerful enemies, so that he can build the temple which his father has planned. He will have room in his life for learning and reflection. He will become a living legend for both his wealth and his wisdom.

Nearly all that the Chronicler tells us about Solomon is already recorded in the books of Kings (1 Kings 1–11). However, as with his account of the reign of David, he does not relate Solomon's failures.

According to the books of Kings, Solomon was wise in his decisions but unwise in his affections. He not only married a huge number of foreign women, but also committed idolatry by worshipping their pagan gods.

The Chronicler knows about this – and he knows that we know. His concern, however, is to highlight the great and remarkable achievements of Solomon's reign. His purpose is to demonstrate the enduring and eternal rule of God, and to reveal his glory and wisdom to Israel.

By the time the Chronicler writes this book, the reigns of David and Solomon are in the distant past. But God's reign is always *now*, and his purpose is for ever waiting to be discovered.

Solomon's early years
(2 Chronicles 1:1–17)

Solomon makes a good and wholehearted beginning to his reign. He imposes his authority on his people, but he submits himself to God.

The young king goes to Gibeon, where the wilderness tabernacle, the tent of meeting, is kept. There, at the bronze altar, Solomon commits himself to God with a thousand burnt offerings.

That night God appears to Solomon and makes him an offer in return. He can ask for whatever he wants. It is typical of God to invite a specific request from someone who is wholly committed to his will (Mark 10:51; John 16:24). Solomon asks for wisdom and knowledge, so that he can govern God's people well.

It is a superb prayer – far better than the usual pleas for wealth, honour, long life or revenge. God not only grants Solomon's request for wisdom, but promises him wealth and honour as well.

David's victories now enable Solomon's prosperity. The new king has the respect and resources to trade with all the surrounding nations. Chariots and horses are the

As travellers approach Jerusalem, they are met with the awesome spectacle of Solomon's magnificent temple dominating the city. It is built on Mount Moriah, at a site bought for the purpose by his father, David. A thousand years earlier, it was the place where Abraham had been prepared to sacrifice his son – a place of sacrifice and redemption.

status symbols of the day, and Solomon has the very finest from Egypt.

Jerusalem grows wealthy at last, with silver and gold 'as common as stones'. Such an influx of wealth is a sign of God's blessing. The vision of the world's kings bringing tribute to Zion is one of the Bible's pictures of God's universal reign and Israel's superiority (Psalm 72:10; Revelation 21:24)!

The building of the temple
(2 Chronicles 2:1 – 5:1)

Solomon prepares for the building of a temple for God and a palace for himself. He writes to his father's old friend, Hiram king of Tyre.

Solomon asks Hiram to supply cedar wood from Lebanon for the new buildings. Hiram agrees. The trees will be logged and rafted by sea to Joppa, as they were in David's time for his royal palace. Joppa is the nearest port to Jerusalem.

Solomon also asks Hiram to send him a skilled worker. The Israelites have little skill in the arts of metalwork, embroidery and engraving. Hiram responds by sending Huram-Abi, a gifted craftsman whose mother was an Israelite from the northern tribe of Dan.

The temple is built on Mount Moriah. This was Araunah's threshing-floor, where God halted the plague which was about to devastate Jerusalem (1 Chronicles 21:15). David offered a sacrifice here, and bought the site for the temple.

As the building takes shape, Solomon attends to every detail.

A place for us

Mount Moriah was where Abraham once prepared to sacrifice Isaac (Genesis 22:9–14). In the future, it will be the hill to the north of the city where Jesus is crucified (John 19:17). Today the site is covered by the Dome of the Rock, one of Islam's holiest shrines.

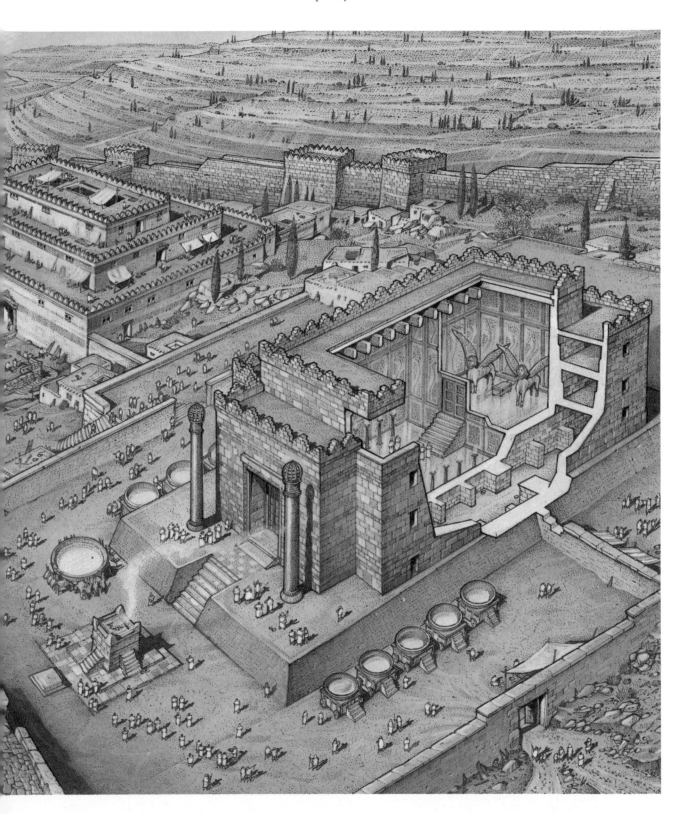

Fire from heaven

Moses and Aaron saw fire fall from heaven when they first set up the altar to God in the wilderness (Leviticus 9:24).

David had the same experience when he first offered sacrifices on the temple site, while it was still the threshing-floor of Araunah (1 Chronicles 21:26).

Elijah will have his prayer answered by fire when he challenges the pagan prophets of Baal on Mount Carmel (1 Kings 18:38).

Each occasion is a public event. 'All the people' see what God has done – and worship him.

The main hall is ninety feet long and thirty feet wide. It is panelled with pine and lined with gold. At one end is the Most Holy Place, thirty feet square, the same width as the rest of the temple.

Two carved cherubim, covered with gold, stand facing the worshippers. Side by side, with wing-tips touching, they span the temple from wall to wall. A curtain, beautifully worked in coloured thread on fine linen, screens off the Most Holy Place. It is in the Most Holy Place that the ark of God will be kept.

Outside, in the courtyard, two great pillars called Jakin and Boaz ('solid' and 'strong') stand north and south at the front of the temple.

Solomon has a huge altar for sacrifice and a vast basin for ablutions cast in bronze. The new altar is four times the size of the old one (which Solomon had used at Gibeon) and twice as high. The basin, called 'the sea', is shaped like a lily and measures fifteen feet across. It stands seven feet high, supported by twelve bronze bulls, and holds 14,500 gallons of water.

The master craftsman, Huram-Abi, works furnishings, decorations and implements in bronze. Solomon commissions some delicate items in gold – the small altar, the tables for the bread of the Presence, the lampstands and lamps, the bowls and dishes.

Finally, the doors of the temple, the hall and the Most Holy Place are all lined with gold. No detail is too small; no effort or expense too great. Nothing but the best is fit for God.

The temple is dedicated
(2 Chronicles 5:2 – 7:22)

When all is ready, Solomon summons the Israelites for a festival in Jerusalem. It is the month of the Day of Atonement and the Feast of Tabernacles.

The ark of the covenant is brought by the Levites from Zion (the part of Jerusalem called the city of David), to the temple. It is reverently installed in the Most Holy Place. This was always David's hope, that the ark which led the Israelites through the wilderness might finally come to rest in a permanent house for God.

As the priests withdraw from the Holy Place, the musicians burst into a mighty psalm of praise. One hundred and twenty priests sound their rams'-horn trumpets, and the temple is filled with the cloud of God's glory.

Solomon blesses the people. He praises God, who has chosen Israel to be his nation, David to be his king, Jerusalem to be his city and this temple to be his house.

This moment, with the cloud of glory filling the temple, sees God's promises fulfilled and David's and Solomon's dream come true. The ark of the covenant, the royal line of David, the city of Jerusalem and the house of God are all brought together for the first time.

On a bronze platform in the temple forecourt, Solomon kneels to pray. He thanks God for fulfilling his promises to David. He prays that David's line of kings will continue to reign in Israel.

Solomon brings to God the situations that may arise in the future – times of dispute, defeat, drought, disaster, pilgrimage, war or exile. He asks that in every kind of need, the temple will be a source of justice, mercy, healing and help; that God's 'eyes will be open and his ears attentive' to his people's prayers.

Solomon calls on God to answer him – to make his presence known. With that, fire falls from heaven and consumes the burnt offerings and sacrifices. The glory of the Lord – the cloud of his presence – fills the temple.

After two weeks of high festival, the people return to their homes. Soon afterwards, the Lord appears to Solomon again one night. He promises to hear and answer his people's prayers when they approach him in the temple. He also promises to sustain the royal line, the city and the temple, if Solomon will keep his laws. But if the Israelites turn to other gods they will be uprooted from their land and their temple will be destroyed.

The magnificent temple is built with the finest materials by the very best craftsmen. Animals are sacrificed every morning and evening, as well as on special occasions, using the altar in front of the building. The focus of the temple is the Most Holy Place, which contains the ark of the covenant – the symbol of God's presence among his people.

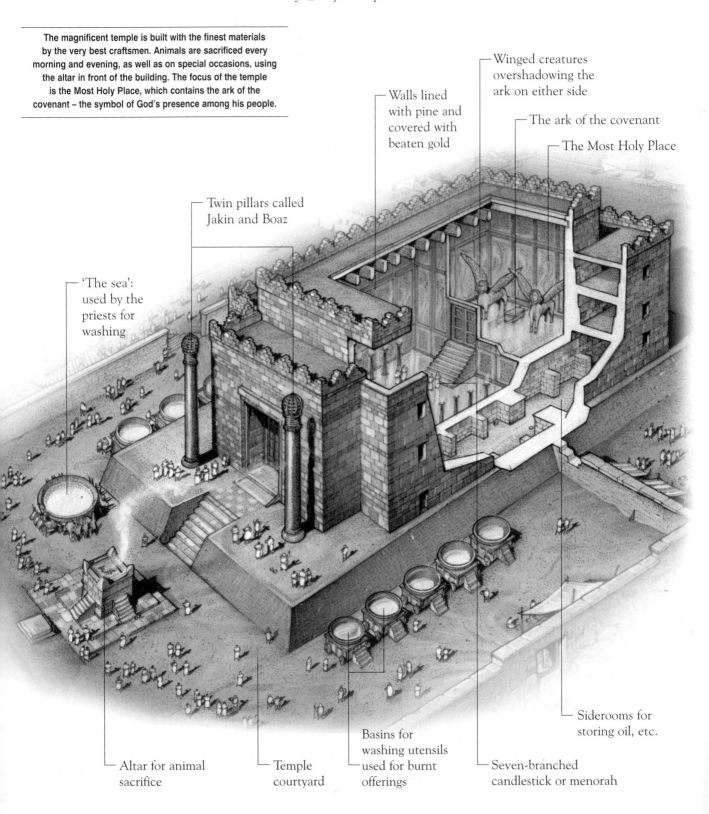

Winged creatures overshadowing the ark on either side

Walls lined with pine and covered with beaten gold

The ark of the covenant

The Most Holy Place

Twin pillars called Jakin and Boaz

'The sea': used by the priests for washing

Altar for animal sacrifice

Temple courtyard

Basins for washing utensils used for burnt offerings

Seven-branched candlestick or menorah

Siderooms for storing oil, etc.

Tearing up the kingdom

During the reign of Solomon, the prophet Ahijah had met Jeroboam on his way out of Jerusalem one day. The prophet dramatically tore his new cloak into twelve pieces. He gave Jeroboam ten of the pieces, as a sign that he would become king of the ten northern tribes.

Two pieces (Judah and Benjamin) would remain to form the kingdom of Judah under the rule of Solomon's son Rehoboam (1 Kings 11:29–39).

The kingdom is to be torn out of Solomon's hand because of his idolatry with pagan gods. However, this will not happen during his lifetime, because of God's promise to David that his kingdom will continue through the reign of his son.

Solomon's greatness

(2 Chronicles 8:1 – 9:31)

The Chronicler concludes his account of Solomon's reign. He makes no mention of the king's foreign wives or idolatries. Instead, he describes Solomon's building and restoration projects, his treatment of foreigners, his faithful worship and his successful sea trade.

When the queen of Sheba comes to visit Solomon, she is overwhelmed by his wealth, wisdom and lifestyle. Like Hiram of Tyre, she recognizes that God must love his people very much to give them such a king. Although Solomon's wealth is impressive, it is his wisdom which is truly remarkable. It is his wisdom which gives his people guidance and justice.

Solomon is now fabulously wealthy. The queen of Sheba brings gold, spices and precious stones. Traders bring gold and fine wood from legendary Ophir. The kings of Arabia bring gold and silver.

Solomon lines the hall of his palace with hundreds of solid gold shields. He furnishes his table with solid gold goblets. He has a throne made of ivory with a footstool of gold. His horses (of which he has thousands) are Egypt's finest. In the end, he has nothing made of silver, because silver has become too common.

Solomon dies after forty years on the throne of David. The Chronicler leaves us in no doubt that this was one of Israel's greatest kings.

Solomon's greatness was all from God. It was God's throne that Solomon occupied. It was God's wealth that Solomon accumulated. It was God's wisdom that he acquired.

Jesus in the Gospels describes himself as 'greater than Solomon' (Luke 11:31). He will give his followers a better wealth than Solomon's (Matthew 6:29) and gifts that are greater than gold (1 Corinthians 12:7–11). He is the wisdom of God, who leads his people into all truth (John 16:13).

The kings of Judah

After the reign of Solomon, the kingdom of Israel is torn apart. The nation divides to form the northern kingdom of Israel and the southern kingdom of Judah.

While the books of Kings give us a parallel history of both kingdoms, the Chronicler tells us only about the southern kingdom of Judah. It is Judah that has David's city (Jerusalem) for its capital, Solomon's temple for its holy place and the descendants of David for its kings.

King Rehoboam

(2 Chronicles 10:1 – 12:16)

King Solomon is succeeded by his son Rehoboam. Where Solomon began his reign by asking God for wisdom and understanding, Rehoboam is brash and ignores all good advice.

Solomon's reign has been hard for the common people. He has taken them from their homes to staff his luxurious palace. He has taken them from their farms and vineyards to work like slaves on his building projects. The elders now counsel Rehoboam to lighten his people's burdens.

But Rehoboam doesn't listen to the advice of the elders. Instead he takes the advice of friends his own age. They say he should increase his people's burden and sharpen their suffering; and this is what he decides to do.

But the people have a champion in Jeroboam. Jeroboam is a leader of the tribe of Ephraim. He was seen as a rival by Solomon and has been hiding in Egypt. Now he returns to challenge Rehoboam.

The prophet Ahijah has told Jeroboam that he will become king of ten of the tribes of Israel (1 Kings 11:26–40). Only the tribes of Judah and Benjamin will remain under the rule of Rehoboam and the descendants of David.

Which nation is 'Israel'?

In the books of Kings, the ten northern tribes are called 'Israel' after the kingdom divides. The two southern tribes are called 'Judah'.

In Chronicles, the name 'Israel' refers to the people of God wherever they are, and is used for both northern and southern kingdoms. Both are part of the true 'Israel', and both have a capacity to either obey or rebel against God.

The thirty-sixth year of Asa's reign

The Chronicler says Baasha, king of Israel, invades Judah 'in the thirty-sixth year of Asa's reign'. This clearly is a mistake as Baasha would have been dead some ten years by then. One possible explanation is that the thirty-sixth year is counted from the beginning of the divided kingdom. It is the thirty-sixth year of Judah's history and the sixteenth year of Asa's reign.

The books of Kings tell us that the division of the nation is God's punishment for Solomon's idolatry with his foreign wives. The Chronicler (who is kinder to Solomon's reputation) says that the split is in fulfilment of God's word through the prophet Ahijah (10:15). The Chronicler explains the division in terms of Jeroboam's rebellion against Rehoboam's headstrong, bullying policies.

At first, Rehoboam gathers his forces to attempt to conquer the northern tribes and unite the kingdom again. However, one of the prophets, Shemaiah, persuades him against this. He explains that the division of the kingdom has been God's doing and is to be accepted.

Rehoboam then strengthens his little kingdom, by fortifying the towns along its southern border. The main threat is from Egypt, whose pharaoh Shishak is likely to prove a friend and ally to Jeroboam.

Priests and Levites come from the northern kingdom to join Rehoboam in Jerusalem. They are offended by Jeroboam, who is setting up his own religion around goat and calf idols. Jeroboam's plan is to combine the worship of the Lord with the idols of Canaan. In this way he hopes to stop the people of the northern kingdom looking to the Jerusalem temple as the centre of their religion.

Rehoboam is well connected to David's line, both through his father Solomon and by his marriages. His favourite wife is Maacah, who is a granddaughter of David's popular but treacherous son Absalom.

Rehoboam is wiser than David in the way he treats his sons. He provides for them so that they aren't resentful, gives them responsibilities so that they aren't restless, and uses their marriages to forge alliances which strengthen the kingdom.

Despite a good start, the southern kingdom slips into idolatry. The Chronicler says that Rehoboam and 'all Israel' (by which he means Judah, which is supposed to be the true people of God) now abandons the law of the Lord (12:1).

God punishes Judah's unfaithfulness with a costly invasion by Shishak of Egypt. Treasures are taken from both the temple and the palace – including the famous gold shields which had lined Solomon's royal hall.

Shishak's own account of his invasion is recorded on the outside wall of the temple of Karnak. The Chronicler tells us that Jerusalem is spared worse punishment, because Rehoboam and the other leaders repent of their idolatry.

The prophet Shemaiah explains that Judah is being abandoned because she has first abandoned God. The Chronicler often shows how God's judgment of a person or people reflects very precisely their own behaviour.

The Chronicler's verdict on Rehoboam is that there is some good in his seventeen-year reign. However, he fails to seek the Lord wholeheartedly. The fatal flaw which is apparent at the very beginning continues to spoil his government.

King Abijah
(2 Chronicles 13:1–22)

Rehoboam is succeeded by Abijah, who is his favourite son by his favourite wife.

Abijah makes a determined attempt to conquer the northern tribes and reunite the kingdom. Drawing up in battle array against Jeroboam, Abijah makes an important speech. He sets out the differences between the northern and southern kingdoms, and claims that God is on the side of Judah.

It is Judah whose king is descended from David. The royal line is guaranteed by God 'by a covenant of salt', an unbreakable promise. It is also Judah that has the true priests and the true worship. Her priests are descended from Aaron, and they have the Levites to assist them. In the temple in Jerusalem, the true God is being worshipped in the manner he has ordained. All this is additional to the record of the books of Kings, and shows the Chronicler's bias to the south. By contrast, Jeroboam has been appointing his own false priests for a false religion.

While Abijah declares a holy war against the north, and urges the men of Israel not to fight God, Jeroboam sends forces to ambush him from behind. Despite this, God enables the armies of Judah to defeat the Israelites and capture some of their towns.

King Asa
(2 Chronicles 14:1 – 16:14)

The Chronicler reports that Asa is a good king. He does what is 'good and right in the eyes of the Lord his God' (14:2).

Asa tackles the pagan worship that is taking place in Judah. He removes the altars of foreign gods and breaks up sacred stones. He even deposes his grandmother Maacah from being queen mother, because she has made an Asherah pole (a fertility symbol of the Canaanite mother goddess).

Asa strengthens Judah's defences, builds up his army and enjoys a period of peace. God then gives him victory against the superior forces of Zerah the Cushite, who invades Judah from Ethiopia. Before the battle, Asa prays, 'Help us, O Lord our God, for we rely on you, and in your name we have come against this vast army.' The prophet Azariah commends Asa for his trust in God: 'The Lord is with you when you are with him.'

Asa continues his purge of Judah's paganism, and repairs the bronze altar in front of the temple portico. When he summons an assembly, the numbers are swelled by people from the northern tribes who make their way to Judah because they hear of Asa's reforms. The whole gathering renews its covenant with the Lord in the Feast of Weeks.

Later in Asa's reign, his faith in God starts to falter. The king of Israel, Baasha, starts to blockade Judah. To counter this, Asa uses temple treasure to buy an alliance with Ben-Hadad, king of Aram (Syria).

The alliance is successful, with Ben-Hadad forcing Israel to withdraw from Judah. However, Asa is condemned by the prophet Hanani for turning to Syria for help instead of relying on God. Asa is in no mood to be

lectured, and puts Hanani in prison. This is the first occasion that the Bible records a prophet being punished.

In the years that follow, Asa's resistance to God continues. Even when he is stricken by a disease in his feet, he seeks the help of physicians (perhaps occult healers) rather than healing from the Lord.

Despite his faults, both the Chronicler and the people of Judah regard Asa as a great king. When he dies, after forty-one years on the throne, Asa is given a funeral of special honour, with a huge fire of burning spices.

King Jehoshaphat
(2 Chronicles 17:1 – 20:37)

Asa's son, Jehoshaphat, is a fine king. He strengthens his fortifications against the northern kingdom, removes the 'high places' of pagan worship and commissions priests and Levites to teach the law of Moses in the towns of Judah.

From the beginning, Jehoshaphat takes David as his example. The Chronicler records that his heart is 'devoted to the ways of the Lord'. Because Jehoshaphat fears the Lord, the fear of the Lord falls on the surrounding nations. The Philistines bring him tribute; the Arabs bring him flocks. His power and wealth – and the organization of his army – are reminders of the great days of Israel's history.

But Jehoshaphat makes a mistake. He involves himself with Ahab, king of Israel. Perhaps he feels that the time is ripe for the two kingdoms to work together again. At first he makes a marriage alliance with Ahab. Some years later he agrees to join him in a military venture – a campaign to recapture Ramoth Gilead from Aram (Syria).

As they discuss their alliance, Jehoshaphat urges Ahab to seek God's counsel. Ahab summons 400 prophets. All of them tell him what he wants to hear: that God will give him victory. Jehoshaphat still has doubts, and asks if there is a more authentic prophet to consult. Ahab admits that Micaiah speaks from the Lord, although he has never enjoyed a favourable prophecy from him.

When Micaiah arrives, he mimics the mindless advice of the other prophets. One of them, Zedekiah, has been capering around with a pair of iron horns, as a sign that the Syrians will be gored to death. But, when pressed, Micaiah predicts that the armies of Israel will be defeated and scattered. The prophets who predict victory are being deceived by God himself, to lure Ahab to his death.

Ahab decides to ignore Micaiah's prophecy, and has him thrown into prison until they return. However, Ahab is alarmed enough to propose that he should go into battle in disguise, and that only Jehoshaphat should be seen wearing royal robes.

When the battle begins, the Arameans prepare to attack Jehoshaphat, because he is the only visible king. He cries out to God for help, and the Arameans realize he is not Ahab. However, an arrow fired at random finds a chink in Ahab's armour, and gives him a fatal wound. He dies in his chariot at sunset. When Jehoshaphat returns to Judah, he is rebuked by the prophet Jehu for his unholy alliance with the king of Israel.

Back in Jerusalem, Jehoshaphat continues to put in place good structures of government. He appoints judges in each of the fortified cities, giving them a careful and solemn briefing that they are to do the Lord's work. In Jerusalem, he appoints priests and senior people to administer the law of Moses. He warns them that the Lord will punish them if they don't tell people not to sin.

A severe military threat now arises. Moabites, Ammonites and Meunites (from Edom) are advancing on Judah. Jehoshaphat calls all the people to fast, and to come together to seek God's help.

Standing in the great assembly, Jehoshaphat leads his nation in prayer. This is one of the great prayers of the Chronicles, second only to Solomon's prayer when he dedicates the temple.

Jehoshaphat praises God as the only God, the God of their ancestors and the ruler of all nations. He recalls how God conquered their enemies in the past, and promised the land to the descendants of Abraham for ever. God also promised that the temple in which they now stand would be the place where he would hear and help in times of need. Now, in this crisis, Jehoshaphat acknowledges their helplessness and appeals to God to save them.

The Lord's answer comes through Jahaziel, who is one of the Levites. He tells Jehoshaphat and all the people not to be afraid. The battle is the Lord's. Jahaziel describes where the army is to take its stand the following day, but assures them they will not have to fight. In the morning, they march out with the praises of God on their lips.

While the people of Judah praise God, their enemies are overtaken by ambushes and infighting. By the time Jehoshaphat and his army arrive at their vantage point, there is nothing to be seen of their enemies but dead bodies. It takes them three days to collect the plunder.

Jehoshaphat reigns for twenty-five years, and the Chronicler rates him as a fine king. His only fault (apart from getting too close to Ahab) has been that he fails to remove all the sites of pagan worship. They spring up as fast as they are suppressed. The attraction of fertility rites and the influence of superstition go too deep, unless the people themselves resolve to turn to the Lord.

King Jehoram
(2 Chronicles 21:1–20)

Jehoshaphat's heir is Jehoram. He begins his reign with an act of sheer brutality, by having his six brothers killed.

While his father had modelled his reign on David, Jehoram takes after his father-in-law, Ahab. Jehoshaphat's involvement with the wicked king of Israel, by making a marriage alliance, is now proving costly for the next generation – and it will prove costlier still.

Jehoram proceeds to lead the people of Judah into idolatry. God only spares him because of his promise to preserve the royal line of David. However, God sets about warning and judging the wayward king, beginning with a letter from the prophet Elijah.

Elijah has been a stern opponent of King Ahab in the northern kingdom, but this is the only occasion when the Chronicler mentions him in connection with the south. It is fitting that it is Elijah who condemns Jehoram for behaving like a king of Ahab's line rather than David's. Jehoram has led his people into religious prostitution – committing idolatry with the Baal-gods of Canaan.

Elijah's message to Jehoram is that God has seen all his wickedness. He is now to lose his family, as he has robbed others of theirs; and he will die a dreadful death.

The Chronicler tells how God stirs up the Philistines and the Arabs to attack Jehoram. They raid Judah, plunder Jehoram's palace, kill his sons and carry off his wives. The king who murdered his brothers is now bereaved of all his sons except one. When the rest of Elijah's prophecy is fulfilled and Jehoram dies of bowel disease, he is buried without any great ceremony or sign of mourning.

King Ahaziah
(2 Chronicles 22:1–9)

Jehoram's youngest and only surviving son is Ahaziah. He becomes king at the age of twenty-one and reigns for just one year.

His mother is Athaliah – a granddaughter of wicked king Omri, and daughter of Ahab and Jezebel. She runs true to her evil pedigree in every way, encouraging brutality and idolatry in her son's brief reign. When Ahaziah is put to death by Jehu, Athaliah has her grandsons slaughtered to secure the throne for herself. She may have some idea of uniting the monarchies – in favour of the north.

Athaliah and Joash
(2 Chronicles 22:10 – 23:15)

One of the royal princes escapes Athaliah's massacre. His name is Joash. He is only a baby when his aunt Jehosheba saves him, by hiding him in the temple, where her husband Jehoiada is a priest. Queen Athaliah rules Judah, unaware that a true heir of David is being raised in the temple nearby.

After six years, the priest Jehoiada becomes the king-maker. With careful secrecy, he makes covenant alliances with the army commanders and summons the Levites and heads of families to Jerusalem. Together, they pledge their loyalty to the young king who is hidden in the temple.

Jehoiada plans his coup with military and religious precision. The prince is to be presented to his people in the temple and crowned as their rightful king. The Levites perform their traditional duty as God's warriors, shielding David's heir with their weapons as they bring him for coronation. The priests bring him forth, like a long-kept secret or the anointing of the shepherd-boy David. They place the royal crown on his head, present him with a copy of the covenant and proclaim him king.

The first Athaliah knows of all this is a sound of cheering coming from the temple. Going to investigate, she is dumbfounded to see the seven-year-old King Joash standing in his place at the entrance. In fury, she tears her robes and cries, 'Treason!' but is powerless to alter events. As she leaves the temple precinct and reaches

The murderous Queen Athaliah usurps the throne, but Jehoiada the priest saves one of the royal princes, named Joash, and hides him in the temple. When Joash is seven years old, Jehoiada anoints him as king, and Athaliah is deposed. The anointing of Joash, from a 12th-century Spanish manuscript.

her palace gate, she is overtaken and killed by her own troops.

King Joash
(2 Chronicles 23:16 – 24:27)

At the beginning of Joash's reign, the young king is only seven years old. Jehoiada the priest is his chief adviser in his early years.

Jehoiada oversees the making of a covenant between himself, the people and the king. They commit themselves to be faithful to the Lord. The temple of Baal is destroyed and its priest executed. The temple of the Lord is placed in the care of the priests and Levites. The people's donations are properly administered for repairs to the fabric and for the commissioning of new furnishings and equipment.

Jehoiada lives to a great age. He has been such an influence for good that, when he dies, he is given a state funeral and buried with the kings.

After Jehoiada's death, Joash falls under a very different influence. Officials from Judah persuade him to adopt Baal-worship, with disastrous results. Jehoiada's son, Zechariah, warns the people that the Lord will reject them if they reject him. On Joash's orders, the faithful Zechariah is stoned to death.

The stoning of Zechariah is a tragedy and a scandal. Because Chronicles is placed as the last book in the Jewish scriptures, Zechariah's martyrdom stands as an appalling rejection of God's messenger. Many Jewish rabbis teach that the destruction of Solomon's temple is God's punishment for the death of this good man. Jesus himself refers to it (Matthew 23:35).

In all, Joash reigns for forty years. Because of his unfaithfulness, God inflicts defeat on him by the armies of Aram (Syria). The king is severely wounded in battle, and murdered in his bed by his own officials. The two men who kill him both have foreign mothers – an Ammonite and a Moabite.

Joash is not a wholly bad king. He begins well but ends tragically. In some ways his reign is like a mini-history of Israel.

King Amaziah

(2 Chronicles 25:1 – 26:2)

The Chronicler says Amaziah does 'what is right in the eyes of the Lord, but not wholeheartedly'.

On becoming king, Amaziah avenges the death of his father, but only executes those who actually committed the murder. He doesn't kill their children, because he discovers that the law of Moses forbids it (Deuteronomy 24:16). This is the first sign that the bloodletting ways of Jehoram and Athaliah are coming to an end.

Amaziah counts his fighting force and finds the numbers much lower than in the days of Asa. He hires mercenaries from Ephraim to increase his military strength, but is warned against using them by 'a man of God', a prophet. Amaziah accepts the prophet's advice, although he regrets the waste of money in paying the Ephraimites and then not using them. The prophet assures the king that God can very easily compensate him for his losses.

God honours Amaziah's trust, and grants him a great victory over the Edomites. Meanwhile, the Ephraimites whom he had sent home prove their unreliability by going on the rampage in the north.

Now Amaziah makes a big mistake. Although he has conquered the Edomites, he brings their gods back to Jerusalem and starts to worship them. He is trying to add the power of the Edomite idols to that of the God of Israel. The king shouts down a prophet who tells him that this is a stupid and dangerous thing to do, and that God will judge him for it.

Amaziah is bold after his success against Edom, and decides to challenge Jehoash of Israel. Jehoash warns him that this will be an unequal fight. Amaziah approaching Jehoash is like a thistle asking to marry a cedar. The cedar will turn into a wild beast and trample him.

Amaziah ignores the warning. The Chronicler explains that this is God bringing about Amaziah's downfall because of his idolatry with the worthless gods of Edom.

Jehoash inflicts a crushing defeat on Amaziah. He breaks down a large section of Jerusalem's wall, ransacks the temple and palace treasures, and keeps Amaziah captive in Samaria for ten years.

During his imprisonment, Amaziah's place on the throne of Judah is taken by Uzziah, his sixteen-year-old son. After his release, Amaziah lives another fifteen years, but his authority is broken. He is a discredited and unpopular king, whose troubles date from the day he turned away from the Lord.

King Uzziah

(2 Chronicles 26:3–23)

Uzziah (Azariah) is one of Judah's great kings. He comes to the throne when he is sixteen years old, to act as regent for his father Amaziah. Amaziah is being held captive in Samaria, the capital of the northern kingdom of Israel.

The ten years of Amaziah's imprisonment are followed by a further fifteen years of co-regency. This means that half of Uzziah's reign overlaps with that of his father. In all, Uzziah reigns for fifty-two years and is the finest king since Jehoshaphat, who ruled Judah 100 hundred years earlier.

Like Amaziah and Joash (his father and grandfather) Uzziah begins his reign well. The Chronicler says that Uzziah does 'right in the eyes of the Lord'. His teacher and counsellor is a man called Zechariah, who is an excellent influence on the king for most of his reign.

The Chronicler says that Uzziah is 'greatly helped'. The name Uzziah means 'The Lord is My Strength'. As king he is also called Azariah, which is possibly a throne-name given him at his coronation. Azariah means 'The Lord Has Helped'.

It is a mark of Uzziah's strength and vision that he recaptures and restores the Red Sea port of Elath. Elath had been developed for industry and trade by Solomon but then lost to the Edomites. Today it is the holiday resort of Eilat.

Uzziah is an all-rounder. As soldier, farmer and administrator, he brings energy and ability to every aspect of his nation's life. He conquers Judah's old enemies – the Philistines to the west and the Arabs to the south. He strengthens Jerusalem's fortifications, provides the army with new equipment and introduces the latest means of defence. He tends his cattle by building watchtowers and digging wells, and takes a lively interest in his vineyards and farms.

Uzziah's reign in Judah runs parallel to Jeroboam II's reign in Israel. Both kingdoms become strong and prosperous at this time, because their enemies are weak. Assyria in particular is experiencing a short-term decline.

Sadly, the last ten years of Uzziah's reign are spoiled

by an act of pride and folly. Although Uzziah has a unique role among his people as their king, he tries also to act as their priest. He enters the temple and prepares to burn incense.

The roles of king and priest are strictly separate – the first is secular and the second is sacred. The king represents God to the people, while the priest represents the people to God. The roles are not to be combined in Israel, unlike some other nations, because there is a danger that they will become confused or their significance lost.

As Uzziah approaches the altar of incense, some brave priests challenge him. As the king rages at them in his defiance, he breaks out in leprosy.

Leprosy is a living death – a highly contagious skin disease which eats the flesh and slowly disables the body. In Uzziah's case it is regarded as a dramatic symbol of sin and a sign of God's judgment.

Because of his disease, Uzziah is forced to live in isolation for the last ten years of his life. Nevertheless, his great achievements and length of reign have made him a landmark for his people. When he dies, in 740 BC, the prophet Isaiah is consoled by a vision of the far greater and eternal kingship of God (Isaiah 6:1).

King Jotham

(2 Chronicles 27:1–9)

Uzziah is succeeded by his son Jotham, who is a good king. He is one of only two kings of whom the Chronicler has nothing bad to say – the other being Solomon's grandson Abijah.

Jotham reigns for sixteen years. He continues his father's sound policies, conquering the Ammonites and extracting tribute from them, and strengthening Judah's defences. At the same time, he is careful not to make his father's mistakes. The Chronicler notes that although the king is good, the people of Judah are corrupt.

King Ahaz

(2 Chronicles 28:1–27)

When Ahaz succeeds his father Jotham, he continues the royal line of David. However, his sixteen-year reign falls far short of the righteousness and justice of his great ancestor.

Under Ahaz, pagan worship becomes rife in Judah. Ahaz himself offers sacrifices to the ancient Baal-gods, even to the extent of burning his own sons. The people of Judah are now behaving in the same way as the Canaanites whom they originally drove from the land.

God's judgment falls on Ahaz in the form of heavy defeats, first by the Arameans (Syrians) and then by the Israelites from the north. The king of Israel, Pekah, takes a terrible toll of human life and seizes a huge number of prisoners.

As the Israelites return to Samaria with their captives, they are met by a prophet named Oded. Oded declares that they have gone far beyond God's will with their atrocities, and commands that the survivors be sent home. These captives are their brothers and sisters, and fellow members of God's people.

The prophet's words are echoed by the leaders of Ephraim. The soldiers give up their prisoners with great grace and generosity. They provide them with food and clothes, put balm on their wounds and transport them back to Jericho on donkeys. Here is the act of kindness to enemies which will one day inspire the parable of the Good Samaritan (Luke 10:33–34).

Ahaz continues to suffer defeats, but they don't make him turn to the Lord. Instead, he appeals to the king of Assyria, Tiglath-Pileser, for help. Tiglath-Pileser merely adds to Ahaz's humiliation by taking his treasures while giving nothing in return.

Ahaz tries worshipping the gods of Damascus, because they have helped Syria defeat him. Finally, he shows all-out defiance of the Lord by closing down the temple and setting up pagan altars on every street corner. When Ahaz dies, he is not buried with the kings of Israel, because he has not been God's king for God's people in any true sense.

Ahaz's reign has been a disaster for Judah. The Chronicler shows how God punishes disobedience with defeat and captivity – and in so doing gives a hint of what is to come. In the past it has been the northern kingdom which has abandoned its loyalty to God; now the southern kingdom is as bad.

King Hezekiah

(2 Chronicles 29:1 – 32:33)

When Hezekiah succeeds his father as king of Judah, his inspiration is the great King Solomon. Hezekiah's vision is to restore the temple and its worship as it was at the beginning. To this end he sets to work on the very first day of his reign.

Hezekiah calls together the priests and Levites. He tells them of his intention to make a covenant with the Lord. After the years of unfaithfulness and idolatry, Judah is now to commit herself again to the one true

God. Hezekiah urges the priests and Levites to dedicate themselves to this holy task, and to thoroughly cleanse both themselves and the temple.

The priests and Levites accept the challenge. They set about clearing the rubbish that has accumulated in the temple during the years of neglect. The priests turn out all the trappings of pagan worship from the sanctuary, and the Levites throw them into the Kidron Valley. When all is clean and ready, they report back to the king.

The king and his officials come to the temple with animals for sacrifice: seven bulls, seven rams, seven male lambs and seven male goats.

The bulls, rams and lambs are for burnt offerings on behalf of the different groups – seven being the 'perfect' number that stands for the relationship of God and humanity.

The male goats are for a sin offering. The king and the assembly lay their hands on the goats before they are killed, to show that it is for their sins that the animals are being sacrificed.

While the offerings are being burned, the Levites play psalms from the days of David, on the instruments which David himself appointed. Even after the offerings are completed, they continue to worship God in psalms, with the priests joining in with their trumpets.

All is now ready for the people to bring their sacrifices and thank-offerings. The number of sacrifices is small compared with the day when Solomon dedicated the temple. In any case, there are not enough priests who are ceremonially clean to cope with the skinning of the animals. The Levites, who have taken the time to prepare themselves properly, are able to help.

With the temple cleansed and rededicated, Hezekiah and all the people praise God. They are full of joy that so much has been achieved so quickly.

Hezekiah sends out an invitation for all Israel and Judah to join in a celebration of the Passover. Sadly, the northern kingdom has now been conquered by the Assyrians (in 723 BC), and only the tribes of Ephraim and Manasseh, Issachar and Zebulun have survived in any numbers.

The Passover is held in the second month of the year, which is a month later than usual. The date is delayed to allow extra time for spiritual, ritual and practical preparation. Hezekiah needs time to send out the messengers with invitations. The priests need time for the lengthy process of consecration. The people who are travelling to Jerusalem need time to make their journeys.

Hezekiah sends messengers throughout the land, from Dan in the north to Beersheba in the south. After more than two centuries of painful division and defeat, this Passover is a festival of reunion and reconciliation. Even those who are not ceremonially clean are welcome to take part. Hezekiah prays that God will pardon all those who are genuinely seeking him.

The festival is so successful that the Feast of Unleavened Bread is extended for a further week. Hezekiah contributes most generously, as befits a true descendant of David. He and his officials donate thousands of animals for sacrifice. These are not burnt offerings but peace offerings – to be offered to God and then shared as food among the worshippers. On their way home, the pilgrims joyfully destroy the sites and symbols of pagan worship.

Now Hezekiah organizes the day-to-day running of the temple. He invites the people of Jerusalem to bring their tithes of grain and produce for the support of the priests and Levites. The response is overwhelming – echoing the glad and generous commitments that were made in the days of David. For four months the offerings are simply piled in heaps, until Conaniah can get the storerooms sorted out!

In Hezekiah, the Chronicler has found his hero. Here at last is a king who seeks God, obeys his law, serves the temple and works hard. He does the right thing with all his heart all the time for the glory of God. And God blesses him.

When Hezekiah has been on the throne for fourteen years, everything he has achieved is threatened with destruction. Sennacherib, the king of Assyria, invades Judah and prepares to lay siege to Jerusalem.

The armies of Assyria are a formidable fighting force. In human terms, Judah stands no chance. But Hezekiah makes safe his water supply, doubles his defences and stockpiles his weapons. Most of all, he encourages his people with the assurance that God is with them and will fight their battles for them.

Sennacherib sends his officers to Jerusalem to intimidate the defenders and destroy their morale. He declares that no god has ever been able to resist the might of Assyria – and that the God of Hezekiah will be no exception. In his pride and ignorance, Sennacherib does not realize that Hezekiah's faith will prove more effective than any army.

King Hezekiah and his prophet Isaiah cry out to God for help. And help comes, in the form of an angel who destroys the Assyrian army in a single night. Sennacherib has no choice but to retreat. He returns to his own land, where his sons assassinate him in the temple of his god.

Before the Chronicler leaves his account of Hezekiah, he gives some final glimpses of this great king.

He records how God spared Hezekiah from death when he was dangerously ill. The books of Kings tell how Hezekiah was suffering from a septic boil, and that Isaiah declared he would die. However, God had pity on him and healed him, promising to add another fifteen years to his life. He made the sun's shadow retreat ten steps on Ahaz's stairway as a sign that this healing was a miracle (2 Kings 20:1–11).

The Chronicler mentions Hezekiah's pride, which aroused God's anger. When envoys came from Babylon to enquire about his healing, Hezekiah failed to give the glory to God. He also foolishly showed off his treasures to his visitors, and talked no doubt about a possible alliance against Assyria. All this gave the impression that Hezekiah was secure in his own strength, when in fact he was totally dependent on God for protection.

King Manasseh
(2 Chronicles 33:1–20)

Hezekiah's son, Manasseh, is twelve years old when he becomes king of Judah. He reigns for fifty-five years – the longest and most wicked of all the reigns.

The Chronicler, like the writer of 2 Kings (2 Kings 21:1–9), describes Manasseh's wickedness. The new king allows back into Israel all the pagan gods and evil practices which had been driven out by Joshua and David. He even sets up pagan altars in the temple itself, and offers his own sons as human sacrifices in the Valley of Hinnom. This terrible place is sometimes known as Gehenna and will be used by Jesus as an image of hell.

It may be that Manasseh is very religious, and that he is enlisting all the forces of foreign gods, astrology and magic to strengthen his kingdom. But this is exactly what God has always forbidden. It is his name only that is to be worshipped in Israel; and he will prove himself greater than all gods in saving and protecting his people.

Unlike the writer of 2 Kings, the Chronicler tells us that God punishes Manasseh. The evil king is taken captive by the Assyrians and led away by a hook through his nose. In exile, he repents and God restores him to his throne. In the closing years of his reign he is able to strengthen the walls of Jerusalem, protect his people and throw out the pagan idols and other trappings of idolatry.

The book of Kings blames Manasseh for the punishment that falls on Judah and the people of Jerusalem in later years. The Chronicler gives a different account. He describes Manasseh's captivity, repentance and the good achievements of his reign. In this way, Manasseh's life can be seen as a miniature of what is to happen to Judah and Jerusalem. They will be conquered by the Babylonians for their sins, and sent into exile, but later restored.

King Amon
(2 Chronicles 33:21–25)

Manasseh is succeeded as king of Judah by his son Amon. Amon is twenty-two years old, and his reign is brief and bitter.

Amon follows the idolatrous ways of his father, but without the repentance which transformed Manasseh's last years. He is assassinated by his own officials. They in turn are slaughtered in a popular movement which brings Josiah to the throne.

King Josiah
(2 Chronicles 34:1 – 35:27)

Josiah, Amon's son, becomes king in 641 BC, when he is eight years old. At this time, Judah is a small and unimportant part of the Assyrian empire, and it is to Assyrian gods that many people look for influence and help. But Josiah's hero is King David. When he is sixteen, he seeks God's help to become a just and godly ruler, like his great ancestor.

By the time Josiah is twenty, the Assyrian power is beginning to wane. The empire has become very large and is proving difficult to control. Josiah takes advantage of this situation to rid Judah of Assyrian gods – breaking down their altars, cutting up the fertility poles of the goddess Asherah and destroying idols.

Josiah's reforms are very thorough, including burning the bones of pagan priests, grinding their ashes to powder and sprinkling them over altars and graves to defile them. However, the worship of Baal-gods has been widespread in Judah for many years; there is no evidence that Josiah's purge is popular.

Josiah's next project is to restore the temple, which has fallen into disrepair. He enlists the money and skills of many of the Israelites from the tribes of Manasseh and Ephraim in the northern kingdom. They have been conquered by the Assyrians in 722 BC, and thousands have become displaced persons. Some have come as refugees to the southern kingdom of Judah, where Josiah puts them to work under the direction of the Levites.

As the work on the temple begins, the high priest discovers the Book of the Law of the Lord. This is probably part of the book of Deuteronomy, which includes the blessings and curses that follow from keeping or breaking the covenant (Deuteronomy 27–28).

When Josiah has the law read aloud to him, he is devastated. God's people have defied and broken it in every aspect, and a terrible judgment must be about to fall. The king consults a prophetess, Huldah, who confirms his worst fears. However, she declares that Josiah himself will be spared the disaster, because he has repented and tried to do what is right.

As events prove, Josiah is the last good king of Judah. He renews the covenant and encourages his people to do the same. He also provides for the greatest Passover celebration since the days of Samuel.

Meanwhile, the international scene is changing. The rising power is Babylon, which is emerging to challenge the dominance of Assyria and Egypt. Pharaoh Neco takes an Egyptian army to support Assyria against the Babylonians at Carchemish. As they pass by Judah, Josiah decides to challenge the pharaoh to battle. It is in this needless skirmish that Josiah is killed at Megiddo. He has been king for thirty-one years.

King Jehoahaz
(2 Chronicles 36:1–4)

Josiah is succeeded as king by his son Jehoahaz. The young man's reign lasts only a few months. He is deposed and deported by the king of Egypt, who puts another of Josiah's sons on the throne instead.

King Jehoiakim
(2 Chronicles 36:5–8)

The new king, Eliakim, is an elder brother of Jehoahaz. The king of Egypt changes his name to Jehoiakim, and demands tribute of silver and gold from Judah.

With the Assyrian empire overthrown, Judah now finds herself squeezed between Babylon and Egypt. Jehoiakim's reign lasts eleven years under the protection of Egypt. However, the king of Babylon, Nebuchadnezzar, defeats Pharaoh Neco in 605 BC and later lays siege to Jerusalem. He takes Jehoiakim captive and raids the Jerusalem temple for treasures to take back to Babylon.

King Jehoiachin
(2 Chronicles 36:9–10)

The next king is Jehoiachin. He reigns for a mere three months, before Nebuchadnezzar exiles him and appoints his uncle, Zedekiah, to be king.

The Egyptian Pharoah Neco (pictured above) rallies his forces to combine with Assyria against the rising power of Babylon. He sends a message to King Josiah, telling him of his intentions, but Josiah regards the foreign troops passing through his territory as unfriendly. He attacks the Egyptian army, but his forces are defeated. Josiah himself is killed.

King Zedekiah
(2 Chronicles 36:11–14)

Zedekiah becomes king when he is twenty-one years old. His country is tossed on the stormy sea of international conflict, but he survives for eleven years. However, he does so without seeking God's help and in defiance of the messages of the prophet Jeremiah.

The fall of Jerusalem
(2 Chronicles 36:15–19)

The Chronicler shows us, in this series of short reigns, the death throes of Judah. She has abandoned God and God is now abandoning her. The armies of Assyria, Egypt and Babylon are all his instruments of judgment. But Judah is corrupt and ready to fall, her people unfaithful and her leaders ungodly.

Zedekiah tries to double-cross Nebuchadnezzar, and so provokes the final assault on Jerusalem by the Babylonians. Jerusalem is destroyed, her population mercilessly slaughtered or captured, and her temple sacked. The Chronicler says that it is God who brings Nebuchadnezzar against his own people, and God who hands them over to their enemy. It is 587 BC.

The exile in Babylon
(2 Chronicles 36:20–21)

Even when the worst has happened – Jerusalem in ruins and her people dead or deported – the Chronicler gives glimmers of hope. After all, he is writing of these events from the other side of the years of exile. He and his readers know that God's people will survive.

Some of the survivors become servants to the king of Babylon. In the past, God made Joseph prime minister of Egypt, and Moses one of its princes. In the future there will be fine servants of pagan kings, such as Daniel and Nehemiah. God hasn't ceased to exist because his people are no longer in their own land and temple. His purpose moves on, even in the darkest of times.

The Chronicler says that the land enjoys her sabbath rests. It seems that Judah's kings have never enforced the sabbath year during which the land could recover strength and fertility. Now, with few people to cultivate them, the fields lie fallow. There is peace after tension and bloodshed. The damage and din of pagan worship have finally ceased.

The decree to return
(2 Chronicles 36:22–23)

After seventy years, a new world power emerges. This is the Persian empire, and Cyrus is its king.

Cyrus is interested in religion and tolerant of all faiths. Just as Nebuchadnezzar was God's instrument for judging his people, so Cyrus is his means of restoring them. One of the new emperor's first actions is to decree that a temple shall be built in Jerusalem. Anyone who wishes to return home to help with this work may do so!

EZRA AND NEHEMIAH

The books of Ezra and Nehemiah tell how the Jews return from exile in Babylonia and rebuild the city of Jerusalem and the temple. This takes place over a long period of time and with great difficulty.

The returning exiles meet strong opposition from their enemies in the region. The Samaritans don't want to see Jerusalem established as a strong, secure city. At the same time, the Jews have to rediscover their nationhood and renew their commitment to God's law.

Nehemiah is appointed governor of Jerusalem by Cyrus, the emperor of Persia. He is granted permission to rebuild the walls of Jerusalem.

Ezra arrives in Jerusalem with a group of returning exiles. It is difficult to tell whether he comes before or after Nehemiah. Ezra is a teacher or scribe who sets God's law at the heart of Jewish life.

Outline

The return from exile and rebuilding of the temple (Ezra 1:1 – 6:22)

Ezra's return and leadership (Ezra 7:1 – 10:44)

The rebuilding of the walls of Jerusalem (Nehemiah 1:1 – 7:73)

Ezra reads the law and the people agree to obey it (Nehemiah 8:1 – 10:39)

Resettlement and Nehemiah's reforms (Nehemiah 11:1 – 13:31)

INTRODUCTION

The book of Ezra continues the history of the Jewish people from the end of the books of Chronicles. It records how two major groups of people return to Jerusalem from exile in Babylon. The first group is led by Zerubbabel, a governor of Judea. The second is led by Ezra, who is a scribe or teacher. Although the book is named after Ezra, he doesn't enter the story until chapter 7.

The people of Israel are suffering from poverty, bewilderment and low morale. The confidence and wealth of the days of David and Solomon are gone, never to return. The new temple won't be as fine as the old one, and will only be built after much discouragement and long delay. Idolatry and immorality have weakened the people's spiritual health and corrupted their society. They have been conquered and displaced for two generations. They have no king, no army and no empire.

Now, at last, there is the opportunity for rebuilding and a new beginning. The prophets have a great sense that God is with his people. Ezra and Nehemiah both believe it is God who moves the Persian king to provide for the temple and give permission for the walls of Jerusalem to be rebuilt. Despite the trauma of the past centuries, God still has a purpose for Israel. He is their king and his law will be their way to a new life.

Personal memoirs

The books of Ezra and Nehemiah are compiled from personal memoirs, imperial edicts, official letters and lists of people. Between Ezra 7 and Nehemiah 13, the memoirs of the two main characters are merged:

Ezra 7:1 – 10:44 Ezra's memoirs 1

Nehemiah 1:1 – 7:73 Nehemiah's memoirs 1

Nehemiah 8:1 – 12:26 Ezra's memoirs 2

Nehemiah 12:27 – 13:31 Nehemiah's memoirs 2

Purity... and understanding

The early chapters of Ezra tell how Zerubbabel brings a group of exiles back to Jerusalem. They offer sacrifices and start to rebuild the temple. Once Ezra enters the story (in chapter 7), there is more attention to the rebuilding of the people themselves. Ezra's hard task is to teach God's law and to lead the people by his own example. In particular, there is a rigorous policy that the Jews should not intermarry with pagan nations.

The books of Ezra and Nehemiah are very strict about the religious purity of the community. Both leaders take action to dissolve mixed marriages. Intermarriage with pagan tribes has led to idolatry in the past, even for wise King Solomon himself. The book of Esther takes a more open view, that God can bless and use a marriage which takes place across a racial boundary. Moses himself had foreign wives.

Scholars have wondered whether the final editing of Ezra and Nehemiah was done by the same person who compiled the books of Chronicles. The Chronicler seems more relaxed about including outsiders in the people of God. 2 Chronicles 30 welcomes the northern tribes after the conquest of Israel. In Ezra and Nehemiah we find a more exclusive view – that only those who have taken part in the Babylonian exile are the true Israel. This fact is simply recorded, without any clue as to whether the writer approves of the statement.

Ezra and Nehemiah are men of great vision and determination. However, they are sometimes narrow and insensitive. At the end of the book of Nehemiah, we see a nation under a dictatorship of strict moral and religious rules. Nehemiah is proud that he has excluded foreigners and evicted his enemy Tobiah from the temple. He is pleased to have forced visiting traders to observe the sabbath rest. He has dealt severely with Jews who have foreign wives and children. But the regime does not convey the real nature and love of God; and it doesn't work.

Nehemiah is a faithful and energetic leader, but we long for more understanding and gentleness in his actions.

Ezra also may be missing a great opportunity when he refuses the help of outsiders (Ezra 4:1–4). Isaiah had prophesied that foreigners would come to love God and serve him in Jerusalem, swelling the number of returning exiles (Isaiah 56:6–8). No doubt Ezra feels that these are desperate times and he needs a pure nucleus to start with.

The search for exclusive holiness continues among the Pharisees of Jesus' day. It is one of the hardest barriers that the early church has to overcome, if the gospel is really to reach all the nations of the world (Acts 10 and 15).

Who came first – Ezra or Nehemiah?

The Bible's order of books has Ezra before Nehemiah. However, in some ways the story would make more sense if Nehemiah came first. That way, Nehemiah rebuilds the walls of Jerusalem and then Ezra comes to teach the people the law of God.

The dates given in the Bible show the Jews returning to their homeland over a period of ninety years. If Zerubbabel returns in 536 BC and Ezra in 458 BC, then Nehemiah's journey to Jerusalem was probably twelve years later, in 445 BC.

We know that Nehemiah was in Jerusalem for twelve years from 445–433 BC. This is from the 20th year of the reign of Artaxerxes I to the 32nd year (Nehemiah 2:1 and 13:6). Nehemiah returned to the Persian court for a while (probably quite a short time), and then came back to Jerusalem to make further reforms.

The traditional view is that Ezra arrived in Jerusalem some years before Nehemiah, in 458 BC. This means that his king, too, is Artaxerxes I (Ezra 7:7). If this date is right, then Ezra comes before Nehemiah, as we would expect from the order of their books in the Bible.

Another theory is that Ezra returned to Judea much later, in 398 BC. This would mean that his king (Ezra 7:7) is Artaxerxes II, not Artaxerxes I. But is it likely that Ezra and Nehemiah would both be living in Jerusalem at the same time, without mentioning each other?

Ezra and Nehemiah

Ezra and Nehemiah were originally one book. They are the last part of the history which tells the story of Israel from Adam to Nehemiah.

It is possible that Ezra is the person who wrote or edited Chronicles. His 'memoirs' in Ezra 7–10 are continued in Nehemiah 8:1 – 12:26. However, the tone of Chronicles is more accepting of foreigners than Ezra is.

The prophets

Two prophets, Haggai and Zechariah, are important figures in the restoration of Jerusalem. Their books give us added insight into the situation at this time. Malachi may also have been written shortly before the return of Ezra and Nehemiah to Jerusalem.

DISCOVERING EZRA AND NEHEMIAH

The return from exile and rebuilding of the temple

Cyrus allows the Jews to return home
(Ezra 1:1 – 2:70)

Cyrus has become king of Persia and has conquered the evil empire of Babylon. One of his first acts is to allow the Jews to return home from exile (1:1–11). He encourages them to rebuild their temple in Jerusalem.

The Israelites once escaped from Egypt, laden with the wealth of their captors. Now the Jews are sent on their way back to Judah, with money, goods, livestock and offerings from their Babylonian neighbours.

The writer is in no doubt that it is God who is doing all this for the Jews. Everything is happening to fulfil the prophecy of Jeremiah. Jeremiah had foretold that the land of Judah would be laid waste and its people made slaves in Babylon for seventy years; but at the end of that time, Babylon herself would be defeated (Jeremiah 25:11–12).

Cyrus is not a worshipper of the Lord. We know from other records that he worships pagan gods, including Marduk and Sin. But he respects the God of Israel. He is careful to return the temple treasures which King Nebuchadnezzar had carried away to Babylon in 597 BC and 587 BC.

THE LIST OF THE EXILES WHO RETURN

The journey from Babylon to Jerusalem takes about four months. This list of leaders, tribes and families is repeated in Nehemiah (Nehemiah 7:6–73), although there are some differences of detail. Here eleven main leaders are listed. In other lists there are twelve, which corresponds to the twelve tribes of Israel.

Zerubbabel is to be the governor. Jeshua (or Joshua) is the first high priest after the exile. He is the grandson of Seraiah, who was the last high priest before the exile. The 'Nehemiah' who is mentioned here is not the governor who will rebuild the walls of Jerusalem, but someone else with the same name.

The families who are returning to Judah are named after their ancestors or their home towns. A huge number – 4,289 – of the returnees are priests. They are looking forward to building and serving in a new temple. Surprisingly, there are only 342 Levites. They include the singers and gatekeepers, who will play an important part in the daily life of the temple. When Ezra returns, he has to call in extra Levites because there aren't enough in his group.

Zerubbabel's title of 'governor' is the Persian for 'the one to be feared'. It will also be used of Nehemiah.

Urim and Thummim are the stones which the high priest uses to give God's guidance. They are kept in the high priest's breastplate and drawn out to indicate 'Yes' or 'No'. There is no other mention of them after the exile.

The first thing the people do on arriving in Jerusalem is to visit the site of the temple, the house of the Lord.

What's been going on?

The Babylonians have conquered the kingdom of Judah and destroyed its capital city Jerusalem. All the leading citizens of Jerusalem have been deported to Babylonia, where they and their families have lived in exile for seventy years.

Now Babylon has in turn been defeated by the combined force of the Medes and the Persians. The city of Babylon fell in 539 BC.

The new Persian king is Cyrus. He is tolerant towards the peoples of his empire. He gives permission for those who have been displaced by the Babylonians to return home. This enables a group of exiled Jews to return to Judea and Jerusalem in 538 BC.

Cyrus wants his subjects to govern themselves, while still paying tribute to his empire. He is willing to encourage national religions and has a great respect for the God of Israel.

This is the moment they have been longing for. They give money for the rebuilding and robes for the priests.

Worship begins again on the temple site
(Ezra 3:1–6)

Although the temple is in ruins, the Israelites rebuild the altar and offer sacrifices there once again. They follow the instructions in the law of Moses – that is, the books of Leviticus and Numbers.

The first major festival they celebrate is the Feast of Tabernacles. This is one of the three great annual feasts, when as many people as possible come to Jerusalem. The festival is sometimes called the 'Festival of Booths', because the people build shelters or 'booths' to recall the days when their ancestors lived in the wilderness. Now it will also remind them of their journey of return from exile.

At last the old pattern of worship and sacrifice is in place. The New Moon sacrifices are not in honour of the moon, but to mark the first day of a new month and make it a holy day.

The foundations of the new temple are laid
(Ezra 3:7–13)

The preparations for building the temple sound similar to the work done by Solomon for the first temple.

Once again the strength and skills of the people of Tyre and Sidon are enlisted to bring cedar wood by sea

Coin of Darius the Great, ruler of Persia from 522 to 486 BC.

The Persian kings

559–530 *Cyrus*

530–522 *Cambyses*

522–486 *Darius I (Hystaspes) (the Great)*

486–465 *Xerxes I (Ahasuerus)*

465–424 *Artaxerxes I (Longimanus)*

424–423 *Xerxes II*

423–404 *Darius II*

404–358 *Artaxerxes II (Mnemon)*

from Lebanon to Joppa. Joppa is the nearest port to Jerusalem. It is a sign of the times that the permission to do this comes from a foreign overlord, Cyrus of Persia.

It is an emotional moment when the foundations of the new temple are laid. While the young Levites carry out the work of building, the old priests weep or shout for joy. Jeremiah had prophesied that one day sounds of celebrations would be heard again in the streets of Jerusalem (Jeremiah 33:10–11). The refrain of their praise is: 'The Lord is good; his love endures for ever' (3:11).

Perhaps the whole song is the one written by David, which is recorded in 1 Chronicles 16:8–36.

Enemies offer to help – and are refused
(Ezra 4:1–3)

The Israelites' enemies offer to help them with the rebuilding. These are people who have been resettled in Samaria by the Assyrians. They come from a variety of races and nations, but claim to worship the God of Israel now that they live in his area.

The Jewish leaders are very firm in their refusal. The new temple and the new Jerusalem are to be purely Jewish. This sounds exclusive and unkind. However, their problem is to keep Israel's vision clear and her faith focused. Mixing with pagan religions has brought disaster in the past. Allowing people to join the work who don't really want it to succeed might prove bad for progress and morale.

Letters of protest to the kings of Persia
(Ezra 4:4 – 6:12)

The opposition hardens against the rebuilding of Jerusalem and the temple. The Israelites' enemies do all in their power to criticize and undermine the project. Their scorn, political lobbying and physical attacks continue through the reigns of several Persian kings.

A LETTER SENT TO XERXES

The writer now mentions some of the letters of protest which are sent to the Persian kings. The first is at the beginning of the reign of Xerxes, in 486 BC (4:6). Xerxes is called Ahasuerus in the Bible and he reigns from 486–465 BC.

SAMARITAN LEADERS WRITE TO ARTAXERXES

The leaders in Trans-Euphrates send a strong letter of warning to another Persian king, Artaxerxes (4:7–24). 'Trans-Euphrates' or 'beyond the river' is the part of the Persian empire to the west of the River Euphrates. It includes the province of Samaria, which is the centre of opposition to the rebuilding of Jerusalem.

The Samaritan leaders warn the king that Jerusalem has been a well-defended city in the past, and that its people have a reputation for being rebellious. If the Jews succeed in rebuilding Jerusalem, they will stop paying tribute to Persia and pull the whole region away from the empire.

King Artaxerxes checks his records and find that what the Samaritans say is true. He orders the rebuilding work to stop immediately, a message which the Samaritans are pleased and quick to deliver. Later, Artaxerxes changes his mind and commissions Nehemiah to rebuild Jerusalem's walls (Nehemiah 2:7–9).

PROPHETS ENCOURAGE THE WORK TO RESTART

It is now the second year of the reign of King Darius of Persia in 520 BC. The work of rebuilding the temple has been halted for about sixteen years. The Israelites have concluded that God doesn't want the work done, and have settled for building their own houses instead (Haggai 1:9).

Into this depressed situation come two great prophets, Haggai and Zechariah. We have books of their prophecies in the Bible, towards the end of the Old Testament.

Haggai challenges the people to return to God again (5:1–2). Every part of their lives is impoverished because they are failing to honour God and complete his house, which is the temple (Haggai 1:5–8).

Zechariah inspires the people with his promises of God's presence in the city and the great days of peace and prosperity that are to come. He, too, urges them to complete the temple (Zechariah 8:9). With their vision renewed, the Israelites set to work and finish the building.

SAMARITAN LEADERS WRITE TO KING DARIUS

Another governor of Trans-Euphrates now writes to another king of Persia. This time the king is Darius, who reigns from 522 to 486 BC (5:3 – 6:12). The governor is Tattenai. He is not hostile like the previous Samaritan governor, but simply asking for information.

Tattenai asks the Israelites who gave them permission to build the temple. He then writes to King Darius, alerting him to the scale of the project, the size of the stones and timbers and the vigour of the work.

Tattenai tells the king that the Jews are claiming Cyrus issued a decree for their temple to be rebuilt. The governor asks Darius to confirm this and give him any further instructions.

The original decree is not found in the archives at Babylon, but a note of the main points has been kept in the summer palace at Ecbatana. The contents agree entirely with the Jews' account of events.

Darius writes to Tattenai with a strong confirmation that the temple is to be completed. He commands that the cost of the building and supplies for the priests are to be met from the revenues of Trans-Euphrates. So the Samaritans are compelled to pay for the work they have been trying to stop!

The temple is completed and dedicated
(Ezra 6:13–18)

The temple is completed on 12 March 515 BC, just seventy years after it was destroyed. Artaxerxes is mentioned among those who have helped the project, although he has not yet been made king. His name may be included because he makes a contribution at a later date.

The celebrations remind us of the festival at the dedication of Solomon's temple, although the number of sacrifices is smaller now because the people are poorer.

The Passover is celebrated
(Ezra 6:19–22)

A month after the dedication of the temple, the Jews celebrate the Passover.

Passover is the most important feast in the Jewish year. By it, the Jews celebrate their birth as a nation. It was during the first Passover night, when they were slaves in Egypt, that God slew the first-born sons of their Egyptian persecutors and 'passed over' the homes of the Israelites. It was this terrible act of judgment which finally persuaded the Pharaoh to release them.

The Levites slaughter the Passover lambs – one for each household. Those who are allowed to take part in the meal are the people who have returned from exile and anyone else who has renounced the pagan practices of neighbours such as the Samaritans.

The lamb is roasted and eaten with unleavened

bread. The bread at the first Passover was made without leaven (yeast), so that it could be prepared quickly, needing no time for the dough to rise. The Passover meal was then eaten in a hurry, with each family member dressed ready to leave Egypt in the morning. Now the Passover meal marks the beginning of a week-long 'Feast of Unleavened Bread'.

The king of Assyria is suddenly mentioned as having assisted with the work! This should, of course, be the king of Persia, who is now ruling the old Assyrian empire.

Ezra's return and leadership

Ezra comes to Jerusalem
(Ezra 7:1–10)

The story moves on sixty years. Zerubbabel and Joshua are now dead, and we have no details of what has happened in the meantime.

Ezra at last enters the book which bears his name. He has an excellent pedigree, being able to trace his family line from Aaron, the first high priest. The 900-mile journey from Babylon takes Ezra and his group four months.

Ezra arrives in Jerusalem in 458 BC. He is a teacher, or 'scribe'. The scribes are secretaries who write letters or make copies of the scriptures in these days before printing. Now they are to become more important in the life of Israel, because they 'keep' the law in every sense. Ezra studies, practises and teaches the law of God. Now he will bring God's law to the heart of Israel's national life.

Ezra's letter from King Artaxerxes
(Ezra 7:11–28)

Ezra is given a powerful mandate by the king of Persia. He is to impose the law of the God of Israel on the whole region of Trans-Euphrates. This is the fifth district of the Persian satrapy, or government, and includes the whole of Palestine and Syria.

Ezra is sent to Jerusalem with money for sacrifices. He also has the king's command that the treasurers of Trans-Euphrates shall provide silver, wheat, wine, oil and salt for the temple. Also, the temple staff are to live tax-free. The king clearly wishes his empire to be protected from the wrath of the God of Israel.

Ezra's main task relates to the law of God. He is to appoint magistrates and judges who are trained in God's law, and to teach those who aren't.

EZRA PRAISES GOD

Suddenly we hear Ezra's own voice (7:27–28). The language changes to Hebrew (until now it has been Aramaic), and we have Ezra's account of events. He praises God for prompting the king to this action, and rejoices that the temple in Jerusalem is to be honoured. He decides to take some leading Israelites with him on his mission.

A list of the leaders who return with Ezra
(Ezra 8:1–14)

While in exile, the Jews have kept their sense of family and nation alive. All the people know to which clan they belong and from whom they are descended. Now Ezra lists the leaders who return with him to Jerusalem, together with their clans. The total number of people is 1,496.

Ezra's leadership
(Ezra 8:15–30)

Ezra is a careful organizer. He assembles the people by the Ahava Canal, to prepare for the journey. They fast and pray, asking God for protection. They have enemies in the region and may well be attacked; but Ezra does not ask the king for an armed escort. They rely completely on God to look after them.

No doubt Ezra is thinking of the exodus from Egypt, when a similar journey to Canaan took forty years. This time he wants the people to live in strict obedience to God. Nehemiah, on the other hand, has no hesitation in asking for the emperor's help. He lists his requests – and they are granted.

Ezra finds there is a shortage of Levites to serve in the temple when they get to Jerusalem. As this is one of the main purposes of the journey, he sends for reinforcements.

Ezra entrusts twelve priests and the twelve newly recruited Levites with the temple treasure. It is worth a fortune.

The exiles arrive in Jerusalem
(Ezra 8:31–36)

When the returning exiles arrive in Jerusalem they rest after their long journey. Then they hand over the temple treasure, weighing and accounting for every item. When they have completed this duty, they fulfil a long-held dream. They offer sacrifices in the temple – whole offerings on behalf of the whole people to a holy God.

Ezra and his colleagues deliver the king's orders to the satraps – the provincial governors of the Persian empire. The governors ensure that the king's orders are carried out. The Israelites are given every assistance in providing for the temple worship and establishing God's law.

The scandal of marriage to pagans

(Ezra 9:1 – 10:44)

Now there is a problem. It is revealed that many Israelites, including priests and other leaders, have married pagan wives. When Ezra hears of this, he is deeply shocked. He tears his clothes and beard as a sign of grief.

For Ezra, the distinctiveness of the community is an important part of religious purity. It is through intermarriage with pagan peoples that Israel has been corrupted by idolatry. It is probably the men of the first group to return from exile who have married foreigners, because of the shortage of Israelite women. They have broken God's law, which says, 'Do not intermarry with them… for you are a people holy to the Lord your God' (Deuteronomy 7:1–6). However, there is a law allowing Israelites to marry foreign captive women (Deuteronomy 21:10–14).

EZRA'S PRAYER

Ezra prays to God (9:3–15). He confesses the people's sin as if it is his own. He freely admits that they have broken God's law, despite the Lord's goodness to them in giving them a new start. He makes no excuses and suggests no remedy.

THE PEOPLE REPENT

While Ezra prays, the people gather round him and weep (10:1–17). One of them, Shecaniah, declares that the answer is in their own hands. All the men are summoned to appear in Jerusalem within three days. Meanwhile, Ezra retreats to fast and pray in the room of Jehohanan. Jehohanan will become high priest one day, succeeding his father and great-grandfather.

The men assemble in the temple forecourt in December. It is raining heavily, as though the weather itself is reflecting their grief.

When Ezra speaks to the men, he solemnly commands them to confess their sin and dismiss their foreign wives. They nearly all agree, but suggest that the matter will be best handled by the elders and judges of their home towns. In the event, the whole process takes three months.

A LIST OF LEADERS WHO MARRIED FOREIGNERS

The book of Ezra ends with a list of the men who have married foreign women (10:18–44). They include priests and Levites, as well as Israelites from eleven clans. Some of them have had children.

However carefully and considerately the divorces are accomplished, this is an agonizing episode in Israel's history. We are not told that God required this inquisition or approved it. Not every human response under repentance is necessarily right. As with Achan's sin after the victory at Jericho, so here: there is a painful backlash to the joy of the return from exile.

The rebuilding of the walls of Jerusalem

Nehemiah receives bad news

(Nehemiah 1:1–3)

Nehemiah is a trusted official in the Persian royal court. He is cupbearer to the king, Artaxerxes I. As Nehemiah begins his story, he is in Susa, where Artaxerxes has a winter palace. Kislev is the ninth month of the year.

News comes to Nehemiah from Jerusalem. The Jews who have returned to their capital after years of exile are struggling to survive. In particular, they are without walls or gates to defend their city.

Nehemiah prays to God for help

(Nehemiah 1:4–11)

Nehemiah is devastated by the news. He is in a difficult position. Some years ago, the king received a report from local officials about Jerusalem, which warned him that the city had a history of rebellion. In their opinion, a restored Jerusalem would make the region ungovernable. Following their advice, the king had issued a command that the rebuilding work should stop. It is very hard to reverse a royal decree!

An example of a Jewish marriage contract, dating from the 19th century.

Nehemiah prays about the problem. He accepts his own part in Israel's disobedience. He draws on the warnings and promises of the books of Moses. The exile has been the fulfilment of a solemn warning, that if Israel was unfaithful to God, he would scatter her people to far countries (Leviticus 26:33). But there is also mercy. If God's people repent, he will gather them back to their homeland (Deuteronomy 30:1–5). Nehemiah asks God to open the way for him to talk to the king – who is, after all, only a fellow human being.

Permission to rebuild Jerusalem
(Nehemiah 2:1–10)

As royal cupbearer, Nehemiah has daily access to the king. His task is to taste the king's wine, to prove that it isn't poisoned. As Nehemiah also serves in the presence of the queen, he has almost certainly been made a eunuch.

After some months of mourning, praying and waiting, Nehemiah has his opportunity. It is Nisan, the first month of the year. The king notices that Nehemiah looks sad. It is a punishable offence to appear sad in the presence of the king. Nehemiah explains that his sadness is because of the desperate state of Jerusalem, his ancestral home.

When the king asks Nehemiah what he wants, the cupbearer sends up the briefest of prayers and begs the royal permission to rebuild the city. He sets a timescale, requests letters of safe conduct and negotiates a supply of wooden beams for the various buildings.

Suddenly all is going well. The king is on Nehemiah's side, but some powerful opposition awaits.

The king's letter comes to the regional governors, Sanballat and Tobiah. We know from a document called the Elephantine Papyrus that Sanballat I is governor of Samaria. Tobiah may be the Persian governor of the Ammonites in east Judea. Neither of them wants to see Jerusalem restored, because they would lose their dominance of the region.

A life-sized figure of a Persian guard on a glazed frieze protects the new palace of Darius the Great at Susa.

Nehemiah surveys the ruins and begins
(Nehemiah 2:11–18)

Once in Jerusalem, Nehemiah inspects the ruined walls. He does so at night, so that no one will guess his plans.

He starts at the Valley Gate, on the south-west corner of the city. From there he visits the Dung Gate to the east, the Fountain Gate on the eastern wall and the King's Pool, which is probably the Pool of Siloam. He also goes some way along the Kidron Valley to review the damage there. He has now seen the worst of the destruction.

After completing his inspection, Nehemiah talks to his officials. He encourages them to work with him to rebuild the city's defences. In this way they will regain their self-respect. He tells them of his experience that God is with them.

Nehemiah defies his enemies
(Nehemiah 2:19–20)

As the work begins, Sanballat and Tobiah arrive to pour scorn on the project. They are joined by Geshem, a powerful Arab chieftain who rules the desert country to the south and south-east of Judah. Jerusalem is almost completely surrounded by enemies.

The critics ask if the Jews are rebelling against their Persian overlord. They are not, of course, but the suggestion is meant to stir up trouble. Nehemiah answers that this is God's work and God will grant them success. Jerusalem's enemies must stay away. They have no part or share in what is going on.

The work progresses well
(Nehemiah 3:1–32)

Nehemiah allocates sections of the wall to different people and groups. There are forty-two sections in all. They are listed in order, anticlockwise from the Sheep Gate on the north-east corner of the city.

Every kind and class of person takes part in the work – men and women, fathers and daughters, priests and Levites, officials and merchants, goldsmiths and perfume-makers. Most of them are working on the stretch of wall near their homes. In each section, the gatehouse is rebuilt and its doors restored and rehung.

Nehemiah organizes defence
(Nehemiah 4:1–23)

Sanballat's scorn turns to fury. To him the task seems impossible, with a puny workforce and damaged materials. Tobiah gives his opinion that even a fox could dislodge the whole structure. But the workers press on, fired up by prayers for help – and revenge. When the enemies threaten to attack, Nehemiah organizes half the people to provide an armed guard while the other half carry on with the work.

Nehemiah is a great motivator. He reminds people that they are fighting for their homes and families – and that God, the greatest fighter of all, is on their side.

Nehemiah secures a fair deal for the poor
(Nehemiah 5:1–13)

As the danger from enemies is confronted, another problem breaks out among the Israelites themselves.

Some of the poor people have had to forfeit their lands and are now having to sell their children into slavery. This is because there is a famine and food is scarce and expensive. In addition, all the Jews are paying taxes to the Persian king, supporting the Persian officials and their Jewish governor *and* providing tithes for the priests and temple.

Nehemiah is angry that wealthy Jews are charging their poorer neighbours 'usury', or interest on loans. This is forbidden in the law of Moses (Exodus 22:25), because all Jews are members of one family. It is wrong to charge interest on a loan within the family.

To tackle the problem of poverty, Nehemiah commands that all land and property shall be returned to its original owners. He also instructs the lenders to return the money and produce that they have taken as interest. This is a mini-Jubilee – good news for the poor and the cancelling of debts.

Nehemiah notes his self-restraint
(Nehemiah 5:14–19)

Nehemiah records that he has not behaved like other governors. He has not claimed a food allowance from the people. He has been sensitive to their poverty and unwilling to add to their burdens. He has been a hard-working governor, overseeing the rebuilding of the city wall and feeding a large number of officials at his own table.

Nehemiah's enemies try to intimidate him
(Nehemiah 6:1–19)

Sanballat and Geshem repeatedly invite Nehemiah to meet with them. Knowing that they plan to harm him, Nehemiah tells them he is busy with something far more important. Next, they send him a blackmail letter, left open so that the messenger can read it. In the letter they claim that the wall is being built in preparation for revolt, and Nehemiah is about to use prophets to proclaim himself king.

Nehemiah gives a simple and straightforward answer. None of what they say is true; it is all the product of their imagination. He denies the charges and prays that he will not be distracted from his task.

Now Tobiah and Sanballat send a false prophet to Nehemiah. The prophet's name is Shemaiah. He tries to frighten Nehemiah into hiding from his enemies in the temple, but Nehemiah has plenty of faith that God will protect him.

If Nehemiah is a eunuch, this suggestion is an attempt to compromise him. The law forbids a eunuch to enter the temple (Deuteronomy 23:1).

THE WALL IS COMPLETED!

The wall is completed on 25th Elul, in early September (6:15). The work has taken only fifty-two days. This is an amazingly short time, and a tribute to Nehemiah's inspiration, the people's dedication and the urgency of the situation.

The surrounding tribes are shaken by Israel's achievement. They had not thought it possible. Nehemiah regards the success as proof of the Lord's help.

Nehemiah appoints guards for the gates
(Nehemiah 7:1–3)

Nehemiah continues to protect Jerusalem by appointing gatekeepers and guards. He chooses only those who are trustworthy (many of them from the temple staff) and gives them clear instructions.

A list of those who first returned from exile
(Nehemiah 7:4–73)

Although the city is now secure, the population is very small. It seems that Nehemiah takes a census of the

people to see how many there are. He uses a checklist of returned exiles, which is the same as the list in Ezra 2.

Ezra reads the law and the people agree to obey it

Ezra reads the Book of the Law
(Nehemiah 8:1–12)

The story moves now to Ezra's memoirs.

The people ask Ezra to bring out the Book of the Law and read it to them. Standing high on a platform in the midst of a great gathering, Ezra reads the law aloud. The Levites also help him by explaining it to the people.

The reading of the law makes the Israelites weep, because they have failed to keep it. However, Nehemiah persuades them to see the joy of it – that God has revealed the right way to live. The law is a gift to be celebrated.

The oldest version of this text, in 1 Esdras, does not mention Nehemiah. This is part of the problem of knowing whether Ezra and Nehemiah were in fact in Jerusalem at the same time.

The people celebrate the Feast of Booths
(Nehemiah 8:13–18)

In the reading of the law the people rediscover the Feast of Booths. This is a week-long festival during which the Israelites live in shelters (booths or tabernacles) made from branches and palms.

The festival is a thanksgiving for the wilderness journey which brought the Israelites to the Promised Land. Living in booths is a reminder of the simple life of daily trust in God. Having found the instructions (Leviticus 23:39–43), they celebrate as never before. There are booths everywhere!

The Israelites confess their sins
(Nehemiah 9:1–37)

The Feast of Booths is followed by a great national act of repentance. The people gather together. They fast as

a sign of sorrow for their sins. They wear sackcloth and sprinkle dust on their heads as a mark of desolation.

For three hours they stand to hear the law of God read aloud to them. Then for three hours they worship God and confess their sins.

We assume it is Ezra who offers a great prayer. He tells of God's goodness in calling Abraham and promising him descendants and a land. He praises God for rescuing their ancestors from Egypt, giving them his law at Sinai and providing for them in the desert. He confesses the many times when, as a nation, they have rebelled and deserved punishment; yet even in judging them, God has been merciful.

Now Ezra comes to the point of his prayer. The Israelites are back in their own land, but they are slaves. They do not own their cattle, or even their own bodies. Their harvest is not their own to enjoy, but the tribute due to a foreign overlord.

They agree to follow God's law
(Nehemiah 9:38 – 10:27)

A binding agreement is made with God and signed by everyone. This is a new start.

Nehemiah's name is the first on the list, but has probably been added later, if his time in Jerusalem was after that of Ezra.

The people's promises
(Nehemiah 10:28–39)

The priests, Levites and ordinary people promise to keep God's law.

They promise not to intermarry with pagan nations.

They promise not to trade on the sabbath.

They promise to allow the land to rest, and cancel all debts every seventh (sabbath) year.

They promise to pay their dues to the temple, to provide for the offerings, sacrifices and maintenance of God's house.

They promise to provide wood for burning on the altar.

They promise to bring their harvest offerings each year.

They promise to dedicate their first-born children to the Lord, and the first-born offspring of their animals.

They promise to bring a tenth of their produce to the temple stores, to provide for the Levites, priests and temple staff.

A Bar Mitzvah ceremony in front of the Western Wall in Jerusalem. A Jewish boy is reading the Hebrew law, which he is now old enough to know and obey.

Resettlement and Nehemiah's reforms

The people who are settled in Jerusalem
(Nehemiah 11:1–24)

Here is a list of the people who are living in Jerusalem, or are deputed to move there. It is decided to increase the population of the city by moving 10 per cent of people from the other towns of Judah.

The people who live in the villages
(Nehemiah 11:25–36)

This is a list of the towns occupied by the descendants of Judah and Benjamin. The Valley of Hinnom and Beersheba mark Judah's northern and southern boundaries.

A list of priests and Levites
(Nehemiah 12:1–26)

The historian lists the priests and Levites who returned from exile in Babylon with the group led by Zerubbabel. Some other details are also included, tracing the pedigree of famous names such as Eliashib and Jonathan, and noting some of the tasks and responsibilities that people had.

The dedication of the wall of Jerusalem
(Nehemiah 12:27–43)

Now we return to the memoirs of Nehemiah.

The rebuilding of Jerusalem's walls has been completed. They are dedicated by the priests with a festival of music – Levites playing instruments, the singers forming two choirs and priests blowing trumpets. The choirs lead two groups around the wall, processing in opposite directions; then all converge in the temple forecourt. It is an occasion of exceptional joy.

Ezra is credited with leading the procession, but this is impossible as he doesn't come to Jerusalem until much later.

Providing for the temple staff
(Nehemiah 12:44–47)

The stores of supplies for the priests, Levites and temple staff are successfully organized. This is how David and Solomon intended it to be.

Zerubbabel and Nehemiah have at last restored the temple, its offerings, music and administration to its original design. They have also organized the arrangements for the Levites to live on the tithes brought in by the other tribes. The Levites in their turn give their tithe to provide for the priests.

Nehemiah's reforms
(Nehemiah 13:1–31)

Foreigners are excluded from Israel.

It is discovered in the book of Moses that the Ammonites and Moabites are to be banned from the assembly of God's people. This command is one of the laws in the book of Deuteronomy (Deuteronomy 23:3–4).

The Moabites became enemies centuries ago, when the Israelites were passing through their land on the way to Canaan. The Moabites hired a prophet called Balaam to curse the strange new people who were so quickly becoming a powerful nation (Numbers 22:4–6). In fact Balaam was a true prophet, and found he could only bless the Israelites and predict their ultimate victory. He even foresaw the 'star' of the Messiah (Numbers 24:17–19).

In the book of Ruth, we have a story which begins with two Israelite brothers marrying Moabite women. It is by her 'mixed' marriage that Ruth, a Moabite, becomes a member of the people of God, and an ancestor of Jesus Christ. After the exile, there is a move against such marriages. Nehemiah ensures that foreigners are excluded from Israel.

TOBIAH IS EVICTED FROM THE TEMPLE

There is also a crisis over Tobiah, who is an Ammonite (13:4–9).

In 433 BC, after twelve years as governor, Nehemiah leaves Jerusalem to visit the Persian court. While he is away, Eliashib the high priest allows Tobiah, the Samaritan governor, to make his home in one of the temple storerooms!

As well as being a foreigner, Tobiah has also been one of the main opponents of the rebuilding programme. When Nehemiah returns, he takes swift action to evict him. The temple room is thoroughly cleaned and restored to its proper use.

There is a strong sense that God's house can be contaminated if non-Jews come into it. Paul will one day be accused (wrongly) of bringing a Gentile into the Jewish part of the temple (Acts 21:27–29).

THE LEVITES ARE PROVIDED FOR

Nehemiah finds that the arrangements which provide for the Levites have been allowed to lapse (13:10–14). This means that the temple staff have dispersed, as the Levites have had to go home to their fields to support themselves.

Nehemiah summons the Levites to return to their temple work, and calls on the people to bring in their tithes. He puts responsible people in charge of the stores.

SABBATH TRADING IS FORBIDDEN

Nehemiah is angry when he sees Israelites working on the sabbath day (13:15–22). The commandment is that God's people shall do no work on the seventh day of the week, but set it aside as a holy day for worship and rest (Exodus 20:8–11). Foreign traders are also bringing their goods and produce into Jerusalem on the sabbath.

Nehemiah sees sabbath trading as inviting God's punishment. He forbids all commercial activity on the sabbath, by both Jews and non-Jews, both inside and outside the city. He uses the Levites to police the situation.

FOREIGN MARRIAGES ARE ANNULLED

Finally, Nehemiah is outraged when he sees the evidence of mixed marriages (13:23–31). Some Israelites have married Philistine women from Ashdod, or taken wives from the nations of Ammon and Moab. Many of their children are unable to speak Hebrew, and have a foreign language as their native tongue.

Nehemiah believes that these marriages will destroy the purity of the Israelite people and their faith. He curses and angrily attacks the men who have behaved in this way, and commands them to stop intermarrying.

Nehemiah reminds the offending Jews that King Solomon made the same terrible mistake, and with disastrous consequences. Foreign marriages were the means by which pagan gods came into Israel. The resulting idolatry was one of the sins which led to the exile.

Even one of Eliashib's sons has married a daughter of his old enemy Sanballat. While Nehemiah has been at the Persian court, Tobiah and Sanballat have forged a close alliance with Israel's high priest. They have achieved a degree of influence through friendship which they never managed by being enemies. Now Nehemiah purges the priesthood and sets them afresh to their tasks and responsibilities.

Nehemiah is a great leader with a deep trust in God –

although we wince when he starts pulling out other men's hair! Perhaps his greatest example to us is the way he so constantly prays for God's help and so consistently seeks to obey God's word.

Nehemiah's rigorous approach may seem harsh to us, but was greatly needed at that time. In the face of Israel's enemies, Nehemiah built a physical wall around Jerusalem. In the face of compromise with foreign nations and their worthless idols, he raised the protection of God's law.

As a result of the work of both Ezra and Nehemiah, the Jews were able to become established again in their homeland. They were able to recover from the nightmare and disintegration of the exile, to serve God once again as his holy and distinctive people.

ESTHER

Here is an exciting tale, full of colourful characters, strong passions and extraordinary coincidences. It is a typically Jewish story. Its purpose is to remind its hearers that God is able to protect his people against any danger, even in a foreign land.

Outline

Esther becomes queen (1:1 – 2:18)

Mordecai saves the king's life (2:19–23)

The plot to destroy the Jews (3:1 – 7:10)

The Jews are allowed to defend themselves (8:1–17)

The origin of the Feast of Purim (9:1–32)

The greatness of Mordecai (10:1–3)

INTRODUCTION

The story

Esther is a Jewess, living in Persia with her cousin Mordecai. She is very beautiful. The king of Persia, Xerxes, falls in love with her and makes her his queen, not realizing that she is a Jew.

Meanwhile, Mordecai makes an enemy. This is Haman, who is one of the most powerful people in the land. Haman plans not only to kill Mordecai, but also to exterminate the Jews in every province of the empire. But Mordecai is in close touch with his cousin, the queen...

Encouraged by Mordecai, Esther risks her life. She goes into the king's presence without being summoned. Mercifully, Xerxes spares her and asks her request. As an answer, Esther invites the king to dine with her, with Haman as their honoured guest.

After the meal, Haman returns home elated at his good fortune. He decides to build a monstrous gallows on which to hang Mordecai. Meanwhile the king passes a sleepless night reading the records of his reign – and is reminded that he owes Mordecai a favour.

When the king and Haman meet the next day, they are delightfully at cross purposes. The king asks Haman's advice on how best to honour a man. Haman (thinking he is the one to be honoured) prescribes a procession fit for a prince – only to find himself having to arrange it all for Mordecai!

At a second banquet, Esther asks the king to spare her life and avert the slaughter that has been decreed for the Jews. The king is furious that such an outrage has been planned, and demands to know the culprit. Esther reveals that Haman, who is dining with them, is the villain. Now Haman is exposed as a coward and a bully. As he pleads for his life, he seals his fate by appearing to assault the queen. Xerxes has Haman hanged on the very gallows he had built for Mordecai.

At last Esther is able to tell the king how she and Mordecai are related. The king gives Haman's estate to Esther and his ring to Mordecai. But how is the extermination of the Jews to be averted? The royal command has gone out to every province of the empire that all Jews are to be killed on a certain day – the 13th day of the month of Adar. The day was chosen by Haman through the casting of *pur* or lots.

The king's order must stand, but Esther and Mordecai persuade him to send out a further decree. At Mordecai's dictation, the scribes and translators dispatch orders that the Jews are allowed to defend themselves. They have the right to kill anyone who attacks them. His task completed, Mordecai leaves the king's presence dressed splendidly in crown and royal robes.

When the 13th day of Adar arrives, the Jews defend themselves with great success, and avenge many scores with old enemies. The date becomes the Feast of Purim for future generations – the last feast in the Jewish year.

Did the story of Esther really happen?

The story of Esther is quite extraordinary, with its pantomime characters and fantastic timing. Esther is a beautiful princess in danger of her life. The Jewish people are threatened with extinction by the wicked vizier, Haman. King Xerxes is as unpredictable as he is powerful, and can command anyone's death at any moment.

But although the story sounds as though it has leapt from the Tales of the Arabian Nights, or the Histories of Herodotus, it is carefully written. The author quotes the place in which the story is set (a provincial capital, Susa) and the date (the third year of the king's reign). If this is a novel, it is based on many accurate facts. The person writing has inside knowledge of the Persian court and government, as well as strong sympathies with the Jewish people caught up in its power play.

The truth of the book of Esther may be even more exciting – that this is an account of God's amazing and timely deliverance of his people. This is, after all, the way the author tells it – and the reason why Esther is a popular and frequently read book among the Jews even today.

In English Bibles, the book of Esther is placed with those of Ezra and Nehemiah. They all record events that take place in the days of the Persian empire.

The book of Esther never mentions God directly. For this reason many scholars (including Martin Luther) have challenged its right to a place in the Bible. All the same, it is very much a Bible story, showing how God uses those who are faithful and brave to do his will. Esther and Mordecai in Persia are like Joseph in Egypt or Daniel in Babylon – all of them raised to high office under a pagan ruler, for the glory of God and the safe keeping of his people.

Living in a pagan world

On a serious note, the story of Esther raises the question of how Jews should maintain their distinctive standards and way of life in a pagan world. The answer seems to be that they must seek the good of their ruler and their neighbours, and put their trust in God in times of persecution. Although the Jews kill many of their enemies at the end of the story of Esther, and see the sons of Haman hanged, there is a strong message in their refusal to take any plunder from their victims. They will defend themselves against injustice, but their welfare and hope is in God alone.

DISCOVERING ESTHER

Esther becomes queen
(1:1 – 2:18)

King Xerxes is the Persian emperor. Xerxes is his Greek name, but he is also known as Ahasuerus or Khshayarshan. His empire is vast, stretching from India to Cush – the Upper Nile in Egypt.

Our story is set in Susa. This is the ancient city of Elam which Darius had rebuilt, and which is now the place where Xerxes has his winter palace.

King Xerxes invites the leading figures of his government and armies to a magnificent banquet. During it he summons Queen Vashti to show off her beauty, but she refuses to appear. This act of female defiance is considered a dangerous example to other wives. The queen is banished by royal decree. Here we see something of the style of the Persian empire as well as the character of its king.

The king is easily led by his advisers when they suggest that he should choose a new queen from among the most beautiful virgins in the empire. Among them – and already living in Susa – is Hadassah, or Esther. Hadassah is the Hebrew word for 'Myrtle', while Esther may be the Persian word for 'Star'. The young woman lives under the guardianship of her older cousin, Mordecai.

The Persian empire... and Xerxes

The Persian empire is founded by Cyrus, who conquers the Babylonians in 539 BC. Cyrus is generous to the religious and national groups in his realm, and gives permission for Jews to return to Jerusalem after their years of exile in Babylonia. However, some Jews remain scattered throughout the Persian empire, and it is part of their story that the book of Esther has to tell.

Cyrus is succeeded as king by Darius, who establishes the administration of the mighty empire. He in turn is succeeded by his son Xerxes, who reigns from 486 to 465 BC.

The Greek historian Herodotus wrote his books in the 5th century BC, not long after the reign of Xerxes. He describes the great king as cruel and unpredictable.

The Persian emperor's own words are recorded on a monument found at Persepolis:

I am Xerxes, the great king, the only king, the king of all countries which speak all kinds of languages, the king of the big and far-reaching earth.

Mordecai

Mordecai, with Esther, is the hero of this story. A baked clay tablet has been found at Borsippa, near Babylon, which names a man called Marduka as a leading official in the court of Susa in the early years of King Xerxes. If Marduka is Mordecai, then perhaps he is already an important person at court, even before Esther becomes queen. This explains the jealousy and racial hatred of other ambitious courtiers, such as Haman. The book of Esther is an early story of anti-Semitism – persecution of the Jews.

In future reigns, under Artaxerxes I and Darius II, there will be many Jews in prominent positions in the Persian government. Perhaps it is Mordecai who paves the way for other members of his gifted race to be entrusted with high office.

Mordecai saves the king's life
(2:19–23)

Meanwhile, Mordecai sits at the king's gate. This may be so that he can keep in touch with Esther, or because he is in fact a royal official overseeing the business of the palace. From this vantage point, Mordecai overhears a plot being made to kill the king (2:19–23). He is able to warn Esther of the danger, with the result that the king's life is spared. Mordecai's good service is recorded in the official history of the reign – to be remembered later in the story!

The plot to destroy the Jews
(3:1 – 7:10)

HAMAN PLOTS TO DESTROY THE JEWS

Esther has complied with all that has been asked of her – and has become queen. Mordecai, on the other hand, now runs into trouble. He is required to bow down before the newly promoted Haman – something he refuses to do. Haman is described as an Agagite. This may mean that he is descended from Agag the Amalekite, and is therefore one of Israel's traditional enemies (1 Samuel 15:32–33). In any case Mordecai is a devout Jew and will bow only to God. This, again, was the same dilemma Daniel and his companions had faced in a pagan culture (Daniel 3).

Haman is furious. However, it seems too small a thing merely to kill Mordecai. He seeks to exterminate the entire Jewish population of the Persian empire (3:1–15). To discover a lucky date for the massacre, Haman has a lot (*pur*) cast to reveal the ideal month and day. The lot falls on the month of Adar, at the end of the year. It is the *pur* which will give its name to the Jewish Feast of Purim – but Haman will not live to see it.

King Xerxes agrees that Haman may issue a royal decree

While Esther awaits her call to the king, she becomes a favourite with Hegai, the eunuch in charge of the royal harem. Like Daniel in the court of Babylon, she acts wisely as befits one of God's people.

Daniel and his friends refused the royal food and wine, in order to keep their self-discipline and devotion to God. Esther adopts a different policy, forging a friendship with Hegai and enjoying his protection and good advice. She also obeys Mordecai in keeping her Jewish identity a secret.

When the time comes for Esther to go to the king, she wins his heart with her pure beauty and unaffected manner. Xerxes makes her his queen, with great celebration.

Esther comes before King Ahasuerus, in a French illustration from the early 16th century.

for the destruction of the Jews. Haman offers a huge amount of silver to pay those who will carry out the massacre. The king declines the money, but gives Haman his personal ring to sign the orders. Haman is now the king's grand vizier, with unlimited powers.

The royal command is sent out to every province in every language of the empire, using the fine postal network created by Cyrus. Once sent, such a decree can never be changed or cancelled. The 'Law of the Medes and Persians' is still a byword for something immutable; but it is more to do with pride than perfection, both then and now.

ESTHER RISKS HER LIFE

As the king's decree becomes known, Mordecai and his fellow Jews cover themselves in sackcloth and dust themselves with ashes. This is a sign of grief and desolation in the face of death.

When Esther hears of Mordecai's state, she sends a eunuch to discover what has happened. Mordecai tells him of the dreadful situation, supplies him with a copy of the decree, and sends a message asking Esther to plead with the king for mercy (4:1 – 5:3).

This is not as easy as it sounds. Esther sends a message back to Mordecai that even the queen cannot

Mordecai and Esther depicted on a mural from Dura Europos, in modern Syria. The mural adorns one of the earliest existing synagogues, dating from c. AD 245.

The survival of the Jews

The story of Esther reminds us that the Jews have suffered hatred and persecution throughout their history, not least in the pogroms and death camps of the 20th century. The Feast of Purim is a celebration of their deliverance, and of the God who keeps his promise to protect them.

go into the royal presence without being summoned. To do so is to risk an immediate sentence of death. Furthermore, she is not sure that she is in favour with the king at this time.

Mordecai's answer is a high point of the story, and the clearest statement of his faith in God's power to deliver them. He warns Esther that she will not escape the massacre herself. God will of course make sure his people survive, but Esther's own branch of the Jewish nation will certainly be destroyed. What has she to lose by going into the king's presence? Might it not be for this very purpose that she has become queen?

Esther, after much fasting and prayer, takes her life in her hands and goes into the king's presence unbidden. To her great relief Xerxes extends his sceptre towards her –

the sign of mercy and permission to approach his majesty. He invites his queen to make her request, but Esther merely opens the way for a special meal together – with Haman.

HAMAN'S HATRED OF MORDECAI

Haman is delighted at the honour of dining with the king and queen. Only one thing spoils his glee, and that is the sight of Mordecai, who stubbornly refuses to bow to him as he passes through the king's gate (5:9:14).

On the advice of his wife and friends, Haman resolves to build the tallest of gallows, and get the king's permission to hang Mordecai on it the very next day.

We cannot help but compare the wisdom and humility of Mordecai and Esther, who seek God's guidance in fasting and prayer, with Haman who is ruled by ambition, jealousy, rage, superstition and peer pressure.

MORDECAI IS HONOURED, AND HAMAN HANGED

By one of those extraordinary coincidences which bring excitement to the story, the king has a sleepless night. To pass the time he sends for the record of his reign and has it read aloud until morning.

The passages of the chronicles which are read include the account of Mordecai saving the king's life. Xerxes has forgotten all about this until now, and is dismayed to find that Mordecai has never been rewarded. He resolves to honour the Jew as soon as possible. At that very moment Haman arrives, and is asked his advice on how this might be done!

Assuming the honour is for him, Haman suggests a procession through the streets, dressed in royal robes and riding a royal horse. The horse is to wear a royal headdress, and is to be led by a noble prince. The king is pleased with the idea, and commands Haman to carry it out in every detail for Mordecai. Haman himself is to lead the horse and shout out Mordecai's fame. Afterwards, it is Haman's turn to cover his head in grief!

That evening the king and queen dine with Haman again, and Xerxes again invites Esther to make her request. At last she feels the time is right. She tells the king about the decree to destroy her people, and pleads that both she and they may be spared.

The king is furious at the situation and demands to know who has engineered it. The culprit is with them at the table, and Xerxes strides out into the garden in a rage to decide what action to take. Left alone with the queen, Haman throws himself on her in desperation and terror. When the king catches him like this, his fate is sealed. Haman is led away with his face covered. He is as good as dead.

When Xerxes hears that Haman has prepared a gallows for Mordecai, he orders that the grand vizier be hanged on it himself. This is typical of the vindication the Jews expect when God saves them from their enemies:

> *They make a pit, digging it out,*
> * and fall into the hole that they have made.*
> *Their mischief returns upon their own heads,*
> * and on their own heads their violence descends*
> * (Psalm 7:15–16).*

A Persian necklace of gold and agate dating from about the 6th to 7th centuries BC.

The Jews are allowed to defend themselves
(8:1–17)

With Haman disgraced and executed, the king gives his estate to Esther. She is finally able to tell Xerxes (who is always the last to know anything) that Mordecai is her cousin. The ring the king had given to Haman is now presented to the Jew. Mordecai is the new grand vizier.

There is one more favour for Esther to ask, and it is that Haman's plan to annihilate the Jews should be averted. Xerxes puts the matter in Mordecai's hands, to publish a further decree granting the Jews the right to assemble together and defend themselves (8:1–17). The first decree may never be revoked, but at least a further decree can give the Jews a fighting chance.

Mordecai leaves the king's presence dressed in royal robes – not this time as a short-lived honour, but as the rightful regalia of his office. As the decree reaches the provinces of the Persian empire, there is joy and celebration in every Jewish community. In Susa itself, perplexity changes to gladness. People of other nations see what has happened, and put their faith in the God of the Jews.

The origin of the Feast of Purim
(9:1–32)

When the 13th day of Adar arrives, the Jews are well prepared. Many of their enemies dare not stand against them, but others do so and are destroyed.

In Susa there is widespread bloodshed, and the ten sons of Haman are among those who are killed. Esther asks the king's permission for the time of revenge to be extended, so that Haman's sons may be hanged the following day. Their humiliation has continued down the ages, with a Jewish tradition that their names are printed vertically. They are still left hanging!

Even though the Jews are carrying all before them, they steadfastly refuse to take any plunder. It is the principle that counts, not the profit.

The author describes how the Feast of Purim comes about (9:1–32). It is a two-day festival on the 14th and 15th days of the month of Adar, the anniversary of the Jews' deliverance from certain death and their revenge on their enemies. The fast and feast, with presents and partying, fall exactly a month before Passover.

Mordecai and Esther write to their fellow Jews in all the provinces of the Persian empire, instructing them

when and how to keep the festival. This is not a feast which is centred on Jerusalem or the temple, but on the celebration of the God who protects his people even in exile.

The greatness of Mordecai
(10:1–3)

The author closes the book of Esther by referring the reader to the official records of the Mede and Persian kings. In them is recorded the extent of Xerxes' empire and the distinguished role of Mordecai the Jew (10:1–3).

Like Joseph in Egypt and Daniel in Babylon, Mordecai is a man who, in the providence of God, has been found worthy of the highest responsibility in a pagan administration.

Persian and Median noblemen await an audience with the Persian emperor. This is a small section of the huge frieze on the staircase of the Apadana or audience hall at Persepolis, one of the most impressive structures of the ancient world. Persepolis was the greatest of five royal palaces created by Darius I, and completed during the reign of his son Xerxes I, the king who features in the story of Esther.

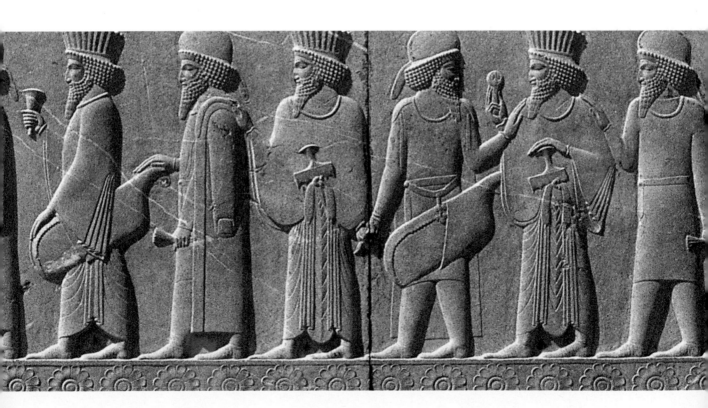

JOB

Job is a good man – an exceptionally good man! He has been blessed with children and great wealth. Indeed he is described as 'the greatest of all the people of the east' (1:3).

One day, and for no apparent reason, Job is plunged into terrible suffering. In a series of disasters, his children are taken from him, his cattle are seized and his property is destroyed. As if this isn't enough, he also loses his health. He is afflicted with painful sores from head to foot. Even his wife urges him to abandon his faith in God. She says to him, 'Are you still holding onto your integrity? Curse God and die!' (2:9).

But Job refuses to curse God. When his friends (Eliphaz, Bildad and Zophar) come to visit him, they at first sit in silence for a whole week. Then, in a complex and beautifully expressed debate, they consider the problem of human suffering. Is our suffering a punishment for our sins? Does God know about our suffering? Does he care about it, or is he the one who inflicts it?

The discussion is lengthy but orderly, with each of Job's friends exploring a point of view and Job answering. Despite his anguish, he maintains both his innocence and his faith. The debate goes round three times, with each friend contributing and Job answering. A young man, Elihu, expresses his exasperation that they have found no answer. Elihu says that God is able to rescue from suffering, but can also use it to punish or teach us. Above all, God is immeasurably great and unknowable.

When all has been said, God himself speaks to Job. He challenges Job to contemplate the vastness and wonder of creation and invites him to consider his own littleness and lack of understanding. Job humbles himself before the majesty and wisdom of God; and the story ends with God upholding Job's righteousness and restoring to him family and fortune.

MELVIN & STEPHANIE
... Close Woodford *Green, Essex* I...
Telephone: *01-505 0722*

Outline

INTRODUCTION

The problem of suffering

The book of Job is one of the world's greatest poems. It probes deeply into human suffering, exploring it from every angle.

Does suffering come because we have done something to deserve it? Is it God's punishment for our sins?

There are many occasions in the Bible when people get what they deserve; but the story of Job is different. While most people can think of a reason for their suffering, Job is convinced that he is innocent.

Three of Job's friends – Eliphaz, Bildad and Zophar – come to be with him. They discuss his situation, each giving their opinion on why this disaster has befallen him.

Job and his friends believe that God rules the world. Both blessing and suffering come from his hand. He rules the world by blessing good behaviour and punishing wickedness. But here is the exception to the rule. Job is a good person – as near perfect as is humanly possible – and yet he is inflicted with every kind of pain.

Even in the depth of his suffering, Job continues to have faith in God. He has enjoyed God's blessing and now he will endure God's trouble. Meanwhile, his friends suspect that he is being punished for some secret sin, and they urge him to confess it and get rid of the guilt. For his part, Job longs to be rescued and restored. He wants everyone to know that this terrible experience is not his fault.

Was Job sinless?

The book of Job never claims that Job is sinless. It simply says that he has done nothing to deserve his suffering. He himself admits that he isn't perfect. God knows, for example, the sins he committed when he was young (13:26). Of course Job is not entirely innocent – no one is. But his suffering is way beyond anything that he can possibly have deserved. If this is punishment for things he did when he was young, then it is out of all proportion to his faults. Here is an almost perfect human being who is undergoing every suffering short of death. Why is God allowing this to happen?

Perspective

The book of Job is not only a beautiful poem, it is also an absorbing discussion. It breaks new ground in the Old Testament's understanding of God's dealings with human beings. It is both a great masterpiece of literature and a superb exploration of our experience of life. It challenges all the popular ideas of why we suffer and how God governs the world. 'What have I done to deserve this?' 'There's no justice.' It also challenges the popular idea that we are being punished for the sins we have committed in a previous life.

Meanwhile, the story takes us behind the scenes to see what is happening in heaven. We find that Job is indeed blameless in the way he lives, and that God is pleased with him. But Satan argues that Job finds it easy to live a godly life because he is blessed with health and wealth. If all that were snatched away, he would soon turn against God. But God has complete faith in Job. He gives Satan permission to test him, but without taking his life.

Satan – evil with attitude

The book of Job tells us more about Satan.

Satan first appears in the Bible as the serpent who tempts Eve in the Garden of Eden (Genesis 3:1–5). The story of Job is older than any of the Bible books – so this is the earliest portrayal of Satan that we have.

The meaning of 'Satan' seems to be 'To Obstruct'. Satan is the one who hinders God's purposes, criticizes human motives and is sceptical that goodness can ever be genuine.

In the Hebrew Bible, 'Satan' can be anyone who adopts the stance of an accuser or adversary – so 'Satan' is not as much a particular person as an attitude (2 Samuel 19:22; 1 Kings 11:14).

In the book of Job, Satan is a member of God's council. When God expresses pride in Job's blameless and upright life, Satan sets out to prove that Job's goodness is shallow. According to Satan, Job is only good because it suits him. Job's righteousness will soon disappear if he is plunged into poverty, bereavement, physical pain and mental anguish.

So Satan is at the heart of the debate about where evil comes from, and whether evil is under God's control. Other religions have tackled the same problem – sometimes deciding that there must be two equal and opposite powers striving for control of the world – good and bad. This is called 'dualism'.

The Bible does not offer us dualism, but nor does it tell us where evil comes from. When Satan appears, he is clearly a part of God's creation who is critical and rebellious, but ultimately under God's authority.

In the books of Genesis and Job, Satan tries to prove to God that human beings are worthless. Satan stirs up criticism and doubt, to spoil the relationship between humankind and God. He wants God and humans to mistrust each other and so fall out.

At the same time, the writer of Job avoids saying that Satan is the cause of Job's suffering. Job is suffering because God allows it. At the end of the book, the writer says, 'They comforted and consoled him over all the trouble the Lord had brought upon him' (42:11). We never really know why God responds to Satan's challenge by allowing Job to suffer.

Who wrote the book of Job?

We don't know who wrote the book of Job, nor when it was written. It has been placed in the Bible after the history books and alongside the Psalms and the writings of Solomon. These books contain deep reflections on the relationship between God and human beings. There are angry outbursts at the silence of God and the pain of the human condition. Some people think that the book of Job is an attempt to understand why God's people suffered so terribly when they were overrun by their enemies and carried off into exile. But, as the history books show us, such suffering was hardly undeserved!

Why do bad things happen to good people?

When tragedy strikes innocent people, it challenges our belief that God is good, wise and powerful.

The book of Job explores these great questions, and gives us some bearings.

First of all, God entirely desires the well-being of his creation. He has pleasure in Job's upright life, and trusts that he will keep his faith even through intense and prolonged trial.

Satan works hard to destroy the trust between human beings and God, but his power is limited.

All the speakers in the poem believe that God is both the creator of the universe and the perfect judge of right and wrong. He is holy and majestic, yet concerned with the smallest detail in the lives of his creatures.

Clearly, God is stronger than evil, but allows evil to have its effect for the time being. This world is a place in which we can make moral decisions and develop godly character. Hardship and temptation play their parts in getting us spiritually fit.

It is true that in this world we often suffer for our mistakes and reap the consequences of our actions. But it isn't always so. There are exceptions. The Bible shows us people who get what they deserve *and* people who don't deserve what they get.

The book of Job shows us undeserved suffering. We cannot simply say that God always blesses the good and always punishes the wicked. Every day we see good people suffering while wicked people prosper.

The New Testament takes the whole matter much further. We see God *involved* in human suffering. God comes to us, not with smooth excuses or brisk retorts, but in the shape of his dreadfully rejected and brutally murdered Son. All our indignant questions and challenges fall silent in the presence of Christ on his cross, the crucified God.

We may not find all the answers to our questions in Job. But, like Job, we have a question put back to us: 'Will we let God be God?'

DISCOVERING JOB

Job's troubles

Job is introduced
(1:1–5)

Job is a man of all-round goodness. He is at peace with God, prosperous in his possessions and blessed with a large family. He lives an upright life and is careful to offer sacrifices for any possible sins of his children.

God gives permission for Satan to test Job
(1:6 – 2:10)

The scene changes. The story moves to God's council in heaven and a conversation between the Lord and Satan. God asks Satan if he has noticed Job's wholesome attitude and lifestyle; but Satan accuses God of giving Job special protection. If God changed Job's circumstances, he would soon start to curse him!

And so God gives Satan permission to test Job in every way, short of taking his life. There follows a series of disasters in which Job's sons and daughters are seized and his servants killed, his sheep consumed by a fire from heaven and his camels carried off by raiders. Finally, a hurricane destroys the house of his eldest son and takes the lives of his remaining children.

Job is devastated by this turn of events. In grief he tears his robe, shaves his head and lies face forward on the ground before God. But, in all his anguish, he refuses to blame or curse God. All that he had was given him by God, and if God chooses to take it away again, so be it.

When Satan finds that Job's faith is still firm, he covers him in sores from head to foot. As Job sits desolate among the ashes of grief and loss, even his wife urges him to curse God and die.

Job's friends
(2:11–13)

As he sits on an ash heap – bereft of his family and covered in sores – Job is visited by three friends. Each of them tries to help him understand why he is suffering so terribly. They all say things that are true and right – but they don't apply to Job! Even today we speak of 'Job's comforters' – people who come alongside us, and think they are being helpful, but leave us feeling rather worse.

Job is already thinking deeply about his situation. He is experiencing acute pain in his mind, body and spirit. However his friends explain the suffering, it is he who is having to endure it. To their credit, the three friends begin by sitting with Job in silence, day and night, for a week. Their silent company and sympathy is probably the best thing they can offer him – certainly better than the words that are to come.

Job's cry of anguish

(3:1–26)

Such is his pain that Job wishes he had never been born. It would have been better to be stillborn or to have died at birth. He desires death like a treasure – to allow him to escape his suffering and be at peace. It is a dreadful torture to have light without sight and life without happiness and freedom.

The shadow of suffering. Job describes the counsel of his friends as a dried-up river bed. The desert travellers leave their route to look for refreshing water – only to be disappointed and distressed.

The speeches of Job's friends

The first round of discussion (4:1 – 14:22)

◆ *Eliphaz's first speech and Job's reply (4:1 – 7:21)*

◆ *Bildad's first speech and Job's reply (8:1 – 10:22)*

◆ *Zophar's first speech and Job's reply (11:1 – 14:22)*

The second round of discussion (15:1 – 21:34)

◆ *Eliphaz's second speech and Job's reply (15:1 – 17:16)*

◆ *Bildad's second speech and Job's reply (18:1 – 19:29)*

◆ *Zophar's second speech and Job's reply (20:1 – 21:34)*

The third round of discussion (22:1 – 31:40)

◆ *Eliphaz's third speech and Job's reply (22:1 – 24:25)*

◆ *Bildad's third speech and Job's reply (25:1 – 26:14)*

The three rounds of discussion

Each of Job's friends speaks in turn and Job replies.

Eliphaz

The first of the friends to speak is Eliphaz. He is probably the oldest and certainly the kindliest of the three. He believes firmly in the holiness of God – and has some

experiences of his own that he is eager to share. Of course, he has no idea (as we do) that the cause of Job's suffering is that God has allowed Satan to test him. Instead he rather suspects that Job has done something to deserve this punishment. Surely no one has ever suffered without deserving it?

Consider now: Who, being innocent, has ever perished?

Where were the upright ever destroyed?
As I have observed, those who plough evil,
* and those who sow trouble, reap it (4:7–8).*

Throughout this debate, Eliphaz and his friends assume that God rules the world in such a way that good is always rewarded and evil is always punished. But Job is a test case which proves otherwise. Sometimes God allows people to suffer who *don't* deserve it.

Meanwhile, Eliphaz prescribes his remedy:

If it were I, I would appeal to God;
I would lay my cause before him (5:8).

Job should take his punishment courageously. It will do him good:

How happy is the one whom
God reproves;
therefore do not despise the
discipline of the Almighty.
For he wounds, but he binds up;
he strikes, but his hands heal
(5:17–18).

Job's reply is that he is indeed bearing the discipline of the Almighty – and nobody knows that better than he does. He needs the support of his friends, not their accusation.

When Eliphaz speaks again (in chapter 15) he increases the pressure on Job to admit his guilt. Job has far too high an opinion of himself:

Are you the firstborn of the
human race…
What do you know that we do
not know? (15:7, 9).

Eliphaz feels that Job has gone quite far enough in criticizing God and dismissing the advice of his friends. He describes the defiance of wicked people, followed by their ruin. He implies that Job fits the description rather well.

Job longs that Eliphaz would stop crafting fine speeches and instead give him the comfort of genuine understanding. It's bad enough being used as target practice by God without also being subjected to the harsh opinions of friends.

When Eliphaz speaks again (in chapter 22) he tries to convince Job that he is guilty of self-righteousness. Probably God isn't that bothered anyway:

What pleasure would it give the Almighty if you were
righteous?
What would he gain if your ways were blameless
(22:3)?

Surely Job isn't being punished for being good. There must be some underlying sin. Perhaps he didn't lend freely to his family, or respond to the needs of the thirsty and hungry, or made the plight of widows and orphans worse. Eliphaz advises him to repent:

Submit to God and be at peace
with him;
in this way prosperity will come
to you (22:21).

But Job knows that he *is* submitting to God. There is nothing more he can do to get right with God. Eliphaz is failing to see that Job really *is* innocent, and to hear the cry of desolation and anger coming from Job's heart.

Bildad

The second of Job's friends is Bildad. From the start, he takes a rigorous approach to the problem. As far as he is concerned, God always acts justly. If Job's children have died, it can only be because they have deserved it. If Job is innocent – as he claims he is – then he can confidently appeal to God and get some action.

If you will look to God
and plead with the Almighty,
if you are pure and upright,
even now he will rouse himself on your behalf
and restore you to your rightful place (8:5–6).

Bildad believes that the world runs in a predictable way. Just as certain laws of nature are always true (for example, that papyrus reeds grow best in marshland) so there is a moral law at work. God can never reject a blameless person – it would be against his nature to do so.

When Bildad speaks again (in chapter 18), he is offended that Job is rejecting all this good advice. Job is being far too arrogant in claiming to be a special case. He warns Job of the terrible fate that awaits the wicked:

They are thrust from light into darkness,
and driven out of the world.

Job accuses God of gradually destroying human hope, just as running water wears away stones and erodes soil.

Job's redeemer

Even in his torment, Job believes that someone will come and prove him right. This person is his 'redeemer':

> *I know that my Redeemer lives,*
> *and that in the end he will stand upon the earth (19:25).*

Mention of a redeemer makes Christians think of the Lord Jesus Christ, who rescues us from sin, delivers us from death and restores our status as children of God. This, of course, is far more than Job can hope for – living as he does many hundreds of years before the time of Christ. But his experience of undeserved suffering helps us to understand what will happen to Jesus. Jesus didn't deserve to suffer either – but he took the punishment that should have been ours.

> They have no offspring or descendant among
>   their people,
> and no survivor where they used to live (18:18–19).

But Job begs his friends to change their minds:

> Have pity on me, my friends, have pity,
>   for the hand of God has struck me.
> Why do you pursue me as God does?
>   Will you never get enough of my flesh (19:21–22)?

In his third speech (in chapter 25), Bildad tries to give a different perspective. He reminds Job that God is perfect. However innocent Job feels himself to be, he can hardly be pure enough for God:

> How then can a mortal be righteous before God?…
> If even the moon is not bright
>   and the stars are not pure in his sight,
> how much less a mortal, who is a maggot,
>   and a human being, who is a worm (25:4–6)!

Job responds with heavy sarcasm. Bildad's track record of good deeds and insight leaves him little reason

to boast – and still less to advise others! Job continues to insist that he hasn't deserved his fate:

> I will never admit you are in the right;
>   till I die, I will not deny my integrity.
> I will maintain my righteousness and never let go of it;
>   my conscience will not reproach me as long as I
>   live (27:5–6).

Zophar

Job's third friend is Zophar. He is indignant that Job still maintains his innocence. He wishes that God himself would intervene to declare the true state of affairs. It is not for human beings to pass judgment on God's ways. His mysteries are too deep for us to probe. Whatever he decides must be right and there can be no appeal.

Like the others, Zophar's advice is that Job should repent:

> If you devote your heart to him
>   and stretch out your hands to him,
> if you put away the sin that is in your hand
>   and allow no evil to dwell in your tent,
> then you will lift up your face without shame;
>   you will stand firm and without fear (11:13–15).

But Job dismisses this advice. The answer to his suffering does not lie in repentance – because he has nothing of which to repent. It is simply not true that he has only to repent and his happiness will be restored:

> I desire to speak to the Almighty
>   and to argue my case with God (13:3).

In his second speech (in chapter 20), Zophar describes the fate of the wicked. They are punished for their sins:

> For they have crushed and abandoned the poor,
>   they have seized a house that they did not build…
> The heavens will reveal their iniquity,
>   and the earth will rise up against them.
> The possessions of their house will be carried away,
>   dragged off on the day of God's wrath.
> This is the portion of the wicked from God,
>   the heritage decreed for them by God (20:19, 27–29).

Job answers that this simply isn't true. God may be a moral God, and the universe may hold consequences for those who are wicked. But Job's point is that people like him are suffering innocently – and the wicked are having a very good time!

> *Why do the wicked live on,*
> *growing old and increasing in power?*
> *They see their children established around them,*
> *their offspring before their eyes.*
> *Their homes are safe and free from fear;*
> *the rod of God is not upon them (21:7–9).*

Job's cry of despair – and hope

Job's friends are eloquent and well meaning. They are rich in their knowledge of God. But in the end they can't relate to Job's trouble. He describes them as 'miserable comforters' (16:2)!

But then, from the depths of his agony, Job makes a ringing declaration of faith:

> *I know that my Redeemer lives,*
> *and that in the end he will stand upon the earth.*
> *And after my skin has been destroyed,*
> *yet in my flesh I will see God;*
> *I myself will see him with my own eyes –*
> *I, and not another.*
> *How my heart yearns within me (19:25–29)!*

A 'redeemer' is a kinsman you can rely on for help. He is the next of kin who pays a debt or avenges a wrong. In the story of Ruth, Boaz is the kinsman-redeemer who cares for Naomi and marries her widowed daughter-in-law.

The God of Israel is a redeemer to his people. He rescues them in time of need. Now Job expresses his faith that this saving God will appear as his redeemer. His vindicator will stand up and tell everyone that Job is right – despite all the mystery of his present suffering.

As Christians, we have problems with suffering. Is it that God doesn't care? Or is the evil in this world too strong for him? But we see, in Jesus on the cross, that God enters into our suffering and bears it and redeems it. Jesus Christ is our kinsman-redeemer – the next of kin we can rely on.

IF ONLY...

Job wishes he could call on God somewhere – go and knock on his door and argue his case:

> *If only I knew where to find him;*
> *if only I could go to his dwelling!*
> *I would state my case before him*
> *and fill my mouth with arguments (23:3–4).*

Job isn't looking to win an argument with God. He simply longs to be in fellowship with him. But God is unobtainable. Remote. High-handed. Job doesn't know where the next blow is going to fall:

> *He stands alone, and who can oppose him?*
> *He does whatever he pleases.*
> *He carries out his decree against me,*
> *and many such plans he still has in store.*
> *That is why I am terrified before him (23:13–14).*

And why doesn't God step in and sort out some of the wrongdoers? What about bullies, kidnappers, murderers and adulterers?

> *Why does the Almighty not set times for judgment?*
> *Why must those who know him look in vain for*
> *such days (24:1)?*

But, despite his indignation and bewilderment, Job clings to his faith in God – and defies the opinions of his friends:

> *As surely as God lives, who has denied me justice...*
> *I will never admit you are in the right (27:1–5).*

Where can wisdom be found?

Humans can tunnel underground for precious metals and jewels, but they won't find wisdom there. It isn't under the ocean either; and it can't be bought for money.

Wisdom belongs to God – then and now (28:1–28). It isn't to be found through any human endeavour of science or engineering. It can't be acquired like knowledge or deduced by reason. There is only one source of wisdom, and that is God. True wisdom is a life lived in the fear of the Lord.

LETTING IT ALL OUT!

Job is going through the worst experiences that anyone can endure. He is poverty-stricken, bereaved, in acute pain, misunderstood by friends and abandoned by God.

And because he is thoughtful and eloquent, we have been able to follow his response. At first he was in a state of shock. Then he was by stages grieving, angry and despairing. But now he has begun to hope again, even in the face of God's silence.

Job clings to his integrity as the only thing left to him – and dares to believe that God has integrity too:

I will not deny my integrity.
I will maintain my
righteousness and never
let go of it;
my conscience will not
reproach me as long as
I live (27:5–7).

JOB'S FINAL PLEA

In a powerful speech Job reviews his life: the days of his prime, his good reputation and the kindnesses he showed to others (31:1–40). Now he is a despised and tragic figure, who has done nothing to deserve his misfortune. Will *nobody* take his side?

Job offers an eloquent and compelling account of his innocence. In every aspect of his life he has been open, honest and generous. God has seen and can judge his every move and motive.

In his sexual behaviour, he hasn't lusted after girls or had affairs with other men's wives.

He has always been fair to his servants, treating them as fellow human beings.

He has not held back from helping the bereaved and the poor; nor has he used bullying or influence to get his way.

He hasn't relied on his wealth instead of trusting God; nor has he paid any attention to astrology.

He hasn't gloated over an enemy's misfortune, or cursed anyone, or refused hospitality to a stranger.

He hasn't concealed secret sins, or harboured guilt, or done anything to make him fear public opinion.

All this is a wonderful statement of Job's moral values in private, public, social and sexual matters. With such a blameless record, small wonder he cries out:

Oh, that I had someone
to hear me!
I sign now my defence –
let the Almighty
answer me (31:35).

Four speeches by Elihu

Now a young man steps forward who has been waiting for his chance to speak. And he is angry! Angry with Job for being so self-righteous, and angry with the friends for being so dim:

Not one of you has
proved Job wrong;
none of you has
answered his
arguments (32:12).

Elihu believes that God is not as remote as Job claims. God speaks in a variety of ways – through dreams and visions, for example, or through healing. And Job should beware of being so scornful of God's justice:

It is unthinkable that God would do wrong (34:12).

Job and his friends are in danger of reducing God – calling him to account for his actions as though he is just another human being. But God is different:

How great is God – beyond our understanding
(36:26)!

Job's wife and friends bring him little comfort in his sufferings. Here Job scratches his sores with shards of pottery, in an illustration from a 12th-century manuscript of the book of Job.

The question Elihu raises is not, 'Why has God done this *to* us?' but, 'What is God doing *in* us?'

The Lord speaks

And now, at last, God speaks (38:1 – 41:34). He speaks to Job out of the storm. A storm, like an earthquake, is nature's echo of the tumult in our human hearts. God is speaking amid the storm of Job's suffering and protest.

God reminds Job of his awesome power, displayed in creation.

God shows Job the vastness of his creation – the foundations of the earth, the springs of the sea, the abode of light and the gates of death. He reviews its splendour: the storehouses of the snow, the networks of stars, the complexities of nature and of the human heart. Look at any of God's creatures – and wonder at the mind and majesty of the creator!

Does Job have any questions about all this? Does he have any advice to offer? Perhaps he would like to take over and run the world better?

> Have you an arm like God…
> Deck yourself with majesty…
> Pour out the overflowings of your anger…

Look on all who are proud, and bring them low;
tread down the wicked where they stand…
Then I will also acknowledge to you
that your own right hand can give you victory
(40:9–12, 14).

God doesn't apologize to Job. He doesn't explain that Satan wanted to test him. He doesn't promise to put everything right in the end. He simply presents Job with the fact that God alone is the creator and he alone has the right and power to judge.

'Look at the behemoth…'
(40:15)

Look anywhere in creation. Look at behemoth, the hippopotamus. Look at Leviathan, the crocodile. Both of them are majestic monsters – beyond human power to create or control! Doesn't the God who made these awesome creatures also have power over the uncontrollable forces of chaos, evil and suffering? And doesn't he have every right, as God, to do things his way?

Job acknowledges God and is restored to life

And so Job submits to God (42:1–17). He is silent in the face of God's awesome majesty and unsearchable wisdom:

I am unworthy – how can I reply to you?
I put my hand over my mouth (40:4).

At the end of the day, Job must let God be God:

I know that you can do all things;
no plan of yours can ever be thwarted…
Surely I spoke of things I did not understand,
things too wonderful for me to know (42:2–3).

Epilogue
(42:7–17)

At last Job's ordeal is over. The poetry of the great debating speeches gives way to the prose of the story. God says that the opinions of Job's three friends have made him angry. They have not been speaking the truth about God. However, the fourth speaker, Elihu, is not condemned. He alone has pointed out that suffering is not necessarily a punishment for sin, nor does it always fit the crime.

God tells Job to pray for his friends as they offer sacrifices and seek forgiveness. Job's prayer counts with God, because it springs from a faithful and integrated life. 'The prayer of the righteous is powerful and effective,' writes James in his New Testament letter (James 5:16).

God restores to Job all that he has lost in family, friends and fortune. Indeed, God grants Job even greater prosperity than he had enjoyed before – and makes him the father of the three most beautiful women in the land. Job, in turn, gives his daughters an equal inheritance along with his sons. He has been a champion of a clear conscience and fair dealing; and he dies at a great age, at peace with his God, his neighbours and himself.

PSALMS

The book of Psalms is a collection of hymns and prayers. They are written by various people over a long period of time. King David wrote some of them, and priests and directors of the temple music wrote others.

The Psalms cover the whole range of our experiences of God, from praising him for our creation and salvation, to complaining about our situation or circumstances. Above all, they are honest with God, and help us to talk to him straight from the heart. Even a lament, when addressed to God, is regarded in the Psalms as 'praise'. The title 'Psalms' means 'praises'.

Outline

Book 1: Psalms 1–41

Book 2: Psalms 42–72

Book 3: Psalms 73–89

Book 4: Psalms 90–106

Book 5: Psalms 107–150

INTRODUCTION

The Psalms were probably collected together after the Jews' return from their exile in Babylon. Psalm 137 recalls those sad and desperate days:

By the rivers of Babylon we sat and wept
  when we remembered Zion.
There on the poplars
  we hung our harps,
for there our captors asked us for songs,
  our tormentors demanded songs of joy;
  they said, 'Sing us one of the songs of Zion!'
How can we sing the songs of the Lord
  while in a foreign land (137:1–4)?

The editors

In the early Middle Ages, scholars called the Massoretes edited the Psalms. They put in vowel sounds (there are no vowels in written Hebrew) and accents, and marked the Psalms for public reading and singing. Their work was carried out between about AD 600 and 1000. They did the same for the poetic books of Job and Proverbs.

Simple and subtle

The Hebrew language is full of fun. It enjoys wordplay and double meaning. It can express the heights of praise as well as the depths of despair. Many of the Psalms have a rhythm, and the lines often run in couplets – the thoughts echoing and complementing each other. When this happens it is called 'parallelism'.

The Psalms are arranged in five sections, or books. The sections don't always follow a theme and are not in order of date. Their arrangement is often informal; but some of David's Psalms are grouped together, and there is an extended collection of praise Psalms at the end.

Each group of Psalms closes with words of praise (a doxology) such as:

Praise be to the Lord, the God of Israel,
  from everlasting to everlasting.
Amen and Amen.

Some of the Psalms are very personal, while others are suitable for a congregation, or for singing at a festival. Jesus knew the Psalms well, and made their words his own. Both Jews and Christians have used them constantly, both for private prayer and public praise.

Who wrote the Psalms?

Many of the Psalms are written by David or associated with him. Book 2 ends with the words, 'This concludes the prayers of David son of Jesse' – but there are other Psalms by David later on in the collection. When a psalm is described as 'of David', it can mean that it is either by him or for him. Half the Psalms (seventy-three of them) are headed 'of David'. Some of these are linked with particular episodes of his life – his exile in a cave, his victories in battle or his repentance after his adultery with Bathsheba.

These are personal poems and prayers which are soaked in the blood, sweat and tears of a great believer, and forged in the heat of his experiences, both good and bad.

Some Psalms (at the beginning of Book 2) are the work of the Sons of Korah – a family which served as temple officials. Psalms 73–83 in Book 3 are by a musician called Asaph, who was a founder of one of the temple guilds.

Over a third of the Psalms are headed 'for the director of music' – perhaps written for use in the daily temple worship, or arranged for a special occasion.

Soul music

In the Psalms we hear a voice which is new to scripture. It is the voice of personal prayer, soul-searching, praise and hope.

During the years of exile, the prophets challenged the Jews to be responsible for their own heart attitude to

God. Without a temple or king, it was up to individuals and local communities to establish their own pattern of worship. The result was a deeper personal faith for some and the development of the synagogue as a place for local prayer and teaching.

A variety of psalms

The Psalms may have been written and collected over a period of 600 years. They include hymns of praise to God for his greatness. They provide songs and chants for pilgrim festivals and royal events. They recall and teach the mighty acts of God in rescuing and helping his people. They express personal prayers of joy and sadness, exaltation and grief.

BOOK 1 (PSALMS 1–41)

Most of the psalms in the first book (or collection) proclaim a truth about God or the godly life. They speak of God as 'Yahweh' (Lord).

In the whole of his creation, the Lord has given a unique place of honour to humankind (Psalm 8). The Lord lives with people who are innocent, honest, trustworthy and generous (Psalms 15, 24). Those who delight in the law of the Lord will be spiritually strong, fresh and fruitful (Psalm 1). All peoples should find their security in the Lord's power and wisdom (Psalm 33).

Many psalms are intensely personal: asking for help against enemies (Psalms 3, 12, 25, 35), or for revival (Psalms 6, 38, 39), or for protection (Psalms 7, 15, 36).

Sometimes the psalmist cries out to the Lord to rescue the good and punish the wicked (Psalms 10, 17), or to look on his longing and count him among the righteous (Psalms 26, 27).

Often, the psalmist sings of love for the Lord and reliance upon him, using images from everyday life: the Lord is a rock, fortress, shield, stronghold, shepherd and light (Psalms 18, 23, 27). Similarly, the psalmist might describe his own plight as caught in a net, fallen into a pit or like a city under siege (Psalms 31, 40).

A psalm may narrate a personal experience of the Lord, which has changed a perspective and brought release (Psalms 32, 34, 37, 40, 41). Some psalms ask that the blessings on an individual may become blessings for the whole people of God, Israel (Psalm 28).

BOOK 2 (PSALMS 42–72)

In this group, the psalms tend to use the word 'Elohim' for God. As one or two of the psalms are repeats from Book 1 (Psalms 53, 70), it may be that this is a collection for people who have a different tradition. We certainly have such preferences and choices in our hymns today.

Here are wonderful psalms of personal devotion, typical of David (Psalms 62, 63). There are prayers for revival (Psalm 42) and rescue (Psalms 43, 54, 55, 58, 59, 69, 70, 71) and forgiveness (Psalm 51). Some psalms remind God of his great deliverance in the past, and ask that he will do the same again (Psalms 44, 60). Others put worries, fears and jealousies in their proper perspective (Psalms 49, 52, 56, 57).

The psalms of the Korahites start to expand from the private and personal to the public and congregational (Psalms 46, 47, 48): 'Clap your hands, all you nations!' There is a great sense of God making himself known and calling people to worship him (Psalm 50). There are mighty praises to God for his acts of creation and deliverance (Psalms 65, 66, 68) and requests for his ongoing mercies (Psalm 67).

BOOK 3 (PSALMS 73–89)

Book 3 has many psalms of Asaph, as though these may have been by him or were in his collection as a choirmaster.

Again, there are psalms for personal use: a reflection on jealousy (Psalm 73) and pleas for guidance (Psalm 86) and deliverance (Psalm 88). But several of the psalms are for public and national repentance and praise. There is a corporate memory of defeat and desecration (Psalms 74, 79), the cry for rescue and restoration (Psalm 80), and celebration that God alone is sovereign and judge (Psalms 75, 76).

Here is the sweep of narrative, recounting God's actions in nature and history (Psalm 78) and his covenant with David (Psalm 89). There is the call for people to turn to God (Psalms 81, 82), the longing for God to overthrow enemies (Psalm 83) and the aching desire for peace (Psalm 85).

In this book, too, there emerges the sense of Zion as God's holy mountain and city – the centre and joy of the whole earth (Psalm 87).

BOOK 4 (PSALMS 90–106)

The fourth book begins with reflection on human life and history in the light of eternity (Psalm 90) and the absolute reliability of God (Psalm 91). There is thankfulness for the blessings of a God-centred life (Psalm 92).

Then follows a group of psalms which praise God for his kingship of the world (Psalms 93–100), and some beautiful psalms of David, brimming with righteousness (Psalm 101), longing (Psalm 102) and praise (Psalm 103). Again, there are psalms which draw on God's provision in nature (Psalm 104) and dealings with Israel (Psalms 105, 106). They evoke wonder and joy.

BOOK 5 (PSALMS 107–150)

Book 5 begins with a review of God's rescue from desperate situations (Psalm 107), and David's determination to honour him (Psalm 108). David also calls down curses on the head of an enemy (Psalm 109)!

There is a psalm in honour of the Lord's chosen king, who will be both priest and judge (Psalm 110), which is followed by praise of God (Psalm 111) and his faithful people (Psalm 112).

There is a selection of songs for Passover, known as the 'Egyptian Hallel' (Psalms 113–118). 'Hallel' lives on in our word 'Hallelujah!', which means 'Praise God!'

The longest psalm is personal – praising God for his law and asking for help in keeping it (Psalm 119). There follows a collection of 'Songs of Ascent', to be sung by Jewish pilgrims as they journey up to the temple in Jerusalem (Psalms 120–134). There are also psalms praising God for his Passover rescue and victory over pagan tyrants and idols (Psalms 135, 136).

Suddenly we are plunged into the painful memory of exile (Psalm 137), but surface to recall the kingship of God (Psalm 138) and his complete knowledge of us (Psalm 139). Next come some psalms of David asking for protection and vindication in the face of his enemies (Psalms 140–143), and praises which testify to God's power and grace (Psalms 144, 145).

The book of Psalms ends with a final Hallel, calling all of creation to praise God (Psalms 146–150).

Hymns of praise

The basis of all praise is that God has created the world. He has conquered the forces of chaos, and defeated all other gods:

> He set the earth on its foundations;
>   it can never be moved.
> You covered it with the deep as with a garment;
>   the waters stood above the mountains.
> But at your rebuke the waters fled,
>   at the sound of your thunder they took to flight…
>   (104:5–7).

However, God has done more than create the world. He has chosen and saved a nation for himself – the people of Israel. A popular theme in the Psalms is the great deliverance of Israel at the exodus, when God brought his people out of Egypt through the Red Sea:

> With your mighty arm you redeemed your people,
>   the descendants of Jacob and Joseph.
> The waters saw you, O God,
>   The waters saw you and writhed;
>   the very depths were convulsed (77:15–16).

After the exodus, there were hard lessons to be learned in the years of wandering in the desert. Some

---

What the scholars say about the Psalms

Hermann Gunkel, in 1904, identifies different types of Psalms. He finds hymns, thanksgivings, laments and epic dramas for royal occasions. He notes how the Psalms belong to the great occasions of national life – the miracle of the exodus, the wonder of the Torah (law) and the majesty of God and of his anointed king.

Sigmund Mowinckel, in the early 1920s, traces the Psalms to the golden age of the monarchy with its festivals and celebrations. He thinks that the Feast of Ingathering and Tabernacles was a time for enacting the glorious victory and kingship of God.

In the Psalms, Mowinckel finds the scripts for great battles with the forces of chaos, the victory procession of God to his holy place (Mount Zion) and the renewing of his covenant commitment with his people.

Suddenly the Psalms come alive – springing from their dusty pages to share the shouts and sobs, laughter and music, dancing feet, clapping hands and swirling robes of God's praising people. God's salvation is to be remembered from the past and celebrated in the present. It is to be enjoyed by everyone now!

Music to our ears

The book we know as 'Psalms' is called 'Praises' in the Hebrew scriptures. Our word 'Psalms' comes from the Greek word 'psalmoi', which means 'music played on instruments'.

psalms recall what happened in those days of friction and discontent:

> *How often they rebelled against him [God] in the desert*
> * and grieved him in the wasteland!*
> *Again and again they put God to the test;*
> * they vexed the Holy One of Israel (78:40–41).*

The Psalms remind Israel of God's ways and his standards, so that they can avoid making the same mistakes in the future. They make history come alive, to encourage repentance and praise in the present, and to give hope for the future.

The Psalms provide songs and prayers for every human situation. Hymns of praise spring from the great things God has done, both for Israel as a nation and for individuals in their own lives:

> *Praise the Lord, O my soul;*
> * all my inmost being, praise his holy name.*
> *Praise the Lord, O my soul,*
> * and forget not all his benefits –*
> *who forgives all your sins*
> * and heals all your diseases,*
> *who redeems your life from the pit,*
> * and crowns you with love and compassion,*
> *who satisfies your desires with good things*
> * so that your youth is renewed like the eagle's*
> *   (103:1–5).*

Some psalms are in praise of Zion – the name for Jerusalem as God's holy city. Pilgrims approaching the capital might sing these hymns as they approach their destination – the city of their king and the temple of their God:

> *Great is the Lord, and most worthy of praise,*
> * in the city of our God, his holy mountain.*

> *It is beautiful in its loftiness,*
> * the joy of the whole earth.*
> *Like the utmost heights of Zaphon is Mount Zion,*
> * the city of the Great King.*
> *God is in her citadels;*
> * he has shown himself to be her fortress (48:1–3).*

God is the true king, not only of Israel, but of the whole earth. It is he who gave his people victory over the pagan nations around:

> *Clap your hands, all you nations;*
> * shout to God with cries of joy.*
> *How awesome is the Lord Most High,*
> * the great King over all the earth!*
> *He subdued nations under us,*
> * peoples under our feet (47:1–3).*

The Lord, the God of Israel, is God of the whole world. The nations are summoned to celebrate the history of Israel – because this is to be their story too. The kings of the nations will assemble as the people of the God of Abraham (47:9).

For most people today, both Jews and Christians, the Psalms provide beautiful expression for personal worship:

> *I love you, O Lord, my strength.*
> *The Lord is my rock, my fortress and my deliverer;*
> * my God is my rock, in whom I take refuge.*
> * He is my shield and the horn [strength] of my*
> *   salvation, my stronghold.*
> *I call to the Lord, who is worthy of praise,*
> * and I am saved from my enemies (18:1–3).*

A large number of psalms are devoted to the pain or longing:

> *As the deer pants for streams of water,*
> * so my soul pants for you, O God.*
> *My soul thirsts for God, for the living God.*
> * When can I go and meet with God (42:1–2)?*

Most of these psalms emerge into confidence and praise. They sing with the wisdom that comes from knowing God's rescue at first hand:

> *Once God has spoken;*
> * twice have I heard this:*

that power belongs to God,
    and steadfast love belongs to you, O Lord.
For you repay to all
    according to their work (62:11–12).

Some psalms are concerned with royal occasions and the special status of the king. They are written for coronations, weddings and anniversaries, but they can also look forward to the Messiah. This one, for example, is quoted by the Gospel writers when Jesus is baptized:

He [God] said to me, 'You are my Son;
    today I have become your Father.
Ask of me,
and I will make the nations your inheritance,
    the ends of the earth your possession.
You will rule them with an iron sceptre;
    you will dash them to pieces like pottery' (2:7–9).

Jesus and the first Christians knew the Psalms and drew inspiration from them. Quotations from them are an integral part of the Gospels and letters of the New Testament. But this is also a book of prayers for us to use today. Here are beauty and honesty, praise and petition, laughter and tears. Here is soul music to which we can tune the song of our own spirit.

The Psalms help us to enter into the supreme privilege of being human, which is to praise God from our own hearts and with our own lips: 'Praise the Lord, O my soul!'

The king

The king has an important part to play in the Psalms. He is God's Son – holy and set apart as the Lord's anointed servant. On rare and special occasions he may even act as a priest, offering prayers and sacrifices to God on behalf of his people. Of course, all Israel's kings are merely human – but their special status points forward to the Messiah. He will be the perfect king and great high priest.

DISCOVERING PSALMS

A selection of Psalms:
    Psalm 1 The good life
    Psalm 2 God's supreme rule
    Psalm 8 Glory in the heavens and humankind
    Psalm 19 The cosmos and the commandments
    Psalm 22 Pain and praise
    Psalm 23 The Lord, my shepherd
    Psalm 51 A plea for forgiveness
    Psalm 73 True wealth
    Psalm 95 A call to worship
    Psalm 100 The gladness of access
    Psalm 103 Amazing grace
    Psalm 107 Thanks for the memories
    Psalm 119 The way of life
    Psalm 121 All-round protection
    Psalm 139 'All yours!'
    Psalm 150 Hallelujah chorus

The good life
(Psalm 1)

The first psalm provides an introduction to the whole collection. It describes the happiness of people who delight in God's law – chewing it over like a dog with a bone. The law feeds and refreshes them, enabling them to live good, happy and fruitful lives. The truth that they hold in their hearts shapes their everyday behaviour, so that they avoid those who plot wickedness, do wrong or scorn godliness.

By contrast, those who reject God's law are like chaff. They have no substance or stability. Like the husks which the wind blows away when grain is winnowed, they will never survive in the furnace of God's judgment. They will have no place among God's people.

Here is a choice which everyone must make and there is no escaping. Either we go the way of God's law or the way of the wicked. The first leads to life, but the second leads to destruction.

God's supreme rule
(Psalm 2)

The nations of the world think they can overthrow God's purpose and his anointed king – but their plans are paltry and pitiful. They stand no chance, as God well knows. Once he has stopped laughing at their feeble efforts, he gives a ringing declaration of his authority: 'I have installed my king on Zion, my holy hill.'

This is a psalm about the certain triumph of God's kingdom, through his partnership with the king, his obedient servant and Son. It may look back to the day of coronation, when God endorsed and enthroned his chosen king David. It certainly looks forward to the coming of Christ (which is the Greek word for 'anointed one').

These verses are quoted many times in the New Testament, and especially at the baptism and transfiguration of Jesus (Mark 1:11 and Matthew 17:5). Paul quotes them in a sermon about the resurrection of Jesus (Acts 13:33). The disciples see the hostility of kings and rulers when Herod and Pilate conspire to crucify Jesus, the Lord's anointed (Acts 4:25–28).

For Christians, this psalm has many glimpses of Jesus. For Jews, it is about the crucial kingship of David and his descendants. Here is the promise that David's line will rule the whole earth, and that all nations must reckon with his God-given authority in the end (Revelation 2:27). They will be wise to bow to him while they still have the chance. They will find both peace and safety in his just and gentle rule.

Glory in the heavens and humankind
(Psalm 8)

Here is a majestic, thoughtful hymn of praise.

The psalmist reflects that God has shown his glory in the vastness and beauty of the heavens. But, just as wonderfully, he allows his name to be praised by the lips of human babies.

God's enemies and critics (of whom the chief is Satan) are dumbfounded that God should share his honour (and risk his reputation) by making humankind in his own image (Genesis 1:26).

Human beings are tiny specks in the scales of creation, yet we are the supreme object of God's compassion. We are also the ones who will share God's eternal glory. Meanwhile, it is to us that God has entrusted the charge and care of his creation in all its variety.

The psalmist closes as he began, with words of wonder, submission and praise. The Lord of creation is *our* Lord!

A dramatic sky (Psalm 18:12) – an image of the judgment and glory of God.

The cosmos and the commandments
(Psalm 19)

There are two great witnesses to the power and perfection of God – they are his creation and his law.

The psalmist describes the heavens as a silent, eloquent declaration of God's greatness. If the heavens are full of wonder, how much more wonderful must their creator be! Not a word is said, but the glorious evidence of his majesty is transmitted continually everywhere and to everyone.

The sun is a supreme example of God's creation. Every day it rises in a blaze of light and heat – like a bridegroom setting out for his wedding. Yet the heavens are a mere tent that God has pitched; and the sun runs the course that God has set.

Now the psalmist turns to the other great witness, which is the law. In its way the law is just as glorious, bright and life-giving as the sun. The two belong together – the sun ruling the cosmos and the law ruling the conscience. Without them, there would be darkness in both the outer world and the inner heart.

The psalmist praises God's law for its perfect revelation of his will. He uses the term 'the Lord', which has a greater sense of relationship than the more general title 'God'. This is God's personal law, with its reliable statutes, true precepts and enlightening commands.

The psalmist finds that God's law helps him to stay pure, gives him a clear conscience and alerts him to moral danger. It is more valuable than gold, more delicious than honey and endlessly rewarding. It keeps him in step with God's will.

Just as there is nothing hidden from the sun, so there is nothing hidden from the law. The psalmist asks God to forgive the faults he is unable to see in himself, because they are so much a part of his human nature and the society in which he is set. Moses taught that some sins are unconscious or accidental – but they are sins all the same. The psalmist begs God's help, too, when he has a strong desire to do wrong.

The psalmist ends with a prayer that his words and thoughts may please God, who sees everything. God is like a rock that shelters from the sun. He is like a redeemer or next of kin, who rescues from the penalty of breaking the law.

Pain and praise

(Psalm 22)

This is the psalm that Jesus cries out as he hangs on the cross. We cannot read it without thinking how completely its words are fulfilled in the suffering and salvation of Christ.

The psalmist feels abandoned by God, as he calls out ceaselessly for help. There is no occasion in David's life that we can link very closely with this description, although he was often in danger and persecuted for long periods of time.

Despite his pain and dereliction, the psalmist still trusts in God. He doesn't curse God or deny him. He knows that the Lord is holy, righteous and enthroned as king. He recalls that God has rescued and delivered others in the past.

The sufferer describes himself as 'a worm' – reduced and diminished, devoid of any sense of worth or significance. He is despised, mocked, insulted, taunted… Yet he never sinks into self-pity, never blames himself for his fate and never seeks revenge.

So many of these details only make sense when they are fulfilled in the crucifixion of Jesus: the animal behaviour of the crowd, the blasphemous taunts about God's rescue, the dislocation of the body stretched in torture, the desperate thirst, pierced hands and feet, the disposal of the clothes… (Matthew 27:33–46).

In all that is happening to him, the sufferer continues to confide in God. He calls out for deliverance from the enemies which surround him. He remembers God's lifelong care of him, right from the moment he was born. He lifts up his heart in hope… then suddenly makes a bold declaration: 'He has listened!'

Now the psalmist's words turn from pain and abandonment to praise and hope. He knows that he will live to celebrate God's deliverance – sharing a sacrificial meal of thanksgiving with the poor and needy.

His good news will travel, so that all the families and nations of the world will hear it. Even the wealthy and self-sufficient, even the dying, even the countless generations yet to come, will hear about this saving God and put their trust in him.

Ancient doors. The great doors of the temple are flung open to welcome not only the pilgrims, but the Lord himself, the king of glory.

The Lord, my shepherd

(Psalm 23)

This is the best known and most popular of all the Psalms. It speaks of God's love and faithfulness in every circumstance of life, both now and in the future.

We are invited to imagine the eastern shepherd at work. He is the leader, provider and protector of his flock. He knows every animal by name, and values each one more than his own life. As David was a shepherd-boy, and Jesus describes himself as the 'good shepherd', these verses take us to the heart of pastoral care.

Walking ahead of his sheep and calling them to follow, the shepherd finds fresh pasture to graze and safe places to drink. Even when the flock has to squeeze through a narrow defile, the sheep have nothing to fear. The shepherd can haul them to safety with his staff, or beat on the rock wall with his rod to let them know he is near.

The shepherd tends his sheep in every way. He clears the pasture of stones and levels the potholes – then stands guard while they eat. He checks their heads for sunburn and treats their wounds with soothing oil. When they are thirsty, he fills the drinking trough to the brim. At night he takes them into his own home.

This is how God is with his people, says the psalmist. He is like a shepherd, and I am in his constant care. His goodness and love will never fail me. In old age and in the face of death, I will continue to live with him.

A plea for forgiveness

(Psalm 51)

David is in extreme mental anguish and heart-guilt. He has committed adultery with Bathsheba and then arranged for her soldier–husband, Uriah, to be killed in battle. Now the prophet Nathan has confronted David with his crimes – and he is devastated (2 Samuel 11–12).

This is the greatest of the psalms which deal with sorrow and repentance. David cries out to God for mercy, cleansing and a new start. Although he has ruined the life of a beautiful woman and destroyed a brave and faithful man, his main crime has been against God.

David is aghast that he could have done such a thing. He accepts that it is all entirely his fault. He doesn't blame ignorance, depression or unruly passion. He doesn't plead that Bathsheba was half-responsible, or accuse Uriah of neglect. It is from his own sinful nature that these acts have sprung – from the sin ingrained in him and in all humanity from birth.

There is no sacrifice that David can offer for the sins of adultery and murder. Unless God forgives him and recreates him, he is lost. But he is not despairing. He holds on to what he knows of God – that he is compassionate and yearns for his people with the utmost love. David prays that his gracious God will wipe away this appalling sin and thoroughly cleanse his heart and soul.

David is asking God for a miracle. He begs to be 'cleansed with hyssop' – as a leper is sprinkled with the blood of a sacrifice, using a bunch of hyssop (a common herb). This is a sign to the leper that he is now fully restored to health and can rejoin the community (Leviticus 14:1–9). David pleads that the bones of his soul, so shattered in shame, may be mended by forgiveness and dance for joy.

David asks for nothing less than a pure heart, which God alone can create in him. He asks that God will restore him to fellowship, giving him a fresh delight in his saving love. He prays for a new spirit within, so that he may be gladly obedient in the future.

David realizes – and tells God – that he will have so much to offer others if he comes through this nightmare of guilt and grief. The fact that we have this psalm is proof that his prayer is answered. It has helped countless numbers of Jews and Christians to confess their sins and find forgiveness, new life and peace with God.

David realizes that, in worship, it is the heart attitude that counts. Sacrifices are meaningful and helpful only if they are offered with genuine repentance, commitment and love. It is this complete openness that God delights to see, and which he will never reject.

The psalm closes with a prayer which is probably added later. It asks that God will restore Jerusalem, his holy city of Zion. The people who endure the years of exile in Babylon, or who long to see Jerusalem and the temple rebuilt, may be making David's confession and prayer their own. The book of Nehemiah tells us how this prayer, too, is answered (Nehemiah 12:43).

True wealth

(Psalm 73)

This great psalm is written by Asaph, who is the founder of one of the temple choirs.

Asaph has been eaten up by a jealousy that has almost robbed him of his faith. He has seen that proud and wicked people lead comfortable and successful lives, without shame or punishment for their sins. He has agonized whether he has made the wrong choice in devoting himself to God.

Asaph has watched unbelievers. They are healthy, wealthy and self-confident. They buy their way out of problems or employ others to shoulder their burdens. They get away with murder, cruelty and unbridled greed. They mouth arrogant opinions, despise goodness and plot evil. They talk of the universe as though they made it themselves and own it. People flock to them, because they admire their attitude and aspire to their achievements.

Meanwhile, Asaph has devoted himself to a godly life. He has spent much time and effort keeping his conscience clear and his actions pure. But he feels it has got him nowhere. It seems that trusting God is for no-hopers who can't face up to life in the real world. But, of course, to express such doubts would be to betray his faith and mislead his fellow believers…

After long days of heart-searching, Asaph brings his problem to God in prayer. At last, in the sanctuary of the temple, he sees an entirely different perspective.

The truth about the proud and wicked is that they are far from God. Their deaths may be peaceful, without fear, pain or regret; but they will awake to the reality of eternal judgment.

Soon it will be God's turn to express his opinion of them – which is that he doesn't know them. Their much-vaunted standard of living is a fleeting and futile dream. Their primrose path is really a road to ruin.

Asaph reflects on his new-found understanding. He has been blinded by envy and ignorance, knowing no more of God than a stubborn and stupid animal. Now he sees that he is truly rich.

Asaph has a friendship with the living God which will never fail or end. God is all he needs or can ever need. He may not have houses or lands or the admiration of others – but he has God, whose presence and protection is priceless, and whose purpose is to share his glory with all who love him.

And yes, holiness is exciting, and God is good to those who keep their hearts pure.

A call to worship

(Psalm 95)

This psalm begins with an invitation to worship God together. For centuries it has been called the 'Venite', from the Latin word meaning 'come'. It is a summons to all-out praise, with joyful singing, loud shouts and every kind of music.

God is 'the Rock of our salvation' – the one on whom all our security and peace is built. He is supreme over all the other false and mistaken gods that humans may worship – gods of the depths, the heights or the turbulent seas. The God of Israel is the One who created these things, and who holds them even now in the palm of his hand.

God's majesty and power prompt us to honour him – bowing, kneeling or lying face down in his presence. We belong to him and he cares for us like a shepherd with his sheep.

God has shown himself to be a sure defence. Jerusalem's walls.

Suddenly there is a solemn warning. God's word is not only for certain people in the past. It is also for us – now. Today may be the day when *we* hear his voice and receive his command. If so, we must not be resistant like the Israelites on their desert journey to Canaan.

At Meribah, the Israelites argued with God. At Massah they tested him. Despite their great deliverance from Egypt and the miracles of manna, quail, water and protection, they refused to believe that God could bring them safely to their Promised Land (Exodus 17:1–7).

God turned those rebellious people back to the desert, to wander for forty years until the older generation died out. Because of their unbelief they never entered their 'rest' – the freedom, peace and plenty of Canaan. Even Moses, their great and godly leader, was ruled out.

It is an awesome privilege to receive God's word. We ignore or resist it at our peril (Matthew 7:26–27). Today there is still a 'rest' for us to enter into and enjoy. It is nothing less than the salvation Jesus has won for us on the cross. The writer of the letter to the Hebrews takes these verses and urges us to enter God's rest – by hearing and believing the gospel (Hebrews 4:1–2).

The gladness of access

(Psalm 100)

This psalm is often known as the 'Jubilate', which is Latin for 'O be joyful'. It is one of the most popular and often-used psalms for public worship. Many other anthems, hymns and worship songs are based on it, the most famous being William Kethe's 'All People That on Earth Do Dwell'.

Here is an invitation to the whole earth (not just separate 'lands') to offer a great shout of joy to the Lord, and to enter his presence, singing with uninhibited joy! It may originally have been a psalm for bringing a thank-offering.

The joyful shout is that of a crowd offering loyalty and welcome to a king. It is not to be given lightly, as it implies a total commitment. The people of Israel shouted in such a way when Saul became their king (1 Samuel 10:24). It is a fanfare of human hearts and voices.

This is a psalm of vast and eternal perspective. God has made us and we belong to him. We are his people, his sheep. His love and purpose cover the whole context of our lives, both now and for ever. To worship this God is also to serve him with our whole self (Romans 12:1).

Knowing that the Lord is God is a sure foundation for our praise. We are secure in his creation and saving love. We are sure of his welcome. We belong to him.

It is because God has made us and he welcomes us that we can come into his presence with such confidence and praise. The courts are the courts of the temple, where nothing unholy is allowed – and yet we may enter. This is God's house, his place – and we can come in!

Finally, the psalmist realizes that this privilege is ongoing. God's nature doesn't change, so his goodness will continue. His love will last for ever. This invitation to acknowledge him is to all people, in every place and age.

Amazing grace
(Psalm 103)

Here is one of the greatest psalms. Beginning with his own heart and experience, David reviews the quality of God's love for all people. He calls on the whole of creation to praise this endlessly merciful and gracious God.

'COUNT YOUR BLESSINGS'

David begins by talking to himself (103:1–5). He urges his soul to praise the Lord. It is easy, but very wrong, to ignore or forget the infinite goodness of God.

The Lord blesses David in so many ways, forgiving his sins and healing his diseases. The Lord redeems him, like a close, reliable and generous relative coming to his aid. Even 'the pit' of despair, disaster and death is not beyond God's saving reach. The Lord gives every appetite its proper satisfaction, and restores the spring of youth, like the strong and soaring eagle.

David is in good heart. He is not burdened with problems, besieged by enemies or racked with guilt. He is free to stand and survey the great vistas of God's mercy and love. This psalm inspired H.F. Lyte to write the wonderful hymn, 'Praise, My Soul, the King of Heaven'.

THE QUALITY OF MERCY

God's character is clear from the way he has dealt with his people (103:6–18). His heart goes out to the needy. He secures justice for the oppressed. He rescued Israel from captivity and gave them his law. He was patient and considerate with their complaining; and even his anger was strictly limited.

This is what God is like. Even when he disciplines, his motive and goal are love. He doesn't prosecute without mercy, or hold long-running grudges, or insist on the fullest punishment. His love is as high as the heavens; his forgiveness as wide as space. The New Testament reveals that God's forgiveness is not because our sins don't matter to him, but because he himself bears the cost of them.

God's love is gut-felt like a father's love, and is as close as a mother's womb. We are human, fallible and finite – formed from dust and as short-lived as a flower. But God's love gives us a lasting value and meaning; his goodness will continue to future generations. The last word is not our futility, but God's faithfulness.

CREATION PRAISE!

David calls on the whole of creation, in heaven and on earth, to praise the Lord (103:19–22). Angels and humans alike owe their existence and service to God. Finally, David returns to his own first thought: that he, from his own soul, can add his voice. No one else can offer my praise.

Thanks for the memories
(Psalm 107)

God's people should thank him. He has been good to them. He has rescued and gathered them from all parts of the world and from every trying circumstance. He has been a 'redeemer' – a strong, reliable next of kin. And he loves them.

This psalm could be based on the exodus or the

A God who saves and satisfies

Here is a God of action. He can be seen in what he does. He turns situations around: rivers become deserts and vagabonds become prosperous farmers. Nobles are reduced to poverty, while the needy are made rich. This is the God of reversals, of whom Hannah sang when her barrenness ended (1 Samuel 2:6–8); and Mary, too, when she was pregnant with Jesus (Luke 1:52–53). He is a God who is worth praising.

The disciples of Jesus saw him do these works of God. He fed a multitude in the desert and called himself 'the bread of life' (John 6:35). He rescued his disciples in a storm – and brought their boat swiftly to land (John 6:18–21). He offered himself as 'living water', the only remedy for spiritual thirst (John 7:37–38).

The Christian church looks forward to a 'city', which will be a perfect community centred on God. Abraham journeyed and died in the hope of it. Jesus died and rose to establish it. It is the new Jerusalem, which God himself will give (Hebrews 11:10; Revelation 21:1–5).

return from exile. It describes how God saved his people from four contrasting situations: desert, darkness, disobedience and disaster.

DESERT

The desert is a place of wandering and rootlessness (107:4–9). It is a place where survival is a struggle and death is always near.

The Israelites experienced the desert in body and spirit during their wilderness wanderings – on the way to Canaan and in the return from Babylon. But they found that God answered their cry for help. He rescued them from distress. He brought them out of trouble by the most direct route. Instead of the trackless wilderness, he gave them a secure and settled city.

DARKNESS

The darkness the psalmist describes is that of prison and slavery (107:10–16). It is also the spiritual darkness of rebellion against God. It is the gloom of living with guilt and its consequences, without choice or hope.

Israel knew this darkness during the long years of slavery in Egypt and the generation of exile in Babylon. Many individuals knew it through their own fault: their darkness fell when they rejected the light of God's law.

But God heard the cry of those in prison. He released the chains of captivity and broke open the confines of despair.

DISOBEDIENCE

God's people became fools. This does not mean that they were ignorant or unintelligent. It means that they wilfully rejected God's way (107:17–22). Their foolhardy attitude almost cost them their lives. But God heard their cry for help. By his powerful word he rescued and healed them.

DISASTER

Finally, the psalmist describes God's people who were almost lost at sea (107:23–32). They were at the mercy of the awesome forces of wind and water. But they cried out to God – and he rescued them. He hushed the storm to a whisper. He brought them safely to land.

Streams in the desert are rare and often dry up, leaving isolated pools (Psalm 17:33–35): Ein Avdat, a river in the Negev desert.

Here is an image of circumstances beyond human control, when chaos reigns and all is lost. But the Lord, with sovereign power and love, is strong to save.

DIRE STRAITS AND DIVINE REVERSALS

The psalmist has described four kinds of extreme need. In each of them, God has answered the call of his people. He has not only rescued them from their trouble, but positively transformed their situation for good.

The psalmist summarizes God's activity in the world (107:33–42). The water of life is his blessing and gift; so is security, plenty and fertility. But hardship, dearth and suffering can be a sign of his displeasure.

'WHOEVER...'

The psalmist closes by pointing out that these memories are not just history (107:43). They are lessons for today – for whoever will listen and learn.

The way of life
(Psalm 119)

This is the longest psalm. It is a prayer to God which sings the praises of his law, and reflects on the security and happiness of those who live by it. To keep God's law is to walk in the light, to run on the freeway:

> *I run in the path of your commands,*
> *for you have set my heart free (119:32).*

The psalm uses several different terms for God's word: law, statutes, precepts, decrees and commands. By one term or another, God's word and way are mentioned in every verse.

The whole psalm is carefully constructed around the twenty-four letters of the Hebrew alphabet. Each letter introduces an eight-verse section or stanza. Each stanza extols a fresh aspect of God's wonderful law, its beauty and benefits. It is like a great love poem.

God's law is his truth, his teaching. It has been revealed so that we may live fully, safely, wisely and well. It is found in all the scriptures, but in the Pentateuch (the books of Moses) in particular.

When Moses presented the people with God's law, he urged them to 'choose life'! He wrote all the laws in a

Book of the Law and gave directions that it should be kept beside the ark of the covenant (Deuteronomy 31:26).

The psalmist refers to God's guidance as *law, precept, statute* and *commandment*.

The psalmist has great delight in God's *law*. It thrills him to have God's truth in his mind and God's wise counsel in his heart:

Your statutes are my delight;
they are my counsellors (119:24).

God's *precepts* are important points of detail. They are to be applied, checked and attended to. They enable the fine-tuning of a well-ordered life:

The psalmist knows God as someone who does not sleep, and whose care is given through every hour of the day (Psalm 121). Upper Galilee, looking south-west from the town of Safed.

You have laid down precepts
that are to be fully obeyed (119:4).

God's *statutes* are binding and permanent landmarks for living. Their permanence is expressed by writing them down and preserving them for future generations. Their truth will never lessen and their relevance never wane:

Your statutes are for ever right;
give me understanding that I may live (119:144).

The *commandments* emphasize God's authority. He is the creator, the Lord. These are his 'maker's instructions' – not a matter of opinion, but a necessity. The psalmist humbles himself to receive them:

I wait for your salvation, O Lord,
and I follow your commands (119:166).

FREEDOM AND PROTECTION

Loving God's law is not to be confused with legalism. Legalism binds us in fearful and obsessive effort, lest we fail to do everything correctly. But love for God's law sets us *free*.

God's law protects us from the opinions of others, and from self-deceit. It steers us away from wrongdoing, hurtful consequences and guilt. It releases us to do right:

> *How can young people*
> *keep their way pure?*
> *By guarding it according*
> *to your word (119:9).*

DISCOVERY AND DELIGHT

The psalmist loves God's law because he loves God. He can't get enough of God's guidance, because it is so good! For him, it is a constant voyage of discovery; a feast of delectable insights:

> *Open my eyes that I may see*
> *wonderful things in your law*
> *(119:18).*
> *How sweet are your words to my taste,*
> *sweeter than honey in my mouth (119:103)!*

LIGHT AND LIFE

To know God's law is to have a light for the path of life:

> *Your word is a lamp to my feet*
> *and a light for my path (119:105).*

It gives access to wisdom – like a door opening. This is wisdom which we could never discover by our own efforts; and yet the simplest person can understand it:

> *The unfolding of your words gives light;*
> *it gives understanding to the simple (119:130).*

A CRY FOR HELP

As the psalmist ends his prayer, he cries out for help. He knows God's law is good and right, but he hasn't been able to keep it. He has strayed away and become lost,

like a sheep. He asks that God will be his shepherd and come to find him:

> *Seek your servant,*
> *For I have not forgotten your commands (119:176).*

God's law is wonderful, permanent and true, but it is only with his constant help that we may live by it.

The people who trust in God will be blessed and experience his generous provision (Psalm 144:11–15). Olive trees at Zippori, near Nazareth.

All-round protection

(Psalm 121)

This is a psalm for pilgrims as they make their way up to Jerusalem. It's a journey where one is aware of the hills, as a place of refuge or a source of danger.

The psalmist looks at these hills. They are the last resort in times of trouble: 'Flee to the mountains!' says Jesus (Mark 13:14). They are the natural defences of Jerusalem, which (as the city of Jebus) was the last stronghold in Canaan to fall to the Israelites.

The hills stand for stability, permanence and protection; but the psalmist doesn't rely on them. His protector is the One who *made* the hills!

The care which God gives to his people is for every individual at all times. God never sleeps; his attention never wavers. There is no circumstance which is beyond his control. The Lord himself guarantees safety in every enterprise, for the whole of life. And the cover starts now.

'All yours!'

(Psalm 139)

This is a psalm about the completeness of God's knowledge and care for every individual.

'O LORD, YOU KNOW!'

David is amazed at how completely God knows him (139:1–16). It is as though God has sifted through him in painstaking detail, to know him in every part.

God has always been at work in David's life. He formed him in his mother's womb. He sees his every action and knows his every thought. There is nowhere David can go which is beyond God's saving presence and love. The vastest distance, the deepest darkness – even death itself – are no barriers to God.

'STILL WITH YOU'

David turns his wonder to praise (139:17:18). God thinks about him constantly! This gives him total security. When he wakes, whether in the morning after sleep or at resurrection after death, he is still with God.

AN OUTBURST

Suddenly David flashes with anger at the violence and blasphemy of the wicked (139:19–22). If God is so powerful, why doesn't he rid him of them? After all, they are God's enemies too.

There is no answer. But the psalm prompts us to realize that God has also made these enemies. Like David, they are never beyond God's reach. He doesn't destroy them, because his patient love waits for them to become friends.

'LEAD ME'

The outburst over, David invites God to test his inner thoughts and worries (139:23–24). He wants more of God's perfect knowledge of him. He wants all of God's way to life.

Hallelujah chorus

(Psalm 150)

The Psalms end with a glorious summons to 'Praise the Lord!' – which is the meaning of 'Hallelujah!'

All of God's creatures, on earth and in heaven, are called to praise him. He is to be praised by humans in his sanctuary, the temple. He is to be praised by angels in the mighty heavens, which are the vastness of his making.

God is to be praised both for his own greatness and for the great things he has done. He has created the universe. He has rescued his people and made them his own.

God is to be praised with the full orchestra: the blowing of ram's-horn trumpets, plucking of strings and shaking of tambourines. This is a triumph of heart over art. Hands and feet, hearts and voices are to join with every kind of instrument – played with gusto.

Isaiah speaks of a day when every knee will bow before God and every tongue will pay homage to his name (Isaiah 45:23). The writer of the book of Revelation hears 'every creature in heaven and on earth and under the earth and on the sea, and all that is in them', singing God's praise (Revelation 5:13–14).

This is the ultimate purpose and fulfilment of all God's creatures, angels and humans: to unite in praising him.

PROVERBS

Proverbs are sayings which distil God's truth for everyday life. They are usually brief, always perceptive and often amusing. They are essential advice for good living. Above all, they introduce wisdom as the perfect companion – attractive, liberating, constant and delightful.

God's truth is true for the whole of life, whoever we are and wherever we live. The Proverbs show how God's truth applies to our everyday situations – at home and at work; in marriage and family; in government and commerce; and in the heart attitudes which shape our reactions, lifestyles and habits. In all these areas, the Proverbs light the way to life and post hazard signs on every road to ruin.

Outline

The first collection of proverbs (1:1 – 9:18)
The second collection: proverbs of Solomon (10:1 – 22:16)
The third collection: sayings of the wise (22:17 – 24:22)
Further sayings of the wise (24:23–34)
The fourth collection: more proverbs of Solomon (25:1 – 29:27)
Other collections of proverbs (30:1 – 31:9)
Epilogue: the treasure of a wise wife (31:10–31)

INTRODUCTION

The book of Proverbs is a collection of wise sayings. It ranges over every aspect of life, showing that there is always a choice between acting wisely and acting foolishly. The two ways of life are presented like people – Wisdom and Folly – who each call us to follow their path.

At the heart of all wisdom is 'the fear of the Lord' (1:7). To fear God is to be in awe of his majesty and reliant on his truth. He is our creator, and he knows what is best for us. The Proverbs are everyday examples of God's truth in real life.

The Proverbs point to Jesus

Proverbs are the light of God's wisdom, broken into a myriad beautiful colours. This is the light which will be seen in its purity and completeness when Jesus comes. He is the light of the world. He is wisdom in person (John 1:9; 1 Corinthians 1:24).

The 'Wisdom' books

The writings of wise people are included in the Bible alongside the works of prophets and priests. They are known as the 'Wisdom' books – Job, Ecclesiastes and Proverbs.

Job explores the mystery of suffering, especially when it is undeserved. He cries out, 'Why?'

The book of Ecclesiastes reflects on the meaninglessness of life, because nothing seems to last. The preacher asks, 'What does it all mean?'

The Proverbs draw our attention to God's wisdom, which reaches into every part of life. They teach us 'how to live wisely and well'.

Famous proverbs

Some proverbs are best known from the King James Bible, which was published in England in 1611 and became known as the 'Authorized Version'. Here are some of them:

Whom the Lord loveth he correcteth (3:12).

Go to the ant, thou sluggard; consider her ways, and be wise (6:6).

Wisdom is better than rubies (8:11).

A virtuous woman is a crown to her husband (12:4).

He that spareth his rod hateth his son (13:24).

Righteousness exalteth a nation (14:34).

A soft answer turneth away wrath (15:1).

Better is a dinner of herbs where love is, than a stalled ox and hatred therewith (15:17).

A word spoken in due season, how good is it (15:23)!

Pride goeth before destruction, and an haughty spirit before a fall (16:18).

A friend loveth at all times, and a brother is born for adversity (17:17).

A good name is rather to be chosen than great riches (22:1).

Train up a child in the way he should go: and when he is old, he will not depart from it (22:6).

Boast not thyself of tomorrow, for thou knowest not what a day may bring forth (27:1).

Faithful are the wounds of a friend (27:6).

A continual dropping in a very rainy day and a contentious woman are alike (27:15).

He that maketh haste to be rich shall not be innocent (28:20).

Where there is no vision, the people perish (29:18).

Who can find a virtuous woman? For her price is far above rubies (31:10).

Wisdom

Wisdom gives life! Wise people are life-givers, because their searching sayings, shrewd comparisons and teasing riddles make us *think*. They make truth intriguing and attractive.

The most famous wise person in Israel's history is King Solomon. But there were wise men and women in Israel and other nations for centuries before his time. Egypt and Arabia, Babylon and Phoenicia all honoured the wise and treasured their wise sayings.

There is something special about the wisdom of Israel. In Israel, wisdom springs from the mind and will of the living God. This makes Israel's wisdom very different from the fear for safety and the hope of good luck which shapes the behaviour of pagans. In Israel, all forms of magic and fortune-telling are rejected as guides to behaviour. In Israel, all forms of immorality – unfaithfulness, indecency and permissive sex – are always wrong. God himself may be hidden, but the way to live a godly life is absolutely clear. Wise behaviour and good behaviour will always be the same thing.

Who wrote Proverbs?

The book of Proverbs is made up of at least five separate collections of wise sayings. Three authors (or collectors) are named – Solomon, Agur and Lemuel. Some proverbs are simply described as 'the sayings of the wise'. The last section makes no mention of an author at all.

Of all the authors, Solomon is by far the best known. He is the son of David and has inherited his father's gift for words. While David is associated with the Psalms, Solomon is associated with the Proverbs. Many of the Proverbs in the third collection (22:17 – 24:22) have also been found in Egyptian writings from as far back as 1300 BC. Agur (whose collection we have in 30:1–33) may be an Arab writer. His style is similar to the book of Job, which comes from the same area. We know nothing more about Agur or about King Lemuel; nor do we know when all the collections were compiled together into one book. A reasonable guess is that the final collection was made after Israel's years in exile, and probably in the 5th century BC.

Solomon

The book of Kings tells how King Solomon was the wisest of the wise people.

God gave Solomon very great wisdom, discernment, and breadth of understanding as vast as the sand on the seashore, so that Solomon's wisdom surpassed the wisdom of all the people of the east, and all the wisdom of Egypt… his fame spread throughout all the surrounding nations. He composed three thousand proverbs, and his songs numbered a thousand and five. He would speak of trees, from the cedar that is in the Lebanon to the hyssop that grows in the wall; he would speak of animals, and birds, and reptiles, and fish. People came from all the nations to hear the wisdom of Solomon; they came from all the kings of the earth who had heard of his wisdom (1 Kings 4:29–34).

DISCOVERING PROVERBS

The first collection of proverbs

Solomon, the son of David and king of Israel, gives us his fatherly advice. At the heart of it all is 'the fear of the Lord', which he describes as 'the beginning of knowledge' (1:7).

Solomon shows us that life is all of a piece, that belief and behaviour belong together. There are many choices to be made between wisdom and folly and between life and death. Solomon describes wisdom as like a woman calling out in public for people to listen to her advice (1:20–23). To those who listen and take her words to heart, she promises a safe, confident and contented life (1:33).

Solomon urges his son to trust in God completely:

*Trust in the Lord with all your heart
    and lean not on your own understanding;
in all your ways acknowledge him,
    and he will make your paths straight* (3:5–6).

The whole of life belongs together, and all our relationships overlap.

Between God and human beings: God is to be honoured with the first and best of our produce:

*Honour the Lord with your wealth,
    with the firstfruits of all your crops;
then your barns will be filled to overflowing,
    and your vats will brim over with new wine*
        (3:9–10).

Among human beings and between human beings and nature: We are to be open, prompt and compassionate in our dealings with one another:

*Do not withhold good from those who deserve it,
    when it is in your power to act.
Do not say to your neighbour,
    'Come back later; I'll give it tomorrow' –
when you now have it with you* (3:27–28).

A warning against adultery
(5:1–23)

Solomon warns his son not to fall into adultery. Another man's wife may look and sound perfect, but an affair with her will end in bitterness, injury and death. It is best to keep a long way from her door! The consequences of adultery are terrible. It will ruin your whole life.

But what is the alternative?

The greatest defence against adultery is a truly devoted marriage. 'Drink water from your own cistern,' says Solomon (5:15). At its heart, a good marriage is exclusive of others, although many will benefit from its warmth and example. As in the Song of Songs, the author encourages good sex with the right person. 'May her breasts satisfy you always, may you ever be captivated by her love' (5:19). Compared with married sex in the security of committed love, an affair with a fellow cheat is cheap, furtive and futile. Even if it stays a secret from other people, it is all known to God. 'For human ways are under the eyes of the Lord' (5:21).

How to handle a crisis
(6:1–5)

Solomon tells his son what to do when a business deal goes wrong. He is to make every effort to get out of debt and not to give up until he is forgiven or free.

Advice for a sluggard
(6:6–11)

We meet the sluggard – the lazy person who never really gets organized. Such a person puts off decisions and evades responsibilities. The sluggard wastes the life, gifts and opportunities that God has given.

Solomon chooses a favourite picture from the world of nature. 'Go to the ant, you sluggard; consider its ways and be wise!' (6:6).

The ant is the harvester ant, which is found in Palestine – always busy, hard-working and effective. The harvester ants store food in the summer to last them through the winter – as Agur will again point out later in the book (30:25). By contrast, the sluggard, with heavy sleeping and many little naps, is storing up poverty for the future. When the sun shines, the sluggard likes to

---

**As God is honoured with the firstfruits of the crops,
so he will bless the people with abundant harvests.**

stretch out and relax, while the ant uses the fine weather to do its work.

The scoundrel
(6:12–15)

Solomon tells his son how to recognize crooks – by their cunning speech and crafty signals. They are always planning mischief for others, but one day they will get what they deserve.

Solomon isn't afraid to predict consequences. He has noticed how things turn out. Lazy people fall on hard

times. Honesty and faithfulness bring great rewards. Villains will face a day of reckoning.

Another warning against adultery
(6:20 – 7:27)

Solomon teaches that adultery begins not in a bed, but in the mind. 'Do not lust in your heart after her beauty,' he warns (6:25). A thousand years later, Jesus will say the same: 'Anyone who looks at a woman lustfully has already committed adultery with her in his heart' (Matthew 5:28). It's the thought that counts. Eyes and

---

Special proverbs

Every proverb is a gem, but here are some special treasures:

Ill-gotten treasures are of no value,
but righteousness delivers from death (10:2).

Hatred stirs up dissension,
but love covers over all wrongs (10:12).

The Lord abhors dishonest scales,
but accurate weights are his delight (11:1).

A gossip goes about telling secrets,
but one who is trustworthy in spirit keeps a confidence (11:13).

For lack of guidance a nation falls,
but many advisers make victory sure (11:14).

Like a gold ring in a pig's snout
is a beautiful woman who shows no discretion (11:22).

A generous person will be enriched,
and one who gives water will get water (11:25).

A wife of noble character is her husband's crown,
but a disgraceful wife is like decay in his bones (12:4).

A heart at peace gives life to the body,
but envy rots the bones (14:30).

Those who oppress the poor insult their Maker,
but those who are kind to the needy honour him (14:31).

A gentle answer turns away wrath,
but a harsh word stirs up anger (15:1).

The eyes of the Lord are everywhere,
keeping watch on the wicked and the good (15:3).

Better a meal of vegetables where there is love,
than a fattened calf with hatred (15:17).

Commit to the Lord whatever you do,
and your plans will succeed (16:3).

Starting a quarrel is like breaching a dam;
so drop the matter before a dispute breaks out (17:14).

He who finds a wife finds what is good
and receives favour from the Lord (18:22).

A stupid child is ruin to a father,
and a wife's quarrelling is a continual dripping of rain (19:13).

The human mind may devise many plans,
but it is the purpose of the Lord that will be established (19:21).

Wine is a mocker and beer a brawler;
whoever is led astray by them is not wise (20:1).

The human spirit is the lamp of the Lord,
searching every inmost part (20:27).

The horse is made ready for the day of battle,
but victory rests with the Lord (21:31).

A good name is more desirable than riches;
to be esteemed is better than silver or gold (22:1).

Train children in the right way,
and when old, they will not stray (22:6).

ears must be defended. They are the doors through which temptation comes.

The consequences of adultery are terrible. 'Can fire be carried in the bosom without burning one's clothes?' (6:27). 'A man who commits adultery lacks judgment; whoever does so destroys himself' (6:32).

As an example, Solomon describes a foolish young man getting involved with a brazen prostitute. The young man thinks he is free to take advantage of the woman's invitation and the husband's absence; but he is 'like a deer stepping into a noose' or 'like an ox going to the slaughter' (7:22).

Solomon tells how to avoid adultery. Firstly, we are to control our hearts – not letting ourselves drift in a wrong direction. Secondly, we must stay away from obvious temptation (the young man just happened to be going past the prostitute's door at twilight!). Finally, we should look at what has happened to others – the multitude whose lives have been wrecked.

Wisdom's call
(8:1–36)

Solomon has already described wisdom as like a woman calling out to people in the street. Unlike the prostitute, Wisdom speaks the truth. The prostitute leads to destruction and death, but Wisdom guides to truth and life. Her instruction makes us truly wealthy – more than any amount of silver, gold and precious stones.

There is nothing secret about Wisdom. She is to be found on the highways and at the city gates – freely available to all. There is no talk of only finding her in church, or through reading books, or by making a pilgrimage to a guru. Wisdom is found in everyday situations, wherever there is the choice between right and wrong.

The wisdom we first met at the street corner is infinitely greater than we first imagined. The Lord God prized Wisdom and made her supreme before ever he created the universe. When God made the world, Wisdom was with him – attending to every detail. 'I was the master worker at his side' (8:30), delighting in God's

Pleasant words are a honeycomb: sweet to the soul and healing to the bones (16:24).

presence and rejoicing in his creativity. The greatest joy of all was the creation of the human race.

Wisdom is an indispensable part of the way the world works. If we want to enjoy this world as our maker intends, we must live by the same wisdom with which he made it. When Jesus comes, he will be seen as this wisdom in person:

He is the image of the invisible God, the firstborn over all creation. For by him all things were created: things in heaven and on earth, visible and invisible, whether thrones or powers or rulers or authorities; all things were created by him and for him. He is before all things, and in him all things hold together (Colossians 1:15–17).

Jesus Christ is none other than the wisdom of God (1 Corinthians 1:24).

Solomon sums up Wisdom's invitation by stating a simple and wonderful fact:

Whoever finds me finds life (8:35).

The invitations of wisdom and folly
(9:1–18)

Solomon describes Wisdom and Folly as like hosts inviting people to dine. The food and drink which Wisdom offers are understanding and the fear of the Lord. Even the simplest people are invited most warmly to share them. Folly, by contrast, is slovenly and ignorant. Her food and drink are exciting only because they are stolen. Hers is an invitation as old as the serpent's to Eve (Genesis 3:6); and the consequences are the same.

The second collection: proverbs of Solomon

Here is a second collection of Solomon's proverbs. In this collection there are no hymns in praise of wisdom or warnings against folly. Instead, there is a wonderful variety of one-off sayings. They contain all kinds of advice and insight on how to understand the ways of the world and live a good life.

Solomon teaches that self-control is very important, especially in the things we say. There are many things which are beyond our knowledge, and which are known only to God. We must be humble in the face of these deep mysteries of life. Now and again a proverb reminds us that God is working out his purposes – in us, around us and sometimes despite us.

Some underlying principles

MAKING PEACE

We belong to one another and are responsible for the poor. Regardless of worldly wealth, it is the righteous who are truly rich. Conflict is harmful when it is unresolved. Hatred makes for discord, but love makes for peace (10:12).

REAL WEALTH

Our quality of life does not depend on whether we are rich or poor. However, the truth is that poor people have a harder life and fewer friends than rich people (10:15). What we do with our money says a lot about us (10:16).

STRAIGHT TALK

The words we say with our tongues indicate our inner thoughts; the thoughts of our hearts. God cares about our business dealings; he loves to see honesty and fairness (11:1).

GAINING BY GIVING

We gain by giving – both of our goods and of ourselves (11:25). The things we say can cause terrible hurt, or lasting healing (12:18).

A WHOLE WORLD

Good people honour and care for the whole of God's creation. They treat their animals as their neighbours (12:10).

The advice of the Proverbs is summed up in a single saying:

Commit to the Lord whatever you do,
and your plans will succeed (16:3).

The third collection: sayings of the wise

Here are thirty sayings which are perhaps to be learned by heart. They are written like a father speaking to his son. They show how to live wisely, with dignity, respect and self-control.

Scholars think that these sayings come from an Egyptian collection. They are very like the 'Instruction of

---

A wise word, even if it is a rebuke, adorns a listening ear, just as precious ornaments adorn the ears themselves. Gold earrings from about 400 BC.

A sharper focus

Most proverbs are written as couplets, or set in pairs. Just as seeing with two eyes gives a better perspective, so the pairing of Proverbs gives a sharper understanding. The second statement often puts the same point but in an opposite way – enabling us to compare wise and foolish, rich and poor, righteous and wicked, proud and humble.

Amenemope', an Egyptian wise man, and there are many parallels between the two. The Egyptian text seems to be much older. Amenemope lived long before the time of Solomon.

Some gems

Do not wear yourself out to get rich;
have the wisdom to show restraint (23:4).

Do not speak in the hearing of a fool,
who will only despise the wisdom of your words
(23:9).

Like many other proverbs, this teaching is echoed in the teaching of Jesus and especially in the Sermon on the Mount. 'Do not give dogs what is sacred; do not throw your pearls to pigs. If you do, they may trample them under their feet, and then turn and tear you to pieces' (Matthew 7:6).

It is important to discipline children; but the real joy comes when children share their father's values of their own free will:

The father of the righteous will greatly rejoice;
he who begets a wise son will be glad in him (23:24).

And there is warning. Prostitutes and unfaithful wives are dangerous predators. They riddle society with lies, guilt and broken relationships.

A warning against getting drunk
(23:29–35)
The father warns his son against becoming a drunkard. Red wine, like a wicked woman, can be seductive and

damaging. He describes the living nightmare of a drink problem.

No need to be jealous
(24:1–2, 19–20)
The father advises his son not to be envious of the friendships or successes of wicked people. They are troublemakers whose lives won't last long.

Further sayings of the wise

This little collection contains excellent advice about fairness, honesty, priorities and hard work.

It is best to sort out your land (which is going to support you) before you start your family (24:27)!

The fourth collection: more proverbs of Solomon

These are Solomon's proverbs, which have been arranged and copied by the scribes of King Hezekiah. It seems that they have grouped them by topic, to avoid repetition.

Hezekiah was the godly king of Judah whose twenty-nine year reign coincided with the ministry of Isaiah.

The collection opens with advice to kings to be thorough in their government (25:2) and for their courtiers not to be proud (25:6–7). There is a feast of observations which give guidance on relationships:

A word aptly spoken
is like apples of gold in settings of silver (25:11).

Like a bad tooth or a lame foot
is reliance on the unfaithful in times of trouble
(25:19).

There is also some very practical, hard-won wisdom, such as 'too much honey makes you sick' (25:16)!

Caring for enemies
(25:21–22)
Here is advice we have met before, and which Paul will repeat in his letter to the Romans (Romans 12:20). By treating your enemies with kindness and generosity, you

'heap coals of fire on their heads'. They burn with shame when they think of the way they have treated you.

Fools, sluggards and mischief-makers
(26:1–28)

Solomon draws on a host of pictures from everyday life to warn against getting involved with unreliable people.

Fools are weak and will let you down like 'the legs of a disabled person' (26:7). The sluggard is attached to the bed 'as a door turns on its hinges' (26:14). Mischief-makers, with quarrels, gossip and deceit, are downright dangerous, 'though their speech is charming, do not believe them' (26:25).

Right attitudes
(27:1–27)

Now the collection turns to personal attitudes. We mustn't assume what the future holds (27:1). It is better to be praised by someone else than to praise ourselves (27:2). Faithfulness in friendship, wisdom and prudence are fine qualities. But beware of being jolly too early in the day, or of a wife who picks fights (27:14–16).

Solomon takes us to the shepherd to see the benefit of good work. Doing today's work well gives satisfaction in the present and provides for the future (27:23–27).

Deep thoughts
(28:1 – 29:27)

The Proverbs now probe the realities of government and justice:

> *When a land rebels it has many rulers;*
> *but with an intelligent ruler there is lasting order*
> *(28:2).*

The northern kingdom of Israel has discovered this truth the hard way. She has been ruled by a series of nine

kings, of whom eight have been assassinated. Meanwhile, the southern kingdom of Judah has enjoyed the stable rule of David and his descendants.

A thin veneer of sincerity that disguises a spiteful heart is rather like a glaze on cheap pottery (26:23). These pots from Shikmona in Northern Israel are of Phoenician origin.

SMILE!

The Proverbs take a long-range view of life – smiling at its ironies and reverses (28:8). The wealth amassed so ruthlessly by one person is generously given away by another!

GOODNESS WORKS

God sees, values and blesses the person who leads a good life (28:18–28). Faithfulness, fairness and hard work are richly rewarded. The person who relies on God's wisdom will always be safe. The people who are generous will find themselves provided for.

CHAOS AND ORDER

A society may fall into wickedness, but goodness will prove stronger in the end (29:16–18). Every parent can contribute to the health of society by raising children well. The antidote to anarchy is to live humbly in the light of God's law.

Other collections of proverbs

Sayings of Agur
(30:1–33)

Agur is another of the wise men of Judah. He speaks towering wisdom from a humble heart. He has a simple faith, plainly expressed:

> *Two things I ask of you, O Lord;*
> *do not refuse me before I die:*
> *Keep falsehood and lies far from me;*
> *give me neither poverty nor riches,*
> *but give me only my daily bread.*

Otherwise, I may have too much and disown you
  and say, 'Who is the Lord?' (30:7–9).

He is a fascinated observer of the world around him.
He wonders at its mysteries:

There are three things that are too amazing for me,
  four that I do not understand:
the way of an eagle in the sky,
  the way of a snake on a rock,
the way of a ship on the high seas,
  and the way of a man with a maiden (30:18–19).

OUTCOMES

Agur warns against behaviour which leads to trouble
(30:20). He is amazed that a woman can commit
adultery as though it's as harmless as eating a snack.
He warns about the consequences of foolish, proud or
wicked behaviour:

As churning the milk produces butter,
  and as twisting the nose produces blood,
  so stirring up anger produces strife (30:32–33).

Sayings of King Lemuel

(31:1–9)

This little collection of sayings was passed on to
King Lemuel by his mother! Lemuel is not mentioned
anywhere else in the Bible and is not a king of Israel.

Lemuel's mother warns him against wasting his
energy on women, or befuddling his wits with wine.
Instead, he should speak up for the powerless and protect
the poor. This is a brilliant insight into Israel's standards
for political authority – and finds many of her kings
falling short!

Epilogue:
the treasure of a wise wife

The book of Proverbs ends with a poem in praise of the
perfect woman. It is as though the lady Wisdom of the
early chapters has got married and is now running a
home. She is trustworthy, hard-working and far-sighted.
She is good at business, clever with her hands and
generous to the needy. She looks good, speaks wisely and
teaches well. Her secret is that she fears the Lord and

the outcome is that her family is proud of her.

Many modern women have no desire at all to be
super-competent in all these ways. But at least they
may accept the compliment to their sex. The book of
Proverbs ends with an example of all the good qualities
praised in the book, and describes them in the form of
a woman.

ECCLESIASTES

Ecclesiastes is a book of wise sayings. They come from a man called Qoheleth (pronounced *Kohellet*), which means 'teacher'. He is outstanding among wise people, and is strongly linked with Solomon. Although the book may sound like Solomon, most scholars believe it was written much later.

The Teacher has looked long and hard at life on earth – and found nothing of lasting value. His opening cry is 'Meaningless! Meaningless! Utterly meaningless! Everything is utterly meaningless' (1:2).

But there is more to his message than despair. The Teacher wants us to stand back from short-term goals and pleasures and find our long-term trust in God.

Ecclesiastes takes its place alongside the other 'wisdom' books of the Bible – Job and Proverbs. Together they show us that 'the fear of the Lord is the beginning of knowledge' (Proverbs 1:7). The Teacher wants to bring us to hope in God by showing us how empty and pointless life is without him.

The Teacher clearly believes in God, but probes human experience to see if faith in God makes any difference. He sounds listless, disillusioned and cynical. We have to realize when he is merely putting a point of view to test us – to make us think. He exposes the selfishness and blind ambition which blights our lives – and reminds us that our time is short.

Outline

INTRODUCTION

A humdrum world

The Teacher says that, in spite of the wonders of creation, life in this world is tedious. There is so much drudgery and dreary routine:

> It is an unhappy business that God has given to human beings to be busy with. I saw all the deeds that are done under the sun; and see, all is vanity and a chasing after wind (1:13–14).

Life isn't fair

The Teacher says that life is unpredictable. Even what we have can be snatched away at any time. Whether our lives are a success or failure in human terms, we all end up in the grave:

> Those to whom God gives wealth, possessions, and honour, so that they lack nothing of all that they desire, yet God does not enable them to enjoy these things, but a stranger enjoys them (6:2).

A longing for more

The frustrations of life make us cry out for meaning. Sometimes we think we see a purpose or glimpse a pattern. But God is too great for us. We cannot read his mind. His thoughts are too deep:

> God has made everything beautiful for its own time. He has planted eternity in the human heart, but even so, people cannot see the whole scope of God's work from beginning to end (3:11).

The Teacher says that even wisdom and knowledge have their limits. In the end, wisdom just shows our stupidity and knowledge reveals our ignorance. In the end, neither wisdom nor knowledge can show us God. We are still left guessing. We are still in the dark.

God

For all that he sounds world-weary, the Teacher is utterly serious about God. God is completely different from us, and his ways are beyond our understanding. We must not be frivolous and shallow when we talk of him:

> God is in heaven
> and you are on earth,
> so let your words be few (5:2).

The Teacher urges us to take our worship and our vows seriously. God is the creator. We are merely a tiny part of his creation. We must realize our littleness and ignorance:

> As you do not know the path of the wind,
> or how the body is formed in a mother's womb,
> so you cannot understand the work of God,
> the Maker of all things (11:5).

God has not made us to be robots, mindlessly reacting to his signals. We can think, reflect and judge. We are responsible for our behaviour. Most of the troubles we experience are our own fault:

> God made human beings straightforward, but they have devised many schemes (7:29).

The Teacher's conclusion

We should enjoy life while we are young – knowing that our youth won't last for ever. We should learn to fear God and keep his commandments while we have our health and strength. This will stand us in good stead when we grow old, and our sight, hearing, strength and courage fail:

Fear God and keep his commandments; for that is the whole duty of everyone (12:13).

Some of the Teacher's sayings

A cord of three strands is not quickly broken (4:12).

When you make a vow to God, do not delay in fulfilling it (5:4).

Whoever loves money never has money enough (5:10).

As they came from their mother's womb, so they shall go again, naked as they came (5:15).

A good name is better than fine perfume (7:1).

Wisdom preserves the life of its possessor (7:12).

Cast your bread upon the waters, for after many days you will find it again (11:1).

Remember your Creator in the days of your youth (12:1).

Some thoughts on time

The Teacher sees 'time' as a period of opportunity. There are different stages and chapters of our lives, and we must accept the freedoms and limitations that come with each of them. Above all, there is time for everything God wants us to do!

> There is a time for everything,
> and a season for every activity under
>   heaven:
> a time to be born and a time to die,
> a time to plant and a time to uproot,
> a time to kill and a time to heal,
> a time to tear down and a time to
>   build,
> a time to weep and a time to laugh,
> a time to mourn and a time to dance,
> a time to scatter stones and a time to
>   gather them,
> a time to embrace and a time to
>   refrain,
> a time to search and a time to give
>   up,
> a time to keep and a time to throw
>   away,
> a time to tear and a time to mend,
> a time to be silent and a time to
>   speak,
> a time to love and a time to hate,
> a time for war and a time for peace
>   (3:1–8).

DISCOVERING ECCLESIASTES

Meet 'The Teacher'
(1:1)

The writer introduces himself in a mysterious way. He calls himself 'The Teacher'. The Hebrew word is Qoheleth, which has often been translated 'The Preacher'.

The writer says he is 'the son of David, king in Jerusalem'. This sounds like Solomon, the son who succeeded David as king, and to whom God gave the gift of wisdom.

Solomon's name is given to other books in the Bible (the books of Proverbs and the Song of Songs) – but not to Ecclesiastes. If the writer is Solomon, why doesn't he say so? Is he writing in a private way, presenting his 'other side' – like a president giving a history lecture, or a prime minister writing a novel? Or is this someone else, who wants to put his wisdom in the super-league alongside Solomon's? We don't know.

Later in this chapter, the writer says, 'I have acquired great wisdom, surpassing all who were over Jerusalem before me' (1:16). This echoes what the Bible tells us about Solomon: 'God gave Solomon very great wisdom, discernment, and breadth of understanding as vast as the sand on the seashore, so that Solomon's wisdom surpassed the wisdom of all the people of the east, and all the wisdom of Egypt. He was wiser than anyone else… He composed three thousand proverbs, and his songs numbered a thousand and five' (1 Kings 4:29–32).

There is further information about the Teacher towards the end of Ecclesiastes. He 'taught the people knowledge, weighing and studying and arranging many proverbs. [He] sought to find pleasing words, and he wrote words of truth plainly' (12:9–10). This makes him sound like a scholar and teacher rather than a man of action and affairs of state, such as a king. But it is possible to be both.

'Vanity of vanities'
(1:2)

The Teacher says that everything there is – creation, history, human life – amounts to 'vanity'. By vanity he means something that is 'in vain' – pointless, fruitless and empty. Life amounts to nothing. It is all meaningless.

This isn't merely a sound bite to attract our attention. It's his conclusion. He's serious.

But what about the reality of God and the joy of leading a godly life? Is the Teacher saying that's vanity as well? No he isn't. He is talking about everything in this world *apart from* God – everything 'under the sun' (1:9). He is talking about life as most people live it, with our perpetual striving for possessions, pleasure, security and success.

The Teacher will reveal himself, in the end, as a person of deeply worked faith. But first he is going to make us take a long, hard (and scary) look at our situation.

The world is boring
(1:3–11)

The Teacher surveys the scene. Life on earth is tiring, tedious and predictable. People live and die, the sun rises and sets; air circulates and water runs downhill. So where's the benefit? What's the point? It's so boring!

The Teacher says there's nothing new to discover or do. That's not true, of course – human history has been a continuing adventure of enterprise and discovery. But the Teacher is challenging us to look at our endless stress and busyness. What's it all about? It's all been done before. We don't know or care about the people in the past, and in the future no one will know or care about us.

There is no meaning in anything
(1:12 – 2:25)

The Teacher describes how he set out to discover the meaning of life. Is it to be found in wisdom? Is wisdom any better than foolishness? After all, wisdom can be worrying and knowledge can be disturbing; but fools seem happy and carefree.

The Teacher reckons that everything is futile. At base, nothing changes – and what will be will be. He sums up the situation in a proverb: 'What is crooked cannot be made straight, and what is lacking cannot be counted' (1:15).

The Teacher tells how he tried to laugh away the problems and experimented with drink. Then he tried being constructive: building houses, planting vineyards and planning gardens and parks. He made a fine collection of fruit trees, all carefully irrigated. He gathered people and animals: slaves and flocks and herds. He acquired enormous wealth in gold and silver and treasure. He was surrounded by music and sated with sex.

It was fun! But it had no meaning. The pleasure was in the effort, not in the result. Wisdom is better than madness only because it is aware of itself. Wisdom knows what it is doing: 'The wise have eyes in their head, but fools walk in darkness' (2:14).

In so many ways, the wise person and the fool are both the same. The wise person dies just as certainly as the fool. The Teacher has come to regret his wealth and achievements. They give him no advantage in this life and might be inherited by a fool when he dies. The pain and strain and sleepless nights are a waste of time. Like chasing the wind.

A glimmer of light
(2:26)

Suddenly the Teacher gives a glimpse of what he really believes. He has been describing life without God as a ceaseless quest for fulfilment which is doomed to failure. But *with* God there is the joy of wisdom and knowledge.

There is a world of difference between life as a mindless drudgery and life as a God-given gift. Without God we invest our life in 'gathering and heaping', like an occupational therapy to fill the time. Working so hard

without purpose or hope is empty and meaningless. But *with* God there is an exciting dimension to life which is endlessly intriguing and fulfilling.

A time to enjoy
(3:1–15)

The Teacher considers the way the world is. Life is made up of seasons and opportunities. The seasons come round again, but opportunities may not. Being born and dying are things we do only once, and about which we have no

choice. For other things – planting and building – we must choose the right moment for success. Other actions and reactions must be appropriate to a relationship or circumstance: to kill or to cure, to break or to mend, to make love or to wage war.

The Teacher says that God has given us this context of rhythm and reliability, crisis and change. We take our place in an unfolding drama and purpose, having missed the beginning and being unable to guess the end. We have our defining moments of usefulness or success, but our contribution is tiny and brief. It is God who knows the purpose and sees the whole. It is his work alone that endures.

Having confined us to a prison of time and circumstance, the Teacher opens a door to freedom in the present. Enjoy! Food and drink and all the varied activities of daily life are God's good gifts. When our life engages with God's love, we experience something of eternal value.

A big question
(3:16 – 4:3)

The Teacher advises that life is to be enjoyed, but for many people that is impossible. What about those for whom life is a misery, because of exploitation, persecution or disaster? Life isn't fair.

The Teacher wants to believe that God will sort everything out, punishing the wicked and rewarding the good. But that hasn't happened. Maybe God is allowing humans to behave like animals until they come to their senses and realize their dignity. But *are* humans a higher form of life than animals? Don't both die and disappear, without significance or hope?

Sometimes life is so bad that death seems better. And many must wish they had never been born.

Alienation
(4:4–12)

As well as injustice and suffering, there is the problem of alienation. People can't relate to each other and society becomes fractured by isolation and loneliness. For some, their driving envy or ambition make more enemies than

---

The Teacher searches for the meaning of life, but his efforts come to nothing. The cycle of the earth continues from day to day and from generation to generation (1:4–5). Morning mist, Tir'an Valley, north of Cana, Galilee.

friends. Others are marginalized because they can't or won't compete. Both the tycoon and the drop-out are too self-absorbed to build a united and caring society.

The Teacher pleads for a balance which he describes as 'a handful with quiet' (4:6). Everyone should have enough to be content, without the extremes of overwork or underachievement.

The Teacher sees single people without any dependent relatives, who work all hours and still don't feel they have enough. He advises that it's better to work with a partner, to share in times of success and help in times of hardship. Partners can also encourage each other – and stand together against a foe.

Be wise
(4:13–16)

The Teacher offers some more advice. It is better to be poor and wise than old but foolish. He has seen a young man come from prison to replace a king, because the young man was wise while the old king was foolish. The new young king will be popular for a while; but experience shows that his novelty will fade. As with everything else, there's nothing new.

Mind how you come
(5:1–2)

The Teacher advises on how to approach God. It is better, when coming to worship, to remember the greatness of God. Don't rush in with your contribution and your noise, as though you are the centre of attention. Instead, wait quietly so that God can speak to you.

And mind how you go
(5:3–7)

Just as worries come out in our dreams, so do fools come out with chatter (5:3).

The Teacher warns us not to let our words run away with us when we make our vows to God. We should keep the promises we make to God – and do so as soon as possible. God is angry when we make a vow and then don't fulfil it – or pretend it was a mistake. We should say what we mean and mean what we say (5:4–7).

The balance of power
(5:8–9)

The Teacher has a word about social order. A hierarchy of authorities can lead to corruption and abuse – the poor being oppressed by those with power or privilege. It's not surprising, because power corrupts (5:8).

But, overall, an authority structure is a good thing, because it imposes duties on people. The Teacher summarizes the benefit in a proverb: 'A king for a ploughed field' (5:9). A king is the price you pay for a settled and ordered society. If there is a clear leader, the needed work is done.

The poverty of riches
(5:10–17)

The Teacher talks about wealth. The person who loves money will never be satisfied, but always crave more (5:10). And when wealth increases, so does expenditure – so the rich have to watch their assets being consumed (5:11). By contrast, poor labourers are well off, because their work results in a good night's sleep – unlike the wealthy who are kept awake by worry and indigestion (5:12).

There is another problem with wealth. It can be lost very suddenly (5:13). A ruined person's children inherit nothing (5:14). In any case, death takes us from our riches. We leave this world as naked as we arrived and can take none of our profits with us (5:15).

A preoccupation with wealth makes rich people poor. It robs them of the simple joys of life, shutting them in a gloomy world of stress, illness and dissatisfaction (5:16–17).

'Whoever loves money never has enough; whoever loves wealth is never satisfied with his income' (5:11). Horde of coins found in an oil lamp.

Simple pleasure
(5:18–20)

The Teacher offers a better attitude to life than being eaten up by envy. Why not enjoy each day as it comes, with its food and drink and work? After all, God gives us life a day at a time. See all that you have as God's gift and savour every moment. You will find you have no time to be jealous of others or to worry about growing old.

They were robbed

(6:1–6)

The Teacher returns to a situation that puzzles him. He has seen people acquire wealth and then not have the chance to enjoy it. Why should someone they don't even know reap the benefit (6:1–2)? It seems to the Teacher that it would have been better to be stillborn, because in that state is peace. Ignorance is bliss. You may have 100 children and live 2,000 years, yet still end up in the same place as the baby that had no life at all (6:3–6).

Life sentences

(6:7–12)

The Teacher sums up the basic dilemmas of human life. We work to eat, but for ever get hungry (6:7). In this, the wise and the foolish are both the same. Poor people may lead better lives than the rich, but never receive any advantage or reward (6:8). It is better to delight in seeing something than to become obsessed with the desire to possess it (6:9).

The Teacher says there is nothing new left to discover, either outside us in the world or within our human nature. We can't argue with someone stronger than us and that's a fact (6:10). The more we talk, the more meaningless everything becomes; for who really knows what is best for us in this fleeting life? And no one knows what is to come (6:11–12).

Get real – get wisdom

(7:1–13)

The Teacher has presented us with bleak realities. Life is constraining, perplexing and short. But now he changes the pace and starts to gather some fragments of truth.

Little by little, the Teacher puts in place a foundation for living, although not everything he writes is reassuring. He doesn't say, 'This is what God wants,' but rather, 'This is hard-won common sense.'

Firstly, a good name is more precious than any material luxury (7:1). Secondly, it is wise to accept the certainty and finality of death. This may mean that we are sad at heart, but that in itself can be liberating – it frees us from pretending to be happy (7:2–4). Foolish people may try to lighten the situation with laughter, but their cackling is like the fierce and futile crackle of a flash-fire (7:5–6).

The Teacher advises us to notice the influences that change us. Hardship can make us wise, because it forces us to wrestle with resentment and longing. A bribe, on the other hand, can make us foolish – undermining our integrity at a stroke (7:7).

It is better to judge something by its end result than to be misled by the promise of its beginning. Patience is a better attitude than pride, because patience is open and looks forward, while pride is closed and looks back (7:8).

The Teacher warns against anger. Only fools let anger take root in their hearts (7:9).

It is vain to hark back to 'the good old days'. They weren't that good, and you fail to live fully in the present (7:10).

Wisdom has great value. It is just as much an advantage in life as owning money or land. Wisdom is an asset which gives protection and independence (7:11–12).

The Teacher advises a realistic, almost fatalistic, approach to life's problems. If God has made a thing in a particular way, it is futile to try to change it (7:13).

Stay cool?

(7:14–22)

The Teacher's tone turns sarcastic. Why not simply stay cool? Life may be easy or life may be tough; but either way, stand well back. Don't get too involved. This is just the way things are (7:14).

Don't be surprised when good people suffer and wicked people prosper. Life doesn't fit into neat patterns of punishment and reward (7:15).

Be good but not too good. No one's perfect, so why strain yourself (7:16, 20)? But don't just throw your life away by deliberately being evil or playing the fool (7:17). Try to find a balance. That way you've covered both bases. Fear God and do what you like (7:18).

But seriously, when you overhear someone say something bad about you, remember you have said the same of others. And when you see a fault in someone else, notice it in yourself as well (7:21–22).

Wisdom is deep

(7:23 – 8:1)

The Teacher has found it hard to discover wisdom and define it. He feels as though he has dug deep, but mined only a few nuggets. He is sure that wisdom is the key to life and that wickedness and folly lead to disaster (7:23–25). A deceitful and manipulative woman, for example, is definitely to be avoided (7:26)!

The Teacher believes that God has made humans 'straightforward' (7:29). Men and women can stand upright physically and live upright morally. They *can* but the Teacher finds they *don't* (7:28).

Only the wise person has really got it all together. Wisdom shines out in a joyful face and a relaxed manner (8:1).

Living in the circumstances
(8:2–15)

The Teacher points out that everyone has to live within the limits of status and circumstance. There is no avoiding the commands of those in authority, so it's wise to obey them promptly and without fear (8:2–5).

But rulers don't have it easy either. The future is uncertain for them as well. They can't control the elements, or avoid death, or evade a battle. If they act wickedly, wickedness won't defend them (8:8).

But what about the wicked? How do they get away with it – even to the extent of being admired and praised by the community they exploited (8:10)? The Teacher is sure they will be judged by God. It may not happen quickly, but it will happen certainly (8:11–13).

The Teacher notes again that good people don't get the rewards they deserve in this life, while some wicked people win all life's prizes. It doesn't make sense (8:14). Again, he recommends enjoyment as the rule of this God-given road (5:18; 8:15).

A glimpse of God
(8:16–17)

The Teacher pauses to state a conclusion – which is that he can't find one! Except that he believes it is God's work he is surveying and God's meaning he is pondering. No one knows the purpose and end of it all – and if they claim to, don't believe them.

All the same
(9:1–6)

The Teacher sees that life is the same for everyone. It isn't clear whom God loves and whom God hates, because all are treated the same (9:1–2). There is no distinction between the good and the wicked, or those who keep the law and those who don't, or those who practise religion and those who don't (9:2).

The only thing that is certain is that everyone dies in the end. Everyone shares the same fate – and the same wicked, crazy human nature (9:3). But if one has to choose between life and death, it is better to be alive. While we are alive we have awareness, hope and a share in what's going on (9:4–5). The dead have nothing – no passion and no power (9:6).

Good cheer
(9:7–10)

The Teacher urges us to live life joyfully. It pleases God if we enjoy our food and drink, wear fine clothes and indulge in life's luxuries (9:7–8). Marriage, work – everything is to be enjoyed! Life is for living, so we must live it while we can. When we come in the end to Sheol (the world of the dead) there will be no such dimensions to existence (9:9–10).

Just our luck
(9:11–12)

The Teacher has found no rhyme or reason to human success. Races aren't always won by the fastest, nor are battles always won by the strongest. Wise, intelligent and skilful people can all suffer setbacks (9:11). Disaster can overtake anyone at any time, and without warning (9:12).

A sad case
(9:13–18)

The Teacher tells a story. There was a wise man who was very poor, but his wisdom saved his little city from being conquered. Sadly, everyone forgot him afterwards (9:13–16). Quiet wisdom is superior to bombastic speeches and heavy armaments. But a fool can do a lot of damage (9:17–18).

Seeds of sense
(10:1–20)

The Teacher offers some proverbs which make sense of life as we find it.

A moment of foolishness can ruin a lifetime of achievement – like a fly spoiling an ointment (10:1).

Wise people and fools lead very different lives. The wise seek the right, while the fool does wrong; yet the wise may sink and the fool may rise (10:2–3, 5–7).

If your boss is angry with you, stay calm. Don't flare up or walk out. Your steadiness and maturity will do a lot to put the matter right (10:4).

Life has consequences. If we live dangerously, we are likely to get hurt (10:8–9). However, wisdom can help us stay safe, by learning from the past and anticipating the future (10:10–11).

Our words matter. They reveal us as wise or foolish, and shape our relationships. All the more reason to speak from wisdom – and to know what we don't know, whether it's the future or the way to town (10:12–15).

A mature ruler is the key to a people's well-being. If a ruler is disciplined in his own life, he can give a good structure to the lives of others (10:16–18).

Laziness will show through the holes in your roof (10:18)!

Everything has a purpose: feasting covers sadness and money covers need (10:19). Be careful what you think. It's amazing how other people will get to hear of it (10:20).

Just do it!
(11:1–10)

The Teacher has been advising caution, but now he commends some positive actions.

Be generous and share what you have. You will receive back the benefits many years later (11:1). Spread your assets to benefit several causes, for you don't know what's going to happen to them or you (11:2).

You can't help the onset of rain or the fall of a tree, but if you're too cautious you'll never do anything (11:3–4). There is so much of God's work that we don't understand – even the basic things about creation (11:5).

Rather than avoiding risk, make time and chance work for you. If you've done your main work in the morning, then use your spare time for another project which may do just as well (11:6).

Life is too good to waste a single day. Be glad of it, right into old age. After all, you'll be dead a long time (11:7–8)!

Are you young? Then delight in the health and strength of your body. There's a whole world to be explored, and you have the energy and enterprise to do it. Your senses and emotions will lead you – but remember there's a reckoning with God (11:9). Don't lose your early years to worry or pain, because this is a time to be free (11:10).

The heart of the matter
(12:1–8)

Finally, the Teacher tells us what he really thinks and believes.

The best advice for living is to begin with God. Commit yourself to God and build your relationship with him while you are young (12:1). Then, when troubles come or old age creeps on, you'll have a firm grasp of your creator's presence and purpose (12:13–14).

The Teacher describes the ageing process in exquisite images. Our appetite and desire begin to fade (12:2). Heaven and earth seem to close down, as we sink into a twilight world, where we can no longer stand, or work, or see, or hear as we used to do (12:3–4). We become frail, anxious and vulnerable as our defences and resources crumble (12:6). We glimpse a funeral; and one day those mourners will be ours (12:5). At the end, our bodies return to dust and our breath or spirit returns to God (12:7).

Is all empty and meaningless? Not at all. All is created, God-given and God-intended. And you aren't dead yet. You're young! Your time to know God is now.

In conclusion
(12:9–14)

The book of Ecclesiastes closes with a description of the Teacher himself. He not only taught and collected proverbs, but put plain truth in beautiful words (12:9–10).

Wise sayings are short and sharp – much better for guidance than many long books (12:11). The point of all things is to know God – to live our lives in the light of his holiness and will (12:13). One day we, with everyone who has ever lived, will find the meaning of our lives at his judgment seat (12:14).

SONG OF SONGS

The Song of Songs is about the longing of love and the joy of sex.

The Song is a collection of love songs. No one is quite sure how many songs there are, or whether they form a continuous story. A woman (the beloved) and a man (the lover) adore one another and tell each other of their love. There are also some friends or attendants who join in with their questions and praises.

These songs may have been sung for many years before they were written down. They may have been used as part of a marriage ceremony or the lengthy celebrations afterwards. They are a lovely, pure antidote to the lewdness and immorality of pagan sex, and especially of the Canaanite fertility rites.

Both Jews and Christians have found in the Song a picture of God's love for his people. This is why it was included in the Bible. But in fact the Song never mentions God. It is good to have the Song in the Bible for its own sake, as a book which describes the tender, mutual and wholesome enjoyment of sex between a man and a woman.

Outline

Introduction

A continuous story?

Some scholars think that the poems of the Song make up a story. King Solomon tries to get a beautiful country girl, a Shulammite, to join his harem in the royal palace. But her true love is a shepherd, and she is eventually reunited with him.

Love is good

The Song of Songs speaks to a society where sex has been abused and degraded. The Israelites are constantly tempted by the permissive and promiscuous sex which other nations so clearly seem to enjoy.

The Song shows that love is good – God's own holy flame within humankind (8:6). The desire and pleasure of sex are his gift. The human body is a treasure trove of sensual delights, to be rightly reserved for, and gladly given to, the right partner when the time is ripe.

The Song's repeated advice is: 'Do not arouse or awaken love until it so desires.' It goes as deep as any proverb (2:7; 3:5; 8:4). A sexual relationship is not to be contrived, manipulated or forced. The Song portrays a love which flourishes on assured commitment, a sharing of souls and mutual delight.

The 'Song of Solomon'?

The Song of Songs is sometimes called the 'Song of Solomon', because it was thought to be by him or to belong to his collection. Solomon was certainly a writer of poems and proverbs, and had a vast knowledge of plants and animals. However, his love life had nothing of the excited adoration and delighted faithfulness which is portrayed here.

Solomon was married many times, with 700 wives and 300 concubines. His sex life was busy but disastrous. By marrying foreign princesses he forged alliances with other nations, which secured peace and good trade for his country. Unfortunately, his wives brought pagan idols into the royal household and Israel's public life. This damaged Solomon's own devotion to God and weakened the faith of his people (1 Kings 11). It also damages his reputation as the wisest person who ever lived.

The meaning of the Song

The 'Song of Songs' means 'the most excellent song'. The Jews did not include it in their scriptures (our Old Testament) until AD 70. Even then, some rabbis felt it was unsuitable because it doesn't mention God and its images are very sexy.

The main argument for including the Song in the Bible has been that it portrays God's love for his people. The love between the man and the woman is seen as a picture of the covenant marriage between God and Israel.

Christians, too, have seen the Song as a beautiful image of the love between Christ and his church. The scholars of the Middle Ages (many of them monks) went to great trouble to find parallels between the lover, Christ, and his beloved, the church. Bernard of Clairvaux did particularly well, finding eighty-six such meanings in the first two chapters alone!

It is true that the prophets picture the covenant as a marriage between God and his people. Hosea, Jeremiah and Ezekiel all accuse Israel of being an unfaithful bride. Even so, they never portray the covenant as an overtly physical and sexual relationship. That would be much too close to the rites of the pagan fertility cults.

It is best to see the Song as a collection of poems in praise of sexual love. By including them in the Bible, the scriptures refuse to let the devil have all the good sex. They remind us that sex is God's gift for creation and recreation, the marriage covenant and mutual joy.

Like all God's gifts, sex is to be used according to his laws and the wider teaching of scripture. Both Christians and Jews believe that the right place for sex is the safe and loving context of lifelong marriage.

DISCOVERING THE SONG OF SONGS

Two lovers
(1:1 – 2:7)

The woman longs for her lover, her king. She is dark and beautiful, suntanned by her open-air life. Her brothers have made her look after the vineyards, which means she has had no time to groom herself. Now she looks for an opportunity to be near her lover by finding where he rests his sheep.

The man and woman are utterly absorbed in each

The woman describes herself as dark skinned and lovely. Her lover declares that she has stolen his heart with one glance of her eyes.

other's beauty, fragrance and touch. Their descriptions of one another draw on lovely images from the world of nature. She reminds him of one of Pharaoh's finest mares, or a lily among thorns. For her, he is like a scented sachet of spices, or a beautiful and sweet apple tree, where she is shaded and refreshed.

Spring in the air
(2:8–17)

The signs of spring are all around and love too is awakening. The lover is like a strong and graceful young stag, bounding over the hills. The beloved is like the peaks in which he delights and the lilies where he grazes.

A restless night
(3:1–5)

The woman dreams that she has lost her lover. She is looking for him and can't find him. There are ancient myths which tell stories like this, which deal with anxiety, loss and grief. At heart they express a fear of death. But this story has a happy ending. Suddenly she finds him and all is well.

A royal procession
(3:6–11)

A grand procession is coming up from the desert. Is this King Solomon arriving for his coronation, or one of his many foreign brides arriving for her wedding?

This may be a song which was first used for royal occasions and has now become a part of other wedding celebrations. Every bride and groom are a royal couple on their wedding day.

A natural beauty
(4:1–7)

The lover praises his partner's beauty. She is altogether lovely and every part of her is perfect. Her eyes are like gentle doves, her hair flows like goats down a hillside, her teeth are like newly washed sheep and her lips like scarlet ribbon. He looks forward to spending the night exploring her fragrant mountains!

The secret garden
(4:8 – 5:1)

The lover calls his bride to come from the remoteness and dangers of mountain ranges to the intimacy and safety of his love. He calls her his 'sister', which is a common term in Egypt for one so dearly treasured.

The man is absorbed in the wonder, taste and smell of his beloved. She has captured his heart.

The woman likens the stirring of love to the coming of spring. Flowers appear on the earth, trees are in blossom, birds sing and the whole landscape surges into life.

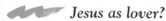

Jesus as lover?

The Song of Songs has often been used by Christians to illustrate Jesus' love for his church. He stands at the door asking to be let in (Revelation 3:20).

The New Testament pictures Christ as the church's bridegroom, but it is misleading to think of Jesus and Christians having a sexual desire for each other. Jesus describes his love in terms of service and sacrifice. He asks his friends to respond not with love songs but with obedience and faith (John 15:12–14).

The bride is a virgin who, like a locked garden, is to be discovered and delighted in. She is an orchard of pleasures, a Persian paradise. The bride calls the winds from north and south to carry the fragrance of her garden to her husband and draw him to her choicest fruits.

When they finally come together, their lovemaking is like breathing in myrrh, feasting on honey and drinking both wine and milk. Every sense is sated and every longing satisfied.

The woman asks her lover to wear her love like an ornament so that others may see it. This ornate bridal crown is from Arabia.

Longing and loss

(5:2–8)

As the girl sleeps, she hears her lover at the door. He is eager for her, calling to be let in. Ready for love, she opens the door, only to find that he is not there. The song takes on a nightmare quality as the young woman searches the streets for her lover and is abused by the night watchmen.

Simply the best

(5:9–16)

Now it is the woman's turn to describe her man. He is far more handsome than other men and glowing with health. His head is noble, his hair luxuriant, his eyes limpid but striking, his cheeks fragrant and his lips sweet. His body is strong, well proportioned and finely formed. She adores him and is proud of him, both as a lover and as a friend.

Inside knowledge

(6:1–3)

The woman's friends offer to help her find her lover, but she knows very well where he is. He is already browsing among her lilies!

An awesome beauty

(6:4–10)

The lover describes his woman in terms of awe bordering on fear. She has the beauty of Tirzah, the old capital of the northern kingdom. She is formidable, like an army in full array.

Parts of this description echo the worship of Ishtar, the Canaanite goddess of love and war. She was as 'fair as the moon, bright as the sun' and as terrifying as an army. Now the same phrases are used to praise this strong, independent and beautiful woman – a woman who commands the admiration and respect of her lover.

Awakening desire

(6:11 – 8:4)

The bride is a Shulammite woman. Her name comes from 'Salem' – the old name for Jerusalem. She dances, stately and regal, for the delight of her lover. He desires her so much that he wishes he could scale her like a palm tree and take her breasts like bunches of grapes. For her part, she would gladly be consumed by him.

The woman calls her lover to go with her to the countryside and make love amid the signs of spring.

Mandrakes are 'love plants' which open in May, and are used as an aphrodisiac to heighten sexual hunger. She wishes she could kiss her lover openly, as she would be able to if he were her brother. She longs to take him home and give herself to him in love.

Love is…

(8:5–7)

The friends see the woman approaching, leaning on her lover. She recalls how they first made love in his family home, where he himself was conceived and born. She asks him to wear her love like an ornament over his heart and on his arm. She reflects that true love endures for ever, as strong as death. It blazes like the fire of God. Rivers cannot quench true love, and a fortune can never buy it.

Chastity and fulfilment

(8:8–14)

The friends ask advice concerning their young sister. How may they best protect her virginity until she is married? If she protects herself, like a wall, they will adorn her with silver. If she is vulnerable, like a door, they will take care to cover her.

The bride likens herself to a wall. She has kept herself a virgin for her true love. Now she is mature, and ready to give herself fully to him. She thinks of Solomon, hiring out his vineyard for money. She too has a vineyard – herself – which is hers alone to give. She will never yield herself for money.

The Song ends with her joyous call for her lover to come away with her, and play the gazelle on her fragrant mountains.

ISAIAH

Isaiah is a prophet who lives in Jerusalem in the 8th century BC.
He is called to be a prophet in 740 BC and his ministry lasts for some forty years. He is a valued counsellor to two of Judah's kings – Ahaz (736–716 BC) and Hezekiah (716–687 BC).

At this time Judah is threatened by the military might of Assyria. Isaiah is sure that God will protect his people and that Jerusalem will be kept safe. He advises quietness and confidence in the face of the crisis.

At the same time, Isaiah delivers probing messages on the state of society and religion in Judah. He looks forward to a perfect Judah, ruled by a perfect king.

Outline

Prophecies to Judah before the exile (1:1 – 39:8)
Prophecies to Judah and Jerusalem (1:1 – 12:6)
Prophecies against foreign nations (13:1 – 23:18)
Future judgment and hope (24:1 – 27:13)
Promises and judgments for Judah (28:1 – 33:24)
God will judge the nations (34:1–17)
A blossoming desert and a highway home (35:1–10)
Assyria threatens Judah (36:1 – 39:8)
Prophecies to God's people during their exile in Babylon (40:1 – 55:13)
God still cares for Israel and will forgive (40:1 – 48:22)
God will rebuild Jerusalem (49:1 – 55:13)
Prophecies to Israel after the exile (56:1 – 66:24)

INTRODUCTION

The prophecies in the book of Isaiah cover three periods of Judah's history:

Chapters 1–39: Isaiah's ministry in Jerusalem
Chapters 40–55: prophecies for the exiles in Babylon
Chapters 56–66: prophecies for the return from exile.

Israel and Judah

After the reign of King Solomon the nation of Israel divides into two kingdoms. Ten tribes in the north become the kingdom of Israel with Samaria as the capital city. The tribes of Judah and Benjamin form a smaller kingdom of Judah in the south, with Jerusalem as the capital. It is in Jerusalem that Isaiah lives.

Both Israel and Judah are little 'buffer' states between the greater powers of Assyria to the north and Egypt to the south. If Assyria pursues her ambition to conquer Egypt, her advance will crush the Hebrew states.

In this situation Isaiah advises the king to stay neutral. Judah should rely on God to defend her – and avoid all foreign alliances. A foreign alliance means compromising with pagan gods – an unthinkable act of unfaithfulness to the Holy One of Israel.

Isaiah's ministry in Jerusalem

(1:1 – 39:8)

The prophecies of Isaiah are not necessarily in the order in which they were first delivered.

Isaiah warns the people of Judah that they are guilty of sin. Their worship is shallow, their greed is breaking up society and they are failing to protect the poor and the weak.

They will suffer severe punishment when God will use Judah's enemies to discipline her. But beyond these dark days is a perfect future when God's reign will bring justice and peace to the whole world.

Politics and religion

Isaiah refuses to separate politics and religion. Each time there is a military threat to Jerusalem, Isaiah urges the king to trust in God for defence.

King Ahaz decides to compromise with the Assyrians.

He asks for, and receives, help against Syria and Israel. The Assyrians protect him by capturing the Syrian capital, Damascus. To show his gratitude, King Ahaz has an Assyrian altar designed and installed beside the altar of the Lord in Jerusalem. So he hopes to get the best from both religions (2 Kings 16:11–14).

King Hezekiah, on the other hand, destroys the pagan shrines. With Isaiah's encouragement, he learns to bring his fears to God and rely on him for help.

God's voice in the situation

Isaiah's prophecies span a period from 740–701 BC. We can trace his ministry through the dates and episodes that are mentioned in his book.

He is called to be a prophet when King Uzziah dies and his son Ahaz becomes king of Judah (6:1).

When Syria (Aram) and Israel (Ephraim) join forces to march on Jerusalem, Isaiah and his son meet King Ahaz. Isaiah says of the danger:

It will not take place,
it will not happen…
If you do not stand firm in your faith,
you will not stand at all (7:7, 9).

Isaiah invites the king to ask God for a sign – but the king refuses. He doesn't want to acknowledge that Isaiah's advice may be right. But Isaiah declares a sign anyway:

'The young woman is with child and shall bear a son, and shall name him Immanuel' (7:14). 'Immanuel' means 'God With Us'. By the time this child knows wrong from right, the nations they fear will have vanished.

When the Assyrians capture the Philistine stronghold of Ashdod, they are clearly too close for comfort. There is an overwhelming temptation to make an alliance with Egypt in the face of this threat.

But God tells Isaiah to go stripped and barefoot in the streets of Jerusalem for three years! This is how the Egyptians will look when they themselves are led away captive. There is no future in relying on them (20:1–6).

When the Assyrians threaten to attack Jerusalem in Hezekiah's reign, the question is: 'Whose god is the stronger?' The Assyrian field commander taunts:

If you say… 'We are depending on the Lord our God'
– isn't he the one whose high places and altars
Hezekiah removed (36:7)?

He goes on to make a counter-claim:

The Lord himself told me to march against this country and destroy it (36:10).

In desperation King Hezekiah turns to Isaiah for a word from the Lord. Isaiah promises the king that the Assyrians will hear a report of action elsewhere and be distracted away from Jerusalem.

When the Assyrian emperor sends a threatening letter to Hezekiah, the king spreads it before the Lord in prayer (37:14). Isaiah assures the king that his prayer has been heard, and that God will protect Jerusalem:

I will defend this city and save it, for my sake and for the sake of David my servant (37:35)!

With that, the Assyrian camp is swept by plague. The Assyrian king, Sennacherib, returns home – to be murdered by his sons (36:1 – 37:38).

Prophecies for the exiles in Babylon
(40:1 – 55:13)

We come to the second main section of the book of Isaiah.

Jerusalem has now fallen to the Babylonians. Most of her population has been carried off into exile in Babylonia.

The prophecies in this section are full of comfort and hope. The destruction of Jerusalem and the exile of her people are God's punishment for sin. But God hasn't forgotten or abandoned his people. His plan is to teach them his ways, renew their commitment and bring them joyfully home to Zion (Jerusalem).

God will summon Cyrus of Persia to conquer Babylon and rescue his people. Meanwhile, there is an opportunity for Israel to reflect on her suffering – and her calling.

Although it is possible that Isaiah of Jerusalem could have uttered these prophecies, most scholars think they are by someone else. The scholars' name for this unknown prophet is 'Deutero-Isaiah' (or 'Second Isaiah').

Prophecies for the return from exile
(56:1 – 66:24)

This is the final part of the book of Isaiah. The prophecies here are addressed to the people who have returned from exile.

Back in Jerusalem, God's people must still live by faith. All the old lessons of obedience to God and hope in his future are to be learned and applied by the next generation.

Jerusalem is at the centre of God's plan for the whole world. All the nations will be able to see God at work in the rebuilding of the city and her righteous community. God is bringing about a new creation – a glorious kingdom of peace and everlasting joy.

The Holy One of Israel

Although the book of Isaiah falls into three sections, it explores the same great themes throughout. Isaiah teaches that God is holy. He is the Lord and judge of all the nations. And Israel – even an Israel that has dwindled to a few scattered survivors – is the focus of God's love and the means by which the world will see God's glory.

DISCOVERING ISAIAH

Isaiah's prophecies are delivered to Israel at three distinct stages of her history: before, during and after the exile in Babylon.

Prophecies to Judah before the exile

Prophecies to Judah and Jerusalem
(1:1 – 12:6)

JUDAH'S WORSHIP IS FALSE

Isaiah challenges the credibility gap between the worship people offer and the lives they actually live. God is sick of burnt offerings. They are just a front behind which people commit crime and oppress the poor. And yet God longs that his people should relate to him again:

'Come now, let us reason together,' says the Lord.
'Though your sins are like scarlet,

Isaiah declares that, even though the donkey or ox know their master, Israel is unable to recognize the Lord (1:3).

Today Jerusalem – tomorrow the world

Isaiah exhorts his people, the 'house of Jacob', to live in the light of God's truth. This is the light which will shine out to the whole world (2:5).

God once called Abraham, to make him a great nation and to bless all the nations of the world through him (Genesis 12:1–3). Now he promises to establish Jerusalem as a geographical centre where all may find God's truth.

---

they shall be white as snow…
If you are willing and obedient' (1:18–19).

THE MAGNET OF ZION

One day God will establish Jerusalem as the centre of his universal reign of peace.

Isaiah describes Jerusalem as 'Mount Zion' rising higher than any other mountain. She will be the place where God lives and from which he reigns. All the nations will make pilgrimage to her, and God's wise judgments will be issued from her.

God's wise ruling will bring peace to the nations, so that the weapons of war can be turned into implements for farming and fruit-growing (2:4).

Micah has the same prophecy as Isaiah (Micah 4:1–3). Either one has copied from the other, or both have used a popular poem or song.

WARNINGS OF JUDGMENT…

Although Isaiah foresees a perfect future for Jerusalem, her present state is compromised and corrupt. She harbours superstition and deals with pagan powers (2:6). She relies on wealth and military might (2:7). She worships gods of human origin (2:8).

Isaiah declares that God will humble these proud and self-important people. Soon they will hide in caves and grovel in the dust, to escape the awesome judgment of God (2:9–11, 19).

Isaiah lists the heights and strengths of the natural world – the cedars of Lebanon, the oaks of Bashan and all the mountains and hills. He mentions the towers and fortifications built by people, and their powerful ocean-going ships. All will be humbled on God's Day of Judgment (2:12–17).

God is going to bring famine and drought on Jerusalem (3:1), and deprive her of every kind of leader (3:2–3). Instead, her rulers will be immature and ineffective. Her social order will collapse in violence and abuse (3:4–5).

God stands up in court to accuse his people (3:13).

He blames the rulers of Judah for the coming disaster. They have ruined 'the vineyard' (the land God gave to his people) and exploited the poor (3:13–15). The women, too, are proud, permissive and self-indulgent. Just as they have spoilt themselves, now he will spoil them (3:16 – 4:1).

... AND A MESSAGE OF HOPE

Suddenly, Isaiah reveals that God's Day of Judgment will also be a day of glory. The 'branch of the Lord' will appear – that is, a king from the family tree of David (4:2). There will be survivors in Jerusalem whom God will himself cleanse from immorality and bloodshed (4:3–4).

God will make Mount Zion a great landmark, with a pillar of cloud by day and of fire by night – the signs of God's presence on Israel's journey through the wilderness (4:5). Over everything will be a canopy, so that Zion becomes a great tent or tabernacle – a place of shelter where God is present: an image of the perfect temple (4:6).

JUDAH IS LIKE A VINEYARD PRODUCING BITTER GRAPES

Israel and Judah are like a vineyard God has planted (5:1–7). They are a chosen people in a promised land. God has done everything to ensure their safety and success. But when he comes looking for a vintage crop, his hopes are dashed. Instead of righteousness and justice he finds bloodshed and distress.

Surely God is within his rights to abandon such an unrewarding project.

GOD IS GOING TO SHOW HIS HOLINESS BY JUDGING HIS PEOPLE

God is going to judge those who have grown rich at the expense of others, by squeezing them off their land (5:8).

Isaiah warns the people of a terror to come and advises them to go to the rocks and hide in the ground from the dread of the Lord and the splendour of his majesty. Caves in Mount Arbela, near the Sea of Galilee.

He is going to lay waste their houses and bring dearth on their vineyards and fields (5:9–10).

God condemns those who live only to get drunk. Their festivals are music and wine, without any celebration of God's goodness and purpose in their lives (5:11–12). Because of such people, both rich and poor are starved of the knowledge of God – and Israel will be led away to exile (5:13).

Sheol (the place of departed spirits) is a cavernous mouth, swallowing the leaders of Judah and her people down into death (5:14).

God takes issue with those who have turned his values upside down. They pretend they want the day of God's judgment to come – as though they welcome his action in the world (5:19). They are liars and posers – brave with the booze and busy with injustice (5:22–23). God will destroy them like a field fire after the good crop has been harvested (5:24).

GOD IS SUMMONING ASSYRIA TO JUDGE ISRAEL

God is Lord of all the nations. He will summon a nation from far away to execute his judgment on Judah and Jerusalem (5:26–28). This is Assyria – powerful, swift and well equipped – bounding towards Israel like a lion to its prey (5:29). A storm is about to break over God's people – a destruction which none can escape (5:30).

ISAIAH'S VISION OF GOD AND HIS CALL TO BE A PROPHET

Isaiah is called to be a prophet in 742 BC – the year of King Uzziah's death. Uzziah has enjoyed a long reign, but lived in isolation as a leper during his last years.

Isaiah has an awe-inspiring vision of God (6:1–13). The Lord is enthroned in his temple, surrounded by seraphs – the winged beings that worship and serve him continually.

God is utterly holy. He is infinitely higher than his creatures. He is completely pure in his character.

Isaiah, in stark contrast, sees himself as a moral leper. He is riddled with sin, and can have nothing to do with this holy God.

But, as Isaiah cries out in despair, a seraph touches his mouth with a live coal from the altar. God in his mercy reaches out to purge Isaiah's sin and remove his shame. His lips are consecrated to speak God's word.

When he hears God asking, 'Whom shall I send?' Isaiah gives the heartfelt response, 'Send me!'

God commissions Isaiah to a difficult and unrewarding task. He has to take God's message to people who will listen but never understand. Their senses will be dulled by self-interest. They won't allow God's word to reach their hearts because they don't want to change their lives. This is the experience of many prophets, from Jeremiah to Jesus (Jeremiah 5:21; Ezekiel 12:2; Mark 11:17–18).

A SIGN OF HOPE: A BABY CALLED IMMANUEL

A sign of hope for King Ahaz

Isaiah is evidently well respected in Jerusalem, and no doubt a familiar figure at court. Two kings – Ahaz and his son Hezekiah – consult him on important matters of state.

In 735 BC Judah's northern neighbours, Aram (Syria) and Israel (Ephraim), move to attack Judah. They are putting pressure on Judah to form an alliance with them against Assyria.

Isaiah advises King Ahaz against such an agreement. If Judah is to keep her political independence and her own religion, she must resist all temptations to compromise. She must simply trust God.

A baby called Immanuel

Isaiah invites Ahaz to ask for a sign of God's protection. The king declines, because he doesn't want to get involved with God. But Isaiah gives him a sign anyway:

The virgin will be with child and will give birth to a son, and will call him Immanuel (7:14).

The name means 'God With Us' – the assurance of victory.

By the time the child is old enough to make choices, Israel and Syria will be deserted. But Judah will have another enemy to contend with – Assyria.

GOD WILL USE ASSYRIA AS HIS WEAPON

Disaster looms

Isaiah predicts that Assyria and Egypt will mass against Judah like swarms of bees and flies. This happens in 735 BC. Ahaz will be humiliated – like having a body shave (7:17 – 8:4).

Isaiah's wife gives birth to a son. The prophet gives him the name 'Quick to the Plunder, Swift to the Spoil'. This will be the Assyrians' approach when they sack Damascus (capital of Syria) and Samaria (capital of

'They will call him Immanuel'

The naming of the baby in Isaiah's prophecy becomes a pointer to the birth of Jesus (Matthew 1:23). There has been much discussion as to whether Isaiah's baby had a virgin mother. The Greek version of the Hebrew Bible uses a word which means 'virgin'; but the original Hebrew word means 'young woman'.

Israel). The name matches that of the baby 'Immanuel'. One name assures Ahaz of God's presence and the other of the defeat of his enemies.

Troubled waters ahead

One of the places Isaiah meets King Ahaz is 'at the end of the aqueduct' (7:3). Jerusalem relies on its gently flowing water supply – a symbol of God's grace. But Isaiah sees that people are rejecting their God – and will soon be overwhelmed by a tidal wave from Assyria (8:5–10).

Fear only God

God tells Isaiah not to be infected with the plans and fears of the people among whom he lives (8:11–12). The only thing that matters is God's holiness, and to fear him alone (8:13).

God will be a rock of sanctuary for his faithful people, but a stumbling block to the spiritually blind. They will trip over God's will and fall headlong to their doom (8:14–15).

Isaiah wants his words sealed up and kept by his disciples, so that what he has said will be seen to come true (8:16–17).

LIGHT OR DARKNESS

Isaiah has around him a small community – his 'children'. Their faith is a sign to the wider community of Israel, because they live with reference to the Lord God of Mount Zion, the true Jerusalem (8:18).

Many people are looking to spiritualism and the occult for guidance – as Isaiah says, consulting 'the dead on behalf of the living' (8:19)! But there is no light in those dark rooms – only spiritual famine, physical exile, exasperated rage and outer darkness (8:21–22).

GOD WILL RAISE UP A KING LIKE DAVID

David was Israel's greatest king, and there was always hope for another one like him. He combined wisdom and strength with a compassion for people and the ability to establish peace.

Here Isaiah celebrates the birth of a royal heir, or perhaps a coronation (9:1–7). The king's reign will be an extension of God's rule. These words enjoy lasting fame as a prophecy of the birth of Jesus. They are a superb description of the Christ.

GOD'S HAND RAISED IN JUDGMENT

Isaiah sees that God is stretching out his hand to judge his people and punish them for their sins.

God spoke to the northern kingdom of Israel through his prophets, Amos and Hosea (9:8). They warned Ephraim (Israel) of judgment and everyone heard; but they were proud and determined to survive (9:9). When the destruction was past, they planned to build bigger and better than before (9:10).

God punished the northern kingdom through her old enemies, the Arameans and the Philistines (9:11–12). Israel was destroyed 'head and tail' – leaders and prophets, the virile and the defenceless (9:13–17).

Israel was torched for her wickedness (9:18–19). The different tribes consumed each other – even the brother tribes of Ephraim and Manasseh, which were both descended from Joseph (9:18–21).

Isaiah speaks against the cruel and cunning judges of his day. They twist the law to rob the poor and cheat the helpless (10:1–2). Where will they hide when the judgment comes (10:3–4)?

In all these events God is reaching out his hand in judgment – and he hasn't withdrawn it yet. There is more punishment to come (10:4).

BUT GOD WILL ALSO HUMBLE ASSYRIA

God is using Assyria as his instrument to punish Israel. Assyria is the club in God's hands (10:5). But Assyria is arrogant and takes the glory of God's victory for himself (10:13). Now God is going to rein in proud Assyria, weakening him with sickness and destroying his splendour in the fire of his holiness (10:16–17).

A SMALL PART OF ISRAEL WILL SURVIVE

Isaiah has a son called 'Shear-Jashub', which means 'A Remnant Will Return' (7:3). By his naming of his son, the prophet expresses his hope that God's people will survive. Although the coming punishment will be terrible, a small group will return from exile and (more importantly) return to the Lord.

COUNTDOWN TO CONQUEST?

The Assyrians are advancing on Judah and Jerusalem from the north – and moving swiftly. Aiath is probably Ai, fifteen miles from Jerusalem (10:28). Supplies are checked and stored at Michmash and the advance continues across a steep valley – over the border of Judah and up to encamp at Geba.

Gibeah is a fortified town which guards the approach to Jerusalem – but its inhabitants have already fled (10:29). Anathoth, five miles north-west of Jerusalem, is captured (10:30), and the Assyrian horde sweeps on to Nob, within a mile of Jerusalem (10:32)!

In the face of the emergency, Isaiah speaks of the sovereignty of God. The Lord will lop off these powerful branches of Assyria and cut down even the tallest trees (10:33). God has set his heart to bless a different stump altogether – the root of Jesse, which is the royal line of David (11:1).

The prophet paints a graphic picture of the relentless approach of the all-conquering Assyrian army (5:26–30). Detail from the bronze decorations on the great door of the palace of Shalmaneser III at Balawat.

A DESCENDANT OF DAVID

Judah is like a tree about to be felled: cut down by God's judgment because of its disease. There will be nothing left of David's dynasty but a stump – 'the stump of Jesse' (the name of David's father).

Isaiah prophesies that, against all the odds, a new shoot will grow from the old stump. It will become strong and significant: a fruitful branch. So he describes the Messiah who is to come (11:1–9).

The Messiah will be endowed with the fullness of God's Spirit – wisdom and understanding, counsel and power, the knowledge and fear of the Lord – and delight in doing God's will.

David's great descendant won't judge by appearances, for he will understand people's hearts. He won't rely on hearsay, because he will know the truth at first-hand. He will find in favour of the poor and needy. He will rule with the authority of his word. Even the divided realm of animals and humans will find peace and harmony under his government.

These words of Isaiah are the Bible's finest description of the leadership style of Christ and the well-being of his perfect kingdom.

A SONG OF PRAISE FOR GOD'S SALVATION

God's people will experience a new exodus. God will rescue them and bring them home from all directions (11:11).

Isaiah allows his future hope to shine into the present crisis (12:1). He will trust in God and take complete comfort in God's protection and salvation (12:2). He calls the inhabitants of Jerusalem to praise God already for what he is certain to do (12:3–6).

Prophecies against foreign nations

(13:1 – 23:18)

All nations are under God's rule, and subject to his judgment. He knows their ways, humbles their pride, sets limits on their power and uses them for his own great purpose.

Isaiah shows God's command of all the nations – the whole earth is God's kingdom. He delivers God's judgments of punishment and hope in the form of 'oracles' or public announcements. An oracle is a 'lifting up' of the voice.

PROPHECIES AGAINST BABYLON AND ASSYRIA

Isaiah declares that God will send his armies on the day of his wrath (13:3, 9) to execute his judgment on the nations of the earth (13:5). He will use the Medes to overthrow the terrible power of Babylon (13:19).

Babylon (herself the conqueror of Assyria) will be defeated in 539 BC. In the Bible she is a symbol of all worldly power which is opposed to God, and the spiritual descendant of the tower of Babel (Genesis 11:1–9).

When God has restored his people to their land, they

will be able to sing of Babylon's fall (14:1–23). This is the Lord's triumph (14:24–27).

GOD'S JUDGMENT ON THE NATIONS

Isaiah declares God's judgment on the Philistines (14:29–32), Moab (15:1 – 16:14), Damascus (17:1–14), Ethiopia (18:1–7) and Egypt (19:1–15). However, there is a prediction of hope for Egypt (19:16–25). She will have an altar to the Lord God at her centre and a pillar of the Lord's protection at her border (19:19–20).

NAKED AND BAREFOOT

In 711 BC, an Assyrian force is sent by King Sargon to capture Ashdod. Ashdod is a Philistine city which had revolted against the Assyrian empire and thrown out an imposed king (20:1). Ashdod has hoped for support from Egypt and Ethiopia – and indeed from Judah – but the proposed rebellion never materializes.

At this time, God tells Isaiah to go about Jerusalem naked and barefoot. Isaiah does this for three years – acting the part of a captive (20:3). This will be the fate of anyone who rebels against Assyria or trusts the support of Egypt! Egypt herself will be defeated and her people deported (20:4–5).

DESERT STORM FOR BABYLON

Isaiah delivers further oracles about the surrounding nations.

The first oracle begins with a vision of 'the wilderness of the sea' (21:1). The forces of Elam (Persia) and Media are sweeping up like a desert storm, dark and destructive (21:1–2). Isaiah realizes that this is the force that will overwhelm Babylon – and he is appalled (21:3–4). Babylon's commanders are taken by surprise as they feast (21:5).

Isaiah sees himself as a watchman, on the lookout for invaders (21:8). God tells him that Babylon has fallen and her idols lie shattered (21:9). Isaiah reports Babylon's fate to Israel, his 'threshed and winnowed one'. God's people have suffered so much upheaval and distress at Babylon's hands (21:10).

THE SILENCE OF NIGHT

Isaiah speaks an oracle concerning Dumah – a place in Edom whose name means 'Silence'. Someone is asking the watchman what time it is – how long will the night of judgment last? The answer is: 'Inquire and come back' – which is an invitation to return to the way of God (21:12).

BRIEF RESPITE

Isaiah speaks to the peoples of the Arabian desert. The oasis at Tema must give water to the Dedanites. They are fleeing from the destruction of the Assyrians (21:14–15). But any relief will be short-lived. In 703 BC the whole area of Kedar is conquered by Sennacherib (21:16–17).

CRISIS FOR JERUSALEM

Isaiah has an oracle for 'the valley of vision' – that is, Jerusalem, where he himself lives (22:1). Jerusalem is surrounded by mountains.

Isaiah weeps for his city (22:4). He foresees an attack and destruction which features Elam, an ally of Babylon (22:6). People are both taking up weapons and partying. The weapons are kept in the House of the Forest – a hall in the royal palace (22:8; 1 Kings 10:17). The partying is a last celebration before people die – or perhaps because there is a lifting of a siege (22:13). Isaiah knows that the fun is out of place because worse is to follow.

Isaiah has messages for two individuals – Shebna and Eliakim (22:15–25). Shebna is the royal steward who has been busy with his status symbols: his chariots and his tomb. Isaiah says that God will demote him and throw him out – far into the desert (22:18).

Eliakim will be promoted in Shebna's place and people will rely heavily on him (22:24). He will have the authority of the royal key and make high-level decisions (22:22). Even so, he is merely human and will ultimately fail (22:25).

Isaiah sees a time when God's judgment on Egypt will result in the drying up of the Nile and the withering of the normally rich vegetation growing on its banks (19:5–8).

TYRE

Isaiah predicts that the Chaldeans (Babylonians) will destroy Tyre – the wealthy seaport whose trading reaches around the known world. This will be God's judgment on her pride (23:9) and will last for a lifetime (23:15). Afterwards her prosperity will be restored, but she will consecrate her wealth to the Lord (23:17–18).

Future judgment and hope
(24:1 – 27:13)

GOD'S WORLDWIDE JUDGMENT...

Having spoken to individual nations, Isaiah now addresses the whole world. God is going to judge all alike – priest and people, owner and slave, buyer and seller (24:2). The earth is to fall under God's curse (24:3–13).

Far away to east and west the praises of the survivors, the 'remnant', can be heard. They are praising God, the Righteous One, for his splendour (24:14–16). But Isaiah still grieves under the weight of his people's sins (24:16).

A cosmic judgment is about to fall. God will call all powers in heaven and on earth to account (24:21–22). The light of sun and moon will be dimmed by the glory of God shining out from Mount Zion (24:23).

... AND VICTORY

Isaiah praises God for his power and justice (25:1–5). He will establish a community of joy and plenty, life and peace on Mount Zion, the new Jerusalem (25:6–8). All sadness and tears – and death itself – will be things of the past (25:8). This is the God and this is the salvation for which his people have waited so long (25:9).

A LONGING FOR GOD

Isaiah looks forward to the secure strength and welcome of God's city (26:1–2). This is his steadfast hope (26:3–4). He longs for God to bring down the proud, give justice to the poor and set the feet of the righteous on a level path (26:5–8).

Isaiah acknowledges that his people have achieved nothing without God (26:16–18). And yet God will call the dead to life (26:19). In the midst of failure, Isaiah glimpses God's resurrection power – the shining dew of a bright new dawn.

As God raises his people to life, he will also punish the wicked and destroy Leviathan, the chaos monster (26:20 – 27:1).

PEACE WITH GOD

At last God rejoices over a fruitful vineyard. This is his people as he has longed them to be – a blessing to the whole world (27:6). What a change from the days of frustration, bitterness and destruction in the past (5:1–7)! The only thorns now are the enemies which the Lord will destroy (27:4).

Israel has come a long way, through much suffering and destruction (27:7–11). But now God is harvesting his people from their far-flung places of exile, and bringing them home to Jerusalem (27:12–13).

Emerging from a time of judgment, God's redeemed people will flourish like flowers blooming in the desert (35:1).

Promises and judgments for Judah
(28:1 – 33:24)

Isaiah condemns drunken leaders, hard-hearted worshippers and the futility of seeking protection from Egypt. God is about to shatter the security of complacent women and strong men. But beyond God's judgment lies his promise of mercy, healing and peace.

Jerusalem – God's own city

Jerusalem always had an eternal quality. The mysterious priest–king Melchizedek had come from there. It was called Salem in those days. Melchizedek met Abraham with bread and wine, gave him a blessing and accepted 10 per cent (a tithe) of the plunder from a recent victory (Genesis 14:18–20).

During the conquest of the land of Canaan by Joshua, Jerusalem was never captured. It remained securely in the hands of the Jebusites. It was David who finally captured it and made it his capital city.

David also made Jerusalem God's capital – bringing the ark of the covenant there and making plans for a temple (33:20–22). It was the city 'where God's name dwelt', and where God promised that the line of David would reign for ever. One day Jerusalem would become fully and gloriously 'Zion' – the centre of God's kingdom on earth.

Small wonder that the inhabitants of Jerusalem think God will never let his

city fall – and certainly not to a pagan army.

Now Isaiah brings the unthinkable message that God himself will lay siege to Jerusalem – and use foreign armies to do so. Calling Jerusalem 'Ariel', Isaiah speaks for God:

Woe to you, Ariel, Ariel,
   the city where David settled!…
I will besiege Ariel…
  I will encircle you with towers
  and set up my siege works against
    you (29:1–3).

The inhabitants of Jerusalem have forgotten that God's protection is conditional on obedience to his commandments. God and his people are married by their covenant. He expects them to be holy as he is. But Isaiah preaches that this once-faithful city has become a prostitute. Her leaders are drunken, idolatrous and corrupt. Her orphans and widows are neglected.

Jerusalem has been unfaithful to God:

See how the faithful city
  has become a harlot!
She once was full of justice;
  righteousness used to dwell in her –
  but now murderers (1:21)!

Meanwhile, the temple worship continues. Sacrifices are offered morning and evening, and festivals are very well attended. But they are a sham. They make God angry!

When you come to appear before me,
  who has asked this of you,
  this trampling of my courts?
Stop bringing meaningless offerings!
  Your incense is detestable to me.
New Moons, Sabbaths and
  convocations –
  I cannot bear your evil assemblies
  (1:12–13).

God will judge the nations
(34:1–17)

God is going to massacre all the nations and unravel his work of creation (34:1–4). The storm will break on Edom, the long-time adversary of God's people (34:5–10). She will become a wasteland, her strongholds overgrown and inhabited only by wild animals (34:11–17).

A blossoming desert and a highway home
(35:1–10)

Meanwhile, another desert will spring into bloom (35:1–2). This is the desert across which God's people will travel when they return from exile to their homeland (35:10).

Isaiah encourages the weak and faint-hearted. God is acting to save them (35:3–4)! The personal handicaps of body and spirit are being healed; the hazards of nature

---

Assyria and Babylon

When Isaiah's ministry begins, the Babylonians are known as Chaldeans. They are ruled by Assyria – having been conquered by Tiglath-Pileser III in 745 BC. Assyrian rulers call themselves kings of Babylon. But Assyria will overreach herself and her power will wane. Babylon will take over as the new superpower in the region.

When Jerusalem is destroyed it will be at the hands of Babylon in 587 BC.

The names of Israel and Judah

The name 'Israel' is used for the northern kingdom after the death of Solomon in about 922 BC. This land and its people are also called 'Jacob' and 'Ephraim' after famous ancestors. The capital of Israel is Samaria and the main centres of worship (for festivals, pilgrimages and sacrifice) are Bethel and Dan.

The southern kingdom at this time is called Judah, and its capital and worship centre (the temple) is Jerusalem.

But 'Israel' can also mean 'God's people'. After the northern kingdom is conquered by the Assyrians in 721 BC, the name of Israel is used for the people of Judah.

---

reversed (35:5–7). God is making all things new – a new creation.

Across the desert stretches a highway – a broad route home for God's holy people. No one will be able to lose their way (35:8). The road will be safe from all danger (35:9), and resound with the joyful praises of the free (35:10).

Assyria threatens Judah
(36:1 – 39:8)

This is an account of the siege of Jerusalem in King Hezekiah's reign. It is also found in 2 Kings 18–20.

The Assyrian commander is confident of an easy victory over Jerusalem – and King Hezekiah is terrified. Nevertheless the king accepts Isaiah's assurance of God's protection – and the Assyrian army disappears without a blow being struck.

God uses Isaiah to cure Hezekiah of a life-threatening boil. In celebration of his recovery, Hezekiah gives a deputation from Babylon a guided tour round his royal treasures. Isaiah warns that one day they will return to carry them off. The foreign threat is no longer Assyria, but Babylon.

Prophecies to God's people during their exile in Babylon

God still cares for Israel and will forgive
(40:1 – 48:22)

WORDS OF COMFORT – THE EXILE IS NEARLY OVER

The scene changes. The Babylonians have captured Jerusalem in 587 BC. Many of God's people have been deported to Babylonia, where they are in exile from their beloved homeland.

The messages in these chapters are the prophet's words of comfort and hope for God's stricken people. The God of Israel hasn't been defeated by Marduk or any of the other gods of Babylon. He himself has been punishing his people for their sin. Now the punishment is coming to an end, and God is going to bring his people back home.

GOD IS HERE!

Zion is to proclaim good news to the cities of Judah: 'God is here!' God will come to his people with majestic strength and goodness. He will care for his people like a shepherd, paying special attention to the weak (40:11).

Suddenly Israel's problems shrink in the perspective of God's mighty power. Job had a similar experience of seeing his suffering in the light of God's majesty and eternity (Job 38:1–7). The waters of creation (and even of chaos) are a mere pool in the palm of God's hand (40:12). The heavens are a hand's breadth; the earth and mountains little more than dust in his scales (40:12).

This mighty creator God has no need of advice from his creatures on matters of guidance, justice, knowledge or understanding (40:13–14). The forests of Lebanon and all its animals would not amount to a sufficient sacrifice for him (40:16).

THE CREATOR WHO CARES

It seems ridiculous to compare the living God to an idol, which is made by people and has to be propped upright (40:18–20). God is the Lord of earth and heaven, time and space: he appoints and removes princes (40:23), sets all the stars in place (40:26) and knows

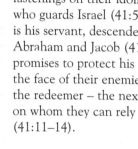

Those whose hope is in God will soar like eagles and discover that he provides them with an unnatural strength and stamina (40:30–31).

every detail of the lives of his people (40:27). He himself is tireless, and is able to revive and sustain all who look to him for strength (40:28–31).

GOD STANDS BY HIS SERVANT

God calls the nations together to take counsel (41:1). He has a question for them: who has stirred up 'a victor from the east' (Cyrus of Persia, 44:28) and allowed him to conquer so many nations? The answer: it is the Lord (41:4).

While other nations rely on the skill of their artisans and the fastenings on their idols, it is God who guards Israel (41:5–10). Israel is his servant, descended from Abraham and Jacob (41:8). God promises to protect his people in the face of their enemies. He is the redeemer – the next of kin on whom they can rely for help (41:11–14).

ISRAEL WILL BE USED TO JUDGE THE NATIONS

God is going to turn his servant, the lowly 'worm' Jacob, into a threshing sledge (41:14–16). A threshing sledge is a heavy piece of machinery which is rolled over the harvested grain to crush it. The

Is there more than one 'Isaiah'?

The prophet Isaiah had a long life and ministry in Jerusalem, 150 years before the exile in Babylon. It is possible that he could have foretold events so many years ahead, but most scholars think that these messages to the exiles in Babylon are by someone else. If they are, their author is clearly a close disciple of Isaiah, and uses similar teaching and language.

Isaiah in Jerusalem has been speaking of Assyria as the enemy – and the place from which exiles will return. Now these prophecies in Babylon talk of the Chaldeans (Babylonians) as Israel's oppressors, with their gods Bel and Nebo.

Another difference between the prophecies in Jerusalem and the prophecies in Babylon is that Jerusalem has now fallen. Instead of threats of judgment there are words of comfort and hope. The prophet looks forward to Israel's return from Babylon – a deliverance like a great second 'exodus'. The new emperor, Cyrus of Persia, is a welcome conqueror. He will do God's work of rescuing his people.

Because we don't know his name, the prophet in Babylon is called 'Second Isaiah', 'Deutero-Isaiah' or 'Isaiah of Babylon'. He writes beautiful, stylish Hebrew, as he sings the praise of the God of Israel in creation and history.

'Isaiah of Babylon' lives with the people in exile. He may be suffering for the messages of hope he brings. There are chapters here which describe just such a 'suffering servant'.

grain is then tossed up in the wind, so that the husks can be blown away while the grain itself falls to the ground. The sledge is a symbol of judgment. God is going to use Israel to judge the nations (41:15–16).

GOD IS ACTIVE, WHILE IDOLS ARE 'NOTHING'

God has compassion on the poor and needy. He will ease their journey across the desert by providing water sources and planting shady trees (41:17–20).

God challenges the gods of the other nations to explain what has happened in the past, or predict what will take place in the future. Of course, they are unable to do so, because they are nothing (41:21–24).

It is God who is stirring up the emperor Cyrus to come from the north (41:25). He declares it now, so that he will be seen to be right (41:26). He can communicate this to his faithful people, but not to deluded idol-worshippers (41:27–29).

THE FIRST 'SERVANT SONG'

God introduces his servant to the watching world. In the previous chapter, this servant is Israel, whom God has chosen and will support (41:8). Now, however, an individual person begins to emerge…

God's servant will be inspired and empowered by God's Spirit (42:1). He will deliver justice to the nations, as David did for Israel (42:1). His style will be gentle and affirming, not loud or bullying (42:2–4). He will not grow tired or discouraged, but will continue his task until he has established God's justice and truth (42:4).

God commissions his servant to do his work. He is to be a light to the nations (42:4–5) and an expression of the covenant relationship between God and his people (42:6). The servant is to release people from physical and spiritual darkness, such as blindness and imprisonment (42:7). The God of the exodus is revealing the vision of a new deliverance (42:8–9).

CREATION PRAISE!

The whole of creation sings a new song to God, in praise of his supreme initiative (42:10). Sea and coastlands, desert and towns rejoice together (42:11–12). Even old enemies like Kedar and Sela give vent to joyful shouts (42:11).

Although the Lord's servant is gentle and quiet, God himself rides out bellowing fury against his enemies (42:13). Like his people, God has been waiting patiently for this moment (42:14). Now he breaks out in passionate activity – transforming nature, rescuing the blind and wreaking havoc among idol-worshippers (42:14–17).

GOD PROMISES DELIVERANCE

The prophet sees the return of Israel from Babylon as a great 'second exodus'. The mountains and valleys will be levelled to make a royal highway across the desert. The exiles will come home (40:3–5)! One day John the Baptist will echo these words. He will call for people to

The 'suffering servant'

Four poems movingly describe a person enduring pain, rejection and death. His agony is undeserved. He is going through this suffering on behalf of others, so that they can be spared.

The poems are to be found in 42:1–4, 49:1–7, 50:4–9 and 52:13 – 53:12.

Sometimes the 'servant' seems to be Israel (by which the prophet means Judah in exile). But it is hard to see how Israel's suffering is undeserved.

Sometimes the servant is clearly an individual – perhaps the prophet himself

or someone the people know. Is this 'Isaiah of Babylon' being rejected by his people, or punished by the Babylonians?

One day Jesus will find inspiration in these poems. He is the perfect servant of God who brings justice and healing to the nations (42:1–9). He is also the innocent person who will be 'led like a lamb to the slaughter' (53:7) as he undergoes rejection, torture and death for the sins of the world.

The identity of the servant is a puzzle. The Ethiopian who meets Philip was still working on it centuries later, and is pointed to Jesus (Acts 8:32–34). It is best to turn it as a jewel in our

hand, and see sometimes Israel, sometimes the prophet, sometimes Jesus.

Later still, Paul sees himself and his missionary colleagues as obeying the mission of the servant in taking the light of the gospel to the Gentiles. He actually quotes Isaiah 49:6 (Acts 13:47).

make a highway in their hearts for the Messiah to arrive and rule (Luke 3:4–6).

In the event, some Jews remain in Babylon where they are settled, rather than sharing the hardship of rebuilding Jerusalem. The returning exiles are still not their own masters, for Judah becomes a province of the Persian empire.

In all this great upheaval, the prophet encourages Israel to know that God is with them. Their punishment is over, and God's future is opening up for them. One day all the nations will look to Israel's God for justice and salvation.

A NEW EXODUS

God declares that he will send for his people in Babylon and compel the Chaldeans to release them (43:14). He is the God of the exodus from Egypt, who parts the sea and drowns enemy armies (42:16–17). But there is no need to look back to the past, because the same God is even now at work in the present (43:18–19).

God is about to do a new thing. He is going to bring back his people from their exile in Babylon. He will make a way across the wilderness, protect them from attack by wild animals and provide rivers for their refreshment (43:19–21).

GOD'S OFFERING TO HIS PEOPLE

God takes Judah to task for not offering him the worship of sacrifices and other gifts. Instead, they have brought him the burden of their sins (43:22–24). But God is determined to forgive Israel, to break the weary cycle of sin and punishment (43:27).

Now God is going to end Israel's spiritual drought, just as he sends rain on thirsty land. He is going to pour his Spirit upon their descendants, so that they will delight to be called 'the Lord's' (44:3–5).

GOD DECLARES HIMSELF TO ISRAEL

God is Israel's true king and only redeemer – both her ruler and her Saviour. He was there at the beginning and will be there at the end (44:6). He is unique as God, for all other gods are powerless frauds and delusions. God also predicts the future, which no other god, pagan prophet or medium is able to do (44:7).

God speaks to Israel's anxieties – her insecurity, lack of faith and fear of the future. He tells her there is no need to be afraid; he has always confided in her what is to happen. There is no other god who is working to save her; no other rock on which she can seek security (44:8).

IDOL-WORSHIP IS NONSENSE

God exposes idol-making as a shameful deceit (44:9–11). The blacksmith gets thirsty and tired as he forges an idol. How can he be making something stronger than himself (44:12)? The carpenter who so carefully draws a human shape and selects a suitable tree, then uses half the wood for an idol and the other half for his fire (44:13–17) – how can his handiwork save him?

The problem with idol-worship is that it is so unthinking. The people who make idols and bow down to them won't face the fact that what they are doing is nonsense (44:18–20).

GOD'S JOY IN DELIVERING HIS PEOPLE

God calls his people to return to him. He has forgiven their sins and recovered them from disaster (44:21–22). Heaven and earth rejoice that God has acted to save Israel and to reveal his glory in her story (44:23).

God declares his power. It is he who has created the cosmos and established truth (44:24–25). He endorses the predictions of his prophets that Jerusalem will be restored and the population of Judah return.

God is the Lord of nature (44:27) and the Lord of history (44:28). Even the emperor Cyrus, the world's most powerful ruler, is like a shepherd caring for people on God's instructions (44:28). With all these assurances, God promises that Jerusalem and her temple will be restored (44:28).

GOD COMMISSIONS CYRUS

Cyrus, the Persian emperor, is anointed by God for a divine purpose – just as Israel's kings were anointed for a holy task (45:1).

God will give Cyrus victories over wealthy King Croesus and the mighty Babylon (45:1–2); but Cyrus's most important work will be to restore the exiled Israelites to their land, capital and worship (45:4–6).

Cyrus is to be God's agent, even though he is unaware of it (45:5). God moves in the great events of nature and history: light and darkness, well-being and disaster, are all his work (45:7–8).

It seems strange and shocking that God will use a pagan emperor to restore his holy people; but God is the Lord of all nations and rulers. Those who criticize what God is doing are like clay questioning the potter that shapes it (45:9). God has raised up Cyrus for this great purpose and he will help him succeed (45:13).

Cyrus of Persia

In a series of brilliant military campaigns, Cyrus wins an empire stretching from Asia Minor in the west to India in the east. He conquers Mesopotamia, and takes Babylon without a struggle in 539 BC. The prophecies in this section of Isaiah date from the years of these campaigns: 550–539 BC.

GOD – THE ONLY LORD AND SAVIOUR

The peoples of other nations will bring their wealth and pay homage to Israel – just as if they have been conquered (45:14). They will acknowledge that Israel's God is the only God, although he is invisible (45:15). Idol-makers will be exposed as deluded frauds, while Israel's God will keep her eternally safe (45:16–17).

God declares that he is the creator of order and truth (45:18–19). While idols are dumb and ignorant, God makes his purposes known (45:20–21). He calls all nations to turn to him, acknowledge him as Lord, and receive his salvation (45:22–25).

NO CONTEST

The famous idols of Babylon are loaded onto animals. 'Bel' (like 'Baal', and also known as Marduk) and 'Nebo' (Marduk's son) are being carted off into captivity (46:1–2). Their powerlessness is exposed for all to see.

By contrast, the living God has always carried his people – and always will (46:3–4). How can anyone persist in comparing the God of Israel to pagan idols? Idols are merely metal objects that have to be carried around or propped in a corner – incapable of helping themselves or anyone else (46:5–7).

The true and only God is fulfilling his age-old purpose (46:8–10). He is summoning the Persian emperor Cyrus, like a bird of prey, to rescue and restore Israel (46:11–13).

GOD WILL JUDGE BABYLON

Isaiah sings a lament for Babylon. She sees herself as a beautiful young woman – the loveliest of kingdoms, for ever secure (47:5, 8). But God is going to humiliate her, reveal her true nature and put her to hard labour (47:2–3).

Babylon is proud and cruel. She talks as though she is God (47:8), relies on the occult for guidance (47:12) and has been merciless to captive Israel (47:6). Now God is going to reduce her to ruin (47:1). Her stargazing astrologers and fortune tellers will vanish in the fire of judgment like burning stubble (47:12–14).

'NEW THINGS'

Isaiah speaks God's word to Israel. Israel claims to rely on God and honour his name, but still continues to sin in thought and deed (48:1–2).

God had long warned Israel that he would punish her, and now he has done it. She can't blame her idols (48:3–5). Now God wants to tell Israel new things – things which have not been so long predicted that they have become dull (48:6–8).

God is going to spare Israel further punishment, because he wants her to live for his glory (48:9–11). He is the living God, the eternal creator and Lord of all (48:12–13). Now he is bringing Cyrus to conquer Babylon (48:14).

The Lord's servant speaks. He has always made himself known – through creation and in wisdom. Now God is sending him to work, in the power of his Spirit (48:16).

If only Israel had obeyed God instead of rebelling! She would have enjoyed prosperity, success and growth (48:17–19). But it is not too late. God commands Israel to leave Babylon – and to do so with joyful praise. God is releasing his people from captivity. He will provide for them on their desert journey home (48:20–21).

God will rebuild Jerusalem

(49:1 – 55:13)

THE SECOND 'SERVANT SONG'

God's servant announces himself to the world (49:1). The Lord God has called him before he was born, to be his spokesperson – his mouth 'like a sharp sword' – to deliver his message of judgment and love (49:2).

The servant's name is Israel; but this is not the Israel that has failed and is in exile. This is Israel as she should be: the suffering servant of God who restores his people (49:3–6).

But the servant's task is to be greater still. He is to reveal God's glory to the nations and give light to the whole world (49:5–6). The rulers of the nations will bow down before this mysterious, rejected, glorious servant who so perfectly expresses the purpose of God (49:7).

MAKING UP

God is restoring his relationship with his people. He calls them from the prison darkness of exile (49:8) and transforms the landscape to ease their journey home (49:9–11). They come from three directions – north, west and south (Syene is Aswan in Egypt). The whole of creation rejoices in God's love for his people (49:12–13).

Does Zion (Jerusalem) still feel that God has forgotten her? God assures her of his enduring love – greater than the love of any nursing mother (49:14–15). Look at the progress of the building work and the steady influx of people (49:17–18)! God is filling sad Jerusalem with children – and foreign kings and queens to look after them (49:19–23).

Will God be able to free all his people? Isaiah says that God is fighting all Jerusalem's enemies – and will defeat even the strongest (49:24–26).

God regrets the years of Israel's exile. It wasn't because of divorce or debt that she was deported, but for rebellion against God (50:1). He called and no one answered (50:2). However, all that is in the past. Now the God of creation and judgment is rescuing his people (50:2–3).

THE THIRD 'SERVANT SONG'

The Lord's servant is a teacher with the ability to encourage. He listens to God and passes on to others what he hears (50:4–5). His work results in him being punished and tortured (50:6). We see why Jesus draws on these songs to understand his own suffering (Mark 10:33–34).

'YOUR GOD REIGNS!'

Isaiah reminds Israel of her experiences of God in history.

God raised the nation of Israel from the unlikely beginnings of elderly Abraham and barren Sarah (51:1–2). Now he will turn Israel's barren wilderness into the Garden of Eden (51:3). The light of his justice shines out; his salvation reaches all peoples. Heaven and earth are short-lived, but his deliverance is for ever (51:4–8).

God is going to act with sovereign power. He once subdued the mythic forces of evil – Rahab (Egypt), the dragon (Satan) and the sea (Chaos). Now the God of the exodus from Egypt is rescuing his people again – from exile in Babylon – and bringing them home with joy (51:9–11). Israel need not fear any foe, nor famine or death, because she is God's own people (51:12–14).

Jerusalem has drunk deeply of God's wrath. She has been made dizzy by devastation and sent sprawling by destruction. She and her children lie unconscious with no one to pity or help (51:17–20). But God will intervene. He will take his cup of wrath from her and give it to her enemies instead – those who have trampled her (51:21–23).

Isaiah gives Zion (Jerusalem) her wake-up call (52:1). This is more than another day – it is a new life, a resurrection. Jerusalem is to receive again her beauty, holiness, dignity and freedom (52:1–2). This is God's doing, who called his people from captivity in Egypt and Assyria (52:3–6) without question or payment. He is the Lord (52:3–5).

What a wonderful sight – the running feet of the messenger, springing through the mountains. He brings God's declaration of peace, salvation and victory (52:7). The watchmen burst into a song of joy which is echoed by the ruins. God has acted! The Lord himself has comforted his people (52:8–10).

The newly holy nation prepares to leave Babylon. She returns from exile like a procession of priests (52:11). All is done with dignity, without haste or fear (52:12).

THE FOURTH 'SERVANT SONG'

God's servant is to be raised up (52:13). He has been rendered almost unrecognizable by what he has suffered. The nations and their rulers fall silent at the sight of him (52:14–15).

There seemed nothing special about the servant when he first appeared – like a root out of dry ground. No majesty. No beauty (53:1–2). He suffered in so many ways – sorrow, rejection, illness – that people dismissed him as hopeless and worthless (53:3).

But now we see the servant's suffering in a new light. It was our suffering he was carrying – and we thought God was giving him what he deserved (53:4). The servant was wounded and crushed for our sins – so that we can be healed (53:5). He has been our scapegoat, our sacrifice, our sin-bearer (53:6).

The description of what happened to the servant is, for Christians, a description of what happened to Jesus – and for the same reasons. In his suffering he was meek and unprotesting, like a lamb being shorn or sacrificed (53:7). It was John the Baptist who recognized Jesus as 'the Lamb of God, who takes away the sin of the world' (John 1:29).

Like the servant's trial, Jesus' trial was unfair and his fate undeserved. Crucifixion was the ultimate cut-off from dignity, life and hope (53:8). Most strangely, the servant's grave was 'with a rich man' – and Jesus on his death will be given the tomb of Joseph of Arimathea (Matthew 27:57–59).

Isaiah sees that all this is God's will. Through this innocent suffering and death will come a great forgiveness and mighty resurrection (53:10–11). This terrible death endured means life and victory for all (53:12).

TRANSFORMATION!

Jerusalem is to rejoice. She was barren, but is now teeming with children. She needs more space to live, and can spread throughout the world (54:1–3). God the creator of all is her husband, restoring their relationship after the miseries of suffering and separation (54:4–8).

The punishment is over and God renews his promises to Israel – as he did to Noah after the flood (54:9–10).

God is going to transform ruined Jerusalem. Her foundations, walls, gates and towers will be of precious stones (54:11–12). Her children will receive God's own teaching and enjoy prosperity (54:13). This is a heavenly city – a place of righteousness, truth and peace (54:14–17; Revelation 21:10–11).

AN OPEN INVITATION

Isaiah calls everyone who is hungry to God's feast. The siege of sin and suffering is lifted. The gates of plenty are thrown open (55:1).

'Why spend your money on junk food?' he asks, 'Why waste your life on vain ambitions? Instead, come into the

---

Free for all! Isaiah imagines a give-away at a bread market. God invites his people to draw sustenance from his words. This free gift of salvation will feed their souls on the richest of food and they will be satisfied (55:1–3; echoed by Jesus in John 6).

life and love of God – the fulfilment of the kingdom of David' (55:2–3). You will become part of God's mission to the world. God will make you radiant so that others may be drawn to his light (55:4–5).

This is a moment of opportunity. It is time to turn to God while he is so approachable, so near (55:6). It is time to receive God's mercy, share his thoughts and catch the wave of his purposes (55:7–11). The freedom, joy and peace of God's people will cause the whole of creation to rejoice (55:12). Peace will break out – a peace which will be for ever the hallmark of God's reign (55:13).

Prophecies to Israel after the exile

Here are encouraging words for the people rebuilding Jerusalem. God's glory is shining around Israel, and the whole world will be drawn to her light. Jerusalem will be at the centre of God's new creation, where injustice and discord will be replaced by joy and peace (65:17–25).

Again we hear the servant speaking (61:1–11). He proclaims God's grace and favour to everyone in need. Jesus will turn to these words when he teaches at the synagogue in Nazareth. God's jubilee of forgiveness and freedom has arrived – in person (Luke 4:18–21).

All are welcome
(56:1–8)

God's salvation is not exclusively for Israel. All who are serious about God's justice and keep the sabbath are welcome to his new community (56:1–2).

Isaiah particularly mentions foreigners and eunuchs. They have been excluded from Jewish worship because of physical or moral defects. But now God wants to include them.

The foreigner or pagan 'outsider' must not assume that God will reject him from his people; nor must the eunuch dismiss himself as a dead and fruitless tree (56:3). The eunuch who lives in God's way will be remembered, even though he has no children (56:4–5). Foreigners, too, who love God and keep his law, may come and worship in his temple (56:6–7).

God's mission, through the Jews, was always to bless the world and draw all nations to him. This was the purpose of God's call to Abraham (Genesis 12:1–2); it will be understood by Jesus (John 10:16); and it is here in the prophecies of Isaiah: 'My house [temple] shall be house of prayer for all peoples' (56:7).

When the watchmen sleep...
(56:9 – 57:13)

The prophets who should be guarding Israel are silent – asleep like dreaming dogs (56:10). Israel's leaders are like drunken shepherds – indulging themselves rather than caring for their people (56:11–12).

As a result, the wild beasts of idolatry invade Israel unchecked (56:9). Trees become the sites of cultic prostitution and rocks are used for child sacrifice (57:5–6). God has tried to ignore Israel's wrongdoing, but he can do so no longer (57:11). The idols will not protect them from God's judgment. Only those who hide in God will be allowed to live in his holy community (57:13).

God is determined to forgive
(57:14–21)

The cry goes up to build the road home from exile (57:14); but God needs also to prepare people's hearts for his holy presence (57:15). God wants to put aside his anger and forgive even those who don't deserve forgiveness (57:16–19).

True fasting is love in action
(58:1–14)

God tells Isaiah to shout out like a trumpet (58:1). He is to declare that the Israelites are fasting in the wrong spirit. They look sincere and eager, but really they are trying to manipulate God (58:2–3).

While they take time off to fast and pray (perhaps on the Day of Atonement), they are still making their employees work (58:3). Going without food is supposed to make them humble before God; but it makes them bad-tempered and violent towards each other (58:4–5).

God's idea of a fast is very different. True fasting means putting ourselves out to serve others: releasing people from injustice and oppression; sharing our food and home and clothes; and helping our relatives (58:6–7). When we do these things, God's blessing is upon us and he answers our prayers (58:8–9).

It is important to keep the sabbath for God's sake, and not just use it as an extra day off. It is a day to delight in the Lord (58:13–14).

Sin separates but God saves

(59:1–21)

Israel's sins are blocking her off from God and preventing God from saving her (59:1–1). All is bloodshed and lies (59:3), dishonesty and the creeping poison of corruption (59:4–5). Society cannot hold together when there is such a complete breakdown of moral standards (59:6). Everyone is bent on doing evil (59:7–8).

Israel is in deep moral darkness (59:9–12), blocked off from the light of God's truth, righteousness and justice (59:13–15).

God sees this desperate situation, and that there is no one to take action (59:15–16). He decides to intervene – coming to the rescue himself armed with radical goodness, intent on salvation and swathed in righteous anger (59:17). He will sweep in like a cleansing flood, giving justice, righting wrongs and punishing the guilty (59:18–19).

And what will be the fate of Israel? He will act as her redeemer: her next of kin who saves her and pays her debts (59:20). He forges an everlasting bond with his people, to put his Spirit of truth within them (59:21).

The panoramic glory of Zion

(60:1–22)

The glory of God dawns over Jerusalem like the sunrise (60:1). She becomes a beacon to a world in deep darkness (60:2) and nations are drawn to her light (60:3).

The procession of returning Israelites becomes an influx of people and wealth from all the nations (60:4–7). They bring animals for sacrifice and gifts to beautify the temple (60:7).

Jerusalem's glory and the news of what God has done for her make her the wonder of the world (60:8–16). Her gates are open day and night, so that the royal delegations may flow in (60:11). All nations are judged by their response to Jerusalem (60:12) and old enemies come to pay homage (60:14).

Everything is richer, stronger, better (60:17). The aim of government is righteousness and its driving force is peace (60:17). Jerusalem is surrounded by salvation and accessed with praise (60:18). The glory of God is her perpetual light, and darkness and grief are no more (60:19–20).

Finally, Jerusalem's people will be righteous – planted as God's own, to grow and flourish (60:21–22). Is it all a dream? No – God himself is going to make it a reality (60:22).

The Lord's anointed

(61:1 – 62:12)

God's servant speaks again – this time with the words which Jesus will take to refer to himself (Luke 4:17–21).

God is sending his servant to his people in exile. He has anointed him to deliver good news of rescue, comfort and freedom (61:1). The year of God's salvation has arrived at last – the joyous Jubilee which dispels injustice, mourning and despair (61:2–3). God's people will become splendid examples of righteousness (61:3). They will rebuild and restore the ruins of long ago (61:4).

God's people will be given their true status as his priests and ministers (61:6). Foreigners will be their slaves and the wealth of nations will support them (61:5–6). God is going to give his people double honour, to make up for their double shame (61:7).

God will bring about all that he holds dear. He will establish justice in the world and set his restored people as the centrepiece of his blessing (61:8–9).

Israel rejoices in all that God is doing for her. She is robed in his saving goodness (61:10). She will grow in his purity and praise (61:11).

Seeing red

(63:1–6)

Isaiah has an awesome vision of God returning from his work of judgment. He is majestic and dreadful – stained with the blood of his enemies (63:1).

God has been to punish Edom (which means 'red') and her capital Bozrah (which sounds like 'grape-harvester') (63:1–2). He has acted alone in this, because there was no one fit to help (63:3–5). It was a lone feat of ruthless, righteous wrath (63:6).

A cry from the heart

(63:7 – 64:12)

Isaiah cries out to God to have mercy on his people. He has been so good to Israel in the past, caring for them in person (63:7–9).

Israel has rebelled against God and become his enemy (63:10); but now she remembers the mighty deliverance of the exodus. She longs for those great days to return (63:11–15). Even if her ancestors, Abraham and Israel, disown her, will not God have mercy (63:16)?

Israel attributes everything to God – even her own hard heart, her disobedience and lack of faith (63:17). Now she begs God to rescue, restore and rule her (63:17–19).

Israel asks God to intervene by his mountain-moving

power (64:1) and like fire in his awesome holiness (64:2). He is the only One who can act in this way, revealing himself in justice to those who wait for him (64:3–5).

Israel admits her sin and guilt – even her best actions are filthy (64:5–6). She feels that she is dying in sin, and that God has turned away and left her to her fate (64:7). And yet she pleads that she is still in God's hands. He can still reform her, like a potter with clay (64:8).

Israel asks God to have pity on her desolate cities – and especially on the ruins of her temple. Is God's silence really final (64:10–11)?

Choices and consequences
(65:1–16)

God says that he has been open to those who haven't looked for him (65:1). The apostle Paul understands this to refer to non-Jews (Romans 10:20). Equally, God has held out his hands to people who did know him, but were rebellious (65:2) – which Paul takes to mean Israel (Romans 10:21).

The sins which have offended God and provoked his punishment are pagan offerings and attempts to commune with the dead (65:3–4). The stench of incense and disgusting foods offends him (65:4–5). God has promised that he will pay back these outrages – and he will do so (65:6–7).

And yet, even in his judgment, God will spare a remnant – like a few good grapes that deserve to survive (65:8). He will retrieve some descendants of Israel to reoccupy his promised land (65:9). The pastureland of Sharon will once again have flocks. The Valley of Achor ('bitterness') will be a place of peace (65:10).

However, God will sentence to death all who worship the Syrian gods of fortune and destiny (65:11). There will be a world of difference between the fate of those who turn to God and those who rely on idols (65:13–16).

God's new creation
(65:17–25)

God describes the new world that he is creating – so wonderful and different that the present pain will be completely forgotten (65:17).

Jerusalem, which has seen so much suffering and destruction, will become a community of joy and delight (65:18–19). Bereavement and early deaths will be things of the past: to live to 100 will be quite normal (65:20)!

There will be peace and stability. Families will be able

to build and plant – enjoying the fruits of their labour through many generations (65:21–23). There will be a new closeness to God and a readiness to speak with him (65:24). The animal world will be at rest, with natural enemies feeding side by side – rather than one eating another (65:25). Only the serpent, the ancient symbol of evil, will continue to be cursed (65:23).

God's judgment and salvation
(66:1–24)

God announces himself. He is the One who has heaven as his throne and the earth as his footstool (66:1) What significance, then, does this 'house', the temple, have? Everything comes from God anyway (66:2).

What God looks for in worship is the obedient response of a humble heart (66:2, 4). Without the offering of the heart, a sacrifice is just mindless pagan butchery (66:3). God has no pleasure in receiving worship which is a pretence. He feels mocked –

and will mock in return (66:4–5).

Isaiah describes a miracle: a woman gives birth to a son without going into labour. It is unheard of, and yet God is going to bring his new nation to birth in an instant (66:7–9).

Isaiah calls all those who love Jerusalem (and have grieved over her) to rejoice (66:10). She will suckle and

earth: Tarshish in Spain, Put and Lud in Ethiopia, Tubal in the north and Javan, which is Greece (66:18–19). They are bringing the Israelites with them – like an offering – on every kind of transport (66:20–21). They will form an enduring community – the worshipping nucleus of the entire world (66:22–23).

At the last, God's restored people will look at the corpses of their enemies – and see the sad and sickening fate of those who resisted God to the end (66:24).

Sunrise over Jerusalem. Isaiah sees a thick darkness covering the earth, but God's glory appearing like a sunrise illuminating his people. Nations and rulers will be drawn to the brightness.

nurture her children (66:11). She is the mother of all, giving wealth and well-being, support and comfort to her people (66:12–13).

The other side of God's blessing is that he will punish and destroy his enemies (66:14). He loathes the eating of unclean foods (66:17).

God is drawing people from the far reaches of the

JEREMIAH

Jeremiah is a prophet of disaster and hope. He lives in the southern kingdom of Judah during the years leading up to the fall of its capital city, Jerusalem. For forty years he preaches that this catastrophe is going to happen if the people don't repent and turn to God.

Jeremiah's warnings come true when the armies of Babylon, directed by King Nebuchadnezzar, invade Judah. In 587 BC they destroy Jerusalem and her temple. The king and many of the people are taken away to exile in Babylonia.

But Jeremiah also has a message of hope. He predicts that one day the people will return and that the nation will be restored. He also promises that God will make a new deal with his people. His law will no longer be 'outside' them, written on tablets of stone. Instead, it will be 'within' them – written on their hearts.

In Jeremiah we see the pain and passion of a prophet at work. God's word burns within him, so that he *must* preach. But his message makes him unpopular. At times he is cruelly persecuted. He has a hard life – crushed between the pressing truth of God and the resistance of his people.

Outline

God calls the young Jeremiah to be a prophet (1:1–19)
God's messages to Judah and Jerusalem (2:1 – 25:38)
Episodes in Jeremiah's life (26:1 – 45:25)
Prophecies against the nations (46:1 – 51:64)
The fall of Jerusalem (52:1–34)

INTRODUCTION

When did Jeremiah prophesy?

Jeremiah prophesies during the reigns of the last five kings of Judah: Josiah, Jehoahaz, Jehoiakim, Jehoiachin and Zedekiah.

Jeremiah is born towards the end of the reign of Manasseh. Manasseh has led the people of Judah in Baal-worship and occult practices. He has introduced idols into the temple and even sacrificed his own sons on pagan altars. Although Manasseh eventually repents of these acts, his son Amon is an idol-worshipper as well (2 Chronicles 33).

When the young king Josiah comes of age, he sets out to restore the worship of the Lord. He wants to be a king like his ancestor David. He demolishes the pagan altars and destroys their images (2 Chronicles 34:1–7).

Jeremiah is a similar age to his king. When he is called to be a prophet in 627 BC, he pleads that he is 'only a child' (1:7).

Assyria and Babylon

Judah is a small kingdom, tossed between the superpowers of Assyria to the north-east and Egypt to the south-west. Judah's twin kingdom, Israel, has rebelled against Assyria and been overrun; her capital city, Samaria, captured in 722 BC and her people dispersed.

In the early years of Jeremiah's ministry, Assyria dominates the region. But Jeremiah's message is that Babylon will arise and conquer all.

Judah, too, has defied Assyria during the reign of Hezekiah. Hezekiah formed an alliance with Egypt and rebelled against Assyria, but the punishment was swift and terrible. The Assyrians devastated Judah in 701, although Jerusalem itself was protected by God, thanks to the faith of Hezekiah and his prophet Isaiah.

While Josiah is pursuing his reforms, Assyria's power begins to fade. Her strong ruler, Ashurbanipal, has died in 627, and the province of Babylon has broken away as

---

Countdown: the decline and fall of Judah

640/39 *Josiah becomes king of Judah at the age of eight.*

628 *He begins his reforms at the age of nineteen.*

627 *Jeremiah starts to preach.*

622 *The Book of the Law is found in the temple.*

612 *The Assyrian empire falls to the forces of Babylon.*

609 *Josiah is killed in battle at the age of thirty-nine. Jehoahaz becomes king of Judah for three months. Jehoiakim is made king of Judah by Pharaoh Neco of Egypt.*

605 *The Babylonians defeat the Egyptians at Carchemish. Daniel and other young leaders are deported to Babylon.*

604 *Jeremiah's scroll is read to King Jehoiakim – and burned.*

601 *Jehoiakim rebels against Babylon.*

598 *Jehoiakim is deposed and dies.*

597 *Jehoiachin is taken off to exile in Babylon, along with 3,000 skilled workers and the temple treasures. This is the first phase of captivity. Zedekiah becomes king at the age of twenty-one.*

588 *Zedekiah rebels against Babylon. Nebuchadnezzar besieges Jerusalem.*

587 *Jerusalem falls to the Babylonian army. Eight hundred and thirty-two of her people are taken into exile. This is the second phase of captivity, but Jeremiah is spared and released. Gedaliah is made governor of Judah, and Jeremiah stays with him at Mizpah; but Gedaliah is assassinated by Ishmael. The survivors from Judah go to Egypt, against Jeremiah's advice; they take Jeremiah with them.*

582/1 *There is a third phase of deportation, with 745 people taken away to exile in Babylon.*

561 *A new king of Babylon releases King Jehoiachin from prison, but keeps him in the royal court. He has been in exile for thirty-seven years.*

539 *Babylon falls to Cyrus, king of Persia.*

539/8 *Cyrus frees the Jewish exiles and allows them to return home.*

an independent power. Her founder, Nabopolassar, defeats his Assyrian masters in 626 and establishes the beginnings of the Babylonian (Chaldean) empire. His famous son is Nebuchadnezzar.

Josiah's reforms

When Josiah has completed the destruction of pagan altars and idols, he commissions a team to restore Solomon's temple. This results in the discovery of the Book of the Law – the long-lost law of Moses. The effect of hearing the law is dramatic. Josiah leads the nation in repentance. The covenant with God is renewed and the Passover celebrated in a week-long festival (2 Chronicles 34:8 – 35:19).

Jeremiah plays a key role in Josiah's reforms. He travels the land, proclaiming the covenant and presenting people with its commands and blessings (Jeremiah 11:1–8). Paganism is deep-seated and Jeremiah has his first taste of opposition and rejection. At Anathoth, where he was raised as the son of a priest, there is a plot to kill him. We begin to see his loneliness, as people reject him as a killjoy:

> *I never sat in the company of revellers,*
> *never made merry with them;*
> *I sat alone because your hand was on me*
> *and you had filled me with indignation (15:17).*

The heart of a true prophet

Jeremiah is often angry with both the people and God – but his message consumes him:

> *O Lord, you deceived me and I was deceived;*
> *you overpowered me and prevailed.*
> *I am ridiculed all day long;*
> *everyone mocks me.*
> *Whenever I speak, I cry out*
> *proclaiming violence and destruction.*
> *So the word of the Lord has brought me*
> *insult and reproach all day long.*
> *But if I say, 'I will not mention him*
> *or speak any more in his name,'*
> *his word is in my heart like a burning fire,*
> *shut up in my bones (20:7–9).*

Jeremiah has the heart of a true prophet. His calling makes him lonely in a crowd; yet he loves his people and longs that they will turn to God. He begs God to spare them:

> *You are among us, O Lord,*
> *and we bear your name;*
> *do not forsake us (14:9)!*

Jeremiah's work continues in this way for twenty-three years. He is protected from harm by Josiah – now in his prime and a true king and father to his people.

Changes in Judah's history

But now international affairs change the course of Judah's history. Assyria is hard-pressed by the rising power of Babylon, and the king of Egypt decides to intervene. He marches to support Assyria in the hope of increasing his influence in Palestine. But Josiah wants Assyria to remain weak, and he rides to intercept the Egyptians – only to be killed in battle at Megiddo.

The Egyptian king uses his new-found power to remove Josiah's successor (Jehoahaz) and install another son, Jehoiakim. But in 605 the Egyptians themselves are swept away by the Babylonian armies of Nebuchadnezzar, at the battle of Carchemish.

It is in 605 BC that God tells Jeremiah to have all his prophecies written on a single scroll. Jeremiah's secretary Baruch writes them down, and they are read in public in the temple.

The new king's staff bring the scroll to his attention and he demands that the prophecies be read to him. Jehoiakim is completely unmoved by the warnings they contain. As each section is read, he cuts it away and throws it on the fire (36:23). But Jeremiah and Baruch sit down and write the whole document again – with some further material for good measure!

Jeremiah's messages are regarded as treason. He is preaching against the temple and the city. He is challenging the new wave of paganism and undermining public confidence. Without a king to protect him, Jeremiah is much more severely persecuted. He is beaten, put in the stocks (20:1–2) and threatened with death (26:16).

Now Nebuchadnezzar takes control of the whole region and demands tribute from Judah. When Jehoiakim rebels, he is deposed and dies. His successor Jehoiachin (Jeconiah) also resists the Babylonians, but is soon defeated. He is taken into exile along with thousands of his leading citizens and all the treasures from Solomon's temple.

Judah under King Zedekiah

The next king is Zedekiah. He immediately lays plans to break Babylon's grip. But Jeremiah knows that Babylon's triumph is God's judgment on Judah. They will be wise to submit to it. He enacts Babylon's control by wearing a yoke on his neck – and warns of dire punishments if Judah tries to throw it off (27:8). When envoys from the surrounding kingdoms come to pay their respects to Zedekiah, Jeremiah sends them away with an extraordinary message: the Lord, the God of Israel, is the supreme God, and Nebuchadnezzar is his servant (27:6)!

Jeremiah also writes a letter to the Jewish exiles in Babylon. He advises them to settle down and 'seek the peace and prosperity of the city to which I have carried you' (29:7). This is a stark contrast to the feelings of Psalm 137. Jeremiah declares that it is *God* who has carried them off to Babylonia, when actually it was Nebuchadnezzar! Their exile is to last for seventy years, after which God will answer their prayers and bring them home.

Even with the Babylonian army threatening Jerusalem, Zedekiah is determined to resist. He consults Jeremiah privately from time to time, asking him for a word from the Lord. No doubt he and his advisers hope for a last-minute rescue, as happened with the Assyrian threat in Hezekiah's reign.

Jeremiah is arrested for trying to leave the city. Although he is on personal business, it looks as though he is deserting to the Babylonians. The king has him placed under guard in the courtyard of the palace (37:21). However, his enemies still object to his messages, which they see as disloyal. They seize him and lower him into a cistern, where he might be lost for ever (38:9). Fortunately he is rescued by one of the king's servants, who is an Ethiopian.

When Jerusalem finally falls, the Babylonian commander seeks out Jeremiah. He gives him his freedom and offers to take him to Babylon. The Babylonians treat Jeremiah as an ally, as he has so long preached submission to Nebuchadnezzar. But Jeremiah chooses to stay in Judah, with the poorest survivors of the catastrophe (40:7).

Meanwhile, King Zedekiah has tried to escape. He is captured, blinded and carried off to prison in Babylon. The last thing he sees is his sons being killed in front of him (52:10–11).

No happy ending

Jeremiah hopes to settle with the new governor Gedaliah at Mizpah. Together they will care for the shattered people of Judah and rebuild their community. But Gedaliah is assassinated by Ishmael, who wants the royal throne.

After much bloodshed, Ishmael is driven off. The survivors ask Jeremiah for a word from the Lord. They promise to do whatever he says. When God speaks, it is to assure them of his protection. There is nothing to fear from Babylon. He will bless and restore them if they stay in their land; but if they take refuge in Egypt, they will die (42:17).

The survivors have learned nothing from their terrifying ordeal. They accuse Jeremiah of lying. He and Baruch are trying to get them all killed or exiled. Far from agreeing that Jeremiah has been right all along, they reject him all over again. They defy God's message and leave for Egypt, taking Jeremiah with them.

There is no happy ending to the book of Jeremiah. We leave him in Egypt, still speaking God's word to a resistant and disobedient people. They revive their pagan practices, burning incense to the Queen of Heaven. The God of Israel has failed them, but they always had plenty when they worshipped her. When the time of captivity is over, thousands of Jews return from exile in Babylon. But nothing more is heard of those who went to Egypt.

DISCOVERING JEREMIAH

God calls the young Jeremiah to be a prophet

Jeremiah is a priest's son. He comes from Anathoth – a settlement of priests on the eastern border of Judah by the open wilderness.

Josiah has been on the throne twelve years and is now about twenty. Jeremiah and his king are a similar age. When God calls him, Jeremiah pleads that he is only a child and unable to speak. But God has known and chosen him from before his birth (1:6–7).

Jeremiah is to serve God as his prophet through forty stormy years. In the north, the Assyrian empire will fall and the Babylonian empire will rise. To the south, the power of Egypt will be both a threat and a refuge. And Judah herself, like her kings, will swing between godliness and paganism.

In all this, Jeremiah is to devote himself to speaking God's messages. He must warn the people of judgment, defeat and exile. Jerusalem and her temple will be destroyed. The king descended from David will become a prisoner. The whole nation will be gutted and displaced. Jeremiah's message is not only unbelievable – it is unacceptable. No one will want to listen.

But Jeremiah is God's choice. God touches his mouth and gives him the words to say. He promises to strengthen and protect this hesitant young man against all that his enemies will try to do to him. And he does. He appoints him to an earth-moving, kingdom-toppling, life-giving ministry (1:10).

To a prophet's eyes, ordinary things take on special meaning. Jeremiah sees an almond tree about to blossom – the first sign of spring (1:11). The Hebrew word for 'almond' sounds like 'watchful'. God is awake and alert to fulfil his plans. Jeremiah sees a boiling pot, tilting its contents from the north. In the same way God is about to pour out his punishment on Judah through fierce invaders (1:13–14).

God's messages to Judah and Jerusalem

Jeremiah starts preaching in 627 BC, which is the thirteenth year of Josiah's reign. The king is twenty-one years old. The messages in these chapters (2:1 – 25:38) come from the remaining years of Josiah's reign, and the following reigns until 605.

Josiah dies in battle at the age of twenty-nine. His son Jehoahaz becomes king for a few months, but is soon deposed by the king of Egypt. The king of Egypt (Pharaoh Neco) puts another son on the throne instead. This is King Jehoiakim, who reigns for eleven years.

Jehoiakim is deposed and taken captive by King Nebuchadnezzar of Babylon. His son Jehoiachin succeeds him on the throne of Judah. He is eighteen years old. Almost immediately, he too is deported to Babylon. His uncle, Zedekiah, becomes king in his place.

Jeremiah prophesies throughout these reigns. Chapters 2–20 contains messages delivered between 627 and 605 BC. In 605, Jehoiakim is king of Judah and Nebuchadnezzar is the new king of Babylon.

God tells Jeremiah to collect his prophecies into a single scroll, which his secretary Baruch writes out for him (36:1–2). This is probably the scroll which is read to King Jehoiakim the following year – and which the arrogant king cuts up and burns.

Israel forsakes the God who loves her
(2:1 – 3:5)

God is like a husband to his people. He remembers the delight of his young love when he rescued her from Egypt, married her in the wilderness and brought her home to a fertile land. But now Israel and Judah have behaved like prostitutes. They commit spiritual adultery by worshipping other gods.

Jeremiah can't believe what he sees. God's people reject him – for what? They lust after fertility gods and goddesses – erecting phallic poles on hilltops and holding orgies under trees. This is like exchanging spring water for the foul contents of a leaking cistern. Idols are made by human beings and they don't work.

God's people are unholy in their behaviour. They are also unfaithful in their politics. They no longer trust God to protect them. Instead they rely on alliances with other nations, such as Egypt and Assyria. But they don't need to be slaves to anyone. They are God's children! And these so-called allies are treacherous. They will just as soon tear them apart.

In all this, the people still call on God as their Father and friend. But their hearts are hard and their eyes are cold. Their actions deny their words.

Jeremiah calls to God's people to return
(3:6 – 4:2)

God shows Jeremiah that the northern state of Israel has behaved like an unfaithful wife. She has played the whore as her people have worshipped Baal ('master') in fertility rites on hills and under trees. Now God has divorced her. The ten tribes of Israel have been captured by Sargon II of Assyria and taken from their land.

God tells Jeremiah to call Israel to return to her true master, who is God (3:14). God promises to give Israel good shepherds – that is, leaders who will nurture and protect her people. God's presence will become far more meaningful to them than in the old days of the ark of the covenant (3:16). Jerusalem herself will become

God's throne where the nations of the world will acknowledge him; and Israel and Judah will be reunited and come into God's blessing (3:18).

Visions of invasion from the north
(4:3 – 6:30)

God urges his people to make a true, deep repentance, like a circumcision of the heart (4:4). Only this will avert the disaster that is about to fall on Judah.

The crisis is breaking. The trumpet must sound the alarm, so that people can take refuge (4:5–6). God is bringing a fearsome army from the north, which is springing forth like a hungry lion from its thicket (4:7). Judah's leaders will be stunned and helpless in the face of

---

Jeremiah reminds his listeners that God had given them a pleasant and fertile land to live in, but they have been unfaithful to him. They have committed spiritual adultery by worshipping other gods. As a consequence, the land he gave them has become defiled. Fertile land in Samaria, west of Sebastiye.

the threat (4:9), and fatally deceived by those who have been prophesying that all would be well (4:10).

The enemy will sweep in like a roasting wind: not useful or refreshing, but inescapable and withering all in its path (4:11).

Jeremiah calls on Jerusalem to repent. The terror is approaching. The alarm is sounded from Dan, the northernmost tribe. The names of Judah's cities are on the lips of the invaders (4:14–16). Jeremiah is doubled up with the pain and overwhelmed by the tumult of invasion (4:19–21). God's people have brought this on themselves by their wanton rebellion (4:22). The prophet sees a desolate and deserted landscape (4:23–26); and yet God will still leave room to be merciful (4:28).

To Jeremiah, Judah is like a woman dressing herself for seduction; but she will soon be writhing in anguish as her enemies have their way (4:29–31).

Is there any hope for Jerusalem? Is there a single person, poor or rich, who could be the reason for sparing the city from destruction (5:1–5)? There is no one. And so Jerusalem will be besieged, as though wild animals are lying in wait outside her walls (5:6). This is God's punishment for her wilful idolatry and rampant immorality (5:7–9).

The people of Jerusalem have been deceived by false prophets. They have believed messages that all will be well and Jerusalem can never fall (4:12–14). But now Jeremiah's words are to be like a fire, igniting God's judgment on his people (5:14). This judgment will be executed by the forces of a mighty, foreign nation, which will consume and destroy all that Judah holds dear (5:15–19).

Topheth

The altars of Topheth in the Valley of Ben Hinnom are the scene of the grossest act of all – child sacrifice. People think they are making the supreme offering – but God has never asked them to do such a thing. Now judgment is on its way and must run its course. Only on the other side of judgment will there be mercy and renewal.

'Topheth' rhymes with the Hebrew for 'shame' and is used to mean 'spit'. The Valley of Ben Hinnom becomes 'Gehenna', the rubbish dump outside Jerusalem. Jesus uses its ever-burning fire as a picture of judgment.

Jeremiah preaches in the temple
(7:1 – 8:3)

Eighteen years have passed since Josiah began his reforms and Jeremiah began to prophesy. Now, in his late thirties, Jeremiah stands at the gate of the temple and preaches to the people as they arrive for worship.

The same sermon (or a similar one) is mentioned in chapter 26, where we are told it is preached at the beginning of Jehoiakim's reign (about 608 BC). In that account, Jeremiah is nearly executed for his radical and hard-hitting words.

Jeremiah accuses the pilgrims of treating God's temple in a mindless, shallow way. They assume they can get forgiveness just by walking through the door. They believe God will never desert them, because he will always protect his temple.

But Jeremiah challenges the behaviour and beliefs of his hearers. Are they true believers? If so, why do they abuse foreigners and the weakest members of society? Are they God's people? Then why do they break his commandments and honour pagan idols?

People are coming to the temple for automatic forgiveness and a sense of safety. But God says they are treating his house as a criminals' hideout. One day Jesus will say the same, when he clears the temple of traders and money-changers (Matthew 21:13).

Will God always protect his temple? No! Look how the shrine at Shiloh was destroyed by the Philistines. And remember what happened to Ephraim (the northern tribes of Israel) when they were defeated by Assyria and dispersed. God didn't step in to save either the place or the people. Nor will he save Jerusalem when the time comes for judgment to fall.

God looks for obedience. Pilgrimage and sacrifice are nothing without the offering of hearts and lives.

Jeremiah is forbidden to pray for the people. They have gone too far. Whole families worship the Queen of Heaven – the moon, or the Canaanite goddess Astarte – each doing their bit to light the fire and bake the cakes.

Judah's resistance and Jeremiah's anguish
(8:4–22)

God's people are in full rebellion against him. It is as though they have fallen and not got up, or gone astray and not turned back (8:4). They have become perpetual backsliders – being dragged along on their backsides, wilfully resisting the right way with all their strength. They no longer have any instinct for God's will (8:7).

The so-called wise people and the priests are singled out for blame. They have busied themselves with getting rich, giving their people casual assurances that all will be well (8:8–11). The leaders will be punished for their shameless behaviour (8:12). God has looked for a harvest from them, but they are like empty and blighted fruit trees (8:13).

Meanwhile, the sounds of approaching invasion are heard from the north (8:16). God is releasing a swift and lethal enemy upon his people, like a brood of adders, to punish them (8:17).

In the face of all this, Jeremiah is grief-stricken. He has no pleasure at all in being right. He is in anguish for the plight of his people, and longs that a remedy might be found for their condition (8:18–22).

Jeremiah preaches about sin and punishment

(9:1–26)

Jeremiah has run out of tears for his people and has nowhere to escape from their wickedness (9:1–2). There is no truth or trust to be found, either in neighbourhoods or families (9:3–4). God is going to punish, but only because he wants to refine and reform them (9:7–9).

The Lord likens the people of Judah to a thriving olive tree. Because they have broken their covenant with him they have laid themselves open to destruction.

Jeremiah sees again the desolation that lies ahead. The landscape will become deserted and Jerusalem destroyed in the judgment that is about to fall (9:10–11). All this will be God's doing, because of the idolatry his people have committed with the pagan gods of Baal (9:12–16).

The only thing that matters is to know God. This is more important than any human wisdom, strength or wealth (9:23). To know God is to realize and embrace his standards and his ways. He is endlessly patient and merciful, just and good. Now he is moving to put his values in the hearts of all peoples (9:24–26).

Jeremiah preaches against idolatry

(10:1–16)

People like a god they can see and touch. But the commandments have always stood against this for the Jews (Exodus 20:1–4). They are not to reduce God to the shape of a creature or the size of a doll. He is eternal Spirit and not to be imaged – the great, invisible, holy Lord. The only image of God is the One he himself has given – a living and self-giving human being: Jesus Christ.

Jeremiah ridicules the whole process of manufacturing an idol. Cut, chiselled and bejewelled, it is no more effective than a scarecrow. It can't speak or walk by itself. It has no power to punish or save.

Why trade idol-worship for a relationship with the living God? He isn't a part of the creation – he is the Creator. He isn't a bolt of lightning or a shower of rain – he is the founder of the universe.

Get real! Idols are a con, as everyone who makes them knows. Worship the only maker that matters – the One who made *you*.

Jeremiah's pain and prayer

(10:17–25)

Jeremiah tells the people under siege that it is nearly time to leave for exile (10:17–18). He himself is in great distress. His life is like a collapsed tent and there are no leaders to put things right (10:19–21). Away to the north he hears the advancing foe – the Babylonian armies which will wreak such terrible destruction (10:22).

Jeremiah pleads with God. Humans are unable to live as they should and deserve to be corrected. But Jeremiah prays that God's punishment won't completely destroy him. He prays that God's anger would be poured out on the nations that have oppressed Israel (10:23–25).

The reason why

(11:1–17)

God speaks to Jeremiah of all that has happened in Israel's history. God rescued his people from the furnace of

Egyptian oppression (11:4) and made a covenant agreement with them. They were to obey him and he would bless them (11:7); but they have utterly betrayed his trust (11:9–10). Now God is about to punish his people, and they must turn to their Baal-idols for help (11:11–13).

Jeremiah is forbidden to pray for his people. They are like a much-loved wife who has now gone too far in her adulterous affairs. They are like a once-beautiful fruit tree, which is now fit only for destruction (11:14–17).

Jeremiah's own people plot to kill him
(11:18–23)

Jeremiah has been given an insight and a message which have plunged him into trouble. He feels that he got involved quite innocently, like a lamb being led to be slaughtered (11:18–19). Now his own neighbours, the people of Anathoth, are plotting to destroy him (11:19). Jeremiah asks God to avenge him (11:20) and is promised that he will (11:21–23).

Anathoth is Jeremiah's birthplace and the home of a frustrated priestly line. Abiathar was a high priest in the time of David, who was banished to Anathoth by Solomon for trying to make someone else king. This was also God's judgment on the corrupt family of Eli, the priest at Shiloh, from whom Abiathar was descended (1 Kings 2:26–27).

The descendants of Abiathar are no doubt angry that they are barred from the temple in Jerusalem. This anger is now focused on Jeremiah, a priest's son, who is predicting the destruction of all that they hold dear (11:19).

Jeremiah complains and God answers
(12:1–17)

Jeremiah knows that God is right, but he still wants to complain about his situation (12:1)! Like Job and David before him, Jeremiah sees wicked people prospering. They are even people who claim to be religious, but the things they say are very different from the things they do (12:2).

For his part, Jeremiah has tried to be genuinely faithful – as God knows (12:3). He begs that God will intervene to judge the wicked, because the whole land is suffering from their evil influence (12:4). In addition, Jeremiah feels discouraged already, because his own family and home town have rejected him, so what chance does he stand in Jerusalem (12:5–6)?

God reveals that he, too, is estranged from his loved ones. He has come to hate his own people and is giving them up to defeat by their enemies (12:7). His own land

has been trampled by those who should have treasured it, abused by idolaters and laid waste by violence (12:10–12).

God swears that he will judge the neighbouring nations that oppress Israel. He will pull them up like weeds (12:14). But then he offers mercy. If pagan nations will learn God's ways from Israel, instead of corrupting her, they will be saved (12:15–16).

Warning signs
(13:1–27)

God gives Jeremiah some striking images of the judgment which is to come.

God tells Jeremiah to buy a linen loincloth (13:1). The prophet is to wear the loincloth without moistening it with water – so it is stiff and uncomfortable. Afterwards, he hides it in the cleft of a rock near the Euphrates (or, more likely, Perath, which is three miles from Jeremiah's home town of Anathoth). When he next goes to find it, the loincloth is ruined (13:7). God says that his people will be similarly ruined, for their stiffness and pride in failing to cling to him (13:9–11).

God gives Jeremiah a saying: 'Every winejar should be filled with wine.' God is going to treat the people of Jerusalem like large winejars and fill them to the brim. They will be thrown into chaos like a group of helpless drunkards (13:12–14).

Jeremiah again takes issue with Israel's pride. He urges them to humble themselves and turn to God's light before the darkness of doom overtakes them (13:17).

Jeremiah is given a message for the young King Jehoiachin and his mother Nehushta. They are to step down from their thrones, because God is taking their crowns from them (13:18). They may think of fleeing to the south when the enemy invasion comes, but the towns of the Negeb ('the Dry') will be shut against them. No one will escape captivity and exile (13:19).

Jerusalem is to be overrun by the forces of Babylon, whom she had once considered as an ally (13:20–21). Now she is to be humiliated and violated – the fate of a prostitute – because of her shameless acts of Baal-worship (13:22–27).

Dry land and lying prophets
(14:1–16)

Judah languishes in drought, which is a sign of God's punishment for sin (14:1; Deuteronomy 28:23–24). There is great suffering in town and country (14:3–4) and among the creatures of the wild (14:5–6).

Jeremiah grieves that God has become a stranger to his people; and yet he should be at the very centre of Judah's community (14:8–9). The people have wandered away from God and are now realizing what life is like without his blessing (14:10).

Jeremiah is forbidden to pray for the people (14:11–12). They are being deceived by the calming words of lying prophets (14:13–14). These prophets promise that there will be no judgment by sword or famine; but God assures Jeremiah that he is going to afflict them with both (14:15–16).

Jeremiah pleads with God
(14:17 – 15:9)

Jeremiah feels God's grief for the people of Judah. He sees her like a young daughter, violently done to death (14:17). He has visions of slaughter in the countryside and famine in the city (14:18). But the cause of this physical disaster is spiritual. It is the treachery of the prophets and priests, who have failed to guide and lead the people in God's way (14:18).

Jeremiah begs God to remember his kingship and covenant with his people – and to have mercy and send rain (14:19–22). He stands before God to plead for the people, just as Moses once did (Exodus 32:11–14) and Samuel (1 Samuel 7:5). But God is adamant that his punishment is to fall in the form of plague, violent death and captivity (15:1–2).

Judah is to be destroyed by enemy swords, the bodies dragged away by dogs instead of having proper burial, the corpses picked clean by birds or torn by wild animals (15:3). This horrible fate will come because of the cruel and idolatrous deeds done in the reign of King Manasseh (2 Kings 21:10–16). Judah's fate is to be a warning to all the other nations of the world (15:4).

Jeremiah's pain and God's assurance
(15:10–21)

Jeremiah wishes he had never been born. He is an innocent bystander who has been caught in the fierce clash between God and his people (15:10). He has committed himself to feed on and deliver God's word (15:16), but it gives him terrible pain. He feels betrayed – like someone who comes to a water source and finds it dry (15:18).

God promises to strengthen Jeremiah for the task of being his mouth and speaking his messages (15:19). His prophet may suffer verbal and physical attack, but God will defend and deliver him. God will make Jeremiah immensely strong – like a bronze wall (15:20–21).

The Lord warns Jeremiah that deadly diseases will devastate the land, and there will be no opportunity to mourn or bury the dead. Bet She'arim burial cave with memorial.

A great grief
(16:1–21)

God tells Jeremiah not to marry or have children. A wife and family will only swell the number of victims in the plague and carnage to come (16:1–4). Jeremiah is not to take any part in mourning the deaths of others, or in celebrating marriages (16:5–9). These expressions of community life no longer apply, because the relationship between God and his people has been severed (16:10–12). God is evicting his people from their homeland and sending them far away to exile in a foreign country (16:13).

And yet God gives a strong promise for the future. A day will come when he will bring his people back again, in an act just as great as the rescue from Egypt in the days of the exodus (16:14–15).

The bare facts
(17:1–18)

Judah's sin is deeply engraved on the hearts of her people (17:1). Even the children have memories of the pagan fertility rites enacted at landmarks around the country (17:2–3). Now God's judgment is that they are to pay for these sins with their possessions and their freedom (17:3–4).

People who trust in themselves instead of God will endure a living death – like a lonely shrub in the desert (17:5–6). But those who trust in God will be like trees with their roots in streams – fresh and secure in times of drought and constantly fruitful (17:7–8).

The human heart is supremely secretive and cunning. No one can understand it, except God. He sees, he knows and he judges (17:9–10).

Wealth made unfairly is like a chick that a partridge hatches. It flies away (17:11)!

God's throne is Israel's glory and hope and spring of life. Those who reject God's reign will be listed among the dead (17:12–13).

Jeremiah asks God to heal and rescue him. He has been hurt by the scorn of those who reject his message of judgment. He longs for God's word to come true, to vindicate his prophet and punish his enemies (17:14–18).

Keep the sabbath!
(17:19–27)

God tells Jeremiah to stand at the various gates of Jerusalem – the People's Gate used by the royal princes and the other gates used by travellers and traders (19:1). He is to warn everyone, as they come and go with their burdens of produce or responsibility, that they should keep the sabbath day as a day of holy rest (17:20–22).

The city gates are a focus of status, access and business. If God is honoured, then these gates will see royal processions and pilgrimages (17:24–26). If God is not honoured, and business continues on the sabbath day, then these gates will be torched and the royal palaces razed to the ground (17:27).

Potter and clay
(18:1–23)

Jeremiah is told to go and see the potter at work. He watches the craftsman at his wheel, moulding a lump of clay into a pot.

As he watches, the potter changes his mind. This particular pot isn't working out and he decides to change the shape. He has every right to do so, of course. He's the potter!

The potter is a picture of God. He is skilful and caring in all his making. But, as Jeremiah realizes,

God is free to change his mind.

At present a judgment hangs over Jerusalem, ready to fall. But there is time to repent. God is free to change his mind – both about his blessings and his punishments. There is nothing fatal and final about God's promises. They are opportunities to change. Remember, Jonah preached certain judgment on Nineveh – but the people listened, repented and were spared!

The image of God as a potter is often used for individual piety – to reflect on the way God can mould our lives. But for Jeremiah it is an image of God's international sovereignty in history.

Why does a potter choose one lump of clay rather than another and why does he mould it and save it, or crush and discard it? Jeremiah sees in the potter God's sovereign right to do as he wills.

Judah is to be broken like a clay jar
(19:1–15)

God tells Jeremiah to buy an earthenware jug from a potter (19:1). He is to take it, with some of Judah's leaders, to the Valley of Ben Hinnom. This is a place just outside Jerusalem, which has been used for pagan worship. Its 'high place' is called Topheth, where children have been sacrificed (19:2–5). In the future it will be the city's rubbish dump, with an ever-burning fire which Jesus will use as an image of hell. The Potsherd Gate may be the place where broken pots are dumped (19:2).

Jeremiah is to pronounce God's judgment and disaster on Judah – and smash the pot to smithereens (19:3–10). Clay on the potter's wheel can be remoulded, but once it has been baked and broken it can never be mended. So God passes full and final judgment on his people for their idolatry and bloodshed (19:11).

After his dramatic action, Jeremiah makes the same announcement in the temple court (19:14–15).

Jeremiah is punished in the stocks
(20:1–18)

The temple's security officer is a man named Pashhur. He punishes Jeremiah for his outburst by striking him and putting him in the stocks overnight. Stocks are a wooden trap. To be locked in them is a sign of public disgrace – and a warning to others (20:1–2).

When Jeremiah is released, he condemns Pashhur and gives him a new name: 'Terror-All-Around' (20:3). Soon it will be Pashhur's turn to be exposed as a fraud. He will be forced to watch while his fellow citizens are killed and their possessions plundered. His predictions of peace have been utterly wrong; now he and the friends he has deceived will be dragged away into exile (20:4–6).

God will fight for Babylon against his own
(21:1–14)

Chapters 21–45 contain Jeremiah's prophecies and prayers during the twenty years between King Josiah's death and the destruction of Jerusalem (609–587 BC).

Jeremiah's prophecies are fulfilled. Judah is invaded by the armies of Babylon, and the leading citizens of Jerusalem are deported. Zedekiah becomes king of the poor and pathetic people who are left. He himself is a puppet ruler, put in place by the Babylonian emperor.

Zedekiah is the last in the line of twenty-one kings who have ruled Judah since the reign of Solomon. He becomes king at the age of 21, when Nebuchadnezzar of Babylon promotes him in place of his nephew Jehoiachin. Zedekiah's name was Mattaniah at first. He is given a new name to show that he has a new master. He reigns for eleven years (597–587 BC).

Zedekiah looks for an opportunity to rebel against Babylon, but Jeremiah advises against it. Jeremiah sees the situation as God's punishment, to be patiently borne (27:5–7).

Although Zedekiah makes an agreement with Babylon, he is encouraged to revolt by the possibility of support from Egypt. His rebellion provokes a massive offensive from Babylon, whose armies lay siege to Jerusalem in 587 BC and capture it in July the following year.

God judges the kings of Judah
(22:1–30)

God tells Jeremiah to go to the royal palace. He is to preach to the king, Zedekiah, who sits on the throne as a successor of King David (22:1–2).

Jeremiah must challenge the king to rule by God's standards of justice and compassion (22:3). If he does so, his royal line will continue in peace and prosperity. If

not, then the palace will be destroyed and become deserted (22:4–9).

God says of another king, Shallum, that he has been exiled and will never return (22:10–12). Shallum is Jehoahaz, who became king after his father Josiah was killed in battle at Megiddo. Jehoahaz had mourned for his father, but really he should be mourning for himself (22:10); he will never see his homeland again (22:12).

God condemns someone who has built a large and luxurious palace, but only by oppressing and exploiting the poor (22:13–17). This is king Jehoiakim, the brother who succeeded Shallum. A godly king is not to be known by the fine cedar panelling of his house, but by his concern for the poor (22:15–16). Jehoiakim will die and his corpse be thrown out like a dead donkey (22:18–19).

God's judgment is to be announced all over the country – in Lebanon to the west, in Bashan to the north-east and Abarim to the east (22:20). The people have had their chance to repent (22:21). Now the wind of judgment will round up and sweep away the shepherds (leaders) and those who have been immoral will be taken captive and exiled (22:22).

God says of King Coniah that he would discard him, even if he were 'the signet ring on his right hand'. A royal signet ring is a symbol of authority, as well as being a treasured and intimate possession (22:24–27). Coniah is King Jehoiachin, who succeeded his father Jehoiakim. He reigned for just three months before being taken away to Babylon. God declares that Jehoiachin will become a dead end, exiled and childless (22:30).

The shepherd king
(23:1–8)

The leaders of God's people are often called 'shepherds'. They have the responsibility to guide, feed and protect the nation in their care.

But King Zedekiah and his officers are failing in their trust. They are destroying and scattering God's flock. Now God himself will take action to gather his people, provide for them and increase their number. He will appoint shepherds who will give them peace and security.

God promises that one day he will give his people a king like David. This will be the Messiah, who will be a branch of David's royal line. Unlike most of Judah's kings, he will be wise and righteous. Through him, God's people will share his righteousness – and be saved.

The lying prophets of Judah
(23:9–40)

There are other prophets at work besides Jeremiah, but not all of them have a genuine word from the Lord. Many of the prophets and priests are corrupt and compromised. They defile the temple with their vice. They pretend to be holy, but in fact they commit adultery and condone evil.

The false prophets make up messages from their own imagination. They promise the people God's peace and safety – but their message is not from God. They claim to have meaningful dreams, steal each other's insights and even begin their sayings with 'the Lord declares'. But their words are empty, misguided and useless.

The tragedy is that if they had only listened to God ('stood in my council') they would have had life-giving, life-saving words for his people. The nation is sick and heading for destruction because the prophets have failed in their task.

Good and bad figs – exiles and survivors
(24:1–10)

God shows Jeremiah two baskets of figs. The figs in one basket are good, but in the other they are bad (24:1–3). God declares that the people who have gone into exile are like good figs. These are King Jehoiachin (Jeconiah) and Judah's leaders (24:1). God will bless them and bring them home (24:4–7). The bad figs are King Zedekiah and the people left in Jerusalem (24:8). God is going to inflict on them further punishment (24:9–10).

Jeremiah might assume that the 'bad figs' are those who have been exiled and the 'good figs' are those who have survived in Jerusalem. In fact it is the other way round.

Jeremiah predicts seventy years of captivity
(25:1–14)

Jeremiah has preached to the people of Judah and Jerusalem for twenty-three years, and they haven't listened (25:1–7). Now Nebuchadnezzar has become king of Babylon (25:1), and he will be God's servant in judging and destroying them (25:8–10). The land will lie waste and its people languish in exile for seventy years (25:11–14).

God's judgment on all nations
(25:15–38)

Jeremiah is to deliver God's judgment to all peoples – like a cup of wine seething with God's anger (25:15–17).

Jerusalem is to drink first, then the rest of Judah (25:18). After them, God's judgment will fall on all the nations of the region and beyond – the Egyptians, the Philistines, the Arabians… Last of all 'Sheshach' is to be judged. Sheshach is a coded word for 'Babel' – that is, Babylon (25:26).

God is like a lion attacking a fold of sheep (25:30, 38); but the sheep are his own people – all the nations of the earth (25:31). There is to be a great judgment and destruction (25:31–33). The shepherds (leaders) will be thrown into confusion (25:34–36) and the fields and folds destroyed (25:36–37).

Episodes in Jeremiah's life

These events are not in the order in which they happen!

Jeremiah's life is threatened
(26:1–24)

It is 609 BC – the beginning of King Jehoiakim's reign (26:1). God tells Jeremiah to preach in the temple court. By preaching to the people who have come there to worship, he is in a way addressing the whole of Judah (26:2).

Jeremiah tells the people that there is still time to turn to God and be spared the coming disaster. If they don't repent, the temple itself will be destroyed and become like the ruined shrine at Shiloh (26:3–6).

When Jeremiah has finished speaking, a crowd gathers round him. They are led by the priests and rival prophets – and they demand Jeremiah's death (26:7–9). Some royal officials arrive to hear what has happened (26:10–11) and Jeremiah repeats his message to them (26:12–15). The officials believe that Jeremiah is a true prophet (26:16). Some elders recall that Micah delivered a similar message in his day (26:17–18).

Micah had prophesied that Jerusalem would be destroyed, but his king, Hezekiah, had repented and the city had been spared. Another prophet, Uriah, had preached a message of God's judgment in the days of King Jehoiakim. Uriah fled to Egypt, but was brought back and executed (26:22–23).

Jeremiah's trial ends, and he leaves under the protection of Ahikam. Ahikam's father, Shaphan, may be the court secretary we encounter later (36:10); his son is Gedaliah – the person Nebuchadnezzar will appoint as governor of Judah after the destruction of Jerusalem (39:14).

Jeremiah wears a yoke

(27:1–22)

The year is 594 BC – the beginning of King Zedekiah's reign (27:1). Judah has been defeated by the Babylonians. Her king and national leaders have been deported. However, there are strong hopes that Judah will be able to rebel – perhaps in alliance with Egypt – and throw off the Babylonian oppressors.

God tells Jeremiah to make a yoke – a heavy wooden collar used for controlling oxen. The prophet is to wear the yoke across his own shoulders (27:2). Then he is to send a message back with the foreign envoys who have been to Jerusalem to plot a rebellion against Babylon (27:3).

Jeremiah's message is that the Babylonian rule has been brought about by God. It will continue for three generations (27:4–7). Those who submit to this yoke will be spared; those who throw it off will be punished by God with death, hunger and disease (27:8–11).

Jeremiah gives the same message to King Zedekiah, and to the priests (27:12–16). But the king and priests listen to false prophets and clairvoyants, who say that all will be well (27:9, 14). They say that the great bronze pieces in the temple – the pillars and the 'sea' (the great basin for washing) – will remain in Jerusalem (27:16–22). But it is all wishful thinking. They will be carried off as plunder to Babylon (27:22).

Jeremiah confronts a false prophet

(28:1–17)

A rival prophet called Hananiah confronts Jeremiah in public debate (28:1). He tells Jeremiah that God is going to break the yoke of Babylon, and return King Jehoiachin (Jeconiah) and the other exiles to Jerusalem (28:2–4).

Jeremiah welcomes Hananiah's prophecy – if it is true. But the only way to know if a prophecy is true is to wait and see if it is fulfilled (28:5–9)! Hananiah is so angry at this sarcasm that he seizes the yoke from Jeremiah's neck and breaks it (28:10). This, he says, is God's sign that the yoke of Babylon will be broken within two years (28:11).

Later, Jeremiah visits Hananiah (28:12). He tells him that his prediction of a successful rebellion is not from God. Hananiah is guilty of preaching a lie (28:13–15). Jeremiah declares God's judgment on Hananiah; within two months, the false prophet is dead (28:16–17).

Jeremiah writes to the exiles

(29:1–14)

Jeremiah sends a letter to the exiles in Babylonia (29:1–3). Instead of assuring them that their captivity will be short, he advises them to settle down. They are to build houses and plant gardens and make a life for themselves (29:4–6). They are also to work hard and pray for the city where they are exiled (29:7). They are not to believe the vain hopes of false prophets and clairvoyants (29:8–9).

Jeremiah is blunt. God is telling him that the period of exile in Babylon will be seventy years (29:10). But God will not forget them and has wonderful plans for their future (29:11). This future will begin when they turn to God with their whole heart (29:12–13). When they finally do this, God will not hide from them (29:13–14). He will gather them from all the places where they are scattered – and bring them home (29:14).

Facing off false prophets

(29:15–32)

In Babylon there are false prophets who are preaching that Babylon will be destroyed (29:16–19). Jeremiah condemns them. Their message is not from God (29:19) and their behaviour is disgraceful (29:21–23). God will cause two of these false prophets – Ahab and Zedekiah – to be executed by Nebuchadnezzar (29:21).

Jeremiah also has to deal with a troublemaker called Shemaiah (29:24). Shemaiah has written to the priests in Jerusalem, telling them to suppress the prophets (29:24–26). Shemaiah names Jeremiah in particular, because he has advised the exiles to accept their punishment and make their lives in Babylon (29:27–28).

Jeremiah pronounces God's judgment on Shemaiah. None of his descendants will live to see the exiles return home (29:29–32).

God promises a new covenant

(30:1 – 31:40)

Jeremiah has a dream. God will bring both Israel and Judah back from captivity and restore them to their land! God promises his people will return home, and he will make a new covenant with them. This covenant will be written on their hearts.

There is a tough time ahead, as this deliverance is brought to birth. Babylon's yoke will be broken. God's people will be released. They will once again be ruled by a king like David.

Meanwhile, there is punishment to be endured. Sin can't simply be brushed aside. God's people are guilty, hurting and apparently abandoned by God. But here and now he promises to heal and restore them. He makes a simple, total commitment:

So you will be my people,
and I will be your God (30:22).

The return from Babylon is going to be like a new exodus. The survivors will, like the Hebrew slaves, 'find favour in the desert' (31:2). Israel will be newly married to God, with great rejoicing. Vineyards will be planted in Samaria – the country that was laid waste over a century earlier. And those who guard Ephraim (Israel) will call people to make pilgrimage to Zion (the heavenly Jerusalem).

All the lost people of Israel will converge on Jerusalem as God brings them home. No one will be left behind because they are useless or weak. Just as they went into exile weeping with despair, now they will return with tears of joy (31:9).

God will take the utmost care of them on the way – treating long-lost Ephraim as his first-born son. Young and old, men and women, priests and people – all will enjoy the freshness, gladness and plenty of Zion (31:12–14).

There has been great grief at the loss of the northern tribes. Ephraim and Manasseh (the two half-tribes descended from Joseph) were lost in defeat and exile. Jeremiah thinks of Rachel, the mother of Joseph and Benjamin, weeping for her children. But now she can dry her tears. They will return. Ephraim, 'the unruly calf', is turning back to God.

Jeremiah wakes from his sleep refreshed. Here at last is a time to build and plant. There will be no more laying the blame for suffering on the sins of a previous generation. Everyone will be equally blessed by God's grace, and equally responsible for their behaviour (31:29–30).

God will make a new covenant with his people. It won't be a covenant like the one on Mount Sinai – defined by laws written on stone. It will be a covenant given and sustained by God's grace and written on human hearts.

In this new covenant, everyone will know the Lord

for themselves and *want* to keep his law. The past is forgiven. This is a new start. A fine, enlarged Jerusalem will be built – a glimpse of the glorious Jerusalem that is to come. This is a God-centred community that will never fall again.

Jeremiah buys a field
(32:1–44)

The year is 587 BC. Jerusalem is besieged by the armies of Nebuchadnezzar and Jeremiah himself is in prison. But he is dreaming that the Jews will return from exile and that their land will be restored.

God tells Jeremiah to expect a visit from his cousin Hanamel. Hanamel wants to sell a field, which by law must be bought by his next of kin (Leviticus 25:25). Jeremiah is that person.

It's an extraordinary situation. Jeremiah is being asked to buy a field which will be immediately seized by Babylonian invaders. Any day now, the Jews will cease to

'Now' and 'then'

Is Jeremiah speaking of the return from exile in Babylon, or the gathering of all peoples into Christ's kingly rule? We have to say 'both'.

There was a return to Judah by exiles from Babylon in 538 BC. But it didn't include the exiles of the northern kingdom of Israel ('Ephraim') and it wasn't crowned with the rule of a king like David.

But the return of the exiles was a miracle of God's power to rescue and forgive. It is a glimpse of the great gathering of both Jews and Gentiles on the Last Day. The new covenant is for the whole world. It is sealed in the blood of Christ, who will return in glory to be God's Messiah – the king who is greater than David.

own any property. Their legal deeds and agreements will be worthless…

But Jeremiah agrees! He counts out the money, puts the documents in a clay jar (for long-term storage) and explains his crazy action. He has bought the field because God has told him to do so. It's a sign of his promise that the Jews will return from exile at some time in the future – and resume their everyday life with houses, fields and vineyards (33:15). His purchase is a sign of hope for when the exile is over.

Jeremiah prays. Is Jerusalem going to be spared after all? Is this land deal a sign that normal life will be restored quite soon? Nothing is too hard for God (32:17). But it isn't to be. Judah is being punished for her immorality and idolatry – and God is on the side of the Babylonians.

But then comes the good news. After the calamity, God will give prosperity. There will once again be buying of fields and signing of deeds all over the country. And Jeremiah has acted on God's word as though it's already done.

God promises that Israel and Judah will be restored

(33:1–26)

While Jeremiah is still in detention, he receives a wonderful promise for the future (33:1–3). The houses of Jerusalem and the palaces of her king, so brutally destroyed by the Chaldeans (Babylonians), are to be restored (33:4–6). God will give healing and forgiveness, prosperity and joy to Jerusalem – for all the nations of the world to see (33:7–9).

Normal life will be resumed in the towns of Judah: weddings and harvests will be celebrated (33:10–11) and shepherds will tend their flocks (33:12–13).

God promises that one day he will unite the kingdoms of Israel and Judah under one king. This king will be a strong and healthy branch from David's family tree. Like David, his reign will be just and righteous; and his people will be secure (33:14–16).

There will always be a king descended from David and there will always be a high priest from the Levites to offer sacrifices (33:17–18). God is doing this to honour

Jeremiah is confident that God's people will return from exile. He buys a field less than five miles from the city, even though it is about to fall to invaders.

his covenant promises to David and the Levites – a bond he can never break (33:19–26).

Jeremiah tells King Zedekiah his fate
(34:1–7)

The Babylonian armies are laying waste the towns of Judah and Jerusalem's destruction seems certain (34:1, 6–7). Jeremiah goes to King Zedekiah to tell him what will happen. Jerusalem will be burned to the ground, but Zedekiah himself will be spared and taken to Babylon (34:2–3).

Jewish slaves should be set free
(34:8–22)

Some of the people of Judah have become slaves – through misfortune or debt. But if the nation is conquered by the Babylonians, the entire population will become slaves. King Zedekiah thinks to win God's favour by declaring that Hebrew slaves (those of Judean race) shall be set free (34:8–10). However, the crisis passes and the reform doesn't last (34:11).

God reminds Jeremiah of the old law of Moses: that every seventh year all slaves shall be freed (Deuteronomy 15:12–18). This is because the Israelites had themselves been rescued from slavery in Egypt (34:12–14). Now, if they do not release their brothers and sisters from slavery, God will release punishment on them (34:15–17).

Those who split from their covenant with God will be split themselves – cut in half like a sacrifice (34:18–20). When the Babylonians execute God's judgment (34:21–22), the king and his officials will be severed from their city (34:21–22) and the land will be parted from its inhabitants (34:22).

The Recabites – an example of obedience
(35:1–19)

It is, perhaps, 598 BC – towards the end of King Jehoiakim's reign. Babylonian raiding parties are active in Judah. Among those taking refuge in Jerusalem is a group of nomads called Recabites.

God sends Jeremiah to meet the Recabites and invite them to the temple to drink wine (35:1–5). The Recabites tell Jeremiah that their ancestor forbade them to drink wine, or build houses, or plant crops. Instead, they live very simply in tents (35:6–10). They have only come to live in Jerusalem because of their fear of the Babylonian armies (35:11).

Jeremiah is greatly impressed by the obedience of the Recabites. God tells him to use them as an example of faithful, upright living. Why can't the people of Judah obey the commands of God in such a straightforward way (35:12–19)?

King Jehoiakim burns Jeremiah's scroll
(36:1–32)

It is 605 BC. God tells Jeremiah to write down all his messages on a scroll (36:1–2). For this great work, Jeremiah enlists the help of a scribe called Baruch (36:4).

Jeremiah is banned from the temple at this time, so he asks Baruch to go there and read out his prophecies (36:5–6). Jeremiah never ceases to hope that people may hear God's word and repent (36:7–8).

In December 604 BC, the Babylonians are advancing through the towns of Philistia. They capture and destroy Ashkelon. Perhaps because of this, the inhabitants of Judah and Jerusalem hold a fast – a day without food, for mourning and prayer (36:9). It is on this occasion that Baruch gives a public reading of Jeremiah's prophecies in one of the rooms of the temple (36:10).

Soon Baruch is asked to read the prophecies to the royal officials (36:11–16). They are shaken by what they hear and advise Baruch to take Jeremiah into hiding (36:16–19). Then one of the royal officials, Jehudi, reads the prophecies to King Jehoiakim (36:20–21).

It is winter, and the king is sitting beside a fire burning in an iron brazier. As Jehudi reads out God's word from Jeremiah, the king slices the scroll with his penknife and throws the paragraphs into the flames (36:22–23). The warnings of judgment don't alarm the king at all – except that he orders Jeremiah and Baruch to be arrested (36:24–26).

God tells Jeremiah to write out all the prophecies again on a new scroll (36:27–28, 32). God gives him further messages, including predictions about King Jehoiakim. Jehoiakim's sons will not succeed him on David's throne; and when he dies his corpse will lie unburied (36:30).

Jeremiah is put in prison
(37:1–21)

The scene changes and the story moves to a later time. The Babylonians have been laying siege to Jerusalem, but have left to deal with a challenge from the Egyptian army. The people of Jerusalem had been hoping that the Egyptians would come to their rescue (37:5).

Baruch – faithful secretary

Baruch is the brother of Seraiah, the quartermaster to King Zedekiah. He becomes a faithful secretary to Jeremiah, writing down the prophet's messages at his dictation (36:4) and courageously reading them in public (36:8).

Baruch stays with Jeremiah and shares his fate when Jerusalem is destroyed. He is accused of influencing Jeremiah in favour of the Babylonians, and taken with Jeremiah and other survivors down to Egypt (43:3, 6).

Baruch is only the scribe who writes down Jeremiah's messages. But there are short links of narrative in the book of Jeremiah which may well be his work.

There has been a change of king. Jehoiakim is in exile, and in 597 BC Zedekiah is appointed as puppet king by Nebuchadnezzar of Babylon.

King Zedekiah asks Jeremiah to pray to God and find out what is going to happen (37:3). Jeremiah predicts that the Egyptians will return home and the Chaldeans (Babylonians) will complete the siege and destruction of Jerusalem (37:6–10).

During the lull in the siege, Jeremiah tries to leave Jerusalem on business. He is accused of trying to go over to the Babylonians. For punishment, he is imprisoned in the cistern of the house of the secretary of state (37:11–16). It is dark and airless.

King Zedekiah sends for Jeremiah and asks him privately about his messages. Jeremiah has no good news for him – only that God will give him over to the king of Babylon (37:17). But Jeremiah asks for better prison conditions and is transferred to the court of the guard. There he is given a regular allowance of bread, right through the siege of Jerusalem (37:20–21).

This clay tablet is part of the Babylonian Chronicle. It records the accession to the throne of Nebuchadnezzar II, the battle of Carchemish between the Babylonians and the Egyptians, the fall of Jerusalem in 597 BC and the installation of Zedekiah as king of Judah.

Jeremiah is lowered into a muddy cistern
(38:1–13)

Jeremiah continues to make predictions which sound disloyal and defeatist. He advises people to surrender to the Babylonians, and says that the fall of Jerusalem is certain (38:1–3). Jeremiah's enemies complain to the king, who gives them permission to ill-treat him (38:4–5).

Jeremiah is lowered into a cistern, where he sinks in the mud and is left to starve (38:6). Fortunately he has a friend – an Ethiopian eunuch – who tells the king what has happened and is allowed to haul him out (38:7–13).

Jeremiah advises the king to surrender
(38:14–28)

King Zedekiah again seeks Jeremiah's advice. This time he promises to take notice of his words and protect him (38:14–16). Jeremiah tells the king that the only way out is to surrender to Babylon (38:17–20). If he doesn't, he will find himself well and truly stuck – and Jeremiah knows how that feels (38:21–22)!

The king insists that their conversation must remain a secret (38:23–28).

Nebuchadnezzar captures Jerusalem
(39:1–18)

In July 587 BC, after a siege lasting a year and a half, the Babylonians breach the walls of Jerusalem (39:1–2). They capture the city and set up a ruling council in a gatehouse (38:3). Meanwhile, King Zedekiah and his officials escape by night through the Fountain Gate. They flee towards the Arabah – the Jordan Valley to the north of the Dead Sea (39:4).

The king and his staff are pursued and caught. They are brought before Nebuchadnezzar in his camp at Riblah (39:5). Nebuchadnezzar forces Zedekiah to watch his sons being slaughtered, and then has him blinded and deported to Babylon (39:6–7). The other nobles are also killed and Jerusalem is sacked and burned (39:8).

When all is done, only the poorest people are left

living in the ruins. The Babylonian captain allows them some fields and vineyards (39:9–10). Nebuchadnezzar gives special instructions that Jeremiah is to be well treated (39:11–12). He is placed in the care of Gedaliah, who will become the governor of the survivors (39:14).

Jeremiah's message of reassurance to Ebed-Melech is recorded. Ebed-Melech is the Ethiopian friend who rescued Jeremiah from the boggy cistern (39:15–18).

Jeremiah is rescued and given his freedom
(40:1–6)

By some mistake, Jeremiah is shackled and is being led away with the other prisoners (40:1). The Babylonian captain releases him and gives him complete freedom to go or stay. He also gives him food and a present (40:2–5). This treatment by an enemy is an extraordinary contrast to Jeremiah's treatment by his own people.

Jeremiah settles with governor Gedaliah
(40:7–16)

Jeremiah goes to join Gedaliah at Mizpah, a few miles from Jerusalem (40:6). Gedaliah has been made governor of the 'remnant' – those who remain in the land after most of the population has been deported.

Gedaliah's policy is to accept the defeat and cooperate with the Babylonians (40:7–9). A number of survivors gather to him and they start to cultivate and harvest the land (40:11–12).

Gedaliah is warned that there is an Ammonite plan to assassinate him, but he doesn't believe it (40:13–16). The Ammonites may be wanting to move into the land left vacant by the departed exiles.

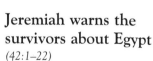

A relief of the head of a pharaoh, king of Egypt. Jeremiah warns that there is no refuge with him, because Egypt, too, will be defeated by the Babylonians (46:25).

Gedaliah is assassinated by Ishmael
(41:1–18)

In October (perhaps of 586 BC) a group of men arrives at Mizpah (41:1). They are led by Ishmael – the assassin about whom Gedaliah has been warned (40:14). As Gedaliah shares a welcoming meal with them, he and his companions are slaughtered (41:2–3).

The following day, some pilgrims arrive from the north. From their shaved heads and self-inflicted wounds, they are in mourning for the temple that has been destroyed (41:4–5). Ishmael massacres them too (41:6–7).

Ishmael rounds up the survivors and prepares to return to the Ammonites (41:10). He is intercepted and defeated by Johanan (41:11–15), who decides to take the group to seek safety in Egypt (41:16–18).

Jeremiah warns the survivors about Egypt
(42:1–22)

The group of survivors from the destruction of Jerusalem has gathered near Bethlehem (41:17). Their leader, Johanan, intends to take refuge from the Babylonians in Egypt. But first they ask Jeremiah for a word from God (42:1–3). They promise to do whatever God says (42:4–6).

After ten days, Jeremiah answers their enquiry. God says that they should stay in their own land, where he will keep them safe and restore them. There is nothing to be afraid of from the Babylonians (42:7–12). But if the survivors are determined to go to Egypt, then the very things they dread – starvation, disease and violent death – will follow them there (42:13–22). As always, God wants his people to trust him, rather than using force, deceit or political alliances.

The survivors ignore Jeremiah's advice

(43:1–7)

Despite their promise to do whatever God tells them, the survivors reject Jeremiah's advice (43:1–2). They accuse Jeremiah's secretary, Baruch, of trying to hand them over to the Babylonians (43:3). Insolent and obstinate, they make their way south to Egypt (43:2, 4, 7). Jeremiah and Baruch go with them. Either they want to share the people's troubles, or they are forced to go.

Jeremiah prophesies that Nebuchadnezzar will conquer Egypt

(43:8–13)

The group of survivors arrives at Tahpanhes in Egypt, on the eastern boundary of the Nile Delta.

God tells Jeremiah to bury some large stones at the entrance to the Pharaoh's palace. Jeremiah predicts that Nebuchadnezzar will conquer Egypt and build his palace on this very spot (43:8–10). The king of Babylon will also destroy the temples of the Egyptian gods (43:12–13).

The Jewish refugees commit idolatry

(44:1–30)

The survivors from the fall of Jerusalem continue their idol-worship in Egypt (44:8). They worship the Queen of Heaven, baking cakes for her and pouring out drink offerings (44:19).

Jeremiah warns this last remaining group from Judah that God will wipe them out entirely (44:11–14). The people refuse to listen to Jeremiah (44:15–16) and continue to revive their old acts of idolatry (44:17).

God's promise of safety to Baruch

(45:1–25)

As Baruch writes down Jeremiah's prophecies (45:1), the prophet adds one which is just for him (45:2). God knows that Baruch has suffered sorrow and pain through being caught up in the persecution of his master (45:3). Perhaps he hoped at one time to find himself on the winning side and to become famous; but now all seems lost (45:5).

God confides to Baruch that there will be further destruction yet, because the work of judgment is still going on. But he promises that, whatever happens, he will always keep Baruch safe (45:5).

Prophecies against the nations

These messages have no particular date. They have been collected together for the finished book of Jeremiah. In the Septuagint (the Greek version of the Hebrew Bible), they are placed in chapter 25.

Jeremiah prophesies to the nations which surround Judah. His messages address Egypt (46:1–28), Philistia (47:1–7), Moab (48:1–47), Ammon (49:1–6), Edom (49:7–22), Damascus (49:23–27), Kedar and Hazor (49:28–33), Elam (49:34–39) and Babylon (50:1 – 51:64).

The God of Israel and Judah is the true God of all the nations. He is at work in their circumstances and histories, and he will punish them for their sins.

The longest prophecy concerns Babylon. God has used Babylon to bring his judgment on Judah, but now Babylon herself will be judged. God is going to bring nations from the north – the Medes and the Persians – to attack her (50:9; 51:11). Everyone who sees her destruction will be appalled (50:13).

Jeremiah tells Seraiah, the chief priest (and Baruch's brother), to read out the prophecies against Babylon when he arrives there with the exiles (51:59–60). After he has read them, Seraiah is to tie the scroll to a stone and fling it into the middle of the River Euphrates – the lifeline of Babylonia (51:63). The sinking stone will be a sign that Babylon will sink into oblivion, when God judges her for her wickedness (51:64).

The fall of Jerusalem

The book of Jeremiah ends with a detailed account of Jerusalem's fall (52:1–27). The story has already been told in chapter 39, but it all goes to prove that Jeremiah has been a true prophet.

The numbers of people taken into exile are recorded (52:28–30), with the years counted in Babylonian time. The seventh year is 598–597 BC, the eighteenth year may be 587–586 BC and the twenty-third year 582–581 BC. Where the numbers don't agree with those elsewhere (2 Kings 24:14), it is possible that this record only counts the men, and not their wives and children.

A king, Jehoiachin, survives in Babylon
(52:31–34)

Nebuchadnezzar is succeeded as king of Babylon by King
Evil-Merodach. The new king treats Jehoiachin kindly,
releases him from prison and invites him to dine at his
table (52:31–32).

After the terrors and traumas of conquest and
deportation, there is a glimpse of a new start, a new
relationship and a definite future for the royal line
of King David (53:34).

LAMENTATIONS

Lamentations are grief-stricken poems. They are the laments or dirges with which the Jews mourn the terrible destruction of Jerusalem by the Babylonian armies in 587 BC.

God has used his people's enemies to punish them for their sins. Even so, the poems cry out to God for mercy and dare to believe that he will restore them to their land again one day.

Outline

The first poem (1:1–22)

The second poem (2:1–22)

The third poem (3:1–66)

The fourth poem (4:1–22)

The fifth poem (5:1–22)

INTRODUCTION

The worst has happened. Jerusalem is in ruins. God's chosen people, the Jews, have lost their city and their land. Now they may also lose their nation and their faith.

The Lamentations are funeral songs for the way of life and the people that have been lost. The songs accept that this disaster is God's punishment, and they look to him as their only help and hope.

The Lamentations give a vivid picture of a desperate situation. All the people of Jerusalem and surrounding Judea have been killed, captured or ruined. Solomon's temple has been torn down. The city's great buildings and fine houses have been reduced to rubble.

The poems admit that this destruction is well-deserved and long overdue. God has punished his people for their sins, by letting their enemies conquer them. But God is also merciful. His people dare to hope and pray that he will accept their repentance and restore them.

A day of grief

The Jews remember the destruction of the temple on 9th Ab – that is, in mid-July. On this day, the 'Lamentations' are read aloud to the east of the temple site.

The temple was destroyed twice in its history. The temple built by Solomon was destroyed by the Babylonians in 587 BC. The temple built by Herod the Great was destroyed by the Romans in AD 70.

Patterns with letters

There are five poems in Lamentations. The first four are cleverly shaped. Each sentence of the first four poems begins with one of the twenty-two letters of the Hebrew alphabet.

The other poem also makes patterns with the letters, and there is much play on the sounds of words.

Who wrote Lamentations?

We don't know for sure who wrote these poems. The Jewish teachers simply call them 'Wailings'. The Vulgate (Latin) version of the Bible calls them 'Lamentations' and says that they are written by the prophet Jeremiah.

Jeremiah had a long and painful career predicting that Jerusalem would suffer God's judgment. He was ridiculed and ill-treated for his prophecies – the king himself shredded and burned his writings. When Jerusalem fell, Jeremiah was caught up in the disaster and migrated to Egypt with a group of survivors.

It is very likely that Jeremiah wrote the Lamentations. If not, then they are the work of someone who sees the destruction of Jerusalem in the same way as he did.

The fall of Jerusalem

The story of the fall of Jerusalem is told in 2 Kings 25.

The king of Babylon, Nebuchadnezzar, lays siege to Jerusalem for two years. At the end of that time, with no food left in the city, the Jewish king Zedekiah and his army try to break out.

The effort is useless. The armies of Judah are overtaken and destroyed by the fast and furious forces of Babylon. Zedekiah is captured, forced to watch his sons killed and then blinded. He is taken to Babylon as a prisoner in chains.

Is this the end of 'the house of David' – the line of kings, descended from David, which God said would last for ever? The author believes that God has not forgotten his covenant promise.

All the leading citizens of Jerusalem are deported. Only the very poor people are left to live in the ruins and look after the land. The Babylonians put a governor in charge, but he is killed by rebels. A group of survivors, including the prophet Jeremiah, goes south to Egypt to find protection and a better life. Jeremiah doesn't approve of this move, but goes with the people to care for them.

Is this the end of the Jews – God's own people? Are God's promises withdrawn and the covenant cancelled? The author believes God still loves them and is with them, even though he is angry. It is his nature to forgive.

Because of the Lord's great love we are not consumed,
*   for his compassions never fail.*
They are new every morning;
*   great is your faithfulness (3:22–23).*

The last poem ends with a prayer:

Restore us to yourself, O Lord, that we may return;
    renew our days as of old
unless you have utterly rejected us
    and are angry with us beyond measure (5:21–22).

The third poem expresses firm faith and a sure hope. The best approach is to wait patiently for God to rescue them:

The Lord is good to those whose hope is in him,
    to the one who seeks him;
it is good to wait quietly
    for the salvation of the Lord (3:25–26).

Bitter weeping in Jerusalem (1:12). A young man mourns the assassination of Izaak Rabin, Israel's prime minister.

DISCOVERING LAMENTATIONS

The first poem

Jerusalem is like a desolate widow
(1:1–7)

The first poem (1:1–22) begins with an agonizing howl of grief: *'How!?'* How terrible is this tragedy of God's city and temple in ruins! And how has such a dreadful thing happened?

    Jerusalem was loved by God and had many children; but now she is a widow (1:1). She was a princess; but now she is a slave (1:1). She had many lovers – nations with whom she could form alliances; now she is alone and her friends have betrayed her (1:2). Her roads used

to be thronged with pilgrims, her priests singing and the young girls dancing; now the roads are deserted, the priests groan and the young girls weep (1:4). The princes, which were her pride, are now like starving stags being hunted down (1:6). All she has are her memories – which are of shame and helplessness and loss (1:7).

Jerusalem is being punished for her sin
(1:8–11)

Jerusalem's idolatry has been exposed like sexual sin (1:8–9). She feels violated by the pagan soldiers who have trampled her sanctuary (the temple), and touched the sacred vessels with their unholy hands (1:10). She feels degraded and worthless – her once-proud people scratching around for food like beggars (1:11).

Jerusalem cries out for sympathy
(1:12–22)

Jerusalem acknowledges that she deserves God's punishment (1:18); but will no one have pity on her (1:12)? God has seared her with the fire of his judgment, tangled and turned her in her efforts to escape, and left her prostrate and stunned (1:13). She feels guilty, rejected and totally alone (1:16–17). She also wants her enemies to become as desolate as she is (1:20–22).

Surviving in the ruins. A solitary worshipper waits on God (3:25–26).

The second poem

The Lord is against his people
(2:1–9)

God has vented his anger on Jerusalem. Never mind that she was his daughter, his footstool (2:1); God's rage has obliterated all such niceties. He has ruthlessly demolished the kingdom, its strongholds and rulers (2:2). He has withdrawn his protection when her enemies attacked (2:3) and has himself taken part in the assault (2:4–5). The temple and the royal palaces lie in ruins (2:7); the ramparts and gates are destroyed (2:7); the royal princes are in exile and the prophets are silenced (2:8–9).

The agonies of famine
(2:10–13)

The writer looks around. What he sees makes him weep until he has no more tears. His stomach writhes and he can't control his bowels (2:11). The scene is one of abject poverty, famine and despair. The plight of the mothers with their little children is pitiful (2:12).

True and false prophets
(2:14–17)

The writer notes how dreadfully the false prophets have failed the people. By preaching that all was well, they have prevented any chance of repentance (2:14).

Prayer and tears
(2:18–22)

The writer urges Jerusalem (the wall that surrounds her) to weep out all her grief (2:18) and to pray for the starving children (2:19).

The poem becomes a prayer, arguing with God. It's not right that mothers should be driven to eat their children; that priests and prophets should be slaughtered in the temple (2:20); that every kind of person lies dead in the streets – old and young, men and women (2:21). It seems that God has invited all Jerusalem's enemies round for a party – to destroy all that she holds dear (2:22).

The third poem

A lament of desolation...
(3:1–21)

The writer records his own suffering. He feels as if God has beaten him day and night, plunged him into darkness and chained him in prison (3:1–9). He has been subjected to every kind of attack – ambush, abduction, isolation and target-practice (3:10–12). He has been pierced, scorned, and saturated with envy and self-pity (3:13–15). He is crushed and humiliated; all vestiges of peace, happiness, dignity and hope have vanished (3:16–18). He can think of nothing but his own loneliness and anguish (3:19–20). And yet there is one thing of which he is certain...

... and a song of assurance
(3:22–42)

The writer is certain of God. God's mercies are as sure as the sunrise (3:22–23). The Lord is all he has – and all he will ever need (3:24). He finds it good to wait for God – to accept his punishment and expect his forgiveness (3:22–30). God's punishment is a sign of his care (3:33): what else can he do when tyranny and injustice are rife (3:34–36)? Are we to protest because God punishes our wickedness (3:39)? It is time to turn to God – to beg his forgiveness (3:40–42).

Rejected by God and people
(3:43–54)

The writer addresses God. God has been merciless (3:43) and remote (3:44). He has made his people the scum of the earth (3:45). They have fallen foul of insults, anxiety and traps (3:46–47). The writer's eyes gush tears when he thinks of what has befallen the young women (3:48–51). He himself has been subject to such ill-treatment that he thought he must be dying (3:52–54).

A prayer for revenge
(3:55–66)

Very wonderfully, when the writer cried to God from the deepest place of despair, the Lord answered (3:55–57). Now he asks God to take revenge on the enemies who have plotted against him and taunted him (3:58–66).

The fourth poem

From riches to rags
(4:1–10)

A great change has taken place in Jerusalem. The gold of the temple is tarnished and her sacred stones – once so reverently cut and built together – are littered around the streets (4:1). The unique and priceless inhabitants of Jerusalem (Zion's children) are as worthless as clay pots (4:2). An unnatural cruelty has seized people, so that they no longer care for their children (4:3–4). People who were once prosperous, stylish, healthy and handsome are now destitute and shrivelled (4:5–8).

It would have been better to have been killed outright than to endure this lingering death by starvation (4:9). Once-loving mothers have cooked and eaten their own children (4:10).

An unbelievable defeat
(4:11–20)

The rulers of the nations look in disbelief at the destruction of Jerusalem. They can't believe that God has allowed it to happen (4:11–12). The writer lays the blame on Jerusalem's false prophets and corrupt priests (4:13). They walked through the streets in clothes soaked with the blood of innocent people (4:14). Now they have been expelled and are treated like lepers (4:15–17).

Judah waited in vain for Egypt to come to her rescue (4:17). Now everyone is watched and controlled by the Babylonians (4:18). When the time came for flight, the Judeans were easily overtaken and captured (4:19). The king himself was surrounded and seized – the one who personified God's presence and rule (4:20).

God will punish Edom too
(4:21–22)

The neighbouring nation of Edom may rejoice for a while – having withheld support from Judah and been awarded land by Babylon; but her turn for judgment will come (4:21). Her shame will be exposed for all to see (4:22).

The fifth poem

A pitiful state
(5:1–18)

God's people are reduced to a pitiful state. They have lost their homes, lands and loved ones (5:2–3). They must buy or bargain for the bare necessities of life: bread, water and firewood (5:4, 6). Danger, discomfort, abuse and torture are their daily experience (5:9–13). There is no pleasure of conversation or music or dancing (5:14–15). They have lost their authority and security because of sin; their hearts, like Mount Zion, are deserted and full of fear (5:16–18).

'Restore us to yourself, O Lord'
(5:19–22)

The laments end with a heartfelt cry to God: 'Restore us to yourself, O Lord, that we may be restored' (5:21). Even if God has finally abandoned his people and his covenant, the writer has no doubt that he is still the only God – and therefore the only hope of forgiveness and new life (5:19).

EZEKIEL

Ezekiel is a prophet who shares the early years of exile with God's people in Babylon.

Ezekiel has amazing visions. One is of God moving around in a chariot–throne – with wheels that go in all directions and are full of eyes. Another is of a valley full of dry bones – which collect into skeletons, develop bodies and become a mighty army!

Ezekiel's message is that God is with his people even in exile. God has not abandoned them. He has both the purpose and the power to restore them to their homeland, nationhood and covenant faith.

Outline

Israel's sin and God's judgment (1:1 – 24:27)

Prophecies against surrounding nations (25:1 – 32:32)

A perfect future for Israel (33:1 – 48:35)

INTRODUCTION

Ezekiel writes his own story. His visions and messages are all in the order in which they happen. He gives us a well-organized record of all his experiences, paying great attention to detail.

As a young man, Ezekiel is a priest, married and living in Jerusalem. In 597 BC, the Babylonian armies of Nebuchadnezzar besiege the city. Jerusalem is captured, and the temple of Solomon is ransacked of its treasures.

Ezekiel is taken captive, along with many of Jerusalem's citizens. King Jehoiachin and 10,000 of his soldiers, skilled workers and business people, are all deported to Babylonia, 700 miles away.

Ezekiel finds himself living on a barren plain, near the Kebar River. The Kebar may be an artificial canal taking water from the River Euphrates to the land south-east of Babylon.

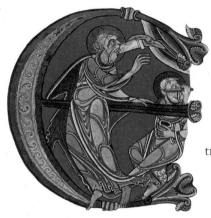

Ezekiel eats a scroll with God's words written on it. He is to take the divine messages deep into his own life.

After four or five years, when Ezekiel is about thirty, God calls him to be a prophet. His messages are to correct and encourage God's people in exile.

Ezekiel's attention is always on what God is doing – in the punishment of Judah, the fall of Jerusalem and the destruction of the temple. In the days before fast news networks, Ezekiel receives visions of what is happening back home.

Of all the prophets of the Old Testament, Ezekiel is the strangest. Like Isaiah, he has a tremendous sense of God's holiness. Like Jeremiah, he acts out some of his prophecies. Like Daniel, he sees visions which leave him speechless. Like Hosea, he experiences heartbreak. But in addition to all these, he seems in some way psychic. He goes into trances, is struck dumb for months and feels himself transported great distances. At one point he visits Jerusalem in a vision and interacts with the people there.

Ezekiel is also a deeply sensitive and passionate man. He is often sad – mourning the fate of the kings of Israel (19:1–14), the death of his wife and the tragic fall of Jerusalem (24:15–27). His last message is dated in the twenty-seventh year of exile, when he is in his early fifties. We don't know what happens to him after this.

Life in exile is not a prison-camp existence. The people are allowed to settle down and form communities. They have their own elders, who organize worship and teaching. Jeremiah advises the exiles to establish a normal life, build houses, plant fields and raise families.

Babylon is an impressive place. The famous 'Hanging Gardens' are one of the seven wonders of the ancient world. The stepped towers, known as 'ziggurats', are formidable temples to seemingly powerful gods. These structures are descendants of the original tower of Babel which tried to reach to God (Genesis 11:1–9). And everywhere are carvings of strange, winged, lion-like creatures – symbols of the might and mobility of Babylon.

The exiles, who have been so proud of Jerusalem, now find themselves dwarfed by the size and scope of Babylon's buildings and businesses. And where is the God of Israel in all this? Is he still alive, or has he been defeated too?

DISCOVERING EZEKIEL

Israel's sin and God's judgment

Ezekiel's vision of God's chariot

(1:1–28)

Ezekiel can name the very day and place when his visions of God begin.

The year is 593 BC. He is thirty years old. If he were in Jerusalem he would be taking up his priestly duties in the temple. As it is, he is in exile in Babylon, where he has been for five years. And the place? He is on the plain of the Kebar River – the Babylonian 'grand canal'.

Something like a windstorm comes sweeping in from the north. The sky grows dark, the wind builds up to a hurricane and lightning starts to flicker around the landscape.

At the heart of the darkness, Ezekiel sees something dazzling, like white-hot metal. There are four living creatures – of human form, but with wings and hands and burnished legs. Each has four faces – a human being, a lion, an ox and an eagle. They move, wing-tip to wing-tip, in a hollow square and with lightning speed. They are like fiery torches, with fire passing constantly between them. And they travel everywhere in an instant – wherever the Spirit of God takes them – without deviation and in perfect unison.

And then Ezekiel sees the wheels: one for each creature – vast, moving in all directions and full of eyes! Here again is perpetual harmony in motion, for the spirit of the living creatures is in the wheels. The sound of beating wings is overwhelming – like rushing waters and the roar of an army.

Above the creatures is an expanse – a platform, a firmament. This is the throne of God. The unity, harmony, mobility and glory are his. He appears like a human being, but dazzling, full of fire and surrounded by the brilliance of storm and rainbow.

Ezekiel is unable to stand. He falls face down in the presence of the Lord.

What does this awesome vision signify? God is transcendent above his creation. He is indescribably glorious. He is everywhere present and active – all-seeing, all-knowing. Suddenly Ezekiel begins to understand the exile of God's people in a new, altogether different, perspective. God is not absent. God is not powerless. God is overwhelmingly here and now.

The call of Ezekiel

(2:1 – 3:15)

The Spirit of God lifts Ezekiel to his feet. God speaks to him as 'son of man' – one small human standing in the presence of the Lord.

God tells Ezekiel that he is sending him as a messenger to his own people, his fellow exiles. There will be no barriers of race or language, but they will still refuse to listen to him. They are a rebellious people – worse than the heathen.

Ezekiel will need to be tough and resolute. God will make Ezekiel's forehead 'harder than flint' (3:9). Isaiah and Jeremiah (his older contemporaries) are similarly fortified (Isaiah 50:7; Jeremiah 1:18).

God gives Ezekiel a scroll, covered on the front and back with messages of woe (2:10). For several years his only words will be warnings of the destruction of Jerusalem. The young prophet is to eat the scroll, taking in these messages and making them his own. He finds it 'as sweet as honey'. John has a similar experience in his vision (Revelation 10:10). The messages may be bitter, but obedience is sweet.

Now Ezekiel is caught up in his new work, and he confesses to feeling angry and bitter. He may feel trapped in a hard and lonely ministry; but it is more likely that he already shares God's own indignation at Israel's rebellion. He moves to the exiles' settlement at Tel Abib ('mound of green barley ears'), where it takes him a week to recover from his ordeal.

To be a watchman

(3:16–27)

God commissions Ezekiel to be a watchman – that is, one who is alert to approaching danger. He is to warn the people of Israel that they are responsible for their sins. Even righteous people are to be warned – and God will hold Ezekiel responsible for telling them.

This idea is new: that people are accountable to God as individuals. In the past, people have been treated as a nation or group.

Ezekiel is to lose his freedom for a while. He is to stay at home and be silent, unless God gives him a message to speak. His mouth is dedicated to the delivery of God's word. Apart from the word of the Lord, he has nothing to say. The enforced silence lasts for six or seven years, until the news of the fall of Jerusalem reaches the exiles (33:22).

Actions speak louder than words
(4:1 – 5:17)

Ezekiel doesn't always speak his messages. Sometimes he acts them. He lies on his side, cuts his hair and remains silent, to convey aspects of suffering and grief.

He draws an outline of Jerusalem on a clay tile, and builds a model siege around it. He pretends he is God laying siege to Jerusalem – 390 days for the sins of Israel and forty days for the sins of Judah. It's a terrible shock to realize that God is set against his own people in this way.

Ezekiel allows himself only a small amount of food and water each day. He cooks in disgusting conditions. Neither the exiles in Babylon nor the people under siege in Jerusalem can enjoy a life of plenty or purity. It is dreadful for Ezekiel, a priest, to have to portray such a state of affairs!

One day Ezekiel packs his bags and then, at night, digs his way out of his house. This is how King Zedekiah will try to escape from Jerusalem (12:3–14).

Prophecy against the mountains of Israel
(6:1–14)

Ezekiel is to pronounce doom on the land of Israel – the mountains and hills, valleys and ravines (6:2–3). The whole landscape has been defiled by idol-worship. There are pagan altars on the 'high places' (hilltops or platforms) and incense-burning and immoral rites under green trees (pagan symbols of fertility). God is going to bring judgment in the form of war, famine and plague (6:11). The sites where the Baal-gods have been worshipped will be littered with corpses (6:5), and the survivors will be scattered to other countries (6:8).

Israel's day of doom
(7:1–27)

The time has come for God's judgment on Israel (7:2–3). She is to be punished for her idolatries and disgusting practices (7:4). The day of doom approaches, when revellers will be plunged into chaos (7:6–7). Just as a rod grows buds, so Israel's pride has developed; her violence has become full-fledged wickedness (7:10–11). Now God is going to judge every single person (7:12) – those who

buy and those who sell, the city dwellers and the country folk (7:12–15).

God's weapons of judgment will be war, famine and plague (7:15). Those who escape will go into mourning (7:18); their money will be useless (7:19) and the women's ornaments will be snatched by strangers (7:20). God will even allow pagan invaders to trample his holy temple (7:22). Prophet, priest and king will all fall silent in the face of the disaster that God will bring upon them (7:25–27).

A visit to Jerusalem
(8:1 – 11:25)

On one occasion Ezekiel feels himself being carried off by his hair, to visit Jerusalem in a vision.

He sees an idol in the temple; the leaders of Israel performing secret rites; women mourning for Tammuz (a pagan god who dies and rises); and men worshipping the sun. In a Passover-type operation, God has all such people killed – but spares those who are innocent.

The awesome chariot–throne that Ezekiel saw by the Kebar River is in Jerusalem as well. As Ezekiel watches, the chariot bears God's glory away from the temple. His presence will no longer be there.

Ezekiel watches the leaders of Jerusalem plotting their wicked schemes. He recognizes some of them and prophesies against them. He watches as one of them, Pelatiah, drops dead (11:1–13)!

When Jerusalem is besieged again, Ezekiel is the first to know. God tells him:

Son of man, record this date, this very date, because the king of Babylon has laid siege to Jerusalem this very day (24:2).

Later, the terrible news is confirmed:

In the twelfth year of our exile, in the tenth month, on the fifth day of the month, someone who had escaped from Jerusalem came to me and said, 'The city has fallen' (33:21).

Prophecies against Jerusalem
(12:1 – 24:27)

Ezekiel has announced God's judgment on Jerusalem. Now he tries to persuade the people that this is indeed going to happen. They are a 'rebellious house' – refusing to listen to God's warning or change their ways (12:2–3).

LEAVING AT NIGHT

Ezekiel is to pack his bags and dig his way out of his house at night (12:7). This is to act out the king's attempt to escape when the disaster strikes (12:12). The king will be caught and carried off to exile in Babylon (12:13).

TREMBLING WITH FEAR

Ezekiel is to shake with fear as he eats and drinks (12:17–20). This is how it will be for everyone when the Babylonian invasion sweeps through the land.

YOU'D BETTER BELIEVE IT!

People like to say of Ezekiel's prophecies, 'It'll never happen.' Now God assures them that all the predictions will be fulfilled in their lifetime (12:21–28).

PEACE SMASHED TO PIECES

Ezekiel condemns the false prophets who have assured people there will be peace. Their visions have been like whitewash on the great wall of Israel's sins (13:10). Now God is going to bring judgment on that wall – a deluge of rain, huge hailstones and a stormy gale (13:11). The wall of sins will be broken down and destroyed – and the uselessness and deceit of the whitewash exposed (13:12–16).

DESIGNING WOMEN

Ezekiel preaches against women who bind people with superstition (13:17–23). They sew wristbands and make veils, which people wear in the hope of being safe from evil powers. By doing this, the women are introducing a layer of false judgment, fear and hope into people's lives. Their activities are nothing to do with God's standards or purpose (13:22). He will destroy their charms and release their captives (13:20).

A Bedouin woman adorned with jewellery. Israel is like a woman whom God has made beautiful and rich, who now gives herself to pagan idols (16:11–15).

BLOCKED HEARTS

Some elders come to consult Ezekiel. He realizes that they can't receive God's word because they have allowed idol-worship and sin to occupy their hearts (14:3–5). Such people must repent and dispose of their idols, or God will turn away from them (14:6–8). If a prophet is taken in by one of these enquirers, both of them will be judged for abuse of God's word (14:9–11).

GOD HAS THE RIGHT TO JUDGE

In the past, God might spare a people or land for the sake of a righteous person who lived there: a Noah, a Daniel or a Job (14:14). Now God announces that he will still spare righteous people, but their presence will not prevent him destroying the rest (14:15–20). There will be some who escape the destruction of Jerusalem, but it will not be because they are righteous. When people see the evil ways of the survivors, they will understand why God acted as he did (14:21–23).

FIT FOR NOTHING

The wood of the vine is useless. It won't even make a coat-peg. It is even more useless when it has been charred by fire. This is how God sees the inhabitants of Jerusalem – the vine he planted in the Promised Land. The people of Jerusalem are to be charred in the fire of God's judgment and discarded in exile (15:1–8).

JERUSALEM – GOD'S WANTON WIFE

Ezekiel tells Israel's life story from God's point of view. God first came across Israel as an abandoned baby, unwashed and unloved (16:4–6). He blessed her with life and, when she came of age and beauty, made a marriage covenant with her (16:7–8). This was the covenant at Mount Sinai when God gave Israel his law. He was an adoring, considerate and generous husband who shared his splendour with her (16:9–14).

But Israel devoted her beauty and blessings to other lovers – the neighbouring nations and their pagan idols (16:15–19). She sacrificed her own children to these gods, and forgot all that the true God had done for her (16:20–22). She gave herself over to a series of liaisons – political alliances and mingling of faiths – with Egypt, Philistia, Assyria and Babylon (the Chaldeans). There were platforms for idol-worship, like beds, in every square and at the end of every road (16:23–29). And yet Israel wasn't a whore, because she paid her lovers for the privilege of their alliances (16:30–34).

Now God is going to expose Israel's shame and turn her lovers into enemies (16:35–39). She will be destroyed by them as God's judgment on her unfaithfulness (16:40–43). There is a strand of paganism and immorality in Israel which comes from her Hittite origins (16:44–46). Her sisters are Samaria and Sodom, who are proud and pagan enough – but Israel is worse than either of them (16:44–52).

God promises to restore Sodom and Samaria – and Israel along with them (16:53–58). God will punish Israel by breaking his covenant with her and allowing her to be defeated and exiled; but afterwards he will renew his commitment to her and forgive all she has done (16:59–63).

A RIDDLE OF TWO EAGLES

Ezekiel tells a story of two great eagles, which represent Babylon and Egypt (17:11–15). Babylon has carried off the leading shoot of Judah, but left an offshoot in Jerusalem (17:3–6). The offshoot grows well, but leans towards Egypt for sustenance (17:7–8). God sees this as rebellious and doomed to failure (17:11–21). It depicts the time in 588 BC, when King Zedekiah of Judah looked to Egypt for help in lifting the Babylonian siege of Jerusalem.

God promises to select and tend a new sprig from the tree of Israel. This shoot will grow on a prominent height and become a landmark and shelter for all the nations of the world (17:22–24). It is a picture of Mount Zion and the kingdom of God.

THE SOUL THAT SINS WILL DIE

People are saying that they don't deserve their punishment. It's all the fault of their parents. As the saying goes:

The parents have eaten sour grapes, and the children's teeth are set on edge (18:2).

There is a lot of truth in this idea. Israel has always had a strong sense of belonging together, and of being blessed or punished together.

But now Ezekiel declares that each generation is responsible for its own actions. People cannot claim innocence just because their parents were wicked. From now on, each person will stand alone before the judgment of God – not hiding behind someone else's goodness, or blaming someone else for their faults. If anyone dies, it will be for their own sin and no one else's. God's new community will be made up of individuals – each of whom has chosen to do right.

A LAMENT OVER THE KINGS OF ISRAEL

God tells Ezekiel to raise a lament for the princes of Israel (19:1). They have been like young lions – one getting caught in Egypt and another captured and taken to Babylon (19:2–9). These images describe the fates of kings Jehoahaz and Jehoiachin.

Ezekiel pictures a strong and healthy vine. This vine has been pulled up and transplanted to a desert situation. Its strength to rule is gone (19:10–14). This is a reference to King Zedekiah, whose rebellion provoked the Babylonian assault on Jerusalem.

ISRAEL'S PAST…

Some elders come to consult Ezekiel. God asks Ezekiel to challenge their motives (20:1–3).

In the beginning, when God chose the Israelites to be his own people, he commanded them to reject the idols of Egypt; but not one of them did so (20:5–8). God considered punishing Israel there and then, but brought her out of Egypt to prove his power to the other nations (20:9–10).

God led the Israelites through the wilderness and gave them his holy laws, but they did not keep them. Again, God considered abandoning them to death in the desert, but he spared them (20:11–22). He warned them that the consequence of breaking his law would be exile among the nations (20:23–24). There was confusion over the offering for first-born children, which was sometimes interpreted as child sacrifice (20:25–26).

Finally, since the Israelites came into their own land, they have defiled it with idolatry (20:27–29). So why should the elders be allowed to consult God? Their ancestors have never taken any notice of what God has said (20:30–31).

... AND GOD'S FUTURE

God will never allow his people to settle for idolatry. He is determined to be their king. He will rescue them from captivity and bring them into the wilderness once again. There he will judge them like a shepherd checking his sheep; and he will renew his covenant with them (20:32–38).

The Israelites can choose to worship idols if they wish. What God will not tolerate is the mixing of idol-worship with the worship of the one true God (20:39). God will establish his holy mountain as the centre for Israel's worship, where all can bring their offerings. It will be a place of repentance and forgiveness – a place to realize the grace of God (20:40–44).

JUDGMENT BY FIRE AND SWORD

Ezekiel is given four prophecies of judgment: one by fire and three by sword (20:45 – 21:32).

Fire in the Negeb

Ezekiel is to preach to the south of Jerusalem, to the forest of the Negeb – the 'dry land'. God promises to kindle there a terrible fire for all to see (20:45–49). Ezekiel himself feels the pain and frustration of such an image. His words are frightening and puzzling, but not understandable.

God's sword against Jerusalem

Ezekiel is to prophesy towards Jerusalem that God is coming to wreak judgment with his sword (21:1–17). The sword is polished and sharp, and is being wielded against God's own people. It will not be sheathed until its task is completed.

Nebuchadnezzar's sword at the crossroads

Ezekiel is to mark a junction in the road. It is the junction where Nebuchadnezzar will pause, to decide whether to march on Jerusalem or Rabbah (the city of the Ammonites – modern Amman). Nebuchadnezzar will choose from arrows with the names of cities written on them; he will consult the teraphim (little idol figures) and inspect the liver of a sacrifice. He will choose Jerusalem and call up the equipment for laying siege to her (21:18–23).

The choice of Jerusalem is no mistake. The time has come for God's judgment on Israel's guilt, which is freshly exposed. Jerusalem's king must prepare to be deposed, and her people must contemplate the unthinkable: that the city will become a ruin (21:24–27).

Ammon's sword turned back

Ezekiel is to prophesy against the Ammonites (21:28–32). They plan to join the attack on Jerusalem, but God tells them to return the sword to its sheath. They themselves are to be judged and destroyed in their own land – and will disappear for ever.

THREE PROPHECIES CONDEMNING JERUSALEM

She is guilty

The time has come for judgment to fall on Jerusalem. The city has brought it on herself with violent bloodshed and vile idolatry (22:1–5).

Jerusalem's crimes affect many sections of the population: murderous princes, despised parents, exploited foreigners, neglected widows, abused religion and broken sabbaths. There is every kind of sexual deviation: orgy, incest, abuse and adultery. There is malpractice in business: bribery, double accounting and extortion. But the heart of all the trouble is that the people have forgotten God and his law (22:6–12).

God announces his verdict. The people of Jerusalem are sentenced to exile – even though their defeat will reflect badly on God's reputation among the other nations (22:13–16).

She is worthless

Jerusalem has become worthless in God's sight (22:17–22). However valuable she once appeared, all her precious qualities will vanish in the furnace of God's judgment.

She is unholy

Jerusalem is spiritually filthy – like an unwashed land in drought. Her leaders are murderous as they intimidate and steal. The priests have failed to teach God's law or observe God's holiness. The officials are corrupt. The prophets are shallow and dishonest. The common people are bullies and thieves. There is not a single righteous person with whom God can start again. He sentences them to the consequences of their behaviour (22:23–31).

THE SHAMELESS SISTERS

God describes two sex-obsessed sisters. Their names are Oholah and Oholibah. In telling of their sexual awakening in Egypt and their insatiable lusts ever since, Ezekiel is describing the idolatry of the fertility religions. He is describing Samaria and Jerusalem (23:1–4).

Samaria was the capital of the northern kingdom of Israel. Jerusalem is the capital of the southern kingdom of Judah. Oholah (Samaria) lusted after the Assyrians and their gods. The Assyrians violated her, seized her children, and killed her. Oholibah (Jerusalem) not only lusted after the Assyrians, but also the Chaldeans (Babylonians). She played the whore with the Babylonians, but was disgusted by them. God was, in turn, disgusted by her (23:5–21).

Now God is gathering all Jerusalem's hoped-for lovers into an invading army. They will attack from the north in huge numbers, well-organized and well-armed. They will execute God's judgment on Oholibah for her abandonment of God's law. She will drink the same cup of horror and desolation as her sister (23:22–35).

Ezekiel weighs the crimes of Oholah and Oholibah. They have committed adultery with other nations and idolatry with other gods. They have offered their children as sacrifices and then entered God's holy temple with blood on their hands. They have entertained foreign suitors by playing the whore and used holy incense and oil for their seductions. Any righteous judge would find them guilty.

God declares that Oholah and Oholibah are to be destroyed, together with their children and their houses. God is holy, and lewdness and idolatry are to be eradicated from his holy people (23:36–49).

THE COOKING OF JERUSALEM

It is January 588 BC. God tells Ezekiel that Nebuchadnezzar, the king of Babylon, has laid siege to Jerusalem. Jerusalem is like a large copper cauldron, placed on the fire of God's judgment to cook. The pieces of meat in the cauldron are her citizens (24:1–5).

The cauldron is rusty. The rust colours the meat, making it look bloody. The contents are poured out on bare rock, so that the earth doesn't soak up the blood. The citizens of Jerusalem, too, will be slaughtered and thrown out at random – to lie without burial (24:6–8).

Finally, the cauldron itself is left on the fire to melt down completely, destroying the rust within it. So God destroys the filth of Jerusalem, her blood-guilt and immorality. He will not turn back now or change his mind (24:9–14).

THE DEATH OF A WIFE

God tells Ezekiel that he is about to take away the delight of his eyes; but he forbids him to mourn or weep. The prophet must put on his turban and sandals as usual, and not give any outward sign of grief. That evening, Ezekiel's wife dies (24:15–18).

Ezekiel's bereavement parallels the tragedy of Jerusalem, who is God's wife. Jerusalem is also the great love of the people in exile. Ezekiel explains to the people that, when the news comes of Jerusalem's death, they are not to give any signs of mourning. But within and between themselves they must pine and groan, because of the sins which have caused this great tragedy (24:19–24).

When the news arrives that Jerusalem has been destroyed, Ezekiel will be able to speak freely again. The worst has happened and his prophecies have come true.

Now he will be able to teach and prepare the people for God's new future (24:25–27).

Prophecies against surrounding nations

God gives Ezekiel prophecies to utter against seven nations: Ammon, Moab, Edom, Philistia, Tyre, Sidon and Egypt. The God of Israel is the Lord of all the earth, and his standards apply to all nations. It is not just Israel who comes under his judgment.

A picture of desolation. The sites of great cities will become pasture for camels when God's judgment falls (25:5).

Ammon, Moab, Edom and Philistia
(25:1–17)

Ammon has rejoiced at Israel's fate. Now God will cause her to be overrun by tribesmen from the east – the Nabateans. Her capital, Rabbah, will become grazing for their camels (25:2–7).

Moab has concluded that the invasion of Judah means that Israel is no different from the other nations. She is wrong and will be invaded herself by the Nabateans (25:8–11).

Edom has taken advantage of the Babylonian invasion of Israel – perhaps by gaining part of southern Judah. Now God will take revenge on her (25:12–14).

The Philistines were always hostile to Israel, and joined in her destruction. Now God will avenge himself on them and destroy their coastlands (25:15–17).

The Lord of all

The surrounding nations may gloat over the fate of Israel at the hands of her own God. But ultimately it is the God of Israel who will judge them too.

Tyre
(26:1 – 28:19)

The proud and magnificent port of Tyre has rejoiced at Jerusalem's fall. She expects to gain from it in plunder and trade (26:2). But, after his destruction of Jerusalem, Nebuchadnezzar will turn his attention to Tyre. He will lay siege to her for thirteen years.

God is against Tyre and will subject her to overwhelming waves of attack. The armies of Babylon will crash over her. She will be broken down and eroded until she becomes merely a bare rock on which to dry fishing nets (26:3–21).

God tells Ezekiel to lament the destruction of such a thriving community. She is like a great trading ship, laden with merchandise, which sinks within sight of the shore (27:1–36). Tyre's pride has been her downfall. Her king has thought himself a god (28:1–10). He was indeed exquisitely wealthy and wise, but his power and pride corrupted him (28:11–19).

Sidon
(28:20–26)

Sidon is to fall under the judgment of God, by plague and sword (28:20–23).

GOD'S PURPOSE IN JUDGING THE NATIONS

God's judgment and destruction of the surrounding nations show his sovereign holiness. He is cutting back the 'briers and thorns' of Israel's enemies, to make a safe place for her to live (28:24–26).

Egypt
(29:1 – 32:32)

In January 587 BC, God declares to Ezekiel his judgment on Egypt. Pharaoh, king of Egypt, is like a great dragon or crocodile ruling the River Nile, his lair. God will hook him up and fling him out (29:1–5).

Egypt is condemned because she was an unreliable support in Israel's need – like a reed staff which breaks when leaned on, tearing the shoulders and buckling the knees (29:6–7). God will punish Egypt by laying waste her land and scattering her people for forty years. Afterwards he will restore her, but only as a shadow of her former power. Israel will never again look to depend on her (29:8–16).

On New Year's Day 571 BC, Ezekiel receives his last recorded prophecy. It is placed here, because it concerns Egypt and Tyre. Nebuchadnezzar has lifted his siege of Tyre around 574 BC. It has been a long and unrewarding venture, lasting thirteen years. Now Nebuchadnezzar will hope to make good his losses (and pay his soldiers) by invading Egypt (29:17–20).

Ezekiel prophesies a day of God's judgment on Egypt – a 'day of the Lord' (30:3). The Babylonian armies of Nebuchadnezzar will sweep through every part of the land (30:4–19).

God will ensure victory for the Babylonians. Pharaoh Hophra's 'arm' was 'broken' in 586 BC, when he tried to relieve the Babylonian siege of Jerusalem. Now God will break both Pharaoh's arms, but strengthen Nebuchadnezzar's (30:20–26).

In June 587 BC, God gives Ezekiel an oracle for Pharaoh and his armies. Egypt is like a mighty cedar of Lebanon, taller and more beautiful than the cedars in the garden of Eden (31:1–9). But Egypt is proud, and her cedar is to be cut down by foreigners – the Babylonians (31:10–14). Pharaoh and his armies will go down to Sheol, the world of the departed (31:15–18).

PHARAOH'S FATE

In March 585 BC, God tells Ezekiel to raise a lament for Pharaoh, king of Egypt.

Does Pharaoh think himself like the winged lion of Babylon? He is more like a cumbersome crocodile thrashing around in muddy waters (32:2). God is going to bring the armies of Babylon to capture and overthrow him (32:3–16). Other nations and their rulers will be appalled at Egypt's destruction (32:9–10).

In the same month, Ezekiel is given a further lament. Pharaoh and his hordes have been put to the sword and now lie buried in Sheol. There they keep company with the dead of many other pagan nations: Assyria, Elam, Meshech and Tubal, Edom and Sidon (32:17–32).

A perfect future for Israel

Responsible to God and the people
(33:1–20)

God tells Ezekiel that he is to be a watchman for Israel – the only one keeping a lookout against attack. He feels an enormous sense of responsibility to tell the people what God is doing, and to warn them of God's judgment. If he fails in his duty, the people will be lost.

Ezekiel is to act as a watchman by warning people. They must stop their wickedness or they will die. They must respond to God *now*. It doesn't matter whether they have acted well or badly in the past. The important thing is to turn to God in the present – and live.

The turning point: 'The city has fallen!'
(33:21–33)

And now comes a turning point in Ezekiel's ministry.

For six or seven years Ezekiel has been silent, except when speaking the Lord's messages. Now, at last, the news arrives which Ezekiel has long predicted, 'Jerusalem has fallen!'

Ezekiel already suspected as much, because the previous evening God had enabled him to speak freely again. This was the sign that Jerusalem ('their stronghold, their joy and glory') was taken away – just as Ezekiel had suffered such a loss when his wife died (24:25–27).

The news of the disaster is terrible, but suddenly Ezekiel is popular. He is a prophet whose word has come true!

The Lord speaks to Ezekiel about the survivors in Judah. Although they are poor and living in the ruins, they are claiming the land of Israel as their inheritance. If Abraham could claim it and he was only one person, how much more do they have the right to it, as they number so many?

The question is whether the land belongs to the people who are in exile (who were the leaders of Judah when they were deported) or to the poor and ignorant survivors who are squatting in the ruins and hiding in caves.

Ezekiel declares that the survivors have no right to the land, because they continue to worship idols, ignore the food laws and commit murder, violence and adultery. They will suffer further judgment. Jeremiah's vision of the two baskets of figs deals with the same issue – and

comes to the same conclusion: it is the exiles who are the 'good figs' (Jeremiah 24:1–10)!

But Ezekiel also has a warning for the exiles. They are eager to hear his messages (now that they know his words are from the Lord), but they treat his words like a beautiful tune rather than a call to change their lives. They listen and enthuse – but go away and do nothing.

From now on, Ezekiel will have messages of renewal and restoration. He will prepare the exiles for their return home.

God will be the shepherd
(34:1–31)

Ezekiel looks forward to Israel being restored. If the failings of the past are to be avoided, there must be a new standard of leadership.

In the ancient Near East, a common description of a leader is the shepherd. He walks ahead of his sheep, leads them to pasture and defends them from wild animals. Both Moses and David are described as 'shepherds' to their people – and both served their apprenticeship looking after real sheep.

Ezekiel delivers the Lord's judgment on the kings who have been Israel's shepherds in the recent past. They have behaved scandalously: exploiting their people, neglecting the weak and allowing the nation to be scattered. They have used and abused the flock as their own, when in truth it was God's.

Now the Lord himself will rescue his people. He will search for them and bring them back from the nations to which they have been scattered. 'Scattering' is one of Ezekiel's favourite terms for the exile. God is to bring his people home, not only from Babylonia but also from Egypt, Phoenicia and Arabia.

When the Lord restores his flock, it will be a day of both rescue and judgment. He will tend the injured and weak, but the sleek and strong he will destroy. This will be the fate of those ruthless and greedy members of society who grow fat at the expense of the rest. Ezekiel hints at the social justice and freedom from oppression which are such an important theme in the prophecy of Amos.

Here is the just and gentle rule of God. He is the good shepherd. God's longing to search for the lost must be the seed thought for a famous parable of Jesus (Luke 15:4–6), and the source of his deep compassion (Matthew 9:36).

Finally, God will place his people in the care of

David, who will be a 'prince' among them. The actual descendants of David have failed in their kingship; but now God promises to appoint a ruler with David's qualities who will shepherd Israel for ever. This will be the Messiah – the perfect ruler of the restored community.

A judgment on Edom
(35:1–15)

God tells Ezekiel to prophesy against Mount Seir, which is the home of the Edomites.

The Edomites nurse an ancient enmity with Israel. This enmity dates back to the rivalry between Esau and Jacob. The Edomites are descended from Esau and the Israelites from Jacob.

The Edomites have failed to help when Judah was invaded and Jerusalem besieged by the Babylonians. They hoped to take possession of the 'two countries' of Israel and Judah (35:10) once the Babylonians had withdrawn.

Now God is going to judge Edom. Just as Edom has rejoiced over the destruction of Israel, so God will make all nations rejoice over the destruction of Edom (35:14–15).

Israel's coming home!
(36:1–38)

Ezekiel is to prophesy to the mountains of Israel: the peaks that have been abused by fertility rites and trampled by pagan armies. God has seen enough of their suffering. He is angry at the derision of other nations, who laugh at Israel's defeat and say her God doesn't care (36:1–3).

God now declares to the whole landscape of Israel that she will flourish once again. Her people are coming home (36:6–8)!

God is concerned to put the record straight. He is not restoring Israel because her goodness has earned it. He is restoring Israel because his holy name has been insulted. Now he is going to gather his people and cleanse them from idolatry (36:22–25).

NEW HEART, NEW START

God is going to work a miracle of his grace. He will change Israel's heart from stone to flesh, from hardness to softness, from death to life (36:26). The law which was engraved on stone and so always 'outside' people will now be planted within them (36:27). Israel will become a

renewed people in a restored land, replanting and rebuilding to the glory of God (36:28–38).

'Prophesy to these bones'
(37:1–28)

Ezekiel is in a valley – either literally or in a vision. The valley floor is covered with a deep layer of bones –

Shepherd and sheep. God is angry with shepherds who have cared only for themselves and not for the flock. He promises that he will shepherd the flock himself.

as though an army has been massacred there. It is a picture of Israel – dead and dismembered by defeat and dispersion.

The Lord puts the question to Ezekiel: 'Son of man, can these bones live?' He replies, 'O Sovereign Lord, you alone know.'

Israel's survival and revival is in God's hands. The situation is beyond human help. Only God can make these bleached and crumbling bones rise to form an army again. Only God can resurrect his people Israel

and restore to them their land and temple.

The Lord commands Ezekiel to prophesy to the bones: to tell them that God will reconstitute them into skeletons, clothe them with muscles and flesh, put breath in them and bring them to life! Ezekiel does so. As he watches, the bones come together and are formed into corpses, but the army is still lifeless.

God commands Ezekiel to prophesy to the breath. 'Breath' means 'wind' as well as 'spirit': invisible, powerful and life-giving. In Hebrew it is 'ruach' – the wilderness wind; the image of the Spirit of God.

Ezekiel summons the breath to inspire the dead – and the mighty army springs to life! This is the power of God's word and Spirit, in partnership with the faith and obedience of his prophet.

Israel will rise again, at the word of the Lord. The God who brought creation into being by his powerful word will restore his people to their life and land.

Prophecy against Gog
(38:1 – 39:29)

Ezekiel's prophecies of the restoration and renewal of Israel are interrupted by oracles about a great battle in the far future. We don't know why the compiler has inserted them here.

These two chapters are unique. They describe an invasion of foreign powers against the people of God, even after the Messiah's reign of peace has begun. Ezekiel prophesies defeat and destruction for these pagan hordes – the massed armies of Gog.

Gog is the commander of an alliance which is bent on the destruction of Israel. His name may come from 'Gygyes', king of Lydia, or the place name Gagaia, a land of barbarians. Gog is described as prince of Meshech and Tubal (probably Phrygia and Cappadocia, to the east of Asia Minor). Some scholars have tried to identify Gog as a historical conqueror such as Alexander the Great.

The nations attacking Israel are from Persia, Cush (Ethiopia), Put (North Africa), Gomer (north of the Black Sea) and Beth Togarmah ('the uttermost north' – perhaps Armenia). They will sweep in like a storm and cover the land like locusts. But God himself will curb them with hooks through their jaws, as he tamed the chaos monster.

Israel is living in quiet prosperity at this future time, enjoying the peace of the Messiah's kingdom. When the invasion takes place, God will defend her with an earthquake, confusion, plague, bloodshed, storm and burning sulphur. His victory will show the world that he is the great and holy God (38:16).

Israel's triumph will be complete. It will take seven months to bury the bodies of the enemy (outside God's land, in the valley of Hamon Gog) and the captured weapons will provide firewood for seven years.

Other prophets predict an end-time battle between the forces of evil and the people of God. Joel speaks of God's defeat of 'the northern army' (Joel 2:20) and

Jeremiah of 'a besieging army… coming from a distant land' (Jeremiah 4:16). Amos and Zephaniah both describe a 'Day of the Lord' which features darkness and destruction (Amos 5:18–20; Zephaniah 1:14–18).

These prophecies are 'apocalyptic' in style. They reveal the true state of things in cosmic images of God's judgment and victory. They assure God's people of his purpose and power to bring all things to a glorious and successful conclusion. This enables believers to live confidently through many terrible trials.

The book of Revelation, at the close of the whole Bible, describes a final invasion by the forces of Satan against God's people and city. The writer identifies Satan's allies as Gog and Magog (Revelation 20:7–9)! Their reputation has travelled a long way from the oracles of Ezekiel.

A vision of the perfect temple

(40:1 – 43:27)

It is now twenty-five years since Ezekiel was taken from Jerusalem to exile in Babylon, and fourteen years since the news arrived that Jerusalem and her temple were destroyed.

Since that dreadful day, Ezekiel's fellow exiles have

recognized him as a true prophet. God has given him many visions and messages of restoration and renewal. Israel will be gathered and cared for by God himself. He will raise her to new life, like a living army from a pile of bones.

Ezekiel's final visions are of a new temple, beautifully and perfectly built; and of the Lord returning to dwell among his people. As Ezekiel is both priest and prophet, this is a fitting climax for his book.

In a vision, Ezekiel is taken to Israel and set on a 'very high mountain'. Immediately we think of Mount Zion, with Jerusalem 'lifted up' to her heavenly status as God's holy city.

Ezekiel is met by a man whose appearance is 'like bronze' – an angelic messenger, equipped with a linen cord and measuring rod. He tells Ezekiel to take in every detail of the new temple's design. Together they tour the temple complex, viewing and measuring the walls, gates, porticoes, courts and rooms.

They come to the centre of the temple area and measure the outer and inner sanctuaries. The Most Holy Place is twenty cubits square, while the temple building is 100 cubits square. Everything is square and symmetrical – the perfect proportions expressing the holiness of God.

Ezekiel notes that some of the walls are decorated with palm trees, while the walls and floors of the sanctuaries are finished in wood. The walls around the outer and inner sanctuaries are decorated with palm trees and cherubim.

The destruction and restoration of God's people are depicted on a wall-painting from Dura Europos. It decorates one of the earliest-known synagogues in modern Syria (c. AD 245).

The temple building

Ezekiel's angel guide measures out the temple building in cubits. This is the 'long' cubit, which is about twenty-one inches. The measuring rod is about ten feet and three inches long, which is the thickness and height of the wall surrounding the temple area.

This outer wall is the 'dividing partition' which separates the sacred space from the secular. There was no such wall in Solomon's temple, but it is now introduced to emphasize the separation of holy things.

Ezekiel is shown the wooden altar for the bread of the Presence, the accommodation for the priests and the rooms for the washing and preparation of sacrifices.

When they come to the east gate, Ezekiel has a vision of the glory of the God of Israel. The Lord returns to his temple from the east, the direction of the sunrise, and enters through the east gate. He is awesome in appearance, as when Ezekiel first saw him by the River Kebar. Ezekiel falls on his face before him.

Nineteen years after Ezekiel's vision of the Lord departing from his temple, the prophet witnesses the glorious return. The glory of the Lord fills his temple.

The Lord tells Ezekiel that this temple is to be holy – the place where he will live among his people. There is to be no repetition of the pagan practices which brought judgment and disaster before.

Ezekiel is to describe the temple to the Israelites, so that they may catch the vision of its holiness and perfection.

Next, Ezekiel is introduced to the laws which will govern the worship of the temple and its administration. He is shown the altar of burnt offering and told of the week-long sequence of sacrifices by which it is to be consecrated.

Regulations for the restored community
(44:1 – 46:24)

THE PRINCE, THE LEVITES AND THE PRIESTS

The east gate

The man (the angel guide) brings Ezekiel to the outer gate of the sanctuary, facing east. This gate is to remain shut, because it is the one through which the Lord God returned to his temple. It is sacred to him and is not to be used by humans. Is it shut because the Lord will never leave his temple again?

The prince

The prince is the only person who will be allowed to sit inside this east gate within the sanctuary – but he must enter and leave by the portico. The human ruler of Israel is to have a privileged but much more humble role than the kings of the past. He is not to be seen as God's representative in the way that David or Solomon were.

Once again, Ezekiel sees the glory of the Lord filling the temple, and falls on his face in awe of his presence.

Reforms

Ezekiel is given detailed instructions about the way the new temple is to be used. There are to be some important changes to avoid the mistakes and abuses of the past.

Access to the temple is to be restricted to members of the community of Israel.

In the past, foreigners have been allowed in – people who didn't share the race and faith of Israel ('uncircumcised in heart and flesh'). Sometimes such people have even been put in charge of the sanctuary. This must change.

In future, the people who come to the sanctuary must be members of the true Israel, the community of faith in the Lord. This isn't a racist ban. It is an attempt to keep the use and care of the sanctuary holy. Only those who know and mean what they're doing are to be allowed in.

These rules may have been drawn up after the time of Ezekiel. His 'perfect temple' was never built, and perhaps some of the old abuses began to occur again. If so, these regulations may have been introduced to guard Ezekiel's vision and protect the temple and its worship from defilement.

Levites and Zadokites

The Levites are not allowed to serve in the temple as priests. Instead, they must do the work which was previously done by foreign slaves. The slaves cannot now enter the sanctuary because they are not circumcised and don't share Israel's faith.

The Levites are to lose their priesthood because they worshipped pagan idols in the years leading up to the exile. Now they are to look after the temple in practical ways. They are the 'lay' administrators and gatekeepers.

God chooses the descendants of Zadok to be his priests. Zadok was the high priest who was appointed by David to serve alongside Abiathar. When Solomon became king, Abiathar was banished and Zadok became the sole high priest. Through Zadok, the priests trace their family line back to Aaron. They will be the priestly group throughout the time of the second temple – the one that will be built after the exile.

The Zadokite priests are given rules about their robes, hair length, wine, marriage and contact with dead bodies. All these rules are designed to show a difference between things that are holy and things that are common.

The priestly robes are to be made of linen, which is lighter than wool. Linen will help to prevent them perspiring. They must change out of these robes before mixing with ordinary people after the services.

The priests must keep their hair trimmed (neither shaven too close nor worn too long); and they are not to drink wine before entering the inner court (the sanctuary). They are to be clean, cool, tidy and sober for their sacred work. Cleanliness and godliness go together. Their outward behaviour should express a pure heart and dedicated life.

The rules for priests cover the same aspects of life as the vows of the Nazirites. The Nazirites (of whom Samson was one in the days of the judges) were to wear their hair long, abstain from strong drink and avoid contact with dead bodies (Numbers 6:1–21).

Ezekiel is seeing a vision of a reformed, holy and disciplined priesthood. When the exiles start to return to Judah and Jerusalem, their leaders will emphasize certain ways to express holiness. These will include circumcision, keeping the law and avoiding intermarriage with non-Jews. The prophet Haggai, the priest Ezra and the governor Nehemiah will commend and pursue these policies.

A priest is not to go near a dead body, unless it is that of a close relative. A corpse is dead and decaying, but priests are to be symbols of health and wholeness.

The priests are not to own any land. God himself is their inheritance – all they have and all they need. The grain and meat that are brought for sacrifices will supply the priests with food.

DIVISION OF THE LAND

God has just told Ezekiel how the priests are to be provided with food. Now he describes how the land is to be divided when Israel returns from exile (45:1–12).

First of all, an area of land is to be set aside and devoted to God. On this land the temple will be built, together with accommodation for the priests. On the surrounding plots, the Levites, the prince and 'the city' (the state) will have allocations. In this way, the temple will be protected by a sacred buffer zone.

After the exile, the prince is to have a set and limited allocation of land. There is to be no more seizing of other people's property, as there was when King Ahab took Naboth's vineyard (1 Kings 21).

All the rest of the land is to be divided between the tribes for their towns, families and farms.

The Lord commands Israel's princes to act fairly. They are not to use their powers and privileges to bully and cheat. In particular, the weights and measures are to be set at an agreed standard. The ephah (for dry goods) and the bath (for liquids) are both to be 'a tenth of a homer'. An ephah is a little less than five gallons. Ten ephahs make a 'homer', which is six bushels of dry goods or 48.4 gallons of liquid. The word 'homer' means 'donkey-load'.

OFFERINGS AND HOLY DAYS

The people are to allocate a proportion of their grain, oil and sheep to the prince (45:13–25). These are 'special gifts', like a tithe: a sixtieth of their wheat and barley, a hundredth of their oil, and one out of every 200 sheep.

There is no mention of wine. In the days before the exile, wine was poured out as an offering and also drunk at the festivals. Perhaps it has been abused and the custom is discontinued. The priests are forbidden to drink when they are on duty (44:21).

The prince, in turn, is to provide the sacrifices which will be offered in the temple on behalf of all the people.

The holy days in the new regime are to be New Year's Day, Passover and the Feast of Tabernacles. There is no mention of the Feast of Weeks or the Day of Atonement – although the latter may be suggested by the extra sacrifice which is to be offered a week after the New Year (45:20).

THE PRINCE'S PLACE

Ezekiel understands that the prince's status is to be strictly limited in the future kingdom (46:1–2).

The prince will be responsible for providing the offerings and sacrifices for the new temple. He will also be permitted to enter the inner court through the east gate – but only on the sabbath and at the New Moon (the first day of each month).

The prince will have a clear view of the worship being offered in the sanctuary, but he himself must not go further than the threshold. This regulation prevents Israel's human ruler from taking on the role of priest, as has happened sometimes in the past.

OFFERINGS ON VARIOUS OCCASIONS

Ezekiel is given details of the sacrifices which are to be offered on the sabbath (every seventh day) and at the New Moon (the first day of the month) (46:3–15).

The burnt offerings are the same on each occasion: six male lambs and a ram. With the ram is offered a grain offering of an ephah (twenty-two litres) of flour. With the lambs, the prince may offer as much grain offering as he pleases, together with a hin of oil (six pints) for each ephah of flour.

At New Moon there is an additional sacrifice of a young bull, together with an ephah of flour. All these sacrifices are similar to those offered in the years before the exile.

Ezekiel is also given instructions for annual festivals, daily sacrifices and any occasion when the prince may wish to make an extra (freewill) offering.

THE ROYAL LAND

If the prince wants to give land to his sons, he may do so. He must allocate the land out of his own share and not seize land from other people. The land transferred to a son will continue to belong to that branch of the family (46:16–18).

If the prince gives land to one of his servants, that land will revert to royal ownership at 'the year of freedom'. The 'year of freedom' is probably the Jubilee, every fiftieth year, when debts are cancelled and land restored to its original owner or family (Leviticus 25:13).

A VISIT TO THE KITCHENS

The man (Ezekiel's angel guide) shows Ezekiel the temple kitchens (4:19–24). These are situated in the rooms at the four corners of the outer court – which is all part of the symmetry and perfection of the temple.

The kitchens have ledges for fires, where meat can be boiled and bread baked. The sacrifices and offerings are to be cooked by the priests and eaten by the worshippers.

It is important to keep the food preparation separate from the crowd of worshippers in the outer court. The offerings are sacred and might become defiled. Equally, some unclean people might contract holiness!

The river from the temple
(47:1–12)

The man (the angel guide) brings Ezekiel back to the entrance of the temple. This is the east gate, the main entrance, through which the glory of the Lord had entered. Here Ezekiel sees water welling out from under the threshold, flowing from the south side of the temple.

Because the east door is kept closed, the guide takes Ezekiel out of the temple by the north door and round the building on the outside. Arriving at the front of the east gate, Ezekiel sees the water emerging and flowing away.

The guide takes Ezekiel along the course of the river,

The significance of the new temple

Ezekiel was a priest before he was called to be a prophet. He looks forward to the return of Israel to Jerusalem and the rebuilding of the temple. But the temple he visits in his vision will never be built.

This is a temple with supernatural features. It is situated on a 'very high mountain'. It has a 'river of life' flowing from its sanctuary. The vision is for inspiration rather than reality.

The Christian understanding is that Christ has fulfilled the Old Testament institutions of temple, priesthood and sacrifice. Jesus Christ is the true temple, where God dwells among his people. He is the great high priest and perfect sacrifice (Hebrews 10:19–21).

So what does this vision mean for Ezekiel? It is an inspiration to return, to rebuild and to hold high the holiness of God. Ezekiel is expressing the centrality and glory of God among his people, in the very best way he can imagine.

John, the writer of the book of Revelation, does not see Ezekiel's temple in the heavenly city, because 'the Lord God Almighty and the Lamb [Jesus Christ] are its temple' (Revelation 21:22).

measuring off distances of a 1,000 cubits (500 yards).
At first the water is only ankle-deep, but at the next
sounding it is up to their knees. Another 1,000 cubits
and the water is waist-deep – after which it becomes
impossible to cross on foot. Ezekiel notices a great
number of trees growing on the banks.

This is no ordinary river. It is not fed by other
streams in the usual way. All the water flows from a
single source, which is God's sanctuary. The river is a
picture of the blessings which flow from God and give
life, fruitfulness and healing to the desert of this world.

The guide tells Ezekiel that this river flows eastwards
through the mountains to the Arabah ('the depression').
This is the Jordan Valley which runs down to the Dead
Sea.

The Dead Sea is the lowest point on the earth's
surface. Normally there is no way of escape for the fresh
water which flows into it. The water evaporates in the
desert heat, leaving an ever-increasing deposit of salt.
But the guide tells Ezekiel that this supernatural river
will turn the salt water fresh and make the Dead Sea
teem with fish.

The guide describes the paradise which the water
from the temple will create. People will stand fishing
along the shores of the Dead Sea 'from En Gedi to
En Eglaim' – a distance of eighteen miles. All kinds
of trees will grow along the river's banks – bearing fruit
continually and producing leaves for use in healing.

The water which flows from the temple reminds us of
the river which flowed from the Garden of Eden to give
life to the world (Genesis 2:10). The writer of Revelation
will also remember Ezekiel's vision, in the description of
'the river of the water of life' (Revelation 22:1–2). This
is the same supernatural river, but now flowing from the
throne of God to make his people fruitful and to give the
nations peace.

Boundaries and divisions
(47:13 – 48:29)

Ezekiel has been given a vision of a new temple. This
temple is blessed with the presence of the glory of the
Lord, and from it flows life for the world. This is the
prospect for the people of Israel when they return home
from exile. It will be like a new exodus – and a new
Promised Land.

The Lord gives instructions for the setting of the
boundaries of the land and its division between the
tribes. The first exodus was completed by Joshua's

allocation of the territory (Joshua 13–21). Now Ezekiel's book closes with a more stylized ('perfect') version.

THE BOUNDARIES OF THE LAND

Israel's northern boundary is to run to the north of Damascus, near Riblah, to the Great Sea (the Mediterranean) just north of Tyre. This is an extension of Israel's historic boundary and includes an area won by David in his conquest of the Arameans. Although it has a natural line of defence, it will prove impossible to retain (47:13–23).

The eastern boundary is to run along the line of the Jordan river, from Hauran in the south to Damascus in the north.

The southern boundary will be on a line with the 'brook of Egypt', the Wadi el-Arish, from a little below the Dead Sea to the Great Sea (the Mediterranean).

THE DISTRIBUTION OF THE TRIBES

When Joshua divided up the Promised Land between the tribes of Israel, he did so by casting lots (Joshua 18:6). Now the allocation of land is made by God's command, although the details are left to the tribes to agree between themselves (48:1–29).

The land is to be divided by a series of boundaries running from east to west. Each tribal territory is to be the same size, so that the allocation is fairer than before.

The tribes which were previously settled to the east of the River Jordan are now relocated to the west. Israel's territory is consolidated and no land is retained on the far side of the Jordan.

In the centre of the land is the special section reserved for the temple and the priests, the Levites and the prince. Seven tribes will have lands north of the central area and five will have lands to the south.

The tribe of Judah's plot is to be the closest to the temple to the north, while the tribe of Benjamin is to be closest to the south. This is a reversal of the arrangement before the exile, when Judah's land was to the south of Benjamin.

The tribe of Levi has no land, except the area adjacent to the temple. The Lord himself is their portion and inheritance. The tribe of Joseph is represented by

---

The Dead Sea is too salty to support life. In Ezekiel's vision, the river flowing from the temple brings life to the Dead Sea, growing trees on its banks and fish in its waters (47:1–23).

---

two tribes which are named after his sons, Ephraim and Manasseh (Genesis 48).

The foreigners (aliens) who live in Israel are to be treated as part of the community and allocated land by the tribes among which they live. This is the most generous treatment of foreigners in the Old Testament. It is a glimpse of the blessing and inclusion which is always God's will for them.

The central portion of land, which includes the temple, is to be an offering to the Lord. It is 25,000 cubits (seven miles) square – exactly ten times the size of the temple square. The vision of the holy city in the book of Revelation will add the same height, so that the whole place is a perfect cube – a heavenly 'holy of holies' (Revelation 21:16).

The 'new Jerusalem'
(48:30–35)

Ezekiel's vision ends with a description of the holy city. It is built on a square, with four walls and twelve gates.

Each gate is named after one of the tribes of Israel. The tribes are those which are descended from the original sons of Jacob (Genesis 29–30). Ephraim and Manasseh are assumed into their father Joseph, and Levi takes his rightful place to make the twelve.

In a vision in the book of Revelation, John will see the heavenly city with twelve gates named after the tribes of Israel, but also with twelve foundations named after the apostles of the Lamb (Revelation 21:12–14). He gives Christian completion to Ezekiel's Jewish vision. One of the names of Jesus Christ is 'Immanuel', which means 'God With Us' (Revelation 21:3).

The name of the city will be 'the Lord is there'. In Hebrew this is 'Yahweh Shammah' – words which sound like 'Jerusalem'. Ezekiel has not mentioned Jerusalem until now. It is the final glory of the holy city that God is present in her.

So Ezekiel concludes his book. For twenty-five years, Ezekiel has served as prophet and priest-in-exile to the people of Israel in Babylon.

He began with a vision of the Lord's chariot–throne, which revealed the God of Israel as supremely glorious and everywhere active.

He saw the Lord withdraw from the temple and predicted the fall and destruction of Jerusalem.

He promised the exiles that God would make a new covenant with his people, to give them a new heart and dwell with them for ever.

He received a vision of the future, with a new temple, priesthood, land and city, all reflecting and expressing God's perfect holiness.

In the dark days of exile, Ezekiel is realistic about God's judgment and certain of a future restoration for Israel. His awareness and portrayal of the glory of God is unsurpassed in the Old Testament. His prophecies and visions hold high the hope that God will one day bring all things to completion and make all things new.

Daniel

Daniel is one of the Bible's holiest and wisest men. He and his friends are Jews living in exile. As young men they are captured during an attack on Jerusalem and taken to live in Babylon. There they are educated in the pagan court of King Nebuchadnezzar, but refuse to compromise their Jewish faith.

This book tells how God protects Daniel and his friends in a series of desperate situations – including the fiery furnace and the den of lions. Just as Joseph became prime minister of Egypt, so Daniel becomes a leading figure in both the Babylonian and Persian empires.

The second part of the book describes Daniel's strange visions. They depict the rise and fall of empires – and the ultimate victory of God.

Outline

Daniel at the royal court (1:1 – 6:28)
Daniel's dreams and visions (7:1 – 12:13)

INTRODUCTION

Daniel is a strange book – a mixture of history and visions. It is very difficult to know who wrote it and when.

The 'history' part of the book describes the adventures of the young Daniel and his friends. They have been deported from Jerusalem to Babylon in 597 BC and bravely maintain their faith in the God of Israel.

However, the 'visions' in the book concern a much later situation – the revolt of the Jewish Maccabees in the second century BC. The Maccabees rebel against attempts to introduce the Greek culture and gods to Jerusalem.

Daniel's story is inspiring for everyone who wants to stand for God in a pagan society. Was the original account of Daniel's faith retold and applied to later situations? Or was it the persecution of the Jews in the time of the Maccabees which led to the writing of Daniel's story and visions?

By telling of Daniel's faith, courage and influence in the past, the Jews could make connections with their later sufferings. 'Daniel' became a legend for oppressed people in every age.

A great disaster has overtaken the people of Judah. Their capital city, Jerusalem, has been captured, and their king, Jehoiakim, has been deported. Holy treasures have been taken from the Jewish temple and devoted to the pagan gods of Babylon.

All this is devastating for the Jews. They thought their

God was all-powerful and would always protect them. It poses an enormous question: is their God in charge or not? Should they persist in worshipping the God of Israel, or should they give up and join in with the Babylonians?

We follow the story of the young man Daniel and his three friends – Hananiah, Mishael and Azariah. They are among the exiled Jews in Babylon. When they are selected for special training and privileges in the pagan court of Nebuchadnezzar, they resolve to keep faith with the God of the Jews.

Illustration from the *Bouquechardière Chronicle*. Antiochus IV Epiphanes, Seleucid king of Syria and his army before Jerusalem, as soldiers plunder the Jewish temple.

The story of Daniel came into its own during the time of the Maccabees. The Jews were then back in their own land, but dominated by the emperor Antiochus IV Epiphanes. He was determined to impose a Greek way of life on the Jews.

Between 175 and 163 BC, Antiochus Epiphanes suppressed all Jewish customs, including the circumcising of baby boys, the keeping of the sabbath as a day of rest and the reading of the Jewish law. He took over the Jerusalem temple and installed a statue of Zeus, the king of the Greek gods. In these oppressive conditions, the story of Daniel inspired the Jews to hang onto their faith in the one true God and to trust that he would rescue his people.

Persecution in the time of the Maccabees

When Alexander the Great died, his empire broke up into four main parts. Judah came to be ruled by a Hellenistic (Greek-style) king of Syria called Antiochus. He added the surname 'Epiphanes' because he claimed to be the 'epiphany' or manifestation of Zeus.

Antiochus tried to make the Jews live like Greeks. Some of the priestly class and aristocracy cooperated, but the common people rebelled. Strict Jews suffered terribly as they saw an image of Zeus set up in the temple, and pigs sacrificed on pagan altars around the country. Innocent families, who refused to defend themselves (and would certainly not fight on the Sabbath) were tortured and killed for upholding Jewish traditions.

At last the Jewish resistance found a leader in a priest named Mattathias. He and his five sons fought a guerrilla war in the hills. One of the sons was Judas 'The Hammer' Maccabeus – and their struggle became known as the Maccabean revolt.

But the Jews were divided in their approach. One group trusted solely in God to defend them. They were the Hasideans, the 'holy ones', who tried to avoid conflict by withdrawing to the desert. They were pursued and slaughtered in a sabbath-day massacre. Meanwhile, the Maccabees were more worldly wise. They realized they would have to defend themselves, however much they trusted in God and regardless of the day of the week.

The Maccabeans and the surviving Hasideans joined forces. They forced Antiochus to back down. Jewish society was once again founded on Jewish law, and the temple was restored. The rededication of the temple on 14 December 164 BC became the feast of Hanukkah in the centuries that followed.

Judas Maccabeus and his descendants became the ruling family in Judah. Their line is known as the Hasmonean dynasty. They ruled until the Roman general Pompey captured Jerusalem in 63 BC.

The Hasidean (strict Jewish) tradition continued in various forms. Some may have founded the Essene community, living in the desert by the Dead Sea at Qumran. The traces of their settlement, and their 'Dead Sea Scrolls' which survived in earthenware jars in the caves, were among the exciting finds of the 20th century.

Other Hasideans may have continued to live holy lives in the midst of Jewish society. Perhaps they became the Pharisees of Jesus' day.

Although the Hasmoneans became the ruling class, the memory of Judas Maccabeus must have inspired the Zealots, who were later to plot the overthrow of the Romans.

DISCOVERING DANIEL

Daniel at the royal court

Taking a stand over food
(1:1–21)

Daniel and his companions are plunged into the Babylonian way of life and given Babylonian names. Daniel becomes Belteshazzar. The other three become Shadrach, Meshach and Abednego. They ask to be excused the rich royal food and drink. Whether this is because the food has been prepared in pagan temples or because they are thinking of their starving compatriots, we don't know. Perhaps they want to stay physically and mentally alert to avoid temptation and compromise. In any case, to eat the royal food is to accept a close and cooperative relationship with the king. Sharing a meal is the sign of making a covenant; and this they are not prepared to do.

At the end of three years of training, and despite living only on vegetables, the young men are the brightest and fittest of their generation. They enter the king's service, where they prove wiser than all the magicians and enchanters of Babylon. Their wisdom isn't painstakingly gathered from ancient proverbs, but received directly from the living God. Daniel is particularly gifted at understanding visions and dreams.

Explaining Nebuchadnezzar's dream
(2:1–49)

One day Daniel has the opportunity to interpret King Nebuchadnezzar's dream. He does so with tact and humility towards the king, and complete trust in God to reveal the mystery.

The dream is of an enormous, dazzling statue. It's not clear whether this statue is an image of Nebuchadnezzar himself. The head is gold, the chest and arms are silver, the belly and thighs are bronze, the legs are iron and the feet are a mixture of iron and clay.

While the king watches, the statue is smashed to pieces by a rock. The rock is from God, 'cut out, but not by human hands'. After destroying the statue, the rock grows to become a mountain which fills the whole earth.

Daniel explains the dream to the king. The statue is a

model of the Babylonian kingdom and the empires which will follow. The gold head is Nebuchadnezzar. His kingdom is the first and the finest. After him come kings and kingdoms of lesser quality.

It is possible to identify the great empires which followed Babylon. The silver chest and arms are the Medes and Persians; the bronze belly and thighs are the Greeks; the iron legs are the Romans. By this interpretation, the rock is the impact of Christianity on the world – coming from God to establish his everlasting kingdom.

Whatever the details of the dream, the overall message is clear. God is in control of the rise and fall of earthly empires. All kings are under his rule and his kingdom will ultimately reign supreme.

Daniel's friends in the fiery furnace
(3:1–30)

King Nebuchadnezzar seeks to unite his people in the worship of a gold statue. The event is heralded by a big band making a mighty crescendo of sound. The penalty for disobedience is to be thrown into a furnace.

Daniel's three companions refuse to worship the statue. They decide they must make their stand against the excessive demands of the state, and they are not afraid:

> If we are thrown into the burning furnace, the God we serve is able to save us from it, and he will rescue us from your hand, O king. But even if he does not, we want you to know, O king, that we will not serve your gods or worship the image of gold you have set up (3:17–18).

Their brave stand brings to mind the witness of Peter and the apostles when the Jewish Council tries to silence them:

> We must obey God rather than any human authority (Acts 5:29).

Daniel's friends are condemned to die in the fiery furnace, but they pass through the fire unharmed. Peering into the fierce blaze, Nebuchadnezzar sees a fourth figure walking freely with them. This fourth person 'has the appearance of a god' (4:25). The king declares his faith in the God of the Jews, and promotes the friends to high positions in his government.

The pride and fall of Nebuchadnezzar
(4:1–37)

The king has another dream – this time of a great tree. The tree is huge, beautiful and fruitful – but a heavenly messenger declares it must be cut down.

Daniel, after much heart-searching, warns the king that the fate of the tree is a picture of his own future. Nebuchadnezzar's pride stands between himself and God, and he will be humbled for 'seven times' (perhaps seven years).

As the dream is fulfilled, Nebuchadnezzar becomes for a while like an animal, living in the open fields and eating grass. But in the end his sanity is restored, and he praises God.

> I... praise and exult and glorify the King of heaven, because everything he does is right and all his ways are just. And those who walk in pride he is able to humble (4:37).

The persecuted Jews of the 2nd century told this story. As they suffered terrible atrocities at the hands of Antiochus Epiphanes, the memory of Nebuchadnezzar helped to cut their oppressor down to size.

King Belshazzar's feast
(5:1–31)

We move on to another story about Daniel, and another king, Belshazzar. Belshazzar abuses the gold and silver cups from the Jerusalem temple. He calls for them to be used at a drunken feast for toasts to the gods of Babylon. This is not only a frivolous bit of fun. He is seriously mocking the God represented by the goblets, as though God is powerless and defeated.

Suddenly, at the high point of the revel, a finger appears and writes some letters on the wall. When the wise men and enchanters fail to interpret the signs, the king calls for Daniel.

Daniel reads and interprets the markings on the wall:

MENE, MENE, TEKEL, PARSIN

Mene, Tekel and Parsin are three coins: a mina, a shekel and a half-shekel. Each is smaller than the last. This alone tells Belshazzar that his kingdom is counting down to its end.

Daniel explains that each coin has a root meaning:

'Mene' means 'numbered'. The days of Belshazzar's reign are numbered.

'Tekel' means 'weighed'. Belshazzar has been weighed and found to be short in God's judgment.

'Peres' (a single parsin) means 'divided' or 'Persia'. Belshazzar's kingdom is going to be divided between the Medes and the Persians.

So God's judgment falls on Belshazzar's outrageous behaviour. That night the king is killed and Darius the Mede takes over his realm. We know nothing of Darius other than what the Bible tells us. History shows that the Medes and Persians joined forces around 500 BC and took over the old Babylonian empire. Some scholars suggest that 'Darius' may be the throne-name for the first Persian king – Cyrus.

Daniel in the den of lions
(6:1–28)

In the reign of Darius, Daniel is arrested for refusing to pray to the king. Again, there would be many parallels for the Jews of the early 2nd century BC. They were being forced to worship the image of Antiochus Epiphanes,

The Persian king, Darius, holds court before his attendants and guards in a bas relief from Persepolis.

who claimed to be Zeus in human form.

Daniel is sentenced to death in the lion's den, but God protects him by shutting the lions' mouths. King Darius, like Nebuchadnezzar before him, realizes the power and majesty of the 'God of Daniel'. Daniel's enemies have gone against the Persian policy of religious freedom by attacking him. He has done nothing wrong.

Daniel's dreams and visions

Daniel is gifted in telling people the meaning of their dreams. He also has visions of his own.

The second half of the book describes some of Daniel's extraordinary visions. This kind of writing is called 'apocalyptic' – which means that it 'reveals' what is going on behind the scenes of history. Some of Ezekiel's book is written in this way, as well as the second part of Zechariah and (in the New Testament) the book of Revelation.

Daniel's dream of four beasts
(7:1–28)

Daniel has a fantastic vision of four beasts. They emerge out of a churning sea:

- a lion with wings which walks like a human being and is given a human heart
- a bear with three ribs in its mouth
- a leopard with wings and four heads
- a nightmare creature with iron teeth and ten horns, more terrifying and destructive than the others.

While Daniel watches, a little horn emerges among the horns of the fourth creature. It uproots three of the other horns – and then starts looking around and boasting!

The vision continues with God, the Ancient of Days, taking his throne in heaven and sitting in judgment on the earth. The first three beasts are disarmed and the fourth is killed and destroyed.

Finally, someone 'like a son of man' comes with clouds of glory into the presence of God. He is given authority, glory and sovereign power. He is made king of a realm which embraces all nations and languages. His is a universal kingdom which will last for ever.

Daniel understands the vision. The beasts are kingdoms which will come and go. Perhaps they are easily recognized by their descriptions:

◆ a winged lion for Babylon and later emperors, Nebuchadnezzar and Belshazzar
◆ a voracious bear for the Medes and their king, Darius
◆ a four-headed leopard for the Persians and their emperor, Cyrus
◆ a ten-horned monster for the Greeks and their emperor, Alexander the Great.

Another theory has the bear for the empire of the Medes and Persians, the leopard for the Greek empire (which split into four, like four heads) and the ten-horned monster for the empire of Rome.

For the Jews of the 2nd century, the outrageous, boasting little horn would represent the insufferable Antiochus Epiphanes!

Daniel views the glory of God's ultimate power and judgment. God disarms the most awesome of earthly empires – and destroys their strutting despots.

The vision of 'one like a son of man' is deeply moving for both Jews and Christians. God has a special place for human beings, made in his image. The human race, the crown of his creation, will also

Part of the remains of Persepolis, with its complex of palaces, throne room and royal tombs. Created by King Darius I, it was burned down in 330 BC by the soldiers of Alexander the Great, perhaps as a reprisal for the Persian sacking of Athens, or simply as the result of a drunken party.

Daniel and Joseph

There are many similarities between the story of Daniel and the story of Joseph.

Both Joseph and Daniel find themselves, through no fault of their own, as strangers in a foreign land. Joseph is in Egypt. Daniel is in Babylon.

Both Joseph and Daniel prove their loyalty to God by their personal standards: Daniel refuses the comforts of court; Joseph refuses to sleep with his master's wife.

Both Joseph and Daniel are able, with God's help, to interpret their ruler's dream. Both are promoted to positions of power in their adopted country.

Both Joseph and Daniel suffer unjustly and almost disappear from history – Joseph in Pharaoh's prison and Daniel in the lion's den.

Both are heroes of faith: trusting God despite many setbacks and proving his guidance in all circumstances.

Father's judgment throne. It is his kingdom which will be established everywhere and for ever.

Daniel's vision of a ram and a goat
(8:1–27)

Daniel's next vision is of a ram which conquers territory in three directions. This ram is charged and swiftly overthrown by a goat with a prominent horn. But just as the goat is at the height of its power, its horn is broken off – and four other horns grow in its place.

As Daniel watches, a small horn grows from one of the four horns, and extends its power towards the 'Beautiful Land'. It causes damage in heaven and imposes its terrible power on the saints on earth.

By now we are more familiar with the imagery of Daniel's visions. The ram is the Persian empire – suddenly attacked by the Greeks under the brilliant command of their 'large horn', Alexander the Great. But Alexander is 'broken off' when he dies while still a young man. His empire is divided between his four generals – the 'four horns' that grow in the place of the large one.

One of the generals is Seleucus. He has a vast kingdom which he and his descendants (the Seleucids) rule from Antioch in Syria. One of their successors is the evil Antiochus IV Epiphanes – 'the horn which started small' but has sinister designs on the 'Beautiful Land' of Judah.

Antiochus tries to force Hellenism (the Greek way of life) on the Jews. He does so with immense cruelty, including torture and bloodshed. He desecrates the temple with pagan sacrifices and a statue of Zeus.

Daniel is given a detailed description of Antiochus. He is a master of intrigue who prospers by deceit. He has come to power by no effort of his own – that is, he has simply benefited from the victories of others.

Daniel is assured that the time of Judah's suffering is limited. All the same, he is stunned by the sheer power of evil depicted in the vision.

Daniel's prayer
(9:1–19)

Daniel may have some scriptures in mind, and in particular the prophecy of Jeremiah. The scriptures are a lifeline for the faith of the exiles. Perhaps their meetings for prayer and study (they have no temples or sacrifices in exile) are the origins of the synagogues which Jesus and Paul will know so well.

From Jeremiah's prophecy, Daniel understands that

be at the heart of his heaven. The beasts won't win!

For Christians, Jesus is the Son of man. He used the title 'Son of man', with Daniel's meaning, to describe himself. He is our perfect representative before the

A book of twos

The book of Daniel is a book of two halves. The first half deals with the experiences of Daniel as a Jew living in exile in Babylon. The second half is an account of his extraordinary visions. The stories and visions complement each other.

Daniel is also a book of two languages. The beginning and end (1:1 – 2:3 and 8:1 – 12:13) are in Hebrew, while the middle (2:4 – 7:28) is written in Aramaic.

the desolation of Jerusalem will last for seventy years. He devotes himself to pray about this. He confesses the sins of his people. He acknowledges that the Jews have deserved God's judgment. He pleads that God will forgive and restore them. His prayer is a model of intercession, like the great prayers of Moses and Nehemiah (Deuteronomy 9:25–29; Nehemiah 9:5–37).

The seventy 'sevens'
(9:20–27)

As Daniel prays about the end of the exile, the angel Gabriel comes to speak with him.

Gabriel reveals that there is a greater plan and a longer timescale than simply the restoration of Jerusalem after seventy years. He speaks of 'seventy sevens' or seventy 'weeks' of years. This means 'a very great length of time' rather than a carefully counted 490 years.

The seventy 'sevens' will give time for the rebuilding of Jerusalem, for people to put their lives in order and to await the Anointed One, their Messiah. But the Anointed One will be 'cut off', and the city and the temple will be destroyed. War and desolations will continue until the end of time. In particular, 'an abomination that causes desolation' will be set up 'on a wing of the temple' – perhaps beside the altar.

Here is a prophecy which provides a pattern for future events. The sequence will repeat in the years to come.

The first sequence will see the suffering of the Jews under Antiochus in the early second century BC.

Alexander the Great (356–325 BC) established an empire which stretched from Italy to India and included Egypt and Persia.

The second sequence will see the rejection of the Christ and the destruction of Jerusalem in the first century AD.

Jesus warns against trying to calculate the particular times and dates when God will act:

It is not for you to know the times or dates the Father has set by his own authority (Acts 1:7).

We must not make this passage a happy hunting ground for cranky theories.

At one level, Gabriel predicts the return of the Jews to their land and the rebuilding of Jerusalem. An invading ruler (Antiochus) will win cooperation from many (the Jewish priests and ruling families) for a 'seven' (seven years?). But he will cause havoc by stopping the temple sacrifices and introducing an abominable idol.

We don't know who the 'Anointed One' is in this scenario, unless it is a high priest, Onias, who is 'cut off' (perhaps murdered) by Antiochus in 170 BC.

At another level, and on a longer timescale, Gabriel makes a prediction which fits the time of Jesus. This makes sense of the 'Anointed One' (the Messiah or Christ) who will be 'cut off' (crucified). The city of Jerusalem and the temple will be destroyed – a judgment carried out by the Roman armies of Titus in AD 70.

When Jesus himself predicts this tragedy, he links it with this part of Daniel:

Coded messages and magic numbers?

Some of the book of Daniel is strange and difficult for us to understand. We are not familiar with the numbers and images which would have been like a coded message for Jewish readers.

For all we know, the creatures in the dreams may have been as easily recognized as a lion for England, or an eagle for America.

Again, it was common for names to have a number. This number was calculated by adding the values of the different letters. 'Nebuchadnezzar' is spelled differently in Daniel from other places in the Old Testament. This enables the letters to add up to 423 – the same as the total for Antiochus Epiphanes. It could be that some of what is said about Nebuchadnezzar is to encourage hope that God will overrule Antiochus.

The important thing to realize is that the 'code language' is referring to events which were taking place at the time of writing. It is not describing upheavals and cataclysms in the distant future.

*When you see the 'abomination that causes desolation'
standing where it does not belong… then let those
who are in Judea flee to the mountains (Mark 13:14).*

Daniel's vision of a man

(10:1 – 11:45)

Daniel meets a heavenly being – an angel who appears
like a glorious man. The vision is terrifying, and Daniel is
overwhelmed.

The angel has been sent in response to Daniel's
earnest prayer. The angel himself is engaged in the
spiritual war in heaven. This war is waged in parallel
with the battle between good and evil on earth. He has
been striving against the king of Persia – helped by
Michael, the guardian angel of the Jews. Angels and
human beings are involved together in a conflict which
spans earth and heaven.

In New Testament times, Paul teaches that we are in
a struggle against invisible powers of evil:

*For our struggle is not against flesh and blood, but
against the rulers, against the authorities, against the
powers of this dark world and against the spiritual
forces of evil in the heavenly realms (Ephesians 6:12).*

The ultimate battle for both earth and heaven
takes place when Jesus dies on the cross. The book
of Revelation describes how:

*The great dragon was hurled down – that ancient
serpent called the devil, or Satan, who leads the whole
world astray (Revelation 12:9).*

Michael and his angels are involved in this conflict
in heaven, as Jesus defeats the powers of darkness by his
death and resurrection on earth.

In chapter 11 the angel gives Daniel more details of
the history which has already been enacted in the visions
of the beasts.

After Alexander's death, his empire is split between
four generals. One of them, Ptolemy, becomes the ruler
of Egypt. His descendants are the Ptolemies and they are
'the kings of the South'.

Another general, Seleucus, rules Syria and Babylonia.
His descendants are the Seleucids, who are 'the kings of
the North'.

As the Seleucids rule from Antioch, they start to take
the name Antiochus. Antiochus the Great, for example,

gives his daughter in marriage to the reigning Ptolemy
in 194 BC. This is described in 11:17 and attracts our
attention because the daughter is none other than the
famous Cleopatra.

The angel's narrative gives an extraordinary
impression of human aggression and intrigue. Antiochus
IV Epiphanes appears in 11:21 and his unspeakable
treatment of the Jews is again foretold. But his time is
limited. Those who are faithful to God should resist him,
even if it costs them their lives.

The end-times

(12:1–13)

As Daniel's final vision draws to a close, he is told of the
end of the world. There will be a period of great distress,
but God's people will be delivered. Those who have died
will be raised to life and judged. The righteous will be
vindicated. The wicked will be sentenced.

There is great hope here that God will put all to
rights. There will be life beyond death and glory after
suffering. But as for the details and the timing, like
Daniel, we must wait and see.

HOSEA

Hosea is a prophet in pain. For many years he has struggled with a broken marriage. But, through his agony and anger, he has realized what love is. He has discovered the heart of God.

God tells Hosea to marry a prostitute, which he does – and they have three children. But his wife, Gomer, is never faithful for long. She leaves her husband and commits adultery with other lovers. She is exploited and abused, and eventually falls into slavery. But Hosea never stops loving her. He goes through every stage of grief and desire for revenge, to arrive at a deeply committed love for his wretched wife – and a longing to restore her.

It is through his experience of a broken heart that Hosea realizes how God must feel about his people Israel. After all, God rescued Israel from Egypt and was married to her by covenant at Sinai. But Israel has been appallingly unfaithful – wantonly chasing after other gods. Now judgment is about to fall on Israel, and she will suffer the terrible consequences of her behaviour. But God's love for her is as deep as ever, and he will rescue and restore her.

Outline

The marriages of Hosea to Gomer, and God to Israel (1:1 – 3:5)
Israel's unfaithfulness to God (4:1 – 13:16)
A message of hope for the future (14:1–9)

INTRODUCTION

The background to Hosea's prophecies

Hosea is a prophet in the northern kingdom of Israel, during the time when the nation is divided from the kingdom of Judah in the south. His name, like Joshua, means 'The Lord Saves'. From the kings mentioned in the opening verse, it seems that he preaches his message for thirty years before Israel's downfall. Only one king of Israel is mentioned (Jeroboam II), but several kings of Judah are named. This is probably because Hosea believes that the kings of Judah are the true royal line descending from the great King David.

We can date Hosea's messages to the 8th century BC, after those of Amos and before the fall of Samaria (the capital of Israel) in 722 BC. This is a period when Israel is prosperous, proud and pagan – and thoughts of God and judgment seems ridiculous. But it is because Hosea's words prove true that his prophecies are remembered and his promises treasured.

The rising superpower is Assyria. Under the command of their emperor, Tiglath-Pileser III (745–727 BC), the armies of Assyria first threaten, and then conquer, Damascus and Samaria. King Pekah of Israel tries to resist Assyria by making an alliance with Syria, but the effort is useless. This episode is described in Isaiah 7. Damascus falls in 732 BC, and part of Israel is overrun. Another of Israel's kings, Hoshea, tries to get help from Egypt, but without success. The Assyrians lay siege to Samaria for three years, and capture it in 722.

Hosea's message

God's message to Israel through Hosea is that his people are committing spiritual adultery. They are worshipping the 'Baals' – the pagan gods of Canaan. 'Baal' means 'Lord', and the gods of that name are thought to have power over rain, crops and fertility. The Baals are worshipped in blood, with animals being sacrificed and people gashing themselves. There are also festivals at which worshippers have sex with the sacred prostitutes at the Baal shrines. Hosea tells Israel (whom he often calls 'Ephraim') that God feels terrible pain and anger at this rejection. He is also exasperated that Israel has looked for help from Egypt and other alliances, instead of turning to him.

An Assyrian army lays siege to a fortified city. Attacking archers and those on the ramparts exchange fire, while other Assyrian soldiers tunnel through the wall. A relief from Nimrud (865 BC).

DISCOVERING HOSEA

The marriages of Hosea to Gomer, and God to Israel

Hosea's wife and children
(1:1–11)

When the Lord began to speak through Hosea, the Lord said to him, 'Go, take to yourself an adulterous wife and children of unfaithfulness, because the land is guilty of the vilest adultery in departing from the Lord' (1:2).

So Hosea marries Gomer, daughter of Diblaim, and she conceives and bears him a son.

God may have called Hosea to marry one of the sacred prostitutes of Baal. Certainly she is a person who has already led an immoral life. They have three children, and each is given a special name. Their first son, Jezreel, is named after the place where Jehu had broken the power of paganism in the reign of King Ahab. This is described in 2 Kings 9 and 10. Their daughter is called 'Lo-Ruhamah' which means 'Not Loved' – because God's love for his unfaithful people is now exhausted. Their third child, another son, is named 'Lo-Ammi', which means 'Not My People', and means that God is disowning Israel altogether. But, even as the Lord gives Hosea such heartless names for his children, a note of hope creeps in. There will come a day when the people of Israel will once again be called 'children of the living God'.

Israel's adultery and restoration
(2:1–23)

Now Hosea draws the parallel between his marriage to Gomer and God's marriage to Israel. Israel has enjoyed

'I will bring her into the wilderness and speak tenderly to her' (2:14). Despite Israel's unfaithfulness, the day will come when God will renew their relationship.

God's gifts of grain, wine, oil, silver and gold – and claimed they are blessings from Baal! God will punish Israel by blighting the harvest and humiliate her for her unfaithfulness.

But now comes a gentle note of longing. God will take Israel back to the desert days of their first love, and woo and win her all over again. The Valley of Achor (where Achan sinned – this story is told in Joshua 7:24–26) will become a door of hope. The marriage between God and his people will be closer, deeper and richer than ever before, drawing the whole of creation into its truth and harmony.

Hosea's reconciliation with his wife
(3:1–5)

Inspired by his vision of God's love for Israel, Hosea goes in search of his wife and brings her back from slavery. He pays the price of a slave – half in silver and half in grain. There is to be a period of waiting before they are intimate again – just as Israel will be without signs of God for a while, when she is defeated and her people dispersed. But eventually there will be a joyful reunion of husband and wife; and the people will return to God and his king. Christians see this fulfilled in the coming reign of Jesus Christ.

Israel's unfaithfulness to God

Hosea's prophecies are all against Israel (4:1 – 13:16). He condemns the lawlessness of Israelite society, with its widespread deceit, brutality and immorality. The world of nature is also suffering because of human sin. Hosea singles out the priests and condemns their corrupt leadership and influence. He criticizes the rituals at the ancient pilgrim sites of Gilgal and Bethel. The sacrifices and words of faith are just a shallow sham. He sarcastically renames Bethel ('house of God') as 'Beth Aven' ('house of wickedness'). For Hosea, a *real* knowledge of the Lord is everything. He mimics the cheap and cheerful repentance of the people, as they chirrup, 'Come, let us return to the Lord.' In God's sight their devotion is as fleeting as the morning mist. God cares nothing for sacrifices if they don't signal a changed life and a fair society.

God also looks on Israel's politics with contempt. The kings and princes are hot with wine and burning with passion and deceit. They undermine each other with intrigue and assassination. None of them turns to God for guidance or strength; and the nation appears ageing and ridiculous on the international scene. Israel is as weak and brainless as a dove as she appeals first to Egypt, then to Assyria for protection. Meanwhile God, like a mighty eagle, is about to swoop in judgment.

Hosea has a strong sense of Israel's history. He harks back to the time when Israel was newly rescued from Egypt. Then she was an exciting discovery for God – like finding grapes in the desert, or the first figs of the season. Israel was like a dear son whom God could teach to walk, guiding him with reins of love, easing his problems and stooping to feed him. But now all the youthful promise has vanished. The love of God for Israel is blighted by idolatry and made barren by disobedience.

Looking forward, Hosea sees certain disaster. Any hope of safety through military strength or political alliance will be crushed by the invading armies of Assyria. But even as God contemplates a sweeping revenge, he is moved to mercy:

> *How can I give you up, Ephraim?*
> *How can I hand you over, O Israel?...*

Israel's love for God is like an early-morning mist, or a dew that soon disappears (6:4). First light in the Tir'an Valley, near Cana, Galilee.

*for I am God and no mortal
the Holy One in your midst (11:8–9).*

Hosea recalls how God had dealt with Jacob, the cheat who became 'Israel'. After all his thrusting ambition and aggressive self-seeking, Jacob had come to terms with God at Bethel. Now Jacob's descendants must do the same. Israel has taken on the values of Canaan, whose traders are notorious cheats. Israelites are getting rich by deceit – and then being deceived by riches.

Hosea sees that God will reduce them again to the simple life of the desert, or the Feast of Tabernacles, when they live in tents. Pagan altars will become like discarded rubble, and Israel will know once more the touch of a God who really cares.

Hosea's style is quite fragmented and some of what he says is hard to understand. The places and episodes to which he refers are outside our own general knowledge. But Hosea's images are powerful and his phrases are pithy. We can at least follow his tremendous mood swings. He shows us God, sometimes burning with anger and resolving to exterminate his people once and for all:

*Like a lion I will devour them;
    a wild animal will tear them
        apart (13:8).*

But at other times, God's heart is almost breaking with longing love:

*My heart is changed within me;
    all my compassion is aroused.
I will not carry out my fierce anger (11:8–9).*

A message of hope for the future

Hosea's prophecy closes with an urgent call to Israel to return to God and seek his forgiveness (14:1–9). She must abandon all hope of help from Egypt or mercy from Assyria – and reject the gods of paganism made by human hands.

For his part, God promises a new start and a new life for Israel. She will grow beautiful and strong, famous and fragrant – a landmark, shelter and blessing to the nations of the world.

Hosea describes the people of Israel as a flock of frightened birds, not knowing which way to fly to escape disaster. God will throw his net over them and bring them down (7:11–12). A wall-painting of Egyptians netting birds in the Nile marshes, from the reign of Tuthmosis IV.

JOEL

Joel's book is small, but packed with big ideas. It is a prophecy written down as a poem. It dates from a time when Jerusalem has been all but wiped from the face of the earth, but promises that she will be rescued and renewed. She will fulfil her eternal destiny as Zion, God's city. Chapter 2 contains one of the Old Testament's most precious jewels: the prophecy that one day God's Spirit will be free for all.

Outline

A devastating plague of locusts (1:1–20)

God's judgment and mercy (2:1–32)

The nations judged and Jerusalem saved (3:1–21)

INTRODUCTION

We don't know very much about Joel. His name means 'The Lord is God' and he prophesies in Jerusalem around the year 400 BC.

The Jews have returned from exile in Babylon (538 BC). They have no king, but the national life is focused on Jerusalem. They have built a new temple under the leadership of Zerubbabel (515 BC) and rebuilt the walls under the leadership of Nehemiah (444 BC).

Joel seems particularly interested in the temple and concerned for the worship. He may have been a priest or a 'temple prophet' who worked there.

Joel declares that a terrible plague of locusts is in fact the judgment of God. He calls on God's people Israel to repent of their sins. When they do so, he promises that a long drought and dearth of the harvests will end. There will be grain and wine for the offerings in the temple once again.

Joel also has a greater message. The locusts are an image of an enemy army invading from the north. Joel sees in them a picture of the great and terrible 'Day of the Lord'. This is the time when God will judge all the nations and establish his eternal kingdom of peace with Jerusalem at its centre.

Joel's prophecy may originally have been in verse, and sung to the pilgrims in the temple. Many of his ideas and phrases are the same as older prophets, especially Ezekiel, Isaiah and Zephaniah. His phrase 'the Lord roars from Zion' is an echo of the prophecies of Amos before the destruction of Jerusalem.

DISCOVERING JOEL

A devastating plague of locusts
(1:1–20)

Joel's prophecy begins with the news of a terrible plague of locusts (1:1–20). Wave upon wave of hungry insects have swarmed over the land like a devouring army. Trees have been stripped of leaf and bark. Fields, vineyards and orchards are all ruined. Farmers and vine-growers are in despair, and the priests have nothing to offer to the Lord.

Joel, like a true prophet, calls the priests and people to turn to God. The devastation of the locusts and the effects of the drought are such that only God can help.

God's judgment and mercy
(2:1–32)

Joel sees more in this crisis than a cloud of locusts. He sees the gathering clouds of God's judgment on the world. He calls for the trumpet to sound the alarm, for here comes another invasion of locusts, even more thorough and all-consuming than the last. Darkness and fire envelop the land as millions of the horse-like creatures swarm over it, turning paradise to desert. But the most terrifying news of all is that God himself is at the head of this invincible army. This is the Day of the Lord; and he is sending a plague of locusts not on his enemies, but upon his own people!

The Lord appeals to his people through Joel. This terrible Day has not yet arrived. The nightmare has not yet become a reality. There is still time to repent and get right with God. The Lord would love to see his people turn to him, so that he can change his plan from punishment to blessing.

Joel calls for the entire community to gather for fasting and prayer. Even the very old, the very young and the newly married are to come and pray. Fasting (going without food) is a sign of utter concentration on God, and often goes with loss of appetite at times of worry or grief. The priests are to beg God to spare his people, especially as other nations will judge God by whatever happens to Israel.

Joel promises that if the people truly repent (tearing their hearts and not just their clothes), then God will sweep away the armies of locusts and restore the crops. The autumn and spring rains will bring life to pastures, trees and animals, and the joy of harvest will fill hearts and stomachs. The word Joel uses for the autumn rains can also mean 'teacher'. God is going to bless his people by teaching them his truth and guiding them in right living.

The last part of chapter 2 is so important that it forms a separate chapter in the Hebrew Bible.

God's Spirit will be given to everyone – men and women, young and old, rich and poor. The whole community will be alive to God – able to perceive his will in visions and dreams, and speak his word in prophecy. This mighty blessing of God's people will go hand in hand with a tremendous upheaval throughout creation. There will be darkness and fire, blood and smoke. And then the dreadful Day of the Lord will come. At the centre of it all, Jerusalem will be both the focus of judgment and the place of refuge.

The nations judged and Jerusalem saved
(3:1–21)

Joel now delivers God's message about the distant future. The nations who have ill-treated Israel will be summoned and judged. Joel sees this taking place in the Valley of Jehoshaphat – perhaps the Kidron Valley where armies have camped when besieging Jerusalem. Joel names some of Israel's enemies – the Phoenician and Philistine traders who have stolen the temple treasures and sold God's people to be slaves in Greece. These words help us to date Joel's prophecy to the early 4th century BC. Joel predicts that the Jews will get their revenge. This will come about when the Persian emperor Alexander captures Sidon in 345 BC and Gaza in 332 BC. The Jews will trade their captured enemies in Arab slave markets.

Joel ends by describing Zion, God's city – high and holy, safe and secure. Just as God's judgment has been described in images of war and devastation, now his blessing is pictured in terms of peace and plenty. The Lord reigns in Zion, and all is well with his people for ever.

The outpouring of God's Spirit

In the New Testament, Peter sees Joel's words being fulfilled. On the great Day of Pentecost, God pours out his Spirit on his apostles. This story is told in Acts 2. The writer of the Acts of the Apostles describes the Spirit as sounding like a violent wind and looking like flames of fire. Those who receive the Spirit are able to praise God in languages other than their own. Peter explains to the crowd that the outpouring of God's Spirit is a sign that Jesus is the Christ, and that God will judge the people who killed him.

Amos

Amos is a new kind of prophet in his day. He preaches the astounding message that God is about to destroy his own people. It may be because his words are so shocking that they are kept and written down. Amos is the first prophet to have his work recorded in a book. Amos preaches that God is the judge of all nations, including Israel. But the special relationship that exists between God and Israel doesn't mean that Israel will be spared as a favourite. On the contrary, Israel will be judged first of all – and by the highest standards.

Outline

God will judge the surrounding nations (1:1 – 2:5)
God will judge Israel, his own people (2:6 – 6:14)
Visions of doom, and a word of hope (7:1 – 9:15)

INTRODUCTION

Who is Amos?

Amos is a shepherd from the southern kingdom of Judah. His home town is Tekoa, about twelve miles south of Jerusalem. He preaches at a time when Israel is divided, with a northern kingdom of Israel and a southern kingdom of Judah, sometime around 760 BC.

Although Amos comes from the south, he does his preaching in the north – probably at the ancient shrine of Bethel. In chapter 7 we read how the priest of Bethel, Amaziah, treats Amos as a traitor and tells him to go back home. But Amos stands his ground. He explains that he never expected to be a prophet, but God called him and gave him his message for Israel.

Amos denounces society

Amos speaks to a society which is both very prosperous and very religious. Israel is wealthy during the rule of Jeroboam II, but her religion is meaningless because she is ignoring God's law.

There is a great gulf between rich and poor. Amos expresses God's anger at those who exploit and crush their fellows:

They sell the righteous for silver,
  and the needy for a pair of sandals –
they… trample the… poor into the dust of the earth,
  and push the afflicted out of the way (2:6–7).

The rich and powerful enjoy their pilgrimages and offer generous sacrifices. But God does not want offerings from people who are greedy and immoral unless they also mean to change their ways and keep his law:

I hate, I despise your festivals… (5:21).

Hate evil and love good,
  and establish justice… (5:15).

DISCOVERING AMOS

God will judge the surrounding nations

Amos begins his prophecy with a description of God roaring like a lion about to attack. The Lord is fiercely angry with each of the nations that surround his people – as well as with Judah and Israel themselves (1:1 – 2:3).

Damascus, the capital of Syria, is criticized for her aggression and cruelty. God's judgment will fall on her when she is conquered by Assyria in 732 BC.

Gaza, a Philistine city, is condemned for her pitiless slave trading. She will fall to Assyria in 734 BC. Other Philistine strongholds, *Ashdod*, *Ashkelon* and *Ekron* are also sentenced. They will be defeated by successive Assyrian emperors.

The port of *Tyre* has also been involved in slave trading, breaking every law of humanity. She will become subject to Assyria, and eventually be captured in 573 BC.

Edom, Judah's neighbour to the south, is found guilty of remorseless and uncontrolled anger. 'Teman' is Edom by another name, and Bozrah its capital.

Amman has been utterly barbaric in its treatment of pregnant women. God will avenge them with fire and storm.

Finally, *Moab* has desecrated the body of the king of Edom. Even though this action is nothing to do with Israel or Judah, it affronts God. God's moral standards apply to everyone, and he will destroy Moab's ruler in return.

All the nations, capitals and kings that Amos has mentioned are pagan. They don't acknowledge the God of Israel or observe his law. But God still holds them responsible for their actions and decides their fates.

God will judge Judah
(2:4–5)

Up to this point, the people of Israel are delighted with Amos' message. God is to judge and punish all their enemies. But now comes the shock. Amos declares God's judgment on his own people, Judah and Israel.

Judah's sins are not those of brutality or bloodshed. Her guilt lies in her rejection of God's law and her preference for worshipping pagan gods. For this she will be conquered by Nebuchadnezzar in 586 BC, and led captive to Babylon.

God will judge Israel, his own people

Sins of social injustice and pagan immorality
(2:6–16)

Israel's sins are her social injustice and her pagan immorality. Innocent people are cheated of justice when their judges take bribes:

> *They sell the righteous for silver,*
> *and the needy for a pair of sandals (2:6).*

Fathers and sons have sex with the same girls – possibly as part of the pagan fertility rites. Honour and respect has broken down in a chaos of greed and abuse.

Amos reviews Israel's history, telling it from God's point of view. God rescued his people from Egypt, gave them victory over their enemies and taught them what was holy. But Israel has behaved shamefully in return – commanding God's prophets to be quiet, and getting the Nazirites (holy ones) drunk. Now God is going to crush his people with inescapable judgment. The strongest, the fastest and the bravest will all alike be overrun.

True religion

The challenge of Amos is that our worship of God should come from our hearts and affect both our personal lives and our social structures. Beautiful music and perfect offerings are nothing without the desire to treat all people fairly and the resolve to live moral and generous lives.

If we don't offer our hearts to God when we worship him, and if we aren't determined to change our ways, then our prayers are a pretence and our lives are a lie. Amos teaches that this angers God and provokes his judgment.

Judgment to come
(3:1–15)

Amos explains that God's judgment is inevitable. The process has already begun. The lion has roared his rage and is about to attack. For Amos, the lion's roar is God's word of judgment – the message that has become his prophecy.

Amos is able to give some graphic details of the disaster to come. Israel's defences will be destroyed and ransacked. Only a few people will be spared – just as a shepherd might pick up a few remains of a lamb after a lion has mauled it. In particular, the centres of Israel's sin – the altars given to paganism and the luxury homes built on exploitation – will be razed to the ground. The 'horns of the altar' – where people would cling in prayer for help – will be cut off.

'Prepare to meet your God, O Israel'
(4:1–13)

Amos is devastating in his judgment of the well-to-do women of Samaria. He calls them cows. Their pampered lives are maintained by other people's suffering; and this offends God. God doesn't excuse their ignorance, make allowance for their feminine frailty or blame their husbands. They themselves are guilty and they will be led off to slavery.

Amos attacks popular religion. He sees the crowds of pilgrims at Bethel and Gilgal. Sacrifices are plentiful, tithes are all in order and freewill offerings are attracting widespread admiration. But Amos sees the pride and boasting that underlie the worship. The shrine is the place to be seen at, and pilgrimages have been taken over by people showing off.

While pilgrims have been pretending to worship, God himself has been attempting to get through to them. He has tried to attract their attention and prayer by sending bouts of famine and drought, crop disease and locusts, sickness and war. But, despite all their hardships, the people never search their hearts or turn to God. Now they will have to reckon with him whether they like it or not: 'Prepare to meet your God, O Israel' (4:12).

God is sick of the insincere and cynical sacrifices offered by his people. Instead he wants to see them concerned for justice and righteousness. Below, modern Samaritans offer animal sacrifices.

A lament for Israel
(5:1–27)

Amos howls a lament for the death of Israel. He forecasts that she will lose her life in battle. Her towns and villages will be decimated. But still the Lord urges her to turn to him for rescue. There is no safety in the pilgrim centres of Bethel or Gilgal – those places are defenceless and unable to help themselves. They will be ruined and their populations exiled.

Israel has destroyed God's standards – turning sweet justice sour, and throwing lofty righteousness to the ground. Now the Lord of the universe, who turns darkness to light and summons mighty floods, is going to bring down change on Israel. Again, Amos recites Israel's sins: that she has trampled the poor so that a few may live in luxury, and allowed corrupt judges to rule the law courts. Everything is fixed by bribery. And yet, if only Israel would turn to God and step into his light, it may not be too late for God to change his mind.

As for those who look forward to the Day of the Lord – they are in for a shock. They assume the Day of the Lord will be a day of glory for Israel. In fact it will be a day of darkness and dismay. God tells Israel how much he hates her phoney religion with its sham sacrifices. Her songs of praise are just a din. God wants to see justice flowing like a great river and righteousness like a stream that never runs dry. In the old days in the wilderness, Israel offered sacrifices with the love of her heart. Now she relies on politics and paganism. God will send her processing off into exile.

The complacency of Israel
(6:1–14)

Amos addresses the comfortable and complacent people of Israel. They are enjoying peace and prosperity. Their borders have been made secure by the victories of Jeroboam II, and vigorous trade has brought great wealth. But God sees only pride. Those who think they are the top nation will find themselves top of the list to be judged – and first to be sent into exile. Israel has abused God's standards – like trying to haul a plough over rocks. She has claimed God-given victories as though she had won them by her own efforts. Now God is raising up an enemy who will demolish Jeroboam's little achievements.

The affluent members of Israelite society have their complacency shattered, as they are the first to go into exile. Amos attacked the selfish lifestyle of those who 'reclined on beds inlaid with ivory', while the poor groaned under the unfairness of their lives. A winged sphinx in ivory from Fort Shalmaneser, Nimrud (9th to 8th centuries BC).

Visions of doom, and a word of hope

Visions of destruction
(7:1–17)

God shows Amos three terrible pictures of Israel's destruction. In the first, a plague of locusts strips the land bare. In the second, the land is entirely engulfed in flames. Amos cries for mercy. Like Moses before him, he begs God not to destroy his people beyond all hope of survival. The Lord hears and accepts his prayer.

But there is to be a certain judgment. In the third picture, Amos sees God holding a plumb line against Israel. The plumb line is the true standard of God's law, and it shows that Israel should be pulled down and demolished. Amos has no answer to this third vision, for the Lord is doing only what Israel deserves and has brought on herself.

The priest of Bethel, Amaziah, complains to the king

that Amos is a traitor. He objects to the forecasts that Jeroboam will be killed and Israel sentenced to exile. He tells Amos to go back to Judah and get the people there to pay for prophecies against Israel. Amos replies that he isn't a professional prophet. He was a shepherd and fruit-farmer, until God called him to prophesy. The message God gave him was specifically for Israel. If he was to obey God, he had no choice but to journey north and deliver it. Amos goes on to give Amaziah a terrible description of the fate awaiting him and his family.

Israel is ripe for judgment
(8:1–14)

The 'Sovereign Lord' (Amos' majestic, distinctive title for God) shows Amos that Israel is ripe for judgment. Just as the right time comes for harvest, so has the moment arrived when Israel's sins must be punished. She has been obsessed with materialism – squeezing trade into every possible minute, manipulating quantities and prices, and treating the poor as slaves.

But, in God's universe, everything belongs together. The land is going to rebel against the behaviour of its inhabitants. There will be a major earthquake and the sun will go into eclipse. The joy of Israel's religious celebrations will be plunged into the grief of a family funeral. Most terrible of all, there will be no word from God. When people look for guidance, they will find only silence. The dearth of the Spirit will be more dreadful and complete than any physical famine or drought.

Destruction... and restoration
(9:1–15)

The shrine is to be destroyed. Amos sees God directing the work of demolition. The people will find no escape from his anger. There is nowhere to hide from God's judgment, because he is always ahead and in complete control. He is not a local, limited god, or one of merely human origin. He is the all-powerful, ever-present, Sovereign Lord, who governs heaven and earth and directs the history of nations. Israel is to be sifted and sorted along with the rest – because she has behaved no better than they have.

But God has agreed with Amos that Israel's destruction will not be a total annihilation. One day the Lord will restore his people and renew the kingdom of David. Israel will fulfil her calling as God's first nation and other nations will join her in acknowledging the Lord. In the early years of the Christian mission, Amos'

prophecy will be quoted by James at the Council of Jerusalem. It is a mandate for including Gentiles (non-Jews) in the Christian church (Acts 15:13–19).

When God brings Israel back from exile, the whole of creation will celebrate. God will set his people in a land of peace and plenty. The God who has sworn and delivered destruction now promises a perfect future.

OBADIAH

The book of Obadiah is the smallest in the Old Testament, but it packs a very big punch. Its impact is that God will punish the nation of Edom for the part she played at the downfall of Jerusalem. Indeed, a day is coming when *all* the nations of the earth will be judged.

Outline

Judgment on Edom (vv. 1–14)

The Day of the Lord (vv. 15–21)

INTRODUCTION

The country of Edom lies south of the Dead Sea, and to the south-east of Judah. Its people are descended from Esau, just as the Israelites are descendants of Jacob. Esau and Jacob were twins. Esau was the elder brother and the rightful heir of the promises God made to his father Isaac and his grandfather Abraham. However, Esau never took God seriously. Jacob, on the other hand, was determined to supplant Esau, and succeeded in cheating him of his inheritance. The story of Esau and Jacob is told in Genesis 25–36.

Centuries later, when the Israelites asked Edom's permission to use the 'King's Highway' (the most direct route from Egypt to Canaan), they were refused. A long-running enmity was established between Israel and Edom, which features frequently in the Old Testament story. Edom becomes a typical example of people who are insensitive to God and oppose his plans.

We don't know who Obadiah was, but his name means 'Servant of the Lord'. There are other people with the same name in the Old Testament, but none of them is the author of this book.

DISCOVERING OBADIAH

Judgment on Edom
(vv. 1–14)

At the time of Obadiah's prophecy, Edom sits proud and strong in her high mountain setting. Her main cities are Bozrah and Sela (which means 'rocks'). Petra is just such a city (although built later, in the 4th century BC)·and is a favourite with tourists today. Obadiah warns Edom that nowhere is too high for God to reach. In fact Edom is about to be brought down to earth very decisively indeed. Her treasures will be ransacked, her allies will betray her, her wise people will be powerless and her warriors will be destroyed.

This catastrophe is to overtake Edom because she looked on and cheered when Jerusalem was sacked by Nebuchadnezzar in 587 BC. Family ties should have drawn Edom to help Judah, but in the event she sided with Babylon. Psalm 137 records the appalling betrayal:

> *Remember, O Lord, what the Edomites did*
> *on the day Jerusalem fell.*
> *'Tear it down,' they cried,*
> *'tear it down to its foundations!'* (Psalm 137:7).

Obadiah condemns Edom for watching while Jerusalem was looted by foreigners – the Chaldeans from Babylon. He recalls vividly Edom's shameful behaviour towards 'your brother Jacob'. Worse still, the Edomites joined in the looting, ambushed the refugees and handed over survivors to the enemy.

The Day of the Lord
(vv. 15–21)

Obadiah has a far greater vision than revenge on Edom. He opens up a vista of all that God will do, for all the nations and for the whole of time.

> *The day of the Lord is near*
> *for all nations.*
> *As you have done, it will be done to you;*
> *your deeds will return upon your own head*
> *(v. 15).*

Judgment... and salvation

Obadiah's message of judgment on Israel's enemies is only one aspect of Old Testament prophecy. There are several occasions when the prophets speak of Israel's enemies turning to God and receiving salvation. This is true of Egypt and Assyria in Isaiah's prophecy (Isaiah 19:19–25), and of Nineveh, the Assyrian capital, in the story of Jonah, the next book of the Bible.

Just as the Edomites drank themselves to a stupor when they joined in the sacking of Jerusalem, so will the nations drink God's judgment until they fall into oblivion. But at the centre, safe and strong, will be Mount Zion, God's holy city and refuge. The house of Jacob (God's people) will be fully reinstated; 'the house of Joseph' (the northern kingdom of Israel) will also be restored.

God's people will not be passive when the Day of the Lord comes. They will be like the field fires after the harvest, sweeping across the stubble of God's enemies. The godless 'house of Esau' (Edom and all who oppose God) will be utterly destroyed.

Obadiah ends his message with a description of lands being shared out and possessed as the Jewish exiles return, and other peoples move into Edom's space. Mount Zion herself will become the centre of government and justice, from which 'deliverers' (saviours) will administer God's perfect kingdom.

The mountainous landscape of Edom, near Petra (now in Jordan).

JONAH

The story of 'Jonah and the whale' is one of the favourites of the Old Testament. Certainly Jonah is the most famous of the twelve little books known as the 'Minor Prophets'. It is most likely that this is a story with a meaning (like a parable) rather than something which actually happened. Listen to it as though it is being told to you by a wonderful storyteller!

Outline

Jonah runs away from God's call (1:1–17)

Jonah's song of praise for his rescue (2:1–10)

Jonah preaches – and Nineveh repents (3:1–10)

Jonah's anger and God's mercy (4:1–11)

INTRODUCTION

God tells Jonah to go and preach to Nineveh – the capital of Israel's enemy, Assyria. Jonah refuses and takes a ship in the opposite direction. When God sends a storm, Jonah admits to the sailors that it is all his fault. To save themselves, the sailors throw him overboard. God then sends a great fish to swallow Jonah and bring him safely to land.

God repeats his command to Jonah to go and preach to Nineveh. This time Jonah obeys. The entire community repents, from king to cattle, and God spares the city. Jonah is furious! While Jonah sulks, God uses the short life and death of a plant to show how much he cares for the whole of his creation.

Is this a true story?

We know a little about Jonah from 2 Kings 14. He came from Gath Hepher in Galilee, and prophesied in the northern kingdom of Israel during the reign of Jeroboam. In the book of Jonah, he comes across as someone who understands God's mercy, but doesn't see why the heathen should be let off lightly.

It seems most likely that the story of Jonah uses this prophet as a character. It's a tall story – and a very funny one. God sends a storm, a huge fish, a fast-growing vine, a very hungry worm and a scorching wind – all to persuade Jonah first to pursue the right action and then to have the right attitude. The story is great fun and makes one of the Bible's most important points: that God loves non-Jews, and even his enemies.

God's love for everyone

It took wind and whale, vine, worm and sunstroke to persuade Jonah of God's care for Nineveh. But the message of God's love for all is one of the Bible's greatest themes. God called Abraham with a view to blessing all the nations of the world (Genesis 12:3). Elijah helped a pagan woman (1 Kings 17) and Elisha healed a foreign commander (2 Kings 5). God's people were always intended to bless others – not withdraw into a life of religious pride and exclusiveness.

In the days of the early church, Peter will have to learn the lesson of Jonah all over again. He will be called to put aside his Jewish prejudice and cross the threshold of a Gentile home. It is interesting that he has a vision of God's care for all sorts of people while he is in Joppa – the very port from which Jonah set sail. Jonah and Peter, centuries apart, were drawn to the same conclusion:

I truly understand that God shows no partiality, but in every nation anyone who fears him and does what is right is acceptable to him (Acts 10:35).

Death and resurrection

Jonah gives us one of the Bible's great images of God's power to save. Just as Joseph was rescued from prison to become prime minister, and Daniel was kept safe among lions, so Jonah is preserved in the belly of a great fish. These episodes prepare us for their greatest sequel – the resurrection of Jesus from the tomb. Jesus went down into the depths of death and experienced utter loss of God – but was raised as the ultimate proof of salvation.

DISCOVERING JONAH

Jonah runs away from God's call
(1:1–17)

This is a story of God's love and human prejudice. God wants Israel's enemies, the Assyrians of Nineveh, to hear his word. He calls his prophet Jonah to go and preach to them, but Jonah runs away. He boards a ship at Joppa – the nearest port to Jerusalem – and sails for Tarshish, which was probably in Spain.

God sends a great wind to blow up a storm, so that the sailors are in fear of their lives. The captain wakes Jonah (who is soundly asleep!) and urges him to add his god to their desperate prayers. Jonah tells the crew that there is only one God, and that the storm is overwhelming them because of Jonah's disobedience. In the end, the sailors agree to throw Jonah into the sea – and the storm abates. As the relieved sailors set about their prayers of gratitude, God sends a great fish to swallow Jonah.

Jonah's song of praise for his rescue
(2:1–10)

The fish (called a whale in some translations of the Bible) is Jonah's home for three days and nights. During this time he praises God in a psalm. God has heard his cry for help from the very depths of the sea – and saved him! At the end of his unusual voyage, Jonah is unceremoniously thrown up on a beach.

The port of Jaffa as it is today. In the story of Jonah, this is Joppa, where the prophet finds a ship which he hopes will take him to Tarshish (probably Spain or Sardinia). Jonah's aim is to evade God's command to preach to the people of Nineveh, the capital of the world's proudest and most pagan empire.

Jesus and Jonah

Jesus mentions Jonah and the meaning of his story. For Jesus, Jonah was a local hero – Gath Hepher being only an hour's walk from Nazareth. If Jonah's message was that God loved everyone and not just Jews, then this was something for which Jesus himself lived and died.

For Jesus, Jonah's experience was a vital sign. Here was someone who was buried for three days and nights, but God rescued him. Matthew's Gospel sees this as a foreshadowing of Jesus' burial in the tomb, before being raised on the third day. Jesus announced himself as 'one greater than Jonah' (Matthew 12:41). In Luke's Gospel, the 'sign of Jonah' is that Jesus, like Jonah, is calling a whole generation to repent (Luke 11:29–30).

forgive – but what about the embarrassment to his prophet who has announced destruction? Jonah is so ashamed, he wants to crawl away and die.

God asks Jonah if it is right to be so angry. Is God wrong to show mercy? Isn't it wonderful that Nineveh has repented? But Jonah sits down at a high point overlooking the city, and wills the judgment to fall.

The sun's heat is fierce. God makes a vine grow over Jonah's shelter to make him more comfortable. Jonah is pleased – until God sends a worm to destroy the vine, and steps up the heat with a scorching east wind. Jonah, who has been rescued from a watery grave, is now in danger of death by sunstroke. He is indignant that the innocent vine has died.

Gently, God speaks to Jonah. If Jonah can care so passionately for a plant – which he hasn't sown, and which has come and gone in a day – how must God feel about Nineveh? There are thousands of people in the city who are deeply ignorant of God – to say nothing of their cattle. Isn't God entirely within his rights to want to reach them – and spare them?

Jonah preaches – and Nineveh repents
(3:1–10)

Again, God tells Jonah to go and preach to Nineveh, and this time Jonah obeys. Nineveh is a huge place, which takes three days to walk around. It seems that Jonah has an impossible task, but no sooner does he start to preach than the whole city starts to repent! The king himself leads the way by wearing sackcloth, sitting in the dust and ordering a total fast. The whole community, including the animals, begs God to have mercy. God sees them and answers their prayer by sparing them from disaster.

Jonah goes overboard. From the Cervera Bible – a Portuguese illuminated manuscript from c. AD 1300.

Jonah's anger and God's mercy
(4:1–11)

Jonah is thoroughly angry at this turn of events. He tells God that he knew all along this would happen. That was why he ran away in the first place. It was so like God to

MICAH

Micah is one of the most far-sighted prophets. Living in Judah at the same time as Isaiah, Micah foresees the destruction of both the northern kingdom of Israel and the southern kingdom of Judah. But, beyond the judgment and suffering that is coming to God's people, Micah predicts a new and everlasting kingdom of peace. This will be the universal reign of God's Messiah.

Outline

God will punish Judah as well as Israel (1:1–16)

God condemns Judah's leaders (2:1 – 3:12)

God's future plans (4:1–13)

The Messiah will come to rule (5:1–15)

God states his case against Israel (6:1–16)

Present darkness and future glory (7:1–20)

INTRODUCTION

DISCOVERING MICAH

Who is Micah?

Micah comes from Moresheth, in the rural lowlands of Judah. Although younger than Isaiah, he prophesies during the same period – the reigns of Jotham (751–736 BC), Ahaz (743–728 BC) and Hezekiah (728–696 BC).

Micah foresees a terrible judgment falling on Israel and Judah. God is going to judge his people because of their idolatry and injustice. Micah sees how powerful people oppress and rob the poor (2:1–2). He also condemns the corruption of the rulers, priests and prophets in Jerusalem (3:9–11).

Micah and Isaiah are both prophesying at about the same time, and they have a similar message. However, they live in very different circumstances and speak from different backgrounds. Isaiah lives in Jerusalem and mixes with the upper class, while Micah lives in a tiny village and sees the plight of the poor in the countryside.

Micah's prophecy begins around 725 BC, when he sees that the religion and identity of God's people are collapsing. The northern kingdom of Israel will be captured and overrun by the Assyrian empire. The southern kingdom of Judah will survive for some years, but will also be judged by conquest – this time by the Babylonians. All this will be God's doing, as a punishment for worshipping other gods and abandoning the covenant promises.

But Micah, like all the great prophets, also sees beyond God's judgment. He looks forward to a future when God will restore Israel. God will make Jerusalem a centre of justice and peace which will attract the whole world to his gentle rule.

The Assyrian king Sargon II (right), conqueror of the northern kingdom of Israel. Relief from Khorsabad (c. 710 BC).

God will punish Judah as well as Israel
(1:1–16)

Micah declares that God is about to destroy both Samaria (the capital of Israel) and Jerusalem (the capital of Judah). Samaria's pagan idols and images will be smashed. The wealth which has been made from sacred prostitutes will be seized by foreign soldiers, who will in turn spend it on debauchery. All this will be fulfilled when the Assyrian armies, led by Sargon, conquer Israel in 722 BC.

Micah goes into mourning. He sees that the disastrous events will spread south to Judah and Jerusalem as well. He lists twelve towns which will be besieged and captured – and shows how their names spell out destruction. Beth Ophrah, for example, which means 'house of dust', will see her inhabitants rolling in the dust of death or grief.

Jerusalem and the southern kingdom of Judah will not in fact fall for another 150 years. Then the Assyrians under Shalmaneser V and the Chaldeans under Nebuchadnezzar will seal their fate.

God condemns Judah's leaders
(2:1 – 3:12)

CORRUPTION IN SOCIETY

Micah launches a detailed attack on people who have been seizing land, especially by deceitful means (2:1–13). This is an abuse of the Promised Land, which was carefully allocated so that everyone could share it. Now God is planning to outwit the land-grabbers and give away all their gains.

Micah also tackles the false prophets, who are

assuring people that God can never be angry with them. What about the bullying of defenceless travellers, women and children? He accuses the people of listening to anyone who will make easy promises. A prophet of 'free-drinks-all-round' would suit them fine!

But God won't leave his people leaderless and defenceless. He himself will be the shepherd who gathers the survivors after the years of destruction. He will break open the gates of their Babylonian prison, and lead them out to freedom.

CONDEMNATION OF THE LEADERS

Micah accuses those in government of behaving like cannibals (3:1–12). The very leaders who should be establishing a good and just society are attacking it and tearing it apart. There will be no help for them when they need it.

The prophets have also abused their position. Instead of preaching God's message without fear or favour, they give words of comfort to people who pay – and threaten those who don't! God is going to plunge the false prophets into darkness. They will be utterly discredited, because they will neither see God nor hear from him.

Micah, by contrast, is in a strong position – full of the Spirit of God, and able to deliver a true and clear message. To be filled with the Spirit is to be passionate for justice. Micah exposes the nation's rulers, judges, priests and prophets for what they are: violent, cruel, greedy and false. They assume God won't depose them because they are custodians of his capital city and his temple. How wrong they are! It is because of them that all will be destroyed.

God's future plans

(4:1–13)

Now Micah looks ahead to 'the last days': a golden age for Jerusalem. The terrors of the siege and destruction are long past. The Lord's temple is rebuilt, and God's mountain is raised high above all the mountains of the world.

The nations of the world will come to this mountain in a never-ending stream – knowing they will be taught God's true way of life. Zion (the name for Jerusalem as God's holy city) will be a centre of justice worldwide.

The good government of God will lead to peace, and the weapons of war will be turned into agricultural implements. A farmer works his smallholding in Sebastiye, Samaria.

O little town of Bethlehem

Bethlehem is given her ancient name, Ephrathah. The one to be born in her will spring from a most ancient line: the great King David had come from Bethlehem. Now an even greater ruler will arise, in the same tradition of godly shepherd-kingship. People throughout the world will be safe in his oversight and protection to the end of time.

Weapons of war will be converted for peaceful purposes (for too long it has been the other way round), and all military activity will cease. Everyone will have their own home, livelihood, space for prayer and peace of mind.

God promises to gather the disabled and scattered remains of his people to Mount Zion, where he will be their king for ever. The watchtower of King Jotham's day will again become a lookout point for the protection of God's people.

Meanwhile, there is terrible suffering in store for Jerusalem. She will find herself without king or counsellors and be thrown into exile in Babylon. But God will rescue her in due time. The nations which gloat over her disgrace will find themselves having to reckon with God. Israel, rescued and renewed, will be God's agent in the threshing (judgment) of the nations.

The Messiah will come to rule
(5:1–15)

Micah calls Jerusalem to prepare for a siege. This will be the arrival of Nebuchadnezzar's armies in 587 BC, which will end in the defeat and captivity of King Zedekiah.

But with the downfall of the capital comes a promise of hope. God's plan won't be ruined by the desolation of his people. At some time in the future, the greatest of all kings will be born in the small family town of Bethlehem. God will use the little and the unlikely to change the world.

When the Messiah comes, God will defend his people against enemies such as Assyria, and provide the leaders and weapons to do so. The survivors of God's people will be a great blessing to the world – like refreshing dew on parched grass. They will live among the nations – strong, vigorous and terrifying, like a young lion among sheep. They will overcome all their enemies purely in the strength of God, and without the help of military might, magic powers or pagan gods.

God states his case against Israel
(6:1–16)

God lays it on the line with his people. He rescued them from Egypt. He kept them safe on their dangerous journey through the desert. Do they still not know the kind of God he is? Do they really think he needs thousands of dead animals to keep him happy? Or child sacrifice? No! God has made himself quite clear. What he wants is simply this:

> To act justly and to love mercy
> and to walk humbly with your God (6:8).

So Micah summarizes the godly life: keeping God's law, sharing God's love and going God's way.

God speaks particularly to the northern kingdom. He has seen them getting rich by cheating – and will bring all their greedy efforts to nothing.

Present darkness and future glory
(7:1–20)

Micah weeps for Israel. She feels utterly unloved. Violence, greed and betrayal have damaged every relationship – even in the closest families and between the closest friends. The only reliable person is God. She waits for God to hear and save. Even in deep darkness, she believes her God will bring her out into the light – and wipe the sneer from the face of her enemy.

Micah looks forward to the ultimate reign of God. One day God will turn the whole situation around, and set his people at the centre of the nations and at the summit of creation. Everyone will realize the perfect character and purpose of God – that he is both angry with sin and tender with sinners. The best is yet to be!

NAHUM

Nahum declares that Nineveh is to be destroyed. Nineveh is the mighty capital of the Assyrian empire – an empire which has crushed Judah and struck terror in the heart of all the nations. Now God is going to judge Nineveh for her cruelty and bring an alliance of armies to overwhelm her. She will be wiped from the face of the earth. This is a great contrast to the message of Jonah. Both books show an important truth about God.

Outline

The Lord's anger against Nineveh (1:1–15)

The downfall of Nineveh (2:1–13)

A battle-song against Nineveh (3:1–19)

INTRODUCTION

The book of Nahum is an account of a vision. God has shown Nahum the fate that is about to befall Nineveh. We learn that Nahum is from Elkosh, which is probably a village in Judah. He writes sometime after the destruction of Thebes – the strong and beautiful city on the Nile in Egypt. This had taken place in 664–663 BC. Nineveh itself will be destroyed in 612 BC. This means that Nahum is prophesying at the same time as Jeremiah, Habakkuk and Zephaniah. Unlike the other prophets, Nahum has no charges to bring against Israel or Judah. His fire is entirely concentrated on Nineveh.

DISCOVERING NAHUM

The Lord's anger against Nineveh
(1:1–15)

Nahum begins with a poem (1:2–8). The first letters of each line spell out the Hebrew alphabet. The prophet sings of the passion and power of God. The Lord may be patient and slow to lose his temper, but once his anger is aroused, all the destructive forces of nature are at his command.

God's great wrath is to be poured out on Nineveh. She is to be judged for her deep hostility to God, and her thoroughgoing wickedness. Her allies will be rendered helpless. Her power over Judah will be broken. Her idols will be destroyed. Nahum urges Judah to praise God, as

The Assyrian monarch Ashurbanipal feasts. He destroyed the magnificent Egyptian city of Thebes, but just over fifty years later his own capital of Nineveh would suffer the same fate.

Nineveh

Nineveh is the capital city of Assyria and the centre of a great empire. As Nineveh dominates the region, she represents all that Israel dreads. She is powerful and impregnable, wealthy, pagan and cruel.

Nineveh rules supreme in the late 8th century BC. Historians have found the remains of the emperors' palaces (one with a famous library), the fine temple to Ishtar (goddess of love and war) and massive fortifications.

There are two different approaches to Nineveh in the prophecies of Israel. Nahum declares God's judgment on her tyranny, but Jonah realizes God's mercy towards her people (and animals). In fact the two views don't conflict. What we are discovering is that God cares deeply about the behaviour of all nations, and longs that all should repent and turn to him (Jonah 4:11).

though the runner has already arrived with the news that Nineveh is no more.

The downfall of Nineveh
(2:1–13)

Nahum tells Nineveh to defend herself. We know with hindsight that her attackers were an alliance of Medes, Scythians and Chaldeans. Nahum sees in vivid detail the red shields and cloaks of the Medes, the flashing armour and the forest of spears. Although Nineveh's commander tries to deploy his defenders, the invaders open the sluices controlling the river, and flood the city. Great buildings have their foundations swept away. The palace collapses.

Nahum sees Nineveh, too, as a pool being drained. Her pride, strength and wealth are ebbing away in the slaughter of her people and the plunder of her treasures. Nineveh which had been like a lion's den – secure in its strength and a breeding place of violence – now lies destroyed. And it is the Lord who has brought about her downfall.

A battle-song against Nineveh
(3:1–19)

Nahum chants a battle-song against Nineveh. She is a 'city of blood' – built on slaughter and maintained by stolen wealth. Now she will get the treatment she has handed out to others. The prophet describes her as a prostitute, devoted to paganism and witchcraft, now exposed, stripped and humiliated before the eyes of the world.

If Nineveh doubts that all this can happen, she has only to remember the fate of Thebes. Thebes had been the pride of Upper Egypt. Today the sites of Karnak and Luxor show something of her beauty and power. She was particularly well protected, by the water surrounding her and the political alliances she had forged with her neighbours (to us, Libya and Somalia). Yet she fell to the forces of Ashurbanipal in 663 BC, as the people of Nineveh knew only too well. Some of them had been serving in the victorious Assyrian forces. Now it is Nineveh's turn. Her defences are weak. Her troops are soft. She is ripe for picking. The merchants and administrators who have swarmed in Nineveh like locusts in winter are about to vanish in a moment.

Nahum keeps his final word for the king of Assyria. His leaders are asleep. They no longer care. His people are dispersed. The damage is final and irreversible. Nineveh has at last suffered the fate she so richly deserved.

HABAKKUK

Habakkuk dares to ask God some blunt questions. If God is completely good and totally powerful, why isn't he answering all the cries for help? How can God use evil to carry out his judgments?

Habakkuk sees the corruption and lawlessness of Israel's society, and longs that God will establish his reign of justice. However, the prophet realizes that God is going to use a Babylonian (Chaldean) invasion to discipline Israel. This is a strange and awesome development, because the Babylonians are even worse than the Israelites!

Habakkuk's questions are resolved when he has a vision of God as a warrior of overwhelming glory, conquering all before him. The Lord is king of all the nations, and his judgments will bring about salvation. Like Job, Habakkuk comes to see his little situation in the vast context of God's majesty and purpose.

Outline

Habakkuk questions God (1:1–17)

Babylon is doomed (2:1–20)

God is supreme (3:1–19)

INTRODUCTION

Habakkuk is a prophet who is probably based in Jerusalem at the same time as Jeremiah. Part of his message (chapter 3) is set out as a song, with instructions for the way it is to be sung in the temple. The name Habakkuk may come from the Hebrew for 'hug' or 'hang on tightly'. Certainly, he hangs onto God in this prophecy.

Habakkuk prophesies at a time when the armies of Babylon are invading Palestine. His work is different from that of the other prophets, in that it is entirely addressed to God. When will God intervene to punish oppression and expose idolatry? Why is he delaying his promised kingdom?

God reveals to Habakkuk that he is rousing the Babylonians to wreak his judgment on Judah. It is an astonishing turn of events.

Habakkuk stations himself before God like a watchman (2:1), to await his word. He is rewarded with the assurance that God is working out his purpose. It may seem slow from a human point of view, but it will surely come about.

Habakkuk arrives at a position of settled faith. Whatever happens, God is Lord. There may be total destruction in earthly terms, but with God there is perfect salvation. This realization gives Habakkuk a surge of confidence and praise.

DISCOVERING HABAKKUK

Habakkuk questions God
(1:1–17)

Habakkuk asks God his first big question: 'How long must I call for help but you don't listen?' There is so much evil going on, with no one able to do anything to stop it. So why doesn't God get involved?

God replies that he is about to do something quite extraordinary. He is bringing in the armies of Babylon – the strongest, cruellest and most unscrupulous force on earth. A self-made people who worship their creator.

Judah is a little nation, tossed on the waves of great empires. The empires rising and falling at this time are Assyria, Babylon and Egypt. As Habakkuk writes, Babylon is rising. Her armies are on the march. She has defeated the Assyrians – destroying Nineveh in 612 BC. A few years after this, in 608 BC, Judah is defeated by Egypt at the battle of Megiddo. Pharaoh Neco, the Egyptian king, kills Josiah the king of Judah and appoints his own rulers.

But Babylon is far stronger than Egypt. Nebuchadnezzar defeats Pharaoh Neco at the battle of Carchemish in 605 BC. After twenty years of threat and fear, Babylon will also defeat Judah – and carry her population into captivity in 586 BC.

Habakkuk asks a second question. How can God possibly use the forces of evil to carry out his holy judgments? How can he watch people being treated like fish in a net? Especially when those who gleefully catch the fish not only live in luxury, but worship the net that gives them success.

Babylon is doomed
(2:1–20)

Habakkuk insists on waiting for God's reply. God doesn't give him a straight answer, but tells him to write down a revelation on tablets of clay. This is a message which is to be kept and passed on – which will prove to be right in the end.

God reveals the truth about the Babylonians. They are proud, misguided – and doomed. They will get rich for a while by plundering other nations – but the time will come when they themselves will be ransacked. Crime and bloodshed are no way to establish a society, and God will bring their achievements to nothing.

Meanwhile, the right way to live is by faith in God.

The earth will be filled with the knowledge of the glory of the Lord, as the waters cover the sea (2:14).

Judah is to be destroyed by the Babylonians, a people far more vile and violent than Israel has become. But God will ensure that the Babylonians will themselves be judged and their conquests and achievements brought to nothing. In the end, the world will not be the domain of any human empire, but of the glorious kingdom of God.

Habakkuk chants five warnings against those who steal and murder. God will see to it that they get exactly what they deserve. The warnings seem to apply to individuals as well as nations. They seem to apply especially to Babylon:

♦ Those who have got rich by plunder will be plundered themselves.
♦ Those who have built on the profits of crime will find their very houses giving evidence against them.

Habakkuk has absolute confidence in the sovereignty of God. Not even crop failure and famine will prevent him from rejoicing in his Saviour.

♦ Nothing will last which is built by violence. God will use it for matchwood – and put a sea of justice in its place.
♦ Those who have brought about the shame of others will find that it's their own turn to be disgraced.
♦ Those who make idols are trusting in objects of wood and stone which are powerless to give teaching or guidance.

Talking of the silence of dumb idols, Habakkuk urges the whole earth to keep silence in the holy presence of God.

God is supreme
(3:1–19)

Habakkuk offers a prayer, which is a poem or psalm of great power and beauty. The word 'shigionoth' may come from a Hebrew word meaning 'to wander' – so perhaps he hopes the musicians will improvise.

Like Job before him, Habakkuk's questions have led him to a new view of God. He praises the Lord who brought Israel from the south (Teman is Edom) and gave them the law in Sinai (the region of Mount Paran). God's majesty covers both heaven and earth. He can use all the forces of nature to deliver his judgments, making the sea roar or the sun stand still. He is ready, willing and able to defeat his enemies and deliver his people.

Habakkuk is left shaken and speechless by this awesome revelation of God. God is God and he will save! When and where and how he does it is entirely up to him. Habakkuk realizes he can wait for God. He isn't anxious any more. Food and wine don't matter now that his gladness comes from God.

With this glorious perspective, Habakkuk feels totally renewed and refreshed. He could jump a mountain for joy!

'The righteous will live by their faith'

The message of Habakkuk is that the right way to live is by faith in God (2:4). The future doesn't lie with the passing empires of this world, but with the glory of God. Lasting victory isn't won by armed strength – or even by religion. The victory is God's, and he will share it with his faithful people. Those who serve God now are on the right track, because knowing God is the only thing that will survive in the end. In centuries to come, Paul will quote this saying, 'The righteous will live by their faith,' in two of his letters – to the Romans and the Galatians.

ZEPHANIAH

Like the other prophets, Zephaniah preaches both judgment and hope. Most of his book declares God's certain punishment. But he also promises that God's people will emerge from their days of darkness and scattering.

Zephaniah foresees that God is going to judge not only Judah but all the nations of the world. This is 'the Day of the Lord', and it is approaching fast (1:14). But Zephaniah calls on those who are humble to do what is right and so escape destruction (2:3). In fact, there is the hope that God's judgment will lead to a change and transformation for many peoples (3:9).

Zephaniah's insights link the messages of all the prophets, before, during and after the destruction of Jerusalem and the exile in Babylon. He sees that God's judgment, though terrible, is part of his great salvation.

Outline

God's judgment of the whole world, especially Judah and Jerusalem (1:1–18)

God's judgment of the nations around Judah (2:1–15)

The fate of the present Jerusalem and the vision of a delightful future (3:1–20)

INTRODUCTION

Zephaniah is a young prophet who preaches during the reign of a young king, Josiah. Josiah came to the throne of Judah in 640 BC and reigned for thirty-one years.

The voice of prophecy has been silent for some seventy years – since the days of Isaiah and Micah. Despite the terrible fate of Samaria in 722 BC, the people of Judah have steeped themselves in paganism. King Manasseh has ignored his father Hezekiah's godly example and reverted to the Baal-worship of his grandfather Ahaz. Manasseh's long, evil and violent reign (696–642 BC) has seen Judah following Assyrian practices of nature-worship and astrology. Nature-worship has involved the gross immorality of fertility rites and bloodshed. Astrology has bred widespread superstition and fear.

Now Zephaniah steps forward to be the herald of the new age of King Josiah's reforms. These reforms take place in 621 BC. Josiah's reforms are described in 2 Kings 22–23. Unfortunately they are too little and too late to avert God's judgment.

Zephaniah is the first of the generation of prophets which will include Jeremiah, Habakkuk, Obadiah and Ezekiel. These are the men who will not only proclaim God's judgment on Judah and Jerusalem, but also be caught up in it themselves. Some of them will live right through the disaster as God's representatives and commentators, announcing and interpreting events.

We are told more than usual about Zephaniah's family line. If his father Cushi was a Cushite (Ethiopian), it may have been important to emphasize his true Jewish pedigree. On the other hand, his great-great-grandfather may have been Hezekiah the king.

DISCOVERING ZEPHANIAH

God's judgment of the whole world, especially Judah and Jerusalem
(1:1–18)

Zephaniah, speaking for God, proclaims a great and worldwide destruction. This will be focused particularly on Judah and her capital Jerusalem.

God will destroy the priests and people who are worshipping the Canaanite god Baal, the god Molech (the Ammonite god Milcom, favoured by some of King Solomon's wives) and the sun, moon and stars. The priests have been mixing pagan worship with the worship of the Lord. The royal court has been mixing the Hebrew way of life with foreign dress and superstitions. All this has obscured the truth about God and muddied the purity of his people. Zephaniah calls for absolute silence, as God approaches the very moment of judgment.

Zephaniah shows his local knowledge as he describes God striking the areas of Jerusalem where the traders operate and where the smart people live. The self-sufficient merchants and self-satisfied homeowners will find their wealth swept away. Those who think God won't touch them will be forced to think again.

Zephaniah describes the Day of the Lord. It is approaching rapidly, plunging the world into darkness and war. People will wander in a state of shock, until they are cut down and destroyed. No amount of wealth will protect them when God's jealous rage sweeps in like fire.

'The Day of the Lord' is the day when God will be roused thoroughly and finally to judge the world. The prophets are convinced that the day will come when God can no longer endure the wickedness of the nations or the unfaithfulness of his own people. On that day his love, hatred of evil, and zeal for justice will boil over in wrath. It will be a day of cosmic upheaval, natural disasters, darkness, despair and death.

God's judgment of the nations around Judah
(2:1–15)

Zephaniah calls everyone to gather together and surrender to God. The only glimmer of hope is that God

Lightning strikes

Zephaniah may have the image of a Scythian raid in his mind as he describes the swift, merciless attack of God's Judgment Day. The Scythians were warlike nomads who fought with the Assyrians against the Medes. With their swift horses they could make lightning strikes even as far south as Egypt. Although the Scythians never attacked Jerusalem, the idea of their ruthless power and surprising speed colours Zephaniah's description of God's judgment. The actual destruction of Jerusalem, when it came, was by the Babylonians in 587 BC.

will see their humility and obedience and have mercy.

Zephaniah predicts the fate of the nearby nations. To the west, towards the coast, are the cities of the Philistines – Gaza, Ashkelon, Ashdod and Ekron. They are strong communities, thriving on trade. But Zephaniah warns that God will destroy them, leaving them deserted and in ruins. The coastal plain will become pasture for the sheep of Judah – a glimpse of a future for God's people after the coming crisis.

Moab and Ammon lie to the east of Judah. They are twin nations descended from Lot. They have long despised Judah, and God has been particularly offended by their arrogance and paganism. Now God solemnly declares that he will treat them like Sodom and Gomorrah – inflicting on them the judgment Lot escaped.

Cush is the name for Ethiopia, which is to the far south of Judah. It may be Zephaniah's way of referring to Egypt, which had Ethiopian kings between 715 and 663 BC. He forecasts that God will destroy this southern power – a prediction which may have been fulfilled by Nebuchadnezzar's invasion of Egypt in 568 BC.

Lastly, Zephaniah declares the fate of Assyria and her capital Nineveh. As he speaks, she dominates the international scene with invincible power and legendary cruelty. For half a century she has demanded and received tribute from Judah as the price of peace. She thinks she is God, but Zephaniah proclaims her destruction. Nineveh will become a rubble-strewn ruin, inhabited only by wildlife.

The fate of the present Jerusalem and the vision of a delightful future
(3:1–20)

Zephaniah proclaims, 'Woe to the city of oppressors.' This is almost certainly Jerusalem. He sees that she has no relationship with God, except to resist him. Officials, rulers, prophets and priests are all unworthy of their high calling. But God hasn't changed. His presence and standards have remained steadfast. His judgments of other nations have been intended as a warning to his own people; but Judah has taken no notice.

God declares that time is running out. The day is coming when he will gather the nations and destroy them. Here Zephaniah looks beyond the events of history to the Judgment Day of God.

Zephaniah goes on to describe the world that God will bring in after the fires of judgment. There will be a new unity in God's service, with people coming from as far away as Egypt to worship him. Those who were proud and hostile to God will have been weeded out. The people who remain will be those who are humble and truthful; and they will be able to live in peace.

Zephaniah calls God's people to sing for joy at the prospect of God's reign. Punishment and fear will become things of the past, as God rescues his people from shame, handicap and exile. Israel will know herself truly secure and loved by God, and honoured by all the nations of the world.

HAGGAI

Haggai is a prophet who urges Judah's leaders to rebuild the temple. The people have returned to Jerusalem after the years of exile in Babylon. They have restored their own houses, but the temple is still a ruin. Haggai explains to them that their failure to put God first is resulting in famine and poverty. His message is well received, and a temple is quickly built. Haggai is one of the few prophets who lives to see his words fulfilled.

Outline

God calls his people to build the temple and they obey (1:1–15)

Words of encouragement, teaching and promise (2:1–23)

INTRODUCTION

A call to build the house of the Lord

Haggai dates his messages quite specifically. They are given to him by God between 29 August and 19 November 520 BC. As he calculates his dates by the reign of King Darius I, we realize that Judah is now just a small province in the great Persian empire.

Persia has replaced Babylon as the superpower. Darius I is Emperor Hystaspes of Persia, who reigned from 522–486 BC. It was one of his predecessors, Cyrus, who had given permission for the Jews to return to their land, in 536 BC, and allowed them to govern themselves once more.

In Cyrus' time there had been plans to rebuild the temple, but the work had lapsed. Persia was distracted by its own leadership struggle, which was eventually won by Darius. The Jews were harassed by their Samaritan neighbours and impoverished by poor harvests. People decided to look after themselves and establish their own homes, rather than face the task of rebuilding the temple.

At the time of Haggai, Judah is part of the Persian empire. Haggai's prophecies are delivered during the early years of the reign of King Darius I. It was Darius who began the building of a magnificent new capital at Persepolis, which was eventually destroyed by the army of Alexander the Great. This artist's impression shows a reconstruction of the royal palace at Persepolis.

DISCOVERING HAGGAI

God calls his people to build the temple and they obey

(1:1–15)

Haggai's first message is for Zerubbabel and Joshua. Zerubbabel is the governor of Judah, and Joshua is the high priest's son.

Zerubbabel is a descendant of King David, grandson of Jehoiachin (the last king of Judah) and heir of the royal line. His name means 'seed of Babylon'. He and Joshua had returned from exile with the first group, led by Sheshbazzar, in 537 BC. It was Zerubbabel and Joshua who had organized the laying of the temple foundations, but the work has been at a standstill for sixteen years. (This episode is narrated in Ezra 3.)

Haggai's message contrasts the fine new houses with the state of the temple. People have proudly panelled the walls of their homes, but have neglected to bring timber for the Lord's house. They have excused themselves by saying it isn't the right time.

Haggai calls them to review their way of life. Times are hard. People don't have enough to eat and drink. Their clothes don't keep them warm. Their money goes nowhere… He explains that all this is happening because they have neglected God's house. Worship and lifestyle go together. It *is* the time to build the temple!

Zerubbabel, Joshua and all the people are inspired by God's word to them through Haggai. The work on the temple begins.

Words of encouragement, teaching and promise
(2:1–23)

GOD WILL GLORIFY THE NEW TEMPLE

The work has been going on for a month, when God's word comes to Haggai again. This time it is to encourage the builders. They may feel that their effort is poor when compared with the splendid temple of Solomon. But God is with them. The point of the temple is not human fame, but God's glory. God intends to make this house a focus of his glory for all nations. He will fill it with his presence and peace (2:1–9).

A NEW START

Two months later, Haggai has a particular question for the priests. Does touching something holy make a person holy? Obviously the answer is, 'No.' In the same way, building the temple won't in itself change the people's lives. If they don't mend their ways, they will still be diseased by sin.

Haggai reminds the people of the shortages which prompted them to listen to the Lord, and resulted in the new work on the temple. From this point on, God promises to bless them (2:10–19).

A MESSAGE FOR ZERUBBABEL

On the same day, Haggai has a special word for Zerubbabel (2:20–23). God is going to cause havoc among nations and between peoples. In this upheaval, Zerubbabel will emerge as God's chosen servant and leader.

History doesn't tell us Zerubbabel's fate, but here is God's endorsement of the royal line which will lead on down the centuries – to Jesus Christ.

Three months in the light of eternity

Haggai's recorded ministry spans only three months of 520 BC, but his words break a lethargy which has lasted sixteen years. The prophet has a remarkable ministry of challenge and encouragement.

Haggai urges the people building the temple to see its long-term significance. It isn't just for the prestige of the nation, but for the glory of God. It won't matter that the new temple isn't as impressive as Solomon's. The important thing is that God himself will bring splendour to the building, because it is his house (2:6–9).

ZECHARIAH

Zechariah serves us a spicy mixture of visions and prophecies. Some of his messages are flavoured with the work and words of earlier prophets. Some of his images are new – unique and vivid. They will take their place in the prophetic tradition until the end of time. Jesus and the Gospels will draw on his insights, and his visions will become the mighty vistas of the book of Revelation.

We know very little about Zechariah. His name is a common one, meaning 'The Lord Remembers'. He prophesies in Jerusalem at about the same time as Haggai – both of them urging the national leaders to complete the rebuilding of the temple.

Outline

Visions to challenge and encourage (1:1 – 8:23)
Prophecies of judgment and restoration (9:1 – 14:21)

INTRODUCTION

The setting of Zechariah's prophecies

The Persian emperor, Cyrus the Great, has conquered Babylon. He has passed a decree in the very first year of his reign, allowing all Babylon's captives to return home. He has even encouraged nations to rebuild their temples and restore their gods. No returning group can have been more delighted with their new-found political and religious freedom than the Jews.

Zerubbabel, the living heir of David, has led the return. The foundations of the temple have been laid, but the work has come to a standstill. Perhaps people can already see that the new temple will never compare with the glory of the one built by Solomon. But Zechariah prophesies that God will be the glory of his restored temple.

We know little about Zechariah, but his prophecies are dated around the same time as those of Haggai. He begins in 'the second year of Darius of Persia' (520 BC) and continues for four years. Like Haggai, he encourages the community of returned exiles as they try to rebuild their ruined lives. He draws on the themes of David's kingship and the divine purpose for Jerusalem (to become the heavenly Zion) from before the days of the exile in Babylon.

Some people think that Zechariah's later prophecies (9:1 – 14:21) have been developed by other people. They continue his themes but have material which could refer to a later time, personalities or situations.

A book of two parts

Zechariah's book is in two parts. Chapters 1–8 are an account of the 'night visions' he received between 520 and 518 BC. Chapters 9–14 are prophecies of God's judgment and his coming kingdom. Although the book of Zechariah is in two distinct halves, it has always been treated as a whole. Although the style changes, the messages belong together and match each other. All the same, some of the ideas are very jumbled and obscure. It is quite possible that Zechariah didn't understand them all himself. Many of them make better sense once Jesus appears on the scene; and who knows what others will become clear in due course?

DISCOVERING ZECHARIAH

Visions to challenge and encourage

A call to return to the Lord
(1:1–6)

Zechariah dates his prophecy in 'the eighth month of the second year of Darius'. Darius I is the Persian emperor who reigned from 522 to 486 BC. In our terms, Zechariah is receiving God's word in October or November 520 BC. His message fits between two of Haggai's prophecies (Haggai 2), both in date and content.

Zechariah and Haggai are prophesying in the same place and at the same time. They also strike the same note of urgency. It is now eighteen years since the Jews returned from their exile in Babylon, and time to press on and complete the rebuilding of the temple.

Zechariah begins by calling the people to return to the Lord. They must learn from the mistakes of the past and not repeat the damaging disobedience of their ancestors.

Eight visions
(1:7 – 6:8)

Zechariah has visions of Zion being restored and the king who is to come. He has eight 'night visions'. The first three are about the renewal of Jerusalem. The next five are about the Messiah. Zechariah is wide awake and able to ask questions. An angel acts as his guide and interpreter.

THE FIRST VISION: THE MAN AMONG THE MYRTLE TREES

Zechariah sees a man on a red horse, standing among myrtle trees in a ravine (1:7–17). Behind him are other horses of various colours. Coloured horses appear again in Revelation 6. Red stands for the blood of war; white is for victory and peace; brown, like churned-up mud, is the colour of unsettled times.

The rider of the horse reports to an angel that they have completed a survey of the world and found everywhere at peace. God is now extending this peace to Jerusalem, giving time and opportunity for the city to be restored and the temple rebuilt.

The temple is completed quickly, over a period of

four years. It doesn't compare well with Solomon's temple which it replaces. The walls of Jerusalem will be rebuilt by Nehemiah in 445 BC. Zechariah proclaims an age of prosperity, which will come about in the reigns of the Maccabean princes in 165 BC. The ultimate peace and glory of Zion is still in the future.

THE SECOND VISION: FOUR HORNS AND FOUR SKILLED WORKERS

Zechariah sees four horns and four skilled workers (1:18–21). The four horns are the powers which destroyed Israel, Judah and Jerusalem. They could stand for Assyria, Babylon, Medo-Persia and Greece; or they may symbolize the four directions from which an attack might come. The four skilled workers are God's workers (perhaps temple builders) who will now overcome the forces of ruin with the power of peaceful construction.

THE THIRD VISION: A MAN WITH A MEASURING LINE

Zechariah sees an angel tell a young man not to measure Jerusalem for rebuilding (2:1–13). The new city is to be far greater than the old, and God himself will be its protector and its glory. The Lord calls any stragglers to escape from Babylon and come into the safety of Zion. The vision breaks into a song of joy as God declares that he will draw many nations to be his people, and will himself live among them. God through his Messiah is going to make Jerusalem his centre and Judah his holy land.

THE FOURTH VISION: CLEAN GARMENTS FOR THE HIGH PRIEST

Zechariah sees Joshua, the high priest (3:1–10) He is standing, grimy and guilty, before God. Satan, whose name means 'accuser', is about to present the case for the prosecution, but God interrupts. God declares that he has rescued Joshua from the fires of judgment and is now restoring him as high priest. He forgives Joshua's sin and commands that he be dressed in clean and splendid robes. God tells Joshua that he and his fellow priests are signs of the Messiah, who is the great priest-king to come. The Messiah is 'the branch' of King David's family tree. He is like a jewel that shines in every direction, with seven eyes which see everywhere. Through his Messiah, God will achieve a perfect cleansing of his people, to bring in an age of human dignity, social harmony and universal peace. The name 'Joshua' is the Hebrew for 'Jesus' and means 'God Rescues'.

THE FIFTH VISION: THE GOLD LAMPSTAND AND THE TWO OLIVE TREES

Zechariah is woken up to see a gold lampstand with seven lights on it (4:1–14). The lampstand is a symbol of God's people, holding high his light to the world. There was a lampstand in the tabernacle in the days of Moses, and there were ten lampstands in the temple of Solomon. In the rebuilt temple of Zechariah's day there will be only one.

Zechariah sees that the lampstand is fuelled by oil from two olive trees, one on each side. God is supplying power without the help of either priest or manufacturer. Zechariah is to encourage Zerubbabel to complete the rebuilding of the temple which he began several years ago, and to do so with God's help. The two trees are symbols of Joshua and Zerubbabel, priest and king. They are 'the two who are anointed'. Together they are a sign of the Messiah (the Anointed One) whom God will one day introduce as his supreme priest-king.

THE SIXTH VISION: THE FLYING SCROLL

Zechariah sees God's missile – his powerful word, like a huge flying scroll (5:1–4). This is God's notice, served on every thief and liar. It has power to lodge in the house of an offender and completely destroy it.

THE SEVENTH VISION: THE WOMAN IN A BASKET

Zechariah sees a woman being kept in a large basket (5:5–11). She is wickedness. The prophet watches as she is airlifted off to Babylon. So evil is to be expelled from Israel, and sent where all rebels against God belong. Babylon is called Shinar in Genesis 11. It is where the people so proudly erected the tower of Babel. Wickedness is honoured there, and they will build the woman a house.

THE EIGHTH VISION: FOUR CHARIOTS

Zechariah sees four chariots emerging from between two bronze mountains (6:1–8). The chariots are drawn by powerful horses – red, black, white and dappled. The angel explains that they are God's horses, going north, west and south. There is no mention of the white horse going east as we might expect. The mission of the chariots is to establish God's peace throughout the world. A particular triumph is that God's Spirit is now satisfied in 'the north country' – the lands of the great invading empires are now brought under God's control.

A crown for Joshua

(6:9–15)

Zechariah is told to crown the high priest, Joshua. He is to do this in a private house, in the presence of three witnesses. The witnesses are all returned exiles. Their wealth is to be used to make the crown.

Joshua is to be told that he is the branch – the one who is to branch out, build the temple and be enthroned as a royal priest. Isaiah and Jeremiah have already used 'the branch' as a prophetic code name for the expected Messiah.

Joshua is to be a symbol of the Messiah. His crown is to be entrusted to the witnesses and placed in the temple. So Zechariah understands that the returning exiles have a key role in the unfolding of God's plans. We don't know why it isn't Zerubbabel, the rightful descendant of David, who is to be crowned. Perhaps the emphasis is on God's appointment rather than on human succession.

Motives behind fasting

(7:1–14)

The next part of the book of Zechariah is a record of encounters and teaching which take place two years after the night visions. The date is December to January 518 BC.

A deputation comes from Bethel to ask about fasting. They ask if they should still keep the fast of the fifth month, which remembers the destruction of the temple in 586 BC.

The Lord urges Zechariah to probe the motives behind fasting and feasting. Are fasts and feasts held in honour of God, or have they become an occasion for people to show off? Zechariah must think again about the reasons for God's judgment on his people, which led to the destruction of the temple. If people refuse to listen to God, then they must realize that one day he will refuse to listen to them.

God promises peace for Jerusalem

(8:1–23)

God promises peace for Jerusalem. The scattered exiles will come to live there in great contentment. Meanwhile, the temple must be rebuilt, and people must start to deal truthfully and fairly with each other. The old fasts are to be turned into joyful feasts. People from other nations will come to Jerusalem to find God, because they have heard he is there. The earthly Jerusalem is being transformed into the heavenly Zion.

In 8:23 Christians have glimpsed the Greeks who came

The 'branch'

Zechariah sees that God is preparing the world for the coming Messiah. One day the Messiah's kingdom will extend to all nations and to the whole of creation. God is preparing Jerusalem and her people to be the focal point of this earthly rule – a kingdom of justice and peace.

The Messiah will emerge from the family tree of David. For this reason, Zechariah calls him the 'branch' (6:12). He will be the perfect combination of priest and king, and will care for God's people as an ideal shepherd. The early Christians found many images of Jesus in Zechariah's words: his birth, ministry, lifestyle, kingship and death are all foreshadowed here. Jesus himself will take up the strange, vivid pictures which Zechariah uses to describe the awesome and awful events at the end of the age.

and asked the disciple Philip if they could be introduced to Jesus (John 12:20–21). Zechariah prophesies that one day large numbers of Gentiles will ask the Jews to lead them in God's ways.

Prophecies of judgment and restoration

Destruction of Israel's enemies and the arrival of Zion's king

(9:1–17)

God declares that he will overthrow the cities of the Philistines, which have so long been Israel's enemies. Alexander the Great will conquer this area in 332 BC,

and the Philistines will disappear from history. In fact they will merge with the Jews, and Palestine will be named after them.

Zechariah proclaims the arrival of Zion's king. He echoes the joy of Zephaniah's prophecy in 630 BC. The true heir of David approaches in peace. Instead of a mighty warhorse, he rides a gentle donkey. God will do away with the weapons of war and establish a worldwide kingdom of peace. Some scholars think this is a description of the great Jewish champion, Judas Maccabeus. Christians follow John's Gospel in seeing here Jesus the Messiah, riding humbly into Jerusalem as its true king (John 12:14–15). The chapter closes with

God giving his people victory over all their enemies, making them as safe as his flock and as delightful as his jewels.

At ease in Zion. Zechariah sees a time of security when elderly people will sit peacefully in the streets of Jerusalem once again.

The Lord will return to Jerusalem, and it will be his dwelling place. The city will be attacked by surrounding nations, but the Lord will defend it and confuse its enemies.

Restoration of Judah
(10:1–12)

Zechariah turns again to the present plight of the Jews. They are defeated and demoralized – the victims of strong enemies and weak leaders. But God is going to rescue them. He will take over as their leader and transform their morale. He will gather them in from their places of exile – Egypt, Assyria, Gilead and Lebanon. It will be like the exodus from Egypt all over again, as Israel and Judah are reunited and brought triumphantly home.

The rejection of the shepherd
(11:1–17)

Zechariah announces a coming judgment. It will sweep in like fire. It will destroy like an axe. He hears the shepherds wailing. They are the corrupt rulers who now see their power and privilege vanishing.

God gives Zechariah a heartbreaking task. He is to care for a flock which is not only doomed to die, but is resentful of his control. He calls his shepherd's staffs Favour and Union – but snaps them to demonstrate God's frustration. Favour (the covenant between God and his people) is broken. Union, (the family bond between Israel and Judah) is destroyed. Zechariah is paid thirty pieces of silver for his pains – which he throws down in the temple.

There is a medley of gospel themes here. One day Jesus will come as the good shepherd, challenging all phoney, careless and oppressive leaders. Tragically, he will be rejected by the very people he has come to save. When Judas betrays Jesus to his enemies, he will be paid a familiar sum: thirty pieces of silver.

God tells Zechariah to act out the part of a selfish and lazy shepherd – and to feel God's fury that his people are so exploited and neglected.

Military triumph and spiritual renewal
(12:1–14)

After the searing warnings of judgment come further words of hope. God declares that when the nations of the world are finally gathered to attack Jerusalem, he will confuse and break them. He will make Jerusalem impregnable, and her leaders unbeatable. Every citizen will be at least as great as David.

Spiritual renewal will go hand in hand with military triumph. God will give his people a new desire and ability to pray. They will grieve deeply for the hurt they have caused, especially to God or his servant. Zechariah sees them looking at someone they have killed unjustly – an echo of

Isaiah's suffering servant, and a prediction of the crucifixion of Jesus. Everyone will be united in mourning: families, clans and individuals; royalty, prophets and priests. We read of the suffering servant in Isaiah 52–53.

Cleansing from sin
(13:1–9)

After victory and repentance, God will enable his people to stay pure. Zechariah says they will be given a fountain which will wash away sin. Idols will be abolished and false prophets will be disciplined and reformed. When former prophets are asked about the scars where they once cut themselves, they are to say they are the marks of childhood accidents.

The idea of being hurt by friends leads on to the next prophecy. God's shepherd is to be killed by someone close to him. The flock will be scattered, and two-thirds of it lost. But God will gather the part of the flock that remains, and make it supremely valuable. God and his people will be proud of each other.

God comes and reigns
(14:1–21)

Zechariah has more to say about Jerusalem's victory over her enemies. At first the other nations will crush her, halving her population and wrecking her property. But God will arrive to defend his people, and open up a valley for their escape. This is a new exodus – this time through solid rock!

Zechariah describes a new, unique and everlasting day: a mode of existence in which God is king. The light and the climate will be perfect. Jerusalem will be a source of life for the world, as fresh water flows from her to east and west. God will reign over a perfect world – a world in which he is acknowledged as the only God. Jerusalem will be raised high above the surrounding plain, and her people will live in safety.

Zechariah closes by seeing the Feast of Tabernacles as a harvest festival of nations. God's enemies will be left to their fate like rotting crops. Those who gather to God will find themselves at peace with his creation. Every detail of every day, from the bells on the horses to the pots on the hearth, will express the holiness of God.

MALACHI

Malachi stands like a beacon at the end of the Old Testament. He shines for God's truth at a dreary and dispirited time in Israel's history. Although the Jews have returned from exile and the temple has been rebuilt, there is a strong drift away from God.

Outline

God's love for his people (1:1–5)

Israel's indifference to God (1:6–14)

A last warning for the priests (2:1–9)

God cannot bear unfaithfulness (2:10–16)

Judgment will be hot for the wicked! (3:1–5)

Test God by tithing (3:6–12)

The fickle and the faithful (3:13–18)

The Day of the Lord (4:1–6)

INTRODUCTION

'My messenger'

'Malachi' means simply 'my messenger'. We don't know for sure if Malachi is the name of the prophet who delivered these messages. We have no other example of Malachi being used as a person's name.

Half-hearted worship

The temple has been rebuilt for some time and the worship has become half-hearted. The priests are setting a bad example by offering second-rate sacrifices. The Jewish men are marrying outside the faith – mixing their pure religion with the more exciting aspects of paganism. There is a rising divorce rate, as first marriages are abandoned. God's people have lost their enthusiasm and their nerve. They are not sure that serving God is worthwhile, as proud, ungodly people seem to get on much better without him. As this was the situation in the fifth century BC, at about the time of Nehemiah's reforms, we may date Malachi at about 460 BC.

God complains that the priests are treating him with contempt. Instead of offering him the best of the flock for sacrifice, they are bringing him animals that are blind, crippled or diseased.

DISCOVERING MALACHI

God's love for his people
(1:1–5)

Malachi begins by telling people that God loves them. If they doubt it, they have only to look at the fate of Edom. The Edomites are Israel's neighbours to the south. They are the descendants of Esau. The enmity between the two peoples dates back to the rift between Esau and Jacob in the distant past.

The Edomites were obstructive to the children of Israel when they were making their desert journey from Egypt to Canaan. Most recently, the Edomites have taken advantage of Israel's weakness and joined in the looting when Jerusalem and Judah were overthrown. Now Edom has herself been finally defeated, and her towns will never be rebuilt. Israel, on the other hand, has been amazingly restored – brought back from exile in Babylon, and encouraged to occupy her land again and rebuild her temple. This, says Malachi, is the clearest possible proof of God's love.

Israel's indifference to God
(1:6–14)

But if God is proving his fatherly love for Israel, Israel isn't showing anything like a child's love for God. The priests are bringing disabled and diseased animals to the altar. They wouldn't dream of offering such gifts to an

The whole nation is under a curse. They have withheld from God the honour that is due to him. God challenges them to bring in their tithes, to offer him a tenth of all that the land produces. In return, he will protect their crops from disease, and give them harvests so plentiful that they will be unable to store all the goods.

earthly governor. Some people are promising a good animal and then swapping it for a reject. The prophet says it would be more honouring to God to close the temple altogether. The Lord will look to other nations and other places for pure and wholehearted worship.

A last warning for the priests
(2:1–9)

Malachi has a direct warning for the priests. God will embarrass them by withdrawing his support from their work. He will turn their blessings to curses. He will humiliate them by smearing their faces with offal. They must return to God's standard – the standard set by their ancestor Levi. Levi was the son of Jacob whose descendants were set aside to be a tribe of priests. Levi not only had great reverence for God, but he taught God's truth faithfully, and set an example by his own way of life.

Malachi foretells 'the Day of the Lord'. God's consuming fire will sweep through the land, destroying the wicked and releasing the innocent from oppression.

Malachi outlines a high standard for what the priest is to be and do. He is far more than a caretaker for the temple or an expert in sacrifices. He is to be nothing less than God's messenger.

God cannot bear unfaithfulness
(2:10–16)

It isn't just the priests who are at fault. The people, too, have betrayed God. Men are rejecting wives of the same race and faith, and marrying pagan women – no doubt hoping to combine the best of the different religions. They still make sacrifices to the Lord and swear their devotion to him. This is an awful confusion of God's standards. God himself is unswervingly faithful to his covenant. He wants his people to live to the same high level of commitment in their marriages, and to raise godly children. He states clearly: 'I hate divorce.' To tear a marriage apart is an act of violence.

Malachi tells people that they have tired the Lord with their special pleading – their arguments by which they turn truth on its head to justify their actions.

'Put me to the test!'

God calls on his people to pay their full tithes, to provide for the work of the temple and the support of the priests. The tithe is an ancient tax, based on the idea that everything comes from God and a tenth is offered back to him.

Now the tithe has become neglected, because people feel they are poor and need the money for themselves. But God challenges them to 'put him to the test' – that is, to take the risk of giving a tenth of income or produce to him (3:10). He promises that he will respond with an overflowing blessing. It is impossible to out-give God!

When Jesus is tempted by Satan, he reminds the devil that we should not put God to the test (Luke 4:12). In saying this he is quoting from the law of Moses (Deuteronomy 6:16). Satan challenges Jesus to test God for reasons of doubt; but God invites his people to test him out of faith.

Judgment will be hot for the wicked!
(3:1–5)

Those who long for the Lord to appear in his temple are in for a surprise. He will indeed arrive – suddenly – and they will feel the heat of his holiness. He will be like a furnace, or like a caustic cleanser. He will begin with the priests and make them pure for their holy tasks. Witchcraft and adultery, lying, bullying and injustice will all be purged.

But God will not destroy his people. He never has done and he never will. His way is to cleanse them with the utmost care and at whatever cost to himself.

Test God by tithing
(3:6–12)

At present, people are robbing God. They are failing to offer their tithes. A tithe is 10 per cent of a harvest or a wage which is given to God, to provide for the priests and the upkeep of the temple. Through Malachi, God invites people to test him – to bring in their tithes, and to discover that God will deluge them with blessings. In particular, God will protect their crops from disease and give them abundant harvests.

The fickle and the faithful
(3:13–18)

But people have lost heart. They can't see God, and they can't see the point of taking him seriously. God's law seems to crush all joy out of life, while the proud and assertive go from strength to strength.

But a group of faithful people get together. They compare notes. They resolve to commit themselves wholeheartedly to God. God records their names and their resolutions on a scroll and swears he will stand by them and prove them to be true.

The Day of the Lord
(4:1–6)

Malachi warns that a day is coming, when evil will be destroyed like stubble in a field fire after the harvest has been gathered in. But for those who are faithful to God, there will be the warm sunshine of his deliverance. They will be like calves let out of their cramping stalls to leap in the open pasture in spring. The wicked will be like ash under their feet.

Finally, Israel will do well to remember God's law – the law he gave to Moses. In due course, a prophet like Elijah will come – calling future generations to respect and love each other. If they fail to do this, the land will fall under God's curse.

Many Jews expect Elijah to return before the Messiah himself will appear. Jesus explains that this is fulfilled in John the Baptist, who faithfully announces the kingdom of God and prepares the way for the king (Matthew 11:14). If John is 'Elijah', then who is Jesus?

THE DEUTERO-CANONICAL BOOKS

There are fifteen books or parts of books in the Deuterocanonical Books or 'Apocrypha'. They form a separate section in Protestant Bibles (usually between the Old and New Testaments) and take their place among the Old Testament books in Roman Catholic Bibles.

In AD 382, the great scholar Jerome started work on a complete Latin translation of the Bible – the 'Vulgate'. In doing so, he decided to reject the Old Testament books whose original texts were only found in Greek. He described such books as 'apocryphal' (from a Greek word meaning 'hidden things'), although they had never in fact been hidden or secret.

The books of the Apocrypha are also known as the 'Deuterocanonical Books'. They form a 'second division' of sacred texts in the Bible, being written later than the 'canonical' books of the Old Testament and before the

The Books of the Apocrypha

Tobit
Judith
The Greek Additions to the Book of Esther
The Wisdom of Solomon
Ecclesiasticus (Wisdom of Jesus Son of Sirach)
Baruch
   The Letter of Jeremiah
1 Esdras
2 Esdras
The Additions to the Book of Daniel
   The Prayer of Azariah and the
      Song of the Three Young Men
   Susanna
   Bel and the Dragon
1 Maccabees
2 Maccabees
3 Maccabees
4 Maccabees
The Prayer of Manasseh
Psalm 151

books of the New Testament. They give valuable information about politics and religion at a time when the Jews were under extreme pressure to conform to Hellenistic (Greek) culture. These years shaped the nation of Israel into which Jesus was born.

Martin Luther (from about 1520) decided that 'apocryphal' books should be published as a separate section in Protestant Bibles. The Church of England today accepts them for public reading, but does not draw on them in formulating the church's official teaching.

Tobit is a romantic adventure story about faithful Jews living in the 'Diaspora'. When Jewish communities were 'dispersed' around the ancient world (after the Assyrian and Babylonian conquests) they began to think seriously about their distinctive religion, laws and moral values.

Tobit lives in exile in Nineveh – although the historical and geographical 'facts' are for effect rather than information! He becomes blind and sinks into poverty because he kindly buries the corpse of an executed Jew. Thanks to his brave son Tobias (who is helped by the angel Raphael, disguised as Azariah), Tobit eventually recovers both his sight and his fortune.

Tobit's relative, Sarah, is a virtuous and prayerful young woman. She has married seven times, but each husband has been killed by a jealous demon called Asmodeus. Tobias is again the hero as he overcomes the demon and marries Sarah.

Tobit reminds us of the suffering and vindication of Job. Suffering is a test and righteousness will result in prosperity. The Jews are encouraged to trust God and their own best efforts for a good and successful life.

Judith is a beautiful and devout Jewish widow, who delivers her people from invasion by seducing and assassinating an enemy commander. The historical and geographical details are wildly inaccurate, and Judith's behaviour is sensational. She becomes a liar and a murderer in the just cause of defending her people.

The Greek Additions to the Book of Esther seem to have been introduced to make the Hebrew original more 'religious'. After all, the book of Esther in Hebrew, which may date from the fifth century BC, doesn't mention God at all! The later material portrays God as more active – and the Jews as more racist.

The Wisdom of Solomon was probably written by a Greek-speaking Jewish scholar in Alexandria. It is certainly not the work of the wise King Solomon, but a much later work which attempts to relate Greek and

Jewish lines of thought. The book shows that the Jews have an attractive and coherent alternative to the learned and secular culture in which they have to live. The great questions of 'wisdom' literature are explored: why do the godless prosper and the righteous suffer; will those who are faithful receive justice; and is there a hope of life after death?

> *The souls of the righteous are in the hands of God,*
> *and no torment will ever touch them.*
> *In the eyes of the foolish they seemed to have died,*
> *and their departure was thought to be a disaster,*
> *and their going from us to be their destruction;*
> *but they are at peace (Wisdom 3:1–3).*

Ecclesiasticus or the **Wisdom of Jesus Son of Sirach** is the longest portion of 'wisdom' literature in the Bible. It is very like the book of Proverbs and is written by the person named in the title. His grandson translated the work into Greek, and its Latin title Ecclesiasticus

may indicate that it was used in churches but not synagogues.

Baruch is a collection of several short pieces, all on the theme of the fall of Jerusalem in 587 BC.

The Letter of Jeremiah (Baruch 6:1–73) denounces the foolishness of idolatry.

1 Esdras is an alternative version of the Hebrew book of Ezra. It includes a short extract from 2 Chronicles at the beginning and from Nehemiah at the end.

2 Esdras is an 'apocalyptic' work featuring supernatural revelations. It is different from the other books of the Apocrypha in that it was written later and includes Christian material.

The Additions to the Book of Daniel include **The Prayer of Azariah and the Song of the Three Young Men**, and the stories of **Susanna** and **Bel and the Dragon** (or snake). They are all additions that appear in the Greek text of the book of Daniel. The Prayer and the Song are liturgical hymns, while the stories are popular tales in which Daniel is the hero.

These writings encourage the Jews to remain faithful to their religion, despite the pressures and attractions of the Greek (Hellenistic) culture which is being imposed upon them by Antiochus IV Epiphanes.

The Books of the Maccabees are all independent of each other. 1 and 2 Maccabees record the Maccabean rebellion, while 3 Maccabees is a historical novel about it, and 4 Maccabees is a discussion of reason, which arises out of the martyrdom of the Maccabean rebels.

The Prayer of Manasseh is a short and beautiful confession. It has been composed by someone to supply the words of the prayer of King Manasseh which is mentioned in 2 Chronicles 33:11–13.

Psalm 151 celebrates the young shepherd David's victory over the Philistine giant Goliath. It is included at the end of the Psalms in the Greek Bible.

The Maccabean rebellion

From 200 BC onwards, Judah was dominated by the Seleucid empire, whose emperors raided the temple for money and accepted bribes from those Jews who wanted to become high priests. Two such candidates, Jason and his rival Menelaus, set out to turn Jerusalem into a Hellenistic (Greek-style) city-state.

In 167 BC the emperor Antiochus 'Epiphanes' 'tried to compel the Jews to forsake the laws of their ancestors and no longer live by the laws of God, and also to pollute the temple in Jerusalem and call it the temple of Olympian Zeus' (2 Maccabees 6:1–2). The statue of Zeus was the 'desolating sacrilege' which he commanded to be erected on the temple altar (1 Maccabees 1:54).

The rebellion against these attempts to erase the Jewish culture and nationhood was led by Judas, called 'Maccabeus' ('the Hammer'), and his son Jonathan. After several victories in Judah, Judas occupied the temple area, purged it of non-Jewish worship and rededicated it in December of 164 BC. This was the institution of the Jewish festival of Hanukkah.

Rome

Puteoli

Tyrrhenian Sea

MACEDONIA

Berea   Philippi
         Thessaloni

SICILY   Rhegium

Syracuse

Corinth
ACHAIA   Athe

MALTA

Mediterranean Sea

CRET

THE NEW TESTAMENT

Troas

ASIA

Pergamum

Smyrna

Thyatira

Ephesus

Sardis

Philadelphia

Miletus

Laodicea

Colosse

GALATIA

Antioch

PISIDIA

Iconium

Lystra

Attalia

Derbe

CAPPADOCIA

CILICIA and SYRIA

Antioch

Palmyra

CYPRUS

Salamis

Paphos

Damascus

Tyre

Caesarea

Jerusalem

Alexandria

EGYPT

Nabatean Kingdom

Memphis

Petra

MATTHEW

Matthew's Gospel is the first of the four Gospels we have collected in the New Testament.

Matthew tells the whole story of Jesus, from his remarkable birth in Bethlehem to his death and resurrection in Jerusalem. He includes Jesus' baptism and temptation, his preaching and teaching in Galilee, and many of his parables about the kingdom of God.

This Gospel is a bridge between the Old and New Testaments. Matthew shows how Jesus fulfils Old Testament prophecies, and that his church is the fulfilment of the history of Israel.

Matthew writes for Jewish Christians. He tells them that Jesus had Jewish roots. He also wrestles with the problem that the Jews have rejected Jesus as their Messiah, and now persecute his followers.

Matthew's Gospel is useful for teaching new Christians and instructing Christian leaders. It has five clear sections of teaching, including the famous Sermon on the Mount. It shows how Christians should understand the Jewish law and live out the heart of its meaning.

Finally, Matthew gives a clear call to Christian mission. Jesus, the risen Christ, sends his disciples to preach his gospel and make disciples among all the nations of the world.

Outline

The birth and early life of Jesus (1:1 – 2:23)

The list of Jesus' ancestors (1:1–17)

Jesus is born in Bethlehem (1:18 – 2:23)

Jesus' baptism and temptation (3:1 – 4:11)

The preaching of John the Baptist (3:1–12)

Jesus is baptized by John (3:13–17)

Jesus is tempted by the devil (4:1–11)

Jesus in Galilee (4:12 – 16:20)

Jesus moves to Capernaum and starts to preach (4:12–17)

The calling of the first disciples (4:18–22)

The kingdom comes to Galilee (4:23–25)

The Sermon on the Mount (5:1 – 7:29)

Jesus performs many miracles (8:1 – 9:34)

Engaging in mission (9:35 – 12:50)

Jesus teaches in parables (13:1–52)

Mixed opinions about Jesus (13:53 – 16:20)

Insights for the disciples (16:21 – 17:27)

Jesus predicts his death (16:21–28)

A glimpse of glory (17:1–13)

A lack of faith (17:14–23)

The temple tax (17:24–27)

Caring for one another (18:1–35)

The greatest in the kingdom (18:1–9)

The parable of the lost sheep: our true value (18:10–14)

Dealing with sin (18:15–20)

The importance of forgiveness (18:21–35)

Jesus in Judea (19:1 – 25:46)

Towards Jerusalem (19:1 – 20:34)

Jesus arrives in Jerusalem (21:1–22)

A war of words (21:23 – 23:39)

Jesus predicts the future (24:1 – 25:46)

The final week (26:1–56)

The plot against Jesus (26:1–5)

Jesus is anointed at Bethany (26:6–13)

Judas turns traitor (26:14–16)

The Last Supper (26:17–30)

Jesus predicts that Peter will deny him (26:31–35)

Jesus prays at Gethsemane (26:36–46)

Jesus is arrested (26:47–56)

The trial and death of Jesus (26:57 – 27:66)

Jesus is tried by the Jewish Council (26:57–68)

Peter fails badly (26:69–75)

Jesus is taken to the Roman governor (27:1–2)

Judas hangs himself (27:3–10)

Jesus and Pilate (27:11–26)

A mock coronation (27:27 31)

Jesus is crucified (27:32–44)

Jesus dies (27:45–56)

Jesus is buried (27:57–61)

The tomb is guarded (27:62–66)

The resurrection and mission of Jesus (28:1–20)

Empty tomb and risen Lord (28:1–10)

An attempt to conceal the truth (28:11–15)

The great commission (28:16–20)

INTRODUCTION

Good news for Jews

Matthew is a Jewish Christian, and he writes his Gospel for people like himself. He begins in a very Jewish way, by tracing the family line of Jesus all the way from Abraham, the founder of the nation, to David, its greatest king, and then down to Joseph, the husband of Mary and human father of Jesus.

Matthew says Jesus is 'one of us'. But he is also a Saviour and king for the whole world. At the beginning of his Gospel, Matthew tells how Magi (astrologers) come from distant lands to worship the infant Jesus. He closes his Gospel with Jesus' open-ended command to preach the good news to all the nations of the earth.

One of Matthew's favourite titles for Jesus is 'Son of David'. Jesus is the true heir to David and the rightful king of Israel. Those who believe in Jesus truly belong to Israel and are citizens of the kingdom of heaven. Matthew is the only Gospel writer to use the term 'ecclesia' – the Greek word for 'church'. It means 'called-out' and was used in the Old Testament to describe Israel as God's people.

Matthew assumes his readers know about Jewish tradition and customs, and the meanings of Hebrew words. He passes on Jesus' teaching on matters which will interest them – fasting, divorce, keeping the sabbath day, providing for parents and paying the temple tax. He helps them see the old Jewish law in the new light of Christ.

Matthew is sensitive to Jewish issues, but tough on Jewish leaders. He records Jesus' fury with the scribes and Pharisees. The scribes write out copies of the law and the Pharisees try to live it in perfect detail. But between them they make God's truth too complicated for the ordinary person. Instead of making plain the way to life, they strew the path with legal traps and burden the people with guilt.

The teaching of Jesus

Matthew gives his Gospel a clear shape. He gathers the teaching of Jesus into five main sections, and writes in patterns and rhythms that make it easy to remember. Even today, we know Matthew's version of the Lord's Prayer better than Luke's. We know Matthew's 'Sermon on the Mount' better than Luke's 'Sermon on the Plain'. This means Matthew's Gospel is especially useful for teachers, and for people who are new to the Christian faith.

Matthew also includes some harder teaching. He records what Jesus said about discipline, forgiveness and future judgment. This makes Matthew an important book for church leaders.

The five sections of teaching are:

- The Sermon on the Mount (5:1 – 7:29): how to live the Christian life.
- Instruction for the twelve disciples (10:1–42): how to approach mission and deal with persecution.
- Teaching about the kingdom of heaven (13:1–58): parables which give pictures of God at work.
- Training in right attitudes (18:1–35): caring for the weak and forgiving the wrong.
- Information for the future (24:1 – 25:46): the destruction of Jerusalem and the judgment of Christ.

The Sermon on the Mount and the Sermon on the Plain

Luke's 'Sermon on the Plain' is much shorter than Matthew's 'Sermon on the Mount'. Both begin with the Beatitudes or 'blessings' and end with the parable of the two houses. Almost all of what Luke has to say can also be found in Matthew. Probably Luke is using the material known as 'Q', while Matthew is adding other teachings of Jesus as well.

In both sermons, Jesus is describing a new way of life. He is reversing the values of the world, so that poor is rich and rich is poor; happy is sad and sad is happy; the hungry will be filled and the full will go hungry.

Matthew makes it clear that Jesus is talking spiritually. 'Hungry' means 'hungry for God'; 'sad' means 'grieving over the state of the world'. But Luke keeps it simple. Poor means poor and hungry means hungry!

A focus on mission

Matthew has a special focus on mission. He recalls that Jesus, in his earthly life, had to concentrate on the Jews. Luke's Gospel opens the door to all kinds of 'outsiders', but Matthew forbids even taking the good news to Samaritans (10:5). But Matthew knows that 'Jews first' is not the end of the story. The climax of his Gospel is that Jesus sends his disciples to preach to the whole world. The Jewish monopoly of God's truth is at an end. The Christian gospel is for all people everywhere and for all time (28:16–20).

Matthew and the other Gospels

Matthew is the first book in the New Testament because it makes so many connections with the Old Testament. It forms a bridge between the old and the new: between prophecy and fulfilment, between the law and the gospel, and between Israel and the church.

Although Matthew's Gospel comes first in the New Testament, it is not the first to be written. Matthew clearly has the shorter Gospel of Mark beside him as he writes. He also has some extra sayings of Jesus, which aren't in Mark – but can often be found in Luke.

Papias, a historian writing in AD 130, says, 'Matthew collected the sayings in the Hebrew language.' This collection of sayings may be a missing document which scholars call 'Q'. 'Q' is short for 'Quelle', the German word for 'source'. It could be the inclusion of Matthew's collection of sayings which has led to the whole Gospel being given his name.

Matthew and the Old Testament prophecies

Matthew wants to show his Jewish readers that their scriptures have come true. To do this, he quotes the messages of the Old Testament prophets – always in a form close to the original Hebrew – and declares, 'All this took place to fulfil what the Lord had said through the prophet.' He quotes five prophecies in the early chapters.

MATTHEW 1:23

Jesus is a male child, born of a young woman. Matthew shows that Isaiah had prophesied this would happen: 'The virgin will be with child and will give birth to a son, and they will call him "Immanuel" – which means, "God with us"' (Isaiah 7:14).

MATTHEW 2:6

Micah foretold that the little town of Bethlehem would be the birthplace of the Messiah (Micah 5:2).

MATTHEW 2:15

Hosea recalled that God would rescue his son (the people of Israel) from Egypt. Matthew sees this event repeated when Jesus returns safely from Egypt as a child refugee (Hosea 11:1).

MATTHEW 2:18

Jeremiah foresees the grief of the mother at the slaughter of her children. Matthew links this with Herod's massacre of the innocent babies of Bethlehem (Jeremiah 31:15).

MATTHEW 2:23

Jesus is dismissed by the Jewish leaders as an uneducated preacher from Nazareth – an insignificant northern town. There is no Old Testament prophecy which says, 'He will be called a Nazarene,' but prophets were often rejected for their lack of education or suitable background. The story of Samson being dedicated as a Na*zirite* is a completely different idea which isn't anything to do with Nazareth (Judges 13:5).

By linking the Old Testament prophecies with Gospel events, Matthew shows how the scriptures point to Christ. Some of Matthew's connections may seem far-fetched to us, but the Jews are used to reading scripture in this imaginative way.

Matthew finds other Old Testament echoes:

◆ The light of God's salvation will shine in the heathen lands of the Gentiles (Matthew 4:15–16 and Isaiah 9:1–2).
◆ Jesus is the faithful 'suffering' servant described by Isaiah. He gives healing to others by his own selfless sacrifice (Matthew 8:7 and Isaiah 53:4).
◆ Jesus uses parables – everyday stories and pictures – to give delightful insights into the ways and workings of God (Matthew 12:18–21 and Isaiah 42:1–4).
◆ The prophet Zechariah had promised that God's king would arrive in Jerusalem one day – not clad in armour and mounted on a warhorse, but meekly riding a donkey (Matthew 21:5 and Zechariah 9:9).
◆ Matthew shows how thirty pieces of silver is the age-old price of betrayal – and links it with the history of the potter's field. The potter's field was bought by Jeremiah as a sign of hope that God would rescue his people and restore their land (Matthew 27:9 and Zechariah 11:12–13; Jeremiah 19:1–13; 32:6–9).

Mediterranean Sea

Tyre

Caesarea Philippi

GALILEE

Ptolemais

Chorazin

Capernaum

Bethsaida

Cana

Sea of
Galilee

Sepphoris

Tiberias

Nazareth

Gadara

Nain

THE GREAT PLAIN

Caesarea

Salim

River Jordan

Sebaste

SAMARIA

Sychar

Gerasa

Antipatris

PEREA

Joppa

Lydda

Bethel

Jericho

Jerusalem

JUDEA

Bethany

Qumran

Bethlehem

WILDERNESS OF JUDEA

Hebron

Machaerus

Gaza

Dead
Sea

IDUMEA

Map: Israel in New Testament times.

Judgment

Another of Matthew's major themes is God's judgment. He writes of judgment on individuals, on the Jewish leaders and on the church.

Matthew teaches that God will judge all human beings at the end of time. Those who are righteous will be welcomed into the kingdom of heaven. Those who are wicked will be sentenced to eternal punishment.

Matthew describes the Last Judgment in the parable of the sheep and the goats. On Judgment Day Jesus, the Son of man, will be the judge. He will separate the righteous from the wicked like a shepherd sorting sheep from goats. But how will he decide which is which?

Jesus says that those who meet human need are in fact caring for him. Those who ignore human need are in fact neglecting him. Both the righteous and the wicked will be surprised at his judgment. They have no idea that their everyday behaviour has such an eternal consequence.

Matthew also warns that God will judge the Jewish leaders. The parable of the tenants is about humans rejecting God's authority. The tenants of a vineyard are like the rulers of Israel. They rebel against the landowner (God) by ill-treating his messengers (the prophets) and even killing his son (Jesus). What can God do but give his kingdom to others – 'to a people who will produce the proper fruits' (21:43)?

Finally, in the parable of the wedding banquet, Jesus warns Christians to remember their salvation. Like guests wearing wedding clothes, they are dressed in the righteousness of Christ. His story describes how one guest is thrown out because he presumes to come in his old clothes (22:1–14)!

The Son of man

Jesus often uses the term 'Son of man' to refer to himself. It can mean simply 'a man' or 'a human being'. However, it has a special meaning in the Old Testament books of Ezekiel and Daniel. Daniel has a vision that 'one like a son of man' becomes God's representative on earth. After suffering, he is given dominion and glory and kingdom by the Ancient of Days. In calling himself the 'Son of man' Jesus gives a very strong clue to who he is.

DISCOVERING MATTHEW

The birth and early life of Jesus

The list of Jesus' ancestors

(1:1–17)

Matthew traces the family line of Jesus. He begins with Abraham, the father of the Jewish nation, and shows how Jesus comes from the royal line of Judah and King David. There are famous names along the way – and a few surprises.

The list of ancestors includes four women, none of whom is a Jew. They have all come into the family through strange circumstances. Tamar was Judah's Canaanite daughter-in-law, who tricked him into making her pregnant (Genesis 38). Ruth was a Moabite widow when she met her future husband, Boaz (Ruth 2:11–12). And was Rahab the prostitute from Jericho (Joshua 2:1)?

Bathsheba was King Solomon's mother, the former wife of Uriah. She was a Hittite and an adulteress. Her affair with King David marked the downturn of his authority in both his family and his nation. There are some shameful episodes in this family history – and there is wonderful proof that God graciously redeems our failures.

There are several differences between the list of ancestors compiled by Matthew and the one compiled by Luke. Is Matthew tracing the 'official' succession to the throne, to show that Jesus is the true king of Israel? He conveys to us that a time of preparation is now fulfilled, by arranging Jesus' forebears in three sets of fourteen: from Abraham to David, from David to the exile and from the exile to the birth of Jesus.

Jesus is born in Bethlehem

(1:18 – 2:23)

Matthew tells us Joseph's story of Jesus' birth. (We have Mary's story in Luke's Gospel.)

Mary and Joseph are pledged to be married – a commitment as serious as the marriage itself. When Mary is found to be pregnant, Joseph thinks of sparing her shame by getting a quiet divorce. That way only two witnesses need know. In the old days she would have been stoned to death for adultery. But Joseph has a dream. An angel tells him that this baby is God's own son, and will become the Saviour of his people.

Both Matthew and Luke want us to know that this child is the Son of God. The baby is announced by angels, conceived by the Holy Spirit and given the name Jesus – the Greek version of Joshua, which means 'The Lord [God] Saves'.

Matthew is not arguing the case for virgin birth as much as telling it the way it was. He confirms it with a prophecy from Isaiah. Isaiah also gives us the name Immanuel, which sums up the purpose of this amazing birth. Jesus is to be 'God With Us' (Isaiah 7:14).

The visit of the Magi – wise men or astrologers from the East – is depicted on many a Christmas card. The idea that there were three of them arises from their three gifts: gold and frankincense and myrrh.

Now Matthew gives us a fix in place and time. Bethlehem, a few miles from Jerusalem, is the birthplace of Jesus. Herod, an Edomite, is the king of the Jews at the time. This is Herod the Great – famous for his mighty building projects (the palace and temple) and legendary cruelty (the massacre of the Bethlehem children).

Herod the Great dies in 4 BC, which enables us to date the birth of Jesus fairly accurately.

Herod is shaken by the Magi's news that a new king has been born. He himself is only half-Jewish and worried by any true claim to his throne. To secure his position, he orders the deaths of all infants in Bethlehem under two years old. It seems that Jesus is a child rather than a baby by the time the Magi visit him.

THE VISIT OF THE MAGI

The Magi or wise men are probably astrologers. They may come from Persia or Babylonia, where astrology is a well-developed science. Their gifts sound Arabian and are clearly valuable. Gold is fit for a king, incense signifies a priest and myrrh (for embalming) suggests one who will die.

The Magi have seen a star – a supernova, comet or conjunction of planets – which means a king has been born to the Jews. Saturn (for Israel) and Jupiter (a king) are merged in the night sky on three occasions in 7 BC.

The mention of a star reminds us of Balaam's ancient and beautiful prophecy of a coming king:

> *I see him, but not now;*
>   *I behold him, but not near.*
> *A star will come out of Jacob;*
>   *a sceptre will rise out of Israel (Numbers 24:17).*

While the Magi follow a star, Herod's scholars search the scriptures. Both arrive at Bethlehem as the birthplace of the new king. Bethlehem is where Israel's greatest king, David, was born. Now Micah's prophecy is fulfilled, that David's great descendant, the Messiah, will also be born here (Micah 5:2).

The early church saw the worship of the Magi as the submission of the 'old gods' of astrology and spells to the king of kings. The Magi are the first Gentiles to worship Jesus and offer him their treasures. Herod's soldiers are the first Jews to try to kill him. But God is protecting this child's life. Both the Magi and Joseph are guided to safety by dreams.

'They offered him gifts' (2:11). The adoration of the Magi, from a 10th-century German manuscript.

THE ESCAPE TO EGYPT AND THE MASSACRE OF THE CHILDREN

Joseph and Mary take Jesus to Egypt. In this way they narrowly escape Herod's massacre (2:13–18).

Egypt has been both a refuge and a prison for God's people in the past. Here Moses escaped death when a tyrant Pharaoh was murdering the Hebrew babies. From here God rescued the Hebrew slaves to make them a nation and give them a land. Jesus is retracing his people's steps. He is the one who is greater than Moses.

THE RETURN TO NAZARETH

Once Herod has died, Joseph brings his family home to Nazareth (2:19–23). We know from Luke's Gospel that this was already their home town.

Nazareth at this time is little more than a village, with a mixed population of Jews and Gentiles. It isn't famous or fashionable – and there is no reference to it in the scriptures. If you want to change the world, you shouldn't start from here!

Jesus' baptism and temptation

Now Matthew brings his story forward some thirty years, to the time when Jesus is about to enter public life.

The preaching of John the Baptist
(3:1–12)

John the Baptist is a striking figure. Dressed like Elijah, he is the first prophet to appear in Israel for 400 years. His camel-hair coat is in stark contrast to the fine clothes of Israel's smooth and cultured religious leaders.

John's message is as stark and striking as his appearance. He calls the Jews to repent and prepare for the coming of their God.

There will be no escaping the great judgment that is about to fall. It will be like a field being harvested or a rotten orchard being cleared. No Jewish pedigree or religious rank will give protection. Only a deep and practical repentance will do.

John baptizes the people who respond to his preaching – plunging them into the waters of the River Jordan. This is a washing-away of sins – the drowning of an old life. But it is nothing to what the Messiah will do when he comes. He will baptize with the Holy Spirit!

Jesus is baptized by John
(3:13–17)

One day Jesus comes to be baptized. John recognizes Jesus as one who is far greater than he is. It is Jesus who should be baptizing him…

But Jesus takes his place with John's converts, and all who are looking for the coming of God's kingdom. By being baptized, Jesus takes his stand with all who belong to the true Israel – those who obey God from their hearts.

After Jesus has been baptized, he sees the Spirit of God descending – like a dove coming down and settling on him. And God speaks. He declares that Jesus is his Son whom he loves and is pleased with.

In David's day, God's chosen king was described as his son (Psalm 2:7). This became a way of referring to the Messiah. God's delight in Jesus echoes Isaiah's description of the suffering servant. This servant leads a blameless life and dies for the sake of others (Isaiah 42:1).

The descent of the Spirit and God's firm and loving words commission Jesus for his life's work. From now on he embarks on the mission and ministry of the Messiah, God's servant-king.

Jesus is tempted by the devil
(4:1–11)

After his baptism, Jesus spends forty days and nights in the desert.

He continues to relive the experiences of God's people – now tasting their forty years of wandering in the wilderness.

The Judean desert, where Jesus spends forty days and nights in fasting and prayer. In so doing, he echoes the wilderness experience of the Israelites, when their faith in God was tested by hunger, thirst and danger.

They had doubted God's calling, and fell to grumbling and idolatry. Will Jesus succeed where they failed?

A battle rages within Jesus as the Spirit leads and Satan sows doubt. What does it mean to be God's Son? And what kind of Messiah must he be?

The devil tempts Jesus to misuse his power. By turning stones to bread, he can meet his need for food – and find a way to win the world.

But Jesus has been thinking of the manna in the wilderness. Human beings need more than bread to sustain them. True life comes with hearing and doing whatever God wants (Deuteronomy 8:3).

The devil challenges Jesus to test God. If Jesus throws himself from the top of the temple, will God care? Will he send angels to catch him?

Jesus answers with another lesson from the wilderness years. It is wrong to test God (Deuteronomy 6:16). Testing God is not a sign of faith but of doubt.

Finally, the devil makes a sensational offer. He will give Jesus all the kingdoms of the world, in return for his worship.

It's a devastating temptation, because Jesus has indeed come to win the world. But again he responds with words of scripture: 'Fear the Lord your God, serve him only' (Deuteronomy 6:13).

Jesus in Galilee

Jesus moves to Capernaum and starts to preach
(4:12–17)

Jesus hears that John the Baptist is in prison. John has been arrested for condemning the king's adultery. Jesus avoids a similar fate by returning north to Galilee. Here he starts to preach – with the very same call to repentance that John has delivered so bravely.

Jesus makes his home in the bustling town of Capernaum, at the northern end of the Sea of Galilee. This is where Matthew himself lives, and where he will soon become a disciple. He sees another of Isaiah's prophecies coming true. Gentile Galilee, which for centuries has been trampled by armies and darkened by paganism, is now to receive the light of God's salvation.

The calling of the first disciples
(4:18–22)

Galilee is a densely populated region, with dozens of thriving villages. Through it run busy trade routes from north to south and from east to west. The people are vigorous, enterprising, open-minded and ready for change. It's an excellent place to start a revolution – or preach the gospel.

Jesus begins by gathering a small group of followers. He calls two sets of brothers – Simon Peter and Andrew, James and John – to join him as his disciples. They have made their living by fishing the fresh waters of Galilee. Now Jesus will train them to fish for people!

We see both the attractiveness of Jesus and the enterprise of the brothers, as they promptly respond to his call. Not many will follow Jesus so readily.

The kingdom comes to Galilee
(4:23–25)

So Jesus begins his public life. He preaches and teaches the good news of God's kingdom in the towns and villages of Galilee. He heals all kinds of illness and disability. He announces the kingdom of God, and demonstrates God's power to rescue and restore broken lives.

The Sermon on the Mount
(5:1 – 7:29)

Jesus doesn't only teach in synagogues. Sometimes he likes to get away from the crowds and teach only his disciples.

Matthew describes Jesus taking his disciples into the hills. Like all rabbis, Jesus sits down to teach and his disciples gather round him to listen. Many people have wondered if the mountain is important. Is Matthew telling us that Jesus is a new Moses, delivering a new law – like Moses on Mount Sinai?

The Sermon on the Mount is Matthew's great account of Jesus' teaching to his disciples. Here Jesus describes the attitudes and behaviour he wants of his followers.

The Sermon on the Plain in Luke's Gospel is shorter, and contains about half of Matthew's material.

THE BEATITUDES

Jesus starts by telling his disciples how to be happy. His list of eight happy attitudes turns popular values upside down (5:3–12).

Most people assume happiness is:

- achieving our goals of wealth and success; leaving others behind.
- always being fun to have around – the life and soul of every party.
- being strong, or beautiful, or rich, or clever; being independent, secure and in control.
- getting our terms agreed, our rights established and ensuring that justice is done.

To our shame, we also find happiness in:

- taking revenge on our enemies.
- indulging our greed and lust.
- picking fights and winning arguments.
- and (better still) avoiding all trouble or misfortune!

Jesus' conditions for a happy life are exactly the opposite.

He says the poor in spirit are happy, because they depend completely on God – which is heaven on earth.

He says those who mourn are happy, because God shares their heartbreak and will surely comfort them.

The meek have a special happiness because they are free of pride and ambition; God will give them the world.

Those who hunger and thirst for goodness are happy, because God himself will satisfy their longings.

Those who show mercy are happy, because they in turn will be treated kindly.

The pure in heart are happy, because they will meet God face to face.

Those who make peace are happy, because they take after God and do his work.

Those who are persecuted for doing good are happy, because they share the real cost of God's kingdom.

Jesus describes a happiness which doesn't depend on possessions, circumstances or good luck. It's a happiness God gives us *now* which nothing can take away. It's a happiness which looks forward to wonderful rewards when God's kingdom finally comes.

Jesus adds a blessing for those who suffer for their faith in him. He promises that God will make it up to them, with a reward which is far greater than anything they can imagine. And persecution is a compliment of sorts. It means we're being treated like the old prophets.

SALT AND LIGHT

Jesus says his disciples are like salt and light (5:13–16). They are very distinctive – and have a strong influence on their surroundings.

Salt is used to flavour or preserve food. True Christians will promote goodness and hinder corruption in society. Those who lose their distinctiveness are like useless salt which is thrown out on the path.

Light is utterly different from darkness. It shines out to conquer gloom, reveal a situation or show the way. Jesus says his followers give spiritual light to this world – their good deeds shining out for the glory of God. So – don't fail the Father by hiding away!

THE FULFILMENT OF THE LAW

Jesus hasn't come to change or cancel the commands and teachings of the Old Testament. He has come to fulfil them by living them completely. The law stands – right down to its smallest letter – until Jesus fulfils the purpose for which it was given (5:17–20).

Jesus is against nit-picking legalism. The Pharisees have developed the law into a mass of little rules – because they are trying so hard to obey it perfectly. But Jesus says his disciples must do better than the Pharisees. They must obey the law by letting it govern their inner thoughts and motives, not just their outward actions.

THE HEART OF THE COMMANDMENTS

To explain what he means, Jesus takes two of the Ten Commandments: 'You shall not murder' and 'You shall not commit adultery' (5:21–30).

Murder is when one person kills another. But Jesus points to the invisible anger which lies behind a murder. Even a mild insult like 'Idiot' ('Raca') or 'Fool' is, in thought, a mini-murder.

The Mount of the Beatitudes, where it is thought that Jesus delivered his famous Sermon on the Mount.

Jesus says there's more to this commandment than simply not murdering. We must tackle our anger by forgiving each other. Even if we are at the most sacred moment of our year – poised to offer a gift to God – forgiveness is more important. We must leave our gift and make peace with the person with whom we are so angry.

Adultery is when a husband or wife cheats on their partner by having sex with someone else. Simple. But Jesus tackles the 'come-on' look which first starts an affair. *That's* when the commandment is broken and adultery takes place. Better to gouge out your eye or cut off your hand than take that road to destruction.

Jesus is exaggerating to make his point. He doesn't really expect a church full of one-eyed, left-handed Christians. But he's serious about our need for self-discipline: if an action will be wrong, don't look, don't touch – and don't think it!

DIVORCE

Divorce in Jewish society is quick and easy for the husband, and extremely unfair to the wife. A man can discard his wife for the slightest reason – simply by giving her a certificate.

But Jesus teaches that there is only one reason for divorcing a wife – when she herself has cancelled the marriage by committing adultery. To divorce her for any other reason is wrong, because the marriage is still valid in God's sight (5:31–32).

A discarded wife will be forced to remarry in order to have a home. The new marriage makes both her and her second husband adulterers.

OATHS

Some Jews have found a way of breaking promises. They distinguish between an unbreakable oath, which is made in God's name, and lesser oaths, which are made on other objects and may be easily broken.

Jesus has no time for this trivial tampering with truth. If a Christian makes a promise, it is automatically in the Lord's name and needs nothing added. The disciples are to give a simple 'Yes' or 'No' – and let their Christian honour defy the devil's deceit (5:33–37).

Matthew and the law

In the early days of Christianity, there is a great debate about the Jewish law. Does being a Christian mean you keep the law more than ever – or are you now released from its demands?

The Pharisees say Jesus breaks the law. They accuse him of working on the sabbath day, because he heals diseases and disabilities, delivers from evil spirits and lets his disciples harvest handfuls of grain. But Jesus says the sabbath is a day of sheer freedom to honour God, not a day of rigid inactivity to honour the law.

Matthew gives a lot of attention to a Christian understanding of the Jewish law. He does this particularly in the Sermon on the Mount (5:1 – 7:29).

Perhaps he shows us Jesus teaching on a mountain to help us connect with Moses receiving the Ten Commandments on Mount Sinai.

Matthew's main point is this: Jesus has not come to abolish the teachings of the Law and the Prophets. He has come to fulfil them. All the Old Testament scriptures will continue as God's guide to a good life. Jesus has come to live them out in perfect obedience and joy.

If the Jewish law still applies, should Christians behave more like Pharisees? Jesus accused some Pharisees of studying the law for reasons of pride, fear and a desire to find loopholes. They were so concerned to interpret the details of the law correctly that they forgot more important matters like justice, mercy and

faithfulness. Both Jews and Christians need to study the law to find the love of God behind it – and to keep it as gladly and wholeheartedly as possible. For a Christian, keeping the law is like walking with Jesus. The yoke of legalism is a chafing burden, but the yoke of Christ is a joyful freedom (11:28–30).

AN EYE FOR AN EYE

Now Jesus announces a truly Christian difference. He reminds his disciples of the old laws of compensation (Exodus 21:24). If someone blinds you in one eye, you can blind one of theirs in return. If someone knocks out one of your teeth, you can knock out one of theirs. But *only* one! The penalty is to be exactly fair.

But now, says Jesus, the Christian way is to forgive (5:38–42). If someone insults you with a terrible blow on the cheek, disarm them by offering the other as well. If someone sues you for your coat, overcome their greed with your generosity – and give them your cloak for good measure. If a Roman soldier forces you to carry his pack for a mile, surprise him by giving him an extra mile free! Give and lend as a matter of course – because that is how God treats you.

LOVE FOR ENEMIES

For centuries the Jews have prized the commandment, 'Love your neighbour' (Leviticus 19:18). A neighbour is any fellow Jew – so the law leaves plenty of room to hate foreigners!

But now Jesus springs the greatest surprise of all. The Christian way is to love our enemies (5:43–48). This is what God does, and we are to take after him. Our heavenly Father doesn't limit his blessings to good people – but sends sun and rain on good and bad alike.

Jesus says that loving people who will love us in return is something any sinner can do. Greeting our own kind is no different from paganism. The challenge is to cross the old lines of pride and prejudice – and accept other people in a way which shows the perfect love of God.

Unselfish love – wanting the best for others, even our enemies – is Christianity's greatest gift to the world. We never knew such love until Jesus came.

GIVING, PRAYING AND FASTING

Jesus teaches his disciples how to do good – for the right reason and in the right way!

It's important to do 'acts of righteousness' (such as giving to the needy, praying and fasting) without showing off. We're not doing these things so that people can admire us. We're doing them for God (6:1–18).

The Pharisees make every effort to do good – but they like to be seen doing it! They give to the needy in a blaze of publicity. They pray where others can still see them and be impressed. They make sure they look pale and wretched when they're fasting.

Jesus calls all this 'hypocrisy' – a public performance, like acting. And, like acting, it may only be pretending. The reward is a round of applause – but not from God!

So how should Christian disciples behave? Jesus assumes we will give to the needy, pray and fast; but the key to being genuine is to keep such actions secret.

When you give to the needy, says Jesus (not 'if', but 'when'!), then barely mention it even to yourself. When you pray, go into your smallest room and shut out the watching world. Jesus suggests a storeroom, because it has no windows and has a lock on the door. When you

The Lord's Prayer

When we pray, we are to talk to God as 'Abba', our dear Father. No one was ever so intimate with God before Jesus came. Now he teaches us to do the same. God is our Father. We can pray this prayer together.

We are to pray that God's name (the way we think of God and what he does) will be honoured as utterly holy.

We are to pray that God's kingdom will come here on earth. May the whole world welcome his reign of love, justice and peace, as heaven already does.

And what should we ask for ourselves? Jesus tells us to ask God for our daily bread – that he will give us the food and clothes and strength we need, without our worrying.

We must ask him to forgive our debts – especially our sins. And, if we ask for forgiveness, it's only right that we should already have forgiven those who have wronged us.

We must ask to be kept from temptation – the kind of test which would overwhelm and destroy us. May God protect us from the power and plans of the devil.

Jesus adds a comment on forgiveness. Prayer is an active engagement with God. Prayer makes us check our attitudes and change our ways. For example, we can hardly expect God to forgive us if we are not forgiving others.

fast, go about your everyday life as normally as possible – with your face washed and your hair tidy.

Our religious acts express our love for our heavenly Father. Giving, praying and fasting are for his eyes only. Only he sees what we do in secret.

How to pray

How shall we pray? Jesus tells us not to babble endlessly. The length of our prayer doesn't matter. It's what's in our heart that counts (6:7–15).

Some pagans try to wear God down until he gives them what they want. Jesus reminds us that God is our Father. He already knows what we need – and loves to give.

Jesus teaches his disciples a prayer. It has become known as the 'Lord's Prayer', and is used constantly by Christians throughout the world.

TREASURES IN HEAVEN

What are we living for? What are our ambitions?

Jesus urges his disciples to live for God.

This world's treasures don't last. Our fashionable clothes will be eaten by moths. Our expensive possessions break down or get stolen. It's important to have our true wealth in heaven, where there is no decay or loss (6:19–24).

Jesus has already spoken of the wonderful rewards that await us. God will bless us beyond anything we have earned or deserved by our little acts of loyalty and obedience to him.

It's important to be clear about this. Just as good eyes enable us to see well, so a good heart will enable us to live well.

Jesus says we must choose between God and money. Money is attractive to us. It makes us feel good because it gives power and choice. But the desire for money can take us over, and we end up worshipping it as our god. This is materialism – a devotion to money and the things it can get us.

Jesus tells us straight. We can only worship God *or* money. There isn't room in our lives for both.

DO NOT WORRY

If we don't set our hearts on money, then what's to become of us? How will we get food to eat and clothes to wear – and all the other things we need?

Jesus says this is where we must learn to trust God (6:25–34).

He tells his disciples to look around – at the birds in the sky and the wild flowers in the fields. Do birds strive furiously for a standard of living? Are flowers consumed with anxiety about the future? No. But the birds are fed and the flowers look glorious, because God looks after them.

So Jesus invites his followers to live in a world where our heavenly Father provides for us. We may have to work, but we don't have to worry. The frantic pursuit of food and drink and clothes is a sign of insecurity. It's the lifestyle of people who don't know God.

Jesus draws on the simple and elegant beauty of nature – even weeds – to encourage us to trust our creator for our daily needs. Wild flowers, Galilee.

What really counts is God's kingdom – his reign in our lives and in our world. If we put God and his kingdom first, everything else will follow – and find its proper priority and place.

JUDGING OTHERS

Jesus warns his disciples against passing judgment on people (7:1–6). God will measure us by the very same standard we apply to others.

Jesus thinks of his days as a carpenter. You can't see to remove a tiny speck of sawdust from someone's eye if you have a great plank of wood in your own. So it is with judging others. We pick on a tiny blemish in someone else's behaviour, when there's a far greater fault in ourselves.

We must also be wise when we speak about God. Sharing the gospel with people who don't want it is like throwing pearls to pigs.

ASK, SEEK, KNOCK

Jesus encourages his disciples to develop their relationship with God. We will find him to be a loving and generous Father. We have only to ask to receive his help, only to seek to find his way and only to knock to discover his welcome (7:7–12).

Are we afraid that God will trick us or disappoint us? Will he take advantage of our weakness, or suddenly let us down? Jesus says that a human father, with all his failings, knows how to be kind and consistent with his child. Won't our heavenly Father, who is perfect, be better still?

'Do as you would be done by!'

Jesus sums up his teaching on how to treat people (7:12). We must behave towards others as we would like them to behave towards us. Give generously and receive joyfully. Forgive and be forgiven. Don't judge and don't be judged. This is the golden rule. This is the love of God in action.

DECISION TIME

The teaching of Jesus is inspired and exciting. A life of joyful obedience opens before us – a life which finds its happiness in God's love and its purpose in the work of his kingdom. But will we follow where he leads (7:13–14)?

Jesus is not interested in merely entertaining us with stories or intriguing us with wise sayings. He looks for us to make a choice. He invites us to join him on the narrow road that leads to life.

A WARNING

Jesus gives a warning about false prophets (7:15–23). These are people who claim to come from God, but don't. They are fierce and dangerous – like wolves disguised as sheep. We must look carefully at what they actually do.

You tell a good prophet like you tell a good tree – by the fruit! Jesus says there are plenty of prophets, exorcists and miracle-workers around who are nothing to do with him. So beware!

THE WISE AND FOOLISH BUILDERS

Jesus ends his teaching with a challenge. *You will only know the truth if you do it!* For Jesus, the truth is to be lived.

Living the truth is like building a house on a foundation of rock. Storms, hurricanes and flood water can do their worst, but the house will always stay standing (7:24–29).

To hear the teaching of Jesus and ignore it is like building a house on sand. It has no proper foundation. When the trials of life come beating down and doubts come flooding in, the life without truth will collapse.

The crowds are buzzing. They like Jesus – his vitality, his wisdom, his humour, his directness… Most of all, his words spring confidently and naturally from his life. He is so different from their other teachers!

Jesus performs many miracles
(8:1 – 9:34)

JESUS' POWER IN ACTION

Matthew tells us some of the amazing miracles that Jesus performs (8:1–34). He has power to heal incurable diseases, control the forces of nature and command evil spirits to depart. These are the proofs that he is the Christ.

JESUS HEALS A PERSON WHO IS PARALYSED

A paralysed man is brought to Jesus by his friends (9:1–8). Jesus sees that the man's real problem is not paralysis but guilt. He assures the invalid that his sins are forgiven – and then heals his paralysis.

Some teachers of the law are indignant that Jesus has presumed to forgive someone's sins. This is something only God has the right and power to do. But the healing of the paralysis is proof that Jesus does indeed have God's authority to act in this way.

THE CALLING OF MATTHEW

Matthew is a tax collector. He works for the local king, Herod Antipas. It seems likely that he is a customs official, sitting in a toll booth and checking goods as they cross the border.

Tax collectors are among the most hated people in society. They have power to stop, search and tax everyone and everything. They can take the clothes off your back or the wheels off your cart! But it's not because of their power that the tax collectors are despised. It's because they betray their own people to make themselves rich.

And Jesus calls Matthew to be his disciple (9:9–13)! In the Gospels of Mark and Luke he is called Levi – but he is clearly the same man. Simon Peter also has two names.

Matthew invites Jesus to dinner, where they are joined by other social outcasts known as 'sinners'. These are people who, because of their work or morals (or both), can't lead a religious life. They are 'unclean'.

The Pharisees are offended that Jesus is keeping such company. Sharing a meal with them is a sign of fellowship. But Jesus tells them he *must* mix with sinners, just as a doctor must mix with the sick. The Pharisees prove their religion by keeping clean. Jesus proves his love by getting dirty.

TO FAST OR TO FEAST?

The disciples of John the Baptist come to Jesus with a question. Why don't his followers fast as they and the Pharisees do (9:14–17)?

Jesus replies that they don't fast because they aren't sad. They're enjoying the presence of Jesus – like a wedding party with the bridegroom there. One day he will be taken from them and they'll be sad. Then will be the time for fasting.

The gospel is like new wine. The Jewish leaders are like shrivelled old wineskins. The gospel needs new and more flexible structures to contain it. Will the disciples of Jesus be the bottles?

LIFE, HEALTH AND PEACE

Matthew tells us about some people Jesus helps. Each one reaches out to Jesus from a hopeless situation, and experiences his extraordinary power to save (9:18–34).

A ruler comes to Jesus with the tragic news that his daughter has died. In Luke's Gospel we know this man is Jairus, the ruler of the synagogue in Capernaum. He believes that if Jesus will only lay his hand on his daughter she will live. But, as the Pharisees see it, to touch the girl's corpse will make Jesus 'unclean'.

Jesus is on his way to the ruler's house when a woman in the crowd touches his cloak. She wants healing for her continual menstrual bleeding, which has troubled her for twelve years. She is 'unclean' and should not be in a public place. She should certainly not be touching a rabbi. But she is healed immediately, and Jesus tells her that her faith has cured her.

Jesus continues to the ruler's house, clears the funeral party from around the door and raises the girl to life.

Later, two blind men follow Jesus, calling on him as 'Son of David' to help them. The title has strong political meaning, and will make Jesus a focus of Jewish opposition to the Romans. Jesus heals them discreetly in the privacy of a house – responding to their faith, but asking them to be quiet about him in future. However, they are just as noisy afterwards!

A demonized man is brought to Jesus. He is dumb, but Jesus heals him by commanding the demon to leave. The crowd is amazed, but the Pharisees are not impressed. They explain Jesus' power over demons by saying he is in league with them. This is an appalling slander and blasphemy against the Holy Spirit who is at work in these acts of rescue.

Engaging in mission
(9:35 – 12:50)

For a second time, Matthew sums up all that Jesus is doing – travelling, teaching, preaching and healing in the towns and villages of Galilee.

A HUGE TASK

Jesus is drawn by the needs of the people, which he feels as a pain in the pit of his stomach (9:35–38). They are like sheep, distressed and defenceless, without a shepherd to care for and protect them. In John's Gospel Jesus actually describes himself as 'the good shepherd' – the One who gives his life for the sheep (John 10:11).

The work is vast and the moment is urgent – like a harvest which must be gathered while the crop is ripe and the weather good. Jesus asks his disciples to pray for more workers. They will soon become the answer to their own prayers.

JESUS SENDS OUT THE TWELVE

Jesus calls his disciples together. There are twelve of them – like a mini-Israel, with her twelve tribes. They are to be the nucleus of the new people of God.

Matthew lists the Twelve and calls them 'apostles' – those who are 'sent'. The learners are becoming missionaries. Jesus gives them his authority to do the very same work that he has been doing: driving out evil spirits, healing all kinds of illness and even raising the dead (10:1–16).

Jesus gives the apostles their instructions:

They are to concentrate on the people of Israel. Matthew is aware that the gospel is for the whole world, but the mission to the Gentiles is still in the future.

They are to travel without money or baggage – relying on God to provide for them. The people they visit will give them food and shelter.

They are not to charge for their work, nor accept any money. The gospel is to be free for all.

The apostles' visit will be a judgment on each home and community. If they are welcomed, their peace will rest on the place. If they are rejected, they must leave – shaking the dust from their feet, and abandoning the people to their fate.

Those who reject the apostles are rejecting the gospel of God's kingdom – a crime far worse than anything done in Sodom and Gomorrah. These were the wicked 'cities of the plain' which God destroyed in Abraham's day (Genesis 19:24–25).

WARNINGS OF PERSECUTION

Jesus warns his disciples that they will be persecuted for their faith. He paints a dark picture of their suffering and trials in years to come (10:17–42).

The apostles will be persecuted at every level of government, from synagogues and local councils to Roman courts and royal palaces. They will be flogged and imprisoned. But their mission to Israel will open out to become a mission to Gentiles too. And God will never abandon them; his Spirit will always be with them and speak through them.

People will disagree about the gospel. It will split even the closest relationships. The apostles will be hated because of the message they bring. But they must proclaim the good news clearly and bravely. The only person they need to fear is God. This is a spiritual battle: evil is being challenged, secrets are being exposed and eternal choices are being made.

Jesus assures his apostles, in the strongest terms, of their ultimate safety and eternal life. God already knows every hair of their heads. Jesus looks forward to presenting them to his Father with great pride.

The apostles are to be Jesus' faithful ambassadors in all kinds of difficult situations. When people meet them, they meet him. And there will be blessings in heaven for anyone who helps them – even if only by giving them a drink.

JESUS AND JOHN THE BAPTIST

Again the disciples of John the Baptist come to see Jesus – this time with a question from John himself (11:1–19).

John wants to know if Jesus is really the Christ, or whether they should look for someone else. John has a personal interest in this. The Messiah (Christ) is expected to release captives from prison – and John is *in* prison!

John's problem is this: Jesus is performing miracles, but there is no sign of the mighty judgment with Holy Spirit and fire which John himself had promised and expected. And Jesus is not at all a holy man by Jewish standards – he doesn't appear to fast and he keeps bad company.

Jesus sends a message back to John. He quotes words from the prophet Isaiah. There *are* signs of the Messiah's work in the ministry of Jesus. The blind are seeing, the deaf hearing, the lame leaping and the dumb shouting (Isaiah 35:5–6)! Best of all, the poor are hearing the good news that God's kingdom is coming (Isaiah 61:1).

As John's disciples leave, Jesus pays tribute to his faithful cousin. He is the greatest of the prophets – the one who Malachi predicted would prepare the way for the Messiah (Malachi 3:1). Even so, he is the last of the old order of Law and Prophets – an Elijah rather than a Simon Peter.

Jesus reflects how people resist making a commitment – like children refusing to join in each other's games. John plays a dirge and Jesus plays a dance – but neither is acceptable. People complain that John starves and Jesus stuffs – and so find reason to reject them both! But both are true expressions of the wisdom and purpose of God.

TOWNS WHICH REJECT JESUS

Jesus continues to be exasperated. The towns in which he has preached and worked so many miracles are still resisting the gospel (11:20–24).

Three lakeside towns in particular – Korazin, Bethsaida and Capernaum – have had a unique opportunity to turn to God. They have seen and heard the Messiah.

The pagan cities of Tyre and Sidon, given the same chance, would surely have repented. If Sodom had received a visit from Jesus, it would never have been destroyed. But these Galilean communities have rejected God – and will themselves be rejected by him on Judgment Day.

AN INVITATION TO REST

Jesus turns from frustration to praise. God is Lord of all. Even the way people respond to the gospel is in the Father's hands. He hides his truth from those who know everything (or think they do) and makes it clear to 'little children' – the humble people who know nothing but their need of God. How typical of the Father to work this way!

Jesus thanks his Father for the task he has been given. Only Father and Son know each other completely: mind to mind, heart to heart, they are God. And Jesus is commissioned to make his Father known – inviting sinful humans to share their life and love.

Jesus commits himself wholeheartedly to his Father's will – and invites us to do the same (11:25–30). Those who are tired of life, or weighed down by dead religion, can come to him for rest. Like a skilled and careful carpenter shaping a yoke, he will fit us with the gentle, liberating purpose of God. Our yoke goes across his shoulders too, for he shares it with us – setting the direction of our life and taking the strain.

A CHALLENGE ABOUT THE SABBATH

The sabbath is a day of rest (12:1–14). God himself established it in the fourth commandment as a weekly space from the burden of work (Exodus 20:8–11). It's a day for a taste of heaven.

In Jesus' day, some of the Pharisees have trussed the sabbath in a web of legislation – which they vigorously enforce. They criticize Jesus for allowing his disciples to 'work' when they pick and munch ears of corn.

Jesus answers with a story of David. Once, when David and his companions were hungry, he asked a priest for bread. The only bread was in the sanctuary – the loaves placed in the presence of God. But David decided that their needs were more important than a mere religious custom – and commanded the priest to feed them.

Jesus agrees with David. He confronts the fussy Pharisees with divine common sense. The sabbath is a day for liberty and liberation – not legalism! To prove it, he does some 'work' of his own on the sabbath, and heals a man with a shrivelled hand. It is this act of defiance that makes some Pharisees want to kill him.

JESUS, GOD'S SERVANT

Jesus has to avoid his enemies, but the time has not yet come for them to have their way (12:15–21). He continues quietly to heal the sick. Matthew sees in Jesus the gentle servant described by Isaiah – devoting himself to God's work without any kind of self-assertion or show of force (Isaiah 42:1–4).

A BLASPHEMOUS SUGGESTION

Jesus heals a demon-possessed man. His action prompts people to wonder if he is the Son of David – the coming Messiah who will deliver Israel by the power of God (12:22–37).

But some Pharisees, full of envy and spite, have a different explanation. They say Jesus has power over demons because he works for their prince, Beelzebub.

This was the very compromise with Satan which Jesus rejected during his temptation in the desert.

Jesus argues that if Satan is now expelling his own agents, then his evil empire must be collapsing. But if Jesus is overcoming demons by the power of God's Spirit, then the kingdom of God is taking them all by surprise. His critics insult the Holy Spirit when they attribute this work to the devil. It's an unforgivable lie against God, and they will be judged for it.

THE SIGN OF JONAH

Some of the Pharisees ask Jesus for a sign, to prove who he is (12:38–45). Jesus answers that the only sign they will be given is the sign of Jonah – the sign of resurrection.

Jesus is amazed at the resistance of the religious leaders. The citizens of Nineveh recognized the truth of Jonah's message, and the queen of Sheba recognized the greatness of Solomon's wisdom. But the Jews can't see that someone greater than Jonah and Solomon is with them now.

JESUS' TRUE FAMILY

When Jesus' family come to see him, they find themselves kept outside the house where he is. Jesus has a closer bond with his followers than he has with his mother and brothers. The kingdom of God comes before every other relationship (12:46–50).

Jesus teaches in parables
(13:1–52)

Matthew has given us two sections of teaching so far – the Sermon on the Mount and the training of the Twelve. Now, in a third section, he collects together seven of Jesus' parables.

Parables are brilliant picture-stories which give images of God's kingdom at work. Jesus uses parables to teach large crowds, because everyone loves a story – and a story can make people think. Even so, some of the hidden meanings are too obscure even for his disciples.

THE PARABLE OF THE SOWER

Jesus tells how a farmer sows seed in his field (13:1–23). The seeds have different fortunes, according to where they fall. Some fall on the path and are eaten by birds. Some fall on rock where they sprout briefly and wither. Some fall among thorns and have no room to grow. But some fall on good soil and produce a marvellous harvest.

Parables

Parables may be quite short stories or sayings – even a proverb or riddle. They can be understood on several levels, and may apply to the present or the future. Jesus was brilliant at telling them, and his followers kept them and passed them on. We still have to puzzle them out today.

Sometimes we are not looking at what Jesus meant, but at what Christians have thought he meant. It gets complicated! But if we look for what a parable is saying about our attitude to God we won't go far wrong. It also helps to realize that Jesus is making one main point and doesn't expect us to find meanings in every little detail.

Jesus later explains that this is a parable about preaching the gospel. The good news is sown in people's hearts, where it may be snatched by Satan, withered by persecution or choked with worry. But an open and obedient heart is like good soil. Such a heart grows a record harvest for God.

THE PARABLE OF THE WEEDS

A farmer discovers that his enemy has sown weeds in his wheat field (13:24–30). He can't destroy these weeds without damaging the good crop – so he lets both grow together until he can separate them at harvest time. This parable is explained a little later (13:36).

THE PARABLES OF THE MUSTARD SEED AND THE YEAST

A mustard seed is the smallest of seeds, but it grows to be a large tree and a shelter for the birds. A small amount of yeast can leaven a large amount of flour (13:31–35).

With these everyday images, Jesus gives a glimpse of the growing power of the kingdom of God. Its beginnings are almost invisible, but it spreads dramatically. In the end it will fill the whole world.

THE PARABLE OF THE WEEDS EXPLAINED

Jesus explains that the parable of the weeds is about the presence of evil in the world (13:36–43). At the moment good and evil grow together – but one day God will separate the two. He will harvest the world with judgment.

THE PARABLES OF THE HIDDEN TREASURE AND THE PRICELESS PEARL

A man finds treasure hidden in a field – and sells everything he has to buy the field! A merchant comes across the finest of pearls – and sells everything else to get it (13:44–46).

So Jesus conjures a picture of the kingdom of God. It's worth more than anything else in the world, and worthy of every sacrifice we have to make to enter it.

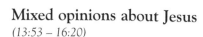
A hoard of Roman coins. Jesus describes the kingdom of heaven as treasure discovered in a field.

THE PARABLE OF THE FISHING NET

The last parable is about God's judgment (13:47–52). Jesus says the angels will be like fishermen sorting the catch from a dragnet. They'll keep the good and discard the bad.

In his parables Jesus uses ordinary objects and situations, as well as giving old stories a new twist. A good teacher must convey the truth in a variety of ways – including some fresh thoughts mixed in with the ancient wisdom.

Mixed opinions about Jesus
(13:53 – 16:20)

Jesus starts to travel further afield. He moves away from the lakeside towns, where he has been so disappointed by the lack of response to the gospel. He goes back home to Nazareth for a while, but his own friends and neighbours reject him. Then he receives the terrible news that John the Baptist has been executed.

John's death puts pressure on Jesus. He tries to find space away from the crowds – but they still manage to find him. They need teaching, healing – and food! They are also looking for a popular Messiah, who will replace their cruel and corrupt king. They dream of a major uprising against the Romans.

A COOL RECEPTION AT NAZARETH

Jesus goes to Nazareth, where he was brought up. He teaches in the synagogue (13:53–58). The people are amazed at his wise words, but in the end they turn against him. They know his family very well. He's nothing special.

Jesus seems to understand their rejection. A prophet may be widely respected and even famous – but never in his home town.

THE DEATH OF JOHN THE BAPTIST

Herod Antipas hears of Jesus. The reports trouble him, because he has recently executed John the Baptist (14:1–12). Something about Jesus reminds him of John. He is worried that the prophet has sprung to life again, with supernatural powers.

Matthew tells us briefly what happened to John. John was imprisoned for speaking out against the king's adultery. The king was afraid to harm him further, because John was so well known as a prophet. But the queen (rather like Jezebel in the old days) was his sworn enemy. She took advantage of the king's drunken promise – and had John beheaded.

Two generations of Herods

When Herod the Great dies, in 4 BC, his kingdom is divided among his three sons: Archelaus, Antipas and Philip. Herod Archelaus is soon deposed for misusing his power, and the Romans take over the government of Judea and Samaria. One of the governors of Judea is Pontius Pilate.

Herod Antipas is a tetrarch, ruling the little kingdom of Galilee and Perea, but he himself is governed by the Romans. During his long reign he builds the city of Tiberias in honour of the Roman emperor.

It is Herod Antipas who imprisons John the Baptist. We can guess something of his crafty character when Jesus calls him 'that fox' (Luke 13:32)! He is eventually deposed by the emperor Caligula in AD 39.

The third son, Philip, rules the territory to the north and east of the sea of Galilee until his death in AD 34.

JESUS FEEDS 5,000 JEWS

Jesus withdraws to get time to himself. He must avoid arrest. He needs to mourn John's death. He wants to train his disciples. But the crowds find him, and his heart goes out to their need. They are hungry and far from home, and Jesus feeds them with a miraculous supply of bread and fish (14:13–21).

All the Gospels tell us about this miracle of the loaves and fishes. Jesus is surrounded by a huge crowd of needy people. He cares for them like the good shepherd he is – healing, teaching and feeding them by the power of God.

Matthew highlights the miracle by telling us there were twelve baskets of scraps left over – a sure sign that there was plenty and some to spare. Twelve is the number that stands for the people of God – the twelve tribes of Israel and the twelve apostles of Jesus.

This feeding is like the old days, when Moses led the people through the wilderness and God gave them manna to eat. It is also a taste of the future, when God's people will feast with him in his kingdom. In the meantime it is a glimpse of the Christian church, meeting in the presence of Jesus to break bread and share his life together.

JESUS WALKS ON WATER – AND SO DOES PETER

There has been some risk in feeding the 5,000. It looks as though Jesus can raise and support an army. John's Gospel says that the people try to make him king.

Jesus defuses the situation. He sends the disciples away from the excitement, disperses the crowd and withdraws to pray. It is a tough decision. Conjuring bread and ruling the world are two of his greatest temptations!

The disciples, rowing their boat across Galilee, have a hard battle against the wind and waves. Towards dawn, Jesus walks across the water to join them. Peter, in his usual impetuous way, wants to walk out to meet him – and nearly drowns. The first Christians treasure this story. It shows Jesus' power over the forces of nature and the storms of life. It also portrays his readiness to rescue a failing follower (14:22–36).

CLEAN AND UNCLEAN

The Pharisees have a careful routine of handwashing before they eat food. For them, clean hands make a pure heart. But Jesus doesn't worry about such details – and nor do his disciples. It is empty legalism (15:1–20).

Jesus points out that some of the Pharisees' traditions actually break God's law. For example, they disobey the fifth commandment (support your elderly parents) by putting their money out of reach, in a special fund for God!

Jesus teaches that there is a difference between physical and spiritual dirt. Nothing we eat can make us spiritually unclean. Food simply passes through our body and doesn't affect our soul. It is the sin already inside us – in our heart or will – that makes us unclean. Every one of God's laws is broken at the command of the human heart. No amount of handwashing (or any other ritual) can prevent it.

A CANAANITE WOMAN'S FAITH

Jesus and his disciples are taking a break in a Gentile area, away from the pressure of the crowds and the Pharisees.

A Canaanite woman comes to Jesus (15:21–28). She's a descendant of the pagan people who were Israel's enemies in the old days. She begs Jesus to deliver her daughter from demon possession – perhaps a form of mental illness or epilepsy.

Jesus ignores the woman at first – and then refuses her request. He explains that his ministry is only for Israelites. She asks him, on her knees, to make her an exception – but he still refuses. He teases her with a racial taunt, that the Israelites are God's children and the Gentiles mere dogs. And there she has him, for she claims that the dogs may at least have some crumbs from the children's table!

Jesus is delighted to lose the argument. This woman has a wonderful faith. He gladly heals her daughter.

Jesus walks across the waters of Galilee, to join his struggling disciples in their boat. Peter tries to join him but starts to sink. A Byzantine fresco (AD 1072–78) by San Angelo Formis, Capua.

JESUS FEEDS 4,000 GENTILES

Jesus returns to the Sea of Galilee, to its north-east coast. This is still Gentile territory, known as the Decapolis or 'ten towns'. Here Jesus heals people among great crowds of Gentiles, and feeds them from a few loaves and fishes (15:29–39).

There is something different about Jesus' ministry to Gentiles. Matthew doesn't tell us that Jesus taught them, but only that he gave them the Messiah's blessings. There is sight for the blind, healing for the lame and speech for the dumb – just as Isaiah once prophesied (Isaiah 35:5–6).

Matthew also conveys a difference from the feeding of 5,000 Jews. He records different numbers of loaves, fishes and people, and a larger kind of basket. But clearly the blessings that the Jews have been receiving are being opened up to Gentiles as well. This is a taste of things to come. The healing of the Canaanite woman's daughter is the start of something big!

PHARISEES AND SADDUCEES

The Pharisees and Sadducees are two important Jewish groups (16:1–12). The Pharisees believe in a pure Jewish race and religion, and resent the Roman government. The Sadducees work with the Roman government, so that they have some share of political power. Both groups see Jesus as a threat, and join forces against him.

Jesus remarks that the Jewish leaders can forecast the weather from the signs in the sky, but they refuse to recognize the signs of the Messiah. He warns his disciples to avoid the 'yeast' effect of such people – and he's not talking about making bread! He's referring to a pervading attitude of unbelief in God.

JESUS IS THE MESSIAH

At Caesarea Philippi, Simon Peter acknowledges that Jesus is the Messiah (16:13–20). Other people may say that Jesus is merely a prophet – even one of the great prophets reappearing. But Peter believes Jesus is the One the prophets foretold: the Messiah, God's anointed king.

Peter may have a high opinion of Jesus, but Jesus also has great praise for him. He tells Simon how fortunate he is, because only God could have revealed this wonderful secret to him.

Jesus will build his church on Peter's faith. Peter, whose name means 'Rock', is the foundation stone of Jesus' new community. This community will live for ever, because it will invade and break open the gates of death and hell. Peter will have a central role in ruling the church, by making the ways of heaven known on earth.

Jesus warns his disciples not to tell anyone that he is the Messiah. There is danger of a double misunderstanding about the kind of Messiah he is.

The first misunderstanding is that thousands of people expect the Christ to be a military leader, like Judas Maccabeus. If the crowds believe that Jesus is the Christ, they will rally to him as their champion. They will revolt against the Romans and plunge the country into a ruinous and bloody war. Jesus is not this kind of Christ, and the disciples must not give the impression that he is.

The second misunderstanding is by the disciples themselves. They hope that Jesus will be revealed as the Son of man, bringing God's kingdom in clouds of glory. This is true, but it is not the whole truth. They have still to learn that the Christ must *suffer*. It will be the hardest lesson of their lives.

Insights for the disciples

Peter's naming of Jesus as the Messiah is a turning point. From now on Jesus' thoughts run towards Jerusalem and his coming death. He starts to spend more time with his disciples. He repeatedly warns them that he must suffer and die. Three of the disciples are granted a glimpse of Jesus' true glory on the Mount of Transfiguration, while the rest have difficulty healing an epileptic child. And Jesus demonstrates a unique approach to paying tax.

Jesus predicts his death
(16:21–28)

There is a change of mood. Far from celebrating that he is the Messiah, Jesus starts to warn his disciples of the dreadful suffering that lies ahead. The elders, chief priests and lawyers of the Jewish high council, the Sanhedrin, will have him killed. But on the third day Jesus will be raised to life.

Peter takes Jesus aside and tries to dissuade him. It is unthinkable that the Messiah should suffer. Jesus must get this death wish out of his head immediately. But it is Peter who is wrong. His mind is on worldly glory, and so he becomes Satan's mouthpiece. He has gone from rock to stumbling block in a matter of minutes.

Jesus gives his most solemn call to real discipleship.

To follow him will mean taking the same path of self-denial and suffering – the way of the cross. But it is also the only way to life. Those who commit themselves totally to Jesus will one day see his glory as the Son of man, welcome his kingdom and receive his reward. Indeed, there are those who will glimpse his glory in this life – as we are about to discover.

A glimpse of glory
(17:1–13)

Jesus takes his closest friends – Peter, James and John – up a high mountain. This may be Mount Hermon, which is 9,400 feet high, and not far from Caesarea Philippi.

There, on the mountain, the disciples see Jesus in his heavenly light – and Moses and Elijah talking with him. They are the two greatest prophets of the Old Testament – and Jesus is the One who fulfils all prophecy. Peter wants to put up tents, so they can stay there and make the moment last – but it is not to be. And then God himself speaks, as he did when Jesus was baptized: 'This is my Son, whom I love.'

As they make their way down the mountain, Jesus again urges his disciples to keep his secret. His passion and death must run their course without triggering a misguided Jewish rebellion.

Peter, James and John were privileged to get a glimpse of Jesus' glory as he talked with Moses and Elijah, two of the greatest figures of the Old Testament. Mount Hermon was possibly the site of that meeting.

The disciples ask Jesus about Elijah. Will he appear again in Israel before the Messiah comes? Jesus says that John the Baptist was the Elijah figure – and he was treated in the same way that Jesus himself is about to be treated.

A lack of faith
(17:14–23)

Meanwhile, the rest of the disciples have been unable to heal a boy who is possessed by a demon – perhaps epilepsy. Jesus is frustrated by their lack of faith. Even the smallest amount of genuine faith is enough to deliver from evil, because it relies on the mighty power of God.

As they prepare for the Passover pilgrimage to Jerusalem, Jesus again predicts that he will be killed. This time he warns them that he will also be betrayed.

The temple tax
(17:24–27)

It is the time of year when the temple tax is collected. The tax is due at Passover, but can be paid in advance. The amount is a half-shekel per male Jew (about two days' wages) and the rabbis are exempt.

Jesus points out that earthly kings don't tax their own children. As the temple tax is for God's house, then surely God's children should be excused. But Jesus is willing to pay the tax, to avoid offending people and causing misunderstanding. He tells Peter to go and catch a fish – and find the payment in the fish's mouth. How? Jesus knows these things!

Obedience to the state and payment of tax will be the policy of the first Christians. Both Peter and Paul teach this in their letters (Peter in 1 Peter 2:13–17 and Paul in Romans 13:6–7).

Caring for one another

For his next section, Matthew gathers together some of Jesus' teaching about relationships. The disciples are the beginning of a new community. They are to have the highest consideration and care for one another.

The greatest in the kingdom
(18:1–9)

The disciples ask Jesus about their status in the kingdom of heaven. What sort of people is God looking for?

In answer, Jesus shows his disciples a little child. God is looking for people who will abandon their obsession with power, influence and ambition. Instead, like children, they will simply love and trust their Father. These 'little ones' (faithful people of all ages) are the greatest in the kingdom of God. They are the ones Jesus describes in the Sermon on the Mount – the 'meek' and 'poor in spirit' (Matthew 5:3–10). Anyone – inside or outside the church – who harms their faith by misleading or tempting them will be severely punished.

The parable of the lost sheep: our true value
(18:10–14)

Jesus describes God's care for the weak. They are very precious to him. They have angels who represent them before God in heaven. God is like a shepherd with a flock of 100 sheep. He will leave ninety-nine of them to find just one which has wandered away.

Dealing with sin
(18:15–20)

While thinking of the sheep that wanders off, Jesus teaches how to deal with an offence or complaint.

If a fellow believer wrongs you, it is best to deal with the matter privately, one to one. If this fails, then bring in two or three others to understand and influence the situation. Only in the last resort should the whole church get involved. If the person who is in the wrong persists, he or she is to be avoided, just as the Pharisees avoid tax collectors.

Jesus has already given Peter authority to make heavenly decisions on earth (Matthew 16:19). Now he gives this responsibility to the whole church. Jesus himself is with them when they meet to do his will.

The importance of forgiveness
(18:21–35)

Peter asks Jesus how many times he must forgive. Seven seems a generous number before finally resorting to punishment. But Jesus teaches endless forgiveness – seventy-seven times if necessary.

He tells the story of a man who owed millions of pounds. The man should have lost everything he had, including his home and family – but he was forgiven. However, the same man then found someone who owed him a fairly small amount – and threw him into prison!

For Jesus, forgiving and being forgiven are the keys to healthy relationships. We must readily forgive others – remembering the huge debt that God has already forgiven us. Jesus includes this among the priorities of the Lord's Prayer (Matthew 6:12–15). If we refuse to forgive others, then God will refuse to forgive us.

Jesus in Judea

Towards Jerusalem
(19:1 – 20:34)

JESUS GOES SOUTH

Until now, Jesus has been in the northern area of Galilee. From here, he goes south to Judea and its capital Jerusalem (19:1–2). This brings him into conflict with the Jewish authorities, and eventually leads to his death.

THE GROUNDS FOR DIVORCE

The Pharisees ask Jesus about divorce (19:3–12). Does he agree that a man can divorce his wife for the slightest reason?

Jesus takes the opposite view. He answers that marriage is a solemn and permanent commitment. God himself has given the bond of marriage, which unites a man and his wife as one person or self. Divorce is an undoing of the work of God.

The Pharisees ask a further question. If divorce is wrong, why did Moses allow men to give their wives certificates of divorce (Deuteronomy 24:1)?

Jesus explains that divorce and its certificates arise because people persist in breaking their marriages. But this is not the way of life that God intended. A man who casually dismisses his wife and takes another is committing adultery.

Now the disciples have a question. Would it be better not to marry at all?

Jesus answers that it is sometimes better not to marry. Some people are naturally single, while others remain single because they have been damaged by the hurts of life. Some (like Jesus himself, perhaps) would normally marry, but choose to stay single in the service of God. Each person must do only what is right for them.

JESUS BLESSES THE CHILDREN

Some parents bring their little children to Jesus for his blessing (19:13–15). There is a Jewish custom of bringing children for blessing on the evening of the Day of Atonement – but this is the exception. Usually children are kept out of the way of adults.

Jesus is different. When he realizes his disciples are trying to keep the children away, he makes a special point of welcoming them. Children, in their weakness and simple trust, are his role models for all believers.

THE COST OF COMMITMENT AND ITS REWARDS

A man comes to Jesus. He is young and very rich. He asks Jesus what good thing he must do to get eternal life.

Jesus answers that only God is good. If we want to take part in God's goodness, then we must keep his commandments (19:16–30).

The young man assures Jesus that he has always kept the commandments; but he knows he still lacks complete commitment.

Jesus challenges the young man to give away his great wealth and become his disciple. But this is the one thing the young man can't do. His wealth is a prison. His possessions own him.

As Jesus watches the young man leave, he remarks that it is very hard for the rich to enter the kingdom of heaven. In fact it's impossible – like a camel (a huge animal) trying to get through the eye of a needle (a tiny hole or gate).

This surprises the disciples. They are used to thinking that wealth is a sign of God's blessing. Peter points out that at least they have left everything to follow Jesus. Jesus assures them that any sacrifice of relationships or possessions will be repaid a hundred times in the world to come. And they – the Twelve – will be the judges of Israel.

The kingdom of God brings surprises. Important people (like the rich young man) will be last and the unimportant (like the little children) will be first.

THE SAME SALVATION FOR ALL

Jesus has just said that 'Many who are first will be last, and many who are last will be first' (Matthew 19:30). Now he gives an example (20:1–16).

He tells a story of a landowner who hires workers for his vineyard. He hires them at different times of day, so that some work many more hours than others. But when he comes to pay them, he gives each the same amount.

This seems very unjust to the labourers. Those who have worked just one hour receive the same pay as those who have toiled all day! But it's not that the landowner is being unfair. He is being generous. And so it is with the salvation God gives. There is no such thing as partial salvation. Even the last and least in God's kingdom are completely saved.

JESUS AGAIN PREDICTS HIS DEATH

For a third time Jesus tells his disciples he must die (20:17–19). Now he adds the detail that the Gentiles (in this case, the Romans) will execute him, and that he will be crucified. But, just as surely as he is to die, he will also be raised to life.

MRS ZEBEDEE ASKS A FAVOUR

All the talk of the first being last has worried the mother of James and John. Her sons were among the first to follow Jesus. Now she asks that they will take the highest places in the new kingdom (20:20–28).

Jesus knows that his glory will be revealed in his suffering. His glory will be the cross. Can James and John share this cup of pain? Anyway, the places of honour are not his to give. Even in this he is subject to the Father's will.

The other disciples are angry that James and John have sought special favours. Jesus tells them all that they still have the wrong idea of greatness. He is the Messiah who has come to give his life for others. They, too, must learn to serve.

JESUS HEALS TWO BLIND MEN

Jesus is leaving Jericho – the last major town before he reaches Jerusalem. The Son of David is on his way to the city of David, and a large crowd follows his progress (20:29–34).

Sitting by the roadside, two blind beggars shout for help. They shamelessly call Jesus 'Lord' and 'Son of David'. In spite of their blindness, they recognize who Jesus is – more than many people with sight.

Jesus – the Messiah with the open road before him and the crowd at his heels – stops! He calls to the beggars. He asks what they would like him to do for them. He listens to their request, is pleased to comfort them and heals their sight. In Mark's Gospel there is just one beggar and his name is Bartimaeus. Perhaps he became a well-known member of the church.

Jesus arrives in Jerusalem
(21:1–22)

Matthew does not tell us of any other visit by Jesus to Jerusalem. This is the climax of his story so far – that the Messiah comes to his city and his temple, with the humility and authority of God himself.

THE TRIUMPHAL ENTRY

From the brow of the Mount of Olives, with Jerusalem spread before him, Jesus sends ahead to borrow a donkey and her colt. He will ride into the city as Zechariah had

The temple

Herod's temple was built largely between 19 and 9 BC, although work was continuing throughout the lifetime of Jesus. Herod the Great was not himself a Jew. He was an Idumean, a descendant of Edom. The temple was the finest of many great building projects with which Herod hoped to impress and please both Romans and Jews.

The temple was built on the same site as Solomon's temple, Mount Moriah. This was the place where Abraham had almost sacrificed Isaac. Between AD 66 and 70 the Jewish resistance to Rome flared up and came to a climax in the Jewish wars. Jerusalem was besieged and conquered by the Roman army, and the temple destroyed by fire in AD 70. The triumphal Arch of Titus in Rome shows sacred objects such as the golden candlestick and the table of showbread being carried into Rome in a victory procession.

prophesied, 'gentle and riding on a donkey, on a colt, the foal of a donkey' (Zechariah 9:9). He is not coming to his people as a victorious general, but as a peacemaking king (21:1–11).

The large crowd welcomes Jesus, paving the road with cloaks and branches as a sign of royal welcome. On their lips is a cry of praise and longing: 'Hosanna!' The festival shout means 'Save us!' (from Psalm 118:25).

Jesus' arrival rocks the city. The pilgrims explain that this is their northern hero, 'the prophet from Nazareth in Galilee'.

JESUS CLEARS THE TEMPLE

As Matthew tells the story, Jesus makes straight for the temple. There he drives out the traders and money changers, whose tables and stalls clutter the court of the Gentiles (21:12–17). This is a purge! Over the years, the sale of animals and

An artist's impression of the court of the women in Herod's temple, with the Holy Place visible behind the Gate of Nicanor.

birds for sacrifice, and the exchange of street money for temple coins, has taken over the visitors' courtyard. Priests and traders have made the place a hub of commerce, with no hope of quiet prayer.

As Jesus arrives there is no mistaking the fulfilment of Malachi's prophecy: 'The Lord will suddenly come to his temple' – and vigorously reform it (Malachi 3:1–3).

Jesus proclaims his authority by quoting scripture: 'My house will be called a house of prayer.' This comes from Isaiah's prophecy that foreigners will be welcomed to the temple (Isaiah 56:6–7). 'Den of robbers' comes from Jeremiah's charge that the worshippers themselves are thieves and hypocrites (Jeremiah 7:9–11).

Jesus performs another of the Messiah's tasks by healing the blind and lame. Such people are no longer excluded from the temple, but tended and healed. Even the children add to the atmosphere of excitement by chanting their 'Hosannas'. This angers the priests, who now join the ranks of Jesus' enemies.

JESUS CURSES THE FIG TREE

On his way into Jerusalem the following day, Jesus looks for fruit on a fig tree (21:18–22). Finding none, he curses it and it withers. A tree which is all leaves and no fruit is a picture of futility – like Israel without faith and the temple without prayer. A terrible judgment is about to fall.

The disciples are amazed that the tree withers so quickly. Jesus assures them that the same power is available to them, through prayer and faith.

A war of words

(21:23 – 23:39)

Having cleared the temple courts of traders, Jesus teaches there. He is intriguing, controversial – and very popular. Soon the Jewish leaders come to challenge and cross-question him.

ON WHOSE AUTHORITY?

The chief priests and elders (the senior religious figures) ask Jesus who is giving him authority to preach and heal (21:23–27). Jesus hasn't trained in their schools or learned from their teachers. He isn't one of them. If he claims to come from God, they will charge him with blasphemy – or insanity.

Jesus (as he likes to do) answers their question with his own. Where did John's authority to baptize come from? If they say, 'From God,' then why did they not respond to John's message? If they say, 'From people,' they will fall out with the crowd, who believe John was a prophet.

THREE ATTACKING PARABLES

Jesus tells three parables which expose the corruption of Israel's religious leaders (21:28 – 22:14).

The first parable: the two sons

Jesus describes two sons who work in their father's vineyard. The first refuses to go to work, but then changes his mind and goes. The second says he is going to work, but doesn't (21:28–32).

By this story, Jesus portrays the sinful 'outsiders' (the first son) who are so surprisingly coming to faith. Such people repented when they heard John's preaching, and have welcomed the coming of Jesus. Meanwhile, the religious 'insiders' (the second son) are claiming to be right with God, but their faith is a sham.

Jesus says that the sinners who are living a new life are entering the kingdom of God ahead of the religious experts. They are, in effect, taking their place.

The second parable: the wicked tenants

Jesus tells another story. This time the religious leaders are like tenants in a vineyard (21:33–46). The vineyard is Israel – so lovingly planted and protected by God (Isaiah 5:1–5). The tenants have the care of the vineyard while the owner is away.

Jesus says that when the owner of the vineyard sends his servants to receive the fruit, the tenants ill-treat them. The servants are the prophets. And when the owner sends his son, they kill him.

Jesus asks his hearers to complete the story. They say the owner will come and throw out the wicked tenants. He will give the vineyard to new tenants, who will respect him and give him his share of the crop.

Jesus adds a saying from the Psalms: 'The stone the builders rejected has become the capstone' (Psalm 118:22). In Hebrew, the words for 'stone' and 'son' are similar. The owner's son, so dreadfully discarded, will turn out to be the keystone of the new Israel that God is building.

The third parable: the wedding banquet

In his third story, Jesus describes a king preparing a banquet (22:1–14). It is a wedding feast for his son. But the guests refuse to come! They busy themselves with their own lives – and even ill-treat and kill the king's messengers.

In his anger the king destroys the people who have murdered his servants. Then he sends his invitation to as many ordinary folk as can be found – good and bad alike – until the wedding hall is filled.

Jesus is picturing God as the king and the banquet as his kingdom. There are those who have long been invited to the banquet – the people of Israel, and especially their leaders. When those who are invited spurn the invitation, then God welcomes others in – sinners, outsiders and Gentiles.

But the new guests must also meet a standard. When the king finds someone without wedding clothes, he has him thrown out. The wedding clothes are the new attitude of repentance and faith – without which no one can take part in the kingdom of God. God's generous call must be matched by our wholehearted response.

HARD QUESTIONS

Matthew now tells us of three questions which different groups put to Jesus (22:15–40). The first two are certainly designed to trap him. The Pharisees join with the Herodians to ask Jesus if it's right for Jews to pay Roman taxes. The Sadducees then ask an elaborate question about the resurrection of the dead.

The first question: is it right to pay taxes to Caesar?

Judea is part of the Roman empire. The Jews resent this. They see themselves as God's own people, owing neither tax nor service to foreigners.

But the Romans impose a poll tax on every Jewish male. It is paid in Roman coins – a denarius, engraved with the emperor's head and the words 'son of god'.

The Pharisees and the Herodians are unlikely allies. The Pharisees have little to do with politics, except to avoid involvement with pagans as much as possible. The Herodians are supporters of the Jewish puppet king, Herod Antipas. Herod owes his position and power to his collaboration with Rome.

The two groups approach Jesus with flattery. He's his own person. He'll speak his mind. Then they put a question which is designed to lose him support. Is it right for Jews to pay the Roman tax? If Jesus says it is, all patriotic Jews will reject him. If he says it isn't, the authorities will arrest him for making trouble.

Jesus asks for one of the Roman coins. He gets them to look again at the portrait of Caesar. Taxes are the

price people pay for government – administration, roads, defence against enemies and protection from criminals. All this is Caesar's business and is to be paid for in Caesar's coin. But human beings are made in God's image, and should offer themselves to him alone.

The Pharisees and Herodians have tried to embarrass Jesus by exposing his divided loyalties. They leave with a challenge to sort out their own: 'Give Caesar his money, but give yourselves to God!'

The second question: what kind of resurrection?

The Sadducees are the Jewish ruling class. They are an elite group with an intellectual and sceptical faith. Their breeding, marriages, religion and politics are all geared to keep them in power.

While the Pharisees avoid all contact with Gentiles, the Sadducees are prepared to compromise with the Romans in order to have some influence in government. While the Pharisees believe in the resurrection of the dead and a future life, the Sadducees live for this life only.

The Sadducees come to Jesus with a question about the resurrection. Under the Jewish law, if a man dies without children, his brother must marry his widow. In this way he can raise a son and heir for his dead brother. This is called levirate marriage, and enables a man's name to live on after his death (Deuteronomy 25:5–6). It's a kind of 'resurrection' without involving heaven or an afterlife.

The Sadducees hope to show that resurrection is ridiculous and impossible. Supposing a woman has a number of levirate marriages. To which of the brothers will she be married in heaven?

Jesus shows that they are simply ignorant. They don't know their scriptures, the nature of heaven or the power of God. In heaven there is no death and no need to have children. Relationships won't be defined and restricted by marriage and sex.

Jesus reminds the Sadducees of what God said to Moses at the burning bush (Exodus 3:6). He introduced himself as 'the God of Abraham, the God of Isaac and the God of Jacob'. He is the *living* God, and those who have faith in him will share his eternal life.

The third question: which is the greatest commandment?

The Pharisees ask Jesus which is the greatest commandment. This is a frequent point of discussion among Jewish teachers, because there are so many commandments in the law. What is the central thread which runs through these hundreds of regulations?

Jesus answers by twinning two commandments: 'Love the Lord your God' (Deuteronomy 6:5) and 'Love your neighbour as yourself' (Leviticus 19:18). All the other commandments depend on these two. They are also the heart of the message of the prophets.

Love is expressed in action. We show our love for God by obeying his law. We show our love for our neighbours by treating them as we would like to be treated ourselves.

JESUS ASKS A QUESTION IN RETURN

Having answered the Pharisees' question, Jesus asks one of his own (22:41–46). What do they think about the Christ? Whose son is he?

If the Pharisees answer that the Christ is the 'Son of David', they are obviously expecting a human king. Their picture is of a great leader, descended from David, who will reign over Israel and make her a world power. Meanwhile, they reject the 'Son of David' who is Jesus, standing in front of them. He is nothing like the Christ!

Jesus refers the Pharisees to a psalm in which David speaks of the Messiah:

The Lord says to my Lord:
'Sit at my right hand' (Psalm 110:1).

'The Lord' is God and 'my Lord' is the Messiah. How can the Pharisees say the Messiah is David's son if it is clear that David calls him 'my Lord'?

The Pharisees are silenced. They don't understand that the Messiah, descended humanly from David, is also the Son of God (Romans 1:3–4).

Phylacteries

The Pharisees tie large phylacteries to their foreheads and left arms. A phylactery is a small leather box containing scrolls of texts from Exodus and Deuteronomy. It is worn at times of prayer. But some Pharisees wear large ones – all the time.

A LAMENT FOR THE JEWISH TEACHERS

Jesus wants the crowds to do what their teachers say, but not what they do! They teach the law of Moses, but they don't practise it. They make the law a huge burden, rather than a joyful freedom (23:1–36).

Jesus utters seven 'woes' on the teachers of the law and Pharisees. Woes are the opposite of blessings or beatitudes. They pronounce grief and disaster.

The Pharisees' religion is all for show, so that people will admire them. Jesus condemns them as hypocrites, which means actors or pretenders. They are more sinister than actors, because they don't admit that they're acting. People think they are genuine, but Jesus sees through them.

The Pharisees fringe their garments with long tassels to show they are rabbis or respected teachers. 'Rabbi' means 'my great one'. They like to be called 'rabbi', 'father' and 'teacher'. They are seeking a kind of glory and status which is due to God alone.

Jesus pronounces 'woes' on the teachers and Pharisees because:

◆ they don't enter the kingdom of God themselves – and they keep others from God by blocking the way with their impossible rules.
◆ they go to enormous trouble to make converts, and then burden them with legalism and pretence.
◆ they make complicated rules about swearing and oaths – as though truth could come from anything other than God.
◆ they tithe even the leaves of herbs, but neglect the things God really wants – such as justice, mercy and faithfulness. Their efforts to keep the law are elaborate and misguided – like straining out a gnat but swallowing a camel!
◆ they wash cups and dishes with the greatest care – as though clean habits make holy lives. But they never tackle the greed and selfishness in their hearts, which is the real source of pollution.

These Pharisees and teachers are blind guides, incapable of leading others. They are like whitewashed tombs, putting a mask of purity on the face of corruption. Jesus sees them trying to escape from God's anger, like vipers wriggling away from a stubble fire. But judgment is about to overtake them.

Jesus holds the religious leaders responsible for the death of every innocent person, from Abel to Zechariah. They build fine tombs to honour the prophets and martyrs of the past; but it was their ancestors, people like

Jesus and the Pharisees

The Pharisees are a group of Jews, numbering about 6,000, who try to lead perfect lives. In order to do this they have developed hundreds of rules covering every aspect of human behaviour.

To make sure they are ritually 'clean' the Pharisees wash their fingers with carefully measured amounts of water. To make sure they don't work on the sabbath they refuse to carry loads, or walk more than a certain number of paces, or even cook food on that day. Jesus teases them that they even tithe the leaves of their herbs!

But the Pharisees are sincere. They are trying to keep the Jewish people holy despite the occupation of their country by pagan Romans. They also believe that God is at work in the world through his holy angels, and that he will raise good people from death at the end of time. Jesus respects their faith in a holy God – and their desire to obey God completely.

However, some of the Pharisees have become religious snobs. They are proud of their purity and disapprove of lesser mortals. They are also control freaks, who criticize Jesus for 'working' on the sabbath when he heals people. In becoming obsessive about God's law,

they have lost sight of God's grace.

The Pharisees think they are pleasing God by keeping sinners out of his kingdom. But Jesus shows that God is welcoming them in! He makes contact with many who are 'unclean' through sin, suffering and circumstance, and helps them to realize God's love.

---

them, who persecuted and killed them.

Abel was the first person to be murdered – killed out of jealousy by his brother, Cain (Genesis 4:8). Zechariah (actually son of Jehoiada) was the last martyr recorded in the history books of the Old Testament. He was stoned to death for speaking out against the evil King Joash (2 Chronicles 24:20–22).

A LAMENT FOR JERUSALEM

After his long outburst of anger against the Pharisees and teachers, Jesus grieves for Jerusalem (23:37–39). He has longed to gather and protect his people, but his love has been spurned. Soon he will leave the temple for the last time, and the presence of God will no longer dwell there. Jesus will not return unless and until the people welcome him as their Lord and God.

Jesus predicts the future

(24:1 – 25:46)

Jesus tells his disciples of the terrible judgment which is to befall Jerusalem. He also describes the events which will bring in the end of the age and the final return of the Son of man.

THE SIGNS OF THE END

The temple, started by Herod the Great, is a most impressive building. But Jesus warns that within a generation it will be totally destroyed (24:1–14). This

will happen in AD 70 when the Roman armies of Titus capture Jerusalem. Jesus' prediction will be quoted against him at his trial.

The disciples ask Jesus privately about the timing of these events. When will the temple be destroyed? What will be the signal that he is about to return?

Jesus says there will be many false alarms. People will claim to be the Messiah. There will be international conflicts, and natural disasters such as famines and earthquakes. But these are not signs of the end. They are just the beginning. They are the first of the contractions which will bring the new age to birth.

The disciples themselves will be persecuted, executed and universally hated. The church will go through hard times, with desertions, betrayals and deceits. But, despite all this, the gospel will be preached to the whole world.

THE LOOMING CRISIS

The sign that the temple is about to be destroyed will be 'the abomination that causes desolation' (24:15–28). In time past, this was a huge idol of the Greek god Zeus which Antiochus Epiphanes set up in the temple in 167 BC. The prophet Daniel had foreseen it in his visions (Daniel 11:31).

Now something like 'the abomination' is to appear again. Emperor Gaius will try (and fail) to install a statue of himself in the temple in AD 40. The Roman legions will parade their standards in the temple before

destroying it completely along with the city in AD 70. For the Jews, this will be the ultimate desecration of their holy place.

Jesus says that when 'the abomination' appears, the people are to run for their lives. There won't be time to collect any belongings from their homes. It will be particularly hard for pregnant women. They must pray that the crisis doesn't come in winter, when the weather is cold and the roads muddy; or on the sabbath day, when it is forbidden to make any long journey.

THE COMING OF THE SON OF MAN

All this is only the judgment and destruction of Jerusalem. The cosmos will be plunged into darkness, the heavens will be rolled up like a scroll and the stars will shrivel like figs. This was how the prophet Isaiah described the fall of Babylon and the judgment of the nations, and Jesus repeats his awesome words (Isaiah 13:10; 34:4).

Many will claim to be the Messiah in these turbulent times, but they are frauds and impostors. One day Jesus will return, and there will be no mistaking his arrival (24:29–35). It will be as unmistakable as sheet lightning, which flashes across the entire sky. It will be as obvious as vultures gathering to devour the carcass of a dead animal.

The return of Jesus Christ, the Son of man, will bring in the end of the age and the end of the world. The nations will be plunged into grief. They will see the Son of man coming in power and great glory. He will harvest his people from every corner of the earth and from every part of heaven.

'BE READY!'

When will these things happen, and what is the timescale? Jesus says that the destruction of Jerusalem will take place within a generation (24:36 – 25:13). As to the date of his return, only God the Father knows which day and hour that will be. But Jesus says it will be on an ordinary day when everyone is getting on with life as usual. That is how it was when the world was destroyed by a flood in the days of Noah. That is also how it will be when the Son of man comes. His harvesting judgment will separate those who are his from those who are not – even choosing between colleagues, friends and neighbours.

In the face of this uncertainty, Jesus urges his friends to be ready – just as a houseowner would be prepared if he knew when a burglar was coming. As it is, a thief invariably takes us by surprise. The best attitude is that of the faithful servant, who is always attending to the master's business. At whatever time the master comes home, he will find his good servant ready and waiting. By contrast, the wicked servant uses his master's absence to ill-treat his fellows and neglect his duties. The master will punish him.

Jesus gives another picture of people who aren't ready for his coming. There are ten bridesmaids waiting for a bridegroom to arrive at his wedding banquet. Five of them are wise and are prepared for a long wait. They have brought extra oil to keep their lamps alight. Five are foolish, and by midnight all their oil is used up. They leave their post to try to buy some more, only to miss the arrival of the bridegroom. They find themselves shut out of the feast.

In this story, Jesus describes himself as the bridegroom. The bridesmaids are believers who are awaiting his return. The wedding feast is an image of heaven, and the oil may be a symbol of holiness or the Holy Spirit.

USE YOUR TALENTS NOW

Jesus says that his return will bring a judgment. He tells the story of a man who gives some talents of money to each of his servants (25:14–30). The talents are each worth hundreds of pounds, but they are not equally distributed. While one servant is entrusted with five, another has two and another only one.

In the master's absence, the servants have to decide what to do with his gifts. The servant with five talents invests them to make five more. The servant with two talents makes two more. The servant with only one talent digs a hole in the ground and hides it.

When the master returns, he congratulates the two servants who have made a profit with their talents, but is angry with the third. The third servant accuses his master of being hard and unpredictable, and explains that he hid the talent to keep it safe and give it back. However, the master accuses him of being both wicked and lazy. He gives the talent to the servant who now has ten, and throws the useless servant out!

Jesus promises that everyone on earth will be aware of his return. He will gather from every nation those who belong to him, and separate those who have chosen to reject him. An illustration of the Last Judgment and the resurrection of the dead, from the Psalter of Ingeborg (c. 1210).

This story is about God and the responsibility he gives to his people. He expects them to be enterprising with the resources entrusted to them, even though he seems to be absent. For Christians, this is a picture of our attitude to the gospel. When Christ returns, he will be delighted with those who have shared the good news with others, and angry with those who have wilfully kept it a secret. We may not have much (perhaps just 'one talent') but it can still be invested in the service of Christ.

SHEEP AND GOATS: THE LAST JUDGMENT

Jesus gives a more extensive picture of the final judgment (25:31–46). He does so in the form of a story.

Jesus describes himself on Judgment Day. He is the Son of man, enthroned in glory and surrounded by angels. All the nations of the world are gathered before him for judgment. He separates them into two groups, like a shepherd sorting sheep from goats. The sheep on his right are the righteous, who are to be welcomed into the kingdom of heaven. The goats on his left are the wicked, who are to be cast into hell.

How does Jesus judge who are 'sheep' and who are 'goats'? He makes his decision according to how they treat people in need – and especially those who are his disciples.

Paul teaches that Christ's people are his body (1 Corinthians 12:27). Those who feed them when they are hungry, give drink to them when they are thirsty, clothe them when they are naked, welcome them when they are strangers, tend them when they are sick and visit them in prison, are in fact ministering to Christ himself.

They are showing by their actions that they are welcoming the gospel and the kingdom of God. Those who neglect or reject such people are really neglecting or rejecting Christ.

Sometimes these words are taken to mean that we must care for people in need, regardless of whether they are Christians. For Jesus, there is the closest possible link between loving God and loving our neighbour. It is by selfless service to our neighbour (the person we have the opportunity to help) that we show our love for God. Such love may be that 'one talent' of the previous parable.

There *will* be a Judgment Day for each one of us, and it is Jesus Christ who will be our judge. On that day he will endorse a choice that we have already made. We have shown our love or rejection of him many times, in our response to the needs of our fellow human beings, and in our treatment of his messengers.

The final week

Matthew now comes to the last days of Jesus' life. He follows quite closely the story as we have it in the earlier and shorter Gospel of Mark.

From this point Jesus gives no teaching, but devotes himself to the suffering and death which he came to accomplish. While evil people think they are trapping and destroying Jesus, he is in fact going to the cross of his own free will. As events unfold, Matthew frequently points out the ancient prophecies which are being fulfilled.

Passover

Passover is the major feast of the Jewish year. The Jews remember how God secured their release from slavery in Egypt. In a single night he slew the first-born of every Egyptian family, but 'passed over' the families of the Hebrews.

The festival is held on the 14th day of the month of Nisan. Lambs for every household are sacrificed in the temple in the late afternoon. They are roasted and eaten at a family meal that evening, which is now 15th Nisan, as the next day begins with sunset.

The Passover food includes unleavened bread and bitter herbs. The original Passover bread was unleavened because it was made in haste, with no time for the yeast to raise the dough. The bitter herbs are a reminder of the bitterness of slavery. During the meal the head of the house retells the story of the Passover. The family celebrates God's goodness in rescuing his people from slavery and making them his own nation.

It is no accident that the death of Jesus takes place in Jerusalem at Passover. His self-offering and death are the fulfilment of this great festival of deliverance. Jesus is the perfect lamb of God, who is giving his life to atone for the sin of the world. Because of his death, the judgment of God will now 'pass over' all who turn to him. His rescue is from slavery to sin and death. His freedom is eternal life with God.

The plot against Jesus

(26:1–5)

The plan to kill Jesus comes from the high priest and other Jewish leaders. The fact that Jesus is in Jerusalem for the Passover festival gives them the opportunity they seek. But Jesus has the support of the common people, and his arrest could cause rioting and bloodshed.

Jesus is anointed at Bethany

(26:6–13)

While the Jewish leaders plot to take Jesus by surprise, we see that he is already preparing himself for death.

Jesus stays in the village of Bethany, near Jerusalem, as the guest of Simon the Leper. Simon may be someone Jesus has healed in the past, but whose disease has lingered on as a nickname. Bethany is the village where Lazarus lives with his sisters, Martha and Mary, and where Jesus raised Lazarus from death (John 11).

As Jesus reclines on a couch at supper, a woman pours a jar of perfume over his head. This is the action of anointing, and she may intend it as a sign that Jesus is Christ, the Anointed One. Mark and John in their Gospels tell us that the perfume is nard or spikenard, which comes from India and is used for embalming dead bodies. It is extremely expensive. When the disciples protest at the waste of money, Jesus says that the woman has prepared his body for burial.

Judas turns traitor

(26:14–16)

Judas now goes to betray Jesus to the authorities. He agrees to do so for thirty pieces (or shekels) of silver – about 120 denarii, or four months' wages. In the prophecy of Zechariah it is a paltry sum of money. It is used to pay off and dismiss the shepherd who has tended the ungrateful sheep of Israel (Zechariah 11:12–13).

Judas has not been at all prominent among the disciples until now. Matthew does not tell us why Judas betrays Jesus. The most likely reason is that Jesus is failing to seize power by force and become the Messiah that people expect. Judas may be trying to save his own life, or simply trying to make some money. John gives us a glimpse of Judas' character. He tells us that Judas keeps the common purse and steals from it (John 12:5–6).

The Last Supper

(26:17–30)

Jesus has arranged to borrow a room in Jerusalem. This is the 'upper room', where he plans to eat the Passover with his disciples.

This is the first day of the Feast of Unleavened Bread – the day before the lambs are killed in the temple. It may be that Jesus knows his arrest is imminent, and decides to share the Passover meal with his disciples a day early. If this is so, there is no roast lamb – but the true Lamb of God is with them.

During the meal, Jesus tells the disciples that one of them will betray him. They are shocked, and protest. When Judas asks if it is him, he calls Jesus 'Rabbi' ('teacher'), rather than Lord. Jesus responds that Judas is indeed the one. Judas is fulfilling a prophecy of betrayal by a close friend (Psalm 41:9), but there is still no excuse for his action.

Jesus, as the host, takes the unleavened bread and blesses God. The traditional prayer is: 'Blessed art thou, O Lord our God, King of the Universe, who bringest forth bread from the earth.' On this occasion Jesus departs from the Passover tradition and gives a new meaning to the bread. He says to his disciples, 'Take and eat; this is my body.' This is a stunning reinterpretation of the broken bread. It becomes a symbol of the broken body of Jesus – the central focus of the Holy Communion, or Eucharist, in the Christian church.

After the breaking of bread comes the sharing of wine. There are four special cups of wine at a Passover meal, and this is the third of them. Jesus takes the cup, gives thanks to God and offers it to his disciples. He declares that this is his blood, which is poured out for many. This pouring-out was predicted by the prophet Isaiah in his description of the suffering servant (Isaiah 53:12). The life of Jesus, poured out as he dies on the cross, will seal a new covenant between God and humankind.

The old covenant was sealed with the blood of a bull sprinkled over the people (Exodus 24:8). It was a covenant that depended on the keeping of the law, and it was broken almost immediately. Now Jesus is making a new covenant, which is a covenant of forgiveness. This forgiveness is secured by offering his own life as a sacrifice for the sins of the whole world.

The fourth cup of wine at the Passover meal looks forward to the Messiah's banquet in the kingdom of God. Jesus says he won't drink it until that great day comes. Having finished the meal, they sing a hymn – the last

Matthew is telling us that the destruction of Jerusalem within a generation is a judgment on the Jews for their rejection of Jesus. His blood is to be 'on them and on their children'. This has sometimes been taken as an eternal curse on the Jews for killing the Messiah. But Matthew only sees the punishment falling on one generation. Furthermore, it is the Roman governor who sentences Jesus, and the Roman soldiers who put him to death.

Although Pilate believes Jesus is innocent, he still has him flogged. This is the cruellest of beatings, and can kill a person who isn't strong enough to endure it.

A mock coronation

(27:27–31)

The Roman soldiers give Jesus a mock coronation. These are tough and cynical mercenaries, probably drawn from nations which hate the Jews. Jesus is to receive the rage and spite of Gentiles just as he did the blows and insults of the Jewish leaders.

The Roman battalion numbers about 600 soldiers. When they are all assembled, they strip their prisoner and dress him in a red cloak. This is his royal robe. They also place a staff in his hand as a sceptre and press a circle of thorns on his head for a crown. They would usually grant their victim's last request and then kill him. In the case of Jesus, their orders are to take him out of the city for crucifixion.

Jesus is crucified

(27:32–44)

The place where Jesus is to be executed is called Golgotha, which means 'the place of the skull'. Today it is possible that the Church of the Holy Sepulchre stands on the site, just outside the old city wall of Jerusalem.

Jesus is unable to carry the crosspiece. It is far too heavy for his tortured body and bleeding back. The soldiers pull a visitor from the crowd, Simon from Cyrene in North Africa. They force him to carry the beam.

When they arrive at the place of execution, Jesus is offered a drink of wine mixed with gall. This may be a drug to dull the pain, or a foul mixture to add to the cruelty (Psalm 69:21). Either way, Jesus refuses it.

Matthew doesn't dwell on the act of crucifixion. Instead, he conveys that Jesus is going through the extremes of suffering described in the most desolate psalms. His drink is bitter. His clothes are divided by the gambling soldiers. He is insulted by passers-by, teased about his 'temple' saying and challenged to save himself.

The cruellest mockery of all is that God doesn't seem to care. He is living through the physical and spiritual hell described in Psalm 22.

As Matthew tells the story, the situation is steeped in agony and irony. The charge above Jesus' head is that he is 'King of the Jews' – which is true. The sarcastic suggestion of the crowd is that he is the Son of God – which is also true. The priests declare that, although Jesus has saved others, he cannot save himself – which is also very true.

Jesus is enduring physical pain, mental torture, undeserved abuse, social rejection and gross injustice. The robbers hanging either side of him are probably political rebels. If so, then Jesus is being linked with a crime he has always rejected and avoided.

Jesus dies

(27:45–56)

Jesus hangs on the cross from midday until mid-afternoon. As he does so, darkness covers the land. This is not an eclipse of the sun, as the moon is full at Passover time. We don't know whether the darkness is caused by dust or cloud cover, but for Matthew it signals God's judgment. Darkness was one of the plagues which preceded the exodus (Exodus 10:22). The prophet Amos says of the Day of the Lord:

> *I will make the sun go down at noon*
> *and darken the earth in broad daylight* (Amos 8:9).

After three hours, Jesus cries out with great passion, 'My God, my God, why have you forsaken me?' These are the opening words of Psalm 22 – the prayer of a person who feels cut off from God. The word for God is the Hebrew 'Eloi', and the bystanders think Jesus is calling for Elijah. The Jews expect the prophet Elijah to appear at the end of the age, or to help in time of need.

Someone gives Jesus a drink of wine vinegar, soaked into a sponge. This is a common drink, and may be provided by the soldiers. Matthew is echoing another psalm: 'They put gall in my food and give me vinegar for my thirst' (Psalm 69:21).

Finally Jesus gives one last loud cry and dies. As he does so, the earth is shaken by a quake; the great temple curtain is torn and the graves of holy people break open.

The temple curtain screens off the Most Holy Place – the heart of God's presence among his people. Only the high priest is allowed into this sanctuary, once a year, on the Day of Atonement. He takes with him the blood of the sacrifices he has made for his own sins and the sins of the people. Now the thick sixty-foot curtain is ripped from top to bottom – torn open from God's side. The death of Jesus has opened the way for all people to enter the presence of God.

Matthew uses the quake as a sign of the mighty upheaval that is taking place in earth and heaven. Death itself is being conquered and the new age of eternal life is breaking in. He describes how the tombs of holy people are burst open. These people appear in 'the holy city' after Jesus' resurrection. Jesus' victory is to be shared by all faithful people – including the saints who lived in the past.

The women who have come with Jesus from Galilee are also watching at a distance. Matthew mentions three of them by name: Mary of Magdala, Mary the mother of James and Joseph, and the mother of James and John. This last woman is called Salome in Mark's Gospel. John's Gospel tells us that she is the sister of Mary the mother of Jesus. Two Marys – Mary of Magdala and 'the other Mary' – will also witness Jesus' burial and be the first to visit the empty tomb.

Jesus is crucified – perhaps the most painful form of execution ever devised. It was reserved for slaves. A Byzantine fresco (c. 1072–78) from the Basilica of San Angelo Formis, Capua.

Jesus is buried
(27:57–61)

As far as the Jewish law is concerned, Jesus is an executed criminal. He must be buried before sunset (Deuteronomy 21:22–23).

Matthew lists the witnesses of this awesome event. They are men and women, Gentiles and Jews; people who have known Jesus for years, and people who have possibly never heard of him until that day.

The centurion and his squad of soldiers see all that happens – and are terrified. They have heard the Jews scorn Jesus as the Son of God, but now they are firmly convinced that he is someone special.

The Romans will leave the body on the ground for the vultures. The Jews will throw it in an unmarked trench.

A wealthy member of the Jewish Council now offers his help. He is Joseph of Arimathea, who is himself a disciple of Jesus and has had no part in the plot to kill him. He takes prompt and selfless action.

Joseph goes to Pilate, the Roman governor, to ask for permission to take Jesus'

The perfect sacrifice

In the letter to the Hebrews, Jesus is seen as the perfect high priest offering the perfect sacrifice. He gains access to the Most Holy Place, the presence of God, not with the blood of animals, but with his own blood:

He did not enter by means of the blood of goats and calves; but he entered the Most Holy Place once for all by his own blood (Hebrews 9:12).

On the cross, Jesus pays the ultimate price of human sin. His sacrifice is completely acceptable and sufficient – and will never need to be repeated. Paul writes, 'He himself is our peace, who… has destroyed the barrier, the dividing wall of hostility' (Ephesians 2:14). Jesus is making peace between God and humanity, and between Jew and Gentile.

body. He wraps it in a clean linen cloth and lays it in his own new tomb. After the dreadful and traumatic events of the day, Joseph's dignified and generous act allows Jesus a decent and reverent burial. The tomb is cut into rock, with a great stone across the entrance to keep out thieves and wild animals.

Matthew describes Joseph as a rich man. The prophet Isaiah says of the suffering servant: 'He was assigned a grave with the wicked, and with the rich in his death' (Isaiah 53:9).

The tomb is guarded
(27:62–66)

The chief priests and Pharisees are anxious about the influence of Jesus even after he is dead. Although it is a holy day, the Passover sabbath, these strict Jews go into the presence of Pilate, the Gentile governor. They warn Pilate that Jesus, although he was an impostor, promised to rise from death. They ask for a guard to be placed at the tomb at least during the danger period of the next few days.

Pilate agrees that the tomb may be guarded – probably by the Jewish temple police. Later these men will report that they fell asleep at their posts. This doesn't sound like Roman soldiers.

Only Matthew records this story about the guards. He is answering the rumour that the disciples stole the body of Jesus and that the resurrection was a hoax. He assures us that no such theft was possible. The tomb is sealed and guarded.

The resurrection and mission of Jesus

Empty tomb and risen Lord
(28:1–10)

The sabbath is over. It is the first day of the week. Mary of Magdala and 'the other Mary' go to look at Jesus' tomb. The 'other Mary' is the mother of James and Joseph (27:56). Matthew has already told us that they are two women who watched as Jesus died and also saw where he was buried (27:61).

There is a violent earthquake – as there was when Jesus died. An angel of the Lord appears, rolls back the stone from the entrance to the tomb and sits on it. The guards are paralysed with fear. Matthew attempts an imaginative description of the actual event – something from which the other Gospel writers hold back.

The angel explains to the women that Jesus is no longer in the tomb. He shows them the place where his body had been laid – as they well remember. He urges them to tell the other disciples that Jesus is risen from death and will see them in Galilee.

None of the Gospels describes the actual resurrection of Jesus. Matthew gives the most dramatic account of the events surrounding it, with a violent earthquake and dazzling angel. The angel's appearance is like lightning and his clothes as white as snow. This is how some of the Bible writers describe the indescribable – the glory of heaven appearing on earth. This angel is God at work.

As time goes by, there will be more sensational versions of this story, as people strive to convey a unique and world-changing event. Compared with these, Matthew's account is relatively simple and restrained. Even so, he conveys the earth-shaking power and stunned bewilderment of the first Easter morning.

As the women hurry from the tomb, Jesus meets them. Matthew doesn't describe his appearance, but says that the women worship him and are able to hold his feet. He is present with them, alive and tangible.

Jesus' greeting is downbeat and informal, like saying,

'Hello.' He tells the women not to be afraid, and sends a message to his disciples, whom he calls 'my brothers'. The denials and desertions of the last few days have done nothing to dim his love for them or change their relationship. He promises to meet them in Galilee.

It is exciting that Jesus asks women to be his witnesses. Their evidence would not be allowed in a Jewish court. It is also striking that he prefers to appear in Galilee, rather than Jerusalem. The risen Christ is challenging assumptions about people and places.

Matthew has already quoted Isaiah's words about Galilee, which is regarded by strict Jews as cosmopolitan and corrupt:

> *The people walking in darkness*
> *have seen a great light;*
> *on those living in the land of the shadow of death*
> *a light has dawned (Isaiah 9:2).*

While Jerusalem rejects and kills God's Messiah, Galilee is a place of new beginnings.

An attempt to conceal the truth
(28:11–15)
Matthew concludes his story about the guards. They go to the chief priests and tell them what has happened. The priests bribe them to say that the disciples stole Jesus' body while they were asleep. Matthew is concerned that, years later, this damaging lie is still being circulated among the Jews.

The great commission
(28:16–20)
The eleven disciples meet with Jesus on a mountain in Galilee. It was on a mountain that Jesus gave them his new commandments. Matthew likes to show Jesus as the new Moses.

Matthew captures the moment when the disciples first see Jesus in his risen life. The truth dawns on them slowly – some worshipping, while others hesitate.

Jesus tells them that he is now the Lord of all things. Satan had once offered him 'all the kingdoms of the world and their splendour' (4:8). Now Jesus has all authority both on earth and in heaven.

Jesus commissions his disciples to continue his work. They are to go to all nations now – not just Israel, as in the past. The gospel is for the Gentiles too. They are to baptize all people, as a sign that they belong to Christ

and are clean and ready for his return. This baptism is to be in the name of the one God, who is Father, Son and Holy Spirit. This is the first time that Jesus has included himself in the name of God.

The disciples are to teach everyone to obey Christ's commands. The good news is to be expressed in good lives – lives which show truth, purity and love.

Finally, Jesus promises to be with his disciples in this great task. Just as God promised Moses and Joshua that he would always be with them, so Jesus promises to strengthen his disciples. Their mission is to continue to the end of the age – that is, until he returns. The Lord of all will be with them always.

MARK

The Gospel of Mark is a vivid account of the life of Jesus. This is the shortest of the four Gospels we have in the New Testament, and many scholars think it was the first to be written.

Mark tells us about the life and death of Jesus – the Messiah who is truly the Son of God. Jesus teaches and heals with astonishing power and authority. However, his closest followers don't really understand him – and the Jewish authorities reject him absolutely. Jesus himself is convinced that he must suffer and die before being raised to life in triumph. The twin peaks of the Gospel are when two people recognize Jesus' real identity. The first is Simon Peter, who declares, 'You are the Christ.' The second is the Roman soldier in charge of Jesus' execution, who says, 'Surely this man was the Son of God!'

Outline

Jesus arrives (1:1–8)

John the Baptist prepares the way (1:1–8)

Jesus is baptized (1:9–11)

Jesus is tempted (1:12–13)

Jesus begins his ministry (1:14 – 3:6)

Jesus calls disciples to follow him (1:14–20)

Jesus teaches and heals people (1:21–39)

Jesus heals a man suffering from leprosy (1:40–45)

Jesus forgives sins (2:1–12)

Jesus calls Levi (2:13–17)

A time to feast! (2:18–22)

The sabbath debate (2:23 – 3:6)

The mission and miracles of the Messiah (3:7 – 9:50)

Nowhere to hide (3:7–12)

The twelve apostles (3:13–19)

Jesus and Beelzebub (3:20–30)

Jesus' family (3:31–35)

The parable of the sower (4:1–20)

Some more parables (4:21–34)

Jesus calms a storm (4:35–41)

'Legion' (5:1–20)

A dead girl and a sick woman (5:21–43)

A prophet without honour (6:1–6)

Jesus sends out the Twelve (6:7–13)

The death of John the Baptist (6:14–29)

Jesus feeds 5,000 people (6:30–44)

Jesus walks on water (6:45–56)

The difference between dirt and sin (7:1–23)

The Syro-Phoenician woman (7:24–30)

Jesus heals a man who is deaf and dumb (7:31–37)

Jesus feeds a crowd of 4,000 (8:1–21)

A blind man receives his sight – gradually (8:22–26)

The secret is out (8:27–30)

Dying to live (8:31–38)

A glimpse of glory (9:1)

The transfiguration (9:2–13)

A difficult healing (9:14–29)

A solemn warning (9:30–32)

Who is the greatest? (9:33–37)

No fear of competition (9:38–41)

Drastic measures (9:42–50)

The road south to suffering (10:1–52)

Jesus is asked about divorce (10:1–12)

Jesus welcomes some children (10:13–16)

A rich young man (10:17–31)

The road to death – and life! (10:32–34)

Ambition (10:35–45)

Blind Bartimaeus (10:46–52)

Jesus comes to Jerusalem (11:1 – 13:37)

The triumphal entry (11:1–11)

Jesus judges a fig tree... and the temple (11:12–26)

Jesus is cross-questioned (11:27–33)

The parable of the tenants (12:1–12)

A trick question about tax (12:13–17)

A trick question about resurrection (12:18–27)

The key commandment (12:28–34)

The riddle of the Messiah (12:35–37)

A warning (12:38–40)

A poor widow (12:41–44)

Jesus foretells the future (13:1–2)

Signs of the times (13:3–31)

When will Jesus return? (13:32–37)

The longest night (14:1 – 15:47)

The Passover plot (14:1–2)

A woman anoints Jesus (14:3–9)

Judas Iscariot (14:10–11)

The Last Supper (14:12–25)

Jesus predicts Peter's denial (14:26–31)

In the Garden of Gethsemane (14:32–42)

Jesus is arrested (14:43–52)

Jesus before the Jewish Council (14:53–65)

Peter denies Jesus (14:66–72)

Jesus is tried by the Roman governor (15:1–15)

Jesus is mocked by the soldiers (15:16–20)

Jesus is crucified (15:21–32)

Jesus dies (15:33–41)

Jesus is buried (15:42–47)

After sunrise (16:1–8)

INTRODUCTION

The writing of Mark's Gospel

Mark may have written his account of Jesus for the Christian church in Rome.

During the reign of Emperor Nero (the AD 60s) Christians were cruelly persecuted for their faith. In particular, they were accused of causing the Great Fire which destroyed a large part of the city. This was the fire during which Nero is said to have played his fiddle – because it suited him to clear the slums of Rome for his rebuilding programme.

In Palestine at this time, the Jews were attempting to overthrow their Roman overlords. This conflict ended in total defeat for the Jews and the tragic destruction of the temple in AD 70. Of course, the first Christians were bound to wonder what the world was coming to! Mark records what Jesus said about suffering – and about the signs of the last days.

Mark shows us Jesus' power

Mark starts his story from the time when Jesus is baptized by John the Baptist. Luke, in his Gospel, tells us that John is Jesus' cousin. Mark shows us Jesus teaching and healing around the towns and villages of Galilee, and calling and training twelve disciples. His message is that the kingdom of God is arriving!

Jesus is able to drive out evil spirits and cure people of disease and disability. Mark reports the amazement on people's faces and the buzz of excitement that Jesus might be the long-awaited Messiah.

While ordinary people welcome Jesus, the religious authorities are hostile. They say Jesus is mixing with bad characters and breaking some of the commandments. They explain Jesus' power over evil by saying he works for the devil. Even Jesus' family begin to wonder whether he is in his right mind.

Jesus uses parables (thought-provoking stories) to give some ideas of what God's kingdom is like. For example, God's kingdom may be almost invisible, like a mustard seed. But, like a mustard seed, it will grow very large. In the end there will be no mistaking it.

Mark shows us how Jesus is stronger than every power in the world of nature and the realm of the spirits. He calms a storm, banishes demons and calls a dead girl back to life. He miraculously provides food for very large crowds – and even walks on water.

Why do Christians suffer?

Mark was probably writing his Gospel for Christians enduring great persecution. They must have asked the questions: is Jesus the Messiah? Has the kingdom of God come? If so, why are we having such a bad time? It's as though they are engulfed in a storm of suffering.

In answer, Mark tells how the disciples were once caught in a storm at sea, while Jesus lay asleep in the stern of their boat. When they woke him in their panic, he was able to calm the wind and the sea instantly. Mark says that Jesus warned his disciples they would suffer persecution for his sake. If they are following him only for power and glory, they had better think again.

DISCOVERING MARK

Jesus arrives

John the Baptist prepares the way
(1:1–8)

Mark tells us that this is the 'gospel'. It is the God-talk or 'good news' about Jesus Christ. This story of misunderstanding, rejection and death will have a happy ending.

Jesus is the Messiah and Son of God – but not in the way that most people expect. He will not be a military leader. He will not crush the Romans and set up a Jewish state. Jesus the Messiah will seem utterly defeated before he wins. But he is God's Son, and he will carry out his Father's work.

John is dressed like Elijah – the great prophet who lived 800 years ago. He preaches in the desert. He baptizes all who want to turn to God. Baptism is a complete drenching with water. It is the sign of a spiritual wash. Someone being baptized is drowning to their old sinful life and starting fresh and clean with God.

John is looking forward to the arrival of God's Messiah. For all his power and popularity, John sees himself merely as the Messiah's lowliest slave. All John can do is give people a wash – but the Messiah will immerse people in the Holy Spirit, the very life of God.

The Son of God

Mark refers to Jesus as the 'Son of God' on just a few very special occasions – at his baptism, at his transfiguration and as he dies on the cross.

The Jews regard their whole nation as God's 'Son'. But now, at Jesus' baptism, the voice of God declares, 'You are my Son, whom I love.' Jesus is God's only Son – as unique and precious as Isaac was to Abraham. And, like Isaac, Jesus will be obedient to his Father, even to the point of death.

Jesus is baptized
(1:9–11)

Jesus comes from the north to the River Jordan, and is baptized by John. He has no sin to be washed away, but he joins with all those who are turning to God. As he comes out of the water, he sees heaven opened and the Holy Spirit descending on him. The Spirit has the gentleness and purity of a dove fluttering down and settling on Jesus. A voice from heaven says, 'You are my Son, whom I love.' It may be that only Jesus sees the Spirit and hears the voice. But we are let in on the great secret – that the Son of God is here.

Jesus is tempted
(1:12–13)

No sooner is Jesus baptized than he is driven by the Spirit into the desert. He wrestles with Satan for forty days. In the other Gospels we learn that Satan attacks Jesus with wrong ideas of how to act as God's Son in trying to change the world.

The desert is one of the Bible's important places – and forty is one of its special numbers. The Israelites were in the desert for forty years, training to be God's own people.

Satan is first mentioned in the opening chapters of the book of Job. He is an angel who confronts God and criticizes his people. He is 'the accuser', who argues that the human race has failed and should be destroyed. Mark shows a battle between Jesus and Satan, with Jesus overpowering demons, disease and death.

Jesus begins his ministry

Jesus begins his public life by preaching the same message as John: 'The kingdom of God is near.' But he adds: 'Repent and believe the good news!' He visits the towns and villages of Galilee. This region has a very mixed population of Jews and Gentiles.

Jesus calls disciples to follow him
(1:14–20)

Jesus calls others to join him. The first four are two pairs of brothers: Simon (later called Peter) and Andrew, James and John. They are all fishermen. The call of Jesus is so strong that they leave their families and businesses to follow him. They are the first disciples – 'learners', or apprentices.

Jesus teaches and heals people
(1:21–39)

In the lakeside town of Capernaum, Jesus teaches in the synagogue. He frees a man from an evil spirit. This is the first example of Jesus being stronger than the power of evil. Later he heals Simon's mother-in-law of a fever. That evening, after the sabbath rest is over, people carry their sick friends and relatives along to the house to be healed.

Jesus is already getting too busy to preach. Early the next day, after prayer, he decides to move on to other villages. His first priority is to announce the kingdom of God.

Jesus heals a man suffering from leprosy
(1:40–45)

A man comes to Jesus. He is suffering with leprosy. This is a skin disease which spreads very quickly and has no cure. But Jesus heals him. He ignores custom and common sense to reach out and touch the man. Instead of Jesus catching the leper's illness, the leper catches Jesus' health. The power of God is stronger than incurable disease.

The remains of a synagogue at Capernaum. Built in the 3rd century AD, it probably stands on the site of the one in which Jesus amazed worshippers by his teaching and rebuking of an evil spirit.

Jesus tells the cured leper to report to the priest, who will give him permission to live a normal life once again. Jesus also cautions the man very sternly not to tell anyone what has happened. But the news spreads, and Jesus is driven out of town by the number of people clamouring to see him.

Jesus forgives sins
(2:1–12)

Back in Capernaum, the pressure of life continues. There is such a crowd around Jesus that one man is lowered through the roof to get to him. This man is suffering from paralysis, but Jesus sees that his real problem is guilt. He tells him that his sins are forgiven. Some teachers of the law are outraged by this, because forgiving sins is something only God can do. To prove his point, Jesus goes right ahead and cures the man of his paralysis as well.

Jesus calls Levi
(2:13–17)

Jesus calls a tax collector, Levi, to become one of his disciples. Tax collectors are hated because they have absolute power to take money from people. The money they collect goes to maintain the Roman empire, with its armies, navies, magistrates, administrators and roads. The Jews treat tax collectors as the scum of the earth. But not Jesus. He shocks religious people by mixing freely with tax collectors, like a doctor visiting the sick.

A time to feast!
(2:18–22)

Jesus tells the Pharisees to loosen up! The kingdom of God is arriving. This is a time to be happy and take risks. Their dried-out legalism is like an old garment which will tear, or an old wineskin which will burst.

The sabbath debate
(2:23 – 3:6)

The Pharisees criticize Jesus. He is allowing his disciples to work on the sabbath. They are harvesting and preparing food! Jesus reminds the Pharisees that the great King David had helped himself to the high priest's holy bread when he and his companions were starving. The sabbath is meant to be a pleasure. The Pharisees have made it an obstacle course of legal barriers and pitfalls. Now, 'The Lord of the sabbath is with them, to show how the day is to be enjoyed.'

On another occasion, Jesus heals a man with a shrivelled hand on the sabbath. The critics are waiting to pounce, but Jesus challenges them. Isn't healing and deliverance what the sabbath is all about?

Miracles

Mark describes some of Jesus' miracles. They prove that the kingdom of God is a reign of healing and release. They also reveal who Jesus is.

But miracles depend on faith. Those who believe that Jesus has God's authority are healed. When Jesus goes home to Nazareth, he is far too ordinary for their taste. They have very little faith in him – and he can do very little for them.

Jesus' enemies agree that he can deliver people from evil spirits. But they explain it by saying that Jesus is working for the devil.

As well as miracles of healing and deliverance, Jesus feeds large crowds, walks on water and destroys a fig tree with a curse. All these actions show God at work – feeding, rescuing and (in the case of the fig tree) judging his people.

From now on there is no pleasing the Pharisees. They form an unholy alliance with the Herodians, with the aim of killing Jesus. The Herodians are the servants of Herod Antipas, the local king.

Jesus is a target of hatred by both the religious and secular authorities. But the evil spirits know who he is. They cry out, 'You are the Son of God' (3:11).

The mission and miracles of the Messiah

Jesus spends the first part of his ministry preaching and healing around the towns and villages of Galilee.

Nowhere to hide
(3:7–12)

People are coming from as far away as Jerusalem in the south and Tyre on the coast to hear Jesus preach and to beg him to heal them. The pressure is so intense that Jesus has a boat on stand-by in case he needs to escape. While everyone wonders what his miracles mean, the evil spirits have no doubt.

The twelve apostles
(3:13–19)

Jesus chooses twelve men to share his life. He calls them 'apostles', which means 'those who are sent'. First he will teach them to preach and heal and cast out evil spirits. Then he will send them out to do God's work. The number twelve reflects the number of tribes of Israel. This is the start of a new people of God.

Simon is listed first. He is given the nickname 'Peter' – the Greek word for 'Stone'. Peter is to be a foundation stone of the church. James and John are nicknamed 'Boanerges', which means 'Sons of Thunder' – perhaps a teasing reference to their stormy tempers. Bartholomew sounds like a surname and may be the same person as Nathanael. Matthew is thought to be the same person as Levi. There is another Simon in the group, and he is described as 'the Zealot'. The Zealots are a group who will later dedicate themselves to overthrowing the Romans.

The kingdom of God

The kingdom of God is wherever God reigns. It is not in any particular territory except the hearts of men and women. The Jews think of God as their king and long for the day when the whole world will acknowledge him. The Old Testament prophets foretell that one day God will reign from Mount Zion in Jerusalem, and that all nations will enjoy his justice and peace.

Now Jesus announces that this kingdom of God is very close. People can turn to God and enter his kingdom now. The kingdom is arriving because Jesus is here. He is sharing love with outcasts, healing the sick and rescuing those in the grip of Satan. He is also warning that God's judgment will fall on those who wilfully reject him.

So has the kingdom of God come yet? Jesus declares that it is arriving with his own arrival. He teaches that it will increase. He promises that it will be completely established one day.

The apostles are all very different from each other, in personality and temperament, politics and background. Andrew and Philip, for example, have Greek names, while the rest are Jewish. Matthew the ex-tax collector will live side by side with Simon the Zealot. And included in the group is Judas Iscariot, who will one day betray Jesus.

Jesus and Beelzebub
(3:20–30)

The teachers of the law come from Jerusalem – their headquarters. They explain Jesus' power over demons.

They say he is possessed by Beelzebub, the prince of demons. But Jesus has the perfect answer for them. If Satan is overthrowing his own agents, then the kingdom of hell is collapsing. But Jesus is angry. To say a work of God is the work of Satan is an outrageous lie and a dreadful blasphemy. It is unforgivable.

Jesus' family
(3:31–35)

Jesus' mother and brothers come to see him. They have to stand outside the crowded house where he is teaching.

When he is told they are waiting for him, he seems to snub them. In fact he has a commitment to God which comes even before his family. His closest relatives are those who are joining him in doing God's will.

The parable of the sower
(4:1–20)

For the first time in Mark's Gospel we are able to listen to Jesus teaching. He sits in a boat, so that the crowd doesn't overwhelm him, and teaches the people along the shore.

He describes a farmer scattering seed. The seed lands in various places – on a path, on rock, among thorns and on good soil. The birds snatch it from the path, the sun scorches it on the rock and the thorns choke it! But the good soil produces a wonderful harvest.

This is a parable. Jesus tells many such stories. He leaves it to his hearers to make the connection between his everyday images and the kingdom of God.

Later, the Twelve ask Jesus what these parables mean. He explains that the good news of the kingdom is like a secret being shared. Some people are spiritually blind and can't see it. Some are spiritually deaf and can't hear it. Some refuse to believe in God and block it out. He reminds them that the prophet Isaiah had to live with this frustration. Isaiah also delivered God's message to people who couldn't or wouldn't receive it (Isaiah 6:9–10). Now Jesus is doing the same.

He explains the parable of the sower. The seed is a picture of God's good news being broadcast. The different places it falls are people's hearts. Some hearts are hard, some shallow, some overcrowded and some open and deep. In spite of all the setbacks, the good news is going to produce a record harvest.

Some more parables
(4:21–34)

Jesus tells some other parables. The good news is like a light which is destined to shine out. If the disciples share the gospel generously, they will receive abundant blessings. God's kingdom is coming like a crop growing – slowly but surely, day and night. Its beginning may be small, like a mustard seed which is almost invisible, but in the end it will be unmissable and unmistakable – a landmark and a shelter.

The parable of the growing seed is exclusive to Mark. It pictures the kingdom of God as being already here in a small way – almost hidden, but with amazing potential.

Jesus calms a storm
(4:35–41)

Jesus and his disciples are caught in a sudden storm. The Lake of Galilee is famous for such storms, and they are very dangerous. Jesus is unworried. He stays sound asleep in the stern of the boat. In the end the panic-stricken

---

'The country of the Gerasenes' is across the Sea of Galilee from Capernaum. Here Legion was delivered from the evil spirits which tormented and isolated him. This view is of Golan and the Sea of Galilee from Susita (ancient Hippos).

A sign of life

Jairus' daughter has been brought back to this life, to enjoy the rest of her years on earth. The miracle is a sign that Jesus has power over death – just as he has power over wind and waves, disease and demons. From now on, death is not the end of life. For the Christian, death is only a falling asleep – awaiting the new life that God will give through his Son, Jesus Christ.

In John's Gospel, Jesus raises his friend Lazarus from death. On his way to the tomb, he assures the dead man's sister: 'I am the resurrection and the life. He who believes in me will live, even though he dies; and whoever lives and believes in me will never die' (John 11:25–26).

disciples have to wake him. Astonishingly, Jesus stands up in the boat and simply commands the wind and the sea to settle down – like telling a dog to be quiet.

From being terrified of the storm, the disciples are now in awe of Jesus. Who is this, who can even control the forces of nature? In the Psalms it was God who 'stilled the storm to a whisper' (Psalm 107:29).

The first Christians would have valued this story because it teaches that Jesus is very near and able to help – even when he seems to be absent (or asleep!).

'Legion'
(5:1–20)

The story of Jesus controlling a physical storm is followed by a story of him controlling a spiritual storm. He heals a man who is possessed by a host of demons.

Jesus and his disciples meet a man whose life is a living hell. He is possessed by so many demons that his nickname is 'Legion' – a legion being 6,000 Roman soldiers! These demons give him incredible strength. He is a terror to all, and a danger to himself. He lives, desolate and abandoned, among the tombs.

The evil spirits in Legion recognize Jesus. Jesus commands them to leave the wretched man and permits them to go into a large herd of pigs. The pigs stampede down a steep bank into the sea, where they are drowned.

When the local people see what has happened, they stop being afraid of Legion and start being afraid of Jesus.

They beg him to leave their region. Legion wants to become a disciple, but Jesus sends him home to his family.

The region of the Gerasenes is hard to place. There is a town called Gerasa, but it is about thirty miles away from the lake. Perhaps Mark is thinking of Gadara, which is only six miles from the lake. The Decapolis is the Greek name for a group of ten towns on the east bank of the Jordan River.

Jesus is stronger than a horde of devils. While Satan inflicts torment and destruction, Jesus brings sanity and peace. Pigs are, for the Jews, unclean animals – so the unclean spirits are banished to live in unclean beasts. The herd destroys itself, just as Legion had been doing under the influence of the demons within him.

A dead girl and a sick woman
(5:21–43)

Jesus returns to Capernaum and a hero's welcome. In the crowd is Jairus, the administrator of the local synagogue. His twelve-year-old daughter is desperately ill. Although he is an important man, he abandons his pride to beg Jesus for help.

Jesus agrees to go with Jairus, but they are delayed by the crowd. Suddenly Jesus is aware that he has lost some of his power. A woman has touched his cloak and has been cured of chronic bleeding. She has had the problem for twelve years. The law has forced her to live apart from her husband and friends and she has spent all her money on doctors. None of them has been able to help her. She certainly should not be mixing in a crowd, but when she touches Jesus' cloak she is healed immediately.

Jesus insists that the woman is found and brought forward. He explains that her faith has healed her. She doesn't have to feel guilty that she has stolen a cure, nor be afraid that her problem will recur. He sends her away with the words: 'Be healthy!'

Meanwhile, precious time has been lost. A message comes that Jairus' daughter has died. But Jesus encourages Jairus to have faith. Arriving at the house, he tells the chorus of funeral mourners to go away. The child is only asleep.

Jesus speaks to the little girl in Aramaic: 'Talitha koum!' – 'Little Lamb, get up!' Her recovery is instant. She gets up, walks around – and is ready for something to eat!

Once again, Jesus urges that this miracle be kept secret. It is an impossible request, as the whole town seems to know of the crisis and its happy outcome.

Peter, James and John are Jesus' closest friends. They form an inner group within the Twelve. They are with Jesus when he raises Jairus' daughter to life, as well as on other important occasions. They will be with him on the mountain when he is transfigured in glory – and in the garden of Gethsemane when he is racked with fear. It is thought that Peter in particular passed on his memories to Mark.

A prophet without honour
(6:1–6)

Jesus and his disciples go to Jesus' home town. Here are the people who were his friends and neighbours, who were at school with him or came to his carpenter's shop. They have heard of his fame and are impressed by his teaching; but they are disappointed in him. They know him too well. He is too ordinary. They refer to him as 'Mary's son' – a little joke they have about his father. For them Jesus is far from unique. For a start, he has brothers and sisters…

Jesus knows that prophets are never accepted in their own home town. His friends miss out, because their lack of faith blocks God's power to help them.

Five loaves and two fish?

There have been many attempts to explain the feeding of the crowd. Some people think that everyone shared the food they had with them. But that would hardly be a miracle. All four Gospels tell this story, and they are all certain that something miraculous took place.

As Jesus directs the crowd to sit down in groups of hundreds and fifties, some would think of the prophet Elisha. He fed 100 men from just twenty barley loaves (2 Kings 4:42–44). Others, seeing 5,000 men sitting in ordered ranks, would remember how God fed the Israelites in the desert with manna and quail (Exodus 16; Numbers 11). For Christians, the way Jesus takes the bread, thanks God, breaks and shares it, is a reminder of Holy Communion. The twelve baskets of scraps seem like a promise of enough for all future generations.

Jesus has already been rejected by the teachers of the law and the Pharisees. Now he is spurned by his friends and neighbours. In John's Gospel we read, 'He came to that which was his own, but his own did not receive him' (John 1:11). The people of Jesus' home town are a sample of the whole Jewish nation. They are rejecting the very person they are waiting for.

Jesus sends out the Twelve
(6:7–13)

Jesus now sends his disciples to extend his work. They go in pairs, so that they can support and encourage each other, and so that people will have the word of two witnesses.

Jesus gives them the power of God over evil spirits. They travel like pilgrims, without food, money or baggage. They depend entirely on God and the hospitality of strangers. If their message is rejected, they must shake the dust of the place from their clothes and feet – a sign that they will have nothing more to do with that town. Their message is not that 'Jesus is Lord', because they hardly understand that themselves as yet. They preach the same message as John the Baptist and Jesus – that the kingdom of God is arriving and that people must repent. They prove that the kingdom of God is present by demonstrating God's power: driving out demons and healing the sick.

The death of John the Baptist
(6:14–29)

While the disciples are away, Mark tells how John the Baptist died.

John had been arrested by King Herod – that is, Herod Antipas, the son of Herod the Great. John had spoken out against the royal marriage, when Antipas had stolen and married his brother's wife. The wife, now called Herodias, became a powerful and vicious enemy of John the Baptist, just as Jezebel had been of Elijah. Herodias seized her opportunity at Herod's birthday banquet. When Herod offered her daughter a reward for her dancing, she demanded that John's head be cut off and brought to her on a plate. It was a tragic and pointless death, and a warning of what lay ahead for Jesus.

Jesus feeds 5,000 people
(6:30–44)

When the Twelve return, Mark calls them 'the apostles' – a Greek term for people who have been on an official

Clean and unclean

The debate about clean and unclean food is an important issue for the Christians reading this Gospel. Jewish Christians have been brought up with the laws of Moses, which list some foods as 'clean' and some as 'unclean'. The best-known 'unclean' meat is pork. Gentile Christians – those from non-Jewish backgrounds – do not share these scruples. Here Mark says that Jesus declares all foods 'clean'. In other words, Jesus discards some of the fussy detail from the law of Moses, and lifts the burden of guilt from those who are anxious about their diet.

mission. Jesus tries to make space for them to rest and share their news, but they are besieged by crowds of people.

Jesus aches with pity for the crowd. He sees them as leaderless and helpless – like lost sheep. First he feeds their hearts and minds with his teaching; then he feeds their bodies by miraculously creating bread and fish. Although there are only five loaves and two fish to begin with, there is enough for everyone – and twelve baskets of scraps left over.

Jesus walks on water
(6:45–56)

Jesus sends the disciples off in their boat, in the direction of Bethsaida. It is hard work rowing, as the wind is

against them. In the early hours of the morning, Jesus follows them – walking across the water to join them in the boat. The moment he arrives, the wind drops!

Christians will treasure this story. Jesus knows our troubles and comes to help. The episode ends with many ordinary people recognizing Jesus and receiving his healing.

The difference between dirt and sin
(7:1–23)

The Pharisees link sin with dirt. For them, washing is a mark of holiness. Now they criticize Jesus' disciples for not washing their hands before eating food. Jesus quotes the prophet Isaiah, who says that human rules can hide a hostile heart (Isaiah 29:13).

Jesus shows how the Pharisees have taken one of God's clearest commandments, and confused it by adding extra conditions. God has said, 'Honour your father and mother'; but the Pharisees have devised a rule of 'Corban', which means 'devoted to God'. Under this rule, any money that is already set aside for God can't possibly be used to support elderly parents.

Jesus teaches that nothing we eat can make us sinful. Sin is in our hearts already. Food goes into our stomachs, not into our hearts (or wills). Immorality, pride and greed are not caused by food. They spring from the evil that is already present in human nature.

Feeding and walking

Mark describes Jesus walking on water straight after the feeding of the 5,000. He wants us to read the two stories together. Jesus is able to feed his people and rescue them in times of trouble.

How does Jesus do such things? Some people think that Jesus was never really a human being. If he was God in human disguise, then walking on water would be simple. Others have said that Jesus was walking in the shallows, or wading along a hidden sandbank. But that

would never impress the disciples who know every part of the lake.

The Jews know that God can do the impossible. For example, he can make a path through the sea – as he did at the exodus:

*Your path led through the sea,
 your way through the mighty
  waters,
 though your footprints were not
  seen (Psalm 77:19).*

Mark is telling us that Jesus is God.

As he approaches the boat Jesus says, 'It is I.' But the disciples cannot grasp the truth. They don't understand that this is God providing bread for his people and coming to help them in their distress. Like the Pharisees, they simply don't believe.

The Syro-Phoenician woman
(7:24–30)

Jesus leaves Israel and goes towards Tyre – a cosmopolitan area on the Mediterranean coast. He needs a break. However, a Gentile woman seeks him out and begs him to drive a demon out of her daughter.

Jesus resists the woman's request. His task is to feed the children (Israel). He must not get sidetracked into tossing little crumbs to dogs (Gentiles).

The woman accepts what Jesus is saying, but still tries to persuade him. Of course, Israel must be fed; but isn't it quite natural for Gentiles to benefit too – even if they are no better than dogs under the table?

Jesus can't possibly refuse her request. She returns home to find that her daughter has been freed from the evil spirit.

Jesus heals a man who is deaf and dumb
(7:31–37)

Jesus travels north some twenty miles before heading south and coming again to the area of the 'ten towns'. He is still in Gentile territory when he heals a man who is deaf and tongue-tied. Like many healers of his day, Jesus uses his fingers – and his saliva. Jesus sighs deeply as he channels the power of God to this needy person. The actual word Jesus uses is 'Ephphatha!' ('Be opened!'). This is not a magic spell, but a divine command.

The tradition of the elders

'The tradition of the elders' was the mass of legal detail which the Pharisees had added to the Torah (God's law). These extra regulations were passed by word of mouth from teacher to pupil, getting ever more elaborate. In the end, instead of explaining the law, they made it too complicated for ordinary people to keep.

Mark tells the story of the Syro-Phoenician woman right next to the teaching about food. He is comparing clean and unclean food to clean and unclean people. Just as Jesus declares all foods 'clean', so he has come to make all people 'clean'. The kingdom of God is not only for the Jews. It is for all the peoples of the world.

Mark describes Jesus healing deafness. The prophet Isaiah foretold that one day 'the eyes of the blind will be opened and the ears of the deaf unstopped' (Isaiah 35:5). These are physical cures with spiritual meanings. One day people will no longer be spiritually blind and deaf. The lines of communication with God will be open.

Shrine niches at Caesarea Philippi, where pilgrims have honoured the moment when Peter acknowledged Jesus as 'the Christ'.

Jesus feeds a crowd of 4,000
(8:1–21)

Mark tells of a second occasion when Jesus feeds a large crowd. This time there are some 4,000 people who have been with Jesus for three days in the wilderness. They are hungry, and Jesus feeds them all

Caesarea Philippi

Caesarea Philippi lies at the foot of Mount Hermon, at the source of the River Jordan. The emperor Caesar Augustus gave the town to Herod the Great. It was Herod's son Philip, the Tetrarch, who named it Caesarea – and had his own name added to distinguish this town from a city on the coast with the same name.

from seven loaves and a few small fish.

Jesus gives thanks and breaks the bread just as he did before. The disciples assist with the distribution of the food, and everyone has plenty. There are seven large baskets of scraps left over.

Nobody really knows why Mark has included two similar stories. Some think that the numbers are important, but there is no agreement on what they might mean. One idea is that Jesus is feeding Gentiles, to match his earlier feeding of Jews. But Mark doesn't say this himself.

The Pharisees want Jesus to prove his identity by performing another miracle, but Jesus refuses. He never responds to demands for signs from heaven. Instead he looks for faith – and faith never asks for proof. Jesus is exasperated by their wilful unbelief.

Meanwhile, the disciples haven't brought enough bread. Why carry loaves when they have the amazing conjuror Jesus with them? Jesus warns them against demanding signs. It is a form of unbelief, and unbelief spreads and spoils, like yeast in flour. Jesus had created bread to show he was the Son of God, not so that they needn't buy loaves any more. Both the Pharisees and the disciples are slow to understand the meaning of Jesus' miracles.

A blind man receives his sight – gradually
(8:22–26)

It is at this point in the story, with both the Pharisees and the disciples suffering from spiritual blindness, that Mark tells us of an unusual healing. Jesus cures a man of blindness, but only in two stages. The disciples, too, are about to receive their spiritual sight in two stages. Very soon, Simon Peter will acknowledge that Jesus is the Messiah. But the disciples will still fail to see that being Messiah involves suffering and death. They won't fully recognize Jesus until after his resurrection.

The secret is out
(8:27–30)

At Caesarea Philippi – a town in the far north – Jesus asks his disciples the key questions: Who do people think he is? And – more to the point – who do *they* think he is?

Most people think that Jesus is a great prophet, but Peter declares, 'You are the Christ.' It is the most momentous statement he will ever make, for the Christ is God's anointed king – the Messiah for whom the Jews hope. But if Peter is expecting applause and instant promotion, he is disappointed. Jesus insists that they keep this secret to themselves. There will be a disaster if excited crowds try to make him king and end his mission with a bloodbath.

Dying to live
(8:31–38)

Instead of planning his coronation, Jesus insists that he, the Son of man, must suffer. He will be rejected by the very people who should welcome him. He will be killed. But after three days he will rise again.

Peter thinks this is wrong. He isn't following Jesus just to see him die. He is looking forward to making him king. When he presses this point, Jesus turns on him. Peter is talking like Satan when he urges Jesus to seize an earthly empire. It is typical of Satan that he tries to subvert God's purpose.

From now on, Jesus often talks about the suffering and death that lie ahead. He also makes it clear that his disciples must suffer too, and make sacrifices.

Now Jesus sets out on the journey which will take him to Jerusalem. He and his disciples will be travelling from the far north back to Galilee and Capernaum. From there they will go south through Judea and Trans-Jordan. Eventually they will come to Jericho, and go on from there to Jerusalem. This journey will eventually take Jesus to the cross.

Jesus says that those who follow him must share his suffering. They will give up everything for the sake of Jesus and his gospel. They will be disgraced and condemned in the eyes of the world. It may look as though they are wasting their lives – but they will be rewarded with eternal life in the kingdom of God.

A glimpse of glory
(9:1)

Jesus says that some of those who are with him will live to see the kingdom of God 'come with power'. He may mean that they will witness his resurrection from death – or receive the gift of the Holy Spirit. Mark follows this promise with a glimpse of glory.

The transfiguration
(9:2–13)

Peter, James and John are allowed to see Jesus as he really is, shining with heavenly light. They watch him as he talks with Moses and Elijah – two giants of the Old Testament. It was through Moses that God gave his people the law. Elijah was the greatest of the prophets. But Jesus is even greater than these heroes. As the cloud of God's presence surrounds them, they hear a voice saying, 'This is my Son, whom I love. Listen to him!'

Peter wants the vision to last. He offers to make shelters by plaiting branches, as the Jews do for the Feast of Tabernacles. But the moment passes. Moses and Elijah return to heaven – leaving Jesus to resume his road to Jerusalem and the cross.

On the way down the mountain, the disciples ask Jesus about Elijah: will he come back to herald the Messiah? Jesus explains that John the Baptist did Elijah's job – and the fate he suffered was a taste of what lies ahead for Jesus.

A difficult healing
(9:14–29)

The crowds are astonished at the sight of Jesus. Like Moses, he may have had an afterglow from his encounter with God. However, he is soon down to earth with a bump!

The disciples have been struggling to deliver a boy from an evil spirit. Jesus traces the fault to their lack of faith. They have forgotten that this is God's work, and have focused instead on whether they can do it themselves. The boy's father begs Jesus to help him break through the barrier of unbelief.

As Jesus banishes the evil spirit, the boy is left for dead. But Jesus takes him by the hand and lifts him up – just as he did with Jairus' daughter. It is a gesture of resurrection.

When the disciples ask Jesus why they have failed, he tells them that prayer is the key to deliverance. It is through prayer that we admit our need of God and access his power to help.

A solemn warning
(9:30–32)

Once again, Jesus tries to prepare the disciples for the harrowing events that lie ahead. He is indeed the Son of man, but his road to glory must pass through death. Mark is very frank in admitting that the disciples can't understand what Jesus is talking about.

Who is the greatest?
(9:33–37)

The disciples ignore Jesus' talk of betrayal and death and give themselves to dreams of power. They hope for the top jobs in God's kingdom when it comes. They argue about which of them will be the most important.

But Jesus shows them a little child – someone without any power or influence. The greatness of God's kingdom is to be found in putting others first. In Aramaic, the word for 'child' and 'servant' is the same. When we count the weak and powerless as more important than ourselves, we come close to the heart of God.

No fear of competition
(9:38–41)

Someone is using Jesus' name to drive out demons. The disciples think he should be stopped, but Jesus is unconcerned.

The first Christians were probably worried about the use of Jesus' name as a word of power. Here Jesus teaches that no harm will ever come of it. There is, after all, only one source of power for good.

Drastic measures
(9:42–50)

Jesus warns his followers that they are responsible for their actions. If they mislead younger believers, or commit any sinful action, they will be punished. It would be better to amputate a hand or foot than use it to do something wrong – and so forfeit a place in God's kingdom. The choice is right or wrong – heaven or hell.

Jesus' picture of hell is based on the valley of Gehenna – the refuse dump where Jerusalem's rubbish is destroyed. Instead of being rotten, Jesus' followers are to have the qualities of salt: tasty, healing and agreeable.

The road south to suffering

Until now, Jesus has lived and worked in the northern part of the country, in Galilee. Now he starts to journey south to Jerusalem, where he knows that suffering and death await him.

Jesus is asked about divorce
(10:1–12)

Divorce is common among the Jews of Jesus' day. However, there is much debate about when it should be allowed.

The experts disagree. Followers of Rabbi Hillel allow a man to divorce his wife for any slight reason, such as burning the dinner. Followers of Rabbi Shammai only allow a man to divorce his wife because of her adultery. In both cases, it is the men who have the right to divorce and the women who are discarded.

Jesus talks about the law of Moses. Moses allowed a man to divorce his wife, provided he gave her a proper certificate. For Jesus, this is second best. Divorce has to be allowed on occasions, because of human failure. God's intention is to make husbands and wives 'one flesh' (or one 'self') for the rest of their lives. A husband should not try to split something God has joined.

Jesus treats men and women as equal. He talks of a woman divorcing her husband, as well as a husband divorcing his wife. He warns that divorce lays people open to adultery, as they break their God-given marriage and take a different partner.

Jesus welcomes some children
(10:13–16)

The disciples think they are doing Jesus a favour by keeping children away from him. Children are not important. They have no strength or influence. But Jesus is indignant. For him, children are a model of simple trust – just the kind of people he wants in his kingdom. He welcomes the little ones and blesses them with enthusiasm!

A rich young man
(10:17–31)

Jesus has just included children in his kingdom. Now a rich man counts himself out. At first he is keen. He begs for the key to life. He has kept all the law, but he still wants to do more. Jesus loves him and calls him to become a disciple there and then. Suddenly the man's eagerness vanishes. His real god is exposed. He is unable to leave his comfort zone of money and possessions to follow Jesus.

'It is easier for a camel to go through the eye of a needle than for a rich man to enter the kingdom of God,' says Jesus. He may be thinking of a merchant's camel being completely unloaded before it is pulled and shoved through a small gate or door. Anyway, it's an amusing and effective saying!

Peter needs reassurance. He and the other disciples have sacrificed everything to follow Jesus. How will they ever be rewarded? Jesus promises Peter that he will have many material resources and a far greater family than he ever had before. One day Paul will sum up the blessings and sufferings of the Christian life: 'Poor, yet making many rich; having nothing, and yet possessing everything' (2 Corinthians 6:10).

The road to death – and life!

(10:32–34)

Jesus sets out for Jerusalem – the city where prophets are stoned and God's messengers killed. Everyone is in awe of his single-mindedness. He describes for his disciples, in detail, the dreadful fate that awaits him – and that he will rise again!

Ambition

(10:35–45)

The disciples are busy with their own thoughts. When Jesus comes to power, which of them will get the top jobs?

James and John are particularly ambitious and confident. They ask Jesus if they can sit on the left and right of him in his glory – little realizing that his glory will be to hang on a cross!

The other disciples are angry and jealous. Jesus tries to change their minds about power. For him, power is shown in service. He is the Son of man – to be supremely honoured by God; but he will show his supremacy by giving himself up. He will offer up his life in payment for the sins of the world.

James' and John's request is 'prayer gone wrong'. They say, 'We want you to do for us whatever we ask' – as if Jesus is an Aladdin's genie. But the right prayer is to say to God, 'We want to do for you whatever *you* ask' – or, in other words, 'Your kingdom come.'

Jesus describes his suffering as though some words of the prophet Isaiah are in his mind:

He was pierced for our transgressions,
he was crushed for our iniquities;
the punishment that brought us peace was upon him,
and by his wounds we are healed (Isaiah 53:5).

He will be pierced and crushed for the sins of others; not for anything he has deserved. And somehow his wounds, so undeserved yet willingly borne, will heal the world.

Blind Bartimaeus

(10:46–52)

They come to Jericho – the lowest town on the earth's surface. The last person in the lowest town is Bartimaeus. He is blind and a beggar.

James and John are blinded by ambition; but blind Bartimaeus can see who Jesus is. He greets Jesus with a political slogan: 'Son of David!' He may as well have come straight out with it and shouted 'Messiah!'

Jesus stops and asks him what he wants. Bartimaeus says, naturally enough, that he wants his sight. Jesus heals him and Bartimaeus uses his newly healed eyes to follow Jesus.

Jesus comes to Jerusalem

The triumphal entry

(11:1–11)

Jesus comes to Jerusalem. His arrival is triumphant and tragic. Instead of invading with armed forces, he rides peaceably on a colt. Instead of taking lives, he gives his own. The common people welcome him, but the authorities are hostile. The Jewish leaders should form a delegation to make Jesus their king. Instead, they conspire to have him killed.

Jesus journeys the fifteen miles from Jericho and approaches Jerusalem from the Mount of Olives. This is the first time that Mark has brought us to the city. Jerusalem is going to be judged by the way she receives Jesus.

Jesus borrows a colt with care and courtesy. He chooses a colt rather than a horse, because he has come to make peace, not war.

People lay their cloaks on the colt and along the road, to pave the way for Jesus and give him a royal welcome. They cut branches as a sign of festival and shout, 'Hosanna', which means, 'Save now!' They sing the festival psalms, which the pilgrims chant on their way up to the temple.

A fig tree. When Jesus searched such a tree for figs, he found none. For him, it was a symbol of barren and fruitless Israel.

Money changing

Every Jewish man has to pay a temple tax by the first day of the month of Nisan – a fortnight before Passover. Because the temple is holy, the tax cannot be paid in Greek or Roman coins. At this busy time of year, money changers set up their stalls in the court of the Gentiles. Here they provide the special Tyrian coins – at an exchange rate which gives them a good profit. Jesus quotes the words of Jeremiah: 'Has this house, which bears my Name, become a den of robbers?' (Jeremiah 7:11).

O Lord, save us;
  O Lord, grant us success.
Blessed is he who comes in the name of the Lord…
With boughs in hand, join in the festal procession
  up to the horns of the altar (Psalm 118:25–27).

This is a celebration that God can save his people. This is a welcome for his Messiah.

Jesus goes to the temple and looks around, before going to spend the night at the village of Bethany, two miles from Jerusalem.

Jesus judges a fig tree… and the temple
(11:12–26)

On his way into the city from Bethany, Jesus looks for fruit on a fig tree. There is none to be found, and he curses it. By the following day it is dead.

The fig tree is a symbol of Israel, which Jesus is examining. Are there any signs that God's people are producing the fruits of faith? He is disappointed and angry to find they aren't.

Jesus discovers that the temple courtyard has been turned into a market. Dealers are exchanging everyday money for temple coins, while others are selling animals and birds for sacrifices. Business and commerce have taken over the place of prayer. Visiting pilgrims are being harassed and exploited.

In a demonstration of pure anger, Jesus expels the traders and calls the temple to order.

The prophet Malachi had warned that one day God would visit his temple and judge what goes on there.

'Suddenly the Lord you are seeking will come to his temple… But who can endure the day of his coming?' (Malachi 3:1–2).

Jesus is cross-questioned
(11:27–33)

The Jewish authorities challenge Jesus. By what right does he clear the temple courtyard and teach here? If Jesus answers that God is telling him to do these things, they will treat him as someone who is mad – or stone him for blasphemy.

Jesus answers their question by asking one of his own. Who gave John permission to baptize? If they admit that John the Baptist was a true prophet, they will have to explain why they rejected him. If they deny that John was God's prophet, they might get stoned for blasphemy themselves! The discussion ends in deadlock.

The parable of the tenants
(12:1–12)

Jesus tells a story about a man who plants a vineyard and rents it to some farmers. At harvest time, he sends his servants to collect some of the fruit. But the tenants beat the servants and finally kill the owner's son. The story ends with a question: 'What will the owner of the vineyard do?'

The vineyard is an image of Israel. The prophet Isaiah described how God had planted her and protected her with the greatest care. But when God came to inspect his vineyard, he found its fruit was bad. 'He looked for justice, but saw bloodshed; for righteousness, but heard cries of distress' (Isaiah 5:1–7).

Jesus takes Isaiah's idea and makes it personal to himself. The rulers of Israel, God's tenants, are about to reject him, the owner's son. But he quotes a psalm: 'The stone the builders rejected has become the capstone' (Psalm 118:22). Israel's leaders will sentence Jesus to death, only to discover that he is the key to life.

A trick question about tax
(12:13–17)

The Pharisees and Herodians try to trap Jesus. They ask him if it is right to pay tax to Caesar. Judea has been a Roman province since AD 6, and the Jews have always hated paying taxes. God, not Caesar, is their king.

Jesus asks for a denarius – a silver coin which is used for paying the Roman tax. He gets his questioners to admit that the coin is marked with Caesar's image. There

The shape of things to come

Jesus warns his disciples of coming events. In the near future, Jerusalem will be captured and the temple destroyed. In the long term there will be wars, earthquakes and famines. There will also be crazy religious leaders – false prophets and phoney messiahs. But, through it all, the followers of Jesus must be a faithful and steadfast witness to the gospel; and, at the end, Jesus will return.

'The abomination that causes desolation'

The 'abomination that causes desolation' is mentioned at the end of the book of Daniel (12:11; Mark 13:14). In Daniel, the abomination was the placing of an altar for the Greek god Zeus on the Jewish altar of burnt offerings. This had been done by the Emperor Antiochus Epiphanes in 168 BC. Now Jesus warns that there will be some further act of desecration. Mark may be referring to the day when the Roman armies will march their standards into the temple and offer sacrifices to their gods. This will be a sign that Jerusalem and the temple are about to be destroyed.

is nothing wrong in giving Caesar his due – after all, it is an expensive business to run an empire, and the Jews receive many benefits. But human beings are made in the image of God. They should pay Caesar his taxes, but give themselves to God. Brilliant!

A trick question about resurrection
(12:18–27)

The Sadducees come to Jesus with a more spiritual question. They are members of a Jewish elite who keep strictly to the ancient law of God. They have no time for new and trendy ideas, such as life after death and angels.

The Sadducees concoct an absurd case, to prove that resurrection is impossible. If a woman marries seven brothers in this life, which of them will be her husband in heaven?

Jesus tells the Sadducees that they know nothing of the power of God. God has better things in store than a rerun of this life. In their own favourite scriptures, God says, 'I am the God of Abraham, the God of Isaac and the God of Jacob.' The living God would hardly name himself after dead humans. Those who honour him continue to live in his presence after death.

The key commandment
(12:28–34)

After the trick questions comes an honest one. A teacher asks Jesus about the most important law. It is a good question, because the Jewish law has become very elaborate. On one estimate, the Ten Commandments have spawned 613 lesser laws – 248 of them positive and 365 negative. The ordinary person needs a clear path through this jungle of legislation.

Jesus says there is one central commandment from which all the others spring: 'Love the Lord your God with all your heart and with all your soul and with all your mind and with all your strength' (Deuteronomy 6:4–5). It is used as a daily prayer by every pious Jew. Then Jesus adds another commandment, which he says is equally important: 'Love your neighbour as yourself' (Leviticus 19:18). For Jesus, love for God goes hand in hand with love for others.

The riddle of the Messiah
(12:35–37)

Now Jesus asks a question. If the Christ (Messiah) is said to be the son of David, how is it that in Psalm 110 David describes him as his Lord?

Both Peter and Paul in their letters describe Jesus as the 'Son of David'. The Jews hope that the Messiah will be a king who is directly descended from David and able to restore the kingdom of Israel. But the kingdom of Jesus is very different from that of David. It is not based on race or political power. It is universal and eternal.

The crowd love to hear Jesus dealing so clearly with these difficult sayings – and see him getting the better of their self-important teachers.

A warning
(12:38–40)

Jesus warns people about the teachers of the law. They love to show off in the way they dress, the people they know and their position in society. But Jesus says that they are 'devouring widows' houses'. They are charging too much for helping poor people. They only serve for money, and they only pray to impress.

A poor widow

(12:41–44)

In the temple there is a treasury. Here it is possible to watch people paying in their gifts – placing money in one of the thirteen trumpet-shaped chests. Some of the contributions are quite impressive! But Jesus notices a poor widow. She gives only two tiny coins, but it is the greatest gift of the day – because it is all she has. She has given her whole self to God.

The poor widow's coins are 'lepta' – sometimes called 'mites'. They are the smallest coins in everyday use. Two of them together pay a farmworker's wage for about ten minutes' work.

Jesus foretells the future

(13:1–2)

The disciples are admiring the magnificent temple in Jerusalem. Its huge stones, dazzling marble and radiant gold express the presence of God among his people. Jesus stuns his friends with the news that the temple is soon to be destroyed.

Signs of the times

(13:3–31)

The disciples ask Jesus when the crisis will come. Jesus answers that there will be many trials and disasters, both natural and as a result of human activity. His followers will be arrested and tried for their faith, and families will be divided. Something abominable will be placed in the temple and the people of Judea will have to flee for safety.

Jesus describes these times of stress as 'birth pains' – the anguish of an old world dying and a new age being born. He quotes the well-known words of Isaiah, describing universal darkness and cosmic chaos. Then, he says, the Son of man will appear. He will come suddenly, with clouds and great glory – just as predicted in Daniel's famous vision (Daniel 7:13–14).

Jesus gives his disciples their bearings in history. Even when the cosmos is plunged into chaos, God is in control. Jesus and his promises will outlast heaven and earth. Nothing in life or death can harm those who

belong to him. They may have to share his suffering now, but in the end they will also share his victory.

When will Jesus return?

(13:32–37)

Many of the first Christians expected Jesus to return in their own lifetime. The people reading Mark's Gospel must have wondered if Jesus would come to save them from their suffering and persecution. Mark helps them understand why they are having to wait and watch.

Jesus says it is impossible to predict or calculate when he will return. This is a date which only God the Father knows. For Christians, the best advice is to be ready – like servants waiting for their master to come home.

Small alabaster jars were commonly used as perfume bottles. This one could be similar to the one used to anoint Jesus in Mark 14:1–9.

The longest night

The Passover plot

(14:1–2)

The chief priests and the teachers of the law want to arrest Jesus and kill him. Their problem is that it is the Passover festival. The population of Jerusalem swells by thousands of pilgrims at this time of year, and Jewish national fervour runs high. Jesus, as a possible Messiah, will be a popular figure, well protected by the crowds.

The Passover meal is eaten on the evening of the 15th day of the month of Nisan. The lambs for Passover are sacrificed in the temple that afternoon. The Jewish day starts at sunset – so the lambs are killed on 14th Nisan but eaten on the 15th.

The Feast of Unleavened Bread was originally a separate festival, but is now celebrated at the same time as Passover.

A woman anoints Jesus

(14:3–9)

During supper at Simon the Leper's home, a woman anoints Jesus. She breaks a jar of perfume and pours it over his head. The perfume is made with aromatic oil from India and is fabulously expensive. The other guests are shocked at her extravagance. Just think what could have been done with the money!

But the woman doesn't see it that way. Here is the Messiah, and he is soon to die. This is her last chance to honour him – and prepare his body for burial. Like the widow in the temple, she does what she can, with all her love and money.

Judas Iscariot
(14:10–11)

Judas, who betrays Jesus, is one of the twelve disciples. Why does he do it? Is he, as treasurer, outraged by the waste of money? Or is he, as a rebel, frustrated that Jesus hasn't sparked off an uprising against the Romans? We don't know. As he betrays his master, Judas is fulfilling the prophecy that Jesus will be 'handed over' to the authorities (10:33). He won't appear as a witness at Jesus' trial. He merely tells the authorities where Jesus can be found, away from the protection of the crowd.

The Last Supper
(14:12–25)

As Jesus arranges his last meal with his disciples, we sense that he is in control. He knows about the room, just as he knew about the colt. He also knows who will betray him.

As Mark tells the story, this is a Passover meal. There is no mention of roast lamb or bitter herbs, but Jesus' thoughts are on the meaning of the festival.

When Jesus breaks the unleavened bread, he gives it to his disciples as a symbol of his broken body. When he passes the cup, he likens the wine to his blood. It will be poured out so that many may share its benefits.

The oldest account of the Last Supper is not in the Gospels at all, but in one of Paul's letters:

The Lord Jesus, on the night he was betrayed, took bread, and when he had given thanks, he broke it and said, 'This is my body, which is for you; do this in remembrance of me.' In the same way, after supper he took the cup saying, 'This cup is the new covenant in my blood; do this, whenever you drink it, in remembrance of me' (1 Corinthians 11:23–25).

From earliest times, Christians have broken bread and shared wine to remember the death of Jesus. Sometimes this is called the Eucharist ('thanksgiving'); sometimes it is 'Holy Communion' or 'the Lord's Supper'. In breaking and pouring and sharing, the church looks back to the death of Jesus in much the same way as the Jews look back to the exodus from Egypt.

The Gospels of Matthew and Luke agree that the Last Supper was a Passover. John's Gospel has a different timescale, with Jesus dying on the cross as the Passover lambs are being sacrificed in the temple. The timing may vary, but the message is the same.

Does Jesus mean that the bread is actually his body and the wine really his blood? Some Christians believe that the bread and wine at Communion or Mass become the body and blood of Jesus in a special way, although they don't change in appearance. Other Christians eat and drink the bread and wine as a way of remembering that Jesus' body was broken and his blood shed for them when he died on the cross. When Jesus says, 'This is my body,' he means, 'I am sharing my life with you.' In passing the cup of wine, Jesus is showing that a new covenant commitment is being made between God and his people. It is a covenant which is signed and sealed by Jesus pouring out his life.

Even as he faces death, Jesus looks forward to new life in the kingdom of God. When he next drinks wine with his disciples, they will be celebrating God's victory and the dawn of the Messiah's reign.

Jesus predicts Peter's denial
(14:26–31)

Jesus and his friends sing a hymn – one of the Passover psalms about the exodus – and walk to the Mount of Olives which is nearby. Jesus knows his disciples will soon be scattered, as sheep are when their shepherd is killed. He recalls some words of prophecy (Zechariah 13:7). Peter insists that he will stay with Jesus whatever happens. But Jesus knows differently. Peter's bravado will evaporate in a matter of moments.

In the Garden of Gethsemane
(14:32–42)

They go to Gethsemane which is a grove of olive trees near the foot of the Mount of Olives. Its name means 'oil-press'. Jesus has with him Peter, James and John – the close companions who were at his transfiguration.

Jesus is in terror of the torture that lies ahead. In the next few hours he will endure extreme physical and mental pain – and suffer the terrible separation from God that is caused by human sin. In his prayer, he begs that he won't have to drink this cup of poison. Nevertheless, he will do whatever God wants. Meanwhile, the disciples keep falling asleep – although Jesus has asked them to stay awake and keep him company.

Jesus calls God 'Abba', which is Aramaic for 'dear Father', or 'Dadda'. This is Jesus' own way of speaking to

Pontius Pilate

Pontius Pilate is appointed prefect of Judea by the Roman emperor in AD 26 and rules until AD 36. He is in charge of the Roman army stationed on the coast at Caesarea, and with a contingent in Jerusalem in the Fortress of Antonia. An inscription found in Herod's theatre in Caesarea mentions Pilate by name.

As Roman governor, Pilate appoints the high priests, controls the temple funds and has power to overturn the decisions of the Sanhedrin. The historians who mention Pilate (Josephus, Eusebius, Tacitus and Philo) describe him as a cruel man who is insensitive to the beliefs and customs of the Jews (see Luke 13:1).

God and is unknown in other Jewish prayers. Paul knows of 'Abba' as a term used by Christians; but this is the only time it comes up in one of the Gospels.

Jesus is arrested
(14:43–52)

Judas arrives with the temple police. They have been sent by the Jewish authorities to arrest Jesus. Judas shows them which one is Jesus by greeting his master with a kiss. Jesus is immediately arrested. One of his supporters (John tells us it is Peter) puts up a brief fight. Then they all desert him. One vivid memory is of a young man wriggling out of his robe and running for his life! Some people think that this is Mark himself.

Jesus before the Jewish Council
(14:53–65)

Jesus is taken to the house of the high priest and put on trial. The ruling council is called the Sanhedrin. It has seventy-one members. This is an emergency session. In later years there will be a rule forbidding the council to meet at night. There is already a regulation that they must not meet on a festival or sabbath. They must also allow a cooling-off period before confirming a 'guilty' verdict. In the trial of Jesus, all these rules are ignored.

Jesus is accused of threatening to destroy the temple, but no two witnesses tell the same story. The high priest cuts through the confusion by asking Jesus directly: 'Are you the Christ?' Jesus says, 'I am.' He tells the court that one day they will have to reckon with him as the Son of man, God's own glorious representative and judge (Daniel 7:13, 14).

Jesus' claim is considered blasphemous by the high priest. He reacts by tearing his clothes. In the past this was a sign of grief; now it shows outrage for what they have just heard. The council agrees that Jesus must die.

What was the charge against Jesus? He was accused of saying something against the temple. 'I will destroy this temple made with human hands and in three days will build another, not made with hands.' It sounds like a mixture of things Jesus said. He predicted that the temple would be destroyed. He also said of himself that he would be killed, but rise to life three days later. Two sayings may have become confused (John 2:21).

The Jews find Jesus guilty of blasphemy, but they don't have the power to pass a death sentence. For this reason, Jesus is sent to the Roman governor for judgment and execution.

Peter denies Jesus
(14:66–72)

Peter is staying as near to Jesus as he dares. He is warming himself by a fire in the outer courtyard. A servant girl accuses him of being one of Jesus' disciples, but he vigorously denies it. Others can tell by his clothes and his accent that he is from Galilee. Soon he is cursing and swearing that he has absolutely no connection with Jesus. At the height of his protest the cock crows – just as Jesus had predicted (14:30).

Jesus is tried by the Roman governor
(15:1–15)

Jesus is now taken to the Roman governor, Pontius Pilate. The governor has no interest in whether Jesus is the Son of God. Instead, he asks if Jesus is the king of the Jews. Jesus does not give a straight answer. Pilate must decide for himself.

Both the Jewish high priest and the Roman governor state the truth about Jesus – but don't believe it.

At Passover time, the governor has the custom of releasing a prisoner. He suggests that this year he release Jesus. However the crowd, encouraged by the priests, shout support for Barabbas. Barabbas has proved himself to be a man of action. He is a rebel and a convicted murderer. The people clamour for Barabbas to be released and for Jesus to be crucified.

Pilate gives in to the pressure, although he knows Jesus is innocent. He has Jesus flogged – tied to a post and whipped front and back. The whip is a cruel instrument of torture, made from multiple strands of leather, each set with fragments of metal and bone.

Jesus is mocked by the soldiers
(15:16–20)

The Roman soldiers – perhaps as many as 600 of them – have Jesus at their mercy. They give him a mock coronation, with a robe of royal purple and a crown of twisted thorns. They tease and taunt him as 'King of the Jews' – not knowing that they are proclaiming the truth.

Jesus is crucified
(15:21–32)

Jesus is taken outside the city to be executed. He is so weak from the beatings that a passing African, Simon from Cyrene, is forced to carry the heavy crosspiece. The place for crucifixion is called Golgotha – the Aramaic word for 'skull'.

Crucifixion is surely the most painful form of death ever devised. It gives us the word 'excruciating'. The victims are stripped of all their clothes and nailed or roped naked to a wooden cross. There they hang day and night, in burning heat or bitter cold, until they die. Their friends may keep

An eastern rock tomb, formed from a cave with a stone to roll across the entrance. This is typical of a number of tombs in the Jerusalem area dating from New Testament times.

them alive with food and drink, or dull their pain with drugs. Eventually, they die of heart failure.

Jesus refuses the offer of a painkilling drink. He must endure every degree of human suffering in body, mind and spirit.

Left and right of Jesus are criminals, perhaps associates of Barabbas. They have the places of honour that James and John had requested (10:37). But even the bandits reject Jesus – although Luke tells us that one of them accepts him.

For Mark, this is Jesus' enthronement. Jesus has been anointed by a woman, paraded on a donkey, crowned as a joke and now exalted on a cross. In John's Gospel this is the moment when Jesus' glory is most clearly seen – not in light and power, but in complete obedience and sacrifice. This is God himself suffering the worst that human nature can devise.

The tenants are killing the owner's son.

All the old temptations come flooding back – for Jesus to save himself, prove himself and seize worldly power.

Jesus dies
(15:33–41)

Jesus hangs on the cross for three hours – from midday until mid-afternoon. The world is plunged into darkness as the dreadful drama reaches its climax.

The women

Mark tells us for the first time that there were several women in Jesus' group. He names three of them in particular. There is Mary from Magdala, a town on the west shore of Galilee, south of Capernaum. In Luke's Gospel, this Mary is mentioned soon after a prostitute has washed Jesus' feet – but the two are not necessarily the same person. (The story of the sinful woman is told at the end of Luke 7 and Mary Magdalene is mentioned in the opening verses of Luke 8.) A second Mary is described as the mother of James the younger (or 'small') and of Joseph. A third woman is named as Salome.

Matthew in his Gospel doesn't mention Salome, but instead refers to 'the mother of Zebedee's sons', the disciples James and John.

On the verge of death, Jesus cries in Aramaic, 'My God, my God, why have you forsaken me?' – the opening words of Psalm 22. He is totally desolate. As if it weren't enough to be deserted by friends and tortured by enemies, Jesus now feels abandoned by God.

The onlookers think Jesus is calling for Elijah to rescue him. One of them gives Jesus a sip of cheap wine to try to keep him alive a little longer – to see if Elijah will come and save him. But Jesus utters one last loud cry, and dies.

As Jesus finally offers up his life, the curtain in the temple is torn from top to bottom. This is the curtain which separates the Most Holy Place (the 'Holy of Holies') from the Holy Place. Only the high priest is allowed past this curtain, for within is the utter presence of God. The high priest enters once a year, on the Day of Atonement, and only after sacrificing a bull for his sins. Now, through the perfect sacrifice of Jesus, the way into God's presence is open to all.

The Roman officer in charge of the execution is deeply moved. He says, 'Surely this man was the Son of God!' Until now, only the voices of God and evil spirits have declared who Jesus really is. This moment of recognition by a Gentile who sees Jesus die is the summit of Mark's Gospel.

Jesus is buried

(15:42–47)

It is nearly the sabbath – which begins at sunset. Whenever possible, a burial must take place the same day as death. It is important to dispose of the body of Jesus before the sabbath rest begins.

Joseph of Arimathea comes to the rescue. He is a leading Jew who may have been a member of the Council which condemned Jesus. Now he assists with the burial. He gets Governor Pilate's permission to take the body, and himself provides a rock tomb. Jesus is laid to rest and Joseph blocks the entrance to the tomb with a large stone. The two Marys are witnesses to the burial and note the site of the grave.

After sunrise

Once the sabbath rest is over, the two Marys and Salome set out to embalm Jesus' body with fragrant spices (16:1–8). They know that there is a stone blocking the tomb – and that the body will already be starting to decay. But, when they arrive at the tomb, the stone has been rolled away and the body has gone!

An angel tells them not to be terrified, because Jesus has risen from death. They must tell the other disciples, especially Peter. Jesus is going ahead, like the good shepherd he is, to meet up with them again in Galilee.

The women flee from the tomb in a state of shock. They are too frightened to tell anyone what has happened.

And there – quite suddenly – Mark's Gospel ends. There are a few more verses in some Bibles, but these have been written later by someone else.

We don't know whether the last page of the Gospel has been lost in some way, or if Mark was interrupted and didn't finish. Or did he mean to end abruptly, and leave his readers as amazed and bewildered as the women?

Even in this brief account of the first Easter morning, we see that death and the grave have not held Jesus. This good news is entrusted to three women. Their evidence would never be allowed in any Jewish court of law – but God chooses them as his witnesses. We are allowed to guess that Peter will be forgiven for his denials and restored to his place as the leading disciple. And Jesus will meet with his friends in Galilee – the unfashionable, half-pagan north country where the disciples were first called to follow him.

LUKE

Luke is the name of a doctor who travelled with the apostle Paul. He wrote two of the books we have in the New Testament – the Gospel of Luke and the Acts of the Apostles.

In his Gospel, Luke gives us a careful account of the life of Jesus. He has talked to some of the people who knew Jesus, and collected their sayings and stories.

Luke gives us facts – information to help us pinpoint the time and place in which Jesus lived. He describes some of the hopeless cases of disability, disease and demon possession which Jesus was able to cure. He shows how Jesus is indeed the Saviour of the world.

Luke wants us to discover the joy of being welcomed and accepted by God – and to take up the challenge of becoming disciples of Jesus.

Outline

INTRODUCTION

Luke – doctor and historian

Luke was not a Jew. He was a Gentile doctor who travelled with Paul on his first journey to Europe and, later, to Jerusalem and Rome. In the Acts of the Apostles, he records the day he joined Paul – probably around AD 49: 'After Paul had seen the vision [a man from Macedonia], we got ready at once to leave for Macedonia' (Acts 16:10).

Luke loves people and adventure and miracles. He writes good Greek. His way of saying things is more stylish than Mark's. As a Gentile himself he is always interested in Gentiles. At the same time, he knows a lot about the Jewish scriptures and Jewish customs.

What's new in Luke?

Luke has done careful research, and seems to have set events in the order in which they happened. Mark and others have already written about Jesus, but Luke has gathered some fresh material.

He tells us the story of Jesus' birth and traces his family line (humanly speaking) back to Adam.

He gives a unique glimpse of Jesus at the age of twelve.

He sets his story in world history by mentioning dates and names and places.

He includes stories (called parables) which are much longer and more detailed than in the other Gospels. Luke's 'exclusives' include such famous tales as the good Samaritan, the rich fool, the great banquet and the lost ('prodigal') son.

Finally, Luke sets a large part of his Gospel (from the end of chapter 9) in the form of a journey to Jerusalem.

Where did Luke get his information?

Luke has used Mark's Gospel. About half of Mark's Gospel is to be found in Luke, with all but one of the episodes in the same order. Half the time, Luke uses Mark's actual words.

Another large part of Luke's Gospel (about 200 verses) can also be found in the Gospel of Matthew. These verses are usually sayings and teachings of Jesus, such as Matthew's Sermon on the Mount, which becomes the Sermon on the Plain in Luke. It seems that neither Matthew nor Luke are copying from each other, but have the same collections of sayings in front of them. The scholars have called this collection of sayings 'Q' which is short for 'Quelle', the German word for 'source'.

So Luke has used two existing documents, Mark and 'Q'. These two documents account for half his Gospel. The rest of the material is his own. He has collected the stories of eyewitnesses and written down the sayings they recited.

Luke also has some of the same little details we find in John's Gospel – that it was the high priest's servant's right ear that was injured, that there were two disciples named Judas and that Joseph's tomb had never been used.

When did Luke write his Gospel?

Luke may have written his Gospel during a two-year stay in Caesarea between AD 57 and 59, while Paul was in prison there. Or he may have collected material in Caesarea and written the final version in Rome. If Luke used Mark's Gospel, which was probably written in the AD 60s, then only the later date is possible.

Luke and Acts

In his Gospel, Luke describes the earthly life of Jesus. In the Acts of the Apostles, he shows that the life and work of Jesus continue in the church. The same Holy Spirit who was present in the baptism and ministry of Jesus is now active in his followers. One day Jesus will return in a visible way – but meanwhile he is already present. The church is his body and the Holy Spirit is his life within it.

Good news for all

Luke records how Jesus welcomed people who were on the fringe of society, or living in its underworld. Strict Jews excluded certain people from their community – but Jesus *included* them. He searched out those very people and made them his friends. While the Jews tended to keep their knowledge of God to themselves, Luke declares that Jesus is 'a light... to the Gentiles' (2:32). The gospel is good news for the poor and the poorly, the diseased and the downtrodden; for friends and foes, Jews and Romans, tax collectors and Samaritans. Women, too, so often excluded or disadvantaged, have a special place in this Gospel. God is delighted – and angels sing for joy – when the sick are healed, the disabled are cured and the lost brought safely home.

Luke shows that Christianity is a true and dignified faith. It springs from roots in the Jewish scriptures and is the fulfilment of all the Jewish hopes. But Christianity is more than a religion for a particular nation or group. This new faith is for the whole world in every age.

DISCOVERING LUKE

'Dear Theophilus'

Luke dedicates all his work – both the Gospel and Acts – to Theophilus. The name means 'friend of God', and we can guess that Theophilus was a Roman man – perhaps a Christian, or at least interested in the Christian faith.

A famous Roman historian, Tacitus, records that Christians were hated in Rome. When a fire destroyed a large part of Rome, in AD 64, it was the Christians who were blamed. Other accounts say that Christians were suspected of cannibalism, because they spoke of eating the flesh and drinking the blood of Christ. The Romans assumed that Jesus was a criminal, because a Roman governor, Pontius Pilate, had sentenced him to death. And many Roman husbands were suspicious of their Christian wives, because they attended 'love feasts'!

In the face of all this, Luke sets out the facts about Jesus for his Roman reader. He shows that Jesus Christ was not a criminal. Jesus came to start a revolution – but not a political one. His is a revolution of love.

Jesus is born

A childless couple
(1:5–23)

Before Luke can tell us about Jesus, he must tell us about his cousin John. This was the man who became John the Baptist. Like Jesus, his birth was quite extraordinary.

The story begins in Judea, where Herod the Great is king of the Jews. One of the many priests at this time is a man called Zechariah. Zechariah and his wife Elizabeth are a faithful old couple, steeped in Jewish tradition. Their only sadness – but it is a very great sadness – is that they are childless.

One day it is Zechariah's turn to burn incense in the temple. It is a great privilege to send up holy smoke as a sign of the people's prayers. There are so many priests that this duty comes round only once or twice in a lifetime.

'Hail, Mary, full of grace'

The prayer 'Hail Mary, full of grace' is based on the greetings of Gabriel and Elizabeth to Mary. It has led many Christians, especially Catholics, to revere the mother of Jesus. She is remarkable in her obedience and courage to fulfil the will of God.

While he is in the temple, Zechariah has a vision. The angel Gabriel tells him that he and his wife will have a son. The child will grow up to be a man of God as great as Elijah – and will have the task of preparing the people for the coming of God.

An elderly couple having a son is the sort of miracle that happened in Old Testament times. Abraham and Sarah had Isaac against all the odds. Two of the judges – Samson and Samuel – were also born to apparently barren mothers. It is a sign of God doing the impossible. Now, after a long silence, God is on the move again. Zechariah finds all this very hard to believe – and is struck dumb for his lack of faith. On the greatest day of his life, he is unable to bless the crowd.

Mary
(1:24–45)

When Elizabeth is six months pregnant, the angel Gabriel visits a young woman in Nazareth, a town in Galilee. This is Mary. She is engaged to Joseph, who is a descendant of King David. Their engagement is as solemn a commitment as marriage.

Gabriel tells Mary that, young though she is, she is going to have a baby. She will become pregnant by God's

Holy Spirit – the same Spirit who hovered over the water at the birth of creation. In this way the child will be the Son of God. He is to be called Jesus. The name is the same as Joshua and means 'God Saves'.

If John is to be a prophet like Elijah, then Jesus is to be a king like David. But he will be greater than David, because his kingdom will last for ever.

Mary goes to visit Elizabeth, who is her elderly cousin. The baby within Elizabeth leaps for joy at Mary's approach. This is the joy that everyone will have when the Messiah comes.

Mary is shocked. To be pregnant outside marriage is a scandal. As she has never slept with Joseph, her pregnancy will be seen as proof of adultery. She may even be stoned to death. And yet she accepts God's will. This is Mary's greatness – that she is completely willing for God to use her life, despite physical pain or social embarrassment.

Mary's song and Zechariah's prophecy
(1:46–80)

In her wonder at being chosen to be mother of the Messiah, Mary praises God. Her song is a medley of Old Testament themes, including much of Hannah's song when she gave her son Samuel to God (1 Samuel 2:1–10). Both Hannah and Mary praise the God of surprises, who turns the world and its ways upside down. The Christian church has come to call Mary's song 'the Magnificat' – after the Latin word for 'glorifies'. Zechariah's prophecy about his son John (1:67–79) is called 'the Benedictus', because it begins with the Latin word for 'blessed'.

The birth of Jesus
(2:1–20)

Jesus is born in Bethlehem. Mary and Joseph make the journey south – some eighty miles – because the Roman

The virgin birth

The story of the virgin birth must have come from Mary herself. The promise that a virgin would have a child was one of Isaiah's prophecies: 'Therefore the Lord himself will give you a sign: The virgin will be with child and will give birth to a son, and will call him Immanuel' (Isaiah 7:14).

In Hebrew, the word 'virgin' means 'young woman'. It doesn't mean a woman who has never had sex. It was when the Hebrew was changed to Greek that a word meaning 'a young woman who hasn't had sex' was used. In any case, Luke refers to Joseph as Jesus' father – so making an important link with King David.

Both Matthew and Luke emphasize

that Jesus' mother was a virgin. In saying this, they are telling us that Jesus is God's son, and is both human and divine.

emperor has ordered a census. Bethlehem is King David's birthplace, and the registration point for his descendants. Here Jesus is born – with a manger as a makeshift cradle in the crowded town.

The first people to hear the news are some shepherds. They are usually the last to be told anything, because they are out on the hills with their flocks. Luke is telling us that this birth is good news for all kinds of people – not just for the great and the good, the clever or the religious. Heaven is split open as the angels sing God's praise. Their joy is echoed by the shepherds – and reverberates throughout the Gospel.

The fields near Bethlehem, where shepherds tend their sheep.

Jesus is named
(2:21–24)

Jesus' birth is followed by three ceremonies. He is circumcised and given his name when he is eight days old. Jesus is the Greek word for the Hebrew Joshua and means 'The Lord Saves'. Because Jesus is the first-born son, his parents make the special offering of five shekels to mark his redemption. This is a link with the Passover when the first-born sons of the Hebrew families were all spared from death. Finally, there is a ceremony of purification for Mary after the mess and stress of childbirth. She offers a humble sacrifice of doves or pigeons.

Simeon and Anna
(2:25–40)

In the temple, two elderly people recognize the baby Christ. An old man, Simeon, declares that Jesus will be 'a light to… the Gentiles'. He wisely warns Mary of the conflict and pain that lie ahead. Anna is a venerable widow, steeped in prayer. She proclaims the wonderful news to all who will listen. Luke is showing that senior, devout, temple-centred Jews are among the first to realize that Jesus is the fulfilment of all their hopes.

The boy Jesus
(2:41–52)

Luke tells a unique story about Jesus as a boy. His parents lose him in Jerusalem – and eventually find him in the temple. When Mary reproaches her teenage son for causing them such worry, Jesus answers that it was quite obvious where he would be. He was in his Father's house. As Jesus enters adult life (for Jewish boys this is at the age of twelve or thirteen), he is already calling God his Father.

Popular songs

Luke gives us the words of several songs in these opening chapters of his Gospel. Mary's Song (1:46–55), Zechariah's Song (1:68–79), the Angels' Song (Luke 2:14) and Simeon's Song (2:29–32) all sound typical of Hebrew verse and remind us of the Old Testament psalms. They have travelled across the world with the Christian faith, and found their way into many collections of hymns, prayers and spiritual songs.

In the Anglican Book of Common Prayer, the songs are known by the Latin words with which they begin: Mary's Song is the Magnificat, Zechariah's Song is the Benedictus and Simeon's Song is the Nunc Dimittis. They are used every day in Morning and Evening Prayer. The Angels' Song is the Gloria, which provides a high point of praise in the Communion service.

The Messiah appears

John the Baptist

(3:1–20)

Luke's story moves on nearly twenty years. Tiberius Caesar is now emperor, and Herod the Great's kingdom has been divided into smaller states, called 'tetrarchies'. John has become a prophet who preaches and baptizes by the River Jordan. He is preparing the hearts and minds of Jewish people to receive their Messiah. He plunges in the river those who want to repent of their old life and start afresh.

John warns of a great judgment about to befall Israel. God's own people have become like a diseased and fruitless tree – fit only to be cut down. John sees his hearers as snakes trying to escape from a stubble fire. They must change their ways! It is no longer enough to claim Jewish descent, because God will judge people by their actual deeds – not by their race or religion. A holy calling must be proved by a holy life.

John is a spiritual giant – one of the all-time greats, like Elijah; but he dismisses any idea that he is the Messiah. The coming Christ will be infinitely greater, dealing not with muddy Jordan water, but with Holy Spirit and fire. John will be his lowliest servant.

Finally, John confronts the king, Herod Antipas, about his affair with his sister-in-law, Herodias. The couple are committing adultery, having both deserted their partners. Herod responds by arresting John and having him imprisoned in the fortress of Machaeras, on the east coast of the Dead Sea.

The baptism of Jesus

(3:21–22)

One day, as John is baptizing, Jesus joins the crowd. As he is being baptized, the Holy Spirit descends on Jesus like a dove, and God the Father's voice is heard saying, 'This is my Son, whom I love.'

At his baptism, Jesus is recognized and anointed as God's chosen king.

Jesus never uses the title Messiah to describe himself, although he accepts it in the high priest's question (Mark 14:61–62). The danger he wishes to avoid is that people will assume he is a military leader. Even his disciples find his style of leadership difficult to understand. Jesus sees himself pictured in the prophecy of Isaiah, where God's servant endures undeserved suffering, so that others may be forgiven and healed (Isaiah 40–55).

The family line of Jesus

(3:23–38)

Luke traces the ancestry of Jesus all the way back from Joseph to Adam. He shows how he is a descendant of the great King David and, like Adam, a true 'son of God'.

The temptation of Jesus

(4:1–13)

By his baptism, Jesus is commissioned for his life's work. Immediately, he is subjected to fierce temptation by the devil. He spends forty days and nights in the desert – working out with prayer and fasting how he shall rightly use his power and status.

The devil tries to undermine Jesus' sense of being God's Son. He tempts him to use his power to turn stones to bread and feed himself. He tempts him to build a world empire – taking all the power of Caesar but using it for God. To do this would entail an endless series of compromises with evil. He tempts him to throw himself from the pinnacle of the temple in Jerusalem, to land dramatically in the court of the Gentiles – always assuming that God's angels will catch him!

Each of these temptations attacks Jesus at one of his strong points – his power to work miracles, his longing to change the world and his need to spread his message. But, in each case, Jesus answers Satan with words of scripture. He draws on the hard-won lessons that the Israelites learned in their wilderness years with Moses.

If Jesus is to fulfil the calling of Israel, he must worship God alone (Deuteronomy 6:13). He must rely on God's word for his life, just as he relies on bread for his body (Deuteronomy 8:3). There is to be no complaining, no cheating and no turning back (Deuteronomy 6:16).

Jesus wins this first struggle with the devil, but Satan will return.

These temptations are crucial for Jesus. In the months that follow, he will feed a multitude, refuse to become king and resist the taunts to escape from the cross. These are the very choices he made in the desert.

Jesus is rejected at Nazareth
(4:14–30)

Back home in Nazareth, a north-country town in the hills of Galilee, Jesus is invited to read the scriptures in the synagogue. He chooses part of Isaiah, where the prophet is announcing that God will rescue his people. He describes something like a Jubilee, when invalids are healed, debts cancelled and prisoners released (Isaiah 61:1–9).

Sitting down to teach, Jesus says simply, 'This is happening now – before your very eyes. I am the Jubilee!' Knowing that the people of Nazareth will want him to do them favours or make them famous, Jesus reminds them of the old prophets. Although there were many widows in Israel, Elijah healed only one – and she lived far away in Sidon, which is Gentile territory. Although there were many lepers in Israel, Elisha healed only Naaman, who was the pagan army commander from Syria.

God works in mysterious ways and to his own priorities and timing. His Son will take after him. Angrily, the citizens of Nazareth try to execute Jesus for blasphemy, but he walks away.

A sense of history

Luke attempts to give some bearings in world history. He mentions a Roman census, for example. A census is the counting of a population – usually for taxation or military service. We know that a governor of Syria named Quirinius conducted a census in Palestine in AD 6–7 – but this is too late for the birth of Jesus. Jesus was born while Herod the Great was still alive – and Herod died some ten years earlier, in 4 BC. An early Christian writer, Tertullian (AD 196–212), mentions a census at the time of Jesus' birth, but gives the governor's name as Saturninus.

Jesus heals at Capernaum
(4:31–44)

Jesus makes his home in the lakeside town of Capernaum (Tell Hum) straddling the trade routes on the north-west shore of the Sea of Galilee. He delivers a man from demon possession and cures Simon's mother-in-law of fever. He does each miracle simply by speaking – commanding both the demon and the fever to release their victims. The man and the mother-in-law are cured instantly and completely. These are the signs of God at work.

In the evening, once the sabbath rest has ended, people come in large numbers for healing and deliverance. The following day, Jesus decides to move on. Healing is good and deliverance is necessary – but preaching the good news is his top priority. Jesus is not called to heal a few sick people, but to rescue a world of sinners.

The training of the disciples

Calling disciples
(5:1–11)

Jesus is now a popular teacher. He borrows a fishing boat to speak to the people who are thronging the shore. Later, he helps the owner of the boat, Simon, make a fabulous catch of fish – after a luckless night and in broad daylight. Simon realizes that this is an act of God, and begs Jesus to go away. But Jesus calls Simon and his business partners, James and John, to become his followers. They will bring their fishermen's gifts of patience and hard work to the task of catching men and women for God.

Healing disease and disability
(5:12–26)

Jesus heals a man of leprosy, which is a dreadful and highly contagious disease. Astonishingly, he reaches out and touches the man, with no fear that he himself may be contaminated. The cure is instant.

On another occasion, Jesus heals a paralysed man. The invalid is lowered through the roof into a crowded room where Jesus is teaching. Jesus offends the strictly religious people by forgiving the man's sins – something only God has a right to do. Forgiving sin is far harder than curing paralysis – but Jesus is able to do both. Perhaps the man's physical condition is rooted in his sense of guilt.

The calling of Levi

(5:27–32)

Jesus calls a tax collector, Levi, to follow him. It's a shocking choice. Tax collectors are utterly despised by the rest of the community. The Jews resent any tax which is not for the support of the temple or priests. Levi and his kind raise money to pay for pagan government – the local king and the wider Roman empire. They are thought to be greedy and dishonest, imposing extra taxes to make themselves rich.

Jesus is criticized for mixing with Levi and his disreputable friends. The Pharisees avoid such people, in case they catch their sinful habits. But Jesus says that he has come to make contact with sinners, just as a doctor must visit and heal the sick.

A time for joy

(5:33–39)

Jesus and his new disciples are getting a reputation for partying! This is very different from the lifestyle of John the Baptist and the Pharisees. They show their religious seriousness by fasting and avoiding strong wine. Jesus explains that he and his friends are celebrating. You don't fast at a wedding. It's time to break the mould of stiff and starchy religion because the Messiah is here! It's a time for rejoicing.

Lord of the sabbath

(6:1–11)

Luke narrates two events which both happen on a sabbath. In the first, Jesus' disciples are picking and eating heads of grain. The Pharisees see this as breaking the fourth commandment, which forbids any kind of work on the sabbath day. The second is when Jesus heals a man whose hand is shrivelled – again, on the sabbath.

In both episodes, Jesus defies the bullying, killjoy attitude of the Pharisees. They are using God's law to build a religious obstacle course – instead of enjoying the wealth of nature and the wonder of healing. Jesus reminds them of the time David 'broke' a religious convention – and claims that he, as 'Lord of the sabbath' has every right to do the same.

Choosing the Twelve

(6:12–16)

Jesus prays through the night before selecting twelve 'apostles' from his group of disciples. He includes the original fishermen (two pairs of brothers) and gives Simon the new name Peter, meaning 'Rock'. Matthew, which means 'Gift of God' is probably the new name of Levi the tax collector. He is chosen along with Simon the Zealot, a person of entirely opposite political views! While Peter becomes known for his certainties, and Thomas for his doubts, Judas Iscariot is remembered as the one who betrays Jesus.

The Sermon on the Plain

People come from far and wide to hear Jesus. He heals and delivers from evil spirits; but most of all he wants to teach. He sees his followers as pathetic in the eyes of the world – poor, hungry, sad and despised. But God is welcoming them into his kingdom!

Blessings and woes

(6:20–26)

In the blessings and woes, Jesus takes all the ingredients of a happy life – wealth, food, fun and popularity – and warns that they will all be reversed. Only when we are dissatisfied with what the world has to offer can we look forward to the real blessings of the kingdom of God.

Jesus assures his followers that they are on the right track. The pain and sorrow they are experiencing are because they are longing for God and homesick for heaven. They can be happy in their hearts, because they know God's kingdom will come. They will be its citizens.

Love for enemies

(6:27–36)

Jesus explains how to live God's way. God gives and forgives. He blesses friends and enemies alike, without resentment or reserve. Jesus urges his followers to extend the boundaries of their love to include their enemies, and turn loans to gifts – just as God does.

THE GOLDEN RULE

'Do to others as you would have them do to you' (6:31).

Most religions have teaching which forbids doing harm to another person. A famous Jewish teacher, Rabbi Hillel, has already said, 'Don't do to someone else what you would hate done to you.'

Now Jesus opens the doors of generosity, kindness, love and service. Instead of just limiting harm, he positively promotes goodness. Instead of 'Don't do what you would hate,' he says, 'Treat others as you would like to be treated.'

Don't judge!

(6:37–42)

Jesus tells his followers not to judge – that is, not to condemn and reject people. Criticism builds barriers and separates people from one another. We can never know all the facts. Sometimes we're seeing in somebody else the thing we don't like in ourselves. We must take the great plank out of our own eye before trying to deal with a tiny speck in someone else's.

A tree and its fruit

(6:43–45)

Just as we can tell a tree by its fruit, so we can tell people by their actions. The way we speak shows clearly what's in our heart.

The wise and foolish builders

(6:46–49)

Jesus ends his Sermon on the Plain with a story about two builders. One takes care to build a house with its foundations securely on rock. The other builds without any foundations at all. No doubt both houses look similar at first – but when a flood comes, the house without a foundation collapses. Jesus says that those who build their lives on his teaching will withstand the storms of life.

Close encounters

A centurion's faith

(7:1–10)

Jesus receives a plea for help from a Roman army officer. The centurion, with command of 100 soldiers, is well known in Capernaum. He has sympathy for the Jews and has been generous in building a synagogue for them. Now he asks that Jesus will heal his servant.

The officer understands that Jesus may not want to go into a Gentile house. He sends a further message to say that he believes Jesus can heal at a distance. As a

An orange tree with fruit. Jesus uses fruit trees and vines as examples of integrity. Good fruit can only grow on healthy trees.

commander himself, he knows what it is to be obeyed – and he confidently expects that Jesus has similar power to give orders to illness. Jesus is amazed at the man's faith, which is finer than any he has found among the Jews.

A widow's son

(7:11–17)

Near the town of Nain, Jesus is met by a funeral procession. A widow is burying her son – her only child. She has lost both the love of her life and her source of livelihood, for widows are poor and powerless.

But God cares for widows, and Jesus is his Son. Against all convention, Jesus touches the coffin and bids the young man, 'Get up!'

The story has many echoes of Elijah restoring a dead boy to his widowed mother (1 Kings 17:17–24). For the widow of Zarephath the miracle was a sign that Elijah was from God and spoke God's word. Luke hints at this story in his choice of words – and in the reaction of the onlookers.

Jesus and John the Baptist

(7:18–35)

John the Baptist is in prison. He feels abandoned. If Jesus is the Messiah, then surely his first act of Jubilee must be to release his cousin from jail? He sends his disciples to ask Jesus to explain the delay.

Jesus responds with an unmistakable demonstration of God's power. He heals the handicapped, cures diseases and delivers from evil spirits. He sends John's disciples to tell what they've seen – and to encourage the prophet to be patient.

When they have gone, Jesus pays tribute to John. He is none other than the prophet that Malachi had foretold – the one who would appear to announce the Messiah (Malachi 3:1; 4:5, 6).

Jesus says there's no pleasing people. They find fault with John's fasting and solitude – and with Jesus' feasting and partying. Time will prove them both true to God in their character and calling.

Jesus is anointed by a sinful woman
(7:36–50)

Jesus is having dinner at Simon the Pharisee's house, when they are interrupted by a prostitute. She walks around the couches and cushions and comes to where Jesus is reclining. She stands over him clutching a jar of perfume and crying. Her tears fall on Jesus' feet. She wipes them away with her hair, and kisses and anoints his feet with the perfume.

This is a very intimate and embarrassing situation – given the way Pharisees treat prostitutes and their regard for foot-washing as menial work.

Simon is surprised that Jesus allows the woman to caress him. But Jesus understands her motives and emotions. She is pouring out her love for God with a passion the Pharisee can hardly guess at. Jesus tenderly accepts her generosity, and assures her of God's forgiveness.

Travelling light
(8:1–3)

Luke gives us a glimpse of Jesus and the Twelve as they travel through towns and villages. They are accompanied by women whom Jesus has healed – notably Mary from Magdala, whom he rescued from demon possession. Some of the women are well connected or have money of their own, and they help to support the group.

The parable of the sower
(8:4–15)

Jesus tells a parable about the mixed fortunes of seed when it is sown. Some falls on the path, where it is trampled or eaten. Some falls where there's no depth of

soil – or where the soil is already full of weeds. But some falls on good soil and grows to produce an excellent crop.

Later, Jesus explains to his disciples that the seed is a picture of God's word. When the message of God's kingdom is sown in human hearts it has a mixed reception. Sometimes the devil snatches it away. Sometimes it is defeated by hard times, or choked by cares. But a humble heart is like open, fertile ground – and there God's word can produce a wonderful harvest.

The story helps the disciples understand the difficulties of their task. Both Satan and circumstances are working against the kingdom of God. But there are still those who welcome the gospel and respond to it. Through them, God's purpose will succeed beyond all expectations.

A lamp on a stand
(8:16–18)

It is stupid to light a lamp and then hide it. Those who have the light of Christ should let their faith shine out, so that others can come to him.

Jesus' mother and brothers
(8:19–21)

Jesus says that those who believe in him are his real family. This is very radical. In Jewish culture the family has the strongest claim on a person's loyalty. But the gospel puts us in a new relationship with God and one another. Jesus called the fishermen from their families and businesses to follow him and become his disciples. Clearly he is being as single-minded himself.

Jesus calms a storm
(8:22–25)

The disciples are caught in one of Galilee's sudden storms. They are afraid they will capsize and drown – yet Jesus sleeps peacefully through it all. When they wake him, he quiets the tempest with a word of rebuke – and asks the disciples why they haven't trusted God in the crisis.

The disciples realize that Jesus has God's power over wind and water. As the psalm says, 'You rule over the surging sea; when its waves mount up, you still them' (Psalm 89:9).

'Legion'
(8:26–39)

Jesus has power to heal uncontrollable bodies and deranged minds. He meets a man whose nickname is

---

Demon possession

A person 'possessed by demons' was unable to control themselves, because of some physical or mental illness. For Jesus, all forms of illness are contrary to God's will. He comes to rescue people from evil and restore them to the health and peace of the kingdom of God.

'Legion', because of the army of demons within him. Just as Jesus has calmed the storm on Galilee, so he stills the chaos in this maniac's life. He commands the demons to leave Legion and enter a herd of pigs, which then stampedes into the sea.

Legion is restored to sanity and dignity; but the people of the region beg Jesus to go away. They can't face up to the changes he makes. They have already lost their pigs. If Jesus stays, what else will have to go?

A dead girl and a sick woman
(8:40–56)

Jesus returns to Capernaum. Last time he was met by messengers from a centurion. Now a well-known figure comes in person. He is Jairus, the president of the local synagogue. His twelve-year-old daughter is dying. Jesus agrees to go to her immediately.

As Jesus tries to make his way through the crowd to Jairus' house, he is delayed by a woman who is ill. She suffers from continuous menstrual bleeding. For twelve years, she has been unable to lead a normal life, or even leave her home. The law of Moses declares that anything she lies or sits on, and anyone who touches her, becomes unclean (Leviticus 15:25–27). Now she breaks the taboo and dares to touch Jesus under cover of the crowd. She only tugs his cloak from behind – like a child asking a rabbi for a prayer – but she is healed instantly.

Jesus realizes that healing power has been drawn from him. He stops to find the woman and speak to her. He assures her that her faith has healed her and that she hasn't won her healing by deceit. But, while he is speaking, the news arrives that Jairus' daughter has died.

Jesus encourages Jairus to have faith that all will be well. When he comes to the house, he tells the mourners to stop their lament. He tells them that the girl is only asleep. Then he takes his closest disciples and the child's parents to the bedside. He reaches for the young girl's hand and calls her to get up. Luke says that her spirit returns. She gets up immediately and is ready for food.

In a busy and interrupted day, Jesus calmly and compassionately meets a host of demands. He gives his undivided attention to each person in need. He overcomes uncleanness with his purity. He dispels the fear of death by declaring it merely a sleep.

Jesus sends out the Twelve
(9:1–6)

Jesus commissions his twelve disciples to preach and heal. He gives them power over demons and diseases. He entrusts them all – from impetuous Peter to sly Judas Iscariot – with the work and reputation of the kingdom of God. He insists that their lifestyles should match their message. They must travel simply, trusting God to feed and defend them. They must stay where they are welcome and leave when they are turned away. They are to be totally identified with God and his gospel.

Herod is curious

(9:7–9)

Herod Antipas is the local king – one of Herod the Great's three sons. He listens to news of Jesus with interest. People are saying John the Baptist is alive again – which Herod knows is impossible, as he's seen his head on a dish. But he is superstitious and uneasy!

When we wonder what Jesus was like, we can note that people linked him with two great prophets – John the Baptist and Elijah.

Jesus feeds 5,000 people

(9:10–17)

A large crowd of people follow Jesus and he teaches them. However, as the evening approaches they find themselves hungry and far from home.

Jesus feeds 5,000 men (and, no doubt, some of their wives and children as well) from just a few loaves and fish. He thanks God and then breaks and shares the food – using the disciples to organize the distribution. This pattern of thanking, breaking and sharing is familiar to all Christian people through the service of Holy Communion.

Jesus is like Moses – feeding God's people in the wilderness. He is teaching his disciples that God is able to meet great need out of tiny resources. Luke hints that this is a Messiah's banquet for the new Israel, because there are twelve baskets of broken pieces left over – the same as the number of the twelve tribes and the twelve apostles.

All four Gospels tell the story of Jesus feeding thousands of people from a few loaves and fish. John's Gospel mentions that the food was 'five small barley loaves and two small fish' – intended as lunch for just one young lad (John 6:5–13).

Peter's confession of Christ

(9:18–27)

Jesus asks the disciples what people are saying about him. They tell him the gossip: that Jesus is a great prophet – perhaps John the Baptist or Elijah come back to life. But then Jesus asks the disciples for their personal opinion: 'Who do you say I am?' It is Peter who courageously answers, 'The Christ of God.' 'Christ' is the Greek word for 'anointed'. Peter believes that Jesus is God's anointed king, the Jewish Messiah.

The Messiah is the great leader who the Jews hope will come to rescue and rule them. He will be a descendant of

King David, and will establish an everlasting kingdom of justice and peace. Some wonderful rewards await his followers!

But Jesus quickly explains that he must first suffer and die. The Christ (Jesus prefers to call himself the 'Son of man') will be rejected by the Jewish leaders and killed. But on the third day after his death he will be raised to life.

The followers of Christ must be prepared to suffer too. Jesus says they must 'take up their cross' – as though they are being led out to be crucified. They must die to all their worldly ambitions, and place their hopes and reputations on a glory that's to come.

The transfiguration

(9:28–36)

It is six days since Peter recognized Jesus as the Christ – and Jesus promised then that some of his disciples would see his glory. Now he takes his closest disciples – Peter, James and John – up a mountain to pray.

As Jesus prays, his disciples see him in a glorious heavenly light. Moses and Elijah appear. They are two of the Old Testament's greatest heroes and represent the Law and the Prophets. Moses led the exodus from Egypt in the old days and there were stories that he never died. Elijah didn't die in the normal way, but was taken into heaven by a fiery chariot (2 Kings 2:11–12). Will Jesus be given this way of escape? No. They talk about the events that await him in Jerusalem.

Jesus will be making a 'departure' or 'exodus', by dying on the cross to pay for sin, and rising from the grave to conquer death. It will be the greatest deliverance since the exodus from Egypt, with Jesus as the sacrifice instead of the Passover lambs. Instead of a new nation finding freedom, a worldwide church will spring to life.

Peter wants to put up three tents – like they did in the wilderness – to enshrine the glory of God. As the shining cloud of God's presence envelops them, the disciples hear God say, 'This is my Son.' Jesus is the One whom Moses and Elijah hoped for. Now the disciples must listen to Jesus only. He is the fulfilment of the Jewish scriptures.

The healing of a boy with an evil spirit

(9:37–45)

The next day the disciples come down to earth with a bump. After the glory of the mountain top, they are met by a despairing father and a demented child. An evil spirit keeps seizing the boy, causing him to scream, lose

The way out

Jesus has come to be the Saviour of the world. Just as God's people were once rescued from slavery in Egypt, so now the whole human race can escape the clutches of sin and death. Jesus is achieving a new 'exodus' – a triumphant way out. Luke uses this word during his account of the transfiguration, where it is translated 'departure' (9:31).

Luke sees a mighty plan of God unfolding. It has its roots in the story of Israel. It takes shape in the message of the prophets. Now God's power to rescue his people from slavery and exile will be realized completely in Jesus.

control of himself and foam at the mouth. The disciples have been unable to help – and Jesus is exasperated by their failure. He heals the boy.

Jesus tells his disciples again, and very earnestly, that he is about to suffer. But he is frustrated by their lack of understanding.

Who will be the greatest?
(9:46–50)

Jesus is preoccupied with the fate that awaits him in Jerusalem. His disciples are full of their own importance – arguing who is to be the greatest in this brave new kingdom of God.

Jesus tries to get his disciples to grasp the values of the kingdom of heaven. He makes a little child stand beside him. The child is small and without strength, money or influence. Jesus says that to honour such a person is to honour him.

The journey to Jerusalem

From now on Jesus has Jerusalem and the approaching crisis on his mind. Luke links the episodes and teaching of the next ten chapters into one continuous journey.

The route of this journey is a roundabout one. It begins with the usual short cut which takes pilgrims through Samaria on their way from Galilee to Jerusalem. Jesus also visits Bethany and Jericho – and even backtracks up to the borders of Galilee again.

Luke is reminding us that Jesus is now focused on his approaching death and resurrection. He is to be 'taken up to heaven' – which is what happened to Elijah. But he must first go down into death before being raised to life and ascending to glory. John's Gospel has the same idea when speaking of Jesus' 'hour' approaching.

Samaritan opposition
(9:51–56)

Once again, the disciples fail to understand the humility of Jesus. When a Samaritan village rejects him (because he is set on going to their rival capital, Jerusalem) James and John want to destroy the settlement by fire from heaven. They are still thinking of Elijah, having recently seen him on the mountain. Elijah called down fire on his enemies – twice, in quick succession (2 Kings 1:10–12). But this is not Jesus' way. He has not come to curse his enemies, but to bless them.

Samaritans ascending Mount Gerizim. Samaritans are of mixed race and religion, but they worship the same God as the Jews. They claim Mount Gerizim as the true mountain of God (John 4:20), rather than the temple mount ('Zion') in Jerusalem.

Jews and Samaritans

There is a long history of hatred between Jews and Samaritans. The Samaritans believe that the books of Moses (the first five books of the Bible) are the only true scriptures. They regard Mount Gerizim as the site of the true temple.

Some Jews (like Jesus and other pilgrims from Galilee) are willing to pass through Samaria – but they are advised to shake its dust from their sandals and clothes afterwards. Those who want nothing at all to do with Samaritans take a longer route, through Perea.

The cost of following Jesus
(9:57–62)

Jesus meets three would-be disciples, but none of them can commit themselves to follow him. One man will miss his home. Jesus says he himself has nowhere to lay his head – until that day when he will rest it on the cross. Another man asks if he can delay joining Jesus until his father has died. Jesus says that the gospel must come

before even the highest family duty. A third wants only to say goodbye to his family; but Jesus says there's no going back. The kingdom must be the first priority in a disciple's life. You can't plough a straight furrow if you keep looking behind you.

Jesus sends out the seventy-two
(10:1–24)

Jesus sends seventy-two disciples ahead of him. They are to go like spiritual commandos on a mission – urgently, with simple equipment and a powerful message.

Time is short – like the opportunity for harvest, when the crop is ripe and the weather is fine. This is when all hands are needed for the work. The time is right for the gospel to be preached.

The disciples aren't to waste time on lengthy greetings, or fuss about their food or shelter. They are to get straight to the business of healing and preaching. If they are welcomed, then God's peace will rest on the people and homes that they visit. If the disciples are rejected, they are to declare God's judgment on the whole town.

Why did Jesus appoint seventy-two missionaries? He is probably following the example of Moses, who commissioned seventy elders (plus Eldad and Medad) to share his work (Numbers 11:24–29).

When the seventy-two return, they have some great stories to tell. They are excited – and so is Jesus – that they have power over demons. After the tensions and misunderstandings of recent weeks, there is joy in seeing Satan's power broken. This wicked prosecutor, who is always accusing humankind, has been thrown out of heaven – thanks to the work of God's kingdom on earth.

Jesus reminds his disciples that there is something even more wonderful than defeating their enemy. Their own peace with God and future home in heaven are secure. This is a high point for Jesus, too. At last he sees spiritual progress and power in the ordinary people who are his followers. He is ecstatic with joy that God's purpose is being fulfilled.

The parable of the good Samaritan
(10:25 37)

A lawyer asks Jesus which laws will lead to eternal life.

Jesus puts the question straight back to the questioner – and the lawyer answers very well. The key commandments are to love our God and our neighbour – and the lawyer quotes them correctly (Deuteronomy 6:5 and Leviticus 19:18).

United with the Father and the Son

Whoever listens to you listens to me, and whoever rejects you rejects me, and whoever rejects me rejects the one who sent me (Luke 10:16).

These words sound like an extract from John's Gospel. Jesus is totally at one with his Father, and prays that his followers may be united with them both.

I pray... that all of them may be one, Father, just as you are in me and I am in you... I in them and you in me (John 17:20–23).

But who does the law mean by 'neighbour'? Where does it draw the line between friend and foe, brother or sister and stranger?

To answer this question, Jesus tells a story. A Jew is robbed and beaten on the dangerous road from Jerusalem to Jericho. Two fellow Jews – a priest and a Levite – refuse to help him. They have their religious duties to attend to in Jerusalem, and must avoid touching blood or dead bodies. But a Samaritan (a hated half-breed and heretic) stops to save the man's life and provide for his future care.

Who is the neighbour? The religious person? The legal expert? The fellow Jew? No! The neighbour is the person who acts in a neighbourly way – the person who helps.

Jesus has turned the question round. It is no longer, 'Who is my neighbour?' but, 'To whom can *I* be a neighbour?'

At the home of Martha and Mary
(10:38–42)

Martha and Mary are the sisters of Lazarus – the man Jesus raises from death in John's Gospel (John 11:38–44). They live in the village of Bethany, not far from Jerusalem.

Martha is busy and hard-working, as she welcomes Jesus to her home. Mary quietly sits at Jesus' feet to listen and learn – an unusual sight in these days when only men are educated.

Luke lets us feel the tension rise, as Martha gets more and more flustered with the cooking – and indignant that Mary is leaving her to do it all by herself...

Suddenly Martha explodes! But Jesus refuses to take her side. Mary may look lazy, but in fact she is doing something supremely important. She is taking in God's truth – which is the only food that matters.

Jesus' teaching on prayer
(11:1–13)

The disciples ask Jesus to teach them to pray. In response, he outlines a model prayer, which has become known as the 'Lord's Prayer'.

The prayer begins surprisingly, by calling God 'Abba' – 'Dear Father'.

The Jews have several names for God, and a hundred ways of avoiding saying his holy name. No one has ever presumed to call God 'Daddy'. Jesus is inviting his friends to share his own intimate relationship with God. This is not like any prayer that has ever been before. This is love talk.

The disciples are to pray that God's name be kept holy and honoured, and that his kingdom will be established on earth.

They are to ask God to provide for their needs day by day; that he will forgive their sins, and not put them to hard testing.

This is a very short, simple and basic prayer. It honours God for his love, holiness and purpose. It asks that everyday physical, spiritual and moral needs may be met: food, forgiveness and protection.

Jesus encourages his disciples to pray. He gives several pictures of the Father's goodwill.

God is better than a neighbour. If a neighbour will eventually and reluctantly answer a call for help, won't God most willingly hear our prayer?

God is better than human parents. If human parents, with all their faults, will never trick their offspring, won't God give good gifts to *his* children?

Jesus tells his friends that they can surely trust God and ask him for things. They should knock on his door and long for access to him. They should ask him especially for his Holy Spirit. They won't get everything they want – but their needs will always be met, and God's gifts are always good!

Jesus and Beelzebub
(11:14–26)

Even Jesus' critics agree that he is able to cast out demons. However, they claim he can do it because he is in league with 'Beelzebub' – the 'Lord of the Flies' or prince of demons. Jesus says that if the devil is now casting out his own demons, his kingdom must be in a state of collapse. The truth is that Satan is being defeated by the power of God.

The people who criticize Jesus are denying that God is at work. They are insulting the Holy Spirit. It's not enough merely to cast out an evil spirit, because it will return with reinforcements. The human heart needs not only to be emptied of Satan, but also to be filled with God's Holy Spirit.

A cry from the crowd
(11:27–28)

A woman in the crowd calls out to Jesus, 'Blessed is the mother who gave you birth and nursed you.' She believes that Jesus is the Messiah, and that Mary is the most privileged of mothers.

Jesus replies that there is a greater blessing for those who hear the word of God and obey it. He has said before that his 'mother' and 'brothers' are those who hear God's word and put it into practice (8:19–21). The new relationships in the kingdom of God are more important to Jesus than his natural family.

In this and the next passage we hear Jesus' frustration that people are missing the opportunity to welcome God's kingdom into their lives.

The sign of Jonah
(11:29–32)

Jesus knows that the crowds are coming in the hope of seeing miraculous signs, rather than to change their ways. The only sign they will get is the 'sign of Jonah' – that is, a man preaching. Jonah was a prophet who preached to the great and wicked city of Nineveh, and the whole community repented. Jesus is greater than Jonah, yet people are refusing to repent.

The queen of Sheba travelled many miles to visit Solomon and hear his wisdom. She responded wholeheartedly to all she saw and heard (1 Kings 10:1–9). Now Jesus is greater than Solomon. He is the wisdom of God (1 Corinthians 1:24). What will the queen of Sheba say to those who have the privilege of seeing and hearing Jesus – but turn away?

The lamp of the body
(11:33–36)

Jesus says that good eyes give light to the whole body. Light is a symbol of spiritual truth which shines in the human mind, heart and life. But Israel has lost her spiritual sight. She has covered up the light of God's truth. She is blind to the presence of her Messiah.

Jesus attacks the Pharisees
(11:37–54)

Jesus confronts the Pharisees. He tells them that their lives are warped and shrivelled by legalism.

The Pharisees have twisted God's truth into a complex legal puzzle. They carefully clean their dishes, to ensure their ritual purity. They count out their tithe to the last leaf of mint. Their manners are absolutely correct. All this obsessional behaviour is their idea of holiness.

Jesus says they are burdening people with unnecessary rules. They are neglecting true justice. They are ignoring the life-changing love of God. People like them have killed God's prophets – and then honoured them with impressive tombs! They have closed the door of the knowledge of God – and thrown away the key.

Be different from the Pharisees!
(12:1–12)

Jesus tells his disciples that the Pharisees are hypocrites. Hypocrisy means acting or pretending. The Pharisees are obsessed with looking holy – which is not the same as *being* holy. They strive for one another's good opinions, when really they should care only for what God thinks of them. By rejecting Jesus, they are bringing God's rejection on themselves.

The struggle with legalism continues in the history of the church. Jesus assures his followers that when they are put on trial over these complex issues, the Holy Spirit will be with them to guide their defence.

The parable of the rich fool
(12:13–21)

A man asks Jesus for help. He and his brother are arguing over the property they have inherited.

Jesus tells a story of a farmer who was rich and getting richer. He went to bed with his head full of dreams – expansion, savings, security, comfort, luxury, retirement…

But he died that night!

True wealth isn't in our possessions, but in our relationship with God. Worldly wealth doesn't last, but with God we are for ever rich.

Do not worry

(12:22–34)

Jesus continues on the theme of possessions. He teaches his disciples not to worry about their length of life, their food or clothes. If we worry all the time, we're insulting God – and no different from pagans.

The world of nature constantly speaks to us of God's amazing provision – even for birds and flowers. If we put God first, then everything else will find its proper place. We can start to enjoy heaven – now.

Watchfulness

(12:35–48)

Jesus is talking about living on earth in the light of heaven. His disciples must be like servants, who wait for their lord when he comes home late. He will be delighted to find them still awake and ready for him – and will surprise them by waiting on them!

This teaching is kept by the church long after Jesus has been taken up into heaven. Christians are waiting for Jesus, the Son of man, to return and establish his kingdom. But how long will he be?

Jesus tells them that faithfulness is the key. When he comes, he will reward those who have served him to the best of their ability, and punish those who have neglected their responsibilities.

The crisis is approaching

(12:49–59)

Jesus knows that he is plunging the world into crisis. For him, a baptism of suffering and death lies ahead. The division of opinion about him will even split families.

He tells the people that they can read the signs of the weather, but they aren't reading the signs of the times in which they live. Israel is on a collision course with God – and with Rome. They are heading for a judgment which will go against them. They had better seek God's forgiveness now, before it is too late.

'Go out into the roads and lanes, and compel people to come in.' A stone door at the Cave of the Ascents, Bet She'arim.

Warnings

(13:1–9)

Some people ask Jesus about recent tragedies. What dreadful thing had the Galileans done, that God allowed the Roman governor to mix their blood with their sacrifices? And was God behind the collapse of the tower of Siloam? Did the victims deserve such a death?

Jesus says these people were not selected for special punishment. They were no more guilty than anyone else. Such events are a warning to get right with God in case our own time comes. Israel is about to be judged – like a tree with a last chance to produce fruit.

A crippled woman healed on the sabbath

(13:10–17)

One sabbath, Jesus heals a woman who has been bent double for eighteen years. The synagogue ruler immediately criticizes him for healing on the sabbath, when it isn't an emergency.

Jesus answers that his critic treats animals better than humans when it comes to the sabbath. This woman is a daughter of Abraham who has suffered long enough – and the sabbath is the ideal day to set her free!

The parables of the mustard seed and the yeast

(13:18–21)

The mustard seed is the smallest seed – yet it grows into a tree and becomes a shelter for birds. The kingdom of God will become a landmark and refuge for the nations.

A small amount of yeast can transform a large amount of flour. In the same way, the kingdom of God will change the world.

Who will be saved?

(13:22–30)

Jesus describes the present situation. It is as though a door is open, through which God's family may enter his house. The door is narrow, to exclude all greed, pride and hypocrisy; and one day God will close it altogether.

Jesus is saying bluntly that the Jews can't take their

salvation for granted. They must repent. Some Gentile believers will surprise them by going into the Messiah's banquet ahead of them.

Jesus' sorrow for Jerusalem
(13:31–35)

Some Pharisees warn Jesus that Herod (Antipas) is trying to kill him. Jesus replies that he will be leaving the area, as he is intent on going to Jerusalem.

Jesus weeps with grief and frustration. He loves Jerusalem, and yet she has killed so many of God's prophets, and will reject Jesus himself. But she will have to reckon with him in the end.

Table talk
(14:1–14)

Jesus is dining with Pharisees. He notices again how much they care about their place in society – and even at table! He recommends his disciples to take the lowest place at first.

Invitations to dinner are a way of dividing society. The custom is to invite your own class of people, who will then invite you in return. The poor are left out. But Jesus says real happiness is found in inviting the poor.

The parable of the great banquet
(14:15–24)

All devout Jews assume they will one day take their place at the Messiah's banquet. Jesus isn't so sure!

He tells a story about a man who prepares a great feast – but nobody comes! Every guest makes a feeble excuse. One is inspecting a field, another is trying out oxen, a third has just got married…

The master is furious. He sends his servant to invite the poor and disabled from the streets and the countryside. He fills his house with the people that society has rejected.

In the same way God will bypass the Jews who scorn his invitation. He will invite the scum of Jewish society instead – the tax collectors and prostitutes – and fill the empty places in heaven with Gentiles!

The cost of being a disciple
(14:25–35)

A large crowd is now heading for Jerusalem with Jesus. Their hope is that his pilgrim's progress will become a military campaign. Jesus spells out the true cost of following him.

To be a disciple, you must prefer Jesus to every member of your family – including yourself! You must estimate the cost, just as you would with a building project. You must assess whether you are able to succeed, just as you would before a battle.

Jesus looks for followers who are like salt – promoting goodness and preventing evil. Without total commitment, they will be useless.

The parables of the lost sheep and the lost coin
(15:1–10)

Jesus is under attack for the company he keeps. Why does he spend so much time with sinners? Their lives are a mess and their morals a disgrace.

To answer these opinions, Jesus tells three stories: the lost sheep, the lost coin – and the lost son.

When a shepherd loses one of his sheep, he leaves the rest and goes to rescue it. When a woman loses a coin (a drachma – a silver coin worth a day's wages) – perhaps part of her dowry from her father – she carefully sweeps the house until she finds it. And when sheep or coins are safe again it's an excuse for a party!

Jesus has come to find and rescue those who are *lost*. Some, like sheep, have stupidly wandered off. Others, like the coin, have been lost through no fault of their own. But Jesus shares the company of such people – so that they may share his salvation. It's a costly mission – but for everyone who repents, there's a celebration in heaven.

What's wrong with money?

Jesus says we can't serve God and money. By money he means 'mammon' or 'gain' – a god of enormous power.

Money has a tremendous attraction, because it gives security, power and choice. We don't need to rely on God for every mouthful of food and every stitch of clothing when we've got money! And money can stave off boredom, win us popularity and afford us treats…

But money makes us self-centred and self-sufficient. Money offers us status and influence, making us the centre of our world and the envy of our friends. It is the very opposite of trusting God and serving him alone.

The parable of the lost ('prodigal') son

(15:11–32)

Jesus' third story is the longest of all his parables.

A man has two sons. One day the younger son demands his share of his father's property. This would normally come to him only after his father's death; but the father agrees, and the young man leaves home with his fortune.

Before long all the money has gone, the country is in the grip of famine and the young man has to take a job feeding pigs. Pigs are unclean animals for Jews and pork is a forbidden food. This job is the pits!

The young man comes to his senses and sets out for home. He resolves to beg his father to let him be a servant on the family estate. But the father sees him the moment he comes over the horizon – and runs to forgive him and welcome him home. Soon the young man has the ring of a son on his finger and the shoes of a freeman on his feet. His father calls everyone together for a party.

But the older son is out in the field – and not at all pleased that his brother has returned. He feels taken for granted and shabbily treated. His father goes in search of him and tries to persuade him to be happy…

The older son is Jesus' picture of the Pharisees. They have 'stayed at home with God' – but without much sense of joy and freedom. And they are jealous and critical when sinners are so joyfully welcomed back.

The parable of the shrewd manager

(16:1–15)

Jesus tells a story about a manager who may be fired.

A manager is being investigated by his employer, who wants an account of his work. Realizing he is certain to lose his job, the manager gets various customers to mark down their bills! In this way he hopes to make friends who will look after him in the future.

Although the manager is a thoroughly bad character, Jesus commends his realism. At least he faces the crisis and takes immediate action. Jesus says that those who reject the love of God had better see what friends they can make with money.

The rich man and Lazarus

(16:16–31)

Jesus tells a story which shows the importance of choosing for God *now*.

There was once a rich man who lived in luxury – while a beggar named Lazarus sat at his gate.

One day they both died – and their fortunes were reversed. Lazarus went to heaven – and the rich man went to hell!

In hell, the rich man asks father Abraham to send Lazarus down with a drink, but Abraham says it can't be done. There's a gulf between heaven and hell, which no one can cross.

In desperation, the rich man asks that Lazarus at least be sent to warn his brothers what's in store for them. But Abraham says they have all the warning they need – in the scriptures. What's more, says he, they won't be convinced even if someone should rise from the dead.

This parable has many important messages – about heaven and hell, death and judgment, and the plight of the hungry in an unfair world. But Jesus' main point is urgency. The rich man's five brothers have the scriptures and have heard their message. Like the shrewd manager they must act quickly to save themselves.

Sin, faith, duty

(17:1–10)

Jesus says it is a terrible thing to introduce someone to sin. At the same time, he encourages limitless forgiveness.

The apostles ask for a lot of faith, but Jesus says that even a little goes a long way. Faith as tiny as a mustard seed can uproot a tree and replant it in the sea – a double impossibility!

Jesus reflects on being a servant. A servant is at his master's disposal – always ready to do his duty, and never needing to be cajoled or thanked. Are Christians as reliable in their service of God?

Ten healed of leprosy

(17:11–19)

Jesus heals ten lepers, but only one returns to thank him. And he's a Samaritan! Not for the first time, Jesus is impressed by a foreigner's faith – and Luke is glad to report it.

The coming of the kingdom of God

(17:20–37)

Jesus is asked when God's kingdom will come. He replies, 'It is within you.' God rules wherever he is welcomed as king.

Both Jews and Christians look forward to the 'Day of the Son of man', when God's Messiah will be given all authority to rule heaven and earth. For Christians, this is the Lord's return – and Jesus says it will be visible, universal and unmistakable. If anyone needs to say, 'There he is!' that *won't* be him!

Jesus Christ will return on an ordinary day – just as Noah's flood and the destruction of Sodom began in the midst of everyday life. Suddenly whole communities were plunged into judgment – and so it will be when Jesus returns. But the judgment of Jesus also applies to every individual. Even between husband and wife, it is possible that 'one will be taken and the other left'.

The parable of the persistent widow
(18:1–8)

Jesus encourages his disciples to pray and keep on praying.

He tells them a story of a nagging widow. She has trouble getting justice out of her local judge – who has no interest at all in hearing her case. But, by wearing him down, she eventually gets her way.

Jesus says that God isn't like that judge. He isn't reluctant, lazy or indifferent to our requests. He loves to hear from his people, and to answer their prayers. All the same, Jesus wonders whether faith on earth will survive with such reluctant, lazy and indifferent disciples.

The Pharisee and the tax collector
(18:9–14)

Jesus tells another story about prayer. The last one was about persistence. This one is about humility.

Two men go to the temple to pray – but only one really prays.

A Pharisee, standing at the front, gives a glowing report of himself to God. He finds himself honest, good and pure. He fasts regularly and tithes to perfection. Oh yes, and he's very glad he's not a lousy tax collector…

Meanwhile, the other man – who *is* the tax collector – stands at the back with downcast eyes. He prays, simply and directly, 'God, have mercy on me, a sinner.'

This is a very daring story! Remember how the piety of the Pharisees is so greatly admired, and the tax collectors are despised and shunned. To think that God might prefer a tax collector's prayer to that of a Pharisee!

The little children and the rich ruler
(18:15–30)

Some parents bring babies to Jesus for his blessing. The disciples think Jesus won't want to be interrupted – for this is a society which generally ignores women and children. But Jesus loves the children's simple trust – for him they are a glimpse of heaven.

A rich young ruler also wants the secret of eternal life. He has kept the commandments for years, so what's he missing?

Jesus tells him to get rid of his possessions, and have wealth in heaven instead. Sadly, the man can't bring himself to do it. His possessions own him – although they don't make him happy.

Later, as Jesus and the disciples talk about this, Peter remarks that they've left everything. But Jesus puts this great sacrifice in perspective. He says they've gained, here and now, immeasurably more than they've given up – and with eternal life still to come.

Jesus again predicts his death
(18:31–34)

Luke records that Jesus predicts his death a third time. The crucifixion won't be an accident, and the resurrection shouldn't be a surprise. Jesus has told his disciples repeatedly that suffering and death await him – and that he will rise again.

A blind beggar receives his sight
(18:35–43)

Just outside Jericho, Jesus encounters a blind beggar. He is shouting a nationalist slogan: 'Jesus, Son of David!' It's enough to cause a riot, if it catches on. He is sowing the idea of a triumphant march on Jerusalem.

Jesus knows that, behind the shouting, is a cry for help: 'Lord, I want to see.' As always, the man's point of need is the Lord's point of delivery. 'Receive your sight,' says Jesus, 'Your faith has healed you.'

Zacchaeus
(19:1–10)

Jesus comes to Jericho – the 'city of palms' lying deep in the Jordan Valley. About half of Israel's priests live here, and no doubt many of them are interested to see Jesus. But Jesus is determined to move on to Jerusalem, which is now only seventeen miles away.

The chief tax collector in Jericho is Zacchaeus. He taxes the Jews on behalf of the Romans and is extremely unpopular. He takes money from his fellow Jews to help pay for the Roman occupation of their country. He also makes a fortune by charging more tax than is necessary and keeping the excess for himself.

Zacchaeus wants to see Jesus. No doubt he has heard that Jesus is friendly to people like him, whom everyone else rejects and excludes as a sinner.

There is a large crowd lining the road, and Zacchaeus is a short man. He is too proud to ask to be allowed to the front, and too unpopular to be invited. But he is cunning. He runs ahead of the crowd and climbs a sycamore-fig tree…

The sycamore-fig is a large tree with wide, low branches. From here Zacchaeus hopes to see Jesus without being seen – but he is wrong. When Jesus comes to the place, he stops, looks up and invites himself to the taxman's house for dinner! Zacchaeus is delighted.

Here is the gospel in action. Jesus comes to Zacchaeus, like a shepherd to a lost sheep. He finds him, accepts him and helps him to discover a new life. Our point of need is God's point of salvation.

The righteous residents of Jericho condemn Jesus for keeping bad company. But Jesus has said before that he is like a doctor who must mix with the sick in order to heal them (Luke 5:31–32).

Zacchaeus is a changed man. He immediately gives half his wealth to the poor and promises to repay all the money he has stolen. The law requires him to add an extra 20 per cent (Leviticus 6:5) – but Zacchaeus tops it with an extravagant pledge to repay four times over. He is as cured of greed as the blind man was from darkness.

Jesus declares that Zacchaeus is 'saved'. The greedy tax collector, so at odds with his neighbours, has come home to the love and forgiveness of God. He is a true son of Abraham now – not by race but by faith. Just as Abraham showed his faith by his actions, so Zacchaeus is proving his new life in his deeds. This is exactly what the Messiah has come to do.

The parable of the ten minas
(19:11–27)

As Jesus approaches Jerusalem there is mounting excitement. It is in Jerusalem that the Jews expect the

Messiah to declare himself and establish the kingdom of God. The people who are travelling with Jesus feel that they are poised on the threshold of a great revolution. Jesus tells a story which gives a very different perspective.

A nobleman has to visit a far country, to be appointed king. Before he leaves on his journey, he gives ten of his servants some money. The amount is a mina – the sum a labourer would earn in 100 days. He commands the servants to make good use of the money while he is away.

Jesus adds a topical twist to the story. The nobleman's subjects don't want him to be their king, and send a delegation to protest. Something like this had happened when Herod the Great died. Herod's son, Archelaus, went to Rome to be appointed king of Judea, but was opposed by a delegation of Jews. As a result, Emperor Augustus made Archelaus ruler of only part of his father's kingdom, and refused to grant him the status of king.

When the king returns, he asks his servants to account for their money. The first two have invested or traded with great success and are rewarded with greater responsibilities. The third has merely hidden his mina in a cloth to keep it safe. He has no gain to show for it – not even the interest it could have earned in a deposit account at the bank.

The king is angry with the third servant – and especially when the man accuses his master of being hard, privileged and unpredictable. The king commands that the mina be given to the servant who has made the most use of his own mina – and that his enemies be killed.

In telling this story, Jesus gives insight into his kingship. He is not coming to Jerusalem to declare himself the Messiah and establish the kingdom of God. Rather he is about to go away for a long time. While he is absent, his disciples must make good use of what he is giving them, which is the gospel.

When Jesus returns as king, he will call his disciples to account for what they have done. If, like the Pharisees, they have hidden God's good news from those who need it, they will be severely judged.

The final week

The triumphal entry
(19:28–44)

Jesus approaches Jerusalem. He wants to arrive in the city in a particular way – a way which will convey both his kingship and the style of his rule. He sends two disciples to borrow an animal for him to ride. It is a colt, the male foal of an ass.

The colt has never been ridden before, and is reserved and ready for Jesus. Soon he will also be given the use of a new tomb (23:53). Luke is showing that Jesus is in command of events. Even as he goes to his death, there are people who are offering him their best, as they recognize and honour him as Lord.

The prophet Zechariah describes how a king will come to Jerusalem one day. He will be 'gentle and riding on a donkey, on a colt, the foal of a donkey' (Zechariah 9:9). He will not come with military might to impose his rule by force, but with gentleness to establish his reign of peace.

Jerusalem from the Mount of Olives. This is the view which pilgrims enjoy when they first come in sight of the city. It is a moment of great exultation – but Jesus weeps (19:41).

As Jesus rides towards Jerusalem, the crowds spread their coats as a carpet on the road. They are welcoming him as their Messiah and inviting him to ride over their lives. As Jesus rounds the Mount of Olives and comes within sight of Jerusalem his followers bless him with words from a psalm (Psalm 118:26).

The Pharisees protest that Jesus is allowing such praises to be spoken. He replies that this is a glorious day of fulfilment. It was for this moment that Jerusalem was built – to welcome her Messiah. If the people remain silent, then the stones themselves will burst into praise.

But when Jesus comes within sight of the city, he starts to weep. Jerusalem was built to be a holy city, the royal seat of God's chosen king and the centre of a worldwide kingdom of peace. Sadly, she has turned her back on God and is about to reject and kill his Messiah. This rejection is going to result in God's judgment within a few years.

Jesus at the temple
(19:45–48)

Jesus has ridden into Jerusalem as its longed-for Messiah. Now he visits the temple. He comes as its Lord to judge and cleanse it (Malachi 3:1–3).

Jesus enters the outer courtyard of the temple. This is the court of the Gentiles, where non-Jewish visitors are able to come and pray. Instead of the quiet wonder of pilgrims waiting on God, he finds the busy street scene of a cattle market.

The priests have taken over the Gentile area for Jewish use. There are kiosks where people can change money, and stalls where they can buy sacrifices. The 'dirty' coins of everyday use have to be exchanged for 'holy' coins with which to pay the temple tax. This is a tax of half a shekel per year on every male Jew. Sacrifices of birds, goats and lambs also have to be carefully checked by the priests – and many pilgrims prefer to buy a creature that has already been approved 'without defect' (Leviticus 3:1).

Jesus begins to drive out the traders. The temple exists to draw all nations to the God of Israel. Now the Gentiles' space is taken up by the human requirements of Jewish religion. This is a scandal. Jesus quotes the words of the prophets: Isaiah's 'house of prayer' has become Jeremiah's 'den of robbers' (Isaiah 56:7; Jeremiah 7:11).

Having cleared the temple area, Jesus puts it to its proper use. He teaches God's word there – to the delight of the people and the fury of their religious leaders.

The authority of Jesus is questioned
(20:1–8)

The Jewish leaders challenge Jesus' right to teach. He has no qualification. He has never been authorized.

Instead of answering by claiming God's authority, Jesus asks them a question in return. Did John the Baptist do God's work or was his baptism merely his own invention?

The priests and teachers can't answer this question without getting caught. If they admit that John's baptism was a true work of God, then they should have accepted it at the time. If they deny it, the people will stone them for blasphemy.

When the authorities can't answer Jesus' question, he declines to answer theirs.

The parable of the tenants
(20:9–19)

Jesus tells a story about a man who planted a vineyard and rented it to some tenants. His Jewish hearers will immediately recognize that Jesus is referring to Israel. Israel is the 'vineyard' which God planted in Canaan when he gave his chosen people their Promised Land (Isaiah 5:1–7). The 'tenants' are the priests and teachers who should be caring for God's people.

Jesus describes how the owner of the vineyard sent his servants to ask for fruit. This is a picture of God sending his prophets to demand righteousness and justice. But the tenants beat and abused the servants, and sent them away empty-handed. Finally, the owner sent his son, in the hope that the tenants would at least respect him. But the outcome was even worse. The tenants saw their chance to seize the vineyard for themselves, and killed the owner's son.

The people listening to Jesus are horrified. God will have no choice but to punish a nation that rejects and murders his son. But Jesus quotes a prophecy from the Psalms. The stone which was once discarded will prove to be the keystone (Psalm 118:22). The builders (the religious leaders) may reject a stone (the Messiah), but they will find it is the most important stone of all – the one which holds the whole building together.

Paying taxes to Caesar
(20:20–26)

The authorities try again to trap Jesus – this time with a question about tax.

The Romans impose a poll tax on every Jewish male. This tax has to be paid annually in Roman coinage – the silver denarius with the emperor's head engraved upon it. The Jews resent this tax for two reasons. It reminds them that they are no longer a free nation, and it confronts them with an image of Caesar, their pagan ruler.

The Jews believe that their only king is God. Their second commandment forbids the making of images, which leads to idolatry (Exodus 20:4).

The Jewish leaders send spies to ask Jesus about this taxation. Is it right to pay it or not? If he answers that it is, then he is betraying his nation. If he answers that it isn't, he may be arrested as a dissident. This is perhaps the cleverest of the questions put to Jesus, and he shows his brilliance in the way he handles it.

Jesus knows that the questioners are insincere. He asks to see one of the silver coins, and they produce one readily enough. They are not so concerned about the issue that they refuse to touch the money. Jesus asks them about the image and inscription, and they answer that it is Caesar's. 'Then give to Caesar what is Caesar's,' says Jesus, 'and give to God what is God's.'

The Roman empire provides the Jews with many benefits – strong government, sound laws, a stable economy and secure trade routes. In return for this, it is reasonable and right to pay tax. But, as human beings, the Jews are made in the image of God. They have a duty to God, which is to offer their very selves to him in worship and service.

God's people, both Jews and Christians, are citizens of two kingdoms. They belong to a secular state, whose God-given task is to govern and protect its people. They also belong to the kingdom of heaven, which crosses all boundaries of time and place.

God's people owe a duty to the state, but owe their hearts to God. As long as the state doesn't play God and religion doesn't become an oppressive regime, it is possible and right to honour both.

The resurrection and marriage
(20:27–40)

The Sadducees come to Jesus with a question about resurrection.

The Sadducees are an elite and scholarly group who form the ruling party among the Jews. They accept only the books of Moses (the first five books of the Bible) as scripture. They disagree with the other leading party, the Pharisees, who believe in the resurrection of the body, the existence of angels and demons, and the hope of life after death.

The Sadducees want to prove to Jesus that the idea of resurrection is nonsense. They describe an imaginary case in which a woman marries each of seven brothers. This is possible under the law of Moses. A widow may marry her brother-in-law, to produce children for her dead husband's family line (Deuteronomy 25:5–6).

The Sadducees' question is this. If there is a resurrection and an afterlife, whose wife will this woman be? Does not God's law imply that the only life we have is now, and that we continue only through our earthly children? Life after death will produce absurdity and confusion.

Although the example is extremely unlikely, Jesus takes the question seriously. He states that resurrection is a privilege, not a right. The choice of those who will enter life in the new age will depend on God's judgment.

Jesus emphasizes that life in the new age will be very different – more like the life enjoyed by angels. There will be no death, and no need to marry or have children. The emphasis will not be on *having* children, but on *being* children – the children of God.

The Passover lamb

The Passover lambs are killed in the temple on the 14th day of the month of Nisan. They are eaten after sunset, which by Jewish reckoning is the following day – 15th Nisan. This is the night of the spring full moon. It is also the first day of the Feast of Unleavened Bread, which is a week-long harvest festival.

Luke measures the days in a different way, because of information he has copied from Mark's Gospel. Mark uses Greek and Roman reckoning for the days, which means that the next day begins at midnight.

Luke, along with Matthew and Mark, describes the Last Supper as a Passover meal. John has a different timing, as he places the crucifixion on the same day as the Passover lambs are being sacrificed in the temple. This is to convey to us that Jesus is the Lamb of God, who takes away the sin of the world (John 1:29).

After the destruction of Jerusalem in AD 70, a group of Jewish Zealots took refuge in the rocky fortress of Masada. Here they withstood a Roman siege for over a year, before committing suicide rather than surrendering.

To show how little the Sadducees have thought about all this, Jesus gives an example from their own scriptures. When God introduces himself to Moses, he describes himself as 'the God of Abraham, the God of Isaac and the God of Jacob' (Exodus 3:6). As he is the God of the living, this implies that these great men of the past are alive with him.

Whose son is the Christ?

(20:41–44)

Now Jesus asks the Sadducees a question. He quotes one of the psalms, which is about the Messiah (Psalm 110:1). In this psalm, David refers to the Messiah as 'my Lord' – and yet the Messiah is expected to be a *descendant* of David, and therefore 'lower' than him in status. Jesus asks the Sadducees how the Messiah can be both David's 'Lord' and 'son'?

God had promised David that his descendants would reign for ever. This promise held true for hundreds of years, until the defeat of Judah by Babylon in 586 BC. At that time, the great institutions of Israel – the king, the temple and the holy city of Jerusalem – were all disrupted or destroyed.

During and after the years of exile, the Jews continued to treasure God's promise to David. It took the form of a future hope – that one day a descendant of David would emerge to be king of the Jews. He would be a strong, just and victorious king, like his great ancestor.

Luke doesn't record the Sadducees' answer. As with their discussion about resurrection, Jesus is opening their minds to the wonder and reality of the new age. The kingdom of heaven is more real than any kingdom on earth. The Messiah will not merely inherit the throne of David, but share the throne of God.

True religion

(20:45 – 21:4)

Jesus warns his disciples about the teachers of the law. They enjoy the status of being religious leaders. They wear special robes, receive respectful bows in the street and are given the best places in church and society. But they are hypocrites. They exploit widows by taking over their property. Their long prayers are merely to impress

an audience. They are heading for judgment.

Jesus' warning is not only about Jewish leaders. His words are a caution for all religious people.

Nearby, some rich people are putting money into the temple treasury. This takes place in the Court of Women, for all to see. Like long prayers, large gifts can be made to impress spectators rather than to honour God.

As Jesus watches, a poor widow puts in two lepta. These are the smallest copper coins, worth almost nothing. To most observers, the widow's gift seems pitiful and pathetic. To Jesus, it is the greatest and most generous gift of the day – because she has put in all she has.

Signs of the end of the age

(21:5–38)

The disciples are admiring the recent work on the temple.

Herod the Great organized the renewal and extension of the 'second temple' – the temple which was built when the Jews returned from exile in Babylon. Herod's design is impressive, with dazzling white stone and burnished gold finishes. The project is carried out between 19 BC and AD 64, which includes the lifetime of Jesus.

Jesus solemnly predicts that one day this temple will be completely destroyed. The disciples ask when this will be, and whether there will be a warning sign.

In his reply, Jesus describes two crises. One will be the destruction of Jerusalem, which will happen within a generation. The other will be the coming of the Son of man, which will happen at the end of the age.

As for warning signs, Jesus says that there will be false messiahs who proclaim that God's judgment is about to fall. They are to be ignored. There will also be news of wars and revolutions, as well as natural disasters such as earthquakes, famine and disease. These will all be signs of the times, but the end of the world will not happen immediately.

Even before these alarming events, the followers of Jesus will be persecuted. They will be put on trial and imprisoned by both Jewish and Gentile authorities. They will be betrayed by their own families, and some will be killed. But Jesus promises to be with them to counsel and protect them. Even death will not harm them. If they endure, they will enter eternal life.

Jerusalem will be surrounded and destroyed by pagan armies. This happened in the past, when the Babylonians laid siege to the city in 586 BC. Jesus recalls that horrific event by using some of the language and descriptions from that terrible day. Now it is to happen again, when the Roman armies surround and destroy Jerusalem in AD 70.

On both occasions God uses Gentile forces against his own people, to punish their sin. This time the judgment will fall because Jerusalem has rejected and killed God's Messiah. It is a judgment that is first signalled when Jesus clears the temple of traders, and when the temple curtain is torn as he dies (23:45). It will be completed when the Roman armies of Titus overrun the city and level the temple site.

As Jesus speaks, the world is about to enter a period of Gentile power. This had been foretold in the book of Daniel (Daniel 12:7). The calling to be God's people will pass from the nation of Israel to the worldwide Christian church. It will be an age of stress, fear and cosmic upheaval. In the end, all the powers of heaven and earth will be shaken. But then the Son of man will appear, coming in the cloud of God's glory to judge the world and save his people.

Ever since the death and resurrection of Jesus, the world has been living in its final age. It is an age of both turmoil and hope. For Christians, it is a time for purity, self-control, prayer and expectancy. When things are at their worst, we look for the Lord's return.

Judas agrees to betray Jesus

(22:1–6)

Passover is approaching, when Jerusalem will be crowded with pilgrims. It is always a festival of national fervour, as the Jews remember their deliverance from slavery in Egypt and their birth as a nation.

The Jewish authorities want to get rid of Jesus. They are afraid he will spark off a revolt against the Romans. But Jesus is hugely popular, and always protected by a crowd of supporters. The leaders find their opportunity when Judas agrees to act as an informer. He will tell them where they can arrest Jesus in some lonely place.

There are many possible reasons why Judas betrays Jesus. He loves money. John tells us that Judas is an eager but dishonest treasurer (John 12:6). Is he so desperate for money that he will sell his master?

It seems more likely that Judas is disillusioned with Jesus – disappointed that he didn't seize power after his triumphant arrival in Jerusalem. He may also fear (as Thomas does) that Jesus will surrender and they will all be killed – in which case he is trying to save himself.

Luke says that Satan enters Judas. This betrayal is the work of the devil; but Judas is still responsible for his action.

The Last Supper

(22:7–38)

Jesus sends Peter and John to prepare their Passover meal. He has a private arrangement to borrow or hire a guest room. The two disciples are to follow a man carrying a water jar – a rare sight in the East, where such work is left to women.

This man will lead them to a house with a large upper room, where they can share the Passover away from official hostility and the public gaze. Like the unbroken colt and the unused tomb, this room is furnished and ready. Again, Luke shows us that nothing is taking Jesus by surprise.

The Passover meal has a menu of roast lamb, unleavened bread, bitter herbs and wine. Each food dish is a reminder of the exodus from Egypt.

The roast lamb commemorates the lamb which was slain for each household and its blood painted on the outside door.

The unleavened bread recalls the bread that was made and eaten in haste, with no time for the dough to rise.

The bitter herbs are a relish to eat with the bread, and a symbol of the bitterness of Israel's slavery in Egypt.

NEW COVENANT, NEW KINGDOM

Jesus and his disciples eat the Passover meal, reclining on cushions around a low table. Jesus tells them that he has looked forward to this meal. They won't share another Passover until they meet again at the Messiah's heavenly banquet, which will fulfil the Passover dream.

As host, Jesus alters the traditional ceremony. He gives thanks for the food and explains its meaning. He takes a cup of wine and passes it round. He himself will not drink wine again until God's kingdom is completely established. He takes the bread, gives thanks to God for it, breaks it and gives it to his friends. This is his body, offered up and broken for them. When they break bread together in future, they are to remember his sacrifice.

At the end of the meal, Jesus takes another cup of wine. This wine is his blood poured out. The blood of an animal was poured out in sacrifice, to pay for and cover a person's sin. Now the perfect life of Jesus is to be poured out for the sin of the whole world. This is a new covenant – a covenant which is not achieved by keeping God's law, but by receiving his grace (22:14–30).

Jesus knows that he is to suffer and die – and that the one who will betray him is present at the meal. Although

Judas' treachery is a fulfilment of scripture, it will still be his own wilful and woeful deed. Meanwhile, it is not at all obvious which of the disciples would behave in such a way. They fall into their old dispute about who are Jesus' strongest supporters and who will receive the greatest reward.

Jesus explains that power-seeking is a pagan attitude. God's kingdom reverses such worldly values. Jesus isn't their Lord by lording it over them, but by serving them. They must be the same – the oldest as the youngest and the leader as a slave. It is this kind of kingdom that his disciples are to share with Jesus, and they will serve as its rulers and judges. They are to be the leaders of the new Israel.

THE SIFTING OF SIMON

Jesus speaks especially to Simon – repeating his name, as he likes to do, to emphasize his point. Simon is louder than the others in his protests of commitment to Jesus, and yet he will vigorously deny him before daybreak (22:31–38).

Satan, who deceives and accuses humankind, has asked permission to test Simon – just as he once tested Job (Job 1:6–12). Satan wants to prove to God that his faith in humanity is misplaced. But Jesus has prayed for Simon – standing before God to defend his friend against Satan's attack. Jesus' hope is that, when Simon has come through this trial, he will be a rock to strengthen his brothers.

Jesus warns his disciples that they are to be plunged into crisis. In the old days in Galilee, they lived without the clutter and protection of possessions. Now, says Jesus (putting the situation starkly), they will do well to get hold of a sword. Jesus knows that he is about to endure the degradation and death of the suffering servant (Isaiah 53). The disciples produce two swords for Jesus – but he hasn't meant them to take him literally. He is simply warning them to brace themselves for conflict.

Jesus prays on the Mount of Olives

(22:39–46)

Jesus and his disciples leave the upper room where they have shared the Passover meal. They make their way out of the city and across the Kidron Valley to the Mount of Olives. This is a favourite place where they have often come in the past.

Jesus feels Satan's temptation pressing hard on them. It is a temptation to doubt that they are on the right course; a temptation to give in, or run away. The only defence against temptation is prayer – and Jesus urges his friends to pray for one another.

Jesus himself kneels in prayer, instead of standing as he would usually do. He prays that the cup of suffering may be removed. This cup contains not just betrayal, injustice, torture and death – although these would have been awful enough. The ultimate suffering for Jesus is that he carries the sin and guilt of the human race – and this cuts him off from God his holy Father. His agony is so great that his sweat runs off him like drops of blood.

The disciples fall asleep, worn out with grief and worry. When Jesus wakes them he urges them again to get up and pray.

Jesus is arrested
(22:47–53)

While Jesus is still speaking, Judas arrives with a crowd. As he arranged with the priests, Judas has led Jesus' enemies to him where they can make an arrest with little trouble.

When Judas approaches Jesus to greet him with a kiss, Jesus confronts him with the truth. This may look like respect and affection, but it is in fact an act of betrayal. The kiss is intended to show the temple guard which person to arrest.

The disciples ask Jesus' permission to fight, and one swings a sword to sever the ear of one of the high priest's servants. Jesus immediately stops the violence and heals the injury. The kingdom of God is not to be won by bloodshed, even for the best of reasons.

Again, Jesus confronts his enemies with the truth.

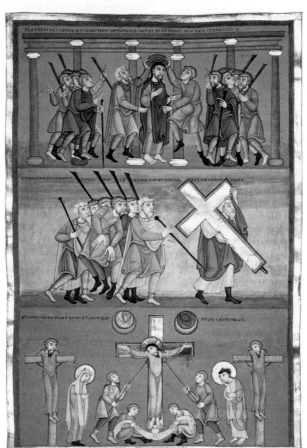

Humiliation, torture and death. Jesus is crowned with thorns, and Simon of Cyrene is forced to carry his cross. Finally, Jesus is crucified. An illumination from the *Golden Gospel Book* of Henry III (c. 1060).

They have had many opportunities to arrest him in the temple, but they did not do so. Now they have come under the cover of darkness, because they are cowards and bullies. But this is Satan's doing, and darkness is his realm.

Peter disowns Jesus
(22:54–62)

The temple guards arrest Jesus and take him to the high priest's house. While the other disciples flee, Peter keeps in touch with Jesus by following at a distance. He joins the group of soldiers and servants around the fire in the courtyard.

In Mark's Gospel, Jesus is put on trial before the Jewish Council during the night. Luke doesn't mention this. Instead he tells only Peter's story. The boldest of the disciples is repeatedly accused of being one of Jesus' followers – and repeatedly denies it. In his way he disowns Jesus just as strongly as Judas has done.

Peter is denying any association with Jesus for the third time when a cock crows. Jesus turns and looks at Peter – and Peter remembers Jesus' prediction. He had said that Peter would deny him three times before dawn. Peter is heartbroken to realize his own cowardice and fickleness of faith.

The guards mock Jesus
(22:63–65)

Although Jesus has not been found guilty of any crime, the guards pass the long night by mocking and beating him. To test his powers of prophecy, they blindfold him and then challenge him to name the person who hits him.

Jesus on trial

(22:66–71)

At daybreak, Jesus is brought before the Jewish Council. This is the Sanhedrin, a council of seventy or seventy-one Jewish elders, under the leadership of the high priest.

Luke gives a brief account of the Jewish trial. When Jesus is asked if he is the Messiah, he refuses to reply. They won't believe him if he claims it, because their idea of a messiah is a victorious military leader.

Instead of using the term 'Messiah', Jesus speaks of 'the Son of man'. This is the person who, in Daniel's great vision, is given God's authority to rule and judge the world (Daniel 7:13–14). Jesus says that they will see the Son of man seated at the right hand of God – in other words, that they will be on trial before him.

The councillors ask Jesus to make himself clear. Is he referring to himself? Does he mean that he is the Son of God? Jesus says that he is – and so gives them the confession they need. They find him guilty of blasphemy – a crime which should be punished with death. The Jews, however, are governed by the Romans at this time, and only the Roman governor can pass a death sentence.

Jesus before Pilate

(23:1–7)

The Jews take Jesus to the Roman governor, Pontius Pilate. Pilate is a pagan and has no interest in a Jewish blasphemy charge. The Jews, however, make no mention of blasphemy.

The Jews accuse Jesus of political opposition to Rome. They say that Jesus has spoken out against Roman taxation and claims to be Christ, God's anointed king. These are the very things Jesus has *not* done! It is because he has not seized political power that the Jewish people are about to reject him.

Pilate asks Jesus if he is the king of the Jews – an idea he must find slightly ridiculous. Although Jesus admits that he is, Pilate still finds no reason to punish him. Jesus can be their king for all he cares. When he hears that Jesus comes from Galilee, he refers him to Herod Antipas.

Jesus before Herod

(23:8–12)

Herod Antipas is the local ruler of Galilee, who is in Jerusalem for the Passover. It is he who imprisoned John the Baptist and had him beheaded. He has wanted to see Jesus for some time, because he has heard about his miracles.

Jesus refuses to entertain the king, so Herod gives him a mock coronation and sends him back to Pilate. By so doing he forges a friendship with the Roman governor. It is in both their interests to keep the Jews under control.

Luke is the only Gospel writer to mention the trial before Herod. In the other Gospels it is the Roman soldiers who abuse Jesus by dressing him as a king.

'Release Barabbas!'

(23:13–25)

Pilate gathers the Jewish leaders to tell them his verdict. He finds Jesus 'not guilty'. Herod, too, has sent Jesus back after treating his kingship as a joke. Pilate proposes to have Jesus lightly whipped and then release him.

The priests and rulers insist that Jesus must be condemned and killed. If anyone is to be released, it should be Barabbas, a rebel and murderer. Their pretence at seeking justice now gives way to raw fury. Jesus, who is innocent, is to be crucified. Barabbas, who is guilty, is to go free.

Pilate asks Jesus' accusers to give him some evidence of their charge. He is shouted down. Even now, Pilate has all the authority he needs to release Jesus and the power to enforce his decision – but he gives in. Both Jewish and Roman laws are powerless in the face of human jealousy and panic. Pilate releases Barabbas to freedom and surrenders Jesus to death.

On the way to the cross

(23:26–31)

As Jesus is taken to be crucified, the Roman guards force a passer-by to carry the crossbar. He is Simon from Cyrene, a port in North Africa.

Simon may be a Passover pilgrim, or a Jew who has lived away from Palestine and now returned. Mark tells us that he is the father of Alexander and Rufus, which implies that the family is well-known in the church (Mark 15:21). Paul greets someone called Rufus and his mother in his letter to the Romans (Romans 16:13).

The heavy crossbar is dragged behind Jesus to the place of crucifixion. Once there, Jesus will be nailed to it and hauled up onto an upright stake. To carry this beam for Jesus is to share his disgrace – and a picture of discipleship (9:23–24).

Jesus is as good as dead, and is insulted and abused by the crowd. Some women follow him, wailing a funeral lament. Jesus turns and talks to them. He calls them 'daughters of Jerusalem' – women of the city that has rejected God's prophets and is now killing his Son.

Jesus tells the women to weep for themselves. When the judgment comes, they will wish they had never had children and that they themselves were dead. He quotes some words of the prophet Hosea, where people pray to be killed by a cataclysm (Hosea 10:8). If Jesus can be treated like this when he is innocent (like a healthy tree) what will happen to those who are guilty (like dead wood, fit only for burning)?

Jesus is crucified
(23:32–43)

Two criminals are also being crucified with Jesus. Perhaps they were friends of Barabbas. They are hung to the left and right of Jesus – completing his total identification with sin and sinners. In the past he has shared his life with them; now he shares their death.

The place of execution is called the Skull. It is to the north of Jerusalem, outside the city wall. Jewish law forbids the death sentence to be carried out within the city boundary.

As the soldiers hammer Jesus' hands to the cross, he begs his Father to forgive them. They have no idea how

The torn curtain

The tearing of the temple curtain is not just an unusual coincidence. It is a dramatic sign.

The Most Holy Place is the inner sanctum of the temple, where God dwells in darkness and mystery. Only one person is allowed beyond the great curtain, and that is the high priest. Once a year, on the Day of Atonement, he enters the sanctuary, holding before him the blood of sacrifice for sins. Now, by the perfect sacrifice of Jesus, the way into the presence of God is open to all.

The writer of the letter to the Hebrews understands that Jesus is the perfect high priest who offers the perfect sacrifice of himself. He opens the way into the holy place of heaven, through the torn curtain of his own body (Hebrews 10:19–20).

brutal and ignorant they are. Having stripped Jesus, the soldiers share out his clothes by throwing dice. Psalm 22 says, 'They divide my garments among them and cast lots for my clothing' (Psalm 22:18). The body of Jesus is being destroyed and his belongings dispersed.

Luke describes the crowd and its various reactions. Most people are watching to see what will happen. The Jewish leaders have Jesus where they want him. They defy him to save himself now. So much for his claim to be the Christ! The Gentile soldiers join in the mockery, and offer the royal personage a drink. It is revolting wine vinegar (Psalm 69:21).

Above Jesus' head there is a notice stating his crime. He is the king of the Jews. It is ironic that Jesus is being crucified for the truth. He is dying on behalf of his people.

One of the criminals curses and abuses Jesus for being unable to rescue them. The other answers that the two of them are getting what they deserve, but Jesus is innocent. He hopes that Jesus does indeed have a kingdom somewhere – and asks to be remembered there. Jesus promises him that he will join him in paradise this very day.

'Paradise' is a Persian word that has been adopted by Greeks and Jews. It means a 'delightful garden' – a place of beauty and refreshment. The scholars who translate the Old Testament into Greek use 'paradise' to describe the Garden of Eden – and it becomes a picture of heaven.

Even in the throes of death, Jesus offers life, peace and hope to a sinner. It is for this kind of person that he came to earth. It is by his death that salvation for sinners is now made possible. The criminal on the cross next to him will be the first to benefit.

Jesus dies
(23:44–49)

It is the sixth hour – high noon. For three hours, darkness envelops the land. Luke says that the sun stops shining – as though the world of nature cannot bear to look at what is happening. An old age is closing – but a new one is about to begin. The temple curtain, which shrouds the Most Holy Place, is torn in two.

Jesus summons a last cry. It is a prayer of commitment to God before falling asleep. He dies with his Father's name on his lips.

The Roman centurion in charge of the execution is greatly moved. Like Pilate and the criminal, he declares that Jesus was an innocent man. There has been a flagrant miscarriage of justice. Many people leave the scene, deeply ashamed of themselves.

Jesus is buried
(23:50–56)

Jesus has been executed as a criminal. His body must be buried before nightfall in a field or tip. However, a friend comes forward with an offer of help. He is Joseph of Arimathea, a member of the Jewish Council who has disapproved of its actions. Like Simeon at the beginning of Luke's Gospel, Joseph is waiting for the kingdom of God to come (2:25). He offers a tomb nearby, cut in the rock and never yet used.

The body of Jesus is wound in a linen sheet and placed in the tomb. It is Friday, the day of preparation for sabbath. They must hastily complete the work of burial before sunset, when the sabbath rest begins. The women who have followed Jesus all the way from Galilee see where his body is laid. They go home to prepare spices and perfumes to embalm the corpse, but can do no more until the sabbath is over.

The 'garden tomb' in Jerusalem, which General Gordon declared to be the burial site of Jesus. Whether genuine or not, modern pilgrims find it a place of deep reflection and peace.

The new beginning

The resurrection
(24:1–12)

The women return to the tomb as soon as they can – at first light on the first day of the new week. Luke names Mary of Magdala, Joanna and Mary the mother of James as the leading figures. He is the only Gospel writer to mention Joanna – perhaps because he has met her and heard her story.

The women come to mourn their Lord, and to complete the work of embalming his body. But the tomb is open, and the body is nowhere to be seen!

Two men appear in shining clothes. They are angels, and remind us of Moses and Elijah who were with Jesus at his transfiguration. These two heavenly beings have come to bear witness to a heavenly truth. They ask what,

for them, is an obvious question: why are the women looking in a tomb for someone who is alive? Don't they remember how, back in Galilee, Jesus foretold his crucifixion and resurrection?

The women remember what Jesus had said. They take the angels' message to the eleven disciples (now without Judas), but are met with blank disbelief. The tomb may be empty, but it proves nothing. Only Peter, impetuous as ever, runs to see for himself. He finds the linen cloths which had been used to wrap the body – but the body itself is not there.

On the road to Emmaus
(24:13–35)

The scene changes. It is afternoon on the same day. Two of Jesus' disciples – Cleopas and perhaps his wife – are on their way home. Their village is Emmaus, which is about seven miles from Jerusalem.

The two are deep in conversation about all that has happened. It has been a Passover from hell, seared by horror and littered with broken dreams. Their supremely gifted leader, their prophet and Messiah, has been brutally put to death. That was Friday. This morning, all was rumour and confusion – an empty tomb and a sighting of angels – but nothing more than hysteria and wishful thinking.

As they walk, a stranger joins them. It is the risen Jesus, but they are somehow kept from recognizing him. He is, after all, the last person they expect to see. Not only do they believe he is dead, but they are also disillusioned with him. And the setting sun is in their eyes.

Jesus asks them what they are talking about, and Cleopas tells him the whole story. Instead of sympathizing, the stranger calls them foolish and slow! Don't they realize that all these things had to happen to the Christ?

Jesus talks about his death and resurrection in the light of the scriptures. Israel has always suffered – sometimes because of the oppression of others, and sometimes through her own fault. God's people have been summed up in the suffering servant – wounded, abandoned and bearing the pain and punishment of others (Isaiah 53).

There is a pattern of events. The history of Israel has always moved from despair to hope, from slavery to exodus, from exile to return. Surely the experience of the Messiah will be the same – from death to resurrection. But at Passover? Of course!

When they reach the village, the disciples invite Jesus to stay with them. As they share the evening meal, Jesus takes bread, gives thanks to God, breaks it and begins to pass it to them. It is through this familiar gesture – or perhaps the sight of his wounded hands – that they recognize him. Jesus disappears, but they know without doubt that he is alive. It was the scripture lesson which first kindled the fire of hope within them, and the breaking of bread which fanned it into flame.

The end – and the beginning
(24:36–49)

The Emmaus disciples return to Jerusalem immediately. They find that the Eleven already know their amazing news. The risen Christ has appeared to Simon Peter – a detail which Paul first mentions in one of his letters (1 Corinthians 15:5). It seems that Jesus is most readily recognized in the teaching of scripture and the breaking of bread – the sharing of truth and life within the grace of God.

They are still talking when Jesus appears. He greets them with his peace – the Messiah's peace which grants forgiveness, conquers fear and unites earth and heaven.

The disciples think Jesus is a ghost; but he assures them it is he. He shows them his wounded hands and feet, and invites them to touch him. As they watch, he eats some fish. He's real!

Jesus again explains how the scriptures point to him. The messages of Moses, the prophets and the Psalms all agree. It was the Messiah's destiny to suffer, die and be raised to life. Now the disciples have a complete gospel to proclaim – not just the dawning of the kingdom, but the triumph of the king.

The outcome of the resurrection of Jesus is that the whole world may be saved. He commissions his disciples to be his witnesses.

The disciples are to go to all the nations of the world, preaching the good news of the gospel. Jesus will ask his Father to send them the Holy Spirit. The Spirit is the personal presence and power of God, to guide and enable

their mission. They must wait in Jerusalem until the Spirit comes – an event Luke will describe in his sequel, the book of Acts.

The ascension
(24:50–53)

Jesus leads his disciples out towards the village of Bethany. There he takes his leave. As he raises his hands in blessing, he is taken up into heaven. The disciples worship Jesus as their Lord, and return to Jerusalem with great joy.

Luke ends his story where he began – in the temple. It is a temple doomed to destruction, but it has its spiritual successor – living stones, holy priests and lively sacrifices – praising God within its courts (1 Peter 2:5).

JOHN

John's Gospel is sometimes called the Fourth Gospel, and is different from the Gospels of Matthew, Mark and Luke. While the others take a similar view of Jesus, through stories of his teaching and miracles, John's Gospel takes only a few episodes and develops them in more detail. As a result we get to know Jesus in greater depth – and especially in his relationship with God his Father.

It is through John's Gospel that we can measure the length of Jesus' public life. John mentions three Passovers – the annual festival for which all male Jews go to Jerusalem if they can. Jesus travels to Jerusalem three times, and it is at the third Passover that he is arrested, tried and crucified.

John shows us Jesus dealing with a selection of people – all very different from each other. There is Nicodemus, a leading Pharisee and national Council member. There is a disgraced Samaritan woman. There is a lame man, a persecuted blind man and a dear friend who is dead and buried. Jew or Gentile, good or bad, well or sick, alive or dead – Jesus brings life, light and hope to them all.

Outline

The prologue (1:1–18)

The signs of life (1:19 – 12:50)

John the Baptist (1:19–28)

Jesus the Lamb of God (1:29–34)

Jesus' first disciples (1:35–42)

Jesus calls Philip and Nathanael (1:43–51)

The first sign: Jesus turns water to wine (2:1–11)

Jesus clears the temple (2:12–25)

Jesus talks with Nicodemus (3:1–21)

Jesus and John the Baptist (3:22–30)

Jesus and the Samaritan woman (4:1–42)

The second sign: Jesus heals an official's son (4:43–54)

The third sign: Jesus heals a man at the Pool of Bethesda (5:1–15)

Life through the Son (5:16–47)

The fourth sign: Jesus feeds 5,000 people (6:1–15)

The fifth sign: Jesus walks on the water (6:16–21)

Jesus teaches: 'I am the bread of life' (6:22–59)

Hard choices (6:60–71)

Doubts and dilemmas (7:1–13)

Jesus teaches at the Feast of Tabernacles (7:14–44)

Pride and prejudice (7:45–52)

Jesus and the woman caught in adultery (7:53 – 8:11)

Jesus in debate with his Jewish critics (8:12–59)

The sixth sign: Jesus heals a man born blind (9:1–41)

Jesus teaches: 'I am the good shepherd' (10:1–21)

The unbelief of the Jews (10:22–39)

The seventh sign: Jesus raises Lazarus from death (11:1–44)

The Jewish leaders plot to kill Jesus (11:45–57)

Mary anoints Jesus at Bethany (12:1–11)

Jesus enters Jerusalem (12:12–19)

Jesus and some Greeks (12:20–36)

The unbelief of the Jews (12:37–50)

The glory of the cross (13:1 – 20:31)

The Last Supper (13:1–30)

The farewell talk (13:31 – 16:33)

The prayer of Jesus (17:1–26)

Jesus is arrested, tried and crucified (18:1 – 19:42)

The resurrection of Jesus (20:1–31)

The epilogue (21:1–25)

Breakfast by the sea (21:1–14)

Jesus and Peter (21:15–17)

Peter and John (21:18–24)

The great and untold story (21:25)

INTRODUCTION

The four Gospels

The four Gospels are all biographies of Jesus. But they are biographies with a difference. They don't just look back and remember a great man who is now long dead. They tell about the life, teaching and miracles of someone who is alive today. They are written to convince the reader that he saved people then – and that he can save us now.

The Greeks wrote biographies. They were a way of recording someone's teaching or collecting their sayings. In the case of Socrates, it was a matter of saving a person's reputation by telling his true story. There is something of this in the Gospels, when we consider that Jesus was executed like the worst kind of criminal. How could he possibly be the Son of God?

The four Gospels are all different from each other – although Matthew, Mark and Luke have a similar approach. These three are called the 'Synoptic' Gospels, because they run parallel to each other and it's possible to compare the way they treat certain episodes. John is different, with very few miracles (he calls them 'signs') and long sections of teaching or reflection.

Archbishop William Temple said that while the Synoptic Gospels are like a photo album, John's Gospel is like a portrait. But there is no mistaking that they are all describing the same person – Jesus Christ, the Son of God, the Saviour of the world and the Lord of the church.

The Gospel of John is arranged like the other Gospels, with a large part telling the story of the last week of Jesus' life. In addition there is an opening passage (the prologue) which sets the scene, and a closing chapter (the epilogue).

Who wrote John's Gospel?

We don't know for sure who wrote the Gospel of John. It is named after John, the fisherman disciple and brother of James, who took care of Mary after the death of Jesus. In this Gospel he is referred to as 'the disciple whom Jesus loved'. John lived to a great age in Ephesus, where people remembered his favourite phrase: 'Little children, love one another!' Perhaps this book started with John's memories of Jesus, even if he didn't actually write it himself.

The 'I am' sayings of Jesus

John's Gospel brings Jesus within reach of everyone. Jesus describes himself as 'the light of the world', 'the real bread' and 'the water of life'. These are pictures which make immediate sense – and yet we can spend a lifetime thinking about them. Best of all, Jesus says, 'I am' – which means his life and work are the presence and ministry of almighty God.

There are seven occasions when Jesus says, 'I am…' Each of them takes an everyday idea which is already special for Jews, but can easily make sense to non-Jews.

I am the bread of life. Whoever comes to me will never be hungry (6:35).

Everyone needs bread. It's a staple diet. But the Jews know that there is more to life than food. They think of God's law as spiritual bread – a basic necessity for the whole of life. Non-Jews, too, know all about a feeling of inner emptiness – a void which money and possessions can never fill. To Jews and Gentiles alike, Jesus says, 'I am the bread of life.'

I am the light of the world. Whoever follows me will never walk in darkness (8:12).

Light shows us where we are. It transforms our understanding. The Jews think of God's word as a light: 'Your word is a lamp to my feet,' says the psalmist (Psalm 119:105). The light of God's word reveals the path of truth, so that we can live a straight life.

The Gentiles, too, think of darkness as a picture of ignorance and light as an image of truth. Without truth, we are lost, with no clue as to the right way. But Jesus announces, 'I am the light of the world.'

I am the good shepherd. The good shepherd lays down his life for the sheep (10:11).

For the Jews, shepherds are leaders. They walk ahead of their sheep, calling them to follow. They provide food and water, protection and shelter. The Jews know that their own leaders have often abused their position as shepherds, and behaved in greedy, selfish and cruel ways.

The prophet Ezekiel said as much (Ezekiel 34:1–6).

The Gentiles, both Greek and Roman, only know the kind of leaders who seize power by force, and get their way by bullying their subjects.

Now Jesus comes as the good shepherd – the loving God who leads by serving; who puts himself out for his people. In the end he will even give his life for them.

I am the gate for the sheep (10:7, 9).

The Jews know that a sheepfold doesn't have a gate. When the shepherd puts his sheep in the fold, he halts each animal with his staff and checks it for wounds and sunburn. He knows every one, and will immediately pick out an intruder from another flock. Once the sheep are safely in the fold for the night, the shepherd himself sits across the door, to protect his flock from wild animals and thieves.

Now Jesus teaches that he is 'the gate for the sheep'. Everyone who wants the joy and safety of God's kingdom must come through him for admission. And once they have entered his salvation, he won't allow any enemy to snatch them away.

I am the resurrection and the life. Those who believe in me, even though they die, will live (11:25).

The Jews are divided on whether the dead will one day be raised to everlasting life. The book of Daniel speaks of God's chosen people waking from the dust of death to shine like stars (Daniel 12:1–3). Some believe this, but others don't.

Greeks and Romans believe there is a shadowy world of departed spirits, but it is a dreary existence compared with the real and colourful experiences of this life.

Jesus not only believes in life beyond death, but says that he himself is eternally alive. He is able to give this life to those who trust him. Those who believe in Jesus will continue to be really alive even though they pass through the experience of death. For Jesus, eternal life begins now – and will be fully realized when all his people are raised to life at the Last Day.

I am the way and the truth and the life. No-one comes to the Father except through me (14:6).

The Greeks have an idea of a supreme good – an eternal truth from which all other truths take their value.

The Jews believe that God's truth is like a path which can be found and followed. There is only one God and only one true way of life, which is to keep his law.

Now Jesus reveals that truth is not a remote ideal, or a code of rules. Truth is a person and a relationship. Jesus himself is the 'true and living way'. He is the one road to God and the only guide who can bring us safely to heaven.

I am the true vine (15:1).

The vine is a symbol of Israel. The prophets (Isaiah, Jeremiah and Hosea) thought of Israel as a vine – chosen by God and planted in the land of Canaan. God hoped that his vine would produce sweet grapes – love towards God and one's neighbour. But something went wrong. Israel was rebellious towards God and unjust in her society. The grapes were wild.

Now Jesus says, 'I am the true vine.' He is Israel in person, offering loving obedience to God, and giving his life for the sake of others.

The Gentiles don't share the national pride and ambition of Israel, but they are well acquainted with vines. They know that the vine is the most wizened of trees, as it gives all its strength to the grapes. So Jesus pours out his life to produce the fruit of holiness in his friends.

DISCOVERING JOHN

The prologue

'In the beginning was the Word.' As he begins his Gospel, John echoes the opening words of the book of Genesis. The 'Word' of God is eternal and has always been at work. It is the 'Word' that created the universe and communicated God's will. Now this 'Word' has become a human being, to reveal God's character and show God's love. Jesus is the 'Word' of God, who comes to share our human life.

John tells us that Jesus is the 'Word', eternal and divine. It was through Jesus that everything was created. Jesus is the source of life and light for all people everywhere.

There came a man who was sent from God; his name was John (1:6).

John wants to make a clear distinction between Jesus and John the Baptist. We know (from the Acts of the Apostles) that there were some Jewish groups that focused on John the Baptist rather than on Jesus Christ. Our writer puts John the Baptist firmly in his place: he is not the light! He is merely a witness to the true light, which is Jesus.

He came to that which was his own, but his own did not receive him (1:11).

John tells us the painful fact which will produce so much conflict in this story. Jesus, the light of the world, comes to his own people – the Jews. Although they long for their Messiah, they fail to recognize him. Instead, they criticize, reject and kill him. He is rejected by his own people, but accepted by some. A few believe in him, and he makes them God's children. They change from being children of the devil to become the children of God.

The Word became flesh and made his dwelling among us (1:14).

John tells us something quite extraordinary. The eternal 'Word' of God, the agent of creation, actually becomes a human being. He becomes 'flesh' – that is, he takes our human nature, with all its wayward appetites and frailties. John says that Jesus 'made his dwelling' or pitched his tent among us – just as God had camped with his people in the tent of meeting during their wilderness wanderings.

We have seen his glory (1:14).

John and the other disciples have seen the glory of God in the life of Jesus. He reveals his glory in the signs he performs; but it is seen most clearly and movingly as he dies on the cross. This surprises us, for we expect 'glory' to mean a radiant vision or a dazzling light. But glory also means the true worth and weight of something. The glory of Jesus is seen in his obedience to his Father and his sacrificial love for the world. Centuries before, Moses realized that God is 'compassionate and gracious… abounding in love and faithfulness'. Now we discover that God's Son is 'full of grace and truth'. God is invisible, but Jesus shows him perfectly.

The signs of life

The first part of the Gospel tells of the great 'signs' that Jesus performs. By these signs (the other Gospels would call them 'miracles') Jesus shows that he is truly the Son of God.

John the Baptist
(1:19–28)

The Jews expect a great prophet to come before the Messiah or 'Christ' appears. John the Baptist doesn't claim to be this prophet – although Jesus will later say he was. John prefers to think of himself in the words of Isaiah. He is a voice, an announcer. He clears the road for God's arrival. The baptism he offers is simply a wash to help people get ready. The Christ who is coming will be very much greater than this humble herald!

Jesus the Lamb of God
(1:29–34)

When John sees Jesus he realizes that this is the 'Lamb of God'. The year-old lamb, almost full-grown, is a familiar image of sacrifice. At Passover a lamb is killed for every family or household. Jesus will be sacrificed for the sin of the world. He is the Son of God. When Jesus baptizes, he will pour down the Holy Spirit!

Jesus' first disciples

(1:35–42)

Two of John's disciples are drawn to Jesus. One is Andrew. The other may be John, the writer of this Gospel. The hour when they first meet with Jesus is for ever etched on their memory. It is mid-afternoon.

Andrew is convinced that they have found the longed-for Messiah. He brings his brother Simon to Jesus. Jesus looks at volatile, unstable Simon and immediately renames him Cephas – which means Peter, or 'Rock'! He sees the potential of the most unlikely people.

Jesus calls Philip and Nathanael

(1:43–51)

Next, Jesus calls Philip to follow him. Philip, like Andrew, has a Greek name. He wants his friend Nathanael to join the group, but Nathanael is cautious. Nazareth is not the kind of place to produce a Messiah.

But while Nathanael is about to dismiss Jesus, Jesus has a high regard for Nathanael. He tells him that he noticed him under a fig tree earlier that day. The fig tree is a place for private prayer, and Jesus knows Nathanael is that rare person, a straightforward Israelite, unlike their devious ancestor Jacob.

Nathanael is amazed! He immediately declares that Jesus is the Son of God, the Messiah! Jesus tells Nathanael that he will see the business of heaven going on, not on Jacob's ladder, but on the Son of man. It is Jesus on his cross who will be the bridge between earth and heaven.

The first sign: Jesus turns water to wine

(2:1–11)

John wants us to think of the resurrection when he says that 'on the third day' there was a wedding at Cana in Galilee. Cana is about nine miles north of Nazareth.

A mural depicting the wedding at Cana, where Jesus turns a large quantity of washing water into a vintage wine.

Eastern wedding celebrations are expected to last for several days. It is very embarrassing when the wine runs out too soon! Jesus' mother tells him of the problem, but he seems to refuse her. He says that his 'time' has not yet come. This is the first occasion that we see how Jesus pays complete attention to his Father, God. He only does what his Father tells him to do. There are times when it is right to work miracles and times when it would be wrong. One day it will be time for the greatest sign of all – for Jesus to be lifted up on the cross.

Mary (who is never called by her name in this Gospel) is not discouraged. She advises the servants to do as Jesus says.

Jesus tells the servants to fill six huge jars with water. These are the stone jars which have been used for washing hands and feet, cups and bowls. The number six is just short of the 'perfect' number seven. The long years of Jewish legalism – trying to be right with God by careful washing – are now to give way to the joyful wine of the gospel.

When the master of the banquet tastes the water, he discovers an excellent wine. This is a miracle of new creation, although only the servants and the disciples know what Jesus has done. Jesus is always discreet with his miracles because life becomes impossible when people are clamouring for sensational signs of God's power. But his glory is briefly glimpsed, and his disciples believe in him.

Jesus clears the temple
(2:12–25)

Jesus goes to Jerusalem for Passover. This is the first of the Passovers that is mentioned in this Gospel. He finds that the outer court, which is the area where the Gentiles can come and pray, is entirely taken over by traders. They are busy selling animals and birds for

'Fill the jars with water!'

John tells us that the six water jars contain between two and three 'metretes' – which is about 150 gallons. This is far more than is needed to spare the groom's embarrassment and extend the wedding party. It is a glorious miracle of creation – a call to be joyful, because the Messiah has come.

sacrifice, and exchanging secular money for the approved temple coins. The temple tax has to be paid by every Jewish man over twenty, in Tyrian coins of pure silver.

Jesus is furious that a place of prayer has been turned into a market. He tells them that this is his Father's house – and drives them out!

The other Gospels say that Jesus cleared the temple two years later, after his triumphal entry into Jerusalem. When he was arrested and put on trial, the main charge against Jesus was that he threatened to destroy the temple. We don't know which of the writers is the most accurate or whether Jesus cleared the temple more than once. It is John who recalls Jesus' saying that he would destroy the temple and raise it again. He explains that Jesus is referring to his own body, which will be crucified and raised from death in three days.

The temple has taken forty-six years to build, but it is soon to be destroyed. God and humanity are now to meet perfectly and completely – not in a temple, but in Jesus. The time has come to worship 'in Spirit and truth' rather than in trappings and tradition. The followers of Jesus will be 'living stones', and their bodies 'temples' of his Holy Spirit.

Jesus talks with Nicodemus
(3:1–21)

A man named Nicodemus comes to see Jesus. He is an important national figure: a Pharisee, a strict Jew and a member of the Jewish Council.

Nicodemus comes to see Jesus at night. Perhaps he is trying to avoid being seen with Jesus until he has made up his own mind about him. He acknowledges that Jesus performs miraculous signs, but doesn't accept that Jesus is the Messiah.

Jesus tells Nicodemus that he will only see the kingdom of God – that is, enter into eternal life and enjoy God's reign – if he is 'born again'. It is rare for Jesus to mention the kingdom of God in this Gospel. John usually prefers to talk about 'entering into life'. Nicodemus assumes that Jesus means something impossible – that a person must return to his mother's womb and be reborn. But the second birth that Jesus refers to is 'from above'. It is a spiritual birth.

God's Spirit is like the wind – invisible and powerful. The Spirit blows where he wills, and brings to new birth whom he wills. Jesus is surprised that Nicodemus, a leading Jewish teacher, is so ignorant of the power and life of the Spirit. God doesn't save people because they are Pharisees or Council members, but because they turn to him in repentance.

We enter God's kingdom by turning to God for forgiveness and cleansing. This cleansing is symbolized by water. We are transformed and renewed by God's Spirit, which is something only God can do. He healed the Israelites in the desert when they simply turned in faith to look at the bronze snake held up by Moses. Now Jesus, the Son of man, will be similarly 'lifted up', and all who turn to him in faith will receive eternal life.

Jesus teaches Nicodemus that God's only motive is love. Jesus hasn't been sent into the world to judge, punish and sentence to death. He has come to reveal the light and show the love of God. He longs that people should stop preferring darkness and clinging to shame.

Jesus and John the Baptist
(3:22–30)

Jesus is now baptizing people – or at least his disciples are (4:2); and the crowds are preferring him to John. But John is too great a man to be jealous. He sees himself as the trusted friend who has the privilege of looking after a bride until the bridegroom arrives for the wedding. Now that Jesus the bridegroom is here, John is pleased to direct people to him. His own work is finished.

Jesus talks to a Samaritan woman beside her local well – to the surprise of his disciples. A Byzantine fresco from San Angelo Formis, Capua (1072–78).

Jesus and the Samaritan woman
(4:1–42)

Jesus' popularity is attracting official hostility. He withdraws to Galilee. There are two or three occasions in this Gospel when Jesus decides it is not the right time to be killed or put in prison!

Taking the direct route north, Jesus passes through Samaria. Here he meets a woman at Jacob's well.

It is noon, the hottest part of the day. There is no one else around. There are several reasons why Jesus and the woman should not speak to each other. Jesus is a man

and she is a woman; he is a Jew and she a Samaritan.

The Samaritans are not pure Jews by race or religion. They accept only the first five books of the Bible (the Pentateuch, or books of Moses) and once built their own temple on Mount Gerizim. But Jesus, who has no time for racial feuds and social taboos, simply asks the woman for a drink.

The Samaritan woman comes to the well alone and in the heat of the day because her neighbours despise her. She has had a succession of husbands and is now living with someone else. As they talk beside the well, Jesus introduces himself as one who gives 'living water' – the gift of eternal life.

The woman is intrigued, and soon realizes that Jesus knows all about her. She asks him what he thinks about the old argument over the two temples, and Jesus tells her that the Jews have been right. But it isn't the place that makes worship genuine, it is the Spirit and truth of God. When the woman says that the Messiah will explain it all, Jesus tells her she is already looking at him!

The disciples are shocked to find Jesus alone with the Samaritan woman. The writer remembers how she left her water jar in her haste to fetch her neighbours to see the Christ. As the people come swarming across the fields towards them, Jesus urges his disciples to become labourers in this human harvest.

The second sign: Jesus heals an official's son
(4:43–54)

Back in Cana, a royal official comes from Capernaum to beg Jesus' help. His son is dying. The local people have been clamouring for Jesus to do something miraculous, but he is reluctant to agree. Demanding signs and wonders is in fact the very opposite of having faith.

To keep his help as quiet and unsensational as possible, Jesus simply tells the official to go back home.

He assures him that his son will live. While he is still on the journey, the man receives the wonderful news that the boy has recovered – and it happened at the very time he had been talking to Jesus.

The healing of the official's son is the second 'sign' that John has chosen to record. This time it is the official and his family and staff who come to have faith in Christ.

The third sign: Jesus heals a man at the Pool of Bethesda
(5:1–15)

Jesus is in Jerusalem for one of the Jewish feasts. John doesn't tell us which feast it is.

Near the Sheep Gate, which is in the north wall of the city, there is a pool where people go to seek healing. From time to time there is a movement of the waters – perhaps caused by an underground spring. People believe the stirring is the work of an angel, and that the first person to get in the pool when it happens will be healed.

Jesus stops to talk to a man who has been an invalid for thirty-eight years. He asks him a very direct question: 'Do you want to get well?' Perhaps it suits the man to sit in the shade and watch the world go by, while others carry him back and forth and supply him with food and drink!

The man doesn't say if he wants to get well. Instead he complains that he has no one to help him into the pool. Someone else always gets there first – and so the years go by.

Jesus cuts straight through the pathetic superstition and half-baked excuses. He appeals directly to the man's faith: 'Get up! Pick up your mat and walk.' Amazingly, after all these years, the man is instantly and completely cured.

As he walks through Jerusalem, the healed man is soon in trouble again. It is the sabbath, and he is carrying his mat! When the authorities accuse him of working on the sabbath, the man adopts his usual attitude of blaming someone else. Someone just healed him and told him to carry his mat, so that's what he's doing. He's just obeying orders. He doesn't know the fellow's name and it's not his fault.

When Jesus comes across the man again, he warns him to change his inner attitude. But the man merely reports Jesus to the authorities.

Life through the Son
(5:16–47)

The Jewish authorities, already suspicious of Jesus, now find a point at which to attack him. He has healed an invalid on the sabbath. He has broken God's law by working on the day of rest.

Jesus tackles them head on. He says that he is merely sharing his Father's work, which goes on every day. This enrages his accusers, because what he says seems blasphemous. He is implying that he is God's Son.

For the first time, Jesus explains that he is doing his Father's will. These healings are just the beginning of a life-giving work which will continue until all who believe are raised to eternal life.

If the authorities doubt that Jesus is genuine, then they should remember again what John the Baptist said

---

Jesus – the Saviour of all sorts

John is introducing us to a variety of people. We have met Nicodemus who is very Jewish, orthodox and guarded. He needs to loosen up and let the Spirit change his life.

We have met the Samaritan woman who is chaotic in her private life and clueless in her religion. But she is ready to recognize Jesus and quick to tell others about him.

We have met the royal official who,

behind his usual sense of status and security, is a desperate father seeking help for his son. He takes Jesus at his word, and is wonderfully rewarded.

We have met a long-term invalid, who may well be a scrounger, and who Jesus may not even like. But he is still completely healed – and given some important advice.

With each person, Jesus comes to the point. One is in spiritual darkness, while a second is ashamed and confused. A third is facing personal tragedy, and a fourth is surly and truculent. But with

each individual, Jesus has the patience, perception and power to help. He releases their seized lives and sets them free.

about him. They should consider the work that Jesus does, and search the scriptures for the pointers to the Messiah. They are hostile to Jesus because they are hostile to God – and far too concerned to win each other's approval. Moses himself would disagree with them, because they have turned God's law into a burden, and completely missed the delight of a covenant relationship with God.

The fourth sign: Jesus feeds 5,000 people
(6:1–15)

Jesus is at the height of his popularity in Galilee. The other three Gospel writers cover this period in greater detail. Jesus is pursued by large crowds who want to see him perform miracles. He finds it hard to make time to teach his disciples.

One day Jesus and his disciples are discovered by a huge crowd. Mark tells us that Jesus taught them until late in the day, and there was then the problem of how to feed all the people. John tells us that it is Andrew, the master of introductions, who brings forward a boy with five small barley loaves and two small fish. As the disciples get the people to sit down in an orderly fashion, Jesus thanks God for the food, breaks it and distributes it among the crowd. By an extraordinary miracle, there is not only enough food for everyone, but a considerable surplus. This is a day of plenty – a Messiah's banquet in the wilderness.

This is the only miracle that is recorded in all four Gospels. It is the boldest and most public of the signs that Jesus performs. The people think of the days of Moses, the supply of manna and the promise that one day a prophet will appear. Is this God's moment for the Jews to rise up in rebellion? Five thousand men plus women and children with unlimited food! They see Jesus not as a Messiah meeting hunger, but as a king bringing victory. Jesus realizes that the crowd wants to make him king, so he retreats further into the mountains.

The fifth sign: Jesus walks on the water
(6:16–21)

The disciples take a boat to Capernaum without Jesus. Night falls and the wind starts to whip up the waves on the lake. As they struggle with the wind and the sea, Jesus terrifies them by walking towards them on the water. Mark says in his Gospel that they think he is a ghost But he reassures them and joins them in the boat.

Suddenly they come safely to land.

John has stopped numbering the 'signs' that Jesus performs, but this is the fifth. By it Jesus shows that he is the Lord of the winds and waves. He enacts the words of a psalm:

They were glad when it grew calm
and he guided them to their desired haven
(Psalm 107:30).

Jesus teaches: 'I am the bread of life'
(6:22–59)

Since he fed the 5,000 from just a little bread and fish, Jesus is hounded by crowds wherever he goes. They are

drawn by the promise of food and the prospect of miracles.

Jesus tries to explain that the bread is merely a sign. The 'true bread from heaven' is the eternal life that God gives.

In the old days, God gave the Israelites manna from heaven. It was a daily miracle, but the food didn't last and the people eventually died. Now Jesus declares, 'I am the bread of life' (6:35). Those who believe in him will never be spiritually hungry and will have eternal life.

Jesus shocks his hearers by explaining, 'This bread is my flesh, which I will give for the life of the world.' In the other Gospels this teaching comes at the Last Supper, when Jesus breaks bread and pours wine with his disciples (Mark 14:22–25).

The church sees a special significance in Jesus feeding the multitude and breaking bread at his last meal. He is showing his followers, in the bread, how he gives his life for them and how they can have his life within them.

Christians continue to share the life of Jesus, by eating bread and drinking wine at the Eucharist or Holy Communion. Jesus describes the bread and wine as the spiritual food of his own body and blood. John completely identifies the food with its meaning and effect: it is the eternal life of Jesus within those who believe. Jesus is the real bread from heaven which gives life for ever.

Some of those who hear Jesus are disgusted. They think he is describing some kind of cannibalism. Like the Samaritan woman, they take Jesus literally. She thought that if Jesus was 'living water' she need never come to the well again. These critics want a ready supply of food for their stomachs – not a costly commitment to the broken and shared life of Christ.

Jesus follows his feeding of the 5,000 by declaring that he is 'the bread of life'. The breaking and sharing of bread is a symbol of Jesus, broken and shared for the life of the world (6:25–40).

Hard choices
(6:60–71)

Some of Jesus' supporters now change their minds about him. They have followed him in the hope of military action or plentiful food, and are disappointed. He insists that they must trust him in some spiritual way, by eating his flesh and drinking his blood. Disgusted and disillusioned, they decide to leave.

Left with the Twelve, Jesus asks them if they want to desert him too. Simon Peter expresses his rock-solid commitment. This commitment, it seems, is something that God is giving, because Jesus says, 'I have chosen you.' Even so, one of the Twelve, Judas Iscariot, is possessed and motivated by Satan.

Doubts and dilemmas
(7:1–13)

It is time for the Feast of Tabernacles – the autumn festival which celebrates the grape and olive harvest. It is now six months since the feeding of the 5,000, but Jesus still has little freedom to travel around. In Galilee he is dogged by those who want him to do miracles. In Judea and Jerusalem, he is in danger from those who want to kill him. His own brothers are torn between doubting his claims and wanting a share in his success. Jesus sends them to Jerusalem without him, and then goes secretly himself.

Jesus teaches at the Feast of Tabernacles
(7:14–44)

The Feast of Tabernacles lasts for eight days. After the first few days, Jesus begins to teach in the temple courts. His hearers are amazed at his clarity and directness. He doesn't use complicated arguments and long quotations like their rabbis. Instead, he speaks straight from God.

Jesus asks the crowd (which includes some Jewish leaders) why they are trying to kill him. Do they intend to break one of the commandments by murdering an innocent man? He stands accused of healing an invalid on the sabbath – breaking God's law by working on the day of rest. But aren't babies circumcised on the sabbath, if that is the eighth day after their birth? If a baby can be circumcised, surely a man can be healed! They must stop being bound by legalism and ask instead what God really intends. If God wants invalids to be healed, then the sabbath is the ideal day.

IS JESUS THE CHRIST?

Jerusalem is buzzing with speculation. Is Jesus of Nazareth the Christ (7:25–44)? Isn't he far too ordinary – a northerner without academic qualifications? Surely the Christ will spring suddenly and majestically from nowhere. Yet he performs these miraculous signs. The authorities give orders for Jesus to be arrested, but he delays them by saying he will soon be leaving anyway. He is referring, of course, to his death. They assume he may be taking his mission to Jews who live abroad, or even to Greeks. If so, their problem will go away, at least for a while.

Every morning of the feast, a golden flagon of water is brought to the temple from the Pool of Siloam. While the pilgrims sing hallelujahs, the priests carry the flagon in procession around the altar, and pour out the water before the Lord. The action celebrates how God provided water for his people in the desert, and will one day pour out his Spirit on all humankind.

On the last and greatest day of the feast, Jesus stands up and shouts an invitation. 'Let anyone who is thirsty come to me and drink!' He is the real source of life which this water ceremony is celebrating. He is the One through whom the Spirit will be given.

Pride and prejudice
(7:45–52)

The temple guards are sent to arrest Jesus, but return without him. They were so impressed by Jesus that they found themselves taking his side. The Council bosses accuse the guards of being ignorant – taken in like the uneducated mass of people who follow this peasant from the north.

Nicodemus intervenes. He is a Council member who has met Jesus personally (3:1–21). He reminds the Council that the law does not condemn someone without a fair hearing. But his colleagues turn on him. Is he an ignoramus from the north as well? They tell Nicodemus to search the scriptures. He won't find any prediction that 'the Prophet' (the Messiah) will come from there.

Jesus and the woman caught in adultery
(7:53 – 8:11)

The earliest versions of John's Gospel don't include this episode. The early church fathers, who wrote commentaries on the Gospels, also make no mention of it. But it seems a very genuine episode, and certainly true to all that we know about Jesus.

Jesus is teaching in the temple one morning, when the religious authorities drag before him a woman caught in adultery. The law says that she and her lover must be put to death – probably by stoning. In fact such punishments are very rare, but they ask Jesus to give his judgment. This is an attempt to embarrass Jesus over the law of Moses. Will he apply the law strictly and cause the woman to die? Or will he pardon her, as though adultery doesn't matter? They hope Jesus can't get out of this one!

For a while, Jesus writes on the ground with his finger. Sometimes a judge will draft a verdict or quote a text this way. Or is he writing some names that might remind these accusers of their own affairs? We don't know. Eventually, he invites anyone who is innocent to commence the execution. One by one, the accusers back away.

When only Jesus and the woman are left, he speaks to her for the first time. He doesn't ask her whether she is guilty, but whether anyone else condemns her. As the perfect judge and holy Son of God, Jesus is the only one who can do so – and he chooses to set her free. He has spared her life, but he urges her to change her ways.

Jesus in debate with his Jewish critics
(8:12–59)

During the Feast of Tabernacles, four huge lamps are lit in the Court of Women, one of the temple's outer courts. There is music and dancing, with men holding flaming torches and singing songs throughout the night. Just as Jesus has said, 'Come to me and drink,' at the water ceremony, so he now says, 'I am the light of the world' (8:12) at this celebration of light.

Light has always been for Israel a symbol of God's glory, an image of his perfect law and a picture of his guidance. Jesus has already said he is the bread of life. Now he says he is the light of the world, the light of life. It is an astonishing claim – that he is actually the light that gives life! He is claiming to be the spiritual equivalent of the sun.

The Pharisees challenge Jesus. Where are the witnesses who will agree with what he says? He could be a liar or someone who is mad.

Jesus replies, as he has done before, that he is perfectly entitled to make these claims. The Pharisees are judging and dismissing Jesus by worldly standards. Although they are highly religious, they don't in fact know God in any living way. When they do, they will recognize Jesus. Unless they change their attitude, they will die in their state of spiritual blindness and unbelief.

More than ever we see how Jesus is entirely dependent on his Father, to know his will and do his work. The Father is always with him, and Jesus cares only to please him.

THE CHILDREN OF ABRAHAM

Despite the doubts about Jesus, there are many Jews who believe him. Jesus tells them that his truth will set them free. They think they are free already because they are God's chosen people, descended from Abraham (8:31–59). But Jesus tells them that they are, in fact, slaves to sin. They can't help but obey the orders of their lower nature. Now Jesus can set them free. If they are truly Abraham's children – having not just his genes but

An Eastern shepherd. Jesus describes himself as 'the good shepherd' – one who knows each of his flock individually. He will not only lead, care for and protect his people, but even lay down his life for them.

his faith – then they will show a lively obedience to God. As it is, there is much clearer evidence that their father is the devil.

Jesus is very tough on these would-be disciples. He challenges their racial prejudice and spiritual complacency. He doesn't want people who are merely moral supporters or well-wishers. He wants those whose lives are being changed by God's truth.

Anyone with the same faith as Abraham will be delighted to encounter Jesus. Jesus states bluntly, 'before Abraham was born, I am!' This is too much for Jesus' hearers. They are offended at his claim to be greater than Abraham. They try to stone him for blasphemy, but he hides from them and slips away. In Galilee, too, Jesus had saved himself from attempts to execute him, or make him king (Luke 4:28–30; John 6:14). He escapes, not because he is a coward, but because it is not yet God's time for his sacrifice.

The sixth sign: Jesus heals a man born blind
(9:1–41)

Jesus has announced that he is 'the light of the world'. To illustrate this, John tells us how Jesus heals a man who is blind from birth.

The disciples believe that someone who has been born blind must be bearing a punishment for some sin. They ask Jesus if this sin was the fault of the man himself or his parents.

Jesus doesn't deny that sin can lead to tragedy. However, he explains that in this case the man's blindness is an opportunity for God to bless him.

Jesus is the light of the world, and he intends to do God's work while he has time. Making mud with his saliva, Jesus pastes it on the man's eyes and tells him to go and wash in the Pool of Siloam. He comes back able to see!

Like the invalid by the Pool of Bethesda, this man soon finds himself cross-questioned about what has happened. Jesus has again chosen a sabbath day, and the Pharisees are outraged that he insists on working on the day of rest. They launch an investigation, asking the man his opinion of Jesus and even interrogating his parents. The man sticks to the plain facts of his story, that he was blind and now sees. He adds that this is surely a work of God. The authorities excommunicate him for blasphemy. He is expelled from the synagogue.

This story will have special meaning for Christians who are suffering for their faith, especially where they are disowned by their families or rejected by their faith communities.

The man who has been healed of his blindness has still not seen Jesus. Jesus goes in search of him and finds him. His mission as the Messiah is that the blind may receive their sight. How sad, he says, that many with physical sight are spiritually blind. Some Pharisees, listening in, think they detect a reference to themselves. They are right.

Jesus teaches: 'I am the good shepherd'
(10:1–21)

Jesus is outraged by the treatment that has been given to the man born blind. The religious leaders are doing their people great harm. They are like thieves or robbers breaking into a sheep-pen, rather than shepherds caring for their sheep. But sheep will recognize the voice of their true shepherd – and so will the people of God recognize Jesus.

The prophet Ezekiel once criticized the leaders of Israel. They were like corrupt shepherds who used their sheep for meat and fleece, and yet neglected them most cruelly. God's people are his flock, and he holds their leaders to account. One day he will himself step in and become their shepherd (Ezekiel 34:1–16). This is what Jesus has in mind when he says, 'I am the good shepherd' (10:11). He has come to tend and protect his people Israel, and to call other flocks (the Gentiles) as well. He will lay down his life for them – as every genuine shepherd is prepared to do for his sheep.

Jesus says, 'I am the gate' (10:7, 9). He is the way in to safety and healing with God. He protects his people, just as a shepherd sits across the door of the sheepfold at night. He gives his people perfect freedom – just as sheep may come in to find rest or go out to find pasture.

Jesus is the good shepherd. He is not a thief coming to steal the sheep, nor a hired helper who will run away at the first sight of danger. He knows all his people by name, and will lay down his life for them. Jesus knows that laying down his life is not just a noble thought, but will soon become a painful reality. He lays it down of his

own free will, and in the sure hope that God will raise him to life again.

Some of those who hear Jesus conclude that he is demon possessed or mad. But if so, how can he have done something as wonderful and entirely good as to heal a blind man's sight? Their tragedy is that they can't see the truth.

The unbelief of the Jews
(10:22–39)

It is now the Feast of Dedication. This is Hanukkah, when the Jews celebrate the rededication of their temple in 164 BC, after it was defiled by the Syrian tyrant, Antiochus Epiphanes. The feast falls in the month of Kislev (December), and John tells us it is winter.

Because of the cold, Jesus and others are in the shelter of Solomon's Colonnade. Here the Jews challenge him again as to whether he is really the Christ. They are frustrated that he will not make a clear statement – and yet if he does, they will immediately jump to the wrong conclusion.

Jesus says that his teaching and actions are clear evidence of who he is. The Jews cannot accept that Jesus and his Father are calling people to salvation and giving them eternal life. They find Jesus' claim of closeness to God an outrageous blasphemy, and again threaten to stone him.

There have been so many attempts on his life that Jesus retreats to the east of Jerusalem. He stays in the area where John the Baptist used to preach, beyond the River Jordan. John's teaching had never been confirmed by miracles, but people can see that all he said about Jesus is coming true. This good shepherd who knows his sheep is also becoming the Lamb of God who will give his life for the sins of the world.

The seventh sign: Jesus raises Lazarus from death
(11:1–44)

We are introduced to Lazarus and his sisters Mary and Martha. They live in the village of Bethany on the eastern slope of the Mount of Olives, about two miles south-east of Jerusalem. They are dear friends of Jesus.

The sisters send a message to Jesus, asking for help because their brother is ill and probably dying. Curiously, Jesus delays. It is true that there is danger for him if he goes near Jerusalem at this time, but more importantly he sees that God's glory is going to shine through this situation. After two days he knows that Lazarus is dead – and he sets out to go to them. Thomas (called Didymus, which is Greek for 'Twin'), encourages the others to go with him, even though he is sure it will mean their death.

When Jesus arrives at Bethany, Lazarus has already been buried for four days. This is a well-known family, and many Jews have come from Jerusalem to comfort the sisters. Martha, whom we know as a woman of action from Luke's story about her (Luke 10:38–42), comes out to meet Jesus. She tells him that if he had only been there, her brother would not have died. Even so, she believes God will still answer his prayer.

Jesus assures Martha that Lazarus will rise again. She assumes this is the hope they all share of resurrection at the last day. But Jesus means that Lazarus will rise *now*! He makes one of the amazing statements which reveal him as the Son of God: 'I am the resurrection and the life. Those who believe in me, even though they die, will live' (11:25). Martha responds with great faith: 'I believe that you are the Christ.'

When Mary comes out to meet Jesus, her tears trigger his own emotions. Outrage and grief flood through him at the death of his friend.

Coming to the tomb, which is a cave with a stone across the entrance, Jesus asks for it to be opened up. Martha, who is proactive to the point of being bossy, warns that there will be a terrible smell of decay. Jesus assures her that she is about to see something of the glory of God.

Jesus prays. As always, he talks to God as his Father. He thanks him that his prayers for Lazarus have already been answered. He prays aloud, so that those who are there can share his complete dependence on God for this great miracle. And then he cries, 'Lazarus, come out!' – and out Lazarus comes, with his grave clothes wrapped around him.

The hope of eternal life. An early Christian reliquary, or container for relics, dating from the 5th century. It is covered with a thin layer of silver, on which Jesus is depicted calling Lazarus from his tomb.

This is the seventh and greatest of the 'signs' in this Gospel. The claim of Jesus, that he is the resurrection and the life, is proved by the resurrection of his friend.

Like Jairus' daughter and the son of the widow of Nain, Lazarus is only retrieved into this life. He will continue to grow old until he dies again. Even so, his new lease of life is a pointer to the real thing – the resurrection of Jesus and the promise of eternal life for all who trust in him.

The Jewish leaders plot to kill Jesus
(11:45–57)

Jesus' 'sign' has the effect of dividing people. While some believe in him, others rush off to report him. Soon the chief priests and Pharisees are meeting together in the Sanhedrin, the Jewish Council, to plan their next move.

The Jewish leaders believe that the raising of Lazarus will draw massive support for Jesus. There will be a Jewish rebellion, which the Romans will then crush. The result will be both the loss of the temple ('our place') and the destruction of the nation. The wily (and, as it turns out, inspired) Caiaphas has the solution. Jesus must die so that the nation may be spared. They begin to plot his death.

Jesus withdraws to Ephraim, about twelve miles from Jerusalem, and awaits the Passover. This is the third and fateful Passover of John's Gospel.

Mary anoints Jesus at Bethany
(12:1–11)

Six days before the Passover, Jesus moves to Bethany to stay with Lazarus, Martha and Mary. It may be at the sabbath meal, on the Friday evening, that Mary pours expensive perfume over Jesus' feet. She wipes them with her hair. Judas takes exception to this waste of a rare luxury (and money), but Jesus accepts Mary's act as his anointing for burial. By this time the next week he will be dead.

An expensive perfume

Nard is the oil of the nard plant which grows in India. The oil comes from the root and spike of the plant, which is why it is sometimes called 'spikenard'. Mary pours an entire litra over Jesus, which is eleven fluid ounces. This quantity of genuine nard is fabulously expensive, and Judas will not be the only one who is shocked by her extravagance. Mary cares nothing for their opinions, and provokes further surprise by wiping Jesus' feet with her hair. She is abandoning all reserve in her regard for him.

Jesus enters Jerusalem

(12:12–19)

The next day, Jesus rides into Jerusalem on a donkey. He is fulfilling an ancient prophecy. Jerusalem's king will come to her gently and in peace – not mounted on a proud warhorse, but riding a humble donkey (Zechariah 9:9). The crowds gather to greet him, waving palm branches. Although palms are waved at the Feast of Tabernacles, they have also become a national symbol for the Jews. There are cries of 'Hosanna!' which means 'Give salvation now!'

It seems that Jesus is at last coming into his own. He is arriving in Jerusalem as a king like David, proclaiming peace, releasing prisoners and giving his life for his people. The news has spread that he raised Lazarus from death, and this sensation swells the crowd still further. The Pharisees wonder how they can regain control. They see that 'the whole world has gone after him' – which indeed it has, especially by the time the readers hold this Gospel in their hands!

Jesus and some Greeks

(12:20–36)

While the Jewish leaders plot to kill Jesus, some Greeks are eager to meet him. Philip and Andrew (both of whom have Greek names) introduce them.

The Greeks have come to take part in the Passover worship. They may be Greek-speaking Jews, or visitors from a nearby Gentile town such as Decapolis. It is possible that they are pilgrims from Greece itself, inviting Jesus to travel with them to their country. Somehow their enquiry prompts Jesus to announce that the time has come for him to die. He is to be 'glorified' – that is, his real nature and worth are to be revealed through his death on the cross.

Like a grain of wheat, Jesus must die to himself and be buried in the ground if a harvest is to grow. Jesus pictures his death and resurrection in this way; but the cross casts a sinister shadow across his heart. As a human being with a dread of torture and the fear of the unknown, he longs that the Father will spare him. However, even more than that, he wants God's name to be glorified. It's a longing that we ourselves express every time we say the Lord's Prayer – but with so little cost to ourselves.

For the only time in John's Gospel, the voice of God is heard. To the crowd it sounds like thunder; but Jesus hears words of reassurance and encouragement: 'I have glorified it [my name], and will glorify it again.' God has already been glorified – revealed and honoured – in Jesus' life and work. Now he will be glorified again through his death and resurrection.

Somehow the arrival of the Greeks and their request has brought home to Jesus the nearness of his death. Is it that they bring the temptation to travel and teach far away from Jerusalem, and so escape the pain of betrayal and crucifixion? Or do they remind him that he must be lifted up on the cross in order to draw *all* people, and not just the Jews, to the salvation of God? He knows the answer, and also that his time grows short.

The unbelief of the Jews

(12:37–50)

Jesus' public ministry is now coming to an end. Although he has worked many amazing miracles, most people are still fixed in their unbelief. As the suffering servant of God, Jesus is to be abused and rejected by his own people. God himself will confirm people in their unbelief – blinding eyes and deadening hearts, as he did in the days of Isaiah (Isaiah 6:10). Fortunately, this hardening of hearts will be used by God for his glory in the end. The rejection of Jesus by the Jews will be the stimulus for the gospel to be preached to the Gentiles.

The Jewish leaders who *do* believe in Jesus are afraid to go public with their faith. They prefer the praise of their peer group and the security of their tradition.

Jesus makes a final appeal to the unbelievers. He tells them again that he has come as light for the world. Behind him is the perfect love and justice of God the Father. He has done no more and no less than the Father has commissioned him to do.

The glory of the cross

The Last Supper

(13:1–30)

It is now the last night of Jesus' life, and the eve of the Passover feast. Jesus spends the time with his disciples – sharing a meal with them, teaching them and praying for them. In particular he will enact his whole mission by washing their feet, and prepare them for the future by promising the gift of the Holy Spirit.

There has been much study comparing the Last Supper in John's Gospel with the accounts of the Last Supper in the Gospels of Matthew, Mark and Luke. Unlike the others, John has no account of Jesus breaking bread and sharing wine, which are indications of a Passover meal and the origins of our Holy Communion. John seems to describe a meal on the evening *before* the Passover – a day earlier than the others. This means that Jesus is dying on the cross at the same time as the Passover lambs are being sacrificed in the temple. It could be that Matthew, Mark and Luke are recording a kind of Passover meal, but without the usual roast lamb.

'The disciple whom Jesus loved'

For the first time we have mention of 'the disciple whom Jesus loved'. He is next to Jesus as they recline on mats or cushions, perhaps at a low table. We will meet him again at the foot of Jesus' cross, and when he comes running with Peter to the empty tomb. Indeed, he is usually associated with Peter. From all that we know of the disciples in the four Gospels, the most likely person to be 'the disciple whom Jesus loved' is John, the son of Zebedee.

We know from the other Gospels that John and his brother James were hot-tempered and ambitious. Jesus nicknamed them 'the Sons of Thunder'. If John is now the author or the source of this Gospel, we can only wonder at the amazing change that his friendship with Jesus has made. He is now so humble that he doesn't even include his own name. The only thing that matters to him is that Jesus loves him.

JESUS WASHES HIS DISCIPLES' FEET

At the beginning of their last meal together, Jesus gets up from the table, takes off his outer clothing and wraps a towel around his waist. He then pours water into a basin and washes his disciples' feet (13:1–17). He who is the Lord of glory lays aside all privilege and status, and humbly does the work of a slave.

Simon Peter objects. He is embarrassed that Jesus should wash his feet. Feet are dirty and smelly. To wash them is the task of the lowliest servant. But it seems there is no slave present, and none of the disciples will volunteer for the task.

When Peter protests, Jesus insists: 'Unless I wash you, you have no part with me.' Jesus our Saviour must do for us what we can never do for ourselves – that is, cleanse us from our most intimate and shameful sin.

Afterwards, when he has resumed his place, Jesus talks about what he has done. Although he is their Lord, he has washed their feet. Now they should do the same for one another. He has modelled for them a life of mutual acceptance and forgiveness which must be the mark of his followers for all time.

Peter responds enthusiastically, 'Then, Lord, not just my feet but my hands and my head as well!' But Jesus says, 'One who has bathed does not need to wash, except for the feet.' People bathe before they go to someone else's house, but their bare feet (in sandals) pick up dust in the street. So it is only their feet that need washing on arrival. Jesus' followers are made clean by God's salvation – symbolized in the washing of baptism. After the cleansing of baptism they need only the day-to-day 'foot washing' of forgiveness, after contact with the grime of the world. John makes the same point in his first letter:

If we confess our sins, he [God] is faithful and just and will forgive us our sins and purify us from all unrighteousness (1 John 1:9).

JESUS PREDICTS HIS BETRAYAL

Jesus has washed the feet of all the disciples, including Judas. But he knows the one who will betray him (13:18–30). He has in mind some words from one of David's psalms:

Even my close friend, whom I trusted,
  he who shared my bread,
    has lifted up his heel against me (Psalm 41:9).

Jesus is about to be betrayed, but he will not be taken by surprise. He is not deceived. His arrest, trial and crucifixion will not be a dreadful miscarriage of his plans, but their fulfilment. Jesus is the suffering servant and perfect sacrifice. He is the Lamb of God who has come to take away the sins of the world. But this is not a cold and calculated operation. The disciples see that Jesus is deeply distressed that his betrayal is by one of his closest friends. And it isn't at all obvious which one of them he means.

We can imagine the arrangement at the meal as Peter says to the beloved disciple, and he in turn to Jesus, 'Who is it?' Jesus is also close to Judas. Perhaps Judas is in the place of honour on Jesus' left. Jesus passes him a special morsel of bread. At the Passover meal the host might pass a tasty morsel to his wife or honoured guest. It is at this very moment that Judas finally resolves to betray Jesus. He goes out, as John says, into the night. Judas plans to extinguish the light of the world. His own darkness is complete.

The Last Supper. Jesus shares the last meal with his disciples before his death. They gather round a single table in the upper room, and share from a common dish. From a Byzantine fresco (c. 1072), San Angelo Formis, Capua.

The farewell talk
(13:31 – 16:33)

JESUS PREDICTS PETER'S DENIAL

Jesus has his last opportunity to talk with his disciples (13:31–38). Soon they will be overwhelmed by the traumatic events of the night. He tells them that he is going to be glorified, not by being recognized, proclaimed and crowned as king, but by going obediently to a disgraceful death on a cross.

The glory of Jesus is so different from anything the world, or even his disciples, expect. By calling himself the Son of man, Jesus has implied he will appear in triumph, in clouds and glory to rule the world. But that is not yet.

Peter is high on enthusiasm. There is nowhere Jesus can go that he can't follow or help. He will do anything for Jesus, up to and including giving his life. But Jesus really knows his friend. By first light Peter will have disowned him not once but three times.

'MY FATHER'S HOUSE'

The disciples are anxious and bewildered. Something is about to befall them which is beyond their imagination or power to control. They realize that Jesus is deeply distressed, and they share something of his agony.

Jesus seeks to steady and reassure them. This is a time to trust God. God is his Father, and heaven is his home – with room for everyone (14:1–4). The whole point of Jesus' suffering and death is to prepare a place for them in heaven, and to take them safely there.

JESUS TEACHES: 'I AM THE WAY'

Thomas wants to understand. Jesus is about to disappear, but they have no idea where he is going, nor how to follow him. Jesus answers him very simply: 'I am the way and the truth and the life' (14:6). The way home to God is not a map or a set of directions, but a person – Jesus himself. He is the true and living way. In fact he is the only way. If they know Jesus, then they know God.

Philip blurts out a question which he has been longing to ask. 'Lord, show us the Father!' In these last moments before he leaves them, can Jesus finally and completely reveal God to them? Jesus answers, 'Philip, do you still not realize, even after all this time? You are looking at him!' The Father's character and purpose can be seen perfectly in Jesus his Son. Jesus and his Father are united. That's how his miracles are possible. Now their unity and work are going to include and involve the disciples as well. If they accept the motives and mission of Jesus, God will work freely through them.

JESUS PROMISES THE HOLY SPIRIT

Jesus promises the disciples that they will do 'greater things' than he has done (14:15–31). How can this be possible? He explains that he will ask his Father to give them 'another Counsellor' – another Person like himself to be alongside them. This is the Holy Spirit, the Spirit of truth.

Jesus tells his disciples that the proof of their love for him will be that they obey his commands. It seems strange to turn love into a duty. We can't love if we are forced to! But Jesus is not treating love as a feeling; he is describing an action – a way of life. We will always show our true relationship with God by the way we treat one another:

This is how we know that we love the children of God: by loving God and carrying out his commands. This is love for God: to obey his commands (1 John 5:2–3).

Jesus is going to be taken from his friends. He will be arrested, put on trial, sentenced and crucified. As far as most people are concerned, he will be dead and gone. But he promises not to abandon them. He promises to return to them. He assures them that he will come alive again, and that he will share his new life with them.

When they meet again, they will realize that Jesus is united with his Father, and that they are united with him. They will find themselves included in the love and life of God. This love and life will be shown by readily, joyfully and wholeheartedly obeying Jesus' teaching.

There is so much for the disciples to learn; and so little time for Jesus to teach them. Jesus assures them that the Holy Spirit will be their Counsellor in the future. He will teach them and remind them of everything Jesus has been telling them.

In all the turmoil and heartache of leaving them, Jesus gives his friends his peace. 'Peace' is the everyday Jewish greeting – 'shalom'. But Jesus doesn't use the word lightly. He gives them God's own peace; the settled conviction that God is in control, and that all will be well.

The disciples are sad that Jesus is going away. He tells them they should be glad for him, because his death will

---

A standard of loving

Jesus gives his disciples a new command – one which will be etched on John's memory for the rest of his life. It is simply stated: 'Love one another' (13:34). What kind of love is this? Affection? Friendship? Lust? Jesus explains, 'It is the kind of love that I have had for you.'

The twin commands of loving God and loving neighbour have been known since the days of Moses. What is new is the standard of loving. Jesus shows his love for his disciples by serving them and laying down his life for them. It is the kind of love he has for his Father, and now extends to embrace the whole human race. Loving one another has been a struggle – almost an impossibility

– for the disciples. In the Gospels of Mark and Luke we see their rivalry, jealousy and conflicting ambitions. Now, says Jesus, they are to put one another first.

Alongside to help

The Holy Spirit is sometimes called the 'Paraclete'. This is the Greek word for a legal counsellor, who advises and defends in a court case. The Holy Spirit is the Spirit of God who comes alongside to help.

The Holy Spirit is the Spirit of truth. He knows the truth of God and shares it with us. Because he is invisible, the world cannot believe he exists. Because he is from God, the world cannot accept what he teaches. But the friends of Jesus know him as a constant companion and adviser, because he lives within them.

'I will come to you'

What does Jesus mean when he promises to come back to his disciples (14:18)? Is this when he is raised to life on Easter morning, when he sends his Spirit to them at Pentecost or when he returns in glory at the end of the world?

The most obvious way that Jesus will come to them and they will see him is when he is raised from death a few days later. He will appear to them all on the evening after his resurrection.

True love

For Jesus, love means putting someone else first.

'Love each other' is the only new command Jesus makes. It says as 'do' what the Ten Commandments can only say as 'don't'. Jesus doesn't impose this command on his disciples like a tyrant, but shares it with them as a friend. It is the heart of his confiding to them what God is really like.

Until Jesus came, no one ever showed true love. Now love is revealed as a joyful combination of obedience to God and selfless service of others.

take him to his Father in heaven.

For now, Jesus won't say much more. The prince of this world, the devil, is approaching. For a while Satan will have his way. He will take Jesus down into death; but he won't be able to hold him there. Jesus will die, not because he is overpowered by evil, but because he has freely offered up his life to his Father.

JESUS TEACHES: 'I AM THE VINE'

Jesus describes himself to his friends as 'the true vine'.

The vine is a symbol of Israel. She is the nation God carefully planted in the Promised Land. He tended, guarded and nourished her; but when he came to look for a harvest of goodness, he found only the bad fruit of wickedness (Isaiah 5:1–2).

Now Jesus is the 'true' vine (15:1–17). He is the genuine Israel, who will produce the fruit of goodness and love. His friends are the branches of this vine, and his Father is the gardener who tends them.

The purpose of the vine is to bear fruit. The gardener cuts off the branches which are barren or rotten. He gently cleans the other branches, to keep them free from disease. So it is with God, as he purifies, nourishes and corrects his people.

For the branches, the secret of fruitfulness is to remain fully connected to the vine. Jesus urges his friends to share his life and draw their strength from his teaching. If they do, they will be wonderfully fruitful and bring untold credit to God.

The vine is a picture of love at work. Jesus gives his life for his friends, just as a vine pours life into its fruit. The life of Jesus is rooted in the love of God; a love he produces in his friends by laying down his life for them. Now they must continue his love. The fruit of their love will be in obeying the Father's will, putting one another first and sharing the life of Jesus with the whole world.

THE WORLD HATES THE DISCIPLES

As John writes, he reflects that the world has met the love of Jesus with hate. The world hated Jesus and now it hates his friends (15:18 – 16:4).

Jesus explains to his disciples that the world will treat them in the same way that it has treated him. Where people would welcome Jesus, they will welcome his friends. The rejection of Jesus and his miracles has been an unreasonable and ungrateful rejection of God himself.

Jesus warns his disciples that tough times are ahead. They will be excommunicated from the synagogues and even killed because of their belief in Jesus. He tells them not to be taken by surprise or lose their faith when such things happen. This is all part of the world's rejection of him and his Father.

THE WORK OF THE HOLY SPIRIT

Jesus tells his disciples that it is for their good that he is going. Only when he has ceased to be with them in a human body can he send his Spirit to be with them in a much freer and fuller way.

The Holy Spirit will be their Counsellor, working alongside them and helping them (16:5–15). He will make people ashamed of the way they treated Jesus. He will show the world that Jesus was in the right, and that he is now with his Father in heaven. He will prove to the world that Satan was wrong, his evil work exposed and his power broken.

Jesus promises his friends that the Spirit will teach and guide them. The Spirit will faithfully communicate God's truth to them in the future. He will reveal the wisdom of Jesus in every situation. Just as Jesus has been showing them the Father, so now the Spirit will continue to show them Jesus.

THE DISCIPLES' GRIEF WILL TURN TO JOY

The disciples are puzzled by Jesus saying that they won't see him for 'a little while'. He explains that they will be plunged into grief for a time, but then their tears will turn to joy (16:16–33). Jesus is referring to his death and resurrection. His friends will mourn his death, but then rejoice for ever at his risen life.

There is still a longing among Christians to see Jesus again. Those who are being persecuted are especially hoping that Jesus will return after this 'little while' and turn their grief to joy.

The disciples cannot understand all this in advance of it happening. They have always assumed that Jesus will be a victorious Messiah. Seeing their leader arrested, mocked and crucified is going to be a devastating experience.

'I am the vine, you are the branches. Those who abide in me and I in them bear much fruit, because apart from me you can do nothing' (15:5).

The disciples are beginning to understand. Jesus is enabling them to relate directly to God. They can know God as their Father, just as Jesus does. They can pray to God directly, thanks to the access they have through Jesus.

Suddenly, they think that all they have to do is say they believe in Jesus. If they do, then all will be well. They think they understand – but they don't.

Jesus knows that the disciples still have a long way to go. They will desert him when he is arrested, and scatter to their homes. But the Father will be with him.

Jesus has warned his disciples of the crisis that lies ahead. Now they can know his peace even in the midst of disaster. He is going to triumph over the troubles of the world.

The prayer of Jesus
(17:1–26)

JESUS PRAYS FOR HIMSELF

Jesus prays to his Father (17:1–5). Now that the time has come for him to go to the cross, he prays that his death and resurrection will give glory to God.

For us, 'glory' means to be clothed in splendour, so that power and majesty are fully displayed. For Jesus, his glory will be seen in the humiliation of the cross. It is in his suffering and death that his love, obedience and sacrifice will be most completely revealed.

Through his death and resurrection Jesus will return to his heavenly Father. He will be given again the heavenly glory which was his before the universe was made, and which he laid aside to take our human nature.

JESUS PRAYS FOR HIS DISCIPLES

Jesus prays for his group of friends – the people God has given him to be his disciples (17:6–19). Jesus has shared his life with them and shown them what God is like. He has taught them God's truth and they have accepted it.

The disciples are a unique group. They are now to live in a wicked world while belonging to their Father in heaven. They are the nucleus of the church.

Jesus prays that God will protect his friends, keeping them loyal and guarding their unity. While Jesus has been with them, he has been able to prevent them from falling out. Only one has been lost, which is Judas Iscariot. His betrayal was foreseen in scripture (Psalm 41:9).

As Jesus prepares to leave this world, he knows that his disciples must engage in an awesome struggle. He prays that God will fill them to the brim with his joy – the delight that comes with knowing the Father and sharing his work.

He prays that, although they must continue to live in the world, they will be protected from the malicious attacks of the devil. He prays that they will be constantly cleansed and strengthened by the truth of the gospel.

Jesus is now devoting himself afresh to the purpose of God – setting himself apart from all other ambitions or distractions. He does this for the sake of his friends. It is through his devoted sacrifice that they in turn may enter the holy presence of God.

JESUS PRAYS FOR ALL BELIEVERS

Finally, Jesus prays for all those who will believe in him through the gospel message of the disciples. He prays that the believers of the future will be united (17:20–26).

Unity must always be a distinctive mark of the church. Because Jesus is one with his Father, and believers are one with the Father and the Son, there should be no room for rivalry and faction.

The unity of Christians, their mutual love and shared purpose, must be the clearest evidence of God in their lives. This will prove to the world that God exists and that Jesus is his Son.

Jesus has always encouraged his friends to be specific in their prayers. Now he comes to his own heart's desire. He asks that his friends may join him in the glory of heaven. This is surely a prayer that the Father longs to grant. It is, after all, the purpose of Jesus entering the world, that human beings may become God's children and join him in heaven (John 1:12).

God is spirit. He is holy. He is invisible. The world can never know him or guess what he is like. But now Jesus has come into the world to make his Father known. As he says to Philip, 'Anyone who has seen me has seen the Father' (John 14:9).

And what is the Father like? He is like Jesus his Son. He constantly pours out his love for his creation. He longs to restore the world to its original beauty and peace.

God gives the ultimate proof of his love by sending Jesus, his only Son, to be the Saviour of the world. He wants all people to come to him of their own free will, to become his children and to be eternally united in his love (John 3:16, 17).

Jesus is arrested, tried and crucified
(18:1 – 19:42)

JESUS IS ARRESTED

It is night-time. Jesus goes with his disciples to an olive grove across the Kidron Valley from Jerusalem. This is the Mount of Olives, a favourite place with Jesus, because it is away from the Passover crowds. Judas knows where to find them.

Judas brings a contingent of soldiers through the trees to arrest Jesus (18:1–11). These may be Roman soldiers who have been brought in to quell any trouble from the thousands of Jewish pilgrims. They are armed with weapons and equipped with lights, ready for a fight. But when Jesus says, 'I am he,' they recoil at his authority.

Jesus surrenders without a struggle. He is concerned to avoid harm to his friends. He is also stepping willingly towards the climax of his mission. This is the cup of suffering that he must drain to the dregs. His passion starts now.

JESUS IS TAKEN BEFORE ANNAS

John tells us that Jesus is taken first to Annas, the father-in-law of the high priest (18:12–14).

Annas was high priest himself from AD 6 to 15, and still has enormous influence. He was deposed by the Romans and replaced by Caiaphas, so there may be many Jews who still regard him as their true leader. Caiaphas has already suggested that the death of Jesus would suit the Jews very well. It could divert Roman anger and save the Jews and their temple from destruction (John 11:50).

PETER'S FIRST DENIAL

At first, Peter and another disciple try to stay in touch with Jesus. The other disciple (who may be John) is able to gain access to the high priest's courtyard. But there, accosted by a girl, Peter's courage starts to fail (18:15–18).

John recalls these events in sharp detail: the cold night, the charcoal fire and the girl on duty at the door. He remembers the question she put to Peter, which almost invited the answer, 'No.' Jesus had known that under the slightest pressure Peter would deny he ever knew him.

THE HIGH PRIEST QUESTIONS JESUS

Standing before the high priest, Jesus is given an informal hearing rather than a trial (18:19–24). It would be illegal to try Jesus late at night, and in any case the full Council of the Sanhedrin isn't present.

Annas questions Jesus about his followers and his teaching. He wants to know if Jesus has a secret plan. Is his teaching blasphemous? Has he been plotting a rebellion?

Jesus replies that all his teaching has been open, and often delivered in public in the temple. In any case, Annas should be getting his evidence from witnesses, rather than cross-questioning Jesus himself.

Jesus' criticism of the high priest earns him a slap on the face, but Jesus refuses to be intimidated. He asks for the hearing to be conducted fairly. Annas realizes that he has reached the limit of his authority. He sends Jesus to Caiaphas his son-in-law, who is the official high priest.

PETER'S SECOND AND THIRD DENIALS

Standing at the fire in the courtyard, Simon Peter continues to deny that he has any connection with Jesus – even when challenged by a relative of the unfortunate Malchus (18:25–27)!

The cock crows. The Romans call one of their night watches 'cockcrow', and it runs from midnight until three in the morning. In the space of a few hours both Judas and Peter have betrayed Jesus, each for different reasons and in different ways.

JESUS BEFORE PILATE

John tells us nothing of Jesus' trial before Caiaphas, in the presence of a hastily convened Sanhedrin. He does, however, give us a longer account of the trial before the Roman governor (18:28–40).

The Jews lead Jesus to the governor's palace. The governor is Pontius Pilate. His permanent headquarters is in Caesarea, but it is his custom to come to Jerusalem for the major Jewish festivals.

The Jews won't enter the Roman palace, because contact with Gentiles will make them 'unclean'. They wish to be ritually pure for the Passover ceremonies later in the day, and for the meal in the evening.

Governor Pilate comes out to talk to the Jewish authorities. He has no interest in a blasphemy charge, and suggests that the Jews should try Jesus by their own law. However, the Jews want Jesus executed. They need a verdict from Pilate, because under Roman occupation they have no power of their own to put a person to death.

Pilate is only concerned about Jesus if he is a political threat. He asks him if he claims to be the king of the Jews. Jesus is, of course, the Jews' Messiah

---

John's account of the passion of Jesus

John's account of the arrest and trial and death of Jesus has many details which are not found in the other Gospels.

John does not mention the Garden of Gethsemane, nor that Judas betrays Jesus with a kiss. He does, however, describe how Peter tries to protect Jesus with a sword – and cuts off the ear of a man called Malchus.

As events unfold, John shows that Jesus is in control. He is offering his life of his own free will. The soldiers and officials who come to arrest him draw back and fall to the ground, but Jesus submits without a struggle.

John tells how, when Jesus is on trial, he puts his own questions to the high priest and the Roman governor. In the other Gospels Jesus remains silent. It is John who tells us that Jesus carries his own cross; and that before he dies he commits his mother to the care of 'the disciple whom Jesus loved'.

The main difference between John and the other Gospels is the time of Jesus' death. John has Jesus dying on the Thursday, as the Passover lambs are being killed in the temple. The other Gospels have Jesus sharing a Passover meal with his disciples. This implies that the lambs have already been killed and that the death of Jesus takes place a day later.

The oldest surviving fragment of any Gospel is a tiny extract from the Gospel of John. It dates from about AD 130 and is preserved in the John Rylands Library in Manchester, England. It contains the words of Jesus to Pilate:

For this reason I was born, and for this I came into the world, to testify to the truth (John 18:37).

and king – but his kingdom is not a particular country or nation. The kingdom of Jesus is the kingdom of God.

Jesus tells Pilate that he has come into the world to proclaim the truth. Pilate doesn't believe it is possible to know the truth. Truth is merely a matter of opinion, and can never be proved. He certainly doesn't recognize the truth standing in front of him.

Going outside, the governor tells the Jews that he has no basis on which to charge Jesus. He suggests that he might release him as his annual gesture of goodwill to the Jews at Passover time. How nice to give them back their king! The Jews shout instead for the release of a convicted rebel called Barabbas.

The cautious Jewish leaders and reckless Jewish crowd unite to get Jesus condemned. The leaders have been threatened by his success and the crowd disappointed by his failure.

JESUS IS SENTENCED TO BE CRUCIFIED

Pilate has Jesus flogged (19:1–16). The soldiers give him a mock coronation, with a crown made of twisted thorns and a purple robe. They taunt him with his royal title and, instead of showing respect, hit his face.

Pilate presents Jesus to the crowd. Surely now they will see he is merely human, and no threat to religion or public order. The Jewish leaders continue to bay for his crucifixion.

The governor is no longer in control of this situation, and is starting to panic. Something the Jewish leaders say makes Pilate wonder if Jesus does indeed have divine power. Suddenly he asks where Jesus has come from. Could it be that he is one of the gods? Will this episode bring him some kind of bad luck? Romans – even governors – are very superstitious.

Jesus puts Pilate's power and responsibility in perspective. The Roman governor is only doing what God is allowing him to do. The greater guilt is with the Jewish authorities, who are now in all-out rebellion against God.

Pilate tries to release Jesus, but the Jews remind him of his duty. Jesus has been found guilty of posing as a king – and that is a clear act of defiance against Caesar. The Jews declare that Caesar is their only king. In doing so they become blasphemers themselves. Every Jew knows that God is their true king.

The Jews have lost all shame and the governor has lost all patience. At the sixth hour on the day of Preparation – that is at about midday – Pilate agrees to crucify the king of the Jews at their own request. He sentences Jesus to death.

On which day was Jesus crucified?

The 'day of Preparation' for Passover is a Thursday, with the Passover meal eaten that night. The Jewish day begins at sunset, so 'Friday' starts on Thursday evening.

John's account of events points to the 'Preparation' being on the Thursday. This means that Jesus, the Lamb of God, is being crucified at the same time as the lambs are being sacrificed in the

temple, ready for the Passover meal.

However, it is possible that the 'Preparation' is for the sabbath (Saturday). This would put the day of crucifixion on a Friday, which is how the Gospels of Matthew, Mark and Luke have it.

The choice of Thursday or Friday also affects our understanding of the Last Supper. Is it a Passover meal? It seems very unlikely. If the Passover has to be eaten on the Friday night, then Jesus has already died.

However, in the Gospels of Matthew, Mark and Luke, Jesus takes the Passover bread and wine and makes them a memorial of his body and blood. Perhaps the Last Supper was a Passover style of meal, but eaten a day early and without the lamb.

The Place of the Skull

'Golgotha' is an English version of the Aramaic word for 'skull'. The Latin for 'skull' is 'calvaria', which gives us the word 'calvary'.

Golgotha may be a small hill with hollows which make it look like a skull. Perhaps it is a place of executions and abandoned bones. It need not be a hill. The Romans often executed criminals by the roadside as a gruesome warning to others.

THE CRUCIFIXION

An execution squad takes charge of Jesus (19:16–27). John tells us that he carries his own cross – or at least the crosspiece – on his broken and bleeding back. Outside the city, at a place called Golgotha, he is crucified between two others.

Pilate decides to show his contempt for the Jewish authorities. He has a notice made which declares Jesus to be 'The King of the Jews'. It is written in three languages and fastened to the cross.

The Jewish leaders protest, but Pilate refuses to change his mind. The irony is that Pilate is right. Jesus is being crucified for the truth. He *is* the king of the Jews. The cross is the means by which he is exalted on high for all to see. It is his glorious throne (12:32–33).

The four soldiers who crucify Jesus divide his clothes between them. The undergarment has been woven all in one piece, so they gamble for it rather than tearing it up. They unwittingly fulfil a prophecy from one of the psalms (Psalm 22:18). In the Gospels of Matthew and Mark, this is the psalm which Jesus recites as he hangs on the cross.

While four soldiers share Jesus' clothes, four women share his suffering. One is his mother and another his aunt. One of them may have woven the seamless garment.

Comparing the lists of the women at the cross with those in the other Gospels, it seems that Jesus' aunt may be Salome. She is the mother of James and John.

A Roman coin depicts the head of Emperor Tiberius who rules at the time of Jesus' ministry. He is the supreme secular authority for both Romans and Jews.

Mary from Magdala, a village on the western shore of Galilee, is mentioned in all four Gospels at this point. John has not named her before, but she becomes a key witness now.

The disciple whom Jesus loved is near, and Jesus commits his mother to his care. Jesus calls her 'Dear woman' as he did at the wedding in Cana. John never mentions her by name, any more than he names himself, or his brother or mother.

JESUS DIES

Jesus cries out for a drink (19:28 37). He is parched by the midday heat and loss of blood. He is given some wine vinegar on a sponge to moisten his lips.

Jesus' last words before he dies are, 'It is finished.' It is a cry of victory, not despair. He has fulfilled all the prophecies of his suffering. He has paid in full for the sins of the world. 'Finished' is the everyday Greek word for the payment of a bill.

When Jesus dies, he gives up his spirit. Nobody takes his life from him – indeed, they are surprised that he has died so soon. This is Jesus' self-offering to his Father, the willing sacrifice of himself for the lost human race.

The following day is a special sabbath, falling as it does in the Passover week. The law of Moses says that a body must not be left to hang on a tree overnight (that is, after execution), because it will desecrate the land (Deuteronomy 21:23).

The Jewish authorities ask Pilate for permission to break the legs of the victims so that they can be lifted down from their crosses without any risk of escaping.

Although the soldiers break the legs of the criminals either side of Jesus, they find that he has already died. To make certain, one of the soldiers pierces Jesus' side with a spear. The result is a sudden flow of blood and water from the wound.

The blood and water are a sign that Jesus' blood has coagulated in death, or that his lungs have become congested with fluid. There is no doubt at all that he is dead.

John seems to refer to himself here as a witness of Jesus' death. He can vouch for the fact that Jesus really died and was not merely pretending.

A psalm of desolation

John has already quoted Psalm 69 twice in his Gospel, with reference to Jesus having a 'zeal for God's house' and being 'hated without reason'. It is a psalm of someone crying out to God from a situation of extreme distress.

In this psalm, vinegar adds to the torture of thirst (Psalm 69:21). It is not the same as the wine mixed with myrrh which Jesus was offered on his way to the cross. He refused this because it was a drug to dull his senses (Mark 15:23).

THE BURIAL OF JESUS

A leading Jew asks for permission to bury the body of Jesus (19:38–42). Normally the corpse of a crucified criminal would be left for the vultures. Joseph of Arimathea, who is a member of the Council, offers instead his own new tomb, which is set in a spacious garden.

Like Nicodemus, Joseph has taken a secret interest in Jesus. Now the two of them take his body the short distance to the 'garden tomb'. It is almost sunset.

Nicodemus and Joseph are just in time. The sabbath is about to begin when they will be forbidden to carry burdens. They wrap Jesus' body in strips of linen, with a large quantity of fragrant spices to counter the smell of decay.

Water and blood

The idea of water and blood as two witnesses to the death of Jesus comes up again in John's first letter (1 John 5:6–8). Water seems to stand for cleansing or baptism, and blood for atonement or sacrifice.

John continues to note the scriptures that are being fulfilled. One of the Psalms describes God's protection of the righteous man, so that 'not one of his bones will be broken' (Psalm 34:20). The prophet Zechariah says, 'They will look on me, the one they have pierced' (Zechariah 12:10).

The resurrection of Jesus
(20:1–31)

THE EMPTY TOMB

It is Sunday – the first day of the week. Mary of Magdala comes to the tomb while it is still dark. The first thing she notices is that the grave has been disturbed. The stone has been removed from the entrance.

Mary is shocked and indignant. She runs to tell Simon Peter and the beloved disciple that the tomb has been interfered with. Someone has taken the body – perhaps to put it in Gehenna, the city rubbish dump. It is outrageous – the final indignity.

Peter and the beloved disciple run to the tomb. John is faster and he gets there first. He remembers everything – the confusion, the anger… but resurrection is the last thing on his mind.

Bending down and looking into the tomb, John can see the strips of linen that have enfolded the body of Jesus. There is something about the way they are lying… He doesn't go in. He waits for Peter, who is the leader.

When Simon Peter arrives, he goes into the tomb. The linen strips are lying where the body of Jesus has been. Just so. The linen turban, which was wound around the head, is lying a little apart – where Jesus' head had lain. Just so…

These grave clothes haven't been stolen along with the body. Nor have they been unwound by someone getting up. They have – collapsed? Or are they neatly rolled up, as though they are no longer needed?

As John enters the tomb and sees the evidence, he dares to believe that Jesus has risen from death. They still don't understand how the scriptures foretell the Messiah's suffering and resurrection. For now, they are struggling to grasp a scene which has sent their heads spinning. Explanations will come later.

JESUS APPEARS TO MARY MAGDALENE

Peter and the beloved disciple return home. Mary remains at the tomb (20:10–18). She weeps. Her tears are of grief and indignation. Her master has been put to death before her eyes, and now his body has disappeared.

Looking into the tomb, Mary sees two angels. They ask her why she is weeping – as though they know something she doesn't. Turning round, she sees a man – perhaps the gardener – standing nearby. But it isn't the gardener…

The stranger's questions are to the point: 'Why are

Close encounters of the resurrected kind

The risen Jesus greets Mary by name – as he does Simon and Thomas when he encounters them. Each of them is slow to recognize him. When they last saw him, he was being tortured to death. Now he is 'risen' – and no one has seen a resurrected body before.

In Luke's Gospel, the risen Jesus joins two disciples on their way to Emmaus. Although their hearts are warmed by his teaching of the scriptures, they only recognize him when he breaks bread (Luke 24:30–31).

you crying?' and, 'Who is it you are looking for?' Mary's eyes are clouded by tears and her heart blind with unbelief. Jesus is the last person she expects to see. She doesn't recognize him until he speaks her name.

When Mary realizes that this is Jesus, she exclaims, 'Rabboni' – the Aramaic word for 'greatest teacher', or 'my teacher and God'. She wants to hold fast to him, to prevent him ever going away again. He gently tells her that he is returning to his Father. Just as he laid down his life, he is now taking it up again.

Jesus sends Mary to tell the others. God is their Father too, and Jesus is their brother for ever.

Mary Magdalene tells the other disciples that she has seen the Lord. Jesus has chosen an unlikely witness. Not only does Mary have a history of demon possession (Luke 8:2), but her lone evidence as a single woman would never be accepted in a Jewish court.

JESUS APPEARS TO HIS DISCIPLES

As the resurrection day draws to a close, Jesus appears to his disciples – perhaps in the upper room where they shared the Last Supper (20:19–23).

The disciples are meeting behind locked doors, because they are afraid. They fear being arrested and suffering the same fate as Jesus. As far as we know, there are ten present – the Twelve, less Judas Iscariot who betrayed Jesus, and Thomas who is absent.

Jesus greets them with his peace. His mission is accomplished. All is well. He shows them the signs of his crucifixion – the scars in his hands and side. They are overjoyed to see him alive. He had promised that in a little while they would see him, and that their grief would be turned to joy (John 16:22).

Jesus repeats his blessings of peace. From now on, God's peace will be the gift of Jesus to all his people. Then he commissions his friends to continue his work – just as he himself was commissioned by his Father. His mission is to continue in and through them.

To strengthen the disciples for their task, Jesus breathes his Holy Spirit upon them. The Spirit is the life-giving presence of God. He is the one whom Jesus described as the Comforter – the One who is the Spirit of Jesus himself, drawing alongside to help.

The 'breathing' of the Spirit is John's way of describing the giving of the Holy Spirit to Jesus' disciples. Luke will describe this in another way through the events of Pentecost (Acts 2:1–4).

The disciples are now fully fledged apostles – those who are sent to pioneer and protect the church. They have Jesus' authority to forgive sins – or to declare sins unforgiven. This has been a unique right of Jesus and his Father (Mark 2:7, 10), which is now entrusted to them.

JESUS APPEARS TO THOMAS

Thomas is not with the rest of the apostles when Jesus appears to them. John has already shown us that Thomas is solid and persistent – a man who makes up his own mind. It was Thomas who voted that they should all come to Jerusalem with Jesus, even though he was sure that they would die if they did (11:16).

Because Thomas was not with the others when Jesus appeared, he refuses to believe that Jesus is alive. He demands to see Jesus for himself, and to touch the marks of his crucifixion (20:24–31).

A week later, and again on a Sunday evening, Jesus accepts Thomas' challenge. He appears to his disciples when Thomas is with them, and invites him to reach out and probe his wounds. He urges Thomas to stop doubting and believe. Thomas gladly and humbly accepts that this is truly Jesus, and makes a ringing statement of personal faith: 'My Lord and my God!'

Most readers of John's Gospel can sympathize with Thomas. They have heard about Jesus, but not seen him alive for themselves. They must depend on what the witnesses say, and then take a step of faith.

Jesus has a special blessing for those who believe without seeing, who include ourselves: 'Blessed are those who have not seen and yet have believed.' This is the final Beatitude (Matthew 5:3–11).

John has arrived at the purpose of his Gospel. His aim

has been to present Jesus to us, so that we may believe that he is the Christ, the Son of God. It is by believing in Jesus that we will enter the eternal life of the children of God.

The epilogue

John's Gospel is now complete, but he adds an epilogue. In it he gives two scenes from the ongoing life of the apostles.

Breakfast by the sea
(21:1–14)

It is the time between the resurrection of Jesus and his ascension. The apostles have returned north, where Simon Peter decides to go fishing on the Sea of Tiberias, which is Galilee. Some of the others decide to go with him.

There are seven in the boat, including Thomas (introduced again as Didymus, the twin), and Nathanael

whom we learn is from Cana where Jesus turned water to wine. The sons of Zebedee are also present, although John doesn't mention their names or that he is one of them.

Suddenly, it is like the bad old days. They fish all night and catch nothing. Luke tells of the same thing happening on the day that Jesus first called Simon to be his disciple (Luke 5:4–5).

In the hazy light of dawn, a figure calls to them from

the shore. He tells them to throw out their net on the other side of the boat. They haven't yet recognized Jesus, but his instruction brings memories flooding back for Peter – especially when they make an amazing catch of fish.

The beloved disciple is the first to realize it is Jesus on the shore; but Simon Peter is the one who throws on his coat and jumps overboard. John remembers how the others follow, dragging the great catch about 100 yards to the beach, and counting the fish. There are 153 of them.

If the number of fish has a special meaning, it may stand for the mission of the church. The Jews of these days believe there are 153 nations in the world; and Jesus has promised his disciples that they will 'catch men and women' (Luke 5:10).

After their long night's work, Jesus invites his friends to breakfast. He has prepared food for them, with fresh bread awaiting and fish already cooking on a charcoal fire. He is a Lord who provides. Again, the fire may trigger Simon Peter's memory. It was beside such a fire, in the high priest's courtyard, that he denied three times that he ever knew Jesus (John 18:18).

John mentions that none of the disciples asks Jesus if it is really him. There is clearly something 'the same but different' about his resurrection body.

Jesus and Peter
(21:15–17)

After breakfast, Jesus and Peter talk heart-to-heart. Jesus doesn't call him by his nickname Peter ('Rock'), but by his old name, Simon son of John. Since Peter has so vigorously denied Jesus, they must now re-lay the foundations of their relationship.

Jesus asks, 'Simon, do you truly love me?' He is asking for the kind of committed love that Peter has sworn to him in the past. But Peter is more realistic now. He knows he has failed. He replies, 'Yes, Lord, you know I love you.'

Peter doesn't promise Jesus committed love any more, but only affection. When Jesus asks the question a third time he echoes Peter's three denials. It hurts Peter to admit the poor level of his love; but at least he is now honest with himself.

The Sea of Galilee at sunrise. The resurrection dawn is realized not only in the capital of Jerusalem, but in the ordinary context of everyday life.

Jesus has already answered Thomas' doubt. Now he rebuilds Peter's confidence. He encourages Simon Peter by accepting his revised commitment and giving him responsibility. He commissions him to feed his lambs and take care of his sheep. Peter is to look after people, the flock of God, as an assistant to the good shepherd. Shepherding is Jesus' own picture of the leadership and care of the church (John 10:11).

Peter and John
(21:18–24)

Jesus foretells Peter's death. One day he will 'stretch out' his hands and be led where he doesn't want to go. This is a way of describing crucifixion. In some thirty years' time, Peter will be crucified, probably in Rome in the time of the emperor Nero. Jesus doesn't disguise this from Peter, but encourages him to know that this road of suffering will give glory to God. He repeats his first call to Peter, which is for ever new: 'Follow me!'

Seeing John following them, Peter asks what is to become of him. Jesus says that John may or may not stay alive until his return. Either way, it is no concern of Peter. Peter is to follow Jesus, regardless of the pressure, rumours or opinions of others. We know that John lived to a great age in Ephesus, and can guess that people linked his long life with the hope of Jesus' return.

As John comes to the end of his Gospel, he says that the 'disciple whom Jesus loved' is the one who followed Jesus and Peter as they walked along the beach that morning. It is he who has been an eyewitness of Jesus' ministry and resurrection, and he or his followers have now written this book. He asserts that what he says is true.

The great and untold story
(21:25)

There is so much more that could be said about Jesus, but if it was all written down, the world would be too small to contain it. Jesus is, after all, the Word and wisdom of God, his agent of creation and only Son. How can one small planet ever contain the whole story of his endless glory and eternity?

ACTS

The book of Acts is really part two of the Gospel of Luke. It is written by the same author, and tells us what happened in the early years of the church.

Although the book is called the 'Acts of the Apostles', Luke tells us only of *some* apostles – mainly Peter and Paul. He begins by describing the life of the church in Jerusalem, where Peter is the leading character. Then he tells us how persecution drives the followers of Jesus out of Jerusalem, so that the good news is spread to other places. Finally, he tells us about the conversion of Paul and his missionary journeys.

By the end of his book, Luke has shown us how the gospel of Jesus Christ has travelled from Jerusalem to Rome – from the religious capital of the Jews to the secular capital of the Roman empire. Jesus promises his followers that they will spread the good news about him 'in Jerusalem, in all Judea and Samaria, and to the ends of the earth' (1:8).

Outline

INTRODUCTION

In the Acts of the Apostles Luke shows us how Christianity becomes established in Jerusalem, and how the faith then spreads to other people and cultures. God himself drives and directs this work, through his Holy Spirit.

The first Christians meet opposition from the same Jewish leaders who had executed Jesus. Peter and John are arrested more than once. Stephen is put on trial and stoned to death. The apostles are always at odds with the Jewish Council, because the apostles insist on preaching the gospel.

As the Christian missionaries travel, they are sometimes arrested and punished. In Philippi, Paul and Silas are imprisoned for freeing a young girl from an evil spirit. In Ephesus, Paul's success with the gospel threatens the local trade in idols and magic charms. In both Ephesus and Jerusalem, Paul is at the centre of a full-scale riot.

Throughout his story, Luke is careful to point out that Christianity is the fulfilment of the Jewish faith. The young church is not a threat to Roman authority. When Paul is put on trial in front of Roman magistrates, they find nothing wrong with his life and teaching.

The 'Acts of the Holy Spirit'

The Acts of the Apostles could almost be called the 'Acts of the Holy Spirit'. It is the Holy Spirit who inspires the apostles and their followers, and enables them to speak other languages, praise and pray in 'tongues', prophesy the word of God and preach in a variety of situations. The Holy Spirit is none other than the Spirit of Jesus, enabling his friends to continue his work.

Peter and Paul

Jesus has promised his disciples that they will do the same work as he has been doing (John 14:12). Luke shows how this promise comes true. The activities of the first Christians reflect the ministry of Jesus.

Peter and Paul confront the power of Satan. They win battles over deceit, disease and demon possession. The first Christians also take care of people in need, and organize themselves to share their possessions and protect the weak.

The book of Acts shows us a lively, practical, persecuted church. The first Christians are not perfect, but they are enterprising and full of faith. We see how the Holy Spirit (the Spirit of Jesus) changes people's lives and enables the church to live together as a strong and caring group. The Spirit of Jesus guides the church's mission, and confirms new converts with his gifts.

At first because of persecution, and then through mission, the gospel spreads outside Jewish areas. Soon the good news is being preached in Samaria, Asia Minor and Europe. Both Peter and Paul are involved, as Christianity seems to be rejected by Jews but welcomed by Gentiles. There is a major problem over whether people have to become Jews before they become Christians. This is thoroughly debated by the church's leaders in Jerusalem. They give simple guidelines for non-Jews (Gentiles) who have become Christians.

Luke is a careful historian, and many of his facts can be checked. But his main aim is to tell us what is going on spiritually. God is spreading his kingdom in the lives of men and women through the good news of Jesus Christ. This comes across most clearly in the story of the Day of Pentecost. The Holy Spirit is poured out on the apostles – a blessing which is repeated at each major stage of the church's growth. There is also no need for division or party spirit in the young church. Peter and Paul, and Jews and Gentiles, are all on the same side in this great new work of God.

Luke repeats episodes which are very important. He tells the story of Saul's conversion three times, and the conversion of Cornelius twice. He also gives us the outlines of sermons preached by Peter and Paul. Most of all, Luke shows how the gospel breaks through barriers of culture and race, to reach despised Samaritans, an Ethiopian official, a Roman centurion, an Asian businesswoman, a Philippian jailer and many others.

Luke's book is the main account we have of the

Christian mission in the years between the ascension of Jesus (around AD 27) and AD 60.

What about us?

As we read about the first Christians, we are bound to wonder whether we should be the same. Should we all share our possessions, be baptized in the Holy Spirit and speak in 'tongues'?

Paul tells us that these things are done and experienced by some people sometimes. The Holy Spirit is God's gift to all Christians, but it is not compulsory to speak in other languages or have visions to prove that he lives in us. We are each unique, and God will give us the gifts and experiences of his choice (1 Corinthians 12:4–11).

Luke tells us the message Peter preached on the Day of Pentecost. He gave a ringing call to turn from sin, and a profound promise that God would come and live in our lives by his Spirit. The practical and public step we are to take is to be baptized!

Repent and be baptised every one of you, in the name of Jesus Christ for the forgiveness of your sins. And you will receive the gift of the Holy Spirit (Acts 2:38).

DISCOVERING THE ACTS OF THE APOSTLES

Early days in Jerusalem

Introduction
(1:1–2)

Luke sets out to tell the story of 'what Jesus did next'. As with his Gospel, he again writes for 'Theophilus'. Theophilus is a distinguished Roman who is either a committed Christian or interested to learn more about Christianity. His name means 'Friend of God'.

Luke is the only non-Jewish writer in the New Testament. His two books (the Gospel of Luke and the Acts of the Apostles) provide a quarter of its contents. He writes as a personal friend of Paul – having joined him at Troas on the journey which took them to Europe and Philippi.

Jesus is taken up into heaven
(1:3–11)

After Jesus is raised from death, he appears to his disciples. He proves to them that he is alive, and shows them how the Old Testament scriptures point to him – in the Law, the history books, the Psalms and the Prophets.

Jesus particularly urges his disciples to wait in Jerusalem until God the Father sends them his Holy Spirit. They won't have the grace or power to preach the gospel unless they are first plunged into the Holy Spirit, just as John the Baptist used to plunge people into water.

They must wait – prayerful and ready – for the Holy Spirit. Once they have received the Spirit they will be able to preach the Gospel not only in Jerusalem, but in the rest of Judea, among their old enemies the

---

Events in the life of Jesus following his death. Illustrations include the burial, the appearance of the angels at the empty tomb, Jesus teaching two disciples on the road to Emmaus and his appearances to the disciples in the upper room, and by the Sea of Galilee. The larger pictures at the bottom centre and bottom right illustrate the ascension of Jesus and the outpouring of the Holy Spirit on his disciples at the Feast of Pentecost. From a manuscript (c. 1140) now held at Christ Church, Canterbury.

Samaritans and to the whole world.

The disciples still misunderstand 'the kingdom of God'. They still expect Jesus to declare himself as a military leader who will defeat the Romans and restore the kingdom of Israel. For Jesus, the kingdom of God isn't a little political state of Israel, but a worldwide spiritual realm. It is everyone who welcomes his gospel. This is the gospel the apostles are to go out and preach. One day this kingdom will be complete, and Jesus will return – but only God the Father knows when that day will be.

THE ASCENSION

Forty days after his resurrection, Jesus finally leaves his disciples. He leads them to the Mount of Olives, less than a mile outside Jerusalem. There, says Luke, 'he was taken up before their very eyes, and a cloud hid him from their sight'.

All the New Testament writers know that Jesus ascended to heaven, but it is only Luke who describes it happening. He says Jesus went 'up into the sky' (1:10) – an event as miraculous and unique as the resurrection.

The resurrection and ascension are two parts of the same act by which God the Father raises Jesus to his place in glory. The important idea is not that Jesus 'lifted off' like a space rocket, but that he was received into the glorious presence of God.

As they look, 'two men dressed in white' stand beside them. They are angels. They tell the disciples that one day Jesus will come back – 'in the same way you have seen him go into heaven' (1:11). 'In the same way' means that one day Jesus will return personally and publicly. We know from his own teaching there will be no mistaking his coming. It will be like lightning – sudden, glorious and unmissable.

A replacement for Judas
(1:12–26)

Returning to Jerusalem, the eleven apostles spend much time praying together. Mary, Jesus' mother, is with them, and so are his brothers. This comes as a surprise. When Jesus' brothers were mentioned in the Gospels, they had no faith in Jesus and were trying to restrain his madness (Mark 3:21). Now they are convinced he is the Messiah, and will become key members of his church. James becomes the leader of the church in Jerusalem. Both James and Jude have letters included in the New Testament.

Peter takes the lead in appointing a successor for Judas, the disciple who betrayed Jesus and committed suicide. Peter finds guidance in passages from the Psalms. The Old Testament is now a new and exciting reference book for the apostles. Peter advises that the new apostle should be someone who has been with them throughout the public ministry of Jesus and witnessed his resurrection.

The apostles are all people who have seen Jesus with their own eyes. Only Paul will be added to their number. He will have a unique encounter with the risen Christ.

The disciples shortlist two men and then pray over the final choice. They make the decision by 'casting lots' – letting God have the last word. Although 'casting lots' was a practice used by the Jewish priests, it is not normally used by Christians. This is because we believe the Holy Spirit can give us wisdom, when we humbly seek God's mind together.

So Matthias is added to the core group of twelve apostles. We don't know anything else about him from the Bible. Some people think that Paul was really the twelfth apostle, called by Christ himself on the road to Damascus.

The Holy Spirit comes at Pentecost
(2:1–13)

Pentecost is a harvest festival which falls fifty days after Passover. It is the busiest Jewish feast because it falls in May when travel is easy. Jews travel to Jerusalem from all

---

The ascension of Jesus

When Luke describes the ascension of Jesus, he says, 'he was taken up before their very eyes, and a cloud hid him from their sight' (1:9).

We don't have to think of Jesus going up like a rocket. He 'goes up' as he is received into the high and holy presence of God. He is returning to the home from which he originally 'came down to earth from heaven'.

Luke says that 'a cloud hid him from their sight'. In the Old Testament, the cloud of God's presence and glory surrounded the tent of meeting in the wilderness (Exodus 40:34). In his Gospel, Luke describes how a bright cloud enveloped Jesus when he met with Moses and Elijah on the Mount of Transfiguration (Luke 9:34–35).

The cloud acts as a shield between God and human beings. It is a sign of his presence. The angels tell the disciples that it is in this cloud of glory that Jesus will one day return.

The Feast of Pentecost

Pentecost is the second of the three harvest festivals which the Jews celebrate each year. It is sometimes called the Feast of Weeks, because it falls seven weeks after Passover. At Passover the grain harvesting begins. At Pentecost the first barley loaves are offered in harvest thanksgiving.

Speaking in other tongues

Luke says that the disciples are speaking in languages they have never learned. People from all over the world are hearing God praised in their native tongue. A new, multiracial, multicultural church is being born.

There are other places in the New Testament where we read of people praying or praising God in tongues. They are speaking praises that rise beyond the limits of words.

Paul teaches that 'tongues' are mainly for the benefit of the person who is praying. If what is said is a message for the church, then it must be interpreted (1 Corinthians 14:13). We don't know whether 'tongues' of prayer and praise and prophecy are always known languages, as they were on the Day of Pentecost. The same word for 'tongues' is used in describing both kinds of event.

the countries around the Mediterranean, swelling the city's population by 130,000 people. They offer the first loaves of the barley harvest, and thank God for feeding them with his law. The law was given to them on Mount Sinai, fifty days after the Hebrew slaves escaped from Egypt.

At this particular Pentecost, at nine o'clock on a May morning, probably in AD 27, God pours out his Holy Spirit on the apostles of Jesus.

The apostles are meeting together. The place is large and public, for they are joined by many hundreds of others. They are probably in one of the temple courts.

Suddenly they hear a powerful gale, like the mighty desert wind. This wind is a symbol of the great gale of God's Spirit pouring out upon them. They are swept by fire from heaven – the flames licking each head. These flames are the warming, purging furnace of God. The disciples of Jesus are inspired and purified by the Holy Spirit of God. From this day they will be burning people – alight with the love of Christ and on fire with his love for the world.

Suddenly the apostles start to speak in other tongues – languages from all over the known world. In the old days, when the tower of Babel fell, the languages of the world were confused. Now that tragedy is reversed. Soon a huge crowd gathers around the apostles – everyone hearing God praised in their own language from back home!

Luke tells us there are people from Asia, Greece, North Africa and Rome – all the places where Jews have been scattered by the winds of misfortune, or the tides of trade. Now they stand together again, united in amazement at this great event. Some think the disciples are babbling because they've been drinking the cheap harvest wine. But Peter stands up and calls for silence. He explains that they're not at all drunk – it's far too early in the day for that!

Suddenly the Spirit's here!

At Pentecost, God gives the apostles the power they need for their mission.

Jesus had promised that he would ask God his Father to send his own Spirit. This is the Holy Spirit, who will remind them of Jesus' teaching and show them his truth in every situation (John 14–16).

In Old Testament times the Holy Spirit was given to only a very few

people. Judges, kings and prophets were inspired for special tasks. But most people could never know the power and presence of God within them. God and his law were always 'outside' them. Now all that is changing. This is the dawning of the age of the Spirit!

The prophets Jeremiah and Ezekiel had promised that one day God's people would be given 'new hearts'. They would be able to love and serve God,

not as an unnatural effort, but as a ready joy. Joel, too, had foretold that God's Spirit would be poured out on all people one day.

Peter's first sermon
(2:14–41)

Peter stands up to speak. He explains that they aren't drunk. It is the Holy Spirit of God who is enabling them to babble in this way! He reminds his hearers of Joel's prophecy (Joel 2:28–29).

Joel promised that one day God would pour out his Spirit, freely and without limit. Men and women, young and old, will be caught up in the life of God – having visions of his kingdom and speaking his word.

This outpouring of the Spirit is happening now, before their very eyes.

Peter tells the crowd that Jesus of Nazareth has been raised to life! The miracle-worker whom they all heard about, and many of them saw, was crucified less than two months ago outside this very city. But God raised him from death. Jesus is in fact the Messiah, the Son of God.

Peter quotes from Psalm 16. There David speaks of a holy One who will not die and rot, but be raised to life with God. This is what has happened to Jesus. He is the true successor to David's throne.

The people are horrified at what has happened – and appalled at their own part in it. Many of them were in the crowd that yelled for Jesus' blood. He was the longed-for Messiah – and they crucified him! They earnestly ask Peter what they can do to get right with God again.

Peter calls them to repent and be baptized. They must stop rebelling against God and become followers of Jesus. Their sins will be forgiven, and they and their families will have God's promise of new life. His words meet with a wonderful response, as about 3,000 people join the church that day.

The fellowship of the believers
(2:42–47)

Luke gives us a glimpse of the everyday life of the first Christians. They enjoy a wonderful unity, as they learn

Should Christians act communally?

The first Christians shared everything, including their belongings. Looking at them, we wonder if we should do the same: sell our possessions and live in a community. Jesus told the rich young man to sell all he had and give the money to the poor (Luke 18:22). And many Christian monks and nuns have no personal possessions, but share a simple life together.

Luke shows that the first Christians aren't forced to sell, give away or share their possessions. They have their own homes, and are free to do what they like with their wealth. What's new is that Christ is setting them free from selfishness and greed. He is opening their hearts to be generous with each other and to the poor. After all, everything comes from God.

together from the apostles and share their meals and times of prayer.

God is with them! His presence overflows in the miracles of the apostles and the love of the church members. The church grows, because this way of life is so genuine and attractive.

Peter heals the crippled beggar
(3:1 – 4:4)

One day, Peter and John encounter a lame man. He sits begging at one of the entrances to the temple. Although he asks them for money, they give him something far better. They heal him in the name of Jesus Christ of Nazareth.

When a crowd gathers, Peter explains how the man has been healed. It is through the power of Jesus Christ that this cripple is now bounding around. As with his first sermon, Peter calls on his hearers to repent and change their minds about the Christ. Jesus is alive! He is in heaven and will one day return. The temple guard arrives to arrest Peter and John. They must stop this dangerous story that the Jewish leaders have murdered an innocent man. But Peter's sermon has a powerful effect. Two thousand people join the company of believers that day.

Peter and John on trial
(4:5–22)

Peter and John are arrested and brought before the Jewish Council. These are the same people who found Jesus guilty of blasphemy.

Jesus warned his disciples that they would be brought before councils, and promised that the Holy Spirit would teach them what to say. It is with faith rather than fear that Peter now speaks. He is courteous and clear. He points out that they are on trial for being kind – for healing a person! But, of course, it is because they have healed in the name of Jesus that they are under arrest. Peter tells the Council that they killed Jesus, but God has raised him from death. The healing of the man is proof that they were wrong. They think they have disposed of Jesus – like a rejected building block – but he is the keystone of all life, the creator and Saviour of the world.

Peter and John are not educated or eloquent, but their evidence is conclusive. Before the court stand two brave apostles and one healed man. The Council decides to release the apostles but ban them from preaching. Peter says they will continue to preach, because their call comes from God himself.

Prayer in the face of persecution
(4:23–31)

When the believers are all together, they pray. Their little suffering is part of God's mighty plan. Herod, Pontius Pilate and the Jewish Council may do their worst, but God is still in control. They pray that they may continue to speak with boldness and heal with power, in the name of Jesus.

Crowds of devout Jews praying at the Western Wall of the temple site, as they gather for a religious festival.

Ananias and Sapphira

(4:32 – 5:11)

The believers continue to share their possessions and care for the poor. Some of them sell houses or fields and bring the money to the apostles.

The church has many people to support because of the pilgrims who stayed on in Jerusalem after Pentecost. Also, some believers have lost their jobs or have been rejected by their families because they have become Christians. A huge donation comes from Joseph Barnabas, who sells a field and gives the money to God's work.

A married couple, Ananias and Sapphira, feel that they, like Barnabas, must make an impressive sacrifice. They sell some property and pretend to give the whole amount to the apostles – but secretly they keep part of the money for themselves. When Peter challenges Ananias about this deceit, the wretched man drops dead. So does his wife. Their sin is a terrible blow to the church, which has lived with such openness and honesty until now.

The fate of Ananias and Sapphira reminds us of Achan. After the battle of Jericho he kept some of the plunder and hid it under the ground beneath his tent. His deceit brought defeat on the whole people of God – and resulted in the deaths of himself and his family (Joshua 7).

Is the punishment of Ananias and Sapphira too severe? Hypocrisy (pretending to be better than we are) is the most dangerous spiritual virus which can attack the church. Peter is in no doubt that it must be confronted and purged.

The apostles heal many people

(5:12–16)

The apostles are alive with the power of God. If we were stunned by the judgment of Ananias and Sapphira, now we are amazed at the healing of diseases and the deliverance from evil spirits that the apostles are able to accomplish.

The believers are now meeting in the eastern cloister of the temple, Solomon's Colonnade. They are a distinct group, and people have to decide whether they will join or not. Even so, some people seek healing from Peter's passing shadow – much as a woman once reached out to touch the edge of Jesus' robe (Luke 8:44).

The apostles are persecuted

(5:17–42)

The apostles (not just Peter and John) are arrested and imprisoned – but the Lord releases them! While the authorities are busy checking the locks and changing the guard, their prisoners are already back in the temple preaching! John the Baptist would have loved to live in these days.

The Jewish leaders are jealous. Peter and his companions refuse to be silenced, and are unaffected by official disapproval or public popularity. They have the complete independence which comes from doing God's will. 'We must obey God rather than any human authority' (5:29) is their simple rule.

As the Jewish Council, the Sanhedrin, cross-questions the apostles, we realize that it is the authorities who are on trial. There is a rising tide of public opinion which now blames them for the death of Jesus. As Peter drives the point home ('You had him killed by hanging him on a tree!'), the councillors are cut to the quick. They are on the very brink of having the apostles executed. But wise Gamaliel advises them to wait and see.

Gamaliel is a Pharisee. As such he is more spiritual and tolerant than the shrewd, political Sadducees. Gamaliel was taught by his famous grandfather, Rabbi Hillel, and is in turn the teacher of Saul of Tarsus, who will become the apostle Paul.

Gamaliel reminds the Council that there have been many popular movements and revolts which have claimed to be from God. He casts his mind back over a quarter of a century to recall two rebels in particular: Theudas and Judas the Galilean. Both had widespread support and some brief success, but in the end they were both killed and their followers dispersed. Gamaliel's advice is to leave the disciples of Jesus well alone, and let time and events prove them right or wrong.

Gamaliel's advice is wise. The apostles are cruelly flogged, but then released. As so often happens, the persecution seems to strengthen them and make them all the more joyful and determined. As a famous church father, Tertullian, puts it, 'The more you mow us down, the more we grow!'

The choosing of the seven assistants

(6:1–7)

Luke is holding two sides of the church's story together. He tells us of the pressures which come from outside – the trials and imprisonments of the apostles because of persecution by the Jewish authorities. He also tells us of the difficulties which arise within the church, as they experience the upheaval of growing numbers and tackle the problems of discipline and organization.

The 'inside' story now is of a crisis over the care of widows.

The Jews are used to caring for widows, orphans and others in need. The synagogues organize a weekly collection (called 'the basket') and a daily collection (called 'the tray'). These collections provide ongoing support for widows and orphans (two meals a day) as well as immediate help in case of emergency.

The new community of the church is also caring for its widows. Some are local, from the Aramaic-speaking Jews of Jerusalem and Palestine. Others are 'Grecian Jews' from the Hellenic or Greek culture. Perhaps they had come to Jerusalem for Pentecost – and stayed! Now, sadly, there is some ill feeling between the two groups. The local widows are being favoured and the foreign widows neglected.

The apostles handle this situation well. They call a meeting, so that the problem may be shared. They make clear that their own priority must be to preach and teach the gospel. But the care of the widows is just as much a part of the church's work. It should be delegated to Spirit-filled people – and seven is an ideal number! Although the Seven are not actually called 'deacons', they are carrying out the tasks which will be linked with deacons in the future.

It is a brilliant solution. The community chooses its assistants and the apostles commission them by praying for them and placing their hands on their heads. All the assistants have Greek names. Perhaps the people who first raised the problem have now become the answer. Among them are Stephen and Philip. Stephen will become the first Christian martyr. Philip will become an effective evangelist. But their first duty is to wait at tables.

The trial and death of Stephen
(6:8 – 7:53)

Stephen is an exceptional Christian man. He is one of the Seven who cares for the widows. He is also an outstanding preacher and teacher. His teaching offends the Jews from the Synagogue of the Freedmen (ex-slaves), whose members come from various countries outside Palestine.

The Freedmen can't disprove Stephen's teaching, so they accuse him of blasphemy. He is preaching that the temple will be destroyed and the law of Moses will be abolished.

In fact Stephen is teaching that Jesus has fulfilled the law of Moses. Jesus has lived the perfect life, and offered himself as a sacrifice for sinners. The death sentence of the law has been met and removed by the sacrifice of Jesus on the cross. As Jesus himself said, he did not come to abolish the law but to fulfil it (Matthew 5:17).

Stephen is also preaching that the temple and its priests are redundant. There is no longer any need to sacrifice animals, because Jesus has himself been the perfect sacrifice. There is no longer any need to make pilgrimages, because God meets his people in their hearts by faith. The true meeting place of God and people is not the temple, but Jesus Christ.

As the members of the Council cross-question Stephen, they see that his face is alight with the glory of God. This is the light that shone in Moses' face when he first received the Ten Commandments (Exodus 34:29).

STEPHEN'S SPEECH TO THE JEWISH COUNCIL

To explain his faith in Jesus, Stephen reviews the history of God's people (7:1–53). His hearers know the Old Testament story well, but Stephen has something new to show them.

'Destroy this temple, and I will build it again in three days'

When Jesus was put on trial, the witnesses said he claimed he could destroy the temple and rebuild it. John explains that Jesus was referring to the temple of his body (John 2:19). He would be killed but would rise again on the third day. But the same old lie lingers on, and appears again in the trial of Stephen – that the followers of Jesus are campaigning to destroy the temple.

The New Testament teaches that the temple in Jerusalem is replaced by Christ and his church. 'Do you not know that your body is a temple of the Holy Spirit?' writes Paul to the Christians at Corinth (1 Corinthians 6:19). And Peter writes, 'You are like living stones, being built into a spiritual house to be a royal priesthood, offering spiritual sacrifices acceptable to God through Jesus Christ' (1 Peter 2:5).

He reminds the Council of four heroes of faith: Abraham who never owned any land; Joseph who was exiled in Egypt; Moses who wandered the wilderness; and David who planned the temple. Gradually, Stephen's point becomes clear. God isn't restricted to any place or building. He is a pilgrim God who lives with his people – wherever they are.

The temple is a meeting place for God and human beings. But now it is replaced by Jesus the Messiah. But the Jewish leaders have killed him! They claim to uphold the law, but they break it. They claim to serve God, but they persecute his prophets.

The Jewish leaders are enraged by Stephen's words. They rush on him and drag him out of the city to be stoned to death. But Stephen is focused on heaven, where he sees Jesus standing to welcome him home.

Like Jesus, Stephen faces death with prayer. Jesus had prayed to God the Father, but Stephen prays to Jesus. He commits his spirit to his care, and asks him to forgive his murderers.

Stephen is the first Christian martyr – the first believer to pay for his faith with his life.

As Stephen dies, a young man guards the coats of the executioners. This is Saul, who will become the apostle Paul.

The church is persecuted – and spreads

The church is persecuted and scattered
(8:1–3)

There follows a violent attack on the church in Jerusalem. The general wonder and goodwill is swept aside by cruel persecution. Saul is at the centre of this campaign to stamp out the followers of Christ.

But there is an unexpected benefit. As the believers flee, they take the gospel to other places. Luke tells us how the good news is received in Samaria – and spreads to North Africa.

Philip and the apostles in Samaria
(8:4–25)

Philip is one of the Seven who was appointed to care for Greek-speaking widows in Jerusalem. He is a gifted evangelist. When persecution drives him from Jerusalem, he travels to Samaria.

The Samaritans are traditional enemies of the Jews – but the gospel breaks down the wall of hatred between them. Philip shares the gospel in word and deed. People are freed from evil spirits, cripples are healed and there is a great joy in God's salvation.

SIMON THE SORCERER

A famous magician, called Simon, realizes Philip has a power far greater than his own. When the apostles arrive from Jerusalem, Simon tries to buy the Holy Spirit from them. Peter rebukes him. The power of Christ is not to be used for magic or money.

The word 'simony' comes from this episode. It means 'trying to buy spiritual powers (or influence) in the church by paying money'.

THE APOSTLES VISIT SAMARIA

Although the new Samaritan believers are baptized into the name of Christ, they do not receive the Holy Spirit until the apostles come from Jerusalem. Peter and John are able to see for themselves what God is doing among the Samaritans. These are the people whom James and John had once wanted to wipe out with fire from heaven (Luke 9:54). Now the apostles confirm the Samaritans' faith by laying hands on them. It is then that the Samaritans receive the Holy Spirit.

The link with Jerusalem is very important. The Samaritan believers are not to become a separate Samaritan church. There is only one church of Christ, which embraces people from every nation.

Philip and the Ethiopian
(8:26–40)

Suddenly Philip is directed to the desert road which runs some sixty miles from Jerusalem to Gaza. Gaza is an old Philistine city near the coast, and this is the main road from Jerusalem to Egypt and Africa.

Travelling along the road is a distinguished African. He is the chancellor, or treasurer, to the Candace, the queen mother of Ethiopia. This man is almost certainly a black Ethiopian, and may also be a Jew. He is returning from a pilgrimage to Jerusalem, sitting in his chariot and reading from a scroll of Isaiah's prophecy.

Philip offers to help him understand the scriptures. Together they read about the suffering servant of God, from Isaiah 53. Jesus has taught his disciples that this prophecy refers to himself. Jesus is the servant of God who goes defenceless and humiliated to his death. He is cut off from life on earth, without any descendants to continue his name.

The words of Isaiah have a powerful message for the Ethiopian. Like other men in royal service, he is a eunuch. He has been mutilated to control his behaviour and, as a result, he will never have children. When he goes to Jerusalem, the law bans him from entering the temple courts (Deuteronomy 23:1). Now he reads about someone who was humiliated and cut off, who was none other than the Messiah himself!

The Ethiopian asks to be baptized – which Philip readily agrees to do. The Ethiopian then continues on his journey with great joy. To this day there is a lively and faithful Christian church in Ethiopia.

Philip goes next to Azotus (the Philistine city of Ashdod) and then travels north along the coast to Caesarea. It is at Caesarea that he settles down and will one day (twenty years later) tell his story to Luke.

The conversion of Saul

(9:1–19)

Saul is like a raging bull. Since we first met him, guarding the coats of the people executing Stephen, he has made every effort to crush the church. Now, with warrants of arrest from the high priest, he takes his anti-Christian campaign to Damascus.

Damascus is about 150 miles from Jerusalem, and outside Jewish territory. The journey takes several days – even with Saul striding ahead in his haste. Suddenly he is blinded by a light from heaven – the light of the glory of Christ.

Thrown to the ground, Saul finds himself being questioned by a person he thought was dead. It is Jesus the Christ, whose followers he is persecuting. In a single life-turning moment, Saul realizes that Jesus is the Messiah, and that he lives and suffers with his church.

This is the most famous conversion in history. The church's fiercest enemy is about to become its most gifted and energetic champion. Saul the persecutor will become Paul the apostle. The event is so astonishing that Luke will tell the story three times in this book – once in his own words and twice in Paul's.

Saul, who set out for Damascus as a proud inquisitor, is now led by the hand into the city. There God brings help and healing through Ananias – a Christian whom Saul would have thrown into prison. Now they are brothers in Christ.

Ananias is the first to know of God's call to Saul to be

an apostle and missionary. He has the privilege of seeing Saul healed, filled with the Holy Spirit and baptized.

Saul in Damascus and Jerusalem

(9:19–31)

Saul's turnabout is complete. Soon he is preaching in the synagogues the very message he had come to suppress.

Paul tells us himself (in his letter to the Galatians) that he now spends three years in Arabia. The Arabian border is quite near Damascus. Luke merely touches on this period by his mention of 'many days' (9:23).

Paul needs time to adjust. He has to rethink everything he has ever learned. Stephen was right! Jesus is the Christ!

We know from Paul's sermons and letters that it is an enormous task to think it all through. He now realizes that all the scriptures (our Old Testament) point to Jesus. The death of Jesus was the perfect sacrifice for the sins of the whole world. The church is the body of Christ, and the way to peace with God is not by keeping his law but by receiving his grace. God's people are not exclusively the Jews, but the worldwide company of Christians – both Jews and Gentiles.

When the time comes for Saul to leave Damascus, he has to avoid the hostile Jews by hiding in a laundry basket!

Back in Jerusalem, the Christians are terrified of Saul. Only Joseph Barnabas (the 'Son of Encouragement') stands with him and confirms his story. Barnabas always believes the best about people (15:37–39).

Saul has been a leading Pharisee and a student of Rabbi Gamaliel. He now brings his fine intellect and education to the task of preaching the gospel. Soon he is in ferocious debate with the Greek-speaking Jews – the same group who opposed Stephen – and very nearly meets the same death. Believing that Saul is more use alive than dead, his fellow Christians send him home to Tarsus.

The acts of Peter

(9:32 – 12:24)

Luke now tells us some of the highlights of Peter's ministry at this time. He heals a paralysed man and raises a dead woman to life. He is the key figure in the conversion of the first Gentile, a Roman centurion named Cornelius. And he has a dramatic escape from prison!

AENEAS AND DORCAS

The believers have been driven from Jerusalem by persecution. Now that there is a period of peace, Peter travels around visiting them. Luke tells of two particular incidents, in Lydda (which today is the site of Lod airport) and Joppa (the modern port of Jaffa) (9:32–43).

At Lydda, Peter heals a paralysed man named Aeneas. At Joppa he raises a dead woman to life. Her name in Aramaic is Tabitha, and in Greek, Dorcas. It means 'Gazelle'.

The way Peter performs these miracles reminds us of Jesus at work. When he tells Aeneas to 'Get up and tidy up your mat,' we flash back to Jesus healing the paralysed man who was lowered through the roof (Luke 5:24). When Peter clears the room of mourners and says, 'Tabitha, get up,' we are reminded of Jesus raising Jairus' daughter from death (Luke 8:54).

Jesus promised that anyone with faith in him would do the same work as he had been doing (John 14:12). It is in the name of Jesus, and to the glory of Jesus, that Peter heals and raises to life. This is a resurrection ministry. To both Aeneas and Tabitha, Peter says, 'Get up!'

THE CONVERSION OF CORNELIUS

Luke has already told us of two momentous conversions – the Ethiopian official and the persecutor, Saul. Now he tells us how the first Gentile was converted – a Roman soldier called Cornelius (10:1 – 11:18). The story rests on Peter managing to change his mind about Gentiles!

Cornelius and Peter's vision

Cornelius is a Roman centurion, with command of 100 soldiers. He is stationed at Caesarea. He is what the Jews call a 'God-fearer'. He believes in God, prays regularly and tries to live a good and generous life. One day, as he prays, an angel tells him to send for Peter.

Peter is in Joppa, staying with Simon the tanner. Tanners are often outcasts from Jewish religion, because their daily contact with the carcasses of dead animals makes them ritually unclean. But Peter is staying in his house, which hints that he is less fussy than he used to be.

As Peter prays on the flat roof of the house, he starts to think about lunch. Perhaps the awning that shades him

A Roman centurion. Jews regard Gentiles as 'unclean' spiritually, and avoid contact with them. The apostle Peter shares this belief, until a heavenly vision and an invitation to visit Cornelius, a Roman centurion, oblige him to change his mind.

from the sun becomes a sheet lowered from heaven. With horror, he sees that it is full of 'unclean' animals – creatures which the Jewish law forbids him to eat. But, as he looks, a voice challenges the habit of a lifetime: 'Get up, Peter. Kill and eat.'

The vision is repeated twice more – and each time with the same message: 'Do not call something dirty that God has made clean!' As Peter thinks this over, the messengers from Cornelius arrive at the gate.

Peter has been brought up to treat certain foods as 'unclean'. The Jewish law forbids him to eat certain animals – those that chew the cud, those with cloven hooves, reptiles and some birds. It is the same with certain people. He mustn't mix with Gentiles. They, too, are 'unclean'. He mustn't enter their homes or share their food. But now, through visions and visitors, he is invited to change his mind.

Peter goes with the messengers to the house of Cornelius in Caesarea. There he crosses the threshold into the Gentile world. It is one small step for a man, but a giant leap for the gospel.

Peter at Cornelius' house

This whole adventure is a miracle of timing. Luke shows how God guides both Cornelius and Peter (10:23–48). Through them, the gospel breaks down one of the greatest barriers of the day – the prejudice and racial hatred between Jews and Gentiles. As a result of his experience, Peter realizes a tremendous truth: 'God has no favourites!' (10:34).

Peter speaks to Cornelius and his family and friends. As with his sermon at Pentecost, he begins with the present situation. They are living in a moment of miracle. God is accepting all people who honour him, regardless of nation or status.

Peter tells them about Jesus – his powerful life and terrible death. He tells how God raised Jesus and made him judge of all. It is through Jesus that people can be forgiven their sins. This is the greatest relief and release to Cornelius, who has tried so hard to get right with God.

As Peter speaks, the Holy Spirit comes upon

Joppa

It was in Joppa that the prophet Jonah found a ship sailing for Tarshish (Spain) – and boarded it to escape God's call to preach to pagan Nineveh. Now, from this same port, Peter is called to share the gospel with Gentiles. He obeys, 'without raising any objection' (10:29).

everyone listening. The Roman house, so alien to the Jews, is filled with the sound of Gentiles praising God in strange languages – just as the apostles had done on the Day of Pentecost. Peter doesn't hesitate. He baptizes them all.

The Jews ('the circumcised') who have come with Peter are amazed to see God's holiness embracing Gentiles ('the uncircumcised'). The Jews have enjoyed a special relationship with God, but have missed their call to mission. God called Abraham to bless all the nations of the world (Genesis 12:1–3), but his descendants have behaved like a superior and exclusive sect.

Peter explains his actions

When Peter returns to Jerusalem he is criticized and cross-questioned (11:1–18). The Jewish Christians are used to avoiding Gentiles and calling them 'dogs'. If Gentiles are to become Christians, then surely they must first become Jews. They must be circumcised and learn the law. They must eat Jewish food and keep Jewish festivals.

To answer his critics, Peter tells his story – from his prayer in Joppa to the Pentecost in Caesarea. It is all so clearly the work of God. Surely this is what John the Baptist had meant by 'baptism with the Holy Spirit'...

To their credit, the critics agree. They join Peter in praising God for this amazing breakthrough – that Jesus is for Gentiles as well as Jews.

THE CHURCH IN ANTIOCH

Luke now tells us of the spread of Christianity to the north and west of Judea. Scattered by the persecution which followed the death of Stephen, the believers travel to Phoenicia (now Lebanon), Cyprus and Antioch (11:19–30). Being Jews themselves, they share the gospel with Jews. But in Antioch, some Christians from Cyprus and Cyrene (North Africa) start to share the gospel with Greeks.

The church at Jerusalem sends Barnabas to visit the believers in Antioch. His goodness and encouragement lead to a further growth in the number of believers.

Barnabas realizes that these converts need sound teaching, and he knows the very person to do it. He goes to Tarsus and recruits – Saul!

For the first time we meet Christian prophets in the young church. They speak straight from God – sometimes acting their message in some way.

A prophet named Agabus predicts that there will be famine throughout the Roman empire. For centuries the Romans have over-farmed their land, and dustbowls are starting to develop. North Africa was once the fertile 'breadbasket' which produced grain for the Roman world. We know it now as the Sahara Desert.

The Christians of Antioch realize that their fellow believers in Jerusalem are very poor. They send Barnabas and Saul with gifts to relieve their need.

PETER'S MIRACULOUS ESCAPE FROM PRISON

In Jerusalem there is a fresh outbreak of persecution. King Herod Agrippa I decides to attack the church leaders – executing James and arresting Peter. It is Passover – the

Antioch – a springboard for mission

Antioch is the capital of the Roman province of Syria. The Jewish historian Josephus describes it as 'the third city of the empire' (the first two being Rome and Alexandria). It is a fine metropolis, founded in 300 BC by one of Alexander

the Great's generals, and built in the Greek style.

Antioch will be a springboard for Christian mission. It is a bustling, cosmopolitan centre, where many races meet and mix – not only Greeks, Jews and Romans, but people from India, Persia and the Far East. The followers of Jesus now live and share their faith

amid the hype, immorality and paganism of the real world – and they find that it works! It is here that they first get the nickname 'Christian', which means 'like Christ' (11:26).

same time of year that Jesus was arrested and crucified.

The death of James is a tragedy. Just four years after Jesus called him and his brother John from their fishing boats, he becomes the first apostle to die for his faith. John will live to a great age and die a peaceful death in Ephesus.

With Peter in prison and strongly guarded, the church prays most fervently for his release (12:1–19). Unless God rescues him, he will be given a show trial and executed. But this very night an angel sets him free! It would be convenient to say that one of the guards helped him, but Luke insists it was an angel.

When Peter knocks on John Mark's door, the Christians can hardly believe that their prayer has been answered so promptly and so completely.

HEROD'S DEATH (12:19–24)

Herod Agrippa I's grandfather was Herod the Great – the cruel tyrant who slaughtered the children of Bethlehem in an attempt to kill the baby Jesus. His uncle was Herod Antipas, who executed John the Baptist. Now this latest Herod seeks popularity by persecuting the apostles.

But Herod's time is short. He visits Tyre and Sidon to bully the people there. Posing in front of them (Josephus says, 'in a marvellous silver robe'), the crowd hail him as a god – and he dies! Luke tells us he is 'eaten by worms' – organisms which gather in the intestine and cause an agonizing death.

The chapter which began with the death of James has ended with the death of Herod. The gospel continues to spread.

The adventures of Paul

The first missionary journey
(12:25 – 14:28)

PAUL AND BARNABAS BEGIN THEIR FIRST MISSIONARY JOURNEY

When Barnabas and Saul return from their errand to Jerusalem, they have John Mark with them. He will accompany them on their first missionary journey.

The leaders of the church in Antioch are as cosmopolitan as the city itself. Barnabas is from Cyprus, Simeon (nicknamed 'Black') is from Africa and Lucius is from North Africa. Manaen was brought up with Herod Antipas, and Saul is from Tarsus in Cilicia. Barnabas we

already know for his generosity and diplomacy. Simeon may be Simon of Cyrene, who carried the crosspiece for Jesus on the way to Golgotha. Manaen apparently comes from a privileged background, having been a childhood companion to a royal prince. Saul is a pedigree Jew who has trained as a rabbi and is now awesomely committed to Christ.

As the church prays and fasts, the Holy Spirit guides them. They are to commission Barnabas and Saul for a special task. When Jesus sent out his disciples in twos, it is good to think that he paired them carefully. Barnabas and Saul are very different from each other, but with complementary gifts. Saul is active, single-minded and intellectually sharp. Barnabas is a more relaxed and accepting character, generous and affirming. They make a good team – but will fall out over John Mark.

This is the Holy Spirit's mission. Paul and Barnabas begin by crossing the sea to Cyprus, and journey through the island from east to west – about ninety miles. To begin with, they preach in synagogues, where fellow Jews will welcome them and be able to judge their message.

A leading Gentile called Sergius Paulus, who is the Roman governor of the island, hears the gospel willingly. However, he has an attendant – a sorcerer named Elymas – who proves a cunning enemy. Saul confronts Elymas in the power of the Holy Spirit, and condemns him to a period of blindness. It is at this point that Luke tells us Saul is also called Paul. Saul is a Jew by birth, but he is also a Roman citizen. As he is now travelling among Gentiles, it is natural for him to use his Roman name, which is Paul.

IN PISIDIAN ANTIOCH

Paul, Barnabas and Mark leave the island of Cyprus and cross the sea to the southern coast of Asia Minor (13:13–52). Today this is Turkey.

At Perga, which is about twelve miles inland, John Mark leaves them. Later we learn that Paul regards Mark as a coward and a deserter (15:38). Perhaps the young man is homesick – or resentful of Paul being bossy. Certainly Paul is taking over the lead from Barnabas, who is John Mark's cousin.

Paul is ill. Pamphylia, where they have landed, is hot and wet – infested with mosquitoes. Perhaps Paul has caught malaria. He and Barnabas travel north, 100 miles into and across the Taurus mountains. Here the land is higher and the air cooler. They arrive in Pisidian Antioch, the leading city of southern Galatia. In a later letter, Paul will recall his sickness, and how kind they were when he first arrived:

> *As you know, it was because of an illness that I first preached the gospel to you. Even though my illness was a trial to you, you did not treat me with contempt or scorn. Instead, you welcomed me as if I were an angel of God (Galatians 4:13–14).*

On the sabbath day, Paul and Barnabas attend the service in the synagogue. This is the quickest way to meet people of their own kind, who read the Jewish scriptures and worship the one true God. Perhaps Paul is dressed as a teacher or rabbi. He is invited to speak.

Paul preaches a sermon which is suitable for his Jewish listeners. He talks of how God chose the people of Israel, rescued them from Egypt, looked after them in the desert and gave them the land of Canaan.

God also gave his people a great king, David – a leader in tune with God. He promised to David a descendant who would be the Holy One, the immortal king, the Messiah. Now this Messiah has appeared, just as God promised. He is Jesus, the longed-for Saviour of his people.

Paul tells how the Jewish leaders had Jesus executed, but God raised him to life. He explains how Jesus is a Saviour – not a military leader defeating their enemies, but a perfect sacrifice paying for their sins.

Paul ends his sermon. He urges his hearers to receive the forgiveness that Jesus offers. Or will they laugh at this good news and reject God's saving love?

Paul's message excites great interest. Some want to hear him again, while others are hostile. On the following sabbath, the leading Jews publicly reject Paul. As a result, Paul and Barnabas resolve to take their message to the Gentiles.

The gospel of Jesus Christ is to be preached to the Jews first. Paul sees that this message must start with the Jews, but it mustn't end with them. The gospel is good news for all nations.

As Paul and Barnabas are expelled from the region, they shake its dust from their feet. This is what Jews used to do after crossing Samaria on their way from Galilee to Jerusalem. To shake the dust from your feet and clothes is to reject a place and its people (Luke 9:5). If the people want nothing to do with God, so be it. It's their choice.

IN ICONIUM

Paul and Barnabas travel on foot to Iconium, some ninety miles from Pisidian Antioch (14:1–7). There they speak in the synagogue, and again cause a hot debate. Although the power of their message is proved by many miracles, they have to flee to avoid being stoned.

IN LYSTRA

Paul and Barnabas are now in Lycaonia, where they visit the out-of-the-way towns of Lystra and Derbe. At Lystra they receive a rapturous welcome – thanks to a local legend (14:8–20).

The story goes that two Greek gods – Zeus and Hermes – once visited Lystra in disguise. The only people who welcomed them were two poor peasants. The gods were so angry that they destroyed the town with an earthquake; but the two peasants were spared and became guardians of the temple.

The superstitious folk of Lystra are now always looking out for visiting gods! When Paul heals a lame man, they hail him as Hermes, the messenger god. Barnabas, who is older, they take to be Zeus. Let the sacrifices begin!

Urgently, Paul explains that they are merely human.

Pisidian Antioch

Pisidian Antioch is a Roman colony, situated on the main road from Rome to Asia. The remains of a Roman aqueduct are still to be seen there today. Although Pisidian Antioch is part of the Roman province of Galatia, there is resistance to Roman rule from tribesmen living in the hills around. This would be one of the places where Paul felt in danger of being attacked (2 Corinthians 11:26).

Iconium

A description of Paul was found in Iconium. It dates from about seventy years after his visit there.

Paul is described as small and bald with bandy legs. His nose is large and his eyebrows meet in the middle. But there are times when he has 'the face of an angel'.

There *is* a true and living God. His power is seen in creation. His love is seen in the blessings of nature…

The Lystrans are confused. When Jews arrive from Antioch and Iconium with news that Paul and Barnabas are frauds, Paul is very nearly killed. They have to leave as soon as possible.

DERBE AND THE LONG WAY HOME

Paul and Barnabas visit Derbe, where the gospel makes many converts (14:21–28). Then, instead of going straight on home to Syrian Antioch, they retrace their entire journey.

They visit and encourage the groups of new believers in each town and city. In every church, they appoint elders. They warn them that the Christian way is tough. They commission them with fervent prayer and fasting. It is hard to imagine greater bravery and faith than is shown by these first church-planters.

Finally Paul and Barnabas return to Antioch in Syria, and to the people who first commissioned them. They have many adventures to relate, but the headline news is this: that God has opened a way for the *Gentiles* to receive the gospel. The Christian church is becoming a multinational community with a worldwide faith.

The Council of Jerusalem

(15:1–35)

A NASTY SPLIT!

The church at Antioch is rejoicing that Gentiles (non-Jews) are becoming Christians. But some Jewish Christians arrive from Jerusalem, with hardline teaching on circumcision. They insist that Gentile Christians must also become Jews. They must be circumcised and keep the law of Moses (15:1–4).

Even Peter is confused. He stops mixing with Gentile Christians and withdraws to a 'Jews only' group. So does Barnabas. Ten years after the Roman centurion Cornelius became a Christian, Peter is still wobbly on the subject of accepting Gentile believers.

But Paul stands firm. He confronts Peter with the facts of the gospel. We aren't saved by being circumcised or keeping the law. If we could be saved that way, Jesus need never have died.

Paul's point is this: we are saved by God's grace. Because Jesus died for us, our sins are forgiven and we have peace with God. If we start to add circumcision, food laws, sabbath rules and other regulations, we are saying that the death of Jesus was not enough. We are discounting his sacrifice and adding our own efforts.

The 'circumcision group' have tracked Paul and Barnabas and sown doubt in all the new churches. Paul is furious – as we know from his letter to the Galatians:

> *I am astonished that you are so quickly… turning to a different gospel – which is really no gospel at all (Galatians 1:6).*
> *You foolish Galatians! Who has bewitched you (Galatians 3:1)?*

THE COUNCIL OF JERUSALEM

The question of whether Gentile Christians must also become Jews threatens to split the church. If the 'circumcision group' wins, Christianity will cease to be a gospel of grace. It will be swallowed back into Jewish legalism and disappear for ever.

Paul and Barnabas go to Jerusalem to discuss the crisis with the apostles. This is the Council of Jerusalem (15:5–21).

When Peter speaks, it is clear he has come to his senses. He points out that God makes no difference between Jews and Gentiles in the way they are saved. With both, God looks at the heart, not at ritual. He saves by grace, through faith. It is only faith that counts.

If this is so, says Peter, why burden Gentile Christians with the law of Moses? The law never saves anyone – and Jews find it impossible to keep! (Peter's speech at the Council of Jerusalem is the last we hear from him. From this point Luke will follow the adventures of Paul.)

Next, the Council hears about the Gentile mission from Paul and Barnabas. They listen with close attention to the astonishing evidence that God is reaching out to non-Jews.

Then James speaks. This is not James the son of Zebedee – he has already died, beheaded on the orders of King Herod (Acts 12:2). This is one of Jesus' brothers who becomes known as James the Just (or James the Elder). He is the leader of the church in Jerusalem. We have one of his letters in the New Testament.

James lifts the Gentile story to the light of scripture. He quotes a prophecy of Amos (Amos 9:11–12), that God will restore his kingly power ('David's fallen tent') to draw Gentiles into his kingdom. This is what is happening through David's descendant, Jesus Christ.

James makes a momentous proposal. He releases Gentile Christians from the clutches of the Pharisees. They do not have to become Jews to be Christians!

Instead, he gives the simplest guidelines for living a holy life in a pagan culture:

They are not to eat meat which has been sacrificed to idols. This is a guideline which cares what other people may think. Pagan idols have no power, and to eat such meat is quite safe. But if eating it misleads or offends someone who is not so clear-thinking, it is best not to do it (1 Corinthians 10:28–32).

They are not to be sexually immoral. Gentile Christians are to be pure in their sexual behaviour. Adultery (sex outside marriage) is forbidden in the Ten Commandments (Exodus 20:14). Sex with close relatives is also forbidden (Leviticus 18). They must now resist pressures to be permissive or perverted. Chastity is a virtue which Christianity perpetuates in the world.

They are not to eat the meat of strangled animals, or meat which still contains blood. This guideline echoes the Jewish laws in Leviticus 17. Blood means life, and is not to be eaten. It is the sacred substance poured out in sacrifice. Although Gentiles are used to eating meat containing blood, they are asked not to do so. This is to be kind to Jewish consciences when they share meals together.

James' guidelines deal with the Gentile customs which most offend Jews. It asks them to respect the way Jewish Christians feel, so that the two communities can now become one church.

THE COUNCIL'S LETTER TO GENTILE BELIEVERS

The meeting agrees to James' proposal. The guidelines are written in a letter, and sent with specially chosen messengers (15:22–35). One of them is Silas, who will become a close colleague of Paul.

There is great relief among the Christians at Antioch when they receive the letter. The 'circumcision group' has no official backing from the church in Jerusalem. New believers need not be circumcised after all!

The second missionary journey
(15:36 – 18:22)

PAUL AND BARNABAS DISAGREE

When spring arrives, Paul suggests that he and Barnabas revisit the churches they founded in south Galatia. Paul never abandons young churches. He writes to teach and encourage them, and visits them if possible –

or sends someone on his behalf.

Barnabas wants to take John Mark with them again – but Paul hasn't forgiven the young man for deserting them the last time (Acts 13:13). They argue and decide to split up (15:36–41).

Barnabas and John Mark sail to Cyprus, which is home ground for the cousins. Paul chooses Silas as his new colleague. They are both Roman citizens, which will have some advantages for their mission. Leaving Syrian Antioch, they travel on foot through the Taurus mountains to Cilicia.

TIMOTHY JOINS PAUL AND SILAS

Paul likes working with a team. At Lystra he finds a new junior partner in Timothy – a young man with a Jewish mother and a Greek father (16:1–5). Paul circumcises Timothy. Since the Council of Jerusalem no one needs to be circumcised, but Paul wants Timothy to be able to mix freely with Jewish groups.

EXTRAORDINARY GUIDANCE

Paul, Silas and Timothy journey through Asia Minor (16:6–11). Paul hopes to turn south-west, to the centres of population in Colosse and Ephesus. Somehow their progress is blocked – whether by illness, opposition or a word of prophecy, we don't know. Luke says only that the Holy Spirit prevents them.

Turning north, they travel instead towards the province of Bithynia and the Black Sea. Again, says Luke, their path is closed – by the Spirit of Jesus. In the end they take the only remaining route, which brings them to the north-west coast of Asia Minor at the port of Troas. So much for the mission to Asia!

But now a new mission field opens up. Paul has a vision of a man begging or beckoning for help. From his dress, he is from Macedonia – the Roman province across the Aegean Sea from Troas. So this is where God is leading!

Has Paul just met Luke? And is Luke a doctor from Macedonia? We don't know. But Dr Luke joins the expedition at this point, and starts to tell their story as his own diary.

Suddenly they make good progress – as though the Holy Spirit is now a following wind. They sail to the rocky island of Samothrace, and then on to the port of Neapolis (which today is modern Kavalla). One hundred and fifty miles in two days! From Neapolis they take the paved road ten miles inland – to Philippi.

LYDIA

There is no synagogue in Philippi, so Paul can't start their mission by preaching to Jews. Instead, they join a group of women who are praying by the river on the sabbath. One of the women is Lydia (16:12–15).

Lydia is a businesswoman. She deals in expensive purple cloth – the choice of emperors. Amazingly, she comes from Thyatira – one of the cities in Asia which Paul has been trying to visit! Now the good news will travel there with trade.

Lydia is converted, not by Paul's words alone, but by the Lord opening her heart to welcome the gospel. She and her household – her family and servants – are all baptized. Paul and his friends accept Lydia's invitation to stay at her home. Is this the house where the Philippian church will meet in future?

PAUL AND SILAS IN PRISON

Over many days, Paul and Silas are harassed by a fortune-teller (16:16–40). She is a slave girl with a 'python spirit' – a follower of the Greek god Apollo. Paul is angry at the state she is in, and that her owners make so much money from her demon possession. In the end, he releases her in the name of Jesus Christ.

The slave girl's owners are furious. They drag Paul and Silas before the city magistrates. They accuse them of being Jewish troublemakers who are trying to promote an illegal religion. They make no mention that their fortune-telling racket has been ruined.

Paul and Silas are brutally flogged and chained up in a prison cell. Bloody and in great pain, they sing hymns until midnight.

Suddenly, there is an earthquake. The prison is wrecked and the prisoners are free. Assuming his charges have escaped, the jailer prepares to commit suicide by falling on his sword. But Paul calls out that all is well.

The jailer – a tough Roman veteran – is a changed man. He puts his trust in Christ, welcomes Paul and Silas into his home and gently washes their wounds. Before daylight, he and his family are baptized.

The following day the order comes for Paul and Silas to be released. But Paul has a point to make. He and Silas are Roman citizens. They have been tried, flogged and imprisoned illegally. They demand, and receive, an official apology!

As Paul and Silas move on from Philippi, they leave behind a curious mix of believers. A businesswoman, a slave girl and a jailer – now united in the shared life of Christ, and the nucleus of a local church.

IN THESSALONICA

Paul, Silas and Timothy journey 100 miles south-west, from Philippi to Thessalonica (17:1–9).

Thessalonica is the capital of the Roman province of Macedonia, and a key centre for the gospel. It is a harbour town on the Aegean Sea, and on the main road (the Egnatian Way) from the Adriatic Sea to the Middle East. From Thessalonica, the gospel can travel both east and west. And it has a synagogue.

On three successive sabbaths, Paul teaches the Jews and God-fearers about Jesus. He explains that Jesus, who suffered, died and rose from death, is the Messiah. He is the One for whom the Jewish scriptures hope, and to whom they point.

As so often, Paul's message causes first an argument and then a riot. Some Greeks believe – and the Jews are jealous. Public order is threatened by this message that Jesus is a new kind of king, greater than Caesar. If this idea wins supporters, it will bring down the empire.

Jason and some other believers are arrested. When they are released on bail, it may be on condition that Paul and Silas leave town.

IN BEREA

Paul and his two companions are smuggled away from Thessalonica under cover of darkness. They travel to Berea, some fifty miles to the south-west (17:10–15).

At Berea Paul again teaches in the synagogue, and meets with a more open response. The Berean Jews are willing to search their scriptures, to check if indeed the Messiah should suffer. Luke tells us that many people put their faith in Christ – both Jews and Greeks.

Unfortunately, some Jews come all the way from

Philippi

Philippi is named after Philip of Macedon, the father of Alexander the Great. Founded in the 4th century BC, it has been a Greek colony for half its history. Now it is governed by Romans, and the home of many retired soldiers. Luke describes it proudly as 'the leading city of Macedonia' – perhaps another clue that this is his home town.

Thessalonica to cause trouble. Paul's new friends have to help him escape. They take him to the coast and then 300 miles by sea – to Athens.

IN ATHENS

Paul is alone in Athens, waiting for Silas and Timothy to join him (17:16–43).

As a Jew and a Christian, everything about Athens appals him. Here is a high culture with low morals. Here is a centre of learning, which is littered with idols! All the Greek and Roman gods are worshipped here, in temples, shrines and wayside altars. In the Parthenon stands a gold and ivory statue of Athena – the warrior goddess who gives Athens her name. Her spear-point is visible forty miles away. Paul feels God's anger and frustration that human beings can devote their lives to such worthless symbols.

The pride, beauty and paganism of Athens: the Parthenon building standing on the hill of the Acropolis. 'Parthenos' means 'virgin' and the temple housed the statue of Pallas Athena, the city's guardian goddess.

Paul gets to work. He reasons with Jews in the synagogue. He argues with the speakers in the market place. Soon he is discovered by the rival Epicurean and Stoic philosophers. Some of them tease him, saying he is a 'babbler' – reciting second-hand sayings like a parrot.

Epicureans believe that life is without meaning or final judgment. They live by taking pleasure and avoiding pain. Stoics are committed to life in all its hardship. They live bravely in the face of fate, without question or complaint.

Paul talks about Jesus and his resurrection. The Greek for 'resurrection' is 'anastasis' – which sounds like the name of an attractive and powerful goddess! Paul, who was once mistaken for Hermes, is now suspected of inventing new gods. The philosophers take him to the Areopagus for closer examination.

'Areopagus' means 'hill of Mars'. It is the leading council of Athens and a world-famous forum of debate.

Paul is invited to speak to the assembly. He begins with his impressions of Athens. He tells them he is amazed at the amount of religion and the range of gods. One particular altar – 'To an Unknown God' – has captured his interest. By this altar the Athenians admit that there is a gap in their religious understanding. This is the gap that Paul longs to fill – with the gospel of Jesus Christ.

Paul goes on to describe the living God – the creator of heaven and earth. This God can't be reduced to an idol or confined to a temple. He doesn't need food or drink or any kind of help from humans. He is more self-sufficient than any Stoic, yet he cares for the whole human race. He orders geography and history, nature and time. Unlike the Epicureans, he gives himself for his creatures. He longs that people should appreciate his constant care, and turn to him in faith and trust.

Paul quotes a Greek poet, Epimenides of Crete: 'For in him we live and move and have our being.' This is a glimpse of the truth Paul is trying to convey. He also quotes, 'We are his offspring,' from the Cilician poet Aratus. Aratus was referring to Zeus, but Paul is talking about God who is the Father of all.

Paul puts it to his hearers: Why are you insulting this almighty creator-Father-God by making idols of metal and stone? This ignorance must stop! It is time to discover what God is really like. The person who can show them God is Jesus. He is the One who died and was raised to life. He is the One who will come to judge the world.

Paul's hearers catch the word 'resurrection'. Epicureans don't believe in it, and neither do Stoics. Both groups live for this world alone – with no hope of life beyond the grave. They've heard enough.

Paul has preached to thirty of the finest intellects in the world. Is he disappointed with his sermon and its outcome? He has no need to be. The philosophers of Athens are great talkers. They don't expect to reach conclusions or change their ways.

But Paul has spoken well. He started where they were, with their idols and writers. He challenged their superstition and spiritual ignorance. He spoke clearly of the one and only God, and of Jesus the risen Lord and judge. And some of his hearers have become Christians as a result – including a member of the Council, and a woman named Damaris.

IN CORINTH

Paul moves from Athens to Corinth – from the intellectual centre of Greece to its commercial heart (18:1–17).

Corinth, along with Athens and Ephesus, is a leading city of the Roman empire. It sits between the two halves of Greece, on a neck of land just five miles wide. All traffic between north and south is funnelled through Corinth, and it has two ports, serving gulfs to the east and west.

Corinth is the capital of the province of Achaia. It is famous for its trade. It hosts the famous Isthmian Games, which are second only to the Olympics. And it is a byword for sex. The temple of Aphrodite, the goddess of love, stands high above the city.

What does Paul have to offer this busy, wealthy, vice-ridden metropolis? One day he will write to the Christians at Corinth: 'I came to you in weakness and fear, and with much trembling' (1 Corinthians 2:3).

After Athens, Paul has resolved to preach only Christ and his cross. Obscure ideas and flowery phrases are a distraction from the simple message of the gospel. From now on he will speak plainly.

God is with Paul, and he blesses him with two good friends – Aquila and his wife Priscilla. They have come from Rome with other Jews, after being expelled by the emperor Claudius.

Like Paul, Aquila and Priscilla are tentmakers. The three of them set up in business together, sewing tents and other items from Cicilian goat-hair cloth. This is the beginning of a long and happy association between them. When Paul moves on to Ephesus, Aquila and Priscilla will go with him, and one of the Christian groups will meet in their house.

Paul begins, as usual, by preaching the gospel in the synagogue every sabbath. When Silas and Timothy join him from Macedonia, they bring a gift of money from the church in Thessalonica (2 Corinthians 11:9). This enables Paul to devote himself to preaching and teaching.

As has happened many times before, some of the Jews reject Paul's message. They make it impossible for him to continue his ministry in the synagogue. In Corinth Paul has the perfect solution. He moves next door, taking the ruler of the synagogue with him!

Paul has offered the gospel to the Jews first. Now he takes his message to the Gentiles. He is greatly encouraged by a vision in which the Lord speaks to him and promises to protect him. As a result, Paul decides to stay on in Corinth for a year and a half.

During this time, Paul's Jewish enemies try to get rid of him. They bring him before the proconsul Gallio and charge him with breaking religious law. The Romans allow Judaism, but surely not this strange worship of Christ!

Gallio is the younger brother of the Stoic philosopher Seneca. He is handsome, intelligent – and nobody's fool. He recognizes the spite and nit-picking of the Jews, refuses to hear any more from them – and throws them out.

This is a momentous decision. Gallio's ruling means that Christianity is accepted as a proper religion under Roman law. The crowd which has gathered to mob Paul gives the new synagogue ruler a beating instead.

The temple of Apollo in Corinth. For the Greeks, Apollo is the glorious god of the sun. Now the coming of Christ reveals the true light of the world – and transforms the significance of Sunday.

PAUL'S TRAVELS

When the time comes for Paul to leave Corinth, he makes a vow and shaves his head. This could be out of gratitude for his long period of safety, or a commitment to his future work.

Paul sails with Aquila and Priscilla to Ephesus, where he teaches for a short time in the synagogue. He leaves his friends there, promising to return. He will travel 1,500 miles before he sees them again (18:18–22).

From Ephesus, Paul sails to Caesarea, the main port of Palestine. From there he goes 'up' to Jerusalem and then 'home' to Antioch – the base from which both his missionary journeys began.

The third missionary journey
(18:23 – 21:16)

Luke tells us briefly that Paul now visits the churches in Phrygia and Galatia. Presumably he follows his familiar circuit, through Pisidian Antioch, Iconium, Lystra and Derbe. He has always been concerned to keep in touch and encourage them. But Luke's main interest is in Ephesus.

The Corinth Canal

Today the Corinth Canal allows shipping to take a short cut between east and west, saving a dangerous 200-mile voyage round Cape Malea. In Paul's day the vessels were laboriously dragged overland on rollers!

Living by faith

Paul lives by faith – but this doesn't stop him earning his living. Jesus was a carpenter, and all Jewish rabbis have an occupation. If a person or church is willing to support Paul, he gladly accepts, and gives all his time to his gospel work. If not, then he readily supports himself.

APOLLOS

An excellent teacher has arrived in Ephesus. His name is Apollos (18:24–28).

Apollos is from Alexandria in Egypt. Alexandria has a strong Jewish community and a long tradition of learning. It is here that the Septuagint (the Greek version of the Hebrew scriptures) was prepared by seventy scholars 200 years before the time of Christ.

Apollos is steeped in scripture, and a gifted speaker. But as Aquila and Priscilla listen to his eloquent teaching, they realize there are gaps in his knowledge and understanding. He knows about 'the baptism of John', but does he know about baptism 'in the name of Jesus'?

Aquila and Priscilla invite Apollos to their home and quietly complete his education. When he travels on to Corinth, he is ready to play a full part in the ministry of the church. 'I planted the seed,' writes Paul looking back, 'Apollos watered it, but God made it grow' (1 Corinthians 3:6).

PAUL IN EPHESUS

After Apollos has left for Corinth, Paul returns to Ephesus (19:1–41).

Paul and the disciples of John the Baptist

In Ephesus, Paul discovers some disciples of John the Baptist (19:1–7). They are stuck halfway between the Old and New Testaments, not realizing that the Messiah has come.

Paul explains to them that John looked forward to Jesus, and gives them Christian baptism. Placing his hands on them, Paul prays that they may receive the Holy Spirit. Like the Samaritan believers, they experience a mini-Pentecost, speaking in tongues and prophesying (Acts 8:14–17).

We glimpse that in the early years of Christianity, some believers only know the teaching and baptism of John the Baptist. Others regard John as equal with Jesus.

The Gospels make it clear that John is the last and finest of the old prophets. With Jesus, a new age has dawned – the age of the Messiah and his kingdom. In Ephesus we see a group of John's disciples catching up with this news – and receiving the Spirit of Christ.

The gospel in Ephesus

Paul returns to the synagogue in Ephesus, as he promised (19:8–20). He teaches there for three months, until the Jewish resistance becomes too strong. After this, he holds meetings in a lecture hall – every day for two years.

Ephesus, like Corinth, is a strong commercial centre. As Paul preaches and teaches in the hall of Tyrannus, travellers and merchants receive the gospel – and take it with them around the whole province of Asia.

Paul is not just a dry lecturer. He is a powerful minister of Christ's healing and deliverance. Luke is a doctor, and he records the extraordinary miracles that God works through Paul at this time.

A key area of conflict is with the occult, especially demon possession and magic. Some exorcists, called the sons of Sceva, try to tap into the power of Jesus – and are badly beaten by a demonized man. This strikes fear among the Ephesian sorcerers, who make a public bonfire of their scrolls of spells. Luke says they valued the loss at 150 years' wages – a tremendous act of witness and a sure sign of conversion!

Paul's plans

The mission in Ephesus is now well established, and Paul plans to move on (19:21–22). He wants to visit the churches in Macedonia and Achaia, to collect money for the poverty-stricken church in Jerusalem. After Jerusalem he hopes to visit Rome. And from Rome (as he confides in his letter to the Christians there) he intends to venture on to the western boundary of the empire – Spain (Romans 15:24).

Ephesus

Paul stays in Ephesus for three years – longer than he does anywhere else.

Ephesus is the capital of the Roman province of Asia. With a population of half a million people, she sits on the coast of the Aegean Sea at the mouth of the River Cayster. She is a centre of commerce for the whole of Asia Minor, and a focal point for both Greek and Roman religion.

There are three temples in Ephesus in honour of the emperor, but the most important temple is to the Roman goddess Artemis, whose Greek name is Diana. Her grotesque image is a squat black meteorite carved into the shape of a many-breasted fertility goddess. Her temple is one of the seven wonders of the world – four times the size of the Parthenon in Athens, with 127 graceful columns and a white marble roof.

A flourishing trade surrounds the worship of Artemis. Magic charms and little scrolls of spells are sold, to bring good luck in love and business. These scrolls are known as 'Ephesian letters'!

The riot in Ephesus

The Christian faith (or 'the Way') is bad for the idol trade. A silversmith called Demetrius makes his living from charms of the goddess and her temple. As the good news of Jesus sweeps away superstition, Demetrius sees the danger to his business and the prosperity of the city. Gathering his fellow skilled workers and other traders, he stirs up a riot (19:23–41).

The mob seizes two of Paul's companions, Gaius and Aristarchus. They are rushed off to the theatre – a vast arena holding 25,000 people. Paul wants to go to their defence, but his friends restrain him.

Into this dangerous situation steps the city clerk. He quietens the chanting crowd by assuring them that the reputation of Artemis is quite safe. Gaius and Aristarchus are neither temple-robbers nor blasphemers. If Demetrius and friends have any charges to make, the proper courts are open and the judges are waiting to hear from them. In the meantime, there is no excuse for rioting and the people had better disperse.

Luke is showing his Roman readers that Christianity is not a threat to public order. There have been court cases and riots, but on each occasion Paul and his companions have been declared innocent.

THROUGH MACEDONIA AND GREECE

Paul leaves Ephesus and travels to Macedonia to visit the churches in Philippi, Thessalonica and Berea (20:1–6). He is collecting money to help the church in Jerusalem, and gathering a team to make the journey with him.

Luke gives only a brief account of Paul's activities during this year, and there is much that we don't know. Eventually he comes to Greece (Achaia), where he stays for three months, probably with friends in Corinth. It may be during this time that he writes his great letter to the Romans.

Paul and his friends are about to sail for Jerusalem from Corinth, when they realize Paul's life is in danger from hostile Jews on the ship. They change their arrangements, split the group and Paul returns to Macedonia to spend Passover (or Easter!) in Philippi. From there he sails to Troas to rejoin the others. Luke is once again travelling with Paul, perhaps as the representative of the church in Philippi.

EUTYCHUS

Paul and his companions stay a week in Troas. Their last night is a Sunday, and the believers meet in an upstairs room for a fellowship meal (20:7–12).

Paul's sermon and the discussion which follows run late into the night. A boy called Eutychus is sitting on the window sill. Overcome by the long talk and the stuffy room, he falls fast asleep and topples backwards to his death.

It is a terrible tragedy, but Paul throws himself on the

The amphitheatre at Ephesus, which holds 25,000 people. Here the silversmith Demetrius leads a protest against the influence of the Christian gospel. The Arcadian Way, which in Paul's day is colonnaded and lined with shops, links the city centre to the harbour.

young man and puts his arms around him. Luke remembers all this in detail – and how Paul then declares that the boy is alive! They return upstairs to share the Lord's Supper and talk on until dawn.

The raising of Eutychus reminds us of the way Elijah restored to life the son of the widow of Zarephath (1 Kings 17:21) and Elisha revived the son of the Shunammite woman (2 Kings 4:34). Peter also raised Dorcas to life. Such things happen, as a sign of God's resurrection power – but not often. Even Jesus raised only three people from death – Jairus' daughter, the widow of Nain's son and Lazarus.

PAUL'S FAREWELL TO THE EPHESIAN ELDERS

Paul wants to go to Jerusalem for Pentecost, but he is already late. Luke tells us how the ship from Troas calls at various ports and harbours as it works around the coast to Miletus. Paul chooses to make part of the journey overland – perhaps to get time to himself. Like Jesus, Paul is setting his face towards Jerusalem. He knows that suffering awaits him there, and possibly death.

Paul has no time to visit Ephesus. Instead he asks the Ephesian elders to come thirty miles to see him while his ship is at Miletus (20:13–38).

Paul knows that this is the last time he will see this group of pastors. He opens his heart to them as he says goodbye. He reminds them how eagerly he taught them – both Jews and Gentiles, in public and private, day and night. He never took money from them as he earned his own living and provided for his colleagues. And his message has always been the same – repentance towards God and faith in Jesus Christ.

Now Paul is going to Jerusalem. The prophets in the churches have given many warnings of danger ahead. This doesn't worry him, as long as he can complete the work Christ is giving him to do.

The Ephesian elders must expect trials of their own. They must act as shepherds to the people in their care, tending and protecting their flock. There will be attacks from false teachers ('savage wolves') both outside and within the church. Paul commits them to God, who alone can build them up and bring them to glory.

Paul is a super-achiever. From zealously persecuting Christians, he has become equally wholehearted as an apostle for Christ. He endures hardship, works for his living, makes long journeys, suffers threats to his life, founds churches and forges doctrine. We get the impression of a driven, workaholic, impatient visionary.

But Paul also shows every aspect of the fruit of the Spirit: love, joy, peace, patience, kindness, goodness, faithfulness, gentleness and self-control (Galatians 5:22–23). Out of love for the Lord, he has served the Ephesians with humility and tears. Now they weep for him, as they realize they won't see him again in this life.

ON TO JERUSALEM

The journey to Jerusalem is marked by many moving reunions and farewells (21:1–16). Luke notes the calls and encounters in his journal.

At Tyre Paul is again warned of danger in Jerusalem. At the fine port of Caesarea they stay with Philip and his four unmarried daughters – all gifted prophets. It is here that Agabus comes from Judea and enacts Paul's arrest by binding himself with Paul's belt.

Agabus is a true prophet – it was he who correctly forecast the famine (Acts 11:28). Luke includes himself among those who beg Paul not to go on, but Paul is not to be diverted from his goal. These warnings are not so that he can avoid suffering for Christ, but so that he can prepare himself to go through it. He is following in his Master's footsteps.

When they arrive in Jerusalem they stay with Mnason. Like Barnabas, he is from Cyprus and was one of the first believers.

Paul's arrival in Jerusalem and arrest
(21:17–39)

Paul receives a warm welcome from the church in Jerusalem. He brings with him the collection which the Gentile churches have made for their welfare (24:17). He is greeted by James and the other elders, who warn him to expect trouble from the Jewish leaders.

The Jewish authorities believe that Paul tells Jews to reject the law and customs of Moses. Paul is not, of course, against the Jewish law and customs – it's just that he knows they don't lead to salvation. To give a correct impression, the church elders advise Paul to join with four men who have taken a Nazirite vow.

A Nazirite vow involves shaving the head and going without meat and wine for thirty days. At the end of this time a sacrifice and other gifts are offered in the temple. The hair that has grown during the fast is shaven off and burned on the altar with the sacrifice.

The elders advise Paul to join with the four in the last stage of their vow, to share in their ceremony and pay their expenses. In this way he will be seen encouraging people to keep the Jewish law. Paul isn't concerned for his own safety or reputation; but he agrees to the suggestion for the sake of the church.

The purification week is spent almost entirely in the temple. It is nearly over when Paul is suddenly recognized by old enemies from Asia. They may have been Jews from Ephesus, who have already recognized Trophimus with Paul.

The Jews assume that Paul has been taking Gentiles with him into the temple area. This is strictly forbidden. A stone wall separates Gentiles from Jews, with signs in Greek and Latin warning foreigners not to enter the Court of Israel. Paul has often argued that this dividing wall should be demolished. He firmly believes that the death of Jesus has overcome the separation of Jews and Gentiles and made peace between them (Ephesians 2:14).

Although Paul is innocent, the Jews drag him from the temple and start to beat him. Jesus was accused of abusing the temple, and so was Stephen. Now Paul is close to death for the same reason. His life is saved only by the swift arrival of the Roman guard from the nearby fortress of Antonia.

The soldiers rescue Paul from the mob, and arrest him for his own protection. Paul is badly shaken, but his head is clear. He speaks to the Roman commander, telling him that he is a Greek-speaking Jew and not a notorious terrorist. Then, with the guard to protect him, he asks to address the crowd from the fortress steps.

Paul speaks to the crowd
(21:40 – 22:29)

Paul decides to tell his story. He does so with simplicity and skill. He has people's attention straight away, because he speaks their language and calls them 'brothers and fathers'. Twenty-two years before, he had heard Stephen begin with the very same words.

Paul introduces himself as a very Jewish Jew. He was born in Tarsus, brought up in Jerusalem and learned Jewish law from the famous Rabbi Gamaliel. When the followers of the Way (Christians) first caused a stir, Paul had been eager to stamp them out. He guarded the coats of those who executed Stephen.

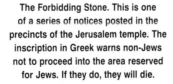

The Forbidding Stone. This is one of a series of notices posted in the precincts of the Jerusalem temple. The inscription in Greek warns non-Jews not to proceed into the area reserved for Jews. If they do, they will die.

Then, one day, Paul met Jesus Christ – suddenly and overwhelmingly, on the road to Damascus. He was converted, baptized and received God's call to take his gospel to the Gentiles.

Suddenly the crowd remembers what it has against Paul. He compromises with Gentiles! He tells them being Jewish doesn't matter! For a moment they were impressed by his pedigree and zeal. Now they find their voice and shout for his death.

The commander decides to retreat into the safety of the fortress, where he can have Paul flogged and get to the truth. But Paul prevents him by stating he is a Roman citizen. It's illegal for him to be tortured without trial. What's more, Paul has his citizenship by birth, whereas the commander had to bribe an official to get his!

Paul's trial before the Sanhedrin
(22:30 – 23:11)

The next day, the commander calls in the Jewish Council, the Sanhedrin. He is interested to hear what they have to say against Paul.

Paul begins by saying he is innocent before God. For this blasphemy, the high priest, Ananias, has him struck across the mouth. Paul is angry and calls Ananias 'a whitewashed wall'! Jesus once called the scribes and Pharisees 'whitewashed tombs', meaning they were pure on the outside, but corrupt within.

When Paul is told that he has insulted the high priest, he quickly apologizes. His eyesight is poor. But his description of Ananias is a good one. The high priest is a greedy, cruel and vengeful man.

Paul knows very well that there are two rival groups in the Sanhedrin – the Pharisees and the Sadducees. He tells them that he is a Pharisee, on trial because he believes in the resurrection of the dead. The Sadducees immediately disagree with Paul, while the Pharisees start to defend him! To prevent any further disorder, the commander withdraws Paul to the barracks.

Paul's situation is now hopeless. If he is released he will be assassinated. If he remains in custody he will never again do the work of an apostle. But that night Jesus speaks to Paul. He assures him that he will live to preach again – and in Rome!

The plot to kill Paul
(23:12–35)

Some Jews plan to kill Paul. They will ask the Sanhedrin to send for him, and then ambush him on his way to the hearing. Paul's nephew learns of the plot and tells the Roman commander. The commander decides to transfer Paul under heavy guard to Caesarea.

At nine o'clock in the evening, and protected by 470 Roman soldiers (half the Jerusalem garrison), Paul leaves for Caesarea – sixty miles away. He takes with him a letter from the commander Claudius Lysias to the governor, Felix.

The commander puts his own action in a good light as he describes the prisoner's situation. Paul is a Roman citizen who has offended the Jews in some way, but done nothing worthy of imprisonment or death.

Luke is showing us yet again how Paul is attacked by malevolent Jews and protected by fair-minded Romans.

Paul's trial before Felix
(24:1–27)

Felix is the governor (or Roman procurator) of Judea. He lives in the vast palace at Caesarea, built by Herod the Great.

The Herods – a bloodstained family

King Agrippa II is a member of the Herod family. He is a Jewish convert who rules a small part of Judea, but has the emperor's permission to appoint the high priest.

The Herods are a bloodstained family. Agrippa II's father was Agrippa I, who executed the apostle James and was eaten by worms (Acts 12:23). His great-uncle was Herod Antipas who beheaded John the Baptist. His great-grandfather was Herod the Great, who built the temple in Jerusalem and the palace at Caesarea, and murdered the Bethlehem babies.

Bernice is Agrippa II's sister and mistress. She has already been married to his uncle and will one day be the mistress of Titus, the emperor who destroys Jerusalem in AD 70. She is the sister of Drusilla, the wife of Felix.

Felix and his brother were slaves who found favour with the emperor and were given their freedom. Felix is the first slave ever to become a governor – a power he wields with heavy-handed cruelty. His third wife, Drusilla, is a young Jewish princess – the daughter of Herod Agrippa I, who was eaten by worms (Acts 12:23). Felix stole her from another king, with the aid of a magic spell.

When high priest Ananias arrives for Paul's trial, he brings with him a lawyer called Tertullus. Tertullus begins by flattering Felix and then tells a pack of lies about Paul.

Paul, claims Tertullus, is a pest who has caused riots all over the world. He is a leading figure in the cult of the Nazarenes, and has recently tried to desecrate the temple.

When Paul speaks, he stays cool and constructive. He points out that he was only in Jerusalem for twelve days, during which time he didn't argue with anyone or stir up a crowd. He belongs to the followers of the Way, but they aren't a sect. They have the same faith in the Law and the Prophets as his accusers. He keeps his conscience clear, because he believes that there is a future resurrection and that everyone will face God's judgment.

Paul explains why he was in Jerusalem. He came to bring help for friends and make offerings in the temple. He advises Felix to talk to those who attacked him, or ask the Sanhedrin about resurrection.

Felix decides to play for time. Judgment must wait

The magnificent city of Caesarea was built by Herod the Great on the shore of the Mediterranean and named after Caesar Augustus. In Paul's day it is the official residence of the Roman governor of Judea, and he is brought here to stand trial before Felix.

until the commander Lysias can give evidence. Meanwhile, he keeps Paul under guard, with his friends (perhaps including Luke) looking after him.

Felix brings his wife to hear Paul preach, but panics when the talk gets round to matters of self-control and judgment! He hopes to receive a bribe for Paul's release.

Paul languishes in prison for two years, until Felix is removed from the governorship. He is dismissed by the emperor for his excessive brutality in suppressing a rebellion.

Paul's trial before Festus

(25:1–12)

The new governor is Porcius Festus. He wastes no time in tackling Paul's case, and summons the Jews to a hearing in Caesarea. This foils their plan to assassinate Paul on his way to Jerusalem.

At the hearing, Luke tells us that the charges are very serious. Paul is accused of crimes against the temple and threats against the government. But the Jews have no evidence.

Festus should dismiss the case, but instead he offers to hear it again in the presence of the Sanhedrin in Jerusalem. Paul realizes that if this happens he has no hope of justice. And so he appeals to the highest secular authority – Caesar himself. Paul is a Roman citizen, and every Roman citizen has the right to take his case to the emperor.

Paul's hearing before King Agrippa

(25:13 – 26:32)

King Agrippa (Herod Agrippa II) and his sister Bernice arrive at Caesarea. They have come to pay their respects to the new governor, Festus. Agrippa is an expert on Jewish matters, and Festus asks his advice about Paul. The king says he would like to hear him.

Paul has appealed to take his case to Caesar – the young Emperor Nero. Festus must now write a letter to brief the emperor, but can't think of any criminal charge to bring against Paul. He hopes King Agrippa, with his special knowledge of Judaism, will be able to help.

Is Paul nervous? Jesus warned his disciples that they would be brought before governors and kings. He promised them that in this situation the Holy Spirit would give them the right words to say (Mark 13:9–11).

Paul tells the king the story of his life. He was well known as a young student in Jerusalem. In those days he was a strict Pharisee, keeping the law of God and looking forward to the coming of the Messiah. When people started to follow Jesus of Nazareth and talk of his resurrection, Paul arrested them and voted for their deaths.

But then Paul met the glorious Christ – in blazing light, on the road to Damascus. Jesus spoke to him by name. He asked him why he was persecuting him by ill-treating his followers. The same question was asked of Saul's namesake, King Saul, by the Lord's chosen king, David (1 Samuel 26:18). Paul was behaving like an ox, kicking against the goads – the pointed sticks used to guide the beast in the right direction.

Paul tells Agrippa that it was there and then, on the Damascus road, that Jesus commissioned him to preach to the Gentiles. His Jewish enemies have seized him only because he believes Jesus is the One whom Moses and the prophets said would come.

This is the third time Luke has recorded Paul's conversion. It is the fullest account of them all.

Festus interrupts to say that Paul is mad! He is taking all this religion too seriously. But Paul appeals to Agrippa, who knows about Jewish prophecy. Agrippa is impressed – but not prepared to commit himself to become a Christian. He certainly finds Paul 'not guilty'.

Festus will live only two more years, Agrippa another thirty. But neither of them will have this moment again – the opportunity to come to faith in Christ through the preaching of the apostle Paul.

The voyage to Rome and shipwreck
(27:1 – 28:10)

PAUL SAILS FOR ROME

Paul is at last on his way to Rome – even though he is being taken there as a prisoner (27:1–44). Luke and Aristarchus sail with him, together with other prisoners. Some are on their way to death in the amphitheatre at Rome.

Luke keeps a diary of the journey. It is fresh in his mind, vivid and exciting – the most detailed record of a storm and shipwreck that we have from ancient times.

At first they sail from Caesarea to Sidon, and then north of Cyprus to Myra. This is only a coastal ferry, and they need to find another ship to take them on to Rome.

At Myra they transfer to a large grain-carrying vessel which is on its way from Alexandria to Rome. This can take up to 500 people. The wind is against them and progress is slow. The gentle breezes of summer are now giving way to the stiff north-westerly winds of autumn. The ship is blown far off course and has to take refuge at Fair Havens, on the south coast of Crete.

Paul is one of the most experienced travellers on-board. Luke has recorded eleven of his voyages, which total 3,500 miles at sea. Paul knows that they have lost time and fair weather. The Jewish Fast (the Day of Atonement) has come and gone, and it is now mid-October. They are late, and their voyage has become very dangerous.

Paul warns the centurion – a fair-minded man called Julius – that some lives will be lost if they continue the voyage. But his advice is ignored by the pilot and the owner of the vessel. They will risk the ship and the lives of its crew in their determination to deliver the cargo.

A soft south wind gives hope that they can move along the coast forty miles, to Phoenix. This will be a better harbour for the winter. But they are mistaken. A hurricane blows up which drives the ship out into open sea, where they are at the mercy of the storm. For two weeks they run before the gale, abandoning cargo and all spare equipment. They attempt to slow their runaway progress with a sea anchor, and pass a rope around the hull to hold the vessel together. In the end, they are forced to give up in despair.

But then Paul speaks. He tells the sailors they will all survive. God has promised Paul that he will live to stand trial in Rome. For his sake, the crew and prisoners are safe. From now on, although he is merely one of the prisoners, Paul is the effective commander of the ship.

About midnight, they sense they are approaching an island. Later they will discover this is Malta. Some of the sailors try to escape in the lifeboat, but Paul insists that they all stay together. Towards dawn, he encourages everyone to have something to eat – and leads by example in saying grace and breaking bread.

At first light they see a cove with a beach. They steer towards it, but run aground on a sandbar. The ship begins to break up. The soldiers want to kill the prisoners to prevent them escaping, but the centurion forbids it. He wants to save Paul's life. By swimming, or clinging to planks of wood, everyone comes safely to shore. Today the place is called St Paul's Bay.

ASHORE ON MALTA

The survivors of the wreck are given a friendly welcome by the islanders (28:1–10). As Paul helps to build a fire, he is attacked by a viper. He shakes the snake from his hand, but the natives think he must be a murderer whom the gods are punishing. When Paul doesn't swell up or drop dead, they change their minds and believe he's a god! Certainly God is protecting Paul from both shipwreck and snake.

The chief official of Malta invites some of the visitors to stay at his house, including Paul and Luke. Paul is able to heal several islanders of illness. Among them is their host's father, who has a fever. There is a sickness known as 'Malta fever' which is caused by microbes in the milk of the local goats.

Paul under house arrest in Rome
(28:11–31)

After spending the winter on the island of Malta, they sail again for Italy via Sicily. After all the delays, they cover the last 200 miles in a single day.

'And so we came to Rome' (28:14). The Christians in Rome hear that Paul has landed. They travel thirty-five miles to meet him at the Three Taverns and greet him as an honoured leader. Paul has longed to see these people, having written to them from Corinth before his fateful journey to Jerusalem. They escort him along the Appian Way to Rome.

Once in Rome, Paul is kept under house arrest. He lives in his own rented home, guarded by a soldier. He

Rome

Rome is the capital city of the mighty Roman empire. With its well-disciplined soldiers and skilful engineers, Rome has conquered the world. Her navy has rid the seas of pirates, her judges have established Roman law and her governors provide firm and fair administration to a host of races and communities.

Of course, the Roman empire is far from perfect. There is widespread superstition and corruption, cruelty and vice. In the book of Revelation, Rome is a powerful, blasphemous beast. But as Luke writes, the 'Roman Peace' is providing an ideal climate for the spread of the gospel and the growth of the Christian church.

Luke always portrays Roman officials as honest and good. He also shows, by his account of Paul's adventures, that God is shifting the focus of the church from Jerusalem to Rome. It is in Rome that he closes his record of Paul – leaving him boldly preaching the gospel at the heart of the empire.

The Roman forum.

immediately invites the leaders of the Jewish community to meet him. He explains to them that neither the Jewish nor the Roman authorities have any case against him.

The Jews return, bringing others, and talk all day. As Paul has found before, there are those who accept his message and those who reject it. God told Isaiah that people would look and listen but deliberately resist salvation (Isaiah 6:9–10).

Paul, as always, has first explained the gospel to his fellow Jews. Now he will tell it to the Gentiles. As he knows from experience, they will listen. Luke tells us that Paul lives in Rome for two years, sharing the good news of Jesus with all comers.

At this point Luke draws his story to a close. He has compiled a thorough account of Paul's career, including a detailed record of five trials. One of the aims of this book may be to show that Paul was innocent of the charges brought against him.

From Paul's later letters we guess that he was released and continued his missionary travels. But when he writes his last letter to Timothy he is again under arrest in Rome and awaiting death. It is thought that Paul was executed in AD 67.

There has never been another missionary like Paul. He bravely proclaimed and tirelessly defended the gospel. And in his own life he reflected the single-mindedness and sufferings of the Lord he loved and served so well.

ROMANS

This is Paul's most important letter. It has helped millions of people to become Christians, and shaped the history of the church.

Paul is writing to Christians living in Rome. He has never been to Rome, but he knows some of the Christians there. He hopes to visit them in the near future, on his way to Spain.

In the churches at Rome there are tensions between Jewish and Gentile Christians. Paul carefully and thoroughly explains the difference that Christianity has made to Jews.

Paul also shows what God is doing in the whole of history. Humankind, descended from Adam, is sinful and spiritually dead. But God still loves humanity. He has sent his son, Jesus Christ, to die for the sins of the world.

Now human beings can be right with God, because their sin is dealt with and forgiven. Just as 'in Adam' everyone has died, so 'in Christ' anyone can receive new life. This new life will show itself in holy behaviour and loving relationships.

Outline

Paul's greeting (1:1–17)

Human sin and God's anger (1:18 – 3:20)

The gospel answer (3:21 – 5:21)

Dead to sin, alive to Christ (6:1 – 8:39)

What about Israel? (9:1 – 11:36)

How to live the good news (12:1 – 15:13)

And finally… (15:14 – 16:27)

INTRODUCTION

The church in Rome

Paul may have written his letter to the Romans in AD 57. For three months he stayed in the province of Achaia (the 'Greece' of Acts 20:3), and probably in the city of Corinth.

The clues lie in Paul's mention of Phoebe, Gaius and Erastus in his greetings (16:1, 23). Phoebe may be taking the letter to Rome with her when she travels there on business. She comes from Cenchrea – the eastern port of Corinth. We know that Gaius was baptized by Paul in Corinth (1 Corinthians 1:14), and an inscription has been found in Corinth for someone called Erastus.

The church in Rome is made up of house churches. The leaders are people like Priscilla and Aquila, Aristobulus and Narcissus, whom Paul greets at the end of his letter (16:3–5, 10–11). The households probably meet in different parts of the city, and include both Jewish and Gentile Christians.

Paul mentions twenty-six people by name. Some are men and women converted through his ministry, others are people with whom he has been in prison and others are his friends or relatives. Some are well placed in society, while others have slave names. Nine of them are women and Paul especially values their care and hard work.

It is now eight years since Emperor Claudius expelled the Jews from Rome. There had been trouble with riots, which Suetonius tells us were 'instigated by Chrestus' (Suetonius, *Claudius*, 25:4). If 'Chrestus' is a reference to 'Christ', then perhaps the Jews and Christians were guilty of causing trouble. The result was that a number of Jews (including Aquila and Priscilla) were expelled from the city (Acts 18:2). Now Jews and Jewish Christians are returning to Rome – perhaps to find the church there dominated by Gentiles.

Paul writes his letter to introduce himself to the Christians he hasn't yet met. He wants to outline his gospel, in case they have believed rumours that he is odd and unorthodox. They may also be wondering why he hasn't kept his promise to visit them earlier.

Paul explains that he is currently on his way to Jerusalem, to deliver the aid money raised in Macedonia and Achaia. After this he wants to visit Rome as he passes through on his way to Spain (15:18–24, 28). In the event, Paul will be arrested in Jerusalem and arrive in Rome as a prisoner. We don't know if he ever went to Spain.

Jewish and Gentile Christians

Paul particularly wants to tackle the tension between Jewish and Gentile Christians. As an apostle to the Gentiles, he has welcomed people to Christ without forcing them to be circumcised. In other words, Paul doesn't believe that Gentiles have to become Jews in order to become Christians.

This approach has always caused trouble with strict Jews. They want to ask Paul what else he has discarded. What about the Jewish law – the sacrifices, food laws and festivals? Or has God now discarded Jewish Israel in favour of the Christian church? In his letter, Paul makes it clear that he believes God's calling to Israel hasn't changed, but that Jewish and Gentile Christians belong together.

Paul's argument with the Jews

The Jews have a special relationship with God. God chose them out of all the nations of the world to be his people. He twice rescued them – from slavery in Egypt and from exile in Babylon. He gave them his law as a guide to the good life. Now, as the Jews see it, all they have to do is to keep God's law and, in return, God will keep them!

Paul corrects this reliance on the law. He shows that the Jews are not made right with God by rigidly keeping his law, but by responding to him in faith.

Abraham is the perfect example of faith. Abraham couldn't keep the law, because he lived long before the law was given to Moses. Abraham had never heard of the law. And yet God declared that Abraham was righteous – because Abraham trusted him. And this happened before Abraham was circumcised – so being right with God didn't depend on circumcision either.

So does the law not matter any more? The law is good, and a perfect guide to right living. The problem is that no one has ever managed to keep it. Measured by the law, everyone is found guilty of sin and worthy of death. The law which was intended to lead to life has proved to be a law of sin and death (8:2).

The Jews have treasured the law, but lost the love.

Strict Jews (such as the Pharisees) observe the law in fine and complex detail. But in doing this they have lost the point of the law – which is to love God and one another. Paul says anyone who loves is keeping the law (13:8).

Paul's worry is this. The Jews are defining themselves as the people who keep God's law – but they aren't keeping it! They are counting themselves right with God because they circumcise their baby boys and refuse to eat pork – but so what? These are just 'works' – human gestures leading to national pride and complacency. The law which should attract other nations to its light has become a barrier to keep them out.

Paul wants to say that God's law is good – as far as it goes – and Israel is very dear to God. But now Christ has come! God's plan of salvation is now completely clear. Life with God is not to be found by keeping the law in an elitist and exclusive Israel. Life with God is to be found by faith in Jesus Christ and forgiveness of sins through his perfect sacrifice. This means that the door of faith has swung open for Gentiles as well as Jews.

The letter which changes lives

St Augustine of Hippo was converted through Paul's letter to the Romans. He was born in North Africa and became professor of rhetoric at Milan. He was torn to the point of tears between the truth of Christianity and his love of wild parties and the attractions of a sinful world.

One day, in the summer of AD 386, he picked up a friend's scroll of Romans and read some words at random:

Let us behave decently, as in the daytime, not in orgies and drunkenness, not in sexual immorality and debauchery, not in dissension and jealousy. Rather, clothe yourselves with the Lord Jesus Christ, and do not think about how to gratify the desires of the sinful nature (13:13–14).

Suddenly all was clear. He remembers, 'A light flooded my heart and all the darkness of doubt vanished away' (Augustine, *Confessions*, 8:29).

A thousand years later, in November 1515, a German monk called Martin Luther was professor of theology in the University of Wittenberg. He was teaching Paul's letter to the Romans to his students, when the truth finally dawned on him! He realized that God's righteousness is not something we achieve by our own strenuous efforts, but something God gives in response to our faith. So Luther began to understand and teach 'justification by faith' – we are put right with God by his mercy and grace in sending Jesus to die for our sin. Luther called Paul's letter to the Romans 'really the chief part of the New Testament, and... truly the purest Gospel'.

On 24 May 1738, an English clergyman by the name of John Wesley went to an evening service at Aldersgate Street in London. There he heard some of Martin Luther's commentary on Romans being read aloud. He remembers, 'He was describing the change which God works in the heart through faith in Christ. I felt my heart strangely warmed. I felt I did trust in Christ, Christ alone, for my salvation; and an assurance was given me that he had taken *my* sins away, even *mine*; and saved me from the law of sin and death' (John Wesley, *Works* (1872), volume 1). From Luther's teaching sprang the great Reformation of the church in the 16th century. And through the conversion and preaching of John Wesley, Christianity experienced revival in England in the 18th century. Both owed their inspiration to this letter from Paul.

Many of the Christians in the church at Rome were Gentiles, who would have come from a background of worshipping the traditional Roman gods. The Pantheon was constructed as a shrine to some of these gods, whose statues occupied niches in the walls. As the sun moved round, it shone through the hole in the roof, illuminating each one in turn.

A systematic letter

This letter is not only the most important of Paul's letters, it is also one of the finest pieces of Christian writing of all time. Paul's letter to the Romans is quite systematic. It gives us a summary of his thoughts at the summit of his career.

Some gems from Romans

SIN

Everyone has sinned, without exception, both Jew and Gentile:

All have sinned and fall short of the glory of God (3:23).

RIGHTEOUSNESS

Everyone is put right with God in the same way – not by keeping the law, but by faith in Jesus Christ:

Now a righteousness from God, apart from law, has been made known… This righteousness from God comes through faith in Jesus Christ to all who believe (3:21–22).

Jews and Gentiles belong together as God's people. All are saved by faith alone, because of God's grace.

THE JEWS

Christians have their roots in the Jewish faith and depend on it for their understanding of God. God has not rejected or discarded his Jewish people. They are still central to his plan of salvation (9:1–11:36):

Did God reject his people? By no means (11:1)!

FAITH

Abraham is the prime example of faith. If we live by faith, we are the true children of Abraham:

He [Abraham] is our father in the sight of God, in whom he believed – the God who gives life to the dead and calls things that are not as though they were… he did not waver through unbelief regarding the promise of God, but was strengthened in his faith and gave glory to God, being fully persuaded that God had power to do what he had promised (4:17, 20–21).

ONE ANOTHER

If we belong to Christ, then we accept one another – without racial prejudice or spiritual one-upmanship:

Accept one another… just as Christ accepted you (15:7).

HUMAN GOVERNMENT

The state has God's authority to govern, although the claims of God's kingdom are higher:

The authorities that exist have been established by God (13:1).

OUR SPIRITUAL STRUGGLE

There is a conflict within every Christian: 'I have the desire to do what is good, but I cannot carry it out' (7:18). But the Holy Spirit comes to our aid: 'the Spirit helps us in our weakness' (8:26).

GOD'S CHOICE

God chooses or 'elects' to save whole nations, not just individual people. Paul quotes Hosea: 'I will call them "my people" who are not my people' (9:25). Paul adds that this 'does not depend on human desire or effort, but on God's mercy' (9:16).

DISCOVERING ROMANS

Paul's greeting

Paul introduces himself to the Christians at Rome (1:1–17). His life's work is to share the gospel with non-Jews, and he looks forward to coming to Rome – the Gentile capital of the world.

In a sentence, Paul believes that 'righteousness from God... is by faith from first to last' (1:17). In saying this, he immediately challenges the Jewish belief that righteousness comes by keeping the law. By 'righteousness', Paul doesn't mean living a perfect life, but being in a right relationship with God. Paul agrees that the Jews were the first to believe in the one true God, but insists that salvation is now open to Gentiles as well.

Human sin and God's anger

God's anger against humankind
(1:18–32)

God is invisible, but his work is clearly seen in creation. Humankind has turned away from the truth about God and instead worships images of his creatures. Men and women have spurned a holy relationship with God and looked for satisfaction in perverted sex. This is particularly true of the Gentiles.

People still have consciences and know what is right, but they encourage one another to abandon all self-control. Now the human race is hostile to God, ignorant of his ways and depraved in its behaviour. Instead of being the living image of God, humans are now the most corrupt animals on earth.

God is angry at this state of affairs. But he has given

Paul's views agree with those of the Old Testament prophets. They declared that religious observance and ceremony are meaningless without a desire to obey God.

human beings free will, and he allows their choice even if it means they go from bad to worse.

A word with the Jews
(2:1–29)

While Gentiles have plunged into idolatry and perversion, the Jews have known better. They can look at the Gentiles and condemn them as godless.

But have the Jews actually lived according to God's law, or have they merely listened to it? Merely listening isn't enough. The Jews have been stubborn towards God and need to repent. One day God's searchlight will also turn on them. Indeed, God will judge them first.

God will judge everyone by whatever light they have: the light of the law (in the case of the Jews) and the light of conscience (in the case of the Gentiles who do not have the law).

Paul intensifies his attack on self-righteous Jews. They are proud of the law, but they break it like everyone else. They are proud of circumcision – but it means nothing without obedience to God. In God's sight, true circumcision is an attitude of heart.

God's faithfulness
(3:1–8)

Having demolished Jewish self-confidence, Paul now gets the Jews to count their blessings.

For one thing, the Jews have access to God's word. For another, they are part of God's plan to save not just the Jews, but the whole world. Even their failures can show how God acts in justice and mercy.

No one is righteous
(3:9–20)

Paul concludes, using quotations from the Old Testament, that both Jews and Gentiles are in the same situation. All have sinned. For Jews, the law has merely shown them the full extent of their sin. If they think otherwise, they are adding pride and self-deception to their long list of failings.

The gospel answer

But now Paul comes to the good news. Forgiveness and peace with God are freely available through Jesus Christ.

Right with God through faith in Christ
(3:21–26)

Paul declares that it is possible to be right with God in a way that is quite different from keeping the Jewish law. It sounds scandalous, but the Old Testament always knew of it.

This righteousness is open to all. Just as Jews and Gentiles are together in sin, so they can be together in salvation.

The means by which human sin can be forgiven is the sacrifice of Jesus on the cross. A sacrifice is the payment of an innocent life for a guilty life. Animals and birds are killed in the temple so that the lives of their owners can be spared. But all these sacrifices are inadequate and have to be constantly repeated. Now Jesus has become the perfect sacrifice – not an animal, bird or human hero, but the Son of God. His perfect life has been freely offered for the sins of the whole world and for all time. His righteousness has been credited to us.

Paul says that through the sacrifice of Jesus we are 'justified'. Our punishment has been borne by Christ, and now it is as if we had never sinned. The sacrifice of Jesus is an 'atonement' – bringing God and human beings together and making peace.

No boasting!
(3:27–31)

So Jews have nothing to boast about. They haven't worked out their own salvation by keeping the law. They are saved by faith in Jesus, just as the Gentiles are. The law is still immensely valuable – but only as a guide to living, not as a way of being saved.

Abraham was saved by faith too!
(4:1–25)

Paul shows how justification by faith worked for Abraham. Abraham was the father of the Jewish race – so what was true for him should be true for everyone.

Abraham was a pioneer of faith. He spent his life believing God for impossible things. He believed God was giving him a land, although he could never conquer or own it. He believed God was making him the father of a nation, although he and his wife were old and childless. And even when he had a son, Abraham was prepared to offer Isaac as a sacrifice, if that was what God wanted.

God counted Abraham's faith as righteousness (Genesis 15:6). It wasn't a righteousness achieved by keeping God's law. God's law wasn't known until the time of Moses. It wasn't a righteousness through being circumcised, or offering Isaac – because both of those experiences were still in the future. It wasn't a righteousness based on Abraham's perfect choices – his mistakes are recorded for all to read. Abraham wasn't perfect – but he had faith.

Paul says this is exactly the kind of faith we must have in Christ. We trust that God will do what he has

A whole new life

Human beings are born with a sinful nature. We are dead to God – and driven by selfish and decadent desires. Because of this, God is angry. He is holy and just. If he is to be true to himself, then he can only condemn us to his judgment.

But God loves us. He hates our sin, but he loves us. What can he do, to be true to both his judgment and his love?

God's answer is to send Jesus, his own dear Son, into the world. Jesus is

God in human life, taking on our sinful nature, temptations and circumstances. In living the perfect life, and dying for the sin of the world, Jesus makes peace between God and humankind.

Here is a sensational free gift! Jesus Christ has paid his life for our sin and secured our forgiveness from God. He has also broken the stranglehold of Satan on our lives – although the struggle with our old nature continues for the time being. Jesus has enabled us to become God's children – the

beginning of a whole new creation, free of all evil, fear, sin and death.

promised – which is far beyond our own ability to achieve. It is not Jews but believers who are Abraham's spiritual descendants.

Peace with God
(5:1–11)

Through Jesus, we have peace with God, the gift of his Spirit and joy in the hope of glory. We may suffer for what we believe – but our suffering makes our hope all the more thrilling. It is absolutely astonishing that God should send his Son to die for us – the only possible remedy for our desperate situation. We didn't design or deserve such a deliverance. It is God's free gift. And if this is how much God loved us when we were his enemies, what a wonderful relationship unfolds, now that we are his friends!

Death through Adam, life through Christ
(5:12–21)

Paul describes how the death of Christ has been the answer to the sin of Adam.

Adam was the first human being, and his sin infected the entire human race. The penalty for that sin was death – even before the law was given, so that people knew what sin was.

Now, through the righteousness of one perfect man, Jesus Christ, life is spreading to the whole human race. Grace wins!

Dead to sin, alive to Christ

Paul explores what it means to live the Christian life. Does being a Christian mean we are permanently forgiven, so that we can now sin as much as we like? Does it mean we won't be tempted any more? Does it mean we are automatically good and holy?

Paul teaches that we are still responsible for our choices and actions. There is nothing automatic about holiness. As Christians, we find ourselves in a lifelong struggle with our old nature, which refuses to die. But Paul has many insights and encouragements to offer.

The Christian and sin
(6:1–23)

We have been baptized into Christ. Our baptism acted out our dying to sin and rising to new life with Christ. We are far too closely identified with Jesus to carry on

sinning. We have died to sin. In theory, we can no more sin than a dead body can!

Of course, we still have free will. We can sin if we want to, but it will be out of keeping with our Christian character. But look at it positively: instead of letting sin dictate our actions, we are free to do right! And which master do we prefer? The only wage sin ever paid was death. But now God *gives* us eternal life. To serve him is perfect freedom.

The Christian and the law
(7:1–25)

What about the law? Do we discard the law because we have died to sin and now live in grace?

Paul uses the picture of a woman being widowed and marrying someone else. She is free to marry again because her first husband has died; her legal contract to him has been cancelled. Paul sees a parallel with our experience: the death of Jesus has cancelled our obligation to sin. Now we are released for a new relationship with God; not bound by the law, but set free by the Spirit.

Paul teaches that the law is good. The law tells us which actions are sinful. Of course, this tends to awaken temptation – but that's not the law's fault.

Paul describes the dilemma of someone who knows that the law is good, but can't keep it. No doubt this was his own experience when he was a devout Jew, delighting in the law, but constantly ambushed by sin. It is from this constant and frustrating failure that Christ has so gloriously rescued him.

The Christian and the Spirit
(8:1–39)

When we belong to Christ, we live in a new dimension. We have a new freedom, a new power, a new Father and a new hope. Paul says we are actually 'in' Christ Jesus! The Holy Spirit within us lifts us out of the gravitational pull of sin and death and sets us in orbit around Christ and our heavenly Father.

Jesus, by his death for us, has met the law's demands in full. When he died, he cried out, 'It is finished!' or 'Paid!' (John 19:30). No further charges can be brought against us. No more condemnation. No more blame. No more penalties. No more guilt.

God has done something for us that the law could never do. The law was beautiful and good – but it sentenced us to death. But God sent his own Son in the likeness of sinful humanity and Jesus gave himself to die for us. Because of his sacrifice, we are forgiven and released.

We are no longer on the dreary religious treadmill of knowing the right and doing the wrong. Instead, God has given us his own Spirit to live within us. The Spirit helps us overcome our old sinful nature, and assures us that we are now God's children.

Instead of crying in desolation and despair, 'What a wretched man I am!' (7:24), we cry 'Abba!' – 'Dear Father!' We have been adopted into God's family and are heirs of eternal glory with Christ.

So what's going on now? Does this mean we lead a perfect life with no problems? No. We still live in the same world, with its wickedness, disasters, pressures and fears. Satan continues to test us – and death awaits us in the end.

But Paul says that we know who we are, and we understand what's happening to us.

We're living in the overlap between the resurrection of Jesus and the final victory of God. We're living in the old cosmos which is in the throes of giving birth to the new creation.

This is a stressful process. The creation is groaning with pain and frustration. We, living in the old creation but part of the new, are groaning with longing for release. The Spirit within us – a Holy Spirit in a sinful nature – is groaning with prayer that God's will be done.

But God is winning. He is reversing the effects of the fall, and recreating his creation. He is transforming us from sinners into his children. If we doubt his commitment, then look again at the love he has already shown us by sending his only Son to die for us. He will surely finish what he has started.

Yes, we are stressed. We are living for God in a world which has rejected him. We share the suffering of Christ. But there is no power in earth or heaven which can stop God loving us now. Every dimension of creation – life and death, the invisible powers of the supernatural and everything that exists in time and space – is subject to the lordship of Jesus Christ.

What about Israel?

Paul turns again to God's purpose for Israel. Jews in Rome will be reading this part of the letter very carefully!

Does the successful gospel mission to the Gentiles mean that the Jewish stage of God's plan is now jettisoned like a burned-out rocket? Paul believes not – and he argues his case very thoroughly.

God's sovereign choice
(9:1–5)

Paul's heart goes out to Israel. He longs that they may turn to Christ and be saved.

The Jews are immensely privileged. They have lived and breathed God's blessings throughout their history. From the call of Abraham to the birth of Christ, they have been at the heart of God's plan.

Surely if God always finishes what he begins, then he will save Israel too. He hasn't divorced the Jews to marry the Gentiles. His purpose is to unite Jews and Gentiles in one new people of faith.

God's amazing grace
(9:6–29)

Paul explains that God hasn't broken his covenant or discarded his people. But we need to think again about what 'Israel' really means.

The true Israel was never the race that shared Abraham's blood group, but the people who shared his faith. And God has always sprung surprises. He chose Jacob instead of Esau, to assert his sovereign right to do so. He hardened Pharaoh's heart, to highlight his own greater power.

In other words, God does what he wants! There are those God has chosen and those he hasn't. If we cross-question God on this, we are like clay criticizing the potter.

Israel's mistake
(9:30 – 10:21)

Israel has forgotten God's sovereign mercy and right to choose. Instead she has defined herself by race and law, and rejected everyone else out of prejudice. In so doing, she has tripped over the grace and mercy of God which he has shown in Jesus Christ – 'a stone that will make people stumble' (9:33).

Now Paul longs that Israel may be saved. The Jews are enthusiastic for righteousness – but they think they can do it themselves. Meanwhile, Christ has closed the road of law – it never was a way to salvation. Instead, he has opened wide the gate of grace. This grace is freely offered to both Jews and

Gentiles. All have the same Lord and receive the same blessings.

This is the good news which Paul is preaching – but not all Jews are accepting it. They don't yet see that this is their God at work, extending to the Gentiles the mercy he has already shown to them.

Israel will be saved

(11:1–32)

Paul is quite convinced that God hasn't finished with Israel. He knows from his own experience that even the most self-righteous and militant Pharisee can be saved.

So why are so many Jews rejecting Christ at the moment? Paul believes their hostility will be useful – because it will show up the grace of God and the faith of the Gentiles. The fact that Jews don't believe allows God to spring another surprise – that he chooses Gentiles. Paul adds excitedly: if Jewish rejection means Gentile selection, what wonderful things await us when the Jews accept Christ!

By preaching to Gentiles, Paul hopes to make Jews jealous. Israel is still the main stock of God's people, into which the Gentiles are now being grafted. Gentiles must be careful not to make the same mistake of pride – or they will find themselves pruned out again.

So God still calls the Jews. Before Christ, the Jews were 'in' and the Gentiles were 'out'. Now, for a time, the Jews are 'out'. But the underlying trend has always been that God is wanting all people everywhere to be saved.

Paul's hymn of praise

(11:33–36)

Paul has come to the summit of his gospel presentation. He surveys the mighty panorama of God's plan – Jew and Gentile, creation and new creation, all united in Christ. He praises the majesty and mystery of our glorious God.

How to live the good news

Paul has set out his Christian beliefs. Now he outlines Christian behaviour. New life 'in Christ' isn't just a beautiful theory, but a daily experience. His Jewish readers will want to see what has happened to sacrifice, community and the law.

Living sacrifices

(12:1–2)

Paul begins with sacrifice. A sacrifice is the offering of an animal in the temple – it's a life paid for human sin. Such a sacrifice is costly – but second-hand and dead. Now, says Paul, make sacrifice direct, personal – and living. Offer *yourselves* to God. This is true worship. And don't be

moulded by the pressures of the world, but allow yourself to be transformed by the mind of Christ.

A humble community

(12:3–8)

Next Paul deals with community life. There is no place for pride. Christian living is humble giving. We belong to one another like different parts of the same body. We each contribute our gifts – speaking God's word, serving, teaching, encouraging, giving, leading, caring. These are God's gifts to us for one another. Instead of pride there is faith, humility, encouragement, generosity, hard work and good humour.

A standard of loving

(12:9–21)

Now Paul recasts the law. As always, it is a guide to loving relationships. But now love is not measured and

Paul condemns the attitude of Jews who regard themselves as righteous merely because they are descended from Abraham. Paul argues that Abraham's righteousness resulted from his faith in God, and it is on that basis that anyone may be saved. He states that the Jewish people are nevertheless significant to God, as he has entrusted them with his laws. A scroll of the law is held aloft during a Jewish festival.

mechanical, but genuine, joyful and from the heart. The old penalty clauses and guidelines for revenge are replaced by blessings and encouragements to make peace.

Matters of judgment and punishment should be left to God. He is the One who is really wronged, and he alone gets perfectly angry. We should bless our enemies – and make them blush!

Be good citizens

(13:1–7)

The Roman Christians must respect their secular government. It has God's authority to punish evil and promote good. Jews who have been dispersed around the world by persecution or business have always honoured the civil authority, and Christians should do the same.

Sometimes a dictator or regime goes beyond God's brief. In that case, Christians must make a stand. But Paul is not thinking of such circumstances. He is talking about paying taxes – and showing respect.

Love your neighbour

(13:8–10)

The commandments still stand. The laws against adultery, murder, theft and covetousness all add up to loving others as we love ourselves. When we love like this, we keep all God's law in its true spirit.

Live in the light

(13:11–14)

It is time to get ready to meet Christ. The darkness of this world and its ways are not for us. Wake up! Live in the light of his coming!

Accept one another

(14:1 – 15:13)

The Christian church is a new community. In Rome, Christians of Jewish and Gentile backgrounds are going into one another's houses and sharing the same meals – for the first time in their lives.

Paul knows that some Christian Jews will still want to keep their food laws and observe their holy days. He describes their faith as 'weak'. They don't realize Jesus has done everything for their salvation. They feel they still have to add some details themselves.

Gentile Christians, on the other hand, may know they can eat anything, and regard every day as holy. If so, their faith is 'strong' – but they must not be proud.

Paul tells Christians of different backgrounds to respect one another's consciences. Everyone should take their lead from the Lord. Those who hold to a strict diet, avoid certain foods or refuse meat that has been killed in pagan temples do this to honour the Lord. Others thank God for everything and eat with grateful hearts. They, too, honour the Lord in their way. Each group should accept the other, as Christ has accepted both.

Paul knows all about food laws. He used to be a Pharisee. Now he can eat anything! But he is careful not to offend anyone with his new-found freedom. If someone will be misled or upset by what Paul eats, then Paul won't eat it. Why should he distress his fellow Christian just to show off his liberty?

Paul gives Jesus as the perfect example. No one was more free to please himself than Jesus, and yet he always put himself out for the needs of others. This is the way that leads to unity and so gives glory to God. And diehard Jews can see their own scriptures coming true. *Gentiles* are being welcomed into the community of faith.

And finally...

Paul tells his Christian readers that they are good in God's sight and able to teach one another (15:14 – 16:27). His own priestly duty is to proclaim the gospel, so that Gentiles may offer themselves as holy and lively sacrifices to God. In so doing, Paul carries on the true work of the temple in Jerusalem, proclaiming the greatness and goodness of God to the whole world.

Paul closes with an update on his own plans, and greetings to his many dear friends.

He commends Phoebe to the Christians in Rome (16:1). She comes from Cenchrea, the port of Corinth, where she is a servant or deacon of the church.

Priscilla and Aquila first met Paul in Corinth. They had been expelled from Rome by the emperor Claudius, along with other Jews. Like Paul, they were tentmakers, and the three worked together both in tentmaking and church-planting (Acts 18:18). Since then they have also lived in Ephesus, but now they are back in Rome – and still with a Christian meeting in their home.

There is a saying, 'You can tell a man by his friends.' Here Paul makes special mention of twenty-four friends, including six women. Half of them have names which could link them with the emperor's household, even though they may be slaves. Andronicus and Junias (a woman?) have been Christians longer than Paul, and he refers to them as apostles (gospel pioneers). Rufus may be the son of Simon of Cyrene, who was forced to carry the crosspiece for Jesus on his way to crucifixion (Mark 15:21).

The number and variety of Paul's friends, the range of their shared experience and the warmth of his greetings tell us much about the great apostle. We glimpse a fellowship of joy and suffering which is loving and hard-working, but vulnerable to division and deceit. Paul ends with praise that God will strengthen them and use them in his mission to the world.

1 CORINTHIANS

Paul founded the church at Corinth between AD 50 and 52. This letter is written from Ephesus a year or two later.

The Christians at Corinth are proud, lively, gifted and quarrelsome. They live in a society which is pagan and immoral, and this seeps into their behaviour. They also argue among themselves about the status of their leaders and the value of their spiritual gifts.

Paul writes to tackle these problems. In doing so he gives us valuable teaching about the church as the body of Christ, and the prime importance of love.

Outline

Paul greets the Christians in Corinth (1:1–9)

Quarrels in the church (1:10 – 4:21)

Scandal, legal action and sex (5:1 – 6:20)

Paul answers some questions (7:1 – 16:4)

Future plans and greetings (16:5–24)

INTRODUCTION

The church in Corinth

Paul arrives in Corinth after his visit to Athens, and stays there for about eighteen months between AD 50 and 52. Luke tells us in the Acts of the Apostles how Paul lives with a Jewish couple, Aquila and Priscilla, and joins them in their business of tentmaking (Acts 18:1–3).

Paul founds the church in Corinth, and then moves on to Ephesus. In Ephesus he gets news from Corinth that various problems have arisen. It is to deal with these problems that he writes the letter we know as 1 Corinthians.

The church in Corinth is reflecting the society in which it is set. There is pride, selfishness, jealousy and immorality. There are splits between different groups and there is rivalry between the leaders.

Some of the questions being raised are very practical – about sex and marriage, living among pagans and paying apostles. Others are more spiritual – understanding spiritual gifts, controlling Christian meetings and believing in the resurrection.

Paul takes each problem in turn and shows how the gospel applies to it. He has a brilliant mind and a warm heart. He gives guidelines for holiness in a pagan society. He puts spiritual gifts in their proper perspective. He teaches about leading worship meetings, and the meaning of the Lord's Supper.

The most famous part of this letter is chapter 13. Here Paul describes love in its many aspects. Even the most sensational spiritual gift is nothing without love.

'I came to you in weakness and fear, and with much trembling'

When Paul first visited Corinth, his confidence was very low. He had travelled from Athens, where he had made very little impact with the gospel. He had found that city steeped in idol-worship, with high-minded philosophers resistant to God's truth. Also, he was lonely.

Paul supported himself in Corinth by working as a tentmaker. He met a Jewish couple, Aquila and Priscilla, who had been expelled from Rome for their faith. They were also leather workers and Paul worked alongside them in their business. They forged a lasting friendship.

When Silas and Timothy arrived from Macedonia, they brought with them a gift of money from the churches. This gift enabled Paul to give all his time to his gospel work.

The book of Acts tells how Paul preached in the synagogue at first, and the leader Crispus was converted. But the Jews rejected Paul's message, and he left the

Colourful Corinth

Corinth is the capital of the Roman province of Achaia, the southern part of Greece. The city stands on a neck of land about five miles wide, which links southern Greece with the mainland to the north.

Across this bridge of land flows trade – by road between north and south, and between seas to east and west. Because of its access to the sea, Corinth has two ports – Lechaeum and Cenchrea – and a slipway for dragging small ships from one side of the isthmus to the other. In modern times the two gulfs have been linked by the Corinth Canal, completed in 1893.

Corinth has a long history. Before 146 BC, it was famous for the temple of Aphrodite, the Greek goddess of love. But in 146 BC the city was destroyed by the Romans, and not refounded until Julius Caesar made it a Roman colony in 44 BC.

The city Paul knows is a busy, wealthy, cosmopolitan centre. The population of 100,000 includes people of many races, classes, cultures and religions. As a Roman colony it has retired soldiers, poor people who have been rehoused from Rome and freed slaves making their way in the world.

People have come to Corinth from many races and nations, thrown together by the search for business and the quest for pleasure. Anything goes! In the ancient world, a 'Corinthian' is a proud extrovert with a larger-than-life appetite for strong drink, wild parties and easy sex. What chance will the good news of Jesus have among such people?

synagogue and moved to the house next door. The houseowner's name was Titius Justus – which suggests he was a Gentile (Acts 18:7).

After this difficult beginning, Paul was encouraged by a vision of Christ. The Lord told him to continue preaching and teaching, and promised to protect him from the attacks of his enemies. When the Jews brought Paul before the Roman governor, he dismissed their charges and threw them out!

Another synagogue ruler, Sosthenes, may be the person mentioned at the beginning of this letter – in which case, he has also become a Christian (Acts 18:17).

The old gods

All the old gods of paganism are alive and well and living in Corinth. Overlooking the city is Acrocorinth, a hill of some 1,850 feet. Built on its summit is the great temple of Aphrodite, the Greek goddess of love. She is a sex goddess like Ashtoreth – whom the Israelites were repeatedly forbidden to worship in the days of the kings Solomon, Jeroboam and Josiah.

At the base of Acrocorinth is the temple of Melikertes, the god of sailors and navigation. He is the nature god Melkart – the Baal-idol brought to Israel by the evil princess Jezebel when she married King Ahab.

Finally, in the centre of Corinth, is the temple of Apollo – god of the arts and homosexuality.

Paul's visits and letters to Corinth

The letters, which we call 1 and 2 Corinthians, aren't the only letters Paul wrote to this young church.

In 1 Corinthians, Paul mentions a previous letter he wrote to them (1 Corinthians 5:9), about sexual purity. In 2 Corinthians, Paul talks about a stern letter he wrote to them, which hurt them and which he regretted sending (2 Corinthians 7:8).

Luke tells us about Paul's first visit to Corinth in Acts 18. But there were other visits. In 2 Corinthians, Paul reminds them of a warning he gave them on his *second* visit, and says he is ready to visit them a *third* time (2 Corinthians 13:2; 12:14).

FITTING THE PIECES TOGETHER

From the information we have, it is possible to suggest a sequence of events. It reveals a stormy relationship between Paul and his readers!

Paul first writes to the Corinthians to teach them about holy living (2 Corinthians 6:14 – 7:1). Then, while he is in Ephesus, he hears from Chloe's people that there are splits and rivalries in the church. He writes 1 Corinthians 1–4 to tackle the problem.

Before he sends this letter, Paul receives further news of scandals and chaotic behaviour at Corinth. He receives a letter from the Corinthians, in which they ask his opinion on matters of marriage and eating 'idol meat'. He adds 1 Corinthians 5–16, and follows the letter by visiting them himself.

This visit turns out badly, with both sides getting hurt. Paul gives the Corinthians stern warnings, but they refuse to respect him as a true apostle. In the end, Paul writes a letter which is so strong that he fears they will reject him completely. Some scholars think this letter is preserved in 2 Corinthians 10–13.

But there is a happy ending. Titus arrives with the good news that the Corinthians regret their behaviour and are longing to see Paul again (2 Corinthians 7:6–7). In his relief, Paul writes a peacemaking letter – which we have as 2 Corinthians 1–9.

DISCOVERING 1 CORINTHIANS

Paul greets the Christians in Corinth

Paul includes Sosthenes in his greeting (1:1–9). In Luke's account of Paul's time in Corinth, Sosthenes is a synagogue leader who gets beaten up by a crowd that was really waiting to attack Paul (Acts 18:17). If this is the same man, he has now become a trusted Christian brother.

Paul highlights the holiness and unity that all Christians share – not by their own efforts, but through belonging to Jesus Christ. He thanks God for their exciting progress and spiritual gifts.

Quarrels in the church

Paul has heard from some of Chloe's people that there are quarrels and splits in the church at Corinth (1:10 – 4:21). The believers are naming themselves after their favourite leader – Paul, Apollos, Cephas (Peter) or even Christ.

The Corinthians want their church leaders to be impressive. Peter has a big personality and Apollos is a brilliant speaker. But Paul disappoints them. He is a small man with poor health and a stammer.

Paul tells the Corinthians that they are looking for the wrong things in their leaders – and in themselves. The message of Jesus is that God takes foolish, humble and weak people and gives them the wisdom and power of Christ.

Jesus didn't look very powerful or sound very eloquent when he hung on the cross. Jews saw his death as a scandal – no Messiah would ever let that happen to him. The Greeks saw his death as ridiculous – not at all godlike!

But, says Paul, the death of Jesus was the wisest and most powerful thing that God has ever done. And if we're looking for something to boast about, then let's boast that Jesus died for us.

Wisdom from the Spirit
(2:6–16)

Paul sees a huge difference between human wisdom and God's wisdom. God's wisdom has nothing to do with pride or cleverness. It is about perceiving spiritual truth. If the secular rulers had possessed such insight they would never have crucified Jesus. And yet God's wisdom is most clearly seen in situations of weakness and suffering.

It is God's Spirit who knows God's wisdom, just as a person's thoughts are known to that person alone. But this same Spirit has been given to every Christian. It is God's Spirit within us that gives us spiritual wisdom and shows us the thoughts and purposes of Christ.

The Greek philosopher Socrates. Paul comments that Greeks are searching for wisdom, and the message of a god who died on a cross makes no sense to them. It is, however, God's means of saving humankind, and makes perfect sense when understood from God's point of view.

Leaders are servants
(3:1 – 4:21)

Paul recalls that when he was with the Corinthians he could only teach them very simple truths – like giving a baby milk. He says they are still childish in the way they squabble over their leaders.

Christian leaders aren't rivals. They are just servants who are doing their bit in God's work. If the church is like a growing crop, then Paul is a planter and Apollos a waterer. But only God makes it grow. If the church is like a building, then Paul laid a foundation in Corinth and others are adding to it.

Christians mustn't be distracted by comparing personalities and gifts. The wonderful truth is that they are *God's* temple, where his Spirit lives and works.

What should the Corinthians look for in a Christian leader? Paul says they should look for someone who is the servant of Christ and a faithful guardian of the gospel. As for himself, he doesn't care what they think of him. The only opinion he values is God's.

The Corinthians are full of their new-found wealth and wisdom. They share the riches and reign of Christ! But Paul believes they misunderstand the Christian life.

Far from ruling the world, Paul feels like a prisoner being dragged along at the end of a victory procession. For him, to be a Christian is to share the public rejection and suffering of Jesus. Paul isn't the cream – he's the scum. And the Corinthians should follow him, because he's their spiritual father. He warns them that he will soon come to challenge their spiritual pride.

Scandal, legal action and sex

Scandal!
(5:1–13)

Corinth is a very sexy place. To be a 'Corinthian' means living to satisfy all your appetites for food and drink and sex. In Corinth everything can be done to excess, because nobody knows you and nobody cares. But the church should be different.

Paul has heard that one of the Christian men at Corinth is having sex with his father's wife. This probably means he is living with his stepmother while his father is still alive. This is forbidden several times by the laws of Moses (in Leviticus 18:8; Deuteronomy 22:30; 27:20). It is a situation which would be offensive even to pagans.

To Paul, this is outrageous. It is a blatant and continuing breach of Christian holiness. But the Corinthians are proud of it! They're not hung up on all the old 'don'ts'. They can do what they like because Christ has set them free!

Paul tells the Christians at Corinth that they should have reacted to this man's behaviour with united grief. It should have upset them deeply that a Christian brother could shame his Lord in this way. They should have expelled him, for his own sake. Much better for him to be punished in this life and come to his senses, than lose his eternal salvation.

Paul reminds the Corinthian Christians that they are *pure*. They are living in the sunlight of Christ. They are an Easter people. At Passover, the spring-cleaning sweeps all the old yeast from a house. Yeast is a symbol of wickedness, because it spreads so completely. Now Christians are to have a new kind of yeast – they must be filled with sincerity and truth. Paul doesn't expect Christians to be perfect – but he urges them to be open and honest.

Paul has written to them before about all this. In a previous letter he told them not to have anything to do with people who are sexually immoral. Some of the Corinthians thought he meant that they shouldn't mix with the rest of society. But Paul now explains that he didn't mean that at all.

Christians *must* mix with unbelievers. That's what Jesus came to do. He had a reputation for sharing meals with tax collectors and other outcasts, and for being a friend of sinners. He told his disciples that they must do the same – like light shining in darkness and yeast mixing with dough. This is how the people of the world will see the gospel lived and hear it explained.

But it is a different matter to mix with evil in the church. The church is a holy people, and its standard of living must express the holiness of God. Paul says that Christians must have nothing to do with church members who are flouting the standards of holiness. It isn't only in matters of sex that Christians must be pure. The same applies to greed for money and possessions, lying, being judgmental about people, drunkenness and robbery.

Paul says that people who call themselves Christians but persistently behave in these ways must be expelled. They must be excluded from the church's fellowship meal. Today we call this 'excommunication' – being banned from attending Holy Communion.

Paul says this discipline is the task of the whole church. It is not just the responsibility of an apostle or leader to take action against an immoral member. Everyone must be involved, acting together as a body.

Lawsuits among believers
(6:1–11)

Paul turns to another subject. Christians are taking each other to court! This is something other people may have to do, but between Christians it should be unnecessary. Paul finds it incredible.

Paul teaches that God's people will one day be judges of heaven and earth – as Daniel prophesied and Jesus promised (Daniel 7:27; Matthew 19:28). If this is the case, then surely the Corinthians can sort out their differences here and now, without going before pagan magistrates. Even the least important member of the church can act as a judge.

If Christians prosecute one another then they have failed to understand the gospel. Paul says it's better to lose your cause than insist on your rights. This is what Jesus taught when he said, 'Turn the other cheek… go the extra mile' (Matthew 5:39–42). Forgiveness and giving way to one another should be the marks of Christian fellowship.

The good-sex guide
(6:12–20)

Paul says that the kingdom of God is for those who have been made pure by Jesus Christ. Sex outside marriage, male prostitution, sodomy and indecent acts all make us impure. Paul knows that the Corinthians used to behave in those ways, but now they are clean.

Paul is being challenged by Christians who say it doesn't matter what they do. They are 'free'. Their bodies don't matter any more, because their souls are safe with God. And anyway, anything they do can be forgiven…

Paul agrees that it is a wonderful thing to be free. Because Jesus died for us we are forgiven our sins and released from guilt. But our freedom isn't a permission to do whatever we like. Paul sees our freedom as a liberty to do what's right. We're not owned, obsessed or driven by any habit or passion, except the power of the new life of Jesus within us.

Paul teaches that our bodies are not just bins for food and tools for sex. Our bodies belong to the Lord. They are part of his own body now. It is unthinkable to use a Christian body, which is part of Jesus, for sex with a prostitute.

Does Paul think our bodies don't matter? Quite the opposite. He believes they matter very much. God made us with bodies and Jesus had one when he shared our life on earth. Our resurrection bodies will be part of our identity in heaven. For now, our bodies are the place in which we meet with God and from which we serve him – in other words, they are temples of God's Holy Spirit.

What's so special about sex?

Paul advises Christians to flee from wrong sex. 'Just run!' – as Joseph did when Potiphar's wife tried to seduce him (Genesis 39:12).

The sex act is unique. It unites our whole self – body, mind and spirit – with the body, mind and spirit of another person. The Bible describes this as becoming 'one flesh' – that is, two persons becoming one 'self' (Genesis 2:24).

Sex is a beautiful and complete commitment. For human beings, it's the ultimate one-anotherness. For Christians, it's a glimpse of the Trinity of God – the continual self-giving of Father, Son and Spirit. For these reasons, the proper use of sex is expressed in marriage – the total togetherness and ongoing commitment of husband and wife.

Paul answers some questions

Paul now turns to some of the matters the Corinthians mentioned in their letter to him. They include questions about getting married and staying single, eating meat which has been offered as a pagan sacrifice and when to use spiritual gifts.

Christians and marriage
(7:1–40)

The Corinthians have asked Paul about marriage. Should Christians get married? Is it purer and more Christian to stay single? If you marry, is it better if you don't have sex?

There are two main views going around in the church in Corinth. One is that sex doesn't affect your spiritual life so you can do whatever you like. The other is that sex is sinful and is to be avoided as an activity of Satan. Paul has to steer between the two.

He begins by saying it's good to be single. This may be what Paul has done himself; but he knows it's not everyone's gift. It is usual for a Jewish rabbi to marry. Paul may have had a wife who died or left him. He has found it best to be single in his kind of work – travelling and teaching, working with a team (or serving prison sentences), without always worrying about a wife and family.

For those whose gift is to be married, Paul prescribes a partnership of one man and one woman. There were marriages in Old Testament times in which a patriarch had more than one wife – but their stories tell of rivalry and jealousy, cheating and revenge.

In an immoral society, the Christian answer is *not* to ban sex and avoid marriage. Paul advises those who marry to have a wholehearted sex life – each knowing that they share their body with their partner.

Paul says it's not super-spiritual to go without sex in marriage – it just opens you to temptation. If you both agree to concentrate on prayer for a while, then do so – but make sure that you renew your sex life afterwards. Christian married couples are to avoid temptation by having sex!

A SEXUAL REVOLUTION

Some people think Paul is unfair to women. He tells men it's better to be single. He tells wives to give in to their husbands. But to sum up his teaching like this is unfair to Paul.

Paul is writing to Christians who are living in a

society that abuses and debases sex. In Corinth a woman can be used as a sex slave or trapped in a loveless marriage. Naturally, the Christians wonder whether sex is dirty, and marriage is second-best.

Into this confusion, Paul brings a sexual revolution. He teaches men to give themselves for their wives. No Greek or Roman had ever heard of such a thing! He teaches wives that they have the same rights and duties in marriage as their husbands. What a liberation for pagan wives! They have been treated as part of their husband's property; now they are released into equal status and mutual love.

A COUPLE THAT PRAYS TOGETHER...

Both Paul and Peter write about married couples praying together (7:5; 1 Peter 3:7). It is one of the most important things they do. Jesus taught the importance of praying in pairs. Did he have marriage in mind when he promised: 'If two of you on earth agree about anything you ask for, it will be done for you by my Father in heaven' (Matthew 18:19)?

WHAT ABOUT THOSE WHO ARE SINGLE?

Some of the Christians at Corinth are unmarried – either because they have never married, or because they are widows (7:8–9). What's best for them?

A Jewish marriage contract. In his first letter to the church at Corinth, Paul sets out his understanding of the purpose and conduct of Christian marriage.

Paul advises those who are single to stay that way. He himself is single, and he finds that he can devote himself completely to the work of the gospel. But Paul realizes that some people are fired up with sexual desire – and it's much better for them to marry than burn with frustration.

It's not unnatural to remain single, and it's not second-best to marry. Both marriage and singleness are right, when they are God's purpose for you.

WHAT ABOUT DIVORCE?

What about those who got married and now regret it (7:10–16)? They feel they have married the wrong person, or they would like their freedom back. Some, of course, have become Christians – and are feeling trapped in marriage to a pagan partner.

To such people Paul gives very direct advice – advice he says is straight from the Lord. He says they must remain committed to their marriages.

Jesus taught that marriage is for life. If a husband or wife divorces a partner and marries someone else, they are committing adultery. They are breaking a union that God himself has made (Mark 10:11–12). Paul sees only two options for a married couple who have fallen out: they must stay separate and single – or they must be reconciled.

Is there a special case for divorce where a husband or wife has become a Christian, and now needs to be released from marriage to a non-Christian partner? Paul says not. A non-Christian partner is blessed by marriage to a Christian – and so are their children. Being blessed isn't the same as being saved, but it means that God's goodness is permeating the relationship.

If the non-Christian partner can't stand the situation, then he or she may leave. Paul much prefers that couples should stay together, but if this means living in a constant state of anger and bitterness, it is better to part. It is not clear from Paul's teaching whether the Christian partner is then free to remarry. Paul says he or she is 'not bound' – that is, not forced to stay with a marriage that the non-Christian partner has rejected.

God wants his people to live in peace. In staying together, and with God's help, it may be that a non-Christian partner will be converted.

FAITH IN THE CIRCUMSTANCES

Paul teaches Christians to accept their situation (7:17–24). If they are married, then they should remain married. If they are circumcised, they shouldn't try to reverse the operation. If they are slaves, they should accept their slavery.

Christian freedom is not to be expressed by breaking our marriage vows, fretting about our condition or rejecting our work. Instead, we are to enjoy a new freedom *in* our circumstances – because we belong to Christ. Every situation is God-given or God-allowed – a place in which we can know his calling and his grace.

Paul warns against the pressure groups that tell Christians to express their faith in violent action. Some people are teaching that divorce, circumcision and rebellion are God's way out of old relationships. But Christians, says Paul, are to work a revolution by accepting their circumstances and having a new attitude towards them. This is how they will bring God's love and healing to every part of their society.

WHAT ABOUT VIRGINS?

The Corinthians have asked Paul's opinion about getting married. No doubt there are those who believe it is more holy to remain a virgin – single and sexually 'pure' (7:25–35).

Paul has no clear teaching from Christ about this, so he answers the question in the light of the overall situation. The coming of Christ has plunged the world into crisis. It is now clear who God is and what God wants – and everyone is called to respond to the challenge.

Paul is writing at a time when many believers expect Jesus to return at any moment. In these days of urgency and stress, Paul suggests that people stay as they are: those who are married should stay married, and those who are single should remain single. Married life presents problems and makes demands – and these will be an added encumbrance and distraction. It is not only single people who are to be single-minded in the last days. Marriage, emotions, possessions and business are all to be held to the light of Christ's coming.

Paul hopes that single Christians will be able to live an undivided life. If they marry, their loyalties and energies will be split between their partner and the Lord. Those who remain virgins can offer single-minded devotion to the Lord.

WHAT ABOUT ENGAGED COUPLES?

Some Christians are already engaged to be married. What is Paul's advice to them (7:36–38)?

Paul says that some couples have become so physically involved or been engaged so long, that they should stop

delaying and get married. This isn't a crime, it's a commitment. Some men have been treating engagement as a means of self-control – putting off sex for as long as possible. Paul says they should admit they're not serious about getting married – and stop posing as super-holy. Either way, engagements are to be resolved, and not become an excuse for indecision. There is nothing wrong with either marriage or singleness, providing they are God's will.

WIDOWS

Marriage is for life, and is ended by the death of one of the partners (7:39–40). Paul says Christian widows are free to marry – but they should only marry a fellow Christian. His own judgment is that widows will find more happiness in the undivided life of being single.

Food and freedom in a pagan society
(8:1 – 11:1)

FOOD SACRIFICED TO IDOLS

In Corinth, animals are sacrificed in pagan temples. The resulting 'idol meat' is shared between the god, the priests and the worshipper. Some is served at banquets and celebrations, while the rest is sold in shops and markets.

The Christians at Corinth have asked Paul how they should treat this meat (8:1–13). Is it impure because it has been offered to an idol? And can the power of a pagan spirit get inside someone who eats it?

Paul cuts the whole issue down to size. Pagan gods are nothing and have no power – so they are no problem. And meat is only food – it doesn't make you closer to, or further from, God.

But Paul gives a warning. It is all right for a 'strong' Christian to eat meat from the idol temples, because he knows there is no spiritual danger. But someone else, who is not so sure, may be offended by this apparently 'un-Christian' behaviour – or even led to believe in idols. Paul would rather not eat meat at all than mislead a 'weaker' Christian.

'Inside information'

There are people in the church who claim to have 'knowledge' (8:9–13). This knowledge gives power and makes the bearer proud. An example of such knowledge is that it is quite safe to eat 'idol meat', because idols are powerless. But pride comes in scoffing at those who disapprove, or taunting those who have superstitious fears.

Paul says that 'knowledge' needs to be balanced by

love – otherwise it merely puffs up people's pride. True knowledge is to know God and be known by him – which leads us to help and support others, and build up their faith. If Christ died for the 'weak' fellow Christian, should we not be willing to restrict our own behaviour for their sake?

THE RIGHTS OF AN APOSTLE

The Christians at Corinth have been comparing their leaders (9:1–27). Some are apostles who were friends or even brothers of Jesus. They like Peter (Cephas), who can fill a room with his presence – and Apollos with his clever mind and brilliant arguments. And others have 'knowledge' – secrets of freedom and power – which they are willing to share with a favoured few… And Paul? They owe a lot to Paul, but he is hardly a front-rank apostle. They say he was converted later.

Paul feels the injustice of their opinion. After all, he is an apostle to them if to no one else, because it was he who brought the gospel to Corinth and founded the church there. Now the Christians at Corinth prefer other leaders. They provide these leaders with food and drink, and allow them to have their wives with them, while Paul continues to support himself with his leather work and tentmaking.

Paul teaches that a minister of the gospel has every right to a living from his converts. After all, soldiers receive food, a uniform and pay in return for their service. Vine-growers can always help themselves to their own grapes, and shepherds drink milk from their goats. Priests and the staff of temples have a share in the sacrifices and harvest offerings; and Jesus told his disciples to stay in people's homes and eat whatever was given them. So why should Paul not be supported by the church?

There is an Old Testament law which allows an ox to eat the grain as it treads out the husks (Deuteronomy 25:4), but Paul has never had his nose in the collection bag – and nor has Barnabas. They haven't wanted anything to get in the way of the gospel – least of all the thought that they preach for money. Paul is compelled to preach the good news – he can't help it – and his reward is to offer the gospel freely to all.

Do the Corinthians find Paul inconsistent and unpredictable? That's because he is not concerned to please them. Once he relied on his Jewish pedigree, fine education and forceful personality to impress – but now he puts himself entirely at the service of others.

Paul has become 'all things to all people', so that he can share the gospel with all sorts. If it helps to be Jewish and have an insider's understanding of the law, then he will adopt that approach. But if he is with Gentiles who are ignorant or suspicious of Judaism, he will discard his Jewishness to help them understand the gospel. And he has a special place in his heart for the 'weak' – those who are laden with guilt and tired of trying to be good. Paul has played that scene himself – many times.

A supreme effort

Remembering that Corinth is the home of the Isthmian Games, Paul appeals to his readers to get spiritually fit (9:24–27)! The goal of an apostle's life is not to live in luxury, supported by admiring converts. Paul has his sights on a crown which God alone will give him – and he bends his body, mind and spirit towards that greatest prize. He wants not only to be saved through Christ, but also to give his very best for his Lord.

WARNINGS FROM ISRAEL'S HISTORY

Paul challenges the pride of some of the Corinthian Christians. He says it is quite possible to belong to the people of God, and yet fail in the Christian life. To show them what he means, he gives examples from the history of Israel (10:1 – 11:1).

When the Israelites escaped from Egypt, they all shared the blessings of God's deliverance and provision. They were all baptized into the leadership of Moses, as they passed with him through the Red Sea to freedom. They were all fed with manna day by day – a picture of Christ, the spiritual food. They all drank the water which gushed from the rock – an image of Christ, who is the water of life. And yet a whole generation rebelled against God and died in the desert. They never entered the Promised Land.

What went wrong? Paul says that they lost their self-control and gave in to idolatry, drunkenness and sexual immorality. They also defied God and complained against him – suffering terrible punishment as a result.

The Corinthians must be on their guard. They, too, have had a great escape from the power of sin and death. They have been baptized into Christ, and enjoy the benefits of the fellowship meal week by week. But they must beware of taking God for granted. It isn't possible to live the life of faith in Christ and still indulge in the excesses of paganism. And they are far too proud – which may lead to a dreadful fall.

The Corinthians are surrounded by every kind of

temptation in their city – but God will always provide a way of escape. They may feel ambushed with nowhere to turn – but there will always be that narrow way to freedom, which is the path of God's rescue through Christ. But Paul is not only talking about the everyday pressures of life in a pagan culture. He is calling the Corinthians to stand firm and faithful in the trials of the last days.

Idol feasts and the Lord's Supper

Paul begs his friends at Corinth to flee from idolatry (10:14–22). There are occasions when they are invited to feast in the temples of idols. Because idols are powerless, they may feel that these are harmless social occasions. But Paul argues strongly against this compromise.

He draws a parallel with the Christian fellowship meal. When they share the cup of thanksgiving, they open themselves to the living presence of Christ. With a sip of wine, they identify with what Jesus did for them on the cross. When they break bread they take part in the living body of Christ.

So, what does this mean for Christians who take part in an idol feast? Are they going to lay themselves open to the powers of evil? Idols, of course, are mere dolls; but behind the worship of idols is the activity of Satan and the demons who are his agents. Paul doesn't want his friends exposed to grave spiritual danger by eating and drinking in association with these dark forces. Those who feast at the Lord's table have no place at the table of demons.

The believer's freedom

The Christians at Corinth place great emphasis on their freedom (10:23 – 11:1). Their catchphrase is 'Everything is permissible.' Christ has set them free from pagan superstition and Jewish legalism. Now they can do anything they like, because all is from God – and all is forgiven!

Paul agrees with them to a certain extent. He can buy meat from the market, or eat what is put in front of him, without needing to know if it was butchered in a pagan temple. But if someone particularly tells him that the meat has been sacrificed to idols, he won't eat it – not because of his scruples but out of respect for the other person's conscience.

So Paul sets a limit to Christian freedom. Christian freedom isn't permission to do whatever we like. Christian freedom is the freedom to do what God wants, and to put the needs and feelings of others before our own. This is what Paul tries to do – and in so doing, he follows the way of Jesus.

Behaviour in worship
(11:2 – 14:40)

HOW TO BEHAVE IN WORSHIP MEETINGS

Having dealt with the issue of Christian freedom in eating idol meat, Paul now turns to the subject of behaviour in worship (11:2–16).

He congratulates the Corinthians for following his teaching so faithfully. There are no prayer books or written instructions and they have to memorize and pass on information by word of mouth. When the teaching is a summary of the gospel, or a description of Jesus at the Last Supper, it is important that the words are passed on with the greatest care and accuracy.

The Christians at Corinth are living out a revolution. In the Jewish temple and synagogues, women have little part to play in leading the worship. Now, in the Christian church, men and women are 'one in Christ Jesus'. People of either sex can lead in prayer or speak a prophecy.

There are other changes as well. Whereas Jewish men cover their heads when they pray, Christian men worship with their heads bare. They stand in God's presence as his free children, made in his image.

But it means something very different if a Corinthian woman has her head uncovered. Her glorious hair is a sight she keeps for her husband. Only prostitutes give the 'come-on' of letting down their hair in public. A woman's uncovered head is, in its way, as shocking as a shaven head. It means she is either an adulteress or a slave.

Paul teaches that Christian worship must reflect God's order of creation and be sensitive to what is right for local people.

There is a decent and orderly way for men and women to behave in worship meetings. Christian worship is not a frenzied free-for-all, with everyone throwing off their inhibitions. The angels look aghast at such irreverence, because they know the deep awe and wonder of God's presence.

In worship, men must honour Christ and offer him their glory. He is their 'head' or source of life. Women in turn must honour their husbands, because God has given men the responsibility of leadership.

A wife is the glory of her husband – a glory expressed in the beautiful crown of her hair. This hair is to be veiled in worship meetings, so that all glory flows to God alone. In wearing their veils, women stand side by side with men, without distraction or embarrassment, to offer prayer and prophecy for the glory of God.

Paul concludes by saying that men and women depend on each other. The creation story tells how woman was taken from man – but, ever since, man has been born from woman. The sex act, too, is an exquisite expression of difference and togetherness. This is how God has made men and women, and we defy common sense when we try to deny it.

Paul writes as a person of his time and culture. His teaching on the relative status of men and women may sound sexist and silly to modern readers. He is, however, straining towards the dignity and harmony that Christ gives to all people and all relationships.

THE LORD'S SUPPER

And now Paul confronts a scandal. The Corinthians are meeting in the Lord's name to share his Supper, but their behaviour is disgraceful (11:17–34). They are a parody of what a church should be.

When the Corinthian Christians come together, they all sit in their groups and cliques. Instead of sharing their food and drink, each person consumes whatever he or she has brought with them. Paul says that if they aren't going to express their life together by mixing and sharing, they might as well stay at home. Sadly, some of the poorer people have little food to bring – and have to watch while others gorge themselves.

Paul reminds the Corinthians of the meaning that Jesus gave to the fellowship meal. He was told about this by the apostles, but his understanding has come from the Lord.

Jesus, on the night of his arrest, shared a Passover meal with his disciples. As host, he took bread, gave thanks to God, broke it, and said, 'This is my body, which is for you; do this in remembrance of me.'

After supper, he took a cup of wine and gave it to them, saying, 'This is the new covenant in my blood; do this, whenever you drink it, in remembrance of me.'

Paul understands that Jesus broke and shared bread, as a powerful indication of his death for all people. Whenever Christians meet, they are to share in the benefits of Christ's death by breaking bread together.

Paul tells how the cup of wine sets the seal on a new covenant – a love-commitment between God and humanity, united through the sacrifice of Christ. When Christians share the memory of Christ's death, they realize afresh his living presence and power.

Paul explains that this breaking of bread and sharing of wine is not just for looking back to the death of Jesus. It is also for looking forward to his coming again. The Lord's Supper is a pilgrim meal for all who are longing for Jesus to return.

Paul warns that Christians who share the Lord's Supper without thinking what it means are desecrating the body of Christ. The body of Christ is the community of the church. We should recognize this body in our life together, especially by our caring and sharing when we meet. This is what Paul means by 'discerning the body'. We must recognize, honour and serve the body of Christ through our Communion fellowship.

The Spirit's body-building gifts

There are several lists of 'spiritual gifts' in the New Testament letters.

In his letter to the Romans, Paul mentions gifts of prophecy, serving, teaching, encouraging, contributing, leading and showing mercy. These are all abilities which help people to know God and minister to each other (Romans 12:6–8).

In his letter to the Ephesians, Paul lists the different roles or tasks of church leaders. Some are apostles. Apostles are witnesses that Christ is truly risen from death and reigns in glory. They are the chief founders and guides of the churches. Others are prophets, who declare God's message to his people, or evangelists, who preach the gospel so that outsiders can understand and respond. Others are pastors and teachers, who care for God's people and train them in Christian living.

All these leaders and ministers are Christ's gift to his church. They guide and tend and teach God's people, so that they can become the healthy and effective body of Christ (Ephesians 4:11–13).

Peter, in his first letter, says that a spiritual gift is to be used for others. It is through such gifts that God's power and love flow through his church. All Christian preaching should be like God speaking. All Christian serving should be done in God's strength. When someone has a spiritual gift, the result is not that he or she becomes famous or proud, but that the church is strengthened and God is praised (1 Peter 4:7–11).

Paul warns that those who treat the bread and wine casually will suffer sickness and even death. The right attitude is to be aware of the risen Christ among his people, to look after one another and to make the Lord's Supper a meal worthy of his name.

SPIRITUAL GIFTS

Now Paul wants to talk to the Corinthians about spiritual gifts (12:1–31). Spiritual gifts are the sign that God's Holy Spirit is at work in a Christian's life. Paul feels the Corinthian Christians are very ignorant on the subject.

The Corinthians are used to the weird and sensational antics of pagan religions – people going into trances, ignoring pain, performing ecstatic dances or making occult predictions. All these strange powers are linked with the worship of idols and the influence of demons.

First of all, Paul gives the Corinthians a simple test for checking the source of a spiritual gift. If someone says, 'Jesus be cursed,' then they are certainly not under the influence of the Holy Spirit. The Holy Spirit is entirely devoted to revealing Jesus as Lord – the only true God. Again, anyone who declares that 'Jesus is Lord' is clearly guided and enabled to do so by the Holy Spirit.

Next, Paul explains that there are many ways in which the Holy Spirit works. Some Christians speak with great wisdom or insight, while others have a strong faith or the ability to heal. Some speak in tongues, which others are able to interpret. These gifts, in all their variety, come from the same Holy Spirit. Again, all the gifts have the same purpose, which is to equip the church, the body of Christ, for service and mission.

Paul is tackling some major misunderstandings. People think that different gifts come from different gods. They shop around the various cults and religions, to get power to survive in this world and the next. Paul says there is only *one* Holy Spirit, and all the varied gifts come from him.

Another misunderstanding is that the gifts of the Holy Spirit are for personal prestige and fame. The Corinthian Christians are proud of their amazing gifts, and look down on those whose gifts are ordinary. Paul says there is no reason to be proud. Firstly, the gifts are *gifts* – they aren't prizes for goodness or effort. Secondly, they may be given to individuals, but they are for the whole church. Even the most sensational gift is only valuable when it builds the church in the understanding, service and mission of Christ.

A *variety of gifts*

Paul gives some examples of spiritual gifts (12:4–11):

There is the gift of speaking a wise word when people are anxious or confused.

There is the gift of knowing the truth about someone – having the kind of insight into their character and motives that Jesus has.

There is the gift of faith – that God is working out his purposes, even when a situation seems hopeless.

There are gifts of healings – healings of sick bodies and minds, broken hearts and damaged relationships. These healings may come through prayer and care, or medicine and counselling – but they will always bring God's reassurance and peace.

There is the gift of working miracles. God enables some people to act with extraordinary powers – to raise the dead, drive out evil spirits or command his will to be done.

There is the gift of distinguishing between spirits – being able to tell whether they come from Satan or from God. The devil is a master of disguise, and poses as an angel of light. God enables his people to tell when Satan is at work.

There is the gift of speaking in different tongues or languages. Some Christians have an ecstatic language with which they pray to God or speak his word. Some speak a foreign language they have never learned.

There is a gift of being able to interpret tongues. When such a language is spoken in public, the sense of it must be made clear to those who are listening.

Paul explains that all these gifts come from the Holy Spirit, who is at work in the church. It is he who decides who will have a particular gift. There is no reason for anyone to boast because they have a gift, or sulk because they haven't.

One body, many parts

How can people with such different personalities, backgrounds and gifts belong together (12:12–31)?

Paul says that the church is like a body – the body of Christ. A Christian may be Jewish or Greek by birth, and slave or free by circumstance. But all Christians are filled with the same Holy Spirit and belong to the same body of Christ, which is the church.

Christians are like parts of a body. They are different from one another, but belong together. Feet are different from hands – and very different from eyes – and yet they belong together and need one another. The eye is deaf – it needs an ear. The ear can't smell – it needs a nose.

And so it is with the church – we are incomplete and disabled without one another's gifts.

Paul makes special mention of parts of the body which are weak or shameful. He often feels weak himself – and knows that some Christians at Corinth are ashamed of him. But he is an apostle and evangelist – a reproductive organ of the church. Just as a body puts on clothes to avoid embarrassment, so the church must take special care of the parts that preach the gospel.

Paul teaches that Christians should not only function together but also *feel* together. In a body, the toothache or a sore toe can make the whole person miserable. So it is with the church. Christians should so feel for one another that they are sad or glad together.

So – *vive la différence!* God builds the church in the way he decides. Of course, there is an order in which the different parts emerge.

Apostles come first. As witnesses to the death and resurrection of Christ, they lay the foundations of the church. Prophets come next, as they speak God's word to particular situations. Then teachers are needed, with the skill and patience to help people understand and live the Christian way.

There are many other indispensable gifts – such as working miracles, healing, helping, administrating or speaking and interpreting tongues… No one person has them all, for God has made us to belong together. It is together that we make up the body of Christ on earth.

LOVE

Now Paul comes to a most important point. Even the greatest gift is worth nothing if it isn't received and used with love (13:1–13).

Paul takes the gifts of which the Corinthians are so proud – and inflates them to amazing proportions. Imagine a gift of tongues which includes every language in earth and heaven, a gift of prophecy that expounds all the knowledge in the universe or a gift of faith that can tell even mountains to move…

Paul says that even these sensational gifts will be nothing without love. If we don't have love, our gift is worthless.

Or imagine being supremely generous – giving away everything we have and then dying a martyr's death! But, says Paul, if we don't do it for love, we have wasted our effort.

Love is…

Paul describes love. It is utterly selfless and enduring – always providing and seeking the best for the loved one.

One of the Greek words for love is 'agape'. Before the days of Christianity, this word was rare. Now Paul uses 'agape' to describe God's own kind of loving. God's love is generous and selfless – poured out on everyone whether they deserve it or not.

In the end, it is only this kind of love that will last. All the gifts that the Corinthians strive for will come to an end. One day prophecy will no longer be necessary, tongues will die out and knowledge will pass into history. But love will survive. Love is the most important quality of all, because it is the essence of God.

Time to grow up!

Paul reminds the Corinthians of what it's like to be childish. When we were children our knowledge was very incomplete, and our behaviour was self-centred and immature. When we grew up, we developed a more complete picture of the world and our place within it.

So it is with growing up as a Christian. When we are young, we are busy with our little gifts and rivalries. When we grow up, we develop the faith, hope and love of the mature Christian.

One day our faith will be replaced by the full knowledge of God; our hope will be fulfilled by the coming of Christ. But love? There will always be love, because God himself is love, and we will live eternally with him.

GIFTS OF PROPHECY AND TONGUES

Now Paul teaches the Christians at Corinth about two particular gifts – prophecy and tongues (14:1–25). These are great gifts, if they are received and used with love.

Speaking in tongues is a way of worshipping God without forming ideas and sentences. Instead, we 'babble' with our lips as our praise wells up from our heart. A tongue is a great blessing for the person who has it – but fellow Christians may feel left out, and non-Christians may be confused or put off.

Prophesying is when we speak God's message clearly – so that the church can understand and apply God's word. If speaking in tongues blesses and builds up one

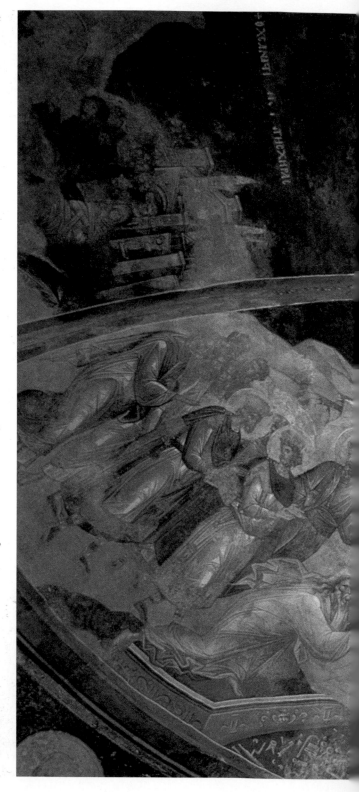

Paul argues that the cornerstone of our faith is the fact of the resurrection of Christ. If he had not been raised from the dead, we would still be condemned to suffer the results of our sin. Through Adam, sin entered the world, but Paul sees Christ as a second Adam, redeeming us from the actions of the first. A mosaic in the funerary chapel of Kariye Camii Church, Istanbul, depicts the Anastasis Christ reviving Adam and Eve from limbo.

person, then prophesying blesses and builds up everyone in the church.

Paul tells the Corinthians that he speaks in tongues more than any of them. But Paul is always concerned for the whole church – and for those who have not yet come to faith. He would much rather speak a few words that everyone can understand, than spout a torrent of tongues. If outsiders find Christians babbling in tongues, they will think they are raving mad. But if they find them sharing God's word, they may realize the truth and come to faith themselves.

ORDERLY WORSHIP

Paul gives some simple guidelines for a Christian meeting (14:26–40).

Everyone can bring something – a choice of hymn, some Christian teaching, a picture of God at work or a tongue and its meaning. Each contribution should in some way strengthen, encourage and build up the church. A few tongues are welcome, but they mustn't drown the other contributions – and they must always be interpreted.

The people who prophesy, who deliver God's message, should speak one at a time. When Christians meet, they must listen carefully to one another and think deeply about what God is saying. God's truth is discovered through humble and respectful working together – not in smart speeches and frenzied competition.

Paul gives a further guideline that women should be silent in church meetings.

Something has been going on that Paul describes as 'disgraceful'. Are women distracting from the worship with their chattering, or arguing with their husbands in public? Are they suffering from a culture that doesn't value or educate them? Are they using their new-found Christian freedom to be pushy and domineering? Are they behaving like pagan prophetesses and delivering strange and ecstatic oracles? We don't know.

We cannot assume that Paul is banning all public ministry by women. Earlier in this letter he has accepted that women pray and prophesy in church meetings (11:5). But both there and here, he is concerned that these meetings should be conducted in a decent and orderly way.

It seems likely that Paul is dealing with a particular problem in that culture or in those days. In another letter, he teaches that Christ has freed us from inequality and prejudice between men and women: 'There is neither... male nor female, for you are all one in Christ Jesus' (Galatians 3:28).

The resurrection
(15:1–58)

THE RESURRECTION OF CHRIST

Now Paul reminds the Christians at Corinth about the basic facts of the gospel (15:1–11). This is the message he himself had received and carefully passed on to them.

The facts of the gospel are that Christ, the Son of God, died to bear the punishment of human sin. The Jewish scriptures (the Old Testament) teach about the seriousness of sin, the importance of sacrifice and the promise of a Messiah (Saviour).

There was no doubt at all that Jesus died and was buried. The wonderful news is that, on the third day after his death, God raised him to life. Again, the scriptures had promised that God's Holy One would not rot in the grave (Psalm 16:10).

This is history. It happened only some thirty years before, and many of the witnesses are still alive. The twelve apostles saw the risen Christ; and so did 500 others, when Jesus appeared to them in Galilee. Paul has visited Jerusalem and met two of the leading apostles – Peter (also called Cephas) and the Lord's brother, James. He heard the story from their own lips (Galatians 1:18–19).

The last appearance of the risen Christ was to Paul himself. Jesus appeared to him in a vision on the road to Damascus, when Paul was on a mission to arrest the first believers. He was stopped in his tracks and blinded by the glory of Jesus. It was this vision which enabled Paul to become an apostle – an eyewitness to the resurrection.

Paul describes himself as the last and least of the apostles – born by an unusual method. He makes up for his abnormality by working extra hard – or rather allowing the grace of God to work in and through him.

THE RESURRECTION OF THE DEAD

Some of the Christians at Corinth are saying there is no such thing as the resurrection of the dead (15:12–34). They believe that the Christian faith is for this life only, without any hope of a future beyond the grave.

Paul strongly disagrees. He argues that if there is no resurrection, the Christian faith collapses. Without resurrection, Jesus must still be dead. If Jesus is dead, then the gospel message is a lie. If the gospel is a lie, then there is no forgiveness of sins, no new life with God and no hope for the future.

If there is no resurrection, says Paul, we are all

helpless sinners facing eternal judgment. If there is no future hope, the apostles are pathetic creatures preaching an empty, powerless gospel. They are either criminal liars or deluded and mad.

But now Paul states what he truly believes – that Jesus Christ *is* raised from death. He is raised, not just for his own victory, but for ours as well. Jesus is the first-fruit of a great harvest. He is the prototype of all who have died and will be raised. Paul is so sure of this that he describes death as merely 'falling asleep', in the certain hope of waking again to new life in Christ.

Paul explains. The entire human race shares a sinful nature and is sentenced to spiritual death. In Bible terms, this is the desperate plight that we have inherited from Adam – the first human. But now all people can be saved through the sacrifice and victory of Jesus Christ. Jesus is the 'new man'. He is the founder of a new humanity – the restored children of God. Just as we inherited spiritual death from Adam, so now we inherit spiritual life from Christ.

But if everyone who trusts in Christ will be raised to life, why have some believers in Corinth died? Paul says that all who have died believing in Christ will be raised to life when he returns. The reign of Christ has begun and his victory is certain – but death will be the last of his enemies to be destroyed.

When Jesus Christ returns, he will overcome all the powers of evil, and present his people to his Father. Just as God placed his whole creation at humanity's feet (Psalm 8:6), so Christ will offer himself and the new creation back to God the Father.

Paul points out that Corinthian Christians are living as though the resurrection is true. Some of them have been baptized on behalf of dead friends or relatives, to include them in the resurrection of Christ. And Paul himself has been involved in fierce fights for the truth of the gospel. In Ephesus he challenged occult powers and risked death at the hands of a mob. Why would he endure such hardship and suffering, if the resurrection is a myth?

Paul urges the Corinthians to stop their slide back into paganism and superstition, and renew their life of holiness and knowledge of God.

THE RESURRECTION BODY

Paul imagines someone asking, '*How* are the dead raised? What is a resurrection body *like*?' (15:35–49). These are silly questions, because they doubt God's power to do something new. To answer them, Paul shows the pattern of death and resurrection in the world of nature.

When we sow a seed or plant a bulb, it looks nothing like the grain or flower that will grow. The seed must go into the ground and die before it can spring up as a beautiful new plant. But although the new growth is completely different, it is the same species that was planted – now gloriously transformed!

God has created physical bodies in amazing variety. Humans and animals, birds and fish, all have bodies to suit their life on earth. In space, too, the sun, moon and stars all have different bodies and degrees of splendour.

From these examples, Paul encourages us to see the power of God. God is able to raise us to new life. He will give us a resurrection body – a body which will be completely different and glorious – and yet it will be *our* body.

Our new body is not an earthly body – it is heavenly. It is not a mortal body – it is immortal. It is a body which will enable us to live in the presence and glory of God. And yet it will be *our* body – just as a plant is related to the seed from which it grows.

Human beings are, like Adam, made from 'dust' – the physical stuff of this earth. The risen Christ, however, has the spiritual body of heaven. In our earthly life we have a natural, physical body like Adam's. In our heavenly life we will have a glorious spiritual body like Christ's.

A DAY OF RESURRECTION!

This transformation from earthly to heavenly has to take place (15:50–58). Our earthly body is not equipped for life in heaven.

Paul reveals a mystery – the open secret of new life through Jesus Christ. We will not go for ever into the sleep of death. Instead, we will all be raised and transformed – together and in a split second – when the heavenly trumpet heralds the Last Day. On that day, our old enemy death will be defeated – its final victory denied and its fatal sting drawn. This great victory comes from God, because Jesus on the cross has cancelled our debt of sin and annulled the death sentence against us.

So, says Paul, take courage! The hope of eternal life gives us a firm footing in this world. It inspires us to serve the Lord with our best efforts. Nothing we do for him is wasted; and we look forward to a very great reward.

The collection for Christians in Judea
(16:1–4)

Now Paul mentions the collection that he is organizing to help needy Christians in Jerusalem. The church in

Jerusalem has always had a large number of widows to support, and to make matters worse the whole of Judea has suffered famine.

Paul wants the Gentile churches to help their Jewish brothers and sisters. And if gifts flow into Jerusalem from the wider world, then some of the Old Testament prophecies will be fulfilled about tribute flowing into Zion.

To collect the aid money, Paul suggests that the Corinthians do the same as the Galatian churches. Everyone makes a gift – little or much, according to their income – on the first day of the week when they meet for worship.

When Paul comes, he will give letters of introduction to those the Corinthians appoint to take the gift to Jerusalem. In this way they can be sure the money will be honestly handled and properly used. In fact, Paul will gather a team from all the churches and they will travel to Jerusalem together – an idea which is forming in his mind as he writes.

Future plans and greetings

Paul talks about his future plans (16:5–24). At present he is in Ephesus, where he is finding good openings for the gospel, and also stiff opposition.

Paul will stay in Ephesus for two and a half years. We know from the book of Acts that he holds daily discussions in the hall of Tyrannus. These meetings share the gospel with people who are visiting Ephesus on business – and take the good news to other parts of the province of Asia.

And the opposition? Paul is involved in battles with occult powers – which end with a great burning of books and scrolls. His successful preaching also causes a riot among the local silversmiths, because they see the gospel destroying their trade in idols and magic charms (Acts 19).

Paul mentions some of the church leaders who are coming and going between Ephesus and Corinth. He asks the Corinthians to be kind to Timothy if he visits them, and respect his ministry. We glimpse that Timothy is unsure of himself and that the boisterous Corinthians might give him a hard time.

Paul also says that he has encouraged Apollos to visit them. Apollos is an impressive teacher and speaker, whom many Corinthians prefer to Paul. But Paul emphasizes that Apollos is a fellow worker, not a rival leader.

Paul sums up his advice to the Corinthians: guard against evil and jealousy; stand firm in the faith of Christ; be mature and brave in your witness; have no other motive than love.

Paul commends three of the Corinthians for their lively faith and practical ministry. The first is Stephanas who, with his family and slaves, was the first person to become a Christian in the province of Achaia. Now he and his household are devoted servants of the church. Two others are Fortunatus and Achaicus, whose visit so encouraged Paul and refreshed him. These are high-quality Christians who should be considered as leaders.

Final greetings
(16:19–24)

Paul signs off lovingly, with greetings from all the churches in the province of Asia. Aquila and Priscilla have special mention – the Christian couple who share Paul's trade of leather working, and have helped him found churches in both Corinth and Ephesus. One of the Ephesian churches meets in their house.

While Paul is loving to believers, he pronounces a curse on those who oppose Christ. He also gives a heartfelt cry for Jesus to return. 'Marana tha!' is a prayer from Palestine in the original Aramaic language. It means 'Come, O Lord!'

2 Corinthians

Paul is hurting. He has felt rejected by the Christians at Corinth. Although he founded the church, they have now been attracted to the new teachers – 'super-apostles' – who have arrived in Corinth since Paul left for Ephesus.

Paul writes to explain that he is a true apostle. He may not have a charming manner, impressive presence and smooth words; but he is genuine. He preaches the gospel of Jesus Christ and bears the suffering involved.

This is a love letter. Paul loves the Corinthian Christians so much that he has been in great pain. It is a heart-to-heart talk about their relationship, with its joys, complaints and misunderstandings. Paul hopes that they will read it and feel as he does:

> As a fair exchange – I speak as to my children – open wide your hearts also (6:13).

Outline

Paul greets his readers at Corinth (1:1–2)

Suffering and strength (1:3–11)

A change of plan (1:12 – 2:13)

A genuine ministry (2:14 – 7:16)

The collection for Christians in Jerusalem (8:1 – 9:15)

A personal defence (10:1 – 13:14)

INTRODUCTION

The church in Corinth

Paul has been away from Corinth for some time. He has been working in Ephesus – some 300 miles away by sea. But it has been possible to stay in touch through letters and messengers.

Since Paul wrote the letter we know as 1 Corinthians, the mood has changed between the apostle and his friends.

The church at Corinth has been joined by some impressive new teachers. Paul calls them 'super-apostles'. He doesn't like what he hears of them – but the Corinthians think they're wonderful!

At some point in the past year, Paul has made a brief visit to Corinth to try to sort out the problem. The visit was a painful one, and Paul followed it with a 'severe' letter. This letter may have survived in 2 Corinthians as chapters 10–13.

There was a long delay while Paul waited for a reply to this letter – a reply which was to come with his friend Titus. When Titus eventually found Paul again, he gave him the good news that the relationship with Corinth was mended.

It's said that Paul was a short man with a bald head and bandy legs; a poor speaker who suffered from fevers and an illness which may have been epilepsy. Compared with the new-style apostles, Paul is a poor advertisement for 'new life in Christ'!

As Paul writes, we can hear him answering some of the criticisms he has felt. He explains that he himself is

Located on the narrow strip of land separating southern Greece from the mainland, Corinth stands at the crossroads of both land and sea routes. In New Testament times it was a large and influential trading centre.

not important. He is just a 'jar of clay' – a plain container for the treasure of Christ within him. He has come to realize that his weakness is a strength – because it forces him to depend on Christ, and shows so well the difference Christ makes to his life.

Being an apostle isn't about dazzling personality and smart words. A true apostle will reflect the love, sacrifice and sufferings of Jesus.

All the same, Paul is clearly wounded at being compared with the 'super-apostles'. Their track record is nothing to his – although they look and sound so impressive. They are like pedlars – offering a cheap and glitzy gospel, while demanding attention and taking money. They are not as much 'super' apostles as 'false' apostles (11:13).

Meanwhile, Paul has a project which requires giving rather than taking. He plans to send help to the poor Christians in Jerusalem who are suffering from famine. He gives the Corinthians the latest news of the collection and encourages them to be generous and cheerful givers.

This letter gives a unique insight into Paul's personality. We feel his pain and longing for acceptance. But he won't compromise the gospel of Jesus Christ for anything or anybody. Nor will he spare himself in the task of challenging, explaining, pleading and encouraging his friends – to clearer understanding, purer lives and warmer hearts. Here is a remarkable, vulnerable, courageous man – serving a supreme, suffering, glorious Lord.

Is there more than one letter in 2 Corinthians?

The letter we know as 2 Corinthians may be a collection of letters. There are some changes of pace and mood which make experts wonder if the pages have been shuffled!

Here is one theory of what might have happened. The simple explanations are usually the best.

Paul has had news of a scandal at Corinth. He interrupts his work in Ephesus and travels 300 miles by sea to visit them. The visit doesn't work out well. Paul leaves, with the Corinthians feeling angry and himself feeling rejected.

Back in Ephesus, Paul writes to express his grief and love (2 Corinthians 2:3–4). Some scholars think that chapters 10–13 may be this letter, now added to a letter which was written later. In these chapters, Paul makes a strong defence of his claim to be an apostle and answers the challenge of the 'super-apostles'.

Titus delivers this 'strong' letter to the Corinthians. Paul is anxious and restless until he receives their reply. He arranges to meet Titus in Troas, but in the end crosses to Macedonia to find him there (2 Corinthians 2:12–13).

Fortunately, Titus brings good news for Paul. The Corinthians have accepted his correction with tears of repentance. They have sent back a message of loyalty and love. Paul is overjoyed (2 Corinthians 7:5–8).

While Paul is still in Macedonia, he writes to the Corinthians again. This is the letter we have as 2 Corinthians 1–9. In these chapters Paul tells of his relief at their change of heart, explains some misunderstandings between them and shares his plans for the Jerusalem collection.

DISCOVERING 2 CORINTHIANS

Paul greets his readers at Corinth

Paul writes from himself and his young companion, Timothy (1:1–2). He introduces himself as an apostle of Jesus Christ. The right to be called an apostle is a major issue between Paul and the Christians at Corinth. An apostle is one of the eyewitnesses of Jesus' resurrection who has been commissioned to preach the gospel and found churches.

Paul was not one of Jesus' original twelve apostles. He was converted some years after the resurrection, through a vision of the risen Christ on the Damascus road. He was commissioned to be 'the apostle to the Gentiles' (Romans 11:13). At Corinth there are now other missionaries and teachers who are calling themselves apostles. They are undermining Paul's status and challenging his authority as their spiritual father.

This letter will be read by members of the Christian church in Corinth and its surrounding area – which is the Roman province of Achaia.

Suffering and strength

Paul has been through a traumatic experience (1:3–11). We know that there was a riot in Ephesus, provoked by the silversmiths who were losing their trade in shrines and magic charms (Acts 19:23–41). We know that there were plots against Paul, especially from 'Judaizers' who felt he was destroying the Jewish law. We know that he was sometimes in trouble with a local governor and flogged or put in prison.

There is no clue as to what has happened to Paul most recently. He says he has been submerged under so much pressure that he felt he was dying. The fact that he has survived has renewed his faith in God, who comforts us in suffering and raises from death.

A change of plan

The Corinthians are saying that Paul is inconsistent (1:12 – 2:13). He promised to visit them but didn't. How can they trust his teaching if he doesn't keep his word?

Paul explains that he had planned to visit them twice, on his way to and from Macedonia. However, his last visit was so painful that he wrote a letter instead. The letter was not written to lord it over them, but to express his great sorrow and love.

Apparently Paul has been involved in disciplining someone in the church at Corinth. It was a difficult case and Paul's own authority was on the line. However, it seems that the person concerned has been punished and Paul is now anxious that he should be comforted and restored to the fellowship. Only Satan benefits from any lingering grudge or division.

Paul returns to his explanation of his recent movements. He was very restless while he was waiting for Titus to return from Corinth with the response to his 'severe' letter. He preached in Troas and was very well received – but couldn't settle without the news he longed for. Instead, he crossed the sea to Macedonia, where Titus later found him.

A genuine ministry

Paul now explains the nature and purpose of his ministry.

'Triumphal procession'
(2:14–17)
Paul praises God for calling him to take part in the victory procession of Christ.

A Roman general would receive a triumphal welcome home after a great victory. His soldiers, prisoners and booty would all be processed before the cheering crowd. Paul likens apostles to the incense which is wafted over the throng of people on these occasions – a fragrant smell for the victors, but the stench of death to the vanquished.

Apostles are good news for those who accept Christ, but an offence to those who reject him. It's an awesome responsibility to be so closely identified with the reputation of Jesus and his gospel. Paul sees himself as nothing less than an ambassador for Christ, speaking for and from God. By contrast, some people (the 'super-apostles' for example) merely peddle the gospel to make some money.

'You are a letter from Christ'
(3:1–6)
What are Paul's credentials for being an apostle? Where are the letters commending his ministry? Paul has the perfect answer: 'You yourselves are our letter.'

The church at Corinth, founded by Paul, is a living letter confirming that his apostleship is true. He is the minister of a new covenant. The old covenant was to do with the letter of the law – a legalism which led to death. The new covenant is the work of the Spirit of God, and leads to liberty and life.

Clay jars. Paul says that a Christian contains something of the glory of God. But, in order to remind us that this gift is from God, yet in a plain, human body, he likens the situation to treasure (or even a light) being kept in a clay jar.

'Ever-increasing glory'
(3:7–18)
The new teachers who have arrived in Corinth have brought with them an old teaching. They want to bring the Gentile Christians under the control of the law of Moses.

Paul reminds the Corinthians that when the law was

given to Moses, his face was radiant with the glory of God. Moses' face was so bright for a while that he had to wear a veil over his face, because people were afraid to come near him (Exodus 34:29–35).

Paul agrees that the law of Moses was glorious, but it had its limitations. For one thing, it condemned us to death, because we failed to keep it. For another, it was

written on tablets of stone and not on our inner hearts. Thirdly, its glory didn't last, because it was surpassed by the work of Christ. The law brought condemnation, but Jesus brought forgiveness.

Paul says that the Jews who live by the law of Moses are still wearing a veil. The veil is over their hearts, preventing them responding to the grace of God. They are stuck in legalism and guilt. But Christ can lift the veil away.

In Christ, says Paul, we can be forgiven our sin, delivered from guilt and restored to a face-to-face relationship with God. Open to God, we reflect his glory – a glory which doesn't fade, but gets ever *more* glorious.

'We do not preach ourselves'
(4:1–15)

Paul is doing God's work. He doesn't need to tamper with the gospel to make it more attractive. He doesn't need to cheat to make it more successful. He serves the gospel straight. If people can't see the light of God's truth, that's because Satan is keeping them in the spiritual darkness of rebellion and deceit.

Paul realizes that his life would discourage most people from becoming Christians. He has suffered many hardships in his work as an apostle, and even now seems on the brink of defeat. Who would want to be so plain and unattractive – especially when the 'super-apostles' are such exciting people?

Paul explains that Christians are like the plain pottery jars which hold a candle. Our lives may look very ordinary, but we contain the light of Christ. The same God who said at creation, 'Let there be light,' has now placed the light of Christ in our hearts. If Paul's poor life offsets the beauty of Christ, then so much the better.

The Corinthian Christians don't understand about suffering and glory. Paul sees his suffering as a little reflection of the suffering of Jesus. He is always dying little deaths – so that the resurrection power of Jesus can be seen in his life too.

Just as Jesus' death meant life for others, so Paul's hardship has been the means by which the Corinthians have received the gospel. If they complain that he is always having a hard time, they should remember that it's for their sake that he suffers.

'Meanwhile we groan'
(4:16 – 5:10)

Paul shrugs off the temporary hurts of this life. He doesn't groan because of his suffering, but because he longs for his new life. His sights are on the eternal glory that's to come.

Paul sees his earthly body as only a tent – a temporary, mobile home in which he lives for a short time. A far more glorious body awaits him in heaven – a permanent, eternal body. His heavenly body is as different from his earthly body as the temple is from the tabernacle.

The only aspect of Paul's earthly life which will also be with him in heaven is the Spirit of God within him. The Spirit is God's down payment or guarantee – the sign and promise of eternal life.

Although our earthly bodies will pass away, the way we behave in them matters to God. We live *in* our bodies, but not *for* them. One day Christ himself will judge us for our earthly actions – and give us an eternal reward or punishment.

'Be reconciled to God'
(5:11 – 6:2)

Paul comes to the heart of what he wants to say to the Corinthians. He is not concerned to impress them or win their approval. He wants only that they should understand and receive the gospel message.

The gospel message is that Jesus Christ died for all people. He died to pay for our sin, so that we can be released into a new life with God. When we accept his death for us, our own old life can die. We die to our self-centred life and rise to the free, loving, God-centred life of Christ.

Because Jesus died and rose for all people, Paul sees everyone in a new light. Everyone can have this new life! God has made this possible at the utmost cost to himself. He gave his own Son to make peace with humanity. Jesus accepted God's anger at human sin, and absorbed all its pain and penalty in his death on the cross.

Paul is not a scruffy pedlar, making money by selling secrets. He is an ambassador of Jesus Christ. He openly declares the terms by which God offers peace to all humankind. On behalf of Christ, he appeals to all people to accept. Jesus took on our sin, so that we can put on his righteousness.

The best time to accept what Christ has done for us is *now*! This is our moment to receive God's grace. God is giving us a window of opportunity between the death and resurrection of Jesus and the Judgment Day to come.

'Open wide your hearts'
(6:3–13)

Paul begs the Corinthians to receive his message – and to open their hearts to him.

Paul tries to make it easy for them. He doesn't lie to them, bully them or charge them money. Nor does he want them to be put off by his sufferings – the beatings and imprisonments by magistrates, the hardships of his travels or the criticisms from other people. Everything is explained by the fact that he is living for God in a hostile world.

If the Corinthians note Paul's troubles, they should also notice his character. He is pure, perceptive, patient and kind. The spirit in him is holy, his love is genuine and his words are true. He fights his battles by the power of God, whether attacking (with the right hand) or defending (with the left).

Paul's life is one of ironies and contrasts. The world may despise and shame him, but God honours him and gives him glory. He endures what people say about him, whether it is bad or good, true or false. He is well known, but dismissed as insignificant. He is at death's door, yet very much alive. He has much grief, but his joy keeps breaking out. He is poor, but his ministry offers lasting treasure. He has nothing, but everything in heaven and on earth belongs to him, because he belongs to Christ.

'Let us purify ourselves'
(6:14 – 7:1)

Paul challenges the Corinthian Christians to live a pure life. Their city is notorious for immorality and 'Corinthian' has come to mean 'fornicator'. But Christians must be different, because they are God's own children.

Paul says that Christians should not be 'yoked

'Come out from them and be separate'

How far should Christians be separated from the society in which they live?

Paul realizes that some Christians are already married to pagans when they become converted. He tells them not to get divorced unless their unbelieving partner wants to do so (1 Corinthians 7:12–15). He also teaches that Christians are free to eat with unbelievers (1 Corinthians 10:27), and non-Christians are welcome to attend Christian worship meetings (1 Corinthians 14:22–25). In these examples, Paul is following Jesus, who mixed with all kinds and classes of people.

So what is the Christian difference? It is on matters of sex and idols that Paul draws the line between mixing and compromise. He forbids Christians to have sex outside marriage, especially with the prostitutes in pagan temples (1 Corinthians 6:15–20). He also strongly forbids joining in the temple meals which are dedicated to idols.

together' with unbelievers. His picture is of an ox and a donkey strapped in the same harness and pulling the same plough. He means that Christians should not marry pagans, or join in their business, work or religion. They are as different as light and darkness. They are as opposite as Christ and Belial (Satan).

In Corinth there are many pagan temples where idols are worshipped. These temples have dining areas where people can share a meal with friends – eating meat which has been sacrificed to the idols and saying prayers to these lifeless gods.

Paul says that Christians must have nothing to do with this custom. They are to be different. As a church and as individuals they are the temple of the living God. God himself lives among them and keeps company with them; so they must live a life worthy of his presence.

'Greatly encouraged'
(7:2–16)

Paul has been waiting anxiously for news of the Corinthians. He sent Titus to them with a 'severe letter', and has been worried about their reaction. Now Titus has returned with wonderful news. The Corinthians have accepted Paul's reproach and put right what was wrong.

Paul is delighted – not because he made the Corinthians sad, but because their sadness resulted in repentance, forgiveness and a clear conscience. He is also pleased and proud that they made a good impression on Titus.

The collection for Christians in Jerusalem

Paul is organizing a collection to help the poor Christians in Jerusalem.

Many of the church members in Jerusalem are Jews who have been disowned by their families when they became Christians. Their number may have been increased by any pilgrims who stayed on in Jerusalem after becoming Christians on the Day of Pentecost. They have always needed to provide for their widows (Acts 6:1–2), and in recent years have been hard hit by famine (Acts 11:27–30).

Paul's plan is that the Gentile churches should make a collection and send it with a delegation to Jerusalem. The churches in Macedonia have already given generously, but the Corinthians have been slow to respond.

'This service to the saints'
(8:1 – 9:5)

Paul describes the good example of the Macedonian Christians – no doubt trying to get the Corinthians to do even better. The Corinthians have so many spiritual gifts – perhaps the grace of giving will now be one of them.

The secret of the Macedonians' generosity is that they first gave themselves to God. It is out of a fresh understanding of God's love and provision for them that they are able to give beyond themselves.

It seems that the Corinthians made a good start and then faltered. Perhaps they weren't able to give as much as they promised. Paul assures them that this doesn't matter. God only asks them to give out of what they have, and not out of what they haven't. He doesn't want any church to bear an unfair burden. His aim is that need and plenty shall be equally shared. Paul is recalling how God provided manna for the Israelites in the wilderness – and that everyone had enough for their daily needs (Exodus 16:14–18).

Macedonia is a Roman province. The churches in Macedonia are at Philippi, Berea and Thessalonica.

Paul is careful to describe how the collection is to be organized. He commends Titus and another brother who are returning to Corinth to finalize the arrangements. Paul will follow later, with a group from Macedonia, to take the collection on to Jerusalem. It is important that everything is done openly and honestly, as this project is an act of witness to a watching world.

'You will be made rich'
(9:6–15)

Paul reminds the Corinthians about the principles of Christian giving.

Giving is like sowing seed: what you get is linked to what you give. The farmer who sows only a little seed will get only a poor harvest, while the farmer who sows generously will reap a rich harvest.

In Christian giving, both the thought and the attitude count. Paul asks the Corinthians to consider carefully what they will give – and then to give it cheerfully.

God himself is a great giver. He provides in all kinds of ways – in crops and food and spiritual gifts. His greatest ('indescribable') gift is that of sending his only Son to be the Saviour of the world.

The Corinthians will discover in their giving that they themselves receive. They will be enabled and

Who are the 'super-apostles'?

The 'super-apostles' are Jewish missionaries who have arrived at the church in Corinth since Paul left. On the surface they are knowledgeable, good-looking and eloquent. Underneath, they are devious and domineering.

The 'super-apostles' manage to mislead the Corinthians, because the Greeks like their gods to be powerful and perfect. They find it almost impossible to accept a God who gets crucified, and Paul (whom one person described as having a bald head, bandy legs and beetle brows) is a most unlikely apostle!

Although the 'super-apostles' present themselves as Christians, they have reworked the gospel for their own ends. The content of their message and the style of their ministry is not at all true to Christ and his gospel.

encouraged to be generous on many future occasions. There will be a harvest of praise to God when people see his grace in their lives.

A personal defence

Paul turns again to an old theme – his authority as an apostle and the challenge from the 'super-apostles'. As he writes, we hear the echoes of the harsh things that have been said about him. We see also how he handles these criticisms – with humility, righteous indignation, plain facts and a dry wit.

'I appeal to you'
(10:1–18)

Paul talks to the Corinthians very personally – not as 'we' but as 'I'. They say he is timid when he is with them and only forceful in his letters when he is away. But they misunderstand his gentleness. He will be bold enough when he next sees them, if he has to be!

The 'super-apostles' look good because they are only comparing themselves with one another. They are taking pride in a church which has already been established – by Paul. Paul has no desire to boast in another person's work. For him the only boast is what God has done for

him through Jesus Christ – which he calls 'boasting in the Lord'.

Paul refuses to compete with the 'super-apostles' for the credit of planting the church at Corinth. His vision is already reaching ahead to new regions – to visit Rome and then take the gospel to Spain. If the work at Corinth expands, it will be because the Christians are supporting Paul's mission to other places.

'False apostles'
(11:1–15)

Paul tells the Corinthians he is indignant. He is angry that the 'super-apostles' have manipulated the gospel to make themselves appear attractive, clever and eloquent.

Paul is also jealous, because the Corinthians are changing their view of Jesus. Paul was a witness to the marriage between the Corinthians and Christ, and he could vouch for their pure devotion. Now they have slipped all too easily into a different spirit and a different gospel.

The Corinthians have been saying that Paul 'lowered himself' by not claiming his pay as a preacher. No doubt the 'super-apostles' charge a good rate for their fine-sounding speeches. But Paul insists on preaching the gospel free of charge. When he was living in Corinth, he earned his own living with his leather work, or received support from the Christians in Macedonia; but he didn't place any burden on the Corinthians.

At last Paul gives his verdict on the 'super-apostles'. They are false, deceitful impostors. They are convincing in the same way that their master Satan is convincing, because they appear as angels of light.

'I also dare to boast'
(11:16–33)

How can Paul show the 'super-apostles' in their true light? He unleashes a dry, sarcastic wit. If the 'super-apostles' can make such a great impression by boasting, he will do a little boasting himself. But he explains that he is talking like a fool. Boasting (as the world does) is unworthy of Christ.

Paul may be teasing and taunting, but he gives us some rare information about himself – and about the 'super-apostles'.

The Corinthians claim to be wise, but they are being duped by these impostors. The 'super-apostles' are taking their minds and their money, as well as bullying and abusing them. Paul says he was obviously too weak to treat them in that way!

The 'super-apostles' are arrogant and pushy. Among the Gentile Christians of Corinth, they boast of their pure Jewish background and their true devotion to Christ. They do it to make the Corinthians feel ignorant and inadequate. The Corinthians then rely on the 'super-apostles' to teach them the Jewish law and show them the 'true' way to follow Christ.

Paul says that he can boast of his Jewish pedigree as well as they can – but he would be a fool to do so. Being a Hebrew is a claim to purity of race. Being an Israelite is a claim to purity of faith (even a Christian faith, as Paul hints in Romans 9:6). Being a descendant of Abraham is a claim to God's exclusive blessing. This is ridiculous! When God chose Abraham to be the father of a nation, it was so that everyone in the world would be *included*, not left out!

The 'super-apostles' show their learning and eloquence to prove their commitment to Christ. Paul shows his sufferings. He lists his imprisonments, beatings, hardships, narrow escapes and daily worries. The book of Acts tells us a few of these, such as his imprisonment at Philippi (Acts 16). But other imprisonments and the shipwreck (narrated in Acts 27) are still in the future. We don't know the half of what Paul endured for the sake of the gospel.

A Jewish lashing is brutal and will kill a weak man. It is delivered to the naked back and front with a many-thonged whip, with sharp pieces of metal and bone in the strands. The fortieth stroke is left out to show mercy. A beating with rods is a Roman punishment, inflicted by the magistrates of a town for some civil offence.

As well as the physical hardships, Paul mentions the mental pain he has been through. He was criticized and betrayed by people both inside and outside the church. He has felt constant anxiety about the welfare of his converts. He has felt pity for the weak – and fury over scandals. These things are as much a pressure on him as cold, hunger and fatigue.

Paul catalogues the many sufferings and hardships he has endured in the course of his service to Christ. This carved ivory depicts a number of scenes from Paul's life.

Paul explains his foolishness. While most people would boast of something to be proud of, Paul will only boast of his weaknesses. For example, what could be more undignified for Paul, as a once-proud Pharisee, than to be smuggled out of Damascus hidden in dirty washing? But this is the sort of thing he will boast about.

'When I am weak'
(12:1–10)

Now Paul's boasting becomes more serious. The 'super-apostles' are claiming that they have had amazing spiritual experiences. Well, Paul can do that too, but not directly. He tells the Corinthians about a man he knows – but we realize he is talking about himself.

Paul describes how, fourteen years before, he had an astonishing vision. He was 'caught up to the third heaven', into the immediate presence of God. For a while he was in paradise. The things he saw and heard are beyond his power or permission to tell.

Does this impress the Corinthians? Of course it does! Wouldn't they like to know more? Of course they would! But they must accept Paul as they actually find him, with all his disappointing shortcomings. Although they would like him to be a 'super-apostle', he is in fact poor of pocket, broken of body and slow of speech. His only glory is that he shares the sufferings of Christ.

Paul mentions in particular that God gave him 'a thorn' in his flesh. This is some physical illness or handicap, such as epilepsy with its sudden seizures, or malaria with its searing headache; but we don't know (or need to know) the precise identity of Paul's 'thorn'.

Paul implored God to take the 'thorn' away; but God refused. Instead, he promised to give Paul the grace to bear it. As a result, the 'thorn' keeps Paul humble and dependent on Christ – and he delights in it! He has found that, when he is weak, he has to rely completely on the strength of Christ, which is the only strength that matters.

Paul's miracles

We don't know what particular 'signs, wonders and miracles' took place in Corinth through the ministry of Paul. The book of Acts tells us some of the miracles God worked through him on other occasions. He healed a disabled man at Lystra (Acts 14:8–10) and delivered a slave girl from an evil spirit at Philippi (Acts 16:16–18). It may be soon after writing this letter that Paul raises a young man to life at Troas (Acts 20:9–10).

'I am ready to visit you'

(12:11 – 13:4)

Paul comes to the end of his 'fool's speech'. He talks in plain language again, without sarcasm or referring to himself as someone else. He says bluntly, 'I am not in the least inferior to the "super-apostles".' The Corinthians should have known this already and defended him against gossip and criticism.

It seems that the Corinthians have been feeling they are an inferior church, because they were founded by Paul who is an inferior apostle. He is not one of the original twelve apostles who knew Jesus personally and had been with him during his ministry (Acts 1:21–22).

Paul assures them that his standing as a true apostle has been proved by the great things God has done through him – signs, wonders and miracles. Then the dry humour creeps back. He tells them the only way they are inferior is that they don't have to pay him for his work!

Paul tells the Corinthians that he is ready to visit them again. This will be his third visit. His first was when he stayed for eighteen months and founded the church. His second was a brief and painful one when he called to tackle a scandal (2:1). Now he plans to visit them again.

Paul assures the Corinthians that his visit will not cost them money. Like a father, he expects to spend on them rather than they on him. Some people have been saying that he is after their funds, and that the collection for the poor Christians in Jerusalem is a trick. But Paul reminds them how honest Titus and his partner were – and he will be the same.

Paul is worried that he and the Corinthians may disappoint each other. He is very ordinary – and they are a turbulent bunch. He also suspects he will find some outrageous behaviour going on, which will shame, embarrass and grieve him. In all this doubt and heartache, we hear Paul's genuine love for this brash and boisterous young church.

Paul's love for the Corinthians will not prevent him challenging their sins – including the situation he dealt with on his last visit. Those who have been saying that Paul is weak are in for a surprise. He will be weak and powerful in the same ways that Christ is weak and powerful – weak in human suffering, but strong in the power of God.

'Finally…'

(13:5–14)

Paul urges the Corinthians to examine their own lives. Is Christ really their Saviour and Lord? Their true faith will be revealed in their behaviour – as Paul's is in his.

Sometimes Paul feels he has failed with the church at Corinth. He wants to be proud of them, but they have many faults. Is this because he didn't work hard or well enough when he laid their foundations? He prays that they will mend their ways, and that he may build them up rather than tear them down.

Paul closes his letter with a blessing. His words have become one of the world's best-known and most frequently used prayers: 'the grace'.

Paul prays that every aspect of God's love may rest upon the Corinthians, his dear brothers and sisters. This letter might easily have ended with final reproaches or a parting curse. Paul's blessing is gentle proof of the grace of God in his own life.

GALATIANS

Paul is angry. The gospel in Galatia has been attacked and undermined by a damaging lie. And it is also being suggested that Paul himself isn't a true apostle.

The Christians in Galatia are mainly Gentiles, but probably include some Jews. Both Jews and Gentiles have simply believed the gospel of Jesus Christ and become Christians.

Now some strict Jews have visited the churches in Galatia. Their message has been that Gentile Christians must be circumcised and keep the Jewish law. In other words, they must become proper Jews before they can become proper Christians.

Paul writes this letter in frustration and rage. He calls the Galatian Christians 'foolish' for believing this nonsense. And he wishes that the teachers who insist on circumcision would go and mutilate themselves!

Outline

Paul introduces himself and greets the Galatian Christians (1:1–5)

The one and only gospel (1:6 – 2:21)

The difference between law and grace (3:1 – 4:31)

Freedom and life in the Spirit (5:1 – 6:10)

From cross to new creation (6:11–18)

INTRODUCTION

Teachers who distort the gospel

This is probably the very first of Paul's letters that have survived to become part of the New Testament. It may have been written as early as AD 48.

Paul first stayed in Galatia because he was ill (4:13–15). The people were very kind to him, and received the gospel willingly. But now they have been visited by Jewish teachers with a different message. These teachers distort the gospel by insisting that Gentile Christians must be circumcised and keep the Jewish law.

Paul quickly sees the danger. If this teaching catches on, it will destroy the gospel. The Jews are adding an extra requirement to simple faith in Christ. They want the Galatians to show their Christian difference in the same ways that Jews have shown their Jewish difference – by circumcision, sabbath-keeping and food laws.

Paul argues that faith in Jesus and his death on the cross is all that is needed for salvation. It was faith, not circumcision, which put Abraham right with God. Being circumcised, keeping the sabbath and eating Jewish food can't possibly add to what Jesus has already done!

Where is Galatia?

Galatia is a Roman province in Asia Minor. The area splits north and south.

Northern Galatia is a mountainous area of Asia Minor, where Celts from Gaul settled in the 3rd century BC. It is called 'Galatia' after the Gauls.

Southern Galatia is a district added by the Romans, including the cities of Antioch (known locally as Pisidia, to distinguish it from Antioch in Syria) and Iconium. These are places Paul and Barnabas visited in AD 47–48, on their first missionary journey (Acts 13 and 14). We don't know if Paul visited the north, nor to which part of Galatia he wrote this letter.

Paul says that we are saved from sin and death and judgment by God's grace. Abraham was the first person to trust God's promises – promises which the whole human race is invited to share. Those who have the same faith as Abraham are his true descendants. Race, sex and status don't matter. God doesn't see Jews and Gentiles, men and women, slaves and those who are free. He sees faith. He sees those who belong to Jesus. He sees his children.

The great debate

Because Christianity comes from a Jewish background, the greatest debate of all is about its Jewish roots. Do Christians have to study and keep the law of Moses? This is thoroughly discussed at the Council of Jerusalem in AD 49.

The Council decides that Gentile Christians need not be circumcised. They must avoid meat that has been sacrificed in pagan temples or killed by strangling (that is, in a way that doesn't drain out the blood).

For Jews, blood contains life. It is sacred to God and not to be eaten. The Gentile Christians must also abstain from sexual immorality – that is, all sex outside marriage. Sexual purity is not just a Jewish hang-up, but a universal law for God's holy people.

When the gospel is first preached, various people try to oppose or adjust it. Jewish legalists try to add their laws. Gentile mystics try to add their secrets. Pagans argue over Christian morality – whether the gospel means free sex for all or no sex at all. And there is the constant threat of suppression by a government or persecution by an enemy.

All these challenges have to be met with clear thinking and brave teaching. And no one is clearer or braver than Paul.

Paul in person

This letter tells us a lot about Paul. We see his personal faith in Christ and his strong sense of calling. We glimpse the three years he spent in Arabia and Damascus, thinking through his new faith (1:17–18).

Paul tells particularly of two visits to Jerusalem. On the first he spends a fortnight with Peter and James, the Lord's brother. On the second, fourteen years later, he meets privately with the church leaders, including Peter, James and John.

Paul is challenging the Jerusalem leaders on their attitude to Christians who are not Jews. He takes a

Gentile companion, Titus, with him as an example. He is pleased to establish that Titus does not need to be circumcised.

Later Paul challenges Peter on another Jewish custom – that Jews don't eat meals with Gentiles. Peter shares meals with Gentiles in Antioch, until some stricter Jews arrive from Jerusalem. Then he starts to eat separately. Paul doesn't let Peter get away with this double standard.

DISCOVERING GALATIANS

Paul introduces himself and greets the Galatian Christians

Paul introduces himself as an apostle (1:1–5). This is what his critics have been trying to deny. After all, Paul wasn't one of the original twelve apostles who were chosen and commissioned by Jesus.

But Paul announces that he is a true apostle because God the Father and Jesus have called and sent him. He hasn't been elected by the other apostles and he certainly hasn't appointed himself. His status comes from the will of God.

Paul begins so strongly because he wants the Galatians to know that what he says to them is true. He greets them with God's grace and peace. He reminds them that Jesus gave himself to die on the cross as a sacrifice for our sins. In doing this he was fulfilling God's will. He was rescuing us from the evil of this world, so that we can live the life of heaven while we are still on earth.

The one and only gospel

Paul attacks those who are altering the gospel
(1:6–10)

Having greeted the Galatians, Paul comes straight to the point. He is astonished that the Galatians have so quickly abandoned their faith in the gospel.

The Galatians have fallen for new teachers who are changing the gospel. They are stripping new Christians of their freedom and putting them in the old prison of the law. Paul curses these teachers in the most solemn terms. It doesn't matter who they are – apostles or angels from heaven – no one has the right to tamper with the gospel. They are doing a terrible thing. They are robbing people of faith.

There is only one gospel, revealed by God himself

(1:11–17)

Paul explains that he received the gospel directly from God. He didn't invent it himself, nor did he learn it from someone else. It was a revelation from Jesus Christ.

Paul tells the Galatians the story of his conversion. He was once the finest and keenest of Jews, vigorously persecuting the Christian church. But then God showed him who Jesus really is – the Messiah, Son of God and Saviour of the world. God turned Paul, on the road to Damascus, from fanaticism to faith. After his conversion, he spent some three years in the desert of Arabia, east of Damascus. There he absorbed the revelation of Jesus and thought through the implications for his life and future work.

Paul didn't depend on the original apostles

(1:18–24)

God had always intended to do this – to call Saul of Tarsus to become Paul, the apostle to the Gentiles. Paul insists that he didn't get his message from the apostles in Jerusalem. He didn't visit Peter and James until three years later – by which time he had fully digested the revelation of the Damascus road.

The apostles in Jerusalem recognize Paul as an apostle to the Gentiles

(2:1–10)

It is not until fourteen years after his conversion that Paul visits Jerusalem again. He goes there because God has told him to go – not because the church leaders have summoned him.

A prophet, Agabus, has predicted that there will be a famine throughout the Roman empire. Paul and Barnabas are sent by the church in Antioch with aid for the Christians in Jerusalem (Acts 11:27–30).

While Paul is in Jerusalem, he checks his gospel message with the original apostles. There is pressure from some Jewish Christians to circumcise Gentile converts. Paul strongly disagrees with the idea. Such people are 'false believers' trying to enslave the new Christians in the requirements of the Jewish law.

Paul has brought Barnabas and Titus with him. Barnabas is a Jew who was a leading and generous member of the Jerusalem church in the early days. Titus is a Greek Christian – one of the people the Jewish pressure group wants to circumcise.

Paul says that the apostles in Jerusalem have nothing to add to his message. The gospel that Paul has received directly from God is the very same gospel of Jesus Christ that they are preaching. They recognize that Paul has been called to be an apostle to the Gentiles, just as Peter has been called to be an apostle to the Jews. They shake hands on their partnership. And there is no talk of circumcising Titus.

Paul has rebuked Peter for hypocrisy

(2:11–14)

Now Paul recounts another episode. Since the handshake with Peter in Jerusalem there has been an argument with Peter in Antioch.

'Antioch' is not the Pisidian Antioch in Galatia, but the capital of Syria in Asia. This Antioch is the home base of the lively church that first sent Paul and Barnabas off on a missionary journey.

Peter has visited the church in Antioch and joined in fellowship with the Gentile Christians. He shared meals with them, eating their food, with no worries that they weren't strict Jews.

But when members of the Jewish pressure group arrived from Jerusalem, Peter changed. He started eating separately from the Gentile Christians because they weren't circumcised. He also influenced others (even Barnabas) to do the same.

Paul saw this behaviour as a double standard. Peter knew very well that the Gentiles were complete Christians. It was he who visited and baptized the Roman centurion Cornelius. But Peter was also a coward who gave in to pressure. Just as he once disowned Jesus by lying to a serving maid, so he now betrayed his Gentile fellowship.

Paul challenged Peter directly and in public. The Christian church must not be split on this issue of circumcision. No Jew has ever been saved by being circumcised, so why should the custom be inflicted on non-Jews? Salvation comes through faith in God's grace, not by keeping the Jewish law.

Paul has made a crucial point. His argument will lead to the Council of Jerusalem, which will decide that Gentile Christians need not be circumcised. If Peter's hypocrisy had infected the whole church, the result would have been a split between Jewish and Gentile Christians. It may even have caused the true gospel to be lost – sunk without trace beneath the waves of Jewish legalism.

Grace and not law is the way to life with God
(2:15–21)

Jewish Christians know that they have been put right with God through faith in Jesus Christ. The Jewish law is good in itself, but no one has ever managed to keep it.

The law, in the end, can only declare us guilty. But trusting in Jesus Christ allows us to be 'justified' – that is, declared 'not guilty'. Jesus has borne the penalty of our sin, so that we can go free.

The Jews made a great effort to keep God's law, and were proud of their achievements. Those Jews who became Christians felt that the law was still the best guide to good living, and wanted Gentile Christians to accept it too. Without it, the Gentile Christians would still be sinners.

Paul argues strongly that faith in Christ is enough. When we come to Christ we die to our old life and rise to his new life. I am no longer right with God through my own efforts, but through Jesus' life in me.

The difference between law and grace

'You foolish Galatians!'
(3:1–5)

Paul can't believe that the Galatian Christians have so quickly lost their way. They have traded the freedom of Christ for the burden of the Jewish law. He calls them 'fools' or even 'idiots', and wonders whether someone has cast a spell on them!

The key question is this: did they receive the Holy Spirit by following the law or by receiving the gospel? And if keeping the law can achieve salvation, why did Jesus go to the cross? The answer is, of course, that they

---

Justified by faith

Martin Luther said that justification by faith is the 'most principal and special article of Christian doctrine'. Without it, Christianity is just another religion – an endless effort to get right with God through self-discipline and ritual.

---

have come to spiritual life only through the death of Jesus and faith in the gospel.

Abraham shows the importance of faith
(3:6–9)

Paul brings Abraham as a witness to the importance of faith. Abraham, after all, is the founding father of the Jewish race – living long before Moses introduced the law.

God invited Abraham to believe that he would give him many descendants and make him a great nation. This was a mighty leap of faith, because both Abraham and his wife were old and childless. But Abraham believed God, and his faith was 'credited to him as righteousness' (Genesis 15:6).

Do the Galatians see what Paul is saying? Being right with God doesn't come from keeping the law. There *was* no law in Abraham's time. Nor does it come from circumcision. Abraham was right with God *before* he was circumcised. So where does righteousness come from? It is God's gift to us when we believe in him.

God wants everyone to be saved through faith. He called Abraham to be the father of a nation, so that he could bless all the nations through him. God's people are the children of Abraham, not because they belong to his race, but because they share his faith.

The law condemns, but faith gives life
(3:10–14)

Paul explains that the law places us under a curse. He quotes from Deuteronomy, to remind us that we have all failed to keep God's law (Deuteronomy 27:26). This is a shock to people who think they have been saving up righteousness by their religion, gifts and good deeds.

Paul says that righteousness comes not by efforts to be good, but by faith. There is nothing new in this – the prophet Habakkuk said the same long ago (Habakkuk 2:4). The law will only give righteousness to those who actually *keep* it (Leviticus 18:5). And no one (except Jesus) has ever managed to do that.

So what hope is there for sinful humans to be put right with God?

Paul explains that Jesus took our guilt and sentence of death upon himself. When people were stoned to death for breaking God's law, they were afterwards hung on a tree. It was a sign of God's utter rejection of them. Now Jesus has been executed by crucifixion – taking our curse to the cross. The result is that God now accepts us

through faith in Christ. He has taken our death and given us life.

Promise is stronger than law
(3:15–18)

Paul continues to argue from the Jewish scriptures – our Old Testament. He quotes prophecies and people well known to the Jewish Christians.

To explain the difference between law and promise, he again takes the example of Abraham. God promised Abraham many descendants. This promise wasn't something Abraham had asked for or deserved. It was a one-sided commitment by God.

God's promise to Abraham was fulfilled in the remarkable birth of Isaac, the growth of the family through Jacob's twelve sons and the survival of the children of Israel, despite famine in Canaan and slavery in Egypt. By the time of the exodus, Abraham's descendants had become a small nation.

It was not until 430 years after the promise to Abraham that God gave his people the law. At Mount Sinai God gave Moses the Ten Commandments and the many lesser regulations for a godly society. But the law didn't replace the promise. Nor did the fulfilment of the promise depend on keeping the law. With God, a promise is a promise. He always keeps his word.

So how is God to keep his promise to Abraham? Where is the 'seed' that will bless the nations and fill the earth? Paul points out that the 'seed' (or offspring) mentioned in Genesis is the word for a single group (Genesis 12:7). The promise is fulfilled in Jesus Christ and all who belong to him.

The law imprisons, but Christ sets free
(3:19–25)

If God's promise is all that is needed for righteousness, why was the law given at all?

Paul explains that the law was given to show our sin. When there was no law, we had no idea what sin was. But once the law was given, it became clear that we were in deep trouble. The law shows us our sin and our need for God's forgiveness.

A highly decorated Torah scroll shows the high regard which Jewish people have for God's law. Paul reminds his Galatian readers that, although God had given the people his law, it did not cancel the earlier promise he made to Abraham that all the nations on earth would be blessed through him. Paul sees that promise fulfilled in Jesus Christ.

But the promise is greater than the law. Paul points out that the law was only given 'second-hand' – through angels and a mediator (Moses). But when God gave the promise, he gave it 'first-hand' from himself to Abraham.

So are the law and the promise against each other? No. Both are concerned for our well-being, but only the promise can give us life. The law shows us our sin and shuts us in a prison of guilt – so that we long for our promised deliverance through faith in Christ.

The Jewish Christians who want Gentiles to be circumcised are assuming that the law is more important than the promise. They are assuming that faith can only be expressed by keeping the rules and regulations of the Jewish law.

Paul says the opposite. All the demands of the law have been met by the death of Jesus on the cross. Now the main line of God's righteousness is absolutely clear. It is free to all through faith in Christ.

From slaves to children
(3:26 – 4:11)

So there is no distinction in God's sight between Jews and Gentiles. Nor does God distinguish between male and female, or slaves and those who are free.

Salvation is offered to all, regardless of race, sex or status. God welcomes as his children all those who belong to Christ. They are the true descendants of Abraham and the heirs of the promise God made to him.

To put it another way, it is as though the law was guiding us while we grew up. This growing up took many hundreds of years for the Jewish people, and is repeated in each of our lives. But the time comes when, by God's Spirit, we are able to call him 'Abba' or 'Father'. We are no longer slaves trying to keep the laws but children delighting in his promise.

Paul is concerned that the Galatians are slipping back into slavery. Before they were Christians, they had rituals and routines to cope with the troubles and dangers of life. Now they are using the Jewish law for the same purpose. They are trying to keep on the right side of God with circumcisions, sabbaths and festivals. Paul wonders if all his efforts to give them the gospel of grace are wasted.

'What has happened to your joy?'
(4:12–20)

Paul knows that something has gone seriously wrong with the Galatians. He remembers their care for him when he

---

Accepting what Jesus has done

We don't like to think that we're helpless – but we are! Pride in what we can do must be replaced by humble acceptance of what Jesus has done for us. If our works could deliver salvation, Jesus need never have gone to the cross.

---

was ill – perhaps with an illness affecting his eyesight. They would have given their eyes to him in those days! But now they seem to have lost all their joy and commitment.

Paul begs his readers to become like him. He longs that they should share his life in Christ, just as he shared their everyday life when he was with them.

The Jewish teachers are paying the Galatians a lot of attention, but they aren't doing them any good. Paul may not be impressive, but at least he is telling them the truth. He feels like a pregnant mother enduring spasms of pain. He is straining to bring the Galatians to birth in the image of Christ.

The example of Ishmael and Isaac
(4:21–31)

Paul gives another example to show the difference between law and promise. He uses the very scriptures which the Jewish teachers are using to impose the law on Gentile Christians.

Paul takes the Jews to the books of the law and the story of Abraham. Abraham had two sons. The first was Ishmael, the child of his slave woman Hagar. The second was Isaac, the child of his wife Sarah. One was born a slave; the other was born free.

Paul says that these sons are a picture of the law and the gospel. The law was given through Moses on Mount Sinai – and that mountain is like a mother that produces children for slavery. The earthly Jerusalem is the same – the capital of a Judaism which is enslaved to ritual, sacrifice and legalism.

But there is another mother, and that is the new Jerusalem which is in heaven. She, like Abraham's wife, is free – and her children are free. They are not the slave children of law, but the free children of promise.

Paul is saying the same as he said before. The real children of Abraham are not the Jews who observe circumcision and keep the sabbath. The real children of Abraham are those who, by faith in Christ, have become the children of God.

Paul is arguing with the Jewish teachers on their own ground – and winning. He wants them to realize the limitations of the law – and accept instead the freedom of Christ.

Freedom and life in the Spirit

Jesus is good news. Good news of forgiveness. Good news of freedom. But Paul warns the Galatians against being caught and burdened by legalism.

The folly of circumcision
(5:1–12)

Paul argues that Gentiles who become Christians must *not* be circumcised. The moment they are circumcised, they will find that they are expected to keep the entire Jewish law. And those who try to keep the law are no longer relying on God's grace.

Paul explains that righteousness comes from God. It is a gift of his Spirit. Circumcision doesn't matter. What counts is faith in Jesus expressed in a life of love.

The Galatians had made a good start in their Christian life. Now something has crept in to spoil their faith and confuse their understanding. Paul assures them that the command for them to be circumcised has not come from God. It is the very opposite of being saved by faith.

Circumcision is an attempt to get right with God by doing something ourselves. The cross of Jesus shows that we can't do anything to save ourselves; we can only trust in what he has done for us.

Free to love
(5:13–15)

Paul reminds the Galatian Christians that they are called to be free. Free from sin. Free from guilt. Free from trying to be good. Free from fear.

Some people have abused this freedom. They have taken the opportunity to indulge themselves, because they believe that God must always forgive them. Paul says that Christian freedom is not permission to do wrong, but liberty to do right. True freedom shows itself in love and service to others.

Loving others was always the aim of the Jewish law – but it proved impossible to do. Now it *is* possible because

Jesus has shown the way and gives his Spirit to help us. We are free – not to break the law, but to keep it. Now we can at last obey God in the right way and for the right reasons.

The flesh and the Spirit
(5:16–26)

Paul encourages the Galatian Christians to live their new life to the full. Their old life was lived in the selfishness with which they were born. Their new life is lived in the selflessness of the Holy Spirit. But the old and the new will always fight against each other.

Paul describes the old life. It is a self-absorbed life of greed, superstition and jealousy. It is marked by wrong sexual relationships, misguided religion, constant strife and destructive habits. These attitudes are so alien to Jesus that he will bar us from his kingdom.

But there is a new life for all who want it. This is the life that the Holy Spirit inspires.

The Spirit enables us to live in love, joy and peace with God. The Spirit gives us patience, kindness and goodness towards other people. The Spirit produces faithfulness, gentleness and self-control in our hearts and behaviour.

Paul calls these lovely qualities 'the fruit of the Spirit'. It is not several fruits, as though our task is to collect them all. It is the single fruit of a Christlike life. And all the Spirit's attitudes are legal. We are no longer bound by the law, but nor will the Holy Spirit ever lead us to break it.

Paul emphasizes that we have a responsibility for our new life. Jesus told his disciples that they must deny themselves and take up their cross and follow him (Mark 8:34). Now Paul says we must crucify our old nature – ruthlessly condemning and rejecting its appetites and desires.

As well as putting our old selfish nature to death, we are positively to 'keep in step with the Spirit'. We are to walk in line with him. This is not a life we can live on autopilot. It demands our continuing attention and response. It is also a life in which we support and encourage one another. There is no place for pride, picking fights or jealousy.

Caring for one another
(6:1–5)

Does 'crucifying' our old nature and 'keeping in step with the Spirit' mean we are now perfect? No. We will never be perfect this side of heaven. Every Christian has an inner struggle between the old nature and the new. Even though we keep on crucifying our old self, it is a long time dying.

Paul teaches the Galatians how to care for one another. If someone falls into sin, those who are mature in the life of the Spirit should gently restore that person. It is a careful process, and not to be done out of curiosity or pride. But how different from being condemned!

Paul describes Christian care as carrying one another's burdens. We each have a load to bear – made up of temptations, failures, problems and sorrows. But we can help one another. This is one way we can obey Jesus' commandment to love one another.

But there is one small load we must always carry ourselves. It is the personal baggage of our own inner attitude – which is a matter between ourselves and God.

The harvest of a lifetime
(6:6–10)

Paul says our life is like a harvest. What we grow will depend on what we sow.

This applies to work and reward. Teachers who sow instruction should receive a harvest of good things from those who learn.

It is also true of our spiritual life. We can't cheat God. If we sow to satisfy our old nature, we will become corrupt and be destroyed. If we sow to please the Spirit, we will grow in holiness and reap eternal life. It's our decision. The crop may seem a long time growing, but every act of kindness is another seed sown.

From cross to new creation

Paul is nearing the end of his letter (6:11–18). He takes the pen from his secretary and writes the last paragraph himself – in large letters. He wishes to make himself very clear.

The people who want the Galatians to be circumcised are concerned for outward appearances. They want to show that Christian converts are coming under the old Jewish law. But Paul says that by cutting flesh they are avoiding the cross of Christ.

The Jewish teachers want the Galatians to keep the law – even though they haven't managed to keep it themselves. They want the Galatians to be circumcised –

even though circumcision does nothing to put a person right with God.

For Paul, the cross is central to salvation. It is to preach 'Christ crucified' that he travels and preaches and suffers as he does. The Jewish teachers want to avoid a crucified Messiah at all costs. They want to get back to the safe routine of circumcision and lawkeeping.

But Paul *boasts* about the cross! It is the cross that shows him his sin and assures him of his salvation. His sin is cancelled. His salvation is certain. Because of the cross, the world and its wickedness have no more attraction for him.

To give his readers the complete picture, Paul makes one last point.

Circumcision is really a very little thing – a small cut which some people have and some don't. It is only a ritual, and eternal life can't possibly depend on it. What really matters, says Paul, is the new person whom God brings to birth by his Spirit. Not a little human incision, but God's new creation.

If anyone counts marks on the body, then Paul already has a fine display. He has the scars of his stoning at Lystra, which some of his readers will remember because they were there. And he will receive many more lashes and beatings before his work is done (2 Corinthians 11:23–25). These are more the marks of Jesus than any circumcision.

Finally, Paul signs off with the grace of Jesus Christ. It will become his customary farewell. And he closes by calling these 'dear idiots of Galatia' his brothers and sisters.

EPHESIANS

Paul is writing to Christians who live in the Greek city of Ephesus. He writes to them about the new life Christ gives – a life of unity, purity and joy.

Through Jesus, God is uniting earth and heaven. The same power which raised Jesus to life is setting people free from sin and making them God's children. And because people belong to Jesus, they can dismantle the ancient barriers which divide them. Jews and Gentiles especially can make peace through Jesus Christ. In Christ, no one is a stranger; everyone belongs.

Paul urges the Ephesian Christians to come out of their old paganism with its dark thoughts, dirty talk and immoral ways. They must discard that life like a set of filthy clothes, and put on the new life of Christ instead.

Outline

Greetings (1:1–2)

God has given us new life in Christ (1:3 – 2:10)

Christ gives peace between Jews and Gentiles (2:11–22)

Paul's work for the Gentiles, and his prayer for the Ephesians (3:1–21)

The life of Jesus lived together in the church (4:1–16)

Put off the old and put on the new (4:17 – 5:21)

New relationships (5:22 – 6:9)

How to fight on God's side (6:10–20)

Final greetings (6:21–24)

INTRODUCTION

Ephesians – a general letter?

This letter is different from some others by Paul. It doesn't have his usual personal messages, and the earliest versions don't even mention Ephesus.

Again, in this letter Paul isn't tackling any particular problem. It isn't a troubleshooting letter like some of his others. At the same time, it is very similar to the letter to the Colossians. A lot of the material overlaps.

It may be that Ephesians is a letter which is taken round various churches in Asia Minor by Tychicus, and read out in several churches. It could be a teaching letter or sermon to Christians whom Paul has never met, and (because he is now in prison) will never get to know. And so he writes some general teaching on the theory and practice of Christianity. He outlines all that God has done for us through Christ, and the difference Jesus makes to our outlook, behaviour and relationships. The Greek is quite formal, and at times complicated. 1:3–14 is all one sentence!

Letters from prison

Paul writes several of his letters from prison. Ephesians, Philippians, Colossians and Philemon all seem to have been written in these circumstances. We know from the book of Acts that Paul is in prison in Caesarea for two years (Acts 24:27) and, later, under house arrest in Rome. The most popular theory is that Paul writes these letters from Rome, while he is waiting to be tried before Emperor Nero. This is in the years between AD 60 and 62.

For two whole years Paul stayed there in his own rented house and welcomed all those who came to see him. Boldly and without hindrance he preached the kingdom of God and taught about the Lord Jesus Christ (Acts 28:30–31).

DISCOVERING EPHESIANS

Greetings

Paul describes himself as 'an apostle of Jesus Christ' (1:1–2). Although he was not one of the original twelve apostles, Paul believes that God has called him just as clearly, to be a pioneering church-planter and leader (Galatians 2:8).

Paul calls the Christians at Ephesus 'saints'. This is not because they are perfect, but because God has chosen them to serve him. 'Saints' means 'those who are set apart' as well as 'holy ones'. He greets them with the twin blessings of grace and peace.

God has given us new life in Christ

Praise to God for spiritual blessings
(1:3–14)

Paul writes his teaching in the form of praise to God. He praises God for choosing ordinary people (not only the Ephesian Christians, but also ourselves) to join his family.

God set his heart on us before the foundation of the world. He has caught us up in the death and life of his Son, Jesus. Because Jesus died for us, God has forgiven our sins and welcomed us into his family – not as servants or slaves, but as his sons and daughters. We belong together – God and humanity, heaven and earth, united with Christ.

The gift of the Holy Spirit 'seals' or confirms what God has done for us – just as a 'sold' notice marks that an item in the market has a new owner. The presence of the Holy Spirit in our lives is our guarantee that we now belong to God.

Thanksgiving and prayer
(1:15–23)

From praise, Paul moves to prayer. He thanks God for the faith that his readers have, and prays that God will strengthen their relationship with him. Their holiness will depend on getting to know God better. They are called to be holy, to be free from sin, to be united in love and to endure suffering. Their hope will depend on God expanding their vision, to see the vast panorama of eternity and the glorious inheritance which awaits them in heaven. They are a resurrection people. The same power that raised Jesus from death is at work in them to give them new life.

God has given Jesus, the king of the universe and the conqueror of death and evil, to be head of the church. Now Christ fills the church with his presence and directs it by his power, just as he already fills and directs the whole universe.

God has voted for us!

God has 'elected' us. He has chosen us not just to exist, but to become his children. Just as he chose Israel out of all the nations to be his special people, so he has chosen us out of all nations and cultures to be his saints – his holy or special people.

God is mending the rift between earth and heaven which came through the fall. He is bringing heaven and earth together again – choosing us who are on earth and blessing us in heaven. God's purpose in all this is that we should live holy lives and be a credit to him.

Grace – the inexhaustible goodness of God

Paul was brought up to obey the law of God. By keeping the Jewish law, he hoped to build a righteous life and earn God's salvation.

Now Paul realizes that salvation comes entirely through God's goodness. It is God who gives us his Son and his Spirit. It is God who calls us to repent of our sins and offers us forgiveness. It is God who helps us to lead holy lives and will give us eternal life.

This full, rich and endless goodness of God to us is called 'grace'. It is not something we have earned or deserved. It is God's love which is seen perfectly in Jesus and received now through his Holy Spirit.

Made alive in Christ
(2:1–10)

Paul explains to his readers that they were spiritually dead. They may have had healthy bodies, lively minds and attractive personalities – but their souls were dead. They were completely unable to respond to God.

But the situation was worse than that. They were not only spiritually dead, but condemned to eternal destruction. God was so angry with them. He was angry with their sin. All their natural God-given desires were warped and exaggerated – so that hunger had become greed and sexual attraction had become lust.

But then came the miracle. God had mercy on the corrupt, captive, helpless human race. Alongside God's wrath is God's love. He has power to save. He raised Jesus from death and seated him in glory – and now he has done the same for those who trust in Christ. What a difference grace makes!

God has done all this for us because of his great mercy, love and kindness. He has saved us from sin and death and given us victory over the powers of evil. We didn't achieve this by ourselves, and we certainly didn't deserve it. But God has done it for us. We are prize examples of what God can do!

For it is by grace you have been saved, through faith – and this not from yourselves, it is the gift of God (2:8).

Christ gives peace between Jews and Gentiles

Paul is writing to Gentiles who have become Christians. For centuries, Gentiles have been excluded from the special relationship between God and Israel (2:11–22).

In the beginning, God made humans in his own image. No person or race was superior to any other. Even when God chose Israel to be his holy people, it was his plan to bless all the nations of the world through their light.

Sadly, the Jews became exclusive. There was a terrible division between Jews and Gentiles. The Jews felt so strongly about their moral and racial purity that they made a point of keeping outsiders away. In Paul's day, a wall forms a barrier to keep Gentiles out of the inner Jewish courtyards of the temple. There are notices warning that trespassers will be executed. Paul calls this 'the dividing wall of hostility' (2:14).

Now Jesus Christ has destroyed this 'wall' and made peace between Gentiles and Jews – those who were 'far away' (the Gentiles) and those who were 'near' (the Jews). Through Jesus and his reconciling death on the cross, both Jews and Gentiles have access to God the Father.

Paul declares the outbreak of peace. The old enmity between Jews and Gentiles is ended. Jesus has broken down the wall of hostility and made peace with God for both Jews and Gentiles.

This peace isn't made by circumcision, special diet or keeping clean. It is a peace which is made by Jesus dying for the sins of Jews and Gentiles alike.

Instead of the human race divided into Jews and Gentiles, there is now one new humanity united in Christ. The Christian church is just the beginning of this new creation – the new humanity in a new society.

The peace of Christ overcomes other divisions as well – such as inequality between men and women or between different social groups. Wherever there is injustice, envy or exploitation, Jesus invites all to make peace with God and with one another. We are no longer divided by our race or sex, our education or status. We are united by faith in Christ.

Paul explains to Gentile Christians that they are no longer outsiders to God and his people. They are fellow citizens of God's kingdom, brothers and sisters in God's

Jews and Gentiles

Paul knows Jews who call Gentiles 'dogs'. Their argument is that Gentiles know nothing about the true God. Gentiles have no covenant with him, no law to govern their behaviour, no coming messiah, kingdom or hope. If a Jewish son or daughter marries a Gentile, the family holds a funeral rather than a wedding. That son or daughter has ceased to exist. In Herod the Great's temple, a wall runs right round the central Jewish courts. This wall, a metre and a half high, keeps the Gentiles at a lower level and far away from the sanctuary. It separates the Gentiles both from the Jews and from God. Notices in Greek and Latin warn that any Gentile who passes this point will be executed.

family and living stones in the true temple of God's church.

As Paul writes, two famous temples dominate the popular imagination. In Ephesus, the temple of Artemis ('Diana of the Ephesians') is one of the seven wonders of the world. In Jerusalem, the temple of Herod the Great is also mightily impressive. But Paul says that God dwells not in a statue of a goddess, nor in an empty sanctuary, but in the lives of his people – his new creation in Christ.

Paul's work for the Gentiles, and his prayer for the Ephesians

Paul, the preacher to the Gentiles
(3:1–13)

What is so special about Paul? Why is he writing this letter from prison? Paul explains that he is in prison for the sake of Jesus – and his readers.

Paul believes that God has revealed a mystery to him. A mystery is something that humans can never discover, but which God makes known.

Both Paul and Peter have had to realize that Jesus is not just for Jews. The gospel is for Gentiles as well – and they needn't become Jews to receive it. This is a major theme of the book of Acts, as the good news spreads beyond Jewish circles – to Samaritans, an Ethiopian and the household of the Roman centurion Cornelius.

Now Paul is a prisoner because of the work he has been doing. Strict Jews have attacked him for preaching that rituals such as circumcision and sacrifice, and even the temple itself, no longer give access to God.

Paul sees that he has received a double gift. God has revealed a mystery to him, and also given him the task of preaching it. The mystery is that Jews and Gentiles are now united through faith in Jesus Christ. The old Jewish picture of a kingdom of God has been replaced with a vision of an international community of faith. Faith in Jesus Christ is all that is needed for salvation.

Paul has only come to this view through immense

Ephesus in Paul's time is a city of about half a million people, and an important centre for trade and culture. This view of Kuretes Street shows the temple of Hadrian on the right and the library of Celsus in the distance.

struggle. He himself was the strictest of Jews – a Pharisee – and a persecutor and murderer of Christians. Only when he was converted on the Damascus road did he realize that, in persecuting Christians, he was hurting the risen Christ. Remembering this, he calls himself 'the least of the least' – a play on his Roman surname, 'Paulus', which means 'Little'.

Now Paul's mission and ministry are to make known the riches of Christ – forgiveness, blessing, peace, unity and the hope of glory. All this is a wealth to be shared. Even the angels and heavenly powers are just beginning to discover the full extent of what God is doing through Christ.

Paul's prayer for the Ephesians
(3:14–21)

Paul prays earnestly that his readers may be strengthened in their faith. He asks that Jesus Christ will make his home and establish his throne in their hearts. He asks that they may realize the vastness of God's love – reaching the most despicable sinner and reconciling the most hostile enemies. He prays that they may be filled with God himself – to become perfect as God is perfect.

All this God is able to do. His work in us isn't limited to the things we can ask for or imagine. He works in us to give a continuing growth and transformation, to give us and all his church a glory that will never fade or end.

Paul concludes his prayer with a timeless affirmation of the power of God. God's plans aren't restricted by our half-hearted prayers and limited imagination. His plans are infinitely greater than we can ever know. God is at work in our lives with the same power with which he raised Jesus from death.

Paul has no doubt that, by God's mighty power, the church will continue to grow and flourish in all the generations to come.

The life of Jesus lived together in the church

Belonging and growing in Christ
(4:1–6)

Paul has shown his readers how they belong together. Now he urges them to live a life which shows their togetherness. It will be a life of united love and holy behaviour.

Paul encourages Christians to live for one another. They must be completely humble and gentle, patient and peaceable.

These are all attitudes which Jesus shows. No one ever thought much of being humble, until Jesus knelt and washed his disciples' feet. He acted as a slave and servant to his friends, putting them first and laying down his life for theirs (John 10:11; 13:14). He describes himself as 'gentle and humble in heart' (Matthew 11:29).

Christians belong together. We all have the same heavenly Father. We all have faith in the same Jesus and are baptized into him. We all have the same Holy Spirit to inspire us and unite us. Paul may be quoting a Christian hymn or creed as he writes, 'One Lord, one faith, one baptism; one God and Father of all...' (4:5–6). The Trinity of God (Father, Son and Spirit) is reflected and lived in his church.

Grace for all and gifts for each
(4:7–13)

All Christians are saved by God's grace and receive his Holy Spirit. God also gives various spiritual gifts to his people, so that they can contribute to the life and work of the church.

Paul quotes a psalm about the victory of God over his enemies (Psalm 68:18). When Jesus ascended to heaven, he was like a general returning from battle, sharing out the plunder with his people. He had come down to the depths of earth, to be born as a man and to die upon a cross. Now he has gone up to the very heights of heaven. So he has visited and conquered the extremities of existence, and now fills the whole universe with his presence and victory.

Paul lists some gifts that help the church to preach and teach God's word. Apostles are sent by God to pioneer church growth in new areas. Prophets speak God's word in a direct and challenging way to particular situations. Evangelists share the gospel clearly, so that people can understand and come to faith in Christ. Pastors and teachers are able to care for and teach local congregations.

There are many kinds of spiritual gifts. There is a different selection in Paul's letter to the Romans (Romans 12:6–8). But all spiritual gifts have the same purpose: to build up and strengthen God's people. Every gift is to be used in serving others, both inside and outside the church.

Carry on growing
(4:14–16)

God wants us to grow up to be 'one new humanity' (2:15) – the mature, strong and loving body of Christ. This may take a long time, because it involves every Christian growing and maturing in knowledge and love.

We are like a body with Christ as the head. The most important aspect of Christian growth is that we learn and live God's word. This is the exercise which gives us strong and settled convictions and makes us fit for useful service.

Put off the old and put on the new

Gentiles live in moral darkness (4:17 – 5:21). They have turned away from the light God has given them in their conscience. They have become hard-hearted towards God and ignorant of his ways. As a result, they throw themselves into a life of selfish greed and lust.

The Christian life is the opposite of paganism. Being a Christian means coming to Jesus and learning his truth and purity. It's like changing clothes – from the filthy old clothes of corruption to the fresh new clothes of Christ. Baptism acts this out – putting aside old clothes and receiving a new white robe. As God makes us new people (something only he can do), we change to new behaviour (something we must do ourselves). Our aim is to become like Jesus.

Paul gives several examples of Christian behaviour. He shows how our Christian beliefs become Christian actions. Each evil thing we stop doing can be replaced by something good which pleases God.

We must stop telling lies and tell the truth instead.

We must only be angry for the right reasons. Jesus was perfectly angry at times. We must get angry about the same things as Jesus and not because we are in a foul mood or not getting our own way. If we realize we are in the wrong, then let's be quick to ask forgiveness and make peace.

We must stop stealing and start giving. If we work, then we can share our strength, skills and earnings with others.

When we talk, we must be true, positive and helpful. We can build people up or tear them down with the things we say. The words that come from our lips show the state of our hearts. Damaging words, such as lies and dirty jokes, are the fruit of a rotten heart.

The devil is interested in our behaviour. He likes to exploit our anger to break our relationships. The Holy Spirit, too, is affected by what we do. He is hurt when we behave in selfish and cruel ways, because he is God's mark of ownership within us. Any wickedness in a Christian is a form of torture for God's Holy Spirit.

We must stop treating one another in spiteful, hurtful and reckless ways. Instead we must treat people as Christ has treated us – with kindness, understanding and forgiveness.

Living as a Christian means copying God – just as a child imitates his or her parents. And, as Jesus shows us, God is absolutely self-giving.

We should treat sex with purity and thankfulness. Pagans wrench sex out of its proper setting of a loving marriage. They take something exclusive and make it common. They take something beautiful and make it ugly. They take an act of selflessness and make it greedy. They crush love with lust.

The leading goddess of Ephesus, Diana, is a goddess of fertility. She is worshipped in orgies of sex. So should the Christians at Ephesus say sex is wrong? Not at all. Paul says his readers should thank God for sex. It is a wonderful gift, but not to be cheapened or abused. And as for immorality – don't even think about it!

Holiness doesn't happen by accident. The Christian life has to be learned from Christ. It's a life of purity in the midst of paganism. It's a life of holiness whose true home is in heaven.

Paul encourages us to lead lives which are worthy of the kingdom of God. We must have nothing to do with adultery and immorality. God's kingdom is a place of purity, and no one who is unclean or unfaithful may enter it.

We must wake up from the sleep of sin and death. Paul quotes a Christian hymn. We must wake up to the life and light of Christ. We have come from darkness to light and from death to life.

God cares about every detail of our lives. He has made us wise, so that we can live his way and use our time and opportunities well. At the heart of the Lord's prayer is, 'Your will be done.'

Instead of getting drunk on wine, we must be filled with the Holy Spirit. Wine makes us lose our self-control and behave like animals. The Holy Spirit *gives* us self-control, making us fully human – like Jesus. Self-control is one of the Spirit's great achievements in our lives (Galatians 5:22–23). Paul says that we must be filled – and go on being filled, moment by moment – with the Holy Spirit.

When Christians meet together for worship, our talking and singing must be for one another and the Lord, full of thankfulness and praise to God.

We are to be humble in all our relationships – putting one another first, as we all put Christ first in our lives.

Good news in the circumstances

Paul is writing to people who are trying to live as Christians in a variety of difficult circumstances. Some feel trapped in loveless marriages, some feel crushed by their parents, some suffer the hardships of slavery. Their relationships are not simple and their circumstances are not fair.

Paul could have said to everyone,

'Jesus Christ sets you free! Abandon your marriages, resist your parents and rebel against those who oppress you!' In fact, he teaches that Jesus can change our attitude to every situation. All relationships, at home and at work, can be transformed if we treat others as Christ has treated us.

As time goes by, Christians will play a key role in strengthening marriage and family life. They will also campaign to abolish slavery and tackle many other forms of injustice. These revolutions come not with violent demonstrations and social upheaval, but with the truth of God challenging and changing our hearts.

New relationships

Paul teaches how 'submitting to one another' applies at home and at work. All relationships – between husbands and wives, children and parents, masters and slaves – are to be transformed by Christ.

Wives and husbands
(5:22–33)

Wives are to submit to their husbands – honouring them and putting them first. This is something many Jewish, Greek and Roman wives are forced to do anyway. For many women, being a wife is no different from being a slave. But Paul is describing something far more wonderful.

A Christian wife is not submitting to her husband because he owns her, or because she is afraid of him. She is submitting to her husband because he is the head of their relationship. The husband is the head of a marriage

The change Jesus brought in

Romans use family life to keep iron control over their women and children. Some Greek thinkers planned to abolish families altogether. The Jews valued family life for training their sons, but excluded their young children and neglected their women.

Into this world came Jesus, who shockingly honoured women and surprisingly welcomed children (Luke 7:36–50; Mark 10:13–16).

just as Christ is the head of the church.

Paul's teaching is not that husbands should dominate their wives. He is saying that husbands are responsible for the well-being, security and happiness of their wives. Christ's headship of his church is shown by being her Saviour, not her tyrant.

And husbands are to love their wives. They are to love their wives, not because they are attractive or useful. They are to love their wives, because they are to be to them like Christ. A husband is to love, care for and serve his wife. Just as Christ brings his church to purity, perfection and glory – so a husband is to give himself so that his wife may know that she is accepted, liberated and fulfilled.

Being practical, Paul says that if a husband loves his wife as much as he loves himself he will do well. After all, this is the great commandment: to love your neighbour as you love yourself. And who is a closer neighbour than a wife? A husband and wife are 'one flesh' or 'one self' – so a husband, in caring for his wife, is caring for himself.

Paul is showing how all relationships are mended and integrated in Christ. Jews and Gentiles have become 'one new humanity' (2:15). Husbands and wives are 'one self' (5:31). And both these transformed relationships give a glimpse of the unity between Christ and his people.

Children and parents
(6:1–4)

Paul has taught wives to submit to their husbands and husbands to love their wives. This is because husbands have an authority, which is to be shown in selfless love. Jesus is their example, and standard of loving.

Now Paul talks to the children! They are part of the church. Their relationship with their parents is 'in the Lord'.

Paul tells children to obey their parents. This is quite natural. Most parents are bigger and stronger then their children anyway – at least to begin with!

Paul adds that this is also one of the Ten Commandments: 'Honour your father and your mother, so that you may live long in the land the Lord your God is giving you' (Exodus 20:12). This law adds the promise that if children honour their parents, then their nation will be strong and stable. One of the signs of the 'last days' is that children are 'disobedient to their parents' (2 Timothy 3:2). When this happens, society starts to decay and break down.

The scandal of slavery

It is estimated that there were 60 million slaves in the Roman empire. Some say the number is impossible to guess. Slaves were the vast majority of the workforce and an indispensable part of the culture. Certainly, slavery was far too extensive a cancer to be removed without the whole society collapsing.

Paul teaches Christian slaves and masters to let Christ transform their relationship. Slaves and masters may be bound together in an unjust system, but at least they can respect one another. Masters can stop being cruel and unreasonable. Slaves can work willingly and honestly. They can all serve Christ.

... and today?

Paul outlines the responsibilities that slaves and masters have to each other because they are Christians. The slave is to serve his master as he would serve Christ – that is, willingly, with all his heart. The master is to treat his slaves as fellow human beings and fellow servants of Christ.

Although slavery was eventually abolished, these attitudes can transform our work relationships today. Employees can see their work as something they do to honour Jesus Christ. Employers can honour Christ in the way they affirm and reward their workforce.

Paul also speaks to fathers. The word he uses can mean 'fathers and mothers'. They are not to exasperate their children, but bring them up in the training and instruction of the Lord.

A Roman father dominates his children. He can punish them, treat them as slaves, sell them or even have them killed. His power over his children is total, and lasts as long as he lives.

Paul teaches parents a different approach. They are not to use their power to oppress or to discourage their children. They are to show their children the love of God and give them the training of Jesus.

So Paul teaches that Christian marriages and families are to be marked by respect and love, obedience and encouragement. Christian homes are to be places of acceptance and training. Jesus is the key to loving discipline – and the perfect example of obedient love.

Slaves and masters
(6:5–9)

Many of Paul's readers are slaves. Their bodies are owned by other human beings, who make them do whatever they want. Some slaves are lucky. They serve the same family for the whole of their lives, and enjoy some respect and family life themselves. Others may be bought and sold several times, or treated with unspeakable cruelty.

Some slaves work as house servants or land labourers. Others are doctors, or teachers, or gladiators or prostitutes. They have no rights to payment, justice or kindness.

What will Paul say to such people? Will he tell them to revolt? Will he command their masters to release them? After all, Jesus 'sets the prisoner free'!

In fact, Paul tells slaves to respect and obey their earthly masters. And he tells masters to treat their slaves in a way that will please God.

Slaves should do their work wholeheartedly and well, for the sake of their heavenly master, who is Christ. Masters should respect their slaves and not bully them. Both Christian slaves and Christian slave owners have the same master in heaven. In God's sight they are equal. God has no favourites. God sees everything, judges everyone and rewards the good.

How to fight on God's side

Paul ends his letter with a call to battle (6:10–20). Christians have a new relationship with one another because they belong to Christ. They also have a new attitude to the devil. He is a devious, wicked and ruthless enemy.

There is a spiritual war going on. This war is being fought between God and Satan in every part of the cosmos, in heaven and on earth.

Jesus wrestled with the devil when he was tempted to doubt his identity and misuse his power. He waged war against the devil when he cast out evil spirits. He told power-hungry and hypocritical religious leaders that they were the devil's children.

Paul also sees the forces of darkness at work in the world. He detects Satan's influence where human rulers are cruel tyrants and human institutions are corrupt and self-serving. And then there are the unseen powers of the occult. The Ephesians themselves had known the bondage and fear of astrology, magic and spiritism. When they turned to Christ they burned their books of spells (Acts 19:19). All this mirrors and reflects a titanic power struggle going on in heaven.

What are puny Christians to do in the face of such a powerful foe? They are to put on God's armour and take their stand in God's strength! The power available to Christians is exactly the same power as God used to raise Jesus from death. It is the power to defy and defeat Satan.

Paul describes the different pieces of Christian armour as though he is equipping a Roman soldier. He may be chained by the wrist to a soldier as he writes or dictates this letter.

The belt of truth holds the Christian together, giving an integrity of belief and behaviour.

The breastplate of righteousness is the protection of Christ's holiness and victory over sin. Dressed in Christ, we can face the enemy.

The Roman soldier has shoes which can grip or graft. They are good for marching or for standing firm. So the Christian must put on the shoes of the gospel – ready to go anywhere with the good news, and able to hold the ground when under attack.

The shield of faith is not the small shield of the gladiator, but the full-length shield issued by the Roman army. These shields protect the soldier's whole body, and link with each other to drive wedges for advance, or form walls for defence. They are covered with hide, to beat out fires or extinguish flaming arrows tipped with blazing tar. In these arrows Paul sees the darts of doubt and temptation which rain down on the Christian, and can only be fended off by faith in God's truth and greater power.

The helmet is an extremely strong protection for the head and neck. For the Roman soldier it is made of iron or bronze. For the Christian soldier it is forged from salvation – the assurance that Christ has rescued us from sin and shares with us his victory.

The Christian's spiritual sword is the Bible – the living and active word of God. It is the only attacking weapon Paul mentions. Properly used, scripture comes right to the point on every issue. God's sword separates truth from falsehood with power and precision, defending us against the devil, and arming us with the gospel.

In this spiritual war, Paul emphasizes the importance of total prayer. Pray in every way on all occasions, and at all times. Christians are to be fully alert to the state of the battle, in constant communication with their commanding Lord and actively supporting their fellow soldiers.

Final greetings

Finally, Paul humbly asks to be included in the prayers of his readers (6:21–24). He doesn't ask them to pray for the opening of his prison door, but for the opening of his mouth. We know, from the closing verses of the book of Acts, that Paul is able to receive visitors while he is under house arrest (Acts 28:30–31). He asks that he may be brave in sharing the gospel and clear in explaining it. Without God's help, Paul knows he will be cowardly and muddled.

Paul posts his letter with Tychicus, whom he trusts to tell the rest of his news. Instead of signing off with best wishes, Paul sends the peace of God and the grace of the Lord Jesus Christ.

PHILIPPIANS

Paul is in prison – but his heart is free and full of joy. He writes to the Christians in Philippi. This is a church he founded himself, and which has always given him loving and generous support.

Paul thanks the Philippians for a gift they have sent him. He assures them that all will be well – although both he and they are going through times of trouble. He begs them to be humble in their attitude to one another, following the example of Jesus. He also urges them to be united in their faith, and to see Christ as the supreme goal of their life and mission.

Outline

Paul greets the Philippians (1:1–11)
He sees a benefit in his imprisonment (1:12–26)
The attitude of Jesus (1:27 – 2:18)
Plans for Timothy and Epaphroditus (2:19–30)
Warnings and priorities (3:1 – 4:9)
Greetings and thanks (4:10–23)

INTRODUCTION

The church in Philippi

Paul founded the church in Philippi when he travelled there with Silas and Timothy in about AD 50. This was in the course of Paul's second missionary journey.

Paul had intended to take the gospel to Asia (modern Turkey), but a series of events hindered him. Luke, who recorded the venture in Acts, saw this as the guidance of the Spirit of Jesus (Acts 16:6–15). They arrived instead at the coastal port of Troas, where Paul had a vision. A man from Macedonia in Greece was begging him to go and help them.

Paul responded to the vision. They crossed the Aegean Sea and brought the gospel to the continent of Europe for the first time.

When they arrived in Philippi, Paul and his friends found a group of women praying by the river. One of them was Lydia, a businesswoman who traded in purple cloth. She became a Christian and welcomed the missionaries to her home.

While they were staying in Philippi, Paul and Silas released a slave girl from an evil spirit. This ended her ability to tell fortunes, and enraged her owners! Paul and Silas were flogged (a punishment that was illegal for a Roman citizen) and thrown in prison, with their feet fastened in stocks. Despite their suffering, they sang hymns until midnight.

When an earthquake threw open all the prison doors, Paul and Silas refused to escape. Instead, they preached the gospel to the jailer and baptized him and his family.

So the church in Philippi was founded – from an extraordinary variety of people (see p. 552).

Where is Paul as he writes?

Paul is writing from prison. He is probably under house arrest in Rome, in about AD 62. This is where Luke ends Paul's story in the Acts of the Apostles (Acts 28:30–31). Paul probably wrote his letters to the Colossians and Philemon around the same time.

Paul is a Roman citizen, and has appealed for his case to be heard by the emperor. Some scholars think that he was released after this and travelled to Spain, before being arrested again and martyred in Rome.

Paul's theme is joy

Paul's theme is one of joy – the happiness and security which come from knowing Jesus Christ. No amount of punishment or imprisonment can rob him of his inner freedom and assurance of eternal life.

Paul is concerned that pride and quarrels are spoiling the Christian fellowship at Philippi. He reminds them of the supreme example of Jesus, who laid aside every shred of status to become the servant and slave of all. Christians must

Stone cross from Philippi.

Philippi – a 'little Rome'

The site of Philippi was just a Greek village until Philip II of Macedon captured it from the Thracians in 360 BC. Philip named the place after himself. In fact he was best known not for the founding of Philippi, but for the son who was born to him four years later, who became Alexander the Great.

The Romans captured Philippi in 168 BC and made it part of their province of Macedonia. The Roman generals Antony and Octavian marched there in 42 BC to avenge the murder of Julius Caesar. They defeated the rebels Brutus and Cassius, and settled many retired soldiers in the city.

Octavian became Emperor Augustus. He made Philippi a Roman colony and it became a 'little Rome'. Its citizens spoke Latin, were governed by Roman law and enjoyed the same rights – as though they were living in Rome itself. They were free from scourging or being arrested, and could appeal to Caesar for justice.

It was Augustus who gave the order for the census which took Joseph and Mary to Bethlehem for the birth of Jesus.

do the same, if they are to be united with one another in faith and service.

Paul also warns the Philippians against teachers who may try to impose the Jewish law on them. He tells them that he himself was an excellent Jew – but that he only found true righteousness in Christ.

One of the treasures of this letter is an early Christian hymn (2:6–11). The hymn is in praise of Jesus, who gave up his glory to lay down his life for us. Now he is exalted to the highest place in heaven and earth.

Overseers and deacons

As Paul writes, we get a glimpse of the way the church is organized.

'Overseers' are sometimes called 'bishops'. They are the elders of the church. They are responsible for its leadership, and especially the preaching of the gospel and the teaching of the scriptures. It is interesting that they are a group and not just one person acting alone.

'Deacons' are servants or ministers of the church. We read in the book of Acts how seven such people were appointed to care for widows (Acts 6:1–7). Serving the church can take any number of forms, from preaching and teaching to pastoring and administration. Being a deacon means meeting a need in the body of Christ.

DISCOVERING PHILIPPIANS

Paul greets the Philippians

(1:1–11)

As Paul begins his letter, we learn that Timothy is with him. Timothy had been with Paul when they first visited Philippi, some ten years ago. Since then he has become a leading member of the church in Ephesus. Both Paul and Timothy see themselves as servants or slaves of Jesus Christ.

Paul writes to all the Christians at Philippi, both members and leaders. He calls them 'saints' – meaning people who are set apart to lead holy lives for God. They do this by living 'in Christ' – their whole lives caught up in his holiness.

Paul greets his readers with 'grace and peace'. 'Grace' is the Greek word for God's overwhelming goodness towards us. 'Peace' is the Hebrew word for the harmony God gives to our lives and relationships.

THANKSGIVING AND PRAYER *(1:3–11)*

Paul writes to the Philippians with great affection. His prayer reaches across to them in love and fellowship, and strains ahead to the day when God's salvation will be complete. As God does everything perfectly, Paul knows that he will complete the work he has begun in them.

Paul is a team player. The Philippians are his partners in proclaiming the gospel. He longs that they should know God more and more deeply, to understand his ways, grow in holiness and share his love.

He sees a benefit in his imprisonment

(1:12–26)

Paul has been through a terrible time. He was arrested in Jerusalem on a false charge: that he had taken a Gentile into the Jewish part of the temple. He was only saved from being killed by the intervention of the Roman authorities.

Paul was taken into custody, partly for his own safety, and held at Caesarea for two years. During this time various governors tried to get some advantage from him – using him to defy the Jewish leaders and hoping for a bribe to release him. Finally Paul claimed his right as a

Roman citizen to have his case heard by Caesar in Rome.

Paul's appeal was granted, but the journey to Rome proved a disaster. The late sailing meant that their ship was overtaken by storms and wrecked on the island of Malta. When he eventually arrived in Rome, Paul was placed under house arrest (Acts 27 and 28).

The apostle has every reason to be frustrated and angry. Precious years of his life have been lost through the lies, cowardice and incompetence of other people. His great vision of taking the gospel to other lands and cultures has been thwarted – certainly delayed and perhaps abandoned altogether. And yet Paul is able to assure his friends that what has happened to him has actually helped to *spread* the gospel!

Paul tells the Philippians how the palace guard have learned why he is in prison. His detention has brought him into contact with some of the finest and most trusted Roman soldiers in the world. As a prisoner, he may even be chained to one of them – with plenty of time to make the gospel known. Christian soldiers will take the gospel with them wherever they go, as business people (such as Lydia) already do.

At the same time, Paul's example has encouraged other Christians in Rome to witness more boldly. Some of these are preachers who see themselves as rivals to Paul. They are probably Jewish Christians who want to insist that Gentile Christians should keep the Jewish law. But Paul rises above these disputes. What matters is that Jesus Christ is being proclaimed, whatever the motive.

A WIN-WIN SITUATION

Paul hopes to survive his present suffering. Even if he doesn't, he knows that death is the gate of glory. This is his winning perspective (1:18–26). If he remains in this life, he can continue to serve the Lord and encourage his fellow Christians. If he dies, then he will go to be with the Lord, which he longs to do. With Christ, even the worst will turn out for the best.

The attitude of Jesus

(1:27 – 2:18)

Paul asks the Philippians to accept the same way of suffering that Christ took, and which he himself has followed. They must put aside their selfishness and pride, and instead lay down their lives for one another.

It is vital that Christians are united. This is all-important for their confidence, fellowship and witness. Together, they can withstand any enemy, confronting their opponents with assurance and hope.

It is a secret of the Roman's army's success that they fight as a single unit. They link their shields to make a wall in defence, or quickly reform into lines or wedges for attack. Will Christians be any less committed to one another than pagan soldiers?

Paul says that the Philippians already have great benefits from belonging to Christ. They are comforted and encouraged by their togetherness in his love. The Holy Spirit enables them to be tender towards one another and share the same deep feeling. But there is something more.

Paul says the Philippians need to have the same *mind*. They need to desire and determine to love one another. For this they must put aside their own ambitions and become humble, like servants. This is a surprising and shocking idea for people who think of slaves as the downtrodden failures of the human race. Nobody wants to be like that. But Jesus was.

A HYMN ABOUT JESUS

Christian humility begins with the example of Jesus. To remind them of what Jesus did, Paul quotes a Christian hymn (2:6–11). It may be a hymn he has written himself.

Jesus is God – equal with God the Father in status and glory. But when he became a human being, Jesus put all his status and glory aside. He didn't cling to it or grasp at it, as Adam and Eve did when they tried to become equal with God (Genesis 3:5).

Jesus did not use his godly nature and power to promote himself in any way. Instead, he 'emptied' himself. He put aside his heavenly glory to become a human being. Then he shed every layer of human status and descended through every level of human dignity:

He became not just a human being but a servant;
not just a servant but a slave;
not just a slave but a dead slave,
degraded and disgraced
by execution on a cross (2:7–8).

But now the scene has changed. God has raised his Son to life. He has given him the highest place in heaven:

Jesus reigns supreme.
His name is the highest authority
in every part of creation;

and every creature must own
that he is 'Lord';
the Lord who continues
to give glory to God (2:9–11).

Here is the truth about God – that his nature is to give and his glory is to serve. This is also to become the nature and glory of his Christlike people, the church.

SHINING AS STARS

The Philippians are saved by faith in Jesus, but they must still work hard to understand and live out his truth (2:12–18). They must not depend on whether Paul is watching, but respond directly to God's will for them.

Complaining and arguing has been a problem in the church at Philippi. This has spoiled their fellowship and dulled their witness. Now Paul calls them to obedience and harmony. They are to shine brightly with God's truth in a dark world, like stars in the night sky.

Paul wants to be proud of the Philippians when he presents them to Christ on Judgment Day. He doesn't want to find that his efforts have produced nothing.

If Paul is to die for his faith, then he will be a mere drink poured over the Philippians' sacrifice. It is their commitment which is all-important – and Paul is pleased to add his small contribution. He is being very modest here, for in fact he has exhausted himself in his efforts to establish their faith.

Paul writes to the church at Philippi reminding them of Christ's willing obedience to his father. Putting aside his status of equality with God, he became human, and suffered even to the extent of dying on a cross. As a result, God elevated him to a position of glory unsurpassed anywhere in the universe, with all creation subject to his lordship. This reliquary depicts the crucifixion and Christ in glory.

Plans for Timothy and Epaphroditus

(2:19–30)

Paul now shares some personal news. Some people think that this may be an extract from another letter, because the tone changes suddenly. Probably Paul is simply changing the subject.

Paul hopes to send Timothy to Philippi soon. He is delaying in the hope that there will be news of his release, so he himself can visit them too.

Timothy is like a son to Paul, and a fellow slave in the service of Jesus Christ. They have worked together for some ten years, and Paul finds him by far the most selfless and reliable of his friends.

Meanwhile, he is sending Epaphroditus back to Philippi. Epaphroditus is their own messenger who has risked his life to bring help to Paul. He has been seriously ill, but is now mercifully recovered. Paul asks the Philippians to give him a hero's welcome home.

Warnings and priorities

(3:1 – 4:9)

Paul seems about to end his letter when he adds an urgent warning. The Philippians are to beware of the Jewish teachers who are insisting that Gentiles be circumcised.

Circumcision has been a sign for the Jews that their sons are members of the Jewish race and faith. Their baby boys are circumcised at eight days old. Now circumcision is being imposed on Gentile men, to show that their 'flesh' (greed, pride and lust) is being cut away and they have become like Jesus.

Paul hates the teaching of the circumcisers. He argues strongly against it, both here and in his letter to the Galatians. In this letter he calls them 'dogs' – the insult the Jews use for Gentiles (Mark 7:27–28). In the letter to the Galatians he wishes they would go and mutilate themselves (Galatians 5:12)!

Circumcision is the cutting away of the male foreskin. It is a sign of commitment and separation. God told Abraham to be circumcised at the age of ninety-nine, and to circumcise the males in his family and household (Genesis 17:9–14). This is the sign of the covenant – the special relationship with God. It is the distinctive mark of the Jews, to show that they are God's own people.

Now Paul claims that the truly 'circumcised' people are those who belong to Jesus Christ. Our true commitment to God is not shown by the outward ceremony of circumcision, but by an inner devotion to God through Jesus Christ. When Jesus died on the cross, he made a total commitment for us all.

Paul sees physical circumcision as unnecessary; a thing of the past. What matters is the new covenant which God has made with us through the sacrifice of Jesus. In this new covenant, we don't put our trust in our own actions or efforts, but in what Christ has done for us.

Paul is making a remarkable break from Jewish custom. To explain what he means, he offers the example of his own life.

Paul has a fine Jewish pedigree. He was born into a Jewish family, circumcised as a baby at eight days old and brought up as a Pharisee. A Pharisee is someone who tries to be holy by keeping the Jewish law in every detail.

As an adult, Paul proved his Jewish purity and zeal by persecuting Christians. The book of Acts tells how he set out to destroy the church by arresting its members and throwing them in prison (Acts 8:3). Luke describes him 'breathing out murderous threats against the Lord's disciples' as he obtained permission to arrest Christians in Damascus (Acts 9:1–2).

In every way – by birth, upbringing and conviction – Paul was the perfect Jew. If Judaism worked, then Paul was right with God. But Paul found that the Jewish law could never save him, because it could never make him righteous. He could never manage to keep it.

Now all the religious credit Paul has amassed through race, ritual and rigour he considers a load of rubbish. Instead, he relies on the perfect righteousness of Christ. In place of exclusive nationality, elitist education and energetic fanaticism, he has faith that Jesus has died for his sins. Paul is righteous only because he shares the righteousness of Jesus. His relationship with Jesus is the supreme joy and privilege of his life.

Although Paul has been granted salvation through Jesus, he isn't yet perfect. The fulfilment of his faith is still in the future. He presses on, like an athlete or charioteer, to win his race and receive the prize of eternal life and glory in heaven.

Some people in Philippi claim to be perfect already. There is no further effort they need to make, because Christ has done everything for them. But Paul begs them to think again. He offers his own way of life as an example for Christians to follow. Those who think they are perfect may be seriously wrong – using their faith as an excuse for greedy and shameful behaviour.

Paul encourages Christians on earth to live as citizens

of heaven – just as the people of Philippi have the same rights as the citizens of Rome. If Christians live in the hope of heaven, then when Jesus returns he will transform their bodies for life in glory.

In the meantime, Paul makes special mention of a local squabble. He pleads with two women in the Philippian church to end their quarrel. Their names are Euodia and Syntyche. Although both have worked with Paul for the sake of the gospel, they have fallen out badly with each other. Paul has already taught that unity is vital to the health of the church, so now he asks these two to 'agree with each other in the Lord'. He also asks one of his trusted colleagues to help them.

Paul urges the Philippians to rejoice in the Lord. This joy doesn't depend on good circumstances or happy feelings. It is the deep satisfaction that comes from belonging to Christ and being united in his love and purpose.

The Philippians are to be gentle, confident and prayerful, as is fitting for people who live together as the Lord's friends and await his coming. If they are anxious about anything, they must turn it to prayer, with thanksgiving. Then God will protect their hearts and minds with his peace – the amazing peace which comes when the love of Christ conquers and embraces all.

Finally, Paul encourages the Philippians to fill their minds with good and beautiful ideals. This will purify their imagination and inspire their actions. Paul tells them to live out the gospel in practical ways. He offers his own life as a model of Christian living. This is not pride as much as good discipling. Paul is a teacher who is willing for his own life to be scrutinized by his pupils, to see how he practises what he preaches.

Greetings and thanks

(4:10–23)

Paul's own joy now breaks out, although he is languishing in prison, longing to see them and uncertain about the future.

He thanks the Philippians for the gift they have sent him. He has learned to be content in all circumstances; but he is overjoyed that they have remembered him and cared for him in this way.

The Philippians have always been generous to Paul, even when other churches gave him nothing. Now he sees their gift as a sacrifice which delights God. He assures them that God will honour their generosity and meet all their needs as well.

And so Paul closes his letter with greetings to everyone at Philippi from all who are with him, especially the Christians who work in Caesar's household. He prays that the grace of Jesus may be with them all.

COLOSSIANS

Paul is in prison – probably in Rome. From there he writes to the Christian church at Colosse in Asia Minor. He has never visited them, but he feels responsible for them. The church at Colosse was founded by one of Paul's converts from Ephesus.

Paul has heard good reports of the Colossian Christians, and he praises God for them. He also warns them against some misleading teaching. There are people who say that the way to heaven can be discovered through mystical worship, strict legalism and self-denial. Paul says that these are *not* what the gospel is about!

The open gospel of Jesus Christ is far greater than any mystery. Christ came to set us free from rituals and superstitions. The whole of life, from the creation of the universe to our everyday relationships, finds its meaning and peace in him.

Outline

Paul greets his readers (1:1–2)

Paul praises God and prays for the Colossians (1:3–14)

Christ unites everything (1:15–23)

Paul's gospel work (1:24 – 2:5)

Choose freedom! (2:6–23)

Raised with Christ (3:1–4)

Putting off and putting on (3:5–17)

Christians at home (3:18 – 4:1)

Final instructions (4:2–18)

INTRODUCTION

The church in Colosse

Colosse is a small town in Asia Minor, about 100 miles east of Ephesus. It lies in the Lycus Valley, not far from the larger and wealthier towns of Laodicea and Hierapolis.

The churches in Asia Minor have been planted by Christian missionaries from Ephesus. Ephesus is the capital city of the region and a focal point for trade. Paul lived there for two years, lecturing every day in the hall of Tyrannus (Acts 19:9–10). People who were visiting Ephesus on business heard the gospel, and took it home with them. One such person may have been Epaphras, who brought the gospel home to Colosse.

The church in Colosse is threatened by exciting but dangerous teaching. We don't know the name or details of this philosophy, but it is sometimes called the 'Colossian heresy'. The only clues we have are in Paul's arguments against it.

It seems that some people are trying to gain power in heaven by worshipping angels. They are also trying to control their own lives and the lives of others by keeping the old Jewish food laws and festivals.

Paul gives his readers a vision of the true greatness of Jesus. Jesus is the Lord of the universe – he is the cosmic Christ. He is the One through whom everything was made – and in whom everything will find its fulfilment.

Paul explains what it means to live a new life in Jesus. He describes how to 'put on' the purity of Christ. He shows how the peace of Christ can apply to all human relationships – in the church, at home and at work.

It is Tychicus and Onesimus who deliver the letter from Paul to the Colossians. Onesimus is a runaway slave who has become a Christian, and whom Paul is sending back to his master, Philemon. It seems that Onesimus comes from Colosse and that the letters to the Colossians and Philemon are written at the same time (4:7–9).

The Lycus Valley in modern Turkey, near the site of Colosse. Another of the towns in this valley was Laodicea, which is mentioned in the book of Revelation.

Did Paul write Colossians?

Some scholars have asked if Paul's letter to the Colossians is really by him, or whether it has been cleverly written to *sound* like him. They argue that the idea of Christ as the cosmic Lord would have come later in the church's history. The 'Gnostic' heresy of mystical secrets (which Paul seems to be challenging) wasn't developed until the 2nd century AD. There is nothing like it in Paul's other letters.

All the same, there are many signs that this letter *is* Paul's own work. His favourite phrases – 'in Christ' and 'in the Lord' – are used to describe the Christian life. We know that the truth of Jesus as the cosmic Lord came to him at his conversion on the road to Damascus.

The new teachers at Colosse may have had an early form of Gnosticism in their beliefs. They are certainly trying to discover the powers and secrets of heaven. But there is a strong strand of Jewish law in their teaching as well. Paul tells them that Christ is supreme over all things in heaven and earth – and his power releases from the bondage of the law.

When did Paul write this letter?

Paul is writing to the Colossians from prison. He asks them to pray that God will 'open a door' for his message. He mentions his 'fellow prisoner' Aristarchus, and adds simply, 'Remember my chains.'

Paul is in prison, but he is able to write letters and receive visitors. This sounds like the time he is under house arrest in Rome, which we read about at the end of the book of Acts (Acts 28:30–31). If the letter to the Colossians is written fairly early in this imprisonment, the year could be AD 60–61.

DISCOVERING COLOSSIANS

Paul greets his readers

(1:1–2)

Paul describes himself as an apostle – one who is commissioned by God to be a pioneer leader of the church. It is because God has called him to be an apostle that Paul works hard, writes with authority and suffers imprisonment. With him is Timothy, his younger colleague and a leader of the church in Ephesus. Paul greets the Colossian Christians as 'holy and faithful'.

Paul praises God and prays for the Colossians

(1:3–14)

Paul has heard good reports about the Christians in Colosse, although he has never visited them. They are living in hope of heaven – a future glory which shines faith and love into their present situation. They are part of a worldwide movement – a movement which first reached them when Epaphras arrived from Ephesus with the gospel.

Paul prays for all the churches, and his prayers are not vague or timid. He prays boldly that they will grow in their faith and lead lives that are pleasing to Christ. With so much talk of 'knowledge', Paul prays that they may have the only knowledge that matters – the knowledge of God's will. For Paul, 'knowing' means both understanding and doing the truth.

Christ unites everything

(1:15–23)

Jesus shows us what God is like. God is invisible, but Jesus is the human image of his Father.

When God made humankind, he made us in his own image, but this likeness was spoiled by sin (Genesis 1:26–27). Now, in Christ, the perfect image of God is clearly seen.

Jesus Christ is the 'first-born over all creation' – the one for whom creation was made and to whom it belongs. As Son of God, Christ existed before the universe. He was the One through whom everything was made. John teaches the same at the beginning of his Gospel (John 1:3). When

Jesus was born as a baby in Bethlehem, the Son of God entered his own creation.

If the Colossians are afraid of the powers of heaven, then here is the answer. There is no power in heaven or on earth that is greater than Jesus Christ. The angels and other spiritual forces were *made* by him and are under his control.

If the Colossians are worried about a split between earth and heaven, then here is the answer. Christ made *both* the visible *and* the invisible parts of creation. He unites them and holds them together. The universe is not 'split'. It belongs to Christ. It is his universe. The infinite variety of creation springs from one creator. The balance and harmony of creation are sustained by one Lord.

What Jesus does for creation he also does for the church. If we think of the church as a body, then Christ is the head. He leads and coordinates his church with wisdom and truth. He founded the church, and by his resurrection pioneered the way to eternal life. He bridges all divides – between earth and heaven, God and humanity, time and eternity, and life and death.

Jesus is the greatest – the creator, coordinator and conciliator of all things.

Paul says that all God's 'fullness' dwells in Jesus. Every aspect of God that can be poured into a human being is found in him.

Jesus is the creator of everything. He is also the Saviour of all. He has conquered every enemy and dismantled every barrier between God and humanity. He has made peace by giving himself as the perfect sacrifice.

The Jews offer sacrifices to pay for their sins. The blood of an animal is poured out on the altar, to show that a life has been paid for a person's sin. Sometimes the meat of the animal is shared as a meal. Through sacrifice, God and his people are united in fellowship, and those who were enemies become friends.

Now Jesus has become the perfect sacrifice for all people and for all time. He has taken the blame and pain of sin upon himself. He has really suffered and really died by submitting himself to torture and death on the cross. By his sacrifice he has won forgiveness, innocence and peace for all. This is the good news of the gospel.

Paul's gospel work

(1:24 – 2:5)

It is costly for Paul to preach the gospel. He suffers insults, beatings and imprisonment. But he has been called to serve the church in this way. He sees his sufferings in the light of the suffering of Christ, for somehow Christ continues to suffer with his suffering servants. Paul, in his own way, suffers for the sake of the Christians at Colosse, even though he has never met them.

Paul explains that his task is to declare the gospel and explain it fully. In the past it was impossible to know the whole purpose of God; but now the truth has been revealed. Forgiveness of sins, peace with God and eternal life are free for all – including Gentiles.

The Colossians are a fine example of God's new work, for God is clearly present among them. They are already enjoying their new life with Christ – and looking forward to the glory that awaits them in heaven.

Meanwhile, Paul makes every effort to encourage and teach the new Christians at Colosse and at nearby Laodicea. His imprisonment, the distance between them and the confusion caused by rival teachers make it a constant struggle. He works by praying for them, writing to them, defending the true gospel and supporting their leaders.

Paul wants to raise Christians in their faith, so that he can present them to God as mature and Christlike disciples. This isn't about introducing them to a succession of secrets and mysteries, as the new teachers might promise to do. There is only one mystery – that Christ is the way to life with God. Whatever they are looking for in wisdom and knowledge, they will find in him.

Although he has never visited them, Paul assures the Colossians that he is with them in spirit. He encourages them with his opinion that they are well set in their faith and well organized for spiritual battle.

Choose freedom!
(2:6–23)

Paul tells the Colossians that to receive Christ as their Lord is just a beginning. They need to become well established in their faith, to develop and gain strength.

He talks to them about the threat of the new teachers. They may sound very clever, but their teaching is empty of truth or power. They are attempting to bind them with the old Jewish traditions and the pride and fear of rituals and routines.

Paul contrasts the new teaching with the reality of Christ. If the Colossians want to enter the fullness of God, then Christ gives them complete and immediate access. He is the whole of God in human form, so that God can be understood and known through him.

WHAT ABOUT CIRCUMCISION?

Paul tells the Colossians that they have already been truly circumcised, not in flesh but in spirit (2:11–15). The Jewish circumcision is a cutting away of the male foreskin, which is a physical separation. The circumcision of Christ is a cutting away of our sinful nature, which is a spiritual separation.

Baptism is the act of spiritual circumcision, in which our selfish nature is cut away. Jesus was circumcised of his whole 'self' when he died on the cross, though the sins he bore were ours and not his. We go down into the waters of baptism to be buried with Christ – to identify

---

The problem – how to get to the 'fullness' of God?

It seems that 'fullness' is a favourite idea of the new teachers. It becomes a major theme with the Gnostics ('those who know') in the 2nd century AD.

The Gnostics teach that God and humans are infinitely far apart. God is an essence of spirit, holy and remote. Humans are made of matter, which is evil and earthbound. The only way for humans to reach God (or enter his fullness) is by mastering the secrets and

passwords of all the realms which separate them from him.

The new teachers at Colosse may have had the seeds of Gnosticism in their ideas. Their way out of earthiness and evil is by circumcision (cutting away part of the body) and by self-control through starvation and beating. They also teach that there is spiritual credit in keeping religious festivals, such as the sabbath (the Jewish rest day) and New Moon.

Paul has no time for this nonsense! He tells the Colossians that all the fullness of God is to be found and

enjoyed in Christ. The created world and the human body are not evil. Jesus took on our human form and was filled with the fullness of God – a fullness which is now for us as well. In Christ we have 'fullness direct'.

our 'selves' with his death. We rise again to the fresh air, to show that God is raising us with Christ to new life.

What has happened to our sins? We owed a debt to God which we could never repay except with our lives. Paul says that God has taken the law which condemned us, and nailed it to the cross. In doing this he has cancelled the law which sentenced us to death. He has also disarmed the critics – the spiritual powers that demand our punishment – and conquered them as well.

THEREFORE...

If the law has been cancelled and the powers of heaven overcome – then Christians are free (2:16–23)! No one can tell the Colossians what to do to get right with God. The rules about foods and festivals were guidelines in the past, to point the way to a God-centred life. But now God himself is among his people, through Jesus Christ. The rules were the pointers, but Jesus is the point.

The new teachers have arrived in Colosse with winsome humility and impressive visions. Paul says bluntly, 'Don't let them rob you!' The false teaching floats into realms of fantasy – completely adrift from the strongly knit truth of Christ.

The Colossians must see through the rules and regulations which are being offered them. Such rules are a magnet to people who want to try to earn their salvation. So many things to avoid! So much effort to be made! A humility to impress your friends! Paul says that these rules are merely of human origin. They actually encourage pride, and are powerless to deal with lust and greed. They will deliver hunger and hallucination – but not salvation.

Raised with Christ
(3:1–4)

If Christians have 'died' to legalism and superstition, what do they 'rise' to? Paul says their hearts and minds must have a new centre and focus. He encourages the Colossians to desire heaven and the kingly rule of Christ. From now on, heaven must become more real than earth. Their real life is now with Christ in heaven.

Putting off and putting on
(3:5–17)

Paul describes the Christian life. He lists first those attitudes and actions which are to be killed off. Then he lists those attitudes and actions which are to be 'put on' like new clothes.

Paul gives his teaching the same shape as baptism. Our old life with its evil habits is to be discarded – like a pile of clothes left on the bank of a river. We go down into the waters of baptism, to enter into the death of Christ. We emerge from the water – perhaps on the other side of the river – to put on our baptismal robe. So Paul describes putting our old ways to death, and dressing ourselves in the grace and forgiveness of Christ.

Paul states that Christ's death on the cross disarmed the powers of evil and made a public exhibition of their defeat. He has in mind the victory parade, when conquering generals would lead their captive opponents in a procession through the streets of Rome for all to see. This carving, on the Arch of Titus, portrays victorious Roman troops parading with treasures from the temple after the defeat of the Jewish revolt in AD 70.

Paul tells the Colossians to 'put to death' their earthly nature. They must face up to their old habits and take decisive action to eliminate them. Paul mentions particularly sexual immorality and greed.

Like Jesus, Paul teaches that immorality takes place in our hearts and heads before we ever do anything wrong (Matthew 5:28). Like Jesus, Paul shows that greed – the desire for money or possessions – is a rival to God himself (Matthew 6:24). This is the kind of behaviour

which arouses God's holy anger because he alone can save us.

Paul gives some more examples. Sexual immorality and greed are sins against ourselves, but now he lists sins against other people. Paul mentions anger and rage, together with the many ways we hurt one another with our words. We also like to dismiss one another on the

grounds of race or religion, culture or class – treating people who don't belong to our group as inferior.

Paul announces a Christian revolution which abolishes all this pride and prejudice. Christ the creator has made everyone equal. Christ the Saviour has died for all. He has no favourites. When people come to Christ it ceases to matter whether they are Greek or Jew, circumcised or uncircumcised, barbarian, Scythian, slave or free.

Greeks and Jews have many reasons to dislike and mistrust each other. Their cultures, which are both ancient and highly civilized, run on opposite values. The Jews are circumcised, while the Greeks are uncircumcised – a physical difference which sums up the religious gulf between them.

'Barbarians' are uneducated foreigners, as far as the Greeks are concerned. They get their name from the Greeks mocking the 'brr brr' sounds of their primitive language. Meanwhile, 'Scythian' is a term the Romans use to insult foreigners.

Another great contrast is between those who are slaves and those who are free. Many millions of people in the ancient world are slaves, without dignity or choice in their lives. They are at the mercy of their owners, who can buy and sell them, split up their families and even have them executed.

It is hard to imagine a greater injustice or source of grievance than slavery. But Paul says that now there is no difference between slaves and their owners. Jesus is Lord and master of both.

As Paul talks of 'putting to death' these deep-seated attitudes, a new character starts to emerge. The Christian is a new self with a new mind – a new person who is becoming like Christ. This is how God intends humans to be.

THE CHRISTIAN'S NEW CLOTHES

Now Paul describes the Christian's new clothes (3:12–14). They are garments of grace and forgiveness, suitable for those who are becoming like Jesus.

Kindness, gentleness and patience are part of the fruit of the Spirit that Paul describes in his letter to the Galatians (Galatians 5:22). They help Christians live in harmony with one another. Compassion and humility may sound like weaknesses. But Jesus showed in his own life that compassion and humility are at the heart of God.

Paul emphasizes forgiveness, as Jesus used to do. Forgiving one another and being forgiven by God belong closely together – indeed, they are inseparable (Matthew 6:14–15).

Once again, Paul gives the Colossians the responsibility for making changes to their lives. The new clothes are beautiful gifts from God, but putting them on is the work of every individual Christian.

The most important item of all is love, which Paul imagines as either an overgarment or a belt. Love unites all the other qualities, and makes the outfit perfect.

Paul urges the Colossians to let peace be the referee in their relationships. The Christian church is like a body, and a healthy body is comfortable within itself. If any part is angry or in pain, then the whole body suffers. Jesus prayed that his followers would be united (John 17:20–21) and gave them his peace as a parting gift (John 14:27).

Paul wants the Colossians to be nourished by 'the word of Christ'. They know some of the teachings of Jesus, and can encourage each other to understand and apply them. They also have his Holy Spirit in their hearts. Every aspect of life can be checked against the example and prompting of Jesus.

In everything Paul emphasizes thankfulness and praise. God has given the Colossians new life, love and hope. The joy of Jesus fills their hearts and overflows in song – both the old Jewish psalms and the new hymns to Christ.

Christians at home
(3:18 – 4:1)

From teaching about life at church, Paul turns to life at home. He has advice for Christian families and workers. He deals with all the 'one-another' relationships – between wives and husbands, children and parents, slaves and masters. It is typical of his clear and Christian thinking that he addresses the more vulnerable partners first.

Paul encourages Christian wives to submit to their husbands – that is, to honour and respect them. This is the way of life that Jesus teaches for all relationships. Without self-giving and service our families cannot survive.

In Greek society, a wife has a formal and isolated existence. She is in charge of the home, but she herself is one of her husband's possessions. Meanwhile, he has freedom to find friendship and sexual pleasure elsewhere.

The Greek wife has to obey her husband anyway, whether she is a Christian or not. What Paul is saying is that she may now submit to her husband out of her own Christian freedom. Paul could easily have given Christian wives permission to escape from their pagan marriages. Instead, he says they are now free to commit themselves to their husbands with love from the Lord.

To husbands, Paul says, 'Love your wives.' Instead of treating them coldly and distantly, husbands are to treasure, affirm and care for their wives. This is unheard of in pagan society, where manhood is expressed by harshness, intolerance and brutality. The Christian husband is to be like Christ to his wife, laying down his life for her.

Paul encourages children to obey their parents – not out of fear, but to please the Lord. There is an authority structure within families, which is given to us by God. The commandment is addressed to children of all ages, saying, 'Honour your father and your mother' (Exodus 20:12). Jesus himself was a junior member of his family (Luke 2:51) and learned the special obedience of sonship (Hebrews 5:8).

Paul warns fathers not to make their children bitter. The Roman father could be far too strict, using his power to provoke and defeat his children. Paul encourages a lighter and more loving touch. Fathers should reflect the fatherly care of God, using their wisdom to be fair and their strength to be gentle. A confident and courteous child is a tribute to a well-judged upbringing.

Paul instructs the Colossian Christians on the responsibilities of husbands and wives to each other, and their attitudes towards their children. A family group with a monogram of Christ, of Roman make (4th or 5th century) now in the British Museum.

Paul's longest section of advice is for Christian slaves. They have nothing of their own, and are completely under the control of their masters. In the past they have worked hard only when they are being watched – to gain credit and avoid punishment. Now Paul encourages them to have a new motive for their work, because their real master is the Lord Jesus Christ. He sees and knows everything, and will give them a full and fair reward.

Paul teaches Christian masters to give their slaves God's care. God is a provider, taking thought for his people and supplying their needs. This is what the masters must do for their slaves. Paul reminds the masters that they are slaves themselves, to their Lord Jesus Christ.

Final instructions

(4:2–18)

As Paul approaches the end of his letter, he asks the Colossians to pray for him. As he waits in prison, he longs that God may 'open a door' for the Christian message. Does he guess that his prayer is being answered even as he writes? The words which are flowing from the pen will carry the gospel to human hearts until the end of time.

Paul cares greatly about the impression that Christians make on outsiders. He warns the Colossians to be wise – not using their Christian freedom to be rebellious or lazy. God will give them many opportunities to share their faith. They must be both loving and challenging in their conversations with everyone.

Paul commends his messenger Tychicus, who will give the Colossians the rest of his news. With Tychicus is Onesimus, a runaway slave who has become a Christian. Almost certainly his master Philemon is a member of the church in Colosse, and Onesimus is now returning home. We have a letter from Paul to Philemon in the Bible.

Paul's friends are always important to him. He makes special mention of his fellow prisoner Aristarchus, who was once seized by a mob in Ephesus (Acts 19:29). He sends greetings from Mark, explaining that he is the cousin of Barnabas. Paul and Barnabas have disagreed about Mark in the past, and it is good to see that the relationship has been mended.

Paul tells the Colossians that their founding father Epaphras prays long and hard for them, and for the other churches in the Lycus Valley. Luke is also with them. He is Paul's travelling companion and diarist, who wrote the Gospel and the book of Acts. It is only here that we learn that Luke is a doctor. Demas is with Paul at the time of writing, but will later desert him (2 Timothy 4:10).

Finally, Paul takes the pen from his scribe and writes his own farewell. He asks them to remember him in prison, and prays that God's grace will be with them.

1 AND 2 THESSALONIANS

These letters are written by Paul to the young Christians at Thessalonica. Paul visited the Macedonian capital briefly, but had to leave before the church was well established.

Now he writes from Corinth to encourage them. In his first letter, he also answers a particular enquiry they have, which is about the return of Jesus and the fate of Christians who have died.

Paul's second letter to the Christians at Thessalonica seems to follow soon after his first. He continues to praise God for their faith, and to teach them about the second coming of Jesus Christ.

Paul counters an idea that Christ has already returned. He says that a 'lawless one' will first appear, leading a rebellion and proclaiming himself to be God. He also continues to challenge Christians who are idle!

Outline

INTRODUCTION

Thessalonica

Paul travels to Thessalonica after his visit to Philippi.
Luke narrates this part of the second missionary journey
in Acts 17:1–9. It is the early summer of AD 50.

Thessalonica is the capital of the Roman province of
Macedonia. Although Paul likes to live and work in the
major cities, his stay here is very brief. He preaches in the
synagogue for only three weeks, before some jealous Jews
stir up a riot against him (Acts 17:1–9). As a result, Paul
and Silas have to leave in a hurry.

They journey on to Berea, but their enemies follow
them. Paul travels on alone to Athens, where he waits for
Silas and Timothy to join him. He then sends Timothy
back to Thessalonica while he himself goes on to Corinth.

In Corinth, Timothy brings good news of the
Christians at Thessalonica. They are holding firmly to
their new faith in Jesus. But they have some questions to
ask Paul – especially about the second coming of Christ.
They wonder whether some of their friends who have
died will now miss the benefits of resurrection.

Paul writes his first letter to the Thessalonians to tell
them of his joy at hearing from them, and to answer their
questions. It is one of the earliest of Paul's letters that we
have. It gives a glimpse of the difficulties and hopes of
the first Christians, and the new way of life to which they
are called. It also shows us Paul's real affection for his
converts – his gentleness, warmth and enthusiasm.

The most important teaching in the letter is about
Jesus' return and the fate of those Christians who have
already died. Paul says that the Lord will come from
heaven in an unmistakable way, and that those who have
died will be raised to life. Then those who are still living
will be caught up into his glorious presence.

Paul wants to reassure those who are worried about
their Christian brothers and sisters who have died. He also
encourages believers to live as 'children of the day' – that
is, as those who are awake and ready for Christ's coming.

Has Jesus Christ already returned to earth?

Paul writes his second letter to the Thessalonians
to answer one particular question. Has Jesus Christ

already returned to earth?

We don't know all the background to this letter, and some of it is difficult to understand. Paul sounds more formal than when he last wrote. His teaching about the 'lawless one' is more complicated and obscure than his usual style.

Something or someone has unsettled the Christians at Thessalonica. There has been a rumour that the Lord has already returned. This rumour is based on something Paul is supposed to have said or written. But Paul denies it. Jesus has not yet returned. The 'lawless one' must first appear and have his day of rebellion before Christ appears to overthrow him.

Paul again tackles the problem of Christians who are idle. He may mean that they are lazy – not bothering to work because Jesus is coming soon. Sometimes the word 'idle' can also mean rebellious. Perhaps these people are refusing to live by the standards of holiness and self-control which honour Jesus Christ.

Thessalonica

Thessalonica is an important city – the second largest in Greece. It stands on the Egnatian Way – one of the great Roman roads. This road runs from east to west across the north of Greece, linking the Aegean Sea in the east to the Adriatic Sea in the west. From the western port, Dyrrhachium (today called Durres), it is a short sea voyage to Italy and Rome.

Excavations of the Roman market at Thessalonica.

DISCOVERING 1 AND 2 THESSALONIANS

Paul greets his readers
(1 Thessalonians 1:1)

Paul, Silas (in Greek, Silvanus) and Timothy were together in Thessalonica and are now writing from Corinth. Silas has been Paul's companion throughout his second missionary journey. Timothy joined them when they passed through his home town of Lystra in Asia Minor.

Paul thanks God for the Thessalonians' faith
(1 Thessalonians 1:2–10)

Paul is delighted that the new Christians in Thessalonica are surviving and flourishing. This is a powerful work of God, motivated by faith, love and hope in Jesus. Only the Holy Spirit can have enabled and sustained such a dramatic and lasting change in their lives.

Paul and his friends have shown the Thessalonians how to be like Christ. There are no Gospels to read at this time. All the teaching is by word of mouth and personal example. Now the Thessalonians are themselves models of Christian faith and life in the Roman provinces of Macedonia and Achaia – which is almost the whole of modern Greece.

A major aspect of the gospel is that Gentiles must stop worshipping their pagan idols. Instead they must serve the living God who is known through his son Jesus. Jesus died and was raised from death. One day he will return to save his people from the wrath of God's judgment on the sins of the world.

Paul recalls his work in Thessalonica
(1 Thessalonians 2:1–16)

There has been some criticism of Paul in Thessalonica. His enemies have accused him of exploiting the new converts. They say he has taken their money in exchange for his spurious teaching. But Paul reminds them of how it really was. Paul and his companions worked hard to provide for themselves so that they wouldn't be a burden to anyone. The message they preached wasn't to play on people's pride or fear, or to trick them out of their money. It was a faithful, gentle sharing of the truth about God.

What's been going on at Thessalonica?

The Christians at Thessalonica are young in their faith. It may be that they have misunderstood something Paul wrote in his first letter. They are very excited by the hope that Jesus Christ will appear again – bringing their suffering to an end and punishing those who are ill-treating them.

Paul told them in his first letter that the Day of the Lord (the return of Jesus) would come with sudden destruction (1 Thessalonians 5:3). Perhaps an earthquake or some other disaster has seemed to fulfil this prophecy. Now the Thessalonians are wondering why they are still suffering persecution (1:5–7). Some of their number have reacted to the crisis by giving up work and are now making a nuisance of themselves while relying on others to support them (3:11).

So Paul writes his second letter. He tells them not to be so easily unsettled. He hasn't sent them any word that the Lord has already come. Instead he reminds them that persecution is a fact of the Christian life – and that Christ will conquer all evil in the end.

Paul thanks God that the Thessalonians received the gospel in the same spirit in which it was given. The proof of their conversion is that they are now being persecuted. Paul himself had suffered at Philippi. Suffering isn't a sign of failure, but the hallmark of the genuine Christian. Now the Gentile Christians in Thessalonica are being persecuted just as the Jewish Christians in Judea were.

Persecution is preventing Paul from visiting the Thessalonians
(1 Thessalonians 2:17–20)

Paul longs to see the Thessalonians again, but is prevented by his enemies. However, he is often with them in his spirit. He is proud of them. He looks forward to presenting them to Christ on his return, as the fruit of his gospel labours.

Timothy has seen the Thessalonians and returned with good news
(1 Thessalonians 3:1–10)

Paul has been anxious about the Christians at Thessalonica, in case persecution and temptation have snatched away their faith. As he has been unable to visit them himself, he

has sent Timothy on his behalf. Timothy has returned with the wonderful news that they are well, faithful – and longing to see him! Paul wishes all the more that he could go back to teach and encourage them.

Paul prays for the Thessalonians
(1 Thessalonians 3:11–13)

Paul sees this work as a spiritual battle. It is Satan who is preventing him returning to Thessalonica (2:18). He prays that God the Father and Jesus will clear the way. Everything is flowing towards the return or 'presence' of Christ. Paul uses a popular Greek work, 'parousia', for the coming of Jesus. He will return with his 'holy ones' – his vast army of angels (Deuteronomy 33:2; 2 Thessalonians 1:7).

A 'parousia' is an official visit by the emperor or some other important person – with crowds lining the roads and the local authorities coming to greet him. It is important to be ready for such a moment – our lives clean (3:13) and our duties done (2:19).

Self-control and love
(1 Thessalonians 4:1–12)

Paul reminds the Thessalonians of the holy lives they are to lead. They are already saints, but they must still work for pure and loving relationships day by day. They have the example of Jesus to follow and the presence of his Holy Spirit to help them.

Sex is a major area of difference between Christians and pagans. While pagans follow their lusts, Christians are to be self-controlled. While pagans take one another's partners, Christians must honour and respect one another's marriages.

Paul reckons the Thessalonians know about love towards their brothers and sisters – unselfishly putting one another first. But he reminds them to live a settled life.

Perhaps some of the Thessalonians are over-excited about the coming of Jesus and want to give up their jobs. Paul encourages them to carry on their daily work and so win the respect of others. Paul, like most rabbis, does the same with his tentmaking and leather work. He doesn't want to be a burden to others.

The coming of Jesus
(1 Thessalonians 4:13 – 5:11)

Paul wants to talk especially about the Christians at Thessalonica who have died. He feels that the believers are mourning as though the dead have missed the glory of God by dying before Jesus' return.

There is no need to grieve! Those who have died have 'fallen asleep' in Christ. They still belong to him. God will raise them to life when Christ appears – even before he calls those still living to join him. Far from being left out of the glory, the dead will be the first to receive it.

Paul describes the coming of Jesus in the way that the Jews have long expected the Son of man to appear (Daniel 7:13). God himself will give the word of command and the archangel will announce it with a trumpet. The details are beyond our imagining, but there will be no mistaking this mighty cosmic event. Paul's teaching here is the same as Jesus', who warned against false alarms and phoney messiahs (Mark 13:21–27).

Paul says that the coming of Jesus will be like the 'Day of the Lord' which the Old Testament prophets foretold. It will be sudden and unexpected: as surprising as burglary and as inescapable as childbirth.

No one knows when the day of the Lord will come. Rather than trying to calculate times and dates, it is better to be ever-ready. Christians will never be taken by surprise if they live as children of the light – children of the day that is about to dawn. So Paul urges self-control, together with the spiritual protection of faith, love and hope. He lists a fuller version of the Spirit's armour in Ephesians 6:10–18.

Paul tells the Thessalonians that God is on our side. Although he must judge the world and punish sin, his longing is to save and spare us. This he does through our Saviour Jesus Christ, who has died for us so that we may live with him. Far from being frightened and fearful, there is every reason to encourage one another.

Christians with attitude!

(1 Thessalonians 5:12–22)

Nobody knows whether the Lord will return today or in the distant future. So how are we to live?

Paul teaches an orderly and constructive way of life. The Thessalonian Christians should respect their leaders, because they represent the care and discipline of Jesus.

The leaders themselves are to be proactive in correcting and supporting their people. They must be firm with those who are idle and gentle with those who are weak. Time may be short, but true pastors take a patient and long-term approach. They must encourage forgiveness, kindness and peacemaking. This is in contrast to the legalism and feuding of pagan society.

The Christian's approach to life is one of joy, prayerfulness and thanksgiving. Everything is continually offered to God – just as Jesus constantly communed with

his Father and obeyed his will.

It is the Holy Spirit who ignites our Christian life. He is a gentle Spirit, and Paul warns the Thessalonians not to quench his fire. When he writes to Timothy, he will encourage him to 'fan into flame the gift of God' (2 Timothy 1:6).

The prophecies the Spirit inspires are to be treated seriously, for he teaches and guides the church. There are charlatans and deceitful spirits around, and it is best to test everything by the character of Jesus. Does this message acknowledge that Jesus is Lord? And is this the kind of thing that Jesus would say (1 John 4:1–3)? Christians are to think things through, and choose what is good.

A closing prayer

(1 Thessalonians 5:23–28)

Paul prays that the God of peace will complete the work of making the Thessalonians holy. Peace is what happens

when we align our hearts with heaven. Peace is a wholeness of body, mind and spirit, so that we are at one with Christ in the will and purpose of God.

Paul greets his readers

(2 Thessalonians 1:1–2)

The second letter to the Thessalonians is again sent by Paul, Silas and Timothy. It seems likely that they are together in Corinth.

Paul thanks God for the Thessalonians' genuine faith

(2 Thessalonians 1:3–12)

Paul continues to thank God for the way in which the Christians at Thessalonica are growing in faith and love. This is all the more remarkable because they are being persecuted for their belief in Christ.

Paul explains that even their suffering proves God to be true. When the gospel is preached it shows up the

In both his letters to the church at Thessalonica, Paul makes reference to the return of Christ from heaven. It will be a mighty cosmic event, announced by the trumpet call of God. He will appear in a blaze of fire accompanied by myriads of angels, and his coming will be followed by the judgment of all humanity. This is Fra Angelico's *Christ Glorified in the Court of Heaven* (probably 1428–30), now in the National Gallery in London.

hostility of evil to good. Those who reject God and the good news of Jesus inflict cruelty on his church. One day God will put the situation to rights. He will reward his faithful people and punish their persecutors. Meanwhile, Paul prays that Jesus will be glorified (seen for who he really is) even through their suffering.

Paul teaches about the coming of Christ and the 'lawless one'

(2 Thessalonians 2:1–12)

Now Paul comes to his main subject. The Thessalonians have become excited and over-anxious about the Lord's return. There is a rumour that Jesus has already come back – a rumour linked with something Paul is supposed to have written or said.

Paul warns the Thessalonians not to be deceived by such stories. There will be no mistaking the coming of Christ when it happens, so they need have no fear of missing it. In any case, there is to be a great rebellion against God, led by the 'lawless one', before Christ returns.

The word Paul uses for 'rebellion' gives us our word 'apostasy' – the rejection of all faith in God. At the end of time there will be a great rebellion against God, leading to the final battle between Christ and Satan. The leader of this rebellion is the 'antichrist'. Is this who Paul means by the 'lawless one'?

Paul describes the 'lawless one' setting himself up in God's temple and proclaiming himself to be God. Such a thing has happened before – as when a foreign ruler, Antiochus Epiphanes, installed a statue of the Greek god Zeus in the temple in Jerusalem (Daniel 9:27). It seems that the 'lawless one' is the last and most terrible of all the evil tyrants who rise up against God.

Paul says that the forces of rebellion are held back at present (2:6), so that their power is restricted and their damage limited. This is the great achievement and benefit of Roman law and government (Romans 13:3–4). But when these dreadful powers are finally unleashed, they will trick people with empty displays of power and ensnare them in every kind of sin.

Those who refuse the truth and love wickedness will have no defence against the powers of evil. God will endorse their rejection of the truth by increasing their delusion.

Paul prays for the Thessalonians
(2 Thessalonians 2:13–17)

God chose the Thessalonians before the beginning of time, called them through the gospel of Christ and saved them by the work of the Spirit. Every Person of the Holy Trinity of God is engaged in this great salvation, which rescues sinners and brings them to glory.

Paul encourages the Thessalonians to hold onto the facts, remembering the truths he has taught them by word and letter. He prays that Jesus and God the Father will strengthen them in their hope and behaviour.

Paul asks the Thessalonians to pray for him
(2 Thessalonians 3:1–5)

Paul values the prayers of his converts – especially that the preaching of the gospel will go well. He also asks for prayer for his own protection. He has been stoned in Lystra and flogged and imprisoned in Philippi. Now he has powerful enemies in Thessalonica and Corinth, especially among the Jews who oppose him.

But God is working his purpose out. Paul knows that the power of God is stronger than that of the evil one. The Lord will keep the Thessalonians safe in his love and fulfil his will in their lives.

Paul warns against idleness
(2 Thessalonians 3:6–15)

Paul is concerned that some Christians at Thessalonica have given up work. They may be making the excuse that they must concentrate on spreading the gospel, because Christ will soon return.

Paul says bluntly that they are idle! Instead of being busy, they are making a nuisance of themselves in other people's business. No one is more urgent and focused than Paul when it comes to preaching the gospel; yet he and his companions always work – at night if need be – to support themselves.

Paul is a leather worker and tentmaker. He is typical of the Jewish rabbis who earn their own living, so that they can teach the law free of charge. Now Paul's rule is that the Thessalonian Christians should do the same. Anyone who won't work must be left in no doubt of the church's disapproval!

A farewell blessing
(2 Thessalonians 3:16–18)

Paul again finishes his letter with a blessing of peace. This is the peace of God himself – peace in the midst of conflict, peace in the face of persecution, peace in the love of God and the hope of eternal life.

He writes a final greeting in his own hand (perhaps the rest has been written down by Silas), so that his readers can be sure it's genuinely from him.

1 AND 2 TIMOTHY

The apostle Paul is writing to Timothy – a younger man who is like a son to him. Timothy is living in Ephesus, where he has some responsibility for correct teaching and sound pastoral care of the church.

In his first letter Paul warns Timothy about false teachers who are active in the church. Their complicated and obscure ideas are distracting and dangerous.

Paul also gives Timothy some guidelines on major aspects of church life. He outlines the principles of Christian behaviour in public meetings. He lists the main characteristics of a potential church leader. He identifies the key issues in caring for certain needy groups.

The second letter to Timothy is written by the apostle Paul from prison. He knows that he faces death in the near future and that this may be his last letter.

Paul reminds Timothy that being a minister of the gospel involves suffering. He encourages him to accept the suffering and do the hard work of being a Christian evangelist and pastor. Timothy must teach the truth of Christ faithfully, and train those who will pass it on to others.

Outline

Paul greets Timothy (1 Timothy 1:1–2)

False teachers (1 Timothy 1:3–20)

True church (1 Timothy 2:1 – 4:10)

Pastoring people (1 Timothy 4:11 – 6:2)

Motives and money (1 Timothy 6:3–19)

A final charge and blessing (1 Timothy 6:20–21)

Paul greets Timothy (2 Timothy 1:1–2)

Paul thanks God for Timothy – and encourages him (2 Timothy 1:3–7)

Suffering, single-mindedness and hard work (2 Timothy 1:8 – 2:26)

Godlessness in the last days (2 Timothy 3:1–9)

Paul's example and Timothy's calling (2 Timothy 3:10 – 4:5)

Paul faces death – and glory (2 Timothy 4:6–18)

Final greetings (2 Timothy 4:19–22)

INTRODUCTION

Paul first met Timothy when he visited Lystra on his first missionary journey. Timothy was a young man from a mixed background: his mother was a believing Jew and his father a pagan Greek. Timothy became a Christian and, a few years later, joined Paul on his second missionary journey.

It was a difficult beginning. Paul circumcised Timothy so as not to offend the local Jews, who knew of the young man's Gentile background (Acts 16:1–3). Paul no longer believed that circumcision was necessary – but he didn't want any barrier to sincere Jews hearing and believing the gospel.

In the following years, Timothy was a constant

When did Paul write the pastoral letters?

It's a puzzle to know when Paul wrote to Timothy and Titus. At the end of the Acts of the Apostles, Paul is under house arrest awaiting trial in Rome. After this, the only clues we have are in the pastoral letters themselves and in the writings of the early church historians.

One theory is that Paul is released after his trial in Rome. He has been accused of speaking against the Jewish law and temple, and of bringing a Gentile into the temple area. The charges against him are weak, and it may be that he is acquitted. The year is AD 62.

Bishop Clement, who is a historian in these early days, says that Paul is able to leave Rome and travel to Spain – the western boundary of the Roman empire. He fulfils his great ambition to take the gospel 'to the end of the earth' (Romans 15:28). He then returns to the centres of population around the Aegean Sea, including Crete.

The churches are being influenced by two strong pressure groups – the Jewish legalists and the Gentile mystics.

The Jewish group emphasizes the importance of Jewish traditions. They tell exaggerated stories of Jewish heroes, memorize long lists of Jewish ancestors and delight in debating the finer points of the Jewish law.

The Gentile group claims special 'knowledge' of the paths through the spiritual realms. Later they will be called 'Gnostics' from the Greek word 'gnosis', meaning 'knowledge'. They are a secret society that shares inside information, such as the secret passwords needed in the life to come.

Paul writes to Timothy and Titus to offer them advice. These false teachers can do great damage to the church, because they distort the gospel. Christians may be misled into legalism or licence – either finding themselves back in bondage to the law, or thinking they are free to do whatever they like. Both extremes misunderstand the gospel. Christ came that we should be free from the guilt and penalty of sin – and free also to do right.

Perhaps Paul writes his first letter to Timothy and the letter to Titus sometime in AD 64–65. He then returns to Rome, where the church is being persecuted by the emperor Nero.

Nero began his persecution of Christians in AD 64. He blamed them for the Great Fire which destroyed large areas of poor housing in Rome, and which Nero wanted levelled anyway. It was for this reason that he is said to have 'fiddled while Rome burnt' – and found it convenient to accuse the Christians of arson.

Paul is once again imprisoned in Rome. His second letter to Timothy is certainly his last letter, before he is beheaded by a Roman sword.

The pastoral letters give us an important glimpse of life in the early church. Some structure and organization is emerging, with mention of 'overseers' and 'deacons'. There are crucial battles being fought over Christian belief and behaviour. And the letters include many early sayings, snatches of hymns and phrases from creeds.

Perhaps the greatest treasure is to have a last letter from Paul – one written when he knows he is soon to die. His readiness to suffer, his steadfast faith and his vision of glory are a priceless witness and encouragement to every Christian.

companion to Paul. He worked with him on several of the great letters, visited Thessalonica and Corinth on Paul's behalf and went with him on the fateful journey to Jerusalem.

By the time of Paul's 'first' letter to him, some years later, Timothy has become a senior figure in the church at Ephesus. He still feels young and inexperienced for such a responsibility, and is naturally hesitant. Paul writes to encourage him to be confident in God, to tackle the issues of doctrine and pastoral care and to be a faithful servant of Jesus Christ.

Despite his adventures, Timothy is quite a shy person. In his 'second' letter, Paul seeks to strengthen his confidence in the gospel. He reminds him of his own example. He encourages him to accept the great responsibility of preaching Jesus Christ in the last days.

The 'pastoral letters'

The 'pastoral letters' are three letters written by the apostle Paul – two to Timothy and one to Titus. They were first called the 'pastoral letters' in the 18th century, because they give guidance about caring for, or 'pastoring', churches.

Paul's earlier letters were much longer, and were to be read to whole churches. These three letters are shorter – written to his companions and co-workers, who are now his link with the churches in Ephesus (Timothy) and Crete (Titus). Timothy and Titus are not the church leaders, as far as we know. This task seems to be fulfilled by the elders and overseers mentioned in the letters.

DISCOVERING 1 AND 2 TIMOTHY

Paul greets Timothy

Paul describes himself as 'an apostle of Christ Jesus'. He is aware of his divine calling, which he neither desired nor deserved. But the outcome is that he no longer lives for himself, but only for Christ.

Timothy is like a son to Paul. Certainly Paul is his spiritual father, having seen him converted, circumcised and commissioned for spiritual ministry in the church. Paul has come to rely on Timothy as a friend, companion and co-worker.

False teachers

Timothy to confront the false teachers
(1 Timothy 1:3–11)
Paul warns Timothy about false teachers in the church. These false teachers are Jews who enmesh their hearers in complex discussions of fables, myths and genealogies. They have taken Old Testament characters and stories, elaborated them out of all recognition and built their own fantasy religion.

Paul admits that these people really want to be teachers of the law – but they're talking rubbish. The law is very good when understood and applied properly. It exposes lawbreakers. It draws the line against serious sin. Ideally, it promotes love. But it was never meant to provide memory games and competitions for righteous people! Paul says the most loving thing to do is to command the false teachers to stop. It will take someone with a pure heart, a good conscience and a sincere faith to do it – because everyone else is handicapped by guilt, fear or superstition.

Paul tells his own experience of God's grace
(1 Timothy 1:12–17)
Paul remembers the days when he himself was hooked on the law. As an energetic young Pharisee, he was so enraged by the followers of Jesus that he became their chief persecutor. But Jesus Christ met him on the road to Damascus – and turned him right round. He forgave

Paul's ignorance and unbelief, poured out his grace upon him and filled him with faith and love.

Paul reckons that if Jesus can do that for him – the worst sinner in the world – then he can do it for anyone!

Paul encourages Timothy to be faithful
(1 Timothy 1:18–20)

Paul knows that he is giving Timothy a tough task. But there has always been something special about Timothy – ever since the Holy Spirit inspired prophecies about him. He may be young and shy, but that means he has to rely on spiritual strengths – faith and a good conscience.

In spiritual warfare it is vital to have holy integrity. The Christian's life must be all of a piece in belief and behaviour. Two people who have failed in this are Hymenaeus and Alexander.

Hymenaeus and Alexander are two leading members of the church whom Paul has had to expel from the fellowship. Hymenaeus believes and teaches that there is no further resurrection for believers after the receiving of the Holy Spirit in this life (2 Timothy 2:18). Alexander is a coppersmith who has done Paul some grave personal wrong (2 Timothy 4:14). Both have been 'handed over to Satan'. They are now without God's protection and may suffer some terrible disease or disability.

True church

Paul teaches that the gospel is for everyone. Jesus Christ has come into this world as a human being so that all people may be saved.

Christian behaviour: prayer, holiness, modesty
(1 Timothy 2:1–15)

Some people think that the church's task is to provoke social upheaval and revolution – protesting and campaigning to destroy the structures of a godless society. Paul calls the church to *pray* for the rulers and governors of the world and to live a holy and peaceable life.

When the church meets for public worship it isn't to be a hotbed of revolution. This isn't the place for fierce argument and fiery rhetoric. It is the place to draw earth and heaven into the peace and purpose of God.

The one God and one mediator, Jesus Christ, are best honoured by united prayer that the world may be one.

The peace and order of the Roman empire are a great help in allowing the gospel to be preached. God has commissioned Paul to tell the whole world of his saving love through Jesus Christ. And Jesus is the perfect go-between, because he is fully God and fully human. No other mediator is necessary – not Jewish angels or Gnostic mystics.

Paul teaches how people should pray in public. The outward gesture ought to express the inner attitude.

Men should lift holy hands in prayer without hiding a clenched fist in their hearts. Women should dress modestly, without flashing their sex or flaunting their wealth. God looks for wholeness in the way we worship – open hearts and loving lives.

The sort of people to appoint as leaders
(1 Timothy 3:1–13)

Paul talks about the qualities needed in church leaders. He uses the words 'overseer' and 'deacon' for their different roles in the church.

The Greek word for 'overseer' gives us our word 'episcopal' – but Paul isn't thinking of bishops as we know them today. He is describing the senior leaders in a local church. In the same way, a deacon is not the curate or church administrator of modern times, but an assistant with a call to help and serve.

Paul says that overseers must be people of Christian maturity and integrity. They have a many-sided responsibility – to lead, teach, provide hospitality, deal with money and relate the church to the wider society. The obvious problems are pride, greed, lust, anger, ignorance, hypocrisy, lack of authority and Satan's snares.

Church leadership begins in the heart and home.

Overseers must be self-controlled in their tempers and habits. They must be faithful husbands and effective fathers. If they can't manage themselves and their families, they have no business trying to lead a church.

It matters, too, what outsiders think of overseers. People judge Jesus Christ and the gospel by what they see of his followers – and especially their leaders. Sometimes outsiders detect false motives and glaring faults that fellow Christians simply overlook. At the same time, outsiders know integrity when they see it and can reject a wicked rumour.

Paul teaches that deacons must have the same qualities as the overseers. They are not expected to teach or offer hospitality to the same extent that the overseers do. But their lives must be upright and self-controlled. They must hold the faith deeply and show that they live it out. Their wives (or women deacons?) must also have a good reputation. They must not be gossips, trading scandal or using their inside information to harm people.

Paul promises 'great assurance' to those who serve well as deacons. It is the assurance of God's presence and help, which we only discover when we *have* to rely on him absolutely.

Women in the church

Paul has something else to say to the Christian women. He knows they are longing to learn and lead. Christ has set them free – which includes being educated in the same way as men, and taking equal responsibility with them in the life of the church.

But Paul cannot accept that women shall have authority over men. He recalls the order in which man and woman were created – Adam first and then Eve (Genesis 2:22–23). He also remembers that it was the woman who was deceived by the serpent, while the man sinned quite knowingly (Genesis 3:4–12). As Paul sees it, men have inherited Adam's authority to lead, and women have inherited Eve's lack of moral judgment.

There has been much argument over Paul's teaching. Some people think he is too influenced by his Jewish background. Some accuse him of being prejudiced against women. Some, on the other hand, believe he is heralding a revolution – releasing women to their full status, role and freedom in Christ. In any case, he can't help being a 1st-century Jew!

We know from Paul's other letters that he accepts the ministry of women in public worship. He assumes that they will prophesy (speak God's word) and

Paul urges women in the churches to dress modestly. Elaborate hairstyles such as this were fashionable among affluent Roman women.

teaches that they should dress modestly (1 Corinthians 11:5). He wants them to be educated, but has some worry about them speaking or calling out in church. Is this because they are ignorant or pushy? We don't know. Paul says husbands should share their understanding with their wives by teaching them at home (1 Corinthians 14:34–35).

Here, in 1 Timothy, Paul teaches that women must not try to seize authority in the life of the church. He would surely say the same to men. He also teaches that women have a God-given role which is as far-reaching as they could ever wish – that of having children and giving them their early security and understanding. Men and women have equal responsibility and complementary roles in the raising and ruling of church and family.

Christian foundations: the completeness of Christ

(1 Timothy 3:14–16)

Paul is writing these instructions so that Timothy knows how to advise the Christian household – made up of living people worshipping the living God. This is a Christian temple in every community – the pillar and foundation of truth for all to see.

Paul quotes the words of a Christian creed or hymn. This is the mystery of godliness – that Jesus Christ has become in himself a living link between earth and heaven. He has taken human nature and been raised to glory – an achievement as astonishing to angels as it is to people.

Paul bursts into praise! This is the whole point of his letter – that the truth of Christ is revealed to the church. If the church will live to her high calling, she will counter false teaching by sharing and showing the gospel.

How to deal with misleading myths

(1 Timothy 4:1–10)

Now Paul discusses a prophecy. The Holy Spirit warns that some believers will be deceived by evil spirits and abandon their faith.

This damage to the church will come from unscrupulous teachers. They will introduce false and unnecessary rules of self-denial – such as staying single or living by a strict diet. Needless to say, they have no instruction from God for this – and no intention of keeping such rules themselves.

Paul is attacking teachers who deny the good things of life. They tell their followers to apply rigid self-control. Behind this is the idea that this world and our bodies are bad. The world must be avoided and our bodies must be punished. If we try hard enough, we will escape from the pull of earthly desires and become spiritual enough to go to heaven. Perhaps the Gnostics of the next century, with their secret information and mystic passwords, have something of this approach.

For Paul, God's creation is *good*. Our bodies are a most wonderful gift. The pleasures of food and drink and sex (in their proper proportion and place) are to be received with thanksgiving and enjoyed with praise. Later on in the letter, Paul advises Timothy to drink a little wine. It will do him good!

In the face of false teaching, Timothy can teach the truth of Jesus. Jesus affirmed our human nature and life in this world by living fully to the glory of God. Timothy will set people free with the truth – cutting through the myths and fables which bring fear and superstition. Physical fitness is good if you can do it – but spiritual fitness is even better. Godliness lasts for ever.

Pastoring people

Take care of yourself

(1 Timothy 4:11–16)

Paul encourages Timothy to give a lead in these matters. He is not to leave it to those who are older or more experienced. He is to keep his own life in good order and be an example to others. Ezra in the Old Testament and Jesus himself each believed in living the truth yourself before applying it to others (Ezra 7:10; Matthew 5:19).

Timothy's basic approach will be to read scripture (the Old Testament) and then explain its meaning and challenge his hearers to change. He is to use his spiritual gift, which was prophesied for him and prayed in at his commissioning by the elders. He is, in his own life, to show the commitment and progress he commends to others – so both he and his hearers will benefit.

Caring for widows, elders and slaves

(1 Timothy 5:1 – 6:2)

Now Paul has practical advice for Timothy. He tells him how to deal with the various groups of people in the church.

Timothy is to be kind, treating members of the church as his own family – which in a way they are. Older people are his parents, younger ones his brothers and sisters. This will help him avoid sexual confusion in his relationship with younger women. In another letter, the care of young wives is left to older women only (Titus 2:3–5).

WIDOWS

Widows are to be given special attention, as they are in Jewish society (5:3–16). The church should encourage families to care for their bereaved parents wherever possible, as part of their Christian duty. Other widows will rely entirely on God, while still others will go looking for pleasure.

Paul refers to a 'list of widows' (1 Timothy 5:9). These are the widows who are to be cared for by the church, but who will also have a ministry of caring for others. Paul says they must be at least sixty years old and known for their good life.

Younger widows are different. They should not be put

on the list for church support. For one thing, they are likely to remarry after a while. For another, they may become idle gossips.

Is Paul speaking from hard experience? Is the church at Ephesus supporting frivolous young widows, who sit around in one another's houses spreading scandal? He recommends that they marry again and find their fulfilment in raising a family.

ELDERS

Timothy is to have a special responsibility for the elders of the church (5:17–25). They are to be honoured for their work as preachers and teachers – and properly paid. They are also to be protected from gossip and slander. If they are guilty of misbehaviour they must be rebuked publicly, because they bear public responsibility.

It is vital that those who preach and teach the gospel shall live a pure and open life. For this reason, time and care must be taken in appointing elders. Some attitudes and actions (both bad and good) don't come to light until much later. Timothy must be careful of his own life, too   but he should certainly allow himself a little wine!

Overseers and elders

Paul describes some church leaders as 'overseers' (3:1) and some as 'elders' (5:17).

'Elders' have been the leaders and administrators of Israel ever since the days of Moses. Now the title is used for the senior people who lead, teach and administer the church. The Greek word for 'elder' is 'presbuteros'. This gives us the word 'presbyter', which is used for a Christian minister. In some branches of the church, 'presbyter' has been shortened to 'priest'.

The Greek word for 'overseer' is 'episcopos'. This gives us the word 'episcopal', which describes the authority and work of a bishop. It seems that, by the 2nd century, some elders or presbyters were given higher responsibilities of leadership, and the name 'bishop' became their superior title.

The famous reformer, John Calvin, believed there were four kinds of ministry to be found in the New Testament: pastors (caring), doctors (teaching), deacons (assisting) and presbyters (leading).

SLAVES

Some of the members of the church are slaves, and some are slave owners (6:1–2). What difference does it make that they are Christians?

Paul says Christian slaves should give their masters the fullest possible respect. They are not to become familiar or casual if their masters are Christians, but serve them all the more gladly as believers.

For Paul, the gospel doesn't demand that slavery should be abolished. Instead, he teaches that, in Christ, relationships of duty become relationships of service and love. Where, in the past, one person has had power over another, the relationship is now one of mutual support and respect.

Motives and money

The motive of money
(1 Timothy 6:3–10)

Paul attacks the false teachers for their pride and greed. Instead of devoting themselves to the basic teaching of Jesus, they love hair-splitting discussions and quarrels. What's more, they are doing it for money – either sponging off their followers or charging fees for their secrets.

Paul says that real wealth is to be found in godliness with contentment – the heart attitudes which produce a pure and happy life. For food and clothes all we need is enough. Constantly wanting more leads to obsession, corruption and ruin.

The motive of holiness
(1 Timothy 6:11–16)

Timothy is to be different. Greed and personal gain have no place in his priorities. His only desire is for spiritual virtues. His only fight is the ongoing fight of faith. His only possession is the hope of eternal life. His whole life is to flow from his first confession of faith, through his stand with Jesus, to his ultimate goal – the glory of God.

Life after wealth
(1 Timothy 6:17–19)

Paul gives some of his most notable teaching about worldly wealth. Timothy is to tell rich people not to rely on their money, but to put their trust in God. God is the giver of everything we need for joy. Money in itself is never enough – it can't buy love on earth and it's of no value in heaven.

So what shall rich people do? Timothy is to tell them to be generous and willing to share. This way they can do good with their money and practise letting it go. They will also store treasure in heaven.

Paul doesn't tell masters to release their slaves; nor does he tell rich people to give away all their money. For Paul, the impact of the gospel is not to dismantle life as we know it, but to transform our relationships within it.

A final charge and blessing

Paul's final words sum up his charge to Timothy (6:20–21). His young friend is to guard the gospel from all attempts to change or destroy it. And he is to avoid the futile arguments and spurious claims of false teachers.

As always, Paul signs off by praying God's grace on Timothy and those who are in his care.

Paul greets Timothy

Paul's greeting is rather formal – announcing himself as an apostle of Jesus Christ (2 Timothy 1:1–2).

Paul often reminds people that he is an apostle. The work he does and the message he proclaims are not of human origin. He is doing God's work at God's command – and his teaching has God's authority. This

letter will find a far wider audience than Timothy. It will become a letter to the whole church.

Paul thanks God for Timothy – and encourages him

Paul remembers the early days when he first met Timothy in Lystra (1:3–7). Timothy had a Jewish mother and a Greek father. His mother and grandmother both became Christians. They had raised Timothy to know the Jewish scriptures, and he had come to faith in Jesus Christ. Since then, Timothy has become like a son to Paul, and he longs to see him again.

Paul is concerned that Timothy has gone rather quiet as far as the gospel is concerned. Is he ashamed of his faith in Jesus Christ, the crucified Messiah? Or is he embarrassed that his hero, Paul, is again in prison?

Paul knows that Timothy is naturally timid – but he urges him not to be a coward. He encourages him to fan into flame the fire of the Holy Spirit within him. This is the Spirit Timothy received when Paul and others prayed for him and ordained him for Christian service.

Timothy may be shy and fearful, but he has the Holy Spirit of Jesus within him. The Spirit strengthens him with power to preach and teach. The Spirit enables him to love fellow Christians and to care for those who do not yet know Christ. The Spirit gives him self-control, to govern and give his life for the gospel.

Suffering, single-mindedness and hard work

A gospel worth the suffering
(2 Timothy 1:8–18)

Paul reminds Timothy of the thrilling gospel message. God has always loved the world, but now his love has been clearly and openly shown by his sending of Jesus. Jesus is the Saviour of the world. There is rescue from sin, forgiveness and eternal life for everyone who believes in him.

It is because the good news is so important that Paul is prepared to suffer as he does. He tells Timothy to guard this wonderful gospel and to accept the suffering that comes with proclaiming it. When he passes it on, he

---

When was 2 Timothy written?

We don't know for certain what happened to Paul in the last years of his life.

At the end of the book of Acts, we left Paul in Rome, where he was under house arrest and awaiting trial. Some people think that he was released and travelled to Spain. He may also have returned to his old mission field around the Aegean Sea, including a visit to Crete.

Eventually Paul travels to Rome again – perhaps to support the Christians who are being persecuted by the emperor Nero. There he is arrested for his gospel activities and put on trial. It could be that this is the final imprisonment, during which he writes his last letter to Timothy.

must keep to the same pattern of teaching that Paul has used, so that the truth will not be diluted or distorted.

Single-mindedness and hard work
(2 Timothy 2:1–26)

Paul calls Timothy to take his place in the front line of Christian mission. He is to be a living link between the generations – training the evangelists and teachers of the future.

This work requires single-mindedness. Like a soldier on active service, Timothy must stay focused on the battle and the commands of his Lord. Like an athlete in competition, Timothy must not compromise or cheat if he hopes to win the prize. But there is a great reward. Like a hard-working farmer, Timothy will be the first to benefit from the sacrifices he has made.

Paul may look like a criminal, shut in prison and confined by chains. But the gospel isn't chained and never will be. If Paul's suffering helps the gospel reach others, he will bear it willingly. He remembers a saying or part of a hymn about death and glory in Christ (2:11–13).

TIMOTHY MUST HANDLE THE TRUTH CORRECTLY

Paul sees great danger in the way some teachers deal with God's truth (2:14–26). They quarrel about the precise meanings of words. They speculate on alternative theories. They are infecting the gospel with lies – with disastrous effects for those who hear them.

For example, two men – Hymenaeus and Philetus – believe that the resurrection of Christians is in the past. What you have is what you received at your baptism. There's no resurrection of your body beyond death, and no life in the world to come.

These theories may please false teachers and impress their followers, but they aren't the gospel. These men are corrupting God's truth, so that it no longer has spiritual power or eternal hope.

Timothy is not to be like these false teachers. He is to be absolutely straight with God's word, so that he won't be ashamed when he presents his work to God.

To be a faithful teacher, Timothy must live a pure life himself. There are all sorts of pots and utensils in a house – but it is the clean ones that are ready for the master to use. So it is with serving Christ. Christians come in all shapes and sizes – but it is the ones who are pure in heart and life who are useful to God.

Timothy must keep his life clean. He must run away from the sexual desires and self-centred ambitions which are typical of young people. He must aim to become a mature and godly man – along with others whose lives are open to the Lord. His teaching must be true and his manner gentle, so that those who learn from him will be saved.

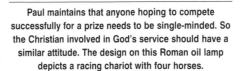

Paul maintains that anyone hoping to compete successfully for a prize needs to be single-minded. So the Christian involved in God's service should have a similar attitude. The design on this Roman oil lamp depicts a racing chariot with four horses.

Godlessness in the last days

Paul describes how people will be in the last days (3:1–9). The last days are the years between the ascension of Jesus to heaven and his return to earth in glory. They are the times in which we live.

Paul says that people will be entirely self-centred. They will love money and pleasure for themselves, but be proud, aggressive and treacherous towards others. They will have no love, respect or forgiveness in their relationships. They will be keen to show off their religion – but they will not let the truth change their lives.

Paul says that the phoney religious teachers will exploit silly women in their own homes. They will take advantage of their weakness, guilt and longings. He likens such teachers to Jannes and Jambres – who were said to be Pharaoh's chief magicians in the disputes with Moses (Exodus 7:11). Such people use their cunning to defy God – but will be exposed as charlatans.

Paul's example and Timothy's calling

Paul's example
(2 Timothy 3:10–13)

Paul offers his own life as an example to Timothy. Timothy has seen for himself how Paul has lived, taught and suffered for the sake of the gospel. Now he must also expect to suffer if he truly follows Christ.

On his first missionary journey, Paul was expelled from Pisidian Antioch, had to escape from Iconium and was stoned and left for dead at Lystra (Acts 13:50 – 14:19). Lystra was where Timothy lived. This was Paul's first running battle with persecution. It was also his first experience of God's continuing protection in the face of many dangers.

Paul sees that living the truth and being persecuted go together in this world. Jesus was the truth in person, and he was crucified. Those who live a lie (who are evil frauds) will go from bad to worse in their deceptions. Those who live the truth will go from strength to strength in their certainties.

The value of the scriptures
(2 Timothy 3:14–17)

The basis of truth is not only in Paul's example, but in the scriptures – what we now call the Old Testament. Timothy was brought up to know these scriptures by his Jewish mother and grandmother. He has also learned from Paul, whose teaching and letters will become part of the New Testament. All these scriptures are 'God-breathed' – expressed by his Holy Spirit through human writers.

The scriptures show us the whole plan of God's salvation. This is something we would never discover or guess by ourselves. God has always loved the world and been grieved by human sin. First he called a people, Israel, to know him. Then he gave them his law to guide them, his kings to rule them and his prophets to deliver his word. Finally he has sent his Son, Jesus, to be the Saviour of all.

The scriptures not only tell us that God saves, but teach us how to live the good life. The scriptures are the main means of knowing God's truth. They correct what is wrong and commend what is right. They lead us to a mature understanding of God's will, and equip us for his service.

Timothy's calling
(2 Timothy 4:1–5)

Paul solemnly commissions Timothy. He does so in the presence of God, and in the light of Christ's return.

Timothy is to preach God's word. He is to speak out what God has revealed about his salvation and his way. Timothy is to do this at all times and in all circumstances. People may refuse to listen. They may prefer more exciting or entertaining teachers. But Timothy is to persevere and fulfil his God-given task.

Paul reminds Timothy of the value of the scriptures and their role in equipping us for life. The Torah (the Jewish law) with a pointer for following the text.

Paul faces death – and glory

'I have finished the race'
(2 Timothy 4:6–8)

Paul knows that he is soon to die. He already feels that his life is being poured out like a drink offering on an altar – a complete sacrifice to God.

Like Jesus, Paul has the assurance that his work is done. As Jesus died, he cried out, 'It is finished!' Now Paul believes he has fought his fight, finished his race and kept his faith to the end. He looks forward to his judgment and reward from Jesus Christ, the Lord he has loved and served and longs to see.

Last words

(2 Timothy 4:9–18)

Paul hopes that Timothy will come quickly to see him before he dies. He needs the cloak which he left at Troas, as winter is approaching and he feels the cold. He also wants his scrolls and parchments – perhaps some scriptures, notes and copies of his letters.

The team which Paul likes to have around him is dispersed. Demas has deserted. Crescens, Titus and Tychicus are away on various errands. The only person left with Paul is Luke, the doctor from Macedonia who is the writer of the Gospel and Acts.

Paul asks that Timothy will bring John Mark with him. The young man who was once a source of friction between Paul and Barnabas (Acts 15:37–39) is now a helpful colleague.

Paul tells Timothy briefly about the first hearing of his trial. Not one of the Christians in Rome came to help him with his case or give evidence in his favour. Alexander the metalworker (who crafts copper bronze) has hurt him badly by speaking strongly against him. But Paul has taken the opportunity to preach the gospel fully, so that his judges and the listening public may hear it!

In all this, Paul has had the overwhelming assurance of Christ's presence and strength. Like Daniel in the lion's den, he has been amazingly protected from harm. He has been able to proclaim the gospel of Jesus Christ at the heart of the Roman empire. And even execution, when it comes, will merely bring him safely to God's heavenly kingdom.

Final greetings

Paul sends greetings to Priscilla and Aquila, the married couple who befriended him in Corinth and helped him found the church in Ephesus (4:19–22). He also greets the household of Onesiphorus – a faithful and courageous servant of Christ who may have recently died. Paul has mentioned him earlier in the letter (1:16–18).

With a few other snippets of news, and his distinctive 'grace', Paul closes. His farewell blessing on Timothy and the church at Ephesus is the last recorded word we have from the great apostle.

TITUS

Paul writes this letter to Titus – the young man he has left in charge of the church on the Mediterranean island of Crete.

Paul is now in the closing years of his ministry. He tells Titus the kind of people he should appoint as church leaders for the future. They must have mature faith and good character. He also advises Titus how to teach the various groups of people in the church – the old and the young, both men and women, and those who are slaves.

Finally, Paul reminds Titus of the difference it makes to be a Christian. Christians should be good members of society – self-controlled, forgiving and reluctant to quarrel. These are rather different qualities from those usually found among the inhabitants of Crete!

Outline

DISCOVERING TITUS

Paul greets Titus

(1:1–4)

Paul is old and was born a Jew. Titus is young and his background is Greek. Now they both belong to Christ. They have the task of bringing others to the faith, hope and way of life that God has made possible through Jesus.

A task for Titus

(1:5–9)

Paul has left Titus in Crete after a visit to strengthen the churches there. His young colleague is to continue the task of establishing the churches on the island – appointing local leaders and correcting false teaching.

Paul describes the kind of people to appoint as church leaders. He calls them 'elders' and 'overseers'. It may be that elders are senior men who form an advisory council, while overseers do the work of leading and teaching. The list of their qualifications is much the same as in the letter to Timothy (1 Timothy 3:2–7).

As the life and organization of the church develop, the 'overseers' will be better known as bishops. In years to come their status and range of responsibility will be much greater. There is no mention of 'deacons' or assistants in this letter to Titus.

An elder must have a good reputation both inside and outside the church. He should have married only once – even if he is divorced or his wife has died. His children must share his faith and not be wild or rebellious.

The overseer's character and manner must express the love of God – gentle, patient and self-controlled. He mustn't be ruled by drink or bad temper. He must be holy in himself and hospitable in his home – so that his own life is a good example of his teaching.

Dealing with heresy

(1:10–16)

An important part of the overseer's task is to challenge lies and heresies (false teaching) in the church. There are people who are actively undermining the truth of the gospel – for example, a strong group of traditional Jews is insisting that Gentile Christians must be circumcised. Such teachers not only do great damage to families and fellowship groups, but make money from their lies.

Cretans have a reputation for being coarse, dishonest and lazy. When such people get hold of wrong religion, they produce a false, bullying and manipulative sect. Titus must deal very firmly with the leaders to rebuke them and bring them to a true faith.

Paul gives some idea of the beliefs of the false teachers. He mentions 'Jewish myths' – the far-fetched stories of Jewish heroes which give a wrong impression of the nature of faith and the power of God. He also speaks of 'the commands of those who reject the truth' – the people who impose strict rules against the everyday pleasures of food and marriage. Like Jesus, Paul teaches that it's the heart that counts in matters of purity – not blaming sin on food, sex or other people's customs.

Teaching various groups

(2:1–10)

Paul outlines the teaching Titus should give to the different groups in the churches. Older men should be self-controlled and dignified, with a well-established faith and persevering love.

Older women are to be as reverent as priests in their daily life. They must control any desire to gossip or drink too much, and teach their children well. They must show younger wives and mothers how to build a secure and loving marriage and family, with purity, hard work, kindness and self-giving.

Paul does not allow women to reject their responsibilities on the grounds that Jesus has made them 'free'. It is always important to Paul what outsiders think of the church. He outlines attitudes and ways of behaving which will show the sense and attractiveness of the gospel.

Titus must challenge the young men to take responsibility for their actions. Titus is one of them, and must set a good example. They should live with such integrity that their critics are left speechless.

Christian slaves are to be respectful of their owners and honest with their property. They, too, can play their full part in making the gospel attractive.

Slavery is part of the way of life in the ancient world. One day Christianity will be the driving force in getting slavery abolished – but not yet.

Did Paul really write the pastoral letters?

The pastoral letters to Timothy and Titus are written in Paul's name. They have his greeting at the beginning and end and contain personal details about his life and feelings.

All the same, some scholars think Paul didn't write them. They believe Paul's name is used to strengthen the teaching in the letters – just as today we might have a 'foreword' by someone famous, to recommend a book by someone we don't know.

Those who think Paul didn't write the pastoral letters give the following reasons:

They say that the letters don't fit the story of Paul's life as we know it from the Acts of the Apostles.

Paul talks about 'overseers' and 'deacons' which were titles for church leaders which came later.

Paul is telling Timothy and Titus how to deal with Gnosticism – a false teaching which didn't trouble the church until the 2nd century AD.

Paul's writing style and the words he uses are different from his other letters.

Those who believe Paul did write the pastoral letters say the following:

It's possible that Paul wrote to Timothy and Titus some years after his house arrest in Rome at the end of the Acts of the Apostles.

Bishop Clement of Rome writes in one of his letters that Paul was released and travelled to Spain – which we know he had long wanted to do (Romans 15:24).

He could have completed this journey in AD 64 and then returned to Crete (Titus 1:5) and Macedonia (1 Timothy 1:3). He could have spent the winter of AD 65–66 at Nicopolis in Epirus (Titus 3:12) and written 1 Timothy and Titus at that time.

In AD 66 or early 67 Paul could have visited Miletus, where he left Trophimus (2 Timothy 4:20). He could have journeyed on to Troas, where he left his cloak, scrolls and parchments at the house of Carpus (2 Timothy 4:13). From there he could have travelled to Rome, where he was arrested and put on trial – writing 2 Timothy from prison before his death.

A pen case and a collection of reed pens from Roman Egypt. Traces of black ink still remain in the inkwell.

Paul may talk of 'overseers' and 'deacons' without meaning the kind of officials who came later. He always tried to leave his churches in the care of suitable leaders. On the first missionary journey, he and Barnabas appointed elders in the churches they founded. Choosing the right people would be even more important to him as he approached the end of his life.

Paul advises Timothy and Titus on how to deal with 'false teachers' with strange ideas. He doesn't mention Gnosticism – but it could be some early version of Gnostic heresy with its myths and secrets. Paul says only that these teachers talk too much, and their beliefs are misleading and powerless.

There may be good reasons for Paul using different words and phrases. He may be choosing a different style of writing in his later life. Or he may have the help of a secretary who influences his style.

Overall, the very personal content of the letters and the passion with which Paul writes make it very probable that the letters are genuinely his.

The reason for godliness
(2:11–15)

Jesus Christ brings a revolution into every life. He shows what God is like, offers salvation and gives power to those who want to change. He has given his life to conquer evil and rescue sinful people into God's family.

The challenge for the Christian is how to lead a pure life in a wicked world. Our hope is not that we will overthrow the evil structures of the world, but that Christ will return in glory and complete his new creation.

Choosing the good
(3:1–11)

Titus is to remind Christians to be good citizens. In what they say and do they are to put others first.

In the past, we were ruled by our strongest feelings and found ourselves hating each other. This was particularly true of the Cretans. Now everything is different in the light of Christ.

Paul says we can be different, because we have experienced the mercy and goodness of God. He has saved us from sin, washed us of guilt and given us his Spirit within. We have a new start and a new hope.

The vain discussions and endless bickering of false teachers are shown up for what they are – a throwback to the darkness and discord of the past.

Finally...
(3:12–15)

For Paul, mutual help and one-anotherness are part of the gospel.

He asks Titus to come to him at Nicopolis, where he hopes to spend the winter. He is sending him one of his co-workers to look after Titus' work while he is away.

He also asks him to help Zenas and Apollos on their way with whatever provisions they need. And he closes his letter with a loving message from everyone to all.

Paul writes to Titus about being saved through the washing of rebirth, an event which is symbolized by the act of baptism. When a person is baptized, he or she is responding to God's love and being identified with the death and resurrection of Jesus. This illumination is from an early 9th-century theological anthology.

PHILEMON

Paul begs a favour. He asks Philemon, a slave owner, to forgive a runaway slave.

While he has been in prison, Paul has met a runaway slave called Onesimus. Onesimus has become a Christian. As it happens, Paul knows the young man's master, Philemon, who is a member of the church in Colosse. Paul now writes to Philemon to ask him to forgive Onesimus and receive him back as a Christian brother.

Outline

Greetings and thanksgiving (vv. 1–7)
Paul's plea for Onesimus (vv. 8–22)
Paul's final greetings (vv. 23–25)

INTRODUCTION

Paul asks Philemon to forgive the slave Onesimus

Philemon lives at Colosse, which is one of three towns in the Lycus Valley. Paul writes from prison, probably in Rome. Almost certainly his letters to the Colossians and to Philemon travel by the same post with Tychicus (Colossians 4:9).

The slave's name is Onesimus – a common name, meaning 'Useful'. However, by running away he has been far from useful, and by coming back as a Christian he gives Philemon a problem. Should he punish him or release him?

It is in the letter to the Colossians that Paul teaches Christian masters to care for their slaves, because they are themselves slaves of Jesus Christ (Colossians 3:22 – 4:1). In the letter to Philemon, a slave owner is actually asked to make a Christian difference by forgiving a slave instead of punishing him.

We don't know what happens next, and whether Philemon agrees to Paul's request. But there is later a bishop of Ephesus called Onesimus.

Jesus and slavery

There were about 60 million slaves in the Roman empire. Even people of well-educated professions, such as doctors, teachers and civil servants may have been slaves. They were the possessions of their owners, who had complete control over their lives.

In centuries to come, Christians will campaign to abolish slavery. Paul, however, never mentions that slavery is unjust, or that it is wrong for one person to own another.

Paul teaches that Christianity changes society by changing attitudes. He doesn't tell Christian wives to divorce their husbands, or Christian masters to release their slaves. Instead, he teaches a new attitude – the dismantling of all social barriers 'in Christ'. Wives and husbands, masters and slaves, are now all 'one' in Christ Jesus.

DISCOVERING PHILEMON

Greetings and thanksgiving

(vv. 1–7)

Paul greets Philemon warmly, along with other friends in his house church. Although separated by distance and circumstance (Paul is in prison), they are united in the love and work of Jesus Christ.

Paul thanks God for Philemon's faith and assures his friend of his frequent prayers. Paul often begins with words of encouragement, before moving on to any confrontation or correction (2 Timothy 1:3–7). Everything he says is in the context of Christian love and service, but this letter must be one of the most persuasive (not to say manipulative) ever written!

Paul's plea for Onesimus

(vv. 8–22)

'Onesimus', the slave's name, means 'Useful'. But, as Paul admits, Onesimus hasn't been very useful in the past. Now all that has changed, because Onesimus has become a Christian, and therefore a Christian brother.

Here is a difficult Christian choice. Paul is asking Philemon to forgive a slave. Onesimus is risking punishment by returning home. Philemon is being asked to treat someone as a person who has formerly been a useless object. All three are struggling with the ground-breaking truth that Jesus doesn't treat people as 'slaves' or 'free', but as God's dear children (Colossians 3:11).

Paul's final greetings

(vv. 23–25)

This letter may be personal, but it isn't private. Paul includes greetings from a number of mutual friends. Epaphras is the founder of the church at Colosse. He is now with Paul in prison. Mark, Aristarchus, Demas and Luke are members of Paul's team who are all mentioned in his letter to the Colossians. The whole church now knows that Philemon is being asked to forgive Onesimus.

Hebrews

Here is a great letter. We don't know who wrote it, but it is full of the greatness of Jesus Christ. Using the themes of Old Testament priesthood and sacrifice, this letter explains what God has done for us by sending Jesus. This is a theme we find in the writings of Paul (Colossians 1) and John (John 1), but here it is expressed most excitingly for people with a Jewish background.

Hebrews is also written for Christians who are being persecuted for their faith. It tells them that Jesus also suffered and knows how life is for them. It lists the heroes of faith in the past, and describes them as a 'great cloud of witnesses' who are urging us on in the race of faith today.

Outline

Introduction: God has spoken by his Son (1:1–4)

Jesus Christ is the greatest (1:5 – 10:18)

Encouragement to enter this great salvation (10:19 – 12:29)

Concluding encouragements and greetings (13:1–25)

INTRODUCTION

The letter to the Hebrews is an original and creative piece of writing. Whoever wrote this letter has thought deeply about the life and death of Jesus in the light of the Old Testament scriptures. The writer gives us a fresh understanding of the uniqueness of Jesus and the completeness of his salvation.

The uniqueness of Jesus

JESUS – THE PERFECT 'WORD' OF GOD

Jesus is the greatest. He is greater than the prophets, greater than the kings, greater than the angels, greater than Moses… He is God's final Word, and his sacrifice is his completed work.

JESUS – THE PERFECT MAN

Hebrews shows how Jesus lived a perfect life, even though he had a body and passions and temptations like our own. The fact that he shared our experience means that he knows what we are going through. He also shows us how to turn suffering into spiritual growth.

If we follow Jesus, we can become perfect too. But the Christian life is marked by suffering. Our salvation is still in the future – when Christ returns. Meanwhile, we may be abused and persecuted for our faith. We need to find in the endurance and victory of Jesus our inspiration to carry on.

JESUS – THE PERFECT HIGH PRIEST

Hebrews shows how Jesus fulfils or replaces the old Jewish practices of priesthood and sacrifice. Jesus is both the perfect high priest and the perfect sacrifice.

Jesus wasn't a priest during his earthly life. But the writer of Hebrews shows that Jesus was doing a priest's work. In his life and death, Jesus was bringing God and humanity together. In fact he did what all the priestly ritual of killing animals and burning incense had failed to do.

The writer is very interested in a character called Melchizedek. Melchizedek was a priest who met and ministered to Abraham, long before the building of a tabernacle and the appointment of Aaron as Israel's high priest. Hebrews sees Jesus as a priest like Melchizedek.

JESUS – THE PERFECT SACRIFICE

Hebrews explains that Jesus' death was a sacrifice. Through his perfect sacrifice on the cross, Jesus has accounted for our sin, defeated death and opened a way to heaven for all.

Who wrote the letter to the Hebrews?

We don't know who wrote the letter to the Hebrews. The King James (Authorized) Version of the Bible assumes that the author is Paul, but this letter is not really in Paul's style. Martin Luther suggested Apollos, whose Jewish learning and eloquence we know from the book of Acts (Acts 18:24). Other possible authors include Silas, who helped with the writing of 1 Peter (1 Peter 5:12), and Clement of Rome.

Whoever the author is, he has a good knowledge of the Septuagint (the Old Testament in Greek). He is likely to be writing from one of the strong centres of Christianity, such as Rome. He has an excellent grasp of the Old Testament and a brilliant understanding of Jesus. This is a well-written, well-organized letter.

When was Hebrews written?

Most scholars think Hebrews was written in the AD 60s. The people receiving this letter have already suffered, and some are still in prison. This points to the letter being written after the persecution of Christians by Emperor Nero. But there is no mention of the temple. Is this because the letter is written some years after the temple has been destroyed – in, say, the mid-80s?

DISCOVERING HEBREWS

Introduction: God has spoken by his Son

Christ is greater than the prophets
(1:1–2)

We have a God who talks! In the past, he spoke through prophets, who delivered his message in a number of different situations. But a prophet's picture of God was always incomplete – flavoured with the prophet's own personality and confined to his particular setting.

But now God has made himself absolutely clear through his Son. Jesus is God's 'Word' in person – for all time and for every place.

The complete works
(1:3–4)

Jesus was with God the Father at the beginning. It was he who was God's agent in creating the universe. Now he has fulfilled all God's purposes.

It is Jesus who has shown us what God is like, by reflecting God's glory (or 'worth') and revealing his nature. It is Jesus who holds creation together in beautiful order and harmony, preventing it collapsing into chaos (Colossians 1:17).

Now Jesus has completed the task of saving us from sin, by offering himself as the perfect and complete sacrifice. His work done, he has resumed his rightful place in heaven: the throne of highest honour, alongside his Father.

Jesus Christ is the greatest

Jesus is greater than the angels
(1:5–14)

People think of angels as superior to humans. They live in God's presence and serve him continually. But Jesus is greater than the angels. He is not a part of God's creation, but a part of God himself. He is God's Son. He sits at God's right hand in glory.

Take the gospel seriously!
(2:1–4)

Once we have received God's word, we cannot plead ignorance. If angels rebelled and were punished, then we must respond seriously to what God is saying in Christ.

Jesus – one of us
(2:5–18)

In coming to earth, Jesus has taken on our human nature. He has fought the devil on his own ground, and destroyed his power. But it was costly. He felt the full force of temptation and the agony of suffering. He knows what it's like for us.

Jesus is greater than Moses
(3:1–6)

Moses received God's law and made it known. In doing so he acted as a faithful servant. But Jesus brings God's grace and forgiveness – and so reveals himself as God's Son.

Beware of unbelief and rebellion
(3:7–19)

Don't make the same mistake as the Israelites. When the going got tough in the desert, they rebelled. As a result, none of them entered God's 'rest' – the Promised Land of

---

Faith and perseverance

Hebrews talks about the importance of faith. Following Christ may be hard; but once we've realized who he is, there's no turning back. The only way is forward. Faith means living on earth in the light of heaven.

The readers of this letter have had a tough time. They have been ill-treated for their faith. Some have suffered imprisonment and loss of property. Now they are tempted to give up. This letter encourages them to persevere – to set their sights on Jesus as their pioneer, and heaven as their goal.

The writer urges his readers not to slip back into their old Jewish ways. The tabernacle, the priests and the sacrifices were all inadequate and temporary – and are now obsolete.

security and peace which is the Bible's image of heaven.

Christians must be careful to act on the good news *today* – in the present moment and situation. It is tempting to delay commitment to Christ, because we want our own way for as long as possible. God respects this hardening of attitude against him, as he has given us free will. But it is our loss.

Don't miss God's rest!
(4:1–11)

When the people of Israel were wandering in the wilderness, there was rest awaiting them in the Promised Land. But they missed it. They reached the threshold and drew back, because they thought the difficulties ahead were too great (Numbers 14:12–23). Because of their unbelief, they spent another forty years in the desert.

Don't be like them! God's rest is still with us, to be entered and enjoyed in this life. It is the rest which comes with hearing, receiving, believing and living the gospel. It is the rest of forgiveness of sins and peace with God through Jesus Christ.

David mentions God's rest (Psalm 95:7–8). He assumes that God's rest is still awaiting us, and we may enter it *today*. The only barrier is if, like the Israelites, we back away in disbelief. God's rest is the real sabbath – the place where we relax in all that God has done for us, and accept completely his purpose for the future. Let's be sure to enter it!

God's word – his judgment
(4:12–13)

God's word is for ever alive and active. When God speaks, it happens – and it happens as exactly and completely as he intends. When he spoke at creation, the universe came into being at his command (Genesis 1:3).

We will all have to face the power and precision of God's word. It is more effective than a sword with two blades. It cuts finer than a surgeon's scalpel. It finds out the

The writer starts his letter by demonstrating the superiority of Jesus over prophets, angels, Moses and the high priests of the Old Testament. Mosaic of an angel from the Chora Monastery, Istanbul, from the first quarter of the 14th century.

division between soul and spirit – between being animal and being human. It separates longings from motives – knowing the difference between our heart and our mind.

Nothing is hidden from God's scrutiny. One day we will be forced to meet his gaze. Our actions and attitudes will be laid bare. His judgment of us will be completely penetrating and absolutely unavoidable. We will have to face God naked and undisguised – as we really are.

Jesus the great high priest
(4:14 – 5:10)

In the days of the tabernacle and temple, the Jews had a high priest. The high priest was a human being like themselves, and knew the temptations of everyday life. In this way he was able to be sympathetic to his people.

Once a year, on the Day of Atonement, the high priest offered a sacrifice for his own sins. He was then allowed through the tabernacle curtain into the Most Holy Place, to offer sacrifices on behalf of everyone else.

Now Christians have a high priest, Jesus Christ, who has passed through the heavens. He had no sins of his own for which to make sacrifice. Instead, he offered himself as the perfect sacrifice for the sins of the whole world.

Encouragement to grow in faith
(5:11 – 6:20)

Christians can so easily get stuck in spiritual babyhood. The author finds his readers are slow learners – ignorant and lazy. He encourages them to grow up to maturity. He is concerned that they may wilfully reject what Christ has done for them – and where can they turn then? They will be like fields of thistles – fit only to be burned.

But the readers of this letter aren't in this state yet. They must realize God hasn't abandoned them. He is committed to bringing them through their suffering. He won't ever let them down. This is their sure anchor of hope.

Christ is a high priest like Melchizedek
(7:1–28)

The writer has already said several times that Jesus Christ is a high priest 'in the order of Melchizedek'.

Now Jesus has become a priest like Melchizedek. He hasn't inherited his priesthood by descent from Aaron. Like Melchizedek, he is a priest straight from God. Jesus lives for ever and his work is complete. Through him there is a perfect bridge between human beings and God. As the writer says, 'Such a high priest meets our need' (7:26). How interesting that the offering of Jesus is celebrated in bread and wine – the very same gifts that Melchizedek brought to Abraham.

Christ establishes a new covenant
(8:1 – 9:28)

Christ is our high priest, not on earth but in heaven. He has taken humankind into the presence of God in a way that could never be done in an earthly tabernacle or temple. The old ritual of sacrificing innocent animals – pouring their blood on the altar and sprinkling the people – is now a thing of the past.

The old covenant of law and sacrifice had failed and needed replacing. Now the perfect priesthood and sacrifice of Jesus has made a new and permanent peace between God and human beings. Jesus has achieved the real reconciliation, of which the old covenant was just a shadow.

The death of Christ was the perfect sacrifice. It superseded the animal offerings of the tabernacle and temple, which had to be constantly repeated. It was the complete offering of a human life to do God's will, and provided humanity with the means of receiving God's forgiveness. *The Crucifixion of Our Lord*, a 15th-century Russian icon from the Cathedral of St Sophia.

The old covenant was based on keeping the law. It failed because of human disobedience. The new covenant is based on grace – God's free forgiveness. God has accepted the sacrifice of Jesus to atone for all sin. Now we can obey God out of love – because his law is in our hearts, not in a book or on tablets of stone.

Christ is the perfect sacrifice
(10:1–18)

We feel the depressing limitations of Jewish sacrifices. They were given so that sin could be paid for with a life – by shedding the blood of an animal. But they didn't work because they did nothing to change the heart of the sinner.

The prophets knew that God hated sacrifices which didn't come from the heart or lead to a changed life. The writer of Psalm 40 realized that God was looking for a *spiritual* sacrifice: the complete offering of a human life to do his will. This is exactly what Jesus did – perfectly, completely and once for all. After his death on the cross, there was no need for any further sacrifice for sin.

Melchizedek

Melchizedek was the priest of Salem (later Jerusalem) who ministered to Abraham (Genesis 14:17–20). He met him on his way home from battle with the Canaanites, offered him bread and wine and accepted a tithe of his plunder. So he showed God's care for Abraham and prayed God's blessing upon him. After this perfect priestly act, he disappeared!

Later in Israel's history came the priesthood of Aaron. Aaron was Moses' brother and he was followed by his sons. This priesthood was bound by the law

The priest Melchizedek, who welcomed Abraham, did not inherit his priesthood by descent. He was appointed directly by God. Melchizedek, priest of Salem, is seen here offering bread and wine in a detail from the Verdun Altar (AD 1181) by Nicholas of Verdun. Champlevé enamel on gilded copper.

and spoiled by disobedience. Aaron and his sons performed religious rituals, but their sacrifices never completely dealt with sin, and had to be for ever repeated.

Encouragement to enter this great salvation

A call to persevere

(10:19–39)

The writer urges his readers to digest and apply this teaching. Jesus has enabled us to come close to God – heart to heart and life to life. So let's do it! And let's live this heart love for God – together.

It's unthinkable to treat this salvation lightly – as though the sacrifice of Jesus is just a mildly interesting event. When we think of how God punished the breach of the old covenant, what hope is there for us if we lightly discard the new? We invite God's fury with such an insult.

Now is the time for Christians to recover their first enthusiasm, to bear the present suffering and be sure of future glory. It won't be long!

The heroes of the faith

(11:1–40)

The writer gives a team-talk on faith.

Faith is trusting God. Faith is believing that God made the world. Faith is Abel giving his best animal for a sacrifice. Faith is Noah building an ark, because he believed judgment was about to fall as a flood. Faith is Abraham, Isaac and Jacob, living as wandering strangers in the land God had promised them… And so the list goes on.

None of these people saw the fulfilment of God's plan – but they all lived in the light of it. At the end of his life, the only land Abraham owned was his wife's grave; and yet he believed God was using him to build a city – a new community to transform the world.

Jesus – our goal

(12:1–3)

The heroes of the faith inspire us to new efforts. Like spectators, they cheer us on to fresh commitment. We want to throw off our sins, see suffering in its true perspective and run the Christian race with joy. But the ultimate inspiration is Jesus. He's been there – done it – triumphed!

The purpose of discipline

(12:4–13)

The Christian life is hard. It's hard being tempted. It's hard living for God in a hostile world. It's hard when other people seem to be getting on perfectly well without God.

But look at it this way. God is raising us as his children – and he want us to be the best. He allows us to go through some tough experiences, to get us spiritually fit and strong. It's a sign that he cares – that he wants us to be holy. Like him.

Living in sight of heaven

(12:14–29)

The writer gives examples of Christian behaviour. Be forgiving, pure, harmonious – and serious about God.

What is heaven like? Is it ominous and scary, like Mount Sinai? No! Heaven is like a perfect Jerusalem – teeming with life, justice and joy. Don't miss this amazing offer!

Concluding encouragements and greetings

The writer ends his letter with some excellent advice *(13:1–25)*. Love for one another as brothers and sisters, hospitality, sympathy, purity, faithfulness and contentment are the marks of Jesus. The Lord is always present to strengthen us. And let us not be ashamed to share his suffering – and offer him our sacrifices of good deeds.

JAMES

The letter of James seems to be written to Jewish Christians who are living in an angry society – a society which is divided by greed and jealousy.

James' writing is more like a series of sayings than a flowing letter. Something about his practical advice reminds us of the book of Proverbs. And there are many similarities to the Sermon on the Mount.

Outline

Greetings (1:1)

Endure trials – they lead to maturity (1:2–18)

Put God's word into action (1:19 – 2:26)

Controlling the tongue (3:1–12)

Genuine wisdom (3:13–18)

Warring world, gracious God (4:1–12)

Carry on regardless? (4:13 – 5:6)

Patience, prayer and healing (5:7–20)

INTRODUCTION

Who is James?

It is thought that this letter was written by James, the brother of Jesus. He is a much-respected leader of the church in Jerusalem. It is possible that he didn't write this material as a letter, but that someone collected his sayings after his death. James was martyred on the orders of the Roman procurator Albinus in AD 62.

The letter isn't mentioned in the early years of the church's history. Then Origen notes it in AD 253 and it is included in the New Testament at the Council of Rome in AD 382.

Two Jameses!

There are two men called James who are leading figures in the New Testament. One is James the son of Zebedee. He is the fisherman who, with his brother John, is called by Jesus to be a disciple. The other is James the brother of Jesus, who is mentioned in Mark 6:3. It is this James who is thought to be the author of this letter.

We know from the Gospels that Jesus' brothers don't believe in him during his lifetime. They come to faith after his resurrection. By the time of the Council of Jerusalem, James is the leader of the church in Jerusalem (Acts 15:13). He is sometimes called 'James the Just'. Jude may be another of Jesus' brothers who has a letter in the New Testament.

A gulf between the rich and poor

In Jewish society at this time there is a gulf between rich and poor. The Sadducees (a group of upper-class priests) are very wealthy. They make money from trade and farming. They welcome the Roman government in Judea, because it makes a stable environment for their businesses.

Some other groups in the same society are very poor – including some of the priests. Widows and orphans are particularly neglected – and some labourers are denied a fair wage.

This bitter division will flare into the Jewish revolt in AD 66. The anger among the poor is as much against the Sadducees as it is against the Romans. The poorer priests will side with the Zealots – the nationalists who want to throw the Romans out of Palestine.

But James is not a hot-headed revolutionary. It is the word of God which will change the world – not violence, bloodshed and vengeance.

The wisdom that comes from heaven is first of all pure; then peace-loving, considerate, submissive, full of mercy and good fruit, impartial and sincere. Peacemakers who sow in peace raise a harvest of righteousness (3:17–18).

James teaches that the rich must not be proud or greedy. He may be speaking of rich Jews or rich Christians. They will show their true religion by the way they care for the poor:

Religion that God our Father accepts as pure and faultless is this: to look after orphans and widows in their distress and to keep oneself from being polluted by the world (1:27).

He is severe with those who put their trust in wealth instead of in God:

Now listen, you who say, 'Today or tomorrow we will go to this or that city, spend a year there, carry on business and make money.' Why, you do not even know what will happen tomorrow. What is your life? You are a mist that appears for a little while and then vanishes. Instead you ought to say, 'If it is the Lord's will, we will live and do this or that' (4:13–15).

James challenges those who have grown rich by exploiting the poor. He tells them their wealth will rot – and so will they!

Come now, you rich people, weep and wail for the miseries that are coming to you. Your riches have rotted, and your clothes are moth-eaten. Your gold and silver have rusted... You have laid up treasure for the last days. Listen! The wages of the labourers who mowed your fields, which you kept back by fraud, cry out, and the cries of the harvesters have reached the ears of the Lord of hosts. You have lived on the earth in luxury and in pleasure; you have fattened your hearts on a day of slaughter. You have condemned and murdered the righteous one, who does not resist you (5:1–6).

James teaches that God is the judge. Those who are oppressed should put their trust in God, rather than planning murder. God will put everything right in his own good time:

Your anger does not produce God's righteousness (1:20).

It is far better to make peace than to pick quarrels: 'If you commit murder, you have become a lawbreaker' (2:11), but, 'Mercy triumphs over judgment' (2:13).

James is very blunt about our duty to the poor. In this he is much more radical than Paul. Paul's advice to people is to let Christ transform their relationships. This can leave the rich with their money and the poor with their hunger. But James says faith must be practical. The rich must look after the poor!

Favouritism

James points out the way we favour the rich. He calls it 'favouritism' (2:1). If someone looks wealthy, we treat that person politely, giving special privileges. If someone looks poor, we treat that person as inferior. James says we are wrong.

The poor are dear to God. They are the neighbours we should love as ourselves.

Double-mindedness

James teaches that it is 'double-minded' to claim faith in God and then rely on money; to trust God but find our real security in what the world has to offer. It is time to defy the devil, to stop striving for our own way and to humble ourselves before God (4:7–10).

Faith and works

The letter of James has been important to Roman Catholics. Here they have found encouragement for the practice of making confession (5:16) and anointing the sick and dying (5:14).

It has not been such a popular book with Protestants. James doesn't say anything about us being saved through faith in what Jesus did for us on the cross. For James, true faith will show itself in good works. Luther, writing in 1522, says James has 'many a good saying', but as far as salvation is concerned, it is 'a right Epistle of straw'! In fact, James applies the gospel principles in very practical, down-to-earth ways. Jesus would be proud of him!

DISCOVERING JAMES

Greetings

(1:1)

James introduces himself as a Christian and a Jew. By saying he is a servant or slave of God, he is claiming to be a church leader. He also speaks of Jesus as Lord (the name of God) and Christ (the Jewish Messiah).

James writes to the 'twelve tribes in the Dispersion'. The Jewish people had been scattered or 'dispersed' first by conquest and deportation and then by trade and business. Now the true Israel, the Christian church, is spread throughout the world by persecution and mission.

Endure trials – they lead to maturity

(1:2–18)

James knows that his Christian brothers and sisters have many troubles. They are tempted and persecuted. But James urges them to welcome their trials joyfully, as tests which will strengthen them. If they treat these attacks as spiritual exercises, they will grow strong and become fully fit in their faith.

James teaches that the Christian way to become wise is to ask God. This is very different from the idea of gaining knowledge through myths and secrets. God gives to anyone who asks – and he does so generously and immediately.

But James urges his readers to ask with firm faith, and not be tossed around by doubt and disbelief.

Christians can take pride in the value God gives them. God lifts up the humble and poor and brings down the proud and rich. Those who are rich will wither in their wealth like a flower in scorching heat.

James continues to think about temptation. There is great happiness to be found in resisting it, because God gives the reward of eternal life. Temptation doesn't come from God, but from our human desires. They seduce and ensnare us in sin which leads to spiritual death.

James says that everything that is good comes from God. God is the origin of good, like a Father of light. His light shines out in the truth of the gospel, which is bringing to life a harvest of believers. Christians are the 'firstfruits' – the first and finest of the crop, presented to God as the start of the new creation.

Put God's word into action

(1:19 – 2:26)

James gives some examples of Christian self-control. A Christian should be much more ready to listen than to speak, and slow to get angry. If we are believers, then we have work to do: clearing out the weeds of wickedness from the ground of our lives and planting the life-giving seed of God's truth.

God's word is active. When we hear it, we must act accordingly. If we don't, it's like looking in a mirror without washing our face or tidying our hair. A mirror shows us what we need to do. When we look into God's word we see truth which must be done; but we only realize God's truth when we do it.

James says that true religion is seen in action; for example, in the way we speak. If we insult, lie and blaspheme, it's clear God has little place in our lives. But if we live a pure life and help people in trouble, we are reflecting the holiness and love of God.

James gives another example of truth in action. Do we, as Christians, give glory to Jesus Christ, or do we worship the wealthy person who walks into our church? And how do we treat a poor person – with contempt, or respect? If we don't obey God's key commandment, to 'love your neighbour as yourself', we break his law just as much as if we murder or commit adultery.

James believes God's word is to be done. Faith can

James points out that the person who looks in a mirror and immediately forgets what he has seen is a picture of someone who hears God's word, but does not obey it.

only be seen when it is turned into action. Faith which is restricted to holy thoughts and good wishes is worse than useless – it is dead. It's not enough to say, 'I believe in God,' because any demon can say the same. The Christian difference is to clothe the naked, feed the hungry and shelter the homeless. We must not merely tell the needy to look after themselves.

The greatest example of faith is Abraham. It is said of him that he 'believed God' and that was enough for him to be counted as right with God (Genesis 15:6). But James points out that Abraham also showed his faith in action: for example, by preparing to offer his son Isaac as a sacrifice. The prostitute Rahab is another example: she showed her faith in God in a practical way. It is impossible to separate faith and works, belief and behaviour. It's like trying to prove the presence of life without a body to show it.

Controlling the tongue
(3:1–12)

James warns his readers to think twice before becoming teachers. A Christian teacher must be both wise and genuine, and this will be proved by self-control.

For example, the things we say can cause immense damage. Just as a boat is steered by a small rudder, so the tongue can change a whole life and influence the course of history. But who is able to control it? James believes the tongue is an endless source of evil: the means by which cruelty, rage and lies spring from a wicked and devious heart. But Christians should be a source of pure speech: praise, truth, wisdom and encouragement. Like Jesus before him, James uses fruit trees as an example (Matthew 7:16–18): pure words can only be the fruit of pure hearts.

Genuine wisdom
(3:13–18)

Those who think they would make good teachers must show goodness and humility in their behaviour. True wisdom isn't self-centred, bombastic and proud. Those qualities come from the devil. But God gives genuine wisdom, which is selfless, gentle and peaceable.

Warring world, gracious God
(4:1–12)

James points out that all human conflicts start with base desires and jealousies. If we want something, the right way to get it is to ask God; but he will search our motives. Greedy grabbing and God's gracious giving are opposites.

James urges his readers to give themselves to God. With God's help we can defy the devil and receive purity and integrity in heart and life. God himself will give us all we need in status and dignity.

It is not for us to pass judgment on anyone else: that's God's business, who will also be judging us.

Carry on regardless?
(4:13 – 5:6)

James has a warning for people who plan their life without God. They assume they can travel and trade for another year, when in fact they can't be sure of another day. All our plans should be subject to God's will. His priority is that we should do the right thing in the present moment, while we have the opportunity.

James warns wealthy people that they are storing up evidence of their selfishness and greed. They have withheld wages and brought death to innocent people. Their riches will soon rot, but their punishment will be eternal.

Patience, prayer and healing
(5:7–20)

James urges his readers to be patient. God is the judge – and he is very near. We should be like Job – trusting that God will rescue us, however hard our situation.

James wants us to bring every circumstance to God. There is no barrier between earth and heaven. God hears our praises and prayers. We can ask him for healing. We can live without pretending to each other. And (like Elijah in the old days) our faithful prayer can change the world (5:17–18).

1 PETER

Peter writes to Christians who live in a wide area of Asia Minor. Today this is Turkey. His readers are being persecuted because of their faith.

Living for Jesus makes Christians different from their neighbours. They feel like outsiders or strangers in a society which used to accept them. Peter encourages his readers to carry on living this different life, even though it means suffering. He reminds them that Jesus suffered too.

Outline

Address and greeting (1:1–2)

Praise for new life and hope in Christ (1:3–12)

God calls his people to be holy (1:13 – 2:12)

Christian relationships (2:13 – 3:7)

Suffering for doing good (3:8–22)

Holy living (4:1–11)

Suffering for being a Christian (4:12–19)

A special word for the elders (5:1–4)

Christian attitudes (5:5–11)

Final greetings (5:12–14)

INTRODUCTION

Peter the fisherman

This letter is headed by the name of Peter, the fisherman whom Jesus called to be his disciple and chief apostle. If Peter wrote it, then he must have done so before his death in the AD 60s. If we think the Greek is rather good for a Galilean fisherman, it's always possible that Silas helped with the writing (5:12).

Peter addresses his letter to the Christians living in Asia Minor, in areas to the north of the Taurus mountains. He writes to them as though they have a strong Jewish background, and encourages them to stand firm in times of suffering and persecution.

We don't know of any particular persecution by the authorities in Asia Minor during Peter's lifetime. We have a letter from a governor called Pliny, who describes the persecution of Christians in Bithynia – but this is much later, around AD 110. Peter can't have written as late as this. He writes from a place he calls 'Babylon', which in Revelation is a coded reference to Rome (Revelation 16:19), but makes no mention of the persecution of Christians in Rome under Emperor Nero (AD 64) and shows no awareness of Paul's martyrdom the following year. However, he realizes that Christians will suffer for their faith and that persecution will spread to the whole church.

Peter has Mark with him, whom he describes as his son (5:13). It is Mark who wrote the Gospel which bears his name, and it is thought that he included many of Peter's memories of Jesus. This letter, too, is full of the spirit of Jesus, the reality and purpose of his sufferings and the certainty of his return.

DISCOVERING 1 PETER

Address and greeting
(1:1–2)

Peter writes to Christians as 'strangers in the world'. This is a familiar idea to Jews who live by God's law in the midst of a pagan society. Now Christians have the sense that this world is not their home. Their real home is in heaven.

Peter mentions all three members of the Trinity: God the Father, the Spirit and Jesus Christ. It is the Father who has chosen his people (his 'elect'); Jesus who is their Lord and Saviour; and the Spirit who is at work in their lives to make them holy.

Praise for new life and hope in Christ
(1:3–12)

Peter blesses and thanks God for the new life and hope he has given through Jesus Christ.

God has chosen his children. They have been 'born again' – this time into God's family. God the Father raised Jesus from death, to give everlasting life to all who believe in him. This is a life of faith, because they can't actually see Jesus; but they can look forward to their salvation – their complete rescue, cleansing and healing in the future. This earthly life is tough, and its wealth doesn't last. For Christians there is also the pain that comes through taking a stand for Jesus, and perhaps being abused or persecuted. But, with the eyes of faith, they can see beyond these short-term sufferings, and live with joyful hope.

The prophets of Old Testament times predicted the suffering and glory of Christ. Isaiah described a 'suffering servant' of God (Isaiah 53); Daniel had a vision of a 'Son of man' entering God's glorious presence (Daniel 7:13); and Micah spoke of God's shepherd king who would be born in Bethlehem (Micah 5:2–5). Now Christians are in a far more privileged position than the old prophets, because they have seen all these prophecies fulfilled in Jesus Christ.

God calls his people to be holy
(1:13 – 2:12)

God has always called his people to be holy. Their way of life is to reflect his holiness.

The people of Israel were to be different from the other nations – living pure lives, guided by God's laws. Now Christians have a further reason to be holy – that Jesus gave his life for their sins. They have been born into a new way of life – a new creation, where evil has no place. Of course, it is still *possible* for Christians to sin, but it is no longer fitting or appropriate for them to do so. They have the imperishable seed of God's word within them, so they can grow up into a pure and eternal life.

THE LIVING STONE AND A CHOSEN PEOPLE

Peter shows how the Old Testament ideas of temple, priest and sacrifice all have new meanings in Jesus (2:4–12).

God is building a spiritual temple, with Christ as the cornerstone – and Christians as stones. He is making a new 'chosen people' – not out of a particular family or race, but out of those who live in the light of Christ.

Now all Christians are part of the spiritual temple and priesthood, offering prayers and spiritual sacrifices. Sacrifices aren't dead animals any more, but the committed lives of Christians who love and serve the Lord.

No wonder Christians feel strange. They are living as God's people in a pagan world. Peter encourages them to live in such a way that the only thing they can be accused of is being good!

Christian relationships
(2:13 – 3:7)

SUBMISSION TO RULERS AND MASTERS

The keynote of Christian behaviour is to 'submit' – that is, to put others first (2:13–25). God, human rulers and fellow Christians are all to be honoured in their different ways.

Slaves are to honour their masters – even those who ill-treat them. Peter says that Jesus himself lived this way, and endured suffering he didn't deserve.

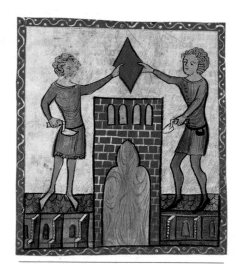

Peter describes Jesus as a living stone. He quotes Psalm 118 which talks of the stone that the builders rejected becoming the chief stone of the building. A book illumination from Westphalia (c. 1350).

WIVES AND HUSBANDS

Wives should honour their husbands (3:1–7). If a husband is not a Christian, he may be won over by his wife's goodness and inner beauty.

Peter is himself showing respect for women by writing to them. In his day women are treated as inferior to men and have no education. Now Peter assures them of their dignity and freedom through Jesus Christ. Their worth doesn't depend on beauty or fashion, but on God's love for them. They are free, not to defy or despise their husbands, but to respect and honour them.

And Christian husbands are also to honour their wives. This is a revolutionary idea for Jews, Greeks and Romans – because all three cultures keep women down. Now Peter says that husbands and wives are partners and fellow heirs of heaven. As husbands care for and support their wives, they will find their physical and spiritual life together is enriched.

Suffering for doing good
(3:8–22)

Christians must put one another first, and form a caring and forgiving community. Their lives must show that Jesus is their Lord – and they must be ready to explain this to anyone who asks.

If Christians find they are ill-treated for doing good, then they must realize that this happened to Jesus too. Peter recalls the suffering servant in Isaiah (Isaiah 53), who accepted punishment on behalf of others. This is how it was for Jesus – and how it will be for Christians.

Peter teaches that Jesus was put to death in his body, but made alive by God's Spirit. When he died, Jesus went and preached to 'the spirits in prison'. It is difficult to know who these spirits are. One early scholar (Clement of Alexandria) thought that Jesus went down to Sheol (the place of departed spirits) to share the gospel with people who never had a chance to understand it. Peter particularly mentions the people in the days of Noah, who were destroyed in the flood. Another idea is that Jesus went to preach to the rebellious angels who are mentioned in Genesis 6:1–4. Jewish writers were very interested in this episode, and developed it with all sorts of fantastic details.

Before Jesus came, the world was gripped by spiritual wickedness. This sprang from the rebellion of Satan and his angels. But Jesus has defeated the powers of evil through his death on the cross. Now Christians share in this victory, and know they are 'saved' from sin and death – just as Noah and his family were kept safe in the ark.

Baptism is a sign of this salvation. It is more than a physical wash. It is a sign of passing safely through death to new life in Christ. Some people think that this whole letter may have been used as a sermon preached at baptisms.

Peter gives instructions to the elders of the church.
They are to care for God's people like shepherds,
willingly serving the flocks that are entrusted to them.

Holy living
(4:1–11)

Christians are to live pure lives in their pagan communities. Peter gives practical examples of the Christian difference. Orgies, drunkenness and idol-worship are things of the past. They are replaced by clear minds and self-controlled lives – lives which are devoted to the love and service of God.

Suffering for being a Christian
(4:12–19)

Peter teaches his Christian friends that suffering is a normal experience. To be a Christian is to be 'like Christ' – and that includes being persecuted for doing good. He encourages them to take suffering as a sign that they're on the right track.

A special word for the elders
(5:1–4)

Peter has advice for the church leaders among his readers. They must remember that Jesus is the chief shepherd, and their service of people should reflect his care. Their temptations will be to please themselves, or to want power or money – so they must remember that their real reward is in heaven.

Christian attitudes
(5:5–11)

Young men will be tempted to be proud or ambitious. Peter advises them to respect those who are older. If God wants them to be leaders, then he will choose them in his own good time. The answer to every worry is to trust God, who knows and cares about everyone and everything. It is the devil who tries to introduce envy and fear – and he is to be resisted by faith.

Body and spirit

Some Greek thinkers are 'Dualists'. They believe there is a battle between Good and Evil in the universe which neither can win. Humans are caught in this struggle, because their 'bodies' are evil but their 'spirits' are good! 'Dualism' believes there is a spark of divine goodness in every human, which needs to escape from the physical body and make its way to union with God.

By contrast, Jewish thinkers believe 'body' and 'spirit' belong together. God created the material, physical world, 'and it was very good' (Genesis 1:31). Human beings are body-spirits who have fallen into sin, but God can redeem.

When Jesus came, he took on human nature, including a physical body. For Christians, this means that physical things (for example, human bodies) aren't condemned to destruction, but will have their place in God's new creation.

Peter sees the resurrection of Jesus as the victory of good over evil. By defeating the power of sin and death, Jesus is the pioneer of God's new creation. Those who trust Christ have 'an inheritance that is imperishable, undefiled and unfading' awaiting them in heaven (1:4).

The devil is a prowler, who seeks to cause doubt and confusion (Luke 22:31). Peter warns his readers to be on their guard. All Christians experience temptation and trial, but Peter says these sufferings are brief and insignificant compared with the glory we will share with Christ in his resurrection life.

Final greetings
(5:12–14)

Peter closes his letter with some personal remarks. Silvanus has acted as his secretary, but now perhaps Peter takes the pen to write a few words himself. Silvanus is called Silas in the Acts of the Apostles. He helped Paul take the gospel to Philippi and Thessalonica (Acts 16 and 17).

Peter sends greetings from the 'sister church in Babylon'. This is probably his way of referring to the Christian fellowship in Rome. He also mentions Mark, whom he calls his son. John Mark once accompanied Paul and Barnabas on a missionary journey, but disappointed them by turning back. It was not until some years later that Paul could describe Mark as 'useful' (Acts 15:37–39; 2 Timothy 4:11). Now Mark has become a colleague of Peter, and will record Peter's memories of Jesus in his Gospel.

Peter ends his letter with words of unity, love and peace, which are the marks of Christ's presence in his church.

2 PETER AND JUDE

The letters of 2 Peter and Jude go together, and even overlap. Most of Jude appears in 2 Peter.

These letters come late in the Bible and are written towards the end of New Testament times. We don't know who they are sent to, or the original situation. But the readers seem to have received a previous letter from Peter – and know of Paul's letters.

2 Peter is in a different style from 1 Peter, and may be written by one of his followers. It is quite common for the 'testimony' or teaching of a great leader to be written down after his death. There have often been doubts as to whether it should be included in the Bible.

Jude is the brother of Jesus who is mentioned in Mark 6:3. His older brother, James, is the leader of the church in Jerusalem. No one knows for certain whether this letter comes from his pen, or whether it is merely written in his name. A letter can be written in someone's name if it comes from his circle of followers and upholds his original teaching. It's a way of saying 'this is true'.

Outline

Christian growth and assurance (2 Peter 1:1–21)

False teachers (2 Peter 2:1–22)

The Day of the Lord (2 Peter 3:1–18)

A letter from Jude (Jude 1–2)

The danger of false teachers (Jude 3–4)

Old Testament examples (Jude 5–19)

In conclusion (Jude 20–24)

INTRODUCTION

False teachers

Both Jude and 2 Peter are concerned with the harm being done by false teachers in the church. These teachers are claiming new insights and experiences which, they say, put them on a higher spiritual level than other people – and allow them to disregard God's law.

In years to come there will be a group called 'Gnostics' ('those with knowledge') who will claim to have secret information on the way to heaven. Armed with these spiritual mysteries, their moral behaviour won't matter any more, and they can behave as permissively as they like.

Jude calls such people 'unspiritual' – merely following 'natural instincts' (v. 19). There is nothing special about them at all – and certainly nothing to distinguish them in the spiritual realm. They are simply excusing themselves from keeping God's law.

Jude's letter doesn't tell us exactly what the false teachers believe, but he states, 'they deny Jesus Christ our only Saviour and Lord' (v. 4). They may think they are so enlightened that they don't need to keep God's law, but they are quite wrong. God's standards haven't changed. Cain's murder of his brother is still viewed as a sin; so are Sodom's sexual perversion, Balaam's opposition to God and Korah's rebellion. Any teacher who says otherwise is an impostor!

2 Peter also deals with the claim that Jesus will *not* now return again. The first generation of apostles is dying out, along with many who believed that they would live to see Jesus return. The idea of Jesus' 'second coming' is being treated by some as a mistake.

The false teachers are saying that there is no need for Jesus to come back. It is now possible for believers to work out their own mystical path to heaven. But the writer of 2 Peter teaches that Jesus *will* return. He explains that God's timescale is very different from ours. If there is a delay, it's to allow time for more people to repent (3:8–9).

The basic truths of the gospel

Peter knows that his death is near, and wants to remind his readers of the very basic truths of the gospel. He particularly wants to insist that Jesus isn't a myth. Jesus is truly the Son of God, as Peter himself realized when he saw his glory revealed on the Mount of Transfiguration (1:12–18).

Jude and 2 Peter show us how Christian writers took up their pens to defend the truth of the gospel at the end of the apostolic age. It is good to have these writings as part of our Bible. They show how the church guards the gospel and confronts the enemies of Christ.

There are many doubts as to whether Peter the apostle or Jude the brother of Jesus actually wrote these letters. But the fact that they were written and sent in their names shows how highly the early Christians valued the gospel truth. They continue to anchor their belief and behaviour in the life and death, resurrection and glory, of Jesus of Nazareth, the Son of God.

DISCOVERING 2 PETER AND JUDE

Christian growth and assurance

(2 Peter 1:1–21)

Peter introduces himself as 'Simeon' Peter – the fisherman whom Jesus called to become his disciple and apostle. He seems to be writing to Gentile Christians, and is full of joy that Jews and Gentiles are now united in Christ (1:1).

Peter wants to remind his readers of God's promises of forgiveness and eternal life in Christ. He also wants to encourage their growth in holiness, understanding, fellowship and service.

God has provided all the resources needed to develop Christian life and holiness (1:3). But we must play our part. To our faith, we must add goodness, knowledge, self-control, endurance, godliness, mutual affection and love (1:5–7). These qualities don't make us right with God (that happened when we first believed), but they produce the fruit of our relationship with him (1:8). We commit ourselves to follow Jesus, become like him and finally enter his eternal kingdom (1:10, 11).

Peter knows that he will soon die. He wants to ensure

The writers of Jude and 2 Peter

Jude's letter is written in good Greek, but with a very Jewish feel to it. He mentions many Old Testament stories, and quotes from the apocryphal book of 1 Enoch when he talks of God's judgment of false teachers.

Peter's letter has more of a Greek atmosphere, but with some vivid echoes of Peter himself. Peter spent his last years in Rome, sharing the leadership of the church there. After Peter's death in AD 64–65, the church in Rome kept in touch with other churches, and wrote letters of teaching and encouragement. It could be that 2 Peter is one such letter. The name of Peter would be an obvious choice to endorse the truth of the contents.

that his readers will remember his teaching (1:12–15). It is sound teaching, based on the things he witnessed. Peter was one of those who saw Jesus revealed as the Son of God, transfigured with heavenly glory on the mountain (Mark 9:1–8). They heard the voice of God the Father acknowledging his Son, in words which echoed a coronation psalm (Psalm 2:7).

The coming of Christ was predicted by the prophets. Their message had been like a lamp shining in darkness, or the Morning Star (Venus) heralding the dawn (1:19). They didn't invent their predictions, but were inspired by God's Spirit – like sailing boats responding to the wind (1:21).

False teachers

(2 Peter 2:1–22)

Peter warns his readers that there are false prophets at work in the church. They are dangerous because they confuse the truth of Christ with lies. They encourage Christians to be 'free' by behaving in impure ways. And they charge money for their teaching (2:1–3).

Peter says that God judges such wickedness. In the past, he cast rebellious angels out of heaven (2:4), punished the ancient world with a flood and destroyed Sodom and Gomorrah with fire (2:4–6). But he was also merciful to those who were righteous, and rescued Lot who was trapped in a godless society (2:7). Peter shows how God separated good from bad. The false teachers need to watch out (2:9, 10).

Peter denounces the false teachers. They are subhuman, arrogant, ignorant, decadent, dissipated and seductive (2:10–14). Like the prophet Balaam, they have sold themselves for money (2:15–16; Numbers 22:31–35). They lack substance – like springs without water or mist in a gale (2:17). They have returned to the sin from which Christ so recently delivered them: 'The sow is washed only to wallow in the mud' (2:17–22).

The Day of the Lord

(2 Peter 3:1–18)

Peter has written a previous letter. This may be the letter we know as 1 Peter, or another letter that has been lost (3:1).

Peter now turns to the question: Will Jesus return? Some laugh at the idea, believing Jesus will never keep his promise (3:2–4). But Peter puts a different view. The God who once judged the world with a flood, is now preparing to judge it by fire (3:5–7). Humans are impatient at God's delay, but their timescale is not the same as God's. If God is slow in bringing the world to an end, it is only because he is allowing more time for people to repent. When he finally acts, he will do so as swiftly and unexpectedly as a thief (3:8–10). Burglary is an image which Jesus also uses to describe the suddenness of his return (Matthew 24:43).

The letters of Peter and Jude were written against a background of persecution of the church by the Roman authorities. This illustration, from a 10th-century German manuscript, shows Emperor Nero on his throne, the beheading of John the Baptist, the fall of Simon Magus and the martyrdom of Peter.

A letter from Jude
(Jude 1–2)

Jude greets his readers as fellow Christians, and is full of generosity and goodwill towards them. He introduces himself as a servant of Jesus Christ, and brother of James. This is not James the fisherman disciple (whose brother was John), but James the brother of Jesus himself.

Jude ('Judas') and James are mentioned in the gospels, along with the other brothers and sisters of Jesus (Mark 6:3). They became believers after Jesus' resurrection, and James became the leader of the Jerusalem church (Acts 15:13–21).

We don't know who Jude is writing to, but he deals with

Peter tells his readers that heaven and earth will be dissolved, and everything exposed to the judgment of God (3:10). Far from causing fear, this should encourage us to holiness. Beyond the destruction of this world lie the heaven and earth of God's new creation (Revelation 21:1).

Peter closes his letter by urging his readers not to be passive believers. While they await the Lord's return, there is much to do in building holy lives and right relationships.

Paul has also written about the delay in the Lord's coming, although his letters have sometimes been misunderstood (3:15, 16). If we treat our salvation carelessly, we will lapse back into immorality, confusion and guilt (3:17). If we aim wholeheartedly for Christian growth, we will develop the love, understanding and likeness of Jesus Christ (3:18).

a particular problem. The church is in danger from false teachers, who are misleading Christians, undermining their commitment to holy living and splitting the fellowship.

Jude uses some illustrations from Jewish literature: the Assumption of Moses (v. 9) and the Book of Enoch (v. 15). These indicate that he is writing to Jewish Christians. It is possible, however, that this letter is not by Jude at all, but by a writer who uses Jude's name to endorse his message. But why choose Jude rather than someone more famous?

The danger of false teachers
(Jude 3–4)

Jude has been meaning to write a longer letter, but now writes a short and urgent warning instead. False teachers have infiltrated the church. They are teaching a deviant

Free – to sin?

False prophets preach a tempting message. They tell Christians there is no need to live a clean life, because God will forgive them anyway. So, carry on sinning! Why not?

Paul deals with this issue in his letter to the Romans. He points out that people who sin are slaves to sin. Christians have been liberated from sin, and are now free to do good (Romans 6:1–2).

form of Christianity. They are giving believers permission to sin, because Christ will freely forgive them. This is a perversion of the truth and a denial of the holiness which Jesus requires (Matthew 5:48). Jude urges his readers to fight this lie, which threatens to destroy the gospel.

Old Testament examples

(Jude 5–19)

Jude gives examples of people who have strayed from the truth in the past. After the exodus, God condemned those Israelites who rebelled (v. 5). In ancient times, he similarly judged rebellious angels who, according to legend, came to earth to mate with humans (v. 6). He destroyed Sodom and Gomorrah, because of sexual immorality (v. 7; Genesis 19:5).

Jude accuses the false teachers of similar immorality, rebellion and lies. By claiming to know about heavenly realms, they slander the angels. He calls them 'dreamers',

2 Peter or Jude – which came first?

Two sections of Jude's letter also appear in 2 Peter. In Jude, verses 4–13 correspond to 2 Peter 2:1–18, and Jude's verses 17–18 are very similar to 2 Peter 3:1–3. So which is the original and which is copied?

It seems likely that Jude has written first and 2 Peter takes extracts for his longer letter. This makes more sense than Jude taking extracts from 2 Peter for a shorter work. It is possible that both are quoting from some other writing, or that Peter wants to endorse Jude's teaching while expressing it less harshly!

because they peddle fantasies (v. 8). Even Michael, the chief angel, didn't voice such misleading and fantastic speculations. Jude refers to a story from the Assumption of Moses, when Michael and the devil argue over the body of Moses. Michael simply answers Satan with words of scripture: 'The Lord rebuke you!' (Zechariah 3:2).

The false teachers are twisting God's truth. Jude likens them to three scandals of the past: Cain murdering his brother (Genesis 4:1–16); Balaam prophesying against God's people (Numbers 22–24); and Korah leading opposition to Moses (Numbers 16).

These false teachers are impostors, like hidden reefs lurking beneath the surface of Christian fellowship. They deceive, like clouds without rain, or trees without fruit or roots (v. 12). They are disruptive and shameful, like waves spewing scum, or misleading stars (v. 13).

Jude quotes a prophecy from the Book of Enoch. God and his angels will judge these false teachers. Their destruction is certain (vv. 14, 15). They may seem attractive and eloquent, but in fact they are domineering and manipulative (v. 16). The apostles have warned about such people, who claim to be spiritual, but in reality are dangerous and divisive (vv. 17, 18; 2 Timothy 3:1–9).

In conclusion

(Jude 20–24)

Jude advises his Christian readers to build themselves up in the true faith. Their resources are prayer in the power of the Holy Spirit, the security of God's love and the mercy of Jesus Christ (v. 21). They must make every effort to rescue those who are going astray, loving the sinner while hating the sin (vv. 22, 23).

Finally, Jude commends his readers to the majestic power and saving grace of God. It is this glorious God who will protect and sustain them in faith and holiness, and bring them home to his presence with great joy (v. 24). Praise him, always and for ever!

1, 2 AND 3 JOHN

John's first letter is written to Christians who are unsure of themselves. Their church members have fallen out with one another and some well-known teachers have left.

Some of the church members are claiming that they have become the perfect children of God. They say they no longer have any problem with sin. Some believe that Jesus wasn't actually human and didn't really suffer on the cross. Some maintain that they are full of love for God – but show no love at all for their brothers and sisters in the church!

The writer tackles these issues and attitudes. He tells his readers how they can be sure that God the Father is *their* Father, and that Jesus is truly their Saviour and Christ. But what if they still sin? And how should they behave towards one another?

John's 'second letter' is like a shorter version of his first letter. He writes to encourage Christians to love one another, and to warn them about the false teachers who are confusing the gospel message.

3 John is the shortest letter in the New Testament. It is from 'the elder' to a church leader named Gaius. The elder praises Gaius for the hospitality he has been giving to travelling preachers. He complains about a man called Diotrephes, who is being a nuisance, and commends someone called Demetrius.

Outline

INTRODUCTION

Who wrote these letters?

We don't know for sure who wrote 1 John. It has no name on it, but from earliest times it was believed to be written by John, the fisherman disciple and apostle of Jesus.

It is just like John not to mention his own name or draw attention to himself. But he says he is a first-hand witness of Jesus' ministry – and his way of writing is *very* similar to that in the Gospel of John.

We think of this writing as a letter – but it doesn't begin or end like one. It may in fact be a sermon or some other form of teaching.

The writer of 2 John refers to himself as 'the elder'. The church has always thought that this is the apostle John, the son of Zebedee, whom Jesus called from his fishing business to be a disciple (Mark 1:19–20). Some scholars wonder if it is another person, called 'John the Elder', who writes these letters. If so, he is obviously close to John the apostle and his teaching.

'The elder' who writes 3 John is either the apostle John, or someone who is close to him. Gaius is one of the leaders in a local church or house fellowship. This fellowship has regular links with 'the elder' and was perhaps started by him.

Why is John writing?

In writing 1 John, the author wants his readers to be sure that they are God's children. For this, they must know God as their Father and Jesus as their Saviour and Lord. John is gentle and tender in the way he writes. His readers are his spiritual children, and he wants to guide and protect them.

There is some teaching going around that God is utterly remote from this world. It claims that God is so pure and holy that he can have nothing to do with the dirty stuff of earth and its vile population of humans.

The teachers of this theory say that the physical world is bad and the spiritual world is good. They tell people how to escape from their wicked physical bodies and find the way through to the heavenly realms. Eventually they will be completely free of evil and emerge into the pure light and spiritual life of God.

In later years this teaching will be called 'Gnosticism', after the Greek word 'gnosis' which means 'knowledge'. This 'knowledge' is the inside information needed to escape from the physical body and pass through the many realms which (it was claimed) separate earth from heaven.

John argues against these ideas. It isn't true that God is utterly remote from us. It isn't true that earthly matter is bad. Jesus himself has come from God and taken an earthly body. He has lived human life 'in the flesh', but without sinning like the rest of humanity.

Some teachers are saying that Jesus was only pretending to be human. If this is so, then he didn't really live and die and rise for us. He hasn't bridged the gulf between God and humans. He hasn't saved humankind from sin and death.

In later years this teaching will be called 'Docetism', from the Greek word for 'seem'. Jesus only 'seemed' to be human. But John insists that Jesus was *fully* human. He knows, because he saw and heard and touched him! But Jesus was also, and is for ever, the perfect Son of God – the Word of life. He is the truth in person. He unites a physical body and Holy Spirit in perfect harmony.

Finally, some teachers are saying that good behaviour doesn't matter any more. There's no need to live a pure life, because we will be leaving our bodies behind us when we die. But John disagrees. He insists that our belief and our behaviour go together. If we love God then we will obey his commands. If we obey his commands then we will love our fellow Christians. What we believe in our hearts will be expressed by our lives.

DISCOVERING 1, 2 AND 3 JOHN

Introduction: 'We were there!'

John's opening words echo the beginning of John's Gospel (1 John 1:1–4).

He begins with the message of Jesus. John and his friends saw and heard and touched Jesus when they became his disciples and shared his life. They were convinced that he was none other than the 'Word' of God – the source and meaning and purpose of life.

The life of God has appeared in a human being, in a place and time, so that we can take *our* place in heaven with God for eternity.

The message of Jesus was never intended to be an exclusive secret for a select group of followers. This is good news for the whole world. Jesus showed his disciples the truth and love of God, so that they could draw others into the family of faith. The message hasn't changed – and neither has its purpose.

Walking in the light

John describes the fellowship of Christians as 'walking in the light'. Sin imprisons us in darkness, but God's presence gives us light!

God is light
(1 John 1:5–7)
How can John sum up all that he has learned about God through Jesus? He puts it as simply and powerfully as he can. God is *light* – vastly brilliant in power, majesty, beauty and holiness. Like light, God makes his presence known. Like light, his power shines out. Like light, he rescues those in darkness.

God's pure character affects the way we live. Light and darkness can have nothing to do with each other. We can't walk in the light of God and still indulge our secret and shameful sins. We must either turn to his light or hide from him.

Because Jesus has died for us, and his blood has blotted out our guilt, we are free to live a holy life. We walk in the light of God, in open friendship with all his forgiven people.

But what if we sin?

(1 John 1:8 – 2:2)

Walking in the light of God doesn't mean we're perfect. No doubt we will still sin, because our human nature is sinful. John says that if we claim we are sinless we are merely deceiving ourselves. Worse than that, we imply that God is lying when his light reveals our sins.

So what can we do when we fall into sin? John says that we can confess our sins to God and receive his forgiveness and cleansing. God will always do this for us – not because we deserve it, but because Jesus has died for our sins. God responds to the request of Jesus to give us his righteousness. This special offer is open to everyone in the world. All we have to do is turn to him.

Love is... obedience

(1 John 2:3–6)

Some people have left the church – claiming that they know more about God than everyone else, and are already living as his perfect children. So how does it feel for those who are left – the readers of this letter? How can they be sure they are right about God?

John tells his readers that they can be sure they know God if they obey his commands. This doesn't mean living to a rigid code of laws, but joyfully responding to God's will.

John isn't talking about being perfect – he has already said that we aren't. He is describing the basic direction and desire of our lives – to please God and go his way. This is what Jesus did perfectly, and we have his example to follow.

Old command – new examples

(1 John 2:7–11)

John is not inventing a new commandment when he says, 'Walk as Jesus did.' He is reminding his readers of what they already know. They are to love one another. The Old Testament law had commanded, 'Love your

neighbour as yourself' (Leviticus 19:18), and Jesus commanded his disciples, 'Love each other as I have loved you' (John 15:12).

But this *is* a new commandment because Jesus has now shown the kind of love involved. He has washed his

In his first letter, John declares that God is light, and that there is no dark side to his character. If we claim to belong to God, we should live in such a way that we also walk in that light.

disciples' feet – acting as their slave even though he is their Lord (John 13:12–15). And he has given his life on the cross – making the supreme sacrifice for everyone in the world.

Christians have a new understanding of the command to love – and a new fellowship in which to live it out. The church is the place where God's people live in his light. Whoever hates a fellow Christian is clearly still in the dark. No doubt John is referring to those members who have recently left the fellowship.

Dear everyone

(1 John 2:12–14)

John greets everyone who will be reading these words – children, fathers and young people. He writes these words like a song or chant – to attract attention and lodge in the memory.

God's 'children' can be any age. They are all those who know God's love and forgiveness through Jesus. 'Fathers' are those who are older and have a deeper understanding of the faith. They have added some years of experience to their first knowledge of God. 'Young people' are those who know the battle with the devil, and are proving that God's victory is real. They have discovered for themselves the power and protection of God's truth.

Reject the world – choose God

(1 John 2:15–17)

John urges his readers not to love the world. This sounds strange, when we know that God loves the world so much that he sent Jesus to be its Saviour (John 3:16). But there is a difference between loving the world for its values and ways and loving the world because you want to change it.

The Bible often gives the choice between loving the world and loving God. Joshua challenged the Israelites to choose between their old pagan gods and the Lord God (Joshua 24:15). Jesus gave his disciples a stark choice. He told them it is impossible to 'serve both God and Money' (Matthew 6:24).

The split

Now John explains to his readers what has happened to split their church.

False teachers have said that Jesus wasn't really the Christ. They have also put pressure on Christians to live a sinless life. But these liars have now left, and those who remain can be sure of the truth: Jesus *is* the Christ, and those who believe in him *are* God's children.

'They did not really belong'
(1 John 2:18–19)

John reminds his readers that they are living in 'the last hour'. This is a time of choice and decision – between God and the world, Christ and Satan, light and darkness. It is a time when the 'antichrist' will appear. The antichrist is a world leader or force who opposes the good purpose of God and tries to seduce the followers of Christ.

John says that 'many antichrists' have appeared already. He means the false teachers who have been undermining the church. They have tampered with the truth about Jesus and made extra rules about Christian behaviour. Worst of all, they have split the church.

These people have now left, but John says that they never truly belonged. Their departure is proof that they weren't united in the truth and love of Christ. Jesus warned his disciples that there would be such lies and betrayals in the last days (Mark 13:5, 12).

The world

When John talks of 'the world' he means human life without God. If we don't know the love and purpose of God, we devote all our time and energy to getting what we want. We are consumed by the things we strive for, lust after and boast about. But the world's possessions can't last and its achievements are short-lived. The person who lives for God has the lasting treasure of salvation, and the promise of eternal life.

Our anointing and promise
(1 John 2:20–27)

John assures his readers that they have full protection against the lies of the antichrists. The greatest lie of all is that Jesus isn't the Christ.

But Christians have 'an anointing from the Holy One'. The Holy Spirit of God has been poured out upon them. Jesus promised his disciples that the Holy Spirit would 'guide [them] into all truth' (John 16:13). John's readers can be sure that the Holy Spirit will give them the wisdom and understanding they need in the face of these subtle and dangerous lies.

'We are children of God'
(1 John 2:28 – 3:3)

And now John thinks about the way forward. He encourages his readers to 'remain' in Christ – to commit themselves day by day to his truth and life. One day Jesus will return to this earth, and we want to be able to welcome him with a clear conscience.

John reminds us of the central, wonderful fact that God loves us and has made us his children. If times are hard, it's because we live in a world that resists God. But the future is glorious. We are to share the family likeness and glory of Jesus. This exciting identity and hope encourage us to live pure lives now.

Taking after our Father
(1 John 3:4–10)

John turns again to the problem of sin. He has already explained that everyone sins, and that if we say we never sin we deceive ourselves (1:8). Now John wants to make his teaching clearer.

He begins by saying that sin is lawlessness. This is the devil's attitude, and he has infected the entire human race with his rebellion against God. We all, quite naturally, break God's law, because we take after our father the devil.

Now Jesus has come to destroy the devil's work and break his stranglehold on our lives. He restores us to life with our true Father, who is God.

When we put our trust in Christ, our old lawless attitude is a thing of the past. Jesus is sinless, and we now belong to him. Once we know the presence and power of Jesus in our lives, it becomes unthinkable that we should carry on sinning.

John is dealing with a big issue. Some people say

Christians must lead perfect lives. Others say Christians can sin and it doesn't matter. Neither is true. John says that our behaviour will take after our spiritual father – either good like God or sinful like the devil. If we belong to Christ, then God's seed (his life and likeness) is for ever planted in us, and we will become increasingly like Jesus.

The standard of loving

Now John talks about the command that Christians should love one another. The two great marks of the Christian life are loving God in obedience and loving our fellow Christians in service.

Loving our brother and our sister

(1 John 3:11–20)

It's a solemn fact that most murders take place within families. The very first murder was when Cain killed his brother Abel. And why? Because he was jealous of his brother's goodness.

In Christ, this age-old attitude is reversed. Now we are to *love* our brothers and sisters – not just our natural brothers and sisters, but also the members of our Christian family, the church. Jesus has shown us how to love by laying down his life instead of taking the lives of others.

Cain (left) and Abel bring their offerings to the Lord. Abel seeks to honour God with his gift, but Cain does not. Cain's offering is rejected and in his jealous anger he murders his brother. An 11th-century ivory.

This kind of loving is intensely practical. It means sharing what we have. It means giving to those in need. It means not just good ideas and holy thoughts, but *action*! We will show the truth by *doing* it.

John says that, when we do right, we feel comfortable with God. No doubt there are some sensitive Christians who still worry about the claims of the false teachers, or fear they haven't done enough for God. John assures them that God knows all about their concern – and overrules their fears.

Christian confidence

(1 John 3:21–24)

John wants his readers to have a confident relationship with God. If there is a barrier of sin, then it can be confessed and forgiven. After that, Christians can live in God's presence with the same assurance that children have with a loving father.

A confident relationship with God means we obey his commands and receive his blessings. If we live in God's way, we can ask him for anything – because the things we ask will be the things he wants to give. Above all, we will believe in Jesus and share his love with one another.

Testing the spirits

(1 John 4:1–6)

John warns his readers not to believe everything they hear. There are many prophets and teachers who journey from church to church – all of them claiming some special secret.

John gives a simple test for what these teachers say. If their message is that Jesus Christ has come 'in the flesh', then this is a true and balanced understanding of the gospel. Jesus is truly the Christ, and has fully entered our human nature and experience.

There are only two spirits who inspire prophets and teachers. There is the Spirit of God and the spirit of the antichrist. The antichrist is the devil who denies Jesus and opposes his work.

Which spirit will win? John assures his readers that the Holy Spirit of God within them is more powerful than the spirit of the antichrist, which is in the rebellious world.

'This is love...'

(1 John 4:7–12)

Again John turns to the theme of love. There is so much more to the Christian life than resisting error and testing spirits. The positive side is shown in the love Christians have for each other. 'Let's *do* it,' writes John, 'Let's live together in the love of God!'

Love is, first of all, something we receive from God. He has shown his love in sending Jesus to die for us. Jesus has won forgiveness of our sins and restored us to life in the family of God. If this is how much God loves us, then surely we can love one another.

The love Christians have for each other is a real experience of God's love. God is invisible, but through the church we can realize and receive his love for ourselves. In John's Gospel, the invisible God is seen in the coming of Jesus (John 1:18). In this letter of John, the invisible God is found in Christian fellowship.

'And so we *know*'
(1 John 4:13–18)

John is writing this letter because the church has been badly shaken. The believers have been worried by false teachers and unsettled by some of their members leaving. Now they need to know where they stand and what they can be sure of in their Christian life.

John tells his readers that they can be sure of the Holy Spirit. The Spirit is the gift of God's presence in each of our lives. They can also be sure that Jesus is God's Son and their Saviour. Owning Jesus as our Lord is another sure sign that we have new life with God.

The heart of all truth is that God is love. Love isn't something God has created, but the heart of his own being. Anyone who shows God's self-giving love is clearly related to him. Such love is 'made complete' when it comes from God through us and brings saving help to others.

If we are afraid of God's judgment, then the cure is love. If we receive and share God's love, we will find no room for fear. Anxiety is the enemy of faith. Jesus expressly tells us not to worry (Matthew 6:25–34; John 14:1).

Getting it together
(1 John 4:19–21)

God never commands us to love without first loving us. We are free to love because we are greatly loved ourselves. Just as secure children have their parents' love in their emotional bank, so Christians have the assurance of their heavenly Father's love.

The love of God checks us when we are tempted to dislike or reject a fellow Christian. Saying we love God

and hating a Christian brother or sister doesn't fit. Loving others isn't just a nice thought. It's God's command.

The quality of *all* our relationships – with family, church, neighbours and strangers – is a sign of our relationship with God. It's very likely that if we're in a bad relationship with someone else, we're also in a bad relationship with God.

Believing in Jesus

John draws two major conclusions, which belong together. The first is that everyone who believes that Jesus is the Christ has been born again as a child of God. The second is that everyone who loves God as Father will also love his children – their fellow Christians.

Faith and victory
(1 John 5:1–5)

Love of God is shown in obeying his commands. Obedience makes life easy. Jesus said his burden is light (Matthew 11:30).

Living in obedience to God is the life of faith – a victory over the ways and wiles of the world. Our faith is in the victory of our Saviour, Jesus Christ, over the power of sin and death.

The whole truth
(1 John 5:6–12)

John describes Jesus as 'the one who came by water and blood'. This is perhaps a phrase from an ancient creed, but its meaning is not very clear to us today.

'Water' brings to mind washing or cleansing – and especially in the waters of baptism. 'Blood' stands for life poured out in sacrifice – the sacrifice of Jesus on the cross. John has already stated that 'the blood of Jesus purifies us from every sin' (1:7).

Both 'water' and 'blood' are signs of cleansing from sin. John emphasizes water and *blood*, as though the blood is more important. While water is a symbol of spiritual cleansing, the shedding of blood is how sin is actually dealt with, cancelled and covered.

In John's Gospel, 'blood and water' flow from Jesus on the cross (John 19:34). A soldier had pierced Jesus' side with a spear, to make sure he was dead. The result was a sudden flow of blood and water – the fluids which had separated and congealed in death.

For the soldiers, the blood and water were proof that Jesus was dead. For the witness who stood there (John himself?), the blood and water were a sign that the sacrifice of Jesus was complete (John 19:35). It was the Holy Spirit who showed him the meaning of Jesus' death.

John says that 'the Spirit, the water and the blood' are the three witnesses who testify that Jesus is the Christ. They are the witnesses that God himself has provided, and their word is more reliable than any human evidence.

The Spirit is God himself bearing witness to his Son. God proves that Jesus is true by giving eternal life to all who believe in him. Jesus is life. Without faith in him, there is no way to receive eternal life.

And so…

John draws his letter to a close. He has given his readers many assurances that their faith in Jesus is well founded and that they are free to live as the loved and loving children of God. In this way, they will have the daily blessing of a clear conscience and the hope of eternal life. Eternal life is not the same as everlasting life. Eternal life means entering fully into the life and love and glory of God.

It's good to talk
(1 John 5:13–15)

John encourages his readers to approach God confidently. We are children with ready access to our Father. We can, of course, 'ask anything', but John reminds us that God answers prayers which agree with his will. Christian prayer centres on what God wants:

> *Your kingdom come,*
> *your will be done (Matthew 6:10).*

Dealing with sin
(1 John 5:16–17)

What about praying for forgiveness for someone who has sinned? Are we asking God to overrule his own holy standard in this case, because we know the person concerned?

John encourages his readers to pray for their brothers and sisters who have sinned – that they may be forgiven and enjoy life with God. This is the main way in which every Christian is a priest, bringing others to God in prayer.

But John says that there are some sins which are unforgivable. These sins lead to death. Jesus said that abusing the Holy Spirit is such a sin (Luke 12:10).

Christians must recognize when people wilfully reject God – and not try to deny God's judgment. Jesus commissioned his disciples to forgive some sins and condemn others (John 20:23). This is what Jesus did, and it is a ministry which his church is to continue.

The bottom line
(1 John 5:18–21)

John sums up his teaching about sin. A true Christian may sin, but won't continue sinning. Sin is possible for the Christian – but it isn't worthy of God's children to behave in this way.

It is very unlikely that any Christian will lapse into determined and permanent rebellion against God. Because we belong to Christ and seek to obey God, our sins are more likely to be short lapses into old habits. Whatever our sins, we deeply regret them. In the grace of God, when such sins occur, we can repent and be forgiven.

John assures his readers that they are God's children. They are living in a world which is in the grip of the devil and death, but Christ is their Saviour and protector. Jesus is also the one who makes God's nature and purpose known to them, so that they understand what he is doing in the world and in the church.

All God's truth is revealed in one person, Jesus Christ – and life is to be found in knowing him. Jesus *is* the true God, so beware of worshipping anyone else or anything less.

The 'elder' greets 'the chosen lady'
(2 John 1–3)

John writes to 'the chosen lady and her children'. This may be a woman who leads a house church or congregation; or it may be John's way of describing God's 'chosen people', the church. Peter has the same idea in his first letter (1 Peter 2:9).

The importance of love
(2 John 4–6)

This is a joyful letter. John's joy is that his readers are continuing to live the Christian life in truth and love. This was always God's command and intention for his people – but each person, group and generation must discover it afresh for themselves. They must 'walk the talk'.

A warning against deceivers

(2 John 7–11)

This joyful letter also carries a warning. John warns his readers that they must not be deceived by false teachers.

The false teachers seem to be travelling from church to church. John says they are 'deceivers' who have gone out into the world – so perhaps they were members of the church at one time. Now they spread the lie that Jesus didn't really take on our 'flesh', or human nature. Instead, they say he was only pretending to be human, and didn't really suffer and die for our sins.

John warns the church not to believe such people, and not to invite them into their homes. He calls the deceiver 'the antichrist'. A false teacher is a part of Satan, just as a true believer is part of Christ.

John recommends that false teachers should be excluded. This is like Jesus telling his disciples to leave a hostile town (Luke 10:10). There must be a clear difference between those who welcome the truth and those who oppose it.

'See you soon'

(2 John 12–13)

John ends his short letter with the hope that he will be able to visit his readers soon. He loves these people as part of his spiritual family. The circle of their joy will be complete when they meet again in the love of God.

The elder greets Gaius

(3 John 1–4)

This is a personal letter – unlike 1 and 2 John, which are written to a group of people. The elder says that he has received good reports about Gaius, and knows that his soul is 'getting along well'!

'Diotrephes loves to be first'

Diotrephes is not a false teacher, but he is setting a bad example. The elder says Diotrephes 'loves to be first', which sounds as though he is pushing himself forward in the local church's leadership. This is an evil attitude, which shows how little he knows about God.

The elder commends him for his hospitality

(3 John 5–8)

Gaius has been giving hospitality to travelling preachers. Some of these may have come from the elder's church, bringing his teaching and encouragement.

Giving hospitality means much more than providing a visiting preacher with food and offering a bed for the night. It means supporting visitors (who may be strangers) with enough money to live on. Gaius has done this for Jesus' sake, just as his visitors are preaching the gospel for Jesus' sake. Both are playing their part in the mission of Christ.

Diotrephes is being disruptive

(3 John 9–10)

The elder says that he has written to the church, but Diotrephes will have nothing to do with him. Diotrephes is a leader who is getting above himself. He is preventing the elder's letter from being read, spreading bad reports about him, rejecting his messengers and excluding his supporters.

Demetrius is trustworthy

(3 John 11–12)

The elder mentions Demetrius as a good example. Everyone speaks well of him. Perhaps he is the one who has brought this letter from the elder to Gaius, to make sure it doesn't fall into the wrong hands.

'I hope to see you soon'

(3 John 13–14)

There is more to say, but the elder hopes to talk to Gaius personally before long. He wishes him God's peace and closes with warm greetings between their groups of friends.

REVELATION

The book of Revelation is the last book of the Bible. It contains the visions of a man called John, who is imprisoned on Patmos, an island in the Aegean Sea. He is probably not the apostle John, the fisherman disciple of Jesus who may have written the fourth Gospel and the three letters of John.

John is in exile because of his faith in Christ. He writes at a time when Christians are being persecuted by the Roman authorities, and many have been martyred. His 'Revelation' is that Jesus Christ is the Lord of heaven and earth, of time and eternity. Through Christ, God is bringing history to its climax and close, and a new creation to birth. The forces of Satan are to be finally defeated and the church is to become the bride of Christ.

Christ speaks to his church through John, to encourage and guide his people. He urges them to persevere through times of darkness and great stress, for after this life they will live with God in his glorious new world.

Outline

INTRODUCTION

Apocalypse now!

'Revelation' comes from a Latin word which means 'unveiling' (or 'wow!'). 'Apocalypse' comes from a Greek word which means the same thing.

In John's visions, it is as though a curtain is drawn aside and scenes of heaven are 'revealed'. John sees the true situation of heaven, and how it affects the unfolding events on earth.

At the centre of heaven is God's throne and 'the Lamb' – the crucified and risen Jesus. On earth there is great disruption and suffering as God pours out his anger on those who have killed his people. There is in fact a great battle going on, both in heaven and on earth, as Satan and his evil allies have their final fling against God and his Christ. But, since the death and resurrection of Jesus, the result has never been in doubt. Satan is a defeated foe.

John describes his visions in the extraordinary picture language which we first met in the book of Daniel. He uses images, symbols and numbers which are difficult for us to decode. But the overall message is clear – that Christ has defeated Satan and broken the power of evil.

Through John, Christ sends messages to each of seven local churches in the Roman province of Asia (western Turkey). He reassures, corrects and encourages them. He gives them the overview of what is going on. The faithful, suffering church is to become nothing less than the perfect bride of Christ – the focus and fulfilment of God's community of heaven on earth. John closes his book of visions with a cry of longing that Jesus will come soon.

The visions of the book of Revelation are similar to the ones in the book of Daniel and other 'apocalyptic' writings. Mighty empires are pictured as terrifying monsters. Vast eras of history are measured by mysterious symbolic numbers. Rather like political cartoons, the meaning of the visions was fairly obvious to the first readers, but rather obscure to us who live so long afterwards.

A circular letter?

The book of Revelation may have been a circular letter, first sent to seven cities in Asia Minor. It tells them that both Christ and Satan have a lively interest in their daily life.

Asia is part of the Roman empire, at a time when there is great pressure to worship the emperor. Some Christians will be asked to choose between Christ and Caesar – and persecuted or martyred if they choose Christ. A likely time for Revelation to have been written is during the reign of Emperor Domitian, between AD 81 and 96.

Images to blow the mind!

Revelation is a fabulous, amazing book. John relates vision after vision, to blow out the walls of our 'little me' Christianity. He opens the eyes of our hearts to the reality and worship of heaven. He shows us the great vistas of God's eternal plan. He sets our daily struggles of faith in the context of the cosmic battle between God and Satan – and assures us that we will share the victory of Christ, which is already certain.

Apocalyptic literature comes chiefly from Jewish writers between 200 BC and AD 100. The main examples in the Bible are Daniel and Revelation. With mind-bending, sometimes nightmarish, images, this kind of writing gives the inside story of historical events, and helps the reader to see politics and history, suffering and victory, from God's point of view.

Having said this, the book of Revelation is not as extraordinary as some of the others. John himself isn't strange or eccentric. He simply shares his vision with other persecuted Christians. In both distant and recent times, this book has reassured Christians who are living in states of anxiety or persecution. They are safe in God's care and will share Christ's victory over evil.

What do the numbers mean?

We can't read Revelation for very long before we start noticing the numbers – seven, four, twenty-four and 144,000 in particular!

Seven is obviously a number with a special meaning. There are seven lampstands representing seven churches. There are seven stars which stand for the angels of the churches. And, later on, there are seven seals on a scroll, seven trumpets sounding warnings and seven bowls pouring wrath.

Seven seems to stand for the completeness of God's work in the world. God rested on the seventh day when he had completed his creation. We have a seven-day week.

God's number is three. He is three-times holy (Isaiah 6:3). He is a Trinity of Father, Son and Spirit. The world's number is four. The Bible talks of the four corners of the world – and the four winds. We have four main points of the compass and observe the year in four seasons. The 'three' of God and the 'four' of the world make 'seven'.

The number four also applies to the four 'living creatures' who worship around the throne of God (4:6–7). Like the seraphs in Isaiah's vision, they have six wings. Like the creatures which attend the chariot-throne of God in Ezekiel's vision, they have the faces of lion, ox, human being and eagle – the leading species of wild and domesticated animals, humans and birds.

The number twenty-four is easier to understand. There are twenty-four elders. They are made up of twelve for the tribes of Israel (the first 'people of God' in the Old Testament) and twelve for the apostles of Christ (the founders of the Christian church in the New Testament).

By now we realize that the numbers in Revelation are symbolic. They are an important aspect of each vision.

A plain meaning

Revelation is one of the most difficult books of the Bible for us to understand. Because it deals in strange visions, dramatic images and mysterious numbers, people have tried to explain it in many different ways.

But it does have a plain meaning. It is a book written for Christians who are suffering for their faith. It encourages them with the message that Jesus Christ is the Lord of all things, and that their time of trial will end in eternal glory.

Although Revelation describes some of the terrible things that will happen to the world, it isn't supposed to be a forecast of current affairs. Jesus told his disciples that there would be times of stress, disaster and persecution in the 'last days', but specifically warned them not to try to predict the time of the end of the world (Mark 13:32).

3 (God) x 4 (the world) = 12 (God's work in the world).

12 (Israel) x 12 (apostles) = 144 (God's people, old and new).

Ten is a number of completeness or perfection – so 1,000 (10 x 10 x 10) is the ultimate full and satisfying number. The multitude of the faithful in heaven is numbered at 144,000. That's (12 x 12) x (10 x 10 x 10) – the perfect number for a perfect people.

Eight visions

The whole book of Revelation is written to a plan of eight major visions. Each of the visions has seven scenes, which follow a similar sequence. The effect is to repeat the central message several times in different forms:

- Seven churches receive a message from Christ.
- Seven seals release trouble on the world.
- Seven trumpets announce terrible judgments.
- Seven bowls pour out destruction from God.

The eighth vision is different from the rest. It isn't another vision of judgment and destruction, but of new creation. Like a Jubilee (fiftieth) Year of celebration and renewal, the new Jerusalem comes down from heaven. Like a resurrection morning, the eighth vision bursts forth – with the dazzling glory of the Lamb and his bride. Like the first day of a new week, this vision is God's new beginning.

Eight scenes

The book of Revelation is made up of eight major scenes Each of the eight scenes contains seven shorter visions.

Scene 1: Christ speaks to his church (1:9 – 3:22)
At first, John sees Jesus in glory, and receives messages for seven churches in the province of Asia.

Scene 2: The worship of heaven and the scroll of history (4:1 – 8:5)
John sees into heaven and watches as Jesus the Lamb unseals a scroll. The scroll is the history of the world in the last days. Each of its seven seals reveals an aspect of God's judgment and victory.

Scene 3: Seven trumpets are sounded (8:6 – 11:19)
After the seven seals come seven trumpets. They teach the same insight over again. They warn of

destruction and death in every part of the cosmos, and the Judgment Day of God.

Scene 4: Seven visions: a woman and a dragon, great beasts defying God, the Lamb and Judgment Day (12:1 – 15:8)

We are shown the tyranny of evil in the world, the suffering of the church and the ultimate triumph of Christ.

Scene 5: Seven bowls of God's anger are poured out (16:1–21)

The bowls are full of God's anger, which brings destruction on the earth. Again, we are seeing the same message and sequence repeated in another way.

Scene 6: The fall of Babylon (17:1 – 18:24)

Babylon is the great prostitute that seduces humankind away from God. Now God sentences her to destruction.

Scene 7: The victory of Christ (19:1 – 20:15)

Jesus is the king of kings, who defeats Satan (Babylon and the beast) and establishes the reign of God.

Scene 8: The new Jerusalem and the wedding of the Lamb (21:1 – 22:6)

God finally establishes the perfect community, in which he himself lives among his people. His heavenly city, the new Jerusalem, is a place of perfect light, harmony, healing and peace.

The key to Revelation is the lordship of Jesus Christ. He was there at the beginning when creation was made. He will be there at the end, when he comes to complete God's new creation.

DISCOVERING REVELATION

Introduction and greetings

John introduces himself as a servant of Jesus Christ (1:1–8). He is writing to seven churches in the Roman province of Asia. The book of Revelation is a letter – the last and longest letter of the New Testament. Like the other letters it was written to a particular situation, but also to us. This letter is Jesus Christ speaking to his church then and now. It is God's word to us.

Like the rest of the Bible, Revelation tells us about God's plan of salvation through Jesus Christ. The Holy Spirit who inspires the writing of scripture is with us to help us understand its meaning. The letter which was written for 1st-century Christians in a remote part of the Roman empire is intended to teach us about our own situation and inspire our Christian living today.

Christ speaks to his church

John's vision of the glorious Christ
(1:9–20)

John has a vision of Jesus 'like a son of man'. This had been Daniel's vision – a human being who fully represents the human race, appearing in clouds and great glory, to be given God's power and authority to reign over all things (Daniel 7:13).

John's vision has far more detail than Daniel's. The Son of man has the same white hair as God, the Ancient of Days. His eyes blaze with the fire of holiness, his feet glow with the strength of bronze. His voice has the multi-levelled sound of rushing water and his mouth speaks truth with power and precision. This is Jesus Christ as the disciples glimpsed him on the Mount of Transfiguration (Mark 9:2–3).

John is in exile, perhaps sentenced to hard labour in the mines of Patmos. His body may be in prison, but his spirit is free.

The glorious Christ stands among seven golden lampstands. These are his churches, which give his light to the world. He also holds in his right hand seven stars.

These are the angels which care for each local church. The face of the glorious Christ is like the sun – the source and appearance of all brilliance.

In the world, the churches are like lampstands. Jesus gave the same picture to his disciples. They are not to hide truth, like putting a light under a bowl. They are to lift it high, where it can give light to everyone (Matthew 5:14–16). In another way, the church is already perfect and gathered – like the seven stars in Christ's right hand. John's vision is of Christ as the living God and Lord of the church.

Letters to seven churches

(2:1 – 3:22)

Each of the letters to the churches has the same shape. They start by recalling the description of the glorious Christ. Then Jesus speaks to each church individually, reviewing its situation and giving a command and a promise. He describes himself in a way which has special meaning for each place. He gives analysis, encouragement and warning in terms which will make sense to the people who live there.

THE LETTER TO THE CHURCH IN EPHESUS

Ephesus is the leading city of Asia (2:1–7). Paul first preached the gospel here, with daily discussions in the lecture hall of Tyrannus (Acts 19:9–10).

The Christians at Ephesus are hard-working and right-thinking. There is a letter from Ignatius, the bishop of Antioch, which praises their brave stand for truth. In particular, they have hated the practices of the Nicolaitans. Nicolaitans are the followers of Nicolas, who may be the deacon from Antioch – one of the seven deacons appointed to serve the church in Jerusalem in Acts 6:5. He may have been guilty of mixing paganism

with Christianity. Nicolaitans are mentioned again in the letter to the church at Pergamum, where they are linked with the false teaching of Balaam – the prophet who was tempted to compromise with Israel's enemies (Numbers 22:10–11).

There is a constant battle to live as Christians in a pagan society. Meat comes from sacrifices in pagan temples. Sex is degraded by permissiveness and perversion. It seems that the Nicolaitans are allowing pagan ways to infiltrate their Christian lives – and Christ hates this dangerous compromise.

But, in their desire to be strict Christians, the Ephesians have lost their first love. Their delight in Christ and one another has faded to a grim but determined sense of duty. Christ urges them to return to their first joy. Instead of the meat of fear and superstition, he will give them the fruit of the tree of life. Instead of seeking satisfaction in obsessive sex, he will give them the peace and plenty of paradise.

THE LETTER TO THE CHURCH IN SMYRNA

Smyrna is the next most important city to Ephesus – and far more beautiful (2:8–11). It is a wealthy city, thanks to its trade, safe harbour, fertile valley and major road to the Far East. Today Smyrna is Izmir, the thriving city of Turkey.

Founded by the Greeks in 1000 BC, Smyrna was destroyed by invaders in 500 BC. It was reborn around 200 BC as a well-planned modern city with a famous street of gold running between the temple of Zeus and the temple of Cybele.

Politically, Smyrna was a staunch ally of Rome. It was awarded the honour of building a temple to the emperor-god Tiberius. In time to come, in February AD 155, Smyrna's Bishop Polycarp will be martyred for his refusal to say, 'Caesar is Lord.'

Smyrna's Jewish community is implacably opposed to Christianity. When Polycarp dies, it will be the Jews who fetch stacks of wood to burn him at the stake. As Jesus Christ looks at the situation of his church, he sees that a 'synagogue of Satan', who are spurious Jews, will inflict great suffering on his people. Christians will be imprisoned and even killed, but Christ will give them victory. Like the city in which they live, they will rise again!

THE LETTER TO THE CHURCH IN PERGAMUM

Pergamum is an important city – not for trade or beauty, but as a seat of government (2:12–17). It has been the

---

Alpha and Omega

'I am the Alpha and the Omega,' says the Lord God in the first chapter of Revelation (1:8). The same description is used of Jesus in the last chapter (22:13).

Alpha and Omega are the first and last letters of the Greek alphabet. The Father and the Son were there at the beginning of the universe – and they will be there at its end.

capital of Asia for nearly 400 years – ever since the break-up of Alexander the Great's empire, when it became the centre of the Seleucid kingdom.

Pergamum has a famous library of parchment scrolls, and parchment gets its name from the 'Pergamene sheet'. The culture and religion is strongly Greek, with an emphasis on the worship of Asklepios, a god of healing. His temples are something like hospitals. For many people Asklepios is the saviour. Also at Pergamum is a huge temple dedicated to Zeus. It is built on three sides of a square, to make a giant chair or throne.

First and foremost, Pergamum is a centre of Roman government, and its main god is Caesar. Christ says to his people, 'I know where you live – where Satan has his throne' (2:13). The Roman governor at Pergamum has 'the right of the sword' – that is, the authority to execute people. But Jesus Christ introduces himself as the one with true authority: 'The one who has the sharp, double-edged sword' (2:12). In the letter to the Hebrews, God's word is said to be 'sharper than any two-edged sword' (Hebrews 4:12). Such a sword is useful for both attack and defence.

The Christians at Pergamum have a tough assignment. The age-old temptation to compromise with paganism, which goes back to the days of Balaam, is now freshly spiced with the teaching of the Nicolaitans. Together they argue that it really doesn't matter how you live, because you will be discarding your body at death and your soul will fly safely to God.

But Christ calls his people to lead pure lives *now*. He will provide for them and strengthen them day by day – just as he nourished his people with manna in the

---

Pergamum is a centre for both Roman government and the worship of Greek gods. Christ promises 'a white stone' to everyone who remains faithful to him: a token of purity and admission to heaven, perhaps. The amphitheatre at Pergamum.

wilderness. Jesus described himself as 'the bread of life' (John 6:35) – a reality celebrated and shared in Holy Communion. For those who remain faithful, Christ promises a white stone – like the symbol of victory given to an athlete or gladiator, or a token of admission to a great event. In status-hungry Pergamum they will joyfully bear the name of Christ.

THE LETTER TO THE CHURCH IN THYATIRA

Thyatira is a busy centre of commerce (2:18–29). Lydia, the purple-cloth dealer whom Paul met in Philippi, came from here (Acts 16:14). There are many wealthy trade guilds, and a shrine where a famous female fortune-teller called Sanbathe gives advice.

Christ introduces himself to the Christians at Thyatira as 'the Son of God, whose eyes are like blazing fire and whose feet are like burnished bronze'. He is a God of penetrating purity and unshakeable power.

The church at Thyatira is loving, faithful and growing in influence. But there is a serious problem with a self-styled prophetess called Jezebel. Jezebel is probably not her real name, but recalls King Ahab's wicked queen from the days of Elijah. This woman, while claiming to speak from God, is leading Christians astray with idol food and forbidden sex. Her immorality is an image of spiritual unfaithfulness. Christ warns that there will be terrible consequences both for herself and for others. Her fascinating secrets are Satan's dangerous lies.

Christ is infinitely more glorious and terrible than the sun god Apollo, whose famous temple stands in Thyatira. Christ will give his church 'the morning star' – the pure point of light which promises the dawn of God's eternal kingdom.

THE LETTER TO THE CHURCH IN SARDIS

Sardis was once a splendid city (3:1–6). Standing 1,500 feet above sea level, she dominated the surrounding countryside. In the 8th century BC she was the capital of the kings of Lydia, of whom the most famous was the wealthy King Croesus. But Sardis' confidence in her wealth and strong position was ill-founded. The Persian troops of Cyrus crept in by stealth one night, and the city was captured. The same thing happened two centuries later, when Antiochus captured the city.

Jesus Christ sees the church in Sardis reflecting the city's history. They have the reputation of a strong and lively church, but in fact they are sleepy to the point of being dead. He urges them to wake up, or he will surprise them by coming to judge them. There are still a few Christians who have not soiled their clothes – they are still faithful to their baptism promises and the white robe they wore that day. They will keep company with Christ and have their names entered for ever in the register of heaven.

Sardis had once been a wealthy and powerful city, but her beauty was now faded and her Christian witness had become complacent. A mosaic on a synagogue floor.

THE LETTER TO THE CHURCH IN PHILADELPHIA

Philadelphia is a young city compared with the other six (3:7–13). Its name means 'brotherly love'. The city's founder, Attalus II, named it after his favourite brother Eumenes. He established Philadelphia to spread the Greek language and way of life to the regions of Lydia and Phrygia.

Jesus Christ tells the Christians in Philadelphia that he has opened a door for them. It is a door to freedom and life. He describes himself as the one who holds the key of David. The door of the house of David, the home of God's people, had once seemed to be only for Jews. Now it is open to Gentiles. The local Jews are jealous and critical of the Christian church and have become agents of Satan. They will be forced to admit that Christians are loved and accepted by God. Christ encourages his people to hold fast during the coming persecution. They will be strong and reliable, like pillars in the temple.

In AD 17, Philadelphia was devastated by an earthquake. The emperor Tiberius gave enormous support to its rebuilding and, as a result, the new city was called Neocaesarea, the new city of Caesar. Now Christ promises to write God's name on the church in Philadelphia. They are his own honoured people.

THE LETTER TO THE CHURCH IN LAODICEA

The city of Laodicea stands in the Lycus Valley on the great trade route between Ephesus and Syria (3:14–22). It was founded by Antiochus of Syria and named after his wife Laodice. In peaceful times it is a prosperous centre, famous for banking, clothing and eye-salve. When an earthquake destroyed the city in AD 61, the people were able to rebuild from their own wealth without any outside help. The local sheep produce a black, glossy wool – ideal for making warm, waterproof coats. A famous medical school supplies ointments for ears and eyes.

When Christ looks at the church in Laodicea, he sees a sorry contrast to the thriving centre in which she lives. The Christians, in spiritual terms, are poor, naked and blind. Christ likens them to the local water supply, which is tepid and sluggish – neither refreshingly cold, nor piping hot.

But Christ hasn't given up on his church. He stands at the door, knocking and calling. They have only to open the door and welcome him in, and he will again share their life, and they will share his reign.

The worship of heaven and the scroll of history

A vision of heaven

(4:1–11)

The scene changes. John sees a door standing open before him. He is invited to pass through it – and finds himself in the presence of God, surrounded by the worship of heaven.

God is at the centre, seated on his throne. John says his appearance is like the beauty, sparkle and lustre of jewels. He is encircled by a rainbow – recalling the grace and mercy he extended to the world after Noah's flood.

God's throne is surrounded by twenty-four others; twelve for the tribes of Israel and twelve for the apostles of Christ. Together they sum up the whole people of God. The elders who sit on the thrones – white-robed and gold-crowned – share God's heavenly reign. From God's throne come lightning and thunder – as there had been on Mount Sinai when God's people stood in his awesome presence and he gave Moses the law (Exodus 19:16–23).

Before the throne burn seven lamps. They recall the seven-branched lampstand which stood first in the tabernacle and the temple. The lamps represent the sevenfold spirit of God – the spirit of wisdom and understanding, counsel and power, knowledge, fear of the Lord and delight in worshipping him (Isaiah 11:2–3). Before the throne is a sea of glass. The cruel sea, dreaded home of sea monsters and all chaos, is now conquered, cleansed and in perfect peace.

Around the throne are four living creatures. With faces of lion, ox, human and eagle, they represent all God's creatures in earth and heaven. Like the seraphs of Isaiah's vision, they have six wings. Like the cherubim of Ezekiel's vision, they are in close attendance on God's throne. They conduct the worship of heaven, giving

The church at Laodicea is described as lukewarm. By contrast, the springs at Pamukkale near Hierapolis (pictured) are piping hot.

Lukewarm Laodicea

Christ speaks to each of the local churches in a way which is especially meaningful to them and their situation.

Christians at Laodicea will recognize the reference to lukewarm water. Their water comes by aqueduct from springs a few miles away. By the time it arrives it has been in the sun for hours, and is warm and tasting of minerals. In contrast, the water at nearby Hierapolis is hot, with healing powers, while the water at Colosse is cool and fresh.

Jesus says of the lukewarm church at Laodicea, 'I wish you were hot or cold – but in fact you make me sick!'

glory, honour and thanks to God – the One, eternal God who reigns for ever:

> You are worthy, our Lord and God,
> > to receive glory and honour and power,
> for you created all things,
> > and by your will they were created
> > > and have their being (4:11).

The scroll and the Lamb
(5:1–14)

As God sits on his heavenly throne, he holds in his right hand a sealed scroll. Written on this scroll is all that is to happen on earth. It is seven-times sealed – and only the Lamb is worthy to open and read it.

And then John sees the Lamb. This is Jesus who was crucified and raised, the perfect and accepted sacrifice, now at the very centre of God's throne. The entire host

of heaven worships him. He is the 'Lion of the Tribe of Judah' – the pride of the Jews. He has seven horns and seven eyes – that is, he has the power, wisdom and insight of God's Spirit. By his utmost commitment to God and creation, he has won the right to unseal the scroll and unfold the meaning of history.

The seven seals

(6:1 – 8:5)

As the Lamb opens each of the first four seals, a horse and rider gallop out. The first horse is white and its rider is given power to wage war and conquer kingdoms. The second horse is a fiery red and its rider is given power to shed blood. The third horse is black and its rider holds a pair of scales. He will spread famine on earth, with shortage of food and high prices. But oil and wine will be spared – a reminder that some people will continue to live in luxury while many starve. The fourth horse is pale and its rider is death.

Together these four riders – the 'Four Horsemen of the Apocalypse' – bring terror and suffering, dearth and death. As each rides out, one of the four living creatures calls, 'Come!' It is a cry of longing that Christ will rescue his people from these terrible events.

When the fifth seal is opened, John sees all the people who have been martyred for their faith. They are themselves sacrifices under the altar of heaven, and cry to God that he will avenge their murder. As John watches, they are each given a white robe – the livery of heaven – and encouraged to wait a little longer.

When the sixth seal is opened, the entire universe is brought to an end. Everyone – high and low, rich and poor – is engulfed in the cataclysm of Judgment Day. This is the day when the full power and wrath of Christ is unveiled and unleashed – the day of the wrath of the Lamb! Jesus had predicted this cosmic collapse with all its darkness and

As the second angel sounds his trumpet, a third of the sea is destroyed, along with a third of the sea creatures and ships. A French illumination of the 11th century.

terror when talking to his disciples (Matthew 24). The description of the stars falling like withered figs goes all the way back to a prophecy of Isaiah (Isaiah 34:4).

The opening of the scroll has revealed the sufferings which will afflict and eventually engulf the world. These are: military aggression, human bloodshed, shortage of food and death by starvation and disease. Far from being excluded from the suffering of humankind, God's people will be caught up in it and even suffer martyrdom as well.

144,000 SEALED

Now John sees the angels of destruction marking God's servants with a seal on their foreheads (7:1–17). Before the great judgment falls and the earth is destroyed, God's people are marked to be spared. The number of those sealed – 12,000 from each of the twelve tribes – symbolizes a complete salvation, with none of God's people missing. Seeing the servants of God being marked for salvation, we are reminded of one of Ezekiel's visions. He saw a man clothed in linen and carrying a writing kit, who went through Jerusalem ahead of God's executioners, marking all those who were to be spared (Ezekiel 9:3–6).

At last John is able to see God's people in their future glory. A multitude too great to count, gathered from every nation, ethnic group and culture, is gathered before God's throne and his Lamb, Jesus Christ. They have passed through the trials of the end times. They have been cleansed from all sin by Jesus' death for them. Now they are safe for ever under his powerful protection and in his perfect care.

THE SEVENTH SEAL

When the seventh seal is opened, there is silence in heaven (8:1–5). Just as God rested on the seventh day of creation and God's people kept the sabbath as a day of rest, so now there is time for absolute stillness and attention to God. Incense is offered to God, together with the prayers of all the saints. Two sequences of visions are now complete: the letters to seven churches and the breaking of seven seals. We, too, fall silent before the great vistas of truth which have been opened before us.

Seven trumpets are sounded

A new sequence begins (8:6 – 11:19). Seven angels sound seven trumpets. They herald and summon terrible judgment. A third of the earth is scorched. A third of the sea is destroyed, with its creatures and commerce. A blazing star crashes to earth, polluting and poisoning a third of all fresh water. The sun and moon lose a third of their light and all the stars are dimmed. Then a nightmare is unleashed – locusts with teeth like lions and stings like scorpions ravage the peoples of earth. They are a host from hell. Like the sea turned to blood (8:8), and the darkness (8:12), the locusts remind us of the plagues of Egypt (Exodus 10). They are led by Apollyon, the Destroyer. Until now the trumpet blasts have heralded disasters in earth, sea and sky. But these locusts are a plague on the human race – for 'five months', a limited time.

The fourth angel blows his trumpet and a third of the sun, moon and stars are put out. The result is darkness for a third of the day and night. A French illumination of the 11th century.

When the sixth trumpet is sounded another army attacks the human race – this time not from hell, but from heaven. Two hundred million mounted troops, commanded by angels, slay a third of humankind. They come from the area of the River Euphrates – the place from which the armies of Assyria swarmed towards Israel as agents of God's judgment in the 8th century BC. John understands that this wave of destruction is God's punishment for human idolatry, immorality and witchcraft. The devastation is intended as a warning to those who survive, so that they have time to repent. But they take no notice.

The angel and the little scroll
(10:1–11)

Now John sees a mighty angel holding a little scroll open in his hand. When he speaks, his voice is like the roar of a lion and the rolling of sevenfold thunder. John is forbidden to write down what he says. The seventh trumpet is about to sound. It will herald the end of all things. All will be fulfilled, just as the prophets foretold.

John is given the little scroll and told to eat it. It is the gospel message which is to be proclaimed in the last days. It is sweet to taste, for it is good news of salvation. It is bitter to preach, because it declares judgment on an unbelieving world.

The two witnesses
(11:1–14)

John is told to measure the inner court of the temple and to count the worshippers there. The temple in Jerusalem was destroyed in AD 70, but Christians understand themselves to be the living temple of God. Although the world is in a state of upheaval, and God's people are under siege, they continue to worship him faithfully and in safety.

God gives power to two outstanding witnesses. Like Elijah they have power to declare drought. Like Moses they have power to call down plagues on humankind. They take their stand, powerful and prophetic – the church at its best, witnessing and suffering for Christ's sake in the face of the world's upheavals. Even so, they will be overwhelmed by the forces of evil ('Sodom' and 'Egypt') just as Jesus himself was. For a short while it will seem that hell has finally triumphed. But God will revive them, striking terror in the hearts of their enemies, and take them to glory.

The seventh trumpet

(11:15–19)

The first six trumpets have heralded judgment and sounded warnings. The seventh trumpet is a glorious fanfare as the kingdom of this world finally enters the kingdom of Christ. The twenty-four elders – the leaders of God's people old and new – fall prostrate in God's presence. They praise God for his mighty power, his keeping of his promises and his destruction of their enemies.

John sees God's temple in heaven opened. There the ark of the covenant stands revealed. For centuries the ark was enshrined in darkness and mystery – first in the wilderness tabernacle, and then in the temple of Solomon in Jerusalem. When Jesus died on the cross, the temple curtain was torn from top to bottom. The Most Holy Place was laid open for all people to gain access to the presence of God. So now heaven is open to earth.

Seven visions are revealed

A woman and a dragon

(12:1 – 13:1)

Another vision begins. John sees a woman clothed with the sun, with the moon under her feet and a crown of twelve stars on her head. She is the human race sharing God's glory and dominion, and crowned with the people of God, the church. Roman Catholic Christians see here a picture of Mary, the mother of Jesus, representing the church.

Suffering for Christ's sake

The theme of suffering runs right through the New Testament. Jesus suffered, and warned his followers that they would suffer too.

As John writes down the messages of Christ for the seven churches in western Turkey, the thought of persecution and martyrdom is never far away. But Jesus himself triumphed through suffering – and now he promises to share his victory with all who keep faith till the end.

The woman is about to give birth to a male child who will rule all the nations. This is the Messiah, the Son of God. But she has a terrible enemy. A great dragon, the ancient Satan, armed with enormous powers of evil, is set to destroy the Messiah at birth. As John watches, God snatches his son to safety, while the woman is given refuge in the desert. This is the drama of history – that Christ has been born and is now ascended to heaven, while his church continues to be cared for by God on earth.

Now John sees war in heaven. Michael, the archangel who fights for Israel, is leading his legions against the great dragon, Satan. Satan is thrown out of heaven, but escapes to wreak havoc on earth. He pursues the woman – God's people – to whom has been born the Messiah. He makes war against her offspring, the Christian church.

Like other visions in the book of Revelation, this is another way of describing the same situation: Satan is a defeated foe, and yet he harasses and persecutes the church.

The beast out of the sea

(13:1–10)

John sees a beast coming out of the sea. With horns and heads and crowns, it reminds us of the monsters of the book of Daniel. Horns stand for power, heads stand for intelligence and identity and crowns stand for authority. This beast represents all worldly power which sets itself up against God.

The peoples of earth worship this beast, with its military might and godless values. His code number is 666. If seven is the number of God, then six is the number of human beings. This beast pretends to have the power and glory of God, but falls short in every way. But the church must stay true to God in patience and faith.

The beast out of the earth

(13:11–18)

Now John sees another beast – this time coming out of the earth. This beast has the appearance of a lamb but the voice of a dragon. He promotes the power of the beast from the sea – the monster of tyranny and dictatorship. He performs mighty miracles – even, like Elijah, calling down fire from heaven (1 Kings 18). The beast from the earth looks like a power for good, but he is in fact a deceiver. He is a picture of a corrupt church serving the interests of worldly governments. In particular he uses the desire for money to bring all people under the control of materialism.

The Lamb and the 144,000
(14:1–5)

While Satan thrashes earth in his death throes, John sees the true situation of God's people. He sees the Lamb, Jesus Christ, standing on Mount Zion – the central place of God's kingdom and community. With Christ is a multitude of 144,000 saints. This number is based on twelves. The twelve tribes of Israel and the twelve apostles of Christ are now multiplied together 1,000 times, symbolizing the complete gathering of the faithful, from Israel and the church.

Instead of the mark of the beast, God's people have on their foreheads the name of Jesus and God his Father. The 144,000 are 'the redeemed'. Christ has rescued them from the power of sin and death by giving his life for them on the cross. For their part, they have committed themselves totally to him. Their lives have been marked by self-control, honesty and a clear conscience. Sex within marriage and the joys of family life are among God's greatest gifts; but here are some who have honoured God by leading single and celibate lives.

The three angels
(14:6–13)

John sees three angels. The first has the gospel of Jesus Christ to proclaim to all the peoples of the world. The second declares the fall of Babylon – the evil beast which has bullied, corrupted and seduced humankind. The third proclaims the consequences of worshipping the beast. Those who worship the beast will receive the full fury of God's judgment. Those who die for their faith in Christ will find peace and rest.

The seven angels with lightning, illustrated in an 18th-century manuscript from Ethiopia.

The harvest of the earth
(14:14–20)

Now John sees someone 'like a son of man' harvesting the earth. Harvest is a picture of judgment. The good grain or grapes are saved, while weeds and stubble are burned.

Both John the Baptist and Jesus imagined Judgment Day as God's harvest time. Jesus told his disciples that only God the Father knows when the Judgment Day will be. Here, in John's vision, an angel brings God's word that the harvest is to begin. The 'son of man' (which may be Christ himself) harvests and gathers God's faithful people. An angel with a sharp sickle harvests ripe grapes, which represent the wicked. They are destroyed in the great winepress of God's wrath. Their blood flows a distance of 1,600 stadia, which is about 180 miles. This is the length of Palestine from north to south.

Seven angels with seven plagues
(15:1–8)

John sees another scene of triumph in heaven. All those who share Christ's victory are singing a heavenly version of the Song of Moses (Exodus 15). The anthem is swollen to cosmic dimensions by the triumph of the Lamb, Christ Jesus.

Seven angels stand dressed in the livery of white and gold, waiting to administer the seven last plagues.

Seven bowls are poured out

Seven angels emerge from the tabernacle of the testimony. They have come from the very presence of God, shining with the glory of his holiness. They bear seven bowls of plagues, which they are told to pour out upon the earth (16:1–21).

When the seven trumpets sounded, seven plagues polluted or destroyed a third of land, sea, fresh water, sky, animals and humans. Those plagues were a punishment and a warning.

Now the bowls of God's wrath cause complete and utter destruction. The land, sea and freshwater springs are polluted, killing those who depend on them for life. This is God's judgment and vengeance for the treatment given to his saints and prophets. The sun becomes unbearably hot, scorching all those caught in its heat – and yet they refuse to repent.

The fifth bowl is poured out on the throne of the beast – breaking his power and plunging his realm into chaos. His subjects, in agony, still persist in cursing God. When the sixth angel pours out his bowl of wrath, the great River Euphrates is dried up. Across its arid bed sweep hordes from the East – the direction from which mighty armies have so often borne down on little Israel.

The plagues of Egypt again come to mind as John sees evil spirits that look like frogs. They spring, unclean, from the mouths of the dragon (Satan), the beast (the evil world power) and the false prophet (the beast out of the earth, which acts as a false church). The frogs work the net of lies, deception and propaganda which entangles world leaders and draws them relentlessly into the last battle – Armageddon.

Armageddon means Mount Megiddo. Megiddo is a town near the plain of Esdraelon, where great battles have been fought in the past. It is here that Sisera was defeated (Judges 5:19–20), and Josiah met his death (2 Kings 23:29).

Armageddon is John's name for the site of the last battle at the end of time. Perhaps, in terms of his own

day, John sees the destruction of Rome by Barbarian hordes – a judgment on her wickedness and cruelty.

Suddenly, Christ himself speaks. It is he who is at work in this final destruction – as unexpected and effective as a thief. He warns his people to be ready for him – like those who know exactly where their clothes are in case of an emergency in the night. Jesus had once warned his disciples to be ready for the destruction of Jerusalem. Now he warns his church to be ready for the final clash of nations and the Judgment Day of God.

A coin of the emperor Domitian, who insisted on being worshipped as 'lord and god'. Many Christians were persecuted for refusing to do so.

The seventh angel pours his bowl of wrath into the air – detonating thunder, lightning and earthquake. The great city – the centre of the world's hostility to God – is utterly destroyed. The landscape becomes featureless; islands and mountains are erased. The world is pounded by giant hailstones and its people wasted by plague.

This is the end of all things.

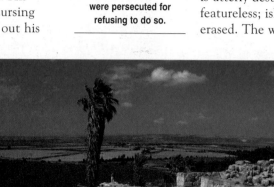

The view across the Plain of Esdraelon from the town of Megiddo where major battles were fought in the past. For John, Megiddo is the site of Armageddon – the final conflict at the end of time.

The fall of Babylon

Babylon's fate
(17:1–18)

As John's vision continues, an angel carries him off to a desert. From here he sees the fabulous glory and the dreadful corruption of worldly powers.

John sees 'a woman sitting on a scarlet beast'. The beast is like the beast out of the sea (13:1–8), and stands for all political powers and worldly governments which oppose God. He is a proud and aggressive scarlet – the colour of Satan – and covered in every kind of insult to God.

The woman is, perhaps, another picture of the beast out of the earth (13:11–18). She stands for human pride – clothed in royal purple and outrageous scarlet. She is bedecked with dazzling jewels. But her appearance is treacherous, for in her hand is a golden cup of poison. Her name is 'Babylon the Great'. She is a symbol of all those human enterprises, from the tower of Babel onwards, which have tried to challenge and displace God. She is the mother of all that is deceitful and disgusting. She is also the foremost enemy of the church. John sees that she has become drunk on the blood of the saints.

The angel tells John that the beast on which the woman rides has astonishing powers of survival. He will seem to be defeated, but will re-emerge. In John's own day, 'Babylon' is the worldwide power of Rome. At other times she has been Nineveh (as in the prophecy of Nahum) or Tyre (as in Isaiah 23). Tragically, she is even Jerusalem, as both Jeremiah and Jesus saw only too clearly (Matthew 23:37).

John describes the beast as having seven heads and ten horns. He explains that the seven heads are 'seven hills' (17:9), which may refer to the seven hills of Rome. He also talks of seven kings, with an eighth still to come. The ten horns stand for ten kings who will enjoy a brief hour of triumph before the beast is destroyed. They will wage war against the Lamb, Christ himself, and will be defeated.

It is difficult to decode the numbers and symbols in

John sees the destruction of Babylon, which in his day is identified with Rome. In its wider sense it represents all kingdoms and authorities that challenge the rule of God. A print of Babylon burning, from the first edition of the Luther Bible (c. 1530).

these verses. Are the seven kings 'with one still to come' a list of Roman emperors? Do the seven hills refer to Rome? And who are the ten kings who fight for the beast against Christ? As John watches, the beast and the ten horns turn on the woman to attack her. At the end of time, evil forces will even destroy each other.

The fall of Babylon
(18:1–24)

An angel proclaims the death of Babylon. She is punished by God for her immorality, greed and persecutions. The kings who have been deceived and compromised by her values watch in horror. The merchants find their trade and livelihood swept away. And it all happens so quickly! The everyday activities of city life are silenced for ever, as God steps in to judge human arrogance and rebellion. This has been the fate of Babylon from the beginning (Genesis 11:1–9).

The victory of Christ

King of kings
(19:1 – 20:6)

A shout of triumph goes up in heaven. The air is full of sound – the din of a great multitude, the roar of rushing waters and loud peals of thunder. The cry is, 'Hallelujah!' – 'Praise the Lord!' The triumph of God over the beast is celebrated in the wedding of the Lamb. His bride is the church, in all her purity and beauty.

THE RIDER ON THE WHITE HORSE

Again, John sees heaven standing open (19:11–21). The scene now is dominated by a rider on a white horse. This is not the rider of worldly conquest we met when the first seal was opened (6:1–2). This is Christ himself, with blazing eyes and crowned head, and his name is the 'Word of God'. He rides ahead of armies of faithful

The binding of Satan

During his earthly ministry, Jesus had talked of the binding of Satan. Satan is like a man who is supremely strong and superbly equipped, but who is overpowered by someone even stronger. When Jesus healed disease and expelled evil spirits, he showed that the power of God is greater than the power of Satan (Mark 3:27; Luke 11:21).

martyrs and witnesses, dressed in white linen – the livery of heaven.

The gentle, patient and compassionate Jesus is also the Christ who judges and rules all things. His sword is his word. What he says is done. As John watches, the beast and his evil armies are overwhelmed and destroyed. An angel summons the carrion birds to devour the flesh of the corpses.

THE 1,000 YEARS

Now John sees Satan bound and thrown into the abyss for 1,000 years (20:1–6).

While Satan is powerless, those who have died for the sake of Christ are raised to new life and reign with him.

Satan's doom
(20:7–10)

At the end of his 1,000-year imprisonment, Satan is released. He resumes his work of deceiving humankind. He summons huge armies from evil warmongering nations – Gog and Magog. They turn the whole world into a battlefield and surround the camp and city of God's people.

The situation looks hopeless, when suddenly the forces of evil are engulfed in fire from heaven. The church is rescued and delivered, not by its strategy or strength, but by the mighty power of God. The devil (the old deceiver), the beast (who pits worldly power against God) and the false prophet (the networker of lies) are all finally destroyed.

The dead are judged
(20:11–15)

John sees the drama of Judgment Day. God presides from his great white throne as the dead come before him and their lives are examined. Everyone is judged on what he or she has done.

It's the deed that counts! The records of human behaviour are in the books that are opened – while each individual salvation is recorded in the book of life. Those whose names are not in the book of life are destroyed, along with death and Hades (the place of departed spirits).

The new Jerusalem and the wedding of the Lamb

The new Jerusalem
(21:1–27)

Now John sees the most amazing sight of all. He has a vision of the new creation – a new heaven and earth. The old is gone – including the sea, which was a symbol of chaos and the lair of monsters.

The centre of the new creation is the holy city, the new Jerusalem. This city isn't laboriously built on earth,

The millennium

Christians have always puzzled over the meaning of the '1,000 years' in Revelation 20. Is it a 1,000-year reign which will begin when Christ returns? Will Satan be bound, while Christ rules the world with his saints? Or is the 1,000 years the long period between Christ's ascension into heaven and his second coming?

In the rest of the Bible, and certainly in the rest of Revelation, the numbers and images are symbolic. They are not supposed to be taken literally. It is very likely that the same is true here. The '1,000 years' are a long period during which Satan's power is restricted and Christ influences the world through his people. Even those who die, beheaded as martyrs, have a vital part to play. By their prayers, their memory and their inspiration, they continue to exert a powerful influence.

The '1,000 years' are the same as the last days. They are the times we ourselves live in. Satan is not yet entirely defeated. We can see his malign influence all around, and yet his power has been essentially broken by the death and resurrection of Christ.

Satan is 'bound', but he is also 'released'. His power is limited, but he is still busily at work. This vision assures us that one day Satan and his dominions will be finally crushed and destroyed. Until then he has an unnerving tendency to re-emerge. His revivals are a macabre parody of the resurrection of Christ.

founded on military victories and defended with constant vigilance. This city comes from heaven itself and is God's gift. John realizes that this city is a picture of the people of God, his church, now ready to be married to Christ.

As he looks, John hears a voice announce, 'Now the dwelling of God is with people…' This is what God has always wanted, but he has been prevented by human sin. In the Garden of Eden, before Adam and Eve's rebellion, God and human beings had lived together in perfect friendship. In the wilderness years, God had shared the life of his people by having a tent among them. When Jesus came, he took on human nature and 'camped' in his own creation (John 1:14). He shared our life on earth, so that we might share his life in heaven.

The book of Revelation ends with John's vision of a new Jerusalem, and the re-establishment of the perfect rule of God. He will reign and his glory will be the light of the city. A Byzantine portrait of Christ in glory from the lid of a 10th-century reliquary.

God speaks from his throne. He proclaims that everything is now perfect – created anew. He promises the water of life to all who thirst. He welcomes into his family all who have remained faithful in times of persecution. The Trinity of God – Father, Son and Spirit – now embraces humans in its life of love. This is what Jesus had prayed for on the night before his death (John 17:24). But all those who have wilfully persisted in evil have no place in God's holy heaven. They are destroyed.

Now John sees the holy city in greater detail. It is altogether glorious, with a beauty and clarity of light like jewels and crystal. To portray its perfection, John describes a vast cube, 1,400 miles long and wide and high! Twelve gates (three on each side) bear the names of the tribes of Israel. Twelve pillars bear the names of the apostles. This is the capital of the whole people of God. The gates of the old covenant and the pillars of the new covenant are part of the same eternal city.

John's vision reminds us of Ezekiel's tour of the new temple (Ezekiel 40–43), when an angel shows him the exact dimensions of the building. It is the perfect house for a perfect God. Now an angel measures out an entire city, where the gates are precious stones, and the walls are 200 feet thick! But the real surprise is that this city, the new Jerusalem, is a picture of the bride of the Lamb, the church of Jesus Christ. It is a picture of… us!

The new Jerusalem would be the perfect place for a temple – but of course there is no need for one. God is completely united with his people now. The business of sacrifice and the remoteness of the Most Holy Place are things of the past. And there is no need for sun and moon, because the glory of God is light and life.

Jesus Christ, the light of the world, is the lamp of

The tabernacle which grew!

As the angel measures the heavenly city, we realize we have met this shape before. It's a cube! The city is 12,000 stadia (1,400 miles) long and wide and high.

The tent of meeting (the tabernacle) in the wilderness was shaped like a cube, and so was the Most Holy Place in the temple. It is the perfect shape for the house of God. But now the presence of God embraces everything, and the place of his dwelling is vastly increased. Measured in 'stadia', it is twelve (the 'three' of God times the 'four' of human beings) times 1,000 (the number of completion, which is 10 x 10 x 10) – in every dimension!

completed, and the fruit of the tree of life is freely available. The leaves of the tree are to be used for the healing of the nations. Grace and giving are the lifestyle of heaven.

Jesus is coming!

As the visions come to an end, John must face again the daily grind of his exile and hard labour. He must wrestle with the pain of persecution and the fear of martyrdom. As he does so, the angel speaks to him the very words of Jesus: 'I am coming soon!' (22:7–21).

There are some final instructions. John is to share the visions, for they are encouragements and warnings which take immediate effect. When Judgment Day comes on the world, it will be too late for people to change their ways. It is vital that we turn *now* from all forms of wickedness – occult practices, immorality, idolatry and deception. We must live holy lives, ready to welcome Jesus at any time.

The Spirit and the bride say, 'Come!' The people of God, and his Spirit within them, are united in their longing for Christ to return. May we who read these words also echo them with our lips, treasure them in our hearts and make them the central hope of our daily lives.

heaven. In his light the nations discover the truth, resolve their rivalries and settle their ancient quarrels. Human rulers cease to glory in themselves and instead offer all their praise to him.

The river of life
(22:1–6)

John sees the river of the water of life. It flows from God's throne and throughout the new Jerusalem. Joel, Ezekiel and Zechariah (three great prophets) had enjoyed visions of such a river – the life-giving grace of God flowing out to transform the world. Jesus himself is the source of this river (John 7:37–39), which is a symbol of God's Holy Spirit.

On the banks of the river grows the tree of life – one of the two forbidden trees that grew in the Garden of Eden. It was to prevent humankind stealing eternal life that God banished Adam and Eve from the Garden (Genesis 3:22–23). Now the great work of salvation is

Index

k

l

m

Picture acknowledgments

AKG London: pp. 23 (Monreale, Sicily), 24 (Collegiate Church, Klosterneuburg, Lower Austria/Erich Lessing), 45 (British Library, London), 90–91 (Judaica-Collection Max Berger, Vienna/Erich Lessing), 108 (Hessische Landesbibliothek, Darmstadt; ms 2505), 120 (Hessische Landesbibliothek, Darmstadt; ms 2505), 125 (Collegiate Church, Klosterneuberg, Lower Austria/Erich Lessing), 138 (wall-painting from Santa Maria de Tahull; Museu d'Art de Catalunya, Barcelona), 155 (from Bible moralise. Codex Vindobonensis 2554, flo. 52v.; Österreichische National Bibliothek, Vienna), 188 (from the Latin Bible; Leon, S. Isidoro; V.I, fol. 130), 272 (Judaica-Collection Max Berger, Vienna/Erich Lessing), 324 (from the Lambeth Bible, fol. 258v.; Lambeth Palace Library, London), 372 (Biblioteca Nacional, Lisbon), 498 (Escorial, Codex Vitrinas 17, fol. 83r., Echternach), 659 (Bayerische Staatsbibliothek, Munich), 665 (Chora Monastery/Erich Lessing), 666 (Collegiate Church, Klosterneuburg, Lower Austria/Erich Lessing), 676 (Hessische Landesbibliothek, Darmstad; ms 2505), 702 (from the Apocalypse of St Severin, ms Latin, 8878, fol. 138v.; Bibliothèque Nationale, Paris/Erich Lessing), 703 (from the Apocalypse of St Severin, ms Latin 8878, fol. 141; Bibliothèque Nationale, Paris) and 709 (Cathedral Treasury, Limburg/Lahn/Erich Lessing).

Ancient Art & Architecture Collection Ltd: pp. 193 (Chellier) and 689.

The Art Archive: pp. 29 (British Library), 32 (Sucevita Monastery, Moldova, Romania/Dagli Orti [A]), 135 (Anagni Cathedral, Italy/Dagli Orti [A]), 158 (Nicolas Sapieha), 411 (Seminary Library, Udine/Dagli Orti [A]), 424 (San Angelo Formis, Capua, Italy/Dagli Orti [A]), (San Angelo Formis, Capua, Italy/Dagli Orti [A]), 510 (San Angelo Formis, Capua, Italy/Dagli Orti [A]), 517 (Musée du Louvre, Paris/Dagli Orti [A]), 520 (San Angelo Formis, Capua, Italy/Dagli Orti [A]), 537 (Victoria and Albert Museum, London/Eileen Tweedy), 588–89 (Dagli Orti [A]), 601 (Bargello Museum, Florence/Dagli Orti [A]), 627 and jacket (spine; front and back [third from top, far right]) (Real Collegiata, San Isidoro, Leon/Dagli Orti [A]), 682 (Seminary Library, Udine/Dagli Orti [A]) and 705 (British Library).

A.S.A.P.: pp. 21 (Richard Nowitz), 36 and jacket (front and back [third from top, second from right]) (Keren Benzian), 88 (Garo Nalbandian), 94–95 and jacket (front and back [second from top, far left]) (Tzur Peli), 112 (Richard Nowitz), 113 (Itzik Marom), 122–23 and jacket (front and back [top, far right]) (Tzur Peli), 130 (Richard Nowitz), 131 (Richard Nowitz), 134 (Sami Avnisan), 146 (Garo Nalbandian), 174–75 (Garo Nalbandian), 178–79 (Garo Nalbandian), 228 (Aliza Aurbach), 240–41 (Richard Nowitz), 251 (Buki Boaz), 253 (Eyal Bartov), 270 (Aliza Aurbach), 284 (Shai Ginot), 286 (Tzur Peli), 319 (Keren Benzian), 320 (Flabio Sklar), 327 (Lev Brodolin), 334–35 (Buki Boaz), 354 (Naftali Hilger), 362–63 (Keren Benzian), 398 (Jacob Kaszemacher), 410 (Garo Nalbandian), 460 (Richard Nowitz), 466 (Richard Nowitz), 478 (Lev Brodolin), 490–91 and jacket (front [bottom, second from left]) (Rafael Macia), 540–41 (Hanan Isachar), 672 (Mike Ganor) and 677 (Garo Nalbandian).

The Bodleian Library, University of Oxford: p. 150 (ms Douce 131, fol. 96v.).

The Bridgeman Art Library, London: pp. 2, 26 (British Library, London, UK), 73 (Lambeth Palace Library, London, UK), 213 (Corpus Christi College, Oxford, UK), 227 (Bibliothèque Nationale, Paris, France), 344 (Musée Conde, Chantilly, France/Giraudon), 434 (Musée Conde, Chantilly, France), 667 (Museum of Art, Novgorod, Russia) and 707 (Bible Society, London, UK).

The British Museum: pp. 2, 4, 204, 313, 364, 374, 378–79, 527, 649 and 658. Copyright © The British Museum, London.

Colchester Musuems: p. 546.

Genut Audio Visual Productions: pp. 568 and 654–55.

Hanan Isachar: pp. 2, 77, 102–103, 139, 151, 164, 243, 277, 368, 371, 415, 482–83, 501, 508, 523, 560–61 and 698. Copyright © Hanan Isachar.

Jon Arnold Images: pp. 2, 40, 42–43, 52–53, 84–85, 108, 111, 121, 222–23, 238, 282–83, 294–295, 314, 340–341, 392–93, 438, 474, 553, 554, 556–57, 563, 566, 572–73, 594, 596–97, 608, 616–17, 624, 631, 640, 699, 700–701, 706 and jacket (front and back [top left; second from top, far right; bottom right]).

Jonathan Adams: pp. 180–81 and 183.

Julie Baines: pp. 10–11 (line drawings only).

Ian Mitchell: pp. 7, 16–17, 115, 402–403 and 408.

Lion Publishing: pp. 310–11 (David Townsend), 417 (David Townsend), 426 (David Townsend), 432 (David Townsend), 515 (David Townsend), 559 (David Townsend) and 687 (Nick Rous).

Mendrea, Dinu, Jerusalem: pp. 2, 67, 101, 114, 119, 123, 154, 206, 224, 245, 262–63, 270–71, 291, 303, 305, 330–31, 355, 375, 382, 393, 397, 450–51, 486, 494–95 (with the kind support of 'Jerusalem Wings') 512–13 and 530–31.

Mendrea, Radu, Munich: pp. 301, 448 and 456–57.

Mendrea, Sandu, Jerusalem: pp. 50, 78, 142–43, 237, 244, 278 and 412. (The photographers Dinu and Sandu Mendrea wish to gratefully acknowledge the kind support of the Israel Nature and National Parks Protection Authority.)

Musée du Louvre: p. 30 (alabaster figure from Mari).

National Gallery: pp. 642–43 (Fra Angelico, *Christ Glorified in the Court of Heaven* [1419–35], tempera on poplar, 32 x 73 cm). Copyright © National Gallery, London.

Powerstock Zefa: pp. 348–49.

Rex Nicholls: pp. 56–57 and 429.

Robert Harding: pp. 216–17 and 387.

Sonia Halliday Photographs: p. 455.

Zev Radovan, Jerusalem, Israel: pp. 3, 39, 46, 60, 87, 106, 133, 136, 137, 140, 153, 162, 165, 199, 203, 214, 215, 254, 256, 264, 281, 306, 336, 347, 350, 353, 356, 396, 422, 463, 578, 581, 634–35, 653, 706 and jacket (front and back [top, second from left; bottom, far left]). Copyright © Zev Radovan.